Do you see a man diligent
and skillful in his business?
He shall stand before kings:

Proverbs
Chapter 22
Verse 29

TAX SHELTERS
and
TAX-FREE INCOME
for
EVERYONE

To my father, Walter,
my wife, Wilma, and
my sons, Bill, Jr. and Steve.

TAX SHELTERS
and
TAX-FREE INCOME
for
EVERYONE

Fourth Edition

by

William C. Drollinger

Epic Publications, Inc.
Orchard Lake, Michigan
1979

Library of Congress Card Number: 72-94179

ISBN 0-914244-04-3

Second printing 1974
Third printing 1974
Fourth printing 1975
Fifth printing 1975
Sixth printing 1977
Seventh printing 1977
Eighth printing 1978
Ninth printing 1978
Tenth printing 1979

Composition by Detroit Offset Printing, Inc.

Presswork and Binding by LithoCrafters, Inc.

PREFACE

Every American, by right of birth, qualifies for certain tax shelters: namely, a personal tax exemption, a unified credit against estate and gift taxes, certain tax-free income, gifts of food, clothing and housing.

Every American who marries acquires another tax shelter, the marital deduction which allows the greater of $250,000 or one-half of his adjusted gross estate to pass tax free to his surviving spouse, and additional tax-free income from the more favorable tax rates of the joint return.

More than 80% of adult Americans have purchased a tax shelter and tax-free income — life insurance protection in which ordinarily the death proceeds are free of income tax and cash values grow tax free.

These tax shelters and tax-free income exist because they are socially and economically desirable. When they no longer serve positive purposes, they will be changed or eliminated as were private foundations and accumulation trusts.

Many social and economic goals of the United States are furthered by the incentives of tax ·shelters and tax-free income. Current examples include: 1) new residential housing construction which has been encouraged by the provision of accelerated depreciation and tax-free cash flow and 2) the construction of pollution control facilities which has been encouraged by the provision of rapid amortization.

The purpose of this book is to identify and explain tax shelters and tax-free income so that the reader may be aware of the benefits as well as the attendant risks and tax aspects of shelters. The book is divided into four parts. Part One is concerned with the investor. Shelters are discussed in general terms followed by examples which describe in detail the structure of the various programs. Part Two dwells on employee benefits which the employer may wish to provide for his employees or which the employee may wish to propose to his employer in contract negotiations. Part Three deals with benefits for corporations — benefits which ultimately acrue to the shareholders. Part Four provides background information which is helpful in gaining a better appreciation of the forms of business organization and various tax entities. It also describes capital gains and losses, and depreciation, amortization, depletion, and investment credit and their relationship to tax shelters and tax-free income.

No attempt is made by the author to recommend programs for investors or to sell or offer to sell investments. The investor should obtain the services of competent advisors to assist him in deciding where to risk his money.

Certain attorneys, accountants, fee-service planners, insurance men, stockbrokers, securities salesmen, investment counselors, tax shelter specialists, bank executives, et al, are qualified financial planners who are capable of recommending tax shelters as part of the investor's overall financial plan. Tax shelters should not be purchased or sold on a package basis but only as they relate to the accomplishment of the overall objectives of the investor to increase his financial security for today and the future.

Financial planning is now a profession, and tax shelters are part of financial planning. It is the obligation and legitimate role of the financial planner to help the investor use tax shelters and tax-free income where they are appropriate to minimize taxes. Tax shelters are a supplement to good financial planning and not a substitute. They must be fitted soundly into the investor's financial plan. This compels the financial planner to sharpen his skills in the area of living planning, to become totally involved in helping the investor fulfill his lifetime goals as well as objectives in event of death. The financial planner will thus become more creative and of greater service to the investor.

To utilize tax shelters in financial planning it will be necessary for planning to be done earlier in the year than was previously necessary. Many tax shelters are available only for a short period of time, and the financial planner must be ready to place the appropriate shelters in the investor's portfolio when the shelters are available. There should be a review of the investor's entire financial plan directly after the filing of his personal income tax return. This review should take into consideration the investor's earning pattern and the availability of after-tax dollars for investment and commitment for various programs.

More industries and more companies within a given industry are registering offerings with the S.E.C. This is a reflection of both the need for additional public money in these programs and the desire of the sponsors to transfer more risk to the investors. In many cases the sponsors will make substantial sums of money in program-selling fees, management fees, product sales, commissions, etc., whether or not the investors make any money or even lose their entire investment. It is therefore important that the financial planner, when necessary, consult with a tax-shelter specialist in given tax-shelter-program areas where they are unknowledgeable, just as doctors and lawyers consult with various specialists in their professions.

In the case of private offerings, the financial planner may suggest restructuring a deal to make it more advantageous to the investor. For example, some financial planners will not permit a client to purchase an interest in a real estate limited partnership without requiring the general partner to repurchase the investment within a certain number of years or forfeit its interest and deed the property to the limited partners, thus providing better assurance of liquidity for the investor.

There is a vast difference between obtaining a tax write-off from an investment and being paid a return on it. If the investor is in a fifty (50%) percent income tax bracket, invests $1,000 and receives a $1,000 deduction, the investment has cost him $500, the amount available to him if he had not invested the money and had paid the tax on it. In many instances the investor would have benefited by not investing where there was a poor return or none at all but merely paid the tax and invested the after-tax dollars elsewhere. Even putting those dollars in a savings account can be a better decision in many cases than simply obtaining a tax deduction.

It is foolhardy for most investors to rely on their own analytical skill in the casual reading of a tax-shelter prospectus which usually contains only what the S.E.C. requires in the way of disclosure. Risk factors are most always stated but projections of benefits are usually absent. Without projections of potential tax write-offs and income and capital gains benefits, it is virtually impossible for the investor to make a reasonable judgment on a tax-shelter offering. Dealer information of this type is made available to salesmen for the sponsor. The investor should be accorded the same information so that he has the opportunity to more fairly evaluate the program and weigh the risks against the benefits.

Investors buy benefits not risks. It is hoped that the S.E.C. will act soon to require the inclusion of projected benefits in the prospectuses and relieve the investor of his disadvantage.

DISCLAIMER

This book and the material in this book is not a prospectus. This material is not an offer or solicitation to sell or buy any securities and is not to be considered sales literature. This material has not been reviewed by any governmental agency.

The programs described in this book are imaginary and any financial, statistical and related similarity between past, present, and future programs is purely coincidental. No program should be purchased on the assumption it is going to perform precisely as shown in these imaginary examples.

This book should not be construed as providing legal and tax advice. The investor should not rely on the legal and tax material in the book. The investor should consult his own financial planner, attorney and accountant for investment, legal and tax advice.

This book has been produced under tremendous time constraints so that it will reflect current tax law. Every effort has been made to avoid errors of fact and law; but, if such exist, the oversights are due to these production constraints. Such errors, if any, should be brought to the attention of the author for correction in the next edition.

ACKNOWLEDGEMENTS

Contributions have been made to this book by many talented individuals in the financial planning industry; however, securities laws preclude us from giving them credit for their work. Should the securities laws change we will give these people due credit in the edition of this book next following the change.

We can, however, acknowledge The Commercial and Financial Chronicle of 25 Park Place, New York, N.Y. 10007 and C. Edward Wall, a specialist in research methodology and information retrieval, now with the University of Michigan for their assistance with this book.

The general introduction which follows is intended to give the reader an overview of tax shelters and tax-free income in preparation for his reading the individual programs described in this book.

With the exception of real estate, the Tax Reform Act of 1976 generally limits an investor's deductions from a partnership tax-shelter program to the amount at risk. To achieve some of the high deductions in the examples shown in this book, partnership borrowings must be with recourse against the investor.

TABLE OF CONTENTS

GENERAL INTRODUCTION

Tax-shelter ventures are new companies engaged in business enterprises which, for various reasons, receive favorable tax treatment under existing tax laws. Some of these ventures are "privately" offered to a limited number of potential investors. Other ventures are "publicly" offered in that they are investments in companies whose initial capital is raised based on an offering circular, or prospectus, cleared by the various State Securities Commissions, registered with the Securities and Exchange Commission, and cleared by the National Association of Securities Dealers for distribution by its member firms.

CHARACTERISTICS OF TAX–SHELTER VENTURES

Tax-shelter companies are usually partnerships or joint ventures so that tax deductions produced by the business will flow directly to investors who can use these deductions in offsetting taxable income from other sources.

These companies are generally organized as limited partnerships with the limited partners being the investors and with a general partner who manages the business of the partnership. It is important that the partnership not be taxed as a corporation so that the deductions will flow directly to investors. A joint venture would also pass losses or gains directly through to the investors, but it would have the disadvantage of not limiting the liability of the investor to his initial capital.

DEGREE OF RISK

Tax shelters usually involve a higher degree of risk than other types of investments. The federal government has found it necessary to encourage investments because of the inherent high risks in certain enterprises such as oil and gas exploration and low-income housing. Tax incentives are necessary in order to attract investment dollars to these areas. This is less expensive for the government than the government covering the total investment itself since the taxpayer contributes some of his money. The 50%-tax-bracket investor is putting up one-half and the government is contributing one-half.

1

LEVERAGE

These investments are often highly leveraged enabling the enterprise to own more depreciable assets through the borrowing of money. This creates a larger initial tax loss and increases the payment of interest which is deductible. Leveraging makes an investment more volatile with respect to potential gain or loss.

LIQUIDITY

Investments in tax shelters are often not very liquid although there is a trend toward providing greater liquidity, even private and public markets in some cases. However, in many investments an investor who wants to get his money out may not be able to locate a buyer, may be prohibited from selling by the terms of the partnership agreement, and may suffer a loss because of early liquidation.

ADDITIONAL CONTRIBUTIONS

Some ventures reserve the right to compel the investor to make additional contributions to the company if more capital is needed. In some cases this feature may result in a benefit and in other cases a loss.

SHARING OF PROFITS AND LOSSES

The sharing of profits and losses between the limited partners and the general partner is usually arranged to maximize the tax benefits for the high-tax-bracket limited partners.

TAX ASPECTS

Tax shelters generally produce a tax deduction or loss in the current year without producing real economic loss. Taxation of income may be deferred to later years or ordinary income may be converted to capital gains.

TYPES OF PROGRAMS

The four major types of programs offered are real estate, oil and gas, equipment leasing, and farming. These will be briefly examined now and studied in detail later.

REAL ESTATE

Real estate investments have been used for income and long-term capital gain. The availability of accelerated depreciation and the ability to borrow a high percentage of the cost of improvements make these types of investments a source of tax losses to be offset against other income and finally result in capital gains on sale of the properties. There are three major goals in real estate investment. Deductions for interest payments and accelerated depreciation on property provide tax shelter for income from other sources. Cash flow available after payment of debt service and expenses can be distributed to limited partners tax-free. Ordinary income can be converted into capital gains through the profitable sale of the properties.

OIL AND GAS DRILLING PROGRAMS

The government encourages the search for more oil and gas reserves by providing tax incentives since locating such reserves is ordinarily a speculative business. The depletion allowance is presently 22%, and there is the right to deduct, as current expense, all intangible drilling costs which can constitute about 70% of total exploration costs.

Drilling programs provide immediate deductions of a substantial part of the investment, sometimes as much as 90% to 100% of the initial investment on programs where the deductible expenses are allocated to the limited partners and non-deductible costs are paid by the general partner.

For an investor in the 50% tax bracket, this may mean that his actual after-tax investment would be only 50% to 55% of the pre-tax commitment. If oil is produced, 22% of the gross income is tax free. Sometimes sponsors of oil programs include liquidity features in which they agree to purchase investors' interests after a few years for either cash or stock at a value determined by an independent petroleum engineer.

Investments in oil programs are probably the most speculative of all tax-sheltered investments from the investment standpoint, but perhaps the least speculative from the tax aspect since most of the tax benefits accrue in the first year and are usually not questioned by the IRS. If the investor will make subsequent investments over the next two or three years, he will get better diversification and increase his chances of participating in a highly successful venture.

3

EQUIPMENT LEASING

Equipment leasing resembles real estate investments in that the equipment such as oil-workover barges, airplanes, equipment containers, railroad cars, office equipment, etc. is usually purchased largely with borrowed funds and leased to a user for a period of years, depending on the economic life of the equipment. At the end of the initial lease term, the lessee may have the right to extend or renew the lease or the lessor (owner) may decide to sell the equipment. The tax shelter arises out of the right to deduct accelerated depreciation and the interest charges on the debt less the rental income.

A problem not confined to leasing is that the combined charges in interest and depreciation decline after a few years to a level less than the annual rent so that an accounting profit develops. This profit must be reported as taxable income even though there is no substantial cash flow to use for paying taxes. Moreover, any gain realized on the sale of the equipment is taxed as ordinary income and not as capital gain. Accelerated depreciation over straight-line depreciation is treated as a tax preference item subject to the minimum tax.

FARMING

There are a number of farming type programs such as tree crops, vineyards, cattle feeding, cattle breeding, and chickens. Various row crops are also beginning to appear. There are certain tax-shelter aspects whereby the investor can write off his investment in the trees and other crops, the equipment used in the business, water, and other management costs. If the venture is successful, it can produce cash flow, part of which comes back at capital gains rates. Furthermore, there may be substantial appreciation of land values.

Farmers have special tax incentives. A farmer may show as a deductible expense many items which by standard accounting practices would be shown as capital improvements. Farmers have also been permitted to use the cash basis of accounting which, for example, would allow a cash purchase of cattle feed as a deductible expense in the year of use or consumption.

CATTLE

Cattle feeding and cattle breeding attract many investors who wish to defer and shelter income. Pure-bred animals are used as seed-stock by commercial breeders who wish to improve the quality of their cross-bred herds. With the per capita consumption of beef in the United States increasing at a rate higher than the rate of population growth, the demand for seed-stock may well exceed supply and therefore increase in value.

Cattle feeding involves purchasing feeder cattle, feeding them to the desired weight in feed lots, and selling the fat cattle to meat packers. Investors use investments in feeder cattle to defer income tax consequences from one year to the next. The deferral is created by deductions for feed, management fees, and interest on any loans to purchase feed or cattle. Income is taken in the following year when the fat cattle are sold.

RATES OF RETURN

Determining the success of prior programs or projecting the success of a current program is not a simple job. Although changes in the law may be made in the near future, current securities regulations are such that prospectuses do not clearly show results of prior activities or projections on a proposed activity. For example, prospectuses of oil programs generally have sections which show success ratios on total wells drilled and also "pay-out tables." These are usually not very helpful in analyzing a program in that an operator could show a very high success ratio in comparing dry holes and productive prospects, but if all the producing wells were producing only enough oil to cover costs, this would not indicate success. If an operator had a low success ratio, but had discovered properties with large oil and gas reserves, this might be a highly successful venture. Early pay-out is not necessarily indicative of a successful program. For example, an operator might purchase producing properties which would create fast cash flow, but this cash flow might end soon. An operator who had made significant discoveries might take two or three years to develop any cash flow due to the fact that he was using revenues from initial wells to further develop these discoveries. Thus, the prospectus showing the early cash flow might be for a program which would turn out to be a failure from the investment standpoint, and the prospectus showing no cash flow might turn out to be a highly successful investment.

5

An experienced analyst, such as a tax-shelter counselor, goes beyond this information and obtains many more detailed facts and figures in order to do a thorough analysis of rates of return. On oil programs, he will probably seek to determine whether the operator has sponsored successful ventures in the past. On real estate, agriculture and other types of programs, he usually gets detailed projections and reviews the reasonableness of these projections.

OIL AND GAS PROGRAMS

The tax-shelter counselor will insist on receiving independent engineers' reserve reports on oil and gas programs. In the past, operators have generally not had independent evaluations done. However, there is now a trend and some proposed securities regulations toward operators disclosing in their prospectuses that they will have independent reserve reports done. A reserve report will estimate the annual cash flow from the sale of oil and gas over the productive life span of the wells. He will use these figures to calculate three basic investment tests:

One is the ratio of total net income to the total investment. This ratio compares the total projected before-tax income which would be allocated to the investors with the investor's total before-tax investments. The criteria for a satisfactory ratio depends on the type of program and on whether the discoveries are mainly oil or gas. The reason for the differentiation between oil or gas is that income from gas discoveries generally takes longer before it starts than with income from oil discoveries. Successful ratios would be in the 2.5 or 3.0 to 1 area.

A second ratio is the return assuming immediate liquidation. This calculation estimates the percentage after-tax return on after-tax investment assuming the program were liquidated in the current year. First, the tax-shelter counselor calculates the net income which would be allocated to the limited partners on an annual basis as estimated in the reserve report. He determines the total present worth of this net income by discounting it at 1% above the current prime rate. He then further discounts this amount by 30% for risk factors. This is a fairly standard method in the oil industry for determining the market value of producing properties. Next, he determines the after-tax investment for the limited partners based on the tax deductions which have been allocated to them. A satisfactory percentage return would be approximately 115% to 120% in the first year and increased by another 15% to 20% for each subsequent year. If the program were successful and if the investor's interests could be liquidated in the first year, he would receive back his after-tax investment, plus a 15% to 20% after-tax profit.

A third ratio is internal rate of return (IRR). Using a computer program, the tax-shelter counselor measures the effective after-tax rate of return on the investor's after-tax investment allowing for the repayment of any borrowings incurred by the program. The computer program assumes the cash flow is reinvested at the same rate as the return from the investment being tested. The result is internal rate of return, which is, in effect, the investment return (or compound interest rate) which, combined with principal payments, would generate the estimated net cash flow year by year of the oil program being tested. A satisfactory IRR for an oil and gas exploration program would be in the 15% to 20% area.

REAL ESTATE PROGRAMS

On real estate programs, the tax-shelter counselor is generally working with projections since there are not many programs available which have been in existence long enough to have developed any significant historical background. Mainly, he is checking for the reasonableness of the underlying assumptions of the projections. He determines their assumed level of rents per project and determines whether or not these are feasible. He checks the vacancy rates that they have assumed in their projections. And he determines whether or not they have been optimistic in their projections for on-going expenses in running the properties. Sometimes, he will rework their projections based on more conservative assumptions and if the rate of return is still commensurate with the investment risk, he may pass favorably on the investment aspects of the program. In real estate programs, he would look for a rate of return of 12% to 15% as indicative of return commensurate with investment risk.

1969 TAX REFORM ACT

In 1969, Congress acted to reduce the benefits of tax-shelter investments. The 1969 Tax Reform Act had three main effects: It provided for a maximum of 50% on earned income

7

in order to reduce the incentive to invest in tax shelters; a minimum tax on certain tax preference items was imposed, and a limitation was put on the deduction of interest paid or incurred to carry tax-shelter investments. The tax benefits of many specific tax-shelter investments were reduced and in some cases eliminated.

It is questionable as to whether or not the maximum tax has significantly reduced the benefits of tax-shelter investments. First, a 50% tax leverage is probably beneficial on good tax-shelter investments, and secondly, investment income is not subject to the maximum. Since many high-tax-bracket individuals also have substantial investment income, higher than 50% tax brackets are still in existence.

The Tax Reform Act of 1976 increases the rate of the minimum tax on individuals from 10 percent to 15 percent. An exemption is provided equal to the greater of $10,000 or one-half of regular income taxes. The carryover of regular taxes that are not used to offset tax preferences in the current year is eliminated. Interest on investment indebtedness is limited to $10,000 per year, plus the taxpayer's net investment income. No offset of investment interest is permitted against capital gain income. An additional deduction of up to $15,000 per year is permitted for interest paid in connection with indebtedness incurred by the taxpayer to acquire the stock in a corporation, or a partnership interest, where the taxpayer, his spouse, and his children have (or acquire) at least 50 percent of the stock or capital interest in the enterprise. Interest deductions which are disallowed under these rules are subject to an unlimited carryover and may be deducted in future years (subject to the applicable limitation).

PARTNERSHIP TAXATION

In order to be attractive as a tax shelter, the "limited partnership" should be treated as a partnership for tax purposes, and not as an association. Taxability as an association depends on how many "corporate characteristics" exist in the structure of the entity. The four main corporate characteristics are: Continuity of life, centralized management, limited liability, and transferability of interest. If an entity had a majority of these corporate characteristics, the entity would be called an association for tax purposes, and the anticipated

8

flow-through of tax benefits would not result. Many programs will attempt to obtain an advance ruling from the IRS as to whether or not the limited partnership would be deemed an association. Most limited partnerships do not have continuity of life and do involve limited liability. Many of them restrict transferability of units.

If the general partner is a corporation, the following characteristics must be present in order to obtain a favorable ruling from IRS:

1. The limited partners must not own more than 20% of the stock of the corporate general partner or its affiliate.

2. The general partner must have, and maintain, a net worth as follows:

(a) If the total investments are $2.5 million or less, the net worth must be the lesser of $250,000 or 15% of the invested amount.

(b) If the total investments are over $2.5 million, the net worth must total at least 10% of the total investments.

(c) If the corporate general partner is also the general partner for other limited partnerships, the net worth requirements are cumulative with respect to all the partnerships.

This is generally not a big tax risk in the "public" offerings, but it could be a substantial risk in the small "private" offerings, and investors contemplating such investments should check this carefully.

ALLOCATING PROFITS AND LOSSES

Allocation of profits and losses is an important aspect of tax shelters. Sometimes, the general partner, who has no need for tax shelter, pays only non-deductible expenses. Sometimes profits are allocated differently from losses. The IRS position on allocation is not entirely clear except that they will follow allocation according to the terms in the partnership agreement as long as the principal purpose of the allocation is not to avoid taxes. They will look at the business purpose; they will want to find substantial economic effects not involving tax consequences; and they will find out whether or not the allocation was made before the amounts could be specifically determined.

9

DEPRECIATION

Depreciation is involved in most tax shelters. It is the declining value of personal or real property as the result of the passage of time, wear and tear, or lessened usefulness. In 1954, the tax laws were changed to permit the calculation of depreciation at rates that allowed larger deductions in the early years of ownership and corresponding lower rates in later years instead of rateably over the assumed life of the property (straight line method). Since then, the determination of depreciation has been adjusted several times by the IRS.

ACCELERATED DEPRECIATION

Accelerated depreciation is available for real estate as well as personal property. New residential rental real property may be depreciated by the double declining or sum-of-years digits methods if 80% of gross rental income for the year is from the dwelling units. Non-residential properties are subject to a maximum of 150% declining balance depreciation. Used properties must be depreciated by the straight-line method, except in the case of used residential rental properties with useful lives of more than 20 years — these may be depreciated by 125% declining balance. A disadvantage of accelerated depreciation is that it leaves a smaller amount to be deducted in later years; and, therefore, it produces a declining tax shelter on properties and may result in taxable income in excess of cash distributions in the later years.

RECAPTURE OF ACCELERATED DEPRECIATION

In the case of residential real estate, the 1976 Tax Reform Act provides for the recapture of all post-1975 depreciation in excess of straight-line, in the same manner as is presently the case for non-residential real estate. In the case of government subsidized housing, the conference agreement provides full recapture of post-1975 depreciation for the first 100 months (8-1/3 years) and a phaseout of the amount recaptured during the second 100 months (up to 16 2/3 years). There will be no recapture thereafter.

MORTGAGE OR INTEREST DEDUCTIONS

A limitation has been placed upon the deductibility of the interest on funds borrowed to acquire or carry investment

10

assets. Under the conference agreement, interest on investment indebtedness is limited to $10,000 per year, plus the taxpayer's net investment income. No offset of investment interest is permitted against capital gain income. An additional deduction of up to $15,000 per year is permitted for interest paid in connection with indebtedness incurred by the taxpayer to acquire the stock in a corporation, or a partnership interest, where the taxpayer, his spouse, and his children have (or acquire) at least 50 percent of the stock or capital interest in the enterprise. Interest deductions which are disallowed under these rules are subject to an unlimited carryover and may be deducted in future years (subject to the applicable limitation). Under the conference agreement, no limitation is imposed on the deductibility of personal interest.

PREPAID INTEREST

The Tax Reform Act of 1976 requires a cash method taxpayer to deduct prepaid interest over the period of the loan to the extent that the interest represents the cost of using the borrowed funds during each such period. This new rule conforms the deductibility of prepaid interest by a cash method taxpayer to the present rule for interest prepayments by an accrual method taxpayer. This rule applies to all cash method taxpayers including the individuals, corporations, estates and trusts, and covers interest paid for personal, business or investment purposes. This rule also applies to prepaid interest on an indebtedness secured by a "wraparound" mortgage.

NON-RECOURSE LOANS

Non-recourse loans are an important aspect of tax shelters. Initially, the tax basis of a partnership interest equals the cost to the investor. The basis is reduced by the limited partner's share of partnership distributions and losses, and increased by their share of partnership income. The tax basis may be increased by the limited partner's proportionate share of liabilities to which partnership assets are subject, but for which no partner in the partnership is liable (non-recourse loans). It is through non-recourse loans that deductions equal to or actually greater than investors' original investments are created.

11

The Revenue Act of 1978 puts further limits on tax shelters—except those involving real estate—by broadening the "at risk" rule adopted by Congress in 1976. That rule was intended to prevent tax shelter investors from taking deductions for losses that exceeded their actual investment or the money they had at risk. The new law, designed to end certain techniques which circumvented the 1976 rule, makes it clear that the restriction applies to all tax shelter activities except real estate.

The new statute also extends the restriction on tax shelter losses to all investors except widely held corporations. Now certain closely held corporations in which five or fewer individuals hold at least 50% of the stock will be subject to the same limitations on losses as individual taxpayers. The one exception applies to companies that obtain at least 50% of their gross receipts from equipment leasing.

CAPITAL GAINS

The 1978 Act increases the amount of any net capital gain which a non-corporate taxpayer may deduct from gross income from 50 to 60 percent. The remaining 40 percent of the net capital gain is includible in gross income and subject to tax at the regular rates. The deducted gain is classified as a tax preference item for alternative minimum tax purposes, but not for purposes of reducing the amount of personal service income which is eligible for the maximum tax.

TAXATION OF OIL PROGRAMS

The main features of Federal income taxation of oil and gas programs should also be summarized. They involve intangible drilling and development costs, dry hole costs, and depletion.

Intangible drilling and development costs are fully deductible as an expense in the year they are incurred. These costs include the costs for drilling, labor, fuel, supplies, and costs for other items which do not have salvage value and which are incurred in preparing wells for production. Intangible drilling and development costs are not treated as tax preference items for purposes of the minimum tax.

For productive wells, the costs of acquiring leases must be capitalized and recovered through the depletion deductions. However, if a lease is not productive and abandoned, the acquisition cost may be deducted in full in the year of abandonment. Geophysical costs are also capitalized for productive properties; but, if the property is deemed worthless, geophysical costs are deductible as ordinary losses.

Under the percentage depletion method, the deduction is 22% per year on the gross income from a particular property, to a maximum of 50% of the total taxable income from that property. Aggregate depletion deduction is not limited by the tax basis of the property; but, to the extent that it does exceed the investor's basis, it becomes an item of tax preference.

NET FARM LOSSES (EXCESS DEDUCTION ACCOUNT)

Investors in farm programs need to watch their net farm losses as they relate to the excess deduction account (EDA). If the taxpayer's adjusted gross income exceeds $50,000 and his net farm losses exceed $25,000, he must establish an EDA. Any excess in this account must be used to convert capital gains from the sale of farm assets to ordinary income. The EDA is increased by farm net losses and decreased by farm net income. When the property is sold, capital gains will be recaptured as ordinary income to the extent that there is any balance in the EDA at that time. No additions to an excess deductions account need be made for net farm losses sustained in any taxable year beginning after December 31, 1975.

MINIMUM TAX

Present law imposes a minimum tax on certain individual and corporate tax preferences. The minimum tax for individuals amounts to 15 percent of the sum of an individual's (or estate's or trust's) tax preferences in excess of one-half of regular income taxes paid or, if greater, $10,000.

The tax preference items included in this base of the minimum tax for individuals are:

(1) Accelerated depreciation on real property in excess of straight-line depreciation;

13

(2) Accelerated depreciation on leased personal property in excess of straight-line depreciation;

(3) Amortization of certified pollution control facilities (the excess of 60-month amortization (sec. 169) over depreciation otherwise allowable (sec. 167));

(4) Amortization of railroad rolling stock (the excess of 60-month amortization (sec. 184) over depreciation otherwise allowable (sec. 167));

(5) Qualified stock options (the excess of the fair market value at the time of exercise over the option price);

(6) Percentage depletion in excess of the adjusted basis of the property;

(7) The deduction for 50 percent of net long-term capital gains;

(8) Amortization of child care facilities (the excess of 60-month amortization (sec. 188) over depreciation otherwise allowable (sec. 167));

(9) Itemized deductions (other than medical and casualty loss deductions) in excess of 60 percent of adjusted gross income; and

(10) Intangible drilling costs on oil and gas or geothermal wells in excess of the amount amortizable with respect to those costs and, for 1977, in excess of net income from oil and gas or geothermal production.

The 1978 Act retains the present law minimum tax with respect to all preference items except capital gains and excess itemized deductions. The Act provides for an alternative minimum tax which is payable by an individual to the extent that the alternative tax exceeds the regular income tax increased by the amount of the existing minimum tax, as revised, on preference items other than capital gains and itemized deductions.

MAXIMUM TAX

Under present law, the highest marginal tax rate applicable to personal service income is 50 percent. However, the amount eligible for this maximum tax rate is reduced dollar-for-dollar by the individual's items of tax preference.

The 1978 Act removes capital gains as a tax preference which reduces the amount of personal service income eligible for the maximum tax rate.

INCOME AVERAGING

Income averaging will be available not only for earned income, but for capital gains, gambling wins, and income from gifts, where income for the current year exceeds the base period by 20% or more; but, if income averaging is used, the taxpayer cannot use the alternative capital gains rate or the earned income ceiling. Income averaging is an alternative which should be considered before recommending the use of tax-shelter products.

INVESTMENT TAX CREDIT

The investment tax credit is intended to encourage modernization of productive facilities by reducing their effective costs. It is also a tool used to stimulate the economy. The credit has been in existence (off and on) since 1962 and is applicable only to the acquisition of special types of property (Section 38 Property). Currently, the credit is equal to 10% of the cost of the new depreciable property, provided the property has a useful life of 7 or more years. If the useful life is less than 7 years, the cost of the property will be reduced before the 10% credit is applied. Property with a useful life of less than 3 years carries no credit. The maximum amount of investment tax credit from all sources available each taxable year to a cash basis taxpayer is $25,000 (or $12,500 in the case of a married person filing a separate return) of his liability for tax (excluding tax preferences and other special taxes) for that taxable year plus 50% of his liability, if any, for tax in excess of $25,000. It should be noted that the investment tax credit is specifically denied to individuals (but not to corporations) who lease equipment under the usual terms of equipment leasing deals.

TAX LAW CHANGES

It must be recognized that tax laws are constantly changing and that the laws discussed in this book are subject to modification.

SOURCES OF TAX–SHELTER PROGRAMS

An investor interested in tax shelters will find them offered through many people in the financial community such as life insurance men, securities salesmen, attorneys, accountants, syndicators, and salesmen for various private offerings.

SELECTION OF SPECIFIC PROGRAM OR PROGRAMS

Whether the offering is private or public, an analysis of the tax and financial position of the investor should be made by a competent advisor to determine whether the investor can benefit sufficiently from tax shelters. If it is decided that it is advantageous for the investor to purchase tax shelters, there should be another analysis to indicate which shelter or shelters are most appropriate and the schedule of purchase or purchases. The type or types of programs may depend to a large extent on the client's reaction to various approaches. For example, some clients have negative reactions toward oil and gas exploration programs, others would not consider cattle investments. Some clients may invest in the program which offers the highest initial tax deduction. The following will discuss briefly the deductibility and other considerations of the main types of tax-shelter programs. The deductibility percentages are only estimates and could vary widely by specific program, but this information may be helpful in constructing an investment plan which satisfies the investor's deductibility needs and utilizes the amounts available for investment.

Oil programs carry a high investment risk. An investor may wish to diversify by program, by drilling area, and by operator. The investor may wish to invest three years running to obtain adequate diversification.

Estimated deductibility — 90% first year

Real estate programs are attractive to many investors, but generally the deductibility amounts are substantially lower in the first year than with other programs. However, they are generally structured in such a way as they continue to produce deductions which can be used to offset income from other sources during the first five or six years.

Estimated deductibility —   50% first year
                                 25% second year
                                 22% third year
                                 20% fourth year
                                 18% fifth year
                                 15% sixth year
                                 10% seventh year

It is interesting to note that an investor who would commit to regular investments each year would after a few years receive a rather high percentage deduction on his regular annual investment. For example, an investor who had invested an equal amount during the past three years might realize a deductibility on this year's investment in excess of 100%. The reason would be that he would realize a 50% deduction on this year's investment, plus a 25% deduction carried forward from last year, plus a 22% deduction from two years ago, plus a 20% deduction from three years ago. This would total 117% of this year's investment amount. Thus, an investor might wish to phase into a tax-shelter investment plan which in the first couple of years would create deductions lower than what he actually needed but which would in later years be more adequate. Moreover, he might wish to combine a real estate program purchase with the purchase of a program which created a higher first year deduction.

Cattle feeding programs are used mainly for investors who wish to defer income tax consequences from one year to the next. Investing in this type of program for only one year does increase the investment risk in that the investor might select a year where cattle prices start high and end up low and thus lose a substantial amount of his investment. From the investment standpoint, it would be better for the investor to plan to invest in cattle feeding over three or four years.

Estimated deductibility: 100% first year

SOURCE OF PREMIUM DOLLARS OR OTHER INVESTMENTS

Tax-shelter investments can be a source of premium dollars for life insurance or other investments. This can come about either through future cash flow or tax savings.

When the investor invests in tax shelters, he is hopeful of a cash flow immediately or in the years ahead. Often the investor will be willing to transfer capital or pay out of income a life insurance premium or other investment amount for the first year or two if he can see a plan for continuing the program beyond this time. Tax shelters can provide the necessary future cash flow.

Some persons are willing to invest in tax shelters as a normal investment transaction while they are reluctant to invest in life insurance or other vehicles. The release of tax dollars by using tax shelters creates a source of dollars for the purchase of insurance or other investments in the following way:

Investment in tax shelter	$10,000
Release of tax dollars otherwise payable	$ 9,000
Tax deduction (assume 90%)	
50% bracket — tax savings available for life insurance premiums and other investments	$ 4,500

17

Some tax shelters such as raw land, improved real estate with quality leases, oil income, and cattle feeding on rising beef markets may be appropriate for investors in any tax bracket. However, other shelters such as real estate where property is to be constructed or is under construction, oil and gas exploration, tree crops, vineyards, cattle breeding, chickens, Scotch whisky, movies, and plays are clearly for high-tax-bracket investors or people with substantial estates who can afford the high risk. These will be discussed in great detail in the following chapters.

PART ONE

TAX SHELTERS AND TAX-FREE INCOME FOR INVESTORS

CHAPTER ONE

REAL ESTATE

Real estate investments have long been among the most attractive types of investments for income and long-term capital gain. Investors in all tax brackets may appropriately invest in real estate. With the introduction of accelerated depreciation and with the opportunities to borrow a significant portion of the total necessary capital, real estate investing became extremely popular for high-tax-bracket individuals since these ventures produced substantial tax losses which could be used to offset income from other sources in the early years and convert current income into capital gains when the property was sold. Investors have the following general objectives with respect to real estate investment: a source of income; a hedge against inflation; a vehicle offering diversification from investments in stocks and bonds; an opportunity to obtain substantial leverage through borrowing; and an investment with tax benefits.

ADVANTAGES OF GROUP OWNERSHIP

Group ownership of real estate properties offers many advantages to investors: Allows for investments in real estate without the management and record keeping responsibilities resting with the investor; allows the investor to participate in both small and large properties rather than just small properties as would be the case if he invested on his own; allows the investor to retain professional management which would probably not be possible if he were on his own; may allow for some diversification as to types and locations of properties; may provide for somewhat better marketability of his real estate investment interests; and may limit his potential risk to the amount of his investment commitment.

FORMS OF GROUP OWNERSHIP

Two of the basic forms of group ownership are real estate investment trusts and real estate limited partnerships. The basic concept of the real estate investment trusts (REIT) is for small investors to be able to participate in the economic advantages that real estate investments offer to large investors. REIT's permit pooling of capital without the disadvantages of double taxation in that REIT's are corporate entities specifically designed for this purpose. If the entity pays out 90% of its income to investors, there is no tax at the corporate level. Although untaxed income may be passed through directly to investors who pay tax on it, accounting losses in excess of income may not be passed through to investors. The only tax advantage of a REIT is the avoidance of double taxation. Shares of REIT's are generally readily marketable especially for those which are listed on national or regional stock exchanges. A REIT is, in effect, a closed-end investment company; and, therefore, the "price" is determined in the open market. The price of REIT shares may be above or below the actual value of the real estate holdings. There are many different types of REIT available. Some emphasize short-term obligations; some emphasize long-term obligations; others emphasize equity pariticipations; and there are those which try to attain a balance among these types.

With real estate limited partnerships, there is no double taxation if the partnership qualifies as such according to IRS Regulations, and accounting losses may offset taxes due on any income distributions and may also offset income from other sources. Limited partnership interests are often not readily marketable. Early liquidation of a real estate limited partnership could lead to serious tax problems. In establishing the "price" of a limited partnership interest, either the general partner or an independent appraiser will actually appraise the properties and allocate the worth of these properties among the limited partners based on their percentage of ownership.

OBJECTIVES OF REAL ESTATE LIMITED PARTNERSHIP

The three main objectives of real estate limited partnerships are to provide tax shelter, provide tax-free cash flow, and to convert ordinary income to capital gains.

A real estate investment can produce tax losses which can be used to offset ordinary income from other sources. The two main aspects of tax shelter in a real estate investment are depreciation and interest deductions. Some ventures will use accelerated depreciation and interest in order to produce substantial tax losses in the early years of the investment. An investor may be able to deduct tax losses over several years which far exceed his original investment in the program since mortgages (or non-recourse loans) may substantially increase the limited partners' tax basis in the investment, providing that these mortgages or loans do not provide for recourse to any individual investor or to the general partner, but are collectible only out of the value of the properties.

In the first several years of a real estate limited partnership, there may be distributable cash flow which can be offset by accounting losses and, therefore, can be distributed to investors on a tax-free basis. The positive cash flow results from the property being depreciated faster than the loan is being repaid. If this is accelerated depreciation, then the difference between deductible loss and positive cash flow can be very impressive in the early years. In later years, depreciation may be lower than the actual loan repayment, and there would be a taxable gain but negative cash flow. If the annual rentals could not be increased, the limited partners would have to pay taxes but would not receive any cash distributions from the limited partnership.

An illustration best shows how to convert ordinary income to capital gains. Assume an investor commited $10,000 to a real estate investment, held his interest for a number of years, and then sold it for $10,000. During that time, he was able to depreciate the property and receive tax deductions from depreciation totaling $6,000. He used the $6,000 of depreciation deductions to offset income from other sources. The tax results of this transaction would be as follows:

Sales Price	$10,000
Adjusted Tax Basis	4,000
Capital Gains	$ 6,000
Original Tax Basis	$10,000
Depreciation Deductions	6,000
Adjusted Tax Basis	$ 4,000

Only 40% of the gain is subject to regular tax rates of 14% to 70%.

The $6,000 of deductions would result in $3,000 of actual tax savings for the 50% tax bracket individual. Assuming he had to pay only 25% on the $6,000 of capital gains, instead of 50% if this were current income, he would save $1,500 of taxes.

If the real estate investment were depreciated on an accelerated basis, and if the property were not held for the proper period of time, there could be some recapture of accelerated depreciation to the extent that it exceeded straight-line depreciation. For example, if $2,000 of the total $6,000 of depreciation were accelerated depreciation, then this $2,000 would be taxable as current income – leaving only $4,000 to be taxed as capital gains.

TYPES OF REAL ESTATE LIMITED PARTNERSHIPS

Two of the main differentiations of program types for real estate limited partnerships are the single property vs. "fund" approach and specified property vs. unspecified property.

There are many limited partnership programs which will invest in only one specific property. These are usually small offerings and often limited to investors from one state. If the program is successful, the investor may have a substantial interest in a highly successful project. If the project were unsuccessful, the investors would lose. Investors could obtain some diversification by investing in several single property limited partnerships, but this would probably require a substantial investment.

The "fund" approach may provide more diversification both by type of property and by location of property. If a large limited partnership invested equally in apartments, mobile home parks, and commercial buildings, and the market dropped for one of these types, an investor might still receive an adequate return. If a large limited partnership had properties throughout the United States, a natural disaster or economic depression in one geographical area might not result in the entire program being unsuccessful.

Other diversification factors would include the size of the property, the types of tenants, whether the property is in the suburbs or the city, age of the property, the range of rental prices, and lease or nonlease operating arrangements.

The "fund" approach could reduce the down-side risk but might also limit the up-side potential. Hopefully, there would be greater efficiency and economy because of the size of the operation.

Some limited partnership offerings show a complete list of the properties which will be included in the partnership in their initial prospectus or offering circular. The advantage of the specified property type of program is that the investor or his advisors can analyze the property before an investment is made. Other limited partnership programs, the unspecified property types (or "blind-pool" or "blank-check" programs), will not describe specific properties but describe in general terms the types of properties which the limited partnerships will buy. This is advantageious to the general partner in that he need not commit to any investments until he knows how many program interests will be sold, and, therefore, how much property he has to buy. It is a disadvantage to the investor because he and his advisors cannot analyze specific properties.

Many limited partnership programs, usually the larger ones, will be partially specified property and partially blind-pool. This permits the investor and his advisors to look at some specific properties and also gives the general partner the flexibility he desires. The risk is that the specified properties will be acceptable investments, but that later the general partner will purchase properties of lesser quality.

PROGRAM STRUCTURE

The overall program structure of a real estate limited partnership involves such facets as the sponsor, forms, offering amounts, payments, assessments, liquidity, cost and revenue sharing arrangements, and other expenses.

The "sponsor" or general partner of a real estate limited partnership is generally a subsidiary of a real estate brokerage firm. The firm may specialize in buying and selling income-producing real estate or may be more widely diversified. Some have subsidiaries which are real estate developers or in property management, leasing, investment counseling, furniture rental, etc. The general partner should be an experienced real estate investment firm with a substantial net worth. If the firm has many subsidiaries offering various types of real estate related services, there could be serious conflicts of interest. For example, if the firm has a subsidiary which supplies electrical equipment for apartment buildings and commercial buildings, and if the limited partnership buys electrical equipment from this entity, there is the risk that the general partner is receiving above-market markups on the electrical equipment.

The investor's interest is in the limited partnership; and, therefore, it is advantageous to the investor if the sponsor has requested a ruling from the IRS that the entity will be treated as a limited partnership for tax purposes and not an association or corporation.

Programs come in a wide range of sizes — from very small offerings (generally single property partnerships) to large offerings involving $20 million or more. It is critical that the general partner has the ability to invest large sums of investment dollars. Since these programs are highly leveraged, a $20 million offering might require the general partner to purchase real estate properties worth $80 million or more. A firm unaccustomed to dealing with such large sums of money might have difficulty properly investing it.

Minimum subscriptions are usually $5,000 to $10,000 with some lower and some higher. Programs with very small minimums usually have higher expenses such as record-keeping and may not be structured to maximize tax leverage since small investors are being sought.

The assessability feature varies by program, and many programs provide for no assessability. As is true with all programs in the field of tax shelters, assessability in a real estate limited partnership is not necessarily an adverse feature. This would be particularly true if the program included properties which were in the development stage since cost overruns may occur. Costs may be higher than anticipated, but potential revenues may also be higher in which case it might be in the best interests of the limited partners to contribute more cash themselves rather than borrowing at what may be unattractive terms. The need for assessments might also arise during the rent-up phase since expenses may be considerably higher than revenues in that period of time.

Liquidity (or marketability) in real estate limited partnerships is not readily available in many programs. The general partner may offer to repurchase units from limited partners who wish to liquidate, but usually there is a penalty for early liquidation. Moreover, the investor may experience adverse tax consequences on early liquidation. If the units were readily redeemable, the limited partnership might have a tax problem in that free transferability of interests is generally considered a corporate characteristic by the IRS. Furthermore, free transferability could also have a negative effect on the overall investment since properties might have to be sold at the wrong time. Some securities brokerage firms have offered to make a market in partnership interests, and it remains to be seen how well they will perform. It can be a complex calculation to determine the fair market value of a unit in that both the underlying value of the property and unused tax benefits are taken into consideration.

Usually, the general partner does not make a direct equity investment in the program. Sometimes, officers and directors of the general partner will purchase limited partnership units for their own accounts and participate in costs and revenues in the same way as any of the other limited partners. There are many methods of compensating general partners, but the three main approaches are as follows:

1. Markup on sales of real estate properties.

Some general partners will purchase the properties themselves and resell them to the limited partnership. In this way, they may generate substantial profits for themselves from the markups on the properties.

2. Brokerage commissions.

Usually, a subsidiary of the general partner will receive brokerage fees both on the purchase and sale of properties for the limited partnership. These fees may range from 4% to 10% and will ordinarily be a percentage of the total purchase price of the property, not just the total equity. In most cases, the seller pays the brokerage fee; but, of course, this is included in establishing the selling price and, therefore, ultimately the limited partners pay this fee when they buy the specific properties. Brokerage fees can be substantial. For example, assume a $20 million real estate limited partnership and assume average brokerage fees of 5%. This $20 million of equity would probably be leveraged to about $80 million of property; and, thus, the general partner would earn $4 million when the properties were purchased for the limited partnership. If the properties could be sold for similar amounts, the general partner would receive another $4 million. The general partner would receive these fees whether or not the venture were successful. Moreover, the general partner might sell and buy properties before the liquidation of the limited partnership, and thus by "churning" the properties, earn more commissions. This would seem to be satisfactory if the general partner at all times acted in the best interests of the limited partners and the fees were commensurate with the value of the services.

3. A share of revenues or profits.

Most limited partnership programs will include the general partner for a certain percentage of revenues from the real estate investments and/or a percentage of profits upon sale of the properties. Sometimes, these sharing arrangements are subordinated to the limited partners receiving a certain percentage return or a certain percentage profit on the sale of the properties. However, defining "return" and "profits" can be a complicated process. A slight difference in the wording of these definitions can result in substantial differences in what the general partner and limited partners ultimately receive in money. A sharing arrangement is important if the general partner is to have an incentive to perform well.

Other expenses include such items as sales commissions to securities dealers, offering costs (filing prospectuses, legal work, blue-sky filings with states, etc.), administrative overhead, management fees, etc. Some general partners pay all of these expenses; others pay none; and still others pay certain expenses and expect the limited partners to pay the balance.

One of the biggest risks in real estate limited partnerships is the risk of paying too much for the property. Under the first two compensation arrangements discussed above, markups on properties and real estate brokerage fees, the general partner or sponsor has an incentive to pay too much for the property. The more the limited partnership pays, the more the sponsor receives. This is a conflict off interest which government authorities are seeking to eliminate.

TYPES OF REAL ESTATE PROPERTIES

There are various types of properties which might be included in a real estate limited partnership. Those which will be discussed are as follows: raw land (unimproved real estate); residential properties such as apartments; Federally subsidized (low and moderate-income) housing; mobile home parks; and also commercial properties.

RAW LAND (UNIMPROVED REAL ESTATE)

Real estate usually experiences four main cycles. First is the undeveloped stage in which real estate is in its crudest form. Second is pre-developed real estate which is close to population centers and will probably have use in the near future. It is between this stage and the next stage where there is the greatest opportunity for increases in value. Third is developed real estate which is being used with buildings and other improvements being added and the property producing income for its owners. Fourth is redeveloped real estate where investors either change the use of existing income-producing real estate or improve the buildings, etc. in order to increase rental income.

Raw land investment involves a certain amount of risk in that the investor must decide if the land is in its undeveloped cycle or in its pre-developed cycle. If it is in the pre-developed cycle, he could receive large gains on his investment.

Raw land does not have much tax leverage. Interest can only include the number of months left in the current year. The only other deductions are property taxes, management fees and certain other expenses.

RESIDENTIAL PROPERTIES

Because of present and predicted future housing shortages, the 1969 Tax Reform Act stressed real estate tax advantages by providing favorable treatment for residential property development, particularly government subsidized or low-income housing.

Regular residential property kept some of the favorable tax aspects. Accelerated depreciation, including 200% of straight-line or sum-of-the-year's digits, can be used on new residential buildings. Used residential buildings may be depreciated at 125% of straight-line. The investor must be the "first user" to qualify for the accelerated depreciation allowances and 80% of gross rents must be received from residential use in order for the project to be called "residential property." The depreciation recapture aspects for regular apartment projects are not as favorable as those for low-income projects. After the property has been held for 100 months, the investor may reduce the amount of accelerated depreciation subject to recapture by 1% per month so that after 200 months

(16 years and 8 months), there is no recapture of accelerated depreciation. Post-1975 depreciation in excess of straight-line is recaptured.

FEDERALLY SUBSIDIZED (OR LOW AND MODERATE–INCOME) HOUSING

The National Housing Act of 1968 and the Tax Reform Act of 1969 combined to create interest in federally subsidized housing as a tax-shelter investment.

Millions of low or moderate-income American families cannot afford standard housing. Low or moderate-income households are generally defined as those who would have to pay more than 20% to 25% of their income for regular unsubsidized housing. The National Housing Act provided certain incentives for building and owning low or moderate-income housing and also in rehabilitating existing low-income housing. Subsidies included the availability of federally insured mortgages and direct interest or rent subsidies for qualified owners and qualified tenants.

The 1969 Reform Act permitted the continuation of 200% accelerated depreciation on new or rehabilitated low-income housing. Moreover, the Act provided more favorable recapture provisions so that the owner could reduce the amount of depreciation subject to recapture by 1% per month after 20 months with no recapture if the property were held for 10 years. This was changed by the 1976 reform act.

There are some definite advantages of participating in a limited partnership which owns low or moderate-income housing. Because of federal subsidies the housing can be rented at rates up to 30% to 40% lower than the general rental market. This can help reduce vacancies. Furthermore, the investor receives substantial tax deductions through accelerated depreciation and the availability of high leveraging (because of the availability of federally insured mortgages). Some low-income programs are projected to return the investor's initial investment in tax savings alone in the first three to four years.

There are also some disadvantages. Low-income projects may result in more rapid actual depreciation in the value of the property than with regular residential housing, and ongoing expenses may be higher. Rents may be considerably more expensive to collect, and maintenance expenses, because of vandalism and crime, may be much higher. The government restricts the amount of cash distributions to owners of such projects, and all rent increases must be approved by HUD which may delay the increase for some time. Good property management may be more difficult to obtain for these types of projects. And there are substantial tax risks involved because of high leveraging and accelerated depreciation.

Usually, these projects are initially developed by private developers who find the land, get it zoned, design the buildings, arrange for sewers and utilities, apply for FHA mortgage insurance and subsidies, arrange financing, and organize the construction of the buildings. If the plans are approved, the FHA will insure the construction mortgage up to 90% of the estimated land, construction, and development costs.

The developer then attempts to sell the project, possibly to a limited partnership. Generally, the developer will sell the project to the limited partnership at full value of the property and receive a 10% free interest in the project. The limited partnership pays 100% for the property and receives a 90% interest. The limited partnership then applies for a 40-year federally insured mortgage covering 90% of the FHA certified costs. The limited partnership can receive no more than a 6% return on its stated equity which is defined as the difference between the FHA determined replacement cost and the amount of the FHA mortgage – which is generally less than the actual cash equity investment. The return may be no greater than 6% and would generally be less than that.

NATIONAL HOUSING ACT–SPECIFIC SECTIONS

Section 236 (interest subsidies) provides for a federally insured 40 year-mortgage of up to 90% of the project cost as determined according to FHA Regulations. The owners may be a profit-making entity, but they must also be a "limited dividend" entity in that their return may not be more than 6%. Also, the government would agree to pay the lending institution on a monthly basis the difference between the principal and interest at market rates (7½ or 8½ or as determined by HUD), and the principal and interest at an interest rate of 1%. Qualified residents would pay the larger of either 25% of their monthly income or a basic rental charge as determined assuming the 1% interest rate mortgage.

Section 221(d)3 (Rental subsidies) mortgages are federally insured, but interest rates are not subsidized. Owners must be "limited dividend" entities; tenants must have income and assets within FHA limits; and, tenants must include the elderly, handicapped, persons displaced by government action or natural disasters, or persons currently residing in substandard housing. Residents would pay 25% of their income toward the rent and the government would pay the owner the difference between the actual market rent levels and the tenant's contributions (but no more than 70% per unit rent).

There are several other subsidized programs. Section 221(d)4 provides mortgage insurance for multi-family housing for moderate income, elderly and displaced persons. Section 202 applies only to Housing for the Elderly. There are also local Public Housing Authority subsidy programs. Under Section 236, federal subsidies are provided for rehabilitation projects. Rehabilitation would include renovation of floors, wiring, plumbing, air conditioning, elevators, etc.

MOBILE HOME PARKS

Mobile home parks are currently an interesting investment which includes certain tax advantages. Mobile homes seem to appeal to families who do not want to live in apartments and cannot afford regular homes. Because of the increased size of these homes, they are far less "mobile" than they were once.; and, therefore, an owner usually sells his home when he moves instead of hauling it to his new location.

There are three main advantages of investments in mobile home parks:

1. Mobile home parks can produce a high cash flow and can maximize the benefits of leverage. Investors purchase the land and improvements such as the recreational facilities, utilities, "pads," swimming pools, streets, etc. The investors do not own the mobile homes; they merely rent the pads.

2. Although mobile home park investors may not depreciate their property at 200% accelerated depreciation as owners of new residential properties are permitted to do, the depreciable portion of the mobile home park owner's investment has a much shorter economic life than do apartments. For example, IRS guidelines provide for new apartment houses to be depreciated over 40 years and new office buildings over 50 years. The average length of the depreciation schedule for mobile home parks is between 12 and 20 years. Therefore,

annual depreciation deductions on mobile home parks may compare favorably to annual depreciation deductions on new apartment buildings. Moreover, there is no recapture of depreciation since mobile home parks are not depreciated on an accelerated basis.

3. While owning an apartment usually involves owning a small piece of land, mobile home parks often contain a large area of land. In future years the value of the land could increase considerably in value and perhaps be changed in usage to the benefit of the investors.

Mobile home parks also have some disadvantages. Zoning regulations with respect to them are usually very strict, and often it is difficult to find a suitable location.

COMMERCIAL PROPERTIES

Commercial properties such as office buildings, shopping centers, industrial properties, hotels, and theaters do not offer as favorable tax treatment as do residential properties. New non-residential buildings may be depreciated on an accelerated basis at 150% of straight-line. Used non-residential buildings may be depreciated at straight-line only. Any accelerated depreciation taken on commercial properties is subject to full recapture regardless of how long the property is owned. However, commercial properties are sometimes included in tax-shelter programs primarily for diversification purposes.

EVALUATION OF REAL ESTATE LIMITED PARTNERSHIPS

A tax-shelter specialist would evaluate a proposed real estate limited partnership program by checking on the experience, reputation, and ability of the general partner, examining projections both on the current program and on prior programs to determine whether the underlying figures and assumptions are reasonable, possibly visiting actual properties, and studying potential conflicts of interest.

The quality of the management is the most important facet of the evaluation. The manager (a sponsor) has the following duties and responsibilities with respect to the limited partnership: Selection of properties; negotiation of acquisitions; structuring the terms; arranging the financing; renting units (or hiring good property managers); reporting to limited partners on both the tax and investment aspects; and planning the sale of properties (timing, sales price and terms).

Unless the program manager has the capabilities of handling all of these responsibilities well, the program could easily fail regardless of how good the structure of the program might be.

The basic underlying assumptions on real estate projections are as follows: Rental amounts – are they reasonable compared with local market conditions?; turn-over rates – high turn-over results in higher expenses even if rental amounts are competitive; vacancy rates – run a "break-even" analysis showing what the vacancy rate could be and still leave enough income to pay debt service and expenses; expenses – they can run as high as 40-50% of gross rental revenues. It would be wise to compare projections on past real estate deals with actual operating results to determine how effective the manager is in projecting future results.

Every program will have certain conflicts of interest. It is important to know how the manager intends to handle possible conflicts. A determination should be made as to whether steps have been taken to reduce the opportunities for management to take advantage of their position and how important the conflicts might be with respect to their effects on future returns to investors. A particularly dangerous situation is where a real estate program buys properties from other programs managed by the same sponsor.

TAX RISKS IN REAL ESTATE PROGRAMS

The main tax risks in real estate investments involve tax law changes, accelerated depreciation and non-recourse loans, and prepaid interest and material distortion.

Tax benefits from real estate investments occur over a number of years and are susceptible to tax law changes. Depreciation, accelerated depreciation, and investment interest are areas of emphasis for tax reform.

The combination of accelerated depreciation and non-recourse loans can lead to adverse tax consequences in future years if the investment projections are not fulfilled. Mortgages do, under current regulations, increase the tax bases of individual limited partners, and they therefore increase the amount of property assets which can be depreciated on an accelerated basis, but premature sale or forfeiture of properties can result in large amounts of depreciation recapture which is taxable to the investor.

The 1976 Tax Reform Act requires a cash method taxpayer to deduct prepaid interest over the period of the loan to the extent that the interest represents the cost of using the borrowed funds during each such period. This new rule conforms the deductibility of prepaid interest by a cash method taxpayer to the present rule for interest prepayments by an accrual method taxpayer. This rule applies to all cash method taxpayers including individuals, corporations, estates and trusts, and covers interest paid for personal, business or investment purposes. This rule also applies to prepaid interest on an indebtedness secured by a "wraparound" mortgage.

INVESTMENT RISKS

Real estate limited partnership investments are subject to all the regular risks of real estate investments such as over-building, severe unemployment, high interest rates, unavailability of mortgage money, increased expenses, competition, natural disasters, etc. In addition, there are four main types of risks which should be considered in connection with these types of investments, namely, inflated purchase price, completion (or development) risk, rent-up risks, and operating risks.

There are many pressures driving up the purchase price of properties going into limited partnerships. If a public developer is selling, he is most interested in a large book profit. If the sponsor is selling his own property to the limited partnership, an important part of his compensation could be the profit he makes on the sale. If the sponsor receives real estate commissions, the higher are his commissions. Some sponsors will tell investors that paying too much is actually to the investors' benefit, since they will have more to depreciate. However, most deals will state that a property will not be purchased for more than its appraised value. The best insurance for an honest appraisal is to deal with a quality sponsor which has sound projections which would result in a return commensurate with investment risk.

If the partnership buys an incomplete project, or develops its own projects, there is the risk of substantial cost over-runs. Labor costs may increase; costs of material may increase; unforeseen delays may occur. Extra costs of completion may very well make the whole project uneconomic in that the rentals might not be able to be increased because of competitive reasons, and therefore would not support expenses and debt service. Some sponsors who buy projects under construction will pay a higher cost for the property but have the developer bear the completion risk.

There are uncertainties as to the timing of achieving rental goals both for the amount of rent per unit and the number of units rented. Some sponsors will pay more for the property and require the developer to assume the rent-up risks.

Once the project has rented-up, risks continue. Property taxes may increase; the rate of lease renewals may decrease; operating expenses (replaced fixtures, etc.) may increase. Some sponsors will make arrangements with developer/property managers to subordinate the annual management fee to other expenses plus possibly a certain return to the partnership, waive or defer lease payments if the developer/manager has a net lease arrangement, or include incentives for the developer/manager to try attaining high profitability by paying him a certain percentage of revenues which are in excess of a certain basic return to the partnership.

This introduction to real estate will provide a background against which specific real estate programs can be examined in the material which follows.

PREFACE TO EXAMPLES

Real estate, as has already been stated, is an investment in which people in all tax brackets can benefit. Those in low brackets can purchase by themselves or acquire from others partnership interests in unimproved real estate with the possibility of capital gain on resale. They can do the same with existing, improved real estate where risk is low and benefit from tax-free income which is generally higher than available elsewhere, equity growth as a mortgage is paid off, and appreciation in land and building values. Some offerings provide a market for resale or have an arrangement to repurchase from the investor should he desire to sell his interest.

There are two broad categories of real estate investment: Privately financed programs, and Federally assisted programs. Private deals usually fall into two areas: Unimproved real estate, also known as raw land, and improved real estate on which structures are built such as homes, apartment houses, office buildings, and factories.

Section 1 of this chapter describes a privately financed raw land offering which is usually a medium-risk tax shelter. Section 2 discusses a privately financed improved real estate offering of existing property such as shopping centers and apartment houses which have been built for a few years and where the investor seeks current income, equity build-up and future capital gains as opposed to a high first-year tax write-off as available on new construction. The second part of Section 2 deals with new construction which has tax advantages not available to existing buildings such as highly accelerated depreciation, certain management fees, loan fees, certain legal fees, and start-up costs. Both existing improved real estate and new construction are considered low-risk tax shelters. Section 3 discusses federally assisted offerings in new low-income housing and rehabilitation projects. These are categorized as high-risk tax shelters.

SECTION ONE

UNIMPROVED REAL ESTATE (RAW LAND)

Raw land is valuable in that it is of finite quantity. If it is located in a new community where there is a good pattern of growth, land should have good potential to increase in value because the community is at the start of a rise and not in the middle or near the top. As population increases, the value of land generally increases.

There is an opportunity for a large capital gain upon the resale of land, but there is also the risk of heavy loss if selection has been poor. It is imperative that the investor seek the advice of an expert in the area of unimproved property investment. His fee would be money well spent.

EXAMPLE OF A PRIVATELY FINANCED RAW LAND INVESTMENT

This is a program in which the investor is interested in long-term capital gain. Write-offs such as interest and taxes are not the major emphasis in this tax shelter. Depreciation is not available on raw land; and, even after it is developed, only the improvements can be depreciated.

54-40 ASSOCIATES

INTRODUCTION TO EXAMPLE

The Managing Partners of the General Partnership will be Able and Baker, herein referred to as the "Managing Partners." It is proposed that individual investors acquire interests in the General Partnership in Fifteen (15) units of Twenty-two Thousand ($22,000.00) Dollars each. In addition, the Managing Partners shall acquire Two (2) investment units of Twenty-two Thousand ($22,000.00) Dollars each, for a total capital contribution of Three Hundred Seventy-four Thousand ($374,000.00) Dollars.

This offering of General Partnership interests is being made on a private basis, and not to the public, to investors who intend to hold such interest for investment, and who have no present intent of selling or otherwise disposing of such interests.

The Managing Partners will receive their profits from the resale of the property to the General Partnership. Upon the execution of the General Partnership Agreement by all the Partners, the Managing Partners shall execute on behalf of the General Partnership the proposed Land Contract between the General Partnership and Managing Partners who are the first Land Contract vendees, which shall provide for the purchase by the General Partnership for a second Land Contract interest in the property.

The name of the Partnership is suggested by its location, being at the interchange of Highway 54 and Highway 40. The subject site is divided by Highway 40 with approximately 100 acres east of the Expressway and 126 acres to the west. Since each parcel has distinct development possibilities, a unique feature has been created in the form of diversification within one investment.

Cities will exert growth pressures as they converge on the site. The area has already sampled this pressure as numberous service stations and a motel are found in the immediate vicinity.

TYPICAL ZONING INFORMATION

Approximately 12 acres are zoned Highway Commercial at the intersection of Highway 54 and Highway 40. This zoning classification allows high end use development such as service stations and motels. The remaining portion of the 100 acre parcel east of Highway 40 is zoned Wholesale and Warehousing district. The Master Plan for Anyfield Township shows a split of the 100 acres between Highway Commercial and General Commercial zoning. The 126 acres west of Highway 40 is currently zoned Agricultural. Preliminary discussions with Anyfield Township officials indicate Multiple zoning would be looked upon favorably. An immediate change in zoning is not practical since the area is not yet ripe for development. The Managing Partners will decide at what point to initiate a rezoning request.

STATEMENT OF RISK FACTORS

This Memorandum is based upon assumptions concerning the

continuing advantages of certain provisions of the Federal Income Tax laws, and the management capabilities of the Managing Partners.

If as a result of some change in circumstances, an investor wishing to transfer his interest may find no immediate market for such interest.

Prospective investors should also recognize the speculative nature of, and risk factors involved in the purchase of unimproved real estate.

SYNDICATION DATA

Purchase Price of 100 Acres	
@ $12,636.96 Per Acre	$1,263,696.00
Down Payment	337,696.00
Land Contract Balance	$ 926,000.00

DETAILS OF LAND CONTRACT PARTICULARS

1. Interest Rate: 7½%
2. Term: Fifteen years to pay balance
3. Payments:
   a. Seminannual with first payment due October, of the first year.
   b. The first six seminannual payments at $34,725 each are interest only and therefore entirely tax deductible.
   c. Thereafter the semiannual payments total $48,642.78 each. A portion of these payments will be deductible as interest.
   d. After the first three years of interest only, the payment schedule is based on a seventeen year amortization with the final payment due in twelve years. Therefore, the final payment of $447,859.90 will be substantially larger than the previous payments.
4. The exact acreage will be determined by a survey. The purchase price will be adjusted to conform to any changes in acreage resulting from the survey.
5. Investors will have no personal financial liability under the Land Contract, other than amounts paid there against.
6. Liberal release clauses in the Land Contract allow for obtaining deed to portions of the property prior to full

payment of the Land Contract balance. This feature gives us the flexibility to sell specific parcels at any time and give a deed thereto to the purchaser.

STATEMENT OF CASH REQUIREMENTS

1. To acquire Equity
   Down Payment $337,696
   Working Fund 36,304
   Total Initial Capital $374,000
   To be made Available in Units of $22,000.00 Each

The Managing Partners are acquiring two investment units of $22,000.00 each.

2. To Finance Land Contract
Each investor would be required to contribute to the Semiannual Land Contract payments:
   Per $22,000.00 Invested
   Semiannual Payments 1 thru 6 (Interest only) $2,042.64
   Semiannual Payments 7 thru 29 . . . . $2,861.34
   Final Payment due 15th year $26,344.70

The interest portion of each year's payments would be immediately deductible. Of course, these payments could be abated or eliminated by the sale of portions of the property.
3. Working Fund
The Working Fund will be used to cover closing costs, and to meet current operating expenses, such as taxes, insurance, land planning, zoning and management fees. The fund has been projected to last between two and three years. Should this fund become depleted, investors would be required to contribute pro rata to restore it to an adequate operating level.

MANAGEMENT STATEMENT

The parcel will be managed by CHARLIE, INC., pursuant to a Management Agreement which provides for a management fee of Four Hundred ($400.00) Dollars per month, for the following services:

1. Provide office functions, including secretarial, telephone,

banking, bill paying, etc.

2. Provide administration prior to sale of property.

3. Provide financial and tax advice on routine matters, as they arise.

4. Prepare periodic interim financial statements.

5. Be directly involved in activities leading to enrichment of overall investment; including but not limited to, preparing the property for resale, all or in part.

6. Other routine matters normally handled by a property management company.

The shareholders of the management corporation are the Managing Partners of the General Partnership. CHARLIE, INC., is engaged in similar management functions for over Forty (40) other Partnerships, in which the General Partners have a financial interest.

TYPICAL DISCLAIMER

CHARLIE, INC., and the Managing Partners of the General Parnership do not intend to assume a fiduciary role as an investment consultant. Sections of this offering are not and should not be taken as legal or tax advice. The decision to become an investor must be a personal one. May we recommend that you contact your attorney and/or tax counsel for their advice regarding your specific situation.

RESALE COMMENTS

CHARLIE, INC., will proceed with a land plan and rezoning when deemed necessary by the Managing Partners. Thereafter, it will test the market periodically to determine the optimum time to sell, all or in part.

It will make no attempt herein to project specific returns on this venture. However, the items referred to in the "Introduction" are all major plus factors that should combine to make this venture quite profitable for all.

RESALE BROKERAGE

An affiliate of the Managing Partners is a licensed real estate broker in Anyfield Township, and, as such, may share in resale brokerage fees. As is customary, a brokerage fee of Ten (10%) percent of the selling price is to be anticipated.

BENEFITS OF A RAW LAND INVESTMENT

1. Taxes, interest (including financing points), and carrying charges are deductible. This can have the effect of converting pretax income to potential capital gains. However, interest costs may be large enough to be either a tax preference item or subject to the interest limitation rules.

2. Land can be exchanged tax-free for other land or improved real estate.

3. Land held for investment can usually be sold on a capital gain basis.

RISKS OF A RAW LAND INVESTMENT

1. The purchase may be a long term investment in which the carrying cost may prove to be a serious cash drain.

2. There may be no present public market for such interest so that the investor may not be able to liquidate his interest in the event of emergency.

3. Transferability may be limited so that in the event of a disposition, the investor could sustain a substantial loss.

4. The investor may have paid too much for the land.

5. The land may have physical or legal problems which drastically limit potential profit.

TAX ASPECTS OF A RAW LAND INVESTMENT

1. Land is never subject to an allowance for depreciation.

2. The costs of clearing land, grading, planting, and landscaping are not generally depreciable since they are part of the cost of land.

3. If taxpayer is a dealer in real estate, gains from the sale of land held for sale to customers will be treated as ordinary income. However, certain land held in his investment account or held for use in his business may qualify for capital gains treatment. If he is not a dealer, a casual sale of land will usually qualify for capital gains treatment. If he is not a dealer and subdivides land into lots or parcels for sale, special rules apply.

Raw land is a medium-risk tax shelter in which large profits are possible. But, if the location of the land is poor or if the timing of the purchase by the investor is imprudent, loss can result. The wise investor would seek the advice of an experienced real estate man in the geographical area of the proposed purchase. For best investment results, one should consider a number of geographical locations with prime growth potential and might consider investing in a number of these areas for diversification purposes.

SECTION TWO

IMPROVED REAL ESTATE

Improved real estate is usually a safer investment than raw land. Ordinarily it is income producing. It is customarily easier to obtain mortgage financing and higher financing on it in many localities. Moreover, it usually has greater resale possibilities. Often it can be a good estate asset to leave a surviving spouse who has need for income.

GENERAL CONSIDERATIONS

There are two general approaches to investments in improved real estate. One emphasizes existing income producing properties and has objectives of profit through current income or long term capital appreciation and secondarily, tax shelter. This method is appropriate for people in all tax brackets. The other stresses the acquisition of properties which are expected to be income producing and has objectives of (1) current tax-sheltered cash distributions, (2) excess tax losses applicable against income from other sources in the early years of operations, and (3) capital appreciation. The latter is generally suited only to persons in the higher income tax brackets.

EXAMPLE OF AN EXISTING, IMPROVED REAL ESTATE PROGRAM

Existing rental real estate sometimes avoids three major risks of new projects, namely, cost over-runs in the development of the property, renting of the space, and unproven management. If these risks are avoided because the project is completely built, leased, and operated by good management, then the investment may be appropriate for most taxpayers. Such a project is described as follows:

In this example, units in a limited partnership, called Frank Real Estate Fund, Ltd., will be sold to raise capital to engage in the business of investing in real estate. The General Partners are Estes Real Estate, Inc. and two of its officers as

43

individual General Partners (the "Special Partners"). A minimum of 90% of such investments will be in income producing improved real property and the remainder in unimproved real property acquired for investment or development into income producing property. A secondary objective of the Partnership is to provide tax shelter for Participants within the investment.

The limited partnership will consist of the General Partner, one or more Special Partners, and one or more limited partners called "Participants". The General Partner will be responsible for the investment policies and direction of the Partnership. Neither Special Partners nor Limited Partners will participate in the management of the Partnership.

The Partnership will pay 100% of the acquisition and management expenditures for investigating, purchasing, and managing real estate. The General Partner is to receive an investment management fee and performance incentive fee.

Most investments will be in office buildings, shopping centers, industrial buildings, and apartments.

Suppose an investor purchased a $5,000 Unit in the limited partnership which then invested in real estate. Assume the partnership purchased a 600 Unit luxury apartment house for $10,000,000. The investor's share might be $18,000 of which his investment (less commissions) is equity and the remainder is mortgaged.

What might one Unit be worth over a ten year period? Some assumptions, per Unit, must be made. (The assumptions used are not intended as a projection, but only to be illustrative. This example, in addition, is highly simplified. Results obtained in an investment could be better or worse than those shown. An additional assumption is that the investor does not have "Tax Preference Income" in excess of the greater of $10,000 or one-half of regular income taxes. In addition, investors should consult their advisers with specific reference to their own tax situation and potential changes in the applicable law.

1. Capital appreciation.

Assume that the value of the property increases by 5% per year or $900 per year - less than recent rates of inflation. At the end of ten years, the investor's share of the property would be worth $27,000.

2. Current income.

Assume that the property produces a cash flow return to the

investor (after all costs and mortgage payments) of 7% per year on his investment or $350 per year distributed to the investor. In addition, for simplicity and to be conservative assume that rentals don't increase at all, so return doesn't increase. (If rents go up, return could increase dramatically. Of course, if rents go down, return would decrease.)

3. Amortization of mortgage.

In addition, the mortgage on the property is being paid, which increases equity in the property. Mortgage payments might be $1,260 per year (per unit) of which, over a ten year period, an average of $280.00 would be equity payments and the remainder interest (which is tax deductible). (Assuming an original 30 year mortgage at 8% interest, and that the apartment is five years old at date of purchase.)

4. Tax shelter.

Assume that the partnership wants to be conservative. It, therefore, uses a 30 year life for tax purposes (although the building might be five years old at time of purchase) and uses straight line depreciation rather than accelerated depreciation. In addition, assume that 10% of the cost, or $1,800, is the cost of the land, which cannot be depreciated. 1/30 of $16,200 can, therefore, be deducted from income each year for Federal Tax Purposes as a depreciation allowance. This is $540 per year.

Using these simplified assumptions, the ten year results would be:

Initial Investment	$ 5,000.00	
Value of Property Purchased	18,000.00	
Initial Equity (Investment less commissions)		$ 4,575.00
Increase in Value of Property – 5% per year		9,000.00
Cash Flow Return Received – 7% per year		3,500.00
Increase in Equity through Mortgage Payments		2,800.00
Total 10 year value of a $5,000 Investment		$19,875.00

In addition, during the ten year period, the investor has been able to take a depreciation allowance which has "tax sheltered" the majority of the income received - 7% per year cash flow return plus the increase in equity through mortgage payments. Because of the depreciation allowance, the partnership may be reporting a loss. The investor's cash flow return, in that case, is considered a nontaxable return of capital (up to his investment). (Even if the partnership reports a small profit, any cash flow return in excess of the profit is considered a nontaxable return of capital.) It decreases the "tax basis" of his units. Upon sale, gain over the tax basis is taxable at capital gains rates.

A $5,000 tax write off, over ten years,

Saves Income Taxes Of:	Bringing The Total 10 Year Value To:
30% Tax Bracket — $1,500	$21,375.00
40% Tax Bracket — 2,000	21,875.00
50% Tax Bracket — 2,500	22,375.00

In addition, gain on sale and depreciation or other tax deductions in excess of the investment of $5,000 are taxed at capital gains rates. Gain on sale is considered to be the difference between the sales price and the investor's cost less any distribution, such as "tax-sheltered cash flow return" in excess of income reported by the partnership.

This is a low-risk tax shelter featuring income which is sometimes part or entirely tax-free and higher than available in most bank accounts and stocks. It further provides equity build-up and possible appreciation for capital gains.

EXAMPLE OF NEW, IMPROVED REAL ESTATE

This tax shelter has more risks than existing improved real estate because of the problems sometimes encountered with development of property, leasing it, and providing on-going management. The more progress that has been made in solving these problems, the greater safety there is in the project and the higher is the income and capital gain potential.

This program is directed toward the high bracket taxpayer who wants a large first year write-off and to get his money out in a few years. All possible expenses, including interest, management fees, loan fees, depreciation, and deductible legal and start-up costs, are put into the early years and the most accelerated depreciation schedule is used to produce the maximum tax write-off. To accomplish this goal the fund purchases new residential real estate such as apartment houses and mobile home parks.

46

When dealing with new rental real estate, there are special risks:

a. Development
b. Rent-up
c. On-going management

By buying the property at a guaranteed cost, the first risk, which is mainly in cost over-runs, was being assumed by the developer. Through the net lease arrangements for the first two or three years, the rent-up risks were also transferred to the developer (he guarantees cash flow for this period). The management risk is shared by the manager and the partnership.

The following is a summary of the program:

Fund: GEORGE REAL ESTATE LIMITED PARTNERSHIP

Sponsor: HAROLD REALTY PARTNERS, LTD. (the Corporate General Partner) and ISSAC and JEROME (Individual General Partners)

Form: Limited Partnership

Payments: $10,000 minimum

Proposed Activities: Investment in improved income-producing real estate and in unimproved real estate for the purpose of development with the objectives of obtaining for limited partners current tax-sheltered cash distributions, tax losses in excess of current cash distributions in the early years, and capital appreciation.

Management Cost and Compensation: (1) All administrative costs (excluding corporate officers' and directors' salaries) will be charged to the partnership;

(2) A management fee of 10% of "net cash receipts" (all cash revenues received by the partnership (except capital contributions, proceeds of loans, refinancing or sale of partnership) less debt service, administrative expenses and other expenses);

(3) 10% of that portion of the proceeds from sale or refinancing of property interests which exceeds the original partnership capital investment in each property.

(4) The managing partner, HAROLD REALTY PARTNERS, LTD., has a real estate broker subsidiary, KENNETH REALTY, INC., which takes commissions (up to 5% of sales price) on limited partnership real estate transactions.

Front End Charges: (1) 8½% of gross proceeds payable to the underwriter, LAWRENCE SECURITIES CORPORATION;

and (2) Offering expenses.

Income Distribution: The partnership anticipates making quarterly distributions of net cash receipts (after deducting all charges and expenses) and estimates return of initial investment through tax savings and tax-free distributions in 4-5 years.

Deductibility: Estimated at 55-60% first year.

Liquidity: Units may be assigned with approval from the general partner. The corporate general partner may buy and sell units for their own account or utilize broker-dealers. There is no assurance that a limited partner will be able to sell his units.

The managing partner projected the following results for the first five years for an investor in the 50% tax bracket:

Investment $10,000	Deductibility	Tax Savings	Cash to the Limited Partner	Total Cash and Tax Savings
Purchased at year-end	55%	$2,750	-0-	$ 2,750
Year 1	22%	1,100	550	1,650
Year 2	20%	1,000	700	1,700
Year 3	17%	850	700	1,550
Year 4	14%	700	700	1,400
Year 5	10%	500	700	1,200
				$10,250

These are fairly conservative numbers but are not guaranteed. If the numbers are correct, the 50% bracket investor should have his money out in 5 years. If the numbers turn out better than projected, he will have his money out sooner.

EVALUATION BY REAL ESTATE ANALYST

A real estate analyst might make the following observations on this program:

I. General comments regarding GEORGE REAL ESTATE LIMITED PARTNERSHIP
   A. Rate of Return

The managing partners claim that investors would receive an annual discounted return after tax of 14% if projects were abandoned in 1986; 19% after tax return if projects were sold at

original price. Using more conservative assumptions, the
investors could receive a 10% return after tax if projects were
abandoned, and a 16% return if they could be sold. These
returns, if achieved, would be attractive.

B. Experience and Expertise of the Manager

The principals have had the credibility in the past to promote
many syndications, raising millions of dollars in equity funds.
Most were formed recently, and, therefore, these investments
are not old enough to enable an evaluation of their economic
success.

The principals appear to have a balanced experience in real
estate, administration and tax aspects - all with substantial
companies.

C. Seller-Developers

The seller-developers of the properties included so far are
publicly held companies with successful development track
records. In all cases, these firms will manage the properties. In
the early years, these firms will guarantee a certain cash flow,
and in later years, their management fees will be subordinated.
(If there is no cash flow to investors, no fees will be paid.)

II. Risks common to most real estate limited partnerships

A. Managing partner's and seller-developers' incentives

Both the managing partner and the seller-developer earn most
of their profits from the sale of real estate. This fact could cause
lack of interest in the critically important property management
phase of a real estate operation.

B. "Blind Pool" investments

There has been some government insistance that managing
partners include descriptions of at least some of the actual
properties which will be included in the limited partnership.
However, a large portion of the offering is still sold on a "blind
pool" basis, meaning that the investor does not know exactly
what properties the managing partner will buy.

C. Sales commissions

The managing partner generally has a real estate broker
subsidiary which takes commissions (up to 5% of sales price) on
limited partnership real estate transactions. The seller-developer
usually stays on to manage the property. This could lead to
possible inflation of the sales prices.

D. Growth of Equity

Institutions lending mortgage money sometimes require

equity ownership in the borrower's company as a condition of granting the loan. This is called an "equity kicker." Because of "equity kickers" on most mortgages and ground leases, the up side appreciation in property value for the limited investors is restricted, and to the extent that properties are under construction or in phases of "rent up", the investors assume considerable development risks in addition to the normal investment risks.

E. Lack of arms-length dealing/conflict of interest

Generally, the managing partner has various subsidiary corporations which can provide services to the partnership. Also, the managing partner may continue to engage in the real estate business, and it is possible that they could purchase properties which might be in competition with the partnership.

F. Summary

Although these risks are inherent in this investment, on balance, the GEORGE venture seems to be reasonably structured from the investor's standpoint.

INSTRUCTIONS TO SALESMEN
FOR THE GEORGE PROGRAM

A salesman for the GEORGE program might be instructed as follows in the investment use of GEORGE REAL ESTATE:

In recommending the GEORGE program to a client the three basic considerations as in any investment suggestion are (1) degree of risk; (2) potential return; and (3) liquidity. There is a historic risk in real estate investments which we need to consider, but if the client has a portfolio which includes basic guarantees and equity investments which provide him with the potential need for liquidity, it is then possible for him to consider the risks of real estate. The anticipated returns on the GEORGE program are such that if the projections are actually experienced, the investor should have received in cash and tax savings economic value equal to his gross investment within four to five years.

The requirement for this investment is that the client be in the 50% income tax bracket. Those entities that may qualify under this restriction include (1) personal investor; (2) corporate investors; and (3) accumulation trusts.

The liquidity of the GEORGE program is very low and any investor that goes into the program should look to it for the long pull. Any early bailout could cause extra tax consequences through the recapture of excess depreciation.

One consideration that might be made is for the investor to consider the possibility of making a gift of the property interest to charity at some future date. A logical time for this would be when the deductions generated from the program become minimal. For example, if after four or five years, when the investor has received his money back in cash flow and tax savings, he might give the interest to charity and if the value of the property remains constant, he could expect a 100% write-off on the interest which would give him in essence a 50% return on his money in four or five years. In the meantime, he has substantially benefited his favorite charity.

Another alternative is to transfer the property by gift at a future date to a dependent. The income from the property will generate a cash flow to his dependent and the final value would be out of his estate and available for the dependent's future use.

SALE OF PROPERTY

When the managing partner of the GEORGE program would elect to sell property, is impossible to determine. One theory is to sell when rental income is maximized. Each one dollar increase in rent theoretically increases the value of the property by ten dollars. If an apartment house has one hundred units and rent is increased ten dollars per unit, rental income is increased by $12,000. Each unit would pay an additional ten dollars per month or $120 per year. One hundred units paying an additional $120 per year is $12,000. That should increase the market value of the apartment house by $120,000.

SUITABILITY OF PROGRAM FOR INVESTOR

Attorneys for the client might differ in their advice regarding the GEORGE program. One might advise against it saying that a high bracket taxpayer should seek more capital gain possibility and a mandatory buy-back within a certain period of time, perhaps 3 to 5 years, to assure liquidity. Another might recommend it saying that it provides some tax advantages which the client can get by just writing a check.

Although new, improved real estate is considered a low-risk tax shelter, it is riskier, for reasons previously mentioned, than existing, improved real estate, and, therefore, should be purchased only by higher tax bracket investors.

BENEFITS OF AN IMPROVED REAL ESTATE PROGRAM

1. Depreciation permits the cost of the improvements to be written off against income while the property may actually be increasing in value.

2. Taxes, insurance, repairs, etc. are deductible.

3. Real estate can be exchanged tax-free for other real estate.

4. Improvements by tenants often increase the value of real estate.

5. If improved real estate is sold at a profit, the taxpayer receives capital gain treatment subject to the depreciation recapture rules.

RISKS OF AN IMPROVED REAL ESTATE PROGRAM

1. A substantial delay in time may occur between the time the investor purchases a limited partnership interest and the time the money is invested in real estate by a partnership. To the extent no investments are made, there may also be a delay in any tax consequences that may be realized.

2. If the Internal Revenue Service treats a partnership as an association taxable as a corporation, distributions to Partners would not be deductible in computing the partnership's taxable income and in addition depreciation taken on Partnership properties would be reflected only on the Partnership's tax return, rather than being passed through to the Partners.

3. Accelerated depreciation leaves a lesser amount to be deducted in later years, thereby providing a vanishing tax shelter. As a result, tax deductions of a Partnership will decrease unless the Partnership acquires new property which will create new sources of depreciation. Tax deductions of a Partnership will also decrease over the terms of the mortgages as payment of interest decreases and payment of principal increases. Payments of interest may be deducted in determining the taxable income of a Partnership. Each partner will be taxed on his pro rata share of Partnership taxable income whether or not actually distributed to him.

4. Most programs provide that units may only be transferred pursuant to a written assignment and subject to the consent of

the General Partner, which will not be unreasonably withheld. Therefore, it can be anticipated that there will be no public market for the units and a Participant may not, therefore, be able to liquidate his investment in the event of emergency. Also, a Limited Partnership unit may not be readily accepted as collateral for a loan.

5. Investments of a Partnership will be leveraged, i.e., the Partnership will finance the acquisition of properties by borrowing. This practice will permit the acquisition of properties of greater cost but it also increases the Partnership's exposure to larger losses. Principal and interest payments on such indebtedness will generally have to be made regardless of cash flow from Partnership investments. There can be no assurance as to whether loans will be available or at what rates of interest. Lenders may require an equity participation in the property being purchased, at nominal or no cost to them, as an inducement to making the loan. Such participation could decrease the benefits to the Partnership of leveraging its investment in a property. In addition, lenders may seek to impose restrictions on the future borrowing, distribution and operating policies of the Partnership.

6. The holder of a unit on any record date during the taxable year may be required to report a share of Partnership income on his personal income tax return even though he received no distributions during the period of his ownership or the amount distributed to him bears no relationship to the amount which he is required to report.

7. A Partnership's investments will be subject to the risks generally incident to the ownership of real property including changes in general or local economic conditions, construction of competing properties, inability to attract tenants, changes in interest rates and availability of mortgage funds which may make the sale of properties difficult or unattractive, changes in real estate tax rates and other operating expenses, and changes in governmental rules and other factors which are beyond the control of the General Partners.

TAX ASPECTS OF AN IMPROVED
REAL ESTATE PROGRAM

The following is a brief summary of some of the Federal income tax consequences to Limited Partners in a Partnership based on the Internal Revenue Code, rules and regulations promulgated thereunder and existing interpretations thereof, any of which could be changed at any time.

There is uncertainty concerning various tax aspects of real estate limited partnerships for several reasons. In particular, the effect of recent legislation on the taxation of real estate limited partnerships depends on future interpretations thereof by the judiciary and the Internal Revenue Service. Further, the applicable rules, regulations and interpretations in the area of taxation are under continuing review by the Internal Revenue Service, and changes in such rules, regulations or interpretations could adversely affect the Partnership and the Limited Partners. In addition, the General Partners understand that the Internal Revenue Service is paying increased attention to the proper application of the tax laws to partnerships, including partnerships investing in real estate. In January, 1978, the Internal Revenue Service announced that it planned to increase its audit coverage of partnership returns from 1.5% to 3% and that most of this additional coverage will be concentrated on high loss returns, with coverage of 24% of partnership returns showing losses of over $25,000.

The availability and amount of deductions taken by the Partnership will depend not only on the general legal principles described below but also upon various determinations relating to particular real property investments as to which no legal opinion is expressed and which are subject to potential controversy on factual or other grounds. Such determinations include the allocations of basis among various components of an investment, the characterization of various expenses and payments made to the seller (such as between interest or purchase price), the characterization of the relationship between the Partnership and the seller of the property, the estimated useful lives of properties, the characterization and purpose of Acquisition Fees paid by the Partnership and various other matters. There can be no assurance, therefore, that some of the deductions claimed by the Partnership or the allocation of items of income, gain, loss, deduction and credit among the Partners may not be challenged by the Internal Revenue Service. Final disallowance of such deductions or reallocation of such items could adversely affect the Limited Partners. Each prospective Limited Partner is therefore urged to consult his own tax advisor with respect to the Federal and state tax consequences arising from the purchase of the Interests offered hereby.

PARTNERSHIP STATUS–FEDERAL TAX RULING

The Partnership obtained a ruling from the Internal Revenue Service to the effect that under existing Federal income tax law and regulations, the Partnership will be treated as a partnership, and will not constitute an association taxable as a corporation, for Federal income tax purposes. The ruling provides that the continued treatment of the Partnership as a partnership for Federal income tax purposes is dependent upon the present law and regulations (see "Possible Legislative Tax Changes"), which are subject to change, and upon the Partnership's continuing to satisfy a variety of criteria, including the General Partners' maintaining substantial assets which could be reached by creditors of the Partnership.

In *Philip G. Larson,* 66 T.C. 159 (1976), the Tax Court suggested that the Internal Revenue Service reconsider its regulations governing the requirements to qualify for partnership tax status. On January 5, 1977, the Internal Revenue Service proposed, but subsequently withdrew, amended regulations which would have made it substantially more difficult for an entity organized as a limited partnership under state law to qualify as a partnership for Federal tax purposes. Under the terms of the proposed regulations the Partnership probably would not have qualified as a partnership for tax purposes. Although the proposed regulations have been withdrawn other proposals relating to partnership taxation have been made. There can be no assurance that other regulations or legislative changes will not be proposed in the future which, if adopted, would cause the Partnership to be treated as an association taxable as a corporation for Federal income tax purposes. In that event all items of income, gain, loss, deduction and credit of the Partnership would be reflected only on its tax returns, would be subject to tax at the partnership level and would not be passed through to the Limited Partners. In addition, all or part of any distributions made to the Limited and General Partners would be taxed as dividends to the extent of current and accumulated earnings and profits of the Partnership and distributions in excess thereof would be treated as a return of capital to the extent of the recipient's basis (which would include only the Limited Partner's cash investment), while the remainder would be treated as a capital gain (assuming the Limited Partner's Interest was a capital asset). Moreover, Partnership losses, if any, would then be allowed only to the Partnership, rather than being passed through to the Limited Partners. In addition, such a change in the Partnership's status for tax purposes could be treated by the Internal Revenue Service as a taxable event, in which event the Limited Partners could have a tax liability under circumstances where they would not receive a cash distribution from the Partnership.

While the Internal Revenue Service does not generally revoke previously issued tax rulings, it might do so when there has been a change in applicable law, regulations or interpretations. Therefore, the Partnership's tax ruling could be either retroactively or prospectively revoked or modified as a result of the adoption of new laws or regulations adversely affecting the Partnership. Further, the ruling will become ineffective if the conditions which were the basis for its issuance, including the condition that the General Partners continue to maintain substantial assets which could be reached by creditors of the Partnership, are not maintained during the life of the Partnership. Under the Partnership Agreement the General Partners are obligated to use their best efforts to maintain the Partnership's status as a partnership for tax purposes and, in connection therewith, to maintain their net worth at a level sufficient to meet Internal Revenue Service standards.

The Partnership does not expect to seek a ruling that any of the joint venture partnerships through which it holds an interest in properties will be treated for Federal income tax purposes as a partnership and not as an association taxable as a corporation. The Partnership expects, in each case, to receive an opinion of counsel that under existing Federal income tax laws and regulations such joint venture will be taxed as a partnership and not as an association taxable as a corporation; however, such opinions of counsel are not binding upon the Internal Revenue Service. In the event any such joint venture partnership were to be treated for Federal income tax purposes as a corporation, the Limited Partners would among other things, not be entitled to include in the basis of their Interests any indebtedness relating to the property owned by such joint venture partnership, any deductions relating to such property could not be passed through to the Limited Partners, such joint venture partnership would be taxable on its income, and distributions from such joint venture to the Partnership would be taxable as described above.

TAXATION OF LIMITED PARTNERS ON PROFITS OR
LOSSES OF THE PARTNERSHIP

Section 701 of the Code provides that no Federal income tax
is paid by a partnership as an entity. Each partner reports on his
Federal income tax return his allocable share (usually as determined by the partnership agreement) of the income, gains,
losses, deductions and credits of the partnership, whether or not
any actual cash distribution is made to such partner during his
taxable year. Thus, an investor's tax liability may exceed the
cash distributed to him in a particular year. A partner is generally entitled to deduct on his personal income tax return his
allocable share of partnership losses, if any, to the extent of the
tax basis of his partnership interest at the end of the partnership
year in which such losses occur. See discussion of limitations on
deductibility of losses below in "Basis of Partnership Interests."
The characterization of an item of profit or loss (e.g., as capital
gain or ordinary income) will usually be the same for the partner as for the partnership.

If in any tax year there is a material change in the law of the
circumstances surrounding the Partnership, the Partnership may
be deemed an association taxable as a corporation, with the
results described above in "Partnership Status—Federal Tax
Ruling."

CASH DISTRIBUTIONS

Cash distributions from a partnership are generally not equivalent to partnership income (if any) as determined for income
tax purposes or as determined under generally accepted accounting principles. If the cash distributions to a Limited Partner by
the Partnership in any year (including his share in any reduction
in liabilities as described below) exceed his share of the Partnership's taxable income for that year, the excess will constitute
for tax purposes a return of capital to such Limited Partner. A
return of capital will not be reportable as taxable income by a
recipient for Federal income tax purposes, but it will reduce the
tax basis of his Partnership interest. If the tax basis of a Limited
Partner should be reduced to zero, his share of any cash distributions for any year (including his share in any reduction in
liabilities as described below) in excess of his share of Partnership taxable income will be taxable to him as though it were a

gain (or recapture) on the sale or exchange of his Interest. See "Sale or Foreclosure of Partnership Properties" and "Sale of Partnership Interests."

A decrease in a holder's proportionate share of non-recourse liabilities (as, for example, when a mortgage is paid off in whole or in part, a liability is discharged through foreclosure, the partnership sells a property subject to a mortgage or non-recourse debt is refinanced with recourse debt) is treated for tax purposes as though it were a cash distribution.

BASIS OF PARTNERSHIP INTERESTS

Generally, the tax basis of any partner's interest in a partnership is equal to its cost, reduced by the partner's share of partnership distributions and losses and increased by his share of partnership income. In addition, the tax basis of an interest in a partnership generally is increased by a partner's proportionate share of liabilities to which partnership assets are subject (to the extent that such liabilities do not exceed the fair market value of the properties subject to such liabilities), but for which no partner or the partnership is liable (such as real estate acquired subject to a mortgage which is not assumed by the partnership or any of its partners). Each partner's proportionate share of non-recourse liabilities for this purpose is determined by the proportion in which such partner shares profits of the partnership. It is anticipated that substantially all of the mortgage indebtedness incurred by the Partnership will be of a non-recourse character so as to be includable proportionately in the basis of the Partnership Interests of all Partners in the Partnership.

Section 704(d) of the Code (as in effect prior to the 1978 Act) generally limits deduction of a partner's share of partnership loss to the amount of the partner's basis and further provides (with respect to partnerships whose principal activity is not investing in real property, other than mineral property) that the adjusted basis of any partner's interest in a partnership for purposes of determining the deductibility of losses shall not include any portion of any partnership liability with respect to which the partner has no personal liability. The effect of this provision is to limit the deductions to the amount that a partner in non-"real estate" partnerships has "at risk" in the activity. This rule, in effect under the Code prior to the 1978 Act, does not affect basis for any purpose except that of determining the deductibility by a partner of losses for tax purposes generated by the partnership. The 1978 Act repeals the applicable portions of Code Section 704(d) for years beginning after December 31, 1978.

For Partnership taxable years beginning after 1978, the 1978 Act provides in Code Section 465 that no taxpayer (whether directly or through investment in a partnership) will be permitted in any year to deduct or offset against other income a loss from any activity, other than holding real property, to the extent that such loss exceeds the aggregate dollar amount which such taxpayer has at risk in such activity. To the extent that such loss is not permitted to be used in any year, it may be carried over by such taxpayer to subsequent years.

Although "holding real property" has not been defined, it is believed that Congress did not intend the change to have any effect on partnerships engaged in real estate activities and that such partnerships and their partners will be treated for tax purposes the same after January 1, 1979, as they were prior to that date. It is expected that such treatment will include considering an investment in a real estate joint venture by the Partnership to be an activity which is "holding real property."

If the Partnership's principal activity prior to the effective date of the 1978 Act were not considered to be "investing in real property," a Limited Partner could not include any non-recourse liability of the Partnership (whether such liability was incurred directly or through joint venture investments) in his basis for purposes of determining deduction by such Partner of his share of Partnership losses. Similarly, to the extent that (after the effective date of the 1978 Act) the Partnership is deemed to be engaged in any activity other than the holding of real property, the losses from such activity will not be deductible in any taxable year to the extent that such losses exceed the amount the Partner is considered to have "at risk" in such activity.

While there has been no judicial or regulatory interpretation of the terms "investing in real property" or "holding real property," it is believed that the Partnership meets the test for deductibility of losses under both Code Sections.

So long as a partnership and joint venture partnerships in which it is a partner are considered to be investing in real property as described above, a partner's tax basis also includes an amount equal to his proportionate share of a partnership's share of non-recourse debt relating to properties owned by joint venture partnerships in which the partnership is a partner (but only to the extent that such liabilities does not exceed the fair market value of the property).

DEDUCTIBILITY OF FEES

No assurance can be given as to the deductibility for Federal income tax purposes of any fees payable to the General Partners or affiliates. If it is ultimately determined that the payment was made to a partner in its capacity as a partner, the Partnership may be unable to sustain the deduction. The Partnership may also deduct a portion of the Acquisition Fee paid for negotiation and evaluation of investments not ultimately acquired by the Partnership, and there is no assurance that any such deduction may not be disallowed by the Internal Revenue Service. Similarly, no assurance can be given that management fees which may be payable to sellers of properties which also participate as joint venturers in the properties will be deductible by the Partnership. In any year such fees are paid, the disallowance of the deductibility of such fees would result in a proportionate increase in the taxable income of the Limited Partners from the Partnership with no associated increase in cash flow with which to pay any resulting increase in tax liabilities.

DEPRECIATION

It is anticipated that when permissible a Partnership will generally use accelerated methods of depreciation. Double-declining balance or sum-of-the-years digits depreciation are now allowed as permissible methods of computing depreciation for new residential rental real property where at least 80% of the gross rental income for the year is from dwelling units, such as apartment houses. Other new buildings are limited to 150% declining balance depreciation. Used buildings are limited to straight-line depreciation except for residential rental property with a useful life of twenty years or more at acquisition which is allowed 125% declining balance depreciation.

In the case of residential real estate, the 1976 Tax Reform Act provides for the recapture of all post-1975 depreciation in excess of straight-line, in the same manner as is presently the case for non-residential real estate. In the case of government subsidized housing, the conference agreement provides full recapture of post-1975 depreciation for the first 100 months (8 1/3 years) and a phaseout of the amount recaptured during the second 100 months (up to 16 2/3 years). There will be no recapture thereafter. Government subsidized housing includes housing (1) with respect to which a mortgage is insured under Section 221(d) (3) or 236 of the National Housing Act (2) under Section 8 of the United States Housing Act of 1937 and (3) with respect to which a loan is made or insured under title V of the Housing Act of 1949.

CONSTRUCTION PERIOD INTEREST AND TAXES

Under the 1976 Tax Reform Act, construction period interest and taxes are to be capitalized in the year in which they are paid or incurred and amortized over a 10-year period. A portion of this amount capitalized may be deducted for the taxable year in which paid or incurred. The balance must be amortized over the remaining years in the amortization period beginning with the year in which the property is ready to be placed in service or is ready to be held for sale.

Under the 1976 Tax Reform Act, separate transitional rules are provided for non-residential real estate, residential real estate, and government subsidized housing. In the case of nonresidential real estate, this provision is to apply only to property where the construction period begins after December 31, 1975. (However, for 1976 only, 50 percent of the construction period interest and taxes for nonresidential real estate need be capitalized.) In the case of residential real estate (other than certain low-income housing), this provision is to apply to construction period interest and taxes paid or incurred after December 31, 1977, and, in the case of low-income housing, to construction period interest and taxes paid or incurred after December 31, 1981.

In addition, the length of the amortization period is to be phased-in over a 7-year period. The amortization period is to be 4 years in the case of interest and taxes paid or incurred in the first year to which these rules apply. The amortization period increases by one year for each succeeding year after the initial effective date until the amortization period becomes 10 years (i.e., the 10-year period is fully phased-in for construction period interest and taxes paid or incurred in 1982, in the case of non-residential real estate; 1984, in the case of residential real estate, and 1988, in the case of government subsidized housing).

ORGANIZATION AND SYNDICATION EXPENSES

Expenses paid in connection with the organization and syndication of a partnership must be capitalized. Organization expenses (but not syndication expenses) may be amortized over a period of not less than 60 months.

RETROACTIVE ALLOCATIONS OF PROFITS OR LOSSES

Items of income, gain, loss, deduction or credit of a partnership may be allocated to a partner only if they are received, paid or incurred by the partnership during that portion of the year in which the partner is a member of the partnership for tax purposes. In determining whether items or income or loss have been received, paid or incurred prior to a partner's entry into a partnership, a partnership may either prorate items according to the portion of the year for which a partner was a partner, or, in effect, separate the partnership year into two or more segments and allocate income, loss or special items in each segment among the persons who were partners during that segment.

Under the Partnership Agreement, income or loss attributable to the period prior to receipt of funds from the escrow account and the first admission of additional Limited Partners is allocated to the General Partners and the initial Limited Partner. Thereafter, income or loss allocable to the Limited Partners is allocated among the Limited Partners pursuant to the Partnership Agreement, which generally provide that Limited Partners are not entitled to an allocable share of losses incurred prior to the date when they are admitted to the Partnership. Such allocations appear to be permissible under the Code. Nevertheless, no assurance can be given that the Internal Revenue Service will not contend that such allocation is a "retroactive allocation" prohibited by the Code, or an impermissable method of accounting.

SPECIAL ALLOCATIONS OF PROFITS OR LOSSES

Allocations of income, gain, loss, deduction or credit among partners pursuant to a partnership agreement will not be recognized unless the allocations have "substantial economic effect." There are presently no regulations which define the circumstances under which an allocation will be deemed to have substantial economic effect. Although the General Partners believe that the allocations of profit and loss among the partners of the Partnership are proper, there can be no assurance that the Internal Revenue Service will not challenge such allocations, particularly to the extent that allocations of profit and loss differ from allocations of cash. If an allocation is set aside, a partner's share of the income, gain, loss, deduction or credit (or item thereof) will be determined in accordance with the partner's interest in the partnership, which is to be determined "by taking into account all facts and circumstances." Such a determination might result in an allocation which is less favorable to the Limited Partners than the allocations set forth in the Partnership Agreement. The Internal Revenue Service could also challenge the allocations of profits and losses among joint venture partners in the case of joint venture investments.

POTENTIAL APPLICATION OF SECTION 183
OF THE CODE

Section 183 of the Code limits deductions attributable to "activities not engaged in for profit." The test of whether an activity is deemed to be "engaged in for profit" is based on facts and circumstances from time to time. The Internal Revenue Service has ruled that this test will be applied at the partnership level.

REFINANCING OF PARTNERSHIP PROPERTY

No gain or loss would be recognized on the refinancing of the permanent mortgage loan for a property so long as the new mortgage is non-recourse and equals or exceeds the unpaid balance of the old mortgage. Any *Sale or Refinancing Proceeds* distributed to the Partners from a new non-recourse mortgage which equals or exceeds the unpaid balance of the old mortgage would not be taxable income to the Partners if at the time of distribution the distributee's tax basis in his Partnership Interest equals or exceeds the amount distributed. To the extent that the amount of any new mortgage exceeds the amount of the existing mortgage, each Partner will increase his basis by his pro rata share of such increase but the total basis of the Partners attributable to the debt to which a property is subject may not exceed the fair market value of the property. Such basis would be decreased by the amount of any cash proceeds of such new mortgage distributed to such Partner. Any such increase in indebtedness will not produce an asset with respect to which additional depreciation deductions can be taken unless the proceeds are specifically used to acquire depreciable property in addition to that already owned by the Partnership.

SALE OR FORECLOSURE OF PARTNERSHIP PROPERTIES

Any profit or loss which may be realized by the Partnership on the sale of any Partnership investments will be treated as capital gain or loss under Subchapter P of the Code (except to the extent of depreciation recapture described under "Depreciation" above), unless it is determined that the Partnership is a "dealer" in real estate for Federal income tax purposes or except to the extent that assets sold constitute "Section 1231 assets" (i.e., real property and depreciable assets used in a trade or business and held for the holding period applicable to long-term capital gain). In the event the Partnership's assets are deemed to be used in a trade or business, a limited partnership's proportionate share of gains or losses from the sale of such assets would be combined with any other Section 1231 gains or losses incurred by him in that year. If his Section 1231 gains exceed his Section 1231 losses, such gains and losses are treated as long term capital gains and losses. If his Section 1231 losses exceed his Section 1231 gains, such gains and losses are treated as ordinary gains and losses. In the event the Partnership is deemed to be a "dealer," any gain or loss on the sale or other disposition of such property would be treated as ordinary income or loss. In general, involuntary transfers of the Partnership's property (such as a mortgage foreclosure) would have the same effect as a sale.

The Partnership has not been organized to operate as a "dealer" in real property and does not presently intend to hold property for sale in a trade or business; however, since a determination as to this matter depends on facts and circumstances existing from time to time, no assurance can be given that the Partnership will not be deemed to be a "dealer" or to hold property for sale in a trade or business at some future date.

Under certain circumstances, the net cash proceeds distributed from the sale or other disposition of property may not be sufficient to pay the tax liabilities of a Limited Partner resulting from such event. Such circumstances might include: (i) the sale of property from which a Limited Partner's share of cash proceeds is significantly less than his share of taxable gain (including recaptured depreciation, taxable as ordinary income) as a result of the fact that in determining such taxable gain the amount of the then existing mortgage on the property is included along with any cash proceeds, while the basis of the property (the amount subtracted from the sales price in determining gain) may have been substantially reduced through previous depreciation deductions; (ii) the sale or transfer of property pursuant to foreclosure of a mortgage, deed of trust or other financing instrument; and (iii) the sale of property at a time when all or part of the net proceeds therefrom may have to be utilized by the Partnership to meet other obligations.

SALE OR TRANSFER OF PARTNERSHIP INTERESTS

Gain recognized by a Limited Partner, who is not a "dealer" in securities, on the sale of an Interest in the Partnership which has been held for more than the applicable holding period (see "Capital Gain and Loss Provisions" below), will generally be taxable as long-term capital gain. In computing such gain, the seller's share of existing mortgage indebtedness is included for purposes of both basis and proceeds. That portion of the selling Partner's gain allocable to "appreciated inventory items" and "unrealized receivables" as defined in Section 751 of the Code would be treated as ordinary income. Included in "unrealized receivables" is depreciation recapture determined as if the selling Partner's proportionate share of all the Partnership's properties had been sold at that time. If a Limited Partner's tax basis, before taking into account his share of the non-recourse mortgage loans, has been decreased below the price he paid for his Interest by tax deductions and cash distributions, his tax liability could exceed the cash proceeds of such a sale.

Prior to the 1976 Act, transfers of interests by reason of death were not subject either to recapture or to capital gains tax. The basis of a partnership interest acquired from a decedent was "stepped-up" to the fair market value of the interest at the date of death of the decedent (or, under an alternative valuation date, six months thereafter). The 1976 Act provided a "carry over basis" for property acquired from a decedent dying after December 31, 1976. (The 1978 Act postpones the effective date to December 31, 1979.) The basis of Partnership Interests acquired from a decedent dying after the effective date of the carry over basis provisions will be the decedent's adjusted basis of the property immediately before the death of the decedent, with certain adjustments. Thus, the sale or disposition of an inherited Interest may subject the holder to substantially more capital gain or ordinary income tax than under prior law.

Generally no gain or loss is recognized for Federal income tax purposes as a result of a gift of property. However, gifts of Interests may result in Federal income tax liability for a Limited Partner if and to the extent that his share of non-recourse liabilities exceeds his adjusted basis for his Interests. Such excess will be treated as gain from a sale of the Interest, and will be subject to the rules described above with respect to the sale of an Interest. Any gift of an Interest may result in the imposition of Federal gift tax and may also be subject to state gift taxes.

NO SECTION 754 ELECTION

Because of the complexities of the tax accounting required, the Partnership does not presently intend to file an election under Section 754 of the Code to adjust the basis of Partnership property in the case of a transfer of an Interest. The effect of such an election would be that, with respect to the transferee Limited Partner only, the basis of the Partnership's property would be either increased or decreased by the difference between the transferee's basis for his Interest and his proportionate share of the Partnership's adjusted basis for all Partnership property. Any increase or decrease resulting from such adjustment would be allocable among the Partnership's assets in accordance with rules established under Section 755 of the Code. After such adjustment had been made, the transferee Partner's share of the adjusted basis of the Partnership's property would equal the adjusted basis of his Interest. If (as presently anticipated) the Partnership does not make such an election, upon the sale of Partnership property or distributions (whether deemed or otherwise) from the Partnership subsequent to a transfer of an Interest, taxable gain or loss to the transferee of the Interest will be measured by the difference between his share of the gross proceeds of such sale or distribution and his share of the Partnership's tax basis in the property (which, in the absence of a Section 754 election, will be unchanged by the transfer of the Interest to him), rather than by the difference between his share of the amount realized or distributed and the portion of his purchase price that was allocable to the property. As a consequence, such transferee will be subject to tax upon a portion of the proceeds which, as to such transferee, constitutes a return of capital, if the purchase price for his Interest exceeded his share of the adjusted basis for all Partnership properties.

DISSOLUTION OF PARTNERSHIP

In the event of a dissolution of the Partnership prior to the expiration of its term, the Partnership might be required to liquidate all of its properties during a limited period of time. This might cause the Partnership to sustain substantial losses (determined in terms of its original cost). Nevertheless, the Partnership might be required to recognize taxable income on such sales as a result of the reduction of its tax basis by depreciation deductions previously taken.

Under Section 708(b) of the Code, if at any time no part of the business of the Partnership continues to be carried on by any of the Partners in the Partnership, or if within a 12-month period there is a sale or exchange of 50% or more of the total interests in Partnership capital and profit, a termination of the Partnership occurs, and the taxable year of the Partnership would close. The properties of the Partnership would be treated as distributed to the Partners, and capital gain or loss and recapture which is taxed as ordinary income may result from such termination. Following the deemed distribution, contribution of the same properties, in the form of undivided interests, would be deemed to be made to a new partnership or to an association taxable as a corporation. The Partnership properties may have a different basis in the hands of the new partnership. In addition, because the properties would have already been used by the Partnership, most or all properties could be depreciated only on the straight-line method by the new partnership.

OTHER POSSIBLE TAX CONSEQUENCES TO INVESTORS

The following is a summary of certain provisions of the Code which, while they are generally not peculiar to the Partnership, may affect an investor depending on his individual circumstances, such as, for example, his tax bracket, the amount of his capital gains or losses, the amount of his personal service income and his other investments.

Capital Gain and Loss Provisions. In any year, a non-corporate taxpayer may deduct net capital losses up to $3,000 (or $1,500 in the case of a married taxpayer filing a separate return) against ordinary income. Within these dollar limitations only 50% of net long-term capital loss in excess of net short-term capital gain may be deducted from ordinary income, while, within such dollar limitations, all of the excess of net short-term capital loss over the net long-term capital gain may be so deducted. The holding period necessary to qualify for long-term capital gain or loss treatment is 12 months.

The 1978 Act makes several changes in the taxation of capital gains. For years beginning prior to 1979 an individual taxpayer could elect to pay a 25% alternative tax on the first $50,000 net long-term capital gain ($25,000 in the case of married persons filing separate returns). This alternative tax is repealed by the 1978 Act for taxable years beginning after 1978.

The 1978 Act also increases the long-term capital gain deduction from 50% to 60% of net long-term capital gains on sales and exchanges occurring after October 31, 1978. It also will eliminate the capital gains deduction as an item of tax preference under the add-on minimum tax and maximum tax. Thus, under the 1978 Act there is no longer a 15% minimum tax on the capital gains deduction, nor do capital gains reduce the amount of income otherwise eligible for treatment under the maximum tax. However, capital gains are subject, as a tax preference item, to the new alternative minimum tax imposed by the 1978 Act. See "Minimum Taxes on Items of Tax Preference" and "Maximum Tax on Personal Service Income" below.

Limitation on Deduction of Investment Interest. In general, interest paid by a non-corporate taxpayer on funds borrowed to acquire or carry investment assets is deductible in a tax year only to the extent it does not exceed the sum of the following items: (1) $10,000 ($5,000 for a married taxpayer filing a separate return); (2) net investment income; and (3) the amount, if any, by which certain deductions attributable to property subject to a net lease exceed the rental income from such property. Net investment income is defined as the excess of the sum of the following items from non-business sources over investment expenses, excluding interest and including straight line depreciation, incurred in earning such income: (i) gross income from interest, dividends, rents and royalties; (ii) net short-term capital gain from investment property; and (iii) the amount of recapture under Sections 1245, 1250 and 1254 of the Code. No offset of investment interest is permitted against long-term capital gain income from the disposition of investment property. Interest deductions which are disallowed under these rules are subject to an unlimited carryover and may be deducted in future years (subject to the applicable limitation).

Interest incurred in real estate ventures, if (as may be the case with certain investments by the Partnership) the property involved is rented under a net lease, is regarded as "investment interest," subject to the above limitations rather than business interest which remains fully deductible. The effect of this provision is that under certain circumstances the full amount of mortgage interest passed through from the Partnership to the Limited Partners might not be allowable as a deduction to some or all of such Limited Partners where property is rented by the Partnership under a net lease. The effect of this provision will depend upon the extent to which the Partnership invests in property leased under net leases and upon an investor's overall tax situation. Section 163(d)(4) of the Code provides that property will be considered to be subject to a net lease if either (1) the sum of deductions allowable for the taxable year solely by reason of Section 162 of the Code (not including depreciation, interest, taxes and reimbursed expenses) is less than 15% of rental income (the "expense test"), or (2) the lessor is guaranteed in whole or in part against loss of income (the "return test").

Minimum Taxes on Items of Tax Preference. Under the Code individuals must pay a minimum tax (the "add-on minimum tax") in each year, in addition to their regular income tax, equal to 15% of the sum of their items of tax preference income in such year reduced by the greater of $10,000 ($5,000 in the case of married taxpayers filing separate returns) or one-half of regular income tax liability for that year (less certain credits). Items of tax preference include the excess of certain itemized deductions over 60% of adjusted gross income ("adjusted itemized deductions"), the excess of accelerated over straight-line depreciation on real property and leased personal property, and 50% of the excess of net long-term capital gains over the net short-term capital losses.

Under the 1978 Act, adjusted itemized deductions and the capital gains deduction will no longer be treated as items of tax preference under the add-on minimum tax for years beginning after December 31, 1978. However, after October 31, 1978 (the effective date of the change in the capital gains deduction) and before January 1, 1979, the 60% capital gains deduction is treated as a tax preference item under the add-on minimum tax.

For years beginning after December 31, 1978, the 1978 Act will provide for an alternative minimum tax to be computed by increasing a taxpayer's taxable income by his adjusted itemized deductions and by the amount of any capital gains deduction. This net amount, reduced by a $20,000 exemption will be subject to alternative minimum tax rates as follows: 10% on the first $50,000, 20% on the next $40,000, and 25% on the remainder. The alternative minimum tax will then be compared to the taxpayer's regular tax liability increased by the amount of any add-on minimum tax. The taxpayer will be required to pay the greater of the two amounts.

The extent, if any, to which any items of tax preference of the Partnership would be subject to either minimum tax will depend on each investor's overall tax situation. Corporations are also subject to the add-on minimum tax, but the provisions applicable to corporations differ in certain respects from those applicable to individuals. Estates, trusts, and electing small business corporations are generally treated as individuals.

Maximum Tax on Personal Service Income. Under Code Section 1348 the maximum marginal tax rate on "personal service income" is limited to 50%; however, all items of tax preference (except capital gains with respect to sales or exchanges after October 31, 1978) reduce the amount of income eligible for the maximum tax. In general, "personal service income" includes "earned income" plus deferred compensation and amounts received as a pension or annuity. The benefits of the maximum tax are reduced to the extent that investment in the Partnership results in tax preference items. Under the 1978 Act, the capital gains deduction will not be treated as a tax preference.

PARTNERSHIP TAX RETURNS AND TAX INFORMATION

The Partnership expects to file its tax returns on a cash basis. The tax return filed by the Partnership may be audited by the Internal Revenue Service. Adjustments (if any) resulting from such an audit could result in an audit of the Limited Partners' own returns. Any such audit of the Limited Partners' tax returns could result in adjustments of non-Partnership, as well as Partnership, income or loss.

Under the 1978 Act, the Code will impose a penalty on a partnership which fails to file a complete and timely partnership information return, unless such partnership shows that the failure to file a complete or timely return is due to reasonable cause. The amount of penalty will be $50 for each month or fraction thereof (up to five months) during which such partnership return is late or incomplete, multiplied by the total number of partners in the partnership during the partnership's taxable year for which the return is due.

In the case of partnerships subject to the registration and reporting requirements of the Securities and Exchange Commission, the 1978 Act will allow the Internal Revenue Service to assess a deficiency (or the taxpayer to file a claim for refund) attributable to partnership items until the later of four years after the date of the partnership return for the year in which the item arose is filed or, if the partnership return does not properly show the name and address of the person to be assessed the deficiency, one year after that information is provided to the Internal Revenue Service.

The Partnership will provide to the Limited Partners (and to any assignees of Interests who have not become substituted Limited Partners) tax information within 75 days after the close of each fiscal year.

REVENUE ACT OF 1978

The 1978 Act does not appear to have any significant tax consequences at the operations level of the Partnership. Certain of the provisions will, however, have tax consequences at the individual investor level. Among changes affecting individuals, (1) the alternative tax on capital gains is repealed; (2) the deduction for net capital gains is increased from 50% to 60%; (3) an alternative minimum tax, applicable only to the extent it exceeds the sum of an individual's regular tax liability plus the current law add-on minimum tax (modified to exclude the capital gains deduction and adjusted itemized deductions), is payable at certain graduated rates, the maximum of which is 25% of an individual's taxable income as increased by adjusted itemized deductions and the net capital gains deduction; (4) the capital gains deduction and adjusted itemized deductions are not treated as tax preference items under the present minimum tax after December 31, 1978, although they would be subject to the new alternative minimum tax; (5) the capital gains deduction is not treated as a tax preference item under the maximum tax after October 31, 1978; and (6) the effective date of the carry-over basis rules enacted as part of the 1976 Act will be delayed until after December 31, 1979.

POSSIBLE LEGISLATIVE TAX CHANGES

In recent years there have been a number of proposals made in Congress, by government agencies and by the executive branch of the Federal government for changes in the Federal income tax laws. Such proposals have varied widely in their scope and in their likely effect on taxpayers investing in real property. Many of such proposals would, if adopted, have had the overall effect of reducing the tax benefits presently associated with investment in real property generally. In early 1978 the Carter administration proposed certain changes in the tax laws which Congress did not incorporate in the 1978 Act. These proposals include the treatment of a large partnership (more than 15 limited partners) as a corporation for tax purposes and a provision to allow the Internal Revenue Service to treat a partnership as an entity for purposes of the audit of partnership-related issues (including statute of limitations, administrative settlement and judicial review) so that individual partners would no longer be able to protest Internal Revenue Service determinations separately.

In addition, it is likely that further proposals will be forthcoming or that previous proposals will be revived in some form in the future. It is impossible to predict with any degree of certainty what past proposals may be revived or what new proposals may be forthcoming, the likelihood of adoption of any such proposals, the likely effect of any such proposals upon the income tax treatment presently associated with investment in real property or the Partnership or the effective date of any legislation which may derive from any such past or future proposals. In view of this uncertainty, potential investors are strongly urged to consider ongoing developments in this uncertain area and to consult their own tax advisors in assessing the risks of investment in the Partnership.

STATE AND LOCAL TAXES

In addition to the Federal income tax aspects described above, prospective Limited Partners should consider potential state tax consequences of an investment in the Partnership. Each Limited Partner is advised to consult his own tax advisor to determine if the state in which he is a resident imposes a tax upon his share of the income or loss of the Partnership. In addition, a Limited Partner may be required to file an income tax or other return in those states where the Partnership acquires real property. The Limited Partner may be taxable on income derived from sources within a particular state (including capital gains on the sale of properties) regardless of whether the Partnership sustains losses from properties located outside that particular state and regardless of the amount of such losses, even though such losses equal or exceed the income derived from sources within that particular state or the total operations of the Partnership result in a net loss. The following states (in which the Partnership has acquired or expects to acquire interests in real property) presently impose a tax on non-resident individuals at the following rates on income from sources within such states: Alabama—5%; California—graduated rates from 1% to 11%; Maryland—graduated rates from 2% to 5%.

The Partnership will advise each Limited Partner of his share of income or loss to be reported to each of the states where the Partnership owns property. Personal exemptions, computed in various ways, are allowed by the various states and may reduce the amount of tax owed to a particular state. The Partnership may be required to withhold state taxes from distributions to the Limited Partners in some instances.

To the extent that a nonresident Limited Partner pays tax to a state by virtue of Partnership operations within that state, he may be entitled to a deduction or credit against tax owed to his state of residence with respect to the same income, and should consult his tax advisor in this regard. In addition, payment of

State taxes constitutes a deduction for Federal income tax purposes, assuming that the tax-payer itemizes deductions.

GENERAL

The foregoing analysis is not intended as a substitute for careful tax planning, particularly since the income tax consequences of an investment in the Partnership are complex and certain of them (including the implications of recent and possible future legislative tax changes) will not be the same for all taxpayers. Accordingly, prospective purchasers of Interests are strongly urged to consult their tax advisors with specific reference to their own tax situation. The cost of such consultation could, depending on the amount thereof, materially decrease any anticipated yield on the investment.

Improved real estate, if well selected, can be one of the finest investments available. It has the attributes of income, appreciation and collateral security for loans together with many tax advantages.

SECTION THREE

FEDERALLY ASSISTED PROGRAMS

Federally assisted low-income real estate programs are usually high-risk ventures. There may be unusually high operating expenses, vandalism, and the tenants may be unable or unwilling to pay rents and/or rent increases. However, such programs have exceptional tax advantages. Some of them provide a 200% first year tax write-off. Rehabilitation expenditures can be amortized over five years. If sale proceeds are reinvested in a similar project, tax on the proceeds may be deferred. Thus, the tax benefits may be great enough to attract the high-tax-bracket taxpayer.

Programs for federally assisted low and moderate income multi-family rental housing are administered by the FHA, a division of the Department of Housing and Urban Development ("HUD"). Investors utilize private placements and public offerings primarily in federal housing programs under Section 236 and 221(d)(4) of the National Housing Act. They may also participate in rent supplement programs under the Section 221(d)(3) Market Interest Rate Program and projects financed by a state or municipal housing finance agency. Investments are also available in housing projects to be rehabilitated and operated with government assistance under Section 236 or Section 221(d)(3).

SECTION 236

Section 236 provides for federal insurance of private, 40-year mortgage loans in an amount, for projects sponsored by profit-making limited dividend entities, up to 90% of the project cost as determined by the FHA pursuant to its regulations. A limited dividend entity is a private entity organized solely for the purpose of providing housing, and whose project rents are calculated so that, after payment of mortgage interest and principal, reserve funds, deposits and expenses, the annual cash distributions are not in excess of 6%

of the initial FHA defined equity investment in the project. The FHA defined equity investment will, in most cases, be significantly smaller than the investment the Partnership makes in each Local Partnership.

In addition to mortgage insurance, Section 236 authorizes monthly rent subsidy payments directly to the mortgage lender on behalf of the project owner. The benefit of this subsidy must be passed on to eligible tenants in the form of lower rents. The amount of the monthly government payment is calculated as the difference between the monthly payment that would be required for principal, interest, and mortgage insurance premiums on the mortgage loan to be insured assuming it were at a market rate of interest (presently limited by HUD to 7%) and the monthly payment that would be required for principal and interest if the mortgage loan carried an interest rate of 1%. The rent subsidy, through interest reduction, may apply to all or a portion of the project. Using the assumed 1% interest rate mortgage loan, a basic rental charge is determined for each dwelling unit. Each eligible resident is required to pay either the basic rental charge or 25% of his monthly income, whichever is the greater, but in no event will he be required to pay more than the fair rental value of his dwelling unit. The fair rental value is the rent that would have to be charged if there were no subsidy payments. In selecting residents, preference must be given to those whose incomes do not exceed levels established by the FHA under standards prescribed by Congress. Residents whose incomes increase beyond such levels are permitted to remain as tenants, and the additional rents collected are paid to the federal government.

An additional feature of the Section 236 program is that normally up to 20% of the dwelling units may be further subsidized pursuant to the rent supplement program under Section 101 of the Housing and Urban Development Act of 1965. This program permits federal payments direct to owners of qualified rental housing projects on behalf of qualified low-income tenants. This benefit must be passed on to the tenant in the form of lower rent. The result of rent supplement payments is to reduce the rents to a level that can be afforded by families eligible for public housing.

Finally, Section 236 permits fees for certain services to be included in determining the project cost, such as architectural, engineering, legal, organizational and loan placement services.

Where there is an identity of interest between the builder and sponsor - for example, where the builder has a partnership interest in the Local Partnership developing a Project, the Project cost on which the 90% mortgage is based may include a "builder-sponsor profit and risk allowance" equivalent to 10% of all project costs other than land. This allowance is normally used by the sponsor to satisfy part of the equity requirement for the Project. If mortgage proceeds are available to fund part of such allowance, such proceeds are applied to pay the builder's overhead and profit, plus certain direct charges. Actual costs incurred by the sponsor for such items and for cost overruns may exceed this 10% allowance, thus requiring additional equity investment. A sponsor may, however, be able to hold such costs below the 10% allowance; in such event the savings would reduce the sponsor's cash equity invested in a given Project.

SECTION 221(d)(3)

The Section 221(d)(3) Market Interest Rate Program is similar to the Section 236 Program except that (i) there are no interest reduction payments and (ii) all housing units receive a full supplement payment under the rent supplement program. Only qualified low-income tenants may live in a Section 221(d)(3) Market Interest Rate Project. As in Section 236 Projects the FHA insures mortgages for 90% of the FHA determined project cost and the annual cash distribution is limited to 6% of the FHA defined equity investment.

SECTION 221(d)(4)

Section 221(d)(4) provides for federal insurance of private, 40 year mortgage loans in an amount up to 90% of the project cost as determined by the FHA pursuant to its regulations. Tenants of Section 221(d)(4) projects are persons of moderate income, and rents allowed to be charged are higher than in the case of Section 236 and Section 221(d)(3) projects. Unlike the Section 236 and the Section 221(d)(3) programs, the Section 221(d)(4) program does not provide for rental or interest subsidies, and the mortgage rate is at the market rate. The cash return to the owners of a Section 221(d)(4) project is not limited by regulation, but increases in the maximum allowable rent for a Project must be approved by the FHA.

Priority for occupancy is given to families displaced by governmental action, but there are no income limitations on eligibility for occupancy. Section 221(d)(4) encourages private enterprise to produce rental housing for moderate income families by limiting the eligibility for FHA mortgage insurance to projects sponsored by private, profit-motivated mortgagors.

The market interest rate program provided for by Section 221(d)(4) permits the FHA to insure mortgages on qualifying projects in an amount not exceeding 90% of the replacement cost of the project as determined by the FHA, including a provision for a "builder and sponsor profit and risk allowance." Mortgages insured under this program may not exceed an amount which entails a debt service in excess of 90% of estimated income after deducting operating expenses. During the period the mortgage is insured, the FHA receives annual mortgage insurance premium payments equal to ½ of one percent of the outstanding principal of the mortgage.

Extensive controls are established by the FHA over construction and operating procedures during the period the mortgage is insured. The FHA inspects construction as it progresses, approves advances of mortgage funds during the construction period and requires certification of costs upon completion.

Regulations issued under this program establish maximum rentals which may be charged. Rents may be increased up to the maximum without the approval of the Federal Housing Commissioner. The FHA will consider increases of the maximum allowable rentals if such increases are necessary to compensate for increased operating expenses.

Under Section 221(d)(4) the amount of annual distributions of cash flow are limited only by the payment of operating expenses, debt service and costs of proper maintenance of the property.

The FHA requires that the owner make monthly deposits to a reserve fund to be used to make replacements of project assets as needed. Property financed under this program may be sold or refinanced at any time without the permission of the Federal Housing Commissioner.

STATE OR MUNICIPAL HOUSING FINANCE AGENCY

Several state and municipal agencies are authorized to make mortgage loans to qualified sponsors for construction of low and moderate income housing within the state or municipality. Such agencies issue bonds and notes to the investing public in order to create a flow of private capital through the agencies into mortgage loans. The agencies enter into regulatory agreements with sponsors which conform a project's construction and operation to the agency's regulations. The regulations control rents, profits, dividends, management of projects, fees, wages, salaries and other matters relating to the operation of the project and its disposition. HUD makes available to qualified state or municipal agencies Section 236 and rent supplement funds which can be allocated by the agencies to their projects. Regardless of the agency regulating a project, it is anticipated that the regulatory pattern will be substantially the same as that required by FHA.

GOVERNMENT SUPERVISION OF PROJECTS

The FHA passes on the eligibility of mortgagors and establishes rules regarding the structure and allowable distributions of profit-making developers. It must approve various aspects of any such project, including the cost and size of individual housing units, and in most cases, require certification of the actual cost of every project. It must approve detailed plans and specifications for each project. FHA regulations determine which items may be included in the amount used to calculate the mortgage loan to be federally insured and subsidized, limit eligibility for residency by income levels and it some cases require that a preference be given to those displaced by certain other housing programs. Certification and periodic recertification of resident income and assets are required, and under some programs rents must be adjusted accordingly. Regulations limit the rent that may be charged and prohibit increases in rent in the absence of specific approval; the FHA gives such approval only to the extent of increases in costs over which the project owner has no effective control. It is empowered to require maintenance and repair activities necessary to keep projects in good condition. It requires a variety of project records and reports, and has extensive access to the premises and records of project sponsors. FHA regulations limit the sale or refinancing of Section 221(d)(3) and Section 236 projects. Compliance with these regulations entails certain direct costs and, if and to the extent that compliance delays completion of construction, added carrying costs.

If projects are developed under state or municipally financed programs, they are subject to substantial regulation similar to that exercised by the FHA. Further, the projects in which the Partnership participates will be subject to local building codes and other local regulation, which may vary widely among localities.

GENERAL CONSIDERATIONS

FHA housing projects provide a low cash flow of 3% to 4% per year of original invested capital; but tax savings are high and continue for almost 20 years. These tax shelters may be appropriate for either corporations or individual who will remain in the 50% Federal income tax bracket or higher for approximately five years.

Tax benefits are available in several ways. It is permissible to use the 200% declining balance or sum-of-the-years digits depreciation, and the basis for depreciation includes the mortgage as leverage. Moreover, the limited partners benefit from capital appreciation, if any, upon the sale or refinancing of the project. If the project is sold to the tenants or an organization representing the tenants, and the proceeds are reinvested in a similar project within the time allowed, the tax may be deferred. This deferral can continue until the limited partner sells or dies. Tax savings and cash flow usually return a limited partner's investment in about 5 years for a 50% tax bracket investor and 4 years for a 60% tax bracket investor from the first installment of his investment.

From this it can be readily seen that the government has recognized the critical need for low-income housing and is offering substantial tax benefits in order to attract high-tax-bracket investors to this tax shelter.

There will be two examples of these projects. First will be an "FHA 236" program involving a new apartment house. Second will be a Rehabilitation project of several older apartment houses.

EXAMPLE OF AN "FHA 236" PROGRAM

This is a program handled by a State Finance Agency. It offers investors 15 limited partnership interests (the units) in MELVIN ASSOCIATES, a limited partnership (the Partnership) organized under State law to acquire, own, construct and operate a garden apartment housing project (the Project) in Anyplace, U.S.A. The financing and operation of the Project is being assisted by the State Finance Agency (the Lender) and the Department of Housing and Urban Development. The general partner of the Partnership (the General Partner) and developer of the Project will be NORMAN INDUSTRIES, INC. Initially the Limited Partners will be entitled to 99% of the Cash Flow from ordinary operations and to 99% of the ordinary profits and losses of the Partnership and the General Partner will be entitled to the remaining 1% thereof. After Participation Change the interest of the Limited Partners in Cash Flow and profits and losses will be reduced to 49.5% and that of the General Partner correspondingly increased. The Limited Partners will be entitled to 49.5% of the residual proceeds from the sale, other disposition or refinancing of the Project and the General Partner will be entitled to the remaining 50.5% thereof. Participation Change is defined to mean the later of the 20th anniversary of the date of Final Acceptance and the date on which the Limited Partners shall have received a distribution of Cash Flow and/or net cash proceeds from a refinancing, sale or other dispostion of the Project which, together with all prior distributions to the Limited Partners of Cash Flow and of such net cash proceeds equals the total purchase price of the Units.

If the Project earns sufficient Cash Flow to distribute the Maximum Limited Partner Distribution, each Investor should receive a distribution of Cash Flow of approximately 4% per annum on the purchase price of his Unit (assuming that there is no upward price adjustment) until Participation Change. After Participation Change, if sufficient Cash Flow is earned, and the maximum distributable Cash Flow remains the same, an Investor should receive a distribution of Cash Flow of approximately 2% per annum on the purchase price of his Unit (assuming there is no upward price adjustment).

The sponsors of MELVIN have applied for and anticipate obtaining a commitment from the State Housing Finance Agency for a 7%, 40-year self-amortizing permanent mortgage loan of $4,250,000. On top of that loan, the sponsors have applied for the entire project (all 200 units) to receive interest reduction payments under Section 236 of the National Housing Act, thereby enabling a reduction in rentals significantly below market rentals.

The State Housing Finance Agency issues mortgage loans and obtains funds by floating both short term notes and long term bonds. Interest rates on the bonds are generally below rates for similar debt securities because of their tax-free status.

PROJECT SUMMARY

Maximum total cost:
(a)	Total maximum purchase price of Units	$ 750,000
(b)	Mortgage loan	4,250,000
(c)	Total	$5,000,000

Unit cost: $50,000.

Schedule of payments per unit: Approximately 25% per year for four years with two payments the first year.

Recoupment: It is estimated that each payment of the purchase price of a Unit made by an Investor should be recouped from anticipated Cash Flow and tax benefits according to the following timetable:

Number of years after payment to
Recoupment of that payment

Payment	50% Tax Bracket	70% Tax Bracket
1	1.25	1.00
2	1.49	1.13
3	2.05	1.34
4	2.46	1.37
5	2.94	1.44

Rate of Return: Based on a pro rata crediting of tax savings throughout each year over a 20-year holding period and a sale of the Project at the end of such holding period for $1.00 and assumption of the mortgage, it is estimated that each Limited

Partner in the indicated tax bracket should earn the following after-tax annual rate of return on his Outstanding Investment:

Limited Partner's Tax Bracket	After-Tax Annual Rate of Return
50%	15.6%
70%	29.0%

Net Investment: Based on a pro rata crediting of tax savings throughout each year over a 20-year holding period, it is estimated that the maximum year-end Net Investment of a Limited Partner is as follows:

Limited Partner's Tax Bracket	Net Investment
50%	$27,500
70%	$18,500

Completion of the project: The General Partner will be obligated to furnish any funds necessary to complete construction in excess of the proceeds of the mortgage loan, the purchase price of the Units and net rental income prior to Final acceptance. If such funds are advanced they will be deemed to be Residual Receipts Obligations which will reduce the interest of the Limited Partners in the proceeds from sale, other dispostion or refinancing of the Project.

Cash distribution loans: The General Partner will agree to loan to the Partnership, so long as the Project is managed by the General Partner or an affiliate, up to $16,000 per year (approximately 59% of the presently projected Cash Flow) for distribution to the Limited Partners if the Limited Partners have not received the maximum Limited Partners' distribution. Any amounts so advanced will be deemed Cash Distribution Loans payable from proceeds of the sale or refinancing of the Project before any distribution of proceeds to the Limited Partners.

Subordinated Loans: If the Partnership should require funds after Final Acceptance, the General Partner may, but is not obligated to, furnish such funds. If such funds are furnished they will be deemed to be Subordinated Loans which do not bear interest but which are payable from Cash Flow before any distribution thereof to the Limited Partners.

An "FHA 236" program enables the high-tax-bracket taxpayer to recover his investment in 4 to 5 years through large write-offs and income. This factor alone may make the investment sufficiently attractive to the high income investor.

EXAMPLE OF A REHABILITATION VENTURE

There is great need for the rehabilitation of old apartment houses in American cities. Congress has responded by offering the rehabilitation tax shelter in which the rehabilitation expenditures can be amortized over 5 years. This shelter provides heavy write-offs for high income investors as shown below.

OLIVER APARTMENTS consist of a total of 190 housing units and are financed by mortgages insured under Section 221(d)(3) and Section 236 of the National Housing Act. The land and buildings to be rehabilitated will be acquired by the Partnership.

Costs of development and financing of the projects:

Costs of development (approximate)

Rehabilitation (including General Requirements)	$1,200,000
Acquisition costs – Existing Structures	700,000
Carrying charges and Financing	200,000
Legal and other organizational costs	50,000
Development fee to builder and Sponsor and payment to General Partners	350,000
Total	$2,500,000

Financing (approximate)

Mortgages	$2,000,000
Investment by Investors	500,000
Total	$2,500,000

SUMMARY OF TERMS

OLIVER APARTMENTS: Section "236" and "221(d)(3)" Rehabilitation Projects; Limited Partnership Interests; 10 Units at $50,000 each

Purpose: Proceeds will be used to acquire five buildings and the land on which the buildings are constructed and to rehabilitate thereon 190 apartment units. The five buildings will be owned by four Partnerships and will constitute four individual Projects for FHA purposes.

Takedown of Monies:

On admission as Limited Partner	$20,000
Following year	$30,000

Allocation of Benefits:

(a) Limited Partners receive 100% of the cash flow, and profits and losses of the four Partnerships through approximately the 20th year.

(b) Thereafter, Limited Partners receive 50% (the General Partners receive the other 50% of the Cash Flow, profits and losses.

(c) Limited Partners receive 50% of the residual proceeds upon the sale of a Project.

Recoupment: It is estimated that the amount of each Limited Partner's investment will be recouped through Cash Flow and tax benefits according to the following timetable:

Number of months after investment payment to recoupment of that payment by tax bracket:

Payment	50%	70%
1	18 months	12 months
2	26 months	15 months

Rate of return: It is estimated that the limited partnership interests will earn the following after-tax annual rate of return:

Limited Partner's Tax Bracket	After-Tax Annual Rate of Return
50%	25%
70%	49%

Construction Guarantees: The General Partners will furnish any additional funds necessary to complete construction of the Projects. Such additional funds will be evidenced by Residual Receipts Obligations and subject to such obligations will not change the respective interests of the Partners.

Subordinated Loans: In the event that the Partnerships should require funds for normal operating purposes in addition to funds provided by rental income, the General Partners agree to make Subordinated Loans up to certain limits.

Subordination of Management Fees: In the event that there is insufficient cash to make the maximum annual allowable distribution to the Investor Limited Partners, the General Partners will loan to the Partnerships up to 50% of the management fees paid for that year.

The General Partners, PAUL, QUIXOTE, and RONALD, have agreed to manage the Projects in consideration of the maximum annual management fee certificable to the FHA as an expense of the Projects.

PARTICULAR ECONOMIC BENEFITS OF OLIVER APARTMENTS

The economic incentives for investment in the Partnerships are (1) an annual cash return, (2) the availability of 50% of the cash from a refinancing, subject to FHA regulations referred to below, and (3) 50% of the Residuals from the sale of the Projects.

1. Cash Return. It is projected that an Investor will receive a distribution of Cash Flow from the Projects of approximately 3% per annum on his investment until Participation Change. If costs increase and the FHA does not permit corresponding increases, the return may be smaller. After Participation Change, an Investor is expected to receive a distribution of Cash Flow of approximately 1.6% per annum on his Investment.

2. Refinancing. 50% of the residuals from a refinancing of a mortgage will be distributed to the Investors. However, no assurance can be given as to the availability or feasibility of refinancing. For 20 years from Final Endorsements, refinancing of the Mortgage is permitted only with prior FHA approval. If a Partnership is receiving rent supplements in respect of low income tenants, after 20 years from Final Endorsement, this restriction on refinancing will continue. Such restriction may continue until maturity of the Mortgage,

which is 40 years from Final Endorsement, if a Partnership continues to receive rent supplements until maturity. The Partnerships have applied to receive rent supplement funds and reserve the right to receive such funds in the future.

3. Residual values. 50% of the residuals from the sale of a Project will be distributed to the Investors. However, no assurance can be given as to the value of the residuals. For 20 years from Final Endorsement, the sale of a Project is permitted only with prior FHA approval. If a Partnership is receiving rent supplement funds between the 20th and 40th years after Final Endorsement, this restriction on the sale of a Project will remain in effect.

BENEFITS OF FHA LOW-INCOME HOUSING PROGRAMS

1. Favorable depreciation of 200 percent declining balance or sum of the years-digits is possible.

2. It provides favorable depreciation recapture of excess of accelerated over straight line on a decreasing amount over the second 100 months.

3. Tax can be deferred on sale of Project to tenants or an approved organization representing tenants if sale proceeds are reinvested properly.

4. Rehabilitation expenditures can be amortized over five years.

RISKS OF FHA LOW-INCOME HOUSING PROGRAMS

1. Tax Considerations: The advisability of investing in a Partnership depends primarily upon the Investor's ability to use the benefits which flow from the present favorable tax treatment available with respect to investment in Projects. The major benefit will result from the ability to apply substantial tax losses generated by Projects against taxable income from other sources. In view of the critical national shortage of residential housing, the Tax Reform Act of 1969 allows a five-year write-off of a rehabilitation expenditures, within limitation.

All or a portion of the benefits an Investor has received or anticipates receiving could be lost and, in some cases, substantial tax liabilities incurred if (1) the Internal Revenue Code of 1954, as amended ("the code") or its current interpretation by the Internal Revenue Service is changed, (2) the Investor does not continue to have income subject to taxation at high rates for approximately 20 years from the date of his investment (7 years from the date of his investment in Rehabilitation Projects), (3) a Unit is sold or transferred by the Investor for any reason except death, (4) an Investor has a substantial amount of items of tax preference in any year or (5) the mortgage on a Project is foreclosed. The risk of mortgage foreclosure can arise from, among other things, high vacancy levels, expenditures exceeding allowable rents, and failure of the mortgagor to meet the conditions of the mortgage loan.

In any event, deductions available to a Partnership from each Project will decline over the years and will be virtually exhausted after approximately 20 years. In addition, it is expected that taxable income will exceed cash distributions at some point, perhaps between the twentieth and twenty-second years after construction. In Rehabilitation Projects, deductions available to a Partnership from each Project will decline sharply in approximately the seventh year; thereafter, Investors may anticipate unsheltered taxable income. In addition, it is expected that taxable income will exceed cash distributions at some point, perhaps the seventh year.

2. Competition: The Federal Housing Administration ("FHA") and comparable state and municipal agencies are limited by various constraints on the maximum amount of mortgage loans they can insure and the maximum amount of financial assistance of other kinds they can provide. These benefits can be made available, therefore, only to a limited number of Projects, and no assurance can be given that a Partnership will be able to locate attractive Projects for which commitments for such assistance are available. In addition, since funds for mortgage financing must be obtained from private sources or from quasi-governmental financing agencies which in turn depend on private funds, there can be no assurance that funds will be available in sufficient amounts and at attractive rates.

It is expected that a Partnership will compete with a large number of other investors for desirable Projects. These other investors, who include wealthy individuals, privately held limited partnerships organized by major investment banking firms and publicly held limited partnerships, may be willing to pay more for a Project than a given Partnership.

3. Project Risks: The FHA does not guarantee the occupancy of the Projects, and no assurance can be given that they will be fully rented. Governmentally-assisted multi-family property is often subject to rising operating costs, vacancy and rent collection difficulties, and adverse economic and social changes. It is difficult to predict the life expectancy of the structures on the properties to be acquired by the Partnership, and the amount of any residual value in these properties is highly speculative.

Rentals obtainable on completion of a Project or upon the expiration of leases may not be sufficient to cover recurring expenses such as maintenance, debt service, taxes and fees. If Project income is not sufficient to meet both operating and extraordinary costs (whether because of excessive vacancies, rental delinquencies or increased costs and expenses), a Local Partnership may be forced to default on mortgage interest and principal payments. If mortgage foreclosure results, a resultant sale of the Project will subject a Partnership to loss of principal and the Investors to the tax consequences of capital gains and depreciation recapture. Such risks of default and foreclosure are increased by, among other things, the fact that these projects may have a relatively large percentage of tenants who have previously lived in substandard conditions. This may in turn result in higher than normal operating expenses, exceeding the estimates upon which initial FHA approved rents are based. As in the case of other residential property, the ability of the developer/manager to estimate accurately and control expenses is crucial. If expenses exceed estimates, the developer must be able to persuade the FHA to agree to rental increases in order to avoid negative cash flow and a consequent default in mortgage payments. While FHA may approve rental increases in the face of unforeseen contingencies, there may be delays in obtaining such approval, and, even when approval is obtained, the tenants, who are generally persons and families of low income, may be unable or unwilling to pay the increased rents.

There recently have been a number of reports of defaults in payments of interest and principal on mortgage loans insured by the FHA pursuant to the Section 236 and 221(d)(3) programs, and in some cases the mortgages reportedly have been foreclosed.

4. Limited Transferability of Units: Some programs have provided a public market for resale of the Units, but others have

not done so. Over the years, the value of a Unit may be expected to decline as the operating losses attributable to it decline, and its sale may result in substantial tax liability to the investor which may exceed the cash received from such sale.

5. Return of Distributions: Substantially all cash distributed during at least the first 20 years of a Partnership's existence is expected to constitute a return of capital. In Rehabilitation Projects substantially all cash distributed during the early years of the Partnership's existence is expected to constitute a return of capital.

6. Government Regulation: A Partnership will be subject to substantial governmental regulation by reason of its investment in the Projects, principally by the FHA. In consideration of mortgage insurance and interest subsidies provided by the FHA, the owners of the Projects must conform to detailed regulations governing such matters as the amount of cash which may be distributed from the Project's operations, eligibility of tenants, maintenance of reserves for contingencies and the like. To the extent a Project is subsidized by a state or municipal agency, comparable constraints may be anticipated.

RISKS OF MODERATE INCOME HOUSING

Moderate income housing is subject to many of the risks just described. The following risk factors, however, are particularly inherent in a project of this nature and should be carefully considered.

Operating expenses, primarily repairs, might exceed projected amounts thereby reducing or eliminating cash flow. While the FHA will, in most instances, grant rent increases to cover justifiable increased operating costs, it generally requires one year of operating experience.Due to this time lag, the continuing impact of inflation on such operating expenses could eliminate the benefits of such an increase. In addition, increased property taxes could cause a reduction or elimination of the cash flow.

As a result of operating income being substantially lower than projected, due to failure to rent by reason of the mix of apartment units (such as too many three-bedroom apartments) or the failure to collect rents or if operating expenses are substantially increased, the project may need additional cash contributions in order to meet working capital requirements. If such additional cash requirements are not provided by the partners (both general and limited) or by additional outside financing, then the project could go into default.

TAX ASPECTS OF FHA LOW–INCOME HOUSING PROGRAMS

1. Usually a Partnership anticipates that it will incur substantial losses for federal income tax purposes, which will decline over the years and will be virtually exhausted after 20 years. A Partner may deduct his share of such losses from his other taxable income, limited, however, to his adjusted basis in his Partnership interest. In a Rehabilitation Project the losses will in most instances be exhausted after 7 years.

2. In the case of residential real estate, the 1976 Tax Reform Act provides for the recapture of all post-1975 depreciation in excess of straight-line, in the same manner as is presently the case for non-residential real estate. In the case of government subsidized housing, the conference agreement provides full recapture of post-1975 depreciation for the first 100 months (8 1/3 years) and a phaseout of the amount recaptured during the second 100 months (up to 16 2/3 years). There will be no recapture thereafter. Government subsidized housing includes housing (1) with respect to which a mortgage is insured under Section 221(d)(3) or 236 of the National Housing Act (2) under Section 8 of the United States Housing Act of 1937 and (3) with respect to which a loan is made or insured under title V of the Housing Act of 1949.

3. The Revenue Act of 1978 provides a three-year extension (until January 1, 1982) of the special 5-year amortization rule for expenditures to rehabilitate low-income rental housing and increases the amount of rehabilitation expenditures that can be taken into account per dwelling unit from $15,000 to $20,000. Rehabilitation expenditures that are made pursuant to a binding contract entered into before January 1, 1982, qualify for the 5-year amortization rule even though the expenditures are actually made after December 31, 1981. In addition, the conference agreement modifies the definition of families and individuals of low and moderate income by providing that the eligible income limits would be determined in a manner consistent with those presently established for the leased housing program under Section 8 of the United States Housing Act of 1937, as amended. These provisions apply to expendi-

tures paid or incurred with respect to low-income rental housing after December 31, 1975.

4. Under the 1976 Tax Reform Act, construction period interest and taxes are to be capitalized in the year in which they are paid or incurred and amortized over a 10-year period. A portion of this amount capitalized may be deducted for the taxable year in which paid or incurred. The balance must be amortized over the remaining years in the amortization period beginning with the year in which the property is ready to be placed in service or is ready to be held for sale.

Under the 1976 Tax Reform Act, separate transitional rules are provided for non-residential real estate, residential real estate, and government subsidized housing. In the case of nonresidental real estate, this provision is to apply only to property where the construction period begins after December 31, 1975. (However, for 1976 only, 50 percent of the construction period interest and taxes for nonresidential real estate need be capitalized.) In the case of residential real estate (other than certain low-income housing), this provision is to apply to construction period interest and taxes paid or incurred after December 31, 1977, and, in the case of low-income housing, to construction period interest and taxes paid or incurred after December 31, 1981.

In addition, the length of the amortization period is to be phased-in over a 7-year period. The amortization period is to be 4 years in the case of interest and taxes paid or incurred in the first year to which these rules apply. The amortization period increases by one year for each succeeding year after the initial effective date until the amortization period becomes 10 years (i.e., the 10-year period is fully phased-in for construction period interest and taxes paid or incurred in 1982, in the case of non-residential real estate; 1984, in the case of residential real estate, and 1988, in the case of government subsidized housing).

FHA low-income housing programs, whether new construction or rehabilitation, should only be considered by investors who can benefit substantially by high tax write-offs and afford to lose their investments if the projects go into default and mortgages are foreclosed.

Real Estate in its various forms as a tax shelter will in all probability continue to be favored in the tax laws by Congress as the need for housing and various other buildings shows no sign of decreasing.

DEFINITIONS CONCERNING REAL ESTATE BUSINESS

EQUITY: That portion of the interests in a Project which represents the fee ownership of the land, buildings, and other improvements comprising the Project.

FHA: The Federal Housing Administration, a division of the Department of Housing and Urban Development.

FINAL ENDORSEMENT: The date upon which the FHA accepts a Project as being completed and the permanent mortgage loan becomes insured.

50% PERCENT BRACKET INVESTOR: A taxpayer at least some of whose income is subject to taxation, after taking into account the losses generated by his investment in the Partnership, at a rate of at least 50% and who does not have items of tax preference, including those generated by his investment in the Partnership, the total amount of which would subject him to the minimum tax for tax preferences or would reduce the amount of "earned income" eligible for the limitation on the maximum rate of taxation on "earned income."

INITIAL ENDORSEMENT: The date upon which the FHA insures a construction loan for a Project.

INVESTOR OR LIMITED PARTNER: A holder of a limited partnership interest in the Partnership.

LOCAL PARTNERSHIP: A limited partnership formed to own the Equity in a given Project. The developer of the Project will generally act as general partner, and the Partnership in each case will act as a limited partner. There will be a separate Local Partnership for each Project in which the Partnership invests, and the sole business of the Local Partnership will be to own and operate the Project.

TAX SHELTER: Tax losses generated by the operation of a Project which are available pro rata to the Partners to offset income from other sources for federal income tax purposes and, under certain circumstances, for state and local income tax purposes as well. These losses occur because non-cash deductions, principally depreciation, when added to cash expenditures, exceed gross revenues of the Project and may be substantially in excess of the amount of cash invested in the Project.

CHAPTER TWO

OIL AND GAS

INTRODUCTION

Oil and gas investments fall into three main categories: Producing property where producing wells already exist; development drilling near producing wells; and exploratory drilling in previously unproductive areas.

Some programs offer investment exclusively in one of these three categories, and other programs are combinations of two and sometimes all three of the categories. Producing wells are usually offered in oil income programs for investors seeking a low-risk oil investment with the opportunity for a reasonably high income, for example, 12% which is partially tax-free because of the depletion allowance. Development drilling is a medium-risk tax shelter for the investor interested in a moderate return through deductions and partially tax-free income. Exploratory drilling is a high-risk tax shelter for the investor who wants a high first-year tax write-off and is willing to gamble against the odds in hopes of his program discovering new oil from which he will receive a large return including some partially tax-free income. Limited partnership interests in these programs may be sold on a capital gains basis. Also, some programs exchange limited partnership interests for stock in public corporations which may be traded on stock exchanges.

TAX ADVANTAGES

The basic tax advantages of oil programs include intangible drilling and development costs and the depletion allowance. Intangibles are the costs for items such as labor, repairs and supplies used in drilling and amounts to 60% to 80% of the cost of completing a well. They are deductible against income in the year incurred. The other costs are capital expenditures and must be capitalized and recovered over a period of years through depreciation. Capital expenditures include acquiring

95

the land to drill and geological, geophysical, and equipment costs. The law permits a depletion deduction of 22% from gross oil and gas sales but limits the deduction to 50% of net income after certain expenses of production have been deducted. The deduction continues indefinitely after the investment has been recovered.

SELECTING THE OPERATOR

As in most investments the key to success with oil is the quality of the management. It is important that the management have a proven record in its previous oil programs. The geologists, the land-men who negotiate the leases, the drilling organization, and the administration must all be efficient and knowledgable. Good management will show a favorable relationship of oil and gas revenues to the investment and be able to handle substantial amounts of investors' money in the oil drilling business. No investment should be considered if the management is not capable of coping with the size of the program it is offering. Also, it is important that the operator be adequately rewarded so that he will have incentive to produce the most favorable results.

There are various ways in which the operator is compensated. The selling fee for organizing the program and offering it to investors is approximately 8% of the amount invested. A management fee of approximately 10% may be charged to cover operational expenses which include office, legal, and accounting charges. The operator may receive a reversionary working interest in future revenues after the investors have recovered their capital investment. This interest is usually between 20% – 30%, and the operator must then pay his proportionate share of operating the property. He may also be granted an overriding royalty such as 1/32 or 1/16 interest in the oil and gas produced and he would bear none of the expenses. Today, the most common arrangement calls for sharing expenses and income. The investor's money pays for intangible drilling and development costs which can be immediately written off, and the operator pays for the items to be capitalized and depreciated over the life of the property. Usually the operator is reimbursed for his overhead and receives 30% to 50% of the income.

In addition to the above basic considerations, it is important for the investor to have some general knowledge of the industry's future. A highly qualified government official discusses this aspect of the oil and gas investment as follows.

STATE OF THE INDUSTRY

How does the future look for the business? What are the chances for success? Those are the traditional questions asked by the investor about any investment he is considering. The following remarks by Gene P. Morrell, Deputy Assistant Secretary – Mineral Resources, Department of the Interior, before the Educational Seminar on Oil and Gas Drilling Programs, New York, N. Y., March 20, 1970, answer such questions about the oil industry and oil investment.

"In 1969, just over three-fourths of the entire energy requirement of the United States was supplied by oil and gas, and approximately the same comment could be made of each of the ten years before that. During this ten-year period, the energy balance has been remarkably stable, with oil consistently accounting for 43% to 45%; gas slowing rising from 29% to 32%; and coal just as slowly sinking from 23% down to 20%. Hydropower has gone along at about 4%, and nuclear power has yet to reach 1% of total energy supply.

"Looking ahead, our fuel resources people in the Department don't see a great deal of change in this balance among energy components over the next fifteen years. Each of the fossil fuels and hydropower will be squeezed to make room for the rising share of nuclear power, but by and large, our projections have oil coming out with 38% of the energy market in 1985 – a decline of five percentage points from last year, and natural gas backing off one point to 31%. Petroleum hydrocarbons will still supply the bulk of our energy requirements in 1985. Now, percentages are great, particularly if you don't want to emphasize your point. What's disconcerting is that when you relate these to absolute numbers and the history of the energy business you find some facts that are a little hard to believe. The fifteen-year supply requirement for oil for the U.S. energy market comes to a hundred billion barrels. This is as much oil as the United States consumed from the beginning of the oil industry in 1859 down to the end of 1967 – just a little more than two years ago. It means finding ten more Alaska Prudoe Bays, this in light of the fact that Prudoe was only the second such find in the past 40 years, the first being East Texas. In the same fifteen years we will need 420 trillion cubic feet of natural gas. This is more – by 80 trillion cubic feet – than all the natural gas our nation has consumed in all its history.

"We make these light-hearted projections, I suppose, on the blythe assumption that the Lord will provide, He always has. Our better sense tells us, as the song goes, that 'It ain't necessarily so.' Not a single foot of gas or barrel of oil was ever provided by a chartist or economist with a calculator and a pencil. It may seem like carrying coals to Newcastle for me to warn this group on the frailties of forecasts, but I do want to be recorded as understanding that demand, particularly for commodities subjected to active competition, is strongly related to supply through price, and this is especially relevant to our domestic energy balance today.

"Ever since anyone can remember, except for such extraordinary episodes as World War II, or other crisis oriented supply problems, the emphasis in the fuel industries has been on sales and markets – a preoccupation with demand, in other words. The general rule that everybody operated by was that you could supply whatever volume you could sell, and this was a correct assumption for many years. Now, much to our surprise, we are finding that our problems are shifting from the sales end to the supply end of the system. We face an impending scarcity of supply of every form of domestically produced energy. The attention given in the press recently to the problem of inadequate reserves of natural gas, and the outlook for reserves will, indeed, put a severe strain on natural gas supplies over the next several years. I hasten to add that those of you who have gas heat in your homes are not going to go home at any time in the foreseeable future and find the furnace cold. But it does mean that the interruptible industrial customers are going to get interrupted sooner and longer, that there is going to be very little new gas available for the expanding needs of present industrial firm customers, and that many new housing developments to be built over the coming years are going to have to use something besides gas for heating.

"The domestic supply position for oil has been eroding along with that of gas, and for many of the same reasons. In the case of oil, however, the ready availability of imports serves to gloss over the extent of this erosion. So, because we haven't felt a supply pinch, we tend to lose sight of the fact that our reserves of oil are just about where they were ten years ago, despite a gain in consumption of 46%; that in five out of the last nine years we failed to replace as much oil in our proved resources as we withdrew from them; and that our productive capacity is declining at the same time that demand is rising, so that indications are all spare capacity will be gone within three or four years. This is the extra capacity on which we have depended ever since the beginning of World War II to give us the oil we needed to get through interruptions to our imports and sudden increases in demand such as occurred at the outbreak of the Korean War or during the Suez Crisis. This is where the U.S. Government has to crank in the element of supply into the economic formula.

"Would you believe that we are short of coal, too? We are. We have hundreds of years' supply of it in the ground – identified, located, and reliably measured, but we haven't produced our full requirements in two years, and the major coal users have been living off fat since 1967. The average supply for utility coal stockpiles is currently around 70 days as against 90 days they customarily maintained in past years, and some individual plants are considerably less than average. Coking plants, which customarily keep a 45-day supply in their yards, now average 35 days. There are many reasons to account for this anomaly of paucity in the midst of plenty, but our subject is oil and gas, and I won't dwell on the problems of other fuels, except to emphasize again that the stringency of energy supply encompasses all forms, including electricity; it is with us now; and it is going to get worse before it gets better.

"Now, the ironic thing about this generalized scarcity of domestic energy is that it does not reflect the physical facts of our energy resources. It is an economic condition, not a physical one; we just haven't drilled enough domestic wells, opened enough domestic mines, or build enough power generating plants to provide the domestic energy we need in the forms we require it.

"The fact is that we have enormous resources of hydrocarbon fuels – solid, liquid, and gaseous – that are available to us at any time we care to make the necessary investment of capital and effort needed to find and extract them.

"The U.S. Geological Survey has published estimates that the amount of total crude oil in the ground underneath the United States and its Continental Shelf out to a water depth of 600 feet is roughly 2,500 billion barrels. Of this, some 400 billion barrels have been discovered, leaving well over 2,000 billion barrels that remain to be found. I should add that of the 400 billion barrels that have been discovered so far, only 90 billion barrels have been produced and another 31 billion barrels have been developed to the point where its production is a reasonable certainty under today's economic and operating conditions. This latter figure, of course, is what the industry calls its proved reserves. The large difference between what has been found and what has been proved up and produced – on the order of 280 billion barrels, is oil remaining in identified fields that is not economically producible at today's levels of costs, prices, and technology. This means that more than two-thirds of the oil we have found so far is not considered recoverable at current prices and technological levels. If either of these two factors improve – and technology is continually doing so – the recovery rate will rise. Historically, it has been doing so at the rate of about half a percentage point a year; that is, thirty years ago, the industry was only recovering 15% of the oil it had found; currently, it is recovering over 30%. The oil industry keeps adding to its knowledge of recovery methods, and every year a substantial amount of oil that was previously considered unrecoverable is found to be worth bringing up with new techniques – and so it is transferred to the proved reserves inventory. But still 60% to 70% of it remains unreachable.

"For an assessment of our gas reserves, I am using the latest estimates of the Potential Gas Committee – a group of eminent petroleum scientists and engineers which has systematically been inventorying the nation's gas established and potential provinces for the past few years. The Potential Gas Committee's estimate is that in addition to the 630 trillion cubic feet of gas that have already been found, not less that 1,225 trillion cubic feet remain to be discovered. The Committee believes that 260 trillion cubic feet of this amount will be found in new pools and extensions of old pools in presently existing fields; that another 335 trillion cubic feet can be found in new fields in known producing provinces; and that the remaining 630 trillion cubic feet — appropriately classed as speculative — may be found in provinces that until now have not proved productive of either oil or gas.

"So the target for those looking for oil and gas in the United States is a big one — over two trillion barrels of oil and over one quadrillion cubic feet of gas. That's the good news. Now the bad news. Whoever goes looking for oil and gas is going to have the very devil of a time finding them. The situation today is like the late stages of an Easter egg hunt after the kids have found all the baskets that were easy to locate. And a study of the participants presents a useful analogy, too. You have some tots who have given up looking and gone weeping back to the house. You have others who are still frantically scratching in and around the places where baskets were found earlier — and occasionally they do find one, but mostly they find frustration. Then you have others who are venturesome enough to strike out into new areas. Most them don't find anything either, but some do, and some of their discoveries are impressive, and lead to great flurries of activity by others in the area where the big new baskets were found.

"Moving the scene back to the oil industry, the 'new places' where people are now looking are Alaska, the Continental Shelf, the deep basins of West Texas and Oklahoma, and, for many independents, such places as the Powder River Basin in Montana and Wyoming, and in central Michigan. In the case of these onshore provinces, it is not so much newness of place as newness of approach, and I'll come back to this important feature a little later.

"If we look across our Northern border into Canada, we also see new frontiers for oil exploration opening up in that country. The possibilities of the Western Canadian Basin which runs the entire North-South expanse of Canada along the Eastern flank of the Rocky Mountains, have in no way been fully explored. Now we have indications of significant discoveries in the Canadian Far North, and in the islands of the Franklin District.

"There has been a great deal of activity on the North Slope of Alaska this past winter; and, of course, each hole put down adds to the store of knowledge as to the oil and gas potential of the region. In general, these jigsaw pieces of information suggest a highly optimistic view of what we can eventually expect out of North Slope production. At this time, we think that there are at least ten billion barrels of recoverable oil in the fields that have already been discovered, and there is good reason to believe that additional discoveries will be made. Tests that have been made indicate that many of the wells that will be drilled in the Prudhoe Bay field can be expected to produce at rates of ten thousand barrels a day or more – rates that are in every sense comparable to those achieved by wells in the Middle East. Depending on transport capability, we might expect North Slope production to reach three to four million barrels a day by 1980.

"This sounds like a lot of oil – and it is. But when you compare it with the nearly twenty million barrels a day that we shall be needing in 1980, you can see that the bulk of our oil supply is going to have to come from places besides Alaska. I am saying simply that while the Alaskan discoveries are a welcome addition to our energy supply, they are by no means the whole answer to our problem of keeping our economy adequately fueled. We shall need all the oil and gas we can find, on-shore and off-shore, shallow and deep, and considering the difficulties and hazards of long-haul transport, we would very much like to find it as close to major market areas as possible. Place utility is important, even to a commodity as easily transportable as oil.

"Now, having given the Department of the Interior view that it is important for the Nation to find oil and gas within its domestic geographical limits, I'd like to spend the rest of my time talking about what I perceive to be the outlook for oil and gas discovery.

"Basically, oil and gas exploration is an exercise in probabilities, which is a polite way of saying it is a gamble, of the rankest sort. With uncanny consistency, year in and year out, we find that wells drilled as rank wildcats – that is, in an area where there is no oil or gas production around – the chances of finding any oil or gas at all are one out of nine. But there are worse things than finding no oil, and one of them if finding just enough oil to encourage the operator to spend several thousand dollars more trying to make a paying well out of it and finally having to give up after throwing much good money after bad. Wells like this are called 'stinkers' – for very good reasons that are apparent to anybody who has ever helped pay for one or been responsible for one paid by others.

"So every year several hundred wells get drilled that are recorded as technical 'successes' – in that they did find a show of oil or gas – which are in reality abysmal commercial failures. In recent years, 15% of all wells originally classified as discoveries were plugged and abandoned within the first year after their completion. I certainly don't want to discourage this group of trying to get investors. The energy needs are such that we must have an increasing number – but I do want you to 'tell it like it is.' There is already enough bad information about the industry floating around without having disgruntled investors among them. They must know they are investing with the possibilities of great return and with the probabilities of no return. Point Number One, then, is that oil and gas discoveries come in all sizes, from the very small to the very large. In the year 1962, the American Association of Petroleum Geologists estimated that out of the 787 wells classified as new field discoveries, only 127, or 16%, found as much as a million barrels of oil. Of these, 119 discoveries estimated as being between one and 25 million barrels of oil; 5 were believed to have found between 25 and 50 million barrels of oil; and only 3 were considered to have found deposits of 50 million barrels or more. The little roulette wheels you have illustrate this principle of diminishing probabilities very well. So while the chances of discovering oil in any amount are rated at an optimistic one out of nine, the chances of finding as much as a million barrels are less than one out of 50, with discovery probabilities diminishing for successively larger fields, until you reach the point where the chances of finding a hundred million barrel field are roughly one out of 3,800.

"Point Number Two is that it is usually better to find oil than to find gas from the well owner's standpoint, although there is now – for the first time in eight years – some basis for hope that this disparity may be remedied. On the basis of average wellhead prices, however, the fact is that oil brings the producer about three times as much revenue as gas for the same heat or energy value, which, of course, is what the consumer pays for. More than that, oil reservoirs always contain gas, which helps push the oil out of the reservoir rock to the wellbore, and thence to the surface, where, when found in sufficient quantities, the gas forms a separate source of revenue to the well owner in addition to the oil.

"Of course, things are not all this one-sided in favor of oil. The development and production expenses for gas fields are much less than for oil fields because fewer wells are required and no costly pumping facilities are needed for gas fields. Moreover, just as oil fields contain gas, gas fields contain liquids which may be extracted from the gas stream to form an important source of additional revenue. Some gas reservoirs actually have such a large content of liquids that this value may exceed that of the gas.

"Under free market conditions, these factors influencing the relative wellhead value of oil versus gas could be expected to be kept in balance by the price mechanism. As you know, the government does control wellhead pricing of all gas moving in interstate commerce. Gas sold in the intrastate markets is not subject to this sort of regulation, however, and the prices of new contracts now being negotiated suggest the order by which interstate gas is presently undervalued. Last week, contracts for Texas gas for use in Texas were being made for 24 cents an Mcf, roughly 50% more than the 16.5 cents set for interstate gas-well gas from the same producing area. At such rates, it is no wonder that more than half of new gas reserves committed to pipelines in Texas last year went to the intrastate market. By and large, this gas went to industrial and power plant uses, since the household heating requirement is relatively small in the comparatively mild climate enjoyed by the most populous regions in Texas. Thus, gas which might have been made available for residential heating in the Midwest and Northeast is being burned under boilers in Texas and Louisiana.

"Point Number Three is that you cannot always find oil or gas to order; that is, it is extremely difficult to selectively look for and find either oil or gas to the exclusion of one or the other, since they both occur in the same geological environment. This concept of selective exploration – usually referred to as directionality – does find some application to oil and gas finding. Just how much application it has is one of the more hotly debated subjects in the industry.

"Certain generalizations are possible, of course. The chances of finding gas are twice those of finding oil at depths below 15,000 feet. No oil has ever been found below 20,000 feet, although large amounts of gas have been found at such depths. A number of areas have shown themselves to be notably gas-prone in character. Western Louisiana and its offshore extension is a case in point. But even in these areas a certain number of wells will reach black oil. Specific formations within a particular geologic province have been found by experience to contain a predominance of gas or oil reservoirs. But, after these relatively few special conditions are taken into account, the only true measure is when the drill bit itself reveals whether a prospect contains oil or gas. And don't forget that eight out of nine will contain neither one.

"The conclusions that I have drawn from observing the economics of petroleum production for several years is that what's good for oil is good for gas, and vice versa. These are joint products, essentially, found and produced by the same operations, by the same people, and at least, to some extent, from the same wells. Both make contributions to the revenue of the producer, and both are chargeable with their fair share of the cost of his operations. To the extent that one fails to contribute its proper share of the producer's income, the difference must be made up by the other, else the production of petroleum hydrocarbons will not yield a return sufficient to attract the investment capital necessary to sustain its operations. Put a little more directly, if the price of oil goes down, the price of gas must go up if the producing segment of the industry is to realize its required rate of return. In this sense, the disparity between the interstate and intrastate prices for gas suggests something of the economic measure by which those who use oil are subsidizing those who use gas. Since these are not mutually exclusive groups, the misallocation has been, in the past, a matter of bookkeeping rather than social concern, and the interdependence of oil and gas finding and following this – price – is a valid concept.

"A couple of more observations are in order. Any extractive minerals industry – and this includes the oil industry – essentially involves a race between depletion and technology. It is a statistical certainty that the largest, richest, most easily accessible deposits of any mineral are going to be found and exploited before the smaller, leaner, less accessible ones. The progression of any minerals industry over the years is therefore a search for deposits that are successively either less valuable, or most costly to find and produce – the Easter hunt analogy I referred to earlier. This continues out to the economic margin permitted by the state of existing technology for discovery and extraction, and as technology reduces these costs, the submarginal deposits become, in turn, worth producing. As a result, you have gas being produced from 20,000 feet depths in West Texas and Oklahoma, gas and oil from wells sited eighty miles or more from the nearest land, off Louisiana and, of course, the on-going development of the phenomenal discovery at Prudhoe Bay – all achievements that would not have been economically feasible with the technology prevailing twenty years ago.

"If I have seemed to equate technology with gadgetry, I did not intend to do so. One of the most refreshing things that has happened to the science of on-shore exploration in recent years has been the renewed interest in geology, particularly subsurface geology, as an approach to oil finding. For forty years, the fair-haired boy of petroleum exploration has been the geophysicist with his reflection seismograph, and tens of billions of barrels of oil have been found by the squiggles on seismic records that indicated the presence of traps which might contain oil or gas. These structural traps, produced by the folding and faulting of the crustal rocks, presented an underground relief profile that could be discerned by such instruments as the seismograph and the gravity meter. But where there were none of these underground humps and bumps, these instruments were largely blind to possible trapping mechanisms. Yet, we know that a vast amount of oil and gas has been found – largely by pure chance – in these so-called stratigraphic traps which present no relief detectable from the surface by instruments now available.

"It is now becoming much too costly to find these stratigraphic traps through random drilling on a hit-or-miss basis. There is, accordingly, a need for an exhaustive kind of detective work which utilizes all evidence that can be related in any way to the occurrence of oil and gas in such formations – including seismic evidence. It is out of such hard intellectual effort, coupled with new and imaginative approaches to oil finding, that have come some significant new discoveries in recent years. The Bell Creek field, in Montana, as an example, was not found by a seismograph or by the blind probing of random drilling, but by creative imagination backed by tough analysis of the subsurface

106

geology in that area.

Here was the case of a big new field — 150 million barrels — found by an independent in a region that had been given up for dead by the majors a few years previous. True, it wasn't another Prudhoe Bay, but is has been a very profitable operation for those who made the discovery and participated in its development. It spawned a whole new search for oil in the Powder River Basin of Southeastern Montana and Northeastern Wyoming, and these efforts were also rewarded by good discoveries: Recluse, Kitty, and Ranch Creek, among others. And there will be other Bell Creeks in the future.

"So the hunt goes on, as it has now these hundred and ten years because men with imagination, brains, and guts were willing to gamble against long odds for big stakes. And just as it seems as though the independent as a breed has come to the end of the trail, something comes along to rescue him from oblivion and send him out again on his tantalizing search for the Big One.

"I think something like that has happened with the advent of the drilling fund as a source of venture capital to the independent segment of the industry. The appearance of this unique channel for matching up investable funds with drillable prospects is contributing greatly to the ability of the independent to continue his historic role as the front runner in domestic oil exploration, and through his successful efforts to find secure sources of oil and gas, it is contributing substantially to the national security of our country and ultimately to the benefit of all the consumers of this Nation."

Mr. Morrell's speech makes it abundantly clear that our tax laws should continue to favor the search for oil and its development once located.

With the introduction and Mr. Morrell's speech as a background we will now consider examples of three typical oil programs. Section 1 will deal with high risk exploratory drilling. Section 2 will discuss an oil income program. Section 3 will illustrate a diversified program featuring a combination of producing wells, development drilling, and exploratory drilling.

SECTION ONE

OIL & GAS EXPLORATION PROGRAMS

There are two basic approaches to investing in oil drilling and exploration programs. One is the direct participation interest which provides ownership of a 1/32 or 1/64 (or other) percentage of each well drilled. The other is similar to a mutual fund in which the investor purchases units of the program for perhaps $5,000 or $10,000 per unit. It is the latter type that is considered in the example below.

The approaches are parallel to real estate investments where the investor has a choice of the small private offering usually with only one or two pieces of property involved or the large public program with greater diversification in types and locations of property. The investors selection between the two approaches or combinations thereof is a matter of personal preference.

There are great risks in all oil drilling and exploration. The types of drilling range from the riskiest wildcat exploration to relatively "safe" secondary oil recovery with development and close-in offset drilling somewhere between those extremes. To reduce risks it may be wise to invest in oil drilling each year for three to five years and perhaps use more than one operator for diversification.

As a rule of thumb, the rate of return on an oil investment can be considered a success if the investor receives his original dollar investment back in two to five years with the possibility of a steady flow of income thereafter. Part of the return of capital is tax savings generated by deductions for intangible drilling expenses the first year. Additionally, income from successful wells is partially sheltered by the depletion allowance.

Once oil is discovered, it is usually desirable to drill development wells to locate reserves that may exist. The investor should be prepared to invest additional funds for this purpose. Often the sponsor of a program will reserve the right to assess the limited partnership participants an amount equal to a certain percentage of their original investment in order to assure the necessary money for development drilling.

If the wells are successful, some investors sell their interests after reserves have been proven. Some sponsors form corporations which offer their stock for the property interest, with the possibility that such stock may be traded publicly.

EXAMPLE OF AN EXPLORATORY OIL FUND

This investment example involves a fund aimed primarily at exploratory drilling. It is a high risk tax shelter and is designed to provide the investor with a high first-year tax write-off, and potential income and capital gains.

The prospective investor, aware of the great risks in this type of investment, should approach a tax-shelter specialist who might analyze the offering as follows:

Victor Oil Drilling Program, a United States Limited Partnership registered with the Securities and Exchange Commission, is offering $5,000,000 in units of $20,000. The Program's funds will be expended on both exploratory and development drilling in the United States. Exploratory drilling is more speculative than close-in or offset drilling, but provides a greater potential return when successful. The program is so structured that the Limited Partners pay the intangible costs and the General Partner pays the tangible costs on exploratory wells to the point of completion. Beyond the point of completion, including all development wells and operations of producing properties, all costs are allocated 70% to the Limited Partners and 30% to the General Partner. As such, investors' deductions will equal approximately 75% of their initial investment. Production income will be shared 70% to investors and 30% to the General Partners.

PROGRAM ORGANIZATION AND INSURANCE

As a Limited Partnership, the Limited Partners will not be held liable for Partnership obligations in excess of their share of the Program's assets and of payments which they have obligated to make. The General Partner will cause the Partnership to purchase casualty, liability, and other insurance of types and coverages as it deems appropriate.

PRESENT AND FUTURE CAPITAL CONTRIBUTIONS

The minimum participation will be one unit of $20,000 and above this amount $5,000 increments will be accepted. Investors' initial capital investment will be payable in two parts, 50% upon signing the Articles of Limited Partnership, and 50% upon a twenty-day notice from Victor.

The program funds will be used for both exploratory and development drilling but with the expectation that as soon as an exploratory well is proven successful development of the property will be carried out as soon as possible in order to prove up maximum reserves. This should tend to increase appreciably overall production and income at minimum risk. Under the terms of the partnership agreement, participants may be required to pay additional capital contributions not to exceed 10% of their initial capital investment. In order to carry out the program successfully, the General Partner also will have the right to use program income, borrow against proven reserves, utilize production payments, and advance its own funds to the program.

COMPENSATION AND COSTS TO GENERAL PARTNER AS OPERATOR

Victor, as General Partner, will receive approximately 7.5% of all costs and expenses paid on behalf of the Program by the participant as direct compensation for its general administrative overhead pertaining to the Program's interests. As noted earlier, the General Partner is contributing all tangible costs on exploratory wells to the point of completion, 30% of all costs beyond this point of completion, and sharing of income in the same ratio. As in most publicly offered programs, the costs and risk of finding oil is borne by the investor. However, there is a 70/30 split of costs between the investor and sponsor on development wells and approximately this same split on completed exploratory wells. This equitable type of sharing costs creates incentive for the operator to find oil, guards against completions of non-commercial producing wells, helps to maintain good cost controls, and does not permit the operator to profit at the expense of the investor should the program be unsuccesful.

APPRAISAL, PROGRESS AND TAX REPORTS

An appraisal report of the Program's results, prepared by an independent engineer, will be made available to participants as soon as possible following completion of the Program's activities. This report will contain, among other information, approximate total future revenues, estimated annual cash flow, and sufficient information to calculate the fair market value of any participant's interests in the Program.

Additionally, the General Partner will furnish to the Limited Partners the following:

1. A monthly progress report covering the Program's activities.

2. Necessary information to complete tax returns.

3. An annual audit of the books of the Partnership by independent chartered accountants.

4. Financial statements of the Partnership prepared on the basis of accounting used for Federal Income Tax purposes.

TAX-SHELTER SPECIALIST EVALUATION

A recent visit to Victor corporate headquarters by an oil expert from the Tax-Shelter Specialist revealed the following:

1. A competent exploratory arm which generates a minimum of 75% of all drilling prospects. Consultants are used only in remote areas to augment technical needs.

2. Good balance on exploration risk spectrum; i.e., close-in lower risk plays balanced with higher risk plays with greater potential.

3. Operates with minimum overhead.

4. Company is regarded highly in industry circles.

5. Good corporate financial position.

RECOMMENDATION OF TAX SHELTER SPECIALIST

We believe the Victor Oil Drilling Program to be a well conceived and structured program for the attendant risk involved. We are satisfied that Victor has a well qualified experienced staff, and that they have integrity and adequate financial capacity to carry out the program. As an exploratory/development oriented venture, operating principally in one of the world's more prospective oil and gas exploration areas, we believe it should be part of a diversified tax shelter program.

REPORT OF INDEPENDENT ENGINEER

One year after the hypothetical program began its operation, an independent engineer was consulted for his analysis of the program. It should be emphasized that there are many ways of evaluating an oil program. The methods used by the engineer in this case are just some of those which might have been employed. The engineer made the following report.

The investor's interest results in the following:

Investment	$20,000
Net Cash Flow After Expenses (25 yrs.)	$55,010
Present Worth (disc @ 8%)	$23,798

These values include only "proven" reserves. Many reserve studies report proven and probable, while others add what they call possible reserves. Additional development wells are being drilled and thus the above reported reserves are not intended to reflect the end result of the program. However, because there is no other base upon which to gain some indication of the program's success, we have calculated the rate of return under two conditions, using just the proven reserves noted above.

PROPERTIES KEPT BY INVESTOR
DURING PRODUCTIVE LIFE.

The 50% Tax Bracket investor's estimated return on investment is 14.3% after tax and 15.8% after tax for the 70% tax bracket investor.

This calculation is made on the computer by imputing the after-tax investment for the first year and the cash flow to the investor (reduced by estimated taxes) in each subsequent year. The result of the calculation is a percentage figure that illustrates the investment return or compound interest rate that, combined with principal payments, would generate the estimated net cash flow year by year of this program. It is assumed in these calculations that the cash flow is reinvested at the same rate as the return from the program being tested.

PROPERTIES SOLD AFTER THE FIRST YEAR.

If the properties are sold approximately one year after the initial investment, the after-tax gain to the 50% bracket client is estimated at 14%, and 58% to the 70% bracket client. One key assumption in these calculations is a 30% discount factor for risk applied to the cash flow discounted value used in figuring the liquidation value. A 5% reduction of this risk discount factor could have nearly a doubling effect on the return. The most frequently applied rate is 30%, but this will not always be the case. It is unknown exactly what rate Victor will apply in any repurchase arrangement. The purchase price will be the Limited Partner's pro rata share in the values of the proven reserves as determined by the estimates of an independent engineer selected by the General Partner plus the value of the other assets of the Partnership determined in accordance with customary practices followed in the petroleum industry.

As a point of emphasis, it is important to say again that these estimates are rough at very best and only reflect what might have resulted from this program if further development activities were not continued. Also, Engineering reports are often optimistic and are not precise. The results could be less than indicated here.

Development work is continuing around the successful exploration wells with a substantial additional investment being made through borrowings. The obligation of the partnership to pay back the debt will reduce the cash flow in the early years and if the development work is unsuccessful, the returns noted above could be less. There is no way of predicting the results from this development drilling, but there remain good possibilities of increasing the production of the successful exploration fields which in turn could increase the investors' return.

LIQUIDATION RETURN CALCULATIONS

		Gross (before Tax)	Net (after Tax)	
			50% Bracket	70% Bracket
Investment		$2,042,000	$1,202,000	$ 866,000
Liquidation Value				
Value of Cash Flow				
Discounted at 8%	$2,429,800			
Discounted for Risk-30%	728,940	$1,700,000	1,366,200	1,366,200
Return on Investment			$ 164,200	$ 504,200
% Return (assuming liquidation in one year)			14%	58%

1. Gross investment $2,042,000
   Deduction at 82% (x $2,042,000) $1,680,000
   Tax Saving at 50% (x $1,680,000) $ 840,000
   Net investment after Tax Saving $1,202,000

2. Gross investment $2,042,000
   Deduction at 82% (x $2,042,000) $1,680,000
   Tax Saving at 70% (x $1,680,000)   1,176,000
   Net investment after Tax Saving $ 866,000

3. Gross Liquidation Value $1,700,000 $1,700,000
   Tax Base
     Investment $2,042,000
     Less: Deductions   1,680,000 $ 362,000
   Taxable Value $1,338,000
   Tax at 25% (x $1,338,860)   334,660
   Net after Tax $1,366,200

BENEFITS OF AN OIL EXPLORATION FUND

1. The investor can convert high pretax income to partially tax-sheltered future income and potential future capital gains.

2. The investor has several ways of reducing taxes on ordinary income: a. The intangible drilling expense write-off against ordinary income which averages 80% of an investment. b. The oil depletion allowance in which 22% of gross income from producing properties is not taxed (not to exceed 50% of taxable income). c. Depreciation on tangible equipment over the useful life of the equipment also is deductible. Reinvestment of earnings in a later partnership would of course compound these tax savings. In the following example we will concern ourselves with the effect of writing off the intangible drilling expenses against the investor's ordinary taxable income in the year that the costs are incurred.

114

Intangible drilling expenses are all those costs incurred (labor, lease of equipment, electricity, water, etc.) in drilling for oil and gas that are not capitalized and amortized over the life of the property such as pipe. The 80% write-off is the equivalent of a subsidy by the Federal Government to the oil investor: The size of the subsidy depending upon the taxpayer's individual tax bracket. The higher the tax bracket the greater the subsidy. Tax money is therefore being used to partially finance oil and gas ventures.

Example:
1. $10,000 investment
2. 80% intangible drilling expense write-off
3. Taxable bracket of 50%

1. Investment	$10,000
2. Initial deduction from ordinary income (80% of investment)	$ 8,000
3. Tax savings (Tax bracket x deduction in #2)	$ 4,000
4. Net cash investment After tax savings (#1-#3)	$ 6,000

3. The investor can achieve additional tax savings through depletion allowance and reinvestment of net cash flow from oil and gas production in subsequent drilling programs.

Example:

Assume gross annual cash flow from oil and gas production of $6,000 with operating expense (pumping cost, labor, etc.) of $1,000.

If the gross cash flow were $6,000 and operating expenses amounted to $1,000, the investor would receive benefit of $1,320 in depletion allowance (22% of $6,000). Therefore, of the $5,000 net cash flow he received, $1,320 would be tax free, giving him an effective depletion allowance of 26.4%.

The illustration above would result in taxable income of $3,680. But, suppose the investor decided to put all of his cash flow back into an additional drilling program; what would be the net federal tax effect?

Re-investment of the $5,000 net cash flow	$5,000
Assume 80% intangible drilling cost write-off	$4,000
Add: depletion allowable	$1,320
Total write-off	$5,320
Write-off "overkill"	$ 320

The $320 in this illustration could be used to reduce taxable income from other sources and no current federal taxes would be due on the income generated by the drilling program.

4. The investor may completely or partially offset a capital gains liability on other assets sold in the same tax year. He thereby keeps the money he would otherwise send to the Federal Government in taxes.

Example:

1. Long term capital gain: $50,000
2. Addition to ordinary income: $25,000
3. Tax bracket = 50%
4. Tax liability = $12,500

Long term capital gain	$50,000
Addition to ordinary income	$25,000
(½ of long term gain)	
Tax liability	
(50% of addition to ordinary income)	$12,500

To eliminate the $12,500 tax you must offset the entire addition to ordinary income ($25,000) by the write-off in an oil venture (write-off approximately 80%)

Addition to ordinary income	$25,000
Oil investment necessary to eliminate tax	
(Divide addition to ordinary income by .80)	$31,000
Summary: Investment in oil venture	$31,000
Investment elsewhere plus original capital	$19,000
Tax savings to investor	$12,500

5. In making a charitable gift to a church, hospital, college, etc., the donor may deduct the full value of the gift (to extent allowed by law) from his ordinary income which produces a savings in tax dollars not sent to the Government. Conservative oil participation units in the past produced a cash surrender value (value of the gift) approximating 80% to 100% of the original investment in one year. For our example we have assumed a 90% cash value factor for the value of the gift. The combination of the investment write-off savings and the gift deduction savings could substantially reduce the donor's out-of-pocket cost of making a gift to a charitable institution. Note that new law under certain circumstances can require recapture of intangible drilling expenses.

Example:
1. $10,000 investment-oil venture
2. 50% tax bracket
3. 80% write-off factor-deduction
4. 90% cash value - 1 year.
5. Gift totally deductible

Initial investment	$10,000
80% write-off intangible drilling expense	$ 8,000
Tax savings (A)	
(50% x deduction)	$ 4,000
90% cash value in one year (gift)	$ 9,000
Tax savings (B)	
(50% x gift)	$ 4,500
Total tax savings (A + B)	$ 8,500
Actual out of pocket cost of gift	
(original investment – savings)	$ 1,500

6. Taxes paid in prior years may be recovered through the carryback of a net operating loss which will result when oil and gas losses exceed other income in the current year. Under Section 172 (b) of the Internal Revenue Code a net operating loss is carried back to the third preceding year. To the extent not used it may then be applied to the second preceding year and then to later years in order. A refund due to a net operating loss carryback may result when an individual has low income in the current year and is able to make an investment larger than his current income.

7. Other investments may have produced capital losses in excess of what can be deducted for tax purposes. These unused losses can be carried over to future years. Investing in oil and gas funds can provide a potential future capital gain situation which can be offset by unused capital losses. Sale of an interest in an oil and gas fund at a gain after the properties have been developed and hald for more than required months results in mostly long-term captial gain. Subject to recapture provisions.

8. The father in a family (high-tax bracket) can make an oil investment to reduce his taxes and then transfer the investment to a ten-year trust (short-term trust) for the benefit of his children. To the extent of income from the drilling investment, taxes are saved by reason of that income's accruing to taxpayers (children) in much lower tax brackets. The father may also make an outright gift of the investment in order to remove it from his estate and thereby save estate taxes. This is subject to recapture provisions.

9. Oil investments can be used in retirement planning. The investor joins a program, and the initial tax deductions are applied against his high tax liability at that time. Since oil and gas generally produce income for 15 to 20 years, a substantial part of the income from the investment will be received when the investor is in his lower retirement tax bracket. He invests while in a high tax bracket and receives most of the oil income when his tax bracket is lower.

10. Oil investments can help level fluctuating income patterns. Writers, actors, sports figures and such often enjoy high earnings one year, and, oftentimes, little or no earnings the next. Income averaging can help but it doesn't cut taxes to their potential minimum as a combination of income averaging and an oil investment could. Especially pertinent is the investment potential which investors in these highly erratic industries – or investors whose professional careers may be limited to a few highly productive years – might obtain at 50 cents, or less, on the dollar.

11. A self-employed individual can combine his HR-10 retirement plan with oil investments to augment his retirement income by reinvesting oil and gas income, thus compounding tax dollars into equity dollars during highly-taxed productive years, eventually taking the income in retirement years. Also, depending on tax bracket, the investor can make part or all of his HR-10 contribution from savings

generated by the oil deduction.

12. Corporations may also participate as oil investors. The following comments illustrate this point:

a. A corporation may reduce its taxable income by deducting intangible drilling development costs. The reduction of Federal income tax caused by these deductions will increase the net income of the corporation.

b. By reducing its taxable net income, a corporation may avoid substantial accumulated earnings tax penalties.

c. Cash otherwise paid out for taxes can be used to develop additional asset values, future sources of tax-sheltered cash flow and higher earnings per share of equity.

d. Corporations may assist their high-salaried key executives in purchasing interests in oil. The corporation may loan cash to an executive for the purpose of purchasing program units, thus achieving the goal of a high salary, without the costs of most other fringe benefits.

e. A corporation may get double tax benefits by purchasing a tax-sheltered interest, and then after holding the interest for required months contribute it to its pension plan and/or its profit sharing trust. The corporation is then entitled to the initial deduction and a second deduction at the time the interest is contributed. These benefits will be partially offset by the long-term gain that must be realized at the time of contribution. This is subject to recapture provisions.

RISKS OF AN OIL EXPLORATION FUND

1. The search for oil and gas, without question, is speculative and may be marked by many unsuccessful efforts. Many wells will be "dry"; even wells which are completed may not produce enough oil and gas to realize a profit. The industry is highly competitive; in searching for oil and gas, a Program must compete with many other companies, including large oil companies having greater resources than the Program. Furthermore, marketing of any oil and gas discovered depends on many variables.

Oil and gas production is subject to regulation and limitation under conservation and other laws. The availability of pipelines and other transportation facilities for the oil and gas discovered by a Program cannot be assured.

There is risk in the oil and gas search; risk in how successfully a Program will be able to sell the oil and gas it does discover.

2. These interests are offered to parties with substantial income subject to higher income tax rates who may benefit from the special treatment presently allowed oil and gas exploration under the Federal income tax laws. There is no assurance that the money invested in the Program will be recovered, or that the special income tax treatment presently allowed oil and gas exploration will continue in the future. The Tax Reform Act of 1969 reduced from 27% to 22% the amount of depletion allowable on producing oil and gas properties and imposed a tax on tax preferences. The effect of the Tax Reform Act of 1969 on tax preferences is covered under "Tax aspects of an oil exploration fund."

TAX ASPECTS OF AN OIL EXPLORATION FUND

GENERAL FEATURES OF PARTNERSHIP TAXATION

Under the present federal income tax law, an organization which is treated as a partnership is not a taxable entity and incurs no federal income tax liability. Instead, each item of partnership income, gain, loss, deduction or credit flows through to the partners, substantially as though the partners had received or expended such item directly. Since the Partnership should be treated as a partnership for federal income tax purposes, each Limited Partner will be required to take into account in computing his federal income tax liability his distributive share of all items of Partnership income, gain, loss, deduction, and credit for each taxable year of the Partnership ending with or without his taxable year, without regard to whether such Limited Partner has received or will receive any cash distributions from the Partnership. Consequently, a Limited Partner's share of the taxable income (and possibly the income tax payable by him with respect to such taxable income) of the Partnership may exceed the cash, if any, actually distributed to such Partner. In addition, actual (or constructive) distributions of cash from the Partnership will be taxable to the extent that such distributions exceed a Partner's adjusted basis for his interest in the Partnership. See "Limitations on Deductions—Adjusted Basis." In most cases such excess distributions will be taxable as long-term capital gain (or short-term capital gain if the distributee has held his interest in the Partnership for twelve months or less at the time of the distribution).

AUDIT OF PARTNERSHIP RETURNS

While no federal income tax is required to be paid by an organization which is classified as a partnership for federal income tax purposes, a partnership must nevertheless file federal income tax returns. These information returns, which will be filed by the Partnership, are subject to audit by the Internal Revenue Service. In this connection, it should be noted that the Internal Revenue Service has recently announced (i) an expansion of the coverage of its national tax shelter audit program (which would include oil and gas partnerships like the Partnership) and (ii) the establishment of a liaison between the Internal Revenue Service, the Securities and Exchange Commission, and state securities commissions. These developments are intended to make audit of partnership returns, such as those of the Partnership, more likely. Any such audit may lead to adjustments, in which event the Partners may be required to file amended personal federal income tax returns. In addition, any such audit could lead to an audit of a Limited Partner's tax return which may, in turn, lead to adjustments other than those relating to the Limited Partner's investment in the Partnership.

The Revenue Act of 1978 amends the Code to extend the period of time in which assessments of deficiencies and claims for refunds may be made for federal income taxes attributable to "partnership items" of partners with respect to "federally registered partnership" (such as the Partnership). Generally, under prior law, the Internal Revenue Service could assess a tax against a partner, or a partner could file a claim for refund for tax, within a three-year period commencing with the date on which the partner files his individual income tax return. The date on which the partnership return was filed did not affect the period of limitations. The Revenue Act of 1978 extends the period of limitations to four years (commencing with the date on which the partnership return is filed) with respect to assessments and claims for refund attributable to partnership items which flow from a partnership and which, by regulations to be prescribed, are deemed more appropriately determinable at the partnership level than at the partner level. This provision also permits the general partner of a federally registered partnership to consent to extend beyond four years the period of limitation with respect to all partners, unless the partnership restricts the authority of the general partner to execute such a consent and the general partner notifies the Secretary of the Treasury of such restriction. The Partnership Agreement denies the General Partners the authority to execute such a consent, and requires the Managing Partner to notify the Secretary of the Treasury of the denial of such authority.

PARTNERSHIP ALLOCATIONS

Certain of the Partnership's deductions and credits resulting from the payment of Partnership costs and expenses with the contributions of the Limited Partners, and any recapture thereof, are allocated to the Limited Partners in accordance with their respective Sharing Ratios. As a result, the allocation of such deductions and credits, and any recapture thereof, is made in a ratio which is disproportionate to the Limited Partners' interest in the Partnership. The capital accounts of the Limited Partners are adjusted to reflect such disproportionate allocations and the capital accounts, as adjusted, will be given effect in distributions made to Partners in the event of dissolution of the Partnership or if a Limited Partner exercises his right to tender for purchase his interest in the Partnership.

The Tax Reform Act of 1976 amended section 704(b) of the Code to provide that special allocations (i.e., an allocation of a partnership item to a partner which is disproportionate to such partner's interest in the partnership) among partners of any item of partnership income, gain, loss, deduction or credit will not be given effect unless the allocation has substantial economic effect. The relevant Congressional committee reports indicate that the purpose of the amendment was to restrict special allocations to situations in which the allocations have "substantial economic effect as presently interpreted by the regulations and case law," but this legislative change could nevertheless result in new criteria being employed to determine if special allocation provisions are valid.

Moreover, the Internal Revenue Service has a formal policy of not issuing rulings with respect to partnership special allocation provisions. The Service has not issued regulations or other administrative guidelines interpreting the partnership allocation provisions of the Tax Reform Act of 1976, and it is possible that such regulations or other guidelines will adopt a more restrictive interpretation of these provisions than that in effect for the corresponding provisions of prior law.

If the Internal Revenue Service should take the position that the allocation of any Partnership item, which is allocated to the Limited Partners in a manner which is disproportionate to the Limited Partners' interest in the Partnership, lacks substantial economic effect, the disproportionate part of the item allocated to the Limited Partners (i.e., the excess over 60%) would not be allowable to them if such position were ultimately sustained.

Further section 613A(c)(7)(D) of the Code requires that the basis of oil and gas properties owned by a partnership be allocated to the partners in accordance with their interests in the capital or profits of the partnership, and it is possible that this provision will be interpreted by the Internal Revenue Service as preventing (i) an allocation of any losses or deductions computed with respect to the basis of an oil or gas property (such as cost depletion or abandonment losses), or (ii) an allocation of gain or loss on the sale or other disposition of an oil or gas property (such as that portion of any gain treated as recapture of intangible drilling and development costs), to the Partners in a manner disproportionate to their respective interests in the capital or profits of the Partnership.

ESTIMATE DEDUCTIBILITY

The nature of oil and gas exploration makes it impossible accurately to predict the portion of the Limited Partners' Exploration Commitments which will be deductible in a particular year. Moreover, it is not possible to predict with any degree of certainty the effect of the Partnership's operations on a Limited Partner's federal income tax liability, principally because of recent legislative changes in the minimum tax on tax preferences and the maximum tax on personal service income, as discussed below. It is suggested that each prospective investor consult his tax advisor as to these matters.

LIMITATIONS ON DEDUCTIONS

A Limited Partner may not deduct from taxable income any amount attributable to his share of the Partnership's losses which is in excess of the lesser of (i) the adjusted tax basis of his Partnership interest at the end of the Partnership's tax year in which the loss occurs or (ii) the amount as to which the Limited Partner is considered "at risk" in respect of the activities of the Partnership at the end of the Partnership's tax year in which the loss occurs. Under current law, the "at risk" limitation applies to an individual Limited Partner, a corporate Limited Partner which is an electing small business corporation (a subchapter S corporation), and a Limited Partner which is a corporation 50% or more of the value of whose stock is owned directly or indirectly by five or fewer individuals.

Adjusted Basis. A Limited Partner's basis for his interest in the Partnership will initially be equal to his cash contribution to the Partnership. It will be increased by his distributive share of Partnership taxable income, by any income exempt from taxation, and by his share of any nonrecourse borrowings of the Partnership (as described below). It will be decreased (but not below zero) by distributions to him from the Partnership, by his distributive share of Partnership losses, by his depletion deduction on his share of Partnership oil and gas income until such deduction exhausts the basis of the property subject to depletion, by his share of any decrease in nonrecourse borrowings of the Partnership (as described below), and by his share of nondeductible expenses of the Partnership which are not properly chargeable to the capital account.

Limitation of Deductions to Amount "At Risk." A Limited Partner's share of losses incurred by the Partnership will not be allowed as a deduction to the extent in excess of the amounts as to which he is at risk. Generally, under this limitation, he will be allowed deductions equal to his equity investment in the Partnership. A Limited Partner is not considered at risk with respect to funds borrowed by the Partnership on a non-recourse basis but such funds may be used to pay expenses which give rise to deductions to a Limited Partner, subject to the "at risk" ceiling on a Limited Partner's total deductible losses. Deductions disallowed as a result of this rule will carry forward, and a Limited Partner could deduct such amounts in the event and to the extent that his at risk investment is increased in any later year—for example, through earnings retained by the Partnership. This "at risk" limitation is not applicable to a corporate Limited Partner (other than a subchapter S corporation or a corporation 50% or more of whose stock is owned directly or indirectly by five or fewer individuals) with respect to liabilities incurred in exploring for or exploiting oil and gas resources.

RECAPTURE OF AMOUNTS "AT RISK"

The Revenue Act of 1978 provides that if a Limited Partner's amount "at risk" is reduced below zero, the Limited Partner must recognize income to the extent that his "at risk" basis is reduced below zero (limited to loss amounts previously allowed to the Limited Partner over any amounts previously recaptured). Distributions to a Limited Partner, changes in the amount of recourse indebtedness attributable to a Limited Partner or the commencement of guarantees or similar arrangements may reduce a Limited Partner's amount "at risk." A Limited Partner may be allowed a deduction for the recaptured amounts included in taxable income if he increases his amount "at risk" in a subsequent taxable year.

TAX EFFECTS OF PARTNERSHIP BORROWINGS

The Partnership may borrow funds to finance its operations. As hereafter described, the federal income tax effects of such borrowings are quite different depending upon whether the loans are on a recourse basis or a non-recourse basis. Regardless of whether any Partnership borrowings are recourse or non-recourse, the amortization of such borrowings with Partnership income will result in a Limited Partner being taxable upon his share of such income although he receives no distributions from the Partnership.

A Partner's share, if any, of any increase in Partnership debt is treated as if such Partner had contributed money to the Partnership, and a Partner's share, if any, of any decrease in Partnership debt is treated as if such Partner has received a distribution of money from the Partnership. Since, as described in "Limitations on Deductions—Adjusted Basis," contributions or distributions of money increase or decrease, respectively, a Partner's adjusted basis for his interest in the Partnership, the allocable deductions which a Partner is allowed (subject to the "at risk" limitations discussed above) as well as the tax effects of sale or liquidation of his interest in the Partnership may be directly affected by such Partner's share of Partnership debt.

To the extent that a Partner is entitled to increase his basis in the Partnership by virtue of Partnership borrowings, reductions in his share of such borrowings may result in a taxable transaction. Thus, if a Partner's interest in the Partnership is reduced (e.g. through disposition of all or part of such interest or by a downward shift in his Partnership percentage) while a Partnership loan which is reflected in his basis is outstanding, or if the Partnership makes payments which reduce the principal balance of any such loan, he will be deemed to have received a distribution of money in an amount equal to all or part of his proportionate share of the loan in addition to such other proceeds as he might actually realize. Any such deemed distribution will result in taxable income to the extent that such distribution, together with other distributions, exceeds the adjusted basis of the Partner's interest.

Recourse Borrowings. If the Partnership borrows on a recourse basis which is not presently contemplated, the General Partners, the Partnership itself, or both, will have personal liability with respect to the debt. A Limited Partner's share of such debt (for purposes of calculating a Limited Partner's basis in his Partnership interest) is determined in accordance with the ratio in which he shares losses under the Partnership Agreement, but cannot exceed the difference, if any, between his actual contribution and the total contribution he is obligated to make under the Partnership Agreement.

Non-recourse Borrowings. On the other hand, if the Partnership borrows on a non-recourse basis neither the Partnership itself nor any Partner will have any personal liability with respect to the debt. In that event, each Partner, including each Limited Partner, will be considered as sharing the debt liability in the same proportion as he shares profits under the Partnership Agreement. Accordingly, a Limited Partner may increase the basis of his Partnership interest by a portion of the Partnership's non-recourse borrowings notwithstanding that he has paid his total contribution to the Partnership. Because of the "at risk" limitation discussed in "Limitations on Deductions," however, any non-recourse borrowings included in a Limited Partner's basis will not have the effect of increasing the extent to which the Limited Partner is allowed to deduct his share of Partnership losses, if the Limited Partner is an individual, a subchapter S corporation, or a corporation 50% or more of the value of whose stock is owned directly or indirectly by five or fewer individuals.

The tax effects described above for non-recourse borrowings will result only if the borrowing is recognized for tax purposes as creating a bona fide debt. The Internal Revenue Service has ruled that under some circumstances non-recourse borrowings may be challenged where the lender has an interest in the transactions greater than that of a mere creditor. Accordingly, the General Partners will not enter into any agreements with non-recourse creditors that would give such creditors any direct or indirect interest in the profits, capital, or property of the Partnership other than as a secured creditor. Similarly, the Internal Revenue Service has ruled that a limited partner may not increase his basis with respect to a non-recourse loan to the partnership by the general partners or an affiliated company.

PARTNERSHIP DEDUCTIONS

The Partnership will determine taxable income or loss on a calendar year basis using the cash receipts and disbursements method of accounting. Under the Partnership Agreement the Partnership will make all elections required to deduct and write off the following costs, which are generally deductible from current taxable income: (a) "intangible drilling and development costs" incurred in drilling wells (including the costs of preparing the location, drill-stem testing, electric logging, chemicals for drilling fluids, and other testing costs and charges to determine whether or not a well is potentially productive) and completing wells (including equipment rentals); (b) the costs of plugging and abandoning dry wells; (c) the costs of oil and gas leases condemned by the drilling of wells, abandoned and expired leases, delay rentals and dry or bottom hole contributions made toward the drilling of wells which are dry and which condemn the Partnership's acreage; (d) the overhead and administrative costs of the Partnership including certain costs of legal, engineering and accounting services to the Partnership; and (e) the costs of operating productive properties.

Prepaid Drilling Costs. The Partnership may be required to prepay certain intangible drilling and development costs under drilling contracts. In that event, the Managing Partner will endeavor to take such steps as may be practicable in order to permit deduction of such prepayments in the year in which they are made, but whether Internal Revenue Service requirements which must be met in order for prepaid intangible drilling and

127

development costs to be deductible by cash basis taxpayers can or will be satisfied by the Partnership in all instances is not certain. Therefore, deductions for prepaid intangible drilling and development costs, if any, claimed in the Partnership's return may be challenged by the Internal Revenue Service, and there can be no assurance that any such disallowance will not be upheld. If disallowed in the year paid, such prepaid expenses would be available as a deduction in the year the work under the drilling contract is actually performed.

Capitalized Costs. For federal income tax purposes, costs incurred in the acquisition and geological evaluation of oil and gas Lease interests are not deductible until the prospect or prospects with respect to which they are incurred are proved worthless or abandoned. Under the Partnership Agreement, the Managing Partner will initially be charged with the costs incurred in the acquisition and geological evaluation of oil and gas Lease interests; however, at such time as the Prospect for which such acquisition costs were incurred has been proven worthless or abandoned before the Partnership has drilled a Commercial Well on it, substantially all such acquisition costs will be reallocated to the Limited Partners who will be entitled to an ordinary loss deduction in the year of worthlessness or abandonment, provided that the special allocation of such losses to the Limited Partners is effective for tax purposes. If an oil and gas Lease is proved to be productive, the costs incurred in the acquisition and geological evaluation of such Lease may be recovered only through depletion allowances; however, if it is subsequently abandoned any unrecovered cost may be deducted in the year in which it is abandoned. In the event of a gain or loss for tax purposes upon the sale of an oil and gas Lease by the Partnership, each Limited Partner would individually report his distributive share thereof.

Organization and Syndication Expenses. No deduction will be allowed to the Partnership or any Limited Partner for any amounts paid or incurred to promote the sale of (or to sell) an interest in the Partnership. However, the Partnership will (as permitted by law) elect to deduct ratably over a period of 60 months certain organization expenses of the Partnership. Syndication fees (the expenditures connected with the issuing and marketing of interests in the Partnership, such as the Dealer Manager's commission, professional fees, and printing costs) must be capitalized and are not subject to the 60-month

128

amortization provision. Such syndication expenses are deductible, if at all, only upon liquidation of the Partnership.

Depletion Deduction. Each Limited Partner may in his federal income tax return deduct an allowance for the greater of cost or percentage depletion on each producing property of the Partnership. The percentage depletion allowance is available only if the Limited Partner qualifies under the "small producers exemption" from the repeal of the percentage depletion allowance described below; otherwise, he will be limited to a cost depletion allowance. Percentage depletion is calculated on the basis of the applicable depletion rate for the year in question (presently 22%) applied to the gross income for the Limited Partner's share of average daily production from each producing property (subject to certain limitations discussed below); however, the percentage depletion deduction may not exceed 50% of the Limited Partner's share of taxable income from the property. Cost depletion is calculated by dividing the adjusted cost basis of the property by the total units of oil or gas expected to be recoverable therefrom (including those sold during the year) and then multiplying the resulting quotient by the number of units actually sold during the taxable year. Cost depletion cannot exceed the adjusted tax basis of the property.

Under the small producers exemption from the repeal of the percentage depletion allowance for oil and gas wells adopted by the Congress in 1975, independent producers and royalty owners are allowed a percentage depletion deduction on a limited amount of domestic oil and gas production. Generally this exemption will cover the first 1,200 barrels of the taxpayer's average daily production of domestic crude oil or, if the prescribed election is made, up to 7,200,000 cubic feet of average daily production of domestic natural gas. This exempt amount of average daily production is reduced by 200 barrels (or 1,200,000 cubic feet of natural gas) a year so that by January 1, 1980, the permanently exempt amount of average daily production will be 1,000 barrels of crude oil or 6,000,000 cubic feet of natural gas. Beginning in 1981 the 22% depletion rate is reduced by 2 percentage points per year until 1984 when the permanent percentage depletion (on the permanently exempt amount of 1,000 barrels of oil or 6,000,000 cubic feet of gas per day) will be 15%.

Special rules are provided in the Code for oil and gas produced by secondary and tertiary recovery processes, retaining depletion at a 22% rate for such production until 1984, but with no increase in the total quantities of oil and gas described above which qualify for percentage depletion.

For purposes of computing average daily production of crude oil or natural gas, a Limited Partner will be treated as realizing production from each oil or gas property held by the Partnership equal in amount to total Partnership production from such property multiplied by the Limited Partner's percentage participation in the revenues of such property. Both the percentage depletion allowance and the cost depletion allowance must be computed separately by each Limited Partner rather than by the Partnership. In addition, under Internal Revenue Service proposed regulations (the "Proposed Regulations"), each Limited Partner would be required to make an annual election on his individual income tax return in order to claim percentage depletion under the small producers exemption with respect to all or any portion of his share of the Partnership's production of domestic natural gas. Each Limited Partner must maintain records of his adjusted basis in each oil and gas Partnership property, make adjustments for depletion deductions to such basis and use such adjusted basis for the computation of loss or gain on the disposition of such property.

Under certain circumstances, related taxpayers are aggregated and treated as one taxpayer in determining the quantity of production (barrels of oil or cubic feet of gas per day) qualifying for percentage depletion under the small producers exemption. Thus, if 50% or more of the beneficial interest in two or more corporations, trusts or estates are owned by the same or related persons, such entities are treated as one taxpayer and are entitled to share only one depletable quantity. Also, members of the same family must share one exemption, but for this purpose a "family" includes only the individual, his spouse and minor children.

The small producers exemption does not apply to any transferee or sublessee (except, under some circumstances certain controlled corporations, business entities under common control, members of the same family, and transferees who acquire properties by reason of death of the transferor) of a proven oil or gas property with respect to production from that property. Under the Proposed Regulations an oil or gas property is considered to be "proven" if the fair market value of the property at the time of the transfer is 50% or more of the fair market value of the property (minus expenses incurred after the transfer for equipment and intangible drilling and development costs) at the time production commences. It is not known at this time whether the Partnership will acquire any properties which would be considered "proven" within the meaning of these rules. This same denial of the exemption to the transferee exists with respect to the transfer of a partnership interest in a partnership which owns a proven oil or gas property, and therefore a transferee of a Limited Partner's interest in the Partnership would not be entitled to claim percentage depletion with respect to his share of production from the Partnership's oil or gas properties which were proven on the date he received his Partnership interest, unless the transfer qualified under one of the exceptions described above. Under the Proposed Regulations, however, it appears that a pro-rata current or liquidating distribution of a fractional or undivided interest in the Partnership's proven oil and gas properties to the Partners will not result in a loss of the small producers exemption for the transferee Partners.

The percentage depletion allowance claimed by a Limited Partner under the small producers exemption is also subject to a limit based on the Limited Partner's taxable income. Such depletion deduction may not exceed 65% of the Limited Partner's taxable income for the year, computed without regard to the percentage depletion deduction and without regard to losses occurring in subsequent years and carried back to the taxable year. If percentage depletion exceeds this limitation, the excess is disallowed as a deduction for the current taxable year, but may be carried over by the Limited Partner and deducted as a depletion deduction, subject to the same 65% limit, in the succeeding taxable year (and subsequent years until used).

The percentage depletion deduction under the small producers exemption is not available to "retailers" and certain "refiners," that is, any taxpayer who, directly or indirectly, sells oil or natural gas through retail outlets or engages in the business of refining crude oil with runs of more than 50,000 barrels per day. A taxpayer is considered to engage in such activity indirectly if another person (including a partnership) related to the taxpayer by a 5% or more ownership engages in such activity. However, under the Proposed Regulations the mere fact that a member of a partnership (such as a general partner) is a "retailer" does not result in characterization of the remaining partners as retailers.

The sale of Partnership oil and gas production through retail outlets, however, could result in denial of the percentage depletion deduction to some or all of the Limited Partners with respect to their shares of the Partnership income from oil and gas production and possibly with respect to any other oil and gas income they may receive. However, a recent amendment to the Internal Revenue Code provides that (i) bulk sales of oil or natural gas to industrial or commercial users are not considered retail sales, and (ii) a taxpayer will not be considered a "retailer" during any taxable year where the combined gross receipts from the sale of oil, natural gas, or any product derived therefrom at all retail outlets operated by the taxpayer and related persons do not exceed $5,000,000.

The foregoing description does not purport to be a complete analysis of the complex legislation relating to the percentage depletion deduction for oil and gas wells, and it is recommended that a prospective investor consult his personal tax advisor with respect to what effect the limited availability of percentage depletion will have upon the advisability of his acquiring an interest in the Partnership.

FARMOUT AND FARMIN TRANSACTIONS

It is contemplated that the Partnership may acquire interests in oil and gas properties in partial or full consideration for its agreement to drill one or more exploratory wells thereon (a "farmin" transaction) and that it may transfer interests in its oil and gas properties in partial or full consideration for an agreement of the transferee to drill one or more exploratory wells thereon (a "farmout" transaction). In Rev. Rul. 77-176, 177-1 C.B. 78, the Internal Revenue Service ruled that any farmout or farmin transaction involving more than one property (as defined in Section 614(a) of the Code) could result in taxable income to both parties, notwithstanding that no cash consideration is given or received.

The Managing Partner, in negotiating farmout or farmin transactions on behalf of the Partnership, will endeavor to take such steps as may be practicable in order to minimize the Partnership's exposure under Rev. Rul. 77-176. However, the application of this ruling in certain fact situations is unclear. Therefore, the Internal Revenue Service may claim that normal farmout and farmin transactions entered into by the Partnership result in taxable gain to the Partnership in excess of amounts reported, if any, on the Partnership's income tax returns. If any such position of the Internal Revenue Service is ultimately sustained, the Partners would be required to include their distributive share of such taxable income in their personal income tax returns, although no cash would be available to the Partnership or the Partners in respect of such income.

SALE OF LIMITED PARTNERSHIP INTERESTS

Generally, a Limited Partner will realize gain or loss on the sale or exchange of his interest in the Partnership measured by the difference between the amount realized on the sale or exchange and the Limited Partner's adjusted basis for such interest. A Limited Partner's pro rata share of Partnership nonrecourse liabilities as of the date of the sale or exchange must be included in the amount realized. Since the amount received on the disposition of an interest includes the amount of nonrecourse debt allocable to such interest, the gain recognized may result in a tax liability greater than the cash proceeds, if any, from such disposition.

Gain or loss on the sale of a Partnership interest by a holder who is not a "dealer" with respect to such interest and who has held it for one year, will in general be treated as long term capital gain or loss. However, there are circumstances in which all or part of the gain realized on the disposition of an interest in the Partnership may be taxed as ordinary income. For example, to the extent that proceeds from the disposition of a Partnership interest are attributable to (i) intangible drilling and development deductions previously claimed by the Partnership which are subject to "recapture" (See "Recapture of Certain Drilling Costs," below), (ii) certain other "tax benefit" items such as depreciation, or (iii) inventory which has appreciated substantially in value, any gain recognized on such disposition will be taxed as ordinary income.

TERMINATION OF THE PARTNERSHIP

The actual or constructive termination of a partnership may have important tax consequences on the partners of that partnership. If a partnership ceases the conduct of its business and sells its assets and makes liquidating distributions to the partners,

133

an actual termination of the partnership will occur for both federal income tax and state law purposes. On the other hand, if 50% or more of the total interests in the capital and profits of the partnership are sold or exchanged within a period of twelve consecutive months, the partnership will be considered constructively terminated for federal income tax purposes (but not necessarily for state law purposes). If the partnership continues in business without actual dissolution and termination, a new partnership between the remaining partners will be deemed to have been created for federal income tax purposes.

Should the Partnership be constructively or actually terminated, Limited Partners will be taxable in the taxable year in which such termination occurs on their distributive share of Partnership income received prior to the date of termination. Such Limited Partners will likewise be entitled to claim their distributive share of deductible items arising out of costs and expenditures paid by the Partnership prior to the date of termination.

Generally, a Limited Partner will not recognize any taxable gain or loss as a result of the pro rata distribution of Partnership assets incident to termination of the Partnership. However, gain will be recognized to the extent that a Limited Partner's pro rata share of the Partnership's cash (and the reduction, if any, in his pro rata share of the Partnership's debt) at the date of termination exceeds the adjusted tax basis of his Partnership interest. In addition, a loss may be recognized at Partnership dissolution if a Limited Partner receives no distributions of any property other than money or property described in section 751 of the Code. Any gain or loss recognized upon dissolution will, in general, be a capital gain or loss. However, if a Limited Partner receives or is deemed to receive more or less than his pro rata share of property described in section 751 of the Code in a distribution, ordinary income or loss may result to the Partnership or to the Limited Partners.

Property distributed in liquidation of a Limited Partner's interest shall have a basis to the distributee Limited Partner equal to the adjusted basis of such Limited Partner's interest in the Partnership, reduced by any cash distributed in the same transaction. A Limited Partner's basis in the assets received upon dissolution will only be recoverable through depreciation or depletion or upon the sale or worthlessness of the property. The potential depreciation and intangible drilling cost recapture of the Partnership and the potential investment credit recapture of each Limited Partner which is not recaptured as a result of the distributions to the Limited Partner taints the distributed property, so that the later sale of an interest in such property by the distributee Limited Partner may result in both ordinary income from depreciation and intangible drilling cost recapture and additional tax liability from investment tax credit recapture.

MINIMUM TAX ON TAX PREFERENCES

A 15% minimum tax is imposed on the amount of a taxpayer's total "tax preferences" to the extent such tax preferences exceed the greater of (a) one-half (or 100%, in the case of a corporation) of the taxpayer's federal income tax liability for the same taxable year computed without regard to tax preferences or (b) $10,000 ($5,000 in the case of married taxpayers filing separately). To the extent that any Partnership item gives rise to a tax preference item with respect to a Limited Partner such Limited Partner will be required to include his distributive share thereof in his minimum tax computation.

There are two types of tax preference which are peculiar to oil and gas (or other mineral) investments. One is the deduction allowable for intangible drilling and development costs (other than costs incurred in drilling a nonproductive well) to the extent such deduction exceeds the portion of such costs which would be deductible if the intangible costs were capitalized and deducted ratably over the 120-month period beginning with the month in which production from such well begins, or, at the election of the taxpayer, over the productive life of the well. The amount of the taxpayer's intangible drilling and development cost deduction treated as a tax preference is reduced by the "net income" of the taxpayer from oil and gas properties for the taxable year. Net income for this purpose is the gross income from all oil or gas properties of the taxpayer less deductions (not including the "excess" intangible deductions described in the preceding sentence) allocable to such properties.

The second tax preference peculiar to oil and gas investments is the amount of the excess of a taxpayer's deduction for depletion over his leasehold cost basis in the related property. For example, if a taxpayer, using the 22% depletion allowance referred to above, deducts $300 for depletion during a taxable year, whereas a $100 deduction would use up the taxpayer's remaining leasehold cost basis in such property, that taxpayer would have a tax preference of $200.

In addition, accelerated depreciation on personal property, the untaxed portion of net capital gains, and in some cases, itemized deductions and other items not ordinarily involved in oil and gas operations, are included among the tax preference items. Under the Revenue Act of 1978, in the case of taxpayers other than corporations, excess itemized deductions and the untaxed portion of net capital gains (60% of net capital gain) will not constitute items of tax preference subject to the 15% minimum tax after January 1, 1979, but to the extent that the sum of these two items exceeds $20,000, such excess will be subject to an alternative tax that would be payable only if such tax exceeds the sum of the taxpayer's regular and minimum tax liabilities.

To the extent that the Partnership items may give rise to items of tax preference each Limited Partner will be required to include his distributive share thereof in his minimum tax computation. A corporate taxpayer (other than a subchapter S corporation or a personal holding company) is not subject to the 15% tax with respect to certain tax preference items such as intangible drilling and development costs.

As the minimum tax computation is rather complicated, a prospective investor should consult his tax advisor in order to determine the extent, if any, to which his participation in oil and gas activities through an investment in the Partnership might cause him to become subject to the 15% tax on tax preferences or increase his liability for such tax.

MAXIMUM TAX ON PERSONAL SERVICE TAXABLE INCOME

The maximum rate of federal income tax on an individual's "personal service taxable income" is limited to 50%. Personal service taxable income is reduced, for purposes of applying the 50% limit, by the total amount of the taxpayer's items of tax preference (other than items of tax preference arising from capital gain income) in the taxable year, including a Limited Partner's items of tax preference arising from Partnership items. To the extent that personal service taxable income is reduced, such income is subject to tax at normal rates applicable to ordinary income. Thus, items of tax preference generated by the Partnership which are allocable to a Limited Partner will decrease the amount of that Limited Partner's personal service taxable income qualifying for the 50% maximum rate on a dollar for dollar basis. Moreover, it is not anticipated that a Limited Partner's distributive share of the net income of the Partnership nor any gain realized on the sale, exchange or liquidation of an interest in the Partnership will be "personal service income" within the meaning of this provision.

RECAPTURE OF CERTAIN DRILLING COSTS

The Code contains a provision for the recapture of intangible drilling and development costs, similar to the provisions with respect to the recapture of depreciation. Under this provision, any gain on the disposition of an interest in productive oil or gas properties (or, as described above under "Sale of Limited Partnership Interests," an interest in an oil or gas partnership owning productive properties) is treated as ordinary income to the extent of the excess of the intangible drilling and development cost deductions which are allocable to those properties (directly or through the ownership of an interest in an oil and gas partnership) over the deductions that would have been allowed had such expenses with respect to successful wells been capitalized and recovered through cost depletion.

Under the Partnership Agreement, the recapture of federal income tax deductions resulting from the sale of Partnership property is allocated to the Partners to whom the deduction giving rise to such recapture was allocated. Since a disproportionate amount of the Partnership's intangible drilling and development costs are to be allocated to the Limited Partners, a similar portion of any gain realized by the Partnership on the sale or other disposition of Partnership oil or gas properties on which intangible drilling costs have been incurred, which constitutes recapture of such costs, will be allocated to the Limited Partners, and must be treated as ordinary income by them. Similarly, that portion of any gain realized by a Limited Partner on the sale or other disposition of an interest in the Partnership which is allocable to the Partnership's oil or gas properties on which intangible drilling costs have been incurred, which constitutes recapture of such costs, will be treated as ordinary income.

POSSIBLE CHANGES IN THE FEDERAL INCOME TAX LAWS

It should be noted that several proposals which could adversely affect the taxation of oil and gas investments have been discussed in Congress in the past few years. No prediction can be made as to whether any of such proposals might be enacted by the Congress, and no prediction can be made as to what additional legislation might be proposed adversely affecting the taxation of oil and gas investments.

OTHER TAX CONSIDERATIONS

The Partnership may operate in state and local jurisdictions which impose a tax on each Limited Partner for his share of the income derived from the Partnership's activities in such jurisdictions. Furthermore, a Limited Partner may incur an income tax, imposed by the jurisdiction of his residence, upon his share of Partnership income without regard to the source of such income. Deductions which are available to a Limited Partner for federal income tax purposes may not be available to a Limited Partner for state or local income tax purposes. In addition, to the extent that the Partnership operates in certain jurisdictions, estate or inheritance taxes may be payable therein after the death of a Limited Partner.

Persons contemplating the purchase of an interest in the Partnership should consult their tax advisors to determine whether any applicable income tax laws of their state of domicile would permit the exclusion of net income earned from the Partnership operations in other states, or permit a credit against state income taxes for income taxes paid to other states where the Partnership may conduct its operations.

COMPETITION, MARKETS AND REGULATIONS

COMPETITION FOR LEASES AND DRILLING RIGS

The Partnership will acquire substantially all its Leases from the Operating Agent for the Partnership which will encounter strong competition from other independent operators and major oil companies in acquiring Leases suitable for exploration. Many of such competitors have financial resources and staffs larger than those available to the Partnership. In view of the current domestic shortage of hydrocarbons, it is anticipated that the cost of acquiring Leases and the equipment necessary to explore such Leases may increase appreciably. Drilling rigs are in high demand, and it is possible that the Partnership may experience delays in securing suitable drilling rigs which could defer the drilling of some exploratory wells with the result that all the Exploration Commitments of the Partners may not be expended during the first year of operation.

MARKETS FOR SALE OF PRODUCTION

The availability of a ready market for oil and gas discovered, if any, will depend on numerous factors beyond the control of the Partnership, including the proximity and capacity of pipelines, and the effect of state regulation of production and federal regulation of gas and crude oil sales.

REGULATION OF PRODUCTION

In most, if not all, areas where the Partnership may conduct activities, there will be some statutory provisions regulating the production of oil and natural gas under which administrative agencies may promulgate rules in connection with the operation and production of both oil and gas wells, determine the reasonable market demand for oil and gas, and establish allowable rates of production. Such regulatory orders may restrict the rate at which the Partnership's Wells produce oil or gas below the rate at which such wells would be produced in the absence of such regulatory orders.

GAS SALES

Sales of natural gas by the Partnership will be subject to the maximum lawful price ceilings set in the Natural Gas Policy Act of 1978 ("NGPA"). The NGPA is very complex; however, generally the act defines certain categories of gas, including "new natural gas" which will qualify for specified maximum lawful ceiling prices. The category of "new natural gas" will qualify for a maximum lawful ceiling price of $1.75 per MMBtu as of April 20, 1977, subject to adjustment for inflation and periodic escalation. Under the NGPA price controls have been extended for the first time to intrastate gas sales; however, gas being sold under intrastate contracts in existence on the day before the date of enactment of the NGPA may continue to be sold at the prices contained in such contracts as of the date of enactment of the NGPA even if higher than the price for "new natural gas," subject to certain restrictions on future escalations. Gas being sold under existing interstate contracts will, with the exception of gas falling within higher price gas categories, continue to qualify for rates set by the Federal Energy Regulatory Commission ("FERC") as of April 20, 1977, subject to an adjustment for inflation. Finally, certain categories of gas will be deregulated as of January 1, 1985, subject to standby authority to reimpose controls under certain conditions. Generally the maximum lawful price ceilings set in the NGPA may be collected only if the Partnership has contractual authority to do so and, in certain instances, has made filings with the appropriate State or Federal agency to collect such rates.

Further, if the Partnership has certain "categories" of gas which were committed or dedicated to interstate commerce on the day before the date of enactment of the NGPA, the sale of such gas will continue to be subject to regulation by FERC under the Natural Gas Act which will require, among other things, that the Partnership obtain a certificate of public convenience and necessity before commencing the sale of such gas, and approval by FERC of the abandonment of such sale once commenced.

No prediction can be made as to what "categories" under the NGPA any gas discovered by the Partnership will qualify for, and accordingly no prediction can be made as to the prices which the Partnership may receive for the sale of any gas it may discover.

Finally, the NGPA establishes certain rules for incremental pricing which will require that certain industrial boiler fuel users bear a larger proportion of the price for higher cost gas. Other bills which were recently enacted will limit the use of natural gas in certain installations. These measures could potentially affect the market for natural gas; however, it is impossible to predict at this time exactly what the impact will be.

140

LIQUID HYDROCARBON SALES

The Partnership's sale of any liquid hydrocarbons it may discover and produce will be subject to the controls imposed under the Energy Policy and Conservation Act of 1975, as amended ("EPCA"). In general the EPCA provides for mandatory crude oil price controls through June 1979 and discretionary controls through September 30, 1981.

Under the EPCA the initial maximum weighted average price for all domestic crude oil is set at $7.66 per barrel, subject to certain contingent upward adjustments. Under a 1976 amendment to the EPCA, however, production from so-called "stripper" properties (i.e., properties which produce less than an average of ten barrels of oil per day during any consecutive twelve-month period beginning after December 31, 1972) is exempt from regulation and may be sold at free market prices.

The Federal Energy Administration ("FEA") which initially administered the EPCA, initially issued regulations designed to result in a weighted average price for all domestic crude oil of $7.66 per barrel. In these regulations, the FEA, in effect, continued the two tier pricing structure which prevailed prior to the issuance of the regulations, with so-called "old" crude oil being sold at lower tier prices and "new" crude oil being sold at upper tier prices. The principal change implemented by these regulations was that "new" crude oil could no longer be sold at free market prices, but must be sold at a price no higher than the upper tier level set by the FEA.

Under the regulations, "new" crude oil is defined as crude oil produced in excess of a particular property's "base production control level" for a particular month and "old" crude oil is defined as all the remaining volumes of crude oil produced from that particular property. A particular property's "base production control level" is defined under the regulations to be either (i) the volume of crude oil produced from the particular property during a particular month in 1972 or (ii) the volume of old crude oil, as the phrase "old crude oil" was defined prior to the adoption of the regulations, produced from the particular property during the corresponding month in 1975. Subject to certain exceptions, during 1975 the volume of "old" crude oil for a property was equivalent to that property's production during the corresponding month of 1972 minus an amount by which production from that property exceeded its 1972 production.

The producer has the right to elect which of these standards it will choose to use for determining its "base production control level."

Under the current regulations "new oil" is being sold at a nationwide average of $12.61 per barrel and "old oil" at an average of $5.65 per barrel. Substantially all liquid hydrocarbons which the Partnership may discover and produce, if any, would be considered "new oil" under the current regulations and therefore entitled to be sold at the higher price.

Under the recently enacted Department of Energy Reorganization Act, the jurisdiction for regulating crude oil prices formerly vested in the FEA has been transferred to the Economic Regulatory Administration, an administrative office within the Department of Energy.

PROPOSED LEGISLATION

The President announced an energy plan on April 20, 1977 including proposals to (i) continue price controls on existing crude oil production at present levels, with adjustment for inflation, indefinitely, (ii) allow crude oil production from future discoveries qualifying under the restrictive definition of "new oil" eventually to receive the 1977 world oil price, with adjustment for inflation, and (iii) apply a crude oil equalization tax to increase the cost of controlled domestic crude oil to world market prices. To date, none of these proposals have been enacted or otherwise implemented; however substantially all of these crude pricing provisions could be implemented by administrative regulation, subject only to Congressional disapproval.

No prediction can be made as to what additional legislation may be proposed, if any, affecting the competitive status of an oil and gas producer, restricting the prices at which a producer may sell its oil and gas, or the market demand for oil and gas, nor can it be predicted which proposals, including those presently under consideration, if any, might be enacted, nor when any such proposals, if enacted, might become effective.

SPECIAL PROGRAM TAX ANALYSIS

SECTION (A)—a synopsis of the Acts' effects on individual investors in the Special Program:

SECTION (B)—a narrative of the conclusions drawn from a detailed review of the Acts and their effects on individual investors;

SECTION (C)—four examples which illustrate the effects and descriptions set forth in Section (A);

SECTION (D)—a synopsis of the tax effect of corporate oil and gas investments, which are generally less widely understood than the tax effects of oil and gas investments for individuals, and a summary of the Acts' effects on corporate investors in the Special Program;

SECTION (E)—a narrative of the conclusions drawn from a detailed review of the Acts and their effect on corporate investors; and,

SECTION (F)—three examples which illustrate the effects and descriptions set forth in Section (D).

For ease of understanding you may wish to review the examples in Section (C) each time they are referenced in Section (A) and the examples in Section (F) when they are referenced in Section (D).

SECTION (A)

SYNOPSIS OF THE ACTS' EFFECTS ON INDIVIDUAL INVESTORS IN THE SPECIAL PROGRAM

1. **The "At Risk" Concept.** Under the 1976 Act the deduction of losses incurred in oil and gas operations is limited to the amount at risk for individuals, electing small business corporations (under Subchapter S) and closely held corporations which have more than 50% in value of their stock owned directly or indirectly by five or fewer individuals.

Applicability: The entire amount of a Limited Partner's investment is "at risk" in this Special Program Partnership. Therefore, Limited Partners will continue to be able to deduct up to 100% of their investment in the Partnership (approximately 60-80% in the first year). Deductibility of 100% or more of the amount of investment is still available over a period of 2-4 years in the Special Program Partnership, even though some Partnership capital is expended on capitalized items such as oil and gas leases, equipment and Partnership syndication costs. Deductibility in excess of 100% of original investment can be generated from a combination of the following: (a) the Partnership's planned normal borrowing for drilling operations equal to 10-15% of Partnership capital (which is recourse as to the Partnership and the General Partners but not the Limited Partners); and, (b) placing some Partnership oil and gas sales revenues "at risk" by investment in additional Partnership drilling operations, which is a deduction generating activity to the extent the Treasury Department permits percentage depletion to be deducted without regard to the amount "at risk." Item (b) results in additional tax losses to the Limited Partner because the deductions generated by such investment commonly exceed the taxable portion of the invested revenue due to the tax shelter provided the Partnership's oil and gas sales income by percentage depletion. The expenditures described in (a) and (b) continue to create deductions under the 1976 Act, even though the Limited Partners are not personally liable for repayment of the borrowing, because the expenditures will not produce sufficient Partnership losses to reduce the Limited Partners' capital accounts to a debit (negative) basis.

2. **The Minimum Tax on Preference Items**. Under the 1976 and 1978 Acts intangible drilling and development cost (IDC) on productive wells (but not on dry holes), in the year the IDC was deducted, are tax preference items for taxpayers other than regular corporations (those which are not Subchapter S corporations or personal holding companies).

For purposes of determining this preference item, the 1976 Act allows the amortization of IDC on productive wells to be reduced (but only for the year in which the productive IDC was incurred) by amortization calculated: (a) on the basis of a 120 month schedule beginning with the first month of production; or (b) on a cost depletion or unit of production basis employing an estimated life of the property.

For individuals, the 15% regular minimum tax is applied against a list of 9 preference items if they exceed an individual's exemptions of the greater of $10,000 or half of his regular tax liability after reduction for applicable tax credits.

144

The Act of 1978 created two alternative preference items: (1) the excluded 60% of capital gains for individuals; and (2) an individual's excess itemized deductions. The Act of 1978 provides that if the alternative minimum tax exceeds an individual's regular taxes plus his regular minimum tax an individual will be subject to the alternative minimum tax. The alternative minimum tax is applied to an individual's taxable income plus the alternative tax preference items, less a $20,000 exemption. The alternative minimum tax rates are 10% on the first $40,000, 20% on the next $40,000 and 25% on amounts exceeding $80,000. For information purposes an explanation of the regular and alternative minimum tax and a list of all regular and alternative preference items is shown on the accompanying "List of Preference Items."

For purposes of the examples in this report, we have employed the regular minimum tax because a Limited Partner can be assured of receiving tax savings from his oil and gas investment at the following rates, unless as explained below, a substantial portion of his taxable income consists of the 40% taxable portion of capital gains.

Tax (savings) Rate	Taxable Income Range
49%	$ 45,800 – $ 60,000
54%	60,000 – 85,600
59%	85,600 – 109,400
64%	109,400 – 162,400
68%	162,400 – 215,400
70%	215,400 and above

Under the Act of 1978, before the alternative minimum tax would apply, and therefore before any reduction in the above rates of tax savings would occur as a result of deduction generating investments, it would be necessary for the Limited Partners' 40% taxable portion of capital gains, (i.e., after the 60% exclusion) to exceed the following percentages of a Limited Partner's total taxable income (after the reduction in taxable income generated by sheltering).

83% of total taxable income at the 49% bracket
78% of total taxable income at the 54% bracket
78% of total taxable income at the 59% bracket

80% of total taxable income at the 64% bracket
88% of total taxable income at the 68% bracket
95% of total taxable income at the 70% bracket

This assumes the Limited Partner is not subject to the regular minimum tax. If the regular minimum tax was a factor, an even greater amount of taxable capital gain would be required before the alternative minimum tax would apply. An example of the calculations used to determine the above percentages of total taxable income at which the alternative minimum tax would begin to apply is shown below.

Applicability: With the deletion of: (i) the 60% excluded portion of capital gains; and, (ii) excess itemized deductions from the list of regular preference items as a result of the 1978 Act, the possibility of the regular minimum tax applying is reduced. If a Limited Partner is subject to a 50% tax rate and does not have preference items which exceed the regular minimum tax exemption of the greater of $10,000 or 50% of his regular income tax liability, no minimum tax will be paid. Therefore, his tax savings and after tax cost of investment will be identical to what they would have been before the 1976 Act. See Example 1. *The 50% tax bracket is applicable to persons relying on the maximum 50% rate on personal service income, but under the Act of 1978 tax rates on total taxable income escalate directly from the 49% bracket to the 54% bracket. For ease in reviewing the Examples referred to herein, we have assumed a 50% bracket.*

As illustrated in Example II, in the event the individual Limited Partner has tax preference items which exceed the exemptions under the regular minimum tax of the greater of $10,000 or 50% of his regular income tax, he will pay the 15% minimum tax on his proportionate share of the unamortized IDC from the Partnership's productive wells. Also, other preference items may become subject to the minimum tax as a result of the reduction in the Limited Partner's minimum tax exemption caused by the decrease in his regular tax liability due to his oil and gas investment.

Based upon how prior Program Partnerships would have been affected by the minimum tax provision of the 1976 Act, Special has calculated that for a Limited Partner in the 50% tax bracket who is subject to this provision, the effect of this tax will raise his after tax cost of investment by 6.47% to 8.66% of the amount invested to a total of 56.47% to 58.66% of the amount invested. Therefore, he will receive the benefit of tax savings equal to 43.53% to 41.34% of the amount invested. See Example II.

Because the minimum tax is levied on only the IDC on productive wells, Special believes that the Acts' effect on the minimum tax is more than offset by: (i) the recent, and the continuing increases in the prices of natural gas under the Natural Gas Policy Act of 1978; and, (ii) the 10% annual oil price increases permitted under the Emergency Petroleum Allocation Act of 1973 (by March 1, 1976 Regulations).

3. **The Maximum Tax on Personal Service Income**. Under the Acts, the amount of personal service income (as opposed to investment income) eligible for the 50% maximum tax rate is reduced by the total items of tax preference (except the 60% excluded portion of capital gains). Therefore, a Limited Partner could have a portion of his personal service income equal to his unamortized IDC on productive wells taxed at rates above 50%. For reference purposes, you may wish to note that for persons filing a joint return the 59% rate is not attained until taxable income reaches $85,600 and the 70% rate is not attained until taxable income reaches $215,400.

Applicability: Limited Partners whose taxable income is subject to the 50% maximum tax rate on personal service income, or who reduce their taxable income by sheltering down to the 49% bracket, would not be affected by this provision. Only Limited Partners with taxable personal service income i.e., after deductions and exemptions, in excess of $60,000 (filing jointly) would be affected by this provision, and even for Limited Partners in this situation the effect of the Act will be limited to the moderate increase in their after tax cost of investment due to the minimum tax (and then only if they have preference items which exceed the statutory exceptions) and the incremental increase in tax on a portion of their personal service income equal to their unamortized IDC on productive wells. A Limited Partner with substantial amounts of unearned income such as is illustrated by Example III will still realize substantial tax benefits from an oil and gas investment because he is probably subject to taxation at rates higher than 50% and any minimum tax or additional tax on his personal service income would merely offset in part the higher tax benefits resulting from

147

utilizing oil and gas deductions against his income otherwise taxable at the higher unearned income rates.

Based upon calculations of how prior Special Partnerships would have been affected by the maximum tax provision, Special calculates that even in the event a Limited Partner has that portion of his personal service income equal to the amount of his unamortized IDC on productive wells taxed at the maximum 70% rate rather than 50%, his after tax cost of investment would only be increased by the amount of his minimum tax plus 4.87% to 7.8% of the amount of his total investment. This additional 4.87% to 7.8% would result from the additional tax paid because of the incremental increase (20%) from the 50% tax rate to the assumed 70% tax rate on an amount of personal service income equal to the unamortized IDC on productive wells. Consequently, Special does not envision a Limited Partner's after tax cost of investment being raised by more than 12.1% to 17% of the total amount of his investment (7.23% minimum tax + 4.87% additional tax = 12.1%; or, 9.2% minimum tax + 7.8% additional tax = 17%). Therefore, we believe his after tax cost of investment would equal 42.1% to 47% of the amount of his investment and he would realize the benefit of tax savings equal to 57.9% to 53% of the amount of his investment. See Example III.

As with the minimum tax provision, it should be noted that the combined effect of the minimum and maximum tax provisions (which produces an anticipated 12.1% to 17% increase in after tax cost as a percentage of total investment) is expected to be more than offset by the continuing increases in the price of natural gas under the Natural Gas Policy Act of 1978, and the 10% annual oil price increases permitted under the Emergency Petroleum Allocation Act of 1973 (by March 1, 1976 Regulations).

4. Taxable Gain on the Disposition of Oil and Gas Properties or Interests. Under the Act of 1976, for properties or interests disposed of after January 1, 1976, intangible drilling and development cost on productive wells which was deducted after January 1, 1976 will now be recaptured as ordinary income on the sale or other disposition of an oil or gas property.

Applicability: When an oil or gas property, or a partnership interest in such properties, is sold or disposed of, ordinary income tax will be paid on the lesser of:

148

a) *the IDC which was deducted in the year incurred, minus the amounts (if any) by which the deduction for depletion would have been increased if the IDC had been capitalized rather than deducted; or,

b) the excess of the amount realized over the adjusted basis of the property in the case of a sale; or, the excess of the fair market value over the adjusted basis of the property in the case of a disposition other than a sale.

The remainder of the gain would be taxed as capital gain. The Act of 1978 increased from 50% to 60% the amount of capital gain which can be excluded from capital gain tax and it also removed the excluded portion of said gains from the list of regular preference items subject to tax.

Although the recapture provision of the 1976 Act somewhat increases taxation on the sale of a Partnership interest, the provisions of the 1978 Act, which provide a greater capital gain exemption and removal of the minimum tax in most cases, should generally cause the net economic effect to be superior to what it would have been even before the 1976 Act. See Example IV.

However, the maximum benefits of a successful oil and gas investment can probably best be realized by retaining the Limited Partnership interest so that the significant tax free benefits of depletable income can be realized. We know of no other investment which can generate tax free income from the investment to the extent possible in oil and gas.

5. **Clarifying Amendments Concerning Percentage Depletion.** The effective date of these provisions is January 1, 1975.

Applicability: Amendments were made to the Tax Reduction Act of 1975 by the Act of 1976 to correct certain

---

*This is the method of calculation employed in Examples IV and VI. It should be noted that studies indicate the provision in item (a) which provides a reduction in the amount subject to recapture is very limited. The effect of this provision is that, if percentage depletion on a property or partnership interest exceeds cost depletion, computed under the assumption that IDC has been capitalized, no reduction will occur. We have prepared Example IV under the assumption that no reduction will occur and we find that the result of this change will have only a minor effect on the net cash received by the Limited Partner.

ambiguities concerning the availability of percentage depletion. It is now clear that a taxpayer (Limited Partner), is entitled to the 22% depletion allowance on his first 1,200 barrels of oil sales per day or his first 7,200,000 cubic feet of gas sales per day in 1979, unless the sales are from proven properties transferred to him after December 31, 1974, or unless he makes more than $5 million of gross annual sales of oil and gas products from retail outlets. Also, in determining the retailer classification, which would otherwise cause the loss of percentage depletion, a specific provision now permits bulk sales of oil or natural gas to industrial and commercial consumers to be excluded from consideration.

A further clarification of the Tax Reduction Act of 1975 by the 1976 Act covered a section of the 1975 Act which disallowed percentage depletion on proven properties transferred after December 31, 1974. The 1976 Act provides that oil or natural gas properties are not to be treated as "transferred" just because there is a change in beneficiaries under a trust if the change occurs by reason of births, adoptions, or deaths involving a single family (the single family group concept). Also, the 1976 Act permits a transfer of property between (a) corporations which are members of the same controlled group of corporations; (b) business entities which are under common control; (c) members of the same family; or (d) a trust and related persons in the same family to the extent that the beneficiaries of that trust are and continue to be related persons in the family that transferred the property. The percentage depletion allowance will continue for only so long as the depletable oil quantity is allocated byetween the transfror and transferee.

In addition, the 1976 Act amended the 1975 Act with respect to the limitation on percentage depletion to 65% of the taxpayer's income. Under the 1976 Act, trusts are now permitted to compute the 65% of taxable income limitation without any deduction for distribution to beneficiaries.

6. Offset of Productive IDC with Net Oil and Gas Income. The Revenue Act of 1978 made permanent the reduction of IDC preference items by the amount of an individual's net oil and gas income. This reduction was previously effective only for one year (1977) under the Tax Reduction and Simplification Act of 1977. Net income from oil and gas properties is gross income from those properties reduced by the amount of deductions (other than unamortized productive IDC) attributable to that gross income. Deductions attributable to properties with no gross income do not have to be taken into account in computing net income from oil and gas properties. Therefore, if an individual has established some net oil and gas income: (i) the amount of his minimum tax payable resulting from productive IDC would be reduced or could be completely eliminated by his net oil and gas income; (ii) his after tax cost of investment would decline; and, (iii) his net tax savings would be increased.

SECTION (B)

CONCLUSIONS REGARDING THE ACTS' EFFECTS ON INDIVIDUAL INVESTORS

Oil and gas investments will continue to provide individual investors with substantial and immediate tax savings. Also continuing is the companion ability to generate significant amounts of tax free income from successful oil and gas investments. This ability is derived from the 22% depletion allowance which is computed on gross income (before operating expenses and production taxes), and can result in 30%-40% of Partnership distributions being received tax free even after giving effect to any preference tax which may be payable on depletable income. Further, as set forth in Examples II and III herein, although the after tax cost of an oil and gas investment may be moderately increased for some investors as a result of the 1976 Act's provisions covering the minimum tax and the maximum tax calculation, we believe that the basic forces of supply and demand as they affect the price of oil, and natural gas, and the positive effect of the 1978 Act in: (i) providing the offset of productive IDC by net oil and gas income; (ii) increasing the capital gain exemption from 50% to 60% (as it would relate to a sale of a Limited Partner's interest); and, (iii) removing the excluded portion of capital gains and excess itemized deductions from the list of regular preference items, more than offset the effects of the 1976 Act.

CAVEAT

IT SHOULD BE NOTED THAT THE ASSUMPTIONS USED IN THE EXAMPLES HEREIN WERE MADE *SOLELY* FOR ILLUSTRATIVE PURPOSES TO REVEAL THE EFFECT OF THE ACTS ON THE SPECIAL PROGRAM AS THEY RELATE TO THE MINIMUM TAX ON PREFERENCE ITEMS, THE MAXIMUM TAX ON PERSONAL SERVICE INCOME, DE-PLETION, IDC RECAPTURE AND CAPITAL GAIN TAX. DUE TO THE RISKS OF DRILLING FOR GAS AND OIL SPECIAL CAN MAKE NO REPRESENTATION THAT THE RESULTS OF FUTURE SPECIAL PROGRAMS WILL BE COMPARABLE TO THE ASSUMPTIONS MADE HEREIN.

SECTION (C)

EXAMPLES OF THE ACTS' EFFECTS
ON INDIVIDUAL INVESTORS

EXAMPLE 1

NO MINIMUM TAX

ASSUMPTIONS

A. The Limited Partner has not used his regular minimum tax exemption equal to the greater of $10,000 or 50% of his regular income tax due before calculating the minimum tax.

B. The Limited Partner is in the 50% tax bracket.

Calculation of Tax Savings and After Tax Cost of Investment

$10,000	Investment
x100%	Total 2-4 Yr. Deductibility
10,000	Total Deduction
x50%	Tax Rate*
$ 5,000	Tax Savings
$10,000	Investment
−5,000	Tax Savings
$ 5,000	After Tax Cost of Investment

Note: Example 1 should be reviewed in conjunction with Examples II and III.

EXAMPLE II

MINIMUM TAX

ASSUMPTIONS

A. For the first year of the oil and gas investment the Limited Partner has already used from other investments, his regular minimum tax exemption equal to the greater of $10,000 or 50% of his regular income tax due before calculating the minimum tax. Therefore he will pay the 15% minimum tax on (a) the amount of his unamortized IDC on productive wells (reduced by any net oil and gas income); and (b) on any other preference items which are subject to the minimum tax as a result of the reduction in his minimum tax exemption caused by the decrease in his regular tax liability due to his oil and gas investment. For a Limited Partner in the 50% tax bracket item (b) could be no greater than 25% of the first year deductibility generated by the oil and gas investment.

---

*The 50% tax rate is applicable to persons employing the 50% maximum tax on personal service income, but under the Act of 1978, tax rates on total taxable income escalate directly from the 49% bracket to the 54% bracket. Please note that for ease in reviewing this example we have assumed the 50% tax bracket.

B. Based upon an analysis of the effects the Act would have had on prior Special Programs, a range of IDC on productive wells equal to 25% to 40% of invested capital was calculated. Therefore, Case 1 assumes IDC on productive wells is equal to 25% of the amount invested and Case 2 assumes said IDC is equal to 40% of the amount invested in both cases it is assumed that the productive wells will be on production for ¼ year in the year of the investment. Therefore, ¼ year of amortization of the IDC on productive wells (using the 120 month option) has been employed.

C. The Limited Partner is in the 50% tax bracket. (a).

D. The Limited Partner has no net oil and gas income.

In the event the Limited Partner has oil and gas income, in a taxable year which commences after December 31, 1976, the Act of 1978 allows him to reduce his IDC subject to the minimum tax by the amount of his net income from oil and gas properties. Net income from oil and gas properties is gross income from those properties reduced by the amount of deductions (other than unamortized productive IDC) attributable to that gross income. Deductions attributable to properties with no gross income do not have to be taken into account in computing net income from oil and gas properties. Therefore, (i) the amount of his minimum tax payable resulting from productive IDC would be reduced or could be completely eliminated by his net oil and gas income, (ii) his after tax cost of investment would decline; and, (iii) his net tax savings would be increased.

CASE 1

Minimum Tax Calculation Assuming
IDC on Productive Wells Equal to
25% of Total Investment

$10,000	$100,000	Investment Amount
x 75%	x 75%	1st Yr. Deductibility
7,500	75,000	1st Yr. IDC
−5,000	−50,000	IDC on Dry Holes
2,500	25,000	IDC on Productive Wells
− 63	− 630	¼ Yr. St. Line IDC Amor.
2,437	24,370	IDC Subject to Min. Tax
+1,875(b)	+18,750(b)	Pref. Items Subj. to Min. Tax Per A(b) Above
4,312	43,120	Total Tax Pref. Items
x 15%	x 15%	Min. Tax Rate
$ 647	$ 6,468	Minimum Tax

CASE 2

Minimum Tax Calculation Assuming
IDC on Productive Wells Equal to
40% of Total Investment

$10,000	$100,000	Investment Amount
x 75%	x 75%	1st Yr. Deductibility
7,500	75,000	1st Yr. IDC
−3,500	−35,000	IDC on Dry Holes
4,000	40,000	IDC on Productive Wells
− 100	− 1,000	¼ Yr. St. Line IDC Amor.
3,900	39,000	IDC Subject to Min. Tax
+1,875(b)	+18,750(b)	Pref. Items Subj. to Min. Tax Per A(b) Above
5,775	57,750	Total Tax Pref. Items
x 15%	x 15%	Min. Tax Rate
$ 866	$ 8,663	Minimum Tax

(a) The 50% tax rate is applicable to persons employing the 50% maximum tax on personal service income, but under the Act of 1978, tax rates on total taxable income escalate directly from the 49% bracket to the 54% bracket. Please note that for ease in reviewing this example we have assumed the 50% tax bracket.

(b) This assumes the maximum amount of preference items subject to the minimum tax as a result of the decrease in the Limited Partner's regular tax liability caused by the oil and gas investment. If the Limited Partner has less than the indicated amount of preference items in excess of the $10,000 exclusion, the amount of minimum tax payable would be reduced and the after tax cost would be even less than shown above.

Calculation of After Tax Cost of Investment

CASE 1

$10,000	$100,000	Investment
x100%	x100%	Total 2-4 Yr. Deduct
10,000	100,000	Total Deduction
x 50%	x 50%	Tax Rate
$ 5,000	$ 50,000	Pre-Min. Tax Savings
$10,000	$100,000	Investment
−5,000	−50,000	Pre-Min. Tax Savings
+ 647(c)	+ 6,468(c)	Minimum Tax
$ 5,647	$ 56,468	After Tax Cost

CASE 2

$10,000	$100,000	Investment
x100%	x100%	Total 2-4 Yr. Deduct.
10,000	100,000	Total Deduction
x 50%	x 50%	Tax Rate
$ 5,000	$ 50,000	Pre-Min. Tax Savings
$10,000	$100,000	Investment
−5,000	−50,000	Pre-Min. Tax Savings
+ 866(c)	+ 8,663(c)	Minimum Tax
$ 5,866	$ 58,663	After Tax Cost

(c) These are the amounts used to calculate the increase in after tax cost as a percentage of total investment.

**Calculation of Increase in After Tax Cost as a Percentage of Total Investment

CASE 1

$$\frac{\$\ \ \ 647}{\$10,000\ \ \text{Increase}} = 6.47\% \qquad \frac{\$\ \ 6,468}{\$100,000\ \ \text{Increase}} = 6.47\%$$

CASE 2

$$\frac{\$\ \ \ 866}{\$10,000\ \ \text{Increase}} = 8.66\% \qquad \frac{\$\ \ 8,663}{\$100,000\ \ \text{Increase}} = 8.66\%$$

Calculation of Net Tax Savings

CASE 1

$10,000	$100,000	Investment
−5,647	−56,468	After Tax Cost
$ 4,353	$ 43,532	Net Tax Savings

CASE 2

$10,000	$100,000	Investment
−5,866	−58,663	After Tax Cost
$ 4,134	$ 41,337	Net Tax Savings

EXAMPLE III

MINIMUM TAX AND MAXIMUM TAX

ASSUMPTIONS

NOTE: Assumptions B and D (but not A and C) are identical to those set forth in Example II.

A. For the first year of the oil and gas investment the Limited Partner has already used from other investments, his regular minimum tax exemption equal to the greater of $10,000 or 50% of his regular income tax due before calculating the minimum tax. Therefore, he will pay the 15% minimum tax on (a) the amount of his unamortized IDC on productive wells (reduced by any net oil and gas income); and (b) on any preference items which are subject to the minimum tax as a result of the reduction in his minimum tax exemption caused by the decrease in his regular tax liability (after taking into account the effect of the additional tax on earned income) due to his oil and gas investment. For a Limited Partner in the 70% tax bracket item (b) could be no greater than 35% of the first year deductibility generated by the oil and gas investment.

B. Based upon an analysis of the effect the Act would have on prior Special Programs, a range of IDC on productive wells equal to 25% to 40% of invested capital was calculated. Therefore, Case 1 assumes IDC on productive wells is equal to 25% of the amount invested and Case 2 assumes said IDC is equal to 40% of the amount invested. It is assumed that the productive wells will be on production for ¼ year in the year of the investment. So, ¼ year of amortization of the IDC on productive wells (using the 120 month option) has been employed.

C. The Limited Partner would otherwise be in the 70% bracket and is relying on the maximum tax on earned income, thus he has a portion of his earned income equal to the amount of his unamortized IDC on productive wells taxed at 70% rather than 50%.

D. The Limited Partner has no net oil and gas income.

In the event the Limited Partner has oil and gas income in a taxable year which commences after December 31, 1976 the Act of 1978 allows him to reduce his IDC subject to the minimum tax by the amount of his net income from oil and gas properties. Net income from oil and gas properties is gross income from those properties reduced by the amount of deductions (other than unamortized productive IDC) attributable to that gross income. Deductions attributable to properties with no gross income do not have to be taken into account in computing net income from oil and gas properties. Therefore, (i) the amount of his minimum tax and the possible effect of the Act on his maximum tax calculation resulting from productive IDC would be reduced or could be completely eliminated by his net oil and gas income; (ii) his after tax cost of investment would decline; and, (iii) his net tax savings would be increased.

CASE 1

Minimum Tax Calculation Assuming IDC on Productive Wells Equal to 25% of Total Investment

$10,000	$100,000	Investment Amount
x 75%	x 75%	1st Yr. Deductibility
7,500	75,000	1st Yr. IDC
−5,000	−50,000	IDC on Dry Holes
2,500	25,000	IDC on Productive Wells
− 63	− 630	¼ Yr. St. Line IDC Amor.
2,437	24,370	IDC Subject to Min. Tax
+2,381(a)	+23,810(a)	Pref. Items Subj. to Min. Tax Per A(b) Above
4,818	48,180	Total Tax Pref. Items
x 15%	x 15%	Min. Tax Rate
$ 723	$ 7,227	Minimum Tax

CASE 2

Minimum Tax Calculation Assuming
IDC on Productive Wells Equal to
40% of Total Investment

$10,000	$100,000	Investment Amount
x 75%	x 75%	1st Yr. Deductibility
7,500	75,000	1st Yr. IDC
−3,500	−35,000	IDC on Dry Holes
4,000	40,000	IDC on Productive Wells
− 100	− 1,000	¼ Yr. St. Line IDC Amor.
3,900	39,000	IDC Subject to Min. Tax
+2,235(a)	+22,350(a)	Pref. Items Subj. to Min. Tax Per A(b) Above
6,135	61,350	Total Tax Pref. Items
x 15%	x 15%	Min. Tax Rate
$ 920	$ 9,202	Minimum Tax

(a) This assumes the maximum amount of preference terms subject to the minimum tax as a result of the decrease in the Limited Partner's tax liability caused by the oil and gas investment. If the Limited Partner has less than the indicated amount of preference items in excess of the $10,000 exclusion, the amount of minimum tax payable would be reduced and the after tax cost would therefore decline.

Calculation of Additional Tax on Earned Income
Per the Acts' Possible Effects on the Maximum
Tax Calculation for Some Investors

CASE 1

$ 2,437	$ 24,370	Earned Income Equal to IDC subject to Min. Tax
x 20%	x 20%	Assumed Max. Increase from 50% to 70% Tax Rate
$ 487	$ 4,874	Add'l Tax on Earned Inc.

CASE 2

$ 3,900	$ 39,000	Earned Income Equal to IDC subject to Min. Tax
x 20%	x 20%	Assumed Max. Increase from 50% to 70% Tax Rate
$ 780	$ 7,800	Add'l Tax on Earned Inc.

Calculation of After Tax Cost of Investment

CASE 1

$10,000	$100,000	Investment
x 100%	x 100%	Total 2-4 Yr. Deductibility
10,000	100,000	Total Deduction
x 70%	x 70%	Tax Rate
$ 7,000	$ 70,000	Pre-Min. Tax Savings
$10,000	$100,000	Investment
–7,000	–70,000	Pre-Min. Tax Savings
+ 723(b)	+ 7,227(b)	Minimum Tax
+ 487(b)	+ 4,874	Add'l Tax on Earned Inc.
$ 4,210	$ 42,101	After Tax Cost

CASE 2

$10,000	$100,000	Investment
x 100%	x 100%	Deductibility
10,000	100,000	Total Deduction
x 70%	x 70%	Tax Rate
$ 7,000	$ 70,000	Pre-Min. Tax Savings
$10,000	$100,000	Investment
–7,000	–70,000	Pre-Min. Tax Savings
+ 920(b)	+ 9,202(b)	Minimum Tax
+ 780(b)	+ 7,800(b)	Add'l Tax on Earned Inc.
$ 4,700	$ 47,002	After Tax Cost

(b) These are the amounts used to calculate the increase in after tax cost as a percentage of total investment.

**Calculation of Increase in After Tax Cost as a Percentage of Total Investment

CASE 1

$ 723	$ 7,227	Minimum Tax
+ 487	+ 4,874	Add'l Tax on Earned Inc.
$ 1,210	$ 12,101	Total Add'l After Tax Cost

$$\frac{\$\ 1,210}{\$10,000} = 12.1\% \quad 12.1\% \text{ Increase} \qquad \frac{\$\ 12,101}{\$\ 10,000} = 12.10\% \text{ Increase}$$

CASE 2

$ 920	$ 9,202	Minimum Tax
+ 780	+ 7,800	Add'l Tax on Earned Inc.
$ 1,700	$ 17,002	Total Add'l After Tax Cost

$$\frac{\$\ 1,700}{\$10,000} = 17.00\% \text{ Increase} \qquad \frac{\$\ 17,002}{\$100,000} = 17.00\% \text{ Increase}$$

Calculation of Net Tax Savings

CASE 1

$10,000	$100,000	Investment
−4,210	−42,101	After Tax Cost
$ 5,790	$ 57,899	Net Tax Savings

CASE 2

$10,000	$100,000	Investment
−4,700	−47,002	After Tax Cost
$ 5,300	$ 52,998	Net Tax Savings

EXAMPLE IV

EXAMPLE OF POSSIBLE FEDERAL INCOME TAX RESULTS FOR INDIVIDUALS ON SALE OF AN OIL & GAS LIMITED PARTNERSHIP INTEREST BEFORE AND AFTER THE TAX ACTS OF 1976 AND 1978

ASSUMPTIONS

A. A Limited Partner invested $10,000 in an oil and gas Limited Partnership in 1979 and has received ordinary deductions of $8,000 ($7,000 in that year and $1,000 from 1/1/80 to 9/30/81). Out of the $7,000 deducted in 1979, $2,500 was expended on productive wells. All leases on which dry holes were drilled were abandoned.

B. On October 1, 1981, the Limited Partner sold his Limited Partnership interest for $12,000.

C. Other long term gains in 1981 did not exceed $40,000.

D. The Partnership's properties had been on production for one year.

E. The Limited Partner had already used his minimum tax exemption.

F. The Limited Partner is in the 50% tax bracket.

	BEFORE THE ACT OF 1976	AFTER THE ACTS OF 1976 & 1978
Total Investment Basis Calculation:		
Total investment	$10,000	$10,000
Less: Share of losses for 1979 to Sept. 30, 1981	(8,000)	(8,000)
Basis for determining gain or loss	2,000	2,000

Calculation of Taxes and Net Cash Proceeds After Payment
of All Taxes:

	BEFORE THE ACT OF 1976	AFTER THE ACTS OF 1976 & 1978
Consideration received	$12,000	$12,000
Less: Basis	(2,000)	(2,000)
Maximum amount of gain	10,000	10,000
Calculation of Ordinary Income:		
Intangible drilling cost on productive wells deducted in prior years	NA	2,500
Less the amount by which the depletion deduction would have been increased if the IDC had been capitalized rather than deducted	NA	– 0 –
Ordinary income	NA	2,500
Calculation of Capital Gain:		
Total gain	10,000	10,000
Less: Ordinary income	NA	(2,500)
Capital gain	10,000	7,500
Net Effect:		
Sales price	12,000	12,000
Less Long term capital gain tax (Before the 1976 Act–$10,000 x 25%) (After the 1976 and 1978 Acts–$7,500 x 40% taxable x 50% tax bracket)	(2,500)	(1,500)
Ordinary income tax (After the 1976 Act–$2,500 x 50%)	NA	(1,250)
Minimum tax on the excluded portion of the capital gain (before the Act of 1976 $5,000 x 10%) (after the Act of 1978 – 0 –)	(500)	– 0 –
Net cash proceeds after payment of all taxes on the sale	$ 9,000	$ 9,250

NOTE: Because in this Example the Investment Tax Credit applicable to a Special Program Partnership interest in the year of the investment would be equal to the recapture of same in the year of the sale, such offsetting effects are not depicted in this Example.

SECTION (D)

SYNOPSIS OF THE ACTS' EFFECTS ON CORPORATE INVESTORS IN THE SPECIAL PROGRAM

A corporation enjoys the same tax incentives from deductible expenditures, depletion and depreciation as an individual with respect to its investment in oil and gas drilling programs. In addition, pursuant to the Act of 1976 a corporation that is not a personal holding company or a Subchapter S corporation does not treat intangible drilling and development costs (IDC) on productive wells as a tax preference item. Further, corporations other than those described in Section (A) 1 above are not subject to the "at risk" provisions of the 1976 Act. Consequently, in some instances, the tax benefits to an individual investor may be somewhat reduced through the application of the 1976 Act's effect on the minimum tax on preference items, and the maximum tax on earned income, but the corporate investor would not be subject to this effect. Through their exemption from the "at risk" provisions of the 1976 Act, qualifying corporations have also retained the ability to generate deductions in excess of their "at risk" investment through the investment of borrowed funds, which they are not liable to repay if the investment fails to generate sufficient funds to repay the lender. As used in this summary, the term "corporation" will refer to a corporation that is not subject to the "at risk" provisions of the 1976 Act.

The tax advantages to a corporation investing in a Special Program may be summarized as follows:

(1) **Deductibility**. The corporation is permitted to deduct all intangible drilling and completion costs, which, together with other deductible items, have historically amounted to 70% to

80% of an investor's capital contribution to prior Special Programs during the first year of a partnership's activities and up to an aggregate of 100% of the investment over the next 2-3 years (subject to the effects of bank borrowing on Partnership revenues). These costs, which to a corporate investor are his allocable share of a Partnership's distributive loss are deductible directly from the corporation's taxable income for its fiscal year within which the Partnership's taxable year ends (i.e., December 31).

Consequently, assuming 100% total deductibility over three years, a $100,000 investment in an oil and gas drilling program will result in $46,000 of tax savings and a $54,000 net (after tax) cost to a corporate investor in a 46% tax bracket. Example V to this report is a comparative example of the tax effect resulting from a corporate investment in a representative Special Program. See Example V. Example VI responds to the questions we have received regarding the effect of oil and gas deductions on a corporation's accumulated earnings and the effect of the Act on gifting a Special Program Partnership interest to a corporate pension plan. See Example VI.

(2) **Depletion Allowance.** In addition to the tax savings discussed above, a companion ability of oil and gas investments is to provide investors (who are not refiners or retailers of oil, gas or products derived therefrom) with significant amounts of tax-free income from successful oil and gas investments. (OF COURSE, DUE TO THE RISK OF OIL AND GAS INVESTMENTS THERE IS NO ASSURANCE THAT SUCH AN INVESTMENT WILL BE SUCCESSFUL.) This ability is derived from the 22% depletion allowance, which is computed on **gross** income (before operating expenses and production taxes) "by property" and is deducted from each property's taxable income on the basis of the individual property's profitability, as discussed below. The benefits to an investor from this non-cash deduction in the calculation of taxable income during the operating (production) phase of the drilling program's life, can be illustrated as follows (assuming a period during which there are no IDC expenditures and the Partnership has no significant debt):

Allocable Portions of Income and Expense

Gross Oil and Gas Revenues	$1,600
Production Taxes, and Operating Expenses	(600)
Cash Received in Distribution	1,000
Depreciation	(40)
Depletion	(350)
Taxable Income	$ 610

The tax shelter provided the cash received in distribution by percentage depletion is, in this example, 35% ($350 ÷ $1,000). It is important to distinguish the depreciation benefit (discussed below) from that derived from percentage depletion. Depreciation also shelters cash distributions, but depreciation is limited to the Partnership's investment in lease and well equipment and the depreciation method by which such costs are recovered. However, percentage depletion is available as a percentage of gross revenues, and continues to be deductible even after leasehold costs are fully recovered, and is limited only to the lesser of 22% of a property's gross revenues from sales of gas and oil or 50% of the property's net income from sales of gas and oil (all depletion is calculated initially on a "by producing property" basis, rather than on the aggregate of Partnership revenues and expenses) but the aggregate percentage depletion so calculated is subject to an overall limitation of 65% of taxable income. In prior Special Programs not substantially affected by debt the effects of the depletion allowance resulted in 30%-40% of Partnership distributions of gas and oil sales proceeds being received tax free.

(3) **Depreciation.** An investor in the Special Program receives, through the allocation of partnership gain or loss, the statutory deduction relating to the depreciation of "tangible" costs relating to the completion of a well, being primarily equipment and related cost items. Special commonly employs the double declining balance method with an eight year life for the calculation of the partnership's depreciation allowance. For prior Special Program partnerships this calculation has resulted in aggregate depreciation deductions, over the first three years, equal to approximately 40% of the partnership's equipment investment.

(4) **Investment Tax Credit (ITC).** In addition to the depreciation allowance, an investor is entitled to a credit against his federal income tax liability equal to 10% of the investor's proportionate share of the capitalized cost of lease and well equipment in the year such items of equipment are acquired and placed in service. Because this is a direct **reduction** of tax, its effect is more than twice as great, to a corporation in the 46% tax bracket, as that of a **deduction** of the same dollar amount from taxable income.

To indicate the effect of depletion and depreciation on an investment financed with oil and gas receipts, Example VII to this report indicates a situation where a corporation realized $5,000 as its share of net oil and gas receipts as a result of an earlier oil and gas investment. As shown in that example, a $5,000 corporate investment in the same year (in anticipation of the $5,000 in cash distributions to the investor) shelters all the taxable portion of the oil and gas income to the corporation. In addition, the deductions generated by the $5,000 investment causes total deductions to exceed taxable income, thus creating tax shelter for other corporate taxable income, i.e. non-oil and gas income. See Example VII.

(5) **Accounting Treatment.** The accounting policies for such an investment do not affect the tax treatment of an investment in an oil and gas drilling program. The accounting treatment must, of course, be determined by the investing company's management based on materiality relative to that company's other assets and operations, the intent of the investment (long-term, short-term, etc.) and other related matters.

The accounting methods for investments are discussed in Accounting Principles Board Opinion No. 18 and its accounting interpretations relating to investments in Partnerships. In accordance with the accounting principles set forth therein, the "cost" method of accounting would probably be appropriate for such an investment by a corporation not principally engaged in the oil and gas business. Under the 'cost' method, income is recorded only as cash distributions are received from the Partnership. The investment would be amortized over the estimated productive life of the Partnerships' oil and gas properties and would be subject to the lower of cost or market

(6) **Amending the Corporate Charter.** It is appropriate for the corporation's Articles of Incorporation to clearly reflect, or be amended to reflect, the fact that one of its specified business purposes is to "engage in the exploration, development and production of oil and gas and related hydrocarbon products." At the time of the amendment, the minutes of the corresponding Board of Directors meeting should also reflect such language. Consequently, the corporate investor should consult its counsel with respect to these legal matters.

SECTION (E)

CONCLUSIONS REGARDING THE ACTS' EFFECTS ON CORPORATE INVESTORS

Oil and gas investments will continue to provide corporate investors with substantial and immediate tax savings. Also continuing is the companion ability to generate significant amounts of tax free income from successful oil and gas investments. This ability is derived from the 22% depletion allowance which is computed on gross income (before operating expenses and production taxes), and can result in 30-40% of Partnership distributions being received tax free. See the discussion of percentage depletion elsewhere. In addition, a corporation enjoys two additional tax advantages in that: (1) intangible drilling and development costs (IDC) on productive wells are not considered tax preference items for regular corporations; and, (2) corporations other than those described in Section (A) 1 above are not subject to the "at risk" provisions of the 1976 Act. Further, although the after tax cost of an oil and gas investment may be moderately increased, for some corporate investors which historically gifted their oil and gas interest to their pension plan, as a result of the 1976 Act's provisions covering the recapture of the productive IDC, we believe that the 1978 Act's reduction in the corporate capital gain tax rate and the basic forces of supply and demand as they affect the price of oil and natural gas sales prices more than offset the effects of the Act of 1976.

CAVEAT

IT SHOULD BE NOTED THAT THE ASSUMPTIONS USED IN THE EXAMPLES HEREIN WERE MADE *SOLELY* FOR ILLUSTRATIVE PURPOSES TO REVEAL THE EFFECT OF THE ACTS ON THE SPECIAL PROGRAM AS THEY RELATE TO THE MINIMUM TAX ON PREFERENCE ITEMS, THE MAXIMUM TAX ON PERSONAL SERVICE INCOME, DEPLETION, IDC RECAPTURE AND CAPITAL GAIN TAX. DUE TO THE RISKS OF DRILLING FOR GAS AND OIL SPECIAL CAN MAKE NO REPRESENTATION THAT THE RESULTS OF FUTURE SPECIAL PROGRAMS WILL BE COMPARABLE TO THE ASSUMPTIONS MADE HEREIN.

SECTION (F)

EXAMPLES OF THE ACTS' EFFECTS
ON CORPORATE INVESTORS

EXAMPLE V

INCOME TAX RESULTS OF A CORPORATION
INVESTING IN A SPECIAL PROGRAM

Tax Treatment Without Investment in Drilling Program	Tax Treatment With Investment in Drilling Program
$100,000 Taxable Income	$100,000 Taxable income used as oil and gas investment
	(70,000) Less: Allocable share of Partnership first year (loss) including depreciation
100,000 Taxable Income	30,000 Taxable Income
x 0.46 Tax Rate (normal and surtax)	x 0.46 Tax Rate (normal and surtax)
$ 46,000 Tax Liability	$ 13,800 Tax Liability
	(1,800) Less: First year qualifying investment tax credit available on investments in tangible equipment
$ 46,000 Tax Liability without investment in Drilling Program	$ 12,000 Tax liability after investment in Drilling Program

$ 46,000	Tax liability applicable to $100,000 of income retained in the corporation
–12,000	Tax liability under the assumption of a $100,000 investment by the corporation in a representative Special Program
$ 34,000	Tax Savings
$ 66,000	Net Cost (first year) to the corporation of its $100,000 investment in the Drilling Program

171

EXAMPLE VI

OTHER TAX CONSIDERATIONS

I. THE "ACCUMULATED EARNINGS TAX"

This tax is applicable to a corporation which has accumulated (and not distributed) earnings that the IRS concludes are in "excess of the reasonable needs of the business." These situations usually occur in the case of closely held corporations.

Although this area of taxation is extremely complex, IRS rules and regulations provide that the corporation ordinarily calculates this tax after recognizing the IRS exemption of $150,000 of accumulated earnings.

A corporation, therefore, may invest in Special Program as part of its tax planning to use the drilling deductions to: (1) avoid the earnings accumulation above the $150,000 exemption; or (2) reduce the earnings accumulations to less than the $150,000 exemption.

The result of the above is that there would be **no** accumulated earnings to which the tax could be applied, as Section 531 of the Internal Revenue Code imposes the tax on "accumulated taxable income," which is defined in Section 535. None of the "adjustments" in Section 535(b) relate to an investment in an oil and gas drilling program.

II. CONTRIBUTING THE CORPORATION'S OIL AND GAS INTEREST TO ITS QUALIFIED PENSION PLAN

After the drilling program's wells have generated sufficient production data, it is the practice of the partnership to have the properties evaluated by an independent petroleum engineer. Assuming that this report evaluates the corporation's proportionate share of the drilling program's reserves resulting from its $100,000 investment as being sufficient to produce total net revenues to the corporation of $200,000 (RECOGNIZING THAT DUE TO THE RISK OF OIL AND GAS INVESTMENTS THERE IS NO ASSURANCE OF SUCH RESULTS), the corporation could transfer its interest to its Pension Plan at the "fair market value," which generally would be permitted to be the estimated "fair market value" based upon the independent engineer's evaluation of future net revenue. (The contribution, naturally, would have to qualify as a proper asset under the then applicable ERISA Rules and Regulations.)

In such an event, based on the previous assumptions, the following are the tax consequences:

$100,000 – Investment in the Special Program
  80,000 – $70,000 assumed first year plus $11,000 assumed second year dry hole and intangible development cost deductions less $1,000 of assumed other items of taxable income during the period
$ 20,000 – Tax Basis

When the corporation donates its interest in the oil and gas program at the end of the calendar year following the year of investment, it is subject to normal corporate tax rates on recaptured productive intangible development costs (IDC), recapture of any investment tax credit, and generally capital gains treatment on the excess of the oil and gas interest's fair market value over the recaptured IDC and the corporation's adjusted tax basis in the interest.

Recapture of Productive IDC and Investment Tax Credit

$ 28,000 – Productive IDC ($80,000 total deduction—less $10,000 of deductions attributable to other deductible items = $70,000 IDC x 40% assumed productive ratio)
$ – 0 –   Less the amount by which the depletion deduction would have been increased if the IDC had been capitalized rather than deducted
$28,000 – Unamortized Productive IDC Subject to Recapture
  x .46 – Corporate Tax Rate
$ 12,880 – Recaptured Income Tax
   1,800 – Recaptured Investment Tax Credit
$ 14,680 – Total Income Tax

Capital Gain

$ 51,456 – Fair Market Value ($200,000 estimated future net revenue–$8,000 assumed distributed in second year of life ÷ 2.5 x .67)*

(20,000) – Tax Basis

(28,000) – Recaptured IDC

3,456 – Capital Gain

x .28 – Corporate Capital Gain Tax Rate

$ 968 – Capital Gain Tax

Based upon the assumptions made herein, the corporation would have generated the following: (i) deductions of $131,456 ($80,000 of IDC and dry hole deductions plus $51,456 from the gift of the fair market value of the oil and gas interest to its pension plan: (ii) tax savings of $46,622 ($131,456 of deductions x 46% tax rate plus $1,800 of investment tax credit less $14,680 of income tax and $968 of capital gain tax) and; (iii) the pension trust has an asset projected to produce $192,000 of income to the pension trust which will be sheltered by cost depletion, depreciation and amortization. The taxable portion of the income will be taxed at an effective rate for unrelated business income, which would normally be substantially less than the corporation's effective tax rate unless the pension plan has unrelated business income in excess of $100,000 annually.

---

*Divided by 2.5 to reflect the return to investment ratio characteristically sought by oil and gas production purchasers and multiplied by 67% to reflect a 33% discount due to the limited marketability of a limited partnership interest.

EXAMPLE VII

THE EFFECT OF DEPLETION AND DEPRECIATION ON A CORPORATE INVESTMENT IN A REPRESENTATIVE SPECIAL PROGRAM

Corporate investor's share of assumed net cash receipts from sale of oil or gas from a prior investment, i.e., gross receipts, less operating expenses	$5,000
Less depletion: In prior partnerships 22% of gross has been found to be equivalent to 30-40% of net (assuming that 22% of gross does not exceed 50% of net calculated on a property-by-property basis within the overall limit of 65% of taxable income, and that the partnership is not substantially affected by debt)	(1,750)
Less depreciation on tangible costs	(120)
Taxable income	3,130
Less intangible development cost and dry hole cost deductions resulting from reinvestment in the same year of the corporate investor's $5,000 net cash receipts from oil and gas production (assumes such costs generate 80% deductibility)	(4,000)
Additional net tax deductions	$ (870)
Investment tax credit	(60)

As shown in the example, through depletion and depreciation, the corporate investor received $1,870 of its net oil and gas income on a tax sheltered basis, and reinvested its total net oil income of $5,000 in a new Special Program, thereby eliminating any tax on the $3,130 of taxable income, generating an additional tax deduction of $870 to apply against other earned income, and receiving a $60 investment tax credit as a direct reduction of its tax bill.

LIST OF PREFERENCE ITEMS AND EXPLANATION OF REGULAR AND ALTERNATIVE MINIMUM TAX

REGULAR MINIMUM TAX

The following are items of tax preference subject to the regular minimum tax. The 15% regular minimum tax is applied to those items if they exceed the greater of $10,000 or 50% of an individual's (100% of a corporation's) regular tax liability.

REGULAR TAX PREFERENCE ITEMS

1) The portion of capital gains recognized as a preference item by corporate taxpayers.
2) the excess of percentage depletion over the basis of the property;
3) accelerated depreciation on real property;
4) the bargain element of stock options;
5)* accelerated depreciation on all personal property subject to a lease (including depreciation under the Class Life Asset Depreciation Range System but not bonus first-year depreciation);
6) the excess of amortization of on-the-job training and child care facilities over regular depreciation;
7) the excess of amortization of pollution control facilities over regular depreciation;
8) the excess of amortization of railroad rolling stock over regular depreciation;
9) excess bad debt reserves of financial institutions;
10)* intangible drilling costs on productive wells reduced (but only for the year in which the productive IDC was incurred) by amortization calculated:
   a) on the basis of a 120 month schedule beginning with the month in which production from the well begins, or
   b) on a cost depletion or unit of production basis employing an estimated life of the well (the Partnership would use whichever of these methods is more favorable). This amount is further reduced by the taxpayer's net oil and gas income.

*Does not apply to corporations.

ALTERNATIVE MINIMUM TAX

The two items of tax preference listed below are subject to the alternative minimum tax. Individuals are subject to this tax only if it exceeds their regular taxes plus the regular minimum tax. The alternative minimum tax is applied to an individual's taxable income plus these alternative tax preference items less a $20,000 exemption. The alternative minimum tax rate is 10% on the first $40,000, 20% on the next $40,000 and 25% on amounts exceeding $80,000.

ALTERNATIVE TAX PREFERENCE ITEMS

1) itemized deductions (excluding medical expenses; state and local taxes and casualty losses) in excess of 60% but less than 100% of adjusted gross income; and,

2) the excluded 60% of capital gains for individuals.

CALCULATION AT THE 49% TAX BRACKET OF THE POINT AT WHICH THE ALTERNATIVE MINIMUM TAX WOULD APPLY AS A RESULT OF SHELTERING CAPITAL GAIN INCOME

The point at which the alternative minimum tax would apply, and after which the rate of tax savings begin to decline as a result of sheltering capital gain income can be defined as that point when the regular tax plus the regular minimum tax equals the alternative minimum tax. Two brief formulas can exhibit this relationship:

X (Regular) = Total Taxable Income (including the 40% taxable portion of capital gain) x the applicable regular tax rate schedule + regular minimum tax

Y (Alternative) = Total Taxable Income + the excluded 60% of capital gain + excess itemized deductions x the alternative minimum tax rate schedule

For a quick reference, we have calculated the percentages above to provide you with general guidelines for selecting the point after which tax savings rates begin to decline. The calculations of this point (shown here for the 49% bracket) began with the lowest end of each tax bracket range of 49% or more.

Tax Rate 49%

Taxable Income	$45,800
Regular Tax	$12,720
(No minimum tax assumed)	

(a) The regular tax on $45,800 of taxable income (the 49% rate) is $12,720.

(b) It is known that the alternative minimum tax on the first $100,000 of alternative minimum tax base is $12,000 ($0-$20,000 exempt + $20-60,000 at 10% + $60-100,000 at 20% = $12,000).

(c) $12,220 regular tax is more than the $12,000 alternative minimum tax; therefore we can calculate the additional amount of alternative minimum tax base needed to make the regular tax plus the regular minimum tax (X) equal the alternative minimum tax (Y) by dividing the excess $720 by the 25% alternative minimum tax rate ($720 ÷ the 25% alternative minimum tax rate above $100,000 = $2,880 additional alternative minimum tax base).

(d) $100,000 + $2,880 = $102,880 total alternative minimum tax base which is total taxable income + the excluded 60% of capital gain.

(e) $102,880 - $45,800 of total taxable income which is necessary to enter the regular tax 49% bracket = $57,080 excluded 60% of capital gain.

(f) $57,080 ÷ 60% = $95,133 total capital gain.

(g) $95,133 x 40% = $38,053 which is the 40% taxable portion of capital gains.

(h) $38,063 ÷ $45,800 = 83%, thus, at the 49% bracket, the taxable portion of capital gains must be greater than 83% of total taxable income before the rate of tax savings is diminished.

THIS SPECIAL PROGRAM TAX ANALYSIS REPORT, AS IT RELATES TO INDIVIDUAL AND CORPORATE OIL AND GAS INVESTORS, SHOULD NOT BE CONSIDERED AS A SUBSTITUTE FOR A THOROUGH REVIEW BY AN INVESTOR AND HIS ADVISORS OF ALL ASPECTS OF ANY OIL AND GAS INVESTMENT UNDER CONSIDERATION FOR THE APPLICABILITY OF THE INVESTMENT TO THE PERSONAL INVESTMENT OBJECTIVES AND TAX POSITION OF THE POTENTIAL INVESTOR.

THIS SUMMARY IS NEITHER AN OFFER TO SELL NOR SOLICITATION OF AN OFFER TO BUY ANY OIL AND GAS INVESTMENT.

THE ASSISTANCE OF ENERGY MANAGEMENT CORPORATION IN THE SPECIAL PROGRAM TAX ANALYSIS IS GRATEFULLY ACKNOWLEDGED.

Energy Management Corporation
Suite 3500/Anaconda Tower
555 Seventeenth Street
Denver, Colorado 80202

Telephone: (303) 825-3328

An oil exploration fund is appropriate for an investor who can afford to lose his entire investment and be satisfied with his high first-year tax write-off.

SECTION TWO

THE OIL INCOME PROGRAM

An oil income program is a limited partnership investment in producing oil and gas properties. Since no drilling activities are conducted, the high element of risk that is usually associated with the oil business is reduced.

While drilling programs meet the investment objectives of many high tax bracket investors, the ownership of producing properties for income is appealing to a different, much larger group. Investors like the attractive return on investment, the low risk and the relatively high cash flows. The conservative valuations normally used as the basis for oil and gas property purchases, plus occasional price increases, pressure maintenance, stimulation methods, and other pluses have generally enhanced the investment profitability; and in some cases, the appreciation has been substantial. Investors also like the modest tax benefits available, but do not depend on them to make the investment attractive.

SOURCE OF PRODUCING WELLS

Some producing properties will probably always be available for an oil income program to purchase. There are many petroleum operators who see themselves as exploration or wildcatters types. They tend to drill many wildcats, make discoveries of new fields, possibly drill up the fields, and then turn around and sell the oil and gas reserves they have found. These companies are very heavily oriented toward the exploration business, but not toward keeping properties for years of production. As the wells are drilled, these operators have tax deductibility against ordinary income. After finding the reserves, they have a capital asset in the ground, which can be sold on a capital gains basis. The capital so generated is then recycled into further exploration activities.

Another common source of producing properties is the disposition by major companies of their geographically isolated and marginally profitable operations. These properties can normally be operated profitably by independents because of their more economical overhead structure and operating procedures. Further acquisition opportunities frequently occur when properties pass into estates, or when properties must be sold as a result of mergers or liquidations.

ESTIMATION OF RESERVES

The risk to the investor is that the program could overestimate the reserves it is buying and pay too much for them.

It is important for the investor to know the basis for his profit. Since the reserves are purchased at a discount against future income, the spread between the discounted purchase price and the ultimate future dollar return represents profit to the investor. The rate of return for the investor is further enhanced through the use of moderate borrowing. The effect of this borrowing is to make the dollars go further. The program can buy more properties. If it paid cash, the rate of return on a straight cash investment would tend to be poorer than the rate of return on equity when a combination of cash plus borrowing is employed. Of course, borrowing depends on the availability of money at current interest rates and involves its repayment. It also increases risks, which makes it unacceptable to some programs.

STRUCTURE OF PROGRAMS

A typical profit or incentive for the program operator would be for it to have a subsidiary corporation act as General Partner in each program and charge a 15 percent management fee. The one-time 15 per cent management fee may be invested jointly with the Limited Partners for a 15 per cent working interest in the properties. Thereafter, expenses and profits are shared proportionately, 15%–85%. Therefore, the degree of the Corporation's gain is in direct proportion to the financial gain produced for the investors.

TAX DEDUCTIBILITY

The front-end deductibility is usually between 20 per cent and 25 per cent of the partnership investment. The program is not structured on tax benefits, but rather is intended to be suitable for investors in modest as well as higher tax benefits.

Since everybody is paying some taxes, however, the 20 per cent to 25 per cent deductibility on the initial investment does reduce the net cost, thus creating a higher yield on out-of-pocket dollars, similar to buying a bond at a discount.

The management fee is deductible. Also deductible are engineering and geological expenses associated with unsuccessful acquisition studies. On the other hand, costs for successful acquisition studies become part of the capitalized investment in the properties, and are recovered through depletion over the life of the producing properties.

DURATION OF PROGRAMS

Partnerships will last as long as the production that is acquired. The average term will be 12 to 15 years, with a good mix of short-lived and long-lived properties.

YIELD FACTORS

The single most important factor in determining the merits of acquisition is the discounted rate of return or yield to the Limited Partners. This involves estimating the reserves and annual cash flow over the property life, and then discounting the Limited Partner's share of cash flow at a certain percentage to determine the maximum purchase price. If estimates of reserves and cash flow prove correct, this will have the effect of producing an attractive yield to the investor.

BALANCING OF PROPERTIES

Balancing of properties can be important in an oil income program, as in an exploration program. A General Partner may intend that each partnership will purchase interests in a number of different properties (usually three or more) to balance the return to investors and minimize any investment risks. Ideally, a portion of partnership capital may be committed to properties having higher rates of production in the early years (to provide revenues with which partnership financing can be repaid plus cash flow for the investors). Some other portion of funds may be committed to properties characterized by more level, longer-lived production which should produce stable income over an extended period of time.

In order to achieve these objectives, a General Partner may make new acquisitions with available partnership funds (ordinarily furnished by the two to three most recently closed partnerships). In those cases where a greater degree of program balance is needed, the General Partner may exchange or trade property interests between partnerships. All partnerships involved benefit from this provision. Ordinarily, any such exchange or trade will be finalized during the first nine to twelve months of partnerhsip activity.

BENEFITS OF AN OIL INCOME PROGRAM

1. It provides partially tax-free income from conservative oil investments. Some programs have yielded approximately 12% income.

2. It eliminates the high element of risk one would ordinarily associate with exploration programs.

RISKS IN AN OIL INCOME PROGRAM

1. Difficulties of Property Purchases: Purchases of producing oil and gas properties are based on available geologic and engineering data, the extent and quality of which will vary in each case. Producing properties available at prices which would permit the investors in a program to earn significant profits on their purchase can be expected to be difficult to locate and acquire. There is no assurance that purchases can be accomplished in such manner as to permit oil income partnerships to achieve their objectives.

2. Competition and Governmental Regulation: Competition for attractive producing property acquisitions is intense. Because others seeking to purchase producing properties may have greater resources, investors in oil income partnerships may be at a disadvantage in this competition. In addition to competition from others for the purchase of producing properties, the partnerships will be subject to the risk that they will pay more for the acquisition of properties than future production warrants. In addition, the oil and gas business is subject to strong governmental regulation which has power to limit the rates at which oil and gas are produced, to fix the prices at which gas is sold and to permit increases in the amount of oil imported from foreign

countries.

3. Limited Tax Benefits: An oil income is not intended to provide any major federal income tax benefits to investors. Neither the deduction for intangible drilling costs nor percentage depletion is an important factor in the Program's design.

4. Absence of Liquidity: The limited partnership interests may be transferable with the consent of the General Partner but no ready public market may exist for such interests. The procedure by which a General Partner will undertake to purchase a Limited Partner's interest after formation of the partnership at a price determined as set forth in the prospectus will not assure a Limited Partner of immediate liquidity with respect to his investment. Because any such purchase will depend upon a number of factors, including the availability of funds for that purpose, there can be no assurance that it will be made.

5. Risks of Reinvestment: Distributions which are reinvested will be treated for income tax purposes as though they had been paid to the reinvesting Limited Partner.

6. Consequences of Borrowing: The Limited Partners of an Oil Income Program partnership will receive taxable income to the extent that the net operating proceeds from a producing property exceed income tax deductions for depletion and depreciation even though the gross receipts are used to repay money borrowed (or to pay production payments created) to acquire such property. During payment of a production loan or a production payment, the taxable income of the partners from the property subject to the loan or payment may be greater than the net cash proceeds therefrom available to them. The investor can deduct only the amount of money he has at risk.

Thus, the oil income program is designed as a relatively low-risk tax shelter for investors in most tax brackets. Much of its appeal is that it also offers an opportunity to obtain partially tax-free income higher than is generally available in other non-oil investments.

SECTION THREE

THE DIVERSIFIED OIL PROGRAM

Diversified oil programs are occasionally offered to give the investor a greater degree of security. Part of the fund's money may go into producing wells which customarily represent a low risk and good income potential. Other money may be used for drilling development wells near established oil wells. Still other money may be used in exploratory drilling where no oil has been previously discovered but providing great reward if oil is found. This makes for a balanced oil investment combining the low risk of the producing wells, the medium risk of development drilling and the high risk of exploratory drilling.

EXAMPLE OF A DIVERSIFIED OIL FUND

The purpose of this example is to explain the format and features of a diversified oil fund. This is done via an hypothetical report of an independent engineer evaluating such a program after one year of activity. Again it must be emphasized that there are many ways of evaluating a program and that the procedure shown here is representative of just one of the methods of analysis that might have been employed.

In this program the investor acquired a limited partnership interest in Uncle Oil Drilling Program which emphasized the purchase of producing properties (approximately 50–60%), with some development drilling (20–35%), and some exploratory drilling (15–25%). After one year of activity, he hired an independent engineer to conduct reserve and economic appraisals.

In preparing a reserve report, the engineer reviewed each property, estimated total oil reserves and expenses involved in producing the oil, did a year-by-year forecast on each well, and estimated revenues from the sale of gas or oil net of expenses. There is some guesswork involved in a report of this nature, and there is always the question as to whether the report is too conservative.

The engineer began his study with this information:

Investments of limited partners $3,400,000
Initial borrowings   624,000
First-Year tax deductibility   58%

The reserve reports indicate total future net income as follows:

Future net income $4,170,044
Present worth of future income discounted $3,553,726
5½% per year (It is customary in the oil
business to discount present worth of future
income by approximately 1% above the prime
rate)

INVESTMENT TESTS

With these figures and with the annual estimated net income figures for the next 25 years as determined by the engineer, we can calculate the three basic investment tests on an oil program:

1. Ratio of total net income to total investments
2. Internal rate of return
3. Return assuming immediate liquidation

These are very rough estimates in that we are using estimated reserves, and further, we are estimating tax treatment in developing our calculations.

CALCULATIONS OF INVESTMENT TESTS

1. Ratio of total net income to total investment

This is the so-called "hard dollar" test, and it compares before-tax income with before-tax investment.

Investments by limited partners $3,400,000
Initial borrowings   624,000
Total investments $4,024,000

Total estimated future net income
  (before tax) $4,170,044

$$\frac{\$4,170,044}{\$4,024,000} = 1.0{:}1$$

A satisfactory ratio for a program of this type would be 2.2:1

2. Internal rate of return (IRR) (50% bracket investor)

This calculation estimates the annual after-tax percentage return on total after-tax investment.

a. Calculate the after-tax investment of the limited partners

(1) $3,400,000 (before tax) x 58% (deductibility) = $1,972,000 (deductions)

(2) $1,972,000 (deductions) x 50% (tax bracket) = $986,000 (tax savings)

(3) $3,400,000 (before tax) - $986,000 (tax savings) = $2,414,000 (after-tax investment)

b. Adjust each estimated annual net income amount (projected in the reserve report) for taxes payable on his return by the 50% bracket investor. Our basic assumptions would be that:

(1) 33% of net income will be tax free due to depletion allowances (22% of gross revenues and depreciation.)

(2) The remaining 67% will be taxed at the 50% rate.

c. Using a computer program, we measure the effective after-tax rate of return on the investor's after-tax investment (allowing for repayment of the borrowings) during the 25 year period. The computer program assumes the cash flow is reinvested at the same rate as the return from the investment being tested. The result is internal rate of return, which is, in effect, the investment return (or compound interest rate) which, combined with principal payments, would generate the estimated net cash flow year by year of the oil program being tested.

d. The result for Uncle Oil Drilling Program was an IRR for the 50% bracket investor of negative 2.4%.

An IRR of 11% would be satisfactory for a program of this type.

3. Return assuming immediate liquidation (50% bracket investor)

This calculation estimates the percentage after-tax return on after-tax investment, assuming the program were liquidated in one year. It should be noted that we use the present worth of future net income discounted by 5½%, and that we discount this figure by another 30% for risk factors. These discounts are standard and the result approximates the market value of the estimated reserves. If Uncle were to liquidate this program, higher or lower discounts could be used.

a. Calculate the after-tax investment of the limited partners. (See "a" in IRR calculation above) $2,414,000

b. Calculate the before-tax liquidation value. The reserve report estimates the present worth of future net income discounted by 5½% per year ($3,553,726).

> (1) We reduce this amount by 30% for risk factors. (This is a standard method used by institutional lenders for calculating liquidation values and is not necessarily the way Uncle would do the calculation.)
>
> $3,553,726 x 70% (30% risk) = $2,487,608
>
> (2) We reduce this amount by the borrowings to determine estimated before-tax liquidation value (or market value of limited partners' interests in the reserves).
>
> $2,487,608 - $624,000 (borrowings) = $1,863,608

c. We calculate the estimated after-tax liquidation value as follows:

$3,400,000 (limited partners' investment) – $1,972,000
(tax deductions @ 50%) = $1,448,000 (investor's tax base)
$1,863,608 (before-tax liquidation value) – $1,448,000
(tax base) = $415,608 (taxable gain)
$415,608 @ 25% (capital gains) = $103,902 capital gains tax
$1,863,608 (before tax) – $103,902 (capital gains tax) =
$1,759,706 (after-tax liquidation value)

d. We calculate the net return percentage by dividing the after-tax liquidation value by the after-tax investments.

$1,759,706 (after-tax liquidation value) ÷ $2,414,000
(after-tax investment) = 72%

A satisfactory percentage for a program of this type would be 111%.

In this diversified program where there is an emphasis on producing wells, it is difficult to show highly favorable results as might appear from an exploratory fund which makes a big oil strike. Also, it is not fair to judge an oil operator like Uncle on the basis of estimated results on one program. Moreover, the limited partnership interests might be exchanged for stock on which the investor might profit.

The benefits, risks, and tax aspects described previously for an oil exploration fund and an oil income fund apply to the exploratory drilling and producing well features of this diversified program.

The diversified program is for the investor who is satisfied with a moderate return from an oil investment compared to the investor seeking a large return from exploratory drilling.

As a tax shelter, oil provides some of the highest risks and some of the greatest potential for profit. It is a complicated investment and even the generally astute investor would do well to seek the counsel of a tax-shelter specialist for specific recommendations.

DEFINITIONS CONCERNING THE OIL INDUSTRY
IN GENERAL

ABANDONMENT LOSS COSTS: Costs of lease acquisition, and nonsalvageable equipment, related to nonproductive wells.

ACQUIRED LEASES: All oil and gas leases acquired by the Program in the Area of Operations (as such Area exists at the time of such acquisition on or after the Effective Date but before the date of dissolution of the Operating Partnership), which are not Excluded Leases.

ACREAGE BLOCK: Oil and gas leasehold interests or contractual rights acquired without the immediate intention of drilling a well thereon, but which shall nevertheless be designated and treated as a Drilling Block hereunder for the purposes of participation in costs and revenues and of ownership of property interests.

APPRAISAL COSTS: All costs in connection with determinations of the Specified Price under the Operating Partnership Agreement and under the Partnership Agreement except Special Appraisal Costs.

BOOKED COST: The tax basis of the general partner for federal income tax purposes, as determined solely and conclusively by its records. The Booked Cost of an oil and gas lease includes costs incurred in the acquisition of such lease (consisting of bonus costs, brokerage commissions and title examination costs and expenses) and geophysical costs charged against the lease which are capitalized for federal income tax purposes.

BOTTOM HOLE CONTRIBUTIONS: Payments made or land transferred pursuant to an agreement wherein an operator contemplating the drilling of a well on his own land secures the promise of another to contribute to the cost of the well if the well is drilled to a specified depth (regardless of whether the well is abandoned as a dry hole or completed as a producer), often in return for an assignment of part of the payee's lease to the payor on completion of the well.

CAPITALIZED COSTS: Those partnership expenditures (1) for acquisition of oil, gas and other mineral leases including lease bonuses, the cost of abstracts, lease acquisition, title examination and title curative work, and geological or geophysical expenses incident to lease acquisition; (2) the cost of all equipment installed in connection with the drilling,

190

testing, completion or production of any well participated in by the Partnership; and (3) all expenditures of a capital nature incurred in connection with such equipment, except that any of the above costs relating to dry holes or leases abandoned without production or abandoned within 180 days after the completion of any well shall be considered non-capitalized costs.

CARRIED INTEREST: A fractional interest in an oil and gas property which by its term relieves the owner of such interst of liability for the acquisition, development and operating costs for such property and permits the co-owners who undertake such liability to recover such costs out of the proceeds from production of oil or gas prior to such owner participating in the revenues and related operating costs.

CARVED-OUT OVERRIDING ROYALTY: A carved-out overriding royalty is created by an operating company establishing or "carving out" an override from its working interest and selling it for cash.

CASING-HEAD GAS: Hydrocarbon gas produced in conjunction with the oil production.

CASING POINT: The objective depth, either a specified depth or the depth at which a specific zone is penetrated, at which point the General Partner must decide whether to set a production string of casing or abandon the well.

COMMERCIALLY PRODUCING WELL: A well which produces income to the lessees from production in excess of the operating costs.

COMPLETION COSTS: In general, includes those costs required to bring a well into production after such well has been drilled to total depth. Such costs include running and cementing a production string of casing, perforating, running tubing, acidizing or fracturing, swabbing and installation of surface equipment used in obtaining, controlling and marketing production.

CONCESSIONS: Working interests granted by governments for the exploitation of designated acreage and are subject to governmental royalties.

DELAY RENTAL: The sum of money payable to the lessor by the lessee for the privilege of deferring the commencement of drilling operations or the commencement of production to the end of specific time periods during the primary term of the lease. Treasury Regulation Paragraph 1.612-3(c)(1) under the

United States Internal Revenue Code of 1954 defines the term as follows: "A delay rental is an amount paid for the privilege of deferring development of the property and which could have been avoided by abandonment of the lease, or by commencement of development operations, or by obtaining production." Subsection (2) of the Regulation allows the payor at his election to deduct such amount as an expense.

DEPLETION: The United State Internal Revenue Code of 1954, in Sections 611 to 613, authorizes a deduction from income for the removal and sale of oil and gas from a well. The taxpayer is entitled to cost depletion or percentage depletion, whichever is higher. Percentage depletion is the method of figuring a depletion allowance on the basis of an arbitrary percentage of income from production.

DEVELOPMENT ACREAGE: Development acreage is acreage believed to be geologically associated with acreage from which oil or gas production has been obtained.

DEVELOPMENT WELL: Any well other than an Initial Well. A well drilled in an area believed to be proven productive because of proximity to other wells already drilled. In an area in which multiple producing horizons may be present, a well may be a development well for a then producing horizon and an exploratory well for another horizon, but, for the purposes hereof, such a well is treated as a development well.

DIVISION ORDER: An agreement among owners of production from oil, gas and mineral leases for the distribution of the proceeds of the sale thereof.

DRILLING BLOCK: One or more leases designated a drilling block by Operating Company for the purposes of drilling wells thereon and believed by it to be located on the same geological structure.

DRY HOLE CONTRIBUTIONS: Money or property given to an operator in payment for drilling of a well on property in which the contributor has no direct interest, but payable only in the event that the well is drilled to a specified depth and is a dry hole.

EFFECTIVE DATE: Date on which operations by the Operating Partnership will commence.

EXCLUDED LEASES: Leases which as of the Effective Date or the date of acquisition by the General Partner (whichever is later) are within any of the following categories:

1. Leases held by production or drilling.

2. Leases on certain structures or features.
3. Leases on designated new field areas.
4. Leases for non-exploratory purposes.
5. Leases requiring third party consent for assignment.

EXPLORATORY LEASES: Leases on acreage that is removed from and not in the vicinity of existing oil or gas production. Wells drilled on such leases are drilled either (1) in search of a new and previously undiscovered reservoir of oil and gas or (2) with the hope of greatly extending the limits of a previously discovered reservoir.

EXPLORATORY PROSPECT: Each leasehold tract or interest acquired by the Partnership for the exploration and production of oil and gas.

EXPLORATORY WELLS: Wells drilled on exploratory leases. Exploratory wells may be subclassified as follows:

1. Wildcat – drilled in an unproved area;
2. Rank wildcat – drilled in an unproved area and located at some distance from any producing oil and gas fields.
3. Step-out – drilled in an unproved area to extend proved limits of a field; and
4. Deep test – drilled within a field area but to unproven deeper zones.

FARM-IN: Refers to a situation covered by a contract with a lease owner (farmor) for the acquisition of a lease or leases under an arrangement whereby an interest in such lease or leases is earned by the farmee by the drilling of a well or wells in accordance with the provisions of such contract. In such contract, an overriding royalty interest is usually retained by the farmor, together with such other rights as may be negotiated between the parties.

FARM-OUT: Refers to a situation covered by a contract with a lease owner (the farmor) for the assignment of a lease or leases under an arrangement whereby an interest in such lease or leases is earned by the party undertaking the drilling of a well or wells (the farmee or farmoutee) in accordance with the provisions of such contract. In such contract, an overriding royalty interest is usually retained by the farmor, together with such other rights as may be negotiated between the parties.

FARMOR: A person who owns a lease or leases and grants rights therein under a contract arrangement.

FARMEE OR FARMOUTEE: The person who obtains rights in a lease or leases under a contract arrangement.

FIXED COST CONTRACT: A contract in which an independent drilling contractor undertakes to furnish all materials and labor and to do all the work required to drill a well to an agreed depth and to test a prospective oil or gas bearing formation for an amount stipulated in the contract.

FUTURE NET REVENUE: The estimated gross income accruing to the interest in question adjusted by its proportionate share of royalty burden and less direct operating expenses (including all assessed taxes except federal income tax) and other applicable costs.

GROSS WELL: One oil or gas well. For example, the ownership of all or any fractional portion of the working interest in single well is termed the ownership of an interest in one gross well.

INITIAL LEASE: Those oil and gas leases to be delivered to the Program on the effective date.

INITIAL WELL: The first well drilled on a Prospect, whether or not such Prospect is unproven or semi-proven property.

INTANGIBLE DRILLING AND DEVELOPMENT COSTS (INTANGIBLES): In general, all costs (except the costs of the leasehold interest) incurred in the drilling and completion of a well for items which have no salvage value.

LEASES: Full or partial interests in the working interest in oil and gas leases, oil and gas mineral rights, fee rights, or other rights authorizing the owner thereof to drill for, reduce to possession and produce oil and gas.

LEASE BLOCK: An area composed of separate, contiguous leaseholds.

LEASE BONUS: The consideration paid by the lessee for the execution of an oil and gas lease by a landowner, usually in cash, although it may take other forms.

LEASEHOLD INTEREST: Full or partial interest in oil, gas, and mineral leases, fee interests or other interests or rights which authorize the owners to drill for, produce and sell oil, gas, and other minerals. A leasehold interest is subject to area limitations, surface and subsurface, of a "property" as that term is defined in Section 614 of the Internal Revenue Code of 1954, as amended and the Regulations thereunder.

LEVERAGE: Involves the use of borrowed funds, generally with properties pledged as security therefor, in order to increase the aggregate funds available to a Partnership without diluting the equity therein of Investors.

LIFTING COSTS: Monthly, recurring operating costs of producing and marketing oil and gas.

NET OPERATING PROFITS: A share of production from a property, measured by net profits from the operation of the property after deducting severance taxes and regular operating costs, but without regard to acquisition, drilling or development costs.

NET WELLS: A measure of interest in wells representing the cumulative total of the percentages of working interest in wells held by a given party. For example, an undivided one-fourth of the working interest in four gross wells equals one net well, and an undivided one-fourth of the working interest in two gross wells equals .5 net wells.

NON-CAPITALIZED COSTS: Those partnership expenditures for wages, fuel, repairs, hauling, supplies, etc., incident to and necessary for the drilling of wells and the preparation of wells for the production of oil or gas, which expenditures are generally termed "intangible drilling and development costs." They shall include the costs of any drilling or development work (excluding amounts payable only out of production or gross or net proceeds from production, if such amounts are depletable income to the recipient, and amounts properly allocable to cost of depreciable property) done for the Partnership by contractors under any form of contract. Examples of such items are amounts paid for labor, fuel, repairs, hauling and supplies or any of them which are used (1) in the drilling, shooting and cleaning of wells; (2) in such clearing of ground, draining, road making, surveying and geological works as are necessary in preparation for the drilling of wells; and (3) in the construction of such derricks, tanks, pipelines and other physical structures as are necessary for the drilling of wells and preparation of wells for the production of oil or gas. These expenditures in general shall include only those drilling and development items which, in themselves, do not have a salvage value. Additionally, non-capitalized costs for purposes of federal income taxation and such other expenditures as are not chargeable to the General Partners as capitalized costs on any well or wells, and in addition, non-capitalized costs shall include costs that would ordinarily be capitalized costs, as defined above, relating to dry holes or leases abandoned without production or abandoned within 180 days after the completion of any well.

NON-PRODUCING PROPERTY: Any property which is not a producing property.

OIL AND GAS: Oil, gas, casinghead gas, gas condensate and other liquid or gaseous hydrocarbons and hydrogen sulfide and helium processed therewith.

OPERATING AGREEMENT: An agreement entered into between a Partnership and a third party (which may be the company) providing for the operation of a producing well and the sale of oil and/or gas derived therefrom.

OPERATING COSTS: The customary expenses of operation of wells and production and marketing of oil and gas therefrom. Such term also includes the cost of reworking any well and shut-in gas royalties paid with respect to leases.

OPERATOR: Any person or corporation engaged in the business of exercising direct supervision over the drilling of or production from a well or lease.

OPTIONAL WELL COSTS: Costs for the drilling and completion of development wells on any Prospect after the expenditure of the aggregate capital of any Partnership.

OVERRIDING ROYALTY: The right to receive, free of costs of development and operations, a share of production from an oil and gas lease during its term, but reserved from the share of production which had initially belonged to the lessee.

PAYING QUANTITIES: Means as to an oil or gas well, when current gross receipts, less all amounts allocable to interests (such as royalties or production payments) held by others, exceed current operating expenditures.

PAYOUT: The time at which the proceeds of production and other items credited to Limited Partners from leases, on a lease by lease basis, equals all costs of drilling, completing and equipping such wells, including lease or lease acquisition costs and the costs of operating such wells until that time, and excluding the management fee to be paid to the General Partner and all expenses of organization of the Partnership and offering of units of participation in the Partnership.

POST-DISCOVERY COSTS: Costs involved in the recompletion, deepening, plugging back or sidetracking of a well previously completed as a commercial producer, construction of facilities incident to the operation but not necessary to the completion of a well, including but not limited to pipelines, gathering systems, treating plants, pressure maintenance and secondary recovery systems. Although some of these costs are capital costs, which must be capitalized for Federal income tax purposes, they will be borne in the same ratio as Operating Costs.

PRIMARY PRODUCTION: Oil is found underground in porous rock formations. The oil trapped in the porous rock constitutes the oil pool or reservoir. When a hole is drilled into the oil-bearing formation, the oil of itself has no inherent characteristic other than weight which would cause it to move from the rock habitat to the well bore. However, "reservoir energy" sufficient to move the oil to the well bore where it may flow or be pumped to the ground surface may be provided by the expansion of the gas which is in solution with the oil or by formation water-drive. Whatever the natural source of this energy is, it is always in limited supply and frequently depleted long before the oil supply has been exhausted from the formation. Primary recovery consists of the period of time when the oil is produced by the energy initially inherent in the reservoir. The primary production phase is ended when there is no longer sufficient reservoir energy to permit recovery of the oil in economically adequate quantities.

PRODUCING PROPERTY: A property on which a completed and equipped well is actually producing oil or gas in paying quantities or is capable of doing so.

PRODUCTION PAYMENT: An economic interest in oil and gas entitling its owner to receive, ordinarily free of cost, a specified sum of money from the proceeds of sale of a specified part of production of oil and gas. After receipt of the specified sum, the interest terminates.

PROPERTY: A geographical area encompassing one or more leasehold interests, working interests or other property interests or prospects owned by a Partnership and includes all interests within such area acquired by the Partnership holding the property. A Property may have any configuration reasonably designated by the General Partner.

PROPERTY INTEREST: A lease or block of leases or contractual rights thereto acquired within a Prospect.

PROSPECT: A geologically related area in which the Program has a group of more or less contiguous leaseholds or other interests which appear to be favorably located for the drilling of a well.

PROVEN ACREAGE: An area so situated with reference to

known or producing wells as to establish the general opinion that because of its relation to them, oil and/or gas is contained in such acreage.

PROVEN LEASES OR DRILLING BLOCKS: Leases or drilling blocks so situated with reference to known oil or gas deposits which, because of their relation to such deposits, are reasonably sure, when drilled, to yield oil or gas therein.

PROVEN PROSPECTS: Leases so situated with reference to known oil or gas accumulations which, because of their relation to such accumulations, are reasonably sure, when drilled, to yield oil or gas in commercial quantities.

REVERSIONARY INTEREST: That percentage of the working interest in a given lease to which the General Partner becomes entitled after payout occurs.

RESERVED OVERRIDING ROYALTY: A reserved overriding royalty is created typically by persons engaging in the oil and gas business who assemble geological data and leases to sell to operating companies and, as a part or all of their compensation, reserve an Overriding Royalty interest in the leases sold.

RESERVOIR ENERGY: The force provided by the expansion of gas in solution in crude oil or by the drive of water contained with the oil which causes the movement of the crude oil to the well bore.

RESERVOIR ENGINEER: A person qualified to evaluate producing properties.

ROYALTY: The landowner's or mineral owner's share of production received by him free of any cost of development or operations, and reserved in connection with the original issuance of the oil and gas lease.

SECONDARY RECOVERY: Energy injection into an oil-bearing formation usually in the form of liquids, or gas, through an input well for the recovery of oil from surrounding wells.

SEMI-PROVEN ACREAGE: An area in which producing wells have been completed (usually at scattered points) but in which the confines of the reservoir have not been determined. The general opinion that oil and/or gas is contained in such acreage is not as certain as it would be in the case of Proven Acreage because Semi-Proven Acreage is more distant from producing wells.

SEMI-PROVEN PROPERTY: A non-producing property which because of its relation to known oil, gas or other mineral deposits has some possibility of yielding oil, gas or minerals therein in commercial quantities but not to the degree that Proven Properties possesses, usually because of its being more distant from known production.

SEMI-PROVEN PROSPECT: A geological prospect in an area in which producing wells have been completed but in which the confines of the reservoir have not been determined.

SHARING RATIO: The sharing ratio in any Partnership of any Investor will be the ratio which his Capital Contribution to that Partnership bears to the Gross Capitalization of the Partnership.

SPECIAL PROJECTS COSTS: The costs incurred in the construction or installation of any plant, secondary recovery system, transmission system, or other facility beyond the usual or conventional surface and tank equipment.

THIRD PARTY WELL: A well drilled on Partnership property as to which the cost of drilling and completing was not charged to the capital accounts of either the Participants or Operator.

TRANSFER WELL: A direction to the purchaser of oil or gas under a Division Order to transfer future payments for a share in the oil or gas produced from one person to another.

TURNKEY BASIS: The completion of all necessary expenditures, whether they are larger or smaller than the budget cost, on a project necessary to bring such project to completion as a fully operating and producing property.

UNITIZATION AGREEMENT: An agreement entered into, either voluntarily or pursuant to regulatory order, under which the owners of oil and gas interests in diverse tracts in a given area agree to combine their interests and to share in stipulated proportions production from the unitized area.

WATERFLOOD: A procedure for secondary recovery by increasing pressure in an oil reservoir by injecting water under pressure into the reservoir for the purpose of increasing oil production.

WILDCAT: A high risk well drilled in a relatively unproven area or to test an unproven zone or horizon, the drilling of which may be considered to be highly speculative as to whether such well will yield oil or gas.

WORKING INTEREST: The lessee's interest under an oil and gas lease which entitles its holder to conduct drilling and production operations.

CHAPTER THREE

EQUIPMENT LEASING

Many types of personal property such as oil-workover barges, containers, airplanes, railroad rolling stock and computers, etc. are used in equipment leasing.

Four major tax factors make these deals interesting:

1. Accelerated depreciation: The 200% declining balance method can be used on new equipment, and it provides a high write-off.

2. Shorter useful lives: New Treasury guidelines for lives of business equipment provide for shorter lives and make faster write-offs possible.

3. Additional first-year depreciation: A limited partner is permitted to write off up to 20% or $2,000 ($4,000 on joint return) of the cost of equipment the first year it is placed in service.

4. Investment Credit: When it is available, the 7% investment credit (now applicable only to corporate investors under most circumstances in leasing arrangements) is an attractive write-off.

Lessees of equipment like the leasing concept because it may increase working capital, provide financing which does not appear on the balance sheet, affords an easy method of financing and avoids the problem of being stuck with obsolete equipment.

The lessor-investors like equipment leasing because taxable income may be deferred and the investment credit is sometimes available. Income is deferred because of accelerated depreciation and interest deductions resulting from high leverage financing. Moreover, the equipment sometimes has a substantial residual value at the expiration of the lease period.

The examples shown below involve oil-workover barges since the chapter follows the one on oil. The first example describes an investment by individuals and the second example shows the results of a corporation investing.

Although the examples pertain to oil-workover barges, the principles involved apply with equal effect to other types of equipment leasing ventures.

INTRODUCTION TO EXAMPLES

There is an unusual tax shelter opportunity in an area of the oil and gas industry — workover barges. These barges have capabilities to operate in shallow waters. When oil and/or gas wells in these waters need reworking, it is necessary that the workover operation be performed from a workover rig mounted on a barge which is floated into a position over the well and then submerged to rest on the bottom. After the barge is submerged and stabilized, the derrick is raised over the well and the workover operations conducted.

Workover rigs are used in three situations: First, a workover rig is often utilized to complete a well after oil has been found and the drilling rig is moved on to drill another well. Second, after a well has been on production, a workover rig is used for many reasons some of which are (1) to repair the casing in the wells, (2) to "cement off" a stratum that starts to produce water, (3) to put an untapped sand on production after the previous producing sands are depleted and (4) the strata which produce oil and gas frequently "get sanded up" and the sand has to be "washed out". Thirdly, a workover rig is necessary to plug and abandon a well when it has ceased to produce.

Each producing oil and/or gas well has to be worked over several times during its producing life; and, as it ages, it requires proportionately more "reworking" to function economically.

EXAMPLE OF INDIVIDUALS INVESTING
IN EQUIPMENT LEASING

In this example it will be assumed that there are ten individual investors who are limited partners. Walter Exploration Corp. is the general partner. The cost of the workover barge will be $2,000,000. Walter will supervise all of the technical services during the design, construction and rigging up of the barge for $130,000. The total cost of one barge, and the equity funds, are as follows:

Projected cost of barge plus construction financing	$2,000,000
Service fee to be paid Walter for technical supervision	130,000
Total Funds Required	$2,130,000
Proceeds of Government Guaranteed Mortgage	1,500,000
Equity Funds Required	$ 630,000

A workover barge is leased to oil producers on a daily rental rate basis with the workover operator furnishing the barge, insurance, crew, crew boats and catering services, etc. The profit per operating day is "built in". There is no risk to the workover operator as needed special equipment is paid for by the producer; if a job becomes difficult and costly, all of the additional expenses are paid for by the producer. In fact, such a job is more profitable to the workover operator.

The cash flow projections indicate that with present prices for the barge's rental and operating costs, the break even point for generating sufficient revenues to pay the fixed rental and overhead allocated to the barge will be 69.0% usage. This means that the barge can be idle 114 days per year and the income still be sufficient to make the fixed rental payment.

Walter, as general partner, will have a 5% equity interest. The limited partners will advance $230,000 in exchange for subordinated installment notes bearing 10.0% interest and payable in ten equal installments commencing in 6 years, and the limited partners will also contribute $400,000 in exchange for 95% of the equity. Walter will give the limited partners a "put" to sell ½ of their 10.0% subordinated notes at par to Walter during the second year and one during the third year. Walter will have a "call" to purchase the subordinated notes from the limited partners at par during the fourth year.

Upon completion of the barge (estimated to be within six months after bid time) the Limited Partnership will lease the workover barge for a 20-year term to an operating subsidiary of Walter to be known as Xavier Barge Corp. Xavier will pay annual rentals to the Limited Partnership of $234,000 escalating to $264,000 in the ninth year and thereafter. Walter will guarantee all rental payments by Xavier. The lease will be a net lease with Xavier standing the cost of all repairs, maintenance, insurance, etc. Xavier will have an option to purchase the workover barge in the seventeenth year, for its then fair market value provided it is in excess of the unpaid principal of the mortgage. Xavier will also have an option to purchase the workover barge at the expiration of the lease term at its then fair market value.

The financial projections reflect the net after-tax cash flow which the Limited Partners will realize as a result of their investment, assuming that the limited partners exercise their put and sell the $230,000 10% subordinated notes to Walter ($115,000 in the second year and $115,000 in the third year) and also assuming that Xavier does not exercise its option to acquire the workover barge from the Limited Partnership for its fair market value in the seventeenth year or at the expiration of the lease.

The financial projections assume that the $1,500,000 government guaranteed mortgage will be amortized over a 20-year period with level principal payments ($75,000 per year) with an effective 8% interest payable on the unpaid balance.

By utilizing the newly enacted Class Lives System of depreciation, the Limited Partnership can depreciate the workover barge using the double declining balance method over a useful life of 9.5 years. In addition, by utilizing a half-year convention, the Limited Partnership can claim 50% of a year's depreciation for the first year, assuming the property is placed in service during the first year. It is assumed that the depreciable basis for the workover barge will be $2,130,000.

The workover barge will qualify for additional first year depreciation of 20% limited to $4,000 of additional depreciation for each limited partner who files a federal income tax joint return. The financial projections are based on the assumption that the partnership will have ten limited partners resulting in $40,000 of total additional first year depreciation.

An individual partner will not be able to claim his share of the investment credit since the 1971 Revenue Act which restored the 7% credit did not permit a non-corporate lessor to claim an investment credit under the facts of this example.

An individual investor will realize an after-tax return (comprised principally of income tax savings derived from depreciation and interest expense) equal to his original investment in slightly over two years. Thereafter (i.e., the following 17 to 18 years) the investor is expected to realize an aggregate after-tax profit equal to approximately 93.0% of his original investment.

The after-tax cash flow during the first 10 years is equal to 19.2% annual rate of return.

The total funds required from investors will be $630,000. An investor can contribute all or a pro rata portion of the $630,000 funds required, but in this example it is assumed that each of ten investors contributes $63,000.

The table on the following page traces the after-tax cash flow of one investment of $63,000.

The high early tax write-offs enable the investor to get his money out of the program in a few years and accomplish the deferral of his income.

EXAMPLE OF A CORPORATION INVESTING
IN EQUIPMENT LEASING

This example is concerned with a corporate investor as a limited partner in a workover barge program. The cost of the workover barge will be $2,000,000. Walter will supervise all of the technical services during the design, construction and rigging up of the barge for $200,000. The total cost of one barge, and the equity funds, are as follows:

Projected cost of barge plus construction financing	$2,000,000
Service fee to be paid Walter for technical supervision	200,000
Total Funds Required	$2,200,000
Proceeds of Government Guaranteed Mortgage	$1,500,000
Equity Funds Required	$ 700,000

Walter, as general partner, will have a 5% equity interest. The Limited Partners will advance $200,000 in exchange for subordinated installment notes bearing 12.5% interest and payable in ten equal annual installments commencing in 6 years, and the Limited Partners will also contribute $500,000

WORKOVER BARGE LIMITED PARTNERSHIP (twenty-year period)

Projected Summary of Limited Partners' after-tax cash flow
for one investment in unit of $63,000 in one workover barge

	Year One	Year Two	Year Three	17-Year Period
Taxable income (loss) (95% of partnership totals)	$(22,754)	$(27,342)	$(19,238)	$211,874
Additional first year depreciation	4,000	–	–	–
Total taxable income (loss)	(26,754)	(27,342)	(19,238)	211,874
Total tax savings (cost) at 50%	13,377	13,671	9,620	105,936
Cash flow (95% of partnership totals)	–	372	1,852	161,214
Total tax savings and cash flow from $40,000 equity	13,377	14,043	11,472	55,278
After-tax proceeds of interest on $23,000 notes	480	1,150	574	–
Proceeds from sale of $23,000 notes	–	11,500	11,500	–
Total after-tax cash flow from equity and debt	$ 13,857	$ 26,694	$ 23,546	$ 55,278
Cumulative total of above	$ 13,857	$ 42,550	$ 66,096	$121,374

Depreciation is computed on the double-declining balance method for the first five years and on the straight-line method thereafter. Salvage value of $100,000 is assumed.

in exchange for 95% of the equity. Walter will give the limited partners a "put" to sell their 12.5% subordinated notes at par to Walter during the second year, and Walter will have a "call" to purchase the 12.5% subordinated notes from the limited partners at par during the fourth year.

Upon completion of the barge (estimated to be within six months after bid time) the Limited Partnership will lease the workover barge for a 20-year term to an operating subsidiary of Walter to be known as Xavier Barge Corp. Xavier will pay annual rentals to the Limited Partnership of $228,000 escalating to $264,000 in the ninth year and thereafter. Walter will guarantee all rental payments by Xavier. The lease will be a net lease with Xavier standing the cost of all repairs, maintenance, insurance, etc. Xavier will have an option to purchase the workover barge in the seventeenth year, for its then fair market value provided it is in excess of the unpaid principal of the mortgage. Xavier will also have an option to purchase the workover barge at the expiration of the lease term at its then fair market value.

The financial projections reflect the net after-tax cash flow which the Limited Partners will realize as a result of their investment, assuming that the limited partners exercise their put and sell the $200,000, 12.5% subordinated notes to Walter in the second year, and also assuming that Xavier does not exercise its option to acquire the workover barge from the Limited Partnership for its fair market value in the seventeenth year or at the expiration of the lease.

The financial projections assume that the $1,500,000 government guaranteed mortgage will be amortized over a 20-year period with level principal payments ($75,000 per year) with an effective 8% interest payable on the unpaid balance.

By utilizing the newly enacted Class Lives System of depreciation, the Limited Partnership can depreciate the workover barge using the double declining balance method over a useful life of 9.5 years. In addition, by utilizing a half-year convention, the Limited Partnership can claim 50% of a year's depreciation for the first year, assuming the property is placed in service during the first year. It is assumed that the depreciable basis for the workover barge will be $2,150,000.

Since the depreciable basis of the workover barge will be

$2,150,000, ($2,200,000 less $50,000 for interest during construction and insurance premium), a corporate limited partner will be entitled to its pro rata share of $142,974 investment credit. However, an individual partner will not be able to claim his share of the investment credit since the 1971 Revenue Act which restored the 7% credit did not permit a non-corporate lessor to claim an investment credit under the circumstances of this example.

A corporate investor may realize an after-tax return (comprised principally of income tax savings derived from depreciation, investment tax credit and interest expense) equal to its original investment in slightly over two years. Thereafter (i.e., the following 17 to 18 years) the corporate investor is expected to realize an aggregate after-tax profit equal to approximately 95% of its original investment.

The after-tax cash flow during the first 10 years is equal to 21.8% annual rate of return.

The total funds required from investors will be $700,000. An investor can contribute all or a pro rata portion of the $700,000 funds required.

The table on the following page traces the after-tax cash flow for a $700,000 investment.

The availability of the 7% investment credit to corporations may increase the number of corporate investors in the equipment leasing field.

Because of the high, early write-offs, the corporation gets its money out of the program after a few years and has deferred receipt of some income.

BENEFITS OF AN EQUIPMENT LEASING PROGRAM

1. Continuous reinvesting can defer high pretax income to a much later tax period.

2. Taxable income can be deferred through accelerated depreciation and interest deductions.

3. Investment credit (when available) is attractive.

4. The additional first-year depreciation allows each partner to write off up to 20% or $2,000 ($4,000 on joint return) of the cost of the property the first year it is placed in service.

5. A taxpayer can elect to amortize the cost of certain

WORKOVER BARGE LIMITED PARTNERSHIP (twenty-year period)

Projected Summary of Limited Partners' after-tax cash flow

for a $700,000 investment in one workover barge

	Year One	Year Two	Year Three	17-Year Period
Taxable income (loss) (95% of partnership totals)	$(238,334)	$(307,868)	$(221,172)	$ 2,024,064
Tax savings (cost) at 50%	119,168	153,934	110,586	(1,012,032)
Investment credit (available to corporations only)	142,974			
Total tax savings (cost)	262,142	153,934	110,586	(1,012,032)
Cash flow (95% of partnership totals)		1,268	10,926	1,617,374
Total tax savings and cash flow from $500,000 equity	262,142	155,202	121,512	605,342
After-tax proceeds of interest on $200,000 notes	2,082	12,500		
Proceeds from sale of $200,000 notes		200,000		
Total after-tax cash flow from equity and debt	264,224	367,702	121,512	605,342
Cumulative total of above	$ 264,224	$ 631,926	$ 753,438	$ 1,358,780

Depreciation is computed on the double-declining balance method for the first five years and on the straight-line method thereafter. Salvage value of $107,500 is assumed.

rolling stock to railroads over a five-year period (60 months).

6. After depreciation and interest deductions decrease and taxable income is generated, the investor can give his limited partnership interest to family members in lower tax brackets.

7. The equipment may have considerable residual value after the expiration of the lease.

8. This tax shelter can be advantageous to high-tax-bracket people nearing the retirement or those with temporarily high incomes. Write-offs in the beginning years offset high income while income generated in later years is subject to lower tax rates.

9. If a partnership purchases used equipment, it may employ, in its first two taxable years, the declining-balance method of computing depreciation, using a rate not in excess of 150% of straight-line depreciation. If new equipment is purchased, the rate will be 200% of straight line depreciation. In either event, a partnership may change to straight-line depreciation at the point (depending upon the useful life of the equipment) when such change is deemed advantageous so long as a proper election is filed by the partnership.

RISKS OF AN EQUIPMENT LEASING PROGRAM

1. Default by the lessee.

2. Accelerated depreciation for personal property on a net lease is a tax preference item. This is depreciation allowable during the tax year for personal property subject to a net lease in excess of depreciation that would have been allowed had the straight line method been used for all tax years. In a net lease the lessor's allowable deductions are less than 15% of gross rents or the lessor either is guaranteed a specified return or is guaranteed in whole or in part against loss of income. Although this is not a preference item as to corporations generally, it is a preference item for corporations electing not to be taxed as such.

3. Under the 1976 Tax Reform Act, interest on investment indebtedness is limited to $10,000 per year, plus the taxpayer's net investment income. No offset of investment interest is permitted against capital gain income. An additional deduction of up to $15,000 per year is permitted for interest paid in connection with indebtedness incurred by the taxpayer to acquire the stock in a corporation, or a partnership interest,

where the taxpayer, his spouse, and his children have (or acquire) at least 50 percent of the stock or capital interest in the enterprise. Interest deductions which are disallowed under these rules are subject to an unlimited carryover and may be deducted in future years (subject to the applicable limitation). Under the conference agreement, no limitation is imposed on the deductibility of personal interest.

Generally these rules are applicable to taxable years beginning after December 31, 1975. However, under a transition rule, present law (sec. 163(d) before the amendments made under the conference agreement) continues to apply in the case of interest on indebtedness which is attributable to a specific item of property, is for a specified term, and was either incurred before September 11, 1975, or is incurred after that date under a binding written contract or commitment in effect on that date and at all times thereafter (hereinafter referred to as "pre-1976 interest"). As under present law, interest incurred before December 17, 1969 ("pre-1970 interest") is not subject to a limitation.

4. Gain from the sale, exchange, or other disposition of depreciable personal property, including a sale and leaseback transaction, must be reported as ordinary income unless the depreciation on the property attributable to periods after 1961 is less than the gain. However, the investor has had the use of that money until it is recaptured in taxes, and this use can be very profitable.

5. If the lease is considered a sale, the investment credit (if and when available) goes to the buyer, and the partnership loses the depreciation deduction.

TAX ASPECTS OF AN EQUIPMENT LEASING PROGRAM

A. *Limited Partner Guarantees*

The Tax Reform Act of 1976 and the Revenue Act of 1978 contain several provisions that apply to tax sheltered investments. The most significant provision in the Tax Reform Act of 1976 pertaining to the Partnership is a rule precluding taxpayers from deducting losses from an activity in excess of amounts "at risk" in the activity.

The amount to which a taxpayer is "at risk" in an activity is the sum of (i) the money and adjusted basis of other property that the taxpayer invests in the activity plus (ii) amounts borrowed for use in the activity but only to the extent that the taxpayer is personally liable for the repayment of such amounts or has pledged property, other than property used in the activity, as security for such amounts.

Since the Partnership is engaging in equipment leasing, which is an activity covered by the "at risk" rules, Limited Partners will be allowed to deduct Partnership losses only to the extent of their "at risk" investment. A taxpayer will not be considered "at risk" with respect to amounts protected against loss through non-recourse financing, guarantees, stop loss agreements, or other similar arrangements.

The "at risk" rules are new and it is not yet clear how the IRS will interpret them and, more particularly, whether the IRS would include the face amount of Guarantees in the "at risk" investment of Limited Partners. The Treasury Department has issued some rulings covering the "at risk" rules that reflect an intention to strictly construe the "at risk" provisions. No ruling of the Internal Revenue Service will be sought on this issue. Instead, the Partnership will rely on the opinion of Counsel that the original guarantees of Partnership debt by the Limited Partners will satisfy the "at risk" provisions of the law.

The Revenue Act of 1978 amended the "at risk" rules so that taxpayers are now required to recapture losses previously claimed if their "at risk" investment is reduced below zero. Therefore, Limited Partners will, in addition to guaranteeing debt sufficient to cover anticipated losses through 1982, be required to guarantee debt in the amount by which the reduction in guaranteed debt exceeds income after 1982.

Although the Federal Income tax treatment of tax shelter investments was changed considerably by the Tax Reform Act of 1976, there can be no assurance that Congress will not make further changes in the tax laws impacting tax sheltered investments as was the case, for example, in the Revenue Act of 1978. Furthermore, if the treatment of a tax sheltered investment is challenged by the Internal Revenue Service it is possible that public opinion and bias against tax shelters will prove to be detrimental to the investor.

211

B. *Partnership Status*

No ruling of the Internal Revenue Service will be requested as to whether the Partnership will be treated as such for Federal income tax purposes. However, it is the opinion of counsel to the Partnership that, under the current Code, Regulations and Rulings of the Internal Revenue Service, the Partnership should be classified as a partnership for Federal income tax purposes and not as an association taxable as a corporation. The opinion of counsel rendered to the Partnership is not binding on the Internal Revenue Service. The opinion is based in part on representations made on behalf of the Partnership as follows:

1. The Limited Partners will not own, directly or indirectly, individually or in the aggregate, more than twenty percent of the stock of the General Partner or any affiliates.

2. The General Partner will act as such for only one limited partnership, the total contributions to that partnership will be less than $2,500,000 and the net worth of the General Partner (based on current fair market value of its assets) at all times will be at least fifteen percent of such total contributions.

For the purposes of computing the net worth of the General Partner in paragraph 2 above, its interest in the Partnership, and accounts and notes receivable from and payable to the Partnership, must be excluded.

To satisfy the net worth test, the General Partner will rely upon a negotiable demand note contributed to it. In its opinion, counsel notes that, for purposes of the Federal income tax issue in question, this Note should be treated as an asset of the General Partner in determining its net worth notwithstanding the fact that current accounting rules require the note to be treated as a subscription receivable, and not as an asset, on the General Partner's balance sheet. Counsel relies upon representations from the General Partner as to its net worth and the collectability of the Note in concluding that the net worth test for the General Partner has been initially satisfied.

Although the Articles of Partnership impose a limit on the extent to which the General Partner may pay dividends, there is no assurance that the General Partner will not have its net worth impaired by business losses or otherwise. The General Partner will attempt to do whatever is required by the Internal Revenue Service to assume that the Partnership will be classified as a partnership for Federal income tax purposes but there can be no assurance that the General Partner will be able to comply with such requirements as they presently exist or as they may be changed from time to time. If partnership status were lost, the tax benefits expected from investment in the Partnership would be lost and substantial tax burdens could be incurred by the Limited Partners, without any corresponding cash distribution, and by the Partnership.

The opinion rendered by counsel to the Partnership (in this paragraph, the "initial opinion") concludes that the Partnership should not be considered as having more than one-half of the characteristics set forth in the Federal income tax regulations to identify entities taxable as corporations. However, the initial opinion also notes that the holders of a majority of the outstanding limited partnership Units may remove the General Partner and elect a new General Partner if the Partnership has previously received an opinion of counsel (in this paragraph the "second opinion") satisfactory to the holders of a majority of the outstanding limited partnership Units to the effect that such action will not jeopardize the tax status of the Partnership or the limited liability of the Limited Partners. The initial opinion notes that, since the Limited Partners have not yet obtained such second opinion, the Articles of Partnership presently require unanimous consent to elect a new General Partner. The initial opinion expressly states that it may not be relied upon as to the status of the Partnership for tax purposes if such second opinion is obtained.

On October 21, 1975 the United States Tax Court issued its opinion in *Phillip G. Larson,* 65 T.C. #10 (1975). The opinion held that two limited partnerships formed under the laws of California were taxable as corporations rather than as partnerships. The Tax Court subsequently withdrew its opinion and reissued it on April 27, 1976 with the opposite result—finding for the taxpayer and holding that the partnership should be treated as such for income tax purposes. The citation to the second opinion is 66 T.C. 159 (1976). On September 14, 1976, the Government appealed the Tax Court's second opinion to the Ninth Circuit Court of Appeals.

The day after the Tax Court issued its initial opinion in *Larson,* the Court of Claims issued its opinion in *Zuckman* v. *United States,* 524 F.2d 729 (Ct. Cl. 1975). The *Zuckman* opinion holds that a limited partnership formed under the laws of Missouri to build and operate an apartment building should be taxed as a partnership and not as a corporation. The *Zuckman* and *Larson* opinions indicate that the Tax Court and the Court of Claims have taken different approaches to the question of whether a partnership is to be taxed as such, notwithstanding that the results in both cases were the same. If the Court of Claims continues to take an approach on this issue which is more favorable to taxpayers, a Limited Partner would be free— provided he paid the tax and then sought a refund—to present his case to the Court of Claims.

On January 5, 1977, the Internal Revenue Service published proposed regulations setting forth new rules distinguishing between partnerships and corporations for tax purposes. Under those proposed regulations, the Partnership would most likely have been treated as a corporation and not as a partnership. The proposed regulations were withdrawn by the Secretary of the Treasury on January 6, 1977. On January 14, 1977, the Secretary announced that the proposed regulations would not be reissued and that the existing regulations would remain in force. However, there can be no assurance that the current administration will not revive the proposed regulation or that they will not be adopted, in substance, by the courts.

In the event the Partnership were treated for Federal income tax purposes as an association taxable as a corporation, the Partnership would be required to pay tax at corporate rates upon its income; items of deduction and credit would be allowed only to the Partnership and would not be passed through to the Limited Partners; and distributions to the Limited Partners would be taxable to them as dividends (at ordinary income rates to the extent of the entity's earnings and profits) and would not be deductible by the Partnership. Accordingly, there would be no tax shelter benefits which could be used by the Limited Partners to offset non-Partnership income.

C. *General Principles of Partnership Taxation*

As long as the Partnership is treated as a partnership for Federal income tax purposes, it will not be subject to Federal income tax but will file partnership information tax returns each year, reporting its operations on a accrual basis using the calendar year as its taxable year. Within 75 days after the end of each calendar year, each Partner will be provided with Federal income tax information relevant to his own Federal income tax return. Each Partner will be required to report on his own return for his tax year, with or within which the Partnership's year ends, his share of the taxable income or loss of the Partnership for the year. Tax payable by a Partner depends upon his share of Partnership taxable income and not upon the absence or presence of a cash distribution by the Partnership. Thus, cash distributions made in years when the Partnership sustains losses are not taxable to a Partner. Likewise, in years when the Partnership generates taxable income, Partners will be taxed on their pro rata share of such income even though cash distributions are expected to be minimal.

A Limited Partner's share of the anticipated Partnership losses may shelter some of his other income from Federal income taxes. Such tax shelter, if realized, will be more advantageous to persons whose income from other sources places them in higher Federal income tax brackets than it will be for those in lower and middle Federal income tax brackets. Investors should be aware that such a tax shelter operates to defer, rather than to reduce, Federal income tax otherwise payable by Partners because of anticipated taxable ordinary income in the later years of the Partnership.

Investors should also be aware that there can be no assurance that all items of deduction will be allowed in the event of an audit. Any adjustments to the Partnership's information return will result in adjustments to their individual tax returns and may result in the audit of other items in their returns unrelated to the Partnership.

D. *Opinion of Counsel*

As noted throughout this "Tax Considerations," the Partnership will not seek a tax ruling from the Internal Revenue Service with respect to the material tax issues relating to the proposed operation of the Partnership. Rather, the Partnership will rely upon the opinions of Counsel. Investors should be aware that these opinions are not binding on the Internal Revenue Service and that the Service is free to challenge the opinions reached by counsel. An opinion of counsel represents only such counsel's best legal judgment and, unlike a tax ruling, has no official status of any kind. No assurance can be given that the conclusions reached in such opinion would be sustained by a court, if contested.

E. *Early Termination of Leases*

Some equipment leases provide for early termination by the lessee. While these provisions vary from lease to lease, early termination may result in an early termination penalty being paid by the lessee. Early termination penalties are taxable as ordinary income even though they are used to reduce the debt secured by the equipment. Consequently, the resulting tax liability could exceed cash available for distribution to Partners.

F. *Legislation*

Since the Revenue Act of 1978 has been enacted, there are no current legislative proposals relating to limited partnership investments in equipment leasing. Although there were significant changes in the Tax Reform Act of 1976 and the Revenue Act of 1978, additional changes in the tax law may be enacted in the future which could eliminate or reduce the anticipated benefits of an investment in the Units. Any legislation which is enacted may or may not be retroactive with respect to transactions entered into prior to the effective date thereof.

G. *Tax Basis*

Initially, the tax basis of a Limited Partner's Unit will be the purchase price paid therefor. Each Limited Partner must then increase (or decrease) such tax basis by the amount of his allocable share of the Partnership's net income (or loss) for the year and by his share of any increase (or decrease) of Partnership indebtedness for which he has assumed personal liability, and must reduce such tax basis by the amount of any cash distributions to him during such year. If the tax basis of his Unit should be reduced to zero, the amount of any cash distribution to a Limited Partner and any reduction in a Limited Partner's share of Partnership liabilities for any year, in excess of his share of the income of the Partnership for the year, generally will be taxable to him in the same manner as sale of a Unit. See "Tax Treatment of Disposition of Units" below.

On his own Federal income tax return, each Limited Partner may deduct his share of the Partnership's loss, if any, to the extent of the aggregate of his tax basis for his Units. A Limited Partner may not deduct losses in excess of his basis for his Units,

216

but may carry forward such excess to such time, if ever, as his basis for his Units is sufficient to absorb such loss.

As previously noted, the Tax Reform Act of 1976 and Revenue Act of 1978 provide that a taxpayer engaged in equipment leasing may not deduct losses in excess of its "at risk" investment. However, the rules set forth in Treas. Reg. § 1.752-1(e) continue to apply to the Partnership (to the effect that each Partner's basis is increased by non-recourse debt to the extent of his interests in the profits of the Partnership).

To the extent Partnership indebtedness is repaid from taxable income of the Partnership, such income will be taxable to the Limited Partners without corresponding cash distributions of such income.

H. *Tax Treatment of Disposition of Units*

(a) Sale

Income or loss on sale by a Partner of his Units will be based on the difference between the amount realized, including his share of Partnership non-recourse liabilities, and the tax basis for his Units. The tax imposed as a result of a sale may exceed the cash proceeds realized. It is likely that all of any such gain will be ordinary income. Loss, if any, would be capital loss.

(b) Gift

A result similar to a sale may be expected in situations where a Partner makes a gift of his Units, except that the "amount realized" by the Partner in such a case will be his share of Partnership non-recourse liabilities only. See "Tax Basis" above. In addition, a gift of a Unit may result in the Limited Partner being liable for gift tax. See Rev. Bul. 75-194, 1975-1 C.B. 80.

(c) Death

The fair market value of a Limited Partner's interest in the Partnership will be included in his gross estate for federal estate tax purposes and will be subject to federal estate tax. Prior to the enactment of the Tax Reform Act of 1976, the basis of an estate's interest in a partnership was adjusted to reflect the fair market value of such interest at death. In some cases stepped up basis allowed an estate to dispose of a partnership interest without suffering a "recapture" of prior losses.

The Tax Reform Act of 1976 eliminated "step-up basis," subject to certain minor exceptions, by requiring that an estate use the basis the decedent had immediately before his death ("carryover basis"). This change eliminates the possibility of avoiding the taxable gain which may result from a disposition of a partner's interest in the Partnership after his death. The Revenue Act of 1978 postponed the effective date of the carryover basis rules to December 31, 1979. Therefore, under current law, the estate of a Partner dying before December 31, 1979 would be able to "step-up" the basis in a Unit to the value at the date of death, while the "carryover basis" rules would apply if a Partner dies after December 31, 1979.

If an estate or beneficiary holds a deceased Limited Partner's interest in the Partnership, such estate or beneficiary would be required to report income or loss from the Partnership in the same manner as if the Limited Partner had not died.

I. *Tax Treatment of Sale of Partnership Property*

In the event of the sale of Partnership property (including a sale or disposition resulting from early termination by a lessee or the enforcement of a security interest) or a casualty loss of the property, the Partnership will realize gain or loss equal to the difference between the amount realized and the Partnership's tax basis in the equipment. The amount realized would include stipulated loss values received (in the event of a casualty loss) termination penalties received (in the event of early termination) and the full proceeds of any sale of the property, including the amount of any indebtedness to which the property is subject which is assumed by the purchaser. Such gain will be ordinary income to the extent of depreciation previously allowable with respect to the property sold.

Since the tax basis of the property is expected to be less than the amount of non-recourse indebtedness to which the property is subject, the income realized on the sale or casualty and taxable to the Limited Partners may exceed any cash realized by the Partnership or available for distribution to the Limited Partners. In such event, Partners would be required to use their personal funds to pay their pro rata share of the excess tax liability.

Tax deferral is one of the investment objectives of a purchase of Units. Investors should note that the tax impact of a premature disposition of the Partnership's property (through casualty or early termination) runs contrary to this investment objective.

Should the amount realized on a sale or casualty of Partnership property be less than its adjusted basis, the resulting loss would generally be deductible as an ordinary loss.

J. *Tax Treatment of Termination of the Partnership*

In the event of termination of the Partnership, the General Partner is required to liquidate the Partnership assets, apply the Partnership funds to the liabilities of the Partnership, and distribute any excess to the Partners. Liquidation of the Partnership assets would have the consequences described under "Tax Treatment of Sale of Partnership Property" above.

K. *Taxation of Leased Property*

As a general rule, the owner of property used in a trade or business or to produce income is allowed to depreciate that property. However, if the property is leased to another on terms such that the lessee has, in effect, the use of the equipment for its entire useful life, the Internal Revenue Service may assert that the lessee, not the lessor, "owns" the property for tax purposes and that the lessee, not the lessor, is entitled to claim depreciation with respect to the property.

The Internal Revenue Service has taken an increasingly aggressive position with respect to the question of whether a lessor has sufficient benefits and burdens of ownership to be treated as an owner entitled to depreciation deductions on leased property. The test used to determine if a depreciation deduction can be taken is whether the lessor has an investment in the leased property and would suffer an economic loss as a result of a decrease in value of the property. *Manuel D. Maverson*, 47 T.C. 340 (1966) *acq.* 1969-1 C.B. 21; *T. W. Blake*, 20 T.C. 721 (1953); *Gladding Dry Goods Co.*, 2 BTA 336 (1925).

In two cases the Internal Revenue Service asserted that taxpayers investing in real estate tax shelters did not own the property involved because actual ownership, as a matter of economic substance, was retained by the lessees. *See Est. of Franklin v. Comm'r*, 544 F.2d 1045 (9th Cir. 1976) and *Frank Lyon Co. v. United States*, _____ U.S. _____ (1978). In *Franklin*, the Ninth Circuit found that the benefits, risks and burdens which the taxpayers incurred with respect to the real estate were not substantial enough to cause the taxpayers to be the

219

"owners" and held that they could not depreciate the real estate. In *Lyon,* however, the Supreme Court reached the opposite result, holding that the "owner" was the owner for tax purposes and entitled to depreciate the real estate.

The Partnership has received an opinion of its counsel that all of the designated leases to be acquired by the Partnership should be treated as leases for Federal income tax purposes. The opinion is based upon current law and notes that the law may change, either as a result of legislation or new court decisions, at any time. The opinion of counsel rendered to the Partnership is not binding on the Internal Revenue Service. The opinion notes that the Internal Revenue Service has been aggressive with respect to the question of whether a lessor has retained ownership of property subject to a lease and that there can be no assurance that the Internal Revenue Service will not assert that the leases should be treated as a sale for Federal income tax purposes.

The Internal Revenue Service has published guidelines for determining whether it will issue a ruling that a lessor is the owner of leased property. Rev. Proc. 75-21, 1975-1 C.B. 715. That revenue procedure provides that, unless other facts and circumstances indicate a contrary intent, for advance ruling purposes only, the Service will consider the lessor in a leveraged lease transaction to be the owner of property if:

(1) the lessor has a minimum unconditional investment in the property at all times during the lease of at least 20% of the cost of the property and can demonstrate that the estimated residual value of the property is at least 20% of the cost of the property;

(2) the lessee does not have an option to purchase the property (other than at fair market value) and the lessor does not have the right to require anyone to purchase the property;

(3) no part of the cost of the property subject to the lease is furnished by the lessee other than for full consideration;

(4) the lessee does not lend the lessor any of the funds necessary to purchase the property; and

(5) the lessor expects to receive a profit from the transaction apart from tax benefits.

The question of whether debt guaranteed by a partner for purposes of the "at risk" rules should be included in a partner's equity investment for purposes of Rev. Proc. 75-21 has not been ruled upon by the Internal Revenue Service. If a partner's equity investment were so increased, it is possible that the equity requirement in Rev. Proc. 75-21 would be satisfied with respect to those leases where associated debt is being guaranteed.

Notwithstanding the advance ruling position of the Internal Revenue Service, courts have not been as restrictive as the Internal Revenue Service and it is possible that the Internal Revenue Service audit position is not as restrictive. See, *e.g., Northwest Acceptance Corp.,* 58 T.C. 836 (1972), aff'd 500 F.2d 1222 (9th Cir. 1974). Thus, the fact that the Internal Revenue Service would not issue an advance ruling with respect to a lease does not necessarily mean that it would attempt to treat the transaction as a sale rather than as a lease.

Although there is an ownership interest, it is possible that ownership of property can be shared in a "joint venture" between two or more parties. There is an issue as to whether the agreements between the Partnership and its brokers might create "joint ventures" for Federal income tax purposes. If such were held to be the case, the brokers might be deemed to own a portion of the leased property for tax purposes.

A joint venture exists if the purported venturers, acting in good faith with a business purpose, intend to and do join together for the purpose of carrying on business and sharing the profits or losses, or both. *Comm'r v. Tower,* 327 U.S. 280 (1946). The issue is factual. The most important indicia are (i) the intent of the parties, (ii) whether profits and losses are shared, and (iii) whether control over the enterprise is exercised jointly. *Herbert M. Luna,* 42 T.C. 1067 (1964).

In Rev. Rul. 75-43, 1975-1 C.B. 383, the Internal Revenue Service held that a corporation rendering services to a cattle feeding operation was not a joint venturer even though the corporation, under a guarantee agreement, was entitled to a percentage of the profits and bore a percentage of the losses from that operation.

It is arguable that equipment brokers who have agreed to re-market the Partnership's equipment will share in profits, since they may be entitled to a portion of cash flow arising from sale or re-leasing of the equipment. They may also have some control over the equipment, from time to time. It is not clear, however, that these circumstances alone will result in a joint venture. The absence of a joint venture is supported by the fact that the cash flow to, and the controls of, the brokers are consistent with their duties as re-marketing agents for the Partnership. Further, they will not be paid fees unless they use their best efforts to obtain lessees or buyers for the equipment.

The Partnership has been informed by counsel that it cannot be predicted with certainty how a court might characterize the relationship between the remarketing brokers and the Partnership because the law concerning the presence of a joint venture in transactions of this nature is not clearly defined. Also counsel has informed the Partnership that the Internal Revenue Service is currently studying its position with respect to the proper treatment of residual fees paid to brokers, for purposes of advance rulings by the Service. Nonetheless counsel does express the opinion that the respective relationships between the brokers and the Partnership should not be treated as joint ventures, although there is a substantial tax risk if the Service takes a restrictive advance ruling position.

L. *Minimum Tax*

A fifteen percent "minimum tax for tax preferences" is imposed by Section 56 of the Code on the amount by which the total of a taxpayer's "items of tax preference" exceeds (i) $10,000 ($5,000 in the case of married taxpayers filing separate returns) or (ii) one-half of the taxpayer's regular Federal income taxes for the taxable year, whichever is greater. The "minimum tax for tax preferences" is not imposed on the Partnership. Rather, each Limited Partner must include his pro rata share of the Partnership's "items of tax preference" in his total "items of tax preference" for the purpose of computing his "minimum tax for tax preferences."

"Items of tax preference" reduce, dollar for dollar, the "earned taxable income" of a taxpayer for purposes of computing the amount of income subject to the maximum tax on earned income under Section 1348 of the Code.

It is expected that the only item of tax preference income generated by the Partnership will be the excess of accelerated depreciation over straight-line depreciation. This item of tax preference is not applicable to corporate taxpayers.

Individual states may have enacted comparable "tax preference" legislation. For example, New York State imposes a tax at the rate of 6% on the sum of the New York items of tax preferences less the current year's taxes paid to New York State and less $5,000 ($2,500 if married and filing separate returns).

The New York items of tax preference are the Federal items of tax preference with certain adjustments. Furthermore, a portion of certain of a taxpayer's itemized deductions otherwise allowable may be disallowed. Such deductions mainly include taxes, interest and charitable contributions. These deductions are allowed in the ratio that the New York adjusted gross income bears to the taxpayer's New York adjusted gross income plus such tax preferences to the extent they exceed $5,000 ($2,500 if married and filing separate returns).

M. *Maximum Tax on Personal Service Income*

The amount of "personal service income" (formerly "earned income") of a Partner which would otherwise be eligible for the 50% limitation on the maximum rate of tax on such income of individuals will be reduced, dollar for dollar, by the amount of the Partner's items of tax preference for the taxable year. Such items of tax preference will include a Partner's share of the Partnership's items of tax preference.

A Limited Partner's share of Partnership taxable income will not constitute "personal service income" for purposes of the maximum tax. A Limited Partner may suffer a tax detriment when Partnership tax losses reduce his income (which would otherwise be subject to the 50% maximum rate) because the Partnership may in subsequent years generate taxable income which is taxable to the Limited Partner at rates in excess of the 50% maximum rate.

N. *Investment Interest*

Section 163(d) of the Code limits the ability of taxpayers (other than corporations) to claim deductions for investment interest. In general, "investment interest" is interest paid to purchase or carry property held for investment and can be deducted each year only to the extent of $10,000 plus "net investment income."

More specifically, Section 163(d)(1) provides that noncorporate taxpayers may deduct investment interest only to the extent of
1) $10,000 ($5,000 in the case of a separate return by a married individual);
2) net investment income; and

3) the amount (if any) by which (i) ordinary and necessary business expenses, (ii) interest, (iii) taxes on real and personal property, and (iv) expenses paid for the production of income exceed rental income produced by the property.

It is not expected that the Partnership will generate amounts described in paragraph 3.

"Investment interest" means interest paid or accrued on indebtedness incurred or continued to purchase or carry property held for investment. As a general rule, the owning and leasing of equipment constitutes a "business" and not an "investment" for income tax purposes. Rev. Rul. 60-206, 1960-1 C.B. 201. However, Section 163(d)(4) of the Code provides that property subject to a "net lease" shall be treated as held for investment and not as property used in a trade or business. Thus, if the Partnership leases are "net leases," the interest paid will be investment interest.

The term "net lease" includes all leases where the lessor's regular business expenses each year are less than 15% of rental income for that year.

"Net investment income" means "investment income" reduced by "investment expenses." "Investment income" is, generally, dividends, interest, rents, royalties, short-term capital gain on investment property and depreciation recapture from the sale of property, to the extent such income is not connected with a trade or business. "Investment expense" is, generally, property taxes, bad debts, depreciation, amortizable bond premiums, depletion and other costs of earning this income (such as safe-deposit box rentals and investment services).

In the case of the Partnership, investment income will consist of the rents and investment expense will consist of the management fees, depreciation and amortization.

Because of high depreciation during the early years of Partnership operations, the Partnership may generate negative "net investment income" as shown above during such early years of operations. Although the negative "net investment income" may reduce investment income which otherwise might be available to "shelter" investment interest, it should not offset the $10,000 amount allowed to each taxpayer each year.

Any investment interest which is disallowed in accordance with the foregoing rules is treated as interest paid or accrued in the succeeding year and may be deducted in such year, subject to the same limitations.

O. *Tax Elections - Effect on Subsequent Purchaser*

Upon the transfer of a Unit, the Partnership may elect, pursuant to Section 754 of the Code and related sections, to make an optional adjustment to its basis in Partnership property for the purpose of determining the new Partner's share of Partnership tax items. If such election is made, the Partnership's basis for its property will be adjusted, only insofar as a new Partner is concerned, to reflect the difference between such Partner's cost of his Unit and his proportionate share of the Partnership's basis in its property. Where the purchase price for the transferred Unit is in excess of the seller's share of the Partnership's basis in its property, such adjustment may be beneficial to the new Partner. On the other hand, where the purchase price is less than such share of the Partnership's basis, an election may prove disadvantageous. An election is binding in the year made and in all subsequent Partnership years. A Partner's ability to resell his Units may depend on whether such election has been made. Whether such election is made for the Partnership will depend upon whether, in the judgment of the General Partner, such election would be beneficial to the majority of the Limited Partners.

P. *Allocation of Profits and Losses*

Section 704(a) of the Code provides that a partner's distributive share of each item of income, gain, loss, deduction, or credit shall be determined by the partnership agreement. However, Section 706(c)(2) of the Code provides that a Partnership may not allocate these items to a partner if the items were incurred prior to the time the partner joined the partnership. To the same effect, see *Comm'r v. Rodman,* 542 F.2d 845 (2nd Cir. 1976). Further, if a partner's allocation pursuant to the partnership agreement does not have a substantial economic foundation, a partner's allocable share of income, gain, etc., shall be determined in accordance with his interest in the partnership (taking into account all facts and circumstances).

Q. *Hobby Losses*

The Tax Reform Act of 1969 added Section 183 to the Internal Revenue Code. Under this section, deductions incurred

225

in any activity may be disallowed or limited to the income derived therefrom if the activity is "not engaged in for profit." In addition to Section 183 of the Internal Revenue Code, courts have held that, under general principles of income taxation, taxpayers will not be allowed to deduct losses from a transaction in cases where an economic profit is not sought. Since the Partnership will seek an economic profit without regard to the tax consequences, and since the Partnership will generate a net cash return to the Partner (without regard to tax results) if the expected residuals are actually realized, neither Section 183 nor the general principles of income taxation should be applicable to investment in the Partnership. However, there is no definitive authority on the question.

R. *Expenses*

The Tax Reform Act of 1976 added a new Section 709 to the Internal Revenue Code. Under this section, any amounts paid to organize a partnership must be capitalized over a period of not less than 60 months. Further, amounts paid to promote the sale of, or to sell, interests in a partnership may be neither deducted nor amortized.

S. *Self-Employment Taxes*

The United States Tax Court has held that a Limited Partner is required to pay self-employment taxes on his share of the income of a limited partnership. *Est. of William J. Ellsasser,* 61 T.C. 241 (1973). Thus, an investor may be liable for the self-employment tax in years (not expected before 1983) when the Partnership has taxable income. In situations where an individual has already paid the maximum amount of employment or self-employment taxes, no additional taxes would be due.

T. *Accumulated Earnings Tax*

Section 531 of the Code imposes an accumulated earnings tax on every corporation formed or availed of for the purpose of avoiding income tax with respect to its shareholders by permitting earnings and profits to accumulate instead of being paid out as dividends.

The tax is imposed upon each year's "accumulated taxable income" at the rate of 27½ percent of the first $100,000 of accumulated taxable income and 38½% on any excess. "Accumulated taxable income" is the taxable income of the corporation reduced by the ordinary corporate taxes (and other adjustments to make the base reflect the economic income) and also reduced by the dividends paid deduction (if the corporation has paid dividends) and the "accumulated earnings credit." Every corporation is permitted to accumulate total surplus of $150,000 (the "minimum credit") without being required to distribute earnings. However, a corporation is not limited to $150,000, but is entitled to a maximum credit equal to the amount of earnings reasonably required in the business.

The tax is imposed only on corporations that are formed or availed of to avoid tax with respect to their shareholders. If a corporation is a mere holding or investment company, that fact alone is *prima facie* evidence that it was formed or availed of to avoid tax with respect to its shareholders.

If a corporation accumulates earnings and profits in excess of the reasonable needs of the business, it is presumed to have done so to avoid tax with respect to its shareholders and has the burden of proving otherwise. Whether earnings are accumulated beyond the reasonable needs of the business is a question of fact. One of the factors considered is the corporation's retention of cash, securities and other assets unrelated to and not essential to the normal operations of the business. An investment in the Partnership may be considered to be the acquisition of an asset unrelated to the Partner's normal business.

U. *Personal Holding Companies*

Section 541 of the Code imposes a tax on the undistributed personal holding company income of every personal holding company. In general, personal holding company income consists of dividends, interest, rents and other passive income. Section 702 of the Code provides, in general, that the character of any item of income, gain, loss, deduction or credit included in a partner's pro-rata share shall be determined as if such item were realized directly from the source from which realized by the partnership. Therefore, it appears that the rental income expected to be received by the Partnership will, in at least some cases, constitute personal holding company income to the Limited Partners.

A corporation will be classified as a personal holding company (unless it qualifies under one of eight exceptions specified in Section 542(c) of the Code) if at least sixty percent of its adjusted ordinary gross income is personal holding company income and more than fifty percent of the value of the corporation's stock is owned, directly or indirectly, by five or fewer individuals at any time during the last half of any tax year. The rental income expected to be received by the Partnership may be sufficient to cause a Limited Partner to be classified as a personal holding company.

V. *Other Tax Aspects*

In addition to the Federal income tax consequences described above, prospective investors should consider potential state and local tax consequences of an investment in the Partnership. A Limited Partner's distributive share of the taxable income or loss of the Partnership generally will be required to be included in determining his reportable income for state or local tax purposes in the jurisdiction in which he is a resident. In addition, New York, and possibly other states in which the Partnership may do business or own properties, imposes a tax on nonresident partners determined with reference to their pro rata share of partnership income derived from such state. However, any tax losses incurred by the Partnership from operations in such states may be available to offset income from other sources within the same state. To the extent that a nonresident Limited Partner pays tax to a state by virtue of Partnership operations within that state, he may be entitled to a deduction or credit against tax owned to his state of residence with respect to the same income. In addition, estate or inheritance taxes might be payable in such jurisdictions upon the death of a Limited Partner.

W. *Depreciation and Recapture*

Upon disposition (through sale or foreclosure) of the equipment, the entire gain on the sale will be taxed as ordinary income unless the sales proceeds exceed the original cost of the equipment. In that unlikely event, the excess may be subject to tax at capital gain rates.

Equipment leasing is a low-risk tax shelter which should be suitable for investors in most tax brackets.

CHAPTER FOUR

FARMING

Heretofore, investment of outside capital in agriculture has been handled mostly by a few well informed investors. They were interested in profit and the tax shelter aspects of agriculture.

Now, agriculture is big business, and many investment programs are offered appealing to all types of investors. Dairy pools offer ordinary income. Fruit and nut orchards can produce capital gains. Beef cattle can convert ordinary income to capital gain or defer ordinary tax from one year to the next. Ranch land can be held for future capital gains. Row crop farming can provide income and tax shelter benefits.

There are many ways of investing in agriculture: Limited partnerships, common stock in agricultural corporations, contracts with management firms, services of brokers, and direct access to the rancher or farmer. Regardless of the direction the investor takes, he should obtain expert counsel before investing. Is it a good investment and is it a good investment for him are two questions which must always be answered.

Five aspects of of farming will be explored: Tree crops, vineyards, cattle breeding, cattle feeding, and chickens and eggs. (Timber will be discussed in a later section.)

SECTION ONE: CROPS

Various types of crops such as grapes; potatoes, carrots and other vegetable crops; almonds; oranges and lemons; cotton, sugar beets and other field crops; figs; pistachios; and walnuts are being offered for public investment. The most interesting programs are those which give the investor an opportunity to participate in the appreciation, if any, of the land on which the crops are grown. To the present time, most of the crop programs offered have involved tree crops, and for that reason tree crops (along with wine) have been selected as the programs for discussion.

TREE CROPS

The principal investment goals of a crop program are as follow: (1) the limited partner investor will receive a substantial tax write-off in the initial year, (2) the property will generate good income from the sale of agricultural products in subsequent years and, (3) the value of the property may increase in value because the partnership will purchase immature groves at a much lower price than that commanded by mature producing groves.

Losses on farming operations are generally deductible. However, individuals whose nonfarm adjusted gross income is in excess of $50,000 will be required to treat future long-term capital gains from farm properties as ordinary income to the extent of farm losses exceeding $25,000 in each year of the farm operation. No additions to an excess deductions account need be made for net farm losses sustained in any taxable year beginning after December 31, 1975.

The 1976 Tax Reform Act requires farming syndicates to capitalize the costs of planting, cultivating, maintaining and developing a grove, orchard or vineyard which are incurred prior to the year the grove, orchard or vineyard becomes productive.

EXAMPLE OF A TREE CROP PROGRAM

Yankee Company offers an attractive farming investment for the taxpayer who desires a high first-year tax write-off, income from the sale of agricultural products in future years, and potential, future capital gain from the sale of real estate.

Yankee Company is a public offering of $4,200,000 of limited partnership interests in nut, citrus, and other fruit groves and grape vineyards being farmed in the United States. The company is managed by Zelda Management Corp., a wholly-owned subsidiary of Albert Corp. It offers to high Federal tax-bracket investors a means of acquiring on a highly leveraged basis, with substantially tax-deductible dollars, a equity interest in agricultural properties, a substantial portion of which is already in commercial production, with both income and capital appreciation potentials.

Yankee was organized to acquire and farm approximately 2,500 acres of nut, citrus and mixed fruit groves and grape vineyards. All but a few acres of the properties, most of which are required for service buildings and other fixed improvements, are presently planted. Approximately 40% of the properties have presently producing groves, with the remaining acreage expected to begin commercial production over the next four years and to reach full mature production over the next eleven years.

The properties involved are 21 noncontiguous acreages, spread across two counties, with a diversified blend of 14 crops which, to a degree, reduce some of the risks of adverse weather, marketing and other conditions.

Zelda Management Corp. is the sole general partner of the Company. Through it Albert will provide overall supervision of the farming operations and the financial support necessary to maintain and develop the properties to their maximum productivity. To accomplish this, Zelda, which is capitalized at $4,200,000, is obligated to make capital contributions equal to the aggregate amounts contributed by the limited partners, or a minimum of $3,000,000 and a maximum of $4,200,000, as they may be needed to conduct the operations of the Company. If operating losses are incurred beyond those anticipated, Zelda then would make capital contributions or loans to the Company, and the limited partners would receive their proportionate share of the additional operating loss deductions. If crop revenues during the early operating years fail to achieve the cash flow necessary to meet fixed obligations and expenses, Zelda would have an annual exposure of more than $3,000,000 to such operating losses. In exchange for this supervision and support, Zelda receives an annual management fee of $25 per acre. Zelda will share in profits of the Company to the extent of 10% plus that percentage which the cash contributed by Zelda to the capital of the Company bears to the total of all cash contributed to the capital by both Zelda and the limited partners. Zelda, as the General Partner, is limited, however, to a maximum 45% interest in future earnings. Zelda may also purchase up to 20% of the units being offered and thus, to the extent of units so purchased, may participate in future earnings as a limited partner.

The offering will consist of 420 Units of Limited Partnership interests, at $10,000 per Unit, and requires the purchase of a minimum of one Unit for $10,000. Additional investment may be tailored to the investors' tax situation in multiples of $10,000 single Unit purchases.

It is believed that the limited partners will be able to deduct from ordinary income against Federal and, where applicable, State income taxes approximately 140% of their total investment over a period of approximately three years, amounting to deductions of an estimated $14.042 per each $10,000 minimum investment. It is possible that additional operating losses might be incurred, as described above, which would be funded by Zelda. In such a situation the tax benefit of up to one-half of those losses would be passed through the Company to the limited partners for their utilization as deductions from ordinary income, thus raising the total amount of estimated available deductions.

For the first year these deductions will consist of depreciation; prepaid interest; a financing fee; a majority of the prepaid farming expenses; and prepaid property taxes and miscellaneous expenses. In future years, with the exception of the financing fee and first year bonus depreciation the same items of deductions will apply plus deduction of the current portion of the farming expenses and the annual management fee.

Under the Tax Reform Act of 1976 investors will be limited to deducting losses from amounts they have at risk in farming operations except those involving trees other than fruit or nut trees. The Revenue Act of 1978 extends the specific at risk rule to all activities except real estate and certain equipment leasing activities of closely held corporations.

232

The deductions applicable to a $10,000 minimum investment for the first year are as follows:

Prepaid Interest	$ 2,408	
Financing Fee	1,506	
Prepaid Farming Fee	1,870	
Prepaid Property Taxes and Miscellaneous	224	
Depreciation	1,020	
Estimated Total First Year Deductions	$ 7,028	70%
Estimated Total Second Year Deductions	4,214	112%
Estimated Total Third Year Deductions	1,844	131%
Estimated Total Fourth Year Deductions	956	140%
Estimated Total Deductions	$14,042	140%

It should be borne in mind that should any of the deductions for prepayments be disallowed in one year, they would be carried forward as deductions in the next year.

Approximately 40% of the Yankee property has currently bearing mature or nearly mature trees and vines. It is believed that substantially all of Yankee's properties will have trees and vines producing crops by the fourth year and should reach the first years of peak production on 90% of the properties by the seventh year and 100% by the eleventh year. The peak producing lives of the trees and vines range from 25 years to in excess of 40 years. Cash flow from crop revenues is expected to exceed operating expenses and capital requirements in the fourth year and should continue to increase until all trees reach maturity.

It is not expected that any public market will develop for limited partnership interests in Yankee Company. A limited partner may assign his partnership interest, or any Unit of it, as a gift to members of his immediate family or to a charitable organization. A limited partner may not otherwise assign his interest before first offering such interest to the Company on the same terms as the contemplated assignment and the Company has rejected such offer.

Based upon the minimum projections, the limited partners' after tax cost by the third year for a $10,000 investment will be approximately $3,000.

$14,042	Total Write-off by third year
50%	Tax Bracket
$ 7,020	Tax Savings

$10,000	Total Investment
7,020	Tax Savings
$ 2,978	After Tax Investment

Based upon the minimum projections, the limited partners' after tax cost by the third year for a $10,000 investment will be approximately $3,000.

There is a known appreciation factor in land since a fully mature producing grove is worth approximately double that of a newly planted grove. Only approximately 40% of the land is in mature production. Each $10,000 investment has an undivided equity interest in the entire 2,500 acres, equivalent to a net equity interest of 5.95 acres per $10,000 investment.

In ten years a $10,000 investor could experience the following increase in land equity and possible appreciation:

Cumulative increase in equity in land due to principal payments on mortgage	$ 8,278
Possible appreciation of land value above cost at 5% per year compounded	11,536
Ten year total	$19,814
Cumulative increase in equity in land due to principal payments on mortgage	$ 8,278
Possible appreciation of land value above cost at 10% per year compounded	$30,096
Ten year total	$38,374

It is estimated that in ten years a $10,000 investor will receive total taxable income of $8,254. If he gives his investment to a low-bracket family member in the fourth year, more of the income will be retained and less paid in taxes.

Tree crops, particularly when the investor can participate in the appreciation, if any, of the real estate on which the crops are grown, is an interesting tax shelter. It is anticipated that more agricultural public programs will be offered in the future for investors desiring tax shelters of this type.

WINE PROGRAMS

Interests in vineyards, heretofore, have been sold in small, private offerings. Now public programs are beginning to appear, particularly those dealing with California wine. For that reason, the wine program selected for discussion below concerns California wine.

The investor in wine programs can benefit from tax write-offs, income from the sale of grapes, and potential, future capital gains from the sale of real estate on which the grapes are grown.

BACKGROUND ON CALIFORNIA WINES

A description of the California wine business provides essential background information for understanding this tax shelter.

The better California table wines are produced from the European wine species, Vitis vinifera, which was originally planted in California in the mid-nineteenth century. In North America, Vitis vinifera has been cultivated primarily in California. Vines generally mature in about seven years and under proper care may have a productive life in excess of 30 years. The growing of different varieties may reduce harvesting pressures in that varieties ripen at different rates and, in addition, may provide a hedge on market demands from year to year.

Most California wineries which maintain their own vineyards also use grapes purchased from other sources. Wine grapes are generally sold prior to harvesting and shipped to the buyer when harvested.

Climatic conditions are considered the most important factor in the production of wine grapes. Quality wine grapes generally grow in moderate climate zones. The better table wine grapes are grown in the cooler wine growing regions, where slow ripening tends to retain in the grapes levels of sugar, acidity and coloring which in fermentation develop the bouquet and flavoring of the better table wines. The method derived by viticulturists of the University of California at Davis and now generally accepted for classifying wine grape growing regions in California, is to calculate heat summation, or the average annual number of "degree days" above 50°F. during the growing season, from April 1 to October 31. For example, if the mean temperature over a five day period were 70°F., the heat summation would be 100 degrees days (70-50=20; 20 x 5 = 100).

California wine growing regions have been divided into Regions I through V, in ascending number of degree days, Region I being the coolest and Region V the warmest. Generally, wine grapes produced in Regions I-III would be considered premium table wine grapes, with Regions I and II most likely to produce grapes from which the better premium table wines are made. The warmer Regions IV and V normally produce grapes for standard table wines, and also produce the sweeter dessert wine grapes. Because of weather variations from year to year, a particular area does not always produce the same quality of grapes.

In addition to overall heat summation, other climatic factors affect wine grapes. Frost during the April-October growing period can cause severe damage. Excessive heat at harvest time may detrimentally affect the physical condition of the fruit as well as the chemical composition of the crushed grapes. Other weather excesses such as rain, wind and fog during the growing period may impair the production and quality of grapes.

Wine is made through the fermentation of crushed grapes, a process involving the transformation into alcohol of some or all of the grape's sugar. Wines are classifed as either sparkling (such as champagne) or still. Still wines are further classified into aperitif, dessert, flavored and table wines, primarily on the basis of their sugar and alcohol content. Table wines generally have a lower sugar and alcohol content than other still wines.

California table wines are classed as either "generic" or "varietal." Generic wines are generally made from a blend of several grape varieties and bear a proprietary name or name of the European prototype which the wine is thought by the vinter to most resemble. Examples of generic table wines are wines labeled as burgundy, chianti, chablis or wine. Varietal wines bear the name of the grape variety from which the wine is principally or exclusively produced. Varietal wines may be a blend, but the named grape must be the source of not less than 51% of the volume of a varietal wine.

California table wines and grapes are further categorized as "standard" or "premium" quality. Standard wine grapes are generally grown in the inland Central Valley and in Southern California. Premium grapes generally are grown in the cooler, coastal wine growing regions of California. Most premium wine grapes are used in the making of varietal table wines. Substantial quantities of raisin and table grapes are also crushed, generally for use in the standard quality wines.

EXAMPLE OF A WINE PROGRAM

Betty Vineyards is a partnership formed to acquire up to 4,000 acres of land in California for the purpose of planting and harvesting wine grapes. The land is not presently planted with wine grapes. The partnership intends to produce and market premium wine grapes and does not presently intend to operate a winery.

Partnership annual profits and losses will be allocated between the limited partners and the General Partner as follows:

1. All profits from operations equal to a six percent annual cumulative return on the limited partners' aggregate Memorandum Investment Account (An account maintained for each limited partner which will reflect each limited partner's original contribution to capital, decreased by cash distributions attributable to proceeds from the sale or refinancing of Partnership fixed assets) will be allocated solely among the limited partners; any remaining profits will be allocated 75% to the limited partners and 25% to the General Partner. The limited partners will bear all annual operating losses of the Partnership, it being intended that the limited partners receive 100% of the operating loss tax deductions anticipated during the development stage of the Partnership's vineyards.

2. Gains and the distribution of proceeds from any refinancing, sale or liquidation of any Partnership assets will be allocated solely to the limited partners until such cumulative allocations total 100% of the limited partners' initial invested capital plus any amount not received on their six percent cumulative annual return, after which such gains and distributions will be allocated 75% to the limited partners and 25% to the General Partner.

3. There will be distribution annually of available cash generated by operations and realized on the disposition or refinancing of assets, except funds which the General Partner

determines to retain as a reserve for anticipated expenditures, including debt service, and to maintain a sound financial condition. It is anticipated that there will not be any distributions of property other than cash.

4. Each limited partner will share in the profits and losses and distributions allocated to the limited partners as a whole in the proportion that his Memorandum Investment Account bears to the total of such accounts of all the limited partners.

The Limited Partnership Units are $1,000 per Unit with a minimum investment of ten Units or $10,000.

The Partnership is to continue until December 31, 2020, but may be dissoved earlier by determination of a majority in interest of the limited partners, and as otherwise provided in the Partnership Agreement.

A limited partner may not withdraw from the Partnership prior to dissolution, and may assign Units only with the prior written consent of the General Partner. Upon the death, incompetency or dissolution of the limited partner, his representatives shall have the rights and obligations of a limited partner for purposes of settling his estate; and such representatives or their assignee may become a limited partner with the consent of the General Partner.

The Partnership will file an annual information income tax return based on the cash method of accounting and utilizing a calendar fiscal year, but will not be subject, as an entity, to the payment of federal income tax. On his personal federal income tax return each limited partner will be required to report and pay income tax on his share of Partnership income or loss without regard to the amount, if any, of distributions made to him. After the Partnership's vines reach commercial production, it is anticipated that cash will become available for distribution to the limited partners; however, distributions, if any, may be less than the limited partner's share of Partnership taxable income and may even be less than the income tax payable thereon. To the extent, if any, that for any year distributions are made which exceed the Partnership's taxable income (whether in liquidation or otherwise), the amount of such excess would be treated as a return of capital reducing the tax basis of the limited partner in his Units. Any such cash distributions in excess of taxable income which exceed the recipient's basis are treated as a sale or exchange of Units resulting in taxable income to the recipient. On his federal income tax return, the limited partner may deduct his share of Partnership losses, if any, to the extent of the tax basis in his Units.

A limited partner's tax basis for his Units is, initially, the cost of the Units plus the limited partner's pro rata portion of Partnership liabilities with respect to which no partner (general or limited) is personally liable. In addition, the basis is increased by the limited partner's proportionate share of the Partnership's annual taxable income and decreased by his proportionate share of the annual Partnership's losses and the distributions for each year.

In preparing its informational income return, the Partnership generally will elect to deduct all cash expenditures to the extent permitted by the Internal Revenue Code. The Partnership will file an election under Section 175 of the Internal Revenue Code to deduct, rather than capitalize, those expenses attributable to soil or water conservation or to the prevention of erosion. The deductibility by each limited partner of his pro rata portion of such expenses is limited, however, in any one year to 25% of the limited partner's gross income from farming for that year. To the extent that the limited partner's pro rata portion of such expenses exceeds 25% of his gross income from farming (from the Partnership or otherwise), such excess may be carried forward to future years. The Partnership will also elect, pursuant to Section 180 of the Internal Revenue Code, to deduct all expenditures for the purchase or acquisition of fertilizer and similar materials used to enrich, neutralize or condition land for farming.

The Partnership intends to elect to utilize, to the extent possible, the class life method of determining the useful lives of its depreciable assets and intends to use the following useful lives for such assets.

Asset	Useful Life
Structures	10
Sprinkler system	
Exposed portion	8
Undergound portion	20
Wells and reservoir liners	20
Pumps	8
Vines, including planting costs	30
Stakes, posts and wires	8

The Partnership intends to use maximum available rates in depreciating its assets. Present law permits the first user of depreciable tangible personal property to use the 200% declining balance method of depreciation. To the extent that the Partnership is not the first user of such tangible personal property, the Partnership may use the 150% declining balance method. New real property may be depreciated under the 150% declining balance method and used real property must be depreciated on the straight-line method.

The Partnership does not intend to make an election under Section 754 of the Internal Revenue Code. Therefore, on the transfer of Units there will be no adjustment to the transferee's pro-rata portion of the tax cost basis of Partnership assets.

The following table sets forth the approximate deductions estimated to accrue to the limited partners for the first four years. In addition to these deductions, the Partnership anticipates that investment tax credits, discussed below, aggregating approximately $50 per Unit will accrue to the limited partners during that four year period. The Partnership must sell a minimum of 5,750 Units but can sell a maximum of 7,000 Units.

Loss Deduction Per $1,000 Unit

Year	Minimum (5.750 Units)	Maximum (7.000 Units)
One	$ 248	$ 245
Two	369	373
Three	455	447
Four	237	252
Total	$1,309	$1,317

In calculating the estimated loss deductions as set forth above, the Partnership has included as present deductible expenses annual prepaid interest on indebtedness incurred to finance the operations of the Partnership, annual prepaid management fees and the prepayment of fertilizer and similar materials.

The 1976 Tax Reform Act requires a cash method taxpayer to deduct prepaid interest over the period of the loan to the extent that the interest represents the cost of using the borrowed funds during each such period. This new rule conforms the deductibility of prepaid interest by a cash method taxpayer to the present rule for interest prepayments by an accrual method taxpayer. This rule applies to all cash method taxpayers including individuals, corporations, estates and trusts, and covers interest paid for personal, business or investment purposes. This rule also applies to prepaid interest on an indebtedness secured by a "wraparound" mortgage. No assurance can be given that items included in the calculation of estimated losses will not be challenged by the Internal Revenue Service. Disallowance of a deduction claimed by the Partnership may lead to an audit by the Internal Revenue Service of the individual returns of each limited partner.

In addition to the estimated losses set forth above, the Partnership anticipates purchasing property which qualifies for the investment tax credit. A credit of 7% of the cost of new (and limited quantities of used) depreciable property which has a useful life of seven years or more is allowed in the year in which the property is placed in service or use. For the Partnership's vines, "use" does not commence until the year that grapes are first produced. The amount of such credit is reduced in the event the useful life of the qualifying property is less than seven years. Under currently applicable regulations, the investment tax credits available to the Partnership each year are to be allocated between the limited partners and the General Partner in the ratio that they share Partnership profits and losses. During years that the Partnership incurs a net loss, anticipated at least through the fourth year, the entire loss and, therefore, all the credits would be allocable solely to the limited partners.

BENEFITS OF A CROP PROGRAM

1. A large portion of the property cost can be allocated to producing trees or vines and irrigation facilities and depreciated over their useful life.

2. If the land is sold for home or industrial development, the unamortized grove or vine costs can be deducted against ordinary income as an abandonment loss. The profit is attributable to the land only and is usually a capital gain.

3. Crop land tends to rise in value because of population growth and the fact that there is only a limited amount of land that can be developed economically.

RISKS OF A CROP PROGRAM

1. The development and operation of nut, citrus and fruit groves and grape vineyards is subject to substantial risks. A purchaser should realize that the full development of such groves and vineyards takes several years and that there can be no assurance that the groves and vineyards will be commercially profitable.

2. Adverse weather conditions can retard the development and operation of the groves and vineyards and in some cases destroy them. Frosts, freezing temperatures and wide variations in temperatures are harmful to all crops and particularly to citrus production. Other temperature variations can cause the regreening of certain citrus fruits resulting in poorer quality and yields. Excessive rainfall or windstorms, particularly when trees are blooming, or severe high temperatures for an extended period of time can also damage crops.

3. Because of the low average rainfall in many areas of production, crops are often dependent on water wells and water delivery and irrigation systems on private property, and Federal, State and local water districts and projects to provide sufficient water to maintain the development of the groves and vineyards. Insects, blight, and diseases can subject the groves, vineyards and crops to serious damage; and, although pesticides have reduced losses from these causes, they have not eliminated this risk. Further, an improper application of such pesticides can result in damage to the crops. Moreover, proposed Federal and existing State legislation may restrict future use of certain of the more effective pesticides.

4. Agricultural production may be adversely affected by labor unrest.

5. Development and caretaking costs for all crops increase with the age of the plants. In addition, future demand for the crops may be adversely affected by various economic and social changes. Crop prices may fluctuate widely from year to year and crop production in excess of market demand can depress selling prices. Harvesting, marketing, storage and other

operating costs are subject to escalation due to inflationary factors. Furthermore, the bearing acreage of many of the crops to be produced may be increased substantially in the near future.

6. Because only a limited number of Units are sold in each offering, and because of the limited transferability of Units, it is not expected that any significant public market will develop for units. Accordingly, an investment in units cannot be expected to be readily liquidated.

TAX ASPECTS OF A CROP PROGRAM

1. Unlike many limited partnership ventures, it is anticipated that after a Partnership's crops reach commercial production, revenues will not be offset by substantial depreciation or other "non-cash" tax deductions; and cash available for distribution to the limited partners would not be expected to exceed, and may well be less than, Partnership profits taxable to the limited partners. In addition, the periods for which Partnership profits are distributed and the periods for which income tax thereon is payable by the limited partners may not coincide. Proposed legislation has been introduced in Congress which, if enacted, would significantly reduce the tax benefits expected to inure from an investment in a crop Partnership. Relevant income taxation principles are also subject to change from time to time by administrative action or judicial decision.

2. On the sale at a gain of depreciable personal property, or depreciable real property held for more than one year with respect to which accelerated depreciation or soil and water conservation expenditures have been taken (within ten years preceding the sale), part or all of such gain may be taxable at ordinary income rates. Similarly, if depreciable real property is sold within one year after acquisition, part or all of the gain may be taxable at ordinary income rates even if straight-line depreciation has been taken. Otherwise, gain on the sale of real property not held primarily for sale to customers in the ordinary course of the Partnership's trade or business will be reportable as capital gain. So long as a Partnership's land is utilized for farming, it will not be considered property held primarily for sale to customers in the ordinary course of the Partnership's trade or business.

However, the method of disposition, including the number of sales entered into by a Partnership, may affect the determination of whether the gain will be taxable as ordinary income or as capital gain.

In the event any property with respect to which the investment tax credit has been taken is sold within seven years and prior to the expiration of the useful life utilized in determining the amount of credit taken, a portion, or all, of such investment credit will be recaptured, increasing the amount of tax payable that year by each limited partner.

The foreclosure of Partnership property upon default of secured financial obligations may result in taxable income to a Partnership, depending on the face amount of the liabilities being satisfied, the fair market value of the property and the basis of the property in the hands of the Partnership. The nature of the gain will depend upon the type of property being foreclosed and the method by which the foreclosure is effected.

3. In the event of a sale or transfer of Units during the year, Partnership profits and losses allocable to the Units transferred for the year of the transfer will be divided among the seller and buyer based on the number of days during the year that each was the holder of the Units. However, in making distributions a Partnership will look only to the limited partner of record as of the last day of the year. Thus, a limited partner who sells Units during the taxable year may be required to report a share of Partnership income even though he receives no portion of the Partnership's cash distribution, if any, for the year; it will be the responsibility of the seller and buyer to make their own adjustments.

On the sale of Units, gain is realized in the amount of the excess of the sale proceeds plus the seller's pro rata portion of Partnership liabilities over the seller's basis in the Units. Gain on the sale of Units held the required months will be long term capital gain, except that the portion of the proceeds of sale attributable to the seller's share of a Partnership's (a) unrealized receivables (including the gain on Partnership properties which if sold by the Partnership would be subject to depreciation recapture), (b) inventory items which have substantially appreciated in value and (c) soil and water conservation expenditures within the prior ten years, will be taxed at ordinary income rates.

4. Under prior law, there were two "at risk" rules designed to prevent a taxpayer from deducting losses in excess of his actual economic investment in the activity involved. The first of these at risk rules—"the specific at risk rule"—applied to four specified activities: (1) farming; (2) exploring for, or exploiting, oil and natural gas resources; (3) holding, producing, or distributing motion picture films or video tapes; and (4) leasing of personal property. The other at risk rule—"the partnership at risk rule"—applied generally to activities engaged in through partnerships. However, there were two exceptions to this rule. First, the rule did not apply to any activity to the extent that the specific at risk rule applied. Second, the rule did not apply to any partnership the principal activity of which was investing in real property (other than mineral property).

The Revenue Act of 1978 extends the specific at risk rule to all activities except real estate (and certain equipment leasing activities of closely-held corporations, as discussed below). For the newly covered activities, the specific at risk rule covers activities which are a part of a trade or business or are engaged in for the production of income. Separate rules for aggregation and separation of activities are provided for the activities to which the at risk rule is extended by the Act. The holding of real property (other than mineral property) is to be treated as a separate activity, and the at risk rule is not applied to losses from that activity. For purposes of this exclusion, personal property and services which are incidental to making real property available as living accommodations are to be treated as part of the activity of holding the real property. Since all the activities currently covered by the partnership at risk rules would now be covered by the new expanded version of the specific at risk rules under section 465, the partnership at risk rule is repealed by the Act.

This provision is effective for taxable years beginning after December 31, 1978.

Under prior law, the only corporations to which the specific at risk rule applied were subchapter S corporations and personal holding companies. The Act extends the application of this rule to all corporations in which five or fewer individuals own more than 50 percent of the corporation's stock. However, the equipment leasing activities of a closely held corporation are not to be subject to the at risk rule if the corporation is actively engaged in equipment leasing, that is, if 50 percent or more of the corporation's gross receipts is derived from equipment leasing. This provision is effective for taxable years beginning after December 31, 1978.

Under prior law, the at risk rule under section 465 may have been interpreted to only require the taxpayer to be at risk as of the end of the taxable year for which losses were claimed. Under this interpretation, subsequent withdrawals of amounts originally placed at risk could be made without the recapture of previously allowed losses.

In order to be consistent with the original intent of the at risk rule, the Act requires the recapture of previously allowed losses when the amount at risk is reduced below zero. Mechanically, this rule works by providing that if the amount at risk is reduced below zero (by distributions to the taxpayer, by changes in the status of indebtedness from recourse to nonrecourse, by the commencement of a guarantee or other similar arrangement which affects the taxpayer's risk of loss, or otherwise), the taxpayer will recognize income to the extent that his at risk basis is reduced below zero. However, the amount recaptured is limited to the excess of the losses previously allowed and which reduced the taxpayer's at risk basis in that activity for taxable years beginning after December 31, 1978, over any amounts previously recaptured. A suspended deduction in the amount equal to the amount of recaptured income would be provided to the taxpayer. This suspended deduction would be allowed in a subsequent year if and to the extent the taxpayer's at risk basis is increased. The provision is generally effective for taxable years beginning after December 31, 1978.

5. The 1976 Tax Reform Act provides that no additions to an excess deductions account need be made for net farm losses sustained in any taxable year beginning after December 31, 1975. In addition, the conference agreement allows divisive "D" reorganizations without triggering EDA recapture. In these reorganizations, the entire EDA account is applied to both corporations. This latter provision applies to reorganizations after December 31, 1975.

6. The 1976 Tax Reform Act requires farming syndicates (1) to deduct expenses for feed, seed, fertilizer, and other farm supplies only when used or consumed (not when paid); (2) to capitalize costs of poultry; and (3) to capitalize the costs of planting, cultivating, maintaining and developing a grove, orchard or vineyard which are incurred prior to the year the grove, orchard or vineyard becomes productive.

The definition of "farming syndicate" includes (1) a partnership or any other enterprise (except a corporation which has not elected to be taxed under subchapter S) engaged in the trade or business of farming if at any time interests in the partnership or other enterprise are offered for sale in an offering required to be registered with any Federal or State agency having authority to regulate the offering of securities for sale or (2) the partnership or any other enterprise (other than a non-subchapter S corporation) engaged in the trade or business of farming if more than 35 percent of the losses during any period are allocable to limited partners or limited entrepreneurs. In general, a limited entrepreneur means a person who has an interest in an enterprise other than a partnership and who does not actively participate in the management of the enterprise.

For purposes of the farming syndicate rules, activities involving the growing or raising of trees are not considered farming unless the activities involve fruit or nut trees. Thus, this provision does not apply to forestry or the growing of timber (or to nursery operations involving the growing of trees).

The provisions of the 1976 Tax Reform Act relating to prepaid feed and other farm supplies and poultry expenses apply generally to amounts paid or incurred after December 31, 1975. In the case of farming syndicates in existence on December 31, 1975, (but only with respect to taxpayers who are members of the syndicate on such date), the provisions apply to amounts paid or incurred after December 31, 1976. The provisions relating to orchards, groves and vineyards do not apply where the trees or vines were planted or purchased for planting prior to December 31, 1975, or where there was a binding contract to purchase the trees or vines in effect on December 31, 1975.

7. With certain exceptions, the Tax Reform Act of 1976 required corporations (and partnerships in which nonexcepted corporations are partners) engaged in farming to use an accrual method of accounting and to capitalize preproductive period expenses. However, subchapter S corporations, family corporations (in which one family owns at least 50 percent of the stock), corporations with annual gross receipts of $1 million or less, and nurseries are not required to use the accrual method of accounting or to capitalize preproductive period expenses.

The 1976 Act provisions generally are effective for taxable years beginning after December 31, 1976. However, the Tax

Reduction and Simplification Act of 1977 postponed the effective date of the required accrual accounting provision until taxable years beginning after December 31, 1977, for certain farming corporations controlled by two or three families.

The Revenue Act of 1978 provides exceptions to the required accrual accounting and capitalization of preproductive period expense rules for certain corporations which are controlled by two or three families. The provisions requiring accrual accounting and the capitalization of preproductive period expenses will not apply to any farm corporation if, as of October 4, 1976, and at all times thereafter, either (1) two families own (directly or through attribution) at least 65 percent of the total combined voting power of all classes of stock of the corporation entitled to vote and at least 65 percent of the total number of shares of all other classes of stock of the corporation, or (2) (a) members of three families own (directly or through attribution) at least 50 percent of the total combined voting power of all classes of stock entitled to vote and at least 50 percent of the total number of shares of all other classes of stock and (b) substantially all of the remaining stock is owned by corporate employees, their family members, or a tax-exempt employees' trust for the benefit of the corporation's employees.

The Act also provides that, with respect to corporations described in the preceding paragraph, stock acquired after October 4, 1976, by the corporation's employees, their families, or a tax-exempt trust for their benefit will be treated as owned by one of the two or three families whose combined stock ownership was used to establish the initial qualification for this provision (as of October 4, 1976). The provision requires that corporations must have been engaged in the trade or business of farming on October 4, 1976, and at all times thereafter, to qualify for this exception.

This provision applies to taxable years beginning after December 31, 1977.

Prior to 1976, farmers, nurserymen, and florists were not required to inventory growing crops regardless of the method of accounting they used for income tax purposes. However, in 1976 the Internal Revenue Service ruled that an accrual method farmer, nurseryman, or florist would be required to inventory growing crops. The changes made by this ruling are to be for taxable years beginning on or after January 1, 1978.

Under present law, corporations and partnerships (in which nonexcepted corporations are partners) engaged in farming are required to use the accrual method of accounting and to capitalize preproductive period expenses (sec. 447). However, subchapter S corporations, family corporations (in which one family owns at least 50 percent of the stock), corporations with annual gross receipts of $1 million or less, and nurseries are not required to use the accrual method of accounting or to capitalize preproductive period expenses. In general, the requirement that preproductive period expenses be capitalized would have the effect of requiring taxpayers to inventory (or capitalize) the costs of growing crops.

The Revenue Act of 1978 permits a farmer, nurseryman, or florist who is on an accrual method of accounting and is not required by section 447 of the Code to capitalize preproductive period expenses to be exempt from the requirement that growing crops be inventoried. The term growing crops does not include trees grown for lumber, pulp, or other nonlife purposes.

The Act also allows those farmers, nurserymen, or florists who are eligible to use an accrual method of accounting without inventorying growing crops to elect, without the prior approval of the Internal Revenue Service, to change to the cash receipts and disbursements method of accounting with respect to any trade or business in which the principal activity is growing crops. If such an election is made, it will be treated as a change in method of accounting initiated by the taxpayer. This election may be initiated only with respect to a taxable year beginning after December 31, 1977, and before January 1, 1981.

With certain exceptions, the Tax Reform Act of 1976 required corporations (and partnerships in which nonexcepted corporations are partners) engaged in farming to use an accrual method of accounting and to capitalize preproductive period expenses. However, subchapter S corporations, family corporations (in which one family owns at least 50 percent of the stock), corporations with annual gross receipts of $1 million or less, and nurseries are not required to use the accrual method of accounting or to capitalize preproductive period expenses.

In addition to the exceptions to the accrual method of accounting and capitalization of preproductive period expenses provided under section 351 of the Act, sod farms are also excepted from these rules. The provision excepting sod farms is effective for taxable years beginning after December 31, 1976.

8. The 1976 Tax Reform Act increases the rate of the minimum tax on individuals from 10 percent to 15 percent. An exemption is provided equal to the greater of $10,000 or one-half of regular income taxes. The carryover of regular taxes that are not used to offset tax preferences in the current year is eliminated.

The Revenue Act of 1978 retains the present law minimum tax with respect to all preference items except capital gains and excess itemized deductions. The Act provides for an alternative minimum tax which is payable by an individual to the extent that the alternative tax exceeds the regular income tax increased by the amount of the existing minimum tax, as revised, on preference items other than capital gains and itemized deductions.

The alternative minimum tax base is the sum of an individual's taxable income, adjusted itemized deductions, and the capital gains deduction.

The following rates are imposed on this amount:

	Percent
$0-$20,000	0
$20,000-$60,000	10
$60,000-$100,000	20
Over $100,000	25

The foreign tax credit and refundable credits are the only tax credits which are allowed against any alternative minimum tax liability.

Publicly offered crop programs will be more numerous as farms become more expensive to operate and more public money is required. Crop programs are a medium risk tax shelter similar to cattle breeding. Cattle feeding is a lower risk, and eggs represent a higher risk. These other programs are discussed in the following sections.

SECTION TWO: CATTLE

Dr. Herrell DeGraff, a keen student of livestock economics, told the audience at the American National Cattlemen's Association the "cows-to-people ratio now is at one of the lowest points in history." He painted a bullish picture of the potential for growth in the beef industry, noting that by 1980 we could need as much as 7 billion pounds more beef than the 22 billion pounds we now produce. He bases that on the assumption that the nation's population could grow to 235 million persons and the per capita consumption may expand to as much as 130 pounds of beef per person if the beef is available. This, he said, potentially calls for 12 million more cows in the beef herd by 1980.

Beef has enjoyed a fabulous market experience in the last 15 years, with consumption per capita increasing by 50% while keeping only 5% more cows. The increase has come through a 5% increase in the calving rate, the shift to beef cows out of dairy cows, the halt in killing of calves for veal, and the coming of the big feedlots. No doubt there is plenty of growth ahead in the beef market. But it will need to be nurtured carefully. Without some planning and thought to the needs of matching supply with growing demand, temporary "bust" situations could easily develop. Cattlemen and those thinking about cattlemen must study their lessons, as Dr. DeGraff put it, if the big growth potential is to be accomplished smoothly.

GENERAL CONSIDERATIONS

The beef cattle industry is divided into five categories — seed stock producers, commercial breeders, feed lot operators, processors and retailers. Seed stock producers, whether purebred or hybrid breeders, initiate genetic improvement by supplying bulls, replacement females and semen for use by other purebred and commercial breeders. The commercial breeders use the approved seed stock to produce feeder cattle which are sold to feed lot operators where they are fed to market weight, and sold to meat packers for processing and sale to retailers and ultimately the consumer.

251

The three traditional domestic breeds of beef cattle are Angus, Hereford and Shorthorn. Recently, exotic breeds such as Charolais, Limousin and Simmenthal have been used for crossbreeding, where cattle of different breeds are mated to achieve predetermined results depending upon the breeders' objectives. By the application of scientific selection processes and crossbreeding, a breeder attempts to produce cattle possessing predictable and inheritable traits such as higher rate of weight gain in terminal cross steers and exceptional mothering ability in first cross heifer calves. Such offspring generally command premium prices from other purebred and commercial breeders who wish to increase the productive characteristics of their herds.

Beef is the biggest single product of the agriculture industry, and the cow herd is the source of production. The two main investor programs available are cattle breeding and cattle feeding. These programs are discussed further below and two examples included which relate to breeding and feeding. Example one is an installment breeding program. Example two is a lump sum investment in both cattle breeding and cattle feeding.

CATTLE FEEDING PROGRAMS

Cattle feeding can be profitable. If an investor buys and sells cattle on a feeding program each month for three years, he may earn an annual return as high as 20% on equity invested. Such a long-term program is preferred in order to level out the fluctuations in cattle prices.

Today two-thirds of cattle slaughtered in the United States are grain fed on feedlots. Feeder cattle, weighing from 400 to 800 pounds and from 6 months to 18 months old, are purchased from commercial cattle breeders or at public auction markets and shipped to feedlots where they are fed for the next 4 to 8 months. They reach a finished condition when they weigh from 950 to 1,150 pounds and are then ready to be sold as slaughter cattle.

Cattle prices fluctuate as much as 5% per day and may experience as much as a 30% change over one year. This means that substantial sums of money can be made or lost by the short-term investor.

FEEDLOT OPERATOR

It is very significant that the feedlot operator be highly capable and have a pattern of success. He must keep good records to know which cattle gain the most weight at the lowest cost and then buy that kind in the future, hopefully, at the right price.

Cattle should be fed well, properly housed, given good medical care, placed in a favorable climate, and sold as soon as finished. Waiting for a higher market often creates a greater loss. Good operators who routinely produce animals having carcasses yielding a better than average percentage of dressed meat are usually paid a premium even in adverse markets. A high yield would result in 63% to 64% dressed meat.

TAX FACTORS

Cattle feeding investments offer the investor the advantages of potentially high profits and the deferral of income from one year to the next or ensuing years. The investor can invest just once in a short-term program or in a long-term continuous feeding program. Usually the investor puts up one-third of the cost of the program and the remainder is financed providing leverage which makes it possible to deduct about 70% to 100% of the investor's "expense" in the year the investment is made. This is governed, however, by the time of year the program begins, since an investment made too early in the year may result in income that will offset some or all of the expenses. May is generally a good month in which to start a program.

Upon investing in the feeding program the investor becomes a farmer and is entitled to use the cash basis of bookkeeping. The 1976 Tax Reform Act requires farming syndicates (1) to deduct expenses for feed, seed, fertilizer, and other farm supplies only when used or consumed (not when paid). The cost of the cattle is not deductible. In the following year, after the cattle are sold, the investor will repay his loan and subtract his cost and additional expenses from the gross sale proceeds. The balance is ordinary income to him. If he reinvests this ordinary income in another feeding program, he will defer the income for still an additional year. He can keep repeating this process of deferring income until he reaches a point in time where his other income is lower.

INVESTMENT STRATEGY

If an investor will invest for 3 years or more, the speculative risk, associated with fluctuating cattle prices, is diminished considerably, and he should derive a reasonable return. Some loads of cattle will probably lose money, but the investor generally should make money on most loads. If he buys and sells cattle each month after 6 to 8 months, he has the advantage of dollar-cost-averaging. Also, he may wish to reinvest the income from slaughtered cattle into more permanent tax shelters such as real estate.

CATTLE BREEDING PROGRAMS

There are two types of cattle breeding programs. In the most typical case, the investor, purchases commercial beef cows which raise male calves for slaughter and female calves (heifers) to increase the breeding herd. From time to time, the herd is culled and the cows and heifers are bred and the bulls sold. The other type of program involves a purebred herd of a major beef brand. These cows are higher priced, and there is an effort to improve the breed through genetic upgrading.

Management expenses are immediately deductible, and there is depreciation on the purchased cows which can later be sold on a capital gains basis. The breeding programs usually last from 5 to 10 years in order for the investor to achieve maximum tax benefits. Only the original purchased herd can be depreciated; and, after 5 years most of the depreciation has been consumed. Cattle acquired after 1969 must be held two years in order to obtain capital gains on their sale.

The conference agreement provides that no additions to an excess deductions account need be made for net farm losses sustained in any taxable year beginning after December 31, 1975. If there is a balance in the account at the time the cattle are sold, it converts a capital gain to ordinary income.

Any depreciation on the cattle taken after 1969 must be reported as ordinary income to the extent of the profit on the livestock when sold.

The following examples illustrate the points made above. The first example describes cattle breeding, and the second example describes a combined program of cattle breeding and feeding.

EXAMPLE ONE: CATTLE BREEDING

Common Breeding Systems is a limited partnership which acquired cattle of various breeds including purebred Black Angus, Charolais, recorded and recordable Angus, Charolais, Limousin, Semmenthal and other crossbred and commercial animals.

Since the U.S.'s per capita consumption of meat has been growing rapidly, farmers and ranchers have been increasing the numbers of their herds and changing their genetic composition in order to meet this increased demand. Since a cattle herd continuously requires new sources of genetic material in order to increase productivity, Common intends to supply beef producers with better animals.

Common will serve as a seed stock source of cattle for purebred and commercial breeders by raising and selling to them a variety of breeds and strains of cattle. To this end, it acquired the above Breeding Herd. Emphasis will be placed upon the breeding and sale of performance and progeny tested purebred and cross bred cattle. The success of the program will be substantially dependent upon experience in using scientific breeding techniques.

To a certain extent, Common will be engaged in commercial breeding resulting from natural mating and the substantial number of commercial animals required to progeny test prospective herd sires. In addition, steer progeny from these commercial test animals will be fed for slaughter in order to obtain performance and carcass data.

Common intends to make use of artificial insemination, identification procedures, computerized recordkeeping and performance and progeny testing in all phases of its operations.

The offering is $10,000,000 – 400 units at $25,000 per unit, payable $2,500 upon subscription and $2,500 at 6 month intervals thereafter. The investor is committed on a recourse basis for the initial and five installment payments or a total of $15,000 per unit purchased. In example two, a program is described in which the investor pays for his interest in a lump sum as distinguished from the installment payment program.

The General Partner will be capitalized with cash equal to 10% of the dollar value of the Limited Partners' units. Thus, the General Partner would be capitalized at $1 million if all 400 units are sold.

The General Partner will receive an annual fee of 3% of Partnership Value (total assets of Common without reduction for indebtedness).

Common's cattle operations are managed by Dorothy Management Company which has an exceptional reputation as a breeder of Black Angus cattle. Dorothy has had considerable experience with other breeds and with the cross-breeding program of Common. Unlike most public cattle programs, Dorothy manages investor herds with its own employees and uses facilities which are either owned by it or leased under long-term arrangements. Dorothy will operate Common's cattle for costs plus 6% for all cattle except registered Black Angus. For registered Black Angus, Common will pay Dorothy $500 per cow unit (cow, or cow plus calf to age 7 months) less an amount equal to $500 times at least 80% of all bull calves born to the registered Angus – the said bull calves to be purchased by Dorothy for that amount.

Under the 1969 Tax Reform Act, an individual engaged in farming may deduct his farm losses from other income. However, if his annual farm loss exceeds $25,000 and his adjusted gross income exceeds $50,000, he must maintain an Excess Deduction Account ("EDA"). If there is a balance in his EDA when cattle are sold, income which would ordinarily have been treated as capital gains will, to the extent of the balance in the EDA, be treated as ordinary income.

Based upon current projections for Common, it is expected that a Limited Partner who acquires one unit will recognize approximately $10,000 of deductible losses per annum for each $5,000 of cash contributed, or a total of $50,000 in losses over the 5 year investment period. Although the anticipated $50,000 loss is twice the $25,000 per unit investment, the tax law permits the deductions since a Limited Partner's cost basis for his unit is increased by his pro-rated share of Common's borrowings, which are anticipated at approximately $25,000 per unit. A Limited Partner can deduct only the amount of money he has at risk.

Assuming that a Limited Partner has no other farming ventures, the EDA account will not become a factor in computing a partner's income. Thus, to the extent Common has capital gains during any year of its operations, such gains will, except for "depreciation recapture," be treated as capital gains by the Limited Partner.

After three years, a Limited Partner may elect to sell his interest to the General Partner who has an option to purchase such interest at 60% in the third year, 70% in the fourth year, 80% in the fifth year, 90% in the sixth year and 95% thereafter of Adjusted Partnership Value (Partnership Value reduced by a Limited Partner's share of Common's debt). Purchases may, at the option of the General Partner, be for cash or 25% in cash plus a 5 year self-amortizing note with interest at the prime New York bank rate.

No income distributions are contemplated before the sixth year and only to a limited extent then with the objective of providing cash flow to the limited partner to help pay taxes on partnership income.

The partnership shall continue for ten years, unless dissolved earlier. It may continue after ten years at a general partner's option except 50% of limited partnership units may vote to terminate.

The purchaser of a unit in Common should be an individual who has current earnings of at least $5,000 over the 50% tax bracket and who reasonably expects to continue to earn income at that rate during the 5 year period of his subscription. If those prerequisites are met, and assuming that the Common Breeding Systems 5 year projections are realized, this purchaser would have an after-tax cost on his Unit of zero dollars at the end of 5 years. Although it is difficult to predict the value of one unit at the end of 5 years, assuming that cattle values continue at present rates, one unit should be worth at least between $20,000 and $25,000 at the end of 5 years – an impressive profit. Compare two individuals, each of whom is in a 50% tax bracket.

	First Man	Second Man
Income:	$50,000	50,000
Annual Investment in Common	5,000	0
Projected Annual Tax Deduction	10,000	0
Taxable Income	40,000	50,000
Taxes Paid (approx.)	20,000	25,000
Net After Taxes	25,000	25,000
	and an investment in Common of $5,000	

Cattle breeding is an interesting tax shelter for an investor desiring high tax write-offs and potential, future capital gains from the sale of cattle.

EXAMPLE TWO: COMBINED CATTLE BREEDING AND FEEDING

This tax shelter is a program featuring cattle breeding and feeding, and is advantageous for the investor in that he can obtain a high first-year tax write-off from the feeding part and potential, future capital gains from the breeding part.

This is an unusual example in that cattle breeding and feeding are combined together. Also, most cattle breeding programs involve installment payments by the investor instead of the lump sum payment described below. However, all of the usual benefits, risks and tax considerations associated with separate feeding programs are described.

Edith Cattle Systems is a limited partnership whose primary purpose is to upbreed an initial herd of cattle and to sell these cattle as seedstock to other breeders. The Partnership will also engage in the feeding of commercial cattle.

Faith Cattle Management Company is the General Partner and Georgina Corporation maintains the herd; both are subsidiaries of Helen Corporation which will "guarantee" the Partnership's ability to obtain the loan for the necessary leverage to generate a 200% first-year deduction.

The offering amount is as follows: Maximum – $5,000,000 consisting of 2000 units of limited partnership interests at

$2,500 per unit; Minimum – $1,000,000 or 400 units.

The minimum investment is $5,000 and is available in increments of $2,500 thereafter.

The management and cost compensation is as follows:

1. The initial herd owned by Georgina will be sold to the Partnership at a substantial mark-up from cost basis, although the final price will be determined by independent appraisals.

2. All male progeny produced by the herd will belong to Georgina.

3. Georgina will receive a cash breeding fee of $50 per year for each female bred during the year, starting in the second year.

4. Georgina will receive commissions upon sales from the Herd (5% of the gross sales price of all cattle sold).

5. When the Partnership is dissolved, Georgina will receive 20% of the net proceeds after the limited partners have recovered their cash investments.

6. Faith will receive a fee for managing the Partnership ($2.50 per month for each female animal, excluding Feeders, 7 months or older).

7. Faith will receive a fee for managing the Feeder Program ($4.00 per head for each Feeder delivered to a Feed Lot, and $2.00 per head for each Feeder sold for slaughter).

There will be a 200% first-year deduction if the Limiter Partner is liable on partnership borrowings.

The Limited Partner has the following liquidity opportunities:

1. Beginning in the third year, General Partner will purchase Limited Partner's interests at 60% of Adjusted Partnership Value (APV), 70% of APV for the fourth year, 80% of APV for the fifth year, 90% of APV for the sixth year, and 95% of APV thereafter. Limited Partner must request repurchase no later than September of a given year, and payments will be made by October 31.

2. The General Partner will repurchase interests of deceased Limited Partners at 100% APV less sales commissions and any prior distributions.

3. The Limited Partner may assign his interest to a third party with written consent from the General Partner.

4. The Partnership is scheduled to dissolve after 10 years.

An investor who does avail himself of the "liquidity feature option" anytime during the first 5-6 years would probably not receive sufficient cash from the liquidation to cover income taxes. The basic reasons for this are: first, the recapture on accelerated depreciation deductions would be high in these years; and, second, the managing partner is, in effect, discouraging early withdrawal by returning only part of the actual partnership value. However, in the event of the death of a limited partner, the general partner will return 100% of the partnership value.

The primary objective of the Partnership is to build a breeding herd which can be eventually sold off in large part at capital gains rates. Secondarily, the program designers wanted to create a first-year 200% tax deduction for Limited Partners and also be able to handle investments on a one-shot basis (instead of spread over a five-year period). To accomplish these objectives, the program designers have established what is, in effect, a feeder "sub-program".

Therefore, in order to obtain the desired $10 million loss in the first year (assuming $5 million of investments), they first calculated the deductions from the breeding herd which approximate $700,000. This leaves the necessity for creating an additional $9.3 million in deductible items from the feeder business — and these deductions will be established through borrowings and purchase of feed and payment of interest and management expenses.

In the second year, the Partnership will recognize a substantial amount of taxable income by selling the feeder animals acquired during the first year. From this income, they will first deduct the losses generated by the breeding herd in the second year of approximately $1.7 million. The remainder of the taxable income (about $10.3 million) must be deferred into the third year through the same mechanics utilized in the first year.

Through the balance of the Partnership, which would terminate in the tenth year, the income from feeder cattle will decline, since each year they reduce that income by losses generated through the breeding herd's deductions for depreciation, management fees and interest.

Assuming the total $5 million offering is sold out, the program will operate as follows:

1. The Partnership will borrow $4 million to purchase the three breeding herds from Georgina. The first-year installment

payment is $400,000, and the loan will be collateralized by the animals in the initial herd and their progeny.

2. The Partnership will use the remaining $4.6 million of equity for investment in feeder cattle and feed. However, to obtain the necessary leverage to create the 200% first-year deduction, the Partnership will borrow an additional $5.7 million on an unsecured basis, guaranteed by Helen Corporation. With this loan, the Partnership will have a total of $10.3 million for investment in feed and feeders.

3. It is a standard practice in the cattle-feeding business to put down 30% of equity and to borrow 70% from the feed-lot operator or his bank. On this basis, the partnership will obtain an additional $17.7 million in borrowings secured by the feeder cattle.

4. Next year, the net taxable income (from the sale of fattened cattle) will be reinvested in feed and feeders, thus deferring taxes for another year. Approximately 90% will be reinvested in feeders. This mechanism will continue, and the investment in the feeder operation will shrink, and the investment in the breeding operation will increase.

5. Assuming the investor is in the 50% income tax bracket and pays the 35% tax rate on capital gains, the operators show the following net cash gains per $2500 unit:

Sixth year — $950 net gain per $2500 unit
Seventh year — $1126 net gain per $2500 unit
Eighth year — $1451 net gain per $2500 unit
Tenth year — $3082 net gain per $2500 unit

Projections are that the feeding operation will break even over the 9-year period. This depends upon cattle and feed prices, efficiency of management, weather, etc. On the breeding side, the breeding business seems to be changing from emphasis on purebred cattle to more emphasis on crossbreeds. Whether the Partnership will be successful in producing marketable breeders is impossible to predict.

Assuming the feeding operation does break even, the assumptions as to the prices obtainable for cull cows, yearling heifers, and mature cows could drop by some 40% and still return a small profit to limited partners. This is a comfortable margin. If the price assumptions on fattened cattle, cull cows, yearling heifers, and mature cows all dropped more than 5¼%, no profit would be available. This is not a comfortable margin and points out the effects of the high leveraging. Being as pessimistic as possible and assuming that the herd sale in the tenth year produced just enough cash to pay off loans with nothing left to distribute to limited partners, the investor would have to pay income taxes of $992 for each $2500 unit.

Assuming no changes in tax laws, the investor will have a zero net investment. There is a reasonable chance that a return from this investment during Years 6 through 10 will exceed the investor's tax liabilities during this period so that he will actually receive a net return after taxes, although this is by no means assured.

The fees are competitive with those in other feeding and breeding programs. The General Partner does have an incentive to operate profitably and meet projections through the "20% of net proceeds after cash investments have been returned to limited partners" arrangement. Although this could result in a $1.5 million return to Georgina after 10 years if projections are met, this represents a fairly small percentage of gross income to Georgina. Georgina's largest return comes from the value of male progeny.

Some cattle funds expand upon Common's program by offering an integrated cattle business combining cattle breeding and cattle feeding with ranch ownership. These funds provide two tax shelter benefits: deferral of current income, and, long term capital gains. Historically, ownership of ranch land has been a rewarding investment, especially where there is a present return on the land while holding it for appreciation.

The type of program selected should reflect carefully developed investment goals.

BENEFITS OF A CATTLE FUND

1. Cattle are usually bred in the summer or fall so that the calf crop will drop in warm weather. Ordinarily a calf crop of 75 percent to 95 percent can be anticipated. Subsequent to the weaning of the calves, the steers are sold and the heifers are kept to enlarge the breeding herd. The new heifers are usually bred when they are two years old. Certain animals are culled from the breeding herd and sold at capital gain rates if the animals are kept longer than twenty-four months. When

steers are sold, the result is ordinary income. The cycle of a breeding herd investment is approximately five to seven years. The costs to raise the animals should have been deducted currently. If the investor has held his annual farm losses under $25,000 the sale of the raised breeding animals will be at capital gain rates. If his Excess Deduction Account has increased over the years, his capital gain will be diminished accordingly. Profit on the sale of purchased breeding animals will be recaptured as ordinary income to the extent of depreciation claimed.

2. Deferral of tax can be accomplished by current deductions to a cash basis taxpayer for expenses necessary to raise and care for animals. Beef feeding programs are able to take advantage of these deductions and provide upwards of 200% first-year tax write-off.

3. For a taxpayer filing a joint return, there is a 20 percent first-year depreciation allowance on the first $20,000 cost of a breeding herd. Accelerated (150%) depreciation is available on the remaining cost of breeders together with the 7 percent investment credit (when available).

RISKS OF A CATTLE FUND

1. Investments in Partnerships should be made only by persons who are in a position to benefit from the tax treatment available to limited partnership investments in the beef cattle business and able to assume the risks inherent in that business. The offering is suitable primarily for investors in high Federal income tax brackets. Moreover, the investment should be judged apart from tax considerations.

2. There is no market for most Units and it is unlikely that any will develop in the future. Often Units are not assignable without the consent of the General Partner.

3. Although Partnerships will seek to reduce the risks inherent in their business, breeding cattle operations will be subject to the following risks, among others: price fluctuations; the ability to sell substantial numbers of animals at favorable prices; conception rates; Calf Crop Percentage; government regulations; disease factors; and the impact of climatic conditions. The Feeder Program will be subject to the following risks, among others: feeder cattle could be purchased when cattle prices, in general, are high, and the

operator might have to sell fattened cattle when prices are low; disease, natural catastrophes and climatic conditions affect feeding operations; the cost of feed could increase substantially; and feed lot charges and interest rates on the necessary borrowings could increase. There can be no assurance that Feeders will be acquired or sold at prices which will produce a profit.

4. To the extent that Partnerships may have undistributed net income which is not offset by Federal income tax deductions (generated through Feeder Programs, breeding cattle operations or otherwise), Limited Partners will be required to report their distributive share of Partnership income on their personal income tax returns even though they may receive no cash distributions from the Partnership.

5. Cattle are usually not insured against loss.

6. A Partnership may borrow substantial funds to finance the purchase of cattle and feed and may engage in hedging transactions, both of which may substantially increase risks to the Partnership.

7. The various aspects of the cattle business in which the Partnership is or may be engaged are highly competitive.

TAX ASPECTS OF A CATTLE FUND

The present tax law creates certain incentives for persons engaging in the cattle and livestock business. By virtue of such incentives, it may be possible for such persons to (i) defer income tax liability to later taxable years, (ii) "convert" ordinary income into capital gains and (iii) reduce current tax liability through the use of investment tax credits.

The Tax Reform Act of 1976 ("Tax Reform Act") limits many of the tax benefits heretofore available to those persons engaging in the cattle business. In particular, certain provisions of the Tax Reform Act made specifically applicable to "farming syndicates" are more restrictive and the Partnership proposed herein will be a "farming syndicate." The discussion in this section attempts to incorporate the provisions of the Tax Reform Act as they now exist. However, as it is a new law with few regulations, rulings or case history, interpretations of that law or changes to that law may change certain of the tax matters discussed herein. In addition, the Revenue Act of 1978 has recently been enacted which also has no regulations, rulings or case history which will leave that law subject to further interpretation. Furthermore, Congress may pass legislation that may reduce most or all of the incentives provided for persons engaged in the cattle or livestock business. (See "LEGISLATION"). In addition, the Revenue Act of 1978 has recently been enacted which also has no regulations, rulings, or case history which leave that law subject to further interpretation.

Tax deferral may be achieved by a taxpayer engaged in the business of farming who, by employing the "cash basis" method of accounting, may deduct some expenses in the year paid, though the income attributable to such expenses is not realized until a subsequent taxable year. However, the Tax Reform Act has placed a limitation upon the use of the "cash basis" method of accounting insofar as it applies to farming syndicates such as the Partnership. (See "Partnership in the Business of Farming" in this Section). "Conversion" of ordinary income into capital gains is possible where gains from sales of qualifying breeding animals are taxed at capital gains rates, though expenses incurred in maintaining and developing such animals had been previously deductible against ordinary income. In addition, investment tax credit with respect to qualifying investment property may be available as an offset against current tax liabilities.

The extent to which such incentives are available is significantly limited by various provisions of the Internal Revenue ("Code"), and administrative regulations and rulings thereunder and by the Tax Reform Act, particularly in the area of cattle feeding and the timing of deductions related to that activity. Moreover, if the General Partner has not requested a ruling from the IRS respecting any of the tax consequences of the Partnership, there is an inherent and substantial risk that such benefits might be challenged in whole or in part by the IRS. Such risk is materially increased by reason that direct authority is lacking in several areas here involved and certain of the tax incidents here discussed are under continuous IRS review.

Whether the aforesaid tax incentives will prove advantageous to a Limited Partner cannot be predicted as the effect of those benefits is dependent upon each Limited Partner's particular financial situation. Accordingly, each prospective investor is urged to consult his personal tax advisor.

The tax consequences to the Limited Partners are dependent upon whether the Partnership (1) is classified as a "partnership" (rather than as an "association") for tax purposes, (2) is deemed to be an activity "engaged in for profit" and (3) is allowed to use the "cash basis" method of accounting.

Classification as a "Partnership." Internal Revenue Regulation ("Reg.") Sec. 301.7701-3(b) provides that a limited partnership may be classified for tax purposes as a "partnership" or as an "association" (taxable as a corporation), depending upon whether it more closely resembles a general partnership or a corporation. Such classification is made irrespective of its designation under local law.

Although restrictive changes to the above cited Regulation were recently proposed and withdrawn by the IRS, there can be no assurance that subsequent changes may not be proposed that could result in the Partnership being classified as a corporation for tax purposes.

If a limited partnership is classified as a "partnership," then the partnership itself is disregarded as a taxable entity, and tax incidents of the partnership are passed through to the partners. Accordingly, the income, gains, deductions, losses and credits of the partnership are proportionately allocated to the partners for inclusion in their individual income tax returns. Cash distributions to a partner are taxable only to the extent that such distributions exceed his basis in the partnership.

If a limited partnership is classified as an "association," then the partnership is treated as a taxable entity subject to taxation as a corporation, and none of the tax incidents of the limited partnership would pass through to the partners. Accordingly, the income is taxed to the partnership when earned and the partners (in effect, shareholders) are taxed on partnership income only when it is distributed to them (in effect, as dividends) and partnership deductions, losses and credits are not includable in the partners' individual returns.

Treatment of the Partnership as a "partnership" is essential to the realization by the Limited Partners of the tax benefits anticipated.

Prospective investors should note that the IRS, in granting advance rulings, respecting the "partnership" status of a limited partnership, would impose, in addition to the foregoing conditions, the further condition that the aggregate deductions from the first two years of Partnership operations not exceed the initial cash investments of the Partners. Whether that further condition might be the basis for an IRS challenge to the "partnership" status of the Partnership cannot be predicted at this time. While, in the opinion of counsel, the Partnership could successfully defend such a challenge on such basis, the possibility of an IRS challenge and success cannot be predicted.

Partnership "Engaged in for Profit." During the early years of the Partnership, the annual expenses of the Partnership may exceed income therefrom. Resulting losses may cause the IRS to question the profit motive of the Partnership and the Limited Partners.

Where an activity is deemed not engaged in for profit, Code Sec. 183 provides that expenses in excess of gross income from such activity will not be deductible, though certain expenses which are deductible whether or not a taxpayer is engaged in a trade or business such as interest and taxes would remain fully deductible. Where, on the other hand, an activity is deemed to be engaged in for profit, all ordinary and necessary expenses from that activity (subject to the limitations of "basis" and "at risk" discussed below) would be deductible, even though such deductions would be in excess of gross income from that activity.

Code Sec. 183 creates a presumption that an activity is engaged in for profit if, in any two of five consecutive taxable years, the gross income derived from such activity exceeds the deductions attributable thereto. Thus, if an activity fails to show a profit in at least two out of five consecutive years, this presumption will not be available. In that instance, the possibility that the IRS could successfully challenge the deductions claimed from the activity would be substantially increased.

Counsel is of the opinion that the Partnership will be engaged in an activity for profit. However, since the intent of each Limited Partner is a factual question to be determined from the facts and circumstances in each instance, no opinion can be expressed as to whether Code Sec. 183 will apply in the case of any Limited Partner. No person should participate in the Partnership unless his objective is to secure an economic profit apart from tax advantages which may be derived by him. Each prospective investor should consult his own tax advisor regarding the impact of Code Sec. 183 upon his particular situation.

Partnership in the Business of Farming. Pursuant to Reg. Sec. 1.471-6(a) a taxpayer engaged in the business of farming may adopt the "cash basis" of accounting. However, the Tax Reform Act placed certain limitations on the utilization of the cash basis of accounting in that deductions of amounts paid for feed, seed, fertilizer or other similar farm supplies will be allowed only in the taxable year in which such feed, seed, fertilizer or other supplies are actually used or consumed. Deductions for prepaid interest have also been eliminated. (See "Tax Attributes of Cattle Feeding and Breeding" in this Section).

Where a partnership is deemed to be in the business of farming and thus eligible for the "cash basis" of accounting, certain tax advantages, such as the deferral of tax liability and the "conversion" of ordinary income into capital gains, are possible. Where, on the other hand, a partnership is deemed not to be in business of farming and thus ineligible for the "cash basis" of accounting (subject to the limitation mentioned above), such tax advantages are substantially eliminated.

If the Partnership is operated in the proper manner, the breeding and feeding of cattle by the Partnership for profit will in the opinion of counsel constitute farming for Federal income tax purposes, and the Partnership will thus be allowed to utilize the "cash basis" of accounting subject to the limitation as to prepayments of feed and interest discussed herein.

The Tax Reform Act placed a qualification on the use of the "cash basis" of accounting for a partnership engaged in the trade or business of farming, if a corporation is a partner in such partnership. In those circumstances, with certain exceptions, it is provided that the taxable income would be computed on an accrual method of accounting with the capitalization of preproductive expenses. However, the Tax Reform Act includes certain exceptions as to corporations and subsidiary corporations which are owned 50% or more by members of the same family which would make the accrual method inapplicable to a partnership that included that type of corporation.

TAXATION OF PARTNERSHIPS

General Principles. A partnership is not itself a taxable entity. The taxable income, gains, losses and credits of a partnership are ascribed to its partners, and must be allocably included by them in their respective individual returns. The character of partnership tax items (e.g., as ordinary income, capital gain, etc.) is "passed through" to the partners. The share of partnership tax items allocable to each partner is determined by the partnership agreement, unless such allocation does not have substantial economic effect.

In any year in which a partnership realizes taxable income, its partners are required to allocably include such income in their respective returns. Such inclusion is required irrespective of whether cash distributions had been received from the partnership during that year. Distributions will be made by the Partnership only when, in the opinion of the General Partner, the cash reserves of the Partnership are in excess of present or anticipated needs of the Partnership and to the extent permitted by financing arrangements. As a result, it is likely that in one or more Partnership years, the Partners will be required to pay taxes on Partnership income, though no distribution will have been received from the Partnership with which such taxes could be paid.

The "At Risk" Concept. The Tax Reform Act introduced the concept of "at risk" for any taxpayer engaged among other activities in the activity of farming. As it is proposed that the Partnership will be engaged in the activity of "farming," the "at risk" provisions included in the Tax Reform Act (as new Section 465 of the Code) provide limitations upon the losses that may be allowed to any taxpayer. The Tax Reform Act provides that a taxpayer shall be considered "at risk" for his farming activities with respect to the sum of (1) the amount of money that he has contributed to the Partnership and (2) the amounts which he has borrowed with respect to such farming activities. A Partner would be considered "at risk" with respect to amounts borrowed for use in the farming activity to the extent that he is personally liable for the repayments of amounts borrowed on behalf of the Partnership or to the extent that he has pledged property, other than property used in the farming activity, as security for such borrowed amounts to the extent of the fair market value of the pledged property. Under this provision, no property would be taken into account as security if the property is directly used in the activity. A taxpayer would not be considered "at risk" with respect to amounts protected against loss through nonrecourse financing, guarantees, stop loss agreements, or other similar arrangements.

As a result, a Limited Partner would be unable to deduct more than 100% of his cash investment in the Partnership unless the investor is "at risk" for additional sums of money. Inasmuch as the Partnership is anticipated to incur tax losses in excess of the amount invested by the Limited Partners during the first calendar year of operation, the "additional" losses cannot be deducted by any Limited Partner unless the Limited Partner is "at risk" for an additional amount of capital equal to his proportion of Partnership losses in excess of his cash investment. In this regard, the opportunity for the Limited Partners to become at risk for an additional amount by guaranteeing Partnership loans may be provided, so that most, if not all, of the estimated losses allocable to the Limited Partners may be deducted by them for tax purposes in the year incurred by the Partnership. However, this guarantee may only be offered in the future depending on borrowing arrangements and compliance with Regulation T and any other applicable rules or regulations. The opportunity to become "at risk" will be purely optional and only those Limited Partners desirous of deducting more than their investments would assume such risks. The assumption of risks by the Limited Partners will be evidenced by their guarantee of certain promissory notes to the Partnership's lender and Limited Partners desiring to guarantee such notes must recognize that they will be liable for the payment of those notes, if the Partnership is unable to repay the notes from operations. To the extent that Limited Partners paid such notes, the General Partner would not be liable to the lender for the repayment but may be liable to the Limited Partners for all or a portion of their repayment.

Although there are no proposed regulations, the IRS may assert that because the General Partner is jointly and severally liable for the debts of the Partnership, any Limited Partner who guarantees debt would have a right of contribution against the General Partner and therefore reduce his "at risk" position. The Revenue Act of 1978 includes a provision that for taxable years after December 31, 1978, a recapture of tax benefits previously attributed to the Limited Partner would be in effect to the extent that a Limited Partner's "at risk" position is reduced below zero.

In any year in which a partnership realizes a taxable loss, its partners may, subject first to the "at risk" rule, allocably include such loss in their respective returns. However, the amount of such loss includable by a partner is further limited to the amount of his basis in the partnership as of the close of such partnership year. To the extent that allocable losses exceed basis or the amount at risk, such losses are placed in a "suspense account," and may be utilized in any subsequent year in which, after giving effect to the partnership tax items for that year, the partner's basis exceeds zero and there is sufficient amount "at risk."

Concept of Basis. The concept of tax basis is central to the taxation of partnerships.

An initial distinction is made between the partnership's basis ("inside basis") in partnership property, and a partner's basis ("outside basis") in his partnership interests. "Inside basis" is, in general, the partnership's cost for partnership property. Such costs determine, among other things, the amount of gain or loss realized upon the disposition of those assets. As "inside basis" determines the measure of partnership tax items, it will affect the amount of income or loss allocable to a partner from disposition of partnership property. (For special adjustments to "inside basis," see "Sale or Exchange of Interest" in this Section.) "Outside basis," on the other hand, is, in effect, each partner's cost for his partnership interest. Such cost determines the amount of gain or loss a partner will realize upon disposition of his partnership interest (realized gain will equal the difference between the amount received and basis) upon cash distributions from the partnership (cash distributions will cause realized gain only after the partner's "outside basis" is zero), but in view of the Tax Reform Act will no longer solely determine the amount of partnership losses deductible by the partner.

A limited partner's "outside basis" is, in general (i) the amount of his cash investment in the partnership, plus (ii) his pro rata share of partnership "non-recourse" liabilities, plus (iii) his allocable share of partnership income, plus (iv) his guarantee of partnership obligations, minus (v) his allocable share of any partnership losses, minus (vi) the amount of any distributions (which concept includes his pro rata share of any repayment of partnership "non-recourse" liabilities) to him from the partnership.

"Non-recourse" liabilities are defined in Reg. Sec. 1.752-1(e) as partnership loans secured solely by the partnership assets, for which loans none of the partners (general or limited) has any personal liability. It is not anticipated that such financing will be available to the Partnership.

ALLOCATION OF PARTNERSHIP TAX ITEMS

Partnership taxable items are allocable to the partners in accordance with the partnership agreement, unless such allocation is determined not to have substantial economic effect in which case such items are to be allocated in accordance with a Partner's interest in the Partnership (taking into account all facts and circumstances). The key factor in such determination is whether the allocation has a "substantial economic effect" independent of tax consequences.

The Partnership Agreement provides, in general, that the income and losses of the Partnership are allocable to the Partners in proportion to their respective Net Cash Investments in the Partnership. The General Partner, however, as compensation for its management of the Partnership, will be entitled to a share of net income in addition to its share as determined by its Net Cash Investment. If any Limited Partners guarantee Partnership debt, losses in excess of the capital contributions of all Partners will first be allocated to those Limited Partners who guarantee such debt to the extent of such guarantee. Profits will then be allocated to those Limited Partners who guaranteed such debt in an amount equivalent to any loss taken in excess of their Capital Contributions. Such allocations will substantially affect the actual dollar receipts of the Partners and, therefore, should have substantial economic effect.

The Partnership Agreement provides in general that the sharing by the Partners in proportion to their Net Cash Investment will be determined by reference to their respective Net Cash Investments as they exist throughout the Partnership year. Such determination is subject to the provision included in the Tax Reform Act which provides that, when Partners enter at different times of the year or when interests are transferred, a Partner's distributive share of taxable items of income, loss and deduction shall be determined by taking into account such Partner's varying interests in the Partnership during the taxable year.

Sale or Exchange of Interest. The sale or exchange of a partnership interest may result in taxable gain or loss to the transferring partner. Any gain or loss will be the difference between the amount received for such interest (which may include the transferring partner's allocable share of any partnership "nonrecourse" financing for which he will be relieved) and the partner's basis (as discussed above) in the partnership at the time of sale.

The transferring partner's gain or loss may be capital or ordinary, or both. Gain realized will be taxable as ordinary income to the extent such gain is attributable to the seller's share of the partnership's "unrealized receivables" (including prior depreciation subject to "depreciation recapture," gain on all feeder cattle and gain on breeding cattle held less than 24 months and "excess farm deductions") and any "substantially appreciated inventory" ("Code Sec. 751 Items"). In addition, the seller will be taxed on his share of the partnership income, if any, to the date of sale. Any remaining gain or loss resulting from the sale will be capital gain or loss if the seller has held the partnership interest for more than 12 months.

The sale or exchange of a partnership interest may result in recapture of any investment tax credit previously claimed by the selling partner, to the extent that such sale or exchange occurs prior to the expiration of the useful life period estimated for the qualifying assets. (See "Investment Tax Credit" in this Section).

Upon the transfer of a partnership interest, the partnership may elect, pursuant to Code Sec. 754 and related sections, to make an optional adjustment to "inside basis" of partnership property for the purpose of determining the transferee partner's share of partnership tax items. If such election is made, the partnership basis for its property, only insofar as a transferee partner is concerned, will be adjusted to reflect the difference between such partner's cost for his partnership interest and his proportionate share of the partnership's "inside basis" for its property. Where the purchase price for the transferred interest is in excess of the seller's share of the "inside basis" in the partnership's property, such adjustment may be beneficial to the transferee partner. Contrarily, where the purchase price is less than such share of the partnership basis, an election may prove disadvantageous. An election is binding in the year made and in all subsequent partnership years. Whether the election has been made, depending upon circumstances, may reduce the ability of the Limited Partners to resell Partnership Interests. Whether such election is made for the Partnership will depend upon whether, in the judgment of the General Partner, such election would be beneficial to the majority of the Limited Partners.

Withdrawal. The withdrawal of a partner from the partnership, in complete liquidation of his interest, will, in general, be treated as a sale or exchange of a partnership interest. The amount and character of any gain or loss realized upon withdrawal will be determined as discussed above.

A variation from the "sale or exchange" treatment, by virtue of Code Sec. 731, is provided where the withdrawing partner receives property other than money in complete liquidation of his interest. In such event, realized gain is immediately recognized only to the extent that money distributed (including money constructively distributed as a result of being relieved of "non-recourse" liabilities) and to the extent that the withdrawing partner's share of "Code Sec. 751 Items," exceeds his basis ("outside basis") in the partnership. Realized gain with respect to property (other than money or to the extent of "Code Sec. 751 Items") received in complete liquidation is not recognized upon distribution, such recognition being deferred until the withdrawing partner disposes of such property. The withdrawing partner's basis in such property, pursuant to Code Sec. 732, is his adjusted basis ("outside basis") in the partnership immediately before such distribution, reduced by the amount of any money received and to the extent of his basis ("outside basis") in the partnership, taxable gain would result.

Dissolution of the Partnership. Upon termination of a partnership, the partnership property (or proceeds therefrom) will be allocably distributed to the partners pursuant to the partnership agreement. Should a partner, through such distribution, receive properties or be relieved of liabilities in excess of his basis ("outside basis") in the partnership, taxable gain would result.

A partnership is deemed terminated for tax purposes if (i) the partnership business is discontinued or (ii) within a twelve month period, there is a sale or exchange of 50% or more of the total interests in partnership capital and profits. In the event of a sale or exchange of 50% or more of such interests, the partnership will be deemed to have constructively distributed partnership property to the partners in their distributive shares. With respect to such constructive distribution, even if no gain is realized by the partners, certain tax disadvantages (in particular, the inability to use accelerated methods of depreciation and the recapture of tax credits) would result.

Pursuant to the Partnership Agreement, the Partnership will continue business for up to a basic seven year period, followed by a liquidation period of up to two years. The sale or exchange of Partnership Interests may be made only with the consent of the General Partner, and the General Partner, by the terms of the agreement, may not consent to any sale or exchange which would result in termination under Code Sec. 708.

ORGANIZATION AND SYNDICATION FEES

The fees for organization and syndication of a Partnership have to be capitalized under the Tax Reform Act. The Tax Reform Act provides certain exceptions for amortization of organization fees paid or incurred after December 31, 1976. These organization fees (as contrasted to syndication fees) could be amortized over a period of 60 months. Syndication fees will be deductible only upon partnership dissolution.

TAX ATTRIBUTES OF CATTLE FEEDING AND BREEDING

Following is a summary of the tax incidents normally experienced by a partner in a "partnership" engaged in the cattle business.

Deductions and Losses. A taxpayer engaged in the business of farming, electing the "cash basis" method of accounting, may deduct from gross income (from whatever source) the ordinary and necessary expenses incurred in the cattle business, subject to the limitations set out below. Additionally, deductions may be claimed for depreciation of purchased breeding animals. However, such deductions are subject in whole or in part, to "recapture" as ordinary income upon the sale of farm property and to the "at risk" rules. (See "Limitation on Capital Gains" and "The 'At Risk' Concept" in this Section).

Deductible Expenses. In employing the "cash basis" of accounting, a taxpayer may, except as discussed below, generally claim deductions for farming expenses in the year paid. The Tax Reform Act, has limited cash basis deductions for "farming syndicates." The Partnership contemplated hereunder to be formed would be classified as a "farming syndicate" under the Tax Reform Act. The Tax Reform Act provides that a deduction, otherwise allowable, for amounts paid for feed, seed, fertilizer, or other similar farm supplies shall be allowed only in the taxable year in which such feed, seed, fertilizer or other similar farm supplies shall be allowed only in the taxable year in which such feed, seed, fertilizer or other farm supplies are actually used or consumed, or, if later, in the taxable year for which an allowable deduction would otherwise occur. Accordingly, deductions heretofore available for feeding cattle, and in particular for feed consumed by said cattle, would be available only to the extent that such feed was actually consumed.

The Tax Reform Act further provides that for a taxpayer using the "cash basis" of accounting, interest paid that relates to a period after the close of the taxable year in which paid should be charged to the capital account and would be treated as paid for deduction purposes in the period to which it applies. Accordingly, there will be no deduction for prepaid interest beyond the close of the taxable year of the Partnership.

The General Partner, in managing the finances of the Partnership, will rely on competent tax advisors and will endeavor to adhere carefully to practices which permit Partnership deductions, when allowed by the new law. Nonetheless, because of the uncertainty of regulations and interpretations under the Tax Reform Act, there is no assurance that such practices will not be challenged by the IRS.

Depreciation. The purchase price of breeding animals is not deductible as such, but is subject to depreciation and deductible over the useful life of the animals. Depreciation may not be taken with respect to Partnership herd progeny, as the Partnership has no "cost basis" for such animals. Similarly, no depreciation is allowable with respect to feeder cattle which are purcahsed by the Partnership for resale, the cost basis of such being recovered upon that resale.

Any accelerated methods of depreciation may be used for depreciable animals not previously used for breeding purposes and having a useful life of three years or more. However, depreciation for "used" animals is limited to the "150% declining balance" or "straight line" methods. Regardless of method, depreciation may not be taken in excess of the salvage value of the animal. The General Partner may use the "200% declining balance" method for "new" animals purchased by the Partnership and the "150% declining balance" method for "used" animals so purchased.

The IRS recognizes a useful life range of from 5.5 to 8.5 years for breeding cattle. Within that range, depending upon the ages of animals purchased, a shorter or longer life may be used for depreciation purposes. A shorter useful life accelerates the depreciation deductions for the animals. However, the use of a life shorter than 7 years will reduce the available investment tax credit with respect to such animals (see below).

No average salvage value is recognized for breeding cattle. The General Partner will determine a reasonable salvage value based on the age of the livestock acquired, the anticipated replacement practices to be followed, and the estimated proceeds upon sale of the animals.

Depreciation on breeding animals is subject to recapture as ordinary income to the extent of actual gain on the disposition of the animals. (See "Limitations on Capital Gains" in this Section).

Investment Interest. Code Section 163(d) limits the amount of "investment interest" annually deductible by a taxpayer. The Tax Reform Act changed the limitations on amounts that could be deducted and also changed certain definitions as to the character of investment interest. Certain carryover rules are provided for interest incurred under a binding contract for pre-1976 interest. Generally, the Tax Reform Act now limits that amount of "investment interest" annually deductible by a taxpayer to $10,000 ($5,000 in the case of a separate return by a married individual), plus the taxpayer's net investment income. Certain additional amounts are allowed under special circumstances as provided in the Tax Reform Act. "Investment interest" is, in general, the interest paid or accrued on indebtedness incurred to purchase or carry property held for investment.

The applicability and effect of Code Section 163(d) will depend upon each Partner's particular financial position and will particularly depend on carryover rules provided in the Tax Reform Act. Prospective Investors are therefore advised to consult their tax advisors in this regard.

Investment Tax Credit. Breeding cattle qualify as "Section 38 Property" eligible for the investment tax credit. The amount of the credit depends on the useful life (for depreciation purposes) of each animal in the breeding herd. The Tax Reform Act extended the temporary increase in the size of the credit from 7% to 10% for herds acquired after January 21, 1975 and before January 1, 1981. The amount of the credit would be computed as follows:

Investment tax credit as
% of Herd Purchase Price

Useful Life	Purchased before January 22, 1975 or after Dec. 31, 1981	Purchased after January 21, 1975 and before Jan. 1, 1981
3-4 years	2 1/3%	3 1/3%
5-6 years	4 2/3%	6 2/3%
7 years or more	7%	10%

The credit, as so determined, is available in full with respect to each "new" animal.

For "used" animals there is a dollar limitation at both the Partnership and Partner level on the aggregate cost of animals for which the credit can be claimed. Under the Tax Reform Act for animals purchased after December 31, 1974 and before January 1, 1981, the aggregate cost may not exceed $100,000 (or, in the case of a married person filing a separate return, $50,000). For animals purchased after December 31, 1981, the aggregate cost may not exceed $50,000 (or, in the case of a married person filing a separate return, $25,000). For the purpose of the $50,000 or $100,000 limitation (or, in the case of a married person filing a separate return, $25,000 or $50,000) the cost of "used" cattle would have to be aggregated with the cost of other used property eligible for the investment credit which was acquired during the same taxable year. Therefore, some or all of the investment credit may be lost by a purchaser.

A partner may apply his allocable share of the investment tax credit against federal income tax otherwise owing subject to the following limitations: in any one year the maximum usable credit may not exceed $25,000 plus 50% of his tax liability in excess of $25,000, for the year 1978 and increasing at the rate of 10% per year thereafter until 1982 to a maximum of 90%. Credit not used in one year may be carried back three years or carried forward seven years. The Tax Reform Act includes a new concept of first-in, first-out in relation to unused credits. As with all other tax consequences of a breeding herd purchase, each purchaser should consult his own tax advisor concerning the availability and impact of the investment credit on his own tax situation.

Claimed investment credits are subject to recapture in whole or in part if the "qualified investment" is disposed of by the

Partnership, or the Limited Partner disposes of his Partnership Interest, before the expiration of the estimated useful life of the investment. While the General Partner will attempt to preserve the tax credits wherever possible, good breeding practices may require premature disposition of purchased animals and recapture of claimed tax credit.

Taxation of Gains. Partnership operations will result in ordinary gains and losses or capital gains and losses which will be allocably includable by the Limited Partners in their individual returns.

Sales from cattle feeding operations will result in ordinary income or loss to the Limited Partners.

Sales from cattle breeding operations will result in capital gains or losses, or ordinary income or losses, depending upon the nature of the animals sold and upon the applicability of certain deduction "recapture" provisions. Generally, sales of cattle owned for breeding purposes, if held for 24 months or more and not held primarily for sale to customers, will qualify under Code Sec. 1231 as capital gains or losses. Sales of cattle not satisfying such holding requirements will result in ordinary income or losses. Capital gains sales are expected to result from periodic sales of breeding animals and from final disposition of the breeding herds. Ordinary income sales may result from annual sales of calves and from sales of culled breeding animals not held for the requisite two year period.

Ordinary income and losses will be taxable to the Limited Partners at the regular income tax rates, as determined by each Limited Partner's individual tax bracket.

The Revenue Act of 1978 provides that the current maximum tax rate of 25% of the first $50,000 ($25,000 in the case of a married individual filing a separate return) of long-term capital gains for any one year for individuals after December 31, 1978 will be subject to the maximum long-term capital gains rate discussed below. Prior to the Revenue Act of 1978, individuals were allowed a deduction equal to 50% of their net long-term capital gains, resulting in a maximum regular income tax rate on such gains of 35%. The Revenue Act of 1978 increases the deduction to 60% of net long-term capital gains and thus reduces the maximum regular income tax rate on such gains to 28%. The 60% deduction, and thus the 28% rate, is effective for sales and exchanges occurring after October 31, 1978. Effective for taxable years beginning after December 31, 1978, individuals' deductions for net long-term capital gains and "excess itemized deductions" will no longer be items of tax preference subject to the "regular" 15% minimum tax. Effective for taxable years beginning after December 31, 1978, individuals will be subject to an "alternative minimum tax" which is payable only to the extent it exceeds the sum of their regular income tax liability and "regular" minimum tax liability. The "alternative minimum tax" is imposed on the sum of (1) the taxpayer's adjusted gross income, or gross income minus deductions, plus (2) the sum of (a) the taxpayer's deductions for net long-term capital gains and (b) his excess itemized deductions (generally itemized deductions in excess of 60% of adjusted gross income reduced by medical and casualty deductions, state and local taxes, and estate taxes which are deductible in computing income in respect of a decedent) in excess of the taxpayer's regular income tax and "regular minimum tax liability for the year (the "excess") at the following rates: (a) 0% on the first $20,000 of the "excess," (b) 10% on the "excess" in excess of $20,000 up to $60,000, (c) 20% on the "excess" in excess of $60,000 up to $100,000, plus (d) 25% on the "excess" in excess of $100,000. Deductions for net long-term capital gains realized after October 31, 1978 (i.e., the 60% deduction) will no longer reduce the availability of the maximum tax on personal service income of individuals.

Limitations on Capital Gains. The benefits of capital gains treatment are limited by "minimum tax," certain provisions of the maximum tax and "deduction recapture" provisions of the Code.

The Tax Reform Act substantially modified the provisions relating to the "minimum tax." A minimum tax of 15% is imposed on the amount by which "tax preferences" exceed $10,000 or one-half of the taxpayer's regular tax liability, whichever is greater. Such tax is payable in addition to the taxes otherwise payable without reference to the minimum tax calculations. "Tax preferences" include excess of accelerated depreciation on real property over straight line depreciation, excess of accelerated depreciation on personal property subject to a lease over straight line depreciation, the excess of percentage depletion over the basis of the property, the bargain element of stock options, itemized deductions (other than medical and casualty deductions) in excess of 60% of adjusted gross income, and intangible drilling costs in excess of the amount deductible if capitalized and written off over 10 years. The Tax Reform Act eliminated the provision relating to the carryover of unused regular taxes.

Certain "deduction recapture" provisions may require inclusion of gains otherwise taxable as capital gains or ordinary income.

Tax preference items (whether or not subject to minimum tax) also reduce the amount of income with respect to which a taxpayer may claim the maximum tax dollar for dollar.

"Depreciation recapture" is required by Code Sec. 1245 whereunder the amount realized from the sale of depreciable assets (such as purchased breeding cattle) will be taxable as ordinary income to the extent that such amount exceeds the "adjusted basis" for the asset. "Adjusted basis" is, in general, the purchase price of an asset less claimed depreciated deductions thereon. To the extent that depreciation methods do not accord with economic realities, such recapture will be required.

Under the Tax Reform Act, further additions to the Excess Deductions Account required by Code Sec. 1251 have been eliminated.

LEGISLATION

The tax consequences discussed herein can be affected by any change in the tax laws which may result from legislation, judicial decision or administrative interpretation. Congress is constantly considering proposals which would adversely affect some of those tax consequences.

The discussion contained in this Section includes the legislative enactments provided by the Tax Reform Act of 1976 and the Revenue Act of 1978 which are major revisions of existing tax laws. As these are new laws, there are at this time no court decisions, few administrative regulations, or rulings relating to the application of the new laws and they will be subject to interpretation over a period of time. The interpretations as imposed by the Internal Revenue Service may differ from the discussions included in this Section.

The tax consequences discussed herein could further be affected by further changes in the tax laws which may result from legislation, judicial decision or administrative interpretation.

STATE TAXATION

The Partnership will conduct operations in several states, some of which impose state income taxes with respect to operations conducted in the state. Accordingly, Partnership income will be subject to taxation in those states which do impose a state income tax. A Partner may also be subject to income tax in his state of residence.

Generally, only income attributable to the income taxing state is taxable thereby, and duplicative taxation is substantially avoided. In general, business income attributable to the taxing state is determined by the percentage of the partnership's (a) property located in that state, (b) compensation paid for services performed in that state, and (c) sales in that state. Greater or lesser percentages are applicable to income derived from property located within or without the taxing state. In general, income from sales of partnership property located outside the taxing state will not be subject to that state's taxation, but will be subject to taxation by the state wherein located, if that state should impose income taxation.

TAX RETURNS AND AUDITS

The General Partner will arrange for the preparation and filing of all necessary federal tax returns for the Partnership, and will furnish all necessary instructions and information to the Limited Partners concerning their allocable shares of Partnership tax items for the preparation of their individual income tax returns. The Partnership will elect to employ the cash basis of accounting and will report its income on a calendar year basis.

The Revenue Act of 1978 extended the period of time during which a deficiency may be assessed against any partnership with interests registered with the Securities and Exchange Commission to four years.

The IRS has informally stated that the informational returns of all "tax shelter" partnerships will be audited annually. If a Partner's individual return is audited, he will bear the expense in responding to that audit, and the resulting adjustments of such audit may relate to non-Partnership, as well as Partnership, tax items.

Cattle programs are somewhat conservative in that cattle breeding is considered a medium risk tax shelter and cattle feeding one of relatively low risk.

The future should see a fairly steady stream of cattle programs as the consumption of beef per capita continues to rise in the United States.

DEFINITIONS CONCERNING THE CATTLE
BUSINESS IN GENERAL

ANGUS: Breed of beef cattle that are black and hornless. Known and regarded for their carcass quality and feed efficiency and disease resistance. Early maturing.

ARTIFICIAL INSEMINATION: The introduction of semen into a cow's reproductive tract with a syringe by a trained technician. Semen is periodically collected from bulls and stored in a frozen state.

BLOAT: A digestive disorder resulting from excess gas in the stomach.

BRANGUS: A breed of beef cattle that are black and polled. This breed is a pure cross between a registered Angus (5/8) and registered Brahman (3/8).

BRED: The impregnated condition of a female which has been mated.

BRED YEARLING: A female yearling that has been bred.

BREED: Cattle with certain distinguishing characteristics fixed by generations of selective breeding and transmittable to successive generations.

BULL: A male bovine animal of any age.

BULL CALF: A male progeny of the Herd prior to 12 months of age and which has not been castrated.

CALF: A male or female bovine animal under one year of age.

CALF CROP: All calves produced by the Herd during a 12 month period.

CALF CROP PERCENTAGE: A percentage determined by dividing the calf crop by the total number of bred females in the Herd at the beginning of a 12 month period.

CALVES: All cattle prior to 12 months of age.

CATTLE: Domesticated bovine animals.

CATTLE BREEDER: Maintains a herd of brood cows for the purpose of raising calves. Cows may be bred through natural service by bulls, or through methods of artificial insemination by trained technicians. Cattle breeders are generally classified into two categories: The purebred breeder, and the commercial breeder. The purebred breeder attempts to develop superior breeds or strains of breeding cattle for sale to other purebred breeders or for sale to commercial breeders. The commercial breeder raises nonregistered cattle that are intended for slaughter after being grown and fattened. Most purebred breeders concentrate on relatively few numbers of cattle and emphasize the development of high quality stock. Most commercial breeders aim to breed the greatest number of pounds of cattle of acceptable quality for the least possible cost.

CATTLE FEEDING: Process of talking calves or year-old cattle and growing and fattening these cattle for slaughter. Cattle are fed out on farms or in large commercial feedlots. Grain is the basic ingredient in fattening cattle.

Depending on a number of factors – such as the size of the animal at the start of feeding, its genetic characteristics, the nutritive value of the feed, weather, conditions of health of the cattle, and many other factors – the amount of feed and grain required to add one pound of weight to an animal will generally range between 6 pounds and 10 pounds. Cattle are usually kept on feed for periods ranging from four to eight months, but this period may be longer or shorter in many cases depending on how big the feeder animal is to start, to what weights it is being fed, and how "hot" or nutritive the feed is.

The feeder can usually estimate in advance how long it will take to fatten an animal to any given weight. The cattle feeder attempts to put weight gains on cattle in order to end up with a finished animal of acceptable quality and to do so with the least cost in terms of grain, labor and other expenses. Expenses faced by the feeder consist not only of the cost of feeder cattle but items such as the cost of grain, supplemental feed ingredients, labor, machinery, pens, land, property taxes, medicines and veterinarians bills, insurance, death losses, and interest charges.

CHAROLAIS: French breed of beef cattle – white to cream colored, large framed with heavy muscling. Lower carcass quality and calving ability.

CLOSED HERD: ,A herd of cattle maintained by adding Heifers and utilizing Herd Sires produced by the herd itself.

COMMERCIAL: Animals which may or may not be purebread but which are not registered with any breed association and animals whose heritage is not fully known.

COW: Adult bovine females that have given birth to at least one calf.

COW-CALF: A cow and her nursing calf, which she usually has at her side for approximately 6 to 8 months.

CROSSBRED CATTLE: Progeny resulting from the mating

of cattle of different Breeds.

CROSSBREEDING: Mating animals of different breeds.

CULL: An animal deemed inferior for breeding purposes and removed from the breeding herd.

CULLING PROCESS: The continuous application of a selective process whose purpose is to retain in a Herd only those animals which possess desirable characteristics from the point of view of breed improvement. In addition, the culling process removes from the Herd animals which by reason of infertility, infirmity or age become unreasonably expensive to maintain in relation to their value or which produce progeny possessing undesirable characteristics or progeny whose estimated value does not justify the cost of maintenance.

CUTABILITY: The yield of edible portions from a carcass.

DOUBLE-MUSCLING: An abnormal enlargement of the muscles of the thighs, shoulders and tongue, with an extremely short-coupled back. The head is thrust forward and the animal assumes a peculiar stance with legs positioned far forward or extended back as the animal seeks a position to relieve cramped muscles.

ENTEROTOXEMIA: Presence in the blood of toxins produced in the intestines.

EXOTIC BREEDS: Breeds which have recently been introduced into the United States from a foreign country.

FAT CATTLE: Feeder cattle which have been fed in feedlots and have reached optimum weights (950 to 1200 pounds) and grades suitable for marketing to meat packers for slaughter.

FEED: The balance mixed feed ration fed to Cattle and consists of Grain plus other ingredients.

FEEDER CATTLE: Cattle, seven to eighteen months of age, which normally weigh between 400 to 750 pounds and which are suitable for placement in feedlots for the purpose of increasing their weight and upgrading their carcass. Lighter weight feeder cattle are sometimes put on pasture prior to being placed in a feedlot.

FEEDERS: Cattle which are to be fed for slaughter.

FEEDLOT OR FEEDYARD: A confined area in which feeder cattle are cared for and fed a scientific ration until such time as they become fat cattle.

FIRST CALF HEIFER: A young female animal, 2 to 3 years of age bred to have her first calf.

FIRST CROSS ANIMAL: The offspring resulting from the first mating of two different breeds. Also designated as F1.

F2: The crossing of two F1 hybrids to produce a second hybrid generation.

FLUSHING: Increase of a female cow's weight prior to and during breeding.

GRADE: An animal which markedly resembles a given breed but which is not eligible for registration.

GRAIN: The principal ingredients (wheat, barley, corn and/or milo) or Feed.

HEDGING: The process whereby a cattle owner contracts in the commodity futures market to sell fat cattle at a future time at a specific price. Normally, the obligations of the purchaser of the contract are met (covered) on the future date by the owner of the contract either (i) delivering his own cattle to meet the conditions of the futures contract or (ii) selling cattle in the open market and repurchasing his futures contract. The normal cattle futures contract covers 40,000 pounds of live cattle of a specified grade.

HEIFER: A bovine female prior to having her first Calf.

HERD: All breeding cattle which are maintained for the Partnership.

HERD BULL OR HERD SIRE: A male animal used to breed naturally or by artificial insemination to females in the herd.

HEREFORD: A breed of beef cattle that are red with white faces — may be horned or hornless. Generally regarded as foragers and range cattle. Lack resistance to certain disease and tend to be less muscular than certain other breeds.

HYBRID: Animals representing two distinct breeds.

HYBRID VIGOR: The mating of animals not closely related usually resulting in offspring exceeding their parents in size and vigor.

INITIAL HERD: All of the females first acquired by the Partnership.

LEVERAGING: The process of borrowing funds from lending institutions to be used in acquiring additional cattle and feed, using as collateral the cattle and feed owned by the Partnership.

LIMOUSIN: French breed of beef cattle — fawn colored, medium size and heavy muscling. A new breed in the United States introduced in 1968. Little knowledge available about breed's weaknesses.

MAINE-ANJOU: A French breed from the provinces of Maine and Anjou characterized by red coloring and an average scale and frame. They are considered a dual-purpose breed of cattle with emphasis on beef.

MUCOSAL DISEASE: A complex of infectious diseases involving both respiratory and digestive systems.

OPEN: Not pregnant.

OPEN 2 YEAR OLD HEIFER: An unbred two year old.

OPEN YEARLING: An unbred female yearling.

PERCENTAGE BULL: A bull containing 50% or more blood of an exotic breed.

PERFORMANCE SELECTED: Cattle which have been added to a breeding herd on the basis of their performance test records.

PERFORMANCE TESTING: The measurement and recordation of various performance criteria such as ease of calving, weaning weight, yearling weight, composition scores, etc. of a group of cattle under uniform conditions of environment including nutrition.

PREGNANT: Carrying young.

PROGENY: First generation offspring.

PROGENY TESTING: The evaluation of herd sires by comparision of their offspring for all performance traits such as feed efficiency, rate of gain, disease resistance and carcass desirability.

PUREBRED: An animal which is eligible for registration with a breed society. An animal whose sire and dam are both members of the same breed. Pure breeding and recording with specific breed associations the ancestors of at least five generations.

QUASI-REGISTERED: Cattle identifiable by breed but incapable of registration or recordation with a breed society.

RECORDED OR RECORDABLE: Animals of various percentages of a breed (1/2, 3/4, 7/8, etc.) whose identification and parentage are recorded or recordable with a breed society.

REGISTERED: Purebred animals whose ancestry is acknowledged by a recognized breed society.

REPLACEMENT HEIFERS: Those female animals that are purchased or born to the herd and used to replace culls or increase the size of the herd.

SEEDSTOCK: A group of breeding animals superior in economically important and heritable traits.

SEMEN: Secretions of the reproductive organs of the male which carry the sperm.

SHIPPING FEVER: An infectious form of pneumonia which commonly occurs after transportation of animals.

SIMMENTAL: A Swiss breed of cattle characterized by brown and white coloring, a large frame and heavy milking.

STEER: A male animal that has been castrated prior to development of secondary sex characteristics. A bull castrated while still a calf.

TERMINAL CROSS: Cross breeding designed to produce an animal used for feed or beef. All such animals are intended for slaughter.

UPBREEDING: In the case of Commercial Cattle it is the process of continually mating animals to achieve a Purebred. In the case of Purebreds it is the constant upgrading of quality within the breed.

YEARLING: An animal ranging in age from 12 to 24 months.

SECTION THREE: CHICKENS AND EGGS

Chickens and eggs are a high-risk tax shelter designed to produce a high first-year tax write-off and deferral of income for the investor.

The purchase price of hens bought for commercial egg production and baby chicks bought for raising and resale may be deducted as an expense, by cash method farmers, in the year these costs are paid, if this is done consistently and clearly reflects income. If the taxpayer deducts the purchase price of chickens as an expense, he must report their entire selling price as income, without deducting purchase price from selling price to determine taxable profit.

The taxpayer may delay deducting the purchase price of hens and chicks until they are sold if he prefers. If he follows this method, he may deduct the purchase price from the selling price to determine taxable profit.

Return on an investment in chickens is in the form of marketable shell eggs. Marketable shell eggs are produced from laying flocks of genetically bred hens and started pullets (young hens attaining egg laying age) approximately twenty weeks of age or older. The total period of lay of a flock is generally twelve months from the commencement of the initial laying period and upon completion of economic egg production, whether due to age or egg market conditions, the hens are sold for processing as salvage fowl. A laying flock will mature at about 26 to 30 weeks of age and during the remainder of its laying period, will have an average rate of lay of approximately 6,500 eggs per 10,000 hens per day. Flocks are generally housed in wire cages, 3 to 8 hens to a cage, which are suspended several feet above the ground and which have watering and feeding devices. Egg production is gathered twice daily, seven days per week. The rate of mortality among hens placed into production averages 20% during their initial laying period. Poultry diseases and severe weather conditions will adversely affect egg production and can increase the mortality rate among the flock.

EXAMPLE OF AN EGG FUND

Ida Farming Program is a limited partnership to be dissolved within five years unless sooner terminated by operation of law or the vote of the Limited Partners. The business of the Partnership will commence upon the sale of the minimum number of Units (1,000) at $2,000 per Unit and will be limited to agricultural activities in connection with the sale and production of shell eggs from Partnership flocks. It is expected that during the existence of the Partnership such flocks will be maintained in facilities owned or operated by farmers under contract with the Partnership.

The principal objective of the Partnership is to engage in the business of farming for a profit; its methods of operations are intended to provide possible cash distributions and tax deferrals for investors, but there can be no assurance that these objectives will be realized.

It is hoped that the program will provide the limited partners with an initial tax write-off equal to twice their initial cash investment and an opportunity for capital appreciation through earnings of the partnership. It is expected that the initial tax deferral can be maintained by increasing the dollar amount of prepaid feed contracts as needed. Assuming no taxable income during the five-year term of the partnership, the limited partners will, upon liquidation, have taxable income in an amount equal to the initial tax deferral, plus any profits or minus any losses.

Jean Egg Farms, Inc., a corporation engaged in the production of shell eggs, is the General Partner of the Partnership. Management of the Partnership is vested in the General Partner. The Partnership's initial laying flocks, all replacement birds and all feed, medication and supplies necessary to maintain the Partnership flocks will be purchased by the Partnership from Kate Foods, Inc., the sole stockholder of the General Partner, or from the affiliates of Kate. A portion of the Partnership flocks will be maintained under contract at farms owned or operated by affiliates of Kate. In addition, the Partnership will sell to Kate all of its marketable egg production and all salvage fowl (laying hens which have ceased economic production). Upon dissolution of the Partnership, all of its assets may be sold to Kate pursuant to a right of first refusal. All contemplated transactions between the Partnership and the General Partner or its affiliates will be at appraised values or at generally prevailing prices for similar products or services.

As a result of the sale of the initial laying flock to the Partnership and the purchase of feed, Kate or its affiliates will realize an approximate profit of between $150,000 (if the minimum number of Units are sold) and $1,754,000 (if all the Units are sold), without giving effect to the sale by Kate to the Partnership of additional laying hens and feed with the proceeds of any borrowed funds.

The General Partner will receive (i) an initial management fee equal to 8% of the gross proceeds of the offering (a maximum of $960,000) and is required to pay all expenses of the offering and (ii) a continuing fee computed and paid weekly for the management of the Partnership's flocks of 1.5 cents per dozen eggs produced and sold from such flocks.

The General Partner may receive a distribution of up to 25% of the gain realized by the Partnership upon the sale of its properties in liquidation.

The net proceeds of this offering after deducting the initial Management Fee will be a maximum of $11,040,000 and a minimum of $1,840,000 and will be applied as follows:

A maximum of approximately $5,553,000 and a minimum of approximately $962,200 for the purchase of the initial Partnership flock consisting of a maximum of approximately 4,809,146 and a minimum of approximately 795,390 laying hens and started pullets.

The balance, a maximum of approximately $5,487,000 and a minimum of approximately $877,800 for the purchase of feed, medication and supplies and the payment of other expenses necessary to maintain the Partnership flocks.

In the event more than the minimum number but less than the maximum number of Units offered hereby are sold, the purchase of flocks and feed and other supplies for the maintenance of the flocks will be decreased proportionately.

Although it is anticipated that the proceeds of the offering will be fully expended in the first year, to the extent there are any sums remaining therefrom the balance of such offering proceeds will be added to the general funds of the Partnership and will be used for Partnership purposes which may include the purchase of additional or replacement flocks, feed and the payment of flock maintenance expenses to contract farmers. The continuing management fee of the General Partner (1.5c per dozen eggs produced and sold) will be paid only from the proceeds of the egg production of the Partnership flocks or other funds realized from operations.

Although no assurance can be given, it is the intention of the General Partner to obtain recourse loans secured by Partnership properties, in an initial aggregate amount equal to the proceeds of this offering. It is not now possible to ascertain the availability of such loans or the terms thereof. If, however, loans can be obtained for the Partnership the proceeds therefrom will be expended for flocks, feed and supplies to be purchased from Kate in proportion to the application of the proceeds of this offering. Thus, the size of the initial Partnership flocks will be increased to a maximum of approximately 9,618,292 and a minimum of approximately 1,590,780 laying hens and started pullets and the balance of the loan proceeds will be applied for the purchase of feed and other supplies. Kate and its affiliates will realize a profit of a maximum of approximately $1,754,000 and a minimum of approximately $150,000 from the sale of the additional laying flocks. feed and supplies to the Partnership.

The Partnership flocks will be housed and maintained at farms owned or operated by unaffiliated farmers as well as at farms owned or leased by Kate. It is anticipated that, initially, between 14% (if the maximum number of Units are sold and an equivalent sum is raised through loans to the Partnership) and 50% (if the minimum number of Units are sold and an equivalent sum is raised through loans to the Partnership) of the Partnership flocks will be maintained under contract at Kate farms. Existing contracts with such farmers and Kate on the flocks to be purchased will be assigned to the Partnership at the time of the sale by Kate. These contracts typically require the owner of the flocks to supply the contract farmer with the chicks, hens, feed and poultry medicine while the farmer is obligated to supply all housing and labor necessary to maintain the hens and to collect the egg production for subsequent processing.

Contract farmers are paid a fee presently ranging from 1.00 cents to 1.65 cents per bird per week until the birds attain 20 to 25 weeks of age and, thereafter, on the basis of per dozen eggs produced ranging from 4.75 cents to 5.50 cents for Grade A and AA eggs and 3.00 cents for all other eggs produced.

The agreement with the contract farmer ordinarily will terminate after a specified period which generally coincides with a particular growing or laying cycle of the flock subject to the contract. The contract is terminable by the owner of the flock in the event the contract farmer fails to perform. During the term of the contract, ownership of the birds, feed, medication and egg production is reserved to the flock owner.

The General Partner will have the right to make certain decisions and elections on behalf of the Partnership which will affect the Federal income tax consequences to the Partners. The following discussion outlines the present intention of the General Partner with respect to some of such decisions and elections. These intentions are based upon the General Partner's assumption that it is in the best interests of the Limited Partners to deduct amounts for Federal income tax purposes at the earliest possible time. This may not be an appropriate assumption with respect to any particular Limited Partner because of his individual tax situation for the year of the deduction, or because of the effect on his subsequent tax years.

The Partnership will report its income and maintain its books and records on the cash basis method of accounting.

The following constitutes the consequences to Limited Partners for Federal income tax purposes of certain practices to be engaged in by the Partnership (assuming the Partnership is treated as a partnership and is deemed to be engaged in the business of farming):

Commencing with the acquisition in the first year of its initial laying flock, the Partnership intends to capitalize the entire cost of all laying hens, started pullets and replacement birds.

During the first year and later years, the Partnership intends to deduct expenses for feed in the year consumed by its flock.

The Partnership will use its best efforts to obtain in the first year and subsequent years, recourse loans secured only by Partnership properties, the proceeds of which will be expended for additional flocks, replacement hens and feed.

As a result of the foregoing it is anticipated that the Limited Partners will be able to fully deduct on their first year Federal income tax return their investment in the

Partnership plus their proportionate share of any recourse borrowings obtained by the Partnership in the first year.

It is anticipated that in subsequent years, except the fifth year, that the income of the Partnership will be substantially offset by deductible expenditures for replacement flocks and feed, thereby resulting in little or no taxable income reportable by the Partnership. However, in the event the General Partner determines that business conditions do not warrant the making of such expenditures, the Partnership may realize significant taxable income in such years.

Under the Revenue Act of 1978 investors will be limited to deducting losses from amounts they have at risk or personally invest in farming operations.

The projections of the program are as follows:

LIQUIDATION POSITION AT END OF FIFTH YEAR

Cash (assuming no prior distribution to limited partners)	$24,000,000
Collection of accounts receivable	3,000,000
Sale of laying flock	11,000,000
Total funds available	38,000,000
Deduct bank loan	12,000,000
Amount available for distribution to general partner and limited partners	26,000,000
Amount distributable to limited partners	23,700,000
Amount distributable to general partner	2,300,000
	$26,000,000
Original investment	$12,000,000
Profit for five year operation	12,000,000
Five year profit percentage	100%
Amount available for distribution	26,000,000
Deduct 140% of original investment	16,800,000
Basis for general partner distribution	9,200,000
	25%
General partner distribution	$2,300,000

BENEFITS OF AN EGG FUND

The investment deters high pretax income to a future tax year and produces a high first-year tax write-off.

RISKS OF AN EGG FUND

1. The business of a Partnership might be limited to activities in connection with the production and sale of shell eggs. This business is highly competitive and, therefore, the Partnership's operations must be conducted on relatively low margins. A small decrease in the market price of shell eggs or a small increase in the costs of production will have a material adverse effect on the earnings of the Partnership.

2. Shell egg prices are extremely sensitive to supply and demand pressures which have caused volatile and uncontrollable price fluctuations.

3. Except in the case of termination and liquidation of a Partnership, the net profits and net losses of the Partnership will be allocated to the Limited Partners and the General Partner in proportion to their capital contributions. The initial and continuing management fees payable to General Partner will be deducted in computing such profits and losses. In this connection, a typical General Partner might distribute by April 1 of each year an amount equal to at least 50% of any taxable income reportable by the Partnership during the prior year, provided such funds are not otherwise reasonably required, in the sole discretion of the General Partner, for the conduct of the Partnership's business. The gain realized upon sale in liquidation of the Partnership Properties would be fully allocated to the Limited Partners unless and until 140% of their initial capital contributions had been distributed to them and the balance, if any, would be allocated 75% to the Limited Partners and 25% to the General Partner.

Allocations to Limited Partners shall be made to the record owners of Units based upon the number of days during the fiscal year of the Partnership each such Unit was so owned by the record owners and not upon the date or dates upon which income may have been earned or losses incurred.

4. Investments in a Partnership may be leveraged. Leveraging, which involves the financing of the ownership of flocks and the purchase of feed through the use of borrowed funds, will enable the Partnership to acquire a larger flock, but also will increase the Partnership's exposure to larger operating losses, due in part to debt service requirements, and the possible loss of flocks securing the indebtedness through foreclosure. Moreover, lenders may seek to impose restrictions

296

on the future borrowing, distribution and operating policies of the Partnership to an extent not presently ascertainable. Partnership is subject to tax, even though no cash is distributed to such Partner.

TAX ASPECTS OF AN EGG FUND

1. Under prior law, there were two "at risk" rules designed to prevent a taxpayer from deducting losses in excess of his actual economic investment in the activity involved. The first of these at risk rules—"the specific at risk rule"—applied to four specified activities: (1) farming; (2) exploring for, or exploiting, oil and natural gas resources; (3) holding, producing, or distributing motion picture films or video tapes; and (4) leasing of personal property. The other at risk rule—"the partnership at risk rule"—applied generally to activities engaged in through partnerships. However, there were two exceptions to this rule. First, the rule did not apply to any activity to the extent that the specific at risk rule applied. Second, the rule did not apply to any partnership the principal activity of which was investing in real property (other than mineral property).

The Revenue Act of 1978 extends the specific at risk rule to all activities except real estate (and certain equipment leasing activities of closely-held corporations, as discussed below). For the newly covered activities, the specific at risk rule covers activities which are a part of a trade or business or are engaged in for the production of income. Separate rules for aggregation and separation of activities are provided for the activities to which the at risk rule is extended by the Act. The holding of real property (other than mineral property) is to be treated as a separate activity, and the at risk rule is not applied to losses from that activity. For purposes of this exclusion, personal property and services which are incidental to making real property available as living accommodations are to be treated as part of the activity of holding the real property. Since all the activities currently covered by the partnership at risk rules would now be covered by the new expanded version of the specific at risk rules under section 465, the partnership at risk rules is repealed by the Act.

This provision is effective for taxable years beginning after December 31, 1978.

Under prior law, the only corporations to which the specific at risk rule applied were subchapter S corporations and personal holding companies. The Act extends the application of this rule to all corporations in which five or fewer individuals own more than 50 percent of the corporation's stock. However, the equipment leasing activities of a closely held corporation are not to be subject to the at risk rule if the corporation is actively engaged in equipment leasing, that is, if 50 percent or more of the corporation's gross receipts is derived from equipment leasing. This provision is effective for taxable years beginning after December 31, 1978.

Under prior law, the at risk rule under section 465 may have been interpreted to only require the taxpayer to be at risk as of the end of the taxable year for which losses were claimed. Under this interpretation, subsequent withdrawals of amounts originally placed at risk could be made without the recapture of previously allowed losses.

In order to be consistent with the original intent of the at risk rule, the Act requires the recapture of previously allowed losses when the amount at risk is reduced below zero. Mechanically, this rule works by providing that if the amount at risk is reduced below zero (by distributions to the taxpayer, by changes in the status of indebtedness from recourse to nonrecourse, by the commencement of a guarantee or other similar arrangement which affects the taxpayer's risk of loss, or otherwise), the taxpayer will recognize income to the extent that his at risk basis is reduced below zero. However, the amount recaptured is limited to the excess of the losses previously allowed and which reduced the taxpayer's at risk basis in that activity for taxable years beginning after December 31, 1978, over any amounts previously recaptured. A suspended deduction in the amount equal to the amount of recaptured income would be provided to the taxpayer. This suspended deduction would be allowed in a subsequent year if and to the extent the taxpayer's at risk basis is increased. The provision is generally effective for taxable years beginning after December 31, 1978.

2. The 1976 Tax Reform Act provides that no additions to an excess deductions account need be made for net farm losses sustained in any taxable year beginning after December 31, 1975. In addition, the conference agreement allows divisive "D" reorganizations without triggering EDA recapture. In these reorganizations, the entire EDA account is applied to both

corporations. This latter provision applies to reorganizations after December 31, 1975.

3. The 1976 Tax Reform Act requires farming syndicates (1) to deduct expenses for feed, seed, fertilizer, and other farm supplies only when used or consumed (not when paid); (2) to capitalize costs of poultry; and (3) to capitalize the costs of planting, cultivating, maintaining and developing a grove, orchard or vineyard which are incurred prior to the year the grove, orchard or vineyard becomes productive.

The definition of "farming syndicate" includes (1) a partnership or any other enterprise (except a corporation which has not elected to be taxed under subchapter S) engaged in the trade or business of farming if at any time interests in the partnership or other enterprise are offered for sale in an offering required to be registered with any Federal or State agency having authority to regulate the offering of securities for sale or (2) the partnership or any other enterprise (other than a non-subchapter S corporation) engaged in the trade or business of farming if more than 35 percent of the losses during any period are allocable to limited partners or limited entrepreneurs. In general, a limited entrepreneur means a person who has an interest in an enterprise other than à partnership and who does not actively participate in the management of the enterprise.

The determination of whether a person actively participates in the operation or management of a farm depends upon the facts and circumstances. Factors which tend to indicate active participation include participation in the decisions in the operation or management of the farm, actually working on the farm, living on the farm, or engaging in the hiring and discharging of employees. Factors which tend to indicate a passive person similar to a limited partner include lack of control of the management and operations of the farm, having authority only to discharge the farm manager, having a farm manager who is an independent contractor rather than an employee, not owning the farm land in fee, and having limited liability for farm losses.

The provision specifies four cases where an individual's activity with respect to a farm will result in his not being treated as a limited partner or limited entrepreneur. These cases cover the situations where an individual—

(1) has an interest attributable to his active participation for a period of not less than 5 years in the management of a trade or business of farming;

(2) lives on the farm on which the trade or business of farming is being carried on;

(3) actively participates in the management of a trade or business of farming which involves the raising of livestock (or is treated as being engaged in active management pursuant to one of the first two exceptions set forth above), and the trade or business of the partnership or any other enterprise involves the further processing of the livestock raised in the trade or business with respect to which he is (actually or constructively) an active participant; or

(4) is a member of the family of a grandparent of an individual who would be excepted under any of the first three cases listed above and his interest is attributable to the active participation of such individual.

The provisions of the 1976 Tax Reform Act relating to prepaid feed and other farm supplies and poultry expenses apply generally to amounts paid or incurred after December 31, 1975. In the case of farming syndicates in existence on December 31, 1975, (but only with respect to taxpayers who are members of the syndicate on such date), the provisions apply to amounts paid or incurred after December 31, 1976.

4. With certain exceptions, the Tax Reform Act of 1976 required corporations (and partnerships in which nonexcepted corporations are partners) engaged in farming to use an accrual method of accounting and to capitalize preproductive period expenses. However, subchapter S corporations, family corporations (in which one family owns at least 50 percent of the stock), corporations with annual gross receipts of $1 million or less, and nurseries are not required to use the accrual method of accounting or to capitalize preproductive period expenses.

The 1976 Act provisions generally are effective for taxable years beginning after December 31, 1976. However, the Tax Reduction and Simplification Act of 1977 postponed the effective date of the required accrual accounting provision until taxable years beginning after December 31, 1977, for certain farming corporations controlled by two or three families.

The Revenue Act of 1978 provides exceptions to the required accrual accounting and capitalization of preproductive period expense rules for certain corporations which are controlled by

300

two or three families. The provisions requiring accrual accounting and the capitalization of preproductive period expenses will not apply to any farm corporation if, as of October 4, 1976, and at all times thereafter, either (1) two families own (directly or through attribution) at least 65 percent of the total combined voting power of all classes of stock of the corporation entitled to vote and at least 65 percent of the total number of shares of all other classes of stock of the corporation, or (2) (a) members of three families own (directly or through attribution) at least 50 percent of the total combined voting power of all classes of stock entitled to vote and at least 50 percent of the total number of shares of all other classes of stock and (b) substantially all of the remaining stock is owned by corporate employees, their family members, or a tax-exempt employees' trust for the benefit of the corporation's employees.

The Act also provides that, with respect to corporations described in the preceding paragraph, stock acquired after October 4, 1976, by the corporation's employees, their families, or a tax-exempt trust for their benefit will be treated as owned by one of the two or three families whose combined stock ownership was used to establish the initial qualification for this provision (as of October 4, 1976). The provision requires that corporations must have been engaged in the trade or business of farming on October 4, 1976, and at all times thereafter, to qualify for this exception.

This provision applies to taxable years beginning after December 31, 1977.

Prior to 1976, farmers, nurserymen, and florists were not required to inventory growing crops regardless of the method of accounting they used for income tax purposes. However, in 1976 the Internal Revenue Service ruled that an accrual method farmer, nurseryman, or florist would be required to inventory growing crops. The changes made by this ruling are to be for taxable years beginning on or after January 1, 1978.

Under present law, corporations and partnerships (in which nonexcepted corporations are partners) engaged in farming are required to use the accrual method of accounting and to capitalize preproductive period expenses (sec. 447). However, subchapter S corporations, family corporations (in which one family owns at least 50 percent of the stock), corporations with annual gross receipts of $1 million or less, and nurseries are not required to use the accrual method of accounting or to capitalize preproductive period expenses. In general, the requirement that preproductive period expenses be capitalized would have the effect of requiring taxpayers to inventory (or capitalize) the costs of growing crops.

The Act permits a farmer, nurseryman, or florist who is on an accrual method of accounting and is not required by section 447 of the Code to capitalize preproductive period expenses to be exempt from the requirement that growing crops be inventoried. The term growing crops does not include trees grown for lumber, pulp, or other nonlife purposes.

The Act also allows those farmers, nurserymen, or florists who are eligible to use an accrual method of accounting without inventorying growing crops to elect, without the prior approval of the Internal Revenue Service, to change to the cash receipts and disbursements method of accounting with respect to any trade or business in which the principal activity is growing crops. If such an election is made, it will be treated as a change in method of accounting initiated by the taxpayer. This election may be initiated only with respect to a taxable year beginning after December 31, 1977, and before January 1, 1981.

With certain exceptions, the Tax Reform Act of 1976 required corporations (and partnerships in which nonexcepted corporations are partners) engaged in farming to use an accrual method of accounting and to capitalize preproductive period expenses. However, subchapter S corporations, family corporations (in which one family owns at least 50 percent of the stock), corporations with annual gross receipts of $1 million or less, and nurseries are not required to use the accrual method of accounting or to capitalize preproductive period expenses.

In addition to the exceptions to the accrual method of accounting and capitalization of preproductive period expenses provided under section 351 of the Act, sod farms are also excepted from these rules. The provision excepting sod farms is effective for taxable years beginning after December 31, 1976.

This is a high risk investment, making it exceedingly important that the investor not invest in a poor egg market cycle and that he not invest so early in the year that income from eggs wipes out the depreciation of the hens.

A publicly offered egg program of this type illustrates the growing need for the farming industry to seek public money in order to help meet rising operating expenses.

CHAPTER FIVE

TIMBER

Because of the large amount of capital usually required to own and grow timber, it is generally held by corporations. However, individuals as well as corporations have been successful with this tax shelter.

GENERAL CONSIDERATIONS

Ordinarily, the taxpayer who cuts timber on his land and sells it in the form of logs, firewood, or pulpwood will have no cost or other basis for such timber, and the sales constitute a very minor part of his farm business. In these cases, amounts realized from such sales, and the expenses incurred in cutting, hauling, etc., may be treated as ordinary farm income and expenses. If he sells standing timber he has held as investment property, it is treated the same as the sale or exchange of any other capital asset. The special rules explained below apply, however, if he owned the timber more than 6 months and he either makes an "Election to Treat Timber Cutting as a Sale," or enters into a "Cutting Contract."

Depletion is to the owner of an economic interest in standing timber what depreciation is to the owner of a depreciable asset. Depletion may be computed under the cost method for all depletable assets.

Cost depletion, in general, is figured by first dividing the total number of recoverable units (board feet determined in accordance with prevailing industry methods) of timber into the adjusted basis of the standing timber to determine the depletion per unit.

For timber, depletion takes place when standing timber is cut. The amount of depletion for each tax year is the number of units cut multiplied by the depletion unit. Depletion of timber must be computed by using only the cost method.

EXAMPLE

The taxpayer purchased a farm in 1950 for $20,000. $1,800

303

of his purchase price was for a tract of standing timber (excluding the cost of the land on which the timber stood). He did not cut any of the timber until the present year. At the time he commenced cutting, it was determined that the entire tract of timber would produce 300,000 board feet. This year he cut and sold 27,000 board feet. His depletion per unit of a thousand board feet of timber is $6 ($1,800 divided by 300 M board feet). His depletion for this year is $162, $6 (depletion per unit) times 27 (units cut).

If he cuts the timber in one year and sells it in a later year, he may not deduct depletion in the year of cutting, unless he elects to treat the cutting as a sale or exchange. If he does not make that election, he determines his deduction for timber depletion according to his method of accounting. If he uses the accrual method, he is allowed the depletion deduction in the year he sells the timber, to the extent of the timber sold. If he uses the cash method, he is allowed the depletion deduction in the year he receives payment of the sales price, to the extent of the amount of timber for which he receives payment.

ELECTION TO TREAT TIMBER CUTTING AS A SALE

Under the general rule, the cutting of timber results in no gain or loss, and it is not until the sale that gain or loss is realized. But if the taxpayer cuts timber he owned for a period of more than 6 months before the beginning of the tax year, he may elect to treat the cutting of such timber as a sale, thus reporting his "gain" or "loss" as income or loss for the year the timber is cut, even though it is not sold until a later year. His "gain" or "loss" in such case is the difference between the fair market value of the standing timber at the beginning of the year in which it is cut and its adjusted basis. This market value then becomes the basis for computing his ordinary gain or loss on the ultimate sale of the logs, pulpwood, or other products. If he elects this method, he must include his gain or loss on the cutting (but not on the sale) in the comparison of gains and losses to determine whether it is treated as capital or ordinary gain or loss.

EXAMPLE

On May 1, 1965, the taxpayer owned 100,000 feet of

standing timber having an adjusted depletion basis of $16 per M. He reports on a calendar year basis. On January 1 of this year, the timber had a fair market value of $40 per M, and the timber was cut during this year. Since he owned the timber for a period of more than 6 months before the beginning of the tax year, he may elect to report the difference between his adjusted depletion basis of the timber and its fair market value as a "gain" on his return for this year. The "gain" would be computed as follows:

Fair market value of timber Jan. 1 . . . . $4,000.00
Adjusted depletion basis of timber $1,600.00

Gain $2,400.00

The fair market value of the timber, $4,000, would then become the basis of the cut timber to him, and the subsequent sale of such timber (including tree stumps or treetops) would result in ordinary income or loss.

CUTTING CONTRACT

If the taxpayer disposes of timber he held for more than 6 months before disposal, under any form of cutting contract through which he retains an economic interest in such timber, such as in pay-for-as-cut contracts, the disposal is treated as a sale of property used in his business regardless of whether he held the timber primarily for sale to customers in the ordinary course of his business. His gain or loss must be included in the comparison of gains and losses, since, unlike the rule for cut timber discussed above, this rule is not elective. The date of disposal is the date the timber is cut; but, if he receives a payment before the timber is cut, he may elect to treat the date of payment as the date of disposal.

Timber is considered to be cut on the date when in the ordinary course of business the quantity of felled timber is first definitely determined. This is true, whether the timber is cut under contract or whether he cut it himself.

Christmas trees (evergreen trees) that are more than 6 years old at the time severed from their roots and sold for ornamental purposes are included in the term timber for the purposes of both rules.

305

BENEFITS OF TIMBER PROGRAMS

1. Timber owners have been accorded special capital gain treatment. They may elect to treat the cutting of standing timber as creating a capital gain even though the timber is not sold at that time. The owners step up their basis to fair market value with capital gain treatment as though they had sold the property to themselves. One-half of their net long-term capital gain is a tax preference item which may be subject to a 10 percent penalty tax. If they sell the timber at no higher value, no further gain would be recognized. If they sell the timber at an additional profit, it would be ordinary income.

2. Costs of growing timber such as taxes, interest, estimating the quantity of standing timber, wages of employees and other expenses are usually deductible as paid.

3. Land on which the timber stands may appreciate in value.

4. Romance of nature.

RISKS OF A TIMBER PROGRAM

Risks Include:

1. Fire, disease, and storms.
2. Price fluctuations depending on building activity.

TAX ASPECTS OF A TIMBER PROGRAM

1. Timber depletion is based on the cost of timber (or other basis in the owner's hands). The basis does not include any part of the cost of land. Depletion takes place when standing timber is cut. Depletion must be computed by the cost method. There is no percentage depletion for timber. The allowance each year is the number of timber units cut multiplied by the depletion unit. The depletion unit is the cost or adjusted basis of the standing timber on hand divided by the total depletable units (M board-feet, cords, etc.)

The depletion allowance is claimed as a deduction in the year of the sale or other disposition of the cut timber unless an election is made. An election may be made, under certain circumstances, to treat the cutting of timber as a sale or exchange. If this election is made, the allowable depletion is subtracted from the fair market value at the beginning of the tax year of the timber cut to determine the gain to be reported on the cutting. The gain is generally reported as long-term capital gain. The fair market value then becomes the basis for determining the ordinary gain or loss on the sale or other disposition of the cut timber.

2. The cutting of timber may be treated as a sale or exchange of a capital asset, if the taxpayer so elects. If he makes this election, any gain or loss recognized on the cutting is a taxable gain or deductible loss that must be included in the comparison of gains and losses.

For this treatment to apply, he must:

a. have owned, or had a contract right to cut, the timber for more than 6 months before the beginning of his tax year;

b. elect to treat the cutting of the timber as a sale or exchange of that timber; and

c. cut the timber for sale or for use in his trade or business.

The taxpayer makes his election on his return for the year in which the cutting takes place by including in income the gain or loss on cutting and attaching his computation of gain or loss to his return. If the timber is partnership property, the election must be made on the partnership return.

Once made, an election remains in force for all later years, unless he can show undue hardship and get the consent of the Internal Revenue Service to revoke his election. It applies to all timber cut during any later year in which he owned or had a contract right to cut the timber more than 6 months before the beginning of that year. A revocation prevents him from again making this election except with the consent of the Service.

He computes the gain or loss on the cutting of standing timber by subtracting the adjusted basis for depletion of the standing timber from its fair market value on the first day of his tax year in which it is cut. The fair market value would then become his basis of the timber cut, and a later sale of the cut timber (including any byproduct or tree tops) would result in ordinary income or loss.

If he owns standing timber and disposes of it under a cutting contract, he must treat the disposal as a sale or exchange, if (1) he held the timber for more than 6 months before its disposal, and (2) he retains an economic interest in it.

The difference between the amount realized from the disposal of the timber and its adjusted depletion basis is considered as gain or loss on its sale. This amount must be included in the grouping of gains and losses.

The date of disposal of the timber is usually the date the

timber is cut; but, if he receives payment under the contract before the timber is cut, he may elect to treat the date of payment as the date of disposal.

The term owner includes a sublessor and the holder of a contract to cut timber.

The term economic interest means that he has acquired an interest in standing timber by investment and, by any form of legal relationship, has derived income from the severance of the timber, to which he must look for a return of his capital investment.

Tree stumps are a capital asset if they are on land held by an investor who is not in the timber or stump business, either as a buyer, seller, or processor. Gain from the sale or stumps sold in one lot by such a holder, is taxed as a capital gain. However, tree stumps held by timber operators, after the merchantable standing timber has been cut and removed from the land, are considered byproducts. Gain from the sale of stumps by such operators is taxed as ordinary income.

The 1976 Tax Reform Act increases the holding period for long-term capital gains and losses from 6 months to 9 months in 1977 and 12 months in 1978 and subsequent years.

For the patient investor with sufficient capital, timber can be an interesting and rewarding tax shelter.

CHAPTER SIX

MOVIES

An investment in a movie fund is designed to defer pretax income to a future tax year. Investors will be limited to deducting losses from amounts they personally invest.

GENERAL CONSIDERATIONS

The production of a feature motion picture film may require six months or longer from inception to completion of the negative. Such time is consumed in completing screenplays, casting, principal photography, editing, scoring and inserting special effects. Production normally commences after the preparation of a screenplay based upon a novel, play, story outline, factual rendition or other original material.

The distribution of feature length motion pictures is characterized by keen competition for motion picture product and bookings in theatres.

In the United States, pictures are licensed for exhibition in theatres on any one or more of the following bases: percentage, modified percentage, flat rental, or variations of percentages and flat rental arrangements. Under a percentage arrangement, the exhibitor agrees to pay to the distributor a percentage of gross box office receipts. In the case of a modified percentage arrangement, the exhibitor agrees to pay the distributor a percentage of gross box office receipts in excess of a specified amount. In the case of a flat rental, the exhibitor agrees to pay a flat price without regard to the box office receipts of the theatre.

EXAMPLE OF A MOVIE FUND

Marie Productions, a limited partnership offers 2,000 units at $3,000 each to develop, acquire and co-produce low to medium budget feature length motion pictures. Assuming this offering is successfully completed, it will be the Partnership's

309

intention to "spread the investment risk", by investing in a number of films. The term of the partnership will be 20 years from date of consummation of contemplated offering.

The General Partner is Nellie Pictures, Inc., a publicly held corporation actively engaged in the production and distribution of theatrical motion pictures. As part of its national distribution organization, Nellie owns and operates six regional sales exchanges in major cities in the United States. Each exchange is engaged in the distribution of Nellie's films in its region. Each such exchange is under the supervision of personnel with extensive experience in the distribution of theatrical motion pictures.

Nellie shall have the sole authority and exclusive control of the Partnership's activities. This shall include the right to:

1. Acquire completed motion pictures.
2. Choose literary properties to be developed into completed screenplays.
3. Acquire completed screenplays.
4. Designate properties for motion picture production.
5. Determine whether to produce or co-produce motion pictures.
6. Determine the method of distribution, including the right to (i) make an outright sale of any motion picture, (ii) distribute the picture through its own facilities or those of its subsidiaries, or (iii) employ unaffiliated distributors.

Nellie's obligations are as follows:

1. If Nellie acts as producer, on behalf of the Partnership, it is obligated to provide all of the services customarily provided by a producer.
2. Nellie shall use from Partnership funds only that amount specifically allocated by Nellie for the purpose of producing any specific motion picture. If the actual cost of such motion picture exceeds the amount allocated Nellie shall be obligated to supplying or arranging for the additional funds required to complete the film at no penalty to the Partnership.
3. If a film is not completed within 30 months from the commencement of principal photography, or, if Nellie shall determine to abandon the project prior to the 30 month period, then Nellie shall be obligated to reimburse the

Partnership for any sums which the Partnership shall have expended in the production of such picture.

4. Nellie shall be obligated to use its best efforts to sell, lease or otherwise dispose of motion pictures acquired, produced or co-produced by the Partnership. All costs of distribution, including prints and advertising will be advanced by Nellie, or distributor, and not by the Partnership.

The activities of the Partnership shall be limited as follows:

1. Not more than $120,000 of Partnership funds may be used for the purpose of acquiring, developing and preparing any specific motion picture property for production, including, among other costs, the preparation of a screenplay, budget, production schedule and any other pre-production costs incurred in connection therewith.

2. Not more than $1,500,000 of Partnership funds can be invested in any single motion picture to be produced, co-produced, or acquired by the Partnership. This does not preclude it from producing, co-producing or acquiring, on a joint venture basis with others, films which require the total expenditure of funds in a greater amount.

The activities and compensation of Nellie shall be limited as follows:

1. For a period of four years from the date of commencement of the Partnership, Nellie, or any of its subsidiaries shall not acquire on an outright basis, produce or co-produce in competition with the Partnership any motion picture or any rights thereto unless the consideration or cost to be paid or incurred to accomplish such production or acquisition shall exceed the remaining capital of the Partnership, or $1,500,000.

2. If Nellie acts as distributor of a picture on behalf of the Partnership, it will be entitled to receive a fee amounting to 40% of the gross receipts derived from the United States; 25% of all sums remitted by sub-distributors licensed for foreign territories; and 50% of the gross receipts derived from various foreign countries where Nellie distributed directly.

3. If Nellie shall make an outright license (flat sum) for the distribution of a picture on behalf of the Partnership, if Nellie licenses the picture to a distributor on a percentage basis, Nellie shall receive a commission equal to 25% of any monies paid to the Partnership.

4. Nellie shall be entitled to 40% of the net profits, as defined, from each of the Partnership's motion pictures.

The manner of distribution of proceeds of each motion picture produced or acquired by, by Partnership to Limited Partners is as follows:

1. Gross receipts
2. Less: distribution fees
3. Less: cost of prints and advertising
4. Return of capital for acquisition or production of film.
5. 60% of remaining net proceeds

The following is an example of how the Partnership would have profited had it invested in a film entitled "Olivia":

Gross revenues	$1,000,000
Less: 40% distribution fee	− 400,000
	$ 600,000
Less: Cost of prints & advertising	− 300,000
	$ 300,000
Less: Cost of acquiring picture	− 150,000
Net profit	$ 150,000

If Limited Partnership, Marie, invested in this film, it would have invested $150,000. Nellie would have advanced $300,000 for prints and advertising.

After the Limited Partners and Nellie were returned all their money and after Nellie received a 40% distribution fee, the Limited Partners would have received an additional $90,000, (60% of net profits, a return of 60% on invested capital). More money may be earned on "Olivia" in the future.

BENEFITS OF A MOVIE FUND

1. Defers high pretax income to a future tax year.
2. Not a rotating fund – monies are returned to Limited Partners as revenues are received.
3. Revenues may come from world-wide theatrical release, as well as, world-wide television, cassettes, and in-flight showings, where applicable.

RISKS OF A MOVIE FUND

1. Investment in the production and acquisition of motion

pictures has historically involved a substantial degree of risk. Such risks typically involve the initial outlay of funds for published or unpublished novels or other screen play materials which may subsequently have to be disposed of at a loss. In addition, the costs of producing films are often miscalculated and may be increased by reason of factors or developments beyond the control of the producers. The ultimate profitability of any motion picture is largely a function of the cost of its production or acquisition and distribution in relation to its ultimate audience appeal, which can rarely be reliably ascertained in advance. It is estimated by management that a substantial number of current motion picture productions are unprofitable. Accordingly, there can be no assurance that the Partnership will produce, acquire or sell any motion pictures which yield profits to the Partnership or which will enable investors to recoup all or any of their capital contributions to the Partnership.

2. The gross receipts of motion pictures are dependent, among other things, upon the availability of a distribution organization which is capable of arranging for appropriate advertising and promotion, selecting proper release dates, and obtaining bookings in theatres. The process of distributing a motion picture entails commercial problems which could adversely affect their ultimate profitability, including competition for theatres, miscalculation with respect to release dates and other contingencies.

3. It is generally known that recoupment of costs of acquisition or production of motion pictures is frequently not accomplished by reason of numerous factors, including generally increasing costs of distribution and production, the difficulty of predicting public reaction to such productions and other materially adverse factors such as labor or artist disputes, equipment breakdowns and similar delays or production disruptions, which often result in production costs exceeding projected estimates.

4. The Partnership intends to engage in a highly competitive business. Competition is encountered in various phases of the motion picture industry. In the production or acquisition phases, competition materially affects the ability of a motion picture company to acquire suitable literary material or completed motion pictures and it may also increase their cost of acquisition. Any productions completed

313

or acquired by the Partnership will, if distributed, ultimately be competing with other productions and indirectly with other forms of public entertainment. Furthermore, the Partnership will be in competition with numerous larger motion picture producers and distributors which have substantially greater financial resources and larger experienced motion picture production and distribution staffs than those which are likely to be available to the Partnership and which have longer established histories of production and distribution of motion pictures. Certain of these larger companies have recently encountered financial difficulties which reflect the highly competitive character of, and recent adverse developments in, the motion picture industry as well as the unpredictability of public reaction to motion pictures.

5. In the event that a substantial portion of the revenues generated by the Partnership is derived from distribution of its motion picture productions in foreign countries, such revenues may be subject to currency controls and other restrictions which will curtail the funds available for distribution to the partners of the Partnership in the United States.

6. The Units will not be transferable by any of the Limited Partners without the prior consent of Nellie. For this reason, as well as other characteristics of such Units, it is anticipated that no organized trading market will develop for the securities offered hereby.

TAX ASPECTS OF A MOVIE FUND

1. The 1976 Tax Reform Act provides that the amount of any loss (otherwise allowable for the year) which may be deducted in connection with one of certain activities cannot exceed the aggregate amount with respect to which the taxpayer is at risk in each such activity at the close of the taxable year. This "at risk" limitation applies to holding, producing, or distributing of motion picture films or video tapes. The limitation applies to all taxpayers (other than corporations which are not subchapter S corporations) including individuals and sole proprietorships, estates, trusts, shareholders in subchapter S corporations, and partners in a partnership which conducts an activity described in this provision.

314

Under this provision, a taxpayer is generally to be considered "at risk" with respect to an activity to the extent of his cash and the adjusted basis of other property contributed to the activity, any amounts borrowed for use in the activity with respect to which the taxpayer has personal liability for payment from his personal assets, and his net fair market value of personal assets which secure non-recourse borrowings.

In general, the at risk provisions apply to losses attributable to amounts paid or incurred (and depreciation or amortization allowed or allowable) in taxable years beginning after December 31, 1975.

With respect to motion picture activities, the 1976 Tax Reform Act also provides that the at risk provision does not apply to a film purchase shelter if the principal photography begins before September 11, 1975, there was a binding written contract for the purchase of the film on that date, and the taxpayer held his interest in the film on that date. The at risk rule also does not apply to production costs, etc., if the principal photography began before September 11, 1975, and the investor had acquired his interest in the film before that date. In addition, the at risk provision does not apply to a film produced in the United States if the principal photography began before January 1, 1976, if certain commitments with respect to the film had been made by September 10, 1975.

In applying the at risk provisions to activities which were begun in taxable years beginning before January 1, 1976 (and not exempted from this provision by the above transition rules), amounts paid or incurred in taxable years beginning prior to that date and deducted in such taxable years will generally be treated as reducing first that portion of the taxpayer's basis which is not a risk. (On the other hand, withdrawals made in taxable years beginning before January 1, 1976, will be treated as reducing the amount which the taxpayer is at risk in the same manner as withdrawals made after that date.)

2. The 1976 Tax Reform Act contains a capitalization rule which requires individuals and subchapter S corporations to capitalize the costs of producing (including the costs of making prints of a film for distribution) motion pictures, books, records and other similar property and permits them to deduct these capitalized costs over the life of the income stream generated from the production activity. This provision applies to amounts

paid or incurred after December 31, 1975, with respect to property the principal production of which began after December 31, 1975.

3. Under prior law, there were two "at risk" rules designed to prevent a taxpayer from deducting losses in excess of his actual economic investment in the activity involved. The first of these at risk rules—"the specific at risk rule"—applied to four specified activities: (1) farming; (2) exploring for, or exploiting, oil and natural gas resources; (3) holding, producing, or distributing motion picture films or video tapes; and (4) leasing of personal property. The other at risk rule—"the partnership at risk rule"—applied generally to activities engaged in through partnerships. However, there were two exceptions to this rule. First, the rule did not apply to any activity to the extent that the specific at risk rule applied. Second, the rule did not apply to any partnership the principal activity of which was investing in real property (other than mineral property).

The Revenue Act of 1978 extends the specific at risk rule to all activities except real estate (and certain equipment leasing activities of closely-held corporations, as discussed below). For the newly covered activities, the specific at risk rule covers activities which are a part of a trade or business or are engaged in for the production of income. Separate rules for aggregation and separation of activities are provided for the activities to which the at risk rule is extended by the Act. The holding of real property (other than mineral property) is to be treated as a separate activity, and the at risk rule is not applied to losses from that activity. For purposes of this exclusion, personal property and services which are incidental to making real property available as living accommodations are to be treated as part of the activity of holding the real property. Since all the activities currently covered by the partnership at risk rules would now be covered by the new expanded version of the specific at risk rules under section 465, the partnership at risk rule is repealed by the Act.

This provision is effective for taxable years beginning after December 31, 1978.

Under prior law, the only corporations to which the specific at risk rule applied were subchapter S corporations and personal holding companies. The Act extends the application of this rule to all corporations in which five or fewer individuals own more than 50 percent of the corporation's stock. However, the

316

equipment leasing activities of a closely held corporation are not to be subject to the at risk rule if the corporation is actively engaged in equipment leasing, that is, if 50 percent or more of the corporation's gross receipts is derived from equipment leasing. This provision is effective for taxable years beginning after December 31, 1978.

Under prior law, the at risk rule under section 465 may have been interpreted to only require the taxpayer to be at risk as of the end of the taxable year for which losses were claimed. Under this interpretation, subsequent withdrawals of amounts originally placed at risk could be made without the recapture of previously allowed losses.

In order to be consistent with the original intent of the at risk rule, the Act requires the recapture of previously allowed losses when the amount at risk is reduced below zero. Mechanically, this rule works by providing that if the amount at risk is reduced below zero (by distributions to the taxpayer, by changes in the status of indebtedness from recourse to nonrecourse, by the commencement of a guarantee or other similar arrangement which affects the taxpayer's risk of loss, or otherwise), the taxpayer will recognize income to the extent that his at risk basis is reduced below zero. However, the amount recaptured is limited to the excess of the losses previously allowed and which reduced the taxpayer's at risk basis in that activity for taxable years beginning after December 31, 1978, over any amounts previously recaptured. A suspended deduction in the amount equal to the amount of recaptured income would be provided to the taxpayer. This suspended deduction would be allowed in a subsequent year if and to the extent the taxpayer's at risk basis is increased. The provision is generally effective for taxable years beginning after December 31, 1978.

4. Under present law, partnerships are required to file an annual information return setting forth the partnership income, deductions, and credits, names and addresses of the partners, each partner's distributive share of partnership income, deduction, and credit, and certain other information required by the regulations. Under prior law, neither the partnership nor any partner was subject to a civil penalty for failure to file, or for late filing of, a partnership information return.

Under the Act, a civil penalty is imposed on the partnership for failure to timely file a complete partnership information return as required by existing Code sections. The penalty is assessed for each month, or fraction of a month (but not to exceed 5 months), that the partnership return is late or incomplete. The amount of penalty for each month, or fraction of a month, is $50 multiplied by the total number of partners in the partnership during the partnership's taxable year for which the return is due. The penalty will not be imposed if the partnership can show that failure to file a complete or timely return is due to reasonable cause. The provision is effective with respect to returns for taxable years beginning after December 31, 1978.

Under present law, partnerships are not taxable entities. Instead, a partnership is a conduit, in which the items of partnership income, deduction, and credit are allocated among the partners for inclusion in their respective income tax returns. Under present law, partnerships are required to file an annual information return setting forth the partnership income, deductions, and credits, names and addresses of the partners, each partner's distributive share of partnership income, deduction, and credit, and certain other information required by the regulations. The Code provides a period of limitations during which the Service can assess a tax or a taxpayer may file a claim for refund. Generally, the period is 3 years from the date the tax return is filed. Under prior law, the income tax return of each of the partners of a partnership commenced that individual partner's period of limitations. Under prior law, the date of filing of the partnership return did not affect the period of limitations. In order to extend the period of limitations with respect to partnership items, the Service was required to obtain a consent for extension of the statute of limitations from each of the partners—not the partnership. Generally, an agreement to extend the period of limitations related to all items on the return of the partner who consented to the extension.

The Act extends the period of time in which assessments of deficiencies and claims for refund of tax attributable to partnership items may be made. These special periods of limitation apply only to partnership items which are attributable to "Federally registered partnerships." A Federally registered partnership means any partnership the interests in which have been offered for sale prior to the close of the taxable year in an offering required to be registered with the Securities and Exchange Commission (SEC) or any partnership which is or has been subject to the annual SEC reporting requirements which relate to the protection of investors. If a partnership is excused from

318

registration or reporting by either a statutory or a regulatory exemption of the SEC, it is not to be treated as a Federally registered partnership.

With respect to deficiencies, the Act provides generally that the Service may assess a deficiency attributable to partnership items within 4 years after the partnership return for the partnership taxable year in which the item arose is filed. If the partnership return does not properly show the name and address of the person to be assessed the deficiency, the period of assessment will not expire until one year after that information is provided to the Service in the manner prescribed by regulations. With respect to credits and refunds, the Act provides generally that the taxpayer may file a claim for credit or refund of tax attributable to partnership items within 4 years after the due date (including extensions) of the partnership return for the partnership taxable year in which the item arose. This provision is effective for items arising in partnership taxable years beginning after December 31, 1978.

A move fund is a high risk tax shelter in that many movies lose money for various reasons including inadequate distribution, poor reaction by the critics and lack of public interest.

CHAPTER SEVEN

PLAYS

A play fund, like a movie fund, is established to defer pretax income to a future tax year. Investors will be limited to deducting losses from amounts they have at risk.

GENERAL CONSIDERATIONS

No one should consider the purchase of an interest in a play without recognizing the speculative nature of, and the risks of loss involved in, the purchase of an interest in an enterprise devoted to a particular theatrical production. An investor purchasing a Limited Partnership interest should understand that he may lose his entire investment or may not receive any return thereon. To an extent, the success or failure of a theatrical venture is dependent upon the ability of the producer thereof. Ultimately, it is for the professional drama critics and the audience to determine whether the production will be a commercial success or failure.

Of the plays produced for the New York stage recently a vast majority resulted in loss to investors. Some plays would have to run a minimum of approximately 200 performances in New York to a full capacity house even to return to Limited Partners their initial contribution. A vast majority of the plays produced recently for the New York stage failed to run that long; of those that did, a mere handful played to capacity crowds.

The total cost of offering a first-class play in the United States, including all production expenses, probably will not exceed $1,000,000. The allocation of that amount might be as follows:

PHYSICAL PRODUCTION

Scenery - Build & Paint)	$150,000.00	
Props)		
Costumes, Shoes, Hair, etc.	150,000.00	
Electrics - Preparation	8,000.00	
- Purchases	3,000.00	
Sound - Preparation & Fee	7,500.00	
Purchases		$318,500.00

FEES

Director, Ass't. Director	7,000.00	
Choreographer, Ass't.		
Choreographer	7,000.00	
Scenic Designer, Asst. Scenic		
Designer	10,000.00	
Costume Designer)	7,500.00	
Ass't. Costume Designer)		
Lighting Designer, Asst. Ltg.		
Designer	6,000.00	
Vocal Arranger	2,000.00	
Dance Music Arranger	3,000.00	
General Manager	5,000.00	47,500.00

SALARIES

Principals	23,700.00	
Chorus	59,250.00	
Stage Managers	10,500.00	
General and Company Managers	9,300.00	
Musical Director	4,500.00	
Musicians	9,500.00	
Crew: Carpenter, Electrics,		
Props	8,250.00	
Wardrobe	3,500.00	
Audition & Reh. Pianists	3,000.00	131,500.00

REHEARSAL EXPENSES

Aud. & Reh. Thtrs. or Halls	$ 6,000.00	
Scripts	1,500.00	
Stage Mgr. & Dept. Expenses	3,000.00	$ 10,500.00

ADVERTISING & PUBLICITY
    Art & Mechanicals; Print Adverti
       tising; Radio-TV Advertising;
       Outdoor Adv'g; Printing;
       Radio-TV Production; Photos;
       Marquee & Front-of-House;
       Press Agent's Expenses $100,000.00 $100,000.00

GENERAL & ADMINISTRATIVE

Office Expenses	4,500.00	
Legal; Legal Advertising	13,500.00	
Bkkpg, Audit & Payroll Svc.	2,000.00	
Payroll Taxes	19,500.00	
Insurance	5,000.00	
Pension, Vacation, Welfare & Hosp'n.	21,000.00	
Prelim. Box Office	7,500.00	
Transportation	12,000.00	
Hauling	9,000.00	
Toll Tel., Messenger, Xerox	5,000.00	
Living Expenses	12,000.00	
Take-in, N.Y. & O.O.T.	42,000.00	
Miscellaneous	4,000.00	
Music Expenses, Orchestrations & Copying	45,000.00	202,000.00

ADVANCES
    Authors   7,500.00   7,500.00

TOTAL ESTIMATED PRODUCTION
    COSTS............................ $817,500.00

BONDS & DEPOSITS*

Actors' Equity Assoc.	$ 40,000.00	
IATSE	4,000.00	
ATPAM	2,500.00	
		46,500.00

RESERVE   136,000.00

        TOTAL CAPITALIZATION 1,000,000.00

EXAMPLE OF A PLAY FUND

The Pauline Company offers 50 Units, Limited Partnership interests, at $20,000 per unit for a total selling price of $1,000,000. The General Partner, Queen, Inc., shall have the right to capitalize the Partnership at such lesser sum as it may deem adequate to meet production requirements, but such sum shall not be less than $900,000.

Aggregate limited partnership contributions are not actually divided into a specified number of units and amounts; but for the purposes of illustration, they may be considered as consisting of 50 units of $20,000 per unit (with the right reserved to issue fractional units). No contribution of less than $2,000 will be accepted, except with the consent of Queen.

Limited Partners will make the entire financial contribution for which they will receive 55% of any net profits of the Partnership. If there are no net profits the Limited Partners will bear the entire risk of loss to the extent of their respective contributions. Any loss in excess of that amount will be borne by Queen. Based upon present estimates and commitments, the Partners' share in net profits, if any, will be computed only after payment to others of about 46% of the gross weekly box office receipts, and deduction of all other expenses from the balance of gross receipts.

The offering is being made by Queen as an incident to its services as the producer of the play. For its services as producer, Queen will receive 45% of the net profits of the Partnership. Queen will make no cash contribution to the Partnership.

The term of the Partnership shall come to an end at a time determined by Queen.

BENEFITS OF A PLAY FUND

1. Defers high pretax income to a future tax year.
2. In addition to granting the producer the right to produce the play, the Production Contract provides, in part, that if the play shall be produced pursuant to the terms thereof, the producer will be entitled to share for the period set forth in the next following paragraph in the proceeds derived from the disposition of certain so-called "subsidiary"

rights in the play, which rights include but are not limited to motion picture, television, stock and amateur rights; second class touring performances, foreign language performances, condensed and tabloid versions, so-called concert tour versions, commercial uses, grand opera, as well as so-called "show album" rights. It should be noted that the Partnership will receive no royalties with respect to publication rights in the sheet music and mechanical and electrical producing rights in the music and lyrics.

If such motion picture rights, or, with respect to the United States and Canada, such other subsidiary rights are disposed of within twelve (12) years after the last public performance of the last first-class run of the play, the Partnership will be entitled to receive 50% of the net receipts derived therefrom. Thereafter, the Partnership will share in the net receipts derived from the disposition of any subsidiary rights as follows:

if within the next succeeding three years, 42%
if within the next succeeding three years, 32%
if within the next succeeding three years, 22%
if within the next succeeding three years, 12%

If any such subsidiary rights are disposed of more than twenty-four (24) years after the last public performance of the last first-class run of the play, the Partnership will not be entitled to receive any part of the net receipts derived therefrom. The first-class run of the play includes the company presenting the play on Broadway and on tour, if any, thereafter.

RISKS OF A PLAY FUND

1. It should be borne in mind that there probably will not be a ready market for the limited partnership interests.

2. Considerable competition exists among producers in the acquisition of theatrical properties for production and in acquiring suitable talent and theatres in connection with the production. To an extent, the success or failure of the theatrical venture is dependent upon the ability of a producer to select not only suitable talent but also to secure a literary property that will appeal to the theatre-going public. Although the conduct and control of the business and affairs of a theatrical limited partnership vests exclusively in the general partner, ultimately it is for the professional drama

critics and the audience to determine whether the production will be a commercial success or failure.

TAX ASPECTS OF A PLAY FUND

The net profits, if any, of the Partnership will be treated by the Partners as ordinary income and any losses resulting therefrom will be treated by the Partners as ordinary losses deductible from ordinary income. The individual Limited Partners will be taxable in any year in their individual capacities upon their pro rata share of the Partnership's income, whether distributed to them or not. Any distributions by the Partnership will not be taxable to a Partner if not in excess of such Partner's adjusted basis for his Partnership interest at the time. In general, a Partner's basis for his Partnership interest includes his initial investment with adjustments for, among others, net profits, losses and distributions.

A play fund, like a movie fund, is a high-risk tax shelter. Most plays are not profitable for the investor for a variety of reasons including poor reviews and lack of audience appeal.

CHAPTER EIGHT

SCOTCH WHISKY

Trading in Scotch whisky is a way of preserving capital and a hedge against inflation. There are good capital gains possibilities in buying new whisky, holding it to maturity, and then selling.

An investment in Scotch whisky means purchasing warehouse receipts for green whisky still in the barrel. These receipts are traded upon sale of the commodity. The investor never takes delivery. A broker sells the whisky to a commercial distiller or other customer hopefully at a capital gain for the investor.

GENERAL CONSIDERATIONS

The Scots have been distilling whisky for centuries and Scotch whisky can only be made in Scotland. There have been attempts to reproduce its unique flavor in different parts of the world, but these have failed.

There are two types of Scotch whisky distilled. Malt whisky, distilled from malted barley only by the age-old pot still method in approximately 100 malt distilleries scattered throughout Scotland, is the source of taste in whisky. No two malts are exactly alike in flavor and bouquet. The proportion of malts in blends varies from approximately 60% to 15%. Malts vary in quality. The proportion of malt to grain in blends has been consistently dropping, giving rise to lighter whiskies. This may continue to increase the demand for grain and decrease demand for the more expensive, less required malt. Trading in malt requires sophistication. Malts have not been subjected to the same degree of cyclical change as grain. Some do not believe profit opportunities in malts are equal to grains. Grain whisky, produced from malted barley together with unmalted barley and other cereals in varying proportions, is produced in approximately 15 relatively large distilling plants, and are relatively neutral in flavor. There are usually no important qualitative differences. Hence traders need no special knowledge of differences. Dealing in grain whisky is similar to buying and selling cotton; it is not ear-marked at this stage for pillow cases, sheets, or particular brands or labels. Most blenders consider grain whiskies interchangeable. Therefore grain whisky could appear under any label of a blended whiskey. Of the Scotch whisky purchased at retail, 95% or more is a blend.

After distillation, the malt or grain whisky is placed in separate oak wooden casks and then stored in a warehouse. At this stage the whisky becomes official "unmatured Bonded Scotch Whisky," and is ready for maturation period, a minimum of three years by Scotch Law, which is an essential and integral part of the process of making Scotch whisky.

A blender, mixing two types of whisky, usually after the maturation period, produces Blended Scotch Whisky. Blends are a more "blind item" than malts. One would need to know what proportion of the blend is malt and what malts are in the blend. It is said that there are nearly 3,000 different brands of blended Scotch whisky on the market; and that some blends contain as many as 40 different whiskies. The blender holds these recipes as a jealously guarded secret that is passed from generation to generation, and each has its own unique flavor.

The Scotch whisky industry operates under a unique financial burden. No Scotch can be sold in the U.S. Market, for example, until it is at least four years old (three years in other parts of the world); so between the distilling processes and the blending/bottling process, comes the aging process of at least three years. Thus, the distiller must have sufficient capital to carry his company over this period, or he must locate persons who wish to purchase raw whisky and hold it until maturity as a long-term investment.

EXAMPLE

Laura Whisky Investment Co. offers warehouse receipts representing various amounts of malt Scotch whisky in Government Bond in the United Kingdom and certain ancillary services. Laura acts as agent of blending companies in the sale of malt Scotch whisky warehouse receipts. The minimum purchase required will be a quantity of malt Scotch whisky of 600 gallons (approximately $1,800 retail price to purchaser) but Laura may accept a purchase in various amounts exceeding said minimum purchase.

Offered for sale are separately identified casks of malt Scotch whisky; not shares of stock in Laura or any corporation. Laura is a sole proprietor and will make available letters containing current information concerning Scotch whisky furnished by blender or the Scotch Whisky Association. Purchasers of whisky are required to pay for storage and insurance.

Laura stands ready to perform services such as furnishing the above mentioned market letters which include information as to market conditions for potential resale, and advising the investor about the availability of insurance. Laura disclaims any contractual liability in the performance of such services.

Laura provides investors with the means of buying Scotch whisky as a commodity in such a manner that there is no entity interposed between the investor and the commodity that would reduce investors earnings. Except as noted with regard to storage and insurance there are no fees or costs or taxes passed on to the investor.

Laura charges up to 15% of the blender's wholesale price at the time of purchase and a .05 cents per gallon service charge if resale is made through Laura. Laura acts as a sales agent only.

Investors may obtain "all risk insurance" against fire, theft, and excess evaporation. A Lloyds of London All Risks Insurance Policy is available, in which case Laura will supply names and addresses of available agents. The annual cost is presently less than 1% of the value of the investment. All risk insurance does not cover damage from nuclear radiation. Future insurance rates may vary substantially. Laura has no control over such rates but will supply current information at the time of purchase.

The investor should ordinarily plan to hold his parcel for a minimum of three years and more likely for four years. The investor is advised not to plan on rapid trading. This should be considered a long-term, management free type of investment. For instance, if the value of Scotch whisky purchased by an investor increases during the holding period, of which no assurance can be given:

1. The investor may buy a quantity of Scotch whisky for investment, hold it for appreciation for at least 36 months and sell it for cash to realize a capital gain; or

2. The investor may buy equal amounts of Scotch whisky in each of four consecutive years. At the end of that time the original purchase attains a maturity of four years and is ready for blending or bottling. The investor then exchanges his original quantity of mature Scotch whisky for an increased

quantity of new whisky, in direct ratio to the prevailing market price, thereby substantially increasing his holdings with no additional capital outlay; or

3. The investor may buy a quantity of new Scotch whisky for four consecutive years. At the end of the fourth year the original quantity has attained a maturity of four years and is ready for blending or bottling. He then exchanges his mature whisky for a similar quantity of new whisky and accepts the difference in value in cash.

In any case, when an individual buys Scotch whisky, he actually purchases a specific quantity of Scotch in casks, which are numbered and gauged under Her Majesty's Customs and Excise supervision. These numbered casks are registered in the name of the buyer in the distillery records and stored under strict government control until the buyer decides to sell his whisky.

Scotch whisky is bought and sold on the original proof gallonage (O.P.G.) basis, at least up to four years old. No statutory law exists, but in accordance with trade practice, Her Majesty's Customs and Excise permit a 9% loss due to evaporation over the first three years, and 2% per annum thereafter. Whisky bought and sold within the period of three or four years is on the basis of O.P.G. irrespective of actual liquid content. The purchaser of 4 year old whisky assumes that a cask contains 11% less whisky than when filled. This is of little concern to a seller as the purchaser pays the current price per evaporated gallon. Evaporation is therefore not a concern in the price structure. Excess evaporation is covered by "all risk" insurance. Claims for excess evaporation are rare.

From time of distillation until maturity, Scotch whisky is stored in Her Majesty's Customs Warehouse under strictest government supervision. Each cask bears, besides the name of its maker and the date of its distillation, its own individual number under which it is registered in the customs' records and by which it can be traced. Storage charges are billed directly from warehouse to purchaser with billing frequency varying from quarterly to annually.

Cost of storage for one hogshead (approximately 60 gallons) is approximately 5 to 9 cents per week. Therefore, storage charges for one hogshead for four years could be from $10.40 to $18.72. Storage charges may vary from those set forth herein. Laura will provide information on current charges at the time of purchase. Other containers are barrels and butts which contain approximately 50 and 110 gallons respectively.

Malt Scotch Whisky, aging and maturing in wooden casks in Scotland, given normal market conditions, normally increases in value as it matures in age. For example, if investor had purchased whisky in 1966 and sold in 1969, his cost and profit would be as follows:

```
Cost of new Fillings (malt) (1966, 600 gals.
   @ $2.60 gal.) ..............................  $1,560.00
Charge by the Company (15% of cost)  ...........     234.00
Warehouse storage (4 yrs.) (average charge for one
   hogshead for four years is $14.56 – billed
   annually or quarterly) ......................     145.60
Insurance, fire & theft (optional) (average charge of
   $2.13 per $100.00 of the value of the whisky
   purchased to insure for four years are billed
   annually or quarterly) ......................      33.23
Casks cost (refundable)  .......................     300.00
Total purchase cost  ...........................  $2,272.83
Sale price of aged whisky (4 yrs.) (1969, 600 gals.
   @ $5.15 gal.) ................................  $3,090.00
Cask refund  ...................................     300.00
Total sale price  ..............................  $3,390.00
Total purchase cost  ...........................   2,272.83
Net profit before taxes  .......................  $1,117.17
```

Purchases are made as follows:

1. Investor executes an order form and pays 10% or more of the total price. All down payments are deposited in Laura's trust fund account within ten (10) days after receipt of order.

2. Ten (10) days after receipt of orders a confirmation of the price, quantity and terms of sale is issued by Laura. Within 10 days, after receipt of such confirmation the balance of the purchase price shall be due and payable to Laura. All such funds are deposited in Laura's trust account and Laura draws its own check payable to the distiller at the Royal Bank of Scotland. Failure to pay the balance in the time specified may result in a loss of the deposit as liquidated damages.

3. A copy of the delivery order and specifications

authorizing the government bonded warehouse to take the specified cask numbers and register them in investor's name is received by Laura as sent from the blending company in Scotland. This document also shows the distiller's name and the date of bonding for verification. Thereafter the casks can only be moved on investor's directive and when accompanied with an identifying signature, such as is affixed to the original delivery order. The investor may sell to whom and whenever he chooses without any further service from Laura.

4. If the quantity of the gallonage set forth in the warehouse receipt varies by more than 10% from the order, investor may rescind the order and Laura will remit all sums received.

5. Investor receives a true certified copy of the specifications of ownership (warehouse receipt).

The investor may have his bank handle the deposit and delivery order and specifications by using a letter of credit until the delivery order and specifications are presented to his bank.

BENEFITS OF A WHISKY INVESTMENT

1. As it ages, Scotch whisky becomes increasingly desired.

2. All transactions (over the required months) are taxed as long term capital gains. There are no other taxes.

3. It is traded in both U. S. dollars and the British sterling, which may protect the investor against further U. S. Dollar devaluation. Whisky is usually bought and sold in pounds sterling. The British devaluation of 1967 had little effect on prices because most whiskey is exported. Export prices in pounds sterling went up immediately following the last devaluation. Since at least half of all Scotch produced finds its way to the U.S. there has been no difficulty in obtaining dollars or pounds sterling for the whisky. Devaluation of the U.S. Dollar, should it occur at a time when English Sterling remains firm, could give the investor a "double hedge", in that the investor would then have a commodity and an item redeemable in sterling. For some investors this may have more interest than any other aspect of this investment.

4. Inflation, creeping or accelerated, should benefit the holder of a commodity, especially a long term commodity.

5. Whiskey (a commodity) is bought and sold in London and free from present or proposed price control, dividend limitation, profit ceilings or controls in the United Kingdom or

the U.S.

6. It may be advantageous to own a commodity that can now be sold in any part of the world using this commodity in bulk.

RISKS OF A WHISKY INVESTMENT

1. Purchasing malt Scotch whisky and holding title while it ages ordinarily increases the value of the investment. The risk exists that the use of malt whisky would decline in the blending process thereby reducing the price of malt whisky.

2. Purchasing grain Scotch whisky and holding title while it ages ordinarily increases its value. There have been two periods since World War II when the resale value of some grain type Scotch was less than its original cost.

3. Market fluctuations may cause a low increase or decrease in the value of aged whisky resulting in an overall loss to the investor. It should be noted that consumption has increased continuously for every year for which data is available.

4. Scotch whisky consumption might suddenly decline due to consumer tastes turning to other hard liquors or for other reasons, and thus reduce demand and price. Such an event would run counter to the trend.

5. It will not be practical for an investor to personally import the whisky because of licensing problems. An investor will ordinarily sell the whisky, after maturity, through an agent.

6. The quantities involved have no significant utility for personal consumption. Many gallons of unblended whisky should only appeal to the desire of an investor to earn, not to consume.

7. All transactions are conducted with the use of lawful money of the United States. Changes in value of the dollar may occur during the period that the Scotch whisky is being held by investor for resale.

8. Changes in value of the pound may occur. However, because whisky is an international commodity, more than half of which is purchased in the United States, devaluation of the pound should ordinarily result in an almost equal increase in price in U.S. dollars, as it did in the past. The change in the English monetary system to the decimal system effective February 15, 1971, should have no effect whatever on the value or price of Scotch whisky excepting that the manner in which

prices are quoted may be changed. An investor might desire to consider as offsetting this risk the possible circumstance of devaluation of the dollar which would leave the investor with what may be an unusual "double hedge" of holding a commodity which is tradeable in English Sterling instead of dollars.

9. The investment is not suited to short term trading. There is very little market for whisky that is less than three years old. In addition, there may be delays in resale which reduce the liquidity of the investments.

10. The investor cannot be certain of obtaining the very best prices because of the time and effort required to obtain market information.

11. If the investor omits to use a letter of credit it is conceivable that he could be victimized by a defalcation. He may, on request, make either or both his deposit or his payment of the balance of the price through his bank by letter of credit, payable against receipt of "delivery order," "specifications" and "invoices." In this manner he can assure himself of certain transfer of documents on the payment of funds.

TAX ASPECTS OF A WHISKY PROGRAM

1. Whisky warehouse receipts in the hands of an investor are capital items and as such are subject to capital gain or loss treatment and are not taxable as ordinary income or loss. The 1976 Tax Reform Act increases the holding period for long-term capital gains and losses from 6 months to 9 months in 1977 and to 12 months in 1978 and subsequent years.

2. U.S. Internal Revenue Code Section 4911 imposes an interest equalization tax on the purchase of stock or debt obligation of a foreign issuer. The purchase of casks of whisky by a United States Citizen in accordance with the procedures set forth above is not the purchase of stock or a debt obligation under current interpretation of said section and, therefore, is not subject to such tax.

3. U.S. Citizens residing in the U.S. are not subject to British taxes on these transactions.

Scotch whisky is for the investor who can wait the long term of 3 to 4 years for his profit. If the investor has any question about his financial ability to wait that length of time, he should not consider this investment.

CHAPTER NINE

MISCELLANEOUS TAX SHELTERS FOR INDIVIDUALS

There are many tax shelters for the investor which belong in a miscellaneous chapter and are described as follows:

ACCIDENT AND HEALTH INSURANCE PROCEEDS

Benefits under an accident or health insurance policy on which the investor has paid all the premiums are exempt from tax.

CORPORATE STOCKS

A corporation may dispose of its own stock (including treasury stock) for money or other property without recognition of gain or loss.

The investor may exchange, without recognition of gain or loss, common stock for common stock in the same corporation, or preferred stock for preferred stock in the same corporation. This rule is not limited to an exchange between a stockholder and a corporation; it includes a transaction between two individual stockholders. It will not apply, however, if common stock is exchanged for preferred, or preferred for common, or if the investor exchanges common stock in one corporation for common stock in another corporation. In a recapitalization between a stockholder and a corporation, the stockholder can exchange his common stock for preferred stock in a nontaxable exchange.

If property is transferred to a corporation by one or more persons solely in exchange for stock or securities in that corporation and immediately after the exchange such person or persons are in control of the corporation to which the property was transferred, ordinarily no gain or loss will be recognized.

To be in control of the corporation the person or persons making the transfer must own, immediately after the exchange, at least 80% of the total combined voting power of all classes of stock entitled to vote and at least 80% of each class of non-voting stock outstanding.

The term property does not include services rendered or to be rendered to the issuing corporation. Therefore, stock received for services is taxable income to the recipient.

If, in addition to securities, the persons transferring property to the corporation receive other property or cash, gain is recognized, but only to the extent of the cash and fair market value of the other property received. No loss will be recognized.

The assumption of liabilities by a corporation is not regarded as the receipt of cash or other property in determining the gain or loss recognized, except when the liabilities exceed the basis of the property transferred.

DEATH

Under the Tax Reform Act of 1976, the basis of property passing from a decedent is "carried over" from the decedent to the estate or heir. Adjustments to basis are made for death taxes, pre-1977 appreciation, and a $60,000 minimum basis. The provision was to apply with respect to property passing from decedents dying after December 31, 1976.

The Revenue Act of 1978 postpones the effective date of the carryover basis provisions so that they will only apply to property passing from decedents dying after December 31, 1979.

FAMILY PARTNERSHIP

The use of the "family partnership" has long been a tool in estate planning to help reduce the tax burden of the family unit. A family partnership is one in which the partners consist of a spouse, ancestor, or lineal descendants, or any trust for the primary benefit of these persons.

When setting up a family partnership, there is generally a gift of an interest in a business by the owner to other family members who thereby become partners, the family members will then split the partnership income between themselves, rather than having the entire income taxed to the original owner.

Some authorities feel that the Subchapter S Corporation has distinct advantages over the family partnership in so far as income-splitting is concerned. A family partnership may be declared invalid by the IRS when the family member is not considered a real partner whereas legal ownership of stock cannot be questioned. A personal service business cannot be set up as a family partnership, but it can be set up as an elective (Subchapter S Corporation). A parent can remain in absolute control of the corporate business through his majority stock ownership, without the threat of dissolution by a family member everpresent in family partnerships. Also, he need not actually distribute any of the corporate earnings as dividends; whereas, in a family partnership, he may even have to distribute the capital to the children under certain circumstances.

There is only one way in which the family partnership is more flexible. It is possible to use trusts as family partners whereas an elective corporation cannot have a trust as a stockholder. The election will terminate if a trust is introduced.

Income already earned by a corporation can be shifted by a gift of stock to another person even though the gift is made near the very end of the corporation's year. This cannot be done with partnership income.

GIFTS, BEQUESTS, OR INHERITANCES

Gifts, bequests, or inheritances the investor receives are not income and, therefore, are not subject to income tax.

Gifts, whether outright or in trust, represent a tax shelter for the donor in that future appreciation of the gifted assets is removed from the donor's estate. The donor also has the advantage of a unified credit against gift and estate taxes and $3,000 annual exclusions. This presumes that the gifts were not made within three years prior to the donor's death and thereby included in the donor's estate.

Gifts of income can be made to lower-tax-bracket family members in irrevocable, ten-year, short-term reversionary trusts as long as income is not used to discharge the grantor's legal obligation of support.

Gifts of income and principal may be made to a "Minor's Trust" for the benefit of the minor who may have all trust assets distributed to him when he attains his majority. This removes assets from the parent's estate.

Gifts of income and principal can be made to family members in irrevocable, long-term, generation-skipping trusts which pay income to one generation and leave the remainder to the next, thereby eliminating estate tax against the generation receiving the income.

Life insurance may be gifted to the donee for the interpolated terminal reserve plus the unearned premium. This is approximately the cash value, and it grows free of income tax.

Life insurance owned by someone other than the decedent-insured may be free of both Federal Estate Tax and Federal Income Tax at the death of the insured.

There is an increase in the gift tax marital deduction in the case of lifetime gifts to a spouse. A donor will be allowed an unlimited marital deduction for the first $100,000 of lifetime gifts made to a spouse and, thereafter, a deduction for one-half of the aggregate lifetime gifts made to a spouse in excess of $200,000. In general, the gift tax marital deduction is to be integrated with the estate tax marital deduction, so that the estate tax marital deduction will be adjusted in certain cases to reflect the marital deduction attributable to lifetime gifts.

INCOME AVERAGING

The income averaging method permits a part of an unusually large amount of taxable income to be taxed in lower brackets, thus resulting in a reduction of the over all amount of tax due. This method operates to tax a part (the averagable income) of the unusually large amount of income in the peak year at the same lower effective tax rate that applies to the first 1/5th of this averagable income.

INSTALLMENT METHOD OF REPORTING INCOME

The installment method of reporting income relieves the investor of paying tax on income that has not been collected, and permits him to include in his gross income only the portion of each collection that constitutes profit. If a sale results in a loss, he may not use the installment method.

The installment method may be used to report gain from the following sales of property:

A casual or incidental sale of personal property (other than property of a kind that would be included in end-of-year inventory) for a price of more than $1,000 if the payments received in the year of sale do not exceed 30% of the selling price; or

A sale of real estate, regardless of the selling price, if payments received in the year of sale do not exceed 30% of the selling price. There must be two or more payments in two or more taxable years, although there is no requirement that the payment be made in any particular year or years.

INSURANCE POLICIES AND ANNUITIES

No gain or loss is recognized or taxes if the investor exchanges:

1. A life insurance contract for another or for an endowment or an annuity contract;

2. An endowment contract for an annuity contract or for another endownment contract providing for regular payments beginning at a date not later than the beginning date under the old contract; or

3. An annuity contract for another if the insured or annuitant stays the same.

JOINT RETURNS

A husband and wife may make a joint return of their combined income, deductions and credits. In most cases, this results in a lower tax than if separate returns are filed and constitutes tax-free income. Under certain circumstances, this practice may also be followed by widows and widowers.

LIFE INSURANCE PROCEEDS

Life insurance proceeds paid to the investor because of the death of the insured are not taxable unless the policy was transferred to him for a valuable consideration. This is true even if the proceeds were paid under an accident or health insurance policy or an endowment contract.

If because of the death of the insured the investor is entitled to receive life insurance in installments, by his election or otherwise, he may exclude a portion of each installment from his income. To determine the excludable portion, he must prorate the amount held by the insurance company (generally the total lump sum payable at the insured's death) over the period in which the installments are to be paid. Amounts exceeding this excludable portion must be included in income as interest.

If insurance proceeds are payable to the investor because of the death of his spouse, and he receives them in installments, he may exclude the prorated amount of the lump sum payable at death plus up to $1,000 of the interest earned each year on the amount held by the insurer.

If death proceeds from life insurance are left on deposit with an insurance company under an agreement to pay interest only, the interest paid or credited to the beneficiary is taxable to him. The $1,000 interest exclusion does not apply to an agreement to pay interest only.

If, as a surviving spouse, the investor elects to receive only the interest from his insurance proceeds, and later changes his election so that he may receive the proceeds from the policy in installments, he will receive the benefit of this interest exclusion from the time of the new election.

LIVING EXPENSES PAID BY INSURANCE

The investor does not include in income amounts received under an insurance contract as reimbursement for additional living expenses he and members of his household incurred because he lost the use of his residence as a result of fire, storm, or other casualty. The amount to be excluded from income is limited to the excess of the actual living expenses he and his household incurred over the normal expenses he would have incurred during this period. Actual living expenses, for these purposes, include only those incurred to maintain him and his family at the same standard of living enjoyed before the loss occurred.

MARITAL DEDUCTION

The Tax Reform Act of 1976 increases the estate tax marital deduction in the case of small and moderate sized estates passing to a surviving spouse. Under the amendment, an estate will be allowed a marital deduction for property passing to a spouse up to the greater of $250,000 or one-half of the decedent's adjusted gross estate.

NONTAXABLE EXCHANGES

Gain from certain exchanges of property is not taxed, nor is loss deductible, at the time of the exchange. The new property is substantially a continuation of the old, unliquidated investment, and in the case of reorganizations, the new enterprise or the new corporate structure is substantially a continuation of the old. Taxation of the gain or deduction of the loss on such exchange is postponed until the investor disposes of the property received in the exchange.

There must be a reciprocal transfer of property, as distinguished from a transfer of property for money only. If the investor receives cash or other property in addition to the property that may be received tax free, the gain, if any, is taxable, but only to the extent of the money received and the fair market value of the other property received.

A loss is never recognized in a nontaxable exchange, even though the investor receives other property or cash.

Exchange of property for like property is the most common type of transaction in which no gain or loss is recognized.

The property traded and received must both be held by the investor for business or investment purposes. Neither property can be used for personal purposes. It must not be property sold to customers, such as merchandise. It must be held for productive use in business and classified as a fixed asset. Machinery, buildings, land, trucks, and rented houses are examples of property to which the rule applies. The rule does not extend to inventories, raw materials, accounts receivable, or other current asset, nor to real estate held for sale to customers by dealers.

The exchange of real estate for real estate and the exchange of personal property for personal property are exchanges of like property. The trade of an apartment house for a store building, or a machine for a truck are like kind exchanges. The exchange of business or investment real property for a lease, in business or investment property, to run 30 years or more is an exchange of property for like property. So are exchanges of city business or investment property for farm business or investment property and improved business or investment property for unimproved business or investment property. An exchange of personal property for real property does not qualify.

These rules and benefits do not apply to exchanges of stocks, bonds, notes, choses in action, certificates of trust or beneficial interest, or other securities or evidences of indebtedness or interest.

If the investor pays cash in addition to the property he gives up, he still has no gain or loss if the above conditions are met. If he receives cash or other property in addition to like property, and the above conditions are met, the investor is taxed on the gain realized, but only to the extent of the cash and the fair market value of the other property he receives.

Assumption of liabilities by the other party, or a transfer of property subject to a liability, will be treated as the receipt of cash.

If the investor disposes of an FHA 221(d)(3) or 236 low-income housing project and reinvests the net amount realized in another similarly financed housing project within the reinvestment period, he may be entitled to make an election under which all or part of any gain from an approved disposition is not recognized.

ORDINARY DIVIDENDS

The first $100 of the total ordinary dividends the investor receives from qualifying corporations is excluded from taxable income.

PERSONAL EXEMPTIONS

Personal and dependency exemptions are tax-free income.

PRIVATE ANNUITY

The private annuity has been called the "gem of the estate planning tools." It glitters as its benefits are enumerated, but there are problems and pitfalls connected with it which limit its appeal and use.

A private annuity is a sale and is created when an individual (usually a family member) promises to pay an annuity to another person in exchange for property transferred by that person. Like any payments made under the annuity principle, a payment made pursuant to a private annuity represents, in part, an income increment taxable at ordinary income rates and, in part, either a return of capital not subject to tax, or a realization of gain taxable at the capital gains rate.

The use of this device should be approached with caution. If the transferor is substantially dependent on the annuity payments, he will suffer if the transferee predeceases him and fails to make adequate provision for him. (In many cases, and particularly where a business interest is transferred, insurance or a reversionary annuity on the life of the transferee will be indicated to protect the interest of the transferor.)

The basis of the transferee is the total of all payments actually made by him, and he gets no deduction for interest paid.

The private annuity allows for the spreading of capital gains, and, as such, it may help achieve the financial objectives of the transferor (annuitant) and other family members. However, the transferor may far outlive his life expectancy and make the purchase very expensive for the transferee compared to that available under the installment sale.

One of the most intriguing aspects of a private annuity is the estate tax consequence. The transferred property will not be included in the transferor's estate if the following conditions are met:

1. The obligation of the transferee terminates at the death of the transferor.

2. There should be no retention by the transferor of a right to income out of or other right over the transferred property.

3. The property was not transferred in contemplation of death.

REAL ESTATE INVESTMENT TRUSTS

An unincorporated trust or association that specializes in investments in real estate and real estate mortgages, meets certain status requirements as to ownership and purpose and the gross income and asset diversification requirements, may elect to be taxed according to the special rules for real estate investment trusts. In any year in which such an electing organization meets these requirements, maintains records to show actual share owners, and distributes 90% or more of its earnings and profits, it is taxed only on its undistributed income and capital gains. Also the minimum tax may apply to it for the year for (1) its tax preference for depreciation in excess of straight-line depreciation on real property and (2) that portion of other tax preference items not distributed to share owners. The distributed income is taxed directly to the share owners.

RETIREMENT INCOME CREDIT

This 15% credit for persons aged 65 or older will be allowed for earned income, such as salary, instead of just for pensions and other forms of retirement income. The maximum amount on which the credit is computed will rise to $2,500 for single persons and married persons filing joint returns where only one spouse is 65 or older, and to $3,750 for couples filing jointly where both spouses meet the age requirement.

ROYALTY INCOME

Royalties from copyrights on literary, musical, or artistic works, and similar property, or from patents on inventions, are amounts paid to the investor for the right to exploit his work over a specified period of time. He may recover his cost or other basis through depreciation deductions over the life of the copyright or patent. If a patent or copyright becomes valueless in any year before expiration, his unrecovered cost or other basis may be deducted in the year it becomes valueless.

SALE OF RESIDENCE

Under present law, the entire amount of gain or loss realized on the sale or exchange of property generally is recognized. However, under a rollover provision of the Code, gain is not recognized on the sale or exchange of a taxpayer's principal residence if a new principal residence, at least equal in cost to the adjusted sales price of the old residence, is purchased and used by the taxpayer within the replacement period. In addition, under prior law, an individual who had attained the age of 65 could elect to exclude from gross income, on a one-time basis, the entire gain realized on the sale of his or her principal residence if the adjusted sales price was $35,000 or less. If the adjusted sales price exceeded that amount, the amount excludible was that portion of the gain which was determined by multiplying the total gain by a fraction, the numerator of which was $35,000, and the denominator of which was the adjusted sales price of the residence.

The Revenue Act of 1978 repeals the provision which relates to the exclusion of gain on the sale of a residence by an individual who has attained the age of 65. It provides instead that an individual who has attained the age of 55 may exclude from gross income, on a one-time elective basis, up to $100,000 of gain from the sale of his or her principal residence. (In the case of a jointly-owned residence, only one spouse must have attained the age of 55.) This exclusion will be available only in the case of gain from the sale of the principal residence which the taxpayer owned and occupied as his or her principal residence for a period aggregating 3 out of the 5 years which precede the sale. (However, a special transition rule is provided by the Act for individuals eligible under the prior law test.) The election for the $100,000 exclusion, which is effective for sales or exchanges after July 26, 1978, must be made in accordance with regulations prescribed by the Secretary.

The Act also provides that gain realized on the sale of a taxpayer's principal residence after July 26, 1978, is not an item of tax preference, under the minimum tax.

Under present law, gain realized on the sale of a taxpayer's principal residence generally is not recognized to the extent the adjusted sales price is reinvested in a new residence. This provision applies where the taxpayer purchases and uses a new principal residence within a period beginning 18 months before and ending 18 months after the sale of the old principal residence. Only the last principal residence purchased and used during the replacement period constitutes the replacement residence for purposes of the rollover provision.

The Revenue Act of 1978 generally provides that taxpayers may use the rollover provision more than one time within the replacement period if the individual relocates for employment purposes. This change is effective only in the case of taxpayers who had a reasonable expectation at the time of the relocation that they would work at the new location for a substantial period of time. The provision applies to both employees and self-employed individuals, and is effective for sales and exchanges of principal residences after July 26, 1978.

SPECIFIC EXEMPTION

A specific estate exemption is replaced by a unified credit.

STOCK REDEMPTIONS

There is a redemption of stock by a corporation when it reacquires its stock in exchange for property, whether or not the stock is cancelled, retired, or held as treasury stock. The important thing is whether the redemption involves merely an exchange for stock (subject to capital gains treatment), or represents a distribution to the stockholders. Each transaction must be analyzed to determine whether an attribution problem exists.

If any of the following conditions are met, redemptions of stock by a corporation, not in complete or partial liquidation, are treated as distributions in part or full payment in exchange for the stock, and gains or losses to stockholders are capital gains or losses:

1) The redemption is not essentially equivalent to a dividend.

2) The redemption is one in which the distribution is substantially disproportionate to the stockholder's holdings.

3) The distribution is in complete redemption of all the stock of the corporation actually or constructively owned by a stockholder.

4) The redemption is of stock issued by a railroad corporation, as defined in the Bankruptcy Act, under a plan of reorganization under section 77 of that Act.

A substantially disproportionate redemption of stock is one in which the shareholder's percentage of ownership of the corporation's voting stock is reduced by more than 20% in the transaction. Additional requirements are that the 20% reduction test must also be met with respect to common stock (whether voting or nonvoting) and that the shareholder must own less than 50% of the voting stock of the corporation immediately after the redemption. The transaction must not be one of a series, the aggregate result of which is not a "substantially disproportionate" redemption with respect to the shareholder.

A distribution of property in redemption of stock that has been included in the gross estate of a decedent may qualify as payment in exchange for the stock, even though the distribution would otherwise be treated as a dividend.

The Tax Reform Act of 1976 permits capital gains treatment of a distribution in redemption of stock by a corporation to a shareholder to pay death taxes only if the value of the stock exceeds 50 percent of the decedent's adjusted gross estate and only to the extent the burden of paying debts, expenses or taxes falls on the interest passing to the shareholder. The tests of present law which permit capital gains treatment of such a distribution if the value of the stock is more than 35 percent of the decedent's gross estate or more than 50 percent of the decedent's taxable estate would be eliminated.

These provisions apply to the estates of decedent's dying after December 31, 1976.

SUBCHAPTER S CORPORATION

A Subchapter S corporation is a small business corporation that has elected not to be taxed as a corporation. A shareholder of a Subchapter S corporation must include in his income his pro rata share of the corporation's taxable income whether the amount was actually distributed to him or not. This becomes a tax shelter when lower-income family members are given or sold stock in such a corporation.

Under prior law, in order to be eligible for a subchapter S election, a corporation could have only 10 or fewer shareholders.

However, after a corporation had been an electing subchapter S corporation for 5 consecutive taxable years, it was allowed to increase its number of qualifying shareholders to 15. In addition, the number of shareholders was allowed to exceed 10 (but not 15) if the additional shareholders acquired their stock through inheritance.

Under the Revenue Act of 1978, the number of shareholders permitted in order for a corporation to qualify for and maintain subchapter S status is increased from 10 to 15 (without regard to any 5-year period). The provision applies to taxable years beginning after December 31, 1978.

For purposes of determining the maximum number of shareholders a corporation may have in order to be eligible for a subchapter S election, prior law provided that stock which was community property of a husband and wife (or the income from which was community property income) under the law of a community property State would be treated as owned by one shareholder. Similarly, a husband and wife were treated as one shareholder if they owned the stock as joint tenants, tenants in common, or tenants by the entirety. Also, a surviving spouse and the estate of a deceased spouse (or the estates of both deceased spouses) were treated as one shareholder if the husbands and wife were treated as one shareholder at the time of the death of the deceased spouse.

Under the Revenue Act of 1978, a husband and wife (and their estates) are to be treated as one shareholder for purposes of determining the number of shareholders in a corporation in determining whether it is eligible to qualify as an electing small business corporation. This treatment is to apply regardless of whether shares are individually or co-owned by the spouses. The provision applies to taxable years beginning after December 31, 1978.

Prior law required that in order for a subchapter S election to be effective for a taxable year, it had to be filed during a 2-month period which began one month before the start of the taxable year. An election was not valid for either the intended year or any future year if it was not filed within this period. Extensions of time for filing the election were not granted. If an election was found to be untimely upon audit several years later, the corporation was taxed as a regular corporation for all the intervening years.

Under the Revenue Act of 1978, the period of time to make a subchapter S election is expanded to include the entire preceding taxable year of the corporation. In addition, the bill will permit all corporations to make an election during the first 75 days of the taxable year for which the election is effective. The provision is effective for subchapter S elections made for taxable years beginning after December 31, 1978.

TAX–EXEMPT INTEREST

Interest on obligations of a State or a political subdivision thereof, the District of Columbia, Puerto Rico, a possession of the United States, or a political subdivision thereof is wholly Toll Road Commissions, Utility Services Authorities, and similar bodies created for furtherance of public functions. (The interest is tax-exempt whether received on a debt evidenced only by an ordinary written agreement of purchase and sale entered into by duly constituted authorities, or received on a conventional bond or promissory note.) It is also exempt if paid by an insurer upon default by the political subdivision. The same is true if the political subdivision, after many years of operation, sells the property, purchased with the bond proceeds, to a private company and the interest is paid out of the payments received from the company.

Interest on arbitrage bonds issued by state or local governments after October 9, 1969, must be included in gross income. An arbitrage bond is an obligation issued by a state or local government for the purpose of buying securities or obligations, the interest on which is expected to be materially higher than the interest on the arbitrage bonds. However, if the bond proceeds are temporarily invested until they are needed for the bonds' original purpose, such bonds are not arbitrage bonds.

Interest on industrial development bonds issued after April 30, 1968, is taxable unless the bonds are used to fund certain exempt activities, or are part of an issue of one million dollars or less and substantially all the proceeds are used to acquire, construct, reconstruct or improve land or depreciable property or to redeem all or part of a prior bond issue that was issued to acquire, construct, reconstruct or improve land or depreciable property.

For bonds issued after October 24, 1968, a tax-exempt limitation of five million dollars may be applied in certain situations. This limitation increases to ten million dollars for bonds issued after 1978. The bond issuer will be able to tell you if the increased limitation applies to the issue in question.

Interest on bonds issued by a community redevelopment agency that is a political subdivision of a state is tax exempt, where the principal and interest payments are secured by property taxes on the increased assessed valuation of the redeveloped property and collected by the local taxing authorities.

State and municipal bonds purchased at a discount. If these bonds were issued originally at a discount, the ratable amount of original issue discount is treated as tax-exempt interest and not included in income. However, any gain attributable to "market" discount is taxable as capital gain upon disposition or redemption of the bonds.

Market discount is computed by subtracting the price you paid for the bond from the total of the original issue price of the bond and the amount of original issue discount that represented interest to any previous holders.

Uniformed Services Savings Deposit Program. Interest on this type of an account with a balance of less than $10,000 is subject to substantial restrictions on withdrawal and is not taxable until actually received or made available to the member of the Armed Forces, whichever is earlier. Interest on an account that has reached and maintained a balance of $10,000 may be withdrawn quarterly and is taxable at that time.

Exempt-Interest dividends received from a mutual fund and designated as such by the mutual fund are not included in income.

Under present law, interest on industrial development bonds is, in general, taxable. However, interest on certain small issues of industrial development bonds is tax-exempt. Small issues are issues of $1 million or less the proceeds of which are used for the acquisition or construction of depreciable property or land. At the election of the issuer, the $1 million limitation could be increased to $5 million under prior law. If this election was made, certain capital expenditures and the total of a series of small issues for a project could not exceed $5 million.

The Revenue Act of 1978 increases the limitation on elective small issues of industrial development bonds from $5 million to

$10 million. In addition, the capital expenditure limitation for facilities with respect to which an urban development action grant (UDAG) has been made is increased to $20 million. However, only $10 million of the funds used to finance an urban development action grant facility may be provided through the use of tax-exempt elective small issue industrial development bonds.

The provision increasing the elective small issues limitation to $10 million applies to bonds issued after December 31, 1978, and to capital expenditures made after December 31, 1978, with respect to obligations issued before January 1, 1979. The provision dealing with urban development action grants applies to obligations issued after September 30, 1979, and to capital expenditures made after September 30, 1979, with respect to obligations issued after that date.

Tax-exempt treatment is provided for industrial development bonds used to provide facilities for the local furnishing of electric energy. Local furnishing has been interpreted by the Internal Revenue Service to mean the furnishing of electric energy to the general populace of an area comprising no more than two contiguous counties (or political equivalents). The Act includes, within the definition of local furnishing of electric energy, the furnishing solely within an area comprising a city and one contiguous county. This provision applies to taxable years ending after April 30, 1968, with respect to obligations issued after that date.

Under present law, an industrial development bond qualifies for tax-exempt treatment where substantially all the proceeds of the bond are used to provide facilities for the furnishing of water if available on reasonable demand to members of the general public.

The Act provides that members of the general public include commercial users. Thus, under the Act, when the proceeds of an industrial development bond are used to provide facilities for the furnishing of water to the general public for any purpose, the interest received on the bond will qualify for tax exemption.

The Act imposes three requirements which the facility must satisfy in order for the bonds to qualify for tax exemption. First, the facility must be for the furnishing of water. Second, the facility must be operated by a governmental unit or a regulated public utility. Finally, the facility must make or will make water available to members of the general public. For purposes of this provision, the general public includes agricultural, industrial, commercial, and electric utility users.

The provision applies to obligations issued after the date of enactment.

Under present law, certain industrial development bonds qualify for tax exemption where substantially all the proceeds of the bonds are used to provide certain "exempt activities" facilities, e.g., mass commuting facilities. However, it has been unclear under what circumstances a refunding issue of exempt activity industrial development bonds would qualify for tax exemption.

Under the Act, a refunding of an industrial development bond in advance of its redemption qualifies for tax exemption, but only if substantially all the proceeds of the refunded issue were used to provide a qualified public facility. A qualified public facility is defied as airports, docks or wharves, mass commuting facilities, parking facilities, or storage or training facilities directly related to these facilities, and convention or trade show facilities which are available for use by the general public.

The provision applies to refunding obligations issued after the date of enactment.

Present law provides that interest on State and local government obligations is, in general, tax-exempt. However, tax-exempt status is denied to arbitrage bonds and certain industrial development bonds. Moreover, in order for such an obligation to be tax exempt, it must have been issued by a State or local government or issued by an authority "on behalf of" a State or local government.

Under prior law, as a practical matter, an issuer has had no appeal from an Internal Revenue Service private letter ruling (or failure to issue a private letter ruling) that a proposed issue of municipal bonds is taxable. In addition, it has been impossible for an issuer to question the Service's rulings and regulations directly.

The Act authorizes the Tax Court to issue declaratory judgments with respect to the tax-exempt status of proposed bond issues. However, relief under the amendment is available only to the proposed bond issuer and only if: (1) the proposed issuer has requested a private letter ruling from the Internal Revenue Service (IRS), (2) the IRS has acted adversely on the request or has failed to act within 180 days, and (3) the proposed issuer has otherwise exhausted all administrative remedies. The Tax

Court determination is to be based on any facts or arguments which the IRS and/or the proposed issuer wish to introduce at the time of trial. Appeal of the decision of the Tax Court will lie exclusively with the United States Court of Appeals for the District of Columbia Circuit.

The provision applies to requests for determinations (private ruling requests) filed with the Internal Revenue Service after December 31, 1978.

Prior to 1969, State and local governments were able to earn arbitrage profits through investing the proceeds of their tax-exempt bonds in higher yielding Treasury obligations. In 1969, tax-exempt status was denied to State and local government obligations (arbitrage bonds) the proceeds of which are invested in materially higher yielding securities or the proceeds of which are used to replace funds which were used to acquire materially higher yielding obligations.

These yield restrictions which were placed on State and local government obligations created a situation where some State and local governments attempted to divert arbitrage profits to third parties which, in some instances, were charities.

On September 24, 1976, the Treasury Department announced regulations which were designed to prevent issuers from diverting arbitrage profits to underwriters and third parties.

The Act, in general, prohibits the Treasury from applying the position taken by the regulations retroactively to prevent arbitrage profits from being donated to a public charity. Thus, under the Act, payment of a refund profit in accordance with a qualified agreement shall not cause the refunding obligation (which gave rise to the refund profit) to be treated as an arbitrage bond or cause imposition of any penalty upon the issuer ("blacklisting") if pursuant to the qualified agreement the refund profit is held (1) in a trust fund, (2) in an escrow account, or (3) by an underwriter or other person.

In addition, where a State or local government accounts to the United States for the refund profit by direct payment or by purchase of low-interest United States obligations because of the Internal Revenue Service's rulings policy, the Treasury shall return such accounted-for refund profits so that it can, within 90 days, be given to the intended beneficiary. Repayment by the Treasury shall be required under the Act, only if on or before January 1, 1977, the State or local government which entered into a qualified agreement requested, in writing, a ruling from the Internal Revenue Service on the tax consequences of paying refund profits to charitable organizations and failed to receive a favorable ruling, and did not pay the refund profit to a charitable organization. The repayment shall be paid out of unappropriated Treasury funds.

UNIFORM GIFT TO MINORS ACT

An adult person may make a gift of securities, money, and life insurance to a minor and still maintain effective control over the subject matter of the gift. If the subject of the gift is life insurance, the custodian shall have all of the incidents of ownership in the policy as if he were personally the owner. The designated beneficiary of any such policy of insurance held by a custodian shall be the minor or, in the event of his death, the minor's estate. It is important that someone other than the donor be the custodian so that the gifted assets will not be included in the donor's estate at his death.

The interest, dividends and capital gains distributions from the gifted assets are taxed to the donee and not to the donor unless used to discharge the donor's legal obligation of support.

VARIABLE ANNUITY CONTRACTS

Variable annuity contracts are considered annuity contracts taxable under Section 72 of the Code. Under the existing provisions of the Code, an increase in the accumulated value of a contract is not taxable to the Owner until received by him either in the form of variable annuity payments or as the results of a redemption.

When variable annuity payments commence, a portion of each payment is excluded from gross income as a return of the investment in the contract. The portion of each payment to be excluded is determined by dividing the investment in the contract by the annuitant's life expectancy. Such "excludable amount" requires adjustment for annuity features such as payments certain and refund guarantees. The variable annuity payments in excess of this amount are taxable as ordinary income.

In the event of a complete redemption prior to the annuity payment date, any gain on the termination of the contract will be taxed as ordinary income. Under certain circumstances, the Owner may be eligible for the tax treatment accorded by Sections 1301-1305 of the Code dealing with income averaging. Partial redemptions, which in the aggregate exceed the investment in the contract, may be taxed as ordinary income. No payment under the contracts is eligible for capital gains treatment under existing law.

This array of miscellaneous tax shelters for individuals clearly indicates that tax shelters are firmly embedded in the law for all taxpayers to enjoy depending upon which areas the IRS decides to favor from time to time.

PART TWO

TAX SHELTERS AND TAX–FREE INCOME
FOR EMPLOYEES

Good employees are difficult to find and require benefits to prevent their being lured to another employer. The talents of insurance men, attorneys, accountants, securities salesmen, actuaries, banks and trust companies, etc., have been directed toward identifying and funding these benefits which are discussed as follows:

PAYMENTS TO BENEFICIARIES OF
DECEASED EMPLOYEES

Up to $5,000 of such payments, made by or for an employer because of an employee's death, are excludable from the income of the beneficiaries. The payments need not be made as the result of a contract. The amount excluded with respect to any deceased employee may not exceed $5,000 regardless of the number of his employers.

This exclusion also covers payments that represent the balance to the credit of a deceased employee under a stock bonus, pension, or profit-sharing plan and received during one tax year of the beneficiary.

Any amount the decedent had a right to receive had he lived cannot be excluded as a tax-free death benefit.

SOCIAL SECURITY, RAILROAD RETIREMENT ACT,
AND UNEMPLOYMENT BENEFITS

Social security benefits received monthly, or in a lump sum, from the Federal Government or from a State under the Federal social security program are not taxable.

Amounts received for basic Railroad Retirement benefits are not taxable.

Unemployment benefits paid by a State from the Federal Unemployment Trust Fund and payments made under the Railroad Unemployment Insurance Act are not taxable.

GROUP HOSPITALIZATION PREMIUMS

Group hospitalization premiums, including premiums for supplementary medical insurance (Medicare), paid by the employer, or former employer if employee is retired, are not included in income if they are not withheld from the employee's pay.

BUSINESS ACCIDENT AND HEALTH PLANS

A form of executive compensation is the employer-financed accident and health plan which may cover disability and/or medical reimbursement.

The contributions made by an employer to accident and health "plans" to provide health and disability benefits for his employees, whether through insurance or otherwise (for payments such as those for medical care, permanent injury, or compensation for the loss of wages), if reasonable in amount, are not taxable income to such employees.

This is an unsettled area of the law, and current cases should be followed to determine what IRS is permitting in so far as what employees may or must be covered and the extent of their benefits.

Assuming the plan is satisfactory to the IRS, the following benefits are tax exempt to the employee:

1. Amounts received as reimbursement for medical and dental expenses of the employee, his spouse, and dependents.

2. Payments for the loss, or loss of use, of a member or function of the body, or permanent disfigurement of the employee, his spouse or a dependent.

3. The 1976 Tax Reform Act generally repeals the present sick pay exclusion and substitutes a maximum annual exclusion of up to $5,200 a year for retirees under age 65 who have retired on disability and who are permanently and totally disabled. (After age 65, these retirees will be eligible for the revised elderly credit.) The maximum amount excludable is to

be reduced on a dollar-for-dollar basis by the individual's adjusted gross income (including disability income) in excess of $15,000 (this amount applies to both single and joint returns). Thus, the disability income exclusion is unavailable if the individual has adjusted gross income of $20,200.

Under prior law, gorss income did not include amounts received under a self-insured accident or health plan as reimbursement for employee medical expenses, unless the expenses were deducted in a prior taxable year.

Under the Revenue Act of 1978, self-insured medical reimbursement plans are subject to rules regarding discrimination as to eligibility and benefits in favor of employees who are officers, shareholders, or highly paid. Reimbursements to an officer, etc., under a discriminatory plan are wholly or partly includible in income.

Under the Act, a plan satisfies the nondiscriminatory eligibility rule if it meets requirements similar to those which must be satisfied by qualified pension plans (sec. 410(b)). In testing the eligibility provisions of a plan, however, part-time employees and seasonal employees may be excluded. Under the Act, employees whose customary weekly employment is for less than 35 hours are considered parttime, and employees whose customary annual employment is for less than 9 months are considered seasonal.

The Act provides that benefits are considered discriminatory unless all benefits provided for officers, etc., are also provided for other employees. However, under the Act, a plan is not considered to provide discriminatory benefits merely because benefits thereunder are offset by benefits paid under another plan of the employer or another employer (insured or self-insured) or by benefits paid under Medicare or other Federal or State law.

The provision applies for taxable years beginning after December 31, 1979.

GROUP LIFE INSURANCE

Group-term life insurance purchased for employees is not included in their income for amounts not in excess of $50,000.

The employee will not be taxed on the cost of group-term life insurance protection in excess of $50,000 if:

357

1. The coverage continues after he has terminated his employment and has reached retirement age or become disabled;

2. His employer is directly or indirectly the beneficiary of the policy for the entire period the insurance is in effect during the tax year; or

3. The sole beneficiary of the excess over $50,000 is a qualified charitable organization for the entire period the insurance is in effect during the tax year.

OPTIONS

If the employee is granted an option to buy stock or other property as payment for his services as an employee, he may realize taxable income when he receives the option. However, if his option is a statutory stock option — a qualified stock option, an option granted under an employee stock purchase plan, or a restricted stock option — special rules generally postpone the tax until he sells or exchanges his shares of stock.

If the employee is granted a nonstatutory stock option that has a readily ascertainable fair market value at the time it is granted to him, he must include in his income for that year the difference between its fair market value and the amount he paid for it, if any. His basis for the option then is its fair market value on the date granted to him.

If the fair market value of the option is not readily ascertainable, he does not realize income until he exercises or transfers the option. When he exercises this type of option, he realizes income to the extent of the difference between the fair market value of the property received less the amount he paid for it.

The fair market value of an option is normally not readily ascertainable unless it is actively traded on an established market.

There are three types of statutory stock options: qualified stock options, options granted pursuant to employee stock purchase plans, and restricted stock plans.

In each case, the employee must be an employee of the company granting the option at all times beginning with the date of the grant of the option until 3 months before the time the option is exercised. Also, it must be nontransferable except at death.

Qualified stock options are those granted as incentives for executive-type employees, enabling them to obtain a proprietary interest in the corporation.

The value of qualified stock options issued to key corporate personnel after May 20, 1976, will be treated as ordinary income rather than capital gains. If the option can be valued when granted, its value will count as income then. Otherwise, the employee will wait until he exercises the option before counting as income the spread between the option price and the market value when he exercises it.

Qualified stock options are items of tax preference and are subject to the 15% minimum tax.

Employee stock purchase plans are designed to permit employees to purchase stock of their employer corporation, usually at a discount. The plan must be nondiscriminatory and must include virtually all employees.

The employee is not required to include any amount in gross income when he receives or exercises the option.

If he holds the stock for more than 6 months and at least 2 years elapse from the time the option was granted to him, the difference between the option price and the value of the stock at the time the option was granted to him must be reported as ordinary income when he disposes of the stock. This amount cannot exceed the gain realized on the sale of the stock. But the excess of the gain realized over the amount reported as ordinary income is capital gain.

The option price to him cannot be less than the lesser of 85% of the fair market value of the stock:

(1) at the time of the grant; or

(2) at the time he exercises the option

If he did not meet the holding period requirements (both 6 months and 2 years), the difference between the option price and value of the stock when the option is exercised must be reported as ordinary income when he sells the stock. This is ordinary income regardless of whether it is greater than the total gain realized. The cost of the stock is increased by the amount reported as ordinary income and the difference between the increased basis and the selling price is a capital gain or loss.

Restricted stock options are options granted to the employee by the employer pursuant to a plan in existence before January 1, 1964.

To get a tax benefit from a restricted stock option the employee must neither dispose of his stock within 6 months of the date of acquisition nor within 2 years of the date the option was granted to him.

If he meets these holding period requirements, and his option price is at least 95% of the fair market value of the stock at the time it is granted to him, the entire gain realized when he sells or exchanges the stock is capital gain.

If he meets the above holding requirements and his option price is between 85% and 95% of the fair market value of the stock at the time the option is granted to him, he must report as ordinary income for the tax year in which he disposes of his stock, either the excess of the fair market value of his stock over the option price at the time it is granted to him or, if less, the excess of the fair market value over the option price at the time of the disposition. The basis for his shares is increased by the amount he includes in his gross income. The difference between this adjusted basis and the amount he realizes from the sale or exchange of his shares is a capital gain or loss.

If he disposes of his shares before he meets the holding requirements, he must include as ordinary income the difference (if any) between the option price and the price of the shares at the time the option is exercised. This is ordinary income regardless of whether it is greater than the gain realized on the disposition. The basis of his shares of stock is increased by the amount he includes in gross income. The difference between this adjusted basis and the amount he realizes from his stock when he sells or exchanges it, is a capital gain or loss.

Restricted stock options are items of tax preference and are subject to the 15% minimum tax.

NONQUALIFIED DEFERRED COMPENSATION

Deferred compensation agreements are designed to avoid high tax rates by delaying the receipt of income until later years. If properly arranged, there is no income tax to the employee prior to the receipt of income. Only each income benefit as received will be subject to income tax. Capital gains taxation on a lump-sum distribution is not available to the employee under nonqualified plans.

QUALIFIED DEFERRED COMPENSATION

Qualified deferred compensation is the "Five Star General" of employee benefits:

1. Contributions to the plan are deductible to the employer, if the employer makes all the contributions.

2. There is no current income taxation to the employee except the cost of life insurance coverage, if any. However, the net amount at risk of life insurance is free of income tax at death.

3. There is no income taxation of trust assets prior to distribution.

4. Lump-sum distributions at termination of employment may receive favorable tax treatment.

5. Pre-retirement annuity death benefits, if paid to a beneficiary other than the participant's estate, are free of Federal estate taxes.

Under prior law, the part of a lump sum pension distribution earned before 1974 is treated as capital gain and, if the taxpayer elects, the post-1973 part is taxed as ordinary income in a "separate basket," with 10-year income averaging. If the election is not made, the distribution is taxed as ordinary income under the usual rules.

Under the 1976 Tax Reform Act, a taxpayer may irrevocably elect to treat all of a lump sum distribution as if it were earned after 1973 so that it is taxed as ordinary income in a separate basket, with 10-year income averaging. The election applies to distributions made after 1975 in taxable years beginning after December 31, 1975.

For capital gain treatment to apply, the distribution must be paid within one tax year. Also, it must be because of: (a) the employee's death or other separation from service, or (b) the death of the employee after his separation from service.

A special averaging method for computing the tax may apply to the ordinary income portion of the distribution if the employee had been a member of the plan for at least 5 years prior to the year of payment. For purposes of computing the limitation, gross income does not include the amounts received as compensation in the same year in which the lump-sum distribution is received if the employee is separated because of death or disability or is at least age 59½ and gross income does not include the capital gain portion of the distribution. The tax on the ordinary income portion of the distribution is limited to 10 times the increase in tax that would result from including 1/10 of the ordinary income portion of the distribution in gross income in the year received.

The two broad categories of qualified deferred compensation are profit-sharing plans and pension plans. A profit-sharing plan is one in which a portion of a firm's profits are set aside annually for future distribution among employees. The plan may provide for distribution after a minimum period of time (at least two years) or at some specific event, such as death, disability, termination, or retirement. A pension plan is one providing for retired employees or their beneficiaries, through the payment of benefits determined without regard to profits.

A stock-bonus plan is one for employees or their beneficiaries providing benefits similar to those of profit-sharing plans, except that the benefits are distributable in the employer's stock, and employer contributions are not necessarily dependent upon profit.

An annuity plan is similar to a pension plan except that retirement benefits are provided under annuity or insurance contracts without a trust.

A bond purchase plan is a nontrusteed pension or profit-sharing plan under which the only investment permitted is in U.S. Retirement Plan Bonds.

Contributions to the plans or trusts may be made by the employer, employees, or both. Voluntary contributions by employees are exempt from tax while in the trust.

The two basic types of products are group and individual. Usually 25 lives or less will tend toward the individual product. More than 50 will probably be group. The facts along with the clients' objectives will influence the decision for the cases between 25 and 50.

Representative group products are as follows:

GROUP RETIREMENT PLAN: The benefits are the same as

individual insurance income at age contracts. For each $1,000 face amount of life insurance and maturity value developed by retirement there will be sufficient to provide $10 of monthly income for life with 60 or 120 payments guaranteed.

GROUP AUXILIARY PLAN: The life insurance provided is of the ordinary life type which develops a much smaller cash value for income purposes, the amount being 30 – 55 percent of that developed under the group retirement plan, The balance of the money needed is accumulated in a separate fund on an actuarial basis.

GROUP DEFERRED ANNUITY: Each year an increment of deferred-annuity income is purchased.

DEPOSIT ADMINISTRATION: Contributions are accumulated in a fund at interest until an employee retires, at which time a lifetime annuity is purchased by withdrawing the necessary premium from the fund.

IMMEDIATE PARTICIPATION GUARANTEE: A variation of the Deposit Administration plan under which annuities are not actually purchased (similar to an uninsured plan) although it offers some basic insurance guarantees. This type of plan is usually only considered by large groups.

SEPARATE ACCOUNT: An arrangement between an insurance company and a client through which a portion of the amount paid to the insurance company for a pension, retirement, or profit-sharing plan is allocated separately for investment purposes.

Many group plans are handled by banks and other institutions with the assistance of an actuary. Common trust funds of the institution are often the investment vehicle.

Plans have been developed which enable each participant to determine how much of the contribution made by the employer on his behalf will be used to purchase guaranteed funds, equities, or insurance.

Some of the plans using individual products are as follows:

FIXED END–BENEFIT, FULLY INSURED AND NON–INTEGRATED: This plan uses insurance to age contracts without regard to social security benefits.

FIXED END–BENEFIT, FULLY INSURED AND INTEGRATED: This plan uses insurance to age contracts and takes social security benefits into account.

FIXED END–BENEFIT, SPLIT–FUNDED AND NON–INTEGRATED: This plan uses ordinary life type products combined with an auxiliary fund without regard to social security benefits.

FIXED END–BENEFIT, SPLIT–FUNDED AND INTEGRATED: This plan uses ordinary life insurance contracts combined with an auxiliary fund and takes social security benefits into account.

MONEY PURCHASE AND NON–INTEGRATED: The annual contribution is a fixed percentage of the employee's earnings without regard to social security benefits.

MONEY PURCHASE AND INTEGRATED: The annual contribution is a fixed percentage of the employee's earnings and takes social security benefits into account.

PROFIT SHARING AND NON–INTEGRATED: Employer contribution is based on profits and employee's earnings without regard to social security benefits.

PROFIT SHARING AND INTEGRATED: Employer contribution is based on profits and employee's earnings and takes social security benefits into account.

VARIABLE END–BENEFIT, SPLIT–FUNDED AND NON–INTEGRATED: This plan uses ordinary life insurance combined with an auxiliary fund without regard to social security benefits. The participant receives the investment result whether more or less than the assumed growth.

VARIABLE END–BENEFIT, SPLIT–FUNDED AND INTEGRATED: This plan uses ordinary life insurance combined with an auxiliary fund and takes social security benefits into account. The participant receives the investment result whether more or less than the assumed growth.

TARGET BENEFIT, SPLIT–FUNDED AND NON–INTEGRATED: This plan has the best features of both a money purchase plan and a fixed benefit plan. It uses ordinary life insurance combined with an auxiliary fund without regard to social security benefits. Employer contributions are based on the typical end-benefit plan, and the participant receives the investment result whether more or less than the assumed growth. The death benefit is the sum of the life insurance proceeds and the participant's share of the auxiliary fund, the same as available under a money purchase plan. Other end benefit plans have a death benefit limited to the greater of the reserve or the insurance proceeds based on $1,000 of insurance for each $10 of monthly income.

TARGET BENEFIT, SPLIT–FUNDED AND INTEGRATED: This plan has the best features of both a money purchase plan and a fixed benefit plan. It uses ordinary life insurance combined with an auxiliary fund and takes social security benefits into account. Employer contributions are based on the typical end-benefit plan, and the participant receives the investment result whether more or less than the assumed growth. The death benefit is the sum of the life insurance proceeds and the participant's share of the auxiliary fund, the same as available under a money purchase plan. Other end benefit plans have a death benefit limited to the greater of the reserve or the insurance proceeds based on $1,000 of insurance for each $10 of monthly income.

SALARY REDUCTION PLAN: This area of the law is unsettled, and the IRS may eliminate this plan at any time. It is customarily an option with a money purchase plan in which employees can have up to 6% of their salary deducted and placed in the pension trust. The employee is not taxed on this part of his income.

THRIFT PLAN: This is a type of money purchase pension plan in which employees contribute a pre-determined percentage of their income up to 6%, and the employer often matches their contribution.

SALARY SAVINGS PLAN: This is a plan for employee voluntary contributions with their after-tax dollars.

SELF–ADMINISTERED PLAN, NON–INTEGRATED AND INTEGRATED: It is a retirement plan under which contributions to purchase pension benefits are paid to a trustee who invests the money, accumulates the earnings and interest, and pays benefits to eligible employees under the terms of the retirement plan and trust agreements. This type of plan is administered by the employer, or a committee appointed by him and the trustee (usually a corporate trustee).

All eligible participants in qualified plans can elect to contribute up to 10% of their compensation and have it placed in the tax-exempt trust. This is, of course, after-tax income.

Insurance products are used as investments in many of the plans mentioned. Years ago it was common for plans to be fully insured. With inflation gaining as a strong factor in the economy the majority of the plans now use part insurance for some guarantees and place the balance in equities such as common stock and real estate. Unimproved land is being given more

365

attention as there is no depreciation write-off to be lost in a tax-exempt trust as would ordinarily be true of improved real estate. Some plans have their investments 100% in equities. However, most plans continue to reflect a desire for investment balance with some insurance for protection against deflation, guaranteed annuity rates at the present price, and the assurance of a substantial benefit in the event of early death together with equities which provide a hedge against inflation and the opportunity for a large growth.

The growth in equities in excess of assumptions in end-benefit plans can be used to make the plan cheaper by using a fixed end-benefit or provide a larger benefit for the participant by using money purchase, variable end-benefit, or target end-benefit.

In money purchase plans a contribution of the lesser of 25% of compensation or $25,000+ is permissible. In end-benefit plans the maximum contribution is the lesser of 100% of compensation or $75,000+. If the employer has both a defined contribution (money purchase) plan and an end-benefit plan, a formula is applied each year for each employee to ascertain whether the limitations have been exceeded. The formula is the sum of a defined contribution (money purchase) fraction and an end-benefit contribution fraction, and this sum must not exceed 1.4.

The contribution toward profit-sharing plans is limited to 15% of covered compensation with provisions for contribution and credit carryovers.

Where an employer has both a pension plan and a profit-sharing plan, his contributions are limited to 25% of covered compensation with provisions for contribution and credit carryovers.

Some of the typical pension formulas are as follows:

FLAT DOLLAR BENEFIT: Each participant receives the same retirement benefit such as $100 per month.

FLAT PERCENTAGE (NON–INTEGRATED): Each participant receives the same percentage of monthly compensation as a monthly retirement income benefit such as 20%.

FLAT PERCENTAGE – INTEGRATED ON A SPECIFIED LEVEL: Each participant receives two portions of benefit. One is based on a percentage of total monthly compensation. The second is based on a percentage of monthly compensation in excess of the specified level. This "integration" level is related to social security wage base and is selected by the employer.

The maximum percentage allowed on the "excess" compensation is 30%. This 30% maximum applies to a participant only if he will have 15 years of service at retirement. Otherwise the maximum percentage that can be used is less. If a participant will not have 15 years of service at retirement, his maximum excess percentage will be 2% times years to retirement.

FLAT PERCENTAGE INTEGRATED ON THE SOCIAL SECURITY TABLE. Each participant receives two portions of benefit. The first portion is a percentage of total monthly compensation. The second portion is a percentage of monthly compensation in excess of a level shown on a social security wage base table. This level varies from individual to individual, based on the date of birth and the table published by the IRS. The maximum percentage allowed on "excess" compensation is 30%. This 30% maximum applies to a participant only if he will have 15 years of service at retirement. Otherwise the maximum percentage that can be used is less. If a participant will not have 15 years of service at retirement, his maximum excess percentage will be 2% times the number of years to retirement.

YEARS OF SERVICE (NON–INTEGRATED): Monthly retirement income is based on the total number of years of service that will be accumulated at the normal retirement age multiplied by a given percent and the total monthly compensation. The years of service may be a non-limited number or there may be a limit placed on the number of credited years of service for purposes of economy or some other reason.

YEARS OF SERVICE INTEGRATED: The benefit can be based on a specified integration level such as $600, or on the IRS – social security table In either case, each participant receives two portions of benefit. One is based on a percentage of total monthly compensation and the second is based on monthly compensation is excess of the integration level (table or specified amount selected by employer). The sum of these two portions is multiplied by the total number of years of service that will be accumulated at the normal retirement age. The years of service may be a non-limited number or there may be a limit placed on the number of credited years of service for purposes of economy or some other reason. If the years of service are limited, the maximum excess percentage when multiplied by years of service cannot exceed 30%. If "years of service" is not limited, the maximum excess percentage cannot exceed .8%.

MONEY PURCHASE (NON–INTEGRATED): A definite percentage of the employee's annual compensation is deposited each year. This formula is also used for some profit-sharing plans.

MONEY PURCHASE – INTEGRATED: Each participant is allowed two portions of deposits. One deposit is based on a percentage of total annual compensation. The second deposit can be based on annual compensation above that shown on the social security table or above a level selected by the employer. The maximum rate of contribution based on compensation over the integration level is 7%. This formula is also used for some profit-sharing plans.

FLAT DOLLAR–MONEY PURCHASE: The amount deposited for each participant is a flat sum and it is the same for each participant.

Some examples of profit-sharing formulas are as follows:

1. A straight percentage formula such as 10 percent of profits.

2. Ascending scale formula such as 10 percent of the first $10,000; 15 percent of the next $10,000; 20 percent of the next $10,000 and 25 percent of all remaining net earnings.

3. Reservation basis such as:

a. 10 percent of profits in excess of $25,000.

b. 20 percent of profits after first setting
aside 15 percent of equity.

c. 15 percent of profits after setting aside
6 percent for dividend earnings.

Formulas using integration with social security may be excess plans in which the retirement benefit or contribution is based only on earnings in excess of a specified amount (generally those earnings not covered by social security) or offset plans in which the end retirement benefit is reduced by social security benefits. Many plans are stepped-up benefit plans as described above in which a higher benefit rate is applicable above a specified level.

KEOGH (HR-10) RETIREMENT PLANS FOR
THE SELF-EMPLOYED

These plans give individuals who are sole proprietors or partners and their employees some retirement tax benefits.

Self-employed individuals can contribute up to $7,500 or 15% of earned income, whichever is less, in a tax-deductible contribution toward the funding of the retirement trust, whose investment income and profits in turn are tax deferred while in the plan. Where the self-employed establishing a plan have partners and/or employees, the law requires that the same percentage of income be contributed for each person covered by the plan.

Participants can also make voluntary contributions up to the limits of the initial tax-deductible contribution allowed for each of them. These contributions are from after-tax dollars but go into a tax-exempt trust.

Tax-deductible contributions are retained in trust until the owner-employee attains 59½ years when he is eligible to retire and receive benefits from the plan. The benefits may be in installments and taxed as regular income. When taken in a lump sum, a special ten year averaging formula may be used. Distributions must commence by age 70½.

Participants can withdraw any after-tax voluntary contributions – but no gains under the trust – without penalty at any time. Participants who terminate employment may leave all of their share, from both employer and their own voluntary contributions, in the tax-exempt trust until later withdrawal.

On the other hand, common law employees are fully vested and may take their share upon termination of employment.

Keogh trust funds may be invested in insurance and in a variety of equity products such as mutual funds, common trust funds, and variable annuities.

There is an exclusion from the gross estate for the value of an annuity receivable by a beneficiary under a self-employed plan to the extent an income tax deduction was allowable when the contribution to such a plan was made.

TAX-DEFERRED ANNUITIES FOR EMPLOYEES
OF TAX-EXEMPT ORGANIZATIONS
AND PUBLIC SCHOOLS

Contributions by tax-exempt organizations, to purchase nonforfeitable annuities for employees, are excludable from the employee's current taxable income only to the extent that the contribution does not exceed the "exclusion allowance."

The "exclusion allowance" is, basically, 20 percent of the employee's compensation for the last 12-month period multiplied by the number of years of service, less the amounts contributed by the employer for annuity contracts which were excludable from gross income of the employee for any prior taxable year. The exclusion may be applied to existing annuities, as well as new annuities which are owned by the employee, with premiums being paid by the employer. In addition, the annuity may be purchased with money from a salary reduction.

In addition to annuities, individual life insurance policies, variable annuities, or group policies issued after December 31, 1962, which provide "incidental" life insurance protection, may be purchased as an annuity contract, to which the exclusion allowance is applied. All life insurance contracts and annuity contracts issued after December 31, 1962 must be non-transferable and nonassignable (except to the issuing company), in order to qualify for the tax deferment.

Tax consequences to the employee are similar to the tax consequences provided under "qualified" pension plans. Although nearly all the tax benefits available under a "qualified" plan are available to the employee, the exempt employer is not bound by some of the restrictions. For instance, the tax-exempt organization can purchase annuities or life insurance contracts for one or more employees on a selective, discriminatory basis and prior approval by the Internal Revenue Service is not needed.

Generally, under present law, the recipient of a "lumpsum distribution" from a tax-qualified pension plan may make a tax-free rollover by transferring the otherwise taxable portion of the distribution to an IRA (an individual retirement account, annuity, or bond) or to another qualified pension plan. However, under prior law, recipients of distributions from a tax-sheltered annuity purchased by an employer that is a tax-exempt charitable organization or a public educational institution were not eligible for tax-free rollovers to IRAs.

Under the Revenue Act of 1978, the recipient of a lumpsum distribution under a tax-sheltered annuity contract is eligible to completely or partially roll over the otherwise taxable portion of the distribution of an IRA or to another tax-sheltered annuity. Subsequently, the amount rolled over to the IRA, plus earnings, may be rolled over to another tax-sheltered annuity, but may not be rolled over to a tax-qualified pension plan. The provisions of the Act apply to distributions or transfers made after December 31, 1978, in taxable years beginning after that date.

RESTRICTED PROPERTY

If the employee receives property for services rendered, the fair market value of the property must be included in income in the year received unless the property is not transferable and is subject to a substantial risk of forfeiture.

If the property is both non-transferable and subject to a substantial risk of forfeiture, it is not taxed until it becomes transferable or when the risk of forfeiture is removed, whichever happens first.

A substantial risk of forfeiture exists when the employee's rights to full enjoyment of the property are conditioned upon his future performance of substantial services.

For example, if the employee receives stock from his employer for work he performed, and there is a provision that the stock will be forfeited unless he completes four years of service, he will not realize any income until he completes four years of service and satisfies the provision.

Fair market value of the property received is determined without regard to any restriction except one that, by its terms, will never lapse.

For example, if the employee receives stock from his employer for services performed with the restriction that he must sell the stock back to the employer at book value when his employment terminates, this will be considered a restriction that by its terms will never lapse and should be considered in determining fair market value.

The employee may elect to report in income the value of any property that he receives which is not transferable and is subject to a substantial risk of fortfeiture that would not normally be subject to tax until the restriction lapsed. If the election is made, any future appreciation will not be taxed as compensation, but will be treated as capital gain. However, if the property is later forfeited, no refund or deduction will be allowed. The election must be made not later than 30 days after the date the property is transferred to him.

Although the IRS occasionally modifies tax shelters for employees, these benefits are strongly entrenched. The Federal government encourages employers to provide such benefits by passing favorable legislation, and the employers strive to retain their employees by providing inducements for them to remain with the company.

PART THREE

TAX SHELTERS AND TAX–FREE INCOME
FOR CORPORATIONS

Tax shelters which are purchased by individuals such as real estate, oil and gas, and cattle feeding and breeding can also be purchased advantageously by corporations. In addition, there are certain specific tax shelters made available to corporations by the tax law as follows:

DIVIDENDS RECEIVED DEDUCTIONS

A corporation is allowed a deduction for a percentage of certain dividends received during its tax year.

A corporation may deduct, subject to certain limitations, 85% of the dividends it receives from taxable domestic corporations (other than dividends on preferred stock of public utility companies). The dividends must be distributions from the earnings and profits of the paying corporations.

Small business investment companies may deduct 100% of the dividends received from a taxable domestic corporation. Small business investment companies are private companies with paid-in capital and surplus of at least $300,000. They are formed and licensed under the Small Business Investment Act of 1958, to provide equity capital to small business concerns.

Members of an affiliated group of corporations may elect, if certain conditions are met, to deduct 100% of dividends received from a member of the same affiliated group.

A corporation may deduct a percentage of dividends it receives from a foreign corporation (other than a foreign personal holding company) that has engaged in a trade or business within the United States for an uninterrupted period of not less than 36 months ending with the close of the tax year in which the dividends are paid if at least 50% of the foreign corporation's gross income from all sources is effectively connected with the conduct of a trade or business within the United States. If the foreign corporation has not existed for 36 months, the period must cover its entire existence up to the close of the tax year.

The deduction is approximately 85% of the portion of

dividends of the foreign corporation attributable to its income effectively connected with the conduct of a trade or business within the United States.

DISTRIBUTION OF APPRECIATED PROPERTY IN STOCK REDEMPTION

Distributions to a shareholder by a corporation after November 30, 1969, of appreciated property (fair market value of the property exceeds its adjusted basis) in redemption of its stock, ordinarily will result in gain to the distributing corporation to the extent of the appreciation. This rule applies even if the distribution is characterized as a dividend to the shareholder. However, the rule does not apply to:

1. A complete or partial liquidation of a corporation;
2. Distributions in complete termination of the interest of a stockholder owning at least 10% of the stock;
3. Distributions of stock of a 50% or more owned subsidiary;
4. Redemptions to pay death taxes;
5. Certain redemption distributions to private foundations; and
6. Certain distributions by regulated investment companies.

WESTERN HEMISPHERE TRADE CORPORATIONS

The term "Western Hemisphere trade corporation" means a domestic corporation all of whose business (other than incidental purchases) is done in any country or countries in North, Central, or South America, or in the West Indies, and which satisfies the following conditions:

(1) if 95 percent or more of the gross income of such domestic corporation for the 3-year period immediately preceding the close of the taxable year (or for such part of such period during which the corporation was in existence) was derived from sources without the United States; and

(2) if 90 percent or more of its gross income for such period or such part thereof was derived from the active conduct of a trade or business.

Under prior law, Western Hemisphere Trade Corporations (WHTC's) are entitled to a deduction which may reduce their applicable corporate income tax rate by as much as 14 percentage points below the applicable rate for other domestic corporations.

The 1976 Tax Reform Act repeals the Western Hemisphere

Trade Corporation provisions for taxable years beginning after December 31, 1979. However, the present preferential rate granted to WHTC's is phased out over a 5-year period, according to the following table:

For a taxable year beginning in—	The percentage shall be—
1976	11
1977	8
1978	5
1979	2

Corporations which presently do not qualify for WHTC treatment will be permitted to qualify and receive the remaining benefits during the phaseout period. Thus, no distinction is made between corporations qualifying for WHTC treatment prior to 1976 and other corporations which first qualify during the phaseout period.

No deduction shall be allowed under this section to a corporation for a taxable year for which it is a DISC or in which it owns at any time stock in a DISC or former DISC.

DOMESTIC INTERNATIONAL SALES CORPORATION (DISC)

In an effort to improve the international financial status of the United States by encouraging exports, new companies called DISCs have been created by Congress. These companies can defer a large part of taxes on export earnings.

The Treasury has issued a summary of DISCs to help acquaint businessmen with the new tax shelter. It is exceptionally comprehensive and is reprinted in its entirety as follows:

The following parts of DISC, a Handbook for Exporters, are reproduced below: Part I, An Overview of DISC; Part II, Basic Questions and Answers About DISC; and Part III, a plain language explanation of the law pertaining to a Domestic International Sales Corporation.

The handbook also includes Part IV, DISC Statute (Title V of Public Law 92–178), which was published in I.R.B. 1972–3, at page 37; and Part V, IRS Technical Information Release 1124 (12-17-71)—Rules for Electing DISC Status, which was published as Revenue Procedure 72–12, I.R.B. 1972–2, 25.

The DISC Handbook may be purchased for $.40 from the Superintendent of Documents, U.S. Government Printing Office, Washington, D.C. 20402.

I. AN OVERVIEW OF DISC

The Revenue Act of 1971 [P.L. 92–178, I.R.B. 1972–3, 14] contains a major structural improvement and simplification for United States exporters. Congress has provided that special export corporations—Domestic International Sales Corporations (or DISCs)—are entitled to special tax treatment for taxable years beginning on or after January 1, 1972. This handbook is intended as an aid in understanding DISC. The Internal Revenue Service will follow the rules and procedures set forth in III, "DISC Explained", until such time as they may be modified in regulations or other Treasury publications.

Under the DISC legislation United States exporters can now receive, through a domestic corporation qualifying as a DISC, tax treatment for their export income more comparable to that afforded by many foreign countries to their exporters. As in the case of a typical foreign corporation, the DISC itself is not subject to United States Federal income tax. The DISC's shareholders are treated as receiving one-half of the DISC's earnings currently, whether or not actually distributed. The remaining one-half of the DISC's earnings may be retained by the DISC and reinvested in its export business, or invested in certain Export-Import Bank obligations or in "producer's loans" to related or unrelated U.S. producers for export without, in general, liability for Federal income tax.

For example, if a DISC has $100,-000 of export earnings, $50,000 is taxed currently to its shareholders as a dividend and $50,000 is eligible for deferral while retained by the DISC. Deferral terminates and tax is imposed on the shareholders of the DISC if the deferred earnings are distributed as a dividend or the corporation no longer qualifies as a DISC and in certain other cases.

The DISC may, as principal or agent, engage in the business of export products manufactured, produced, grown or extracted in the United States. It can export articles produced by related and unrelated producers and can export to related and unrelated purchasers. In addition, a DISC may lease or sublease such products for use outside of the United States. A DISC may also perform engineering or architectural services for foreign construction projects.

As indicated, a DISC may invest its tax-deferred earnings not only in expansion of its export business, but also in certain Export-Import Bank obligations and in "producer's loans" to United States export producers. By the use of producer's loans the DISC may form an economic relationship with its suppliers, sharing in the financing of their facilities, inventory, and research and development.

The DISC legislation contains special rules, designed to provide a simplified allocation method, for determining the earnings of a DISC which purchases from, or acts as commission agent for, a related supplier.

A domestic corporation presently engaged almost solely in the export business might well be able to qualify as a DISC. In cases where an export business is conducted in a noncorporate form, by a sole proprietorship or a partnership, it will be necessary to organize a corporation. Since the profits of a DISC are not subject to tax at the DISC level, but only at the shareholder level, the incorporation of a business as a DISC will not result in taxation at two levels.

A corporation engaged in manufacturing or in non-export sales can organize a DISC for export sales.

II. Basic Questions and Answers About DISC

The following Basic Questions and Answers about DISC indicate in a general way how exporters can use a DISC. For an explanation of the major operational features of the DISC legislation, see "DISC Explained".

HOW DOES A DISC HELP EXPORTERS?

A DISC helps exporters in two major ways:

(1) Federal income taxes are deferred on one-half of the export earnings of the DISC; and

(2) Special rules, designed as a simplified allocation method, are provided for determining the export earnings of a DISC which purchases from, or acts as commission agent for, a related supplier.

WHAT IS A DISC?

A DISC is a corporation, organized under the laws of any state or the District of Columbia, which elects with the consent of its shareholders to be treated as a DISC. It must have equity capital of at least $2,500 and is limited to one class of stock. The DISC must derive at least 95 percent of its receipts in the form of qualified export receipts and have at least 95 percent of its assets in the form of qualified export assets.

HOW LONG ARE TAXES ON ONE-HALF OF THE DISC'S EARNINGS DEFERRED?

Deferral continues as long as the earnings of the DISC are used in its export business, invested in certain obligations issued or guaranteed by the Export-Import Bank, or remain in the United States as "producer's loans" to related or unrelated United States producers.

WHAT IS A PRODUCER'S LOAN?

A "producer's loan" is a loan to a United States manufacturer or other producer for the financing of the assets of that producer that are deemed export related. These assets include plant, machinery, equipment and supporting production facilities; inventory, and research and experimental expendi-tures of the borrower. The extent to which these assets are deemed export related depends, in general, on the portion of the borrower's production which is exported. While DISCs will often make "producer's loans" to their parent companies, a loan to any United States producer whose products are exported can qualify as a "producer's loan".

ARE ASSETS FINANCED THROUGH PRODUCER'S LOANS ALSO ELIGIBLE FOR THE JOB DEVELOPMENT INVESTMENT CREDIT?

Machinery, equipment and supporting production facilities used in the U.S. are generally entitled to the 7 percent job development investment credit, also enacted as part of the Revenue Act of 1971. Where the investment credit would ordinarily apply to the acquisition of assets, the credit remains available even though the assets are deemed export related and are, in effect, financed through "producer's loans".

DOES FOREIGN INVESTMENT END THE DEFERRAL OF TAX LIABILITY?

The DISC legislation provides that certain investments in foreign plant, equipment and real property are attributable to producer's loans. To the extent foreign investment is attributable to producer's loans, deferral of tax on these loans ends. However, the rules for determining whether foreign investment is attributable to "producer's loans" provide reasonable latitude for foreign investment which will not end deferral.

HOW IS A DISC TAXED?

The DISC itself it not subject to Federal income tax. On income which is not entitled to deferral or when deferral ends, the shareholders of the DISC are subject to tax.

WHO MAY OWN A DISC?

Individuals, corporations, partnerships, trusts and estates can own the stock of a DISC. A DISC can handle exports produced by any number of related or unrelated United States producers. It is anticipated that many United States producers will form DISCs as wholly-owned subsidiaries to handle their exports.

WHAT ABOUT INDEPENDENT EXPORT DISTRIBUTORS?

A combination export manager or other independent export distributor which is organized or reorganized in corporate form can readily qualify as a DISC and have one-half of the Federal income tax on its export earnings deferred. A DISC can (1) purchase goods for export from United States producers or distributors or from unrelated DISCs, or (2) sell on a commission basis for such persons. A DISC can also manage the export activities of unrelated DISCs. Where the best course for a business has been to export through an independent distributor, there is no reason why such an arrangement should not continue. It might be advantageous for the business to organize its own DISC which would in turn export through an independent distributor.

HOW CAN A SMALL BUSINESSMAN USE A DISC?

A small businessman can use a DISC with a minimum of difficulty even though a DISC must be a corporation. For example, a small manufacturer can with little difficulty organize a DISC with $2,500 of capital and have it act as a commission agent on export sales.

I HAVE NEVER EXPORTED BEFORE. CAN A DISC BE OF BENEFIT TO ME?

The Government would like to encourage persons to export who never exported before and DISC should prove helpful in this. There is a minimum of formality required to set up and operate a DISC. The Commerce Department has experts in its National Office and its 42 field offices who are available with advice and information for the new exporter. Commerce will provide information on economic conditions, foreign markets, specific export opportunities, and U.S. Government sponsored commercial exhibitions abroad. Financing for U.S. exports is available through commercial banks and the Export-Import Bank which, along with Commerce, will supply information on export loans, guarantees and insurance. The telephone number of the National Office of the Commerce Department is (area code 202) 967–3181.

CAN A GROUP OF SMALL PRODUCERS SET UP A DISC?

Yes. There are no limitations or requirements as to the number of shareholders, and a DISC can handle the exports of any number of United States producers whether related or unrelated. It is contemplated that in many instances several small producers will arrange among themselves to export through a jointly owned DISC.

CAN A WEBB-POMERENE ASSOCIATED BE A DISC?

Yes, provided it is organized as a corporation. If the association is not in corporate form it may reorganize as a corporation and readily qualify as a DISC. A Webb-Pomerene Association which qualifies as a DISC would have one-half of the Federal income tax on its export earnings deferred and could make "producer's loans" to its member companies or other export producers.

BUSINESS NECESSITY REQUIRES ME TO KEEP MY FOREIGN SELLING ORGANIZATION. WOULD A DISC BE OF BENEFIT TO ME?

Yes; for example, a U.S. producer that has a foreign selling subsidiary or an independent foreign distributor which it intends to keep, will generally find it advantageous to have a DISC to act either as agent or principal on sales to its foreign subsidiary or distributor.

I ALREADY HAVE AN EXPORT DEPARTMENT THAT I INTEND TO MAINTAIN. WOULD A DISC BE OF BENEFIT TO ME?

Yes. One of the advantages of also forming a DISC is the simplified allocation method that would be available.

WHAT PROPERTY CAN A DISC EXPORT?

Property manufactured, produced, grown or extracted in the United States (including Puerto Rico and the possessions of the United States) qualifies for sale through a DISC. At least 50 percent of its value must be attributable to United States content. Components and finished products, agricultural commodities and minerals would be qualified DISC exports. However, property which benefits from certain government export subsidies, or which has been declared by the President to be in short supply in the United States, would not qualify. As yet, no property has been declared to be in short supply for this purpose.

WHAT IS AN EXPORT?

In the case of a sale, the property must be delivered outside of the United States for use outside of the United States. In the case of a lease, the place where the property is used determines whether there is an export.

TO WHOM MAY A DISC SELL?

A DISC may sell to any related or unrelated person where the property is to be delivered outside the United States for use outside the United States. A DISC may also sell and make delivery in the United States to a second DISC for export by the second DISC

if the two DISCs are unrelated. Sales to other persons by a DISC for delivery in the United States will qualify only if they are unrelated and it is established that after the sale by the DISC there is no further sale, use or processing within the United States and the property is delivered outside the United States within one year after the sale by the DISC. In general, property sold by a DISC for use by the United States Government will not qualify where the law requires that such property must be produced in the United States.

CAN A DISC ACT AS COMMISSION AGENT?

Yes. In general, the same rules are applicable as when the DISC buys and resells.

CAN A DISC ENTER INTO LEASING TRANSACTIONS?

A DISC may lease or sublease to any unrelated person for use outside of the United States.

WHAT ABOUT SERVICES?

A DISC is permitted to provide related and subsidiary services in connection with sales or leases by it, including transactions on which it receives commissions. In addition, engineering and architectural services, in connection with a construction project or a proposed construction project in a foreign country, produce qualified receipts. Export management services rendered to unrelated DISCs also qualify. Other services do not qualify.

MAY A DISC MANUFACTURE OR GRANT LICENSES?

A DISC may perform packaging and limited assembly operations in the United States or foreign countries, but manufacturing is not a qualified activity. Royalties and fees derived from the license of intangible property are not qualified receipts.

IF A DISC BUYS FROM OR SELLS FOR A RELATED SUPPLIER, HOW MUCH OF THE TOTAL PROFITS CAN BE ALLOCATED TO THE DISC?

In a case where a DISC purchases export products from a related producer or other related supplier, or acts as an export commission agent for such producer or supplier, special rules permit the DISC to pay a transfer price or charge a commission which results in the DISC earning out of the combined taxable income the greater of:

(a) Fifty percent of the combined taxable income of the DISC and such producer or supplier derived from the production and sale, or purchase and sale, of the product exported; or

(b) Four percent of the DISC's sales (or the principal's sales on which the DISC earned commissions).

A DISC is entitled to receive additional income, where either of these formulas is used, equal to 10 percent of the export promotion expenses actually incurred by the DISC, including advertising, sales commissions, salaries, warehousing, and one-half of the freight for shipment on U.S. carriers where the use of such carriers is not required by law.

In lieu of the above rules, a DISC may pay a transfer price or charge commissions under the normal rules applicable to transfers between related persons.

WILL I BE ABLE TO RELY ON THE SPECIAL ALLOCATION RULES IF I WON'T HAVE THE INFORMATION TO APPLY THESE RULES UNTIL AFTER THE END OF THE YEAR?

This should be no problem. The Regulations to be issued will provide that adjustments in prices, rentals, or commissions can be made after the close of the DISCs taxable year. This will permit use of the most favorable pricing formula when the necessary data become available.

WHAT PRICES SHOULD A DISC CHARGE TO A RELATED FOREIGN PURCHASER?

An arm's length price under the normal rules applicable to transfers between related persons.

WHAT IF A CORPORATION FAILS TO MEET THE 95 PERCENT GROSS RECEIPTS TEST OR THE 95 PERCENT ASSETS TEST?

Subject to certain conditions, a corporation may maintain its qualification as a DISC and continue deferral on its qualified income by distributing the non-qualified income or assets as a taxable dividend to its shareholders. If a distribution is not made or the DISC wishes to terminate its status, the accumulated income of the DISC is taxable to the DISC's shareholders over a ten-year period, or such shorter time as the DISC has been in existence.

WHAT IS THE APPROPRIATE ACCOUNTING TREATMENT FOR THE DEFERRED TAXES?

The Accounting Principles Board of the American Institute of Certified Public Accounts has determined that the deferred Federal income taxes on the earnings of a DISC can be treated in the same way as the deferred taxes of a foreign subsidiary. This means that such taxes need not be taken into account for financial statement purposes as long as there is no intention to distribute the income or otherwise act so as to end the deferral of tax liability.

DEFERRED INCOME?

A DISC may use its deferred income to extend financing to its foreign customers, to build up its inventory of products to be exported, to invest in office and warehouse facilities and other property that it uses in its business, to pay its suppliers more promptly, and to invest in certain Export-Import Bank obligations. In addition, one of the most important uses for its tax-deferred income is in "producer's loans" which are described on page 254.

HOW CAN A CORPORATION ELECT TO BE TREATED AS A DISC?

A corporation seeking to qualify as a DISC must file an election, as well as the consent of the shareholders of the corporation, with the Internal Revenue Service. In general, a newly formed corporation can make an election on or before (1) the 90th day after the beginning of its first taxable year, or (2) March 31, 1972, whichever is later. In the case of other corporations, the election can be made within the 90-day period before the beginning of the first year in which it seeks to qualify as a DISC, except that in any event an election made on or before March 31, 1972, will be timely. There are no special requirements for the articles of incorporation or charter.

WHAT SHOULD I DO IF I HAVE FURTHER QUESTIONS ABOUT DISC?

As with questions about other provisions of the Internal Revenue Code, the Internal Revenue Service is available to deal with questions about DISC. The National Office of the Internal Revenue Service will issue advance rulings on proposed transactions or before a return is filed in specific cases involving DISCs. Questions may be addressed to the Commissioner of Internal Revenue, Attention: T:I:C: 3, Washington, D.C. 20224. For procedures relating to the issuance of rulings, see Revenue Procedure 72–3, I.R.B. 1972–1, page 9, which is available from the same address.

Regulations are being prepared by the Legislation and Regulations Division, Office of Chief Counsel, Internal Revenue Service. During the process of preparation, comments or suggestions with respect to the contents of these regulations are invited. These should be addressed to the Commissioner of Internal Revenue, Attention: CC:LR:T, Washington, D.C. 20224.

III. DISC EXPLAINED

In this part all of the major operational features of the DISC legislation are explained in a general way. The Internal Revenue Service will follow the rules and procedures set forth in this part until such time as they may be modified in regulations or other Treasury publications. Any such modifications which may be adverse to taxpayers will apply prospectively only.

A. DEFINITION OF A DOMESTIC INTERNATIONAL SALES CORPORATION (DISC)

A DISC must be in corporate form duly incorporated under the laws of any state or the District of Columbia; must have only one class of stock; must have at least $2,500 of capital stock outstanding at all times as measured by the par or stated value and must, with consent of all shareholders, elect to be treated as a DISC. A DISC should have its own bank account and separate accounting records. While DISCs are encouraged to have their own employees, this is not required where the DISC arranges for employees of others to serve as its officers or otherwise act on its behalf. A corporation that meets the requirements referred to above will be treated as a separate corporation and qualify as a DISC (subject to the 95 percent receipts and assets tests) without regard to such other tests of substance, as the ratio of its debt to its equity, that are relevant in the case of other types of corporations. Debt of a DISC, regardless of the debt-equity ratio, will not be treated as an additional class of stock so long as it is in the form of debt, and wide disparities in funds made available by different groups of stockholders do not justify such treatment. If a related tax-payer makes a loan to a DISC, interest must be charged to the extent required under section 482 of the Internal Revenue Code. *See section 992(a).**

B. OWNERSHIP OF THE STOCK OF A DISC

Individuals, corporations, partnerships ,trusts and estates, including non-resident aliens and foreign corporations, can own the stock of a DISC. Any dividends or gains received (or deemed received) by a nonresident alien or foreign corporation with respect to its stock in a DISC will be treated as effectively connected with a United States trade or business operated through a permanent establishment. *See section 996(g) for rules regarding "effectively connected" income.*

C. ELECTION TO BE TREATED AS A DISC

(1) By the Corporation. To qualify as a DISC, a corporation must elect such treatment by filing an election with Internal Revenue Service. (See Revenue Procedure 72–12, I.R.B. 1972–2, 25.) In general, a newly formed corporation can make an election on or before (1) the 90th day after the beginning of its first taxable year, or (2) March 31, 1972, whichever, is later. In the case of other corporations, the election can be made within the 90-day period before the beginning of the first taxable year in which it seeks to qualify as a DISC, except that in any event an election made on or before March 31, 1972 will be timely. Once an election is made, it will, unless revoked by the corporation, continue in effect for subsequent years

in which the corporation qualifies as a DISC even if the corporation failed in intervening years to meet the tests for qualification. However, if the corporation fails to qualify for five consecutive years, the DISC election will terminate. *See section 992(b) (1) and (2) for the procedure for, and the effect of, making a DISC election.*

(2) Consent of Shareholders. For the election to be valid, all persons who were shareholders of the corporation on the first day of the initial election year must consent in writing. For taxable years beginning in 1972, consents can be filed on or before the 90th day after the beginning of the taxable year. For subsequent taxable years, consents must be filed with the statement of election unless there is reasonable cause for failure to file a particular consent with the election.

In the consent, the shareholder agrees to be treated as a DISC shareholder with respect to distributions or deemed distributions of DISC income. In the case of a foreign shareholder the consent also represents the agreement of the shareholder that any distribution or deemed distribution of gains or other income to the foreign shareholder is effectively connected with the conduct of a trade or business in the United States through a permanent establishment. The consent is binding on all subsequent shareholders of the corporation. *See section 992(b)(1)(B).*

(3) Termination of Election of DISC Status. An election to be treated as a DISC may be revoked by the corporation any time after the first taxable year it is in effect. To be effective for a given taxable year, however, the revocation must be made on or before the 90th day of that year. A revocation made after the expiration of the 90-day period will not be effective until the following taxable year. As noted, there is an automatic termination of an elec-

---

*References in italics are to the Internal Revenue Code of 1954, as amended by the Revenue Act of 1971 (P.L. 92–178, Title V, I.R.B. 1972–3, 37) and are included for purposes of reference only.

tion where the corporation does not qualify as a DISC for a period of five consecutive taxable years. A corporation that has terminated an election may again elect to be a DISC. *See Section 992(b)(3).*

D. ACTIVITIES OF A DISC

The 95 percent gross receipts requirement and the 95 percent assets requirement, which are set forth in subsequent sections, are designed to limit the DISC to export related activities. A DISC may export products manufactured, produced, grown or extracted in the United States which qualify as export property. (See Section I for the definition of export property.) Components and finished products, agricultural commodities and minerals are qualified DISC exports, but see Section G which deals with subsidized exports and other excluded receipts.

The DISC may export as a principal, purchasing and reselling the export property. Alternatively, it may act as a commission agent for export sales. Where a DISC acts as commission agent for a related supplier, the DISC and supplier should define their relationship in writing. They could, for example, provide for orders to be sent in the first instance to the DISC or for invoices to be issued by the DISC on behalf of the principal.

A DISC may also lease or sublease United States produced property or act as agent for such transactions. Services performed by a DISC that are related and subsidiary to its qualified sale or lease transactions (whether the DISC acts as principal or agent) are also qualified activities. A DISC may also perform engineering or architectural services for foreign projects, manage other DISCs, invest in certain Export-Import Bank obligations and invest its earnings from the foregoing activities in producer's loans.

Receipts from the sale or lease of property produced by the DISC do not qualify. A DISC may, however, engage in packaging activities and in limited assembly operations with respect to property it sells, within the United States or in a foreign branch. If the property sold by the DISC is substantially transformed by it prior to sale, the property will be treated as having been produced by the DISC and the receipts from the sale will not be treated as qualified export receipts. Physical operations performed by a DISC are, in any event, considered to be production where the cost added to the product because of the manufacturing, assembly, processing, packaging or similar operations of the DISC is 20 percent or more of the total cost of goods sold. *See section 993(a) for the qualified export receipts of a DISC, section 993(b) for the qualified export assets of a DISC, and section 993(c) for property which is export property.*

For purposes of the DISC legislation, the United States includes Puerto Rico and the possessions and the continental shelf adjacent to the United States. Thus, for example, property produced in a possession could constitute export property and property sold for ultimate use on the United States continental shelf would not be treated as having been exported. *See section 993(g).*

E. GROSS RECEIPTS REQUIREMENT

To be a DISC, a corporation must receive at least 95 percent of its gross receipts from exports and export related investments and activities.

Gross receipts means the total receipts from the sale or lease of inventory qualifying as export property and gross income from all other sources. In the case of commissions, the amount taken into account as gross receipts is the amount of gross receipts received by the principal from the sale or lease (including receipts for related and subsidiary services) on which the commissions were paid.

Subject to the exclusion described in Section G qualified gross receipts are the following:

(1) Receipts from the Sale of Export Property. This generally means receipts from the sale of property, such as inventory, produced in the United States, which is sold "for direct use, consumption, or disposition outside the United States." This requirement is discussed in Section F. *See section 993(a)(1) (A).*

(2) Receipts from the Leasing (Including Subleasing) of Export Property. Leases to unrelated persons of property qualifying as export property which is used outside the United States produce qualifying income. Whether the leased property satisfies this usage test is to be determined on a year-by-year basis. Thus, the receipts on a lease of export property might qualify in some years and not in other years, depending on the place where the lessee uses the property in the years involved. *See section 993(a)(1)(B).*

(3) Receipts from Services Rendered in Connection with a Qualified Export Sale or Lease Transaction. Service income in connection with an export sale or lease qualifies if the services are related and subsidiary to an export transaction for which the corporation received qualified sales or lease income, including commission income, irrespective of the place where such services are performed. In general, a service is related to a sale or lease if it is of a kind customarily and usually furnished with that type of transaction in the trade or business in which the transaction arose and if the agreement to furnish these services is connected with the sale or lease. A service is subsidiary if it is of less importance and

value as compared to the sale or lease. Transportation services or services related to the installation or maintenance of export property would generally qualify as services which are related and subsidiary to the sale or lease. *See section 993(a)(1)(C).*

(4) Gains from the Sale of Qualified Export Assets. This category covers the sale of plant and equipment and other business asets used in the DISC's export business. For purposes of this test, only the gain is treated as a receipt. *See section 993(a)(1)(D).*

(5) Dividends. Dividends from a qualified foreign investment of a DISC in a related foreign export corporation constitute qualified gross receipts. Generally, the investment will be in stock or securities of a foreign selling subsidiary of the DISC which qualifies as a foreign international sales corporation. (See Section L.) *See section 993(a)(1)(E).*

(6) Interest. Interest (including discount) on any qualified export asset is a qualified receipt. Such receipts include, for example, interest on accounts receivable arising out of sales in which the DISC acted as principal or agent, interest on producer's loans, and interest on certain obligations issued, guaranteed, or insured by the Export-Import Bank or the Foreign Credit Insurance Association. *See section 993(a)(1)(F).*

(7) Engineering and Architectural Services. Receipts from engineering or architectural services on foreign construction projects which are either located abroad or proposed for location abroad are qualified receipts. Such receipts by a DISC may be earned by way of a commission where the DISC arranges for engineering or architectural services to be rendered by another United States person. These services would include feasibility studies, design and engineering and general supervision of construction. They would

not include services connected with exploration for minerals. Receipts from the actual performance of construction are excluded. *See section 993(a)(1) (G)*.

(8) Export Management Services. Receipts for export management services provided for unrelated DISCs are qualified receipts. This narrow category of income is intended to permit experienced exporters to provide the management for small or inexperienced DISCs and thereby derive qualified receipts. This category is limited to the furnishing of management expertise and staff for export sales and leasing. *See section 993(a)(1)(H)*.

F. EXPORT REQUIREMENT

In order to assure that DISC benefits are available only where there has been a true export, the legislation contains a two part requirement: a destination test ("direct use, consumption, or disposition outside the United States") and a requirement that the sale not be for "ultimate use in the United States." *See sections 993(c) (1)(B) and 993(a)(2)(A)*.

In the case of sale, the destination test, which is the first part of the export requirement, will generally be considered as satisfied if:

(1) The DISC delivers the property to a carrier or freight forwarder for delivery outside of the United States, regardless of the F.O.B. point or place of passage of title, whether to a United States or foreign purchaser and whether for use of the purchaser or for resale;

(2) The sale is to an unrelated DISC for such a purpose, whether delivery is to be made in the United States or at a foreign destination; or

(3) The sale is to any unrelated person for delivery in the United States if the DISC establishes that after the sale by the DISC there is

no further sale, use, assembly or other processing within the United States and the property is delivered outside the United States within one year after the sale by such DISC.

The second part of the export requirement for sales is that the sale must not be for ultimate use in the United States. This test is applied at the time of the sale. If the property is to be used predominantly outside the United States, the sale is not for ultimate use in the United States.

Property sold to an unrelated person is considered sold for ultimate use in the United States if the property is sold pursuant to an agreement or understanding that the property as such will be used in the United States or if a reasonable person would have believed that the property will be used in the United States. For example, if property were sold to a foreign wholesaler and it was known in trade circles that the wholesaler, to a substantial extent, supplied the U.S. retail market, the sale would not be a qualified export sale.

Where the property exported to an unrelated person is incorporated as a component or material in a second product, the following rules apply:

(1) Where the property exported constitutes a major part of a second product produced outside the United States, or where 20 percent or more of the second product is used in the United States, the sale will be considered for ultimate use in the United States if there is an agreement or understanding that the second product will be used in the United States or if a reasonable person would have believed that the second product will be used in the United States.

(2) Where components or materials are sold to an unrelated party and incorporated into a second product, but do not constitute a major part of the second product and less

than 20 percent of the second product is used in the United States, such components or materials will be deemed to have been used in the United States only if the components or materials were sold pursuant to an agreement or understanding that the second product will be used in the United States. There would be such an agreement or understanding, for example, where a component is sold abroad under an express agreement with the foreign buyer that the component is to be incorporated into a product to be sold back to the United States. There would also be such an agreement or understanding if the foreign buyer indicated at the time of the sale or previously that the component is to be incorporated into a product which is designed principally for the United States market. However, such an agreement or understanding does not result from the mere fact that a product (into which U.S. exports, not constituting a major part of the product, have been incorporated) which is sold on the world market is sold in substantial quantities in the United States.

(3) Components or materials constitute a major part of a product if they represent 20 percent or more in value of a product.

Property sold to a related person, whether or not incorporated into a second product, will be deemed to be ultimately used in the United States if such related person uses, or resells the property or the second product for use, in the United States.

In the case of a lease by a DISC, actual use during each of the DISC's taxable years governs and determines whether both parts of the export requirement have been satisfied. If leased property is used both in and out of the United States in a taxable year, this standard will be applied on the basis of predominant use.

G. EXCLUSIONS FROM QUALIFIED EXPORT RECEIPTS

Receipts from four types of transactions and related services are excluded from the qualified export receipts. These are:

(1) The most important exclusion, "ultimate use in the United States," embodies the second part of the export requirement as discussed in Section F.

(2) The Treasury has been given authority to exclude receipts from sales of products under United States Government programs which subsidize exports. Treasury is presently reviewing those United States Government programs which may give rise to such excluded receipts.

With respect to agricultural products, the Treasury has determined so far that excluded receipts are receipts from any products sold under the P.L. 480 program and under all agricultural programs administered by the Agency for International Development. However, receipts from agricultural products on which subsidies have been paid under the Agricultural Act of 1949 or the Agricultural Adjustment Act of 1938 are not excluded receipts.

Receipts from the sale of products financed through the General Sales Manager Program and receipts from sales as to which the Export-Import Bank or the Foreign Credit Insurance Association has made loans or issued guarantees or insurance are not excluded receipts. *See section 993(a) (2)(B).*

(3) Under similar authority, direct or indirect sales or leases of property or services for use by the United States Government or any instrumentality thereof where the use of U.S. products or services is required by statute or regulations are also excluded. Programs in which the United States Government

merely procures products for resale to foreign governments and others on commercial terms will not produce excluded receipts. Similarly, purchases pursuant to bilateral or multilateral programs open to international competitive bidding will not give rise to excluded receipts. *See section 993(a)(2)(C)*.

(4) A sale by a DISC to another DISC may be a qualified export, except that a sale by a DISC to a DISC that is a member of the same controlled group of corporations is not a qualified export. *See section 993(a)(2). The term "controlled group" is defined in section 993(a)(3)*.

Further guidance on those receipts which constitute excluded receipts will be issued shortly.

H. ASSET REQUIREMENT

To be a DISC, the corporation at the close of the taxable year must have qualified assets with an adjusted basis equal to at least 95 percent of the sum of the adjusted basis of all assets of the corporation.

Qualified assets of a DISC are the following:

(1) *Export Property.* This is the DISC's inventory and property held for lease meeting certain tests described in Section I. *See section 993(b)(1)*.

(2) *Business Assets.* These are assets used primarily in connection with the sale, lease, storage, handling, transportation, packaging, assembly or servicing of export property; or the performance of managerial, engineering or architectural services producing qualified export receipts. Examples include materials handling equipment, warehouses, containers and other transportation equipment, office buildings and office equipment. *See section 993(b)(2)*.

(3) *Trade Receivables.* These are accounts receivable and evidences of indebtedness which arose in connection with the DISC's qualified export sale or lease transactions (whether the DISC acted as principal or agent and including indebtedness arising from related and subsidiary services) or the performance of managerial, engineering or architectural services producing qualified export receipts. Thus, for example, a DISC which acted as commission agent on export sales might purchase accounts receivable arising on such sales from the principal. *See section 993(b)(3)*.

(4) *Working Capital.* This constitutes money, bank deposits and similar temporary investments which are reasonably necessary to meet the working capital needs of the corporation. *See section 993(b)(4)*.

(5) *Producer's Loans.* These are loans of the DISC's profits to any United States export producer whether or not related to the DISC. *See section 993(b)(5)*.

(6) *Related Foreign Export Corporations.* This refers to stock or securities of foreign selling subsidiaries of the DISC where the subsidiaries qualify as foreign international sales corporations or other related foreign export corporations. (See Section L.) *See section 993(b)(6)*.

(7) *Export-Import Bank Obligations.* These are obligations issued, guaranteed or insured (including reinsurance) by the Export-Import Bank of the United States or the Foreign Credit Insurance Association, if the obligations are acquired from the Bank or Association or from the person selling or purchasing the goods or services giving rise to the obligations. A person who purchases obligations issued by the Export-Import Bank from an underwriting syndicate which purchased these obligations from the Bank will be considered to have purchased these obligations from the Bank, provided they

are purchased on or before the 90th day after the obligations were first offered to the public. Also included are obligations of certain domestic corporations organized to finance sales of export property under certain agreements with the Export-Import Bank. Under the last rule, obligations of Private Export Funding Corportaion are qualified. *See section 993(b)(7) and (8).*

(8) Funds Awaiting Investment. These are amounts deposited in banks in the United States at the end of the corporation's taxable year which are in excess of the reasonable working capital needs of the corporation and which are invested, during the period provided for in and otherwise in accordance with Treasury regulations, in other qualified export assets. *See section 993(b)(9).*

I. EXPORT PROPERTY

Generally, the principal function of a DISC will be the selling or leasing of export property for use outside the United States. Export property is property which—

(1) Has been manufactured, produced, grown or extracted in the United States by someone other than a DISC;

(2) Once acquired by the corporation seeking to quality as a DISC, is held primarily for sale or lease in the ordinary course of business for direct use, consumption or disposition outside the United States (see Section F) ; and

(3) Has at the time of sale or lease by the DISC not more than 50 percent of its fair market value attributable to imported articles.

As previously noted in Section D, a DISC may engage in packaging and limited assembly operations with respect to property sold by it. However, property produced by a DISC would not be export property.

With regard to determining the percentage of the fair market value of a product attributable to imported articles, any components or materials imported into the United States and incorporated in a product are to be taken into account at their fair market value upon their importation (i.e., at what would be their full dutiable value in the absence of any special provisions in the tariff laws which result in a lower dutiable value). Even though an imported component has some U.S. content, it is to be treated as if it were 100 percent foreign.

In many cases it will be evident that the United States content requirement has been satisfied. Where there is a question, the content can be determined as follows. Where the DISC is related to a supplier which imports the foreign components or material incorporated into the product sold by the DISC, the content can be ascertained by customs invoices available to the related supplier. Where a DISC deals with unrelated suppliers and causes the suppliers to maintain the records required by the Regulations, the DISC's reasonable conclusion that the United States content requirement has been met will be accepted.

Property which has been declared by the President to be in short supply in the United States would not constitute export property. As yet, no property has been declared to be in short supply for this purpose.

See section 993(c).

J. PRODUCER'S LOANS

Producer's loans are one of the main features of the DISC legislation as such loans enable the DISC to employ its tax deferred income productively. However, this is not the only way in which a DISC can usefully employ its income. It may, also, for example, use its deferred income to extend financing to its foreign customers, to build up its inventory of products to be exported, to pay its suppliers more promptly, and to invest in certain Export-Import Bank obligations.

Under the producer's loan concept a DISC may help finance U.S. production for export through loans of its accumulated DISC income to any related or unrelated U.S. producer for export. When a DISC is a subsidiary, producer's loans will typically be made to the parent corporation. If a loan is qualified when made, it will remain a qualified asset of the DISC until its maturity, but see Section K on foreign investment attributable to producer's loans. A producer's loan will not be treated as a constructive dividend.

A producer's loan must be evidenced by a note, be designated as a producer's loan, have a stated maturity not to exceed five years and, as described below, be attributable to assets used in export production. As indicated below, a producer's loan can be renewed if the requirements are met at the time of renewal. In the case of related companies, the loan must be interest bearing at the rates required by section 482 of the Internal Revenue Code.

Interest on producer's loans constitutes a qualified export receipt for purposes of the 95 percent gross receipts requirement and the producer's loan itself will be treated as a qualified asset for purposes of the 95 percent asset requirement. Nevertheless, such interest is treated as if it had been distributed to the DISC's shareholders, whether or not actually distributed, in the year earned by the DISC. The practical effect of a producer's loan to a borrower who is also the DISC's sole shareholder is an interest free loan, assuming the interest is actually distributed as a dividend by the DISC. The reason for this is that the interest is not taxed to the DISC and is a deduction for the borrower-shareholder and the dividend is

taxed to the borrower-shareholder.

A producer's loan is a loan made out of the tax-deferred accumulated DISC income. The loan need not be traced to a specific investment by the domestic borrower but is subject to certain tests to assure that it does not exceed the investment in assets which can be attributed to production for export. The following paragraphs describe in a general way the method by which this test is applied.

The total amount of producer's loans which can be made to any borrower is limited to the borrower's export-related assets. The borrower's assets taken into account for this purpose are (1) the adjusted basis of United States plant, machinery, equipment and supporting production facilities; (2) inventory; and (3) aggregate research and experimental expenditures incurred in taxable years beginning after 1971, whether or not capitalized. These assets and expenditures are deemed export related in the same proportion that export receipts of the producer (through a DISC or otherwise) bear to the total receipts of the producer. This proportion is determined with respect to the three taxable years of the borrower immediately preceding the taxable year of the borrower in which the loan was made, only taking into account taxable years beginning after 1971. Until three such taxable years have ended, the proportion will be computed on the basis of the years which have ended prior to the year in which the loan was made. Thus, no producer's loans can be made to a borrower until after the end of the borrower's first taxable year beginning after December 31, 1971.

There is a further requirement to have a producer's loan. The borrower must increase its investment in the year in which the loan is made in the categories of assets taken into account by an amount at least equal to the amount of the loan.

If the borrower is a member of a controlled group of corporations, the limitations described in the two preceding paragraphs may be determined, at the option of the borrower, by taking into account the assets and sales of (1) the borrower, or (2) the group of corporations, other than any member of the group which is a DISC.

Thus, if 20 percent of the total receipts of the borrower during the period are export receipts, and the total assets taken into account are $1,000,-000, $200,000 of its assets are deemed export related. The borrower could borrow up to $200,000 from DISCs that would qualify as producer's loans, assuming the increase in investment in those assets is at least equal to that amount.

Specific provisions of the law provide for the estimating of production assets and receipts in the case of films to be produced in the United States.

A loan that is extended at maturity will be treated as a new loan and the DISC and the borrower must meet the above tests on the date of the extension.

As is described in Section K below, if an increase in foreign investment is attributed to producer's loans the amount thereof is treated as if distributed to the shareholders of the DISC. *See section 993(d) regarding producer's loans.*

K. FOREIGN INVESTMENT ATTRIBUTABLE TO PRODUCERS LOANS

In order to prevent the flow of tax deferred funds into foreign investment, the tax deferral on funds loaned by a DISC as producer's loans will end if the funds are deemed to have been invested overseas.

This provision is of concern to a DISC only if (1) the DISC is a member of a controlled group of cor-porations (more than 50 percent ownership), (2) the DISC has made producer's loans to one or more other members, and (3) the foreign investment of the group has been increased.

In such a case, a series of tests must be applied to determine whether the foreign investment is deemed to have been made with producer's loans. If there has been such investment, the DISC's shareholders are treated as having received dividends to that extent.

In order to determine whether foreign investment is deemed attributable to producer's loans and, if so, the amount thereof, three tests must be applied. No foreign investment is attributable to producer's loans if any one of the tests fails to produce a positive amount. If positive amounts result under all of these tests, the smallest of the three amounts is the foreign investment attributable to producer's loans. The three tests are: (i) the net increase in foreign assets by members of the controlled group; (ii) the actual foreign investment by domestic members of the group; and (iii) the amount of outstanding producer's loans by the DISC to members of the group.

In determining the net increase in foreign assets, the assets taken into account are depreciable property and real estate located outside the United States and used in a trade or business (assets described in section 1231(b) of the Internal Revenue Code). Assets used for United States export purposes—e.g., assets of a foreign export sales affiliate—are not treated as a foreign investment for this purpose.

To compute the net increase in foreign assets for this purpose, there is subtracted from the gross amount of the increase, (A) depreciation on the type of assets taken into account; (B) the amount of equity and debt (other than normal trade indebtedness) raised abroad by the controlled group (including foreign members) from persons other than members of the group and United States persons (for this purpose foreign branches of U.S. banks are not treated as United States persons); (C) one-half of the earnings and profits of foreign members of the group and of foreign branches of domestic members; (D) one-half of the royalties and fees paid by foreign members of the group to domestic members of the group.

The net increase in foreign assets is generally computed on a cumulative basis. Transitional rules provide that in determining the net increase, there is to be subtracted foreign capital raised under the Foreign Direct Investment Program prior to 1972 not previously allocated to direct investment, and liquid balances in excess of normal working capital requirements held by foreign members and foreign branches on October 31, 1971.

The second of the three tests is the "actual foreign investment by domestic members" of the group. This is the sum of (A) contributions to capital by domestic members of the group to foreign members of the group; (B) transfers of funds to foreign branches; (C) stock and debt obligations (other than normal trade indebtedness) of foreign members of the group issued to domestic members; and (D) one-half of the earnings and profits of foreign subsidiaries and foreign branches of domestic members of the group.

See section 995(d) concerning foreign investment attributable to producer's loans and section 995(b)(1) concerning the amount deemed to be distributed by reason of foreign investment attributable to producer's loans.

L. QUALIFIED FOREIGN INVESTMENTS OF A DISC

A DISC may acquire and receive income in the form of dividends and interest from certain foreign investments which are related to exports from the United States. In general, these are:

(1) Stock or securities of a foreign export sales subsidiary, referred to as a foreign international sales corporation. This is a foreign corporation controlled by the DISC and which has at least 95 percent of its gross receipts from the sale or lease of United States export property and from services related and subsidiary to such sales or leases. For this purpose, packaging and minor assembly will be permitted, provided that there is no substantial transformation of the exported goods by the DISC and the foreign corporation and provided that the value added by the physical operations of these corporations does not exceed 20 percent of the cost of goods sold. In addition, at least 95 percent of the adjusted basis of the foreign corporation's assets at the close of the taxable year must consist of certain qualified export assets. *See section 993(e)(1).*

(2) Stock or securities of a controlled foreign real estate title holding corporation, holding title to foreign export facilities of the DISC. *See section 993(e)(2).*

(3) Stock or securities of an unrelated foreign corporation, provided that the ownership is in furtherance of an export sale or sales and provided that the direct or indirect stock ownership by the DISC is less than 10 percent of the total combined voting power of the foreign corporation. This exception is intended to be limited to investments that might be required in unrelated foreign distributors or to help finance a customer's purchase of export property. *See section 993(e)(3).*

M. INTER-COMPANY PRICING RULES

(1) *Basic rules.* Two safe haven rules have been provided which can be applied at the discretion of the DISC

and its related supplier (whether or not the related supplier is the manufacturer), in lieu of the rules set forth in the regulations under section 482, in setting the transfer price between the related supplier and the DISC. When these rules are used, section 482 does not apply. Under these rules, which are designed to simplify compliance, the transfer price from the related supplier to the DISC is finally computed only after the DISC sells the goods to a customer. The DISC and its supplier may make adjustments upwards or downwards following the close of the taxable year in which the DISC sells the goods to obtain the most favorable allocation of income permitted by these rules.

Upon the sale of export property to a DISC by a related person, the related person may set a transfer price to the DISC which enables the DISC, out of the combined taxable income from manufacture and sale, or purchase and sale, of such products or product lines, to obtain taxable income up to the greater of:

(a) 4 percent of the qualified export receipts of the DISC plus 10 percent of the export promotion expenses incurred by the DISC (*see section 994(a)(1)*), or

(b) 50 percent of the combined taxable income of the related supplier and the DISC from production and sale, or purchase and sale, of the export's property plus 10 percent of export promotion expenses incurred by the DISC (*see section 994(a) (2)*).

Neither of the above rules permit the related person to price at a loss.

A transfer of inventory to the DISC which the DISC does not sell in the year of the transfer may be accounted for in the year of transfer by the DISC paying the amount of the related supplier's inventory cost, with a corres-

ponding reduction in the related supplier's inventory and an increase in the DISC's assets in that amount. Expenses incurred by the related supplier with respect to such property, such as shipping costs to a DISC's warehouse, would be added to such inventory cost to be recovered by the related supplier from the DISC in such year if the related person would ordinarily include such transportation as part of the cost recovered on a shipment to a branch. On the sale by the DISC to a customer in a subseqent year, the DISC would divide the combined taxable income with the related supplier, and reimburse the related supplier for the supplier's expenses allocable to the export property which were not included in costs originally paid by the DISC.

Examples of inter-company pricing under these special rules follow:

(a) Under the 4 percent rule: This pricing rule can be illustrated by a DISC which sold for $1,000 export property it purchased from a related person, and incurred expenses attributable to that sale of $90, all of which were export promotion expenses. In this case, there could be allocated to the DISC that part of the combined taxable income arising with respect to the export property which did not exceed $49 (4 percent of $1,000, plus 10 percent of $90). This profit element of $49 plus the DISC's expenses of $90 indicates that the transfer price of the related person to the DISC could be $861 ($1,000 less the $90 of promotion expenses and the $49 of DISC profit). If the combined taxable income arising on the sale (i.e., the receipts of the DISC on the sale less the related supplier's cost of goods sold for the property and the other expenses of the related supplier and the DISC) were only $25, then the amount of profit allocated to DISC on the sale could not exceed $25.

(b) Under the 50–50 rule: This pricing rule can be illustrated by a transaction in which the combined taxable income of the DISC and the related supplier was $170, computed on the basis of assumed facts as follows:

DISC's sales price_____	$1,000
Cost of goods sold of related supplier _____	650
Combined gross income_____	350
Direct expenses:	
Export promotion expenses incurred by the DISC_____	90
Direct selling expenses incurred by the related supplier____	60
Total _____	150
Indirect non-production expenses (all borne by related supplier)*_	30
Total direct and indirect expenses of both parties_____	180
Combined taxable income_____	170
Total unallocated expenses (all borne by related supplier)____	$300
Combined gross income as computed above_____	350
Combined gross income of both parties from all transactions (excluding transfer prices paid by the DISC to the related supplier) _____	3,500
Proration of unallocated expenses ($300×$\frac{\$350}{\$3500}$) _____	30

*The indirect expenses prorated to the export income could have, for example, been computed as follows:

In this case, the DISC would be allowed a taxable income of $94 (50 percent of the combined taxable income of $170, or $85, plus $9, representing 10 percent of the export promotion expenses it incurred). Accordingly, the related supplier would be allowed a taxable income of $76. This represents one-half of the combined taxable income of $170, less the $9 allocated to the DISC because of its export promotion expenses.

Thus, the related supplier could charge a transfer price to the DISC of $816 ($650, cost of goods sold; $60, direct selling expenses incurred by it; $30 indirect expenses; and $76, taxable income). The DISC would realize a gross profit of $184 and after deduction of the $90 export promotion expenses, a taxable income of $94.

The same inter-company allocation to the DISC will be permitted whether the DISC takes title as principal or acts as a commission agent (*see section 994 (b)(1)*). The Regulations are to provide for the allocation of expenditures in computing combined taxable income in certain cases (*see section 994 (b)(2)*).

A DISC, or the supplier for which the DISC is acting as commission agent, must sell to a related foreign purchaser on an arm's length basis, under the provisions of section 482 of the Internal Revenue Code, viewing the DISC and any related supplier as a single entity which sells to a foreign purchaser.

(2) *Export Promotion Expenses.* A DISC selling on behalf of a related person, as principal or agent, can obtain an allocation, as stated above, out of combined taxable income of up to 4 percent of the DISC's export receipts or 50 percent of the combined taxable income, whichever is greater. Moreover, to the extent the DISC itself incurs export promotion expenses, it is entitled to an additional allocation of taxable income based on 10 percent of the export promotion expenses incurred by it. Export promotion expenses comprise a DISC's ordinary and necessary expenses paid or incurred to obtain qualified export receipts. In general these include market studies, advertising, salaries and wages of sales, clerical and other personnel, rentals, sales commissions, warehousing and other selling expenses, and one-half of the freight expenses (not including insurance) for shipping export property aboard U.S.

flag vessels and U.S. owned and operated aircraft (unless required by law). Not included are interest expenses, income or franchise taxes, the cost of assembly operations or any expenses which do not directly or indirectly further the distribution of export property for use abroad. If a DISC, itself, actually negotiates and contracts with unrelated persons, for export services to be rendered to it, the expenses will be export promotion expenses. However, intercompany transactions in which the DISC is billed by an affiliate will not be treated as export promotion expenses. *See section 994(c)*.

N. TAXATION OF A DISC AND ITS SHAREHOLDERS

A DISC is not subject to United States income tax on any of its income. Whenever the DISC income is taxable, the tax is imposed not on the DISC, but on the shareholders. *See sections 991 and 995(a)*.

In the usual course of its business a DISC is likely to derive two types of income taxed annually to its shareholders, whether or not distributed currently:

(1) If the DISC has any producer's loans outstanding, the interest on the loans is taxable currently to the shareholders (*see section 995(b)(1)(A)*), and

(2) One-half of the DISC's taxable income (after deduction of interest on producer's loans deemed distributed) is taxable currently to its shareholders (*see section 995(b)(1)(D)*).

In some cases an increase in foreign investment may be attributed to producer's loans and if that occurs deferral will terminate to that extent.

In the normal conduct of business a DISC will often operate by making actual annual distributions of dividends in the amount of any interest on

producers's loans, plus one-half of the remaining taxable income. This will eliminate the necessity for keeping track of income previously taxed to the shareholders. The shareholders will pay ordinary income tax on the amounts distributed, while the DISC continues to hold its remaining income with tax deferred. Thus, if a DISC had $100,000 of taxable income, including $10,000 of interest on producer's loans, the DISC might distribute the $10,000 interest, plus one-half of the remaining taxable income, or $45,000, retaining $45,000 tax deferred. Of course, an actual distribution is not required and a DISC is free to distribute less or nothing at all.

While the foregoing covers the normal operations of a DISC, there are certain special situations in which the DISC is deemed to have distributed a dividend which is taxable to its shareholders:

(1) In order to prevent certain tax avoidance arrangements, part of the' gain that is recognized by a DISC on the sale of section 1245, section 1250 and nonqualified assets received by it from transferors in a tax free transaction will be deemed taxable to the DISC's shareholders. A deemed distribution in this situation is to prevent using the DISC as a conduit to sell off appreciated capital assets or to avoid recapture of depreciation. *See section 995(b)(1)(B) and (C)*.

(2) If, in spite of the procedures for making qualifying distributions of non-qualified assets or income (see Section O which describes such deficiency distributions), a DISC nevertheless disqualifies, or if the DISC status is intentionally terminated, the tax-deferred DISC income that has been accumulated to that point becomes taxable. In such cases, as long as the corporation remains in existence, this income is deemed taxable to the

shareholders over a 10-year period, or such shorter time as the DISC had been in existence. If the income is distributed, it is taxed currently. This deemed distribution of the previously accumulated DISC income continues even though the corporation might again qualify for deferral on new export income. *See section 995(b)(2)*.

(3) As described above, the tax deferral on the principal of such loans will be ended if the funds are deemed to have been invested in foreign assets. Again the mechanism is to treat such income as being distributed to the shareholders. *See section 995(b) (1)(E)*.

(4) If a DISC shareholder disposes of his stock in a DISC (or if the DISC is liquidated), his gain, to the extent of the earnings and profits of the DISC accumulated while he was a shareholder and on which tax was deferred, is deemed to represent a dividend distribution to him. Since he pays the tax on these undistributed profits at the time of the sale, the purchaser from the shareholder will be entitled to receive actual dividends tax free from the DISC to the extent of the earnings and profits on which tax was paid by the selling shareholder. *See section 995(c)*.

O. DEFICIENCY DISTRIBUTIONS

If a DISC fails to satisfy the gross receipts test or the assets test, it can make a deficiency distribution of the taxable income attributable to non-qualified receipts or in respect of the non-qualified assets to avoid disqualification. When made, the distribution must be designated as a distribution to meet qualification requirements. There are two types of deficiency distributions:

(1) Reasonable cause: As long as the failure to qualify is due to reasonable cause, such as failure resulting from blocked currency, expropriation or reasonable uncertainty as to what

constituted a qualified receipt or asset, the distribution can be made any time before or after the close of the DISC's taxable year, including at the time of a later tax audit. A payment in the nature of interest must be made to the Internal Revenue Service.

(2) Reasonable cause assumed: Regardless of reasonable cause, a deficiency distribution can be made if the DISC had 70 percent of its gross receipts for the year and 70 percent of its assets at the end of each month during the taxable year in the form of qualified receipts and assets. However, in this case the distribution must be made within 8½ months after the close of the DISC's taxable year, which is the date by which a DISC must file its information return. *See section 992(c) concerning deficiency distributions*.

One of the uses of the deficiency distribution procedure is to permit a DISC to enter into a transaction which it reasonably believes might be qualified before Regulations have been issued on the point, such as when the status of a U.S. Government subsidy program has not been announced.

P. SOME SPECIAL CONSIDERATIONS

In considering the use of a DISC, a number of special considerations which are set forth in general terms below should be taken into account:

(1) Receipts in connection with sales of export property shipped prior to January 1, 1972, are not qualified export receipts. However, receipts arising on or after January 1, 1972, from export property shipped on or after January 1, 1972, even though the contract to sell the property was entered into before January 1, 1972, can be income of the DISC giving rise to qualified export receipts, if there is an appropriate assignment under which the DISC participates in the transaction as principal or agent.

(2) A DISC may not be included in a consolidated return nor are dividends from a DISC's accumulated DISC income entitled to the corporate dividends received deduction. *See sections 1504(b)(7) regarding consolidated returns and 246(d) regarding the dividends received deduction.*

(3) A dividend distribution by a DISC out of export income is treated by the shareholder as foreign source income, but may not be included by the shareholder in computing the overall limitation under the foreign tax credit provisions of the Internal Revenue Code. A corporate shareholder owning at least 10 percent of the stock of a DISC is entitled to a credit for foreign income taxes paid by the DISC or a subsidiary of the DISC, but only to the extent of the U.S. income tax on the dividend (or deemed dividend) the shareholder receives from the DISC. *See sections 901(d) and 904(f) regarding foreign tax credits.*

(4) Certain types of corporations may not be DISCs. These include tax-exempt corporations, personal holding companies, banks, savings and loan associations and similar financial institutions, insurance companies, regulated investment companies and subchapter S corporation. *See section 992(d).*

(5) A DISC will not obtain qualified export receipts from the lease of property to a corporation which is a member of the same group of controlled corporations. *See section 993 (c)(2)(A).*

(6) Export property does not include any patents, inventions, models, designs, formulas, or processes, whether or not patented, copyrights (other than films, tapes, records or similar reproductions, for commercial or home use), good will, trademarks, trade brands, franchises, or other like property. However, the fact that inventory property sold or leased abroad is protected by a patent, trademark or copyright does not exclude it from constituting export property. Thus, for example, if a book is sold abroad or a film is sold abroad for exhibition abroad, the receipts could constitute qualified export receipts. *See section 993(c)(2)(B).*

(7) The regulations to be issued will provide that for purposes of determining whether a shareholder of a DISC is a personal holding company, the activities of the DISC will be attributed to the shareholder. *See Regulations § 1.951–1(a).*

(8) Upon the death of a shareholder of a DISC, the tax basis which would ordinarily apply to the DISC shares is reduced by the accumulated DISC income attributable to the shares. *See section 1014(d).*

(9) The DISC legislation and this handbook generally used the concept of controlled group and related person with the meaning set forth in section 1563(a) of the Internal Revenue Code, except that in lieu of a relationship of 80 percent a relationship of more than 50 percent is provided. However, it should be noted that in other instances the concept of related person has the meaning set forth in section 482 of the Internal Revenue Code. These different uses will be made explicit in the Regulations. *Compare section 993 (a)(3) with section 994(a).*

Q. DISC TAX RETURN

A DISC must file an annual information return for its taxable year on or before 15th day of the 9th month following the close of the taxable year. Shareholders receiving actual or deemed distributions from a DISC will, of course, report such dividends on their annual corporate or individual tax returns. *See section 6011(e) for regulatory authority concerning the filing of DISC tax returns.*

R. REORGANIZATION OF FOREIGN
   OPERATIONS

The DISC legislation provides that certain foreign Export Trade Corporations can transfer assets on a tax-free basis to DISCs without obtaining an advance determination under section 367 of the Internal Revenue Code and without the realization, as a result of the transfer, of subpart F income. In the case of a transfer of assets by other foreign sales affiliates to a DISC, in connection with a restructuring of export operations, the Internal Revenue Service generally will not consider that there is a United States tax avoidance motive for purposes of section 367.

The 1976 Tax Reform Act requires the tax deferral benefits accorded to a DISC and its shareholders to be computed on an incremental basis. In general, the incremental computation rules allow DISC benefits to the extent that current export gross receipts exceed 67 percent of the average of the DISC's export gross receipts for a 4-year base period. For taxable years beginning in 1976, the base period is the 4 taxable years, 1972, 1973, 1974 and 1975. These 4 base period years remain the same for any taxable year beginning before 1980. (Thus, a 4-year grace period is provided.) In taxable years beginning in 1980 and later years, the base period becomes a 4-year moving base period, and moves forward one year for each year beyond 1979. A small DISC exemption from the new incremental rules is provided for DISCs with adjusted taxable income of $100,000 or less in a taxable year. These small DISCs will continue to receive the full DISC benefits provided under present law. However, the small DISC exemption phases out at $150,000 of taxable income.

Tax shelters for corporations can play an important role in reducing corporate taxes and adding to corporate growth. The same care in selection of shelters that is recommended for individual investors is also advised for corporations. Seek the counsel of a tax-shelter specialist.

397

PART FOUR

FUNDAMENTALS TO UNDERSTANDING TAX SHELTERS

To understand the significance of tax shelters it is essential to have a background in the forms of business organization and various tax entities, capital gains and losses, and depreciation, amortization, depletion, and investment credit. These write-offs reduce the taxable income of the taxpayer.

CHAPTER ONE

FORMS OF BUSINESS ORGANIZATION

The taxes that result from a business activity depend to a great extent on the form of the business organization carrying on the activity. To achieve the best tax results, the investor should seek the counsel of an expert in this area to determine which form would be most advantageous for the investment in question.

SOLE PROPRIETORSHIPS

A sole proprietor is an individual in business for himself. His income from the sole proprietorship is part of his total gross income. Each asset of his sole proprietorship is treated separately for tax purposes. In selling his entire business as a going concern he determines gain or loss separately on each individual asset.

PARTNERSHIPS

A partnership in an association of two or more persons to carry on as co-owners of a business for their joint profit. Most partnerships are general partnerships in which each partner involves himself in the management of the company. However, tax shelters frequently utilize limited partnerships which have one or more general partners and one or more limited partners. A limited partner has no voice in the management of the business, and his liability for partnership obligations is limited to the amount of capital that he has contributed to the company. Often the investor in a tax-shelter partnership is a limited partner.

A partnership is not a taxable entity but determines its income and files its return the same as an individual. A partner, in determining his taxable income, takes into account his distributive share of partnership items. For income tax purposes the term partnership includes (in addition to typical general partnership and limited partnerships) a syndicate, group, pool, joint venture, or similar organization that is carrying on a business and that is not classified as a trust, estate, or corporation.

The 1976 Tax Reform Act imposes a limitation of $2,000 on the amount of additional first-year depreciation that a partnership can pass through to its partners. This provision does not affect the present $2,000 limitation which is applicable to each individual partner. Thus, a partnership can pass through to each partner his pro rata share of the $2,000 bonus depreciation allowance. An individual partner would then aggregate all of the additional first-year depreciation deductions from all partnerships in which he was a member, but the aggregate deduction cannot exceed $2,000 ($4,000 in the case of a joint return). This provision applies to taxable years of partnerships beginning after December 31, 1975.

The 1976 Tax Reform Act requires fees paid in connection with the syndication of a partnership to be capitalized (and thus, syndication fees may not be deducted). Organization fees may be amortized over a 5-year period. The provision relating to partnership syndication fees applies to partnership taxable years beginning after December 31, 1975. The provision with respect to organization fees applies to partnership taxable years beginning after December 31, 1976.

The 1976 Tax Reform Act provides that income or losses will be allocable to a partner only for the portion of the year that he is a member of a partnership and not retroactively to periods prior to entry. In determining the income, loss or special item allocable to an incoming partner, the partnership will either allocate on a daily basis or separate the partnership year into two (or more) segments and allocate income, loss or special items in each segment among the persons who were partners during that segment. This provision applies to partnership taxable years beginning after December 31, 1975.

The 1976 Tax Reform Act provides that an allocation of taxable income or loss, as well as any item of income, gain, loss, deduction or credit, among partners of a partnership will be controlled by the partnership agreement if the partner receiving the allocation can demonstrate that the allocation has substantial economic effect. If an allocation made by the partnership is set aside, a partner's share of the income, gain, loss, deduction or credit (or item thereof) will be determined in accordance with the partner's interest in the partnership. Among the relevant factors to be taken into account are the interests of the respective partners in profits and losses (if different from that of taxable income or loss), cash flow, and rights to distributions of capital upon liquidation. These provisions apply to partnership taxable years beginning after December 31, 1975.

The 1976 Tax Reform Act provides that for purposes of the limitation on allowance of losses under Section 704(d) of the Code, the adjusted basis of a partner's interest will not include any portion of any partnership liability with respect to which the partner has no personal liability. The effect of this provision is to limit deductions which may be passed through to a limited partner to the amount of investment which he actually has and will have at risk in the partnership. It is intended that in determining whether a partner has personal liability with respect to any partnership liability, the rules of section 465 (relating to the limitation on deductions to amounts at risk in case of certain activities) will apply. This provision will not apply to any activity to which section 465 (relating to the limitation on deductions to amounts at risk in case of certain activities) nor will it apply to any partnership the principal activity of which involves real property (other than mineral property).

Under the 1976 Tax Reform Act, this provision would apply to liabilities incurred after December 31, 1976.

Under prior law, gain from a sale or exchange of depreciable property is denied capital gain treatment if the sale is between a husband and wife, or between an individual and a corporation (if over 80 percent of the value of the corporation's stock is owned by the individual, his spouse, and his minor children or grandchildren).

The 1976 Tax Reform Act broadens the provision of present law to cover a sale or exchange of depreciable property between commonly-controlled corporations. In addition, the rules of constructive ownership are broadened to include the taxpayer's parents, adult children, plus any trust, estate or partnership in which the taxpayer is a beneficiary or partner. These provisions apply to sales or exchanges made after the date of enactment, except those sales made pursuant to a binding contract entered into before the date of enactment.

The 1976 Tax Reform Act provides that the amount of any loss (otherwise allowable for the year) which may be deducted in connection with one of certain activities cannot exceed the aggregate amount with respect to which the taxpayer is at risk in each such activity at the close of the taxable year. This "at risk" limitation applies to the following activities: (1) farming (except farming operations involving trees other than fruit or nut trees); (2) exploring for, or exploiting, oil and gas resources; (3) holding, producing, or distributing of motion picture films or video tapes; and (4) equipment leasing. The limitation applies to all taxpayers (other than corporations which are not subchapter S corporations) including individuals and sole proprietorships, estates, trusts, shareholders in subchapter S corporations, and partners in a partnership which conducts an activity described in this provision.

Under this provision, a taxpayer is generally to be considered "at risk" with respect to an activity to the extent of his cash and the adjusted basis of other property contributed to the activity, any amounts borrowed for use in the activity with respect to which the taxpayer has personal liability for payment from his personal assets, and his net fair market value of personal assets which secure non-recourse borrowings.

In general, the at risk provisions apply to losses attributable to amounts paid or incurred (and depreciation or amortization allowed or allowable) in taxable years beginning after December 31, 1975. However, with respect to equipment leasing activities, the conference agreement provides that the at risk rule will not apply to net leases under binding contracts finalized on or before December 31, 1975, and to operating leases under binding contracts finalized on or before April 30, 1976. With respect to motion picture activities, the conference agreement also provides that the at risk provision does not apply to a film purchase shelter if the principal photography begins before

September 11, 1975, there was a binding written contract for the purchase of the film on that date, and the taxpayer held his interest in the film on that date. The at risk rule also does not apply to production costs, etc., if the principal photography began before September 11, 1975, and the investor had acquired his interest in the film before that date. In addition, the at risk provision does not apply to a film produced in the United States if the principal photography began before January 1, 1976, if certain commitments with respect to the film had been made by September 10, 1975.

In applying the at risk provisions to activities which were begun in taxable years beginning before January 1, 1976 (and not exempted from this provision by the above transition rules), amounts paid or incurred in taxable years beginning prior to that date and deducted in such taxable years will generally be treated as reducing first that portion of the taxpayer's basis which is not at risk. (On the other hand, withdrawals made in taxable years beginning before January 1, 1976, will be treated as reducing the amount which the taxpayer is at risk in the same manner as withdrawals made after that date.)

Under prior law, there were two "at risk" rules designed to prevent a taxpayer from deducting losses in excess of his actual economic investment in the activity involved. The first of these at risk rules—"the specific at risk rule"—applied to four specified activities: (1) farming; (2) exploring for, or exploiting, oil and natural gas resources; (3) holding, producing, or distributing motion picture films or video tapes; and (4) leasing of personal property. The other at risk rule—"the partnership at risk rule"—applied generally to activities engaged in through partnerships. However, there were two exceptions to this rule. First, the rule did not apply to any activity to the extent that the specific risk rule applied. Second, the rule did not apply to any partnership the principal activity of which was investing in real property (other than mineral property).

The Revenue Act of 1978 extends the specific at risk rule to all activities except real estate (and certain equipment leasing activities of closely-held corporations, as discussed below). For the newly covered activities, the specific at risk rule covers activities which are a part of a trade or business or are engaged in for the production of income. Separate rules for aggregation and separation of activities are provided for the activities to which the at risk rule is extended by the Act. The holding of real property (other than mineral property) is to be treated as a separate activity, and the at risk rule is not applied to losses from that activity. For purposes of this exclusion, personal property and services which are incidental to making real property available as living accommodations are to be treated as part of the activity of holding the real property. Since all the activities currently covered by the partnership at risk rules would now be covered by the new expanded version of the specific at risk rules under section 465, the partnership at risk rule is repealed by the Act.

This provision is effective for taxable years beginning after December 31, 1978.

Under prior law, the only corporations to which the specific at risk rule applied were subchapter S corporations and personal holding companies. The Act extends the application of this rule to all corporations in which five or fewer individuals own more than 50 percent of the corporation's stock. However, the equipment leasing activities of a closely held corporation are not to be subject to the at risk rule if the corporation is actively engaged in equipment leasing, that is, if 50 percent or more of the corporation's gross receipts is derived from equipment leasing. This provision is effective for taxable years beginning after December 31, 1978.

Under prior law, the at risk rule under section 465 may have been interpreted to only require the taxpayer to be at risk as of the end of the taxable year for which losses were claimed. Under this interpretation, subsequent withdrawals of amounts originally placed at risk could be made without the recapture of previously allowed losses.

In order to be consistent with the original intent of the at risk rule, the Act requires the recapture of previously allowed losses when the amount at risk is reduced below zero. Mechanically, this rule works by providing that if the amount at risk is reduced below zero (by distributions to the taxpayer, by changes in the status of indebtedness from recourse to nonrecourse, by the commencement of a guarantee or other similar arrangement which affects the taxpayer's risk of loss, or otherwise), the taxpayer will recognize income to the extent that his at risk basis is reduced below zero. However, the amount recaptured is limited to the excess of the losses previously allowed and which reduced the taxpayer's at risk basis in that activity for taxable years beginning after December 31, 1978, over any amounts previously recaptured. A suspended deduction

deduction in the amount equal to the amount of recaptured income would be provided to the taxpayer. This suspended deduction would be allowed in a subsequent year if and to the extent the taxpayer's at risk basis is increased. The provision is generally effective for taxable years beginning after December 31, 1978.

Under present law, partnerships are required to file an annual information return setting forth the partnership income, deductions, and credits, names and addresses of the partners, each partner's distributive share of partnership income, deduction, and credit, and certain other information required by the regulations. Under prior law, neither the partnership nor any partner was subject to a civil penalty for failure to file, or for late filing of, a partnership information return.

Under the Act, a civil penalty is imposed on the partnership for failure to timely file a complete partnership information return as required by existing Code sections. The penalty is assessed for each month, or fraction of a month (but not to exceed 5 months), that the partnership return is late or incomplete. The amount of penalty for each month, or fraction of a month, is $50 multiplied by the total number of partners in the partnership during the partnership's taxable year for which the return is due. The penalty will not be imposed if the partnership can show that failure to file a complete or timely return is due reasonable cause. The provision is effective with respect to returns for taxable years beginning after December 31, 1978.

Under present law, partnerships are not taxable entities. Instead, a partnership is a conduit, in which the items of partnership income, deduction, and credit are allocated among the partners for inclusion in their respective income tax returns. Under present law, partnerships are required to file an annual information return setting forth the partnership income, deductions, and credits, names and addresses of the partners, each partner's distributive share of partnership income, deduction, and credit, and certain other information required by the regulations. The Code provides a period of limitations during which the Service can assess a tax or a taxpayer may file a claim for refund. Generally, the period is 3 years from the date the tax return is filed. Under prior law, the income tax return of each of the partners of a partnership commenced that individual partner's period of limitations. Under prior law, the date of filing of the partnership return did not affect the period of limitations. In order to extend the period of limitations with respect to partnership items, the Service was required to obtain a consent for extension of the statute of limitations from each of the partners—not the partnership. Generally, an agreement to extend the period of limitations related to all items on the return of the partner who consented to the extension.

The Act extends the period of time in which assessments of deficiencies and claims for refund of tax attributable to partnership items may be made. These special periods of limitation apply only to partnership items which are attributable to "Federally registered partnerships." A Federally registered partnership means any partnership the interests in which have been offered for sale prior to the close of the taxable year in an offering required to be registered with the Securities and Exchange Commission (SEC) or any partnership which is or has been subject to the annual SEC reporting requirements which relate to the protection of investors. If a partnership is excused from registration or reporting by either a statutory or a regulatory exemption of the SEC, it is not to be treated as a Federally registered partnership.

With respect to deficiencies, the Act provides generally that the Service may assess a deficiency attributable to partnership items within 4 years after the partnership return for the partnership taxable year in which the item arose is filed. If the partnership return does not properly show the name and address of the person to be assessed the deficiency, the period of assessment will not expire until one year after that information is provided to the Service in the manner prescribed by regulations. With respect to credits and refunds, the Act provides generally that the taxpayer may file a claim for credit or refund of tax attributable to partnership items within 4 years after the due date (including extensions) of the partnership return for the partnership taxable year in which the item arose. This provision is effective for items arising in partnership taxable years beginning after December 31, 1978.

CERTAIN FARMING TAX SHELTERS

FARMING SYNDICATES

A farming syndicate may be a partnership, any other non-corporate enterprise, or an electing small business corporation

(Subchapter S corporation), engaged in the trade or business of farming, if:

1) At any time interests in the partnership or enterprise have been offered for sale in any offering required to be registered with any Federal or State agency; or

2) More than 35% of the losses during any period are allocable to limited partners or limited entrepreneurs.

A *limited entrepreneur* is a person who has an interest in an enterprise other than as a limited partner and who does not actively participate in the management of the enterprise.

An interest will not be considered held by a limited partner or limited entrepreneur if an individual:

1) Has an interest that is attributable to active participation in the management of a farm for at least 5 years (where one farm is substituted for or added to another farm, both farms will be treated as one farm);

2) Lives principally on the farm on which the trade or business of farming is being carried on;

3) Actively participates in the management of a trade or business of farming which involves the raising of livestock (or is treated as being engaged in active management under (1) or (2)), and the trade or business of the partnership or any other enterprise involves the further processing of the livestock raised in the trade or business with respect to which the individual is (actually or constructively) an active participant;

4) Who has a principal business activity involving active participation in the management of a farm, any interest in any other trade or business of farming; or

5) Is a member of the family or a grandparent of a person who meets any of the four conditions stated previously and whose interest is attributable to the active participation of that person. For purposes of this condition, the family of a person includes that person's brothers and sisters (whether by the whole or half blood), spouse, ancestors, and lineal descendants.

Deductions are limited for farming syndicates. In the case of any farming syndicate, a deduction for amounts paid for feed, seed, fertilizer, or other similar farm supplies is only allowed for the tax year in which such items are actually used or consumed (or, if later, the tax year for which such amounts are deductible under the syndicate's method of accounting). However, this does not apply to any amount paid for supplies on hand at the end of the tax year which would have been consumed, but were not because of fire, storm, flood, other casualty, disease, or drought. Also, this rule does not apply to any amount required to be capitalized, as an orchard or vineyard expense, as discussed later.

Certain poultry expenses. The cost of poultry (including egg-laying hens and baby chicks purchased by a farming syndicate for use in a trade or business (or both for use in a trade or business and for sale) must be capitalized and deducted ratably over the lesser of 12 months or their useful life in the trade or business. The cost of poultry purchased for sale must be deducted for the tax year in which the poultry is sold or otherwise disposed of.

Farming defined. For farming syndicates the term farming means the cultivation of land or the raising or harvesting of any agricultural or horticultural commodity including the raising, shearing, feeding, caring for, training, and management of animals. Trees (other than trees bearing fruit or nuts) will not be treated as an agricultural or horticultural commodity.

Orchard and vineyard expenses. A syndicate that is engaged in planting, cultivating, maintaining, or developing a grove, orchard or vineyard in which fruit or nuts are grown must capitalize, and recover by depreciation, any amount that:
1) Would otherwise be deductible;
2) Is attributable to the planting, cultivation, maintenance, or development of the grove orchard, or vineyard; and
3) Is incurred before the tax year in which there is a crop or yield in commercial quantities.

However, this does not apply to deductions attributable to a grove, orchard, or vineyard which was replanted after having been lost or damaged (while in your hands) by reason of freezing temperatures, disease, drought, pests, or casualty.

AT RISK LIMITATION

You may be subject to a new at risk limitation, discussed later, if you are involved in one of the following activities as a trade or business or for the production of income:

1) Farming
2) Exploring for, or exploiting, oil and gas resources;
3) Holding, producing, or distributing motion picture films or video tapes; or
4) Leasing personal property, certain other tangible property other than buildings, an elevator or escalator, or certain other real property, that is or has been subject to an allowance for depreciation or amortization.

For applying the at risk limitation to individuals, each film, or videotape, item of leased equipment, farm, or oil and gas property is treated as a separate activity. However, in the case of a partnership or Subchapter S corporation, all of the activities in the same category (for example, all farming activities) are treated as one activity.

Generally, for amounts paid or incurred in tax years beginning after December 31, 1975, any loss from one or more of the specified activities will be allowed only to the extent of the aggregate amount you have at risk for the activity at the close of the tax year. This limitation applies to all noncorporate taxpayers, including shareholders in Subchapter S corporations.

Depreciation and amortization allowed or allowable for any period are treated as amounts paid or incurred in that period. Any loss from the activity that is not allowed for a year will be treated as a deduction allocable to the activity in the first succeeding tax year.

Amount of loss. A loss means the excess of deductions allowed for the year (without regard to the at risk rules), and allocable to a specified activity, over income received or accrued during the year from that activity.

Amounts considered at risk. Generally, you will be considered at risk with respect to an activity to the extent of your cash and the adjusted basis of other property contributed to the activity and amounts borrowed with respect to that activity.

Borrowed amounts. Generally, you are considered at risk for amounts borrowed for use in activity if you are personally liable for the repayment of the amounts, or if the amounts borrowed are secured by property other than property used in the activity. However, in the latter case, the amount considered at risk will be limited to the net fair market value of your interest in the pledged property. The net fair market value of property is its fair market value less any prior (or superior) claims to which it is subject. The amount at risk cannot be increased through collateral if that collateral is directly financed by indebtedness secured by any property used in the activity.

In addition, you will not be considered at risk with respect to borrowed amounts if the lender has an interest, other than as a creditor in the activity, or if the lender is related to you. Members of the immediate family include brothers and sisters (whether by the whole or half blood).

Amounts not considered at risk. You will not be considered at risk for amounts protected against loss through nonrecourse financing guarantees, stop loss agreements, or other similar arrangements.

Nonrecourse financing. You will not be considered at risk with respect to the proceeds from your share of any nonrecourse loan used to finance the activity or to acquire property used in the activity. In addition, if you borrow money to contribute to the activity and the lender's recourse is either your interest in the activity or property used in the activity, the amount of the loan is considered to be financed on a nonrecourse basis and does not increase your amount at risk.

Other loss limiting arrangements. Your capital is not at risk in the business, even as to your equity capital which you have contributed, to the extent you are protected against economic loss for all or part of your capital by an agreement or arrangement of compensation or reimbursement to you for any loss you may suffer. For example, you will not be at risk if you arranged to receive insurance or other compensation for an economic loss after the loss is sustained, or if you are entitled to reimbursement for part or all of any loss by reason of a binding agreement between yourself and another person.

Example 1. In livestock feeding operations some commercial feedlots offer to reimburse investors against any loss sustained on sales of the fed livestock above a stated dollar amount per head. Under such stop loss orders, the investor is to be considered at risk only to the extent of the portion of the investor's capital against which the investor is not entitled to reimbursement.

Example 2. In some livestock breeding investments carried on through a limited partnership, the partnership agrees with a limited partner that, at the partner's election, it will repurchase the partnership interest at a stated minimum dollar amount (usually less than the investor's original capital contribution). In this situation the partner is considered at risk only to the extent of the portion of the amount otherwise at risk over and above the guaranteed repurchase price.

Example 3. You are personally liable on a mortgage but you separately obtain insurance to compensate you for any payments which you must actually make under such personal liability. You will be considered at risk only to the extent of the uninsured portion of the personal liability to which you are exposed. You will be able to include in the amount you have at risk any amount of premium which you paid from your personal assets for the insurance. However, if you obtain casualty insurance or insurance protecting yourself against tort liability it will not affect the amount you are otherwise considered to have at risk.

A government target price program (such as provided by the Agriculture and Consumer Protection Act of 1973) or other governmental price support programs with respect to a product grown by you does not, in the absence of agreements limiting your costs, reduce the amount you have at risk.

Amounts at risk in subsequent years. In applying the at risk limitation, the amount of any loss which is allowable in a particular year reduces your at risk investment (but not below zero) as of the end of that year and in all succeeding tax years for that activity. Thus, if you have a loss in excess of your at risk amount, the loss disallowed will not be allowed in subsequent years unless you increase your at risk amount. Losses which are suspended because they are greater than your investment which is at risk are to be treated as a deduction for the activity in the following year. Consequently, if your amount at risk increases in later years, you will be able to take a deduction for previously suspended losses to the extent that these increases in your amount at risk exceed your losses in later years.

BASIS OF PARTNER'S INTEREST

The determination of the adjusted basis of a partnership interest is ordinarily made as of the end of a partnership's tax year. However, if there has been a sale or exchange of all or a part of your interest, or a liquidation of your entire interest in a partnership, the adjusted basis of your interest must be determined as of the date of sale or exchange or liquidation. The adjusted basis of your interest is determined *without regard* to any amount shown in the partnership books as your capital, equity, or similar account. Your adjusted basis for an interest in a partnership can never be less than zero.

Example. You contribute to a partnership property that has an adjusted basis of $400 and a fair market value of $1,000. Your partner contributes $1,000 cash. While under your agreement each of you may have a capital account in the partnership of $1,000, which will be reflected in the partnership books, the adjusted basis of your interest is only $400 and your partner's basis is $1,000.

The original basis of your interest acquired by a contribution of property, including money, is the money you contributed plus your adjusted basis of the property contributed. If the acquisition of an interest in a partnership results in taxable income to you, the income is an addition to the basis of your interest. Any increase in your individual liabilities because of the assumption by you of partnership liabilities will also be treated as a contribution of money by you to the partnership.

If the property you contribute is subject to indebtedness, or if liabilities of yours are assumed by the partnership, the basis of your interest is reduced by the portion assumed by the other partners, since the partnership's assumption of your indebtedness is treated as a distribution of money to you. The assumption by the other partners of a portion of your indebtedness is treated as a contribution of money by them.

Example. You acquire a 20% interest in a partnership by contributing property that had an adjusted basis to you of $8,000, and was subject to a $4,000 mortgage. Payment of the mortgage was assumed by the partnership. The adjusted basis of your interest is:

Your adjusted basis of the property contributed	$8,000
Less: Portion of mortgage assumed by other partners that must be treated as a distribution of money to you (80% of $4,000)	3,200
Basis of your partnership interest	$4,800

Mortgage exceeds basis. If, in the above example, the property you contributed was subject to a $12,000 mortgage, the adjusted basis of your partnership interest would be zero, and the excess of the mortgage assumed by the other partners over your basis ($9,600 less $8,000) would be treated as a capital gain to you from the sale or exchange of a partnership interest.

If you acquire an interest in a partnership by gift, or inheritance, or under any circumstances other than by a contribution of property to the partnership, your basis must be determined under the general rules discussed earlier in this chapter.

If you pay cash for a partnership interest, your basis will be the amount of cash paid.

Adjustments to basis. The original basis of your interest will be *increased* by further contributions to the partnership and by the sum of your current and prior years' distributive shares of taxable income of the partnership that you have not withdrawn. Your original basis will also be increased by tax-exempt receipts of the partnership and by the excess of the deduction for depletion over the basis of the depletable property.

Your basis will be *decreased* (but never below zero) by the amount of money and the adjusted basis of property distributed to you by the partnership, by the sum of your current and prior years' distributive shares of partnership losses (including capital losses), by nondeductible partnership expenditures that are not capital expenditures, and by the amount of your deduction for depletion with respect to oil and gas wells. If distributions of money or other property are made in a year in which there is a partnership loss, the distribution to the partner must be taken into account before computing the amount of a partnership loss that is allowed to the partner as a deduction.

Partnership liabilities. If the liabilities of a partnership are *increased,* and each partner's share of the liabilities is thereby increased, each partner's increase is treated as a contribution of money by that partner to the partnership. The basis of the partner's interest in the partnership is correspondingly increased.

For example, you and Sue Brown are equal partners and your partnership borrows $1,000. The basis of the partnership interest of each of you is increased by $500 since each is considered to have contributed that amount to the partnership. You use this rule regardless of the partnership's method of accounting.

If the liabilities of a partnership are *decreased* and each partner's share of the liabilities is thereby decreased, each partner's decrease is treated as a distribution of money to the partner by the partnership.

For example, you and Bill Black are equal partners and your partnership repays a $10,000 obligation. The basis of the partnership interest of each of you is decreased by $5,000 since each is considered to have received a distribution of that amount from the partnership.

The term *liabilities* includes the partnership's obligations for the payment of outstanding trade accounts, notes, and accrued expenses, whether or not they are recorded on the partnership books under its method of accounting.

A partner's share of partnership liabilities will be determined in accordance with the partner's ratio for sharing losses under the partnership agreement.

A limited partner's share of partnership liabilities will not exceed the difference between the partner's actual contribution credited to the partner by the partnership and the total contribution which the partner is obligated to make under the limited partnership agreement. However, where none of the partners have any personal liability with respect to a partnership liability (as in the case of a mortgage on real estate acquired by the partnership without the assumption by the partnership or any of the partners of any liability on the mortgage), then all partners, including limited partners, will be considered as sharing this liability in the same proportion as they share the profits.

Assumption of a mortgage liability by a limited partnership does not increase the basis of your interest as a limited partner in the partnership if under the limited partnership agreement you are not liable to creditors beyond your original contributions, even though you agree to indemnity general partners for payments exceeding their pro rata share of partnership liabilities. The general partners will increase their basis of their partnership interests by their share of the liability assumed by the partnership.

Limitation. The amount of an indebtedness may be taken into account only once, even though the partner (in addition to being liable for the indebtedness as a partner) may also be liable in a capacity other than as a partner.

413

Alternative rule. In certain cases, the adjusted basis of your partnership interest may be determined by reference to your share of the adjusted basis of partnership property that would be distributable upon termination of the partnership.

The alternative rule may be used to determine the adjusted basis of your interest if the circumstances are such that you cannot practicably apply the earlier rules or if, in the opinion of the Commissioner, it is reasonable to conclude from a consideration of all the facts that the result produced will not vary substantially from the result under the preceding rules.

Adjustments may be necessary in determining your adjusted basis of a partnership interest under the alternative rule. Adjustments would be required, for example, to reflect in your share of the adjusted basis of partnership property and significant discrepancies arising from contributed property, transfers of partnership interests, or distributions of property to the partners.

PARTNER'S BASIS OF PROPERTY RECEIVED

Except in a complete liquidation of your interest, the basis of property (other than money) distributed to you by your partnership is its adjusted basis to the partnership immediately before the distribution. However, the basis of the property to you may not exceed the adjusted basis of your interest in the partnership reduced by any money you receive in the same transaction.

Example 1. The adjusted basis of your partnership interest is $30,000. You receive a current distribution of property with an adjusted basis of $20,000 to the partnership, and $4,000 cash. Your basis for the property is $20,000.

Example 2. The adjusted basis of your partnership interest is $10,000. You receive a current distribution of $4,000 cash and property with an adjusted basis to the partnership of $8,000. Your basis for the distributed property is limited to $6,000 ($10,000 less the $4,000 cash you received).

Complete liquidation of partner's interest. The basis of property received by you in complete liquidation of your interest is an amount equal to the adjusted basis of your interest in the partnership, reduced by any money distributed to you in the same transaction.

Special rule. When a partnership *distributes unrealized receivables,* or *substantially appreciated inventory items* in exchange for any part of a partner's interest in other partnership property (including money), the distribution is treated as a sale or exchange of property unless the property received was contributed by the distributee partner or the payments were made in liquidation of a partner's interest.

The special rule also applies if the partnership distributes other property (including money) in exchange for any part of a partner's interest in unrealized receivables or substantially appreciated inventory items.

In either case, you have a gain or loss from the distribution, measured by the difference between your basis in the property relinquished and the fair market value of the property received in the distribution. If the special rule applies, the basis of the property treated as received in a sale or exchange will be its fair market value.

The partnership also realizes ordinary income or loss, or capital gain or loss, in such cases.

Distribution in kind. If you receive your share of partnership assets in kind, the distribution will not be treated as a sale or exchange. Thus, if you receive, in kind, your share of the partnership's unrealized receivables or substantially appreciated inventory items, the distribution of these items will not be treated as a sale or exchange.

Basis allocated among properties. A part or all of the basis of your partnership interest must be allocated to properties distributed to you. This allocation must first be made to unrealized receivables and inventory items included in the distribution. The remaining basis must then be allocated to any other properties distributed to you in the same transaction in proportion to their adjusted bases in the hands of the partnership before the distribution. The receivables or inventory items may not take a higher basis in your hands than their common adjusted basis to the partnership immediately before the distribution, unless the distribution is treated as a sale or exchange under the special rule mentioned previously.

Examples. The adjusted basis of your partnership interest is $30,000. In complete liquidation of your interest you receive $10,000 in cash, inventory items having a basis to the partnership of $12,000, and two parcels of land having adjusted bases to the partnership of $12,000 and $4,000.

The basis of your partnership interest is reduced to $20,000 by the $10,000 cash. This $20,000 basis is then allocated to the properties you received. The inventory items in your hands now have a basis of $12,000. To allocate the balance of $8,000, add the bases of the land ($12,000 and $4,000), and take 12,000/16,000 of $8,000 and 4,000/16,000 of $8,000. The bases of the two parcels of land in your hands are $6,000 and $2,000, respectively.

Partner's interest less than partnership basis. If the adjusted basis to the partnership of the unrealized receivables and inventory items distributed to you is greater than your adjusted basis of your interest (reduced by the money distributed to you in the same transaction), the amount of the basis to be allocated to such items is allocated in proportion to the partnership's adjusted basis of the items.

Example. Your basis for your partnership interest is $18,000. In a distribution in liquidation of your entire interest you receive $12,000 cash, inventory items having an adjusted basis to the partnership of $12,000, and unrealized receivables having a basis to the partnership of $8,000. The basis of your partnership interest is reduced to $6,000 by the $12,000 cash you receive. This $6,000 basis is allocated proportionately between the inventory items is $3,600 (12,000/20,000 of $6,000). Your basis for the unrealized receivables is $2,400 (8,000/20,000 of $6,000).

Partner's interest more than partnership basis. If the basis of your partnership interest to be allocated exceeds the adjusted basis to the partnership of the unrealized receivables and inventory items distributed, and if no other property is distributed to which the excess can be allocated, you sustain a capital loss to the extent of the unallocated basis of your partnership interest.

Special adjustment to basis of property received. There is a special rule for determining the partnership basis of property (other than money) distributed to a partner within 2 years after the partner acquires his or her partnership interest through a sale or exchange, or upon the death of a partner.

PARTNERSHIP BASIS OF PROPERTY RETAINED

Generally, a partnership may not adjust the basis of its property as the result of a distribution of property to a partner or as a result of a transfer of an interest in the partnership, either by sale or exchange or due to the death of a partner unless the partnership elects to make an optional adjustment to the basis of its property in that event.

Optional adjustment to basis. The effect of this election is to require the partnership to *increase* the adjusted basis of its property by the excess of the incoming transferee partner's basis for his or her partnership interest over his or her share of the adjusted basis of all partnership property or to *decrease* the adjusted basis of its property by the excess of the incoming transferee partner's share of the adjusted basis of all partnership property over his or her basis for his or her partnership interest. These adjustments affect the basis of partnership property with respect to the incoming transferee partner only in that they become part of his or her share of the common partnership basis.

The election is made by filing a written statement with the partnership return, Form 1065, for the tax year during which the distribution or transfer occurs. For the election to be valid, the return must be timely filed (including extensions). The time for filing an election may be extended in certain cases. The statement must set forth the name and address of the partnership, be signed by any one of the partners, and state that the partnership elects to apply sections 734(b) and 743(b) of the Internal Revenue Code. Once a valid election has been made, it continues to be applicable in succeeding years until revoked.

The election may be revoked only with the approval of the Internal Revenue Service. An application to revoke must be filed with the District Director for the Internal Revenue Service district in which the partnership return is required to be filed not later than 30 days after the close of the partnership tax year for which the revocation is to be effective. The application must be signed by one of the partners and must set forth the grounds on which the revocation is desired. Examples of sufficient grounds for approving the application includes a change in the nature of the business, a substantial increase in assets, a change in the character of the assets, or an increased frequency of shifts of partnership interests. However, no application for revocation of the election will be approved when the purpose is primarily to avoid stepping down the basis of partnership assets upon a transfer or distribution.

Partnership profits (and other income and gains) are not taxed to the partnership. Except for certain items that must be stated separately, a partnership determines its income in much the same way as an individual determines income.

Most elections affecting the computation of income are made by the partnership (not the individual partners). These include elections of methods of accounting, methods of computing depreciation, amortization of certain organization fees, and non-recognition of gain or involuntary exchange. However, the individual partners, not the partnership, make elections as to treatment of foreign taxes and certain exploration expenditures.

A partnership may initially elect to use the calendar year as its tax year without obtaining the prior approval of the Internal Revenue Service. An election of any other tax year, or a change of tax year, requires prior permission (except for adoption of or change to the tax year of all the principal partners or the tax year to which all the principal partners are changing).

Form 1065 must be filed. Every partnership doing business in or having income from sources within the United States is required to file Form 1065 for its tax year. This is principally an information return.

Since the partnership itself is not subject to income tax, no declaration of estimated tax is required of it.

Each partner must report his or her distributive share (whether or not actually distributed) of the partnership income or loss, rather than individual drawings from the partnership during the year, on his or her income tax return.

A partner's distributive share of the partnership *loss* is an allowable deduction on the individual return only to the extent of the adjusted basis of the partner's interest in the partnership.

The partners' distributive shares of separately reportable partnership items are shown in Schedule K and Schedule K-1, Form 1065.

The individual members of a partnership may be required to file declarations of estimated tax.

INCOME FROM A PARTNERSHIP

Partners, in determining their income tax for the year (on their income tax returns), must take into account, separately, the partner's *distributive share* (whether or not distributed) of the following partnership items:

1) Gains and losses from sales or exchanges of capital assets;
2) Gains and losses from sales or exchanges of certain property used in a trade or business, and involuntary conversions;
3) Charitable contributions;
4) Dividends for which there is an exclusion or a deduction;
5) Certain taxes paid or accrued to foreign countries and to possessions of the U.S.;
6) Depletion allowance with respect to partnership oil and gas properties; and
7) Other items of income, gains, losses, deductions, or credits, which are further explained in the discussion of Schedule K, Form 1065, in *Part VIII, Form 1065—Partnership.*

In addition, distributive shares of any partnership items which if taken into account separately by each partner, would result in a tax different than that which would result from not taking the items into account separately, must be shown separately on Form 1065 or an attachment and taken into account separately by each partner.

For example, a credit for the elderly is often available to one or more partners. The partnership must show separately on its return any pensions, annuities, interest, rent, or other income it may receive, so that a qualifying partner may get a full credit.

Tax preference income. For determining the minimum tax on tax preference income, each partner must take into account separately the distributive share of items of income and deductions that enter into the computation of each partner's tax preference items.

Each partner's distributive share of partnership income or loss must be reported on their own individual return, Form 1040, even though the partnership does not distribute any money to them. Generally a partner's distributive share of any item or kind of income, gain, loss, deduction, or credit is determined by the partnership agreement.

However, a partner's distributive share of income, gain loss, deduction, or credit (or item thereof) will be determined by the partner's interest in the partnership (determined by taking into account all facts and circumstances), if:

1) The partnership agreement does not provide for the partner's distributive share of income, gain, loss, deduction, or credit (or item thereof); or

2) The allocation to a partner under the agreement of income, gain, loss, deduction, or credit (or item thereof) does not have substantial economic effect.

An allocation of overall income or loss, or any item of income, gain, loss, deduction, or credit will be controlled by the partnership agreement if the partner receiving the allocation can demonstrate that it has substantial economic effect; that is, that the allocation may actually affect the dollar amount of the partner's shares of the total partnership income or loss independently of tax consequences. Other factors which may affect the validity of an allocation include the business purpose for, and duration of, the allocation and the allocation of related items.

If an allocation made by the partnership is set aside, a partner's share of the income, gain, loss, deduction or credit (or item thereof) will be determined in accordance with the partner's interest in the partnership, taking into account the interests of the respective partners in profits and losses (if different from that of taxable income or loss), cash flow, and their rights to distributions of capital upon liquidation.

Income not distributed to, nor withdrawn by, a partner increases the basis of that partner's interest in the partnership.

Character of items constituting distributive share. The character in the hands of a partner of any item of income, gain, loss, deduction, or credit is determined as if it were realized or incurred directly by the partner.

For example, if a partnership sold corporate stock it had held for more than one year, the partners would treat as long-term capital gain their distributive shares of the gain from the sale. This treatment would even apply to the distributive share of a partner who had a holding period of not more than one year for his or her partnership interest.

Gross income. A partner's gross income includes the partner's share of the gross income of the partnership, that is, the amount of gross income of the partnership from which was derived that partner's distributive share of partnership income or loss. For example, each partner's share of the partnership gross income is used in determining whether an individual income tax return must be filed.

Distributions by the partnership are generally not taxable to the partners unless the distributions are treated as a liquidation, or sale or exchange of all or part of their capital interests, since the partners must include in their income their share of partnership income, whether distributed to them or not. But see *Distributions or Withdrawals* discussed later.

Losses limited. If the partnership has a loss for its tax year, each partner's distributive share of the loss and depletion on partnership oil and gas properties will be allowed only to the extent of the adjusted basis (before reduction by current year's losses) of partner's interest in the partnership at the end of the partnership year in which the loss occurs. Any excess of the loss over the basis will be allowed as a deduction in the succeeding year or years to the extent that the partner's adjusted basis for the partnership interest at the end of the succeeding year exceeds zero (before application of the excess loss). In no event may the partner's basis be less than zero. Basis includes the partner's pro rata share of partnership liabilities.

Example. Mr. Green and Mr. White do business as a partnership. They file their partnership and individual returns on a calendar year basis. The partnership lost $10,000 during last year. Mr. Green's distributive share of the loss was $5,000. The adjusted basis of his partnership interest, before considering his share of last year's loss, was $2,000. He could claim only $2,000 of the loss on his last year's individual return. The adjusted basis of his interest at the end of last year was then reduced to zero.

The partnership showed an $8,000 profit for this year. Mr. Green's $4,000 share of the profit increased the adjusted basis of his interest by $4,000 (not taking into account the $3,000 excess loss he could not deduct last year). His return for this year will show partnership income of $1,000 ($4,000 distributive share less the $3,000 loss not allowable last year). The adjusted basis of his partnership interest at the end of this year is $1,000.

Treatment of partnership liabilities for which the partner (including a corporate partner) has no personal liability. For purposes of the limitation on the allowance of a deduction for a loss by a partner, the adjusted basis of any partner's interest in the partnership will not include any portion of any partnership liability incurred after 1976 for which the partner has no personal liability.

Example. You and another individual form a road paving partnership. Both you and your partner share profits and losses equally. Each of you made a $15,000 cash contribution to the partnership on its formation. The partnership uses the cash method of accounting. The partnership purchased machinery and equipment costing $160,000 for use in the road paving business by putting $10,000 cash down and giving a $150,000 nonrecourse note. For the tax year, the partnership had a $46,000 loss. No portion of the $150,000 nonrecourse loan is includible in the adjusted basis of the partners' interests in the partnership for the purpose of deducting losses. As a result, the amount of each partners' deductible loss would be limited to $15,000.

This rule does not apply to partnerships whose principal activity consists of investing in real property (other than mineral property), or to any activity to the extent deductions are limited to the amounts at risk in that activity. These activities, if conducted as a trade or business or for the production of income, are:

1) Holding, producing, or distributing motion picture films or video tapes;
2) Certain farming activities;
3) Equipment leasing; or
4) Exploring for, or exploiting, oil and gas resources.

Although this rule on limitation of losses will not apply to any corporate partner (other than an electing small business corporation or a personal holding company) with respect to liabilities incurred in any of the four "at risk" activities, it will apply to all corporate partners in all other respects unless the partnership's principal activity is investment in real estate.

Depreciation of contributed property. Generally the partnership's basis for determining depreciation, depletion, or gain or loss on property contributed by a partner is the same as the adjusted basis of the property in the contributing partner's hands. If nonbusiness property is contributed, the partnership's basis is the lesser of the contributing partner's adjusted basis or the fair market value at the date contributed.

Adjusted basis different from fair market value. The fair market value of property, at the time it is contributed, may be different from its adjusted basis in the contributing partner's hands. The partners may (if the partnership agreement so provides) allocate the allowable depreciation, depletion, or gain or loss on the property in a manner that will account for all or any portion of the difference. However, the amount allocated among the partners in this manner may not exceed the total of the amount properly allowable to the partnership for tax purposes. The allocation may apply to all property contributed, or only to specific items.

Example. Partner B contributed $20,000 in cash to a partnership, and the other partner, C, contributed depreciable property with a fair market value of $20,000, an adjusted basis in C's hands of $10,000, and a 10-year life. The partnership's basis for the property is the same as the adjusted basis in C's hands, or $10,000.

If provision has been made in the partnership agreement, the entire yearly depreciation, $1,000, may be allocated to B, who contributed the cash. If the partnership had income of $2,000 before deducting depreciation, with no other deductions, B's distributive share of partnership income would be $1,000 less the depreciation deduction of $1,000 allocated to B, or zero. C's share would be $1,000.

Undivided interests in property contributed. Assumed that all the partners contributed to the partnership their undivided interest in property they owned as tenants in common. Their undivided interests in the property before the contribution were in the same proportion as their interests in the capital and profits of the partnership after the contribution.

In this case, any depreciation, depletion, or gain or loss on the undivided interests is determined as though the interests had never been contributed. In other words, it is as though the property were still held by the individual partners outside the partnership. This rule does not apply if the agreement specifically provides otherwise. If the partner's interests in the capital and profits of the partnership are subsequently changed, this rule no longer applies.

FAMILY PARTNERSHIPS

A family partnership is one whose members are closely related through blood or marriage.

Family member as a partner. Family members will be recognized as partners only if:
1) Where capital is a material income-producing factor, they acquired their capital interest in a bona fide transaction

(even if by gift or purchase from another family member), actually own the partnership interest, and are vested with dominion and control over it; or

2) Where capital is not a material income-producing factor, they contribute substantial or vital services.

Capital is a material income-producing factor if a substantial portion of the gross income of the business results from the use of capital, as when substantial inventories or investments in plant, machinery, or equipment are required.

Capital is not a material income-producing factor, ordinarily, if the income of the business consists principally of fees, commissions, or other compensation for personal services performed by members or employees of the partnership.

A capital interest in a partnership means an interest in its assets that is distributable to a partner upon the withdrawal of that partner from, or the liquidation of, the partnership. The mere right to share in the earnings and profits is not a capital interest in the partnership.

If a family member acquires by gift a capital interest in a family partnership in which capital is a material income-producing factor, there are limitations on the amount that may be allocated to that member as a distributive share of partnership income.

First, the donor of the interest must be allowed an amount that represents reasonable compensation for services rendered to the partnership. The remaining income generally may be divided among the partners according to their agreement for sharing partnership profits and losses. However, the portion of the remaining income allocated to the donee may not be proportionately greater than that allocated to the donor, on the basis of their respective capital interests.

An interest purchased by one member of the family from another member of the family is considered to be created by gift for this purpose. The family, for this purpose, includes only the husband or wife; ancestors, and lineal descendants, and any trusts for the primary benefit of such persons. Brothers and sisters are not included.

Example. A partnership, in which the father sold (considered a gift) a 50% interest to his son, had a profit of $60,000 for the year. Capital is a material income-producing factor. The father performed services worth $24,000 as reasonable compensation, and the son performed no services. The $24,000 must be allocated to the father as compensation. Of the remaining $36,000 income which is attributable to capital, at least 50%, or $18,000, must be allocated to the father since he owns a 50% capital interest, and the son's share of partnership income cannot exceed $18,000

PARTNER'S DEALING WITH PARTNERSHIP

A partner who engages in a transaction with the partnership other than in the capacity of a partner is not treated as a member of the partnership for that transaction. This rule does not apply to certain sales or exchanges of property between partners and partnerships.

Losses will not be allowed if they result from a sale or exchange of property (other than an interest in the partnership) directly or indirectly between a partnership and a partner whose direct or indirect interest in the capital or profits of the partnership is more than 50%.

If the sale or exchange is between two partnerships in which the same persons own more than a 50% interest of the capital or profits, no loss deduction is allowed. However, if a purchaser later sells the property, any gain realized will be taxable only to the extent that it exceeds the loss previously disallowed.

Gains are treated as ordinary income in a sale or exchange of property directly or indirectly between a partner and partnership, or between two partnerships, if more than 80% of the capital or profits interest in the partnership or partnerships is owned directly or indirectly by the same person or persons, and if the property in the hands of the transferee immediately after the transfer is property other than a capital asset.

Property other than a capital asset includes, but is not limited to, trade accounts receivable, inventory, stock in trade, and depreciable or real property used in the trade or business.

Determination of the 50% or 80% ownership in partnership capital or profits is made by applying the following rules:
1) An interest owned, directly or indirectly, by or for a corporation, partnership, estate, or trust is considered to be owned proportionately by or for its shareholders, partners, or beneficiaries;

2) An individual is considered as owning the interest owned, directly or indirectly, by or for the individual's family;

3) The family of an individual includes only brothers and sisters (whether by the whole or halfblood), spouse, ancestors, and lineal descendants; and

4) An interest constructively owned by a person under rule (1) is treated, for applying rules (1) or (2), as actually owned by that person. But an interest constructively owned by an individual under rule (2) is not treated as owned by that person for again applying rule (2) to make another the constructive owner of the interest.

Under these rules, ownership of a capital or profits interest in a partnership may, be attributed to a person who is not a partner in order that another partner may be considered the constructive owner of the interest under the rules.

Guaranteed payments made by a partnership to one of its partnership to one of its partners for services or for the use of capital, to the extent they are determined without regard to the income of the partnership, are treated by the partnership in the same manner as payments made to a person who is not a partner but only for purposes of gross income and deductible business expenses. For other tax purposes, guaranteed payments are regarded as a partner's distributive share of ordinary income. Generally, the payments are deductible by the partnership as a business expense, are included in Schedule K and K-1 of the partnership return, and are reported by the individual partner on Form 1040 as ordinary income, in addition to that partner's distributive share of the ordinary income of the partnership. However, guaranteed payments made to a partner or partners for organizing the partnership, or syndicating interests in the partnership are capital expenditures and not deductible by the partnership.

Example. Under the terms of the partnership agreement, Jane is entitled to a fixed annual salary of $10,000 without regard to the income of the partnership. Her distributive share of the partnership income is 10%. After deducting the guaranteed payment, the partnership has $50,000 of ordinary income. Jane must include $15,000 as ordinary income in her income tax return for her tax year within or with which the partnership tax year ends ($10,000 guaranteed payment plus $5,000 distributive share).

Guaranteed minimum. If a partner is to receive a percentage of the partnership income, with a stipulated minimum payment, the guaranteed payment is the amount by which the minimum guarantee exceeds the partner's share of the partnership income before taking into account the minimum guarantee.

Example. Under your partnership agreement, you are to receive 30% of the partnership income, but in no event less than $8,000. During the year, the partnership has taxable income of $20,000. Your share, without regard to the minimum guarantee, is $6,000 (30% of $20,000). Thus, the amount of the guaranteed payment that may be deducted by the partnership is $2,000 ($8,000 less $6,000). Your income from the partnership is $8,000, and the remaining $12,000 will be reported by the other partners in proportion to their shares under the partnership agreement. If the partnership taxable income had been $30,000, there would have been no guaranteed payment since your share, without regard to the guarantee, would have exceeded the guarantee.

Payments resulting in loss. Assume that a partnership agreement provided for guaranteed payments to a partner. The payments during the year resulted in a partnership loss in which the partner shared. That partner must report the full amount of the guaranteed payments as gross income and must separately take into account the appropriate distributive share of the partnership loss.

Meals and lodging furnished on its business premises by the partnership to a partner are not deductible unless they qualify as guaranteed payments to the partner receiving them. Moreover, the partner to whom the meals and lodging are furnished is not entitled to exclude their value from gross income.

CONTRIBUTED PROPERTY

Generally, gain or loss is not recognized to a partner or partnership upon the contribution to the partnership of property, including installment obligations, in exchange for an interest in the partnership. This rule applies to a partnership in the process of formation as well as to one that is already formed and operating. The holding period to the partnership for the property includes the holding period of the contributing partner.

A transaction may be treated as an exchange of property between partners upon which gain or loss is recognized if property is contributed to a partnership and within a short period:

1) Before or after the contribution other property is distributed to the contributing partner and the contributed property is retained by the partnership, or

2) After the contribution the contributed property is distributed to another partner

Special rule for exchange funds. Gain will be recognized if the property contributed (in exchange for an interest in the partnership) is transferred to a partnership that would be treated as an investment company if the partnership were incorporated. This requires the current taxation of gains realized by investors who transfer appreciated stock or securities (or other property) to an exchange fund operated as a partnership. A loss realized on a contribution of stock or securities (or other property) to a partnership will not be recognized.

A partnership will be treated as an investment company if, after the exchange, over 80 percent of the value of its assets (excluding cash and nonconvertible debt obligations) is held for investment and consists of readily marketable stocks or securities (or interests in regulated investment companies or real estate investment trusts). Whether a partnership is an investment company under this test will ordinarily be determined immediately after the transfers of property under the same plan or as part of the same transaction.

In addition, for the nonrecognition treatment to be denied, the transfers of property to the partnership must be found to result, directly or indirectly, in diversification of the transferors' interests.

These rules are to apply both to limited partnerships and general partnerships, regardless of whether the partnership is privately formed or publicly syndicated.

The basis of the contributing partner's interest in the partnership is the same as the adjusted basis of the property to the contributing partner at the time of contribution increased by the amount (if any) of gain recognized to the contributing partner at such time.

In addition, the assumption of a partner's liability by the partnership may result in income to the contributing partner.

Interest acquired as compensation. A partner may acquire an interest in partnership capital as compensation in whole or in part for services rendered or to be rendered. The net value of such an interest must generally be included in the partner's gross income in the first tax year in which rights of the member become transferable or not subject to a substantial risk of forfeiture. Such a transfer of a partnership interest as compensation for services is subject to the rules under *Compensation in the Form of Restricted Property*.

DISPOSITIONS OF A PARTNERSHIP INTEREST

You may partially or completely withdraw or sell your interest in an existing partnership arrangement as follows:

1) You may receive money or other property from the partnership with a corresponding reduction, in partial or complete liquidation, of your partnership interest; or
2) You may sell or exchange all or part of your interest in the partnership to another partner or to a third party.

These means of withdrawal are discussed later. In addition, a partnership may be terminated by being reorganized as a corporation.

DISTRIBUTIONS OR WITHDRAWALS

When money is distributed to or withdrawn by you (as a partner) it must be included in your income only to the extent that it exceeds the adjusted basis of your interest, unless the *special rule,* discussed under *Disposition of Partner's Interest,* applies. A loss on distributions is recognized to you only upon liquidation of your entire interest in the partnership, and then only if the distribution is in money, unrealized receivables, or inventory items.

When property (other than money) is distributed to you, no gain is recognized to you until you sell or otherwise dispose of the property. But see *Liquidation of Partner's Interest* and the special rule under *Disposition of Partner's Interest* discussed later.

Example. The adjusted basis of your partnership interest is $10,000. You receive a distribution of $8,000 cash and land with a basis to the partnership of $2,000 and a fair market value of $3,000. You realize no gain. Any gain on the land you receive is recognized when you sell or otherwise dispose of the property. Your basis for the land is $2,000.

Unrealized receivables and inventory items received by you in a distribution will result in ordinary income or loss to you, if you later sell or exchange them. However, if you hold the *inventory items* more than 5 years, gain or loss, when realized, will be capital gain or loss if the property is then a capital asset in your hands. See *Disposition of Partner's Interest,* for definitions of unrealized receivables and inventory items.

Example 1. You received, in dissolution of a partnership, merchandise inventory that has a basis to you of $19,000. Within 5 years you sell the merchandise for $24,000. The $5,000 gain is taxed to you as ordinary income. If you had held the inventory for more than 5 years, your gain would have been capital gain, assuming the merchandise was in all respects a capital asset in your hands at the time of the sale.

Example 2. Bill Smith, a partner, in the dissolution of his law firm, received his share of accounts receivable amounting to $17,000. Since he received only his share, the *special rule* explained later under *Disposition of Partner's Interest* did not apply. The partnership used the cash method, so the receivables had a basis of zero to the partner. If the receivables are later collected, or if the partner sells them, the amount received will be ordinary income. The capital gain treatment under the 5-year rule, illustrated in Example 1, does not apply to accounts receivable.

LIQUIDATION OF PARTNER'S INTEREST

When payments are made by the partnership to a retiring partner or the successor in interest of a deceased partner in return for the complete relinquishment of that partner's interest in the partnership, the payments are allocated between *Payments in liquidation* and *Other payments* as described later. For income tax purposes, a retired partner, or a successor in interest to a deceased partner, will be treated as a partner until the interest of the partner in the partnership has been completely liquidated.

Payments in liquidation of a partner's entire interest, to the extent that they are made in exchange for the interest in partnership property, are treated as distributions to the partner by the partnership as discussed earlier. This treatment does not apply to amounts paid for *unrealized receivables,* or *goodwill* in excess of its basis to the partnership, unless the partnership agreement provides for payment for goodwill. See *Other payments.*

Generally, the valuation placed by the partners upon a partner's interest in partnership property in an arms-length agreement will be regarded as correct. If the valuation reflects only the partner's net interest in the property (total assets less liabilities), it must be adjusted so that both the value of the partner's interest in the property and the basis for the interest take into account the partner's share of partnership liabilities.

Unrealized receivables or substantially appreciated *inventory items.* Payments made to a retiring partner for the partner's interest in unrealized receivables or substantially appreciated inventory items (defined later) may constitute ordinary income to the recipient.

The remaining partners' distributive shares are not reduced by payments in exchange for a retired partner's interest in partnership property as described earlier.

Other payments. Payments to a retiring partner in liquidation of an interest that are not considered payments for the interest in partnership property, as described earlier, are treated either as *distributive shares* of partnership income or as *guaranteed payments* irrespective of the time over which the payments are to be made. If the amount is determined by partnership income, the payments to the recipient are taxable as distributive shares. If the amount is not determined by partnership income, it is treated as a guaranteed payment. In either event, the payments are treated as ordinary income to the recipient except in the case of a distributive share of a capital gain.

These payments are included in income by the recipient for that partner's tax year with or within which ends the partnership tax year for which the payments are a distributive share or in the recipient's tax year with or within which ends the partnership tax year in which the partnership or partner is entitled to deduct them as guaranteed payments.

The remaining partners' distributive shares are reduced by payments in exchange for a retired or deceased partner's interest only when those payments are considered as distributive shares or guaranteed payments.

Guaranteed installment payments in satisfaction of a partnership's liability to a previously retired partner that are continued by the former remaining partners after they terminate the partnership are deductible by them as business expenses in the year paid.

Certain Information must be furnished by the partnership and the partners in cases of liquidations of partnership interests.

DISPOSITION OF PARTNER'S INTEREST

The *sale or exchange* of a partner's interest in a partnership ordinarily results in capital gain or loss measured by the difference between the amount realized and the adjusted basis of that partner's interest in the partnership. If the selling partner is relieved of any liabilities of the partnership, the selling partner will include that amount in determining the amount realized for the interest.

Example 1. You become a limited partner in the ABC Partnership by contributing $10,000 in cash on the formation of the partnership. The adjusted basis of your partnership interest at the end of the current year is $20,000, which includes your proportionate share of partnership liabilities, on which neither you, the other partners nor the partnership have assumed any personal liability of $15,000. The partnership had no other liabilities and no unrealized receivables or substantially appreciated inventory items. You sell your interest in the partnership for $10,000 in cash. You had been paid your share of the partnership income for the tax year.

The amount realized by you from the sale of your partnership interest is $25,000, consisting of the $10,000 cash payment and the amount of your share of partnership liabilities of which you are relieved, $15,000. Since the adjusted basis of your interest in the partnership is $20,000, you realize a gain of $5,000, which you will report as a capital gain.

Example 2. The facts are the same as in example 1, except that instead of selling your interest you withdraw from the partnership at a time when the adjusted basis of your interest in the partnership is zero. In this situation you are considered to have received a distribution of money from the partnership of $15,000, the amount of liabilities from which you are relieved. Since the partnership has no unrealized receivables or substantially appreciated inventory items, you will report a capital gain of $15,000.

Special rule. Amounts received by the selling partner that are attributable to the interest in *unrealized receivables* or *substantially appreciated inventory items* result in ordinary income or loss.

Unrealized receivables is a term applied to any rights to certain types of income that have not been included in gross income under the accounting method used by the partnership.

The term *unrealized receivables* includes the ordinary income potential in certain depreciable property owned by the partnership to the extent of the gain that would have been realized if the partnership had sold the depreciable property at its fair market value at the time of the transaction when any of the following partnership transactions occur.

1) A distribution by a partnership to its partners;
2) A payment made in liquidation of an interest of a retiring partner or deceased partner;
3) A sale or exchange of an interest in a partnership by a partner.

The term unrealized receivables also includes the ordinary income potential in a franchise, trademark, or trade name.

Example. You are a limited partner in the ABC Partnership. The adjusted basis of your partnership interest at the end of the current year is zero. Your proportionate share of partnership liabilities, on which neither you, the other partners nor the partnership have assumed any personal liability, is $15,000. Your share of the ordinary income potential in partnership depreciable property is $5,000. The partnership had no other liabilities, unrealized receivables, or substantially appreciated inventory items. You sell your interest in the partnership for $10,000 in cash.

The amount realized by you from the sale of your partnership interest is $25,000, consisting of $10,000 cash and $15,000 of partnership liabilities of which you are relieved. Since the adjusted basis of your interest in the partnership is zero, the entire $25,000 will be reported by you as a gain. The $5,000 which represents your share of ordinary income potential in partnership depreciable property will be reported by you as ordinary income. The remaining $20,000 gain will be reported as a capital gain.

Inventory *items,* as used in this discussion, are not limited to stock-in-trade or the general concept of an inventory. The term includes, for this purpose, all assets of the partnership except capital assets and those that are sometimes treated as capital assets, such as depreciable property. However, a capital asset or or an asset used in the trade or business, such as a depreciable asset, is included in the term *inventory items* if the asset would not be considered a capital asset or properly used in a trade or business if held by the selling or distributee partner.

Inventory items are considered to have *appreciated substantially* in value if at the time of the sale or distribution their aggregate fair market value exceeds 120% of the total adjusted basis of the partnership for such inventory items and if their fair market value is more than 10% of the fair market value of all partnership property other than money.

Example. Assume that you sold your 1/3 interest in your partnership. The partnership used the accrual method, had the following assets, and no liabilities:

Assets	Adjusted basis	Fair market value
Cash..........................	$ 10,000	$ 10,000
Accounts receivable	5,000	2,500
Trade notes receivable	2,000	2,100
Merchandise on hand	4,000	9,500
Land	80,000	100,000
Total assets	$101,000	$124,100

The *inventory items;* the accounts receivable, trade notes receivable, and merchandise, had a total adjusted basis of $11,000 and a fair market value of $14,100. The total value of all assets other than cash was $114,100. Since the fair market value of the inventory items, $14,100, was more than 120% of their adjusted basis, $11,000, and also more than 10% of all assets other than cash, $114,100, there has been a substantial appreciation of inventory items. Thus, you realized ordinary income to the extent that the amount received for your interest in the inventory items exceeds your basis in them. If the amount you received for your interest in the other assets exceeded the basis of your interest in them, you realized a gain to that extent.

Certain information must be furnished by the partnership and the partners in cases of sales or exchanges of partnership interests.

Sale of partner's interest with zero basis. If you sell your partnership interest when your basis for it is zero, the sales proceeds attributable to other than unrealized receivables and substantially appreciated inventory items will be amounts realized from the sale or exchange of a capital asset.

Installment reporting of partnership interest sale. A partner who sells a partnership interest at a gain may elect to report the sale on the installment method. However, the requirements for reporting on the installment method, such as those on the amount of down payment in the year of sale and the type of property sold, must be met.

The income portion of installment payments received by the partner may be treated in part as capital gains and in part as ordinary income where the partnership interest sold includes several classes of assets. Separate computations must be made to the extent needed to assure that the capital gains and ordinary income attributable to these assets are correctly reported. Thus, the income portion of the down payment and of each installment payment must be allocated among:

1) The partner's interest attributable to unrealized receivables (which includes the partner's ordinary income potential in depreciable property) and substantially appreciated inventory; and

2) The partner's interest in other partnership property.

The amounts of income thus allocated are reported concurrently.

In the case of the unrealized receivables, ordinary income potential from depreciation must be reported first before capital gain treatment will be given to the balance of the gain. In other words, all ordinary income potential from depreciation must be fully reported before any capital gain realized on the disposition of that property can be reported. This does not apply to any property that, if sold at fair market value, would not result in ordinary income potential from depreciation.

Year of Inclusion. If you dispose of your entire interest in a partnership, you must include your distributive share of partnership items in your taxable income for your tax year within which your membership in the partnership ends. For the purpose of computing your distributive share, the partnership's tax year is considered ended on the date that you disposed of your interest. In order to avoid an interim closing of the partnership books, the partners may agree that your distributive share may be estimated by taking a pro rata part of the amount of the items you would have included in your income had you remained a partner for the entire partnership tax year.

If a partner dies, the estate or other successor in interest will report in its return the decedent's distributive share of the partnership items for the partnership year within which the death occurred.

For example, if the partnership and the partners all use the calendar year as their tax year, and one of the partners dies on June 10 none of the income of the partnership for that year will be reported in the final return of the deceased partner, but all of it will be included in the return of the estate or other successor in interest.

However, if the partnership year terminated with the death of the partner, the distributive share of income for that year would be included in the deceased partner's final return. But, if the tax year was different from the partnership's, the decedent's final return would include his or her share of income for the partnership year ending within the decedent's last tax year (i.e., the tax year ending with the date of death).

A partner, who sells or exchanges less than an entire interest in a partnership or whose interest is reduced (whether by entry of a new partner, partial liquidation of a partner's interest, gift, or otherwise), will report the distributive shares of the varying interests at the end of the partnership tax year. The partner will determine this share by taking into account his or her varying interest during the partnership year.

FAMILY PARTNERSHIPS

The family partnership is an estate planning device for gifting capital to family members and for splitting income within a family, that is, channeling income to those in lower income tax brackets. It is a partnership in which the partners consist of husband and wife, ancestors, lineal descendants and/or trusts (other than a short-term trust) for the primary benefit of such persons. The income tax of the family unit is reduced through the spreading of income among the members.

The tax advantages include: (1) an estate can be accumulated in the lower income tax bracket of a family member, (2) assets are taken out of the donor's estate and distributed to family members, thereby reducing the donor's estate tax liability, and (3) a portion of the business can be transferred to the family member when the interest is small so that the gift tax liability is kept at a minimum.

A family member will be recognized as a partner only if:

1) Where capital is a material income-producing factor, he acquired his capital interest in a bona fide transaction (even if by gift or purchase from another family member), actually owns the partnership interest, and is vested with dominion and control over it; or

2) Where capital is not a material income-producing factor, he contributes substantial or vital services.

Capital is a material income-producing factor if a substantial portion of the gross income of the business results from the use of capital, as when substantial inventories or investments in plant, machinery, or equipment are required.

Capital is not a material income-producing factor, ordinarily, if the income of the business consists principally of fees, commissions, or other compensation for personal services performed by members or employees of the partnership.

A capital interest in a partnership means an interest in its assets that is distributable to the owner of the capital interest upon his withdrawal from or the liquidation of the partnership. The mere right to share in the earnings and profits is not a capital interest in the partnership.

If a family member acquires by gift a capital interest in a family partnership in which capital is a material income-producing factor, there are limitations on the amount that may be allocated to him as his distributive share of partnership income.

First, the donor of the interest must be allowed an amount of partnership income that represents reasonable compensation for his services to the partnership. The remaining income generally may be divided among the partners according to their agreement for sharing profits and losses. The portion of the remaining income allocated to the donee, however, may not be greater than the portion of the remaining income allocated to the donor in proportion to his respective capital interest.

An interest purchased by one member of the family from another member of the family is considered to be created by gift for this purpose.

ESTATES AND TRUSTS

An estate or trust, unlike a partnership, may be required to pay Federal income tax. A beneficiary will be required to pay tax on his share of the estate or trust income. However, there is never a double tax.

If the taxpayer is a beneficiary of a trust that is required to distribute currently all of its income, he must report his share of the distributable net income whether or not he has actually received it.

If the taxpayer is the beneficiary of an estate or trust and the fiduciary has discretionary powers to distribute all or a part of the current income, he must report all income that is required to be distributed to him (whether or not actually distributed) plus all other amounts actually paid or credited to him, to the extent of his share of distributable net income.

Each item of income retains the same character in the hands of the taxpayer as it had in the hands of the estate or trust. Thus, if items of income distributed or deemed distributed to the taxpayer include dividends of domestic corporations, tax-exempt interest, or capital gains, they will retain the same character in his hands for the purpose of the special tax treatment given those items.

Losses of estates and trusts are generally not deductible by the beneficiary.

The beneficiary must include his share of the estate or trust income in his return for his tax year in which the last day of the estate or trust tax year falls.

CORPORATIONS

Corporate profits are normally taxed to the corporation. Then, when they are distributed as dividends, the dividends are taxed to the individual shareholders. Some corporations (commonly called Subchapter S, Tax-option, or Pseudo-Corporations) may elect not to be taxed as corporations. These corporations are not taxed on their incomes except that a capital gains tax may apply. Their shareholders include in their individual gross incomes their distributive portions of the corporate profits — a tax shelter for a family with low-bracket members as shareholders.

The term corporation, for Federal income tax purposes, includes associations, joint stock companies, insurance companies, and trusts and partnerships that actually operate as associations or corporations.

Unincorporated organizations having certain corporate characteristics are classified as associations and must be taxed as corporations. Such an organization must have associates and be organized to carry on business and divide the gains therefrom, and in addition must have a majority of the following characteristics:

    1) Continuity of life;
    2) Centralization of management;
    3) Limited liability; and
    4) Free transferability of interests.

However, other factors may be significant in classifying an organization as an association. An organization will be treated as an association if the corporate characteristics are such that it more nearly resembles a corporation than a partnership or trust.

The presence or absence of these characteristics must be taken into account in determining whether an organization is an association. Whether the characteristics are present or not is a question of fact in each case. Many tax shelters organized as partnerships would lose their value as a tax shelter to the investor if classified as an association and taxed as a corporation. Write-offs would belong to the corporation and distributions to the investor would be dividends subject to a tax at the corporate level and to the individual. This is such a point of concern that legal counsel for the tax shelter may seek an advance IRS ruling that the enterprise will be taxed as a partnership and not as a corporation. In this way the investor is assured of getting his write-offs.

Most tax shelters take the form of a limited partnership so that the investor as a limited partner will have liability only to the extent of his capital contribution and deductions and income will pass directly to him. However, depending on the objectives of the investor and his circumstances another form of business organization such as a corporation may be more appropriate.

CHAPTER TWO

GAINS AND LOSSES

One of the most common and significant tax shelters is capital gain. It can permit the retention of more profit from the disposition of a capital asset. Capital gain can benefit various tax entities, such as, individuals, corporations, estates, and trusts. This chapter will examine these tax entities showing how capital gain is developed and computed.

GAIN ON DISPOSITIONS OF DEPRECIABLE PROPERTY

Depreciation allowed may cause gain on a disposition of property to be treated as ordinary income.

Gain on certain dispositions of depreciable property used in your business or held for the production of rents or royalties may be treated as capital gain.

However, all or a part of the gain on a disposition of such depreciable property may be treated as ordinary income.

In addition to sales, exchanges, and involuntary conversions, other dispositions (including gifts and distributions by corporations and partnerships) are subject to these rules.

Different rules apply to personal property and to real property in determining what part, if any, of the gain on disposition is ordinary income.

You must keep permanent records of the facts necessary to determine the depreciation allowed or allowable on your depreciable property and in particular the depreciation allowed or allowable after 1961 on personal property and after 1963 on real property, in order to calculate any gain that must be reported as ordinary income. In general, the information needed will be the same as that required for other tax purposes, including the dates of acquisition, cost or other basis, depreciation, and all other adjustments that affect basis.

440

In addition, if you have property that has an adjusted basis reflecting depreciation or amortization taken by you on other property (such as a machine acquired in a nontaxable exchange) or by another person on the same or other property (as in the case of property you received as a gift), your records must contain this information.

PERSONAL PROPERTY (SECTION 1245)

Depreciable personal property includes any property that is or has been subject to an allowance for depreciation and that is:
1) Personal property (both tangible and intangible);
2) An elevator or an escalator;
3) Real property (not included in (4)), to the extent its adjusted basis reflects amortization deductions for certified pollution control facilities or for on-the-job training and child-care facilities; or
4) A special purpose structure or storage facility. This is any other depreciable tangible property (except a building or its structural components) that is (or has been) an integral part of specified business activities, that is a research facility used in connection with those activities, or that is a storage facility used in connection with those activities. The business activities are manufacturing, production, or extraction, or the furnishing of transportation, communications, electrical energy, gas, water, or sewage disposal services.

Building and structural components. This does *not* include a structure that is essentially an item of machinery or equipment. It does not include a structure that houses property used as an integral part of an activity if the use of the structure is so closely related to the use of the property that the structure clearly can be expected to be replaced when the property it initially houses is replaced. The fact that the structure is specially designed to withstand the stress and other demands of the property and can not be economically used for other purposes indicates that it is closely related to the use of the property it houses. Thus such structures as oil and gas storage tanks, grain storage bins, silos, fractionating towers, blast furnaces, basic oxygen furnaces, coke ovens, brick kilns, and coal tipples, are not considered buildings.

Storage facility. This is a facility used principally for the bulk storage of fungible commodities. To be fungible, a commodity must be of such a nature that one part may be used in place of another. Bulk storage means the storage of a commodity in a large mass prior to its consumption or utilization. Thus, if a facility is used to store oranges that have been sorted and boxed, it is not used for bulk storage.

Once property qualifies as depreciable personal property, it remains so even though its function may change. A leasehold of any of the property already described also is depreciable personal property.

TREATMENT OF GAIN

Gain from the sale, exchange, involuntary conversion, or other disposition of depreciable personal property, including a sale and lease-back transaction, must be reported as ordinary income (in Part III of Form 4797), unless the depreciation on the property attributable to periods after 1961 is less than the gain (for elevators and escalators the date is June 30, 1963) In that case, gain to the extent of the depreciation after 1961 is ordinary income, reportable in Part III, Form 4797 and the balance is reported in Part I of Form 4797.

Example. On January 2, 1969, you bought a machine for $6,000. You claimed $600 for depreciation on it each year and sold it for $2,000 on July 1, 1978. Your adjusted basis on the date of sale was $300 ($6,000 less the $600 depreciation deduction for each of the years 1969 through 1977 and $300 for 1978); therefore, your gain was $1,700. Since the gain ($1,700) was less than the total depreciation ($5,700) after 1961, the entire gain must be included as ordinary income.

Depreciation, for determining the treatment of gain, includes additional first-year depreciation, amortization of emergency facilities and pollution-control facilities, and amortization of on-the-job training, child-care facilities, amortization of certain expenditures for certified historic structures, and after 1976 the deduction for the removal of certain barriers for the handicapped or elderly, in addition to normal depreciation based on useful life or class lives.

If you receive property for like property in a tax-free exchange or in an involuntary conversion, depreciation includes that taken on the property you exchange to the extent it is reflected in your adjusted basis of the property you receive. If you receive property as a gift, depreciation taken by the transferor is included to the extent that it is reflected in your basis. Depreciation does not include any adjustments for depreciation or amortization (except amortization of emergency facilities) for periods before 1962. If you acquired property from a decedent you do not include depreciation taken by the decedent for that property.

On other than personal property, depreciation considered must include that for periods when the property was not used as an integral part of an activity or did not constitute a research or storage facility, as described earlier.

For example, if depreciation deductions taken on certain storage facilities after 1961 amount to $10,000, of which $6,000 is attributable to periods before their use in connection with a prescribed business activity, the entire $10,000 must be taken into account in determining ordinary income because of depreciation.

The greater of the depreciation allowed or allowable for periods after 1961, to you or to any other person who held the property if the depreciation was used in determining the adjusted basis of the property in your hands, is generally the amount to use in determining the part of gain to report as ordinary income. However, if you can prove that the depreciation allowed in any tax year was less than the amount allowable, you may use the amount allowed.

This special treatment applies only in determining what part of gain is treated as ordinary income under the rules of this chapter.

Sale of depreciable personal property and other property. A sale or other disposition may include several items of depreciable personal property, or a combination of depreciable personal property and other property. To determine gain or loss on each item, the total amount realized must be allocated among the depreciable personal property and the other property in proportion to their respective fair market values.

Dispositions from multiple asset accounts. In determining ordinary income as a result of depreciation, you may treat any number of units of depreciable personal property in a single depreciation account as one item as long as the total ordinary income resulting from depreciation computed under this method is not less than it would be if depreciation on each unit were computed separately.

Example. In a single transaction you sold 50 machines, 25 trucks, and certain other property that was not depreciable personal property, all of which were recorded in a single depreciation account. After allocating the total received among the various assets sold, you determined that each unit of depreciable personal property was sold at a gain. You may determine the ordinary income because of depreciation as if the 50 machines and 25 trucks were a single item.

However, if 5 of the trucks had been sold at a loss, only the 50 machines and 20 of the trucks could be treated as a single item in determining the ordinary income because of depreciation.

The normal retirement of depreciable personal property in multiple asset accounts does not require recognition of ordinary income because of depreciation if your method of accounting for asset retirements does not require recognition of that gain.

REAL PROPERTY (SECTION 1250)

Depreciable real property includes all real property that is subject to an allowance for depreciation and is not or has not been depreciable personal property (as defined earlier) at any time. It also includes leased property to which the lessee has made improvements that are subject to an allowance for depreciation (such as a building), and the cost of acquiring a lease. A fee simple interest in land is not included because it is not depreciable.

If, as a result of a change in its use, depreciable real property is reclassified as depreciable personal property by a taxpayer, it may never again be considered as depreciable real property by that taxpayer.

The following rules do not apply if:

1) You compute depreciation on the property using the straight-line method or any other method resulting in depreciation not in excess of that computed by the straight-line method, and you have held the property more than a year.

2) You realize a loss on the sale, exchange, or involuntary conversion of the property; or

3) You dispose of low-income rental property that you held for 16-2/3 years or more. (In the case of low-income rental housing for which the special 60-month depreciation for rehabilitation expenditures was allowed, the 16-2/3 years began when the rehabilitated property was placed in service.)

Gain treated as ordinary income. To determine what portion of the gain is to be treated as ordinary income you must use the following procedure:

1) In a sale, exchange, or involuntary conversion of the property, determine the excess of the amount realized over the adjusted basis of the property (in any other disposition of the property, determine the excess of fair market value over adjusted basis);

2) Determine the additional depreciation attributable to periods after 1975; and

3) Multiply the lesser of (1) or (2) by the applicable percentage (as discussed later).

If any gain remains after following this procedure (that is, if (1) exceeds (2)) then:

4) Determine the additional depreciation attributable to periods after 1969 and before 1976; and

5) Multiply the lesser of the remaining gain ((1) less (2)) or (4) by the applicable percentage (as discussed later).

If any gain remains (that is, if (1) exceeds (2) and (4)) then:

6) Determine the additional depreciation attributable to periods after 1963 and before 1970; and

7) Multiply the lesser of the remaining gain ((1) less (2) and (4)) or (6) by the applicable percentage (as discussed later);

8) Add (3), (5) and (7) to arrive at the gain treated as ordinary income and reported in Part III, Form 4797.

ADDITIONAL DEPRECIATION

If depreciable real property is held longer than one year, the *additional depreciation* is the excess of actual depreciation adjustments for periods after 1963 over the depreciation adjustments that would have resulted during the same period had the straight-line method been used for the entire period the property was held. Thus, additional depreciation arises when the taxpayer uses the declining-balance method, the sum of the years-digits method, the units-of-production method, or any other method of rapid depreciation. Additional depreciation does not result from amortization of: pollution-control facilities; on-the-job training and child-care facilities; expenditures to remove architectural and transportation barriers to the handicapped and elderly; or certain rehabilitation expenditures for certain historic structures.

If depreciable real property is held for one year or less, the entire depreciation is additional depreciation.

If the actual depreciation for any portion of your holding period, is less than it would have been for that portion under the straight-line method, the difference may be offset against the *additional depreciation* (excess of actual over straight-line depreciation) for any other portion of your holding period in computing the part of the gain to be reported as ordinary income.

Depreciation taken by other taxpayers or on other property. For determining additional depreciation, include all adjustments reflected in the adjusted basis of depreciable real property because of depreciation deductions for periods after 1963 whether on the same or other property (as in an exchange) and whether allowed or allowable to the taxpayer or any other person (as in a transfer by gift).

Example. Larry Johnson gives his son depreciable real property on which he has taken $2,000 in depreciation deductions, of which $500 is additional depreciation. Immediately after the gift the son's adjusted basis in the property is the same as his father's and reflects the $500 additional depreciation. If the son takes depreciation deductions of $1,000 on the property, of which $200 is additional depreciation, the adjusted basis of the property in the son's hands will reflect depreciation deductions of $3,000, of which $700 is additional depreciation.

The greater of depreciation allowed or allowable after 1963 (to any person who held the property if the depreciation was used in determining its adjusted basis in your hands), is generally the amount to use in determining the part of gain to be reported as ordinary income under these rules. However, if you can show that the deduction *allowed* for any tax year was less than the amount allowable, the lesser figure will be the depreciation adjustment for determining additional depreciation.

Retired or demolished property. The adjustments reflected in adjusted basis generally do not include deductions for depreciation on retired or demolished portions of depreciable real property, unless these deductions are reflected in the basis of replacement property that is depreciable real property.

For example, if a wing of a building is totally destroyed by fire, the depreciation adjustments, reflected in the adjusted basis of the building after the wing is destroyed, do not include any deductions for depreciation attributable to the wing (unless the wing is replaced and the adjustments for depreciation on the destroyed property are reflected in the basis of the replacement property).

The useful life and salvage value for determining the amount that would have been the depreciation if the straight-line method had been used generally is the same as that useful life used under the actual depreciation method employed. If no useful life is used under the depreciation method actually employed (such as with the units-of-production method), or if salvage value is not taken into account (such as with the declining-balance method), the useful life or salvage value for determining what would have been the straight-line depreciation is the useful life and salvage value the taxpayer would have used under the straight-line method.

Example 1. On January 3, 1978, Sue Parks, a calendar-year taxpayer, sells property that she purchased for $10,000 on January 2, 1963. Throughout the period she computed depreciation under the declining-balance method, using a rate of 200 percent of the straight line rate and a useful life of 40 years. Under this method salvage value is not taken into account. If the taxpayer had computed depreciation under the straight-line method she would have used a salvage value of $1,000. The depreciation under both methods is set forth below.

Year	Declining balance	Straight line
1963	$ 550	$ 225
1964	475	225
1965	451	225
1966	429	225
1967	407	225
1968	387	225
1969	368	225
1970	349	225
1971	332	225
1972	315	225
1973	299	225
1974	284	225
1975	270	225
1976	257	225
1977	244	225
Sum of depreciation deductions for periods after 1963	$4,867	$3,150

The additional depreciation for the property is $1,717, which is depreciation actually deducted for the periods after 1963 ($4,867), minus the depreciation that would have resulted for such periods under the straight-line method ($3,150). Of the $1,717, $51 ($501 minus $450 for 1976-1977) is additional depreciation after 1975; $499 ($1,849 minus $1,350 for 1970-1975) is additional depreciation for the years after 1969 and before 1976; and $1,167 ($2,517 minus $1,350 for 1964-1969) is additional depreciation before 1970.

Example 2. Sam Smith, a calendar-year taxpayer, sold depreciable real property on January 3, 1978, that was purchased for $10,000 on January 2, 1968. For the period 1963 through 1969 the taxpayer computed depreciation deductions on the property under the declining-balance method, using a rate of 200% of the straight-line rate and a useful life of 10 years. If the taxpayer had used the straight-line method, a salvage value of $1,000 would be used. As of January 1, 1970, the taxpayer elected to change to the straight-line method and redetermined the remaining useful life of the property to be 9 years and its salvage value to be $120. The depreciation under both methods is set forth below:

448

Year	Actual depreciation	Straight line
1968	$2,000	$ 900[1]
1969	1,600	900
1970	696[2]	898[3]
1971	698	898
1972	698	898
1973	698	898
1974	698	898
1975	698	898
1976	698	898
1977	698	898
Sum of depreciation deductions	[4]9,184	[4]8,984

[1]One-tenth of $9,000 ($10,000 minus $1,000).
[2]One-tenth of $6,280 ($8,400 minus $120).
[3]One-ninth of $8,080 ($8,200 minus $120).

The additional depreciation for the property is $200, that is, the depreciation actually deducted ($9,184), minus the depreciation that would have resulted under the straight-line method ($8,984). The entire $200 is attributable to periods before 1970 since there is *no additional* depreciation after 1969 ($698 actual depreciation annually is less than $898 straight-line depreciation).

Property held by leasee. In the case of a lease-hold improvement by a lessee, the lease period for determining what would have been the straight-line depreciation adjustments and to calculate the additional depreciation, includes all renewal periods but is limited by the useful life of the improvement. This same rule applies to the cost of acquiring a lease.

Renewal period means any period for which the lease may be renewed, extended, or continued under an option exercisable by the lessee. However, the inclusion of renewal periods cannot extend the lease by more than two-thirds of the period that was the basis upon which the actual depreciation adjustments were allowed.

Depreciation attributable to rehabilitation expenditures. A portion of the special 60-month depreciation adjustment allowed for rehabilitation expenditures incurred in connection with low-income rental housing is additional depreciation. If the property is held for one year or less after the expenditures are incurred, the entire special depreciation adjustment is taken into account. If the property is held for more than one year after rehabilitation expenditures are incurred, the additional depreciation is the excess of the special depreciation adjustments attributable to rehabilitation expenditures over the adjustments that would have resulted had the straight-line method and the normal useful life and salvage value been used. See Publication 534.

Example. On January 2, 1979, Fred Plums, a calendar-year taxpayer, sells real property, the entire basis of which is attributable to rehabilitation expenditures of $50,000 incurred in 1971. The property was placed in service on January 3, 1972, and under the special depreciation provisions for rehabilitation expenditures, was depreciated under the straight-line method using a useful life of 60 months (5 years) and no salvage value. If the regular straight-line method had been used, there would be a salvage value of $5,000 with a useful life of 15 years. Depreciation under the straight-line method would be $3,000 each year (1/15 x $45,000 ($50,000 - $5,000)). As of January 1, 1979, the additional depreciation for the property is $29,000 computed as follows:

Year	Actual depreciation	Straight line	Additional depreciation (deficit)
1972	$10,000	$ 3,000	$ 7,000
1973	10,000	3,000	7,000
1974	10,000	3,000	7,000
1975	10,000	3,000	7,000
1976	10,000	3,000	7,000
1977		3,000	(3,000)
1978		3,000	(3,000)
Total	$50,000	$21,000	$29,000

APPLICABLE PERCENTAGE

To determine the amount taxable as ordinary income because of additional depreciation, when real property is disposed of, you may have to use as many as three applicable percentages depending upon whether the property is nonresidential real property, residential real property, or low-income housing. The applicable percentages that must be applied to these types of real property are as follows.

Nonresidential real property. For real property, which is neither residential real property nor low-income housing, the applicable percentage is 100% for periods after 1969. For periods before 1970 the applicable percentage is 100% minus one percentage point for each full month the property was held in excess of 20 full months. Consequently the amount taxable as ordinary income upon disposition decreases the longer the property is held. When the property has been held at least 10 years, the applicable percentage is zero and no ordinary income will result on its disposition because of additional depreciation before 1970.

Example. An office building with an adjusted basis of $200,000 was sold on January 3, 1978, for $290,000. The property was purchased new on January 1, 1969, and was owned for 108 months. Additional depreciation attributable to the property is $18,000, of which $16,000 is for additional depreciation after 1969 ($2,000 yearly for 1970-1977). The applicable percentage for additional depreciation before 1970 is 12% (100% less 88%) and the applicable percentage for additional depreciation after 1969 is 100%. Gain to be recaptured as ordinary income is computed as follows:

1) Excess of amount realized
   ($290,000) over adjusted basis
   ($200,000) $90,000
2) Additional depreciation after 1969 .   16,000
3) Lesser of $90,000 or $16,000, times 100% $16,000
   Additional steps are necessary because (1) exceeds (2)
4) Additional depreciation before 1970 $ 2,000
5) Lesser of $74,000 ($90,000 minus $16,000) or
   $2,000, times 12% .... $ 240

Gain treated as ordinary income (3) plus (5) $16,240

The balance of the gain reported in Part I, Form 4797, is subject to tax under other provisions of the law relating to sales and exchanges of depreciable property.

Residential real property. For residential real property, other than low-income housing, the applicable percentage is 100% for periods after 1975. For residential rental property (80% or more of the gross rental income is from dwelling units) the applicable percentage for periods after 1969 and before 1976 is 100% minus one percentage point for each full month the property was held in excess of 100 months. When this property has been held for at least 16-2/3 years, the applicable percentage is zero and no ordinary income because of additional depreciation will result on its disposition. The applicable percentage for periods before 1970 is 100% minus one percentage point for each full month the property was held in excess of 20 full months.

Low-income housing. The applicable percentage for periods after 1975 for low-income housing (see list of qualifying low-income housing that follows) is 100% minus one percent for each full month the property was held in excess of 100 full months.

For properties described in (2), (3) and (4) as shown later under types of low-income housing, the applicable percentage for periods after 1969 and before 1976 is 100% minus one percentage point for each full month the property was held in excess of 100 full months. However, for property described in (1) the applicable percentage is 100% minus one percentage point for each full month the property was held in excess of 20 full months. The applicable percentage for periods before 1970 is 100% minus one percentage point for each full month the property was held in excess of 20 full months.

To determine the applicable percentage for low-income housing for which the special depreciation for rehabilitation expenditure was allowed, the 100 full months begin when the property was placed in service.

Low-income housing includes the following types of property:

1) Federally assisted housing projects where the mortgage is insured under section 221(d)(3) or 236 of the National Housing Act, or housing financed or assisted by direct loan or tax abatement under similar provisions of State or local laws;
2) Low-income rental housing for which a depreciation deduction for rehabilitation expenditures was allowed;

3) Low-income rental housing held for occupancy by families or individuals eligible to receive subsidies under section 8 of the United States Housing Act of 1937 as amended or under the provisions of State or local laws that authorize similar subsidies for low-income families; and
4) Housing financed or assisted by direct loan or insured under Title V of the Housing Act of 1949.

Foreclosure. If real property is disposed of because of a foreclosure or similar proceedings which began after 1975, the monthly percentage reduction of the amount of additional depreciation is determined as if you ceased to hold such property on the date of the beginning of such proceedings.

Example. Low-Income rental property was acquired by you on June 1, 1976. On April 1, 1987 (130 months after the property was placed in service) foreclosure proceedings were started on the property and on December 1, 1988 (150 months after the property was placed in service) the property was disposed of as a result of the foreclosure proceedings. The low-income rental property qualified for the special additional depreciation monthly percentage reduction, since it was held in excess of 100 full months (this is a one percent per month reduction after 100 months). The applicable percentage reduction will be 30% (130 months less 100 months) rather than 50% (150 months less 100 months) since the percentage reduction would cease to apply on April 1, 1987, the date of the beginning of the foreclosure proceedings.

Gain from disposition of interest in oil or gas property. If an interest in an oil or gas property is disposed of at a gain, all or part of the gain may be treated as ordinary income.

Holding period. For determining the applicable percentage, when it is less than 100% under the previously mentioned rules, the holding period for property acquired generally begins on the day after it is acquired. Thus, if property is purchased on January 1, 1969, the holding period begins January 2, 1969. If the property is sold on January 1, 1978, the holding period is exactly 108 months and the applicable percentage for additional depreciation before 1970 is 12% (100% reduced by a percentage equal to the number of full months in the holding period in excess of 20 months). The applicable percentage for additional depreciation after 1969 is 100% unless one of the exceptions outlined earlier applies.

For property constructed, reconstructed, or erected by the taxpayer, the holding period begins on the first day of the month in which it is placed in service, in a trade or business, in the production of income, or in a personal activity.

For depreciable real property acquired by gift or in a tax-free exchange, the basis of which is determined by reference to the basis in the hands of the transferor, the holding period for the purpose of the applicable percentage includes the holding period of the transferor.

If, however, the adjusted basis of the property in the hands of the transferee immediately after the transaction exceeds its adjusted basis to the transferor immediately before the transaction, the holding period of the excess is determined as though it were a *separate improvement.*

PROPERTY WITH TWO OR MORE ELEMENTS

If depreciable real property consists of more than one separate element, the gain to be reported as ordinary income is the sum of the ordinary income calculated separately for each element.

INSTALLMENT SALES

Gain from a disposition of depreciable personal property or real property may be reported under the installment method, provided you are permitted to use that method. In this case, the income (other than interest) on each installment received must be reported as ordinary income attributable to depreciation, as discussed in this chapter, until all such gain has been reported. Any balance may be either ordinary income or capital gain.

Example 1. Casey Jones sold depreciable personal property for $10,000, to be paid in 10 yearly installments of $1,000 plus 8% interest per year. He realized a gain of $3,000 on the sale, of which $2,000 was gain attributable to depreciation after 1961. If he properly elects the installment method of reporting gain, the entire $300 gain in each of the payments for the first 6 years and $200 of the gain in the 7th year's payment must be reported as ordinary income because of depreciation. The $100 balance of gain included in the 7th year payment and the entire $300 gain in each of the last 3 years' payments may be either ordinary income or capital gain.

Example 2. You sold depreciable real property for $100,000 to be paid for in 10 yearly payments of $10,000 each plus 8% interest per year. At the time of sale, the property had an adjusted basis of $70,000. The additional depreciation attributable: to periods after 1975 was $250; to periods after 1969 but before 1976 was $2,250; and to periods before 1970 was $7,500. The applicable percentage for additional depreciation after 1969 but before 1976 as well as for after 1975 is 100%; for additional depreciation before 1970, it is 40%. Since the $10,000 total additional depreciation ($250 after 1975 plus $2,250 after 1969 but before 1976 plus $7,500 before 1970) was less than the $30,000 gain realized ($100,000 less $70,000). the gain to be treated as ordinary income resulting from additional depreciation is $5,500 (100% of $250 plus 100% of $2,250 plus 40% of $7,500).

If you properly elect to report the sale under the installment method, all the gain reportable in the first year ($3,000) and $2,500 of the gain reportable in the 2nd year must be reported as ordinary income resulting from additional depreciation. The balance of gain reportable in the 2nd year ($500) and the entire $3,000 gain reportable in each of the last 8 years are reported according to the rules later described.

If you dispose of more than one asset in a single transaction, separate computations must be made to the extent necessary for each asset in order that the gains may be properly reported. The income portion of the down payment and each installment payment must be allocated between your ordinary income from depreciation and your other interests that may be entitled to capital gains treatment. The amounts thus allocated can be reported concurrently. The ordinary income from depreciation must be reported in full for each asset before capital gain treatment will be given the balance of the gain.

OTHER DISPOSITIONS

If you make a *gift* of depreciable personal property or real property, you are not required to report income on the transaction. However, if the donee sells or otherwise disposes of the property, the depreciation that you claimed must be taken into account by the donee in determining the gain to be reported as ordinary income.

In the case of depreciable real property for which the applicable percentage is less than 100%, depending on the length of time the property was held, the donee must take into account the holding period of the donor to compute the application percentage. But see also *Holding period under Applicable Percentage* earlier.

Disposition part gift and part sale or exchange. If you transfer depreciable personal property or real property for less than its fair market value, the transaction is considered to be partly a gift and partly a sale or exchange. If the amount realized exceeds your adjusted basis, you must report ordinary income because of depreciation, as discussed in this chapter. Only the balance of your depreciation is carried over to the transferee, to be taken into account in the event of a later disposition.

Example 1. You transfer depreciable personal property to your son for $20,000. At the time of the transfer the property has an adjusted basis to you of $10,000 and a fair market value of $40,000, and your depreciation taken after 1961 was $30,000. You are considered to have made a gift of $20,000, the difference between the $40,000 fair market value and the $20,000 sale price to your son. You have a taxable gain on the transfer of $10,000 ($20,000 sale price less $10,000 adjusted basis) that must be reported as ordinary income because of depreciation. Since you report $10,000 of your $30,000 depreciation after 1961 as ordinary income upon the transfer of the property, only the remaining $20,000 is carried over to your son, to be taken into account by him in the event of a later disposition.

Example 2. You transfer depreciable nonresidential real property to your son for $46,000. At the time of the transfer the property has an adjusted basis to you of $36,000 and a fair market value of $70,000. You have a taxable gain on the transfer of $10,000 ($46,000 sales price less $36,000 adjusted basis) and you are considered to have made a gift of $24,000 ($70,000 fair market value less $46,000 sales price).

Assume that at the time of the transfer the total additional depreciation is $10,000 ($9,500 of which is for periods after 1969 but before 1976 and $250 for periods after 1975) and that you have held the property for a full 108 months. The $9,750 ($9,500 and $250) additional depreciation after 1969, because it is less than the $40,000 gain realized, is reported as ordinary income (applicable percentage of 100%). Since the $250 remaining gain ($10,000 less $9,750) is not more than the $250 additional depreciation before 1970, $30 ($250 multiplied by 12% applicable percentage) must also be reported as ordinary income. The remaining $220 ($250 less $30) is reportable according to the rules later described.

When your son receives the property, the additional depreciation before 1970 in his hands is $220 ($250 less $30 gain to you) and his holding period is 108 full months (the same as yours). His basis for the property is $46,000, the amount he paid. If your son sells the property 10 full months after he receives it from you, his holding period is 118 full months and the applicable percentage for gain attributable to additional depreciation before 1970 is 2%.

If your gift is to a charitable organization, the amount of your charitable contribution of property must be reduced by 100% of the ordinary gain and short-term capital gain that would result had you sold the property at its fair market value at the time of the contribution. In addition, you also may have to reduce the amount of your charitable contribution of property for gifts made before November 1978 by 50% (62½% for a corporation for gifts made before 1979) of the long-term capital gain that would result had you sold the property at its fair market value at the time of the contribution and by 40% for such gifts made after October 1978 (28/46 for a corporation for gifts made after 1978). Thus, the fair market value of depreciable real or personal property given to a charitable organization must always be reduced by the potential ordinary gain because of depreciation.

Bargain sale to charitable organization. A bargain sale is a sale or exchange of property to a charitable organization for less than its fair market value with the result that the transaction is in part a sale or exchange and in part a charitable contribution. The special bargain sale allocation rules following apply only if, without regard to those allocation rules, the sale would result in a charitable contribution for the contributed portion of the property.

In determining whether the sale would result in a charitable contribution, the fair market value of the property must be reduced by the sale proceeds, by 100% of the ordinary gain, and for sales made before November 1978 by 50% (62½% for a corporation for sales made before 1979) of the long-term capital gain. If such reduction applies, that would be realized if the *entire* property had been sold by the donor at its fair market value at the time of the sale or exchange and by 40% for such sales or exchanges made after October of 1978 (28/46 for a corporation for gifts made after 1978). If no contribution results or if, because of the percentage limitations on charitable contributions, no deduction is allowable, the bargain sale is treated as a regular sale.

Allocation to sold and contributed portions. After it has been established that the sale results in a charitable contribution and thus qualifies as a bargain sale, the adjusted basis of the property must be allocated between the portion of the property sold and the portion of the property given to the charity. This allocation is made on the basis of the fair market value of each portion. Gain because of depreciation that would have resulted had the entire property been sold at its fair market value at the time of the contribution is allocated in the same manner.

Example. You sell depreciable personal property to a charitable organization for its adjusted basis of $12,000. The property has a fair market value of $20,000, it originally cost $22,000, and you have claimed depreciation after 1961 of $5,000 for it. Assume that the contribution amount is not required to be reduced by a portion of the long-term capital gain that would have resulted from a sale at fair market value. Without regard to the bargain sale allocation rules, the sale would result in a charitable contribution of $3,000 ($20,000 fair market value less $12,000 sales proceeds and $5,000 depreciation after 1961).

Since the sale qualifies as a bargain sale, you must allocate 60% ($12,000 sale proceeds ÷ $20,000 fair market value) of the adjusted basis to the portion sold and the remaining 40% to the portion given.

Sale price	$12,000
Allocation of basis 60% x $12,000	7,200
Gain on portion sold	$ 4,800
Allocation of depreciation 60% x $5,000	3,000
Gain not from depreciation	$ 1,800

Because the depreciation after 1961 ($3,000) is less than the gain ($4,800), you must include $3,000 as ordinary income. The remaining gain ($1,800) is treated according to the rules relating to sales and exchanges of depreciable property described later.

Gain on portion given:
Value of contribution $8,000
Reduction for gain not long-term capital gain:
This is lesser of:
1) Entire gain on portion given ($8,000 - 40% of
   $12,000), $3,200; or
2) Depreciation (40% of $5,000), $2,000 2,000
Amount of contribution $6,000

TRANSFERS AT DEATH

When a taxpayer dies, no gain is reported on depreciable personal property or real property transferred to the estate or beneficiary.

Also, if the taxpayer disposed of the property while alive and, because of the method of accounting used or for any other reason, the gain from the disposition is reportable by the estate or beneficiary, it must be reported in the manner the decedent would have been required to report it if death had not occurred.

Ordinary income because of depreciation must be reported also in connection with a transfer from an executor, administrator, or trustee to an heir, legatee, devisee, or beneficiary if the transfer constitutes a sale or exchange resulting in gain realized.

Example 1. Janet Smith owns depreciable property that, upon her death, is inherited by her son. No ordinary income because of depreciation will be reportable on the transfer, even though the value used for estate tax purposes is greater than the adjusted basis of the property to Janet at the time of her death. However, if she had sold the property before her death and realized a gain and because of her method of accounting the proceeds from the sale were income in respect of a decedent reported by the son, the son would have to report ordinary income because of depreciation.

Example 2. The trustee of a trust created by will transfers depreciable property to a beneficiary in satisfaction of a specific bequest of $10,000. If the property had a value of $9,000 at the date used for estate tax valuation purposes, the $1,000 of appreciation in value to the date of distribution is gain realized by the trust and ordinary income because of depreciation must be reported by the trust on the transfer.

EXCHANGE OF PROPERTY FOR STOCK

A tax-free exchange of depreciable personal property or real property solely for stock or securities of a controlled corporation will not result in ordinary income as a result of additional depreciation under the preceding rules. In this case, the transferee corporation's basis will be the same as the transferor's adjusted basis on the date of the transfer.

For depreciable real property, the holding period of the transferee corporation will include the holding period of the transferor (but see the special rules explained under *Holding period*). Any additional depreciation at the time of the exchange is carried over to the transferee corporation and must be considered in the event of a later sale or other disposition.

However, if, in addition to the stock, money or other property is received by the transferor and gain to the extent of the money or other property received must be included in income, ordinary income as a result of additional depreciation must be reported, but it may not exceed the gain required to be included in income.

Example 1. You own equipment having a fair market value of $12,000 on which you have claimed depreciation of $10,000 ($3,000 of which was after 1961). The equipment originally cost you $18,000. In 1978, you transfer it to your controlled corporation for stock worth $11,000 and $1,000 in cash. Since the gain required to be included in your income is limited to the cash received, and it is not more than the $3,000 of depreciation after 1961, the $1,000 must be reported as ordinary income. The basis of the property in the hands of the corporation will be $9,000 (your adjusted basis of $8,000, $18,000 less $10,000, plus the gain of $1,000 you are required to report). If the corporation sells the equipment for $12,000 without claiming further depreciation, its gain will be $3,000, of which it will have to report $2,000 as ordinary income (your $3,000 of depreciation after 1961 less the $1,000 ordinary income you report on your exchange).

Example 2. If, in the previous example, you received $3,500 cash and stock worth $8,500, you would report $3,000 as ordinary income because of depreciation and the balance of $500 would be treated as explained later.

Example 3. You transfer depreciable real property to a corporation, in exchange for $1,000 cash and stock in the corporation worth $9,000. Your property has a fair market value of $10,000, and an adjusted basis of $4,000. The additional depreciation is $2,000, ($1,200 before 1970, $700 after 1969 but before 1976 and $100 after 1975) and the applicable percentage for additional depreciation before 1970 is 30%. Ordinary income resulting from additional depreciation is $1,160 (100% of $800 ($700 after 1969 but before 1976 and $100 after 1975) plus 30% of $1,200 (before 1970)). But the ordinary income you are required to report for the year of the transaction is limited to the gain recognized (the cash received), or $1,000. If the cash received were $1,500, you would report $1,160 as ordinary income as a result of additional depreciation, and the balance of $340 would be treated as explained later.

If you transfer property to a tax exempt organization for stock or securities of that organization, you generally must report the amount of ordinary income attributable to depreciation, as determined under the rules discussed in this chapter, for the year the exchange is made.

The preceding paragraph will not apply if you transfer property to an exempt farmer's cooperative or if the organization receiving the property uses it in an unrelated trade or business.

LIKE-KIND EXCHANGES AND INVOLUNTARY CONVERSIONS

Depreciable personal property. A like-kind exchange of your property, or an involuntary conversion, will not result in you having to report ordinary income because of depreciation unless property other than depreciable personal property is received in the transaction.

If you receive property other than depreciable personal property and, therefore, are required to include gain as ordinary income because of depreciation, the amount is limited to the lesser of:

461

1) The gain on the transaction to the extent of depreciation attributable to periods after 1961; or
2) The gain required to be included in income plus the fair market value of property other than depreciable personal property acquired in the transaction.

Example 1. On January 6, 1978, you acquired a new machine for $4,900 cash plus your old machine for which you were allowed a $760 trade-in. The old machine cost you $5,000 on January 5, 1973. For 1973 through 1977 you claimed depreciation of $2,000, $1,200, $720, $432, and $260. Even though $4,612 has been claimed for depreciation after 1961, the $372 gain on the transaction ($760 trade-in allowance less $388 adjusted basis) need not be reported because any tax on the gain is postponed and you received only depreciable personal property of a like kind in the exchange.

Example 2. On January 4, 1977, you purchased office furniture for $1,500. On your 1977 return you claimed $300 additional first-year depreciation and $240 ordinary depreciation computed under the declining-balance method. On January 3, 1978, a fire destroyed the furniture and you received $1,200 as a result of your insurance claim. However, it cost you only $1,000 for the replacement furniture. Since your taxable gain is limited to the $200 unexpended insurance proceeds, which is less than the $540 of depreciation you claimed, the $200 must be reported as ordinary income.

Example 3. In 1978 a fire destroyed machinery you owned. The depreciation attributable to periods after 1961 was $16,000, and the machinery had an adjusted basis of $100,000. You received $117,000 of insurance proceeds, realizing a gain of $17,000.

You immediately spent $105,000 of the insurance proceeds for replacement machinery and $9,000 for stock that qualifies as replacement property, and you elected to postpone tax on your gain. Since $114,000 of the $117,000 insurance proceeds was used to acquire replacement property, the gain required to be included in income is the unexpended portion, or $3,000. In addition, the portion of the proceeds ($9,000) used to acquire the nondepreciable property (the capital stock) also must be included in the computation.

The amount you must report as ordinary income on the transaction on your return is $12,000, computed as follows:

1) Gain on the transaction ($17,000) to the extent
   of depreciation after 1961 ($16,000) $16,000

2) Gain required to be included in
   income........................ $3,000
   Fair market value of property other
     than depreciable personal prop-
     erty (the stock) acquired in the
     transaction   9,000

Total $12,000

Amount to be reported as ordinary income (lesser
   of (1) or (2)) $12,000

If, instead of buying $9,000 in stock you had bought $9,000
worth of depreciable personal property similar or related in use
to the destroyed property, you would report $3,000 as ordinary
income.

Depreciable real property. If you have a gain from a like-kind
exchange of your property, or an involuntary conversion, the
amount to be reported as ordinary income as a result of additional depreciation is limited to the *greater* of the following:
   1) The gain required to be reported under the rules for like-
      kind exchanges or involuntary conversions plus the fair
      market value of stock purchased as replacement property
      in acquiring control of a corporation; or
   2) The gain you would have been required to report as ordi-
      nary income because of additional depreciation had the
      transaction been a cash sale less the cost (or fair market
      value in the case of an exchange) of the depreciable real
      property acquired.
The ordinary income that is not reported for the year of the
disposition is carried over to the depreciable real property acquired in the like-kind exchange or involuntary conversion as
additional depreciation attributable to the property disposed of.
Furthermore, for determining the applicable percentage of the
additional depreciation to be treated as ordinary income, the
holding period is begun anew for the new property.
   Example. The State paid you $116,000 when it condemned
your depreciable real property for public use. You acquired
other real property, similar in use to the property condemned,

for $110,000 ($15,000 for depreciable real property and $95,000 for land) and you also acquired stock for $5,000 to gain control of a corporation owning property similar in use to the property condemned. You elect to postpone tax on the gain. Had the transaction been a sale for cash only, under the rules of this chapter, $20,000 would have been required to be reported as ordinary income because of additional depreciation.

The ordinary income to be reported is $6,000, which is the greater of the following:

1) The gain that would be required to be reported, $1,000 less $115,000) plus the fair market value of stock purchased as qualified replacement property, $5,000 for a total of $6,000; or

2) The gain you would have been required to report as ordinary income because of additional depreciation ($20,000) had this transaction been a cash sale, less the cost of the depreciable real property acquired ($15,000), or $5,000.

Basis of property acquired in involuntary conversions. If only depreciable real property is acquired to replace depreciable real property in an involuntary conversion in which gain is realized, and tax on the gain is postponed, the basis of the replacement property is its cost less the gain on which tax is postponed. If the replacement consists of more than one piece of depreciable real property, the cost of each piece is reduced by an allocable part of the gain.

If the replacement property purchased consists of both depreciable real property and other property, however, the basis must be computed as follows:

1) Determine a tentative basis for the depreciable real property by subtracting from its cost the ordinary income because of additional depreciation that is not required to be reported (if more than one piece of depreciable property is acquired the tentative basis must be allocated to each piece in proportion to its cost);

2) Add the tentative basis determined in (1) to the cost of the other property acquired;

3) Subtract from the total obtained in (2) the excess of gain on which tax is postponed over the ordinary income because of additional depreciation not required to be reported; and

4) Allocate the amount obtained in (3) to each asset in proportion to its cost, as listed in (2).

Example 1. You receive insurance proceeds of $90,000 because of the destruction by fire of depreciable real property (office building) that had an adjusted basis of $75,000, additional depreciation after 1975 of $1,000, additional depreciation after 1969 but before 1976 of $7,000, and additional depreciation before 1970 of $12,000 for which the applicable percentage is 40%.

Your realized gain from the involuntary conversion is $15,000 and under the general rules for dispositions of depreciable real property you would report $8,000 (lesser of $8,000 additional depreciation after 1969 ($7,000 after 1969 but before 1976 and $1,000 after 1975) or your $15,000 gain) plus $4,800 (lesser of 40% of $7,000 remaining gain or 40% of $12,000 additional depreciation before 1970), or $10,800, as ordinary income because of additional depreciation. However, you immediately spend the $90,000 for depreciable real property similar in use to the property destroyed, electing to postpone tax on the gain, and therefore no income attributable to additional depreciation is required to be reported under the special rule for involuntary conversions previously discussed.

The basis of the replacement property is its cost of $90,000 less the $15,000 gain on which tax is postponed, or $75,000. The $10,800 of ordinary income that you would otherwise be required to report is carried over to the replacement property as additional depreciation and a new holding period then begins for the newly acquired depreciable property.

Example 2. John Adams receives $90,000 in fire insurance proceeds for depreciable real property (office building) that had an adjusted basis of $30,000. He uses all of the proceeds to purchase property similar in use of which $42,000 is for depreciable real property and $48,000 is for land. He elects to defer tax on the $60,000 gain realized on the involuntary conversion. $10,000 of this gain is ordinary income as a result of additional depreciation, but is not reported because of the exception for involuntary conversions. The $30,000 basis of the property acquired is determined as follows:

1) Tentative basis of depreciable real property is $32,000 (cost of $42,000, less $10,000 ordinary income not required to be reported).

2) Tentative basis of depreciable real property plus cost of other property (land) is $80,000 ($32,000 plus $48,000).

3) Subtract from the $80,000 determined in (2) the difference between $60,000, the gain on which tax is postponed and $10,000, the ordinary income due to additional depreciation not required to be reported. The difference is $50,000 which, subtracted from $80,000, leaves $30,000.

4) Allocate the result in (3) to both properties according to their cost as considered in (2).

Depreciable real property	$32,000 + $80,000 x
	30,000 - $12,000
Other property (land)	$48,000 + $80,000 x
	30,000 - $18,000

The ordinary income not required to be reported ($10,000) is carried over as additional depreciation to the depreciable real property acquired, and may be taxed on a later disposition. The holding period of the acquired property includes the holding period of the exchanged or involuntarily converted property, but for calculating the applicable percentage on the acquired property a new holding period begins when it is acquired.

Example 3. Assume that the depreciable real property acquired as replacement in Example 2 is sold for $35,000 after being held for 80 months, and at the time of the sale its adjusted basis is $5,000 and the additional depreciation for periods after it was acquired is $2,500. Accordingly, the additional depreciation is $12,500 ($10,000 not required to be reported as explained in Example 2, plus the $2,500 additional depreciation for periods after acquisition). The applicable percentage is 28% (100% less one percent for each month held in excess of 20 months) for additional depreciation before 1970 ($8,000), 100% for additional depreciation after 1969 but before 1976 ($4,000), and 100% for additional depreciation after 1975 ($500). Since the total additional depreciation of $12,500 is less than the $30,000 gain realized on the sale ($35,000 sale price less $5,000 adjusted basis), the amount treated as ordinary income upon the sale is $7,700 (100% of $4,500 plus 40% of $8,000).

DISPOSITION OF DEPRECIABLE PROPERTY AND OTHER
PROPERTY IN A SINGLE TRANSACTION

If you dispose of both depreciable personal property and
other property in a single transaction and realize a gain, you
must allocate the amount realized between the two types of
property disposed of in proportion to their respective fair market values to determine the part of your gain to be reported as
ordinary income because of depreciation. In general, if a buyer
and seller have adverse interests as to the allocation of the
amount realized between the depreciable personal property and
other property, any arm's-length agreement between them will
establish the allocation.

In a *like-kind* exchange or involuntary conversion, if both
depreciable personal property and other property are disposed
of and both types are also acquired in the transaction, the portion of the amount realized on the disposition that is allocated
to the depreciable personal property is deemed to consist of,
first, the fair market value of the depreciable personal property
acquired and, second (to the extent of any remaining balance),
the fair market value of property other than depreciable personal property acquired. The amount allocated to the other
property disposed of is deemed to consist of the fair market
value of all property acquired that has not already been taken
into account.

In the event you dispose of *depreciable real property* and
other property in a single transaction, similar rules apply.

Example. A fire destroyed your property having a total fair
market value of $50,000 and consisting of machinery worth
$30,000 and other property worth $20,000. You received insurance proceeds of $40,000 and immediately used these pro-
ceeds plus $10,000 of your own funds (or a total of $50,000)
to acquire machinery with a fair market value of $15,000 and
other property with a fair market value of $35,000. Assume
that your adjusted basis of the machinery was $5,000 and the
depreciation after 1961 on the machinery was $35,000. Assume
further that you made the election to postpone tax on your gain
arising from the involuntary conversion. You must report
$9,000 as ordinary income because of depreciation arising from
this transaction, determined as follows:

First, the $40,000 of insurance proceeds must be allocated
between the machinery and the other property destroyed, in

proportion to the fair market value of each. Therefore, the amount allocated to the machinery is 30,000/50,000 of $40,000, or $24,000, and the amount allocated to the other property is 20,000/50,000 of $40,000, or $16,000. Your gain on the involuntary conversion of the machinery is $24,000 less $5,000 adjusted basis, or $19,000.

Second, the $24,000 allocated to the machinery disposed of is deemed to consist of the $15,000 fair market value of the replacement machinery acquired and $9,000 of the fair market value of other property acquired in the transaction. (All of the $16,000 allocated to the other property disposed of is deemed to consist of the fair market value of the other property acquired.)

Third, you are required to report as ordinary income, because of depreciation, the lesser of the first or second item under the limitation for tax-free exchanges and involuntary conversions, explained earlier. The amounts to be taken into account are: under the first item, your $19,000 gain on the machinery (since it is less than the $35,000 depreciation after 1961), and under the second item, the gain required to be included in income (none, since you elected to postpone tax on your gain), plus the $9,000 of the fair market value of other than depreciable property acquired, which is deemed included in the proceeds for the machinery disposed of. The lesser of the amounts under the first or second item, $9,000, is the amount you are required to report as ordinary income because of depreciation.

CORPORATIONS AND PARTNERSHIPS

Corporations and partnerships compute ordinary income because of depreciation on the disposition of either depreciable personal or depreciable real property in the manner described earlier for individuals. Although the computations differ for each type of property in arriving at the gain to be reported as ordinary income, once the gain is determined, the treatment of the transaction generally is the same.

Corporate distributions. If the fair market value of depreciable personal or real property distributed by a corporation to its shareholders either as a dividend or in liquidation, exceeds the adjusted basis of that property the corporation must report ordinary income because of depreciation even though the distribution might otherwise be nontaxable.

Example 1. The X-L Corporation distributes depreciable personal property to its shareholders as a dividend. The fair market value of the property is $6,200, and its adjusted basis to the corporation is $4,000. Depreciation claimed by the corporation after 1961 is $2,600. The corporation must report $2,200 as ordinary income because of depreciation (the lower of $2,600 depreciation after 1961 or the $2,200 difference between fair market value and adjusted basis), even though the distribution would not otherwise result in any recognized gain to the corporation.

Example 2. The X-L Corporation distributes depreciable personal property to its shareholders as in Example 1. However, the transaction is a taxable liquidation distribution rather than a dividend and the fair market value of the property is $7,600. The corporation must report $2,600 as ordinary income because of depreciation (the lower of $3,600 difference between fair market value and adjusted basis, or $2,600 depreciation after 1961), even though the distribution otherwise would not result in any recognized gain to the corporation.

Basis of property to distribute shareholder. The basis of the property distributed to a noncorporate shareholder is its fair market value, and no adjustment is made for the ordinary income required to be reported by the distributing corporation. In the case of a shareholder which is a corporation, however, the basis to be used when the fair market value exceeds adjusted basis is the adjusted basis of the property in the hands of the distributing corporation increased by the ordinary income required to be reported on the distribution.

PARTNERSHIPS

Each partner's share of the partnership's ordinary income because of depreciation generally will be determined in accordance with the partnership agreement. If a partnership agreement provides for the allocation of the total gain from a sale or other disposition of property, but not for the allocation or ordinary income because of depreciation, the allocation of that ordinary income must be in the same proportion as the total gain.

If the partnership has elected to make certain special adjustments permitted to reflect the difference between the basis of a

partner's interest in the partnership and that partner's proportionate share of the adjusted basis of partnership property, these
adjustments must be taken into account.

Example. On January 3, 1975, Helen Hood bought the one-
third interest of a partner in the ABC partnership, which had
depreciable personal property consisting of machinery with an
adjusted basis of $30,000. At the time of Helen's purchase, the
partnership had taken depreciation after 1961 of $3,000. A
$5,000 special basis adjustment was elected in respect of Helen's
one-third share of the common partnership's adjusted basis of
the machinery. During each of the years 1975, 1976, and 1977
the partnership deducted $3,000 depreciation, or a total of
$9,000. Helen was allowed to deduct $4,200 for this period,
consisting of her $3,000 distributive share of the partnership
depreciation plus $1,200 depreciation in respect of her special
basis adjustment.

On January 3, 1978, the partnership sold the machinery for
$48,000, realizing a gain of $27,000. The ordinary income because of depreciation to be taken into account by the partnership is $12,000, of which Helen's distributive share is $4,000.
However, the amount of gain recognized by Helen as ordinary income because of depreciation is $4,200, determined as follows:

1) Helen's adjusted basis:
   1/3 portion of partnership adjusted
       basis (1/3 of $21,000) . . . . $ 7,000
   Add special basis adjustment at date of
       sale ($5,000 minus $1,200)   3,800

   Adjusted basis $10,800

2) Helen's adjusted basis plus
   depreciation after 1961:
   Adjusted basis (as above) $10,800
   Add: Helen's portion of partnership de-
       preciation after interest acquired   3,000
   Depreciation for same period in respect
       of special basis adjustment   1,200

   Adjusted basis plus depreciation $15,000
3) Helen's portion of amount realized by
   partnership (1/3 of $48,000) $16,000
4) Ordinary income reportable by Helen (lesser of
   (2) or (3) minus (1)) . . . . $ 4,200

A total of $8,000 of ordinary income because of depreciation ($12,000 less $4,000) will be reported by the other two partners, in the ratio required by the partnership agreement.

Distribution by partnerships. When a partnership distributes to a partner property which, if sold by the partnership to an outsider, would have resulted in ordinary income to the partnership because of depreciation, the distribution will result in ordinary income to the partnership equal to the excess of the total potential ordinary income over the portion of such ordinary income attributable to the partner receiving the property.

Ordinary income because of depreciation will not result to the partnership if the property distributed to the partner had been contributed to the partnership by that partner.

The basis of property distributed by a partnership to a partner, for arriving at the amount, if any, of the potential ordinary income to be recognized upon the distribution, is determined by reference to the adjusted basis of the property to the partnership.

Distribution of depreciable personal property. At the time of the distribution of the property by the partnership, the potential ordinary income, representing the lesser of post-1961 depreciation or the difference between the fair market value of the property at the time of distribution and its adjusted basis, must be determined.

Example. Carl Arden owns a one-third interest in the ABC partnership. The only assets of the partnership are cash, land, and a machine. The partnership bought the machine, which has an adjusted basis of $9,000 and a fair market value of $15,000. Depreciation taken on the machine after 1961 is $9,000 when it is distributed to Carl Arden in complete liquidation of his partnership interest, the basis of which is $10,000. Since, at the time of the distribution, potential ordinary income of $6,000 exists (depreciation after 1961 to the extent of the excess of fair market value over adjusted basis), the partnership (as constituted after the distribution) will be required to recognize $4,000 of ordinary income because of depreciation (two-thirds remaining interest times $6,000 potential income).

The basis of the property to Carl Arden as a result of the distribution equals his basis for his partnership interest of $10,000. However, if he eventually disposes of the property, he must take into account $2,000 ($6,000 potential ordinary income less

$4,000 reported by the partnership) as depreciation after 1961.

Distribution of depreciable real property. At the time of the distribution of depreciable real property by a partnership to a partner, the potential ordinary income that would be recognized to the partnership, if there were an outright sale of the property at its fair market value, must be determined.

That portion of the potential ordinary income attributable to the remaining partners' interest in the distributed property is treated as ordinary income by the partnership in much the same manner as already described under *Distribution of depreciable personal property.* When the distribute partner disposes of the asset, that partner may be required to take into account the potential ordinary income that was not recognized by the partnership upon the liquidation.

A contribution of property by a partner to a partnership generally will not result in ordinary income because of depreciation previously deducted by the contributing partner, and the basis of the property in the hands of the partnership remains the same as its adjusted basis to the partner contributing it. However, if the property is subject to a mortgage that is assumed by the partnership, however, the contributing partner may be required to report ordinary income because of depreciation.

Example 1. Joe Smith contributes property to a new partnership for a one-half interest in it. The property has a fair market value of $10,000, an adjusted basis in Joe's hands of $4,000, and depreciation after 1961 of $3,000. Joe is not required to report ordinary income on the transfer, and the basis of the property to the partnership is $4,000, the same as its adjusted basis to Joe.

Example 2. Assume the same facts as in Example 1, except that the property is subject to a $9,000 mortgage that is assumed by the partnership. Joe is treated as receiving a distribution in money of one-half the $9,000 liability assumed by the partnership, or $4,500, and thereby realizes a gain of $500 ($4,500 less his adjusted basis of $4,000). The ordinary income because of depreciation required to be reported on the transfer is limited to the gain otherwise includible in income without regard to the rules of this chapter. Therefore, the ordinary income Joe is required to report is limited to $500.

GAINS AND LOSSES

If you dispose of an asset in a manner that requires you to report a gain or a loss, the gain may be given preferential tax treatment. However, certain restrictions may be placed on the amount of loss you may claim.

It is important that you properly classify everything you sell or exchange as:

1) *A capital asset;*
2) *A noncapital asset;* or
3) An asset that may be treated as *either capital or noncapital,* depending on the circumstances. This category includes some assets used in your trade or business, and involuntarily converted assets.

HOW TO CLASSIFY ASSETS

Everything you own is a *capital asset* except:

1) Property held primarily for sale to customers or property that will physically become a part of merchandise intended for sale to customers;
2) Accounts or notes receivable acquired in the ordinary course of your trade or business for services rendered or from the sale of any properties described in (1);
3) Depreciable property used in your trade or business (even though fully depreciated);
4) Real property used in your trade or business;
5) A copyright, a literary, musical, or artistic composition, a letter or memorandum, or similar property; created by your personal efforts; prepared or produced, in the case of a letter, memorandum, or similar property, for you; or acquired from a person who created the property or for whom the property was prepared, under circumstances entitling you to his basis (for example, by gift);
6) U.S. Government publications that you received from the Government free or for less than the public sales price or that you acquired under circumstances entitling you to the basis of someone who received the publications free or for less than public sales price, if you sell, exchange or contribute the publication after October 4, 1976; and
7) Obligations of Federal, State, and municipal governments issued on a discount basis and payable without interest at a

fixed maturity date not more than one year from the date of issue.

Whether property is held primarily for sale to customers in the ordinary course of business is a question of fact to be determined in each case. Among the factors to be considered are:

1) The purpose for which the property is acquired;
2) The development of the property between the time of acquisition and time of sale;
3) The number and frequency of sales; and
4) The time the property is held before it is sold.

Example 1. You are engaged in the business of developing and selling luncheonette businesses. You are constantly acquiring new sites, developing and selling the businesses. Upon completion of the construction of a luncheonette and prior to operation, you sell it. Since the businesses are property you hold primarily for sale to customers in the ordinary course of your business, the businesses are not capital assets. Gain or loss from the sale of the businesses is ordinary gain or loss. The result would be the same if you had incorporated the luncheonettes and sold the stock of the corporations.

Example 2. You manufacture and sell to customers steel cable which you deliver on returnable reels having a useful life of 8 years. The customers make deposits on the reels, which you will refund providing the reels are returned within a year. If they are not returned, you retain the deposits as the agreed-upon sales price of the reels; however, most of the reels are returned within the one-year period. You maintain adequate records showing depreciation and other charges to the capitalized cost of reels. Under these conditions, the reels are not property held for sale to customers in the ordinary course of your business. Any gain or loss resulting from their nonreturn may be capital or ordinary, depending on your section 1231 transactions (discussed later in this chapter).

Stocks, stock rights, and bonds including stock received as a dividend are capital assets except when held for sale by a securities dealer. However, see *Losses on Small Business Stock* (Section 1244), later.

Dividends on stock sold. When stock is sold, and a dividend is declared and paid after the sale, the dividend is not gross income to the seller. When stock is sold after the declaration of a dividend and after the date the seller becomes entitled to the dividend, the dividend is income to the seller. When stock is sold between the time of declaration and the time of payment of the dividend, and the sale takes place at such time that the purchaser becomes entitled to the dividend and the dividend is income to the purchaser. However, even if the purchaser has not received legal title to the stock and does not receive the dividend in some cases the purchaser may still be considered to have received the dividend. For example, if the seller retains the legal title to the stock as a trustee solely for the purpose of securing the payment of the purchase price, with the understanding that any dividends received from time to time are to be applied as a reduction of the purchase price, the dividends are considered to be income to the purchaser.

Bonds traded flat. If bonds with accrued interest are traded without allocating between interest and principal, the part of the selling price that represents payment of interest accrued on the bonds while the seller held them must be determined. The portion of the amount received that is allocable to the interest accrued while the seller held the bond is determined by multiplying the selling price by the interest accrued while the seller held the bond and that amount is then divided by the sum of the principal plus the unpaid interest accrued on the bond up to the date of the sale. The interest is taxable as ordinary income and the balance is considered received for the bonds in determining gain or loss on the sale of a capital asset.

Securities purchased to guarantee performance of a contract in the regular course of business or to obtain inventory items are not capital assets. Gain or loss from the sale of such securities is ordinary gain or loss in some cases and in others is reflected in the cost of goods acquired for the year in which the gain is realized or the loss sustained.

Long-term capital gain of a Subchapter S corporation may be subject to a capital gains tax.

Options to buy or sell. Gain or loss from the sale or exchange of a purchased option to buy or sell property that is a capital asset in your hands, or would be if you acquired it, is a capital gain or loss.

Gain or loss from the sale or exchange of a purchased option to buy or sell property that is not or would not be a capital asset in your hands is ordinary gain or loss. Under certain circumstances, this may be treated as a capital gain or loss.

Example 1. You acquire an option on a new home. The property goes up in value, but you decide not to buy it, and you sell the option for more than you paid for it. Your gain is capital gain since the property, if you had acquired it, would have been a capital asset in your hands.

Example 2. Assume the same facts as in Example 1, except that the property goes down in value and you sell the option for less than you paid for it. Your loss is not deductible even though it is a capital loss, since a loss on the sale of your personal residence, which the property would have been had you acquired it, would not be deductible. This would also be true if you had failed to exercise the option and forfeited the money you paid for it.

If you fail to exercise an option to buy or sell, and you incur a loss, the option is considered to have been sold or exchanged on the date that it expired. Your loss is treated in the same manner as already explained.

The capital asset treatment does not apply:

1) To the gain from the sale of the option if the gain from the sale of the property underlying the option would be ordinary income;
2) To a dealer in options, if the option is part of the dealer's inventory; or
3) To loss from failure to exercise a fixed price option, acquired on the same day the property identified in the option is acquired.

If you grant an option after September 1, 1976, on stocks, securities, commodities, or commodity futures and it is not exercised, the amount you receive (if you are not in the business of granting options) is treated as a short-term capital gain regardless of the classification of the property in your hands. However, if you granted the option before September 2, 1976, or on types of property other than stocks, securities, commodities, or commodity futures, and it is not exercised, you realize ordinary income on the amount you receive, even though the option may have been a capital asset that you held. If the option is exercised, you add the option payment to other amounts you receive to compute the amount you realize on the sale of the property. The classification of your gain or loss is then determined by the type of property you sold.

Your holding period for property acquired under an option to purchase begins on the day after *the property* was acquired not the day after the option was acquired.

An invention is generally a capital asset in the hands of the inventor whether or not a patent or patent application has been obtained. The inventor is the individual whose efforts created the property and who would qualify as the original and first inventor (or joint inventor).

If you are an inventor and transfer all substantial rights to patent property, you may obtain *special tax treatment,* as described later, providing the transfer is not to your employer or to a related person.

If you acquire all the substantial rights to patent property before the invention is reduced to practice (tested and operated successfully under operating conditions) for a consideration paid to the inventor, you may, when you dispose of your interest, obtain the special tax-treatment discussed later if you are not the employer of, or related to, the inventor.

However, if you purchase patent property after it is put into practice it may be treated as either a capital or noncapital asset, depending on the circumstances.

All substantial rights to patent property means all rights that are of value at the time they are transferred. The right to prohibit sublicensing or subassignment of rights, or the retention of a security interest (such as a lien), or a reservation providing for forfeiture for nonperformance are not considered substantial rights for these rules and may be retained by the holder.

In the following situations, all substantial rights were not transferred, and the transferor is *not* entitled to the special tax treatment:

1) The rights are limited geographically within a country (limiting the rights to one or more whole countries could be a transfer of all substantial rights);
2) The rights are limited in duration to a period less than the remaining life of the patent;
3) The rights are limited to fields of use within trades or industries, which are less than all the rights that exist and have value at the time of the grant; and
4) The rights are less than all the claims or inventions covered by the patent that exist and have value at the time of the grant.

Special treatment. If you are the inventor, or an individual who acquired all the substantial rights to the patent property (as described earlier), and you transfer all the substantial rights, or an undivided interest in all such rights, the transfer will be considered a sale or exchange of a long-term capital asset. This treatment applies even though you have not held the patent property for more than one year and the payments received are made:

1) Periodically during the transferee's use of the property; or
2) Contingent on the productivity, use, or disposition of the transferee's rights in the property.

Related persons. The special tax treatment does not apply if the transfer is either directly or indirectly between you and a related person with the following modifications:

1) Members of your family include your spouse, ancestors, and lineal descendants, but not your brothers or sisters (whether by the whole or half blood); and
2) An individual and a corporation are considered related parties if 25% of more (rather than more than 50%) in value of the outstanding stock of the corporation is owned, directly or indirectly, by or for that individual.

If you come within the definition of a related taxapyer independent of family status, the brother-sister exception, previously described, does not apply. Thus, a transfer between a brother and a sister, one of whom is the beneficiary and the other the fiduciary of a trust, is a transfer between related parties. The brother-sister exception does not apply, since the trust relationship exists independent of the family status.

Trade secrets are generally eligible for capital gains treatment on sale or exchange. In order for a transfer of a trade secret to constitute a sale or exchange, the transfer must include all substantial rights to the trade secret. The substantial rights which must be transferred consist of the right to use the trade secret in perpetuity or until it becomes public knowledge and no longer protectable and the exclusive right to prevent further disclosure.

Copyrights. Literary, musical or artistic compositions, or similar property are not treated as capital assets if your personal efforts created them, or if you acquired the property in such a way that all or part of your basis in the property is determined by reference to a person whose personal efforts created it. The sale of such property, whether or not it is copyrighted, results in ordinary income.

However, if you acquire such property or a copyright to it in any other manner, amounts received for granting the exclusive use or right to exploit the work throughout the life of the copyright are considered to be received from the sale of property. It is immaterial whether the consideration is measured by a fixed amount or by a percentage of receipts from the sale, performance, exhibition, or publication of the copyrighted work, or by the number of copies sold, performances given, or exhibitions made.

It is also immaterial that the consideration is paid over the same period as that covering the grantee's use of the copyrighted work. If the property was used in your trade or business, the gain or loss may be subject to the treatment described later.

Letters, memorandums, and similar property (such as drafts of speeches, recordings, transcripts, or manuscripts, drawings, or photographs) are not treated as capital assets if your personal efforts created them or they were prepared or produced for you. Similarly, such property is not a capital asset if your basis in the property is determined by reference to the person who created the property or the person for whom it was prepared. For this purpose, letters and memorandums addressed to you are considered prepared for you. If letters or memorandums are prepared by persons under your administrative control, they are considered prepared for you whether or not you review them.

Sale of land. If you are a dealer in real estate, gains from the sale of land held for sale to customers will be treated as ordinary income. However, certain land held in your investment account or held for use in your business may qualify for capital gains treatment. If you are not a dealer, a casual sale of land will usually qualify for capital gains treatment. If you are not a dealer and you subdivide land into lots or parcels for sale, you may be eligible for capital gains treatment under special rules.

A contract for services is not an asset subject to capital gains treatment. If you assign or sell such a contract, and the assignee or purchaser is merely entitled to compensation for services under the terms of the contract for its remaining life, the amount you receive is ordinary income.

COMPUTING CAPITAL GAINS AND LOSSES

If gain or loss is from the disposition of a capital asset, or is treated as such, you have a capital gain or loss.

Long- or short-term. If you hold a capital asset one year or less for tax years beginning after 1977, the gain or loss from its sale or exchange is short term, except for an invention, as discussed earlier, and certain property acquired from a decedent as discussed later. If you hold it longer than one year for tax years beginning after 1977 the gain or loss from its sale or exchange is long term.

Gain from an installment sale of a capital asset qualifying for long-term capital gain treatment in the year of sale will continue to qualify for such treatment in later tax years.

Short-term capital gains and losses are merged by adding the gains and the losses separately and subtracting one total from the other to determine the net short-term capital gain or loss.

Long-term capital gains and losses are merged in a similar manner to determine the net long-term capital gain or loss.

The total net gain or loss is then determined by merging the net short-term capital gain or loss with the net long-term capital gain or loss.

Holding period. To determine whether you held property *over one year,* begin counting on the day following the day you acquired the property. This same day of each succeeding month is the beginning of a new month regardless of the number of days in the preceding month. The day you dispose of the property is considered as part of your holding period.

Example 1. If you purchased an asset on January 5, 1978, you should start counting on January 6, 1978. The 6th of each succeeding month is the beginning of a new month. If you sold the asset on January 5, 1979, your holding period would not be over one year, but if you sold it on January 6, 1979, it would be.

This rule holds true for property acquired on the last day of any calendar month. For example, the holding period of property acquired on March 31, begins on April 1 and the first of each succeeding month represents the beginning of a new month.

Example 2. You are a cash-basis, calendar year taxpayer. You sold stock at a gain on December 31, 1977. According to the rules of the stock exchange, the sale was closed by delivery of the stock 5 trading days after the sale. You received payment of the sales price on that same day. Your gain, therefore, is reportable on your 1978 return. However, it is classifiable as long-term or short-term capital gain depending on whether you had held the stock more than one year. Your holding period ended on December 31.

If you had sold the stock at a loss, your loss would be reportable on your 1977 return, and would be classifiable as long-term or short-term capital loss depending on whether you had held the stock more than 9 months.

Nontaxable exchanges. If you acquire the asset in exchange for another asset and your basis for the new asset is determined, in whole or in part, by your basis in the old asset, then the first day of the holding period of the new asset is the day following the date you acquired the old asset.

Corporate liquidation. The holding period of property received in a liquidation generally begins on the day following the day of a distribution on which gain or loss is recognized. However, in a one-calendar-month liquidation in which the basis of property received is determined in whole or in part by the basis of the stock cancelled or redeemed in the transaction, the holding period of the distributed property includes that of the stock given up.

If you receive a gift of property and your basis is determined by the donor's basis, the first day of your holding period is considered to have started on the same day as the donor's holding period.

If you acquire property from a decedent and your basis for it is determined by reference to its fair market value at the date of the decedent's death or alternate valuation date, you do not have to determine your holding period. You are considered to have held that property for more than one year even though you dispose of it within one year after the decedent's death.

Real property purchased. To determine how long real property has been held, begin counting on the day following that on which title passed, or on the day following that on which delivery of possession was made and the burdens and privileges of ownership were assumed by the purchaser, whichever occurred first. In the case of real property acquired at a Federal tax sale, the purchaser's holding period begins upon the expiration of the prior owner's redemption period (120 days after the tax sale). Delivery of possession of real property under an option agreement is not important until a contract of sale comes into being through exercise of the option. The holding period of the seller cannot end before the date the option is exercised.

Real property repossessed. If you sell real property with the retention of a security interest, and then later repossess the property under the terms of the sale contract, your holding period for a subsequent disposition includes the period you held the property prior to the original sale, and the period after the repossession. Your holding period does not include the time between the original sale and the repossession; that is, it does not include the period during which the original purchaser held the property.

CAPITAL GAIN DEDUCTION AND ALTERNATIVE TAX

If you are a *noncorporate taxpayer* and your net long-term capital gain exceeds your net short-term capital loss, you may claim a deduction equal to 50% (60% of the excess attributable to transactions occurring, and installment payments received after October 1978) of the excess. If you have no net short-term capital loss, your capital-gain deduction is 50% (60% of the excess attributable to transactions occurring, and installment payments received after October 1978) of your net long-term capital gain. The capital-gain deduction may be subject to a minimum tax on tax preferences.

Example. During the year you had the following transactions which occurred before November 1978:

Long-term capital gain	$5,400	
Long-term capital loss	(1,750)	
Net long-term capital gain		$3,650
Short-term capital gain	$2,600	
Short-term capital loss	(3,790)	
Net short-term capital loss		(1,190)
Excess of net long-term capital gain over net short-term capital loss		$2,460

Although you have a net gain of $2,460 from capital transactions, only 50%, or $1,230, is taxed, since you may deduct 50% of the excess of the net long-term capital gain over the net short-term capital loss. This deduction is claimed on Schedule D

(Form 1040) to determine the capital gain includible in adjusted gross income.

The alternative tax for an individual is computed on page 2 of Schedule D (Form 1040). You should figure your tax by using both the regular and alternative methods and then select the method that produces the lowest tax. The alternative tax for individuals will no longer be in effect for tax years beginning after 1978.

Individuals having earned income the tax on which is limited to a maximum rate of 50% compute the alternative tax on Form 4726.

If your net long-term capital gains do not exceed $50,000 ($25,000 for married persons filing separate returns), your alternative tax is computed in the following manner:

1) Reduce taxable income by the net long-term capital gains included in income (after the capital gains deduction);
2) Using the regular tax rates, compute a partial tax on the amount determined in (1); then
3) Add to this partial tax 25% of the total net long-term capital gains.

The total represents your alternative tax. The effect of this computation is to tax your net long-term capital gain at a maximum rate of 25%.

Example 1. You are single and your taxable income (after deducting your excess itemized deductions and personal exemption) is $46,200. This includes long-term capital gains of $4,000, of which 50% or $2,000 is includible in your income because all of your long-term capital gains transactions occurred before November 1, 1978. The 50% maximum tax on earned income does not apply. The regular tax (without regard to the credit for your personal exemption) on $46,200 is $16,590. The alternative tax is computed as follows:

1) Taxable income	$46,200
2) Less: Portion of net long-term capital gains included in taxable income	2,000
3) Balance	$44,200
4) Tax on $44,200	$15,490
5) Add: 25% of total net long-term capital gains (25% of $4,000)	1,000
6) Alternative tax	$16,490

Since the alternative tax ($16,490) is less than the regular tax ($16,590), enter $16,490 on line 4, Schedule TC (Form 1040), and check the box marked Schedule D on that line.

Example 2. Assume the same facts as stated in Example 1 except that $3,000 of your long-term capital gains occurred before November 1, 1978, and $1,000 occurred after October 31, 1978. Of the $3,000 received before November, 50% or $1,500 would be included in income, and of the $1,000 received after October, 60% or $600 would be deducted leaving only 40% or $400 to be included in income. The alternative tax is computed as follows:

1) Taxable income	$46,200
2) Less: Portion of net long-term capital gains included in taxable income ($1,500 plus $400)	1,900
3) Balance	$44,300
4) Tax on $44,300	$15,545
5) Add: 25% of total net long-term capital gains (25% of $4,000)	1,000
6) Alternative tax	$16,545

Since the alternative tax ($16,545) is less than the regular tax ($16,590), enter $16,545 on Schedule TC (Form 1040), line 4, and check the box marked Schedule D on that line.

If your net long-term capital gains exceed $50,000 ($25,000 for married persons filing separate returns), your alternative tax is increased and is determined in the following manner:

1) Determine the regular tax on your ordinary income;
2) Add $12,500 (25% of first $50,000 of net long-term capital gain); then
3) Add the difference between the regular tax on your total taxable income (or the amount of your net long-term capital gains, after subtracting your capital gains deduction, if it is greater than your taxable income), and the regular tax on the sum of your ordinary income; plus an additional amount, this amount is $50,000 multiplied by a fraction, the numerator of which is your net long-term capital gains reduced by your capital gains deduction, and the denominator of which is your total net long-term capital gains.

Example. You are single and your taxable income (after deducting your excess itemized deductions and personal exemption) is $152,200. This includes $40,200 of ordinary income and $112,000 net capital gain ($224,000 long-term capital gain less $112,000 capital gain deduction). Your alternative tax is computed as follows:

Tax on $40,200 ordinary income		$13,290
25% of first $50,000 of long-term capital gain		12,500
Regular tax on $152,200 taxable income.......................	$88,090	
Less: Regular tax on the sum of $40,200 ordinary income and $50,000 times ($112,000/224,000)....	28,310	59,780
Alternative Tax		$85,570

Enter $85,570 on Schedule TC (Form 1040), line 4, and check the box marked Schedule D on that line.

For married persons filing separate returns, the amount of net long-term capital gain that will be taxed at 25% is limited to $25,000 on each return. If either you or your spouse has a net long-term gain in excess of $25,000, follow the computation under *if your net long-term gains exceed $50,000.* Substitute $25,000 for the $50,000 shown in that discussion.

For corporations, the alternative tax on capital gains before 1979 is 30% of the excess of the net long-term capital gain over the net short-term capital loss. For tax years ending after 1978 the rate is reduced to 28%. Because a corporation's income tax for calendar year 1978 consists of a normal tax of 20% on the first $25,000 of its taxable income and 22% on the excess over $25,000, plus a 26% surtax on the excess over $50,000, a calendar-year corporation with taxable income of $50,000 or less will not benefit from the alternative tax computations.

If taxable income exceeds $50,000, the corporation will pay less by using the alternative tax computation on capital gains.

Alternative tax for a calendar-year corporation is computed as follows:

1) From the corporation's taxable income (line 30, page 1, Form 1120) subtract the excess of the net long-term capital gain over net short-term capital loss;

2) Compute a partial tax at the regular rates on the ordinary net income so determined; then

3) To this partial tax add 30% of the capital gain that was eliminated from taxable income in (1).

Example. A calendar-year corporation had taxable income of $60,000 for 1978, which included the following:

Long-term capital gain		$13,000
Long-term capital loss		(3,600)
Net long-term capital gain		$ 9,400
Short-term capital gain	$2,000	
Short-term capital loss	(5,400)	
Net short-term capital loss		(3,400)
Excess of net long-term capital gain over net short-term capital loss		$ 6,000

Regular tax computation:

Normal tax, 20% of first $25,000 taxable income ($5,000) plus 22% of $35,000 remainder of taxable income ($7,700)	$12,700
Surtax, 26% of $10,000 (taxable income in excess of $50,000)	2,600
Regular tax	$15,300

Alternative tax computation:

1) Taxable income	$60,000
Less: Excess of net long-term capital gain over net short-term capital loss (see preceding)	6,000
	$54,000
2) Partial tax on (1):	
Normal tax, 20% of $25,000 plus 22% of $29,000	$11,380
Surtax, 26% of $4,000	1,040
	$12,420
3) Add 30% of the $6,000 capital gain	1,800
Alternative tax	$14,220

Alternative tax for a fiscal year corporation whose tax year ends after 1978 is generally computed by using the 30% rate for the period before 1979 and the 28% rate for the period after 1978.

Deductions subject to a limitation based on taxable income are not adjusted in computing the alternative tax.

Example. If, in the previous example, the corporation had claimed the maximum deduction for contributions (5% of $63,157.90, or $3,157.90), in determining its taxable income of $60,000, that deduction would not have to be adjusted to use the alternative computation.

LIMIT ON CAPITAL LOSSES

This discussion deals with the treatment of capital losses and the limitation on the deduction allowed for them.

Corporations may deduct capital losses only to the extent of capital gains. Any capital loss in the current year that exceeds capital gains is carried back to the 3 years preceding the year of loss and, if not completely absorbed, is then carried over for up to 5 years succeeding the loss year.

A capital loss may not be carried back from or to a year in which the corporation was a Subchapter S corporation. In addition, a capital loss carryback may not increase or produce a net operating loss, in the carryback year.

The carryback or carryover is treated as a short-term capital loss regardless of whether it was a short-term or long-term loss in the year in which it occurred. For example, if a corporation had a net short-term capital gain of $3,000 and a net long-term capital loss of $5,000, it could offset the $3,000 gain. The remaining loss of $2,000 would be treated as a short-term loss when it is carried back or forward.

If a corporation has two or more capital loss carrybacks to the same year, the loss from the earliest year is considered first. Similarly, when there are two or more carryovers, the loss from the earliest year is applied first to reduce the current year's net capital gains, then the next carryover is applied, etc., until all carryovers are absorbed. In computing the capital loss to be carried over from the current year, no net capital loss carryover from earlier years may be taken into account.

Foreign expropriation capital losses of a corporation may not be carried back. Such losses, however, may be carried over to each of the 10 succeeding years.

Limitations. An *individual* may claim a capital loss deduction if capital losses exceed capital gains. The deduction is limited to the smallest of the following amounts:

1) Taxable income for the year reduced (but not below zero) by the zero bracket amount, and computed without regard to either capital gains and losses or deductions for personal exemptions;
2) $3,000 for tax years beginning after 1977; or
3) Net capital loss, as described in the following paragraphs.

Joint and separate returns. The capital loss deduction limitation (2) is $3,000 on a joint tax return. But if a husband and wife file separate returns, the amount in limitation (2) is limited to $1,500 for each return. Neither spouse may use any part of the other's loss on separate returns.

Computing the loss. Net short-term capital losses are considered at 100% in arriving at a capital loss (subject to limitations (1) and (2), above). In other words, net short-term losses can be used to reduce your ordinary income dollar for dollar. Only 50% of the net long-term loss can be used to reduce your income. Therefore, $6,000 of net long-term capital losses are needed to produce a $3,000 deduction; $3,000 to produce $1,500, etc.

Example 1. In 1978 Judy Smith had wages of $8,000, a net long-term capital loss of $1,600, and she did not itemize deductions. Her capital loss is $800 (½ of $1,600).

Example 2. Assume the same facts as in Example 1 except that Judy's long-term loss was $600. In addition, she had a $500 net short-term capital loss. Her capital loss deduction is $800 computed as follows:

Net short-term loss	$500
1/2 of net long-term loss (1/2 of $600)	300
Net capital loss	$800

Your net capital loss for the year is determined as follows:

—If you had a net *short-term capital loss* and a net *long-term capital gain,* your capital loss is the excess of your net short-term capital loss over your net long-term capital gain;

—If you had a net *long-term capital loss* and a net *short-term capital gain,* your capital loss is half the excess of your net long-term capital loss over your net short-term capital gain; or

—If you had both a net *short-term capital loss* and a net *long-term capital loss,* your capital loss is your net short-term capital loss plus half your net long-term capital loss.

Example. You had capital gains and losses for the year as follows:

	Short-term	Long-term
Gains	$700	$ 400
Losses	800	2,000

Your net capital loss is $900, computed as follows:

Shor-term capital loss	$ 800	
Less: Short-term capital gain	700	
Net short-term capital loss		$ 100
Long-term capital loss	$2,000	
Less: Long-term capital gain	400	
Net long-term capital loss	$1,600	
Less: Half of net long-term loss	800	800
Net capital loss		$ 900

Your deduction is limited to this $900 or your taxable income reduced (but not below zero) by the zero bracket amount, whichever is smaller. If your net capital loss was $3,200, your deduction would be limited to $3,000, with a carryover to the next year.

Capital loss carryover. If capital losses exceed the limitations already listed, the excess can be carried over to subsequent years until it is completely absorbed. When carried over, the loss will retain its original character as long term or short term; thus, a long-term capital loss carried over from a previous year will offset long-term gains of the current year before it offsets short-term gains of the current year.

When carrying over an unused long-term loss, 100% of the loss is carried to the next year, and treated as if it had been incurred in that year.

Note. Any capital loss carryover from 1977 to 1978 should be reflected on the space provided on your 1977 Schedule D (Form 1040), page 2, Part V. Schedule D (Form 1040) for 1978 should be used to compute capital loss carryovers to 1979 if you have a capital loss from years beginning after 1969, Form 4798 should be used if you have a capital loss from years beginning before 1970, or a combination of pre-1970 and post-1969 capital losses.

In determining the capital loss carryover, short-term losses are applied first, even if they were incurred after a long-term loss. If, after applying the short-term loss, the loss limitations listed previously have not been reached, the long-term losses are applied until the limitations are reached. Since long-term losses are only deducted at 50%, twice the amount needed to reach the limitation represents the long-term loss absorbed in the year.

Example. On your 1978 return your capital loss deduction limit is $3,000 and you realized short-term losses of $800 and long-term losses of $6,600. Your carryover is computed as follows:

Maximum amount of capital loss deduction.	$3,000
Less: Short-term capital loss	800
Remaining available capital loss deduction	$2,200
Long-term capital loss	$6,600
Amount absorbed to reach $3,000 limitation (line 3, $2,200 x 2)	4,400
Long-term capital loss carryover to 1979	$2,200

If a taxpayer dies after sustaining a capital loss, the loss can be deducted on the final tax return only up to the limits already set forth. No part of the loss may be deducted by the decedent's estate or carried over to subsequent years.

PROPERTY USED IN YOUR BUSINESS

The sale or exchange, or the involuntary conversion, of an asset used in your trade or business is sometimes treated as the sale or exchange of a capital asset, at the end of the chapter.

Property used in your trade or business includes real property and depreciable personal property, but not property you hold for sale to customers.

Real property includes all interests, such as easements, leaseholds, water rights, etc., that are recognized as real property under applicable State law.

Depreciable property includes most assets *used to carry on your trade or business,* on which you expect to recover a substantial part of your investment through depreciation deductions.

Property held primarily for sale to customers, or property that is properly includible in your inventory, is *not* depreciable property. If you look to the sale of property for the recovery of all, or substantially all, of your investment in it, and not to its consumption through use in the course of your business operations, it is property held primarily for sale to customers. Thus, all cars acquired by a car dealer are considered to be part of the dealer's stock in trade unless the dealer can clearly show that a vehicle was purchased expressly and exclusively for use in business (other than as a demonstrator), and that its cost may reasonably be anticipated to be recovered through depreciation rather than resale.

Example 1. Each year an automobile dealer assigns cars from new car inventory to sales-personnel and company officials. The automobiles are used by these individuals for display and demonstration to the public. Regardless of the length of time the automobiles are used by these individuals they are not considered property used in business; they cannot be depreciated; and any gain on their sale is ordinary income because they are held primarily for sale to customers.

Example 2. An auto dealer operates an auto rental service as a part of the business. An auto may be rented for periods ranging from 6 months to 2 years, with the renter having the option to buy it at any time. If the renter does not buy it before the end of the rental period, the auto is turned over to the used car division of the auto dealer's business and sold. Such autos are not "property used in a trade or business," but are held primarily for sale to customers. Gain on these sales must be reported as ordinary income.

Example 3. Mary Jones is in the business of building and selling houses. In 1976, she bought six lots, resold one and built
apartments on five. Shortly after the apartments were constructed in 1977, she began a vigorous selling activity with respect to these properties; selling was handled in the same way as
house sales and by the same sales outlet. Some of the apartments
were rented in that year and in 1978 before they were sold.
Mary has ordinary income on the sales of the apartments because they were property held primarily for sale to customers in
the ordinary course of business.

TIMBER, COAL, OR IRON ORE

The cutting of *timber* may be treated as a sale or exchange of
a capital asset, if you so elect. If you make this election, any
gain or loss recognized on the cutting is a taxable gain or deductible loss that must be included in the comparison of gains and
losses discussed later.
For this treatment to apply, you must:
1) Have owned, or had a contract right to cut, the timber for
   more than one year;
2) Elect to treat the cutting of the timber as a sale or exchange of that timber; and
3) Cut the timber for sale or for use in your trade or business.

Make your election on your return for the year in which the
cutting takes place by including in income the gain or loss on
cutting and including a computation of gain or loss under these
provisions. If the timber is partnership property, the election
must be made on the partnership return.
Once made, an election remains in force for all later years, unless you can show undue hardship and get the consent of the
Internal Revenue Service to revoke your election. It applies to
all timber cut during any later year in which you owned or had
a contract right to cut the timber for more than one year for tax
years beginning after 1977. A revocation prevents you from
again making this election except with the consent of the Internal Revenue Service. The election cannot be made on an
amended return.

Compute the gain or loss on the cutting of standing timber by
subtracting the adjusted basis for depletion of the standing

timber from its fair market value on the first day of your tax
year in which it is cut.

Example. You owned for more than one year 4,000 MBF
(1,000 board-feet) of standing timber having an adjusted depletion basis of $40 per MBF. You report on a calendar-year basis.
On January 1 the timber had a fair market value of $200 per
MBF, and the timber was cut during the year for sale or use in
your business. You report the difference between the fair
market value and your adjusted depletion basis as a gain on your
tax return. This amount must be included in the grouping of
gains and losses to determine if it is to be treated as long-term
capital gain. The gain would be computed as follows:

Fair market value of timber January 1	$800,000
Less: Adjusted depletion basis of timber	160,000
Gain	$640,000

The fair market value would then become your basis of the
timber cut, and a later sale of the cut timber, including any by-
product or tree tops, would result in ordinary income or loss.

Disposing of standing timber. If you own standing timber and
dispose of it under a cutting contract, you must treat the disposal as a sale or exchange if: you held the timber for more than
one year before its disposal; and you retain an economic interest in it.

The difference between the amount realized from the disposal of the timber and its adjusted depletion basis is considered as gain or loss on its sale. This amount must be included
in the grouping of gains and losses to determine whether it is to
be treated as capital, or ordinary, gain or loss.

The date of disposal of the timber is usually the date the timber is cut; however, if you receive payment under the contract
before the timber is cut, you may elect to treat the date of payment as the date of disposal.

The term *owner* includes a sublessor and the holder of a contract to cut timber.

The term *economic interest* means that you have acquired an
interest in standing timber by investment and, by any form of
legal relationship, have derived income from the severance of the
timber, to which you must look for a return of your capital investment.

493

Example. You own standing timber that you have held for more than one year and that has an adjusted depletion basis of $20 per MBF. You had no other gains or losses during the year. If you enter into a contract under which the purchaser has a right to cut and remove the timber for $40 per MBF, you will have a capital gain of $20 per MBF on the disposal of the timber.

Tree stumps are a capital asset if they are on land held by an investor who is not in the timber or stump business, either as a buyer, seller, or processor. Gain from the sale of stumps sold in one lot by such a holder, is taxed as a capital gain. However, tree stumps held by timber operators, after the merchantable standing timber has been cut and removed from the land, are considered byproducts. Gain from the sale of stumps by lot or on a tonnage basis by such operators is taxed as ordinary income.

Coal and iron ore royalties. If you own coal or iron ore in place, have owned it for more than one year and dispose of it under a contract providing that you retain an economic interest in the coal or iron ore, gain or loss is generally treated in the same manner as for timber sold under a cutting contract, already explained. An owner is any person, including a sublessor, who owns an economic interest in the coal or iron ore in place.

The difference between the amount realized from disposal of the coal or iron ore and its adjusted depletion basis (increased by certain expenditures not allowed as deductions for the tax year) is a gain or loss that must be included in the comparison discussed later.

The deductions that are added to the adjusted basis are for expenditures attributable to the making and administering of the contract under which disposition of the coal or iron ore occurs and to preserving the economic interest retained under the contract. The date of disposal is considered to be the date the coal or iron ore is mined. Only cost depletion may be used.

This treatment does not apply to income realized by an owner who is a co-adventurer, partner, or principal in the mining of coal or iron ore.

Special rules for iron ore. This treatment applies only to iron ore mined in the United States. However, it does not apply to domestic iron ore if its disposal is directly or indirectly to:

1) A related taxpayer whose relationship to the person disposing of the ore would result in the disallowance of a loss;

2) A partnership from a partner owning directly or indirectly more than 50% of the capital or profits interests in the partnership or between two partnerships in which the same persons own, directly or indirectly, more than 50% of the capital or profits interests; or

3) An individual, a trust, estate, partnership, association, company, or corporation owned or controlled directly or indirectly by the same interests that own or control the party disposing of the iron ore.

TRANSFER OF A FRANCHISE, TRADEMARK OR TRADE NAME

Amounts you receive on transfer of a franchise, trademark, or trade name will not receive capital gain or loss treatment if you retain any significant power, right, or continuing interest in the franchise, trademark, or trade name.

A franchise is a contractual arrangement that gives the right to distribute, sell, or provide goods, services, or facilities, within a specified area.

Significant power, rights, or continuing interest in a franchise, trademark, or trade name include but are not limited to the following rights in the transferred interest:

1) A right to disapprove any assignment of the interest, or any part of it;

2) A right to terminate the agreement at will;

3) A right to prescribe standards of quality of products used or sold or of services provided and of the equipment and facilities used to promote such products or services;

4) A right to require the recipient to sell or advertise only your products or services;

5) A right to require the recipient to purchase substantially all supplies and equipment from you; or

6) The right to receive payments based on the productivity, use, or disposition of the subject matter of the interest transferred if such payments are a substantial part of the transfer agreement.

LOSSES ON SMALL BUSINESS STOCK
(Section 1244)

Only an individual (not including a trust or estate) is allowed to deduct as an ordinary loss, rather than as a capital loss, the loss on the sale, exchange, or worthlessness of certain stock he or she owns in a small business corporation (defined later). Gain on this stock is capital gain if the stock is a capital asset in his or her hands.

For stock issued after November 6, 1978, these provisions are changed to increase the maximum amount an individual may treat as an ordinary loss and to increase the amount of stock that a qualified small business corporation may issue to $1,000,000. Also, these changes remove the requirements for a written plan, the equity capital limitation, and the no prior stock outstanding limitation.

Ordinary loss on this stock is limited to the aggregate amount of loss, not to exceed $25,000 on a separate return, and $50,000 on a joint return even though the loss is sustained only by the husband or wife. These limitations are increased to $50,000 and $100,000 respectively for stock issued after November 6, 1978. Thus under the original limits, if the wife's loss on such stock is $10,000 in Corporation X and $50,000 in Corporation Y, and the husband does not have a loss, they may deduct $50,000, but only on a joint return. The excess of $10,000 is a capital loss.

Do not offset the gains against the losses that are within the limits, even if the transactions are in stock of the same corporation.

The stock must be issued to the individual sustaining the loss that is, the ordinary loss treatment is only available to the original owner of this stock. For you to claim a deduction loss on stock issued to your partnership you must have been a partner when the stock was issued and remain so until the loss is sustained. You add your distributive share of this loss to your individual loss on the stock before applying the limitation.

If the partnership distributes the stock to the partners, the stock loss no longer qualifies for treatment as an ordinary loss, even if the partner sustains it in an individual capacity.

Small business stock for this purpose is voting or nonvoting common stock of a domestic corporation provided;

1) The stock is not convertible into other securities of the corporation;
2) For stock issued before November 7, 1978, the stock has been issued under a written plan adopted by the corporation after June 30, 1958. The plan must specify the maximum amount in dollars to be received by the corporation in consideration for the stock to be issued under the plan and the period during which it can be offered (That period must end not later than 2 years after the date the plan was adopted.);
3) For stock issued after November 6, 1978, a plan is not required;
4) For stock issued before November 7, 1978, at the time the plan in (2) was adopted (but not necessarily at the time the stock was issued or the loss occurred) the corporation qualified as a small business corporation and no portion of any other stock offering was outstanding;
5) For stock issued after November 6, 1978, the corporation must qualify as a small business corporation when the stock is issued;
6) The stock was issued under the plan in (2) for money or property other than stock or securities. Ordinarily, stock will not qualify if it is received as a stock dividend, in a recapitalization or any other type of reorganization. But see the *Special rule*. Stock issued for services does not qualify; and
7) At the time you sustain the loss on the stock, more than 50% of the corporation's aggregate gross receipts for the 5-year period preceding the year of your loss must have been derived from sources other than royalties, rents, dividends, interest, annuities, and sales or exchanges of stock or securities. In computing aggregate gross receipts for this purpose, gross receipts from the sale or exchange of stock or securities include only gains therefrom.

Item (7) does not apply if the corporation's gross income is less than its deductions for this period (computed without any net operating loss and dividends received deductions). If the corporation has not been in existence for 5 tax years, the period consists of the tax years of its existence before the year of your loss. If the corporation has not been in existence for at least one tax year, the period consists of the entire time of its existence. Unless the corporation is largely an *operating company* during this period you will not be allowed the ordinary loss deduction.

Stock sold through an underwriter is not small business stock unless the underwriter acted as an agent for the corporation.

Special rule. A stock dividend on small business stock received from the corporation in which you own such stock qualifies as small business stock.

If you exchange your small business stock for new common stock in the same corporation in a reorganization qualifying as a recapitalization, the new stock is small business stock.

If you exchange your small business stock for new common stock in the same corporation in a reorganization that constitutes a mere change in identity, form, or place of organization, the new stock is small business stock.

If you hold small business stock and other stock in the same corporation, not all of the stock you receive as a stock dividend or in a reorganization, will qualify as small business stock. Only that part pertaining to the small business stock you hold will qualify.

Example. Your basis for 100 shares of X common stock is $1,000. These shares qualify as small business stock. If in a nontaxable stock dividend you receive 50 additional shares of common stock the basis of which is determined by reference to the 100 shares you own, the 50 shares are also small business stock.

If at the time the stock dividend is received, you also have stock of the corporation that is not small business stock, the shares received as a dividend must be allocated between the small business stock and the other stock. Only the shares allocated to the former are treated as small business stock.

Small business corporation defined. A corporation qualifies as a small business corporation, for stock issued before November 7, 1978, if at the time the written plan is adopted the following requirements are met:

1) The amount of the offering plus money or other property received by the corporation after June 30, 1958, for its stock, as a contribution to capital, and as paid-in surplus, does not exceed $500,000 (Property received is taken into account at its adjusted basis to the corporation for determining gain, reduced by any liabilities to which the

property is subject or that were assumed by the corporation at the time the property was received); and

2) The amount offered under the plan plus the equity capital of the corporation (as of the date the plan is adopted) does not exceed $1,000,000. Equity capital of a corporation is the sum of its money and other property in an amount equal to the adjusted basis of such property for determining gain, less the amount of its indebtedness to persons other than shareholders.

Time for satisfying requirements. Since, for stock issued before November 7, 1978, the small business corporation requirements must be satisfied only at the time the plan to issue the stock is adopted, it is possible that a loss may be treated as an ordinary loss even though the corporation does not qualify as a small business corporation at the time of the loss.

A corporation qualifies as a small business corporation, after November 6, 1978, if the dollar amount of money and other property received by the corporation, as a contribution to capital, and as paid-in surplus, does not exceed $1,000,000. This determination is made when the stock is issued, and includes amounts received for this stock as well as any other stock that was previously issued. Also, property (other than money) is taken into account at its adjusted basis to the corporation for determining gain, reduced by any liabilities that the property was subject to or that were assumed by the corporation. These determinations are made as of the time the property was received by the corporation.

Limitation of loss on contributed property. If small business stock is issued in exchange for property that immediately before the exchange had an adjusted basis, for determining loss in excess of its fair market value, and the basis of the stock is determined by reference to the basis of the property, a special limitation applies to the ordinary loss on the disposition of the stock. For computing the ordinary loss on small business stock, the basis of the stock is reduced by the difference between the adjusted basis of the property and its fair market value. This reduction is made for this purpose only and does not affect the basis of the stock for any other purpose.

Example. Joe Smith transfers property with an adjusted basis of $1,000 and a fair market value of $250 to a corporation for its small business stock. For computing the ordinary loss under this provision, the basis of the stock is its adjusted basis of $250 ($1,000 less $750), the excess of the property's adjusted basis over its fair market value. If Joe later sells the small business stock for $200, there will be an ordinary loss of $50 and a capital loss of $750.

Contribution to capital. For determining the ordinary loss on sale of small business stock, increases in the basis of outstanding stock through contributions to capital or otherwise are treated as applicable to nonqualified stock.

Example. Sally Jones purchases 100 shares of stock for $10,000, which would qualify as small business stock if they were sold. She later makes a $2,000 contribution to capital that increases the total basis of the 100 shares to $12,000. Then the 100 shares are sold for $9,000, resulting in a loss of $3,000 of which only $2,500 ($10,000/$12,000 x $3,000) may be treated as an ordinary loss. The remaining $500 must be treated as a capital loss.

Net operating loss. The loss on small business stock that is treated as ordinary loss is a business loss when determining a net operating loss.

You must file a statement with your return if you claim an ordinary loss deduction for your small business stock. It should show the address of the corporation that issued the stock to you, how you acquired the stock, the nature and amount of your payment for it, and (if you acquired it in a nontaxable transaction and gave other than money for it) the type of property, its fair market value, and its adjusted basis on the date you transferred it to the corporation.

You must maintain records sufficient to distinguish your small business stock from any other stock you may own in the corporation.

The corporation must keep in its records the plan to issue small business stock for stock issued before November 7, 1978. To substantiate an ordinary loss claimed by its shareholders for such stock, the corporation should maintain records that show:

1) The persons to whom the stock was issued under the plan, the date it was issued to each, and the nature and amount of the consideration each gave for the stock;

2) If it received other than money for its stock, the type of

property and its fair market value and adjusted basis in the shareholder's hands on the date the corporation received the property;

3) The stock certificates that represent stock issued under the plan;

4) The amount of money and the basis in its hands of other property received after June 30, 1958 (and before adoption of the plan for stock issued before November 7, 1978) for its stock, as a contribution to its capital, and as paid-in surplus;

5) If before November 7, 1978, its equity capital on the date the plan was adopted; and

6) Information relative to any tax-free stock dividend made with respect to its small business stock and any reorganization in which it rransferred its stock in exchange for its small business stock.

CASUALTY LOSS

A casualty is the complete or partial destruction or accidental and irretrievable loss of property resulting from an identifiable event of a sudden, unexpected, or unusual nature, such as an automobile collision, fire, flood, storm, hurricane, or other similar event. Even if a loss does not qualify as a casualty loss, if it is incurred in a trade or business or in a transaction entered into for profit it is generally deductible as a business loss.

Auto accidents are casualties and damages to a business automobile from a collision caused by the faulty driving of any driver or a person acting for the taxpayer are usually deductible losses if the collision was not caused by the willful act or willful negligence of the taxpayer. Ordinarily, if you have $100 deductible collision insurance, the amount that may be allowed cannot exceed $100, since the insurance company will pay all damages over $100.

Mine cave-in damage to your property is a casualty, and the loss is deductible.

Sonic boom damage from jet aircraft is deductible.

A loss from vandalism, caused by agencies outside your control, is deductible if the loss is sudden and destructive in effect.

Smog damage resulting from a severe, sudden and unexpected concentration of chemical fumes in the atmosphere is deductible as a casualty loss.

General decline in market value. The reduction in value of property because it is in or near an area that suffered a casualty and the area might again be subject to such an event is not deductible. A loss is allowed only for the actual physical damage to property resulting from the casualty.

Loss of potential profits from, for example, ice storm damage to merchantable trees that reduces the rate of growth or the quality of subsequent timber increment is not a deductible casualty loss. To qualify as a casualty the damage must actually result in existing timber being rendered unfit for use.

Progressive deterioration through a steadily operating cause, and damage from a normal process, is not a casualty loss. Thus, the steady weakening of a foundation by normal or usual wind and weather conditions is not a casualty loss. Cost of repairing the damage or of correcting the condition, however, may be either a business expense or a capital expenditure, depending upon all the facts. Such damage may also have an effect upon the useful life of the property, and on the salvage value used in computing the depreciation deduction.

Expenses incident to casualty, such as care of personal injuries and the cost of temporary lights, fuel, moving, or rental of temporary quarters are not a part of the casualty loss. However, if such expenses are incurred in connection with a casualty loss to business property the expenses may be business expenses.

Amount of loss. If your business property is completely destroyed, your deductible loss is the excess of the adjusted basis of the property over the total of any salvage value, insurance, or other compensation received or recoverable, from the loss.

In a partial destruction, the deductible loss is the amount of the decrease in value of the destroyed portion or the adjusted basis of the property, whichever is less, reduced by any insurance or other compensation received or recoverable.

A separate computation must be made for each individual identifiable property damaged or destroyed. Thus, if there is a casualty loss to a building and to trees used in a trade or business, both of which are a part of the same tract of real property, a separate loss must be determined for the building and for the trees.

If you are liable to a lessor for damage caused by casualty to leased property, the amount of your casualty loss is the amount you must pay to the lessor on account of the casualty, reduced by any insurance or other compensation you recover.

The value of the destroyed portion is the difference between the value of the property immediately before and immediately after the casualty. These values should be ascertained by competent appraisals. You may not deduct the cost of repairing, replacing, or cleaning up after the casualty unless it is a business expense.

However, repair costs may be a measure of the value of the destroyed portion of the property if:

1) They are necessary to restore the property to its precasualty condition;
2) The amount spent for repairs is not excessive;
3) They do no more than take care of the damage suffered; and
4) The value of the property after repairs is no more than its value before the casualty.

The cost of debris removal may be used, like the cost of repairs, as evidence of the amount of the casualty loss sustained, if these conditions are satisfied.

Expenditures for protection against future casualties, such as the cost of a dike to prevent future flooding, are not deductible but should be capitalized as permanent improvements.

Example 1. You owned a building used in your business, which cost you $50,000. Exclusive of the land, the building had a depreciated (adjusted) basis of $30,000 when it was partially destroyed by storm. The value immediately before the storm was $60,000 and the value immediately after was $40,000. Since the value of the destroyed portion, $60,000 less $40,000, or $20,000, is less than the adjusted basis, $30,000, the deductible loss is $20,000 less any insurance or other reimbursement received or expected to be received.

Example 2. If, in the above example, the value of the property after the storm had been only $25,000, the adjusted basis, $30,000, would have been less than the value of the destroyed portion ($60,000 less $25,000, or $35,000). In this case your deductible loss would be $30,000 less any insurance or other recovery received or expected to be received.

Federal loan canceled. The portion of a Federal disaster loan that was cancelable under the Disaster Relief Act of 1970 is considered other compensation for the loss. In general, the cancelable portion was the excess of the principal amount of the loan over $500, with a limit of $5,000 on the amount cancelable. This portion reduced your casualty loss deduction. If the loss was deducted for a previous year, the cancelable amount should be treated as discussed later.

Grants received under the Disaster Relief Act of 1974 are not includible in your gross income. However, no casualty loss or medical expense deduction will be permitted to the extent you are specifically reimbursed for such expenses by the grant.

Appraisals should be made by an experienced and reliable appraiser. The appraiser's knowledge of sales of comparable property and conditions in the area, knowledge of your property before and after the casualty, and method of ascertaining the amount of the loss are important elements for proving a casualty loss.

Automobiles. The so-called blue books issued periodically by various automobile organizations are useful in determining the value of motor vehicles. The amount offered for your vehicle as a trade-in on a new vehicle is not usually a measure of its true value.

The basis of property damage, or destroyed by a casualty must be reduced by the allowable loss deduction. The basis must be further reduced by any insurance or other compensation you receive.

Example 1. Your business truck is involved in an accident and, after appraisals have been made, you determine the loss to be $200. You carry $50 deductible insurance and receive $150 from the insurance company. Your deductible casualty loss is $50 ($200 less $150 insurance recovery). The basis of your truck must be reduced by your casualty loss, $50; and further reduced by the $150 of insurance received.

Example 2. Before being partially destroyed by fire, your building had an adjusted basis of $15,000. Its value was $30,000 just before the fire and $20,000 immediately after, and you collected $10,000 insurance. You have no casualty loss deduction since your recovery was equal to the value of the destroyed portion. The basis of your building is reduced by $10,000, the amount of recovery.

Of course, amounts paid or incurred to replace or restore property damaged or destroyed as a result of a casualty that are not business expenses are capital expenditures and should be added to the remaining basis of the property. These adjustments are required to determine your adjusted basis in the property.

Casualty losses are generally deductible only in the tax year in which the casualty occurred. This is true even though the damaged property may not be repaired or replaced until succeeding years. In cases where you are liable for casualty damage to leased property, you deduct your loss in the year you pay the damages to the lessor.

Election for disaster area losses. If you sustained any deductible loss from a disaster that occurred in an area subsequently determined by the President of the United States to warrant Federal disaster assistance you may elect to deduct that loss on your return for the immediately preceding tax year. If you make the election, the loss will be considered as having occurred in the preceding year.

The election must generally be made on or before the later of the due date (exclusive of extensions) for filing your income tax return for the tax year in which the disaster actually occurred, on the due date (*with* regard to extensions) for the return for the tax year immediately preceding the tax year in which the disaster actually occurred. Thus, in the absence of any extensions of time to file, a calendar-year individual taxpayer has until April 16, 1979, to amend his 1977 income tax return to claim a disaster loss which took place anytime during 1978.

The election, once made, becomes irrevocable 90 days after it is made. Reasonable extensions of time to change the election (not exceeding a total of 240 days beyond the original period to change an election) may be granted by Internal Revenue Service Regional Commissioners, District Directors, or Service Center Directors. A revocation of the election is not effective unless the credit or refund which resulted from the election is repaid within the revocation period (a revocation before receipt of the refund claimed is not effective unless the refund is repaid within 30 calendar days after receipt).

The election must be in writing and signed by you, and must be made on a return, an amended return, or a claim for refund. It should specify the date or dates of the disaster and the city, town, county, and State where the damaged or destroyed property was located.

Reimbursement. A deduction for a casualty loss will be denied to the extent that you failed to seek the reimbursement (for example insurance) that you would have been entitled to receive.

If a claim for reimbursement exists, the part of the loss covered by the claim is not deductible. But, if it can be ascertained with reasonable certainty that all or a part of the claim will not be received, the amount not receivable may be deducted for that year. Settlement, adjudication, or abandonment of the claim are examples of reasonable certainty as to the amount of the claim to be received.

Example 1. Your business automobile, having an adjusted basis of $1,500, was involved in a collision and sustained a casualty loss of $400. The car was fully insured for the loss, but because the accident was determined to be your fault you decided not to file a claim for recovery with your insurance company. Because you were entitled to recover the $400 loss from your insurance company, none of the loss may be taken as a deduction on your tax return. Your loss did not arise from the casualty, but rather from your election not to claim or receive insurance proceeds that you were entitled. Also, you cannot deduct the expenses to repair the accident damage if these expenses were otherwise reimbursable.

Example 2. Your business automobile, having a fair market value of $2,000 and an adjusted basis of $1,500, was completely destroyed in a collision with another car in 1978 as the result of negligence of the other driver. As of December 31, 1978, there was reasonable prospect that you would recover the total damages from the owner of the other car. You do not have a deductible loss in 1978. In January 1979 the court awards you a judgment of $2,000, but in July 1979 you can show with reasonable certainty that the other driver has nothing against which you can enforce your judgment. You may claim a $1,500 loss in 1979.

Example 3. You had business property with an adjusted basis of $10,000 completely destroyed by fire in 1978. Your only claim for reimbursement was an insurance claim for $8,000. You may claim a casualty loss deduction of $2,000 in 1978 since the most you could possibly have collected from your claim was $8,000. In 1979 the insurance company offered to settle your claim for $7,000 and you accepted the offer. In 1979 you may claim an additional deduction of $1,000, the excess of your total loss ($10,000 - $7,000 = $3,000) over the amount of the loss claimed in 1978.

Loss of Inventory. The manner of reporting a casualty or theft loss of inventory or items held for sale to customers will depend upon whether you have received or will recover any part of your loss from insurance or other reimbursement. If no recovery or other reimbursement is anticipated, the loss will be automatically reflected in cost of goods sold if your opening and closing inventories are properly reported. This loss should not be claimed again as a casualty loss. If you wish to show the loss separately, an offsetting credit either to opening inventory or to purchases is required.

If your inventory loss results from a natural disaster that has been declared as such by the President of the United States, you may elect to deduct the loss in the immediately preceding year; however, you must adjust the opening inventory for the year of the loss so that the loss will not be reflected again in inventories.

Insurance proceeds received in the year of the loss must be included in gross income if you reflect the loss in closing inventory. However, the recovery should not be included in gross income if you show the loss separately and offset the insurance against the loss. The insurance must be accounted for in your return. If the insurance is not received by the end of the year, you must remove the amount of the loss from cost of goods sold.

If your creditors forgive, in the year of the loss, part of what you owe them because of your inventory loss, this amount must be taken into account as income, or you must make appropriate adjustment to your cost of goods sold. If the indebtedness is not forgiven until after the year of loss, see *if you receive reimbursement for loss in a later year,* earlier in this chapter.

If your suppliers replace damaged or destroyed inventory items in the year of loss at no cost to you, no adjustments should be made. If replacement is made in a later year at no cost to you, see *if you receive reimbursement for loss in a later year.*

Proof of casualty loss. A deduction is allowed only for damages to or losses of property owned by you. You must substantiate the amount of any casualty loss and be prepared to submit evidence showing:

1) The nature of the casualty and when it occurred;
2) That the loss was the direct result of the casualty;
3) That you were the owner of the property, or were contractually liable to the owner of the property for damage to property leased to you;
4) The cost or other adjusted basis of the property, evidenced by purchase contract, checks, receipts, etc.;

5) The depreciation allowed or allowable, if any;
6) The values before and after the casualty (pictures and appraisals before and after the casualty are pertinent evidence); and
7) The amount of insurance or other compensation received or recoverable, including the value of repairs, restoration, and cleanup provided without cost by relief agencies.

THEFT LOSS

A theft is the unlawful taking and removing of your money or property with the intent to deprive you of it. It includes, but is not limited to, larceny, robbery, extortion, and embezzlement. Kidnapping for ransom, threats, or blackmail may be thefts. You must be able to show that the taking of your property was illegal under the law of the State where it occurred, and was done with criminal intent. The mere disappearance of money or property from your person, your home, or your place of business is not a theft. However, an accidental and irretrievable loss of property may qualify as a *casualty,* if it results from an identifiable event that is damaging to property and is sudden, unexpected, and unusual in nature.

The amount of the loss is the adjusted basis of the business property stolen, reduced by the total of any insurance or other compensation received or recoverable.

When loss is deductible. Losses arising from theft are generally deductible only in the year of discovery. You need only prove that there was a theft and the year in which you discovered the property was stolen. You do not have to prove when it was stolen.

If a claim for reimbursement exists, your loss resulting from theft will be reported in the same manner as explained earlier for casualty losses.

Proof of loss of stolen or embezzled property, is substantially the same as described previously for casualty losses.

A theft of nonbusiness property is deductible only to the extent that the loss exceeds $100.

PROPERTY PARTLY BUSINESS AND PARTLY NONBUSINESS

If you own property that you use partly for for business or for production of income, and partly for personal purposes, loss from a casualty or theft must be allocated on the basis of its use. The loss must be computed as though two separate pieces of property were stolen, damaged, or destroyed—one business and the other personal. The amount of loss to be taken into account in computing the deductible loss on property used for personal purposes that is destroyed is the lesser of the decrease in the fair market value or the adjusted basis reduced by insurance or other recovery.

However, the first $100 of the total loss from each casualty or theft of property used for personal purposes is not deductible.

Example. You use half of your house in your business and the other half as your residence. In January it was completely destroyed by fire. Your insurance recovery in full settlement of the loss was $21,000. Your cost basis in the entire house was $25,000, allocable equally to the business and personal parts, and you had claimed depreciation deductions of $1,500 on the business part.

The adjusted basis of the business part is $11,000 (½ of $25,000 less $1,500 depreciation); the loss is $11,000 less $10,500 (½ of the $21,000 insurance recovery), or $500. The $500 loss on the business part is included along with other gains and losses from *Section 1231 Property,* discussed later.

Assuming that the basis of the house attributable to the personal use (½ of $25,000, or $12,500) was less than the fair market value, the loss on the residential portion is $12,500 minus $10,500 (½ of the $21,000 insurance recovery), or $2,000. The first $100 is nondeductible. Therefore, you may deduct $1,900 if treatment as a deduction results after you include it along with other gains and losses from *section 1231* property.

SECTION 1231 PROPERTY

Property used in a trade or business or held for the production of rents or royalties and held more than one year for tax years beginning after 1977, and any other property (including capital assets) held more than one year for tax years beginning after 1977 that is subjected to an involuntary conversion, is known as section 1231 property. In a disposition of depreciable property, ordinary gain attributable to depreciation is determined first according to rules discussed earlier. Any remaining gain is included in the section 1231 computation.

Under certain circumstances, you may elect to defer recognition of all or part of a gain from an involuntary conversion.

The following transactions may result in gain or loss from section 1231 property:

1) Sales and exchanges of real property or depreciable personal property used in a trade or business and held for more than one year,

2) Sales and exchanges of property held for the production of rents or royalties if held for more than one year,

3) Sales and exchanges of leaseholds used in a trade or business and held for more than one year,

4) Sales and exchanges of cattle and horses acquired after 1969 for draft, breeding, dairy or sporting purposes and held for 24 months or more;

5) Sales and exchanges of livestock (except cattle, horses, and poultry) acquired after 1969 for draft, breeding, dairy or sporting purposes and held for 12 months or more;

6) An unharvested crop on land used in farming if the crop and land are sold, exchanged, or involuntarily converted at the same time and to the same person, and the land has been held for more than one year—growing crops sold with a lease on the land, even though to the same person in the same transaction, are not included. Nor is a sale, exchange, or involuntary conversion of an unharvested crop with land included if the taxpayer retains any right or option to reacquire the land, directly or indirectly (other than a right customarily incident to a mortgage or other security transaction);

7) Timber, coal, or domestic iron ore;

8) Property condemned for public use, if it was held for more than one year (This includes business property, and capital assets such as investment property and nonbusiness property. However, since losses from the condemnation of property held for personal use are not deductible, they are not included); and

9) Casualty and theft gains and losses on property held over one year. These include casualties and thefts of nonbusiness property (such as your car or residence, but in case of a loss only the excess over $100), business property, property held for the production of rents and royalties, and investment property (such as notes and bonds). Insurance proceeds or other reimbursement must be taken into account in arriving at the net gain or loss.

INVOLUNTARY EXCHANGES, INCLUDING CONDEMNATIONS

If you have a gain resulting from an involuntary exchange, you may elect to postpone paying tax on all or part of the gain even though the involuntary exchange may not necessarily qualify as a casualty.

An involuntary exchange occurs when your property or part of it is destroyed, stolen, requisitioned, or condemned for public use and other property or money, such as insurance or a condemnation award, is received in payment.

Condemnation is the exercise under the legal power of a Federal Government, a State government, or a political subdivision or instrumentality to take privately owned property for public use upon award and payment of a reasonable price. You have an involuntary exchange if your property is sold or exchanged either under a threat or imminence of condemnation or after the condemnation actually occurs.

Threat or imminence of condemnation exists when you are informed, either orally or in writing by a representative of a governmental body or public official authorized to acquire property for public use, that the body or official has decided to acquire your property, and you have reasonable grounds to believe from that information that steps to condemn will be instituted if you do not sell voluntarily. It also exists if, after you are formally advised by a governmental body of its decision to acquire your property by condemnation if necessary, you sell your property to a designated private nonprofit association that is cooperating in the acquisition of your property for public use for eventual resale to the governmental body.

Also threat or imminence of condensation applies when you learn of a decision to acquire your property for public use through a report in a newspaper or other news medium, provided you get confirmation of the published report from a representative of the governmental body or public official involved and the confirmation gives you reasonable grounds for believing that steps to condemn will be instituted if you do not sell voluntarily. The Internal Revenue Service may ask you to get written confirmation of any oral statement by government representatives or public officials upon which you relied.

To have reasonable grounds to believe that condemnation will occur if you do not sell voluntarily, you must know the identity of the condemning authority. Assume, for example, that the condemning authority is a public utility which, although it does not have intrinsic legal authority, generally can readily obtain the power to condemn by applying to the appropriate State official. You would have reasonable grounds to believe that condemnation will occur if you do not sell voluntarily if, during negotiations prior to the sale, the representative informs you of the imminence of condemnation and also reveals the identity of the condemning authority. However, you would not have reasonable grounds to believe that condemnation will occur in the absence of a voluntary sale if, during negotiations prior to the sale, the representative does not identify the condemning authority. This will be the case whether or not the representative also indicates that your property will be condemned if you do not sell voluntarily.

Building not fit for human use. Sale of a building because the health department declares it to be unfit for human use is not an involuntary exchange.

Tax sale. The sale of your real estate by a taxing authority to satisfy a lien for delinquent taxes is not a condemnation of private property for public use.

Property voluntarily sold by you may receive, in certain situations, involuntary conversion treatment. This treatment is permitted only where all facts and circumstances show a *substantial economic relationship* between this property and condemned property, so that together they constituted one economic property unit. In addition, you must show the unavailability of suitable nearby property of a like kind to that condemned, which would permit you to continue operations on the property retained after the condemnation.

Property not owned by the same taxpayer, even though it otherwise bears a very close economic relationship to property that was condemned, will not be permitted involuntary conversion treatment.

Example. Assume that X Corporation rented its manufacturing plant from your father and an adjacent warehouse building from you. Your father owns 51% of X's stock and the remainder is owned equally by you and your brother. During the year, your father sold his building under threat of condemnation and you sold your building because the entire business had to be relocated. Your voluntary sale is not permitted treatment as an involuntary exchange because, even though they bore a close economic relationship to one another, the two properties were owned by different taxpayers.

Easements. If you grant a perpetual easement under condemnation or threat of condemnation, giving up any beneficial use of the property but retaining legal title, you are considered to have disposed of a property interest. If the perpetual easement is over part of the property, a part of the basis of the entire property is allocated to the affected portion. Gain or loss on a perpetual easement is computed in the same manner as on a sale of the property, and is subject to the rules discussed in this chapter. Thus, the tax on gain may be postponed by acquiring replacement property within the replacement period.

Example. The Department of Agriculture is authorized to acquire any lands or interest in lands for the protection of the historic, cultural, and scenic values of an area. It informed you in writing that unless you were able to agree voluntarily upon terms for the sale of a scenic easement over your property, condemnation proceedings would be initiated. In conveying the scenic easement, you gave up a beneficial use of the property (the government had the right to control the use of the land to protect its aesthetic values); therefore, you disposed of a real property interest under the threat or imminence of condemnation.

DETERMINING GAIN OR LOSS

You will realize a gain or an involuntary exchange, if the net proceeds are more than the adjusted basis of the converted property. You will realize a loss if the net proceeds are less than the adjusted basis of the property; however, in the case of a casualty or theft, a loss is incurred if the net proceeds are less than the decrease in its fair market value and if that decrease is less than the adjusted basis. Gain or loss on the total destruction of business property is determined by comparing the amount of compensation received with the adjusted basis of the property, without taking into account fair market value.

Example. You own a rental building with an adjusted basis of $25,000 but a fair market value of only $20,000. The property is condemned by the State for a highway project. If you receive compensation of more than $25,000, you would realize a gain. You would sustain a loss if you receive compensation of less than $25,000.

Net proceeds means money plus the value of unlike property received, less expenses incurred in obtaining them.

Proceeds from sale of property (not under threat of condemnation) damaged or destroyed by casualty are not the result of a *direct conversion* into money or unlike property. Such amounts, therefore, are not net proceeds in exchange for the converted property. For example, a hurricane uproots a large number of trees on timberland that you own. You sell the damaged timber at a gain and use the proceeds to purchase other standing timber. In such a situation you must report the entire gain on the sale in the year realized. If, on the other hand, you receive insurance proceeds for the damaged timber and use these proceeds to buy replacement property, you may elect to postpone tax on the gain. The insurance proceeds are received as a direct result of the involuntary conversion, whereas the sale proceeds are not.

Condemnation award is the amount of money you are paid or the value of other property you receive for your property that is condemned, or the amount you are paid as the result of a sale of your property under the threat or imminence of condemnation.

Use and occupancy, and business interruption insurance proceeds, which are reimbursing you for lost profits or interest and which are included in a condemnation award, are *not* proceeds from the conversion of property. They must be reported as ordinary income.

The use of any part of the proceeds to pay off the mortgage or other liens on the old property does not reduce the proceeds received. Such a payment is neither an expense, nor an investment in replacement property.

Example. Your property was condemned under State power of eminent domain, and the State awarded you $200,000 for the property, which had a basis of $100,000 in your hands. You received $150,000, and $50,000 was paid directly to a holder of a mortgage for which you were not personally liable. You have a $100,000 gain. The $50,000 paid on the mortgage is considered a part of the award you received, even though it was not paid directly to you and the mortgage was not your personal liability, but was attached to the property.

Lump-sum proceeds received for assets simultaneously involuntarily exchanged must be allocated among the assets according to their respective fair market values at the time of exchange, and separate computations must be made of the gain or loss for each asset having a separately identifiable basis.

Severance damages are compensation in addition to an award for the property condemned, paid to the owner because part of the property is condemned and the value of the remaining part is decreased as a result of the condemnation. Severance damages may be paid, for example, because of impairment of access to or flooding or erosion of the property retained, or because the owner must replace fences, dig new wells or ditches, or plant trees to restore the retained property to its former use.

Severance damages should be designated as such by both contracting parties. When it is not clearly shown that the award includes a specific amount as severance damages, it will be presumed that the proceeds were given in consideration of the property taken by the condemning authority.

Example. You transferred part of your property to the State under threat of condemnation. In determining the total award, you and the condemning authority considered severance damages to residual land. The contract signed by both parties showed only the total award to be paid to you, and did not specify a fixed sum for severance damages. However, when the condemning authority paid you the award, it gave you closing papers that clearly showed the part of the award stipulated as severance damages. The preceding requirements are considered to have been met, and you may treat the amount specified in the closing papers as having been paid by the condemning authority for severance damages.

You may not make an after-the-fact unilateral allocation of the damages. However, you may show the actual apportionment to the severance damages contemplated by the parties. The portion of the total award representing severance damages is a fact to be determined from all the circumstances. Severance damages may be shown even if the award makes no allocation.

Treatment of severance damages. Severance damages first must be reduced by expenses incurred in securing them, and then by any special assessment levied against the part of the property retained, and withheld from the award by the condemning authority. Expenses necessary to restore the retained property to its former use may be, under certain circumstances, considered *Replacement Property* (as defined later) and you may elect to offset these expenses against the amount of the severance damages received. This same treatment can result if you expended the severance damages, together with other money received for the property condemned, to acquire adjacent property that will permit you to continue business operations. If such suitable nearby property is unavailable and you are forced to sell the retained property and relocate in order to continue operations, see *Property voluntarily* sold, earlier.

If there is a balance of severance damages remaining, it is used to reduce the basis of the retained property. Any excess of this balance of severance damages over the basis of the retained property must be reported as a gain in your income tax return for the year in which it is realized. If the severance award is based on damages to a specific portion of the retained property, only the basis allocable to that portion is reduced by the severance damages received.

Consequential damages, and awards of a similar nature, are paid to you because of damages caused by improvements made by a State, city, or other public body, but which involve no actual taking of your property. These damages are awarded for the same reasons as severance damages, such as impairment of access, flooding, or erosion of property, and are treated in the same manner as severance damages.

Relocation and replacement housing payments received under the Housing and Community Development Act of 1974 (or previous Acts) by persons displaced from their homes, businesses, or farms as a result of Federal or Federally-assisted programs are not income, nor are they part of the condemnation award. The payments are taken into account as part of the displaced person's cost of the newly acquired property and are includible in the basis of that property.

You may elect, or you may be required, to postpone paying tax on all or part of the gain realized from an involuntary exchange. See *Postponement of Tax on Gain,* following. If you decide not to make the election, or if you suffered a loss, the gain or loss will be reported in the usual manner. You may have either a capital gain or loss or ordinary income or loss.

Losses by individuals from condemnations of assets not held by investment nor used in a trade or business are nondeductible personal expenses. Therefore, a loss on a condemnation of property held for personal use (such as a personal residence) is not deductible.

POSTPONEMENT OF TAX ON GAIN

If you realized a gain from an involuntary exchange you may elect in some cases to postpone paying tax on all or part of the gain.

Like kind property received. If you receive reimbursement from the condemning authority in the form of property of a like kind to that condemned, or similar or related in service or use, you do not report any gain on the transaction. Your basis for the new property is the same as your basis in the property condemned. This rule would apply if, for example, the condemning authority gave you another piece of real estate in lieu of money for your condemned real estate. You would have no election in this case; but such situations are rare. In the usual case you receive money from the condemning authority, and must acquire replacement property during the replacement period in order to postpone tax on gain.

Money or unlike property received. When you receive money, including insurance proceeds, or unlike property such as State bonds issued for property condemned, you are ordinarily required to report the gain. However, under certain circumstances you may elect not to report the gain and thus defer the payment of the tax. To do this you must purchase, within a specified replacement period, replacement property the cost of which equals or exceeds the net proceeds received from the involuntary exchange.

If the replacement property costs less than your net proceeds from the involuntary exchange, your gain must be included in income to the extent of the unexpended portion. Part or all of this gain may be ordinary gain attributable to depreciation.

Example. A building used in your business, having an adjusted basis of $9,000, was totally destroyed by fire. During that year you received $11,000 from the insurance company and immediately spent $9,500 to replace the destroyed building.

You realized a gain of $2,000 from the destruction of the old building. Since $1,500 of the insurance proceeds were not spent for its replacement you must report $1,500 in your gross income. You may elect not to report the other $500 of gain. If you had spent only $8,500 you would have been required to report the entire gain of $2,000, since the unexpected portion of the insurance proceeds would have been more than your gain.

REPLACEMENT PROPERTY

When you receive money or unlike property for property involuntarily exchanged, ordinarily you must report the entire gain on the transaction unless (for the specific purpose of replacing the old property) you:
1) Purchase replacement property similar or related in service or use to the old property;
2) Purchase a controlling interest in a corporation owning property similar or related in service or use to the old property; or
3) Purchase like-kind property to replace real property that was used in business or for rental or investment and was condemned or sold under threat of condemnation.

You must purchase the replacement property. Property or stock you acquire by gift or inheritance does not qualify. The identical proceeds received by you for the old property do not have to be used to acquire the replacement property.

Advance payment to a contractor for construction of replacement property is not the purchase of replacement property. You will not be considered as having acquired the replacement property unless the construction is complete before the expiration of the replacement period.

Similar or related in service or use for an owner-user means that the property must be functionally the same as the old property. This is the functional use test. Thus, a business vehicle must be replaced by a business vehicle and the replacement must perform the same function.

Similar or related in service or use for a lessor whose property is involuntarily exchanged pertains primarily to the relationship

of the services or uses that the old and replacement properties
have to the lessor.

You, the lessor, must determine:

1) Whether the properties are of similar service to you;
2) The nature of the business risks connected with the properties; and
3) What these properties demand of you in the way of management, service, and relations to your tenants.

Example. You owned land and a building that you rented to
a manufacturing company. The building was completely destroyed by fire and, during the replacement period, you constructed a new building on other land already owned and rented
it out for use as a wholesale grocery warehouse. Since the replacement property also is rental property, the two properties
will be considered similar on related in service or use provided
there is a similarity in your management activities, in the amount
and kind of services that you render to your tenants, and in the
nature of your business risks connected with the properties.

Similar or related in service or use for a lessee. If you received
an award in consideration of a lease you gave up in a condemnation (or under threat of condemnation), you may elect to
postpone tax on the gain you realized if you purchase replacement property within the required replacement period. You
will be considered to have purchased replacement property if
you purcahse a leasehold similar or related in service or use to
the lease you gave up. To qualify, you must actually reinvest
the proceeds in a leasehold, rather than merely enter into a
lease agreement.

Example. You leased improved real property that you used
in your business of manufacturing machine parts. The property
was condemned for public use and the public authority awarded
you $50,000 as damages for the loss of your lease. You were
able to locate improved real property suitable for use in your
business, on which the Smith Investment Company held a lease.
You purcahsed the unexpired portion of the lease from the
Smith Investment Company for $50,000. The purchase of the
leasehold qualifies as replacement property.

Construction, on land you own (or acquire after the condemnation), of new buildings that are used to carry on the
same business as that for which the old leasehold was used, will
qualify as replacement property.

Example. Assume that in the previous example you were not able to locate other improved real property suitable for use in your business, and you purchased unimproved land and constructed new buildings on it at a total cost of $50,000 for use in carrying on the same business of manufacturing machine parts. The new land and buildings qualify as replacement property.

Stock as replacement property. If your property is involuntarily exchanged, and you purchase a controlling interest in a corporation owning property that is similar or related in service or use to the old property, the purchase will meet the requirements of replacement property. The purchase, however, of a controlling interest in such a corporation owning like-kind property will not meet the requirements of the special rule where the old property is real property used in business or for rental or investment, as explained later.

The cost of such stock must equal or exceed the proceeds from the old property for you to postpone the tax on all of your gain.

Controlling interest, as used here, means the ownership of stock possessing at least 80% of the total combined voting power of all classes of stock entitled to vote, and at least 80% of the total number of shares of all other classes of stock of the corporation.

REAL PROPERTY USED IN BUSINESS OR FOR RENTAL OR INVESTMENT

Special rules apply to the replacement of real property used in your trade or business, or held for the production of income or for investment, which is involuntarily exchanged as a result of seizure, requisition, condemnation, or sale under the threat of condemnation. These special rules do not apply to stock in trade or other property held primarily for sale or to the acquisition of a controlling interest in a corporation.

If the condemned property is replaced within the replacement period by other real property of a like-kind that may be used in your trade or business or held for the production of income or for investment, the tax on the gain may be postponed as already described even though the property is not similar or related in service or use to the old property. On the other hand, the fact that replacement property is not like-kind does not preclude you from showing that the replacement property is actually similar or related in service or use to the property converted.

Outdoor advertising displays as real property. You may make an irrevocable election to treat qualifying outdoor advertising displays as real property, provided that no investment credit or additional first-year depreciation is, or has been, claimed against this property. The election applies to tax years beginning after 1970. An outdoor advertising display is a rigidly assembled sign, display, or device permanently affixed to the ground or permanently attached to a building or other inherently permanent structure constituting or used for the display of, a commercial or other advertisement to the public.

Like-kind property generally means real property, and it does not matter whether the property you gave up, or the property you acquired, is improved or unimproved. However, in considering the like-kind test, although the term real estate often is used to embrace land and improvements on it, land and improvements are by nature not alike merely because one term is used to describe both.

The following qualify as like kind property if they are held for use in business or for the production of income:

1) Easements;
2) Rights-of-way;
3) Leasehold for a term of 30 years or more (the term includes the initial term of the lease and all optional renewal periods);
4) Perpetual water rights, if they are considered real property rights under applicable state law; and
5) Any similar continuing interests in real property.

Example 1. You owned unimproved property on which you planned to build warehouses for use in your business. The unimproved property was condemned before the warehouses were built. You purchased improved real property on which there were located a garage, a service station, and automobile salesrooms that you could hold for rental purposes. The purchase of improved real estate to replace unimproved real estate is not a replacement of property that is similar or related in service or use. But since the property purchased was of a like-kind (held for the production of income), it qualifies as replacement property for the election.

Example 2. Assume that in Example 1 the proceeds of the condemnation had been used to buy the stock of a corporation owning the property on which the garage, service station, and salesrooms were located. The stock would not qualify as replacement property and any gain would have to be included in your income for the year in which the gain was realized.

Example 3. Unimproved land that you held for investment was condemned. You used the proceeds of the condemnation to construct an office building to be held for investment on another site that you already owned. The building constructed on land you already owned does not qualify as replacement property (land and improvements are not alike) and accordingly, any gain would have to be included in income for the year in which it was realized.

Example 4. The State condemned a portion of your land upon which your manufacturing plant was situated. The condemned portion had been used as a storage area for your products and also contained a garage that housed the delivery trucks. You received an award for the condemned property, of which none was compensation for damages to the portion of the property that you retained.

Because of the prohibitive cost of acquiring land in the area suitable for storage, you used part of the proceeds of the condemnation award to rearrange the layout of the plant facilities on the remainder of your land to create a new storage area. You used the rest of the award to build a new garage to house the delivery trucks on a small plot of land you owned nearby.

To the extent that you used the condemnation proceeds to restore the plant site so it could be used in the same manner as it was used before the condemnation, it qualifies as replacement property. The garage also qualifies as replacement property.

Property used partly for business. If real property used for both business and personal purposes is condemned, you must allocate the condemnation award to the business and personal portions for the purpose of reinvesting in qualified replacement property.

Example. The authorities condemn your real property, comprising both your residence and your business. On the basis of fair marekt values, the condemnation award is allocated 35% to the portion of the real estate used as a residence and 65% to the portion used for business. To postpone tax on gain resulting from the condemnation, you must reinvest at least 35% of the award in another residence and at least 65% of the award in real estate to be used for business or investment.

If you elect to postpone tax on gain, you must reduce the cost or basis of the replacement property by the amount of gain not taxed.

REPLACEMENT BY OTHER THAN TAXPAYER

The election to postpone tax on gain by acquiring qualified replacement property must be made by the taxpayer who realizes the gain. Thus, if property owned by a partnership or corporation is involuntarily converted, it is the partnership or corporation that must make the election and that must acquire replacement property during the replacement period. The acquisition of replacement property by an individual partner or shareholder does not qualify.

If a taxpayer dies before acquiring replacement property, the entire gain must be reported for the year in which the decedent realized it. The tax on gain from an involuntary exchange may not be postponed by the acquisition of replacement property by the executor of the estate or any person succeeding to the funds derived from the involuntary exchange. An amended return for the year in which the gain was realized may be necessary if the individual had elected to postpone tax on the gain, but died before acquiring the replacement property.

REPLACEMENT PERIOD

To postpone tax on any or all of the gain, you must purchase replacement property within the replacement period.

The replacement period begins, in the case of a casualty or theft, on the date your property was damaged, destroyed, or stolen.

If you elect to postpone tax on the gain from a condemnation, or other disposition of property because of a threat or imminence of condemnation, the replacement period begins on the date of the disposition of the converted property or the date of the beginning of threat or imminence of condemnation, whichever is earlier.

The replacement period ends, in the case of a casualty or theft, or of a condemnation of personal property or of real property held for personal use, 2 years after the close of the first year in which any part of the gain upon the conversion is realized.

Business or investment real property. If a condemnation occurs after 1974, the replacement period for real property (other than inventory) held for productive use in a trade or business or for investment ends 3 years after the close of the first tax year in which any part of the gain resulting from the disposition of the condemned property is realized. However, if condemnation proceedings were begun before October 4, 1976, the replacement period for this type of real property ends 2 years after the close of the first tax year in which any part of the gain is realized.

Example 1. You were notified by the State on March 1, 1975, of its intention to acquire your investment real property by negotiation, or condemnation if necessary. On May 1, 1976, the State paid you the full amount for the property as a result of a negotiated settlement between you and the State. No condemnation proceedings were ever started by the State. Since the property was disposed of after 1974 and no condemnation proceeding began before October 4, 1976, you are entitled to a 3 year replacement period which would end on December 31, 1979.

Example 2. The facts are the same as in Example 1 except that you and the State could not negotiate a settlement, which resulted in the State filing a condemnation suit in order to acquire your property. The suit was settled in court May 1, 1976, and you received full payment for your property on May 15, 1976. Since the condemnation proceeding began before October 4, 1976, you are only entitled to a 2 year replacement period, regardless of the fact that the property was disposed of after 1974. Your replacement period would end on December 31, 1978.

Example 3. You are a calendar-year tax-payer. You were notified by the city council on December 1, 1978, of its intention to acquire your real property (used in your business) by negotiation or condemnation, if necessary. On June 1, 1979, when the property had an adjusted basis of $40,000 to you, the city converted the property to its use and paid you $50,000. The replacement period started on December 1, 1978, the date that you were notified of the intention to condemn the property. Since you did not dispose of the property until 1979, the replacement period ends on December 31, 1982, 3 years after the last day of the year in which the gain was realized.

If replacement property is acquired before the involuntary exchange, but after there is a threat or imminence of condemnation, the benefits are available, provided you still hold the replacement property at the time of the actual exchange. If property is acquired before there is a threat or imminence of condemnation, it will not qualify as replacement property acquired within the replacement period even if you still hold it at the time of the actual conversion

An extension of the replacement period may be granted if you apply to the Internal Revenue Service office or Service Center where you filed the tax return containing your election. The application should be made before the expiration of the replacement period, and should contain all the details concerning the need for the extension. You may file an application within a reasonable time after the replacement period expires if you can show reasonable cause for the delay. No extension will be granted unless you can show reasonable cause for not making the replacement within the regular period.

MAKING THE ELECTION

All details in connection with a condemnation or other inventory exchange of property at a gain should be reported in the tax return for the tax year in which the gain is realized. If you elect to postpone the tax on the gain, the election should be indicated on your return.

If replacement property is acquired before your return is filed, and you elect to report the gain only to the extent of the unexpended portion of the proceeds, you must attach a statement to your return showing the amount realized from the involuntary exchange, your computation of the gain, and any gain to be reported. If you did not spend an amount at least equal to the proceeds in acquiring the replacement property and if you do not intend to do so within the specified replacement period, you must report in your income the part of the unexpended proceeds that represent gain.

If the cost of the replacement property equals or exceeds the amount realized on the involuntary exchange, you are not required to recognize the gain and you may postpone paying tax on that gain.

If replacement property is to be acquired after your return is filed, you still may elect to postpone tax on the gain from the involuntary exchange. In this case, you must attach a statement to your return showing all the facts relating to the involuntary exchange, including your computation of the gain. You also must state that you elect to replace the old property within the required replacement period.

When the replacement property is acquired, a second statement containing the detailed information on the replacement property should be attached to the return for the year in which the replacement is made.

If the replacement property is not acquired within the required replacement period, or if the replacement is made at a cost less than the proceeds received from the involuntary exchange, you must file an amended return for the tax year for which the election was made.

You may change your election. If you have filed your return and paid the tax on the gain, you still may elect to postpone the tax, provided the replacement period has not expired. To do so, you should file a claim for refund for the year the gain was taxed.

Election to report the entire gain. If you do not wish to replace the converted property or wish to replace it but would still like to pay tax on the entire gain in the tax year in which it is realized, you should report the gain in the usual manner.

ESTATES AND TRUSTS

Capital gains and losses of a trust are normally taxable to the grantor, if the income of the trust is taxable to him. Even though the income is not taxable to him, when the grantor retains a reversionary interest in the corpus (as under a short-term trust) capital gains will be taxable to the grantor in the year realized by the trust when applicable state law requires such capital gains to be added to the trust corpus. Presumably, capital gains would also be taxable to the grantor if the terms of the instrument require that they be added to the principal.

Capital gains of an estate or trust (except as previously set forth) are normally includable in the gross income of the estate or trust. However, when capital gains are:

1) Allocated to income under the terms of the governing instrument or local law, or

2) Allocated to corpus but acutally distributed to benficiaries during the taxable year, or

3) Used (pursuant to the terms of the governing instrument or the practice followed by the fiduciary) in determining the amount which is distributed or required to be distributed, the capital gains will be taxed to the beneficiaries.

Capital losses of an estate or trust are deductible only by the estate or trust with certain exceptions: (1) if the estate or trust would be entitled to a capital loss deduction in a taxable year subsequent to the year of termination but for the termination, the deduction will be allowed to the beneficiaries succeeding to the property; (2) if the income of the trust is taxable to the grantor, capital losses are deductible by him.

With certain exceptions for property acquired prior to January 1, 1921, the basis for computing the amount of gain or loss and the period held is as follows:

The capital gain or loss incurred by an estate on assets from a decedent is measured by the difference between the sale price and the value of such asset on date of death. If acquired after decedent's death, the measure is the difference between the cost on date of acquisition (or the adjusted basis) and the sale price. Similarly, the date of death or of later acquisition is used in determining the period held – in order to establish whether the transaction was short-term or long-term.

As to a trust, the capital gain or loss on property received from the grantor is determined as though the sale were made by the grantor (i.e., the trust takes the grantor's basis, both as to amount of gain or loss and for determining period held). As to property acquired by the trust by purchase, the difference between the sale price and the cost to the trustee (or adjusted basis) is the gain or loss; and the time from date of purchase is the period held.

Capital gains and losses, when taxable to an estate or trust, are taxed in the same manner as for individuals.

Capital gains can be very significant in tax shelters such as real estate, oil and gas exploration, farming and timber, and cattle breeding. Some counselors will not permit a client to invest in a tax shelter unless the tax consequence is capital gain. The high-tax-bracket investor generally avoids ordinary income in investments.

CHAPTER THREE

DEPRECIATION, AMORTIZATION, DEPLETION, AND INVESTMENT CREDIT

Some tax shelters exist because of the write-offs available from depreciation, amortization, depletion, and investment credit. These write-offs reduce the taxable income of the taxpayer.

DEPRECIATION

The basis of a building or other tangible and intangible property is recovered by deductions for depreciation. If income-producing property or property used in a trade or business has a limited useful life that can be determined or reasonably estimated, you may deduct its cost or other basis over its useful life. The cost of property with a useful life of more than one year, such as buildings, furniture, machinery, copyrights, patents, and oil wells, may not be deducted entirely in one year.

Ordinarily, you cannot depreciate an asset that does not have a limited useful life, such as land or goodwill.

Each year you may deduct, as depreciation, a reasonable allowance for the exhaustion, wear and tear, and obsolescence of *depreciable property* used in your trade or business or held for the production of income. This enables you to recover your cost or other basis of depreciable property during its estimated useful life. There are several methods of computing depreciation. No asset may be depreciated below a reasonable salvage value (defined later) under any method.

Generally, if your depreciable property is sold, exchanged, or involuntarily converted and if a gain is realized, all or a portion of the gain may be treated as ordinary income.

Tax preference items for the minimum tax include: a portion of accelerated depreciation on real property, a portion of accelerated depreciation on leased personal property, depletion in excess of property's cost or other basis, and excess amortization of pollution control facilities.

528

Various parts of the following discussion may not apply to taxpayers who elect the Class Life Asset Depreciation Range (CLADR) System or the Class Life (CL) System.

DEPRECIABLE PROPERTY

The kind of property on which you ordinarily may claim the depreciation deduction is property with a useful life of more than one year. Examples are buildings, machinery, equipment and trucks.

Must be for business. The depreciation deduction is allowed only for property you use in a trade or business or hold for the production of income. You may not deduct depreciation on property that you and your family use as your personal residence, on your automobile used solely for pleasure or for commuting, or other items used in a similar manner.

If property is used for both business and personal purposes, depreciation is deductible only to the extent that the property is used in your business.

Property held primarily for sale to customers or property that is properly includible in your inventory is not depreciable property used in your business. If you look to the sale of property for the recovery of most, or substantially all, of your investment and not to its consumption through use in your business operations, it is not depreciable property used in your business.

Containers generally are includible in inventory. However, large durable containers, used to ship your products, may be depreciable if they have a life in excess of one year, if they qualify as property used in your business, and if title to them does not pass to the buyer. Factors to be considered are your retention of title as indicated by the sales contract, sales invoice, or acknowledgement of order; and their treatment as separate items on the invoice; and their proper recording of basis in your records.

If deposits on containers are required, your gain or loss because customers fail to return them is ordinary income or loss.

Professional libraries are depreciable if their value will diminish. The cost of technical books, journals, and services that have a usefulness of one year or less is deducted as business expense.

Depreciation on equipment used to construct your own capital improvements is not deductible as an expense. The depreciation allowable for the period of construction must be added to the cost basis of the improvements.

Repairs and replacements. You may deduct, as an expense, the cost of incidental repairs that maintain the property in efficient operating condition, if they do not materially add to the value of the property or appreciably prolong its life. Any expenditure for replacements that arrest deterioration or appreciably prolong the life of the property should either be capitalized and depreciated or charged against the depreciation reserve.

Expenses for the removal of architectural and transportation barriers for the handicapped and elderly. For tax years beginning after 1976 and before 1980, you may elect to currently deduct the cost of the removal of architectural and transportation barriers for the handicapped and elderly. If you do not make this election the cost must be capitalized and depreciated over the useful life of the property.

Tangible property. You may deduct depreciation on tangible property only to the extent that it is subject to wear and tear, to decay or decline from natural causes, to exhaustion, and to obsolescence. Buildings may be depreciated; land may not.

Intangible property. If an intangible asset used in your business has a limited period of usefulness, it may be depreciated. Your unsupported opinion is not sufficient to establish that fact, but your experience and other factors may be used in the determination. All supporting information should be shown on your tax return.

Straight-line method of depreciation must be used for intangible property.

The additional first-year depreciation deduction, discussed later, may not be claimed on intangible property.

Patents and copyrights are examples of intangible property subject to depreciation. The period of usefulness is ordinarily the life granted by the Government for the patent or copyright. If a patent or copyright becomes valueless in any year before it expires, your unrecovered cost or other basis may be deducted in that tax year. No accounting for salvage value is required for a patent or copyright.

Franchises, designs, drawings, and patterns are intangible assets, and, in some instances, you may deduct a pro rata part of their cost or other basis over their life.

Assets, such as customer and subscriptions lists, location contracts, and insurance expirations may be depreciable, if they are recognizable and distinguishable from goodwill. A factual determination must be made that these types of assets have an ascertainable value, separate and distinct from goodwill, and have a limited useful life of which the duration can be ascertained with reasonable accuracy. If both of these facts exist and are determined properly, the value may be depreciated. No deduction, however, is allowable merely because a basis for the asset and a limited useful life have been estimated in the unsupported view of the taxpayer.

NONDEPRECIABLE PROPERTY

Inventories and stock in trade, automobiles used solely for pleasure purposes or for commuting, and a building used only as a residence are never subject to an allowance for depreciation.

Land is never subject to an allowance for depreciation. Also, the costs of clearing land, grading, planting, and landscaping generally are not depreciable since they are part of the cost of land.

The cost of streets, curbs, sidewalks, sewers, and water mains turned over to a local government and dedicated to public use is not depreciable.

Goodwill is an intangible asset that is not subject to depreciation.

Trademarks and trade names usually have an indefinite life, and the purchase price of such intangible property is not deductible, depreciable, or amortizable.

LEASED PROPERTY

Property that is leased is never subject to an allowance for depreciation by the lessee (tenant). Payments under the lease may be deducted as expenses.

Improvements by the lessee, ordinarily are subject to an allowance for depreciation or amortization by the lessee.

Improvements by lessor. Capital expenditures made by a lessor (landlord) for the erection of buildings or other improvements subject to depreciation allowances must be recovered as depreciation deductions over the useful life of the improvements without regard to the period of the lease.

BASIS FOR DETERMINING DEPRECIATION

The basis for determining depreciation is the same as the basis that you would use to determine your gain if you sold the property. Usually, the cost of property is its basis. If you materially improve the property, the additional costs are added to the basis; whereas, casualty losses reduce the basis.

The basis for nonbusiness property converted to business use is the lesser of its fair market value on the date you began using it in your business, or the adjusted basis of the property at that time.

Apportionment of basis. If you acquire property for a lump sum which includes both depreciable and nondepreciable property, you must allocate your total basis between the depreciable and nondepreciable property. The basis for depreciation cannot exceed an amount which bears the same proportion to the lump sum as the value of the depreciable property bears to the value of the entire property at the time you acquired it.

Example. You purchased a building and the land on which it stands for $30,000. If the value of the building is two-thirds of the total value of the land and building, your basis for depreciating the building, before considering salvage, is $20,000 (2/3 x $30,000).

AMOUNT OF DEPRECIATION DEDUCTION

You should take the proper depreciation in each tax year. If you failed to deduct allowable depreciation in past years, you may not deduct the unclaimed depreciation in the current or a later tax year.

If you acquire or dispose of property during the year, and do not use an averaging convention, regular depreciation is allowable for only part of the year. Depreciation begins when the asset is placed in service and ends when the asset is retired from service. An asset is considered first placed in service when it is first available for service.

Example. You order a new frame straightening machine for use in your auto body shop. The machine is installed in your shop and available for use on May 1. The machine is not used until July, because you did not have any frame straightening jobs until then. Depreciation begins as of May 1, when the machine was first available for service.

You are not required to allocate the *Additional First-Year Depreciation,* discussed later.

In the case of a multiple asset account, the amount of depreciation may be determined by using an *averaging convention,* that is, by using an assumed timing of additions and retirements. For example, it might be assumed that all additions and retirements to the asset account occur uniformly throughout the tax year in which case depreciation is computed on the average beginning and ending balances of the asset account for the tax year. An averaging convention, if used, must be consistently followed for the account or accounts for which it is adopted. The averaging convention method may not be used in computing depreciation for large and unusual acquisitions that substantially distort the depreciation deduction for the year. Instead, such assets must be depreciated separately from the multiple asset accounts according to their useful lives.

Cannot exceed basis. The total of all your annual depreciation deductions cannot exceed your cost or other basis (less salvage value) of a property. For this purpose, the depreciation deduction amounts must include any depreciation you were allowed to claim, even if you failed to claim the deduction. *Salvage value* is discussed later.

If you acquire a combination of depreciable and amortizable property, depreciation is allowable only for the portion of the property that is not subject to the allowance for amortization.

USEFUL LIFE

The first step in computing depreciation is to determine the estimated useful life of the asset. No average useful life for an item is applicable in all businesses. The useful life of any item depends upon such things as the frequency with which you use it; its age when you acquired it; your policy as to repairs, renewals, and replacements; the climate in which it is used; the normal progress of the art, economic changes, inventions, and other developments within the industry and your trade or business.

You should determine the useful life of the depreciable property on the basis of your particular operating conditions and experience. If your experience is inadequate, you may use the general experience in the industry until your own experience forms an adequate basis for making the determination.

Can be changed. The estimated useful life may be modified because of conditions you know exist at the end of any tax year. This change may be made when necessary regardless of your method of computing depreciation. However, the estimated remaining useful life of any asset should be redetermined only when the change in useful life is significant and there is a clear and convincing basis for a redetermination.

Boilers fueled by oil or gas. If you expect to retire or replace a boiler that is fueled by oil or gas before the end of its originally determined useful life, then for tax years ending after November 9, 1978, you may file a special application with the Internal Revenue Service to depreciate the remaining basis of the equipment over a shortened useful life.

Agreement as to life. You may enter into a written agreement with the Internal Revenue Service as to the estimated useful life, method and rate of depreciation, and salvage value of any property. You must apply for this agreement, in quadruplicate, to your District Director of Internal Revenue.

Obsolescence. In computing depreciation, you may consider the extent to which the expected useful life of the property will be shortened by technological improvements, progress in the arts, reasonably foreseeable economic changes, shifting of business centers, prohibitory laws, and other causes, apart from physical wear and tear that actually diminish the value of the property or shorten its useful life.

SALVAGE VALUE

Salvage value is the amount (determined at the time of acquisition) that you estimate will be realized upon sale or other disposition of an asset when it is no longer useful in your business or in the production of your income and is to be retired from service. Salvage value is not subsequently adjusted merely because of a price level change. If you customarily use an asset for its full inherent useful life, salvage value may be no more than junk value. But, if it is your policy to retire assets that are still in good operating condition, salvage value may represent a relatively large portion of the original cost or basis of the asset.

Salvage, when reduced by the cost of removal, is called net salvage. You may use either salvage or *net salvage* in determining depreciation but one practice must be consistently followed. However, negative net salvage is not allowable, and the net salvage is zero when the estimated charges for removal exceed estimated salvage value. Your treatment of the costs of removal must be consistent with the practice you adopt. If you redetermine the useful life of an asset, you should at the same time redetermine the salvage value.

If you acquire new or used personal property (other than livestock) with a useful life of 3 years or more, you may reduce the salvage value by any amount up to 10% of the full adjusted basis of the property when acquired.

Example 1. You purchased a new lathe, having a useful life of 10 years for $1,000, for use in your business. Assume the salvage value to you of this lathe at the end of its useful life would be $80. If you wish, you may disregard salvage value and compute your depreciation based on the entire $1,000 cost.

Example 2. Assume the same facts as in Example 1, except that salvage value is $120. You may disregard up to $100 of salvage value and compute your depreciation deduction on $980. The remaining $20 is your salvage value for this asset.

ADDITIONAL FIRST-YEAR DEPRECIATION

You may elect to deduct 20% of the cost of qualifying property (subject to a dollar limitation discussed later) as additional first-year depreciation in addition to your regular depreciation. You do not use salvage value in computing this deduction.

Trusts may not claim the additional first-year depreciation. All other taxpayers may, if they acquire qualifying property.

When allowable. You may take this deduction only in the first tax year that a depreciation deduction is allowable on the property. Ordinarily this is the year in which the property is acquired. However, if it has been your consistent practice to treat property acquired during the last half of a month as property acquired on the first of the following month, then additional first-year depreciation on property acquired during the last few days of your tax year would be deducted in the following year.

Qualifying property. New or used tangible personal property having a useful life of at least 6 years (determined at date of acquisition) is qualifying property. It must be purchased for use in your business or for the production of income.

Tangible personal property includes assets that are accessories to the operation of a business, such as machinery, printing presses, transportation equipment, office equipment, refrigerators, individual air-conditioning units, and grocery counters (even though such assets may be termed fixtures under local law). The adjusted basis of property traded in for like property will not be taken into account in determining the cost of the newly acquired property for purposes of the additional depreciation allowance.

Example. You are allowed $500 on an old truck that you traded for a new $3,000 truck. You paid $2,500 either in cash or notes. Only the $2,500 would be the cost of the qualifying property.

Nonqualifying property. Land and improvements, such as buildings or other inherently permanent structures thereon (including items which are structural components of such buildings or structures), and intangible property, such as patents or trademarks, do not qualify for the additional first-year depreciation deduction. Also, property must be *purchased* in order to be eligible for this deduction (gifts and bequests do not qualify). If property is purchased for personal purposes and later converted to use in a trade or business or to property held for the production of income, it does not qualify for the additional allowance. Moreover, the additional allowance is not allowed on purchase transactions between related taxpayers, related partners and partnerships, and certain members of the same affiliated group of corporations.

Related taxpayer transactions (except that for this purpose, brothers and sisters—whether by the whole or halfblood—are not considered members of the immediate family), will not qualify for the additional allowance. For example, a purchase of property from your husband or your wife does not qualify, but property purchased from your brother or sister will qualify for the deduction.

Transactions between either a partnership and a partner owning directly or indirectly an interest of more than 50% of the capital or profits of the partnership, or two partnerships in which the same persons own directly or indirectly more than 50% of the capital or profits of both partnerships, will not qualify for the additional allowance.

The rules for *constructive ownership* apply in determining the 50% ownership in partnership capital or profits.

If property is acquired by one component member of a controlled group from another member of the same controlled group, the additional allowance is not allowed.

Limitation. The cost of property on which you may take this additional allowance is limited to $10,000 on a separate return and $20,000 on a joint return. For example, if during your tax year you bought $30,000 worth of qualifying property, you may deduct 20% of only $10,000 on a separate return or 20% of only $20,000 on a joint return, if a corporation had purchased the property, its deduction would be 20% of only $10,000.

You may select the items, and the portion of their costs upon which you wish to claim the additional allowance.

Any additional allowance claimed by an estate and allocated to a beneficiary does not affect the additional allowance that a beneficiary may otherwise claim on property not held by the estate.

Computation of deduction. The additional first-year depreciation deduction is determined without adjustment to basis for salvage value and is allowed in full, even though the property is acquired during the year. Ordinary depreciation is then computed on the cost or other basis of the property, less the additional first-year depreciation deduction and salvage value.

Example. You are a calendar-year taxpayer. On July 1, you bought a used piledriver for $14,500. It had an estimated useful life of 10 years and a salvage value of $500 (over and above the 10% of basis that may be disregarded). Your depreciation deduction is computed as follows:

SEPARATE RETURN

Additional first-year depreciation: 20% of $10,000 ($14,500 limited to $10,000)	$2,000
Regular depreciation: 10% of $12,000 ($14,500 less the $2,000 and less $500 salvage) x 1/2 year	600
Total depreciation for the year	$2,600

JOINT RETURN

Additional first-year depreciation: 20% of $14,500 (limitation is $20,000).....................	$2,900
Regular depreciation: 10% of $11,100 ($14,500 less the $2,900 and less $500 salvage) x 12 year	555
Total depreciation for the year	$3,455

The election must be made separately for each tax year for which you claim additional first-year depreciation. You make the election on your income tax return for the year to which the election applies. This tax return must be filed within the time (including extensions) prescribed for filing your return for the first year for which a deduction for depreciation is allowable on the qualifying property.

To make the election you must show the additional first-year depreciation separately on the depreciation schedule, which should be attached to your return. However, you combine your regular depreciation and the additional first-year depreciation amounts to compute your total depreciation deduction for the year.

The items of property selected, as well as the election itself are binding and cannot be changed without the consent of the Internal Revenue Service.

Records. You must keep records that permit specific identification of each piece of property for which the additional first-year depreciation is claimed and that show how, when, and from whom the property was acquired.

Partnerships. The election to claim additional first-year depreciation on partnership property is made by the partnership. However, the amount of the additional allowance is determined separately for each partner. Each partner's additional allowable depreciation is determined by allocating to each partner a portion of the cost of the qualifying property selected by the partnership in the same ratio as is used for determining each partner's distributive share of ordinary depreciation. An allocation of the amount of the qualifying property among the partners may not be modified after the due date of the partnership return (without regard to extensions of time) for the year of the election.

For partnership tax years beginning *after 1975,* the partnership is limited to $10,000 of cost upon which the partnership is allowed to compute the additional allowance.

Each partner's total allowance for additional first-year depreciation is limited to $2,000 ($4,000 if married and filing a joint return), including the amount allocated by the partnership and any additional first-year depreciation to which the partner may be entitled from a separate trade or business.

The basis of the partnership's qualifying property must be adjusted to reflect this additional allowance. This adjustment to the partnership's basis is required, even though a partner may not be entitled to deduct all or any of the amount attributable to the partner from the partnership because the total additional first-year depreciation allowances available to the partner from this and other partnerships or sole proprietorships exceed the limitation of $2,000 or $4,000. Of course, if the partnership elected to claim the additional allowance for a smaller portion of the cost of the qualifying property, the basis would be adjusted only for the smaller additional allowance.

Example. Assume that the partnership of Jones, Smith, and Brown purchased $100,000 of qualifying property on February 10, 1978. The tax year of the partnership began on January 1, 1978. Under the partnership agreement, the allocation of each partner's distributive share of ordinary depreciation is 45% to Jones, 5% to Smith, and 50% to Brown. Jones is married and files a joint income tax return. Smith and Brown are both single. The partnership elects to claim the additional first-year depreciation allowance on the qualifying property. The partnership is entitled to deduct, in the year of purchase only, $2,000 (20% of $10,000) of additional first-year depreciation because a partnership with a tax year beginning after 1975 is limited to $10,000 of cost upon which the additional allowance may be computed. The allocation of the $10,000 and the additional allowance to each partner is computed as follows:

Partners	Jones	Smith	Brown
Shares of ordinary depreciation..............	45%	5%	50%
Maximum amount subject to election ($10,000)	$4,500	$500	$5,000
Additional first-year depreciation allowance ($2,000)	$ 900	$100	$1,000

If any of the partners was a member of another partnership or had an individual business that elected to claim additional first-year depreciation on its qualifying property, and the sum of the additional allowances from the partnership in the Example and any other businesses exceeded the limitation of $2,000 or $4,000, that partner could not deduct the full amount of the additional allowance as computed in these examples. However, the basis of the partnership property still would be adjusted for the full allowance.

Trust as partner. If one of the partners is a trust, the partnership may only use the cost of qualifying property attributable to the non-trust partners. No additional first-year depreciation is allowed to the trust, and no adjustment to the basis of the qualifying property is required for the share of the property allocable to the trust. If in the previous example Brown was a trust, only the qualifying property attributable to Jones' 45% and Smith's 5% could be selected by the partnership for the additional first-year depreciation allowance. The entries in the Example would then appear as follows:

	Jones	Smith	Brown Trust
Partners			
Share of ordinary depreciation.............	45%	5%	50%
Maximum amount subject to election ($5,000)..........	$4,500	$500	- 0 -
Additional first-year depreciation allowance ($1,000)	$ 900	$100	- 0 -

METHODS OF COMPUTING DEPRECIATION

Any reasonable method that is consistently applied may be used in computing depreciation. The three methods most generally used are:

1) Straight-line
2) Declining-balance; and
3) Sum of the years-digits.

Certain depreciable property, such as used property, may be eligible for the additional first-year depreciation, but not for use of the sum of the years-digits method or the declining-balance method using twice the straight-line rate.

Likewise, the sum of the years-digits method or the declining-balance method using twice the straight-line rate may apply to certain depreciable property that is not eligible for the additional first-year depreciation.

Depreciable real property that you acquire new after July 24, 1969, may not be eligible for use of the sum of the years-digits method or the declining-balance method using twice the straight-line rate. (See the sections describing the declining-balance and sum of the years-digits methods.)

The depreciation allowance illustrated in the examples in the following paragraphs does not include additional first-year depreciation, since the depreciable property is not eligible for this additional depreciation in all cases.

Straight-line method. This method is the simplest for computing depreciation. Under this method, the cost or other basis of the property less its salvage value is deducted in equal annual amounts over the period of its estimated useful life.

The depreciation for each year is determined by dividing the adjusted basis of the property, less salvage value, by the remaining useful life. This method must be used for any depreciable property for which you have not adopted a different acceptable method. The straight-line method must also be used for certain boilers that use oil or gas and that are placed in service after September 1978.

Declining-balance method. Under this method, the depreciation, which you take each year, is subtracted from the cost of other basis of the property before computing the next year's depreciation. The same depreciation rate applies to a smaller or declining balance each year. Thus, a larger depreciation deduction is taken for the first year and a gradually smaller deduction in succeeding years.

Within limits, the depreciation rate used is greater than the rate that would be used under the straight-line method. Under some circumstances you may use a rate twice as great as would be proper under the straight-line method. Under other circumstances you are limited to a rate 1½ or 1¼ times as great as the rate you would use under the straight-line method.

Salvage value is not deducted from the cost or other basis of your property in determining the annual depreciation allowance under the declining-balance method. However, you must not depreciate your property below its reasonable salvage value. But see *Salvage Value.*

Twice the straight-line rate may be used to compute depreciation under this method only on the following tangible property:

1) Property having a useful life of 3 years or more that you acquire new after 1953, and, if real property, before July 25, 1969.
2) Property having a useful life of 3 years or more that is constructed, reconstructed, or erected by you after 1953, and, if real property, before July 25, 1969;
3) Real property, any part of which was constructed or financed under a written contract entered into by you before July 25, 1969, and binding on you on and after that date; or
4) Real property that is new residential rental property. (See *Real Estate Depreciation* discussed later.)

Example. Assume you purchased a new machine in January of this year for $2,000, and its estimated life is 10 years. Under the straight-line method of computing depreciation, the rate is 10%. Since this machine meets all the conditions already stated, it may be depreciated under the declining-balance method at a rate twice the straight-line rate or 20%. Your depreciation allowance on this machine for this year is $400, which is 20% of $2,000. Your depreciation allowance the following year is $320, or 20% of $1,600 ($2,000 minus $400).

One and one-half times straight-line rate. The maximum rate you may use under the declining-balance method on used *tangible personal* property (or new property acquired before 1954) having a useful life of 3 years or more, is 1½ times the straight-line rate. The same maximum rate applies to *used* depreciable real property acquired before July 25, 1969, and to *new* real property (other than new residential rental property) acquired after July 24, 1969.

Example. If in the preceding example you had purchased a used machine, the maximum declining-balance rate would be 15% (1½ times the straight-line rate of 10%). Thus, your depreciation for the first year would have been $300, which is 15% of $2,000, and for the 2nd year $255, which is 15% of $1,700 ($2,000 minus $300).

One and one-fourth times straight-line rate. The maximum rate that you can use under the declining-balance method on *used residential rental property* acquired after July 24, 1969, and having a useful life of 20 years or more is 1¼ times the straight-line rate.

You may change from the declining-balance method to the straight-line method without the consent of the Internal Revenue Service. This change may be made at any time during the useful life of the property, unless the change is prohibited by a written agreement. When this change is made, the unrecovered cost of other basis less the estimated salvage value must be spread over the estimated remaining useful life determined at the time of change.

A change from the declining-balance method to the straight-line method may be made only on the original return for the tax year in which the change is made. The change may not be made on an amended return filed after the due date, including extensions, for filing your return.

You must attach a statement to your return for the tax year in which the change is made showing the date of acquisition of the property, the cost or other basis, the amounts recovered through depreciation and other allowances, the salvage value, the character of the property, its remaining useful life, and information as may be required.

After you change to the straight-line method for any property, you generally may not change to the declining-balance or to another method of depreciation for a period of 10 years without written permission from the Internal Revenue Service.

You cannot combine assets in an account on which depreciation was formerly computed by the declining-balance method with assets in an account previously depreciated by the straight-line method. They must be maintained in separate

543

If you used an erroneous method of depreciation for used property and the Internal Revenue Service disallows such improper method, you may adopt the straight-line method, or any other method of depreciation that would have been permissible had you adopted it initially. Moreover, if you filed your first return using an improper depreciation method, and later file an amendment return before the return filing date for the next succeeding tax year, you may use the proper depreciation method on the amended return without obtaining the consent of the Internal Revenue Service.

Sum of the years-digits method. Under this method, as a general rule, you apply a different fraction each year to the cost or other basis of each single asset account *reduced by estimated salvage value.* The denominator (bottom number) of the fraction, which remains constant, is the total of the digits representing the years of estimated useful life of the property. For example, if the estimated useful life is 5 years, the denominator is 15, that is, the sum of $1 + 2 + 3 + 4 + 5$. To save time in arriving at the denominator, especially when an asset has a long life, square the life of the asset, add the life, and divide by 2. Thus, the asset with a 5-year life has the denominator $5 \times 5 + 5 \div 2 = 15$.

The numerator (top number) of the fraction changes each year to represent the years of useful life remaining at the beginning of the year for which the computation is made. For the first year of a 5-year estimated useful life, the numerator would be 5, for the second year 4, etc. Thus, for property with an estimated useful life of 5 years, the fraction to be applied to the cost or other basis, minus salvage value, to compute depreciation for the first year is 5/15. The fraction for the 2nd, 3rd, 4th, and 5th years are 4/15, 3/15, 2/15, and 1/15, respectively.

The sum of the years-digits method may be used only on property that meets the requirements for up to *twice the straight-line rate* under *Declining-balance method,* discussed previously.

Remaining-life plan. You may use the sum of the years-digits method for single asset accounts and group, classified, or composite accounts on the remaining-life plan by applying changing fractions to the unrecovered cost or other basis reduced by salvage.

Under this plan, the denominator of the fraction changes each year to a number equal to the total of the digits representing the estimated remaining useful life of the property. The numerator of the fraction changes each year to represent the years of useful life remaining at the beginning of the year for which the computation is made.

For example, property with an estimated useful life of 5 years is purchased for $6,500 and placed in service January 3, 1978. Assuming a salvage value of $500, the depreciation allowance for 1978 is $2,000, (5/15 of $6,000). The fraction of 5/15 is arrived at as already shown. For 1979, the unrecovered balance is $4,000, and the remaining-life is 4 years.

The sum of the digits 1, 2, 3, and 4 is 10, and the depreciation allowance for 1979 would be $1,600, that is 4/10 of $4,000 ($6,000 less $2,000). For 1980, 1981, and 1982, the depreciation allowances, respectively, would be $1,200 (3/6 of $2,400 ($4,000 less $1,600)). $800 (2/3 of $1,200 ($2,400 less $1,200)) and $400 (1/1 of $400, the unrecovered cost in the last year of useful life).

You can get the decimal equivalents of the sum of the years-digits fractions corresponding to remaining lives from 1 to 100 years from the income tax regulations on depreciation available at your Internal Revenue office, and you may use them in your computations in place of the fractions you would otherwise compute.

You must obtain consent from the Internal Revenue Service by filing Form 3115 if you wish to use the sum of the years-digits method for group, classified, or composite accounts under a plan other than the remaining-life plan.

Nontaxable exchanges. Neither the declining-balance method at twice the straight-line rate nor the sum of the years-digits method may be used on property that you acquire as a separate taxable entity in a nontaxable exchange, even though the transferor used one of these methods before the exchange. The reason is that the original use of the property did not begin with you, as is required.

Any other consistent method of computing depreciation, such as the sinking fund method, may be used for Federal income tax purposes. However, during the first two-thirds of the useful life of the property, your depreciation deductions under any such method must not result at the end of any tax year in accumulated allowances that are greater than the total that could have been deducted if the declining balance method had been used. The limitations on the use of the declining-balance and sum of the years-digits methods apply equally to any consistent method used other than the straight-line method.

If you convert to business or rental use property that you held for personal use, and you were the original purchaser and user of the property, you may select the declining-balance method or the sum of the years-digits method for computing depreciation, subject to the limitations prescribed for each method.

For example, if you bought a new home in 1963 as your residence, and converted it to rental property on or before July 24, 1969, you may compute depreciation on the property under the sum of the years-digits method, or you may use the declining-balance method and apply a rate not in excess of twice the rate under the straight-line method. But, if you acquired the residence before 1964 or if you were not the first owner, you may not use the sum of the years-digits method, and, if you select the declining-balance method, the rate of depreciation may not exceed 1½ times the rate under the straight-line method.

After July 24, 1969. Any realty converted to a business or income producing use after July 24, 1969 is treated as used real property.

Before you select a method for computing depreciation, you should check the limitations to make sure it is available to you. Then, you decide whether you want a fixed deduction each year under the straight-line method, or a larger deduction in the first year with diminishing deductions in succeeding years under the other methods. You may use different methods for each item account and for each group, classified, or composite account. But you must thereafter apply the method consistently to each item of property in each item account, and to each group, classified, or composite account. However, see *Change of method,* discussed later.

Comparative writeoffs under three methods. Assume that a new machine with an estimated life of 5 years is bought on January 3, 1978, for $10,000, its salvage value, which is estimated to be $500, was not taken into consideration in computing depreciation since it was less than 10% of the cost of the machine. See

Salvage value, discussed earlier. Additional first year depreciation is not considered since the useful life of the property is less
than 6 years.

Straight-line method:

Year	Cost	Rate	Deduction	Reserve Dec. 31
First...........	$10,000	20%	$2,000	$ 2,000
Second.........	10,000	20%	2,000	4,000
Third	10,000	20%	2,000	6,000
Fourth	10,000	20%	2,000	8,000
Fifth	10,000	20%	2,000	10,000

Declining-balance method:

Year	Unrecovered Cost Jan. 1	Rate	Deduction	Reserve Dec. 31
First...........	$10,000	40%	$4,000	$ 4,000
Second	6,000	40%	2,400	6,400
Third	3,600	40%	1,440	7,840
Fourth	2,160	40%	864	8,704
Fifth	1,296	40%	518	9,222

Sum of years-digits method, general rule, used for single asset
account only:

Year	Cost	Fraction	Deduction	Reserve Dec. 31
First	$10,000	5/15	$3,333	$ 3,333
Second	10,000	4/15	2,667	6,000
Third	10,000	3/15	2,000	8,000
Fourth	10,000	2/15	1,333	9,333
Fifth	10,000	1/15	667	10,000

Sum of years-digits method, remaining-life plan:

Year	Unrecovered Cost Jan. 1	Fraction	Deduction	Reserve Dec. 31
First...........	$10,000	5/15	$3,333	$ 3,333
Second.........	6,667	4/10	2,667	6,000
Third	4,000	3/6	2,000	8,000
Fourth	2,000	2/3	1,333	9,333
Fifth	667	1/1	667	10,000

Change of method. Generally, any change in the method of computing depreciation is a change in method of accounting that requires the consent of the Internal Revenue Service. However, as previously discussed, certain changes from the declining-balance method to the straight-line method do not require consent. Once you have changed to the straight-line rate you may not change back without getting permission.

A change in your depreciation method should be requested on Form 3115 which requires you to provide certain information concerning the depreciable property which is the subject of the change.

REAL ESTATE DEPRECIATION

Generally, real property that you acquired new before July 25, 1969 can be depreciated under the declining-balance method of depreciation at a rate not exceeding twice the straight-line rate or under the sum of the years-digits method. Used real property acquired before July 25, 1969 can be depreciated under the declining-balance method at a rate not exceeding 1½ times the straight-line rate. The straight-line method can be used for any property qualifying for depreciation.

Limitation on real estate depreciation. You are limited to a rate that is 1½ times the straight-line rate on new real estate (including commercial and industrial buildings) acquired after July 24, 1969. An exception is made for new residential rental housing, if at least 80% of the gross rental income from the building each year is derived from rentals of residential units. A residential unit means a house or an apartment used to provide accommodations, but does not include units in a hotel, motel, inn, or other establishment in which more than one-half of the units are used on a transient basis. You may still use a rate that is twice the straight-line rate for this property.

The 80 percent test is computed each year. Therefore, if your gross rentals are only 75% for 1978, you may use the 150% declining-balance for that year. If your gross rentals are 80% for 1979, you may use the 200% declining-balance or sum of the years-digits method for new residential property. A change in the method of computing depreciation which is permitted or required because of the operation of this test does not require consent of the Service since it is not considered a change in method of accounting.

You may depreciate *used* real estate (other than certain residential property) acquired after July 24, 1969, only under the straight-line method. Used residential rental property with a useful life of 20 years or more, acquired after July 24, 1969, is limited to a rate that is 1¼ times the straight-line rate.

Refer to Publication 534 for a detailed discussion of real estate depreciation.

Low-income rental housing. The taxpayer may elect to compute depreciation of rehabilitation expenditures incurred for low-income rental housing after July 24, 1969, and before 1982, by using a 60-month useful life. Rehabilitation expenditures incurred after 1981 may be eligible for the 5-year life, if these expenditures were incurred pursuant to a binding contract entered into before 1982 or if the rehabilitation was begun before 1982. For this purpose the straight-line method is used, and no salvage value is used in computing depreciation. Rehabilitation expenditures eligible for this treatment are limited to $20,000 ($15,000 for expenditures incurred before 1976) per dwelling unit. The term low-income rental housing means any building in which the dwelling units are held for rent to families and individuals of low or moderate income.

ACCOUNTING FOR DEPRECIABLE PROPERTY

The cost or other basis of every asset subject to depreciation is recorded in an asset account. You may establish as many accounts for depreciable property as you wish. You may either itemize each asset separately, or combine two or more assets into one account.

Single item accounts. Under this accounting practice, each individual item of property is treated as a separate account.

Component accounts. The components of depreciable property (such as wiring or a roof) may be set up in separate accounts and depreciated separately. This method can be utilized for new property. However, to use this method for used property, the cost of acquisition must be properly allocated to the various components and useful lives must be based on the condition of the components at the time of acquisition and based on competent appraisal. The rate of depreciation for the various structural components of a used building acquired after July 24, 1969, is limited to the amount computed using the straight-line method, or the 125% declining-balance method for used residential rental property.

Multiple asset accounts. A number of assets with the same or different useful lives may be combined into one account, using a single rate of depreciation for the entire account. Multiple asset accounts generally are broken down into group, classified, and composite accounts.

In the case of group accounts the rate of depreciation is determined by using the average of the useful lives of the assets.

In the case of classified or composite accounts, the rate of depreciation generally is computed by determining the total amount of one year's depreciation for each item or each group of similar items. The total depreciation amount is then divided by the total cost (or other basis) of the assets in the account. The average rate so determined is to be used as long as subsequent additions, retirements, or replacements do not substantially alter the relative proportions of different types of assets in the account.

Group accounts contain assets similar in kind with approximately the same useful lives.

Classified accounts consist of assets classified according to use without regard to useful life, such as machinery and equipment, furniture and fixtures, or transportation equipment.

Composite accounts include assets without regard to their character or useful lives.

Group, classified, or composite accounts also may be set up on the basis of location, dates of acquisition, cost, character, use, or any other basis you consider necessary for your business.

Reserve for depreciation (Accumulated depreciation). Depreciation allowances are computed separately for each account and should be recorded in a separate depreciation reserve account.

Adjustments to asset or reserve accounts must be shown in detail in the appropriate account.

Redeterminations of life or rate for depreciation should be made in classified or composite accounts whenever additions,

retirements, or replacements substantially change the proportion of types of assets in those accounts.

Idle assets. You must claim a deduction for depreciation on an
idle asset if it is usually used in your business but is temporarily
idle due, for example, to the lack of a market for the item produced with such asset or for other reasonable causes. Such an
asset is treated as being used in your business for Federal income tax purposes.

A manufacturing or processing concern that must include depreciation as part of the cost of goods sold must attach a
schedule to its return showing the details of the depreciation
computation. This depreciation may not be deducted again as a
separate business expense on your return, but you may deduct
depreciation allowances as a separate business expense to the
extent that they are not required to be included in the cost of
goods sold.

ABANDONMENT OF ASSETS

If for some unforeseen change in business conditions, it suddenly becomes necessary for you to prematurely discard or
abandon assets permanently, you may claim a loss measured by
the difference between your unrecovered cost or other basis and
the salvage value (if any) of the property abandoned. This does
not apply to your inventories. The loss must be fully explained
on your tax return. Mere nonuse of property does not constitute abandonment.

When loss is deductible. Your deduction for the loss on premature discard or abandonment of business assets must be claimed
only for the tax year in which the loss of usefulness is actually
sustained, even though sale or other disposition does not occur
until a later year.

Example. You used special machinery exclusively for the
manufacture of one of your products, and the continued profitable use of that machinery suddenly becomes impossible. You
may claim a loss in the year in which you actually discontinue
the use of the machinery.

Demolition. If you abandon a building used in your business
and demolish it to make room for other improvements, your

abandonment loss ordinarily is your undepreciated basis of the building increased by the net cost of demolition or decreased by the net proceeds from demolition. Demolition of a building will prove your intent to abandon. Although if other satisfactory proof is available, you need not demolish it in the same tax year for which you claim a deduction for the undepreciated basis of the building.

However, if you demolish a building in connection with a contract to sell or lease the land, the following conditions apply, regardless of your intent before entering into the contract.

Lease contract. If, under the requirements of a lease or of an agreement that resulted in a lease, you demolish a building on the land that is being leased, you may not claim the demolition loss in the current year but must amortize it over the term of the lease. If the lessee demolishes the building, any loss must also be amortized over the term of the lease.

Sale contract. If you demolished a building used in your business as a condition of the contract to sell land on which the building was situated, even though it had been your intent to raze it at some future date to make way for other improvements, no abandonment loss is allowable. The net costs or the net proceeds resulting from demolition must be shown as an adjustment to basis in computing gain or loss from the sale.

If you acquire improved property and demolish the old building to construct a new one on the property, you are not entitled to any deduction for the demolition. The total cost of land, the old building, and the cost of demolishing and removing the useless building will be your basis for the land.

However, if you buy improved property with the intent to demolish the building after using it for a brief period either in your business or for the production of income, you may allocate a part of the total cost of the building and depreciate that amount over the period of use. The amount you allocate to the building is the present value of the right to receive rent from the property over the period of its intended use. If you demolish the building before you had originally planned, any remaining portion of the amount allocated to the building is then allowed as a loss.

Example 1. On January 3 you bought improved property for $60,000 with the intention of renting it out for about 3 years after which time you intended to demolish the buildings and convert the property to your own use. On April 1 you entered into a 3-year lease and rented the property for $100 a month. Assume that on April 1 the present value of your right to receive $100 a month rent for 3 years is $2,850; therefore, $2,850 of the $60,000 is allocated to the building and $57,150 to the land. You are allowed to take a depreciation deduction of 1/36 of $2,850 each month over the period of the lease.

Example 2. Assume the same facts as already stated, except that after 18 months you and the tenant mutually agree to cancel the lease, and you decide to demolish the building at that time. You have claimed depreciation deductions of $1,425 (one-half of the amount allocated to the building) for the period prior to demolition. The remaining $1,425 is an allowable loss.

CLASS LIFE ASSET DEPRECIATION RANGE SYSTEM

You may elect the *Class Life Asset Depreciation Range (CLADR) system* of computing the reasonable depreciation allowance for all eligible property placed in service after 1970. Eligible property is tangible personal and real property placed in service by the taxpayer after 1970 for which there is in effect an asset guideline class and an asset guideline period.

The election is made each year and applies to all property that is eligible for the election. It may not be revoked for any year once the election has been made for that year. The election is made by filing Form 4832 along with your timely filed income tax return (including extensions). An election to use CLADR system is deemed a change of accounting method to which the Internal Revenue consents.

The CLADR system is designed to minimize disputes between taxpayers and the Internal Revenue Service, as to the useful life of property, salvage value amounts, repairs, and other matters. If you elect to apply the CLADR system, you have certain options as to the application of specified provisions of the CLADR system.

Certain advantages are present if you elect to apply CLADR system. The useful lives of depreciable assets are generally shorter than under the normal methods of depreciation. The salvage value of an asset, as determined by you, will not be increased by the Internal Revenue Service, unless such increase would exceed the salvage value established by you by more than 10% of the unadjusted basis of the account at the close of the tax year in which the account is established. Also, salvage value is not considered in computing the annual depreciation deduction under the CLADR system.

For certain assets placed in service before 1971, an elective class life system is provided for computing depreciation for taxable years ending after 1970.

The CLADR system may not be used for otherwise eligible property for which you compute depreciation under a method other than straight-line, declining-balance, or sum of the years-digits. Nor may you use this system of depreciation for property for which you claim special amortization, such as a certified pollution control facility.

AMORTIZATION

You may deduct each year, as amortization, a proportionate part of certain capital expenditures. Amortization permits the recovery of these expenditures in a manner similar to straight-line depreciation. Only certain specified expenditures may be amortized for Federal income tax purposes.

A corporation's organization expenses or a partnership's organization expenses may be amortized under certain conditions.

Cost of acquiring lease. If a lease or leasehold is acquired for business purposes, the purchaser may recover the cost by amortization deductions ratably over the term of the lease. The cost includes commissions to obtain a lease or to secure a tenant.

Research and experimental expenses may be amortized over a period of 60 months or longer, or deducted currently as business expenses, if they are connected with your trade or business.

Trademark and trade name. Amounts, other than the purchase price, paid or incurred for the acquisition, protection, expansion, registration, or defense of trademarks and trade names may be treated, if you so elect, as deferred expenses and amortized over a period of not less than 60 months. The 60-month period must begin with the first month of the tax year in which the expenses are paid or incurred. The election does not apply to any part of the *purchase price* of an existing trademark or trade name.

To make the election you must attach a statement to your timely filed return for the year in which the expenditures were paid or incurred; indicating that you are making the election and showing the character and amount of the expenditures being amortized, and the number of months (not less than 60) over which the amortization will be taken. A separate election may be made for each trademark or trade name.

Construction period interest and taxes. Individuals, Subchapter S corporations, and personal holding companies are not allowed to deduct real property construction period interest or taxes (except as noted later under *Amortization deduction*) that were paid or accrued in the tax year on property that is expected to be used for a trade or business or in an activity conducted for profit; instead, these amounts must be capitalized and may be amortized.

Construction period interest and taxes means all:
1) Interest paid or accured during the construction period on indebtedness that was incurred or continued to acquire, construct, or carry real property; and
2) Real property taxes paid or accured during the construction period.

The *construction period* is the period beginning on the date on which construction of the building or other improvement begins, and ending on the date on which the item of property is ready to be placed in service or is ready to be held for sale.

Amortization deduction. Individuals, Subchapter S corporations, and personal holding companies are allowed to deduct a portion of these amounts in the tax year paid or accrued and in each subsequent amortization year in accordance with the following table. However, where no year is noted in the table you may elect to either capitalize or fully deduct such amounts that were paid or accrued in that tax year.

If the amount is paid or accrued in a
        tax year beginning in—

Non-residential real property	Residential real property	Low-income housing	Percentage amount allowable for amortization year
1976	–	–	*
–	1978	1982	25
1977	1979	1963	20
1978	1980	1984	16 2/3
1979	1981	1985	14 2/7
1980	1982	1986	12 1/2
1981	1983	1987	11 1/9
after 1981	after 1983	after 1987	10

*For amounts paid or accrued by the taxpayer for tax years beginning in 1976 the percentage of such amounts allowable is 50% and, for each amortization year thereafter, 162/3%.

Amortization year means the tax year in which the amount is paid or accrued, and each tax-year thereafter (beginning with the tax year after the tax year in which the amount is paid or accrued or, if later, the tax year in which the real property is ready to be placed in service or is ready to be held for sale) until the full amount has been allowed as a deduction (or until the property is sold or exchanged).

Bond premium is the amount you pay in excess of the face value of bonds purchased.

The premium must be amortized on tax-exempt bonds, but no deduction is permitted for the amortizable premium in computing taxable income.

The premium on taxable bonds may be amortized at the election of the taxpayer. If you do not elect to amortize the premium, it will be treated as part of your basis of the bond.

You must reduce the basis of the bond by the amortizable bond premium in all cases in which you are required, or elect, to amortize the premium so that the correct gain or loss will be reflected upon the sale or redemption of the bond.

Election to amortize. The only way you may elect to amortize a bond premium is to claim a deduction for amortization on your tax return for the first tax year for which you desire the election to apply, and to attach to your return a statement showing the computation of the deduction.

The election is binding for the year it is made and for later tax years. It applies to all similar bonds you own in the year the election is made, and also to those you acquire in later years.

An election may be revoked only with the written approval of the Internal Revenue Service.

Example. You are a calendar-year taxpayer. On July 3, 1978, you paid $1,120 for a $1,000 taxable bond that will mature on July 3, 1988. You have elected to amortize the bond premium. You are entitled to a $6 amortization deduction for 1978 computed as follows:

Purchase price of bond on July 3, 1978 .... $1,120
Face value of bond at maturity 1,000
Bond premium .... $ 120

6 (months held in tax year) ÷ 120 (months from acquisition to maturity) x $120 (total bond premium) = $6 (Portion of bond premium deductible)

The adjusted basis of the bond is then reduced as follows:

Purchase price of bond at July 3, 1978 .... $1,120
Less: Amortization deduction in 1978 6
Adjusted basis of bond at December 31, 1978........ $1,114

During 1978 you received $15 interest on the bond. This amount is fully taxable and must be included in income on your 1978 return.

A *dealer in bonds* or anyone who holds them primarily for sale to customers in the ordinary course of a trade or business and who could properly include *bonds on hand in inventory* at the close of the tax year cannot claim a deduction for amortizable bond premium; it is part of the cost.

For information on the tax treatment of *callable and convertible bonds,* contact your Internal Revenue office.

On-the-job training and child-care facilities. Any capital expenditure you make in acquiring, constructing, reconstructing, or rehabilitating child-care facilities may be amortized ratably over a 60-month period if you so elect. This amortization is also allowable on any capital expenditures for facilities to be used for on-the-job training of your employees or prospective employees, or for facilities to be used as child-care centers primarily for your employees' children. In order to qualify, the property must be tangible, of a character that is subject to depreciation, and it must be located in the United States.

Amortization begins with the month the property is placed in service and is taken in lieu of any depreciation deduction otherwise allowable. It is available for qualified on-the-job training facilities expenditures made after 1971 but before 1977, and for qualified child-care facilities expenditures made after 1971 but before 1982.

An on-the-job training facility must be primarily a location for providing training. A production facility may not be classified as an on-the-job training facility simply because new employees receive training on machines they will be using as fully productive employees.

A child-care facility must be constructed, renovated, or remodeled specifically for use as such to qualify as a child-care facility. Qualifying facilities include buildings and equipment, or portions of them, actually used for child-care services in which children receive personal care, supervision, and protection in the absence of their parents. General purpose rooms like recreation rooms used by employees during the evening will not qualify, nor will a part of a room simply screened off for use by children during the day. Special kitchen, toilet, and other facilities used for the child-care center or area could be included as child-care facilities.

Making the election. The election to amortize on-the-job or child-care facilities is made by a statement on, or attached to, the return (or amended return) for the tax year, stating that the election is made under section 188 and setting forth information to identify the election and the facility or facilities to which it applies. The election is binding and irrevocable for each item of property to which it applies.

This election must be made not later than the time (including extensions) for filing the return for the first tax year for which the election is being made, or 90 days after the date final regulations under this provision are filed, whichever is later.

Ordinary income rule. Gain realized on the disposition of a facility for which the special amortization and depreciation deduction has been taken is treated as ordinary income to the extent of the amortization deductions taken.

Tax preference item. The amount by which the amortization deductions exceed depreciation deductions otherwise allowable on such a facility (including for this purpose accelerated depreciation deductions) is a tax preference item for purposes of minimum tax.

Investment credit. If an election is made to claim the special amortization deduction, the facility involved is not eligible for the investment credit.

Pollution control facilities. You may elect to amortize the cost of a certified pollution control facility over a period of 60 months. The amortization deduction is available for a pollution control facility completed or acquired after 1968 as a new identifiable treatment facility which is used in connection with a plant (or other property) that was in operation before 1969. However, in the case of a treatment facility that is used in connection with a plant (or other property) that was not in operation before 1969, but was in operation before 1976, only that portion of the basis of the facility which is attributable to construction, reconstruction, or erection after 1975 may qualify for the amortization election.

A certified pollution control facility must be depreciable property that is a new identifiable treatment facility used for abating or controlling water or atmospheric pollution or contamination by removing, altering, disposing, storing, or preventing the creation or emission of pollutants, contaminants, waste or heat and that is appropriately certified by the State and Federal certifying authorities. However, no certification may be made if it appears that the cost of a facility will be recovered from its operations (e.g., sales of recovered waste, etc.).

In addition, you will be entitled to an *investment credit,* if the facility has a useful life of at least 5 years.

DEPLETION

If you own mineral property, an oil or gas well, or standing timber, you may be entitled to deduct a reasonable allowance for depletion.

The only properties subject to the allowance for depletion are mines, oil and gas wells, other exhaustible natural deposits, and timber.

An operating owner or an owner of an economic interest in mineral deposits or standing timber may claim depletion deductions.

You have an economic interest in every case in which you have acquired by investment any interest in minerals in place or standing timber and secure, by any form of legal relationship, income solely from the extraction and sale of the mineral or cutting of the timber, to which you must look for a return of your capital. More than one party may have an economic interest if each qualifies. If you have no legally enforceable right to share in mineral in place, you do not have an economic interest in such mineral.

Depletion, whether cost or percentage, is computed separately for each property. A property is each separate interest you won in each mineral deposit in each separate tract or parcel of land. Various special rules permit taxpayers to aggregate or combine separate properties or to treat such properties as separate.

Partnerships' oil and gas properties. The depletion allowance is computed separately by each partner and not by the partnership. However, the partnership must allocate to each partner that partner's proportionate share of the adjusted basis of each oil or gas property of the partnership. This allocation must be made on the date the partnership acquires the oil or gas property. A partner's proportionate share of the adjusted basis of the partnership's property is determined by the amount of that partner's interest in the partnership's capital or income.

Also, each partner is responsible for keeping separate records of: the allocated share of that partner's adjusted basis in each oil and gas property of the partnership; and the adjustments that must be made to the adjusted basis of that partner's share because of any depletion taken on such property. Also, each partner must use such adjusted basis each year to compute either cost depletion, or in the event of the disposition of such property by the partnership, gain or loss.

DETERMINING DEPLETION ALLOWANCE

There are two methods of computing depletion: cost depletion, and percentage depletion. Percentage depletion does not apply to timber.

Cost depletion of minerals generally is computed by dividing the total number of recoverable units (tons, barrels, etc., determined in accordance with prevailing industry methods) in the deposit into the adjusted basis of the mineral property, and multiplying the resulting rate per unit:

1) By the number of units for which payment is received during your tax year if you use the cash receipts and disbursements method; or
2) By the number of units sold if you use an accrual method of accounting.

The adjusted basis is your original cost (or other basis in your hands) of the mineral property, less all the depletion allowed or allowable on the property. Depletion allowed or allowable each year is the greater of percentage depletion or cost depletion. However, the adjusted basis can never be less than zero.

The number of units in place in a natural deposit is primarily an engineering problem. It is your responsibility to substantiate, by using accepted reserve evaluation methods, the number of recoverable units.

Percentage depletion is a certain percentage of your gross income from the property during the tax year, but the deduction for depletion under this method can not exceed 50% of your taxable income from the property, computed without the deduction for depletion. The use of percentage depletion for oil and gas is not allowed with exemptions for certain domestic production (certain domestic gas wells and independent producers and royalty owners of oil and gas wells). If you are a qualified independent producer or royalty owner of oil and gas, the deduction for depletion shall not exceed 65% of your taxable income (reduced in the case of an individual by the zero bracket amount) from all sources computed without regard to the depletion allowance, any net operating loss carryback, and any capital loss carryback.

Rents and royalties paid or incurred with respect to the property must be excluded from the gross income from the property when percentage depletion is claimed by the payor.

A net operating loss deduction is not deducted from gross income from the property for computing the 50% limitation.

Charitable contributions are not deducted from gross income from the property by a corporation in determining its taxable income for the 50% limitation.

Special rule. For computing the 50% limitation, mining expenses must be reduced by any gain that must be reported as ordinary income. The gain must be allocable to the property and result from the disposition of certain depreciable property.

Even if you have recovered your cost or other basis of the property, you may be allowed a deduction for percentage depletion.

If percentage depletion is less than cost depletion for any year, you should use cost depletion for that year.

Oil and gas wells. The use of percentage depletion for oil and gas is not allowed, with exemptions for certain domestic gas and oil production. The percentage depletion rate is 22% of the gross income from certain domestic gas and oil property.

Income from natural gas sold under a fixed contract, and geothermal deposits, which are determined to be gas wells, in the United States or its possessions qualified for percentage depletion. Independent producers and royalty owners (the small producers' exemption) may use percentage depletion with certain limitations. The use of percentage depletion for geothermal deposits which are determined to be gas wells is repealed effective October 1, 1978, in tax years ending after September 30, 1978.

Natural gas sold under a fixed contract is domestic gas sold by the producer under a contract in effect on February 1, 1975, and all times thereafter before the sale. The price must not have been adjusted to reflect the increase in the liability of the seller for tax because of the change in the law regarding percentage depletion for gas.

The small-producer exemption provides for a 22% rate for a maximum daily average of 2,000 barrels (6,000 cubic feet of natural gas is the equivalent of a barrel of oil) for 1975 and decreases by 200 barrels each year until 1980. After 1979 the number of barrels a day remains constant at 1,000 while the rate decreases 2% yearly until 1984 and thereafter the rate is

15%. For secondary and tertiary production the rate is 22% until 1984.

The small-producer exemption does not apply to any tax-payer who, directly or through a related person, engages in the refining of crude oil and whose refinery runs exceed 50,000 barrels on any day during the tax year. This exemption also is not available to a taxpayer who directly or through a related person sells oil or natural gas, or any product derived from oil or natural gas, through a retail outlet or to certain persons obligated to use a trademark or trade name owned by the tax-payer or a related person in marketing or distributing oil or natural gas.

However, the exemption will apply if the combined gross receipts of all retail outlets do not exceed $5,000,000 from the sale of oil or natural gas (excluding bulk sales of such items to commercial or industrial users), or any other product derived from oil or natural gas, for the tax year. Also, for this purpose, sales of oil, natural gas, or products that are derived from oil or natural gas do not include sales made outside the United States, if no domestic production of the taxpayer or a related person is exported during the tax year or the preceding tax year.

The small-producer exemption does not apply to a transferee in the case of a transfer in any interest in a proven oil or gas property transferred after 1974. However, the term transfer generally does not include a transfer at death, nor does it include certain transfers to controlled corporations, changes of bene-ficiaries of a trust, transfers between business entities under common control or between members of the same family, and transfers between a trust and related persons in the same family.

A producer with a partial interest in property has production from that property proportional to the interest. If a producer's average production for 1978 exceeds 1400 barrels (or 8,400,000 cubic feet of gas) the small-producer exemption must be allo-cated among all of the properties in which the producer has an interest.

Allocation of the exemption must be made among corpora-tions that are members of the same controlled group (the com-mon control test is 50%); among corporations, trusts, and estates if 50% of the beneficial interest is owned by the same or related persons (considering only persons that own at least 5% of the beneficial interest); and among the producers or royalty owners and their spouses and minor children.

If you are a lessee, any part of gross income that you distribute to a lessor or other owner of an economic interest in the property must be excluded from your gross income when you compute your deduction for depletion.

Gross income from oil and gas property is the amount you receive from the sale of the oil or gas in the immediate vicinity of the well. If you do not sell the oil or gas on the property, but manufacture or convert it into a refined product before sale or transport it before sale, the gross income from the property is the representative market or field price of the oil or gas at the well-head as of the date of sale, before conversion or transportation.

Natural gas from geopressured brine. Effective October 1, 1978, in tax years ending after September 30, 1978, independent producers and royalty owners of qualified natural gas from geopressured brine will be able to deduct percentage depletion at the rate of 10%.

Geothermal deposits. Effective October 1, 1978, in tax years ending after September 30, 1978, geothermal deposits qualify for percentage depletion. A geothermal deposit is a geothermal reservoir consisting of natural heat which is stored in rocks or in an aqueous liquid or vapor (whether or not under pressure). It is not considered a gas well and does not include any geothermal deposit located outside the United States or its possessions.

The applicable percentage through 1980 is 22%. The rate decreases by 2% yearly through 1983 and thereafter the rate is 15%.

Mines and other natural deposits. The percentage of your gross income allowable as a deduction is based upon the type of deposit being mined. Some of the more common depletion percentages follow:

Deposit	Percent
Sulphur and uranium; and, if from deposits in the United States, asbestos, lead, zinc, nickel, mica, and certain other ores and minerals	22
If from deposits in the United States, gold, silver, copper and iron ore, and oil shale	15
Coal and sodium chloride	10

Deposits	Percent
Clay and shale used in making sewer pipe or bricks or used as sintered or burned light-weight aggregates	7 1/2
Clay (used or sold for use in manufacture of drainage and roofing tile, flower pots, and kindred products), gravel, sand, and stone	5
Most other minerals and metallic ores	14

Gross income from mining property is the gross income attributable to the process of extracting ores or minerals from the ground, and the treatment processes considered as mining to the extent that they are applied by the mine owner or operator to the mineral or the ore, including transportation that is not over 50 miles from the point of extraction to the plant or mill in which the treatment processes are applied. Treatment processes considered as mining depend upon the ore or mineral mined, and generally include those necessary to bring the mineral to the stage at which it first becomes suitable for commercial use or consumption. This usually means to a shipping grade and form; however, in certain cases, additional processes specified in the law are considered as mining.

Transportation in excess of 50 miles. If the Internal Revenue Service finds that the physical and other requirements are such that the ore or mineral must be transported more than 50 miles to plants or mills where the processes considered as mining are performed, the entire transportation will be included as mining. If you wish to include transportation in excess of 50 miles as mining, you must file an application, in duplicate, setting forth the facts, with the Internal Revenue Service, Washington, D.C. 20224, Attention: Engineering and Valuation Branch, Corporate Tax Division.

To determine your depletion allowance for mineral properties, you should compute it under both the cost and percentage depletion methods for each property, and claim a deduction for the greater of the two amounts.

LESSOR'S GROSS INCOME

A lessor's gross income from the property ordinarily is the sum of the royalties received from the lease, excluding rentals that do not represent payment for units of mineral produced or to be produced.

Bonuses and advance royalties received for executing a contract granting a mineral lease are often overlooked in computing depletion. A bonus or advance royalty is a payment in advance of production received from the lessee for minerals to be extracted, and, as such, is *gross income from the property* subject to the depletion allowance. If on termination of the lease there has been no production, then no depletion has been sustained. Therefore, the depletion deduction taken in advance must be included in income in the year the lease is terminated. A corresponding adjustment must be made to restore to your basis the depletion deduction previously taken. If no depletion was taken in the year a *bonus* was received, then no income results and no basis adjustments are required for the year the lease is terminated.

However, if you sold, exchanged, or by any other means divested yourself of all your interest in the minerals before terminating a bona fide mineral lease, you are not required to include in your income the depletion deduction taken on the bonus.

Note: Proposed regulations state that for tax years ending after 1974, recipients of oil and gas lease bonuses are not permitted to compute depletion on a percentage basis. Recipients of these types of lease bonuses are allowed to use cost depletion only. In addition, advanced royalties received by persons who qualify as small producers (previously defined) are eligible to use percentage depletion only to the extent its use is justified by actual production which occurs in the same tax year. Therefore, in the absence of actual production, small producers who are recipients of advanced royalties are limited to using cost depletion on such payments. Other types of mineral property are still eligible for percentage depletion.

A bonus or advance royalty, paid to a lessor who holds the landowner's royalty or to a sublessor who holds an overriding royalty, may be subject to the allowance for depletion (see the previous paragraph concerning proposed regulations): when paid for the original term of the lease or sublease; when paid to extend the life of the lease or sublease for a period longer than one year; when paid in connection with the renewal of the original lease; or when paid because such payments could not be avoided by drilling or establishing production.

Delay rentals are payments for the privilege of deferring development of the property for a period not in excess of one year, and could be avoided by abandoning the lease, by commencing development operations, or by obtaining production. Since delay rentals are in the nature of ordinary rent, these amounts received by a lessor are ordinary income *not* subject to depletion.

TIMBER

You may compute timber depletion only by the cost method; no percentage depletion exists for timber. You base your computation on your cost of (or other basis in) the timber. Your cost does not include any part of the cost of the land.

Because depletion takes place when standing timber is cut, you may compute your depletion deduction only after the timber is cut and after the quantity of cut timber is first accurately measured in the process of exploitation. At the end of your tax year, include in your closing inventory as a cost item any allowable depletion on unsold products of the cut timber.

To compute your depletion allowance for your tax year, multiply the number of timber units cut by your depletion unit. Your depletion unit is the quotient of your cost or adjusted basis of the standing timber on hand divided by the total depletable units (MBF, cords, etc.).

Example. If you bought a timber tract for $20,000 and the land was worth as much as the timber, your basis for the timber would be $10,000. If your depletion unit was determined to be $10 per MBF (1,000 board-feet), based on an estimated one million board-feet (1,000 MBF) of standing timber, and you felled 500,000 board-feet of timber your depletion allowance would be $5,000 (500 MBF at $10 per MBF).

The depletion allowance is claimed as a deduction in the year of the sale or other disposition of the cut timber, unless an election is made as discussed later, in the above example, if you felled 500,000 board-feet of your timber in 1978 and sold the logs in 1979, your depletion allowance would be deducted in 1979, the year of the sale.

An election may be made, under certain circumstances, to treat the cutting of timber as a sale or exchange. If this election is made, the allowable depletion is subtracted from the fair market value at the beginning of the tax year of the timber cut to determine the gain to be reported on the cutting. The gain generally is reported as long-term capital gain. The fair market value then becomes your basis for determining the ordinary gain or loss on the sale or other disposition of the cut timber.

SALE OR LEASE OF PROPERTY

If you sell all your economic interest in a property, and retain no continuing interest or reverting interest in it, any gain ordinarily is capital gain. However, if you grant operating rights in a mineral property (other than a coal or timber property) and retain a royalty interest in it, you have made a leasing transaction and the proceeds received for the assignment, as well as the collections of any royalty income, are ordinary income subject to a depletion allowance.

Disposal of coal, iron ore, or timber with a retained economic interest may result in a capital gain equal to the difference between the amount realized and the adjusted depletion basis rather than ordinary income under certain circumstances. If you dispose of the coal, iron ore, or timber and are entitled to treat the gain as a capital gain, you are not entitled to a depletion deduction.

INVESTMENT CREDIT

If you acquired new or used depreciable property for use in your business and placed the property in service during the tax year, or made qualified progress expenditures, you may qualify for the investment credit. Also, energy property acquired or constructed after September 1978 may qualify for a new additional investment credit that is determined separately from the regular investment credit. The property must be qualifying property to be eligible. The amount of your investment in qualifying property that is eligible for the regular investment credit depends upon the useful life of the property and whether the property is new or used. The regular credit allowable is 10% of the eligible investment and is limited to the income tax liability shown on your return, or $25,000 plus 50% (60% for

tax years ending in 1979) of the tax liability in excess of
$25,000, whichever is less. (Married persons filing separate re-
turns are limited to a credit of $12,500, plus 50% (60% for tax
years ending in 1979) of the individual tax liability in excess of
$12,500). The energy credit allowable is 10% of the qualified
investment in energy property and is limited to 100% of your
tax liability, except for solar or wind energy property on which
the credit is refundable. If, before the end of the estimated useful life you used in computing the credit, you dispose of an
asset, or if it ceases to be eligible, you must recompute the
credit using the actual useful life and increase your tax liability
for the disposition year by the difference between the credit
taken in all affected years and the recomputed credit.

QUALIFYING PROPERTY

The property must:
1) Be depreciable;
2) Have a useful life of at least 3 years;
3) Be tangible personal property or other tangible property
   (except buildings or their structural components and certain air conditioners and space heating units placed in service after September 1978) used as an integral part of
   manufacturing, production, or extraction, etc.; and
4) Be placed in service in a trade or business or for production of income by you during the year. (However, see
   Qualified progress expenditures, discussed later.)

Property is considered placed in service in the earlier of the
following:
1) The tax year in which, under your depreciation practice,
   the period for depreciation for the property begins; or
2) The tax year in which the property is placed in a condition
   or state of readiness and availability for service.

Tangible personal property. This includes depreciable tangible
property except land and land improvements (such as buildings
and other permanent structures and their components). It does
not include air conditioners or space heating units that are
placed in service after September 1978, except those that are
acquired under a contract which, on October 1, 1978, and at all
times thereafter was binding on the taxpayer. Property in the

nature of machinery is the principal type of property that qualifies as tangible personal property. Buildings, swimming pools, paved parking areas, wharves and docks, etc., are not tangible personal property.

All property (other than structural components) that is contained in or attached to a building and is accessorial to the activity within the building qualifies whether or not it is considered a fixture (i.e., real property) under local law. Assets such as grocery store counters, printing presses, and individual air-conditioning units (except as noted before), normally qualify as tangible personal property.

Assets of a mechanical nature, such as gasoline pumps, even though located outside a building, also qualify. Generally, central heating and air-conditioning systems, plumbing, wiring, etc., are structural components of a building and do *not* qualify as tangible personal property.

An automobile may qualify if you can establish that it is used in your trade or business and has a useful life of 3 years or more. You may claim the investment credit on the automobile even though your deduction for its operating expenses is computed by using the standard mileage rate.

Used partly for business purposes. If a depreciation deduction is allowable for only a part of property that you place in service during the year, only the proportionate part of the property for which depreciation is allowable qualifies for the credit.

Example. You use your automobile 80% in your trade or business and 20% for personal purposes. Only 80% of the basis (or cost) may be considered for the credit.

Other tangible property. This is any other depreciable tangible property except a building or its structural components that is an integral part of the business activities specified later, that is a research facility used in connection with those activities, or that is a storage facility used in connection with those activities. The business activities are manufacturing, producing, extracting, or furnishing of transportation, communications, electrical energy, gas, water, or sewage disposal services.

Integral part. Property is used as an integral part of one of the specified activities if it is used directly in the activity and is essential to the completeness of the activity.

Storage facility. This is a facility used principally for the bulk storage of fungible commodities. To be fungible, a commodity must be of such a nature that one part may be used in place of another. Bulk storage means the storage of a commodity in a large mass prior to its consumption or utilization. Thus, if a facility is used to store oranges that have been sorted and boxed, it is not used for bulk storage.

Gasoline station storage tanks used to store gasoline at a retail gasoline station are qualified property for investment credit purposes.

Buildings and structural components do not qualify as investment credit property. The term building generally means any structure or edifice enclosing a space within its walls, and usually covered by a roof, the purpose of which may be to provide shelter or housing, or to provide working, office, parking, display, or sales space. The term includes structures such as apartment houses, factory and office buildings, warehouses, barns, garages, railways or bus stations, and stores. The term also includes any structure constructed by, or for, a lessee even if the structure must be removed, or ownership of the structure reverts to the lessor, at the termination of the lease.

The term building *does not* include a structure which is essentially an item of machinery or equipment; or a structure which houses property used as an integral part of manufacturing, production, extraction, or furnishing transportation, communications, electrical energy, gas, water or sewage disposal services if the use of the structure is so closely related to the use of the property that the structure clearly can be expected to be replaced when the property it initially houses is replaced. Nor does the term building include certain single-purpose agricultural or horticultural structures, such as greenhouses or poultry houses. Factors which indicate that a structure is closely related to the use of the property it houses include the fact that the structure is specifically designed to provide for the stress and other demands of the property and the fact that the structure could not be economically used for other purposes. Thus, the term building *does not* include such structures as oil and gas storage tanks, grain storage bins, silos, fractionating towers, blast furnaces, basic oxygen furnaces, coke ovens, brick kilns, and coal tipples.

Structural components include the parts of a building such as walls, partitions, floors, and ceilings, as well as any permanent coverings such as paneling or tiling; windows and doors; all components (whether in, on, or adjacent to the building) of a central air conditioning or heating system, including motors, compressors, pipes and ducts; plumbing and plumbing fixtures, such as sinks and bathtubs; electric wiring and lighting fixtures; chimneys; stairs; sprinkler systems; fire escapes; and other components relating to the operation or maintenance of a building. A fire protection system designed to remain in place permanently is also considered to be a structural component of a building.

However, the term structural components *does not* include machinery if the *sole justification* for installation is the fact that the machinery is required to meet temperature or humidity requirements essential for the operation of other machinery or the processing of materials or foodstuffs. Machinery may meet the *sole justification* test even though it incidentally provides for the comfort of employees, or serves, to an insubstantial degree, areas where such temperature or humidity requirements are not essential. For example, an air conditioning and humidification system installed in a textile plant in order to maintain the temperature or humidity within a narrow optimum range which is critical in processing particular types of yarn or cloth is not included within the term structural components.

Rehabilitation expenditures. For tax years ending after October 1978, capital expenditures that you make after October 1978 in connection with the rehabilitation of a building may qualify for the investment credit. For more information, see Publication 572.

An elevator or an escalator qualifies if it either is acquired during the tax year and the original use begins with you; or if you complete its construction, reconstruction, or erection during the tax year. But the cost of structural alterations to the buildings, such as the construction of a shaft or alteration to the floors and walls may not be included in the basis of the elevator or escalator.

Livestock (other than horses) qualifies for the credit. However, special rules apply in determining the amount of investment if during the 1-year period beginning 6 months before the date of acquisition you have disposed of substantially identical livestock for which there is no recapture of investment credit. In this case, the cost of the livestock acquired must be reduced by the amount realized on disposition of the other livestock (except for disposition by involuntary conversion).

LEASED PROPERTY

If you lease property rather than purchase it outright, you are allowed the investment credit provided that the owner elects to pass the credit to you and that the property is considered qualifying new property, both to you, the lessee, and to the owner. A lessor cannot pass the credit for used property to the lessee.

Time for making election. The election of a lessor must be made by filing a statement (with the required information) with the lessee, signed by the lessor and including the written consent of the lessee, on or before the due date (including any extensions) of the lessee's return for the tax year in which the possession of property is transferred.

The credit to the lessee is computed, generally, on the fair market value of the property, whether it was purchased or constructed by the owner. For example, if you leased a machine with a fair market value of $10,000 that the owner had purchased from the manufacturer for a discounted price of $8,000, your basis for computing the investment credit would be the fair market value, $10,000. However, if a lease is between corporations which are component members of the same controlled group the lessee's basis is the owner's basis.

Leased property purchased from lessor. A lessee who leases qualifying new property from a lessor who properly elected to pass through the investment credit to the lessee is not entitled to an additional investment credit upon the purchase of the property from the lessor.

Certain short-term leases. If you leased property, the amount of credit that the lessor can pass on to you is limited if the term of the lease is significantly shorter than the estimated useful life of the property. Under this rule your investment for the credit is the fair market value of the property (or the basis to the lessor if both the lessor and lessee are component members of the same controlled group) multiplied by a fraction—the term of the lease divided by the class life of the property leased—but only if the property:

1) Is new;
2) Has a class life in excess of 14 years;
3) Is leased for a period that is less than 80% of its class life; and
4) Is not leased subject to a net lease.

The useful life to the owner, regardless of the length of the lease period, is the life to be used for determining both whether the property qualifies and the amount of investment subject to credit, if you stop leasing the property before the expiration of the useful life used in computing the credit, the *Recapture Rule* discussed later will apply.

Property leased by a noncorporate lessor. The investment credit is not allowed in every instance for property that is leased by a *noncorporate* lessor. For property that is leased by an individual, partnership, estate or trust, or a Subchapter S corporation, the credit is allowed to the lessor only *if one of the following* is met:

1) *Property manufactured by lessor.* The property that is leased will qualify if it has been manufactured or produced by the lessor. For example, if you manufacture or produce the property in the ordinary course of your business you may claim investment credit for the article if it is qualifying new property even though you lease the property to someone else.

2) *Business leases.* The property that is leased will qualify if:
   a) The term of the lease (including options to renew or extend) is less than 50% of the useful life of the leased property; and
   b) The business expense deductions allowable to the lessor for the property (other than rental and reimbursed expenses) exceed 15% of the rental income from the property for the first 12 months after it has been transferred to the lessee. For the 15% test, investment expenses such as interest, taxes, and depreciation are not considered business expenses.

PROPERTY THAT MAY QUALIFY

Property used in U.S. possessions. Property may qualify if, in general, it is used predominantly within a U.S. possession and is owned by a U.S. citizen or corporation whose income from the possession is subject to U.S. tax. In addition, certain aircraft registered by the Administrator of the Federal Aviation Agency and operated outside the United States under a contract with the United States may qualify for the credit.

NONQUALIFYING PROPERTY

Intangible property, horses, or real property other than that already referred to does not qualify.

Property used primarily for lodging does not qualify. This includes most property used in the operation of an apartment house and most other facilities where sleeping accommodations are provided and rented.

However, property used by a hotel or motel that primarily serves transient guests (the rental period is normally less than 30 days) or property used in nonlodging commercial facilities (like a restaurant available to the public as well as to tenants) is not considered property used primarily for lodging.

Similarly, coin-operated vending machines and coin-operated washing machines and dryers located in apartment houses and other similar facilities are not considered property used primarily for lodging.

Property owned by or leased to a governmental unit, except on a causal or short-term basis, does not qualify.

Property owned by or leased to certain tax-exempt organizations (other than farmers' cooperatives) does not qualify, unless it is used predominantly to produce unrelated business taxable income; or is leased on a casual or short-term basis.

Property for which special 60-month amortization is taken generally does not qualify for the credit. This includes expenditures for rehabilitation of low-income rental housing, and expenditures for child care facilities.

Property used predominantly outside the United States generally will not qualify for the credit.

Boilers fueled by oil or gas. Except as indicated in the next paragraph, any boiler that is primarily fueled by petroleum, petroleum products, or natural gas and that is placed in service after September 1978, does not qualify for the investment credit. This rule does not apply to a boiler that was constructed, reconstructed, erected or acquired by a contract that was binding on the taxpayer on October 1, 1978, and at all times thereafter. Nor does the rule apply if the use of coal is prevented by Federal air pollution regulations or by State air pollution regulations in effect on October 1, 1978.

A boiler fueled by oil or gas will not be prevented from qualifying for the credit if it is used:
1) In an apartment, hotel, motel, or other residential facility;
2) In a vehicle, aircraft, vessel, or in transportation by pipeline;
3) On a farm for farming purposes;
4) In a shopping center, an office building, a wholesale or retail establishment, or any other facility that is not an integral part of manufacturing, processing or mining; or
5) In Hawaii.

BUSINESS ENERGY CREDITS

The Energy Tax Act of 1978 provides a new 10% credit for investment in energy property placed in service after September 1978 that may be claimed in addition to the regular investment credit. Property may qualify for both the business energy credit and the regular investment credit only if the property meets the qualifications for both. For example, certain structural components of a building may qualify for the business energy credit but not for the regular investment credit since, as discussed earlier, structural components of a building generally do not qualify for the regular credit.

Energy property defined. Energy property is any of the following categories of property:
1) Alternative energy property;
2) Solar or wind energy property;
3) Specially defined energy property;
4) Recycling equipment;
5) Shale oil equipment; and
6) Equipment for producing natural gas from geopressured brine.

For the property to qualify as energy property, you must have completed the construction, reconstruction or erection of the property after September 1978. If you acquired the property, you must have acquired and first used it after September 1978, and must have been the original user of the property. The property must be depreciable (or ammortizable) and have a useful life of 3 years or more determined at the time the property is placed in service.

AMOUNT OF CREDIT ALLOWABLE

The amount of your investment in qualifying property that is eligible for the investment credit depends upon the useful life of the property and whether the property is new or used. Moreover, the amount of credit allowable against your tax liability in any one year is limited, but any excess may be carried back or forward (except for certain solar or wind energy credits) as described later.

AMOUNT OF CREDIT AVAILABLE

The credit allowable is the sum of your investment credit carryovers, 10% of the current year's investment eligible for the regular investment credit, 10% of the current year's investment eligible for the business energy credit (discussed earlier), plus the investment credit carrybacks to the year. Subject to the limitation based on tax liability discussed later, you may deduct this amount from the total tax due on your return. Use Form 3468, Schedule B of Form 3468 is used to compute your business energy credit.

The tax liability against which the credit is allowed is your income tax computed without regard to the minimum tax, accumulated earnings tax, tax on lump sum distributions from qualified employee plans, capital gains tax on Subchapter S corporations, personal holding company tax, or increases resulting from early disposition of property on which you claimed credit in a prior year (see *Recapture Rule* discussed later), but after reducing your tax by any foreign tax credit, and the credit for the elderly.

The regular investment credit is limited to the income tax liability shown on the return, or $25,000 plus 50% of the tax liability in excess of $25,000, whichever is less. The percentage of tax liability in excess of $25,000 increases to 60% for tax years ending in 1979; 70% for tax years ending in 1980; 80% for tax years ending in 1981; and 90% for tax years ending in 1982 or thereafter. See however, *Business energy credit limitation,* discussed later.

Example. On your calendar year return you have a tax liability of $42,500. Your maximum investment credit is $33,750 ($25,000 plus $8,750).

For married persons filing separate returns, each is limited to a credit of $12,500, plus 50% (60% for tax years ending in 1979) of the individual tax liability in excess of $12,500. If one spouse has no qualifying investment (or unused credit), the one having the investment (or unused credit) may use the entire $25,000 limitation plus 50% (60% for tax years ending in 1979) of the tax liability in excess of the $25,000 limitation.

A controlled group of corporations may annually apportion the $25,000 among its members in any manner elected by the members.

Alternative limitation for certain airlines. For tax years ending after 1976 and before 1981, the amount of credit that an airline may claim for investment in qualified airline property may be computed under a special limitation that in effect increases the percentage limitation that applies to tax liability in excess of $25,000, as discussed previously. The alternative limitation applied only if your investment in qualified airline property is 25% or more of your total investment in qualifying property (including nonairline property) and, for tax years ending after 1978, only if the percentage computed under the alternative limitation is greater than the percentage allowed for the applicable year under the regular limitation (60% for tax years ending in 1979 and 70% for tax years ending in 1980).

Qualified airline property means investment credit property used directly in connection with the trade or business carried on by you of the furnishing or sale of transportation as a common carrier by air subject to the jurisdiction of the Civil Aeronautics Board or the Federal Aviation Administration.

If 75% or more of the airline's total investment in qualifying property is attributable to qualified airline property, the 50% limit on tax liability in excess of $25,000 is increased by the tentative percentages for each of the years as follows:

If your tax year ends in:	The tentative percentage is:
1977 or 1978	50%
1979	40%
1980	30%

Thus, for example, if an airline's investment in qualified airline property is 75% or more of its total investment in qualifying property for a tax year ending in 1978, its limit on investment credit for the year is $25,000, plus 100% of tax liability in excess of $25,000.

If 25% or more but less than 75% of the total investment in qualifying property is attributable to qualified airline property, the 50% limit is increased as follows:

$$\text{Percentage limit for tax liability in excess of \$25,000} = 50\% + \text{Tentative percentage} \times \frac{\text{Investment in qualified airline property}}{\text{Total qualified investment}}$$

Example. For its tax year ending in 1978, an airline has $200,000 of investment that is attributable to new qualified airline property, and $500,000 total investment in qualifying property. The taxpayer has a tax liability of $30,000 and no carryovers of unused credits to the year. Using the formula, the percentage limit for its tax year ending in 1978 is computed as follows:

$$\text{Percentage limit} = 50\% + 50\% \times \frac{\$200,000}{\$500,000}$$
$$= 50\% + (50\% \times 2/5)$$
$$= 50\% + 20\%$$

The investment credit allowed to the airline for its 1978 tax year would be $28,500; i.e., $25,000 plus 70% of $5,000 ($30,000 liability minus $25,000).

Business energy credit limitation. The business energy credit (discussed earlier) is limited to 100% of your tax liability except for solar or wind energy property. The credit allowable for investment in solar or wind energy property is refundable and therefore may exceed 100% of your tax liability.

If both the regular investment credit and the business energy credit are being claimed, you must apply them against tax liability in a certain order. First, you apply the regular credit against tax liability (subject to the limitations just discussed) without regard to any business energy credits: Next you apply the business energy credit other than for solar or wind energy property against 100% of your tax liability. Lastly, you apply the business energy credit for solar or wind energy property. If the energy credits exceed tax liability and any of that excess is attributable to a solar and wind energy credit, that excess is treated as an overpayment of tax and is refundable to you. If the regular credit and the business energy credit (other than for solar or wind energy property) exceed that applicable limitations, you have an unused credit carryback or carryover which is discussed later.

Qualified progress expenditures. A taxpayer may elect to treat expenditures for property under construction as qualified investment in new property before the property is actually placed in service. Once the election is made it is binding for later years.

To qualify, the property must have a normal construction period of 2 years or more and be investment credit property having a useful life of 7 years or more when placed in service. This determination will be made at the end of the year in which construction begins. However, if the election is not made until a year after construction begins, the determination will be made at the close of the election year.

AMOUNT OF INVESTMENT SUBJECT TO THE CREDIT

The useful life of property is determined at the time you place it in service. You must use the same useful life in determining the amount of the allowable investment credit as you use in computing depreciation or amortization on the qualifying property. For example, if you used the Class Life Asset Depreciation Range (CLADR) System, the class life would be the life used for investment credit purposes.

Property with a useful life to you of less than 3 years does not qualify for the credit. Only one-third of the investment in qualifying property with a useful life to you of at least 3 years but less than 5 years is subject to the credit (except for *Commuter highway vehicles,* discussed later). Two-thirds of the amount invested is subject to the credit if the property has a useful life to you of at least 3 years but less than 5 years is subject to the credit (except for *Commuter highway vehicles,* discussed later). Two-thirds of the amount invested is subject to the credit if the property has a useful life to you of at least 5 years but less than 7 years. The full investment is subject to the credit if the property has a useful life to you of at least 7 years.

For qualifying used property, you may count no more than $100,000 of the cost in determining the credit for any one year. For more details, see *Used property* discussed later.

Example. You purchase new equipment with a useful life of 2 years for $5,000, used equipment with a useful life of 4 years for $15,000, used machinery with a useful life of 6 years for $30,000, and new equipment with a useful life of 7 years for $100,000. All of the property is qualified property so it all is subject to the credit. The amount of your investment that is subject to the credit is computed as follows:

Property	Basis or cost	Estimated useful life	Part to be counted	Amount subject to the credit
New equipment	$ 5,000	2	0	0
Used equipment	15,000	3-4	1/3	$ 5,000
Used machinery	30,000	5-6	2/3	20,000
New equipment	100,000	7	all	100,000
Amount of investment subject to credit				$125,000

Incorrect useful life category. If your estimate of useful life for the asset when it was placed in service was 3 years but less than 5 years (or 5 years but less than 7 years) and it is later established that the estimated useful life should have been 5 years but less than 7 years (or 7 years or more), you may recompute the credit (including carrybacks and carryovers) and file an amended return (use Form 1040X or 1120X if your original return was a Form 1040 or 1120) for the tax year the credit was claimed. The amended return must be filed within 3 years from the date your original return was filed or within

2 years from the time the tax was paid, whichever is later. If the amended return cannot be filed within these periods, you may not change to a different useful life category that would produce a larger credit for the prior year even if, as a result of an examination of the prior year's return by the Internal Revenue Service, the estimated useful life of the asset is increased for computing depreciation deductions.

Pollution control facility. The portion of the adjusted basis of a certified pollution control facility that is the amortizable basis of the property is eligible for the investment credit.

To qualify, the facility must have a useful life of 5 years or more and the special 60-month amortization election must be made. The credit is based upon 50% of the investment constituting the amortizable basis. For tax years ending after 1978, the percentage of investment which is the amortizable basis increases to 100%, except for property financed by industrial development bonds which remains at 50%. The 100% rate also applies to property, the construction, reconstruction, or erection of which was completed by you after 1978, but only to the extent of the property's basis attributable to construction, reconstruction, or erection after 1978. Any portion of the basis that is not subject to the election is eligible for the regular investment credit.

Commuter highway vehicles. If you acquire a commuter highway vehicle, such as a van or bus, to transport your employees to and from work, and if the vehicle has a useful life of at least 3 years, you may under certain conditions make a special election for the investment credit. The election permits you to claim the investment credit on 100% of your investment in the commuter vehicle. Normally, property with a useful life of 3 years is subject to the investment credit on only 1/3 of the investment, as discussed previously under *Amount of Investment Subject to the Credit.*

To qualify, the vehicle must have a seating capacity of at least eight adults not including the driver, it must have been acquired on or after November 9, 1978, and placed in service before 1986, and the vehicle must pass the 80% use test.

Eighty percent use test. To qualify for the election, you must reasonably expect that at least 80% of the vehicle's mileage will be used for vanpooling. For this purpose, vanpooling means transporting your employees between their residences and their pieces of employment on trips during which the number of employees transported is at least one-half of the adult seating capacity of the vehicle, not including the driver. The mileage use that qualifies for vanpooling includes not only mileage travelled on trips that transport the required number of employees, but also mileage that is incidental to such trips such as deadheading.

In determining whether employees are transported from their homes to their places of employment, it is not necessary that the employees be picked up at and transported to their homes. It is sufficient if the employees are transported to and from some central point or points or intermediate location between the employees' residences and their places of employment.

Recapture of credit, if, within 3 years after it is placed in service, you dispose of a commuter highway vehicle on which you made the election, you must recapture the entire amount of the credit as discussed later under *Recapture Rule.* You must also recapture the credit if the 80% use test (discussed previously) is not met during the entire portion of any tax year that is within the first 36 months of the operation of the vehicle.

If recapture results from a change in use from vanpooling to other business use, the amount of credit that is recaptured is: 2/3 of the investment credit claimed, assuming the vehicle has a useful life of 3 or 4 years, 1/3 of the credit claimed, assuming the vehicle has a useful life of 5 or 6 years, and none if the vehicle has a useful life of 7 years or more. If recapture results from a change from vanpooling use to personal use, the entire amount of the investment credit will be recaptured.

The election is made on your return for the tax year in which the commuter vehicle is placed in service.

NEW PROPERTY

You count, as your investment, your basis in the qualifying new property. Thus, if you trade old property to new property in a tax-free exchange, you count the adjusted basis of the old property and any additional amount expended to acquire the new property. The construction, reconstruction, or erection of the property must be completed by you (or for you in accordance with your specifications) during the tax year, and you must be the first user of the property. If you bought a factory-rebuilt machine it would not qualify as new property, since you were not the first user. But, see *Used property,* discussed later.

However, if the cost of reconstruction may properly be capitalized and recovered through depreciation or charged against the depreciation reserve, you may use that cost as the basis of new property even though it is charged against the depreciation reserve.

Example. You bought a used machine that is qualifying property as defined earlier, for $10,000, and in rebuilding it spend $2,500, which must be capitalized. Regardless of whether the $2,500 is added to the basis of the property or is capitalized in a separate account, you use this amount in figuring your qualified investment in new property. But, no part of the $10,000 purchase price may be used for that purpose. But, see *Used Property,* as follows.

USED PROPERTY

The cost of used property that may be taken into account in computing investment in used property is limited to $100,000.

In determining your investment for computing the investment credit, only the cost of your qualifying used property purchased during the tax year is counted. Cost does not include any part of the purchased property determined by reference to the basis of other property you held at any time. Thus, if you trade old property in a tax-free exchange, you count only the additional amount you expend in the trade.

If within 60 days before or after the date of disposition of old property (whether it qualifies or not), you buy (or contract to buy) similar used qualifying property as a replacement in a transaction in which the basis of the used property is not determined by reference to the adjusted basis of the old property, you count only the expenditure in excess of the basis of the old property. But, see *Recapture Rule* later for a different rule if disposition of the old property results in a recapture tax.

Example. You buy a used machine for $5,000 to enlarge your operations. You count the entire $5,000 in computing the credit. However, if you bought the machine to replace an old machine within 60 days before or after an outright sale of the old machine that had an adjusted basis of $4,000, only $1,000 would be counted, regardless of the amount you realized on the disposition of the old machine. If you traded the old machine for the used machine in a tax-free exchange and paid an additional $700, only the $700 would be counted. But see *Recapture Rule,* discussed later.

Property you inherit or receive as a gift does not qualify.

You may count no more than $100,000 of the cost of your qualifying used property in any one year for purposes of the investment credit.

Example. On August 22 you purchase a used machine for $50,000 and on November 3 you purchase used equipment for $60,000, and a new machine for $70,000. Your investment subject to the investment credit is $170,000 ($70,000 for the new machine plus your purchases of used machinery and equipment limited to $100,000).

Partnerships, estates and trusts, and Subchapter S corporations (corporations that have elected not to be taxed) may count only up to $100,000 of qualifying used property.

Example. You are a member of a partnership and your distributive share of all partnership items is 10%. You also are a 25% shareholder in a Subchapter S corporation. In addition, you operate a separate business as sole proprietor. The partnership, the corporation, and you all use the calendar year. The cost of qualifying used property acquired by the partnership is $120,000; the corporation, $120,000; and you, $20.000.

The partnership and the corporation each may count only $100,000 of the qualifying used property. Your share of the qualifying used property from the partnership is $10,000 and from the corporation $25,000. You take into account $55,000 for determining your cost of qualifying used property.

Married persons filing separate returns each may count only up to $50,000 of qualifying used property, unless one of them has no qualifying used property. In that case the other may use the entire amount up to $100,000.

A controlled group must apportion the $100,000 limitation among its members in accordance with their purchases of used property.

Acquisitions from related taxpayers. If the property was acquired from a person or in a transaction described under *Nonqualifying property,* the property does not qualify for the investment credit. Likewise, if the same taxpayer is using the property after the acquisition as was using it before the acquisition, it does not qualify.

For applying the preceding rules, property used by a partnership is considered used by each partner. Also, property used by a taxpayer only on a casual basis is not considered used by the taxpayer before acquisition.

Example 1. You sell depreciable property used in your business to a company that immediately thereafter leases the property back to you (sale-leaseback). The property does not qualify because it is being used, after its acquisition, by the same person who used it before its acquisition.

Example 2. You purchase property that you previously leased. The property does not qualify since you are the same taxpayer who used it before acquisition.

Example 3. You placed machinery in service in your proprietorship business during 1976. During 1978, you sell the machinery to a partnership in which you share one-third of the profits and losses. The machinery is not used property to the acquiring partnership because you are the same person who used the machinery before acquisition. The result would be the same as to you if the partnership had placed machinery in service during 1976 and later sold it to you during 1978.

Example 4. You purchase an interest in a partnership, including a proportionate interest in machinery and other depreciable tangible personal property previously placed in service by the partnership. Your purchase does not result in an acquisition of used property because the partnership property is used, after you acquired your interest, by the same persons (your partners) who used the property previously.

UNUSED CREDIT CARRYBACKS AND CARRYOVERS

You have an unused credit if the sum of the investment credit carryovers to the tax year plus the credit allowable for the tax year exceeds the limitation based on tax liability as discussed earlier. Your unused credit, to the extent attributable to credit allowable for the current tax year, may be carried back to the 3 preceding tax years, and the balance still unused in those years may be carried over to the 7 succeeding tax years (or 10 succeeding tax years in certain cases). The unused credit must be used in the earliest of these years (and thereafter in each of the other 9 years) and is absorbed to the extent allowed as a carryback to a prior year or as a carryover to a later year.

Carryback rule. An unused credit carried back to a prior tax year is absorbed to the extent that limitation based on tax liability for the prior year exceeds the sum of:

1) The investment credit carryovers to that year;
2) The credit earned for the year; plus
3) The investment credit carrybacks of years preceding the year from which the credit is being carried.

Example. You are a calendar-year taxpayer and have $3,000 of unused investment credits for 1978 available as a carryback to 1975. Your income tax for 1975 is $2,500, investment credit for 1975 was $1,000, and unused credit carryback from 1977 was $1,000. The unused credits for 1978 that can be used in 1975 are limited to $500, the amount by which your 1975 income tax ($2,500) exceeds the sum of your 1975 investment credit ($1,000) plus your 1977 investment credit carryback.

Carryover rule. An unused credit carried over to 1978 is used before a credit for 1978 to the extent the unused credit does not exceed the limitation based on tax liability. Credits earned for 1978 are then absorbed in the amount by which the limitation based on 1978 tax liability exceeds the carryovers from 1977 and prior years.

Example. You, a calendar-year taxpayer, have an investment credit of $1,200 for 1978, income tax of $1,500 for 1978, and investment credits of $500 to be carried over from 1977. The unused credits from 1977 are first absorbed to the extent of 1978 tax liability, and then the 1978 credits are absorbed to the extent of the excess $1,000 ($1,500 - $500). Unused 1978 credits are treated as discussed under *Carryback rule.*

A claim for refund based upon your investment credit carryback to a preceding tax year may be made by filing an amendment return (use Form 1040X or 1120X if your original return was a Form 1040 or 1120) for the tax year to which the unused credit is carried.

The amended return form must be filed on or before the 15th day of the 40th month (39th month for a corporation) following the close of the year of the unused investment credit which resulted in the carryback. For example, if you are a calendar-year individual taxpayer, an amended return for taxes overpaid in 1972 as the result of an investment credit carryback from 1975 would be timely filed if filed on or before April 16, 1979.

For an investment credit carryback from a tax year that is caused by a net operating loss carryback (or a capital loss carryback for a corporation) from a later tax year, the amended return must be filed on or before the 15th day of the 40th (or 39th) month following the close of the later tax year from which the net operating loss (or capital loss) is being carried. Thus, if the investment credit carryback from 1975 in the preceding paragraph was caused by a net operating loss carryback from 1978, the amended return would be timely filed if filed on or before April 15, 1982.

Quick refunds. You may, if you prefer, apply for a quick refund of prior year taxes by filing Form 1045 (Form 1139 in the case of a corporation) for a tentative adjustment of tax that is affected by an investment credit carryback. An application for a tentative carryback adjustment must be filed on or after the date of filing the return for the tax year of the unused investment credit from which the carryback results, but may not be filed later than 12 months from the end of that tax year. For an investment credit carryback from a tax year that is caused by a net operating loss carryback (or a capital loss carryback for a corporation) from a later tax year, the application may be filed within 12 months from the end of the later tax year from which the net operating loss (or capital loss) is being carried.

RECAPTURE OF INVESTMENT CREDIT

At the end of each tax year you must determine whether you disposed of any property during the year for which you claimed investment credit in a prior year. If so, you must compare the actual useful life of the property with the estimated useful life originally used in computing the credit. You then determine if all or part of the credit must be recaptured according to the rules discussed here. However, no recapture determination need be made if you held the property for 7 years or more.

DISPOSITIONS

A disposition occurs in any transaction as a result of which you cease to own property. An outright sale of property is the clearest example of a disposition. Another very common type of disposition occurs when you exchange (tradein) worn-out or obsolete business assets for new ones. You also are considered to have disposed of property if the property ceases to be qualifying property, as when business property is converted to personal use.

Not every transaction involving property for which investment credit has been allowed results in a disposition for investment credit purposes. The following are some common events that may or may not be dispositions.

Mortgaging, foreclosure, and bankruptcy. No disposition occurs if property is transferred as security for a loan. However, disposition does occur if there is a transfer of property by foreclosure.

Property transferred to a trustee in bankruptcy (who does not continue the taxpayer's business) to liquidate the assets and make distributions to the creditors is considered disposed of in the year the assets are transferred to the trustee.

Leased property. Generally, the mere leasing of investment credit property by the lessor who took the credit is not a disposition. However, if the lease is treated as a sale for incoming tax purposes it will be treated as a disposition. Also, a disposition will occur if the property ceases to be investment credit property in the hands of the lessor, the lessee, or any sublessee.

Reduction in basis. If the basis (or cost) of investment credit property is reduced, the property is treated as having ceased to be investment credit property to the extent of the reduction on the date the reduction takes place. This would occur, for example, if you purchase property and later receive a refund of part of the original purchase price. It would also occur where you elect a reduction in basis (cost) of property because you realized a gain from the discharge of indebtedness before the close of the useful life of the property whether or not the indebtedness was incurred to purchase qualifying property. For recomputing the credit under the recapture rule discussed later, the actual useful life of the property treated as having ceased to be qualifying property is considered to be less than 3 years.

Retirement or abandonments. Property has been disposed of if it is abandoned or otherwise retired from use. Normal retirements from either single asset or multiple asset accounts are considered dispositions, but will not result in recapture of investment credit since the property was held for its entire estimated useful life.

Ordinary retirements under the CLADR system. The sale of property qualifying as an ordinary retirement under the CLADR system is a disposition and may result in recapture of investment credit if the property was not held for its entire estimated useful life.

Transfer by reason of death. There is no disposition of investment credit property if the property is transferred because the taxpayer died before the end of the property's estimated useful life. The property is treated as if it had been held for its entire estimated useful life.

Gifts. Property transferred by gift is considered disposed of. This includes gifts by a taxpayer prior to the taxpayer's death, even if the value of the gift is included in the taxpayer's gross estate for estate tax purposes (such as a gift in contemplation of death).

Property destroyed by casualty or theft is treated as having been disposed of.

Used Property. If you disposed of used property before the end of the estimated useful life used in computing the credit, you can avoid application of the recapture rule if certain circumstances existed for the year you claimed credit. For that year, the cost of used property placed in service must have exceeded $100,000, thus forcing you to select property for which you claimed credit. Under a special rule, you may reselect property placed in service during the same tax year and substitute its cost in place of the cost of the property disposed of.

To make a reselection of used property you must attach a statement to your income tax return for the year of reselection, containing the following information:

1) Your name, address, and taxpayer account number; and
2) The month and year placed in service, cost, and estimated useful life of both the original used property and the reselected used property.

Election of Subchapter S status. If a corporation elects to become a Subchapter S corporation, the investment credit previously claimed by the corporation may be subject to recapture. However, there will be no recapture if the corporation and each of the shareholders agree to:

1) Notify the Internal Revenue Service of any disposition or loss of eligibility of investment credit property; and
2) Be jointly and severally liable for any investment credit recapture.

For additional information see Publication 589.

Change in form of doing business. A disposition does not occur because of a mere change in the form of doing business, provided that all of the following conditions are met:

1) The property is retained as qualifying property in the same trade or business;
2) You retain a substantial interest in the business;
3) Substantially all the assets (whether or not qualifying property) necessary to operate the trade or business are transferred to the new form of business; and
4) The basis of qualifying property in your hands is carried over in whole or in part to the new form of business.

You are considered to have retained substantial interest in the trade or business if your interest in the new form of business is substantial in relation to the total interest of all persons, or is equal to or greater than your interest prior to the change in form. For example, if you own a 5% interest in a partnership and after incorporation, you retain at least a 5% interest in the corporation, you are considered as having retained a substantial interest in the business.

Property you transferred to the new form of business will cease to be qualifying property to you if:

1) The new form of business disposes of the property before the close of the useful life you used to compute your credit; or
2) You do not retain a substantial interest in the new form of business in any tax year.

If your interest in the business is reduced even though you retain a substantial interest after there has been a mere change in the form of conducting a business, you must apply the rules set out later in *Disposition of interest in a Subchapter S corporation, partnership, or estate or trust* to determine whether any part of your interest has ceased to be qualifying property to you.

591

Example 1. In January 1977 you acquired various items of qualifying property for use in your sole proprietorship business and for which you claimed an investment credit. In March 1978 you transferred all assets used in your business to Ace Corporation in exchange for 45% of Ace's stock. The transfer to Ace Corporation is considered a change in form of operating the business.

Example 2. Assume that in February 1979, Ace Corporation in the preceding example sells one of the items of qualifying property. The item sold ceases to be qualifying property to you on that date, and has no effect on the March 1978 transfer to Ace Corporation. For making the computations under the *Recapture Rule* discussed later, you are considered to have held the property for 2 years and one month (from January 1977 to February 1979).

Sale and leaseback. There is no disposition when investment credit property is sold by the taxpayer who claimed the credit and then leased back to the taxpayer as part of the same transaction.

Disposition of interest in a Subchapter S corporation, partnership, or estate or trust. For a shareholder of a Subchapter S corporation who claimed credit for his or her share of investment in property acquired by the corporation and who sells or otherwise disposes of some part of that interest in the Subchapter S corporation, the property may cease to be qualifying property to the shareholder. This occurs if, after the end of the year for which the shareholder claimed the credit and before the close of the estimated useful life of the property, the shareholder's proportionate stock interest is reduced below 66-2/3% of what it was at the time the credit was claimed.

Under these rules, property ceases to be qualifying property to the extent of the actual reduction in the shareholder's stock interest. However, once this occurs, such property does not again cease to be qualifying property unless the shareholder's proportionate stock interest drops below 33-1/3% of what it was when the credit was claimed.

Similar rules apply to the reduction of a partner's proportionate interest in the general profits of a partnership (or in the particular piece of property) or the reduction of an estate's, trust's, or beneficiary's proportionate interest in the income of the estate or trust.

Example 1. Shareholder C owned 60% of the outstanding stock of a Subchapter S corporation. One hundred dollars was apportioned to C as her share of the basis of qualifying property acquired by the corporation. C later sells half her stock and her proportionate stock interest is thereby reduced to 30%. Since C's interest is reduced below 66-2/3% of what it was when she claimed the credit (66-2/3% of 60%, or 40%), the property is treated as having ceased to be qualifying property to C to the extent of $50. The amount that C must add to her tax liability is determined under the *Recapture Rule* discussed later.

Example 2. Partners A and B share the profits and losses of ABC Partnership equally. During 1976 the ABC Partnership acquired new business assets with a 10-year life and a basis of $90,000. Assume that each partner got a $4,500 credit (10% of $45,000) for 1976. In 1978, A sells one-half of his 50% interest to C. Since this reduces his partnership interest to 25%, which is below 66-2/3% of what it was in 1976 (50% x 66-2/3%, or 33-1/3%), one-half of A's share of basis (1/2 of $45,000, or $22,500) ceases to be qualifying property to A. Under the *Recapture Rule* discussed later, the actual useful life of A's share of basis no longer qualifying is less than 3 years. Consequently, he must add to his 1978 tax liability $2,250 (i.e., $4,500 original credit minus $2,250 recomputed credit).

A's remaining share of basis in property will not cease to be qualifying property unless his partnership interest drops below 16-2/3% (i.e., 33-1/3% of the 50% interest existing in 1976).

Termination of election. No disposition occurs when a Subchapter S corporation terminates or revokes its election not to be taxed.

RECAPTURE RULE

If you dispose of an asset before the end of the estimated useful life you used in computing the credit, you must recompute the credit substituting actual useful life (i.e., the period beginning with the first day of the month you placed the asset in service and ending with the date you disposed of it) for the estimated useful life used originally in computing investment subject to the credit.

You must also recompute the unused credits carried back or carried over to any other tax year that is affected by the reduction in the credit allowed for the year the asset was placed in service. This recomputation of the investment credit is intended to place you in the position in which you would have been had you used the actual useful life in computing the credit.

If you are a shareholder of a Subchapter S corporation, you must recompute the credit if assets are disposed of by the corporation before the end of the useful life used in computing the credit. The same is true if you are a member of a partnership, or a beneficiary of an estate that disposed of assets on which you claimed credit.

If the recomputed credit is less than the credit that actually reduced your tax liability (for the year the asset was placed in service as well as for any carryback or carryover year) you must add to your tax liability for the year the asset is disposed of any excess of the credit allowed for all affected years over the recomputed credit.

Example 1. On September 1, 1975, you acquired three new machines that cost $2,000, $3,000, and $5,000 respectively. Each machine had an estimated useful life of 10 years, and all were placed in service at the time of purchase. On your 1975 return you claimed the full credit of $1,000 against a tax liability of $1,300. However, on October 1, 1978, you sold the machine that cost $3,000.

Since you held the machine more than 3 years but less than 5 years, your recomputed investment subject to credit is $8,000 (100% of $2,000 + $5,000, and 1/2 of $3,000). Thus, your recomputed credit is $800, and you must add to your 1978 tax, $200, the excess of the original credit claimed in 1975 over the recomputed credit.

Example 2. The facts are the same as in the preceding example, except that your income tax liability for 1975 was only $100. You had no income tax liability for 1972-1974, but had $500 tax each year for 1976 and 1977. The original credit for 1975 ($1,000) was claimed as follows: $100 for 1975; $500 for 1976; and $400 for 1977.

If you had used the actual, instead of estimated, useful life, your investment subject to credit would have been $8,000, and your credit for 1975 would have been $800. The amount you must add to your 1978 tax liability—the $200 excess of the credit claimed over the recomputed credit—is computed as follows:

Year	Credit allowed for year	Recom- puted credit	Excess of original credit over recomputed credit
1975	$ 100	$100	$- 0 -
1976	500	500	0
1977	* 400	200	200
	$1,000	$800	$200

Example 3. The facts are the same as in *Example 2,* except that in February 1978 you placed in service a new machine with an estimated useful life of 10 years that cost you $10,000. Your income tax liability for 1978 is $900. The excess for 1978 of the credit earned over the tax liability ($1,000 - $900) is an unused credit carryback to 1975.

If you had used the actual, instead of estimated useful life, your investment credit for 1975 would have been $800. The amount carried to 1976 is $800 ($700 carried over from 1975 and $100 carried back from 1978). The amount carried to 1977 is $300 ($200 carryover from 1976 and $100 carryback from 1978). The amount you must add to your 1978 tax liability— the $100 excess of the credit claimed over the recomputed credit—is computed as follows:

Year	Credit allowed for year	Recom- puted credit	Excess of original credit over recomputed credit
1975	$ 100	$100	$- 0 -
1976	500	500	- 0 -
1977	400	300	100
	$1,000	$900	$100

Example 4. In September 1975 you placed in service machinery with an estimated useful life of 10 years that earned an investment credit of $2,100. You had no tax liability for 1972-74. For calendar year 1975 your tax liability was $2,100, against which you claimed credit of $2,100. Your tax liability for 1976 and 1977 was $250 for each year.

In November 1978 you disposed of the machinery placed in service in 1975 and purchased other new machinery with estimated useful life of 10 years. This machinery was placed in service in 1978 and earned a credit of $1,300. Your 1978 tax is $800 and therefore you have an unused credit of $500.

Since the machinery was held for more than 3 years but less than 5 years, the recomputed credit for 1975 is $700. If the $700 recomputed credit earned had been used for 1975 instead of $2,100, the $500 unused credit for 1978 would have been carried back to 1975, 1976, and 1977. The 1978 unused credit of $500 is carried back to 1975.

The amount that must be added to your 1978 tax liability (the $900 excess of the original credit over the recomputed credit) is computed as follows:

Credit originally claimed for 1975		$2,100
Credit that would have been allowed:		
For 1975	$700	
For 1978 unused credit carryback		
to–1975	500	1,200
Amount added to 1978 tax liability		$ 900

Certain net operating losses. A special rule applies for determining whether a net operating loss carryback is taken into account in determining the recapture amount resulting from disposing of an asset before the end of its estimated useful life used in computing the credit.

Individuals, estates, trusts, or corporations that dispose of investment credit property before the end of the useful life years category used in computing the credit, may use Form 4255, or attach a statement to the return for the year in which the asset is disposed of, showing the computation of the recapture amount and the reduction in any investment credit carryover.

You may not reduce the amount of tax liability created by a recapture by credits allowed for the year in which the asset is disposed of, nor can it be reduced by any carryovers or carrybacks of credit to the year.

Example. You dispose of an asset in 1978 before the end of its estimated useful life originally used in 1974 in computing the credit. Your 1978 tax liability is otherwise zero except that you must add $600 for recapture of investment credit. Also, you purchase a new asset in 1978 that earns a credit of $500, none of which is absorbed by carrybacks. The $500 credit for 1978 may not be claimed against the $600 recapture tax for 1978. In addition, an unused credit carryback from a later tax year may not be credited against the $600 recapture tax.

If the recomputed credit is more than the credit you have actually used to reduce your tax (for the year the asset was placed in service as well as for any carryback or carryover year) you decrease the unused credit by the difference between the original credit available and the recomputed credit.

Example. During 1974, its first year of operation, ABC Corporation purchased for $40,000, various qualifying new assets, each having an estimated useful life of 8 years or more. Although the earned credit for 1974 amounted to $2,800, the investment credit was limited to the corporation's tax liability of $1,000. An $1,800 unused credit was available for 1975, 1976, and 1977 but was not used in any of those years. During 1978, one of the 1974 items, originally costing $5,000, was sold.

Since the item was held for more than 3 years but less than 5 years, the recomputed investment for the item is $1,667 ($5,000 x 1/3). The recomputed investment credit for the remaining investment ($35,000 + $1,667) amounts to $2,567 ($36,667 x 7%). Since $2,567 exceeds the $1,000 credit used to reduce 1974 tax liability, the $1,800 unused credit is decreased by $233, the difference between the original credit and the recomputed credit ($2,800 - $2,567). As a result, the unused credit available for 1978 is reduced to $1,567.

Property traded. If you had previously taken an investment credit on qualified property, and later traded it for other qualified property before the end of its estimated useful life, there will be a recapture of investment credit for the original property, and an investment credit available for the new property in the year of the trade.

Example. On September 1, 1975, you bought a new machine costing $4,000 and having a useful life of 10 years. You are a calendar year taxpayer. On your 1975 Federal income tax return you claimed investment credit of $400. During 1975, 1976, 1977, and the first 9 months of 1978 you took a total of $1,233 in depreciation deductions for the machine. On October 1, 1978, you traded the machine plus $2,000 for a new like-kind machine with a useful life of 10 years that also qualifies for the investment credit. Since you held the first machine for more than 3 but less than 5 years, there will be a recapture of $267. The basis for the second machine is the cash paid, $2,000, plus the adjusted basis of the old machine given up, $2,767 ($4,000 - $1,233); or $4,767. This amount is now subject to the investment credit since the new machine is fully qualified, and has a useful life of at least 7 years. The credit is thus $477.

If you acquired used property in a transaction in which the recapture rule applies to the disposition of your old property, the basis of the used property for computing the investment credit is computed the same as for new property acquired. Thus, if in the preceding example, you had acquired a used machine in the tarde rather than a new one, its basis for computing investment credit would not be limited to the $2,000 cash paid as discussed previously under *Used Property.* Instead, its basis would be the $2,767 adjusted basis of your old machine plus the $2,000 cash paid, or $4,767.

ACCOUNTING FOR INVESTMENT CREDIT IN
FINANCIAL REPORTS

You are not required to use any particular method of accounting when reporting your investment credit in financial reports subject to the jurisdiction of any Federal agency or reports made to any Federal agency. You must, however, disclose the method of accounting you choose in your financial reports and also must use the same method of accounting in all such reports unless the Secretary of the Treasury or the Secretary's delegate consents to a change to another method.

Recordkeeping requirement. In general you must maintain records for each item of qualifying property. They should include the following information:
  1) The month and tax year in which the property was placed in service;
  2) The estimated useful life originally assigned;
  3) The basis (or cost) of the property, and date acquired; and
  4) The date of disposition.
An exception to this requirement may apply in the case of assets that qualify as mass assets.

Mass assets are usually minor in value in relation to the group, numerous in quantity, impractical to separately identify, and are not usually accounted for on a separate basis. Examples of mass assets include electric tools, railroad ties, and hardware. In the case of mass assets, an appropriate mortality dispersion table may be established instead of maintaining records for each asset.

Depreciation, amortization, depletion, and investment credit contribute to the benefits of various tax shelters by creating deductions and tax-free income. From time to time laws change these contributing factors often in an effort to spur or contract growth of a particular sector of the economy. That is why a tax-shelter expert should oversee the investor's existing tax-shelter investments and the consideration of new purchases. The types of tax shelters retained and purchased should be those which are consistent with the investor's objectives and most benefited by the existing tax law.

APPENDIXES

PERCENTAGE DEPLETION RATES

Percentage Depletion Rates for mines, wells and other natural deposits are as follows:

(1) 22 PERCENT—

(A) oil and gas wells;

(B) sulphur and uranium; and

(C) if from deposits in the United States — anorthosite, clay, laterite, and nephelite syenite (to the extent that alumina and aluminum compounds are extracted therefrom), asbestos, bauxite, celestite, chromite, corundum, fluorspar, graphite, ilmenite, kyanite, mica, olivine, quartz crystals (radio grade), rutile, block steatite talc, and zircon, and ores of the following metals: antimony, beryllium, bismuth, cadmium, cobalt, columbium, lead, lithium, manganese, mercury, molybdenum, nickel, platinum group metals, tantalum, thorium, tin, titanium, tungsten, vanadium, and zinc.

(2) 15 PERCENT — If from deposits in the U.S. —

(A) gold, silver, copper, and iron ore, and

(B) oil shale (except shale described in paragraph (5)).

(3) 14 PERCENT —

(A) metal mines (if paragraph (1) (C) or (2)(A) does not apply), rock asphalt, and vermiculite; and

(B) if paragraph (1)(C),(5), or (6)(B) does not apply, ball clay, bentonite, china clay, sagger clay, and clay used or sold for use for purposes dependent on its refractory properties.

(4) 10 PERCENT — asbestos (if paragraph (1)(C) does not apply), brucite, coal, lignite, perlite, sodium chloride, and wollastonite.

(5) 7½ PERCENT — clay and shale used or sold for use in the manufacture of sewer pipe or brick, and clay, shale, and slate used or sold for use as sintered or burned lightweight aggregates.

(6) 5 PERCENT —

(A) gravel, peat, pumice, sand, scoria, shale (except shale described in paragraph (2)(B) or (5)), and stone (except stone described in paragraph (7));

(B) clay used, or sold for use, in the manufacture of

drainage and roofing tile; flower pots, and kindred products; and

    (C) if from brine wells — bromine, calcium chloride, and magnesium chloride.

    (7) 14 PERCENT — all other minerals, including, but not limited to, aplite, barite, borax, calcium carbonates, diatomaceous earth, dolomite, feldspar, fullers earth, garnet, gilsonite, granite, limestone, magnesite, magnesium carbonates, marble, mollusk shells (including clam shells and oyster shells), phosphate rock, potash, quartzite, slate, soapstone, stone (used or sold for use by the mine owner or operator as dimension or ornamental stone), thenardite, tripoli, trona, and (if paragraph (1)(C) does not apply) bauxite, flake graphite, fluorspar, lepidolite, mica, spodumene, and talc (including pyrophyllite), except that, unless sold on bid in direct competion with a bona fide bid to sell a mineral listed in paragraph (3), the percentage shall be 5 percent for any such other mineral (other than slate to which paragraph (5) applies) when used, or sold for use, by the mine owner or operator as rip rap, ballast, road material, rubble, concrete aggregates, or for similar purposes. For purposes of this paragraph, the term "all other minerals" does not include —

    (A) soil, sod, dirt, turf, water, or mosses; or

    (B) minerals from sea water, the air, or similar inexhaustible sources.

For the purposes of this subsection, minerals (other than sodium chloride) extracted from brines pumped from a saline perennial lake within the United States shall not be considered minerals from an inexhaustible source.

DEPRECIATION GUIDELINES

(*Also Part I, Section 167.*)

Rev. Proc. 72–10

SECTION 1. PURPOSE.

The purpose of this Revenue Procedure is to restate under the rules authorized by section 167(m) of the Code, the asset guideline classes, asset depreciation periods and asset depreciation ranges referred to in section 1.167(a)–11(b)(4) of the Income Tax Regulations for the Class Life Asset Depreciation Range System (ADR) that taxpayers may elect for certain assets first placed in service by the taxpayer after December 31, 1970. In addition, this Revenue Procedure restates under the rules authorized by section 263(f) of the Code the asset guideline class repair allowance percentages referred to in section 1.167(a)–11(d)(2) of the regulations that may be used by electing taxpayers in determining, under sections 162, 212, and 263 of the Internal Revenue Code of 1954, the treatment of expenditures paid or incurred in connection with the repair, maintenance, rehabilitation or improvement of certain property described in section 1.167(a)–11(d)(2)(iii) of the regulations. Taxpayers may elect, in accordance with the provisions of section 1.167(a)–11 of the regulations to apply the established asset depreciation periods and asset depreciation ranges to "eligible property" as defined in section 1.167(a)–11(b)(2) of the regulations, and to apply the established asset guideline class repair allowance percentages to "repair allowance property" as defined in section 1.167(a)–11 (d)(2)(iii) of the regulations. Taxpayers may also elect to apply the

asset guideline periods in accordance with section 1.167(a)–12 of the regulations to certain property placed in service before January 1, 1971.

SEC. 2. RULES OF APPLICATION.

2.01 In the case of a building or other structure which is section 1250 property (as defined in section 1250(c) of the Code), in accordance with section 1.167(a)–11(d)(2)(iii) of the regulations each item of such property shall for purposes of applying the asset guideline repair allowance be treated as in a separate asset guideline class. Thus, for example, if the taxpayer has two buildings which would, but for the preceding sentence, be in the same asset guideline class, the repair allowance for each building will be determined by applying section 1.167(a)–11(d)(2)(iii) separately to the unadjusted basis of each building.

2.02 Property which is used predominantly outside the United States may be eligible property if the requirements of section 1.167(a)–11(b)(2) of the regulations are met. In the case of property first placed in service and used predominantly outside the United States during the taxable year of election, an asset guideline period, but no asset depreciation range is in effect. Accordingly, such property shall not be treated as included in the same asset guideline class as property used predominantly inside the United States, for purposes of determining the asset depreciation period under section 1.167 (a)–11(b)(4) of the regulations. Thus, for this purpose each asset guideline class described in this Revenue Procedure has an exact counterpart which consists of property otherwise includable within the class, but used predominantly outside the United States during the taxable year of election. Generally, for this purpose property is used predominantly outside the United States if such property is physically located outside the United States during more than 50 percent of days of the taxable year of election, beginning with the date the property is first placed in service. However, there are ten exceptions to this general rule and these are contained in section 48(a)(2) of the Internal Revenue Code of 1954. The asset depreciation period for property, which is determined in the taxable year of election, will not be changed because of a change in predominant use after the close of such taxable year. Although treated as in a separate class for purposes of determin-ing the asset depreciation period, property predominantly used outside the United States shall be included in the same asset guideline class as property predominantly used inside the United States for purposes of applying the asset guideline class repair allowance under section 1.167(a)–11(d)(2) of the regulations.

SEC. 3. ASSET GUIDELINE CLASSES AND PERIODS, ASSET DEPRECIA-TION RANGES, AND ANNUAL AS-SET GUIDELINE REPAIR ALLOW-ANCE PERCENTAGES.

The asset guideline classes, asset guideline periods, asset depreciation ranges, and asset guideline repair allowance percentages have been estab-lished as set forth below.

Asset guideline class	Description of assets included	Asset depreciation range (in years)			Annual asset guideline repair allowance percentage
		Lower limit	Asset guideline period	Upper limit	
00.0	DEPRECIABLE ASSETS USED IN ALL BUSINESS ACTIVITIES, EXCEPT AS NOTED:				
00.1	Office Furniture, Fixtures, Machines, and Equipment: Includes furniture and fixtures which are not a structural component of the building, and machines and equipment used in the preparation of papers or data. Includes such assets as desks, files, safes, typewriters, accounting, calculating and data processing machines, communications, duplicating and copying equipment	8	10	12	7.5
00.2	Transportation Equipment:				
00.21	Aircraft (airframes and engines) except aircraft of air transportation companies	5	6	7	14.0
00.22	Automobiles, taxis	2.5	3	3.5	16.5
00.23	Buses	7	9	11.0	11.5
00.24	General purpose trucks, including concrete ready-mix trucks and ore trucks for use over-the-road:				
00.241	Light (actual unloaded weight less than 13,000 pounds)	3	4	5	16.5
00.242	Heavy (actual unloaded weight 13,000 pounds or more)	5	6	7	10.0
00.25	Railroad cars and locomotives, except those owned by railroad transportation companies	12	15	18	8.0
00.26	Tractor units used over-the-road	3	4	5	16.5

00.27	Trailers and trailer-mounted containers...............	5	6	7	10.0
00.28	Vessels, barges, tugs and similar water transportation equipment, except those used in marine contract construction..........	14.5	18	21.5	6.0
00.3	Land Improvements:[1]				
	Improvements directly to or added to land that are more often than not directly related to one or another of the specific classes of economic activity specified below. Includes only those depreciable land improvements which have a limited period of use in the trade or business, the length of which can be reasonably estimated for the particular improvement. That is, general grading of land such as in the case of cemeteries, golf courses and general site grading and leveling costs not directly related to buildings or other structural improvements to be added, are not depreciable or included in this class but such costs are added to the cost basis of the land.		20		
	Includes paved surfaces such as sidewalks and roads, canals, waterways, drainage facilities and sewers; wharves and docks; bridges; all fences except those included in specific classes described below (i.e., farm and railroad fences); landscaping, shrubbery and similar improvements; radio and television transmitting towers, and other inherently permanent physical structures added to land except buildings and their structural components.				
	Excludes land improvements of electric, gas, steam and water utilities; telephone and telegraph companies; and pipeline, water and rail carriers which are assets covered by asset guideline classes specific to their respective classes of economic activity...				

[1] This class is established for a three-year transition period in accordance with Section 109(e)(1) of the Revenue Act of 1971 (P.L. 92-178, I.R.B. 1972-3, 14) and will be in effect for the period beginning January 1, 1971 and ending January 1, 1974 or at such earlier date as of which asset classes incorporating the assets herein described are represcribed or modified.

Asset guideline class	Description of assets included	Lower limit	Asset guideline period	Upper limit	Annual asset guideline repair allowance percentage
		\multicolumn{3}{} Asset depreciation range (in years)		

Asset guideline class	Description of assets included	Asset depreciation range (in years) — Lower limit	Asset guideline period	Upper limit	Annual asset guideline repair allowance percentage
01.0 to 79.0	DEPRECIABLE ASSETS USED IN THE FOLLOWING ACTIVITIES: [2]				
01.0	Agriculture: Includes only such assets as are identified below and that are used in the production of crops or plants, vines and trees (including forestry); the keeping, grazing, or feeding of livestock for animal products (including serums), for animals increase, or value increase; the operation of dry lot or farm dairies, nurseries, greenhouses, sod farms, mushroom cellars, cranberry bogs, apiaries, and fur farms; the production of bulb, flower, and vegetable seed crops; and the performance of agricultural, animal husbandry and horticultural services.				
01.1	Machinery and equipment, including grain bins and fences but no other land improvements.	8	10	12	11.0
01.2	Animals:				
01.21	Cattle, breeding or dairy	5.5	7	8.5	
01.22	Horses, breeding or work	8	10	12	
01.23	Hogs, breeding	2.5	3	3.5	
01.24	Sheep and goats, breeding	4	5	6	

Asset class	Description				
01.3	Farm buildings..	20	25	30.0	5.0
10.0	Mining: Includes assets used in the mining and quarrying of metallic and non-metallic minerals (including sand, gravel, stone, and clay) and the milling beneficiation and other primary preparation of such materials..............	8	10	12	6.5
13.0	Petroleum and natural gas production and related activities:				
13.1	Drilling of oil and gas wells: Includes assets used in the drilling of onshore oil and gas wells on a contract, fee or other basis and the provision of geophysical and other exploration services; and the provision of such oil and gas field services as chemical treatment, plugging and abandoning of wells and cementing or perforating well casings; but not including assets used in the performance of any of these activities and services by integrated petroleum and natural gas producers for their own account.............	5	6	7	10.0
13.2	Exploration for petroleum and natural gas deposits: Includes assets used for drilling of wells and production of petroleum and natural gas, inclding gathering pipelines and related storage facilities, when these are related activities undertaken by petroleum and natural gas producers................	11	14	17	4.5

[2] All asset classes defined below include subsidiary assets within the meaning of Section 109(e)(2) of the Revenue Act of 1971 whenever such assets are used in the economic activities specified. However, in accordance with the provisions of that section of the Act, during the period beginning on January 1, 1971 and ending January 1, 1974 or such earlier date as of which asset classes incorporating the subsidiary assets are represcribed or modified, taxpayers may exclude from an election all subsidiary assets in a specified class provided that at least 3 percent of all the assets placed in service in the class during the taxable year are subsidiary assets. See section 1.167(a)–11(b)(5)(vii) for application of 3 percent test.

Asset guideline class	Description of assets included	Asset depreciation range (in years)			Annual asset guideline repair allowance percentage
		Lower limit	Asset guideline period	Upper limit	
13.3	Petroleum refining: Includes assets used for the distillation, fractionation, and catalytic cracking of crude petroleum into gasoline and its other components............	13	16	19	7.0
13.4	Marketing of petroleum and petroleum products: Includes assets used in marketing, such as related storage facilities and complete service stations, but not including any of these facilities related to petroleum and natural gas trunk pipelines............	13	16	19	4.0
15.0	Contract construction: Includes such assets used by general building, special trade, heavy construction and marine contractors; does not include assets used by companies in performing construction services on their own account.				
15.1	Contract construction other than marine............	4	5	6	12.5
15.2	Marine contract construction............ Includes floating, self-propelled and other drilling platforms used in offshore drilling for oil and gas.	9.5	12	14.5	5.0
20.0	Manufacture of foods and beverages for human consumption, and certain related products, such as manufactured ice, chewing gum,				

vegetable and animal fats and oils, and prepared feeds for animals and fowls:

20.1	Grain and grain mill products: Includes assets used in the production of flours, cereals, livestock feeds, and other grain and grain mill products........	13.5	17	20.5	6.0
20.2	Sugar and sugar products: Includes assets used in the production of raw sugar, syrup or finished sugar from sugar cane or sugar beets........	14.5	18	21.5	4.5
20.3	Vegetable oils and vegetable oil products: Includes assets used in the production of oil from vegetable materials and the manufacture of related vegetable oil products........	14.5	18	21.5	3.5
20.4	All other food and kindred products: Includes assets used in the production of foods, beverages and related production not included in classes 20.1, 20.2 and 20.3........	9.5	12	14.5	5.5
21.0	Manufacture of tobacco and tobacco products: Includes assets used in the production of cigarettes, cigars, smoking and chewing tobacco, snuff and other tobacco products..	12	15	18	5.0
22.0	Manufacture of textile mill products:				
22.1	Knitwear and knit products: Includes assets used in the production of knit apparel and other finished articles from yarn........	7	9	11	7.0
22.2	Textile mill products: Includes assets used in the production of spun, woven or processed yarns and fabrics; of mattresses, carpets, rugs, pads, and sheets, and of other products of natural or synthetic fibers........	11	14	17	4.5

611

Asset guideline class	Description of assets included	Asset depreciation range (in years)			Annual asset guideline repair allowance percentage
		Lower limit	Asset guideline period	Upper limit	
22.3	Finishing and dyeing: Includes assets used in the finishing and dyeing of natural and synthetic fibers, yarns, and fabric..........	9.5	12	14.5	5.5
23.0	Manufacture of apparel and other finished products: Includes assets used in the production of clothing and fabricated textile products by the cutting and sewing of woven fabrics, other textile products and furs; but does not include assets used in the manufacture of apparel from rubber and leather.	7	9	11	7.0
24.0 24.1	Manufacture of lumber and wood products: Cutting of Timber: Includes logging machinery and equipment and road building equipment used by logging and sawmill operators and pulp manufacturers on their own account.....	5	6	7	10.0
24.2	Sawing of dimensional stock from logs: Includes machinery and equipment installed in permanent or well-established sawmills.............	8	10	12	6.5
24.3	Sawing of dimensional stock from logs: Includes machinery and equipment installed in sawmills characterized by temporary foundations and a lack, or				

Manufacture of lumber, wood products, and furniture:

minimum amount, of lumber-handling, drying, and residue disposal equipment and facilities 5 6 7 10.0

24.4 Manufacture of lumber, wood products, and furniture:
Includes assets used in the production of plywood, hardboard, flooring, veneers, furniture and other wood products, including the treatment of poles and timber ... 8 10 12 6.5

26.0 Manufacture of paper and allied products:

26.1 Manufacture of pulps from wood and other cellulose fibers and rags:
Includes assets used in the manufacture of paper and paperboard, but does not include the assets used in pulpwood logging nor the manufacture of hardboard 13 16 19 4.5

26.2 Manufacture of paper and paperboard:
Includes assets used in the production of converted products such as paper coated off the paper machines, paper bags, paper boxes, and envelopes 9.5 12 14.5 5.5

27.0 Printing publishing and allied industries:
Includes assets used in printing by one or more of the common processes, such as letterpress, lithography, gravure, or screen; the performance of services for the printing trade, such as bookbinding, typesetting, engraving, photoengraving, and electrotyping; and the publication of newspapers, books, and periodicals, whether or not carried out in conjunction with printing 9 11 13 5.5

28.0 Manufacture of chemicals and allied products:
Includes assets used in the manufacture of basic chemicals such as acids, alkalies, salts, and organic and inorganic chemicals; chemical products to be used in further manufacture, such as synthetic fibers and plastics materials, including petro-chemical processing beyond that which is ordinarily a part of petro-

Asset guideline class	Description of assets included	Asset depreciation range (in years)			Annual asset guideline repair allowance percentage
		Lower limit	Asset guideline period	Upper limit	
	leum refining; and finished chemical products, such as pharmaceuticals, cosmetics, soaps, fertilizers, paints and varnishes, explosives, and compressed and liquified gases. Does not include assets used in the manufacture of finished rubber and plastic products or in the production of natural gas products, butane, propane, and byproducts of natural gas production plants..............	9	11	13	5. 5
30.0	Manufacture of rubber and plastics products:				
30.1	Manufacture of rubber products:				
	Includes assets used for the production of products from natural, synthetic, or reclaimed rubber, gutta percha, balata, or gutta siak, such as tires, tubes, tubes, rubber footwear, mechanical rubber goods, heels and soles, flooring, and rubber sundries; and in the recapping, retreading, and rebuilding of tires-------	11	14	17	5. 0
30.2	Manufacture of miscellaneous finished plastics products:				
	Includes assets used in the manufacture of plastics products and the molding of primary plastics for the trade. Does not include assets used in the manufacture of basic plastics materials nor the manufacture of phonograph records-------------	9	11	13	5. 5

Account	Description				
31.0	Manufacture of leather: Includes assets used in the tanning, currying, and finishing of hides and skins: the processing of fur pelts; and the manufacture of finished leather products, such as footwear, belting, apparel, luggage and similar leather goods..........	9	11	13	5.5
32.0	Manufacture of stone, clay, glass, and concrete products:				
32.1	Manufacture of glass products: Includes assets used in the production of flat, blown, or pressed products of glass, such as plate safety and window glass, glass containers, glassware and fiberglass. Does not include assets used in the manufacture of lenses. .	11	14	17	6.0
32.0	Manufacture of stone, clay, glass, and concrete products, continued:				
32.2	Manufacture of cement: Includes assets used in the production of cement, but does not include any assets used in the manufacture of concrete and concrete products nor in any mining or extraction process......................	16	20	24	3.0
32.3	Manufacture of other stone and clay products: Includes assets used in the manufacture of products from materials in the form of clay and stone, such as brick, tile and pipe; pottery and related products, such as vitreous-china, plumbing fixtures, earthenware and ceramic insulating materials; and also includes assets used in manufacture of concrete and concrete products. Does not include assets used in any mining or extraction processes....................	12	15	18	5.4
33.0	Manufacture of primary metals: Includes assets used in the smelting and refining of ferrous and nonferrous metals from ore, pig, or scrap, the rolling, draw-				

Asset guide-line class	Description of assets included	Asset depreciation range (in years)			Annual asset guide-line repair allow-ance percent-age
		Lower limit	Asset guide-line period	Upper limit	
	ing, and alloying of ferrous and nonferrous metals; the manufacture of castings, forgings, and other basic products of ferrous and nonferrous metals; and the manufacture of nails, spikes, structural shapes, tubing, and wire and cable.				
33.1	Ferrous metals	14.5	18	21.5	8.0
33.2	Nonferrous metals	11	14	17	4.5
34.0	Manufacture of fabricated metal products: Includes assets used in the production of metal cans, tinware, nonelectric heating apparatus, fabricated structural metal products, metal stampings and other ferrous and nonferrous metal and wire products not elsewhere classified	9.5	12	14.5	6.0
35.0	Manufacture of machinery, except electrical and transportation equipment:				
35.1	Manufacture of metalworking machinery: Includes assets used in the production of metal cutting and forming machines, special dies, tools, jigs, and fixtures, and machine tool accessories	9.5	12	14.5	5.5
35.2	Manufacture of other machines: Includes assets used in the production of such machinery				

Class	Description				
	as engines and turbines; farm machinery, construction, and mining machinery; general and special industrial machines including office machines and non-electronic computing equipment; miscellaneous machines except electrical equipment and transportation equipment......	9.5	12	14.5	5.5
36.0	Manufacture of electrical machinery, equipment, and supplies: Includes assets used in the production of machinery, apparatus, and supplies for the generation, storage, transmission, transformation, and utilization of electrical energy.				
36.1	Manufacture of electrical equipment: Includes assets used in the production of such machinery as electric test and distributing equipment, electrical industrial apparatus, household appliances, electric lighting and wiring equipment; electronic components and accessories, phonograph records, storage batteries and ignition systems......	9.5	12	14.5	5.5
36.2	Manufacture of electronic products: Includes assets used in the production of electronic detection, guidance, control, radiation, computation, test and navigation equipment and the components thereof. Does not include the assets of manufacturers engaged only in the purchase and assembly of components.	6.5	8	9.5	7.5
37.0	Manufacture of transportation equipment: Includes assets used in the production of such machinery as vehicles and equipment for the transportation of passengers and cargo.				
37.1	Manufacture of motor vehicles and parts: Includes assets used in the production of automobiles, trucks, trailers, buses and their component parts........	9.5	12	14.5	5.5

Asset guideline class	Description of assets included	Asset depreciation range (in years)			Annual asset guideline repair allowance percentage
		Lower limit	Asset guideline period	Upper limit	
37.2	Manufacture of aerospace products: Includes assets used in the production of aircraft, spacecraft, rockets, missiles and their component parts	6.5	8	9.5	7.5
37.3	Ship and boat building: Includes assets used in the manufacture and repair of ships and boats, but excludes dry docks	9.5	12	14.5	8.0
37.4	Manufacture of railroad transportation equipment: Includes assets used in the building and rebuilding of railroad locomotives, railroad cars, and street railway cars..	9.5	12	14.5	5.5
38.0	Manufacture of professional, scientific, and controlling instruments; photographic and optical goods; watches and clocks: Includes assets used in the manufacture of mechanical measuring, engineering, laboratory and scientific research instruments, optical instruments and lenses; surgical, medical and dental instruments, equipment and supplies; ophthalmic goods, photographic equipment and supplies; and watches and clocks....	9.5	12	14.5	5.5
39.0	Manufacture of products not elsewhere classified: Includes assets used in the production of jewelry; musical instruments; toys and sporting goods; pens, pencils, office and				

art supplies. Also includes assets used in production of motion picture and television films and tapes; as waste reduction plants; and in the ginning of cotton . . . .

Class	Description			
40.0	(cotton ginning, above)	9.5	12	14.5	5.5

Railroad Transportation:
Includes the assets identified below and which are used in the commercial and contract carrying of passengers and freight by rail. Excludes any nondepreciable assets included in Interstate Commerce Commission accounts enumerated for this class.

| 40.1 | Railroad machinery and equipment . . . . | 11 | 14 | 17 | 10.5 |

Includes assets classified in the following Interstate Commerce Commission accounts:

Road accounts:
- (16) Station and office buildings (freight handling machinery and equipment only)
- (26) Communication systems
- (27) Signals and interlockers
- (37) Roadway machines
- (44) Shop machinery

Equipment accounts:
- (52) Locomotives
- (53) Freight train cars
- (54) Passenger train cars
- (55) Highway revenue equipment
- (57) Work equipment

| 40.2 | Railroad structures and similar improvements . . . . | 24 | 30 | 36 | 5.0 |

Includes assets classified in the following Interstate Commerce Commerce road accounts:
- (6) Bridges, trestles, and culverts
- (7) Elevated structure

619

Asset guideline class	Description of assets included	Asset depreciation range (in years)			Annual asset guideline repair allowance percentage
		Lower limit	Asset guideline period	Upper limit	
	(13) Fences, snowsheds, and signs				
	(16) Station and office buildings (stations and other operating structures only)				
	(17) Roadway buildings				
	(18) Water stations				
	(19) Fuel stations				
	(20) Shops and enginehouses				
	(31) Power transmission systems				
	(35) Miscellaneous structures				
	(39) Public improvements construction				
40.3	Railroad wharves and docks.................	16	20	24	5.5
	(23) Wharves and docks				
	(24) Coal and ore wharves				
40.5	Railroad power plant and equipment:				
	Electric generating equipment:				
40.51	Hydraulic.................	40	50	60	1.5
40.52	Nuclear.................	16	20	24	3.0
40.53	Steam.................	22.5	28	33.5	2.5
40.54	Steam, compressed air, and other power plant equipment.................	22.5	28	33.5	7.5

Class	Description			
41.0	**Motor transport-passengers:** Includes assets used in the urban and interurban commercial and contract carrying of passengers by road, except the transportation assets included in class 00.2 above........	6.5	8	9.5	11.5
42.0	**Motor transport-freight:** Includes assets used in the commercial and contract carrying of freight by road, except the transportation assets included in class 00.2 above........	6.5	8	9.5	11.0
44.0	**Water transportation:** Includes assets used in the commercial and contract carrying of freight and passengers by water except the transportation assets included in class 00.2 above........	16	20	24	8.0
45.0	**Air transport:** Includes assets used in the commercial and contract carrying of passengers and freight by air.........	5	6	7	14.0
46.0	**Pipeline transportation:** Includes assets used in the private, commercial, and contract carrying of petroleum, gas, and other products by means of pipes conveyors. The trunk lines related storage facilities of integrated petroleum and natural gasproducers are included in this class........	17.5	22	26.5	3.0
48.0	**Communication:** Includes assets used in the furnishing of point-to-point communication services by wire or radio, whether intended to be received aurally or visually; and radio broadcasting and television.				
48.1	**Telephone:** Includes the assets identified below and which are used in the provision of commercial and contract telephonic services:				

621

Asset guide-line class	Description of assets included	Asset depreciation range (in years)			Annual asset guide-line repair allow-ance percent-age
		Lower limit	Asset guide-line period	Upper limit	
48.11	Central office buildings: Special purpose structures intended to house central office equipment and which are classified in Federal Communications Commission Account No. 212..........	36	45	54	1.5
48.12	Central office equipment: Includes central office switching and related equipment classified in Federal Communications Commission Account No. 221......	16	20	24	6.0
48.13	Station equipment: Includes such station apparatus and connections as teletypewriters, telephones, booths, and private exchanges as are classified in Federal Communications Commission Account Nos. 231, 232, and 234............	8	10	12	10.0
48.14	Distribution plant: Includes such assets as pole lines, cable, aerial wire and underground conduits as are classified in Federal Communications Commission Account Nos. 241, 242.1, 242.2, 242.3, 242.4, 243, and 244...........	28	35	42	2.0

Asset class	Description			
48.2	Radio and television broadcasting...........	5	6	7	10.0
49.0	Electric, gas and sanitary services:				
49.1	Electric Utilities:				
	Includes assets used in the production, transmission and distribution of electricity for sale, including related land improvements and identified as:				
49.00	Hydraulic production plant:				
	Including dams, flumes, canals and waterways. Also includes jet engines and other internal combustion engines used to operate auxiliary facilities for load shaving purposes or in case of emergencies.........	40	50	60	1.5
49.12	Nuclear production plant:				
	Includes jet engines and other internal combustion engines used to operate auxiliary facilities for load shaving purposes or in case of emergencies.....	16	20	24	3.0
49.13	Steam production plant:				
	Includes jet engines and other internal combustion engines used to operate auxiliary facilities for load shaving purposes or in case of emergencies.....	22.5	28	33.5	2.5
49.14	Transmission and distribution facilities....	24	30	36	2.0
49.2	Gas Utilities:				
	Includes assets used in the production, transmission, and distribution of natural and manufactured gas for sale, including related land improvements and identified as:				
49.21	Distribution facilities:				
	Including gas water heaters and gas conversion equipment installed by utility on customers' premises on a rental basis.....	28	35	42	2.0

623

Asset guideline class	Description of assets included	Asset depreciation range (in years)			Annual asset guideline repair allowance percentage
		Lower limit	Asset guideline period	Upper limit	
49.22	Manufactured gas production plant.........	24	30	36	2.0
49.23	Natural gas production plant.............	11	14	17	4.5
49.24	Trunk pipelines and related storage facilities......	17.5	22	26.5	3.0
49.3	Water utilities: Includes assets used in the gathering, treatment, and commercial distribution of water............	40	50	60	1.5
49.4	Central steam production and distribution: Includes assets used in the production and distribution of steam for sale.........	22.5	28	33.5	2.5
50.0	Wholesale and retail trade: Includes assets used in carrying out the activities of purchasing, assembling, storing, sorting, grading, and selling of goods at both the wholesale and retail level. Also includes assets used in such activities as the operation of restaurants, cafes, coin-operated dispensing machines, and in brokerage of scrap metal.........	8	10	12	6.5
65.0	Building Services:[3] Provision of the services of buildings, whether for use by others or for taxpayer's own account. Assets in the classes listed below include the structural shells of buildings and all integral parts thereof; equipment that services normal heating,				

plumbing, air conditioning, illumination, fire prevention, and power requirements; equipment for the movement of passengers and freight within the building; and any additions to buildings or their components, capitalized remodeling costs, and partitions both permanent and semipermanent. Structures, closely related to the equipment they house, which are section 38 property are not included. See section 1.48–1 (e)(1) of the regulations. Such structures are included in asset guideline classes appropriate to the equipment to which they are related. Depreciation periods for assets used in the provision of the services of buildings and which are not specified below shall be determined according to the facts and circumstances pertinent to each asset, except in the case of farm buildings and other building structures for which a specific class has otherwise been designated.

65.1 Shelter, space, and related building services for manufacturing and for machinery and equipment repair activities:	
65.11 Factories...	45
65.12 Garages..	45
65.13 Machine shops...	45
65.14 Loft buildings...	50
65.2 Building services for the conduct of wholesale and retail trade, includes stores and similar structures	50
65.3 Building services for residential purposes:	
65.31 Apartments..	40
65.32 Dwellings...	45

[3] This class is established for a three-year transition period in accordance with Section 109(e)(1) of the Revenue Act of 1971 (P.L. 92–178, I.R.B. 1972–3, 14) and will be in effect for the period beginning January 1, 1971 and ending January 1, 1974 or at such earlier date as of which asset classes incorporating the assets herein described are represcribed or modified. See Sections 1.167(a)–11(b)(3)(ii), 1.167(a)-11(b)(4)(i)(a), and 1.167(a)-11(b)(5)(vi) of the regulations for special rules relating to real property.

625

| Asset guide-line class | Description of assets included | Asset depreciation range (in years) | | | Annual asset guide-line repair allow-ance percent-age |
		Lower limit	Asset guide-line period	Upper limit	
65.4	Building services relating to the provision of miscellaneous services to businesses and consumers:				
65.41	Office buildings................		45		
65.42	Storage:				
65.421	Warehouses.................		60		
65.422	Grain elevators..............		60		
65.43	Banks......................		50		
65.44	Hotels......................		40		
65.45	Theaters....................		40		
70.0	Services: Includes assets used in the provision of personal services such as those offered by hotels and motels, laundry and dry cleaning establishments, beauty and barber shops, photographic studios and mortuaries. Includes assets used in the provision of professional services such as those offered by doctors, dentists, lawyers, accountants, architects, engineers, and veterinarians. Includes assets used in the provision of repair and maintenance services and those assets used in providing fire and burglary protection services.				
	Includes equipment or facilities used by cemetery organizations, news agencies, teletype wire services, plumbing con-				

	8	10	12	6.5
tractors, frozen food lockers, research laboratories, hotels, and motels (except office furniture and fixtures)............	8	10	12	6.5

79.0 Recreation and Amusement:

Includes assets used in the provision of amusement or entertainment services on payment of a fee or admission charge, as in the operation of bowling alleys, billiard and pool establishments, theaters, concert halls, amusement parks, and miniature golf courses. Does not include such assets which consist primarily of specialized land improvements or structures, such as golf courses, sports stadia, race tracks, ski slopes, or buildings which house bowling alleys.................

	8	10	12	6.5
	8	10	12	6.5

SEC. 4. EFFECT ON OTHER DOCUMENTS.

.01 The provisons of Revenue Procedure 62–21, C.B. 1962–2, 418, including subsequent supplements and amendments thereto, are revoked for taxable years ending after December 31, 1970, except to the extent continued in effect for limited purposes under sections 1.167(a)–11(b)(5)(vi) and 1.167(a)–12. See section 1.167(a)–12 of the regulations with respect to the provisions of an elective guideline system for determining the reasonable allowance for depreciation for taxable years ending after December 31, 1970, for certain assets placed in service before January 1, 1971.

.02 Revenue Procedure 71–25, I.R.B. 1971–28, 62 is superseded, since the provisions stated therein are updated, and revised, and restated under the current statute and regulations.

.03 The asset guideline classes, asset guideline periods, asset depreciation ranges and asset guideline class repair allowances set forth in this Revenue Procedure will from time to time be supplemented and revised Taxpayers using this Revenue Procedure should apply it as supplemented and revised.

TAX REDUCTION ACT CONCERNING OIL AND GAS

On March 29, 1975, the President of the United States signed the Tax Reduction Act of 1975. For taxable years ending after December 31, 1974, this new law affects percentage depletion generally for oil or gas produced on or after January 1, 1975. However, percentage depletion is continued at 22% for domestic natural gas which is produced and sold by a producer before July 1, 1976, and which is subject to the jurisdiction of the Federal Power Commission if no price adjustment is permitted after February 1, 1975, to reflect repeal of percentage depletion. Percentage depletion is also continued at 22% for natural gas sold under a fixed price contract in effect on February 1, 1975, which does not permit price adjustment after that date to reflect repeal of percentage depletion.

In addition, an exemption from the repeal of percentage depletion is provided for small independent producers and royalty owners. The exemption is initially for 2,000 barrels of average daily production of oil (or natural gas if elected by the taxpayer, treating 6,000 cubic feet of gas as one barrel of oil). The exemption is reduced gradually until 1980, when the permanent exemption of 1,000 barrels of oil (or natural gas equivalent) is reached. The depletion rate for oil and gas covered under the small producer exemption is 22% for the years 1975 through 1880, and after 1980 is phased down gradually to a permanent rate of 15% in 1984 and thereafter. Percentage depletion at 22% will be allowed on secondary or tertiary recovery production until 1984 to the extent of 1,000 barrels of production.

In the case of partnerships, a partner's share of production shall be the total production from the property multiplied by the partner's percentage participation in the revenues from the property, and the exemption from repeal of the percentage depletion allowance for small independent producers and royalty owners shall be computed separately by the partners and not by the partnership.

The deduction resulting from the small producer and royalty owners' exemption may not exceed 65% of the taxpayer's net income from all sources. Also, the exemption is generally not available with respect to any oil or gas property transferred after December 31, 1974, if the principal value of the property has been demonstrated before the transfer.

The new law also limits the amount of payments of foreign taxes which will be allowed as a credit against United States tax to 52.8% of taxable income from foreign oil and gas extraction in taxable years ending in 1975, reducing to 50% of such taxable income in years after 1976. Any taxes paid in excess of the limits are not allowed as a deduction, and any excess credits within the limits are allowed only to offset United States tax against foreign oil-related income. Beginning in 1976, the amount of creditable taxes with respect to foreign oil-related income can be calculated only under the overall limitation, and not under the per-country limitation. Also, beginning in 1975, any losses with respect to foreign oil-related income are to be recaptured against future oil-related income by limiting the foreign tax credits available with respect to such future income.

In addition to the law signed by the President on March 29, 1975, the House Ways and Means Committee previously had issued tentative decisions on tax reform, including a new minimum tax, payable if in excess of an individual's regular tax. The new minimum tax would be computed by applying one-half of the regular tax rate to "economic income." Economic income is adjusted gross income under present law plus tax preference items under present law, including the excess of percentage depletion over the tax basis of the property and one-half of capital gains, less certain deductions and a basic exemption of $20,000, which exemption is reduced on a dollar-for-dollar basis to the extent economic income less deductions exceeds $20,000. The tentative decisions also include a limitation on deduction of intangible drilling costs to the amount for which the taxpayer is at risk; taxing as ordinary income any gain on the disposition of interests in oil and gas wells to the extent of the excess of the intangible drilling deductions taken with respect to those wells over the deductions that would have been allowed had the expenses been capitalized; and amendment of taxation of capital gains, including elimination of the alternative tax on the first $50,000 of gains.

On January 15, 1975, the President of the United States

proposed an energy program which includes an excise tax on oil production, an excise tax on gas production and a tax on windfall profits of oil producers.

No prediction can be made as to whether the legislation as proposed or under consideration will be enacted into law, or whether other provisions affecting Partners may be proposed and enacted into law.

Deductible Costs

The following is a more detailed list of the costs which, under the present provisions of the Internal Revenue Code and Treasury Regulations, may be deducted by a Partnership:

1. Costs of drilling any well;
2. Costs of running drill stem tests, electric logs and other tests to determine whether a well is potentially productive and should be completed;
3. Intangible costs of completing wells;
4. Cost of operating productive leases;
5. Costs of plugging and abandoning dry holes;
6. Contributions made toward the drilling of offset wells which will tend either to prove or to condemn a Partnership's acreage, when such wells are dry;
7. All unrecoverable costs of properties established to be worthless during the tax year;
8. Administrative costs and other costs attributable to the ordinary and necessary business expenses of operating a Partnership;
9. Interest paid on loans secured by mortgage liens on oil and gas interests acquired by a Partnership;
10. Depreciation of tangible equipment owned by a Partnership.

Depletion Deduction

Present law provides for a deduction for depletion of producing oil and gas wells. Depletion is computed separately on each property and claimed for each property by whichever of the following two methods produces the greater allowance each year:

1. Percentage depletion, subject to the limitations imposed by the Tax Reduction Act of 1975. There is no limit to the

aggregate percentage depletion which may be taken over a period of years, but the excess of the deduction for depletion allowable for the taxable year over the adjusted tax basis of the property at the end of the taxable year (without adjustment for the year's depletion) is one of several tax preference items under Section 57 of the Internal Revenue Code, and will be subject to a special tax of 10% to the extent the total tax preferences of an individual Partner exceed the sum of $30,000 plus the tax imposed for the year.

2. Cost depletion, which may not exceed the unrecovered basis of the property. Cost depletion is computed by dividing the basis of the lease (exclusive of the equipment) by the estimated recoverable reserves of oil or gas, expressed in barrels of oil or in thousands of cubic feet of gas (mcf), to obtain a unit cost per barrel or mcf. The allowance for the current year is then determined by multiplying the number of barrels or mcf sold in the current year by the cost depletion unit.

Income to a Partnership which is used to reduce indebtedness is taxable income, but the taxable amounts will be reduced by depletion.

Net Loss Deduction

A Partner's share of net losses of a Partnership is deductible only to the extent of the adjusted basis of his interest in the Partnership at the end of the year of the Partnership in which the loss occurred. A Partner's adjusted basis shall be equal to his contributions to the Partnership, increased by his share of taxable income, tax-exempt receipts, the excess of the deductions for depletion over the basis of the depletable property and his share of non-recourse debt; and reduced (but not below zero) by distributions, his share of Partnership losses, Partnership expenditures which are not deductible and which are not capital expenditures, and reduction of his share of liabilities.

Borrowed Funds

If a Partnership borrows money and none of the Partners have personal liability with respect to the loan, for Federal income tax purposes all Partners, including Limited Partners, will be considered as sharing such liability (limited to the fair market value of the property securing the liability) in the same proportion as they share Partnership profits, and the Partners' tax bases will be correspondingly increased. Partnership losses arising from the use of borrowed funds may be claimed by a Partner to the extent of his adjusted tax basis, including any increase arising by reason of the borrowed funds. If income in excess of allowable deductions is used for amortization of principal on the mortgage, there will be Partnership income taxable to Partners but not distributed. Satisfaction of any nonrecourse debt by foreclosure will be treated as a sale of the property, resulting in a capital gain except to the extent of any depreciation recaptured or any recapture of investment credit.

Some lenders may require that the General Partners and Partnership be personally liable on the loans. In no event, however, will the Limited Partners be personally liable for loans in excess of their capital contributions. If a Partnership borrows money and only the General Partner has personal liability with respect to the loan, the tax bases of the Limited Partners will not be increased.

Canadian Tax Law

If a Partnership conducts oil and gas operations in Canada, the Partners will be subject to the Canadian Federal and Provincial Income Tax on their share of income earned in Canada, with deductions allowed under the Canadian law. The Partnership itself will not be a taxpaying entity. The Income Tax Act of Canada as adopted on January 1, 1972, permits a Partner to deduct his share of the costs incurred in Canada for drilling, exploration and acquisition of Canadian oil and gas rights from his present and future Canadian oil and gas income, such income including proceeds in the year of any disposition of Canadian oil and gas rights and interests therein. Such deductible costs may be carried forward indefinitely until fully deducted, provided they are deducted in the year in which incurred and in subsequent years to the extent of the Partner's Canadian oil and gas income for each such year. Equipment costs must be capitalized and recovered through the capital cost (depreciation) allowance. A depletion allowance is provided for, the statutory rate being 33-1/3% of the

Partner's aggregate net profits (after allowable deductions) reasonably attributable to oil and gas production in the case of income from working interests. In the case of royalty income, the statutory rate of depletion is 25% of gross income.

Commencing in 1977 the depletion allowance of 33-1/3% and 25% will be replaced by "earned depletion." Expenditures on drilling and exploration (excluding the cost of acquisition of Canadian resource properties) incurred after November 7, 1969, will "earn" depletion at the rate of $1 of depletion for each $3 of expenditure provided that the amount of depletion claimable in any year by a Partner cannot exceed 1/3 of his net oil and gas production income during that year.

Canadian taxes paid by a Partner may as a general rule either be claimed as a deduction for computing United States tax or may be taken directly as a credit against United States tax. A Partner, other than a corporation, is required to file an income tax return only for those years in which Canadian tax is payable or for those years when a return is demanded by the Minister of National Revenue of Canada. Corporate Partners must file income tax returns annually.

On March 13, 1975, an Act to amend the statue law relating to income tax received Royal Assent and became law. The new law:

(a) brings forward the concept of "earned depletion" retroactively to May 7, 1974 and reduces the maximum amount of depletion claimable in any year by a Participant from 1/3 to 1/4 of his net oil and gas production income during that year;

(b) requires a taxpayer in computing his income for a taxation year to include therein the amount paid or payable to the federal or a provincial government or government agency of Canada after May 6, 1974 as a royalty, tax, rental or other levy or payment in relation to the production of petroleum, natural gas or related hydrocarbons from oil and gas wells in Canada and to disallow as a deduction in computing his income such amounts actually paid therefor;

(c) allows a taxpayer to deduct an amount not exceeding 30% of his Canadian resource property acquisition costs and Canadian development expenses as defined (including drilling costs) incurred after May 6, 1974; and

(d) grants an abatement of 10% after May 6, 1974, 12% for 1975 and 15% after 1975 on the basic 50% federal tax rate on oil and gas production profits.

Sale of Partnership Interests or Partnership Property

If a Partner sells his interest in a Partnership, the Partner will realize taxable gain or loss on the sale measured by the difference between the sale price and the adjusted tax basis of the Partner's interest. The sale price includes cash or property received, plus any decrease in a Partner's share of the liabilities of the Partnership, or any decrease in a Partner's individual liabilities. Assuming the Partner has held his Partnership interest longer than six months, gain or loss on the sale will be taxed as long-term capital gain or loss, except to the extent that the sale price is attributable to the Partner's allocable share of substantially appreciated inventory and unrealized receivables, including depreciation recapture. That part of the sale price attributable to those items is considered as an amount realized from the sale or exchange of property other than a capital asset.

If a Partnership sells oil and gas property held for more than six months and not held primarily for sale to customers, a Partner's share of the gain will be treated as a long-term capital gain unless attributable to recapture of depreciation or recapture of investment credit, and a share of loss will be treated as an ordinary deduction from income. Gains or losses from sale of oil and gas properties not held for more than six months will be ordinary income or deductions.

A Partner will not ordinarily recognize gain upon termination of a Partnership and distribution of the assets to Partners. However, should he receive cash in excess of the adjusted basis of his Partnership interest, or should he receive unrealized receivables or inventory items, there would be taxable gain. Gain or loss may also be realized when the Partner sells property received in a distribution.

State Taxes

A Partnership may operate in states which impose a tax on each Partner's share of income from Partnership activities. In addition, the Partnerships may operate in jurisdictions where estate or inheritance taxes may be payable upon the death of a Partner. Partners will also be subject to the tax laws of the state where they reside. The treatment of various items under state and local tax laws may vary materially from Federal income tax treatment, and Partners should consult their own tax counsel on these matters.

COMMODITIES

The number of speculators in commodities has grown substantially since World War II reflecting increasing sophistication among investors.

Commodity markets will become even more significant as demand increases for mined and raised commodities, as populations continue to expand, as additional farm land becomes less available and as mining locations are depleted.

GENERAL CONSIDERATIONS

COMMODITY FUTURES, COMMODITY EXCHANGES AND MARGINS

Commodity Futures

Commodity futures contracts are contracts, usually made on a commodity exchange, which provide for the future delivery of various agricultural or industrial commodities during a particular period of time at a given price and place. The contractual obligations, depending on whether one is a buyer or a seller, may be satisfied either by taking or making physical delivery of an approved grade of the commodity or by making an offsetting sale or purchase of an equivalent commodity futures contract on the same exchange prior to the designated date of delivery. As an example of an offsetting transaction where the physical commodity is not delivered, the contractual obligations arising from the sale of one contract of May 1975 wheat on a commodity exchange may be fulfilled at any time before expected delivery of the commodity is required by the purchase of one contract of May 1975 wheat on the same exchange. In such instance the difference between the price at which the futures contract was sold and the price paid for the offsetting purchase, after allowance for the trading commission, represents the profit or loss to the trader.

In market terminology, a trader who purchases a futures contract is "long" on the futures market, and a trader who sells a futures contract is "short" in the futures market. Before a trader closes out his "long" or "short" position by an offsetting sale or purchase, his outstanding contracts are known as "open trades."

636

Typical agricultural commodities which are the subject of futures contracts are wheat, corn, oats, rye, soybeans, soybean oil, soybean meal, broilers, grain sorghums, barley, flaxseed, cattle, eggs, pork bellies, hogs, potatoes, sugar, cocoa, cotton, orange juice and wool. Non-agricultural commodities which are the subject of futures contracts include copper, platinum, silver, gold, plywood and foreign currencies.

Two broad classifications of persons who trade in commodity futures are "hedgers" and "speculators." Commercial interests which market or process commodities use the futures markets primarily for hedging. Hedging is a protective procedure designed to minimize losses which may occur because of price fluctuations, for example, between the time a merchandiser or processor makes a contract to sell a raw or processed commodity and the time he must perform the contract. In such case, at the time he undertakes to sell the commodity, he will simultaneously buy futures contracts for the necessary equivalent quantity of the commodity. At the time for performance of the contract, he will buy the actual commodity and close out his futures position by selling futures contracts. Thus the commodity markets enable the hedger to shift the risk of price fluctuations to the speculator. The objective of the hedger is to protect the profit which he expects to earn from his merchandising or processing operations, rather than to profit from his futures trading.

The major portion of the total commodity futures trading volume represents trading by speculators who, unlike the hedger, generally expect neither to deliver nor receive the physical commodity. Instead, the speculator risks his capital with the hope of making profits from price fluctuations in commodities. The speculator is, in effect, the risk bearer who assumes the risks which the hedger seeks to avoid. Speculators rarely take delivery of the actual commodities but close out their futures positions by entering into offsetting purchases or sales of futures contracts.

Since the speculator may take either a long or short position in the commodity futures market, it is possible for him to make profits or incur losses regardless of the direction of price trends. Thus, unlike the stock markets where most investors purchase stocks with the expectation of price appreciation, rather than take short positions in anticipation of price declines, a decline in prices on the commodity futures markets can be as advantageous as an increase in prices to the trader who has correctly predicted the trend. All trades made by the Partnership will be speculative, rather than for hedging purposes.

Commodity Exchanges

Commodity exchanges provide facilities for trading in specific kinds or categories of commodities. Among the principal exchanges in the United States are the Chicago Board of Trade, the Chicago Mercantile Exchange, the New York Mercantile Exchange and the Commodity Exchange, Inc. In addition it is contemplated that the Partnership will make trades on the New York Cocoa Exchange, Inc., the New York Cotton Exchange, the New York Coffee and Sugar Exchange, Inc. and certain other exchanges. Among the commodities traded on exchanges are: wheat, cotton, rice, corn, butter, eggs, fats and oils, peanuts, soybeans, livestock, livestock products, frozen concentrated orange juice, copper, silver, cocoa, coffee and sugar.

Certain commodity exchanges are subject to regulation under the Commodity Exchange Act by the Commodity Exchange Commission and by the Secretary of Agriculture. The Commodity Exchange Authority is the governmental agency through which the Secretary of Agriculture effects such regulation. The Commodity Futures Trading Commission Act of 1974 (the "Act"), was signed into law on October 23, 1974. Under the amendments to the Commodity Exchange Act effected by such Act, the Commodity Futures Trading Commission ("CFTC") will on April 21, 1975 replace the Commodity Exchange Authority as the governmental agency having responsibility for regulation of commodity exchanges and commodity futures trading. The function of the Commodity Exchange Authority is, and that of the CFTC will be, to prevent price manipulation and excessive speculation and to promote orderly and efficient commodity futures markets. Such regulation, among other things, provides that futures trading in commodities must be upon exchanges designated as "contract markets" by the Secretary of Agriculture or, under the Act, the CFTC, and that all trading on such exchanges must be done by or through exchange members.

The Act provides for the creation of the CFTC and increases federal regulation of commodity futures trading. Under the Act, futures trading in all commodities traded on domestic exchanges will be regulated. The CFTC will also regulate the activities of commodity trading advisors and commodity pool operators; under this provision, Queenie, Inc., which makes all investment decisions for the Partnership, and the Partnership may be required to register with the CFTC as part of such expanded regulation. The new legislation authorizes the CFTC to regulate trading by commodity brokerage firms, their officers and directors; expands the ability of the CFTC to require exchange action in the event of market emergencies; and establishes an administrative procedure under which commodity traders may institute complaints for damages arising from alleged violations of the Act. It is impossible to predict what impact, if any, the Act will have on commodity futures trading generally or the Partnership.

Before the Partnership commences trading on a particular exchange it will comply with all rules applicable to it. The Partnership will conform in all respects to the rules, regulations, and guidelines of the Chicago Board of Trade and any other exchange on which its trades are executed. THE CHICAGO BOARD OF TRADE HAS NOT AND WILL NOT ENDORSE OR APPROVE ANY PROGRAM, PRACTICE OR OFFERING OF THIS PARTNERSHIP, OR OF ANY OTHER INVESTMENT COMPANY.

Some exchanges limit the amount of fluctuations in commodity futures contract prices during a single trading day by regulation. These regulations specify what are commonly referred to as "daily limits." The daily limits establish the maximum amount the price of a futures contract may vary either up or down from the previous day's settlement price during a particular daily trading session. Once the daily limit has been reached in a particular commodity, no trades may be made at a price beyond the limit. Because the "daily limit" rule only deals with price movement for a particular trading day, it affords protection only against substantial losses which may occur during that particular trading day. It does not afford any protection to the commodity futures trader over a long term since it is possible for commodity futures prices to move the daily limit for several consecutive trading days with little or no trading taking place, thus preventing prompt liquidation of futures positions and subjecting the commodity futures trader to substantial losses.

Pursuant to the Commodity Exchange Act, the Commodity Exchange Commission has established limits, referred to as "position limits," on the maximum net long or net short position which any person may hold or control in particular commodities. The position limits established by the Commission apply to grains, cotton, soybeans, eggs, potatoes and corn. In addition, the several commodity exchanges have established position limits with respect to other commodities traded on those exchanges such as hogs, pork bellies and frozen broilers. Under the Act, the CFTC will have jurisdiction to establish position limits with respect to all commodities. The following are examples of position limits and commission rates of commodities which are likely to be traded by the Partnership and do not represent all commodities in which the Partnership will trade:

Commodity	Limit(1)	Dollars of Initial Margin Per Contract Required(2)	Minimum Commission Rate Per Trade(3)	Ruth Commodities Rate Per Trade(4)
Copper(5)	None (25,000 lbs. per contract)	$2,500 per contract	$36.50	$42.50
Corn(6)	600 contracts (5,000 bu. per contract)	$1,250 per contract	$30	$37.50
Pork Bellies(7)	250 contracts (36,000 lbs. per contract)	$1,000 per contract	$45	$52.50
Live Cattle(7)	300 contracts (40,000 lbs. per contract)	$1,200 per contract	$40	$47.50
Live Hogs(7)	750 contracts (30,000 lbs. per contract)	$ 900 per contract	$35	$42.50
Silver(5)	None (5,000 troy ounces per contract)	$3,000 per contract	$23.00	$30.50
Soybeans(6)	600 contracts (5,000 bu. per contract)	$3,000 per contract	$30	$37.50
Wheat(6)	400 contracts (5,000 bu. per contract)	$1,500 per contract	$30	$37.50

(1) The limits set forth reflect the maximum net long or net short positions on an exchange. Specific commodities may have additional position limits with respect to the maximum net long or net short position in any one contract month or the maximum number of purchases or sales on any one trading day on an exchange.

(2) Unless otherwise noted, based on limits and initial margin requirements in effect by exchanges on February 26, 1975. Margins are periodically reviewed and modified by the exchanges based on market conditions. In addition, Ruth Commodities, the general partner, may impose margin requirements in excess of exchange minimums.

(3) Established for overnight trades by the exchange on which the commodity is traded.

(4) This rate is in effect for all overnight trades by customers of Ruth Commodities, regardless of the number of contracts traded. These rates are subject of change at any time without notice.

(5) Position limit and initial margin requirement established by Commodity Exchange, Inc.

(6) Position limit and initial margin requirement established by the Commodity Exchange Commission and the Chicago Board of Trade, respectively.

(7) Position limit established by the Chicago Mercantile Exchange.

The Limited Partnership Agreement, which must be signed by each Limited Partner or his attorney-in-fact, places certain restrictions on commodity trading by Limited Partners in order to prevent the Partnership from violating position limits applicable to it.

Margins

Commodity futures contracts are customarily bought and sold on margins which may range upward from as little as five percent of the purchase price of the contract being traded. Because of these low margins any price fluctuations occurring in commodity futures markets will create profits and losses which are greater than are customary in other forms of investment or speculation. Margin is the minimum amount of funds, usually in the form of cash, which must be deposited by the commodity futures trader with his clearing broker in order to initiate futures trading or to maintain his open positions in futures contracts. The Partnership will use only cash, and not treasury bills, to fulfill its margin requirements. The minimum amount of margin required in regard to a particular futures contract is set from time to time by the exchange upon which such commodity futures contract is traded and can be reset from time to time by the exchange during the term of the contract. Under the regulations of the Chicago Board of Trade, the Partnership will be required to maintain 125% of the minimum margin levels applicable to regular accounts traded on that exchange.

Brokerage houses carrying accounts for traders in commodity futures contracts may increase the amount of margin required as a matter of policy in order to afford further protection for themselves. A margin deposit is similar to a cash performance bond. It helps assure the commodity trader's performance of the commodity futures contract. Margin could be further described as the "equity" of a trader in his open contracts. When the market value of a particular open commodity futures position decreases to a point where the margin on deposit does not satisfy minimum margin requirements, a margin call will be made by the clearing broker. If the margin call is not met within a reasonable time, the broker is required to close out the trader's position. Margin requirements are computed each day by the trader's clearing broker.

Example

Stella Commodity Fund II (the "Partnership") is a limited partnership organized under the Uniform Limited Partnership Act to trade in commodity futures contracts. The General Partner of the Partnership is Ruth Commodities, Inc. ("Ruth Commodities" or the "General Partner"). The Units of Limited Partnership Interest (the "Units") have not been traded prior to this offering. The Units are offered at $1,000 per Unit for a period of thirty days from the date hereof, subject to extension for up to an additional sixty days at the General Partner's discretion, unless all Units have previously been subscribed for. All funds received from subscribers will be held in escrow by National Bank and Trust Company until the offering is terminated. In the event that Units aggregating at least $1,000,000 have not been subscribed for when the offering is terminated, all amounts paid by subscribers for Units will be returned without interest. At the time of the termination of the offering, the Partnership will, if the minimum number of Units has been subscribed for, commence trading activities. The Units are not transferable except by will or intestacy and in certain other limited circumstances. A Limited Partner may require the Partnership to redeem any or all of his Units at the net asset value thereof as of the next of February 1, May 1, August 1, or November 1, on at least thirty days' written notice to the General Partner, subject to the right of the General Partner to refuse redemption of Units, if, in the sole discretion of the General Partner, such refusal is necessary to prevent termination of the Partnership for federal income tax purposes. All trading decisions will be made for the Partnership by Queenie, Inc. through its computerized trading system, TAM-COM. Ruth Commodities, Inc., the General Partner of the Partnership, will act as sole commodity broker for the Partnership. The initial public offering price of the Units has been determined arbitrarily by the General Partner.

Investment Requirements

The minimum investment in the Partnership is $5,000 (5 Units). Each investor must represent in the Subscription Agreement that he is able to assume the risks inherent in an

642

investment in the Partnership, including the risk of loss of his entire investment.

Use of Proceeds

The net proceeds of this offering (ranging from $9,890,000 to $899,000, depending on the number of Units subscribed for) will be deposited in the Partnership's commodity account with Ruth Commodities and will be utilized by the Partnership to engage in commodity futures trading. It is anticipated that, when the Partnership commences trading, approximately 60% of the proceeds of this offering will be committed as initial margin for commodity futures contracts and the balance of such proceeds will be retained in cash to apply if needed as additional margin.

Subscriptions for Units will be held by National Bank and Trust Company, as escrow agent (the "Escrow Agent"), until the offering is terminated, at which time all subscriptions held by the Escrow Agent will be transferred to the Partnership's commodity trading account maintained at Ruth Commodities. The Partnership will not, however, commence trading activity until subscriptions have been accepted by the General Partner. In the event that less than $1,000,000 of Units have been subscribed for on the date that the General Partner terminates this offering, all subscriptions will be returned without interest.

The Service Contract

The Partnership and Ruth Commodities have entered into the Service Contract, which provides that Ruth Commodities shall perform the following services for the Partnership:

1. Execute all trades on behalf of the Partnership based on the instructions of the Investment Manager.

2. Maintain books, records and financial information (including tax returns) relating to the activities of the Partnership.

3. Administer and perform secretarial and other clerical responsibilities, and furnish office space, equipment and supplies as may be necessary for supervising the affairs of the Partnership.

4. Prepare monthly reports for distribution to the Partners.

5. Administer the redemption of Limited Partners' Units.

Ruth Commodities will receive no compensation for its services to the Partnership under the Service Contract, except that Ruth Commodities will charge the Partnership brokerage commissions on trades in commodity futures contracts.

The Partnership will be responsible for all of the Partnership's debts and expenses, including taxes, fees payable to governmental agencies and commissions, legal fees and accounting fees incurred in the preparation of annual audited financial statements.

The TAM-COM Trading System

Queenie, Inc., will provide trading instructions to the Partnership from its computerized commodity trading system known as TAM-COM. The TAM-COM trading system has been developed during the past eight years by a group of commodity traders and computer technicians. Research and analysis of factors considered by the developers to be relevant to commodity price trends and movements were consolidated into a series of formulas with the aid of computers. The officers of the Investment Manager have discretion to select among different formulas which give different weight to various factors and, accordingly, may produce different trading recommendations. The officers of the Investment Manager also select a diversified portfolio of commodity futures contracts, usually maintaining positions in more than one option month of each commodity and trading on a number of different commodity exchanges. These selections are based on the amount of trading in each commodity, their respective margin requirements and the historical tendency of each commodity to move in narrow or wide price swings. After the selection of the portfolio and the formulas to be employed, TAM-COM determines the dates to start and stop trading in any particular commodity and the daily buy and sell points for that commodity, based on the factors described below.

TAM-COM is a technical system; its instructions are not based on the anticipated supply and demand of the cash (actual) commodity. Instead, TAM-COM calls for purchases or sales when the relationships between price, volume or open

644

interest depict a particular price trend in effect for a given commodity. It also calls for the offsetting of open positions when existing price trends or market conditions (as indicated by the TAM-COM formulas and rule sets) change. These changes are indicated by the price of the commodity moving above or below predetermined price points or upon attaining predetermined objectives. Commodity futures prices are highly volatile and are influenced by, among other things, fundamental factors such as weather, changing supply and demand relationships, and political and economic conditions and events. Such factors may rapidly change the supply of and demand for commodities which are the subject of commodity futures contracts. Because the TAM-COM trading system is based on price trends and not on fundamental factors, its performance is sometimes adversely affected by sudden unexpected changes in these factors.

The TAM-COM trading system is dependent upon, among other things, the existence of trends in the commodity futures markets of a significant duration or well-established periods of consolidation. It is also dependent upon the ability of the broker to execute the TAM-COM orders as given. During the last few years, the commodity markets have gone through some relatively illiquid periods when it has been difficult to obtain execution of orders at or near the desired trade prices. Under such conditions, it is likely that the TAM-COM trading system would be adversely affected by the broker's inability to execute trades in accordance with its instructions.

In nearly all instances, the Partnership's decision as to the purchase or sale of a given commodity traded by the Investment Manager will be that dictated by the TAM-COM trading system. However, from time to time, market conditions may be such that, in the opinion of the officers of Queenie, Inc., execution of trades recommended by TAM-COM would be difficult or extremely risky to the Partnership. In those instances (estimated by Queenie, Inc., to affect less than 5% of the trading decisions) the instructions of TAM-COM may be modified in the discretion of officers of Queenie, Inc.

The use of a computer in developing a commodity trading system does not guarantee the success of the system. The computer is merely an aid in compiling and organizing trading information. Accordingly, there is no assurance that TAM-COM will produce trading advice which will result in profits

645

to investors in the Partnership. Computerized systems designed to render commodity investment advice have been employed only in recent years and have met with varying degrees of success. The TAM-COM trading system is a trend-following approach to commodity speculation, and may not perform well under any or all market conditions.

Performance of the Investment Manager

Queenie, Inc.'s commodity trading advice is rendered through the TAM-COM trading system. This system has been used for trading discretionary commodity accounts. The TAM-COM trading system has been applied to a number of separate commodity trading accounts which have experienced different investment results depending in part on the period during which they traded and the amount of their initial equity. The tables below set forth certain unaudited information relating to the investment results of those accounts which have followed the TAM-COM system, including Stella Commodity Fund. The first table shows the composite results achieved by all accounts traded by the TAM-COM trading system except for Stella Commodity Fund but does not reflect the actual performance of any one account. Accordingly, investors in accounts contained in the first table may have had less favorable results than the first table below indicates. The second table shows actual results of Stella Commodity Fund.

In the tables below, "Equity" means the sum of all cash together with the current liquidating market value of all open commodity positions maintained by the accounts; it includes unrealized profits and losses from open commodity positions. "Additions" and "Withdrawals" mean, respectively, all cash added to or withdrawn from the accounts during each quarter. "Brokerage Commissions" means all brokerage commissions charged by Ruth Commodities to such accounts during such quarter, including clearing, brokerage and exchange fees payable to exchanges and their clearing houses. "Ending Equity" is the total equity in the accounts on the last day of each quarter, net of all operating expenses, including brokerage commissions shown in the table and management fees. "Increase or Decrease in Equity" is the net addition to or subtraction from equity for the accounts for the quarter and is calculated by subtracting (a) the sum of

646

Starting Equity and the net of Additions and Withdrawals during such quarter from (b) Ending Equity. "Cumulative Increase or Decrease in Equity" is the sum of increases and decreases in equity for all quarters shown in the tables.

THE RESULTS SET FORTH BELOW ARE NOT INDICATIVE OF AND HAVE NO BEARING ON ANY RESULTS WHICH MAY BE ATTAINED BY THE INVESTMENT MANAGER IN THE FUTURE.

Quarter	Starting Equity	Additions	With-drawals	Brokerage Com-missions	Ending Equity	Increase or Decrease in Equity	Cumulative Increase or Decrease in Equity
1st yr. Third	$ 35,000	$ 50,000	$ –0–	$ 18,349	$ 122,984	$ 37,984	$ 37,984
1st yr. Fourth	122,984	300,000	76,853	73,283	384,732	38,601	76,585
2nd yr. First	384,732	409,326	56,623	154,486	710,847	(26,588)	49,997
2nd yr. Second	710,847	674,700	153,600	189,091	2,119,241	887,294	937,291
2nd yr. Third	2,119,241	1,274,582	193,567	211,366	3,604,775	404,519	1,341,810
2nd yr. Fourth	3,604,775	125,000	62,535	281,743	2,761,268	(905,972)	435,838
3rd yr. First	2,761,268	954,106	738,738	372,521	7,429,606	4,452,970	4,888,808
3rd yr. Second	7,429,606	325,000	811,779	596,080	6,062,941	(879,886)	4,008,922
3rd yr. Third	6,062,941	29,000	336,345	574,015	9,240,857	3,485,261	7,494,183
3rd yr. Fourth	9,240,857	185,000	596,758	623,347	7,489,769	(1,339,330)	6,154,853
4th yr. First	7,489,769	212,652	5,777,749*	299,999	1,704,577	220,094	5,934,759

STELLA COMMODITY FUND

Quarter	Starting Equity	Additions	With-drawals	Brokerage Com-missions	Ending Equity	Increase or Decrease in Equity	Cumulative Increase or Decrease in Equity
4th yr. First	6,377,696	–0–	–0–	359,324	7,201,761**	824,065	824,065

*Approximately $4,600,000 of the equity in the accounts included in this table was transferred to Stella Commodity Fund.
**After deducting accrued brokerage commissions of $107,905.

The data in the foregoing tables is unaudited; however, in the opinion of Queenie, Inc.'s management the first table fairly presents the composite results of all accounts traded by the TAM-COM trading system and shown therein. The information contained in the second table fairly reflects actual results of Stella Commodity Fund since it commenced operations. As noted above, the results set forth above cannot be interpreted to mean that an investment in the Partnership will have similar results or will experience any profits whatever.

The Management Contract

The Partnership has entered into the Management Contract with Queenie, Inc. This contract provides that the Investment Manager shall have sole responsibility for determining commodity futures contract trades which will be made by the Partnership. The Investment Manager agrees to perform this function to the best of its ability. The Management Contract does not prevent the Investment Manager from rendering its services to persons or entities in addition to the Partnership and does not require that the Investment Manager or its employees devote their full time to the affairs of the Partnership. However, pursuant to an agreement between the Investment Manager and Ruth Commodities, the Investment Manager will, with certain minor exceptions, provide commodity advisory services only for the Partnership, certain other partnerships traded through Ruth Commodities, including Stella Commodity Fund and certain other accounts.

For the performance of its services under the Management Contract, the Investment Manager will be entitled to receive from the Partnership a fee equal to 20% of the Appreciation (as defined in the Management Contract) experienced by the Partnership during each 3-month period ending on a redemption date. "Appreciation" is defined as (i) on the first February 1, May 1, August 1, or November 1 after the Partnership commences trading activites, the excess (if any) of Net Equity on such date over Net Equity initially committed to the Partnership, as adjusted for distributions by the Partnership, and (ii) on any succeeding redemption date, the excess (if any) of Net Equity, as adjusted for withdrawals from and distributions made by the Partnership, over the highest Net Equity, as adjusted as aforesaid, on any previous redemption date. "Net Equity" is defined as the sum of all cash together with the current liquidating market value of all open commodity positions maintained by the Partnership less all liabilities of the Partnership (exclusive of any accrued but unbilled commissions).

If any payment shall have been made by the Partnership to the Investment Manager on account of Appreciation experienced by the Partnership and the Partnership shall thereafter incur a net loss for any subsequent three-month period, the Investment Manager shall be entitled to retain such amounts previously paid by the Partnership in respect of Appreciation. However, no subsequent payment shall be made to the Investment Manager until the Partnership has again experienced Appreciation, as so defined, on a redemption date.

The Management Contract also provides that the Investment Manager, its shareholders, directors, officers and employees shall not be liable to the Partnership, its partners or any of its successors or assigns except by reason of acts of or omissions due to bad faith, willful misconduct, gross negligence or reckless disregard of their duties or for not having acted in good faith in the reasonable belief that their actions were taken in the best interests of the Partnership.

As compensation to the Investment Manager for the right to the use of its advisory services. Ruth Commodities has agreed to pay to the Investment Manager each month an amount equal to 1% of the net equity (computed as provided in the Management Contract) of the Partnership, subject to certain adjustments. The Partnership will not pay any portion of this fee.

Distributions and Redemptions

The General Partner has sole discretion as to the distribution of profits, if any, of the Partnership. The General Partner does not expect to distribute more than twenty percent of the realized profits of the Partnership for any fiscal year, although the General Partner may, in its sole discretion, distribute a greater or lesser percentage of such realized profits, if any. Since the Limited Partners will be taxable on the Partnership's undistributed profits at the end of any fiscal year and the Partnership may thereafter sustain losses offsetting such profits, a Limited Partner may not realize profits on which he has been taxed. If the Partnership earns profits, such profits will be taxable to the partners pro rata in accordance with their respective investments in the Partnership. However, any distribution of profits will not necessarily be adequate to cover the taxes payable by partners resulting from profits of the Partnership. Subject to the limitations on redemption of Units, a Limited Partner may redeem a portion of his Units if he wishes to realize appreciation, if any, in the value of his interest in the Partnership.

A holder of Units of Limited Partnership Interest may cause any or all of his Units to be redeemed by the Partnership at the net asset value thereof as of the next of any February 1, May 1, August 1, or November 1, by giving the General Partner thirty days prior written notice of redemption. The net asset value of a Unit is defined in the Limited Partnership Agreement as the aggregate of the capital accounts of all Limited Partners divided by the number of Units on the effective date of redemption. Net asset value shall include cash plus the liquidating market value of all open positions in commodity futures contracts held by the Partnership, less all liabilities of the Partnership. The right to obtain redemption is contingent upon the Partnership having property sufficient to discharge its liabilities on the date of redemption and on receipt by the General Partner by registered mail of a request for redemption on the form attached to the Limited Partnership Agreement (or any other form approved by the General Partner) at least thrity days prior to the date on which redemption is requested. The General Partner may refuse redemption of Units if, in its sole discretion, based on an opinion of counsel, such refusal is necessary to prevent termination of the Partnership for federal income tax purposes. In the event that redemptions are requested in respect of more Units than the General Partner elects to honor, the General Partner will give priority to requests for redemption in the order received by the General Partner. No redemption of partial Units will be permitted.

Upon redemption of a Unit, a Limited Partner will receive a distribution from the Partnership equal to the net asset value of a Unit as of the February 1, May 1, August 1, or November 1 on which such redemption is made less any amount owing by such Limited Partner to the Partnership. A limited partner of a partnership is liable to the partnership by operation of law for any sum, not in excess of the cash value of a limited partner's interest upon redemption, necessary to discharge the partnership's liabilities to all creditors who extend credit or whose claims arose before any return of the cash value of a limited partner's interest to him. Accordingly, it is possible that the Partnership may have a claim against a Limited Partner after his redemption of Units from the Partnership for liabilities of the Partnership which arose before the date of such redemption, but such claim will not exceed the sum of such Limited Partner's capital and profits, if any. The Partnership will make such claim only in the event that assets of the Partnership are insufficient to discharge the Partnership's liabilities to its creditors.

OPERATING POLICIES

Trading Policies

The objective of the Partnership is to achieve substantial appreciation of its assets through speculative trading in commodity futures contracts. There can be no assurance, however, that this objective can be met. The Partnership will attempt to accomplish its objective by following the trading policies set forth below:

1. Partnership funds will be invested in futures contracts only of commodities which are traded in sufficient volume to assure, in the opinion of the Investment Manager, ease of taking and liquidating positions. During the past 12 months, accounts managed by the TAM-COM trading system have made investments in futures contracts of 19 commodities.

2. The Partnership will generally not trade in any commodity futures contract during a delivery month.

3. Due to exchange rules, the Partnership will not be as highly leveraged as permitted in the case of an investment by an individual investor. For example, the Chicago Board of Trade imposes on investment companies, including the Partnership, margin levels of 125% of the minimum levels applicable to individual accounts.

4. The trading technique commonly known as "pyramiding" in which the speculator uses unrealized profits on existing positions as margin for the purchase or sale of additional positions, will not be employed by the Partnership.

5. The Partnership will not write or purchase commodity options or options to purchase or sell securities.

6. Borrowings will not be utilized by the Partnership.

7. The Partnership may from time to time employ trading techniques such as spreads or straddles. The term "spread" or "straddle" describes a commodity futures trading transaction involving the simultaneous buying and selling of a particular commodity futures contract dealing with the same commodity but involving different delivery dates and in which the trader expects to earn profits from a widening or narrowing movement of the two prices of the commodity futures contracts.

The trading policies described above may be altered without approval by the Limited Partners if the Investment Manager determines in the future that such change in policy is in the best interest of the Partnership. It is the present policy of the Investment Manager, although it is not obligated to do so under the Management Contract, to notify the Limited Partners of any significant changes in operating policies.

Investment Limitation Due to Position Limits

The Commodity Exchange Commission has imposed limits, commonly called "position limits," on the maximum number of contracts which any speculator may purchase or sell for any commodity for any delivery month. The number of positions which the Partnership expects to hold, when combined with positions of other accounts managed by the Investment Manager or other proprietary accounts of Ruth Commodities, may require the Investment Manager to modify the recommendations of the TAM-COM trading system to comply with such limits. Such adjustments may adversely affect the performance of the TAM-COM trading system and the profitability of the Partnership. The Management Agreement provides that if position limits are exceeded by the Investment Manager in the opinion of the General Partner, the CFTC or any exchange or other regulatory body, the Investment Manager will liquidate positions in accounts other than the Partnership or Stella Commodity Fund to the extent necessary to comply with applicable position limits.

Trading Techniques to Defer Taxes

If the Investment Manager deems it desirable, the Partnership may employ trading techniques to defer taxation. This involves the purchase of commodity futures contracts for delivery in one month and a concurrent sale of a futures contract in the same commodity but for delivery in a different month. Then, assuming a fluctuation in the market price of the commodity, a loss position will result in either the long or short contract, depending on the price movement of that commodity, while a corresponding gain position results in the other contract. This loss position is closed prior to the end of the taxable year resulting in a short-term capital loss for that year. At the same time, in order to protect the unrealized gain on the other position against further market fluctuations, a third futures contract is purchased for the

652

same commodity, either long or short, depending on which position is still open. Then in the following taxable year both open positions are closed, which results in a realization of this gain in the second year approximating the realized loss in the prior year. While the market price of contracts relating to the same commodity but having different delivery dates generally fluctuates in the same direction, there are sometimes differing variations in the price of contracts having different delivery dates. Thus, it is possible that the amount of gain subsequently realized will be more or less than the amount of loss previously incurred through use of the tax deferral techniques. In addition, the use of these trading techniques requires the payment of brokerage commissions on all trades involved in the transaction.

Implementation of Trades

Trades will be effected through Ruth Commodities, the sole broker for the Partnership under the Limited Partnership Agreement and the Service Contract between the Partnership and Ruth Commodities.

Benefits of Commodity Investments

1. High profit potential.
2. There are relatively few actively traded commodities to watch compared to the thousands of active stocks on the listed exchanges and the over-the-counter market.
3. Pertinent information is available to all investors from government agencies and the commodity exchanges.
4. Commodity futures market is relatively liquid as they are traded on an auction market which is usually active.
5. Government agencies supervise the activity of most of the commodities traded to prevent fraud and manipulation.
6. Commodity straddles have potential tax advantages. A straddle is the concurrent purchase of one contract month against the sale of another. This can postpone taxes from one year to the next and convert short-term profits into long-term capital gains. If prices rise after beginning a straddle, the investor would lose on one contract and gain on the other. If losses are realized before the year expires, the investor has established losses to offset against gains. If the investor

liquidates the profitable contract early in the new year, the gains have been carried forward to the next year.

Risks of a Commodity Fund

Risks Inherent in Commodity Futures Trading. (1) *Trading is Speculative.* Commodity futures prices are highly volatile, because prices for commodity futures contracts may fluctuate very substantially in a short period of time. Price movements of commodity futures contracts are influenced by, among other things, changing supply and demand relationships, governmental agricultural and trade programs and policies, and national and international political and economic events. Changing crop prospects occasioned by unexpected weather or damage by insects and plant diseases make it continuously difficult to forecast the amount of future supplies of agricultural commodities. (2) *Trading is Highly Leveraged.* Because of the low margin deposits normally required in commodity futures trading, an extremely high degree of leverage can be achieved. As a result a relatively small price movement in a commodity futures contract may result in immediate and substantial losses to the investor. For example, if at the time of purchase ten percent of the price of the futures contract is required to be deposited as margin, a ten percent decrease in the price of the futures contract would, if the contract is then closed out, result in a total loss of the margin deposit before any deduction for the trading commission. (3) *Trading May be Illiquid.* Some commodity exchanges limit fluctuations in commodity futures contract prices during a single day by regulations referred to as "daily limits." Trades which cannot be executed within those limits must be delayed until the next trading session or later. Commodity futures prices have occasionally moved the daily limit for several consecutive days with little or no trading; similar occurrences could prevent the Partnership from promptly liquidating unfavorable positions and subject the Partnership to substantial losses.

Ability to Liquidate Investment in Units is Limited. An investment in the Units cannot be immediately liquidated by a purchaser. The Units cannot be resold and no market for the Units will exist at any time. A purchaser can liquidate his investment only if written notice of his desire to have the

Partnership redeem any or all of his Units is given to the Partnership at least thirty days prior to the next February 1, May 1, August 1, or November 1. The right to obtain redemption of Units is limited by the right of the General Partner to refuse redemption of Units if the General Partner determines, based on an opinion of counsel, that such refusal is necessary to prevent a termination of the Partnership for federal income tax purposes.

No Assurance of Distribution of Profits. Although the General Partner intends to distribute a portion of the Partnership's profits, if any, the Partnership is not required to distribute profits. In the event that the Partnership is profitable for any fiscal year, there can be no assurance that Limited Partners will receive cash distributions even though the Limited Partners will be taxable with respect to earnings of the Partnership.

Substantial Charges to Partnership for Management and Brokerage Services. Under the Management Contract, the Investment Manager will charge the Partnership 20% of the net appreciation (as defined in the Management Contract) of the Partnership experienced during each quarter. Under the Service Contract, Ruth Commodities will charge the Partnership customary brokerage commissions charged by Ruth Commodities to its customers from time to time. It is anticipated that annual brokerage fees may approximate 35% of the net equity of the Partnership. Accordingly, the Partnership will be required to make trading profits of a very substantial magnitude to avoid depletion or exhaustion of the assets of the Partnership from these charges.

Reliance on General Partner and Investment Manager. Purchasers of the Units offered hereby will not be entitled to participate in the management of the Partnership or the conduct of its business. The Limited Partnership Agreement vests all management responsibilities in the General Partner, which has delegated all responsibility for making investment decisions for the Partnership to Queenie, Inc.

Limited Experience of Investment Manager. The Partnership. has entered into a management contract with the Investment Manager under which the Investment Manager will have exclusive responsibility for making trading decisions on behalf of the Partnership. The Investment Manager was organized in 1973 to operate a trading system which had been in use since May 1972;

accordingly, its experience managing commodity investment funds and discretionary commodity accounts is limited.

Trades Determined by Computer Program. Investment advice rendered by the Investment Manager will be based on a series of computerized trading programs known as TAM-COM which has been in operation only since May 1972. Computerized trading programs have been employed during only the past few years for recommending trades in commodity futures contracts and have met with varying degrees of success. No assurance can be given that the TAM-COM trading system or any computerized system will be successful under any or all kinds of market conditions.

Possibility of Taxation as Corporation. The General Partner has been advised by counsel that, under current federal income tax law and regulations, the Partnership will be classified as a partnership and not as an association taxable as a corporation. This status has not been confirmed by a ruling from the Internal Revenue Service and no such ruling has been or will be requested. Furthermore, the facts and authorities relied upon by counsel in their opinion may change in the future. If the Partnership should be treated as an association taxable as a corporation for federal income tax purposes in any taxable year, income and losses of the Partnership would be reflected only on its tax return and taxed at corporate rates rather than being passed through to the partners, and all or a portion of any distributions made to partners could be taxable to the Partners as dividend or capital gain income which would not be deductible in computing the Partnership's taxable income.

No Firm Underwriting Commitment. Since the offering of the Units is being made without any commitment on the part of an underwriter to purchase any of the Units, there can be no assurance that any or all of the Units will be sold.

Statutory Regulation. Although the Partnership and the Investment Manager will be subject to regulation by the Commodity Futures Trading Commission, the Partnership is not required to be registered under the Investment Company Act of 1940 (or any similar state law) and the Investment Manager is not required to be registered under the Investment Advisers Act of 1940 (or any similar state law), and investors are therefore not accorded the protective measures provided by such legislation.

656

Tax Aspects of a Commodity Investment

The Partnership has been advised by its counsel that under the facts as stated herein and the current federal income tax law and regulations as interpreted by the Internal Revenue Service, the Partnership will be treated as a partnership for federal income tax purposes and will not constitute an association taxable as a corporation, and that the allocation among the Partners of items of income, gain, loss, deduction and credit set forth in the Limited Partnership Agreement will be determinative of the Partners' shares of such items for federal income tax purposes. No tax ruling has been obtained from the Internal Revenue Service confirming this federal income tax treatment and the General Partner does not intend to request such a ruling. The following is a brief summary of some of the federal income tax consequences to the Limited Partners based upon the Internal Revenue Code of 1954, as amended, the rules and regulations promulgated thereunder and existing interpretations thereof, any of which could be changed at any time:

1. The Partnership, as an entity, will not be subject to federal income tax, and each Limited Partner will be taxed on his pro rata share of the Partnership's taxable income, whether or not distributed to him. Each Limited Partner will be entitled to include on his personal income tax return for the taxable year in which or with which the Partnership's year ends his pro rata share of the Partnership's net losses, if any, to the extent of the tax basis of his Units, as of the end of the Partnership's year in which the loss occurs.

2. Generally, a Limited Partner's tax basis will be $1,000 per Unit, reduced by the Limited Partner's share of Partnership distributions and losses and increased by his share of Partnership income.

3. If cash distributions to a Limited Partner by the Partnership as a result of the redemption of any or all of his Units by the Partnership during any calendar year exceed his share of the Partnership's taxable income for that year the excess will constitute a return of capital to the Limited Partner. A return of captial will not be reportable as taxable income by a recipient for federal income tax purposes, but it will reduce the tax basis of the Limited Partner's interest in the Partnership. If such tax basis should be reduced to zero, any cash

distributions for any year in excess of his share of Partnership taxable income will be taxable to him as though it were a gain on the sale or exchange of the Units. Loss will be recognized only if, after the distributions following the complete redemption of a Limited Partner's Units, he has any tax basis remaining in the Partnership, in which case he will recognize capital loss to the extent of such remaining basis. If the Limited Partner is not a "dealer" in securities and he has held his interest for more than six months such gain or loss will be long-term capital gain or loss.

4. Because the Partnership will purchase commodity futures contracts, for investment only for its own account, and not for the account of others, and because the Partnership will not maintain an inventory in commodity futures contracts for tax reporting purposes, substantially all of the profits or losses generated by the Partnership will have the character of capital gains or losses which in turn may be either short-term or long-term. Because the commodity futures contracts traded by the Partnership will generally not be held for more than six months, the character of the capital gains or losses will generally be short-term.

5. The 1976 Tax Reform Act increases the rate of the minimum tax on individuals from 10 percent to 15 percent. An exemption is provided equal to the greater of $10,000 or one-half of regular income taxes. The carryover of regular taxes that are not used to offset tax preferences in the current year is eliminated.

6. Under prior law, the maximum marginal tax rate on earned income is limited to 50 percent. Earned income includes wages, salaries, professional fees or compensation for personal services (including royalty payments to authors and inventors). For individuals engaged in a trade or business where both personal services and capital are material income-producing factors, a reasonable amount (not to exceed 30 percent) of his share of the net profits from the business is treated as earned income. The 1976 Tax Reform Act eliminates the $30,000 exemption to the preference offset and the 5-year averaging provision. The new tax preferences are added to the preference offset. The maximum tax is extended to pension and annuity income. In addition, the conference agreement redefines "earned income" as "personal service income." These provisions apply to taxable years beginning after December 31, 1976.

7. The Revenue Act of 1978 increases the amount of any net capital gain which a noncorporate taxpayer may deduct from gross income from 50 to 60 percent. The remaining 40 percent of the net capital gain is includible in gross income and subject to tax at the regular rates. The deducted gain is classified as a tax preference item for alternative minimum tax purposes, but not for purposes of reducing the amount of personal service income which is eligible for the maximum tax. A corresponding increase in the capital gains tax preference also is made for November and December 1978 capital gains under the add-on minimum tax. The increase in the capital gains deduction, the elimination of the maximum tax offset, and the increase in the capital gains tax preference are effective for taxable transactions occurring, and installment payments received, after October 31, 1978.

The Act reduces the alternative tax rate on corporate capital gains from 30 to 28 percent. The minimum tax preference of corporate long-term capital gains will be 18/46 of the gain. This change is effective with respect to taxable transactions occurring, and installment payments received, after December 31, 1978.

8. Under the 1976 Tax Reform Act interest on investment indebtedness is limited to $10,000 per year, plus the taxpayer's net investment income. No offset of investment interest is permitted against capital gain income. An additional deduction of up to $15,000 per year is permitted for interest paid in connection with indebtedness incurred by the taxpayer to acquire the stock in a corporation, or a partnership interest, where the taxpayer, his spouse, and his children have (or acquire) at least 50 percent of the stock or capital interest in the enterprise. Interest deductions which are disallowed under these rules are subject to an unlimited carryover and may be deducted in future years (subject to the applicable limitation). Under the 1976 Tax Reform Act, no limitation is imposed on the deductibility of personal interest.

Generally these rules are applicable to taxable years beginning after December 31, 1975. However, under a transition rule, present law (sec. 163(d) before the amendments made under the conference agreement) continues to apply in the case of interest on indebtedness which is attributable to a specific item of property, is for a specified term, and was either incurred before September 11, 1975, or is incurred after that date under a binding written contract or commitment in effect on that date and at all times thereafter (hereinafter referred to as "pre-1976 interest"). As under present law, interest incurred before December 17, 1969 ("pre-1970 interest") is not subject to a limitation.

9. If the Partnership should be treated as an association taxable as a corporation for federal income tax purposes in any taxable year during which it is in existence, all or a portion of any distributions to Limited Partners could be taxable as dividend or capital gain income to the recipient, and would not be deductible in computing the taxable income of the Partnership. In addition, all Partnership income and deductions would not be passed through to the Limited Partners but would be reflected on the tax return of the Partnership and would be taxable at rates applicable to an association taxable as a corporation.

Commodities are a high risk tax shelter for investors interested in large potential gains and who can afford to lose their entire investment.

CABLE TELEVISION

There has been rapid growth in the number of cable television subscribers in the United States and in industry revenues.

In addition to delivering high quality pictures, cable television performs other services such as fire and burglar alarms, at-home shopping, user response educational programming and high speed transmission and data handling.

CATV Industry

The CATV industry developed in the late 1940's and early 1950's in response to the needs of residents in predominantly rural and mountainous areas of the country where the quality of television reception was inadequate because of geographic location, surrounding terrain, manmade structures, or the curvature of the earth. In more recent years, CATV systems have also been constructed in larger cities, where interference problems or the unavailability of a number of channels create a need for better service. Manmade obstructions and noise in and around large cities create interference problems to which television signals are especially susceptible. Television reception is substantially improved by CATV because of its insulation from outside interference.

Presently more than 13,000,000 subscribers are served by approximately 4,000 CATV systems. Comparable statistics for certain intervals over the last 25 years are set forth in the following table (source: Television Factbook, Number 47).

Jan. 1 Year	Operating Systems	Total Subscribers
1953	150	30,000
1956	450	300,000
1959	560	550,000
1962	800	850,000
1965	1,325	1,275,000
1968	2,000	2,800,000
1971	2,570	5,300,000
1972	2,770	6,000,000
1973	2,991	7,300,000
1974	3,158	8,700,000
1975	3,366	9,800,000
1976	3,651	10,800,000
1977	3,801	11,900,000
1978	4,001	13,000,000

In January, 1977 there were approximately 71,556,200 television households (i.e., homes containing television sets) in the United States (Source: Television Factbook, Number 47). As indicated above, only 13,000,000 or 18.2% of those homes were served by CATV in January, 1978. Although the total number of new customers subscribing for CATV service has increased significantly between 1973 and 1978, the percentage growth rate of new subscribers compared with the number of existing subscribers has diminished. This decrease in annual growth rate percentage from 1973 onward has been due partially to the restricted availability of expansion capital and partially to the fact that most cable television companies went into a period of consolidation. This consolidation has taken the form of obtaining rate increases and updating and extension of existing systems.

CATV Systems

A CATV system is a facility which receives television signals and FM radio signals off the air by means of high antennas or by means of a microwave relay service, amplifies the signals and distributes them by coaxial cable to the premises of its subscribers, who pay a fee for the service.

A CATV system consists of three principal operating components. The first, known as a "head end" facility, is located at a favorable receiving location, such as a microwave terminal, mountain top or tall structure, and initially receives the signal through the use of an antenna array capable of high reception discrimination. A second component, the distribution network, consists of coaxial cables (and associated electronic amplifiers) which originate at the head end and may be branched repeatedly to different sections of the system. This equipment is normally attached to public utility poles, but on occasion the distribution network may be partially or completely underground or on the system's own poles. The third component of the system is a cable which extends from the distribution network and delivers the signal into the subscriber's premises via a small coaxial cable terminating, through a special transformer, at the back of the subscriber's television set.

CATV systems typically offer signals of all three national television networks and such independent and education television stations (both VHF and UHF) as are available at the head end and which are allowed to be carried by the rules of the Federal Communications Commission. Systems with unused channel capacity occasionally utilize one or more of such channels for the distribution of programs and services which are originated by the system and are not available to nonsubscribers. Such locally originated programs may consist of music, news, weather reports, stock market and financial information and live or video tape programs of a public service or entertainment nature. FM radio signals are also frequently distributed to subscribers. Some CATV systems also offer a pay cable channel by which additional programming, usually sports and movies, is made available to subscribers for an additional charge. The subscriber thus benefits from an enlarged choice of television stations and programs as well as from improved reception without the use of a rooftop antenna.

A subscriber generally pays an initial connection charge and a fixed monthly fee. Monthly service fees, which constitute the basic source of revenues for a CATV system, vary from one area to another. Subscribers normally are free to discontinue the service at any time without additional charges.

CATV operations are generally conducted pursuant to the terms of a franchise or similar license granted by the local governing body of the area to be served. Joint use or pole rental agreements are normally entered into with electric and/or telephone utilities serving a CATV system's area and annual rentals generally range from $1 to $5 for each pole use.

In building a new CATV system, there is generally competition for a CATV franchise. The award of a new franchise is not only related to the amount of franchise fees to be earned from the system by the local government body granting the franchise, but also depends on the ability, reputation, and financial condition of the franchise. Another significant consideration is the capacity of the system to be built and the kinds of services to be made available to subscribers. There can be no assurance that the Partnerships will be successful in the competition for any specific franchise they may seek.

After a franchise has been awarded, some delay may be encountered in engineering, FCC authorization and arranging the necessary contracts for the use of existing utility poles. Further delays may result from late delivery of equipment and difficulty in rearranging utility poles to accommodate the cable for the CATV system.

Each of the cable television systems owned by prior partnerships had some subscribers who later terminated the service. However, each of these systems currently has a net increase in the overall number of subscribers. Termination occurs primarily because people move to another home or to another city. In other cases, people terminate on a seasonal basis because of the network summertime policy of re-runs or because they can no longer afford, or are dissatisfied with the service. A part of the cable television system revenues derives from re-connect charges for service to homes that request service after having been previously disconnected. This reconnect charge is generally the same as the charge for an original connection. The amount of past due accounts in systems owned by prior partnerships is not material.

Competition

CATV systems compete with so-called free television, that is, the television signals which the viewer is able to receive directly on his set using his own antenna. The extent of such competition is dependent in part upon the quality and quantity of the signals available by such antenna reception as compared to the services rendered by the CATV systems. Accordingly, it is generally less difficult to obtain a franchise and obtain higher subscriber saturation in areas where there are few or no television signals available, than in larger cities where more adequate television signals are available without the aid of CATV.

CATV systems also compete with translator stations, which receive broadcast signals and rebroadcast them on different frequencies at low power pursuant to an FCC license. CATV systems are also in competition, to various degrees, with other communications and entertainment media, and are dependent upon the continued popularity of television itself. The construction of more powerful transmission facilities near a system or the increase in the number of television signals in such area could have an adverse effect on revenues. A possible new source of competition known as MDS (Multipoint Distribution Service) is now just beginning to emerge. This service has the capabilities of providing directly to apartment houses, hotels and the like, a closed circuit television channel which could provide programming quite similar to a CATV system's pay cable channel. Other intelligence may also be transmitted via the

MDS facilities. MDS, however, is limited as to the number of channels it can provide.

REGULATION AND LEGISLATION

Introduction

The cable television industry is intensively regulated by the Federal Communications Commission ("FCC"), by some state governments, and by most local government authorities. Additionally, the 94th Congress extensively revised the Copyright Act of 1909 with the result that Copyright liability is now imposed on all cable systems. Present FCC regulations, among other things, have requirements with respect to certification of operation; carriage of certain signals; deletion of duplicating programs; records keeping; technical standards; and periodic reporting. Additionally the FCC has regulations governing minimum channel capacity, maintenance of program origination equipment, and maintenance of non-broadcast channels (e.g., access channels for local educational use). However in February of 1978 the Eighth Circuit Court of Appeals struck down these access channel requirements. The FCC has filed a petition for review with the United States Supreme Court and the effectiveness of the court's order pending the appeal has been stayed. Proposed FCC regulations include limitations on multiple ownership holdings of cable television operations. It is also conceivable that regulations may ultimately be proposed and adopted to control the rates which cable systems charge subscribers. Several states have assumed regulatory jurisdiction of the cable television industry, and it is anticipated that other states will do so in the future. Cable television operations are subject to local regulation insofar as systems operate under franchises granted from local authorities.

On June 6, 1978 the Chairman of the Subcommittee on Communications of the House Interstate and Foreign Commerce Committee introduced in the United States House of Representatives a bill entitled "Communications Act of 1978" (H.R. 13015). This bill is a virtual rewrite of the existing Communications Act of 1934 as amended and as introduced, would radically alter the telecommunications policy of the United States. Specifically as relates to cable television, it would prohibit federal regulation of cable television. Additionally the bill would allow any common carriers to provide any telecommunication or telecommunications related service through a separate company. This would have the effect of allowing AT&T and the other telephone companies to engage in the cable television business. Abolition of federal regulation could lead to increased state regulation with significant disparities in such regulation from state to state, and the entry of the telephone companies into cable television could introduce a significant element of competition for cable properties and franchises. The General Partner cannot predict whether or in what form the bill will be enacted or its ultimate effect on the future operations of the Partnerships.

To the extent that such regulations and laws hinder or stimulate the growth of the cable television industry, the business of the Partnership will be directly affected. The following is a summary of Federal laws and regulations materially affecting the growth of the cable television industry and a description of certain state and local laws.

Federal Regulation

The FCC has asserted regulatory jurisdiction over the cable television industry as a whole since March, 1966. In February, 1972, the FCC issued a comprehensive new set of rules for cable television (which became effective on March 31, 1972) designed in part to facilitate establishment of new cable television systems in the nation's larger metropolitan markets, while maintaining what the FCC considers to be the proper and continuing viability of broadcast television. These new rules as subsequently modified and which could be further altered by currently pending legal challenges, are summarized below.

Carriage of Broadcast Television Signals

The FCC rules with respect to the carriage of broadcast signals by cable television systems are based primarily upon the division of television markets into groups based on the size of the viewing population and the location of the system with respect thereto. A market is defined as the area or zone contained with a 35-mile radius of a specified reference point in a community to which a television station is licensed.

Communities not within a distance of 35 miles of such reference points are not considered to be within any market.

The FCC's rules require carriage of all "local" television signals (as defined in the rules) and authorize carriage of a varying number of out-of-market ("distant") signals. The extent of required and permissible signal carriage varies, depending upon the location of the system with respect to any particular television market (as defined above) and the size of such market. In general terms, cable television systems, upon request, must carry the signals of all television stations which are licensed to communities within 35 miles of the cable system, or which are "significantly viewed" (as defined by FCC regulation) in the county or community in which the cable television system is located. In addition to the signals which a cable television system is thus required to carry it may also be permitted to carry the signals of a limited number of distant television stations. Unless the system is outside of all zones or markets, the number of distant signals permitted varies, depending upon the size of the television market in which the cable system is located and the number of local stations which the system is required to carry. Systems located outside of all zones or markets may carry as many distant signals as they desire. The rules contain a very limited restriction with respect to the choice of distant television signals which may be selected by certain cable television systems for carriage. There are no significant restrictions in regard to the carriage of distant foreign language, religious, automated or educational television stations on any cable system. Furthermore all cable systems are entitled to carry any UHF television station whose predicted Grade B contour encompasses at least a portion of the cable community. Cable television systems in operation prior to March 31, 1972 (the effective date of the rules) may continue to carry signals which were lawfully carried pursuant to prior regulations even though such carriage does not comply with the regulations which became effective on March 1, 1972. Systems commencing operation after that date and existing systems which wish to add additional television signals may do so only upon a showing that the signals proposed for carriage comply with the new carriage regulations. See Certification Procedure, below.

Exclusivity

Cable television systems must, upon request of a local station entitled to do so, delete the network or syndicated programming of distant stations when such programming is also being carried by local stations entitled to exclusivity under the Commission's rules. The rules requiring deletion of syndicated programming are generally not applicable to cable television systems located outside the top 100 television markets (as defined by the rules) although the FCC is now restudying this. In some instances, the cable television system may substitute programming of another distant station for the programming which the system is required to delete.

Program Origination

Cable television systems may engage in cable-casting of programs on their systems and may present advertising. Revenues generated by local program origination may not offset related operating expenses and capital costs and such expenses may, therefore, constitute a financial burden for some cable television systems.

The FCC rules allow per program or per channel charges to subscribers for special interest programs. Cable operators engaged in cable-casting or the presentation of programs for which a per program or per channel charge is made are prohibited from presenting lotteries or obscene programming material and are required to comply with the FCC's "Fairness Doctrine" which governs the presentation of conflicting views on controversial issues of public importance, and with the FCC's regulations governing political broadcasts, political advertisements, and sponsorship identification.

Channel Capacity and Access Requirements

The FCC's rules require cable television systems having 3500 subscribers to have a minimum channel capacity of 20 channels and two way capability. Major market CATV systems having 3500 subscribers which commenced operations after March 31, 1972, are required to be in compliance on June 21, 1976. Major market CATV systems having 3500 subscribers which commenced operations prior to March 31, 1972, and systems having

3500 subscribers, but not located within a major market which commenced operations, or will commence operations, prior to March 31, 1977, are required to be in compliance with the rule on or before June 21, 1986. Any CATV system commencing operations subsequent to March 31, 1977, must be in compliance at the time it commences operation.

Effective June 21, 1976, all CATV systems having 3500 subscribers are required to have four dedicated access channels, one each dedicated specifically for the general public, local educational authorities, local government uses, and lease services; but only if there is sufficient activated channel capacity on the system to do so. Access programming can be combined on one composite channel until such time as a demand develops for a full time dedicated channel in these specified categories.

If on June 21, 1976, a CATV system does not have sufficient activated channel capacity to meet the requirements of this rule, it may comply by providing a single composite access channel, and if no separate activated channel is available on this date, compliance may be achieved by providing access service during unused (including blackout) time on broadcast channels. The FCC rules do not prohibit local franchising authorities from imposing the above channel capacity and access requirements on CATV systems having less than 3500 subscribers, but no requirements may be imposed by local franchising authorities in excess of those prescribed by the FCC. The channels for governmental and educational authorities must, for a period of five years, from the date the CATV system first offers services to such entities be made available without charge. The channel designated for use by the public must always be made available without charge and the cable television system must make production facilities (i.e., a studio, etc.) available, but production costs may be assessed for the installation of equipment (including minimum facilities and equipment necessary for the production of public access programming), as well as additional operating expenses. The General Partner is unable to predict the significance of these potential expenditures at this time.

Cable operators may not censor or control programming presented on the above-described access channels but are required, under the FCC's regulations, to promulgate and enforce rules prohibiting the presentation of lotteries, obscene or indecent programming and advertising on certain of the access and leased channels; such regulations must also specify the rates at which leased channels will be made available.

Technical and Reporting Requirements

The FCC rules include technical standards for cable television systems with which all systems must comply. Additionally cable systems using the midband spectrum are subject to recently adopted rules designed to prevent harmful interference by cable systems to aeronautical navigation and safety radio services. Cable television systems must also pay annual fees to the FCC and submit certain annual ownership, operating, employment and financial reports. However, the FCC has suspended the collection of CATV fees and all other fees until litigation is completed with respect thereto.

Franchise Terms

The responsibility for franchising or other authorization of CATV systems is left to the state and local authorities. Although the FCC recommends certain procedures and provisions to be included in the local authorization the only FCC rule relating to such local authorization restricts the amount of fees paid by the cable television operator to the franchising authority to a maximum of 3% of gross subscriber revenue (except under special justification in which case up to 5% may be allowed).

Certification Procedure

Under the rules, all cable television systems with 1,000 or more subscribers must operate pursuant to a certificate of Compliance. A new system must first obtain an authorization issued by the FCC before it is allowed to serve more than 999 subscribers. Certified cable television systems must first obtain a modified certification if they wish to add new signals to their systems except for must-carry signals and certain educational television stations. In order to obtain certification, such existing or proposed systems must show compliance with the relevant rules described above. The FCC rules permit CATV systems, television stations and other interested parties to apply for special relief or waiver of the rules or for the imposition of more stringent standards. These procedures may result in delays or denial of the institution of new or additional cable television services.

Proposed Federal Rules and Laws

The FCC has asked for comments on alternative proposals which, if adopted, would impose limitations on the number of systems which may be under common ownership or upon the number of subscribers served by systems under common ownership. The alternative proposals upon which comments have been requested include (a) a limit on ownership to a maximum of 50 cable television systems (as defined) having 1,000 or more subscribers, (b) a limit on subscribers served by commonly-owned systems to a maximum of 2,000,000 provided that existing systems would be permitted to expand to the extent of 10% of their roster of subscribers, (c) a limit on the number of systems owned in certain size metropolitan areas, and (d) limits on the number of systems which could be owned in the same and/or contiguous states. If one or more of these proposals is ultimately adopted, it might restrict the number of systems in which the Partnership could take an equity position. The FCC has indicated that any rules finally adopted on multiple or common ownership of cable television systems may be retroactive and divestiture of prohibited ownership interests in existing systems may be required in some instances. Numerous interested parties have requested the FCC to make substantive changes in its regulations governing program origination by cable systems; other parties have petitioned the FCC to vacate its stay of such rule and implement it in its present form. In response, the FCC is considering substantive changes to such regulations.

The FCC has proposed rules regulating the carriage of distant radio signals by cable television systems and a rule which would restrict the carriage of certain broadcast signals of distant professional sports events by some cable television systems in certain instances. Other rule making proceedings are pending with regard to various aspects of cable operations. The ultimate affect of these on the future operations of the Partnership cannot at this time be predicted.

Pending Federal legislation would authorize the FCC to regulate numerous aspects of cable operations including the authority to regulate rates.

The General Partner cannot predict whether or in what form any of these proposed regulations or legislation will be enacted.

Communications Satellite System

The FCC has issued rules authorizing systems of domestic communications satellites. One of the uses of such satellite systems could be the transmission of television signals, including syndicated programming to be carried exclusively on cable, to cable television systems located at great distances from the point of signal origination.

Copyright Matters

On September 30, 1976 Congress passed a comprehensive bill on Copyright which, for the first time, subjects cable television systems to Copyright liability for the carriage of distant broadcast signals. The President signed the bill into law on October 19, 1976. In general, the Copyright Law grants CATV systems a "compulsory license" to carry distant broadcast signals without having to negotiate individually with Copyright owners for each program broadcast by the distant stations carried on the CATV system. The Copyright Law requires that in consideration for the compulsory license, CATV systems must deposit with the Copyright Office as Copyright royalty payments, a percentage of the systems' gross revenues from basic subscriber service. Every CATV system must file certain notices and statements of account with the Copyright Office on a regular basis. The Copyright liability attaches for the first time on January 1, 1978 and it is the intent of the Copyright Law to subject CATV systems to Copyright only for the distant signals which the system carries although all systems must pay a minimum royalty whether or not they carry distant signals. The Copyright Act contains specific formulas for calculating the amount of the Copyright fee. In general under these formulas the larger the system and the more distant signals carried, the greater will be the Copyright fee liability.

State Regulation

Several states have subjected cable television systems to the jurisdiction of state governmental agencies. Attempts in other states to so regulate cable systems are continuing and can be expected to increase. It cannot be predicted whether state regulation will have an adverse effect on the growth of cable television and the business of the Partnership.

Local Regulation

A cable television system is generally operated pursuant to a non-exclusive franchise or permit granted by the local governing body of the area to be served. In some states legislation has been adopted which specifically empowers municipal or local governing bodies to regulate various aspects of the CATV business: and in other states, including Colorado, such local bodies have purported to regulate CATV and issue franchises on the basis of "inherent powers." Franchises are granted for a stated term, generally 15 years and in many cases are cancellable for failure to comply with various conditions and limitations, including compliance with national, state and local safety and electrical codes, required rates of construction, limitations as to installation and monthly service charges and conditions of service. Franchises usually call for the payment of fees, often based on percentages of the system's gross subscriber revenues, to the granting authority. All of such state and local regulations are subject to the requirements imposed by the FCC regarding the terms and conditions of franchises.

Miscellaneous

On February 6, 1978 the United States Congress passed a combination pole attachment/CATV fines bill which became law on March 24, 1978. The law gives the FCC adjudicatory authority over pole attachment disputes under certain specified circumstances. The law also specifically empowers the FCC to impose fines upon cable television system operators for willful or repeated violations of the FCC's rules and regulations.

Example

This is an offering of Interests, each in the amount of

$500, in Ursula Fund IV, a limited partnership ("the Partnership"), which will engage primarily in the acquisition, construction, development and operation of cable television systems in the United States. **No specific properties have been selected, nor are any negotiations for such properties being conducted.** An investor must purchase a minimum of 5 Interests, except that certain states require a greater minimum purchase. Vera Intercable, Inc., will be the General Partner of the Partnership.

Under the terms of the Partnership Agreement, the General Partner will have the sole right to control the business of the Partnership, including the making of all determinations on behalf of the Partnership in connection with any CATV systems or rights or licenses with respect thereto in which investments may be made. The General Partner has the sole responsibility for investment policies and direction of the Partnership. Limited Partners do not have the right to participate in the management of the Partnership.

The Partnership will be organized for the purpose of (1) the acquisition, development and operation of existing CATV systems; (2) seeking and acquiring licensing permits or franchises necessary for the operation of CATV systems in areas in which such systems do not exist; and (3) the construction development and operation of such systems. The Partnership has no operating history, nor does it own any franchises or licenses with respect to any CATV systems, any existing CATV systems, or any options to acquire CATV systems or any other assets.

It will be the policy of the General Partner in selecting CATV properties for the Partnership to emphasize potential capital appreciation of a system, with the ability to generate cash flow to the Limited Partners as a secondary objective. There is no assurance that these objectives can be met.

Management Compensation and Fees

The following outlines the fees and compensation to be paid to the General Partner, its affiliates, and others. Except for compensation to the Underwriter and to professional consultants, none of such fees were determined by arms length negotiations.

Upon Consummation of the Offering

Wendy and Company Incorporated (no affiliation) will earn underwriting commissions for the sale of Interests.	$225,000 (Max.), $45,000 (Min.) Plus an expense allowance.

Acquisition Stage

The Xavier Group, Ltd., an affiliate of the General Partner, will receive brokerage fees of a maximum of 6% of the purchase price of a system. Could equal 9% for both a purchase (6%) and a sale (3%), see below.	Assuming maximum leverage $38,400 (minimum interests sold) $231,000 (maximum interests sold)

Operational Stage

General Partner's management fee— (i) base fee of $.50 per mo. per subscriber and subscriber equivalent to a system if the monthly subscriber charge is $6; if more or less, the fee is adjusted proportionately (ii) operating incentive fee of 1.5% of base fee for each 1% aggregate increase in the number of sub. and sub. equivalents up to maximum aggregate increase of 30% of sub. and sub. equivalents.	The amounts of the base and incentive fees are indeterminate.
General Partner's 1% interests in profits and losses.	Amount indeterminate
The Xavier Group, Ltd., will receive brokerage fees on the sale of a system of 6% of the sales price (3% if it	Amount indeterminate

675

earned a commission on the same acquisition).

Yolanda Transmission, Inc., an affiliate of the General Partner, will supply mapping and engineering data
and may lease equipment to the
Partnership, all at competitive industry rates determined by ascertaining
what charges are made for comparable services or equipment by third
parties.

Amount indeterminate

All Stages

Unaffiliated lawyers, accountants
and other professional consultants
will render services to the Partnership for amounts to be agreed unpon
by the parties.

Amount is indeter-
minate except for legal
and accounting fees in
connection with this
offering, estimated at
$51,300.

General Partner will receive reimbursement of expenses incurred for
the Partnership at any time during
the term of the Partnership.

Amount indeterminate

Dissolution

General Partner has 25% share in
assets after all Partnership obligations paid and after Limited Partners
have received an amount which when
added to their prior distributions
equals 100% of their capital contributions.

Amount indeterminate

General Partner's Interest in Profits and Losses

The Internal Revenue Service has recently taken the position
that in order for a limited partnership to be treated for Federal
income tax purposes as a "partnership," and not as an association taxable as a corporation, the general partner must share

in at least 1% of every material item of partnership income, gain, loss, deduction, and credit. Accordingly, the General Partner shall be allocated 1% and Limited Partners shall be allocated 99% of profits or losses.

Reimbursement of Expenses of General Partner

The General Partner shall be entitled to reimbursement from the Partnership for all items of overhead and administrative expense directly identifiable to the operation of the Partnership and expended by the General Partner on behalf of the Partnership, including all legal, auditing, and other fees and expenses of other agents or advisers; costs of insurance; expenses connected with distributions to and communications with Limited Partners and the bookkeeping and clerical work necessary in maintaining the books and records; the cost and expenses of maintaining relations with the Limited Partners, including the cost of printing and mailing checks, statements, proxy solicitation materials, and reports. The General Partner shall also be entitled to reimbursement from the Partnership for general overhead and administrative costs, which shall include, but not be limited to, all direct and indirect expenses and salaries of any full or part-time employees allocable to the operation of the Partnership. Such allocation will be made by the General Partner and will be subject to a fiduciary duty to the Limited Partners to make a fair and reasonable allocation.

Management Fee of the General Partner

The functions which the General Partner will perform include supervision of employees, operation and control over physical assets such as vehicles, antennas, amplifiers, towers, cables, and test instruments and billing for and receiving payments from subscribers. The General Partner will also oversee the following: expansion and construction activities, obtaining pole attachment agreements and agreements with utility companies, development of marketing programs for new subscribers, administration of franchise agreements, new data computations for FCC reports, administration of State and Federal employee FICA and unemployment requirements, administration of employee time keeping requirements, semi-annual employee review and related wage matters, hiring and termination

677

policies, liaison and price negotiations with suppliers, the generation of purchase orders and follow-up through receipt of materials and payment approval, field employment forms, generation, implementation, and management of standard operating procedures, leases, contracts and easements, safety requirements under the Federal OSHA Program; final engineering approval of selected vendor products, day-to-day bookkeeping, accounting, record keeping, and financial reports, and banking relationships.

The management fee will be determined on a system by system basis and will consist of a base fee with an incentive for increasing the total number of subscribers and subscriber equivalents. The base fee will be $.50 per month per subscriber or subscriber equivalent for a system where the monthly charge to subscribers for single set residential television service is $6.00. If the monthly subscription charge is less or greater than $6.00, then the base fee shall be adjusted accordingly and in the same percentage as the $6.00 per month subscription charge varies from any lesser or greater monthly subscription charge. "Subscriber equivalents" are determined by dividing the total operating revenues of a system from all sources other than from single set residential television subscribers by the single set monthly residential television subscription charge. Subscriber equivalents are generated by multiple usage by a single subscriber, burglar and fire alarm taps, channel leasing, advertising revenues, and all other revenue items for which the system charges a fee.

As compensation for increasing the number of subscribers and subscriber equivalents, and thereby increasing the revenues to a system, the General Partner will also receive an operating incentive management fee equal to 1.5% of the base fee for each 1% aggregate increase in subscribers and subscriber equivalents, up to a maximum aggregate increase of 30% of subscribers and subscriber equivalents, computed on a system by system basis. In the event subscribers and subscriber equivalents of any system should increase more than 30%, no additional compensation per subscriber, per month will be paid to the General Partner on account of the Operating Incentive Fee. Thus, a one percent increase in the total number of subscribers and subscriber equivalents of a system would have the effect of changing the total fee from $.50 per month per subscriber or subscriber equivalent to $0.5075 per subscriber or subscriber equivalent. Operating management incentive fees shall accumulate and will be earned by the General Partner only if and when the Limited Partners have received distributions from revenues from routine operations in excess of operating expenses (including interest and excluding depreciation and amortization), on a cumulative basis, equal to at least 1.75% per quarter (7% per year) of their initial capital contributions. In the event the number of subscribers and subscriber equivalents for a system decreases after the fee has increased above the original base fee, the fee for such system shall be decreased at the rate of 1.5% for each 1% decrease in subscribers or subscriber equivalents, but the fee shall not be decreased below the original base fee.

The base fee is payable monthly. The operating incentive fee will be computed quarterly on the basis of an average of the number of subscribers and subscriber equivalents for each system at the end of each month during the preceding quarter.

Participation in Dissolution and Winding Up

On the dissolution and winding up of the Partnership the General Partner is entitled to receive, after payment of all liabilities of the Partnership including any fees due the General Partner, 25% of any remaining Partnership assets, payable only after Limited Partners have received an amount which when added to prior distributions to Limited Partners will equal the amount they initially contributed to the capital of the Partnership.

Compensation of Affiliated Companies

The General Partner expects to engage, on a non-exclusive basis, its affiliated companies to perform specialized work for the Partnership at rates of compensation comparable and competitive with the compensation of any other person who is rendering comparable services or selling or leasing comparable goods which could reasonably be made available to the Partnership. All agreements for any such services will be in writing and will be terminable upon 60 days' notice by the Partnership. Two such affiliated corporations are The Xavier Group Ltd., and Yolanda Transmission, Inc. All of the shares of such companies are owned by Zane International, Ltd.

(a) *CATV Brokerage*. The Xavier Group, ltd., conducts a small, limited CATV system brokerage business involving the buying and selling of CATV systems as representative or agent for parties desiring to acquire or dispose of CATV systems, equipment and instruments. The General Partner may arrange to have The Xavier Group, Ltd., provide services, as broker, to find and negotiate the sale or purchase of a CATV system or systems for the Partnership. The commission paid for such activity will not exceed 6% of the lower of the appraised value or the total purchase price of any such system. On the resale of any property by the Partnership on which The Xavier Group, Ltd., has previously received a commission, any brokerage commission payable to The Xavier Group, Ltd., shall be limited to a maximum of 3% of the total sales price and shall be subordinated and accrued until after payment to each Limited Partner of an amount equal to 100% of his capital contribution. The total brokerage fees payable to The Xavier Group, Ltd., could be as high as 9% on the purchase (6%) and later sale (3%) of a system.

(b) *Data Supply and Construction Services*. Yolanda Transmission, Inc. is a corporation engaged on a limited basis in the business of CATV system development, planning, mapping, the making of television signal surveys, the preparation of CATV engineering data, the leasing of CATV equipment and in assisting in the preparation of construction contracts utilizing said mapping and engineering data which it has prepared. It may also supervise the letting of said construction contracts and may be retained to supervise the construction phases of said contracts. The General Partner may arrange to have Yolanda Transmission, Inc. provide some or all of said services for the Partnership. If Data Transmission, Inc. supplies such information, services or equipment leasing, it will charge the Partnership standard rates which are competitive within the CATV industry for such engineering data, surveys, contracts, supervision or leasing. Such rates may result in a profit to Yolanda Transmission, Inc. Yolanda Transmission, Inc. may also engage in the business of selling antenna, amplifiers, towers, cable and test instruments, and other CATV equipment and instruments to the Partnership. If such equipment is purchased by the Partnership, it will be at a price which is competitive with that charged within the industry.

If any affiliate of the General Partner is engaged at competitive rates to perform specialized services for the Partnership, the expenses of such affiliate shall not be reimbursed by the Partnership.

Underwriting Commissions

Wendy and Company, Incorporated, the underwriter of this offering, will receive underwriting commissions for the sale of Interests. It is not affiliated with the General Partner or the Partnership.

Professional Fees

In connection with the formation and operation of the Partnership and the acquisition of properties, the Partnership will likely utilize the services of non-affiliated lawyers, accountants and other professional consultants. The amount of fees payable for such services cannot be determined, except that the legal and accounting fees in connection with this offering are estimated at $51,300.

FIDUCIARY RESPONSIBILITY
OF THE GENERAL PARTNER

The General Partner is accountable to the Limited Partners as a fiduciary, which means the General Partner is required to exercise good faith and integrity in dealings with respect to Partnership affairs. This is in addition to the several duties and obligations of, and limitations on the General Partner, set forth in the Partnership Agreement. Each Limited Partner or his duly authorized representative may inspect the Partnership books and records at any time during normal business hours. Cases have been decided under the common and statutory law of partnerships to the effect that a limited partner may institute legal action on behalf of himself or all other similarly situated limited partners (a class action) to recover damages from a general partner for violations of its fiduciary duties, or on behalf of the partnership (a partnership derivative action) to recover damages from a third party where the general partner has failed or refused to enforce the obligation. Counsel to the General Partner has advised that comparable relief may be available under state partnership law. Counsel has also advised that on the basis of federal statutes and rules and decisions by federal courts, it appears that (i) limited partners have the right, subject to the provisions of the Federal Rules of Civil Procedure, to bring partnership class actions in the federal courts (to enforce federal rights of all limited partners similarly situated) and partnership derivative actions in the federal courts (to enforce federal rights of the limited partnership), including in each case rights under certain Securities and Exchange Commission rules, and (ii) limited partners who have suffered losses in connection with the purchase or sale of their interests in the partnership due to the breach of a fiduciary duty by the general partner in connection with such purchase or sale, including misapplication by the general partner of the proceeds from the sale of interests in the partnership, may recover such losses from the general partner in an action based on Securities and Exchange Commission Rule 10b-5.

The General Partner may not be liable to the Partnership or the Limited Partners for certain acts and omissions to act, since provision has been made in the Partnership Agreement for indemnification of the General Partner. Purchasers of the Interests may thus have a more limited right of action than they would otherwise have. **Insofar as indemnification for liabilities arising under the Securities Act of 1933 may be provided to directors, officers and controlling persons pursuant to the foregoing, or otherwise, the General Partner has been advised that in the opinion of the Securities and Exchange Commission such indemnification is against public policy as expressed in the said Act and is, therefore, unenforceable.**

It should be noted that the foregoing summary describing in general terms the remedies available under state and federal law to limited partners for breach of fiduciary duty by a general partner, is based on statutes, rules and decisions as of the date of this writing and that this is a rapidly developing and changing area of the law. Therefore, limited partners who believe that a breach of fiduciary duty by the General Partner has occurred should consult with their own counsel as to their evaluation of the status of the law at such time.

Prior Partnerships

The General Partner is also the General Partner of three other limited partnerships which own CATV systems, none of which has operated at a profit since its formation. The following tables provide certain information concerning these systems. Interests in Ursula Fund I are publicly held. Prospective investors should note that they will not acquire any interest in the partnerships described below, nor should the performance of these other partnerships be considered indicative of the future performance of the Partnership whose interests are offered hereby.

VERA INTERCABLE, INC.
Use of Proceeds of Proposed and Prior Limited Partnerships
(As Percentage of Initial Investment)

	Proposed			Prior	
	URSULA FUND IV		URSULA	URSULA	URSULA
	Minimum 100.0%	Maximum 100.0%	Fund I 100.0%	Fund II 100.0%	Fund III 100.0%
OFFERING INFORMATION					
Less Offering Expenses					
Selling Commissions ...	9.0	9.0	8.5	9.5	10.0
Organizational Expenses	18.0	3.6	8.8	5.6	5.3
Amount Available for Investment	73.0%	87.4%	82.7%	84.9%	84.7%
ACQUISITION INFORMATION					
Prepaid Items and Fees					
Related to Purchase					
of Property	-0-	-0-	-0-	-0-	-0-
Cash Down Payment	64.0%	77.0%	74.7%	70.2%	82.5%
Acquisition Fees	7.7	9.2	8.9	-0-	-0-
Reserves	1.3	1.2	(.9)	14.7	2.2
Proceeds Expended	73.0	87.4	82.7	84.9	84.7
Offering Expenses	27.0	12.6	17.3	15.1	15.3
Total Application of Proceeds	100.0%	100.0%	100.0%	100.0%	100.0%

Use of Proceeds of Prior Offerings

OFFERING INFORMATION:	URSULA Fund I	URSULA Fund II	URSULA Fund III
Dollar Amount Offered	$500,000	$220,000	$150,000
Dollar Amount Sold	154,000	132,000	150,000
Less Offering Expenses			
Sales Commissions—non-affiliate	--	12,540	15,000
Sales Commissions—affiliates	13,090	--	--
Organizational Expenses—affiliates	10,000	7,240	8,000
Other Organizational Expenses—non-affiliate	3,628	150	--
Amount Available for Investment	$127,282	$112,070	$127,000

ACQUISITION INFORMATION:	URSULA Fund I	URSULA Fund II	URSULA Fund III
Purchase Price of Partnership Investments ...	$288,750	$ 92,690	$123,750
Mortgages and Other Financing Outstanding ..	$160,000	$ -0-	$ -0-
Prepaid Items and Fees Related to			
Purchase of Systems	$ -0-	$ -0-	$ -0-
Cash Down Payment (Equity)	115,000	92,690	123,750
Acquisition Fees	13,750	-0-	-0-
Acquisition Fee Deferral	(8,750)	-0-	-0-
Reserves	7,282	19,380	3,250
Proceeds Expended	$127,282	$112,070	$127,000
Offering Expenses	26,718	19,930	23,000
Total Application of Proceeds	$154,000	$132,000	$150,000
COMPENSATION ALLOCATIONS (including reimbursements) AND FEES TO GENERAL PARTNER AND AFFILIATES:			
General Partner Management Fees			
Period Ending First Year	$ 6,086	$ 2,310	$ 234
Period Ending Second Year	15,041	4,235	4,222
General Partner Allocated Expenses (reimbursements)			
Period Ending First Year	5,594	2,448	162
Period Ending Second Year	14,033	8,300	8,609
Affiliated Management Fees			
Period Ending First Year	2,153	--	--
Sales Commissions	13,090	--	--
Offering Expenses	10,000	7,240	8,000
System Brokerage	13,750	--	--
Leasing Payments to Affiliate	667	2,380	2,040
Total to General Partner and Affiliates through Second Year	$ 80,414	$ 26,913	$ 23,267
CUMULATIVE INVESTMENT RETURN:			
Cumulative Federal Tax Deductions Available to Limited Partners through Second Year ..	$129,209	$ 34,764	$ 30,109
Cumulative Federal Tax Deductions Available per $1,000 of Investment through Second Year	839	263	201
Cumulative Reduction in Principal of Initial Mortgage through Second Year	18,208	--	--
Cumulative Reduction in Principal of Initial Mortgage per $1,000 of Investment through Second Year	118	--	--
Cumulative Cash Distributions to Limited Partners through (Return of Capital) Second Year	15,400	14,310	7,875
Cumulative Cash Distributions to Limited Partners per $1,000 of Investment through Second Year (Return of Capital)	100	108	53

INVESTMENT OBJECTIVES AND POLICIES

General

The principal objective of the Partnership will be to acquire existing CATV systems and to the extent deemed desirable by the General Partner CATV operating authorities ("franchises"), pursuant to which systems may be developed and expanded. A prime consideration in selecting CATV properties for acquisition will be prospects for capital growth. A secondary objective will be to acquire a system or systems that will be able to provide some cash flow distributions to the Limited Partners. The General Partner will seek to acquire systems which will provide enough operating revenues in excess of operating expenses to allow the Partnership to make cash distributions annually in an amount equal to 7% of the initial capital contributions of the Limited Partners. If so, such distributions may be "sheltered" to some extent with offsetting operating losses resulting from the deduction of noncash expenses, such as depreciation and amortization. No assurance can be given that any of these objectives will be attained or that the tax laws of the United States will continue to allow such treatment.

Nature of Investments

The capital in the Partnership will be used primarily for the acquisition, development and operation of existing CATV systems. The General Partner may, however, also invest Partnership capital for the purpose of seeking and developing licensing permits or franchises necessary for the operation of CATV systems in areas in which such systems do not exist. The General Partner has made no determination of how the proceeds of this offering will be allocated between existing systems and franchises for future systems, although it is expected that more than half of the proceeds will be used to acquire existing systems.

An existing CATV system will be considered for investment if the General Partner determines that the system has the potential for long-term appreciation in value. A secondary consideration will be the potential of the system for production of cash flow distributions to the Limited Partners. The General Partner will generally seek to acquire existing systems which have been in operation for at least one year and have a history of generating cash flow or which the General Partner believes have a prospect of producing cash flow in the near future. Moreover, in making investments in existing CATV systems, the General Partner also intends to give emphasis to the following factors: numbers of existing or potential subscribers and subscriber equivalents; number of homes passed by existing or feasible cable that are not connected to a CATV system; number of dwelling units and housing density in franchise or potential franchise area; terms of existing or potential franchise; and likelihood of population growth in franchise or potential franchise area. No assurance can be given that such objectives will be achieved.

The types of assets (and their depreciable lives, assuming new equipment is involved) normally acquired upon the purchase of a cable television system are land (not depreciable); head-end building (30 years); distribution system which is comprised of coaxial cable (buried or installed on poles), electronic amplifiers, electronic filters, power supplies and numerous mechanical fittings (cable and fitting—10 years, electronics—5-8 years); head-end equipment which is comprised of antennas, tower and electronics (antenna and electronics—5-8 years, tower—10 years); auto/trucks (3 years); furniture and equipment (5-10 years); and the CATV franchise (an intangible which is amortized over its remaining life).

The General Partner will obtain independent appraisals on properties prior to purchase. Such appraisals are only estimates of value and should not be relied upon as measures of true worth or realizable value. Although the Partnership on purchase of CATV properties will not be required to pay only the appraised values, any commission paid to affiliates of the General Partner will be based on the lower of sales price or appraised value. However, the General Partner may, in its discretion, decide to pay more than the appraisal, in which event any brokerage commission to an affiliate would be limited to 6% of the appraisal. The Partnership will not purchase, lease, or sell any CATV system or franchise from or to the General Partner or from or to any affiliate of the General Partner except for sales as part of a future reorganization of the Partnership into corporate form, either alone or with affiliated or unaffiliated entities. The Partnership may on occasion purchase or lease equipment, however, from an affiliated entity.

The prospective investments of the Partnership in CATV

686

properties will not be limited to any specific geographical area, but will be confined to the United States. It is expected that most of the investments will be made in areas having between 1,000 and 30,000 actual or potential sub-scribers. "Potential subscribers" generally means all dwelling units existing or to be built in a particular area, and for purposes of this paragraph reflects the judgment of the General Partner as to what number might ultimately be realized (which is a function of factors such as existing dwelling units and businesses that might become subscribers, geography, area growth, off-air availability and population mix and income). The General Partner will, in seeking to make investments in CATV operations, give attention to areas which indicate potential population growth utilizing standard metropolitan area indices. There is no limitation on the percentage of the assets of the Partnership which may be invested in any one CATV property or group of properties.

It is expected that the Partnership will hold the various CATV properties which it may acquire until such time as sale or other disposition appears to be advantageous in view of the investment objectives of the Partnership. There can be no assurance that advantageous sales could be made in the future.

The proceeds of any sales or refinancings of properties may be reinvested by the purchase of additional CATV systems or development of systems in the discretion of the General Partner.

The extent of the operations of the Partnership, the number of projects in which it acquires an interest, and the geographic diversification it obtains will be substantially dependent upon the amount of capital at the Partnership's disposal.

In determining whether the Partnership will purchase a particular property, the Partnership may obtain an option on such property in order to allow time to determine the desirability of purchasing such property. The amount paid for such an option, which could be as high as 10% of the purchase price, usually is surrendered if the property is not purchased. If the property is purchased, the option price is normally deducted from the purchase price. The General Partner may on behalf of the Partnership enter into joint ventures, general or limited partnerships, and other participations with unaffiliated entities for the purpose of owning and financing CATV properties provided that by such participation the Partnership acquires a controlling interest in such joint venture, partnership or other participation. Also, on behalf of the Partnership, the General Partner is empowered to make loans to owners of unaffiliated CATV systems as part of an arrangement whereby the Partnership acquires an equity interest in a CATV system. Such loans might be unsecured.

In connection with any future sales of properties by the Partnership, purchase money obligations may be taken as part payment. The terms of payment to be accorded by the Partnership will be affected by customs in the area in which the property being sold is located and the then-prevailing economic conditions.

Prohibited Activities

The Partnership will not:

1. Commingle its funds with those of any other person.

2. Make loans to the General Partner or affiliates of the General Partner.

3. Underwrite securities of other issuers.

4. Arrange on behalf of the Partnership for the sale, purchase or lease of any CATV system or franchise · or similar operating authority to or from the General Partner or any Affiliate of the General Partner; provided however that to the extent that a future reorganization of the Partnership into corporate form, either alone or with affiliated or unaffiliated entities, might be deemed to involve the sale of Partnership assets to an "affiliate" of the General Partner, such sale is not prohibited.

5. Make distributions from borrowed funds except to the extent that revenues from routine operations of the Partnership exceed Partnership operating expenses (including interest and excluding depreciation and amortization of intangibles).

6. Acquire any CATV system on behalf of the Partnership without first receiving an independent appraisal as to the value of such system; provided however that the Partnership will not be required to purchase such system at

the appraised value; and further provided that any brokerage commission to be paid to any affiliate of the General Partner shall be based on the lower of appraised value or purchase price.

Borrowing Policies

In order to provide a degree of flexibility in managing the assets of the Partnership, the Partnership may leverage its investments by financing the acquisition or expansion of a CATV system by borrowing. However, in order to limit the exposure of the Partnership to the risks of leveraging the General Partner will restrict any such borrowing to a maximum of 50% of the purchase price or appraised value of any CATV system, whichever is higher. Borrowings of the Partnership may be secured by mortgages or other interests on the property purchased or on other properties held by the Partnership. As a general rule, the General Partner will seek to limit recourse for such indebtedness to only the particular Partnership property to which the indebtedness relates, although there can be no assurance of such a limitation and some borrowings could be with recourse against the Partnership. The Partnership may also take title to properties "subject to" existing mortgages thereon, where the Partnership normally will not assume any liabilities under such circumstances, although the mortgages must be paid by the Partnership in order to maintain ownership of the mortgaged properties. To the extent properties are taken subject to a mortgage, but without recourse to the Partnership, such indebtedness will increase the basis of the Limited Partners' Interests for tax purposes under present tax laws and regulations. If recourse should exist against the Partnership, such indebtedness will not increase the basis of the Limited Partners' Interests for tax purposes. The Partnership Agreement also authorizes the issuance of notes, debentures and other debt securities in connection with the borrowings by the Partnership. Leverage techniques such as the foregoing, while increasing the capital available for investment, increase the risk of loss to the Partnership for which such techniques are utilized. No assurance can be given as to the availability of, or the terms of, credit to the Partnership. CATV properties purchased on a leveraged basis generally will be profitable only if they generate, at a minimum, sufficient cash revenue to service the related debt and to cover operating expenses. While it will not be a policy of the Partnership to grant lenders equity participations in its properties, in the event a lender should receive an equity participation in a property of the Partnership, such participation could decrease the benefits to the Partnership. In order to obtain financing from sellers of properties or others, the Partnership may be required to pay mortgage loan fees.

Any gains made through the use of borrowed funds in excess of interest paid will generally cause the net income of the Partnership to increase at a greater rate than would otherwise be the case. If the performance of investments made with borrowed funds fails to cover the interest cost of the Partnership, the net income of the Partnership will decrease faster than would otherwise be the case.

Borrowed funds may be used for distributions to Limited Partners only to the extent that revenues from routine operations of the Partnership exceed Partnership operating expenses (including interest and excluding depreciation and amortization).

Capitalization

The Partnership has not been formed. The following table sets forth the capitalization of the Partnership if the minimum and if the maximum number of Interests are sold.

Title of Class	Minimum	Maximum
Limited Partnership Interests ($500 per Interest)	$500,000	$2,500,000
General Partner's Capital	0	0

Benefits of a Cable Television Fund

1. It is anticipated that the first year write-off will be at least 30%. Total write-offs over the first five years are anticipated to be about 80%. Prior to, or at the end of that period, it is expected that the system will be sold and the partnership dissolved.

2. Cash flow distributions are expected to be paid quarterly. These cash flow distributions will be non-taxable return of capital. This non-taxable aspect of cash flow distri-

690

butions is expected to continue through at least the first five years of the partnership life.

3. Capital appreciation in a cable television system is measured primarily by the number of subscribers in a particular system. The objective in URSULA FUND IV for subscriber increases is similar to other cable television limited partnerships. Systems acquired by the partnership will hopefully have subscriber increases at the rate of about 20% per year.

Risks of a Cable Television Fund

1. **Risks Involved in the CATV Business.** Extensive capital outlays are normally required in a CATV system before it reaches a cash flow break-even level. While the principal investment objective of the Partnership will be the acquisition and operation of CATV systems with prospects for capital growth, there can be no assurance that such objective will be attained immediately or at all. Accordingly, investment in the Partnership should be considered only by those who can afford an investment that involves a high risk of loss.

2. **Competition.** The CATV business is highly competitive and in seeking to acquire existing CATV systems or to develop new systems, the Partnership will be competing with numerous established companies having much greater financial resources. Because of the limited amount of capital which will be available to the Partnership, it will not be possible to acquire many of the larger CATV systems in the country that might be for sale, although the Partnership might acquire an interest in such a system, if available. While no specific properties are in mind for acquisition by the Partnership, there is always competition in all parts of the country for systems and franchises and the Partnership will directly encounter such competition.

3. **Limited Operating History of The General Partner.** The General Partner is the general partner in three limited partnerships which own CATV systems, none of which has gross assets in excess of $340,000. None of such partnerships has operated at a net profit since inception, and all of which have had negative cash flows. The limited partners in these three partnerships have received distributions from borrowed funds in the form of a return of capital when operating expenses

have exceeded operating revenues. In the future, distributions, if any, to these limited partners will be limited to the excess of any operating revenues over operating expenses of the respective partnerships. The General Partner and its affiliates have engaged in the operation of other cable television systems which have incurred operating losses.

4. **Government Regulation.** The CATV industry is subject to extensive regulation by federal, state and local regulatory and governmental agencies.

5. **No Specific CATV Properties Have Been Chosen or Are Known to be Available.** The General Partner has not acquired or contracted to acquire any CATV properties for the Partnership, nor is it presently negotiating for the acquisition of any CATV systems, operating licenses, permits or franchises with respect thereto on behalf of the Partnership. Consequently the risk to the investor is increased, as it is impossible for him to evaluate the precise way his investment will be placed prior to the actual investing thereof. Furthermore there could be a time lapse between subscription for Partnership Interests and purchase of a CATV system or systems by the Partnership. During such time investors would not receive a return on their investment. In identifying and selecting operating CATV systems for purchase, the General Partner may be limited to those systems for which suitable financial information is available or may be obtained. This may restrict the Partnership from acquiring some systems which might otherwise be appropriate investments for the Partnership. There can be no assurance that any properties which may be acquired will operate at a profit or will increase in value or that desirable properties will be available or can be acquired on economically attractive terms. The potential profitability of the Partnership could be affected by the amount of funds at its disposal. If only the minimum number of Interests in the Partnership is sold, the opportunities of the Partnership will be reduced, thereby increasing the risk of investment.

6. **Reliance on General Partner.** Since the specific CATV properties to be acquired by the Partnership have not yet been determined, the General Partner will have complete discretion in making investments in such properties. Investors will, therefore, have to rely upon the General Partner as to the investments of the Partnership.

7. **Leverage.** Investments of the Partnership may be

leveraged; that is, the Partnership may finance a portion of the cost of acquisition or development of its properties by borrowing a portion of such cost. This practice could enhance the ability of the Partnership to acquire CATV properties of greater aggregate cost, although it would increase exposure of the Partnership to larger losses, since fixed payment obligations must be met on due dates, regardless of liquidity of assets purchased with such borrowed funds, or the receipt of revenues derived therefrom. There can be no assurance that such loans will be available or, if available, what rate of interest will be charged thereon. In addition, lenders from which the Partnership may borrow could seek to impose restrictions on the future borrowing, distributions, and operating policy of the Partnership. In order to limit the exposure of the Partnership to the risks of leveraging, the General Partner will restrict any borrowing to a maximum of 50% of the purchase price or 50% of the appraised value of any CATV system, whichever is higher. In seeking a loan to finance acquisition of a property, the Partnership will attempt to negotiate an interest rate pegged to the prime rate and to negotiate a loan with interest only payable the first year, with periodic amortization of principal and interest for a ten-twelve year period thereafter. It is not expected that loans with "balloon" payments at the end of the term will be sought, nor is it anticipated that refinancing of such loans will be sought. There is no assurance that the Partnership will be successful in negotiating such loans.

8. **Lack of Ready Transferability of Interests**. There is no market for sale of the Interests offered, nor is it likely that such market will develop in the future. Transfer of the Interests will be restricted by a provision of the Partnership Agreement which prevents a Limited Partner from substituting an assignee in his place without the consent of the General Partner. A Limited Partner will not be able to liquidate his investment whenever he desires. Accordingly, an investment in Interests is not suitable for persons who may need to liquidate their investment on short notice.

9. **Federal Taxation**. The share of Partnership income or loss required to be reported on a Partner's personal income tax return may be unrelated to distributions received by him during the period of his ownership. Cash distributions from the Partnership may not be sufficient to pay income taxes, if

any, resulting from Partnership income, and the Limited Partners could have income tax liabilities in years in which there are no cash distributions from the Partnership.

Federal income tax consequences to the Limited Partners are based upon the Internal Revenue Code, rules and regulations promulgated thereunder and existing interpretations thereof, any of which could be changed at any time.

Tax deductions will include depreciation on tangible properties forming part of a CATV system. The Partnership may elect to use an accelerated method or methods of depreciation on particular properties. Accelerated depreciation concentrates maximum deductions in the early years, thereby providing a declining tax shelter as to any particular property. If property which is depreciated for tax purposes is sold at a gain, then all or a portion of such gain may be taxed at ordinary income rates rather than capital gains rates by operation of the "recapture" provisions of the Internal Revenue Code.

Various members of the United States Congress and the Treasury have proposed legislation to reform the Internal Revenue Code. Many of these proposals would substantially affect the tax consequences to the investor of investment of capital in certain ventures by changing (a) the special capital gains tax rate; (b) fast depreciation methods; (c) recapture rules for real property; (d) additional first year depreciation allowances; (e) the tacking on of a mortgage to basis; and (f) other deductions now available to taxpayers. If this legislation passed in some current proposed form, it would materially affect the advantages of making investments in ventures like the Partnership.

The General Partner has received a ruling from the Internal Revenue Service that, based on certain representations about the General Partner and the Partnership when formed, the Partnership will be treated as a partnership, and not as an association taxable as a corporation, for Federal income tax purposes. If the accuracy of such representations is not continued after formation of the Partnership, the Internal Revenue Service could assert the Partnership should be taxed as a corporation. Taxation of the Partnership as a corporation would have a substantial, detrimental financial impact on Limited Partners. Furthermore, an audit of the Partnership's information return may result in an audit of individual Limited Partners' tax returns.

The Partnership will claim certain items as current deductions. The Internal Revenue Service may disallow or capitalize some of these items. In such case, there may be an adverse impact on Limited Partners.

Upon the sale or other disposition of his Interests in the Partnership, a Limited Partner may be subject to substantial Federal income tax liability. Furthermore, on sale or other disposition of Partnership property, under some circumstances a Limited Partner's tax liability may exceed his share of proceeds from such disposition.

10. **Management Fees are Payable Regardless of Profits of the Partnership.** The base management fee will be, and any operating incentive fee could be, payable to the General Partner notwithstanding that the Partnership may not have earned a profit or may be operating at a loss.

Tax Aspects of a Cable Television Fund

It is impractical to comment on all aspects of Federal, state and local tax laws which may affect the tax consequences of participating in the Partnership. Therefore, each prospective Limited Partner should satisfy himself as to the income and other tax consequences of his participating in the Partnership by obtaining advice from his own tax adviser. Furthermore, while the Partnership will furnish each Limited Partner information to enable him to file Federal, state and local tax returns, the preparation and filing of such returns will be the personal responsibility of the Limited Partner. The following statements, however, may be of significance as regards participation in the Partnership.

Federal Income Tax Aspects—Introduction

The following statements, together with the ruling issued the Partnership from the Internal Revenue Service, are based upon the provisions of the Internal Revenue Code of 1954, as amended (the "Code"), the existing applicable regulations thereunder, the existing proposed regulations thereunder, existing judicial decisions and current administrative rulings and practice. It is emphasized, however, that no assurance can be given that legislative, judicial or administrative changes may not be forthcoming which would modify such statements.

695

Furthermore, legislation has been proposed before Congress which would, if enacted in its present form, reduce or eliminate the tax benefits of participating in the Partnership which are described below. Certain of such legislation, if enacted, would modify statements with respect to, among other things, the classification of the Partnership as a "partnership" for Federal income tax purposes, "excess investment interest," the "minimum tax for tax preferences" and the amount of depreciation the Partnership could claim. Any such changes may or may not be retroactive with respect to transactions prior to the effective date of such changes.

The existing tax benefits associated with ownership of limited partnership interests do not eliminate the risks. A substantial benefit to Limited Partners may be the application of Partnership tax deductions against the Limited Partner's taxable income from other sources. Accordingly, prospective Limited Partners who are in the lower or middle Federal income tax brackets should recognize that they may not be able to utilize as fully as persons in the higher income tax brackets the various tax benefits that may be obtained by the Partnership for its partners.

Classification as a "Partnership"

The Partnership has received a ruling from the Internal Revenue Service that the Partnership when formed will be classified as a "partnership" for Federal income tax purposes. The Internal Revenue Service, pursuant to Revenue Procedure 72-13, is currently conditioning the issuance and continuing validity of such rulings on certain conditions, including (a) that the Limited Partners will not own, directly or indirectly, within the meaning of the attribution rules of Section 318 of the Code, individually or in the aggregate, more than 20 percent of the stock of the General Partner or any of its affiliates (as defined in Section 1504 (a) of the Code); and (b) that the General Partner at all times maintains a certain minimum net worth. The General Partner is of the opinion that at the present time its net worth is and at the time of formation of the Partnership its net worth will be, in excess of the required net worth as set forth in Revenue Procedure 72-13; but there can be no assurance that the General Partner will be able to maintain the required net worth at all times during the existence of the Partnership.

696

In the event the Partnership is treated in any taxable year as an association taxable as a corporation and not as a partnership for Federal income tax purposes, no losses of the Partnership could be deducted by the Partners on their personal income tax returns (such losses would be taken by the Partnership against its income, if any). Further, any distributions from the Partnership to Partners would not be deductible by the Partnership and may be taxable to the Partners at ordinary income tax rates (i.e., as dividends) to the extent of any earnings and profits.

Partners, Not Partnership, Subject to Tax

Assuming the aforementioned requirements are complied with, the Partnership, itself, as a "partnership," will not be subject to Federal income tax. Each Partner must take into account separately his distributive share of all items of the Partnership's income, gain, loss, deduction, credit, and tax preference for any taxable year of the Partnership ending within or with his his taxable year, without regard to whether such Partner has received or will receive any distributions from the Partnership. Thus, it is possible for a Partner to have income reported on his Federal income tax return although cash in an amount less than his reported income is distributed to him. Furthermore, the amount of any loss which a Partner may utilize in computing his Federal income tax liability is limited to his adjusted basis in his Partnership interest at the end of the Partnership taxable year in which such loss occurred.

Partner's Adjusted Tax Basis

A Limited Partner's adjusted basis in his Partnership Interests will be the price paid therefore, increased by (i) the amount of his distributive share of its items of income and gain of the Partnership; and (ii) the amount of his share (based on his interest in Partnership profits) of Partnership indebtedness for which no Partner is personally liable, and reduced (but not below zero) by (i) the amount of his distributive share of items of Partnership loss, deduction, and nondeductible expenditures which are not capital expenditures; (ii) the amount of any distributions to him; and (iii) the amount of any reduction of Partnership indebtedness for which no Partner is personally liable.

Distributions from the Partnership

The receipt of a cash distribution from the Partnership by a Limited Partner in respect of, and not in liquidation of, his Partnership interest generally does not entail the recognition of gain or loss for Federal income tax purposes. However, cash distributions in excess of a Limited Partner's adjusted basis in his Partnership interest immediately prior thereto ("Excess Distributions") will result in the recognition by such Limited Partner of gain in the amount of such excess. Such gain will generally be taxable at capital gains rates, except to the extent of the Limited Partner's share of unrealized receivables, substantially appreciated inventory and depreciation recapture.

Section 754 Election

The Internal Revenue Code provides for optional adjustments to the basis of partnership property as the result of a distribution of partnership property to a partner (Section 734) or a transfer of a partnership interest (Section 743), if a partnership election has been made in accordance with Section 754. By making this election, transferees of partnership interests are treated for purposes of depreciation, and profits and losses as though they had acquired a direct interest in the partnership assets and the partnership is treated for such purposes, upon certain distributions to partners, as though it had newly acquired an interest in the partnership assets and therefore acquired a new cost basis for such assets. Once the election is made, it is irrevocable with respect to all current and future transfers and distributions, unless the consent of the Internal Revenue Service is obtained. The tax accounting required to implement such an election is quite complex and costly, as adjustments must be made each time there is a transfer of a partnership interest or a distribution of partnership property. Accordingly, the General Partner does not presently intend to make such an election. One consequence of the absence of such election is that upon a sale of

Partnership property subsequent to a transfer of a Limited Partner's interest, taxable profits or losses to the transferee of the interest will be measured by the difference between his share of the amount realized and his share of the Partnership's tax basis in the property (which, in the absence of a Section 754 election, will be unchanged by the transfer of the interest to him), rather than by the difference between his share of the amount realized and the portion of his purchase price that was allocable to the property. Thus, the absence of such an election may be considered an additional impediment to the transferability of Partnership Interests.

Treatment of Gain on Sale of Partnership Property

Gain recognized by the Partnership on sales or exchanges of properties held for more than six months will generally, under present law, be treated as long-term capital gain except to the extent of depreciation recapture (discussed below), unless the Partnership is deemed to be a "dealer" in such properties, in which case the gain will be treated as ordinary income. The General Partner does not intend to operate the Partnership in such a manner as to make it a "dealer" for tax purposes. In determining the amount received upon the sale or other disposition of any of the Partnership's properties, the Partnership must include, among other things, the amount of any indebtedness to which such property is subject. As a result, the Partnership's gain on such sale, and in some cases, the income taxes payable by the Partners with respect to such gain, could exceed such cash proceeds, and in any event, such income taxes may exceed the amount distributed to the Partners.

Any tax losses from the ownership and operation of CATV properties by the Partnership could decline over time and could eventually result in taxable income in excess of cash flow from normal operations. This would occur as the annual depreciation deductions under accelerated depreciation methods decline from year to year. In addition, under a level payment mortgage, the portion of each payment which represents nondeductible amortization of principal increases from year to year and the portion representing deductible interest decreases. Thus, it may be economically desirable to sell a property, or for a Partner to sell his Partnership Interest, prior to the end of respective useful lives of each of the properties.

Sale of Partnership Interests

Assuming that the Partnership is not a dealer in CATV properties and the Partner is not a dealer in securities, the sale or liquidation of a Partnership Interest, and the receipt of an Excess Distribution, by a Partner who has held such interest for the required months will generally result in the recognition of a long-term capital gain or loss. However, if at the time of the sale of a Partnership Interest, or of the receipt of an Excess Distribution, the Partnership has "unrealized receivables" or "inventory items" which have substantially appreciated in value, the portion of the Partner's gain attributable to such items will be taxable as ordinary income. For this purpose "unrealized receivables" include, among other things, unrealized receivables (in the accounting sense) and Section 1245 and 1250 property (i.e., tangible personal and real property subject to "recapture" of depreciation) to the extent of the amount which would be treated as ordinary gain under such sections had the property been sold by the Partnership at its fair market value. See Depreciation Recapture, below. In the absence of an election under Section 754 of the Code, discussed above, it is possible that on the sale or liquidation of a Partnership Interest a Partner will realize ordinary income in the form of depreciation recapture with respect to depreciation claimed by the Partnership during the time he was not a Partner. As a result, a Partner's gain on the sale or liquidation of such an interest may substantially exceed the cash proceeds of such sale, and in some cases the income taxes payable with respect to such gain could exceed such cash proceeds.

Death of a Partner

On the death of a Partner, any Interest, the value of which is includable in his gross estate for Federal estate tax purposes, will under existing law receive a carryover basis. Presumptively, this is the value reported for Federal estate tax purposes. However, in the absence of an election under Section 754, discussed above, this basis will not affect the basis of underlying Partnership property.

The 1976 Tax Reform Act requires a cash method taxpayer to deduct prepaid interest over the period of the loan to the extent that the interest represents the cost of using the borrowed funds during each such period. This new rule conforms the deductibility of prepaid interest by a cash method taxpayer to the present rule for interest prepayments by an accrual method taxpayer. This rule applies to all cash method taxpayers including individuals, corporations, estates and trusts, and covers interest paid for personal, business or investment purposes. This rule also applies to prepaid interest on an indebtedness secured by a "wraparound" mortgage. In certain cases, the Treasury Department is authorized to treat interest payments under a loan with variable interest rates as consisting partly of interest computed under an average level effective rate of interest and partly of an interest prepayment allocable to later years of the loan. However, the new rule does not change the present treatment of a discount loan by a cash method taxpayer.

The new prepaid interest rule applies to prepayments of interest on and after January 1, 1976, except that it does not apply to prepayments of interest made before January 1, 1977, pursuant to a binding contract or written loan commitment in effect on September 16, 1975 (and at all times thereafter).

Fees and Other Expenses

The Partnership will pay various expenses, including legal and accounting fees, for obtaining subscribers to CATV systems. The Partnership will also pay to the General Partner a management fee and reimburse the General Partner for expenses incurred in managing and operating the Partnership. The General Partner intends to claim all such amounts as currently deductible expenses on the Partnership Federal return. However, should the Internal Revenue Service disallow deductions for the management fee or require any of the expenses deducted by the Partnership to be capitalized, the income tax loss of the Partnership may be decreased or income tax gain may be increased. Furthermore, the Internal Revenue Service has taken the position that the costs of acquiring CATV franchises should be capitalized for Federal income tax purposes, rather than deducted in the year paid or incurred, and the Internal Revenue Service has also taken the position that such costs may be amortized only if the franchise has a determinable useful life, otherwise such costs can be deducted only upon abandonment of the franchise. It is unclear to what extent the Internal Revenue Service's position has been modified by Section 1253 of the Code, which was adopted as part of the Tax Reform Act of 1969, since the proposed Regulations apparently do not cover this question.

Use of Accelerated and Bonus Depreciation

The Code presently permits the use of certain accelerated methods of depreciation for both real and personal property and an additional (but limited) first-year depreciation allowance for tangible personal property. In addition, the new Class Life Asset Depreciation Range (ADR) System, which liberalizes depreciation for assets placed in service after 1970, was recently made available for computing depreciation allowances for assets used in providing cable television services. The useful life range of some CATV assets goes as low as 7 to 10 years for service and test equipment and as high as 9 to 13 years for head-end equipment. The General Partner may utilize accelerated methods of depreciation with respect to the Partnership's properties. There can, of course, be no assurance that the tax accounting assumptions and methods utilized by the Partnership will be accepted by the Internal Revenue Service.

Depreciation Recapture

In general, gain on the disposition of personal property (including tangible property used as an integral part of a CATV system) is taxable as ordinary income to the extent of the depreciation deducted; and gain on the disposition of depreciable real property is taxable as ordinary income to the extent of the excess of accelerated depreciation over straight line depreciation, although, in both cases, the so-called depreciation recapture (i.e., the amount taxable as ordinary income) is limited to the amount of the gain realized upon disposition of the property.

Investment Credit

A credit against a Partner's Federal income tax is allowed
of 10 percent of his distributive share of the Partnership's
qualified investment in certain depreciable personal property
(including tangible property used as an integral part of a
CATV system), subject to certain limitations. The credit is
allowed for the year the qualifying property is placed in
service. The liability for tax against which the credit may be
applied is the income tax as reduced by the foreign tax credit,
the credit allowed individuals for partially tax-exempt interest
and the retirement income tax credit. The investment credit
may not exceed tax liability. If tax liability exceeds $25,000,
the tax credit may not exceed $25,000 plus 50 percent of the
tax liability over that amount. Special rules are provided for
married individuals filing separate returns and affiliated corporations not filing a consolidated return. Any part of the
investment credit which is not applied as a credit against the
tax because of the foregoing limitations may be carried back
three years and carried over seven years. The amount of
"qualified investment" is the sum of the basis of new "investment credit property" and up to $100,000 of the cost of used
"investment credit property" (a special rule applies to the
$100,000 limitation in respect of used "investment credit
property" in the case of partners and partnerships). The cost
or basis that qualifies is limited, however, if the property has
a useful life of less than seven years (2/3 credit if useful life is
five to seven years; 1/3 credit if useful life is three to five
years; and no credit if useful life is less than three years).
Where "investment credit property" is disposed of before the
end of its estimated useful life, the tax for the year of
disposal is increased by the difference between the credit
originally allowed (including carrybacks and carryovers) and
the credit (including carrybacks and carryovers) that would
have been allowed if the computation had been based on the
shorter useful life. A disposition for this purpose includes a
reduction (for example, by a sale, by a change in the partnership agreement, or by the admission of a new partner) of a
Partner's proportionate interest in the general profits of the
Partnership below 66 2/3 percent of such Partner's proportionate interest in such profits for the year in which such
property was placed in service.

Minimum Tax for Tax Preference

Present law imposes a minimum tax on certain individual and corporate tax preferences. The minimum tax for individuals amounts to 15 percent of the sum of an individual's (or estate's or trust's) tax preferences in excess of one-half of regular income taxes paid or, if greater, $10,000.

The tax preference items included in this base of the minimum tax for individuals are:

(1) Accelerated depreciation on real property in excess of straight-line depreciation;

(2) Accelerated depreciation on leased personal property in excess of straight-line depreciation;

(3) Amortization of certified pollution control facilities (the excess of 60-month amortization (sec. 169) over depreciation otherwise allowable (sec. 167));

(4) Amortization of railroad rolling stock (the excess of 60-month amortization (sec. 184) over depreciation otherwise allowable (sec. 167));

(5) Qualified stock options (the excess of the fair market value at the time of exercise over the option price);

(6) Percentage depletion in excess of the adjusted basis of the property;

(7) The deduction for 50 percent of net long-term capital gains;

(8) Amortization of child care facilities (the excess of 60-month amortization (sec. 188) over depreciation otherwise allowable (sec. 167));

(9) Itemized deductions (other than medical and casualty loss deductions) in excess of 60 percent of adjusted gross income; and

(10) Intangible drilling costs on oil and gas or geothermal wells in excess of the amount amortizable with respect to those costs and, for 1977, in excess of net income from oil and gas or geothermal production.

The Revenue Act of 1978 retains the present law minimum tax with respect to all preference items except capital gains and excess itemized deductions. The Act provides for an alternative minimum tax which is payable by an individual to the extent that the alternative tax exceeds the regular income tax increased by the amount of the existing minimum tax, as revised, on preference items other than capital gains and itemized deductions.

The alternative minimum tax base is the sum of an individual's taxable income, adjusted itemized deductions, and the capital gains deduction.

The following rates are imposed on this amount:

	Percent
$0-$20,000	0
$20,000-$60,000	10
$60,000-$100,000	20
Over $100,000	25

Maximum Tax

Under present law, the highest marginal tax rate applicable to personal service income is 50 percent. However, the amount eligible for this maximum tax rate is reduced dollar-for-dollar by the individual's items of tax preference.

The Revenue Act of 1978 removes capital gains as a tax preference which reduces the amount of personal service income eligible for the maximum tax rate. This change generally is effective with respect to taxable years beginning after October 31, 1978. In the case of taxable years beginning before November 1, 1978, and ending after October 31, 1978, the change is effective with respect to so much of the taxpayer's net capital gain as is attributable to post-October 31, 1978 taxable transactions and installment payments.

Excess Investment Interest

Under the 1976 Tax Reform Act interest on investment indebtedness is limited to $10,000 per year, plus the taxpayer's net investment income. No offset of investment interest is permitted against capital gain income. An additional deduction of up to $15,000 per year is permitted for interest paid in connection with indebtedness incurred by the taxpayer to acquire the stock in a corporation, or a partnership interest, where the taxpayer, his spouse, and his children have (or acquire) at least 50 percent of the stock or capital interest in the enterprise. Interest deductions which are disallowed under these rules are subject to an unlimited carryover and may be deducted in future years (subject to the applicable limitation).

Under the conference agreement, no limitation is imposed on the deductibility of personal interest.

Generally these rules are applicable to taxable years beginning after December 31, 1975. However, under a transition rule, prior law (sec. 163(d) before the amendments made under the 1976 Tax Reform Act) continues to apply in the case of interest on indebtedness which is attributable to a specific item of property, is for a specified term, and was either incurred before September 11, 1975, or is incurred after that date under a binding written contract or commitment in effect on that date and at all times thereafter (hereinafter referred to as "pre-1976 interest"). As under present law, interest incurred before December 17, 1969 ("pre-1970 interest") is not subject to a limitation.

Capital Gains Rates

The Revenue Act of 1978 increases the amount of any net capital gain which a non-corporate taxpayer may deduct from gross income from 50 to 60 percent. The remaining 40 percent of the net capital gain is includible in gross income and subject to tax at the regular rates. The deducted gain is classified as a tax preference item for alternative minimum tax purposes, but not for purposes of reducing the amount of personal service income which is eligible for the maximum tax. A corresponding increase in the capital gains tax preference also is made for November and December 1978 capital gains under the add-on minimum tax. The increase in the capital gains deduction, the elimination of the maximum tax offset, and the increase in the capital gains tax preference are effective for taxable transactions occurring, and installment payments received, after October 31, 1978.

The Revenue Act of 1978 reduces the alternative tax rate on corporate capital gains from 30 to 28 percent. The minimum tax preference of corporate long-term capital gains will be 18/46 of the gain. This change is effective with respect to taxable transactions occurring, and installment payments received, after December 31, 1978.

GLOSSARY

Acquisition Fees. Any and all fees and commissions paid by any party to any party in connection with the acquisition of a CATV property by the Partnership, including brokerage commissions and similar non-recurring fees.

Additional Closing Date. Any date, other than the Initial Closing Date, on which the subscribers for Interests are admitted to the Partnership as Limited Partners.

Appraisal of CATV Systems. An independent appraisal of a CATV system is a fair market valuation of a cable system undertaken for compensation by a third party in an arms-length transaction in connection with the purchase or sale of a cable television system. Appraisals are only estimates of value and should not be relied upon as measures of true worth or realizable value.

CATV System (Community Antenna Television System). See Cable Television System.

CATV Properties. The tangible and intangible, real and personal property which is employed in a CATV system, including franchise, pole and management agreements, communications satellite earth station, head-end receiving system, trunk line, distribution lines, subscriber drops, receivers, amplifiers and related electronic equipment, land and/or building on which the head-end is situated (or a lease thereof), inventory, office equipment, vehicles, and supplies.

Cable Television System. Any facility that receives off-the-air television or radio signals or is supplied with television or radio signals by a microwave relay system, satellite relay, or by origination at the system, including special services, or otherwise or by any combination of the foregoing means, and amplifies, controls or processes such signals before delivering them by wired means (usually coaxial cables) to the public for a fee. Reverse Direction Transmission (sometimes called "upstream" services) may be employed to permit many types of two-way signal services, including without limitation such services as pay television, intrusion alarm systems, computer access and fire alarm systems.

Capital Account. The capital account of a Partner will

707

initially be credited with his initial capital contribution and thereafter credited with his share of net profits and debited with his share of net losses and cash distributions.

Distribution Lines. Secondary coaxial cables and electronics connecting trunk line and subscriber drops.

Final Closing Date. The last date on which subscribers for Interests are admitted to the Partnership as Limited Partners.

Franchise or Operating Authority. Authorization issued by a local government entity which allows the construction and operation of a cable television system within the bounds of its governmental authority.

Head-End. The electronic equipment located at the start of a cable system, usually including antennas, preamplifiers, frequency converters, demodulators, modulators, and related equipment.

Initial Capital Contribution. The amount of initial cash investment made by a Limited Partner in the Partnership.

Initial Closing Date. The date on which subscribers for Interests are first admitted to the Partnership as Limited Partners.

Cash Flow. All cash receipts derived from the routine operations of the Partnership, less principal and interest payments and cash expenses (meaning all operating expenses of the Partnership excluding depreciation, amortization and other non-cash items of a similar nature).

Operating Expenses. All expenses incurred in the operation of a CATV system. These include salaries, legal/audit, insurance, property taxes, outside consulting fees, management fees, and overhead allocation, but do not include depreciation and amortization of intangibles.

Pole Agreement. An agreement between the CATV operator and the utility companies or other owners of poles upon which the operator has been granted the right of attaching his fittings for the suspension of his cable.

Potential Subscribers. The number of dwelling units, existing or expected to be built, within a cable television system franchise area.

Profit and Loss. Partnership profits and losses will be determined according to generally accepted accounting principles.

Revenues from Routine Operations. All revenues generated from delivery of cable television services including basic monthly subscription charges for residential television service, pay TV, installation charges, multiple usage burglar and fire alarm taps, channel leasing, advertising, and other revenue items for which a CATV system may charge a fee. This does not include proceeds realized from the disposition of depreciable or amortizable assets.

Saturation Rate. The number of subscribers per number of houses passed by a cable television system, expressed as a percentage.

Subscriber. Person or entity who pays a monthly fee for delivery of signals to a single television set via a CATV system.

Subscriber Drop. A cable which connects the tap or coupler of the feeder cable to the subscribers' premises and T.V. set.

Subscriber Equivalent. Measure of revenue generated by a CATV system from other than subscribers to single set residential cable television service. The subscriber equivalents of any system are determined by dividing the total service revenues of a system from all sources other than from single set residential television subscribers by the single set monthly residential television subscription charge. Subscriber equivalents are generated by multiple usage by a single subscriber, bulk rates for multiple unit residential and commercial establishments, burglar and fire alarm taps, channel leasing, advertising revenues, and all other revenue items for which the system charges a fee.

Subscriber Terminal. The cable television system terminal to which a subscriber's equipment is connected. Separate terminals may be provided for delivery of signals of various classes.

Television Households. A household having one or more television sets.

Trunk Line. The main coaxial cables and electronics of a CATV system which feed signals from the head-end to the distribution lines.

APPENDIX

EXCHANGE TRADED PUT AND CALL OPTIONS

Exchange Traded call options have made it possible to buy and sell options with the same ease and in the same way as securities on the major stock exchanges.

Previously buying and writing of call options was impeded by lack of standardized option contracts and by the absence of a central, competitive marketplace for buying and selling. Buying depended upon being able to locate a seller, and vice versa. This resulted in awkward and sometimes impossible trading.

The issuer of the Options covered by this writing is the Clearing Corporation. The Clearing Corporation is obligated to perform upon the exercise of an Option in accordance with its by-laws and rules and its agreements with the Exchanges. It also serves as the clearing house for Options transactions. The Clearing Corporation's principal executive office is located at 5950 Sears Tower, 233 South Wacker Drive, Chicago, Illinois 60606, telephone (312) 322-6200.

Each of the Exchanges is registered as a national securities exchange under the Securities Exchange Act of 1934, as amended ("Exchange Act"). As of the date of this writing the Exchanges are the Chicago Board Options Exchange, Incorporated ("CBOE"), the American Stock Exchange, Inc. ("AMEX"), the Philadelphia Stock Exchange, Inc. ("PHLX"), the Pacific Stock Exchange Incorporated ("PSE") and the Midwest Stock Exchange, Incorporated ("MSE").

Subject to certain limitations, the holder of a Call has the right to purchase from the Clearing Corporation, and the holder of a Put has the right to sell to the Clearing Corporation, the underlying security covered by the Option at the stated exercise price at any time prior to the expiration of the Option. As of the date of this writing, Puts are available only with respect to a limited number of the underlying securities on which Calls are traded. A list of the underlying securities, exercise prices and expiration months of Options which are traded on a particular Exchange may be obtained from the Clearing Corporation or from the Exchange or a member thereof. Options of a particular series which are traded on only one Exchange may be purchased and written, and positions in those Options may be liquidated in offsetting closing transactions, only on that Exchange. Options of the same series which are traded on more than one Exchange may be purchased and written in opening transactions, and positions in those Options may be liquidated in offsetting closing transactions, on any of the Exchanges on which that series of Options is traded. Except when restrictions on trading are imposed or trading has been halted or suspended. Options of a particular series which are opened for trading continue to be traded until noon Pacific Time, 2:00 P.M. Central Time, 3:00 P.M. Eastern Time on the business day prior to their expiration date.

If the holder of an Option does not liquidate his position in the secondary market by a closing sale transaction, he can generally realize on its value only by exercising it before its expiration. An Option that expires unexercised becomes worthless. Options are exercised by the submission of timely exercise institutions to the Clearing Corporation by the Clearing Member acting on behalf of the exercising holder. Exercise instructions submitted to the Clearing Corporation by Clearing Members are irrevocable. While Clearing Members may submit exercise instructions to the Clearing Corporation at any time prior to the expiration of an Option, *customers wishing to exercise Options must so instruct their brokers prior to an earlier exercise cut-off time on the business day before the expiration date.* The cut-off times fixed by brokers which are not Exchange members may be earlier than the cut-off times fixed by Exchange members. Each customer should determine from his brother the applicable cut-off time, because a customer's failure to instruct his broker to exercise an Option prior to that time will mean that the Option may not be exercised.

Options may be purchased or sold through securities brokers, many of which are members of one or more of the Exchanges. The price (premium) of the Option, which is paid by the purchaser and is received by the seller (writer) of the Option, is determined in the Exchange's auction market. Both purchasers and writers pay the transaction costs, which may include commissions, charged or incurred in connection with their Options transactions. Such transaction costs may be significant.

711

Tax rulings published by the Internal Revenue Service state that (assuming the underlying common stock which is the subject of an Option traded on an Exchange is a capital asset in the hands of the holder or would be if acquired by the holder) upon the sale or expiration of the Option, the holder would recognize capital gain or loss (long-term or short-term depending upon the length of time the Option has been held and the taxable year in which the sale or expiration occurs); and, in the event of the exercise of such an Option, the holder would treat the premium paid as part of the cost of the underlying stock (in the case of a Call), or as a reduction in the proceeds of the sale of the underlying stock (in the case of a Put). The published tax rulings also state that (assuming the writer of such an Option does not grant it in the ordinary course of his trade or business of writing options) upon the expiration of the Option, or upon termination of the obligation of the writer in a closing purchase transaction, the writer would realize short-term capital gain or loss; and, in the event of the exercise of such an Option, the writer would treat the premium received as part of the proceeds of the sale of the underlying stock (in the case of a Call), or as a reduction in the cost of the underlying stock (in the case of a Put).

The risk factors listed below highlight certain significant risks of Options transactions.

1. The purchase of a Put or a Call runs the risk of losing his entire investment in a relatively short period of time.

2. The uncovered writer of a Call is subject to a risk of loss should the price of the underlying security increase, and the uncovered writer of a Put who does not have a short position in the underlying security equivalent to the number of shares required to be purchased upon exercise of the Put is subject to a risk of loss should the price of the underlying security decrease.

3. The writer of a Call who owns the underlying security deliverable upon exercise of the Call, and the writer of a Put who has a short position in the underlying security purchasable upon exercise of the Put are subject to the full risk of their respective positions in the underlying security; in exchange for the premium, so long as such persons remain writers of Options they have given up the opportunity for gain resulting from, in the case of a Call writer, an increase in the price of the underlying security above the exercise price, or, in the case of a Put writer, a decrease in the price of the underlying security below the exercise price.

4. In the event a secondary market in an Option ceases to exist, closing transactions may not be possible. If exercise restrictions are also imposed while there is no secondary market, Options may be unable to be either sold or exercised.

5. If a broker handling accounts of Options customers 'ecomes insolvent or otherwise ceases doing business, his customers may not be able to sell or exercise Options held in their accounts, and their positions as writers of Options may be liquidated.

THE EXCHANGES AND THE CLEARING CORPORATION

The Exchanges

As of the date of this writing, Options are listed and traded on the five registered national securities exchanges named above. The Exchanges and their respective members are subject to the Exchange Act and the regulatory jurisdiction of the SEC. The AMEX's trading floor and principal executive office are located at 86 Trinity Place, New York, New York 10006 and its telephone number is (212) 938-6000; the CBOE's trading floor and executive offices are located at 141 West Jackson Boulevard, Chicago, Illinois 60604 and its telephone number is (312) 431-5600; the MSE's trading floor and executive offices are located at 120 South LaSalle Street, Chicago, Illinois 60603 and its telephone number is (312) 368-2222; the PSE's Options trading floor is located at 301 Pine Street, San Francisco, California 94104 and its telephone number is (415) 393-4000; the PHLX's Options trading floor and executive officers are located at 17th Street and Stock Exchange Place, Philadelphia, Pennsylvania 19103 and its telephone number is (215) 563-4700.

Options of a particular series may be the subject of trading on only one Exchange or on more than one Exchange, and an Exchange may provide a market for Calls covering particular underlying securities without providing for Puts covering the same underlying securities. Options which are traded on only one Exchange may be purchased or written, and positions in those Options may be liquidated in closing transactions, only on that Exchange. Thus, if XYZ January 25 Calls are listed and traded only on the CBOE, an investor desiring to purchase or write an XYZ January 25 Call, or to liquidate a position in an XYZ January 25 Call in a closing transaction, may do so only on the CBOE. Options of the same series which are traded on more than one Exchange may be purchased and written, and positions in those Options may be liquidated in closing transactions, on any of the Exchanges on which that series of Options is traded. Thus, if ABC October 50 Calls are listed and traded on AMEX and PHLX, an investor may purchase such an Option on either of those Exchanges, and if, for example, such a Call is purchased on PHLX, the investor may subsequently liquidate his position as a holder of the Call in a closing transaction on either AMEX or PHLX. A list of the underlying securities, expiration months and exercise prices of particular Puts and Calls which are traded at any given time on any particular Exchange may be obtained from the Clearing Corporation or from such Exchange or a member thereof.

The Clearing Corporation

The Clearing Corporation is a Delaware corporation that is owned equally by the five Exchanges. It is registered as a clearing agency under the Exchange Act, and it and its Clearing Members are subject to the Exchange Act and the regulatory jurisdiction of the SEC. As of the date of this writing, its by-laws provide for a Board of Directors composed of 15 directors: nine Member Directors who are elected by the Clearing Members; five Exchange Directors representing each of the five Exchanges; and a Management Director who is the chief executive officer of the Clearing Corporation. The nine Member Directors, who are selected by a Nominating Committee (or by vote of the Clearing Members where nominees have been proposed by petition), are divided into three classes whose terms are staggered so that three such directors are elected each year. The Exchange Directors are elected for a term of one year. The Nominating Committee is composed of six persons who are officers or employees of Clearing Members and who are selected in the same manner as Member Directors.

GENERAL CONSIDERATION

INTRODUCTORY STATEMENT

This writing covers Calls that are traded on the Exchanges, and Puts that are proposed to be traded on the Exchanges upon receipt of the necessary regulatory approvals. All references in this writing to proposed Put trading are based upon applications presently pending before the Securities and Exchange Commission, and are subject to change.

Subject to certain limitations, each Call gives the holder the right to purchase the underlying security in accordance with the rules of the Clearing Corporation at the exercise price prior to the fixed expiration date, and each Put gives the holder the right to sell the underlying security in accordance with such rules at the exercise price prior to the fixed expiration date.

The "writer" of a Call is a person who, through his broker, has written a Call on an Exchange in an opening sale transaction and has thereby undertaken with the Clearing Corporation to deliver the underlying security represented by the Call upon the assignment of an exercise notice to him against payment of the aggregate exercise price. The Clearing Corporation does not itself own the underlying security, and the writer may not own the underlying security. The writer of a Put undertakes with the Clearing Corporation to purchase the underlying security represented by the Put upon the assignment of an exercise notice to him against delivery of the number of shares of the underlying security represented by the Put.

As consideration for the rights and obligations represented by an Option, the buyer (often referred to herein as "holder") of a Put or a Call pays and the writer receives an amount known as the "premium." The premium is determined in the Exchange's auction market on the basis of supply and demand, reflecting considerations such as the duration of the Option, the difference between the exercise price and the market price of the underlying security, and the price volatility and other characteristics of the underlying security.

The expiration time represents the latest time by which notice of exercise must be received in proper form at the Clearing

Corporation. The expiration time is 8:59 P.M. Pacific Time, 10:59 P.M. Central Time, 11:59 P.M. Eastern Time, on the Saturday immediately following the third Friday of the expiration month. However, under certain circumstances the Clearing Corporation may accept exercise notices filed by Clearing Members after the expiration time as provided in its by-laws. The expiration time should not be confused with the *earlier* exercise cut-off time. *In order to exercise an Option, a customer must so instruct his broker prior to the exercise cut-off time. For brokers who are members of one or more of the Exchanges, the exercise cut-off time is 2:30 P.M. Pacific Time, 4:30 P.M. Central Time, 5:30 P.M. Eastern Time, on the business day immediately preceding the expiration date.* If an outstanding Option is not properly exercised prior to its expiration, it will become worthless.

In order to permit a secondary market in which an existing position as holder or writer of an Option may be liquidated by an offsetting closing transaction. Options issued by the Clearing Corporation have standardized terms which include the expiration time and exercise price for each series of Options, leaving the premium and transaction costs as the only variables.

For the same reason, once an Option has been issued by the Clearing Corporation the contractual ties between the holder and the writer of the Option are severed. Instead, the holder of an Option looks to the Clearing Corporation, and not to any particular writer, for performance in the event of exercise. Since each time an Option is issued to a holder there is a writer of an Option of the same series contractually obligated to the Clearing Corporation (through a Clearing Member), the aggregate obligations of the Clearing Corporation to holders of Options are backed up by the aggregate obligations which writers owe to the Clearing Corporation. Upon exercise of an Option, the Clearing Corporation assigns an exercise notice to a Clearing Member's account with the Clearing Corporation selected at random from among all Clearing Member accounts reflecting the writing of Options of the same series as the exercised Option. The Clearing Member to whose account the exercise notice was assigned is obligated, in accordance with the rules of the Clearing Corporation, to deliver the underlying security in the case of a Call, or to purchase the underlying security in the case of a Put. If the exercise notice was assigned to the Clearing Member's customers' account, the Clearing Member in turn allocates the exercise notice to one or more of its customers who are writers of Options of the same series as the exercised Option.

Under the present practices of Exchanges, each class of Options is assigned to one of three expiration month cycles: the January-April-July-October cycle, the February-May-August-November cycle, or the March-June-September-December cycle. Trading in Options of a particular expiration month normally commences approximately nine months earlier, so that at any given time there are generally open for trading Options in each class having three different expiration months. For example, on the day following the expiration of January Options, trading in Options expiring in the following October will normally be opened (and trading in Options expiring in April and July will previously have been opened).

An Exchange may from time to time change the expiration month cycles to which particular classes of Options are assigned. Such changes would be phased in over a period of months, in connection with the opening of new series of the affected classes, and would have no effect on series of Options which had previously been opened for trading. (Example: if an Exchange decided at the beginning of October to reassign a class on the January-April-July-October cycle to the March-June-September-December cycle, the change would begin immediately after the expiration of the October Options of that class. At that time, trading would be opened in a new series expiring in June rather than July. The January and April Options outstanding at the time of the change would remain unaffected, but as each series expired, a new series would be opened expiring approximately eight months in the future, rather than nine, until all outstanding series were on the new expiration cycle).

Exercise prices are generally fixed at 5 point intervals for securities trading below 50 (although 5 point intervals are occasionally extended to securities trading below 60 or 70), 10 point intervals for securities trading between 50 and 200, and 20 point intervals for securities trading above 200. When trading is to be introduced in a new expiration month, an Exchange ordinarily selects the two exercise prices surrounding the market price of the underlying security on the day of selection. (Example: if the underlying security trades at 27 during the day exercise prices are being selected for a new expiration month, two new series of Options will ordinarily be selected with exercise prices at 25 and 30, respectively). However, if the market price of the underlying security is at or very close to a standard exercise price, three exercise prices might be selected: the exercise price that approximates the market price and the two surrounding exercise prices. The Clearing Corporation has been advised that one or more of the Exchanges may in the future propose to change certain of the exercise price intervals, subject to the approval of the Securities and Exchange Commission ("SEC"). Under the proposals being contemplated as of the date of this writing, 2½ point intervals would apply to securities trading below 25, 5 point intervals would apply to securities trading as high as 80 or 100, and 10 point intervals would be extended above 200.

When significant price movements take place in an underlying security following the introduction of new expiration months in the manner described above, additional series of Options with exercise prices reflecting such price movements may be opened for trading for one or more of the expiration months already the subject of trading. Ordinarily, when the price of the underlying security has moved upward or downward to the mid-point of the interval, an Exchange will introduce additional series of Options having an exercise price at the next appropriate interval with respect to all expiration months then the subject of trading, other than for Options expiring in less than 60 days. (Example: XYZ October 30 Puts have previously been opened for trading; an Exchange will ordinarily open XYZ October 25 Puts, as well as XYZ 25 Puts for the other two expiration months then the subject of trading, when the underlying security price reaches 27½.) However, if the underlying security price has moved upward or downward very rapidly, an Exchange may open two new exercise prices at the same time. (Example: XYZ October 30 Calls have previously been opened for trading and the security price has moved to 22½ before XYZ October 25 Calls have actually commenced trading; an Exchange may open XYZ 20 Calls and XYZ 25 Calls for each expiration month at the same time, or open only XYZ 20 Calls for each expiration month.)

The above examples are illustrative only, and each Exchange will independently determine the time and circumstances under which specific series of Options are to be opened for trading on that Exchange.

Once a series of Options is opened for trading on an Exchange, Options of that series will ordinarily remain open for trading notwithstanding the subsequent introduction of other series having different exercise prices. Thus, if XYZ Octobers are originally opened for trading with exercise prices of 25 and 30, and XYZ October 35s are subsequently introduced, XYZ October 25s and 30s will ordinarily continue to be traded.

Each of the Exchanges has advised the Clearing Corporation that it has established prohibitions on the entry of orders for opening purchase transactions and opening sale transactions with respect to certain Options traded on that Exchange. The Options subject to such prohibitions are those where the closing price of the Option on that Exchange was less than $0.50 per share on the last day on which the Option was traded on that Exchange, and where, in the case of a Call, the exercise price is more than $5 above, or, in the case of a Put, the exercise price is more than $5 below, the closing price of the underlying security in the primary market on the last day on which such security was traded. Not included in these prohibitions are opening transactions that create certain spread positions, certain transactions of market-makers, specialists and registered option traders, and transactions in Options traded on more than one Exchange where such Option was traded on the previous business day on any of the Exchanges and closed at $0.50 per share or higher. Also excluded from these prohibitions are transactions resulting from orders for opening sale transactions where, in respect of such transactions, the writer will be a covered Put writer or a covered Call writer, or where the writing of a Call is covered in the account on a share-for-share basis by securities immediately exchangeable or convertible without restriction (other than the payment of money) into the underlying security, and transactions resulting from orders for the purchase of a Put against a long position on a share-for-share basis in either the underlying security or securities immediately exchangeable or convertible without restriction (other than the payment of money) into the underlying security.

In addition, under the rules of the Exchanges in effect on the date of this writing, an Exchange may impose other restrictions with respect to Options whenever such action is deemed advisable in the public interest or for the protection of investors or in the interest of maintaining a fair and orderly market. Such restrictions may involve the suspension of a particular type or types of transactions (such as opening purchase transactions, opening uncovered writing transactions, or all opening writing transactions) or of all types of transactions, with respect to one or more classes or series of Options. In addition, the rules of the Exchanges in effect on the date of this writing provide that an Exchange may impose trading halts or suspensions in opening or closing transactions, or both, in one or more classes or series of Options whenever such action is considered advisable in the interest of a fair and orderly market, taking into consideration such factors as trading halts or suspensions or other trading irregularities in an underlying security, or other unusual circumstances. Similarly, unusual or unforeseen circumstances may cause normal Exchange operations to be interrupted. In any of these events, the liquidity of the secondary market for affected Options on one or more Exchange could be impaired or eliminated, in which event holders and writers of such Options might find it difficult or impossible to liquidate their positions through closing transactions on the Exchanges.

Adjustment in Terms

Except as stated in the immediately following italicized sentence, the number of shares or other units underlying Options and/or the exercise price are subject to adjustments in the event of dividends, distributions, stock splits, recapitalizations or reorganizations with respect to the underlying security or the issue thereof. *No adjustment is made to any of the terms of Exchange Traded Puts or Calls to reflect the declaration or payment of cash distributions made out of "earnings and profits" as defined in the Federal Internal Revenue Code.* However, if the holder of a Call effectively exercises it prior to an ex-date for any distribution, including a cash distribution for which no adjustment is made, the exercising holder is entitled to that distribution even though the writer to whom the exercise is assigned may receive actual notice of such assignment on or after the ex-date for the distribution. Conversely, the holder of a Put who effectively exercises it prior to an ex-date for a distribution, but delivers the underlying security to the writer to whom the exercise is assigned after such an ex-date, must also deliver the distribution to the writer.

Adjustments to the terms of Options are effective as of the "ex-date" of the event giving rise to the adjustment. Except

720

as noted in the following paragraph, stock splits, stock dividends and other stock distributions which increase the number of outstanding shares of the issuer of the underlying stock have the effect of proportionately increasing the number of shares of underlying stock covered by the Option and decreasing the exercise price.

However, where a stock split, stock dividend or stock distribution results in the issuance of one or more whole shares of underlying stock for each outstanding share of underlying stock, the number of shares covered by the Option is not adjusted. Instead the number of outstanding Options is proportionately increased and the exercise price is proportionately decreased. This may be illustrated by comparing for a single Option covering 100 shares of stock at an exercise price of $60 the adjustments resulting from a 3 for 2 stock distribution with those resulting from a 2 for 1 stock distribution. In the former case, after adjustment the Option covers 150 shares at an exercise price of $40, while in the latter case, after adjustment there are two Options covering 100 shares each at an exercise price of $30. It is important to note that where following an adjustment an Option covers more than 100 shares, the aggregate premium for the Option is determined by multiplying the premium per share by the number of shares covered by the Option. Thus, if an Option covers 110 shares following adjustment for a 10% stock dividend, and the premium is quoted at $5 per share, the aggregate premium for the Option is $550.

In the case of other distributions (other than ordinary cash dividends), recapitalizations or reorganizations by the issuer of the underlying security, or in the case of distributions where the adjustments described in the two preceding paragraphs are not considered by the Clearing Corporation to be appropriate in the circumstances, the exercise price of Options with respect to such security may be reduced by the value per share of the distributed property, or such Options may be equitably adjusted to include the equivalent property which a holder of the underlying security would be entitled to receive, or such other adjustments may be made to the exercise price, unit of trading or number of Options outstanding as the Clearing Corporation determines to be fair to the holders and writers of such Options.

Notwithstanding the foregoing, any adjustment in the exercise price will be rounded to the nearest 1/8 of a dollar and any adjustment in the number of shares will be rounded to the nearest whole share.

Limitations on Exercise

Options are exercisable at any time after issuance until expiration, except as follows:

1. Each of the Exchanges has advised the Clearing Corporation that it has established limits on the aggregate number of Options in each class which may be exercised by a holder or group of holders acting in concert within any five consecutive business days, and that under the rules of that Exchange customers are required to agree not to violate such limits. Puts and Calls covering the same underlying security are separate classes of Options, and are not aggregated for purposes of these limits. At the date of this writing the exercise limits established by each Exchange are 1,000 Options for each class of Options (which in most cases would cover 100,000 shares of an underlying stock), regardless of whether the Options were purchased on the same or different Exchanges or are held in one or more accounts or through one or more brokers. Any Exchange may establish different limits from time to time either across the board for all classes of Options traded on that Exchange or in respect of particular classes of Options. AMEX, PHLX and PSE have further advised the Clearing Corporation that under their rules exceptions may be made to their exercise limits in particular instances involving highly unusual circumstances. Customers should determine from their brokers the exercise limits to which they will be subject before engaging in an Option transaction.

2. Each Exchange is empowered to restrict, wholly or partially, the exercise of particular Options within a class of Options traded on that Exchange, if in its judgment such action is advisable in the interest of maintaining a fair and orderly market in such Options or in the underlying security or securities, or is otherwise deemed advisable in the public interest or for the protection of investors. For the duration and to the extent of any such restriction, the holder of any such Option will be unable to exercise it in contravention thereof if his position is maintained with a

member of the Exchange imposing the restriction. However, commencing ten business days prior to an Option's expiration, no such restriction will remain in effect.

3. The Clearing Corporation is also empowered to restrict the exercise of particular Options except during the ten business days prior to the Option's expiration. For the duration and to the extent of any such restriction the holder of any such Option will be unable to exercise it in contravention thereof irrespective of where his position is maintained. During such ten day period or thereafter the Board of Directors of the Clearing Corporation may impose a restriction on delivery of underlying securities not already owned by a writer of a Call to whom an exercise notice is assigned, or by a holder of a Put who has exercised it. In the event such a restriction is imposed on writers of Calls, or as an alternative to imposing such a restriction on holders of Puts, the Clearing Corporation shall (based on its then estimate of the value of the underlying security) fix a daily settlement value, if any, for such Option. In such case, in lieu of delivery and receipt of the underlying security upon exercise, the parties to the exercise will be obligated to pay and accept the settlement value fixed for the day the exercise notice is assigned, in lieu of receipt or delivery of the underlying security. When a restriction is imposed on holders of Puts based upon the suspension of trading in the underlying security, such restriction may be terminated by the Clearing Corporation when such suspension of trading has been lifted, or when the Clearing Corporation determines that the underlying security has no value. The Clearing Corporation does not intend to impose any restrictions on the delivery of underlying securities unless trading in the underlying security has been enjoined or ordered suspended by a court, the SEC, or another regulatory or self-regulatory authority having jurisdiction over trading in that underlying security.

4. Each Exchange is also empowered to restrict wholly or partially the exercise of particular Options if it determines that the holder thereof (or a group of holders acting in concert) is in violation of the position limits (see below) established by that Exchange.

Position Limits

Each of the Exchanges has advised the Clearing Corporation that it has established limitations governing the maximum number of Puts and Calls covering the same underlying security that may be held or written by a single investor or group of investors acting in concert (regardless of whether the Options are purchased or written on the same or different Exchanges or are held or written in one or more accounts or through one or more brokers), and that under its rules customers are required to agree not to violate these limits. An Exchange may order the liquidation of positions found to be in violation of these limits, and it may impose certain other sanctions. At the date of this writing, positions may not exceed an aggregate of 1,000 Puts and Calls on the same side of the market relating to the same underlying security. Calls purchased are on the same side of the market as Puts written, and together may not exceed 1,000 Option contracts; Calls written are on the same side of the market as Puts purchased, and these in the aggregate may not exceed a separate 1,000 Option contract limit. These limits are illustrated in the following table. Where the table indicates that two positions are "combined," the total number of contracts in the two positions may not exceed 1,000 Options; conversely, where the table indicates that positions are "not combined," then the 1,000 Option limit applies separately to each of the two positions involved.

	Long Call	Short Call	Long Put	Short Put
Long Call	Combined	Not Combined	Not Combined	Combined
Short Call	Not Combined	Combined	Combined	Not Combined
Long Put	Not Combined	Combined	Combined	Not Combined
Short Put	Combined	Not Combined	Not Combined	Combined

Illustrative of the foregoing, an investor or group of investors acting in concert may purchase up to 1,000 Calls covering a particular underlying security and at the same time may write up to 1,000 Calls covering the same underlying security (long Call and short Call positions are on opposite sides of the market and are not combined for purposes of position limits). An investor or group of investors acting in concert that has purchased 700 Puts covering a particular underlying security may at the same time write up to, but not more than, 300 Calls covering the same underlying security (long Put and short Call positions are on the same side of the market, and are combined for purposes of the limit).

Notwithstanding the foregoing, any Exchange may establish different limits from time to time either across the board for all classes of Options traded on that Exchange or in respect of particular classes or series of Options traded on that Exchange. For example, position limits in an Option class may be increased temporarily following a stock split which results in an increase in the number of outstanding Options of that class. AMEX, MSE, PHLX and PSE have further advised the Clearing Corporation that under their rules exceptions may be made to their position limits in particular instances involving highly unusual circumstances. Position limits differing in some respects from those described above may be imposed on brokers and their customers by regulatory or self-regulatory organizations other than the Exchange Customers should determine the then current position limits from their brokers before engaging in an Option transaction.

Certificateless Trading

Ordinarily no option certificates are issued by the Clearing Corporation to evidence the issuance of Options. Rather, the Clearing Corporation maintains a daily record of Options issued in each of the accounts of its Clearing Members, and each Clearing Member is required to maintain a continuous record of his respective customers' positions in Options. The ownership of Options is evidenced by the confimations and periodic statements which customers receive from their brokers, and which show for each Put or Call held (and written) the underlying security and the number of shares or other units thereof subject to the Option, the exercise price and the expiration month. Confirmations and statements of account furnished to customers are matters between brokers and their customers, and although the Exchanges do have general authority over their members, neither the Exchanges nor the Clearing Corporation are responsible for inaccuracies or omissions in confirmations or statements of account.

Since the only evidence of a customer's position as a holder or writer of an Option is found in the records of his broker, the customer must continue to maintain an account with his broker so long as he has an Option position, and the Option may only be exercised, or the position liquidated in a closing transaction, through the broker handling the account in which the Option position is held. A customer may transfer his account to another broker by making a written request to his former broker to transfer his account to a new broker who has agreed to accept the account.

For a customer who desires documentary evidence of his ownership of an Option, the Clearing Corporation will, upon request, and upon payment of a charge (currently $2.00) by the Clearing Member, issue a non-negotiable certificate to the Clearing Member maintaining the customer's account. The certificate, which is only issued by the Clearing Corporation in the name of a Clearing Member, indicates that the Clearing Member is the holder of an Option, and provides a space for the Clearing Member to certify to his customer that the Option is held for the account of such customer. The transfer of the certificate does not change the ownership of the Option except with the consent of the Clearing Corporation.

Underlying Securities

The underlying securities as to which Options are available are determined from time to time by the respective Exchanges on which the Options are to be traded. The Clearing Corporation and the Exchanges have agreed that all securities selected as underlying securities for Options will be registered and listed on a national securities exchange pursuant to the Exchange Act (or will be exempt from such registration). The issuers of underlying securities are subject to the reporting and disclosure requirements of the Exchange Act and of their listing agreements with securities exchanges. These issuers are generally required, among other things, to file with the SEC and with the exchanges on which their securities are listed annual reports describing the business of the issuer and containing financial statements, quarterly financial reports, and current reports of certain significant events. They must also generally file and distribute proxy statements to their stockholders. These materials are maintained for the three most recent fiscal years in the public files of the SEC and such exchanges. Each Exchange has agreed to maintain in its public reference files, with respect to the issuers of the underlying securities selected by such Exchange for Options trading, copies of the annual, quarterly and current reports and proxy statements which are in the public file of the SEC, and to make such materials available to the public for inspection or copying.

The Exchanges at present have generally uniform standards governing the selection and maintenance of underlying securities for Options trading. Except as set forth below, underlying securities selected for Options trading must have the following characteristics at the time of selection:

(A) A minimum of 8,000,000 shares owned by persons other than directors, officers, principal stockholders and others required to report their stock holdings under Section 16(a) of the Exchange Act.

(B) A minimum of 10,000 shareholders.

(C) Trading volume on all markets on which the stock is traded of at least 2,000,000 shares per year in each of the two previous calendar years.

(D) The market price of the underlying security shall have been at least $10.00 per share each business day of the six calendar months preceding the date of selection as measured by the lowest closing price recorded in any market on which the underlying security traded on each of the subject days.

(E) The issuer of the stock has been subject to and has complied in all respects, including timeliness, with the requirements of Sections 13 and 14 of the Exchange Act for at least the last three fiscal years.

(F) The issuer and its significant subsidiaries have not during the past three years defaulted in the payment of any dividend or sinking fund installment on any preferred stock or in the payment of any principal, interest or sinking fund installment on any indebtedness for borrowed money, or in the payment of rentals under long-term leases.

(G) The issuer and its consolidated subsidiaries had an aggregate net income, after taxes, but before extraordinary items net of tax effect, of at least $1,000,000 in each of three of the last four fiscal years, including the most recent fiscal year.

Except as set forth below, if one or more of the following conditions occurs with respect to an underlying security, an Exchange shall not open for trading additional series of Options relating to such security until the security again meets the initial selection standards set forth above:

(1) The issuer and its consolidated subsidiaries failed to have net income after taxes but before extraordinary items net of tax effect of at least $250,000 in more than one of the preceding four fiscal years.

(2) The issuer and its significant subsidiaries have defaulted in the payment of any dividend or sinking fund installment on preferred stock, or in the payment of any principal, interest or sinking fund installment on any indebtedness for borrowed money, or in the payment of rentals under long-term leases, and such default has not been cured within six months of the date on which it occurred.

(3) The issuer has failed to make timely reports under Section 13 and 14 of the Exchange Act, and such failure has not been corrected within thirty days of the date on which the report was due to be filed.

(4) Less than 7,200,000 shares of the underlying security are held by persons other than directors, officers, principal stockholders and others required to report their stock holdings under Section 16(a) of the Exchange Act.

(5) There are less than 9,000 holders of the underlying security.

(6) The volume of trading in the underlying security on all markets is less than 1,800,000 shares in the preceding calendar year.

(7) The market price per share of the underlying security closes below $10.00 on a majority of the business days during the preceding six-month period as measured by the highest closing price recorded in any market on which the underlying security trades.

Under the rules of the Exchanges, in exceptional circumstances any Exchange may select for Options trading underlying securities which lack initial selection characteristics (A), (B), (C) or (D). In addition, in exceptional circumstances and in the interest of maintaining a fair and orderly market or for the protection of investors, any Exchange may open additional series with respect to underlying securities which fail to meet maintenance conditions (4), (5), (6) or (7). Any Exchange may alter its standards governing selection and maintenance from time to time pursuant to the provisions of the Exchange Act. In addition, an Exchange may determine to discontinue trading in Options covering one or more underlying securities, in which event the Exchange ordinarily will not introduce new series of such Options, and may, depending upon the circumstances, also prohibit opening transactions or all transactions in such Options already the subject of trading.

In selecting securities for Options transactions and in continuing the listing of Options covering securities previously so selected, the Exchanges ordinarily rely on information made available by the issuers of the underlying securities, including information on the SEC public file. Accordingly, the selection of an underlying security for Options trading and the continued listing of Options covering an underlying security should not be relied upon as a representation by the Clearing Corporation or an Exchange that the underlying security or its issuer, in fact, meets the requirements for such selection or listing.

Issuers of underlying securities do not participate in the selection of underlying securities for Options transactions and do not become subject to the regulatory jurisdiction of any Exchange solely by virtue of being selected for Options transactions on that Exchange. Such issuers have no responsibility regarding the issuance, the terms or the performance of any Option, and Option holders have no rights as security holders of such issuers. Further, the Clearing Corporation does not participate in the selection of underlying securities, and it relies upon the representation of the Exchange selecting a particular security that the requirements for such selection appear to be met.

Hours of Trading

Subject to restrictions on trading of certain Options that might be imposed by one or more Exchanges and the possibility that an Exchange may discontinue or interrupt the trading of Options or of a particular class or series of Options, Options are ordinarily traded on the Exchanges during the same hours in which underlying securities are traded in their primary markets. However, an Exchange may open or continue the trading of an Option at times when the underlying security is itself not being traded, and the Exchanges have advised the Clearing Corporation that they are participating in a pilot program under which the trading of Options is continued for a short period (ten minutes, as of the date of this writing) after the close of each day's trading in the underlying securities. The pilot program is scheduled to expire early in 1979, but may be extended or made permanent in its present form or with modifications.

Options are traded on each trading day as described above until the business day immediately prior to the day on which the Options expire, when trading in expiring Options ceases at noon Pacific Time, 2:00 p.m. Central Time, 3:00 p.m. Eastern Time. The Clearing Corporation has been advised that immediately following the time that trading in expiring Options ceases, some or all of the Exchanges may conduct "closing rotations." A closing rotation is a procedure that permits brokers and dealers on the floor of an Exchange to make bids, offers and transactions in particular Options, one series at a time, for the purpose of facilitating an orderly close. During a closing rotation (which typically takes several minutes to conduct, but may at times take a substantially longer period), customer orders already represented on the trading floor may be executed, but it may be difficult or impossible for new customer orders to be executed or for pending customer orders to be cancelled. Prior to the pilot program referred to in the preceding paragraph, some of the Exchanges conducted closing rotations at the close of each day's trading for non-expiring Options. The Clearing Corporation has been advised that daily closing rotations (but not the closing rotations for expiring Options described above) have been discontinued during the term of the pilot program. Daily closing rotations may be resumed if the pilot program is not made permanent.

Order Placing and Execution

Under the rules of the Exchanges in effect on the date of this writing, before an investor may purchase or write Puts or Calls on an Exchange through a broker who is a member of the Exchange, his account with the members must be approved by the member for Options transactions. Before approving a customer's account for Options transactions, Exchange members are required under Exchange rules to exercise due diligence to learn the essential facts as to the customer, his investment

730

objectives, and his financial situation. Exchange members may require customers to meet minimum financial or other requirements before approving their accounts for Options transactions, and may impose special requirements for particular types of Options transactions, such as uncovered writing transactions. Under Exchange rules, an Exchange member who recommends an Option transaction to a customer is required to have reasonable grounds, on the basis of the information known to the member, for believing that the recommendation is not unsuitable for the customer. Brokers who are not Exchange members may not be subject to some or all of the foregoing requirements. Customers are required by each Exchange to agree that Options transactions in their accounts will be handled in accordance with the rules of the Clearing Corporation and the rules of such Exchange and that the customer will adhere to the position and exercise limits established by the Exchange. The enforcement of an Exchange's rules in the foregoing and all other respects is the responsibility of that Exchange and not of the Clearing Corporation. The Clearing Corporation has been advised by the Exchanges that their rules permit customers and other non-members to demand arbitration of certain disputes with Exchange members. Information regarding the arbitration procedures of a particular Exchange may be obtained from that Exchange.

Options may be purchased or written by placing an order with a broker, as for other types of securities. Orders should specify whether the order is for Puts or Calls, the underlying security, expiration month and exercise price, the number of contracts to be purchased or written and whether the purchase or sale is an "opening" or "closing" transaction. The Exchanges have advised that in addition to many of the types of orders found generally in securities markets (that is, markets orders, limit orders, contingency orders, etc.), "spread orders" and "straddle orders" are available in connection with Option trading.

When a broker receives an order to buy or write an Option of a particular series, the order is transmitted for execution to the floor of the one of the Exchanges on which such Options are traded. The Exchanges have advised the Clearing Corporation that if agreement as to the premium is reached between a buyer and a writer or their agents on the floor, then a trade binding on the parties (but not yet on the Clearing Corporation) take place. Reports of trades that have been agreed upon on the Exchanges (referred to as "matched trades") are filed with the Clearing Corporation on the trade date, or as soon thereafter as the parties to trades that do not match are able to reconcile their differences and report matched trades.

The Clearing Member for the buyer on a matched trade is required to pay the premium to the Clearing Corporation prior to 7:00 A.M. Pacific Time, 9:00 A.M. Central Time and 10:00 A.M. Eastern Time, of the first business day following the day on which the Clearing Corporation receives the report of the matched trade.

If the transaction is then accepted by the Clearing Corporation, the transaction becomes effective at 10:00 A.M. Pacific Time, Noon Central Time and 1:00 P.M. Eastern Time on the next business day. This is the time that the Option is issued by the Clearing Corporation in the case of an opening purchase transaction, or that the writer's prior position is liquidated in the case of a closing purchase transaction. An exception to the foregoing is that if the Clearing Corporation receives a report of an opening purchase transaction matched as of the last trading day prior to the Option's expiration, the Option will be deemed to have been issued by the Clearing Corporation on the last trading day.

Even though an Option will not ordinarily be issued until the business day following the date of the transaction in which it was purchased, it may nonetheless be exercised on the date of purchase, subject to the condition that the exercise will not be effective unless the purchase transaction is accepted by the Clearing Corporation on the following business day.

Acceptance and Rejection of Transactions by the
Clearing Corporation

An Option transaction is automatically accepted by the Clearing Corporation if a report of a matched trade is filed with the Clearing Corporation and if the Clearing Member for the buyer has paid its total net premium obligations to the Clearing Corporation for all Options purchased through the Clearing Member's account. If the Clearing Member does not make this payment, the Clearing Corporation may reject the transaction, notwithstanding that the customer may have paid the premium to his broker. The Clearing Corporation's general policy is to accept all opening and closing purchase transactions, even though the premiums have not been paid, but the Clearing Corporation may in its discretion elect to reject any such transaction if it deems it in the best interest of the Clearing Corporation to do so. Transactions where matched trade reports are not filed will be automatically rejected.

If a transaction is rejected for nonpayment of the premium, the Clearing Corporation will promptly notify the writer's Clearing Member. The writer will then have the remedies available under the rules of the Exchange where the transaction occurred. Under these rules as in effect at the date of this writing, if the writer was engaging in an opening writing transaction, his Clearing Member may either cancel the transaction or write a new Option, charging any loss to the defaulting Clearing Member. If the writer was engaging in a closing sale transaction, he may instruct his broker either to cancel the transaction (thereby continuing his position as a holder of an Option) or to enter into a new closing sale transaction, charging any loss to the defaulting Clearing Member. Neither the Clearing Corporation nor any Exchange will have any responsibility when a transaction has been rejected for nonpayment of premiums or because of any delays or errors in the filing by members of matching trade reports, nor will the Clearing Corporation have any responsibility arising out of any delays or errors by an Exchange in the filing of reports of matched trades.

THE SECONDARY MARKET IN OPTIONS

General

As mentioned elsewhere in this writing, the Exchanges have each advised the Clearing Corporation that the secondary market in Options on such Exchange is designed ordinarily to permit investors with existing positions as holders or writers of Options traded on such Exchange to liquidate their positions in offsetting "closing" transactions. Since holders and writers of Options are not contractually linked to each other, but instead have rights or obligations running to the Clearing Corporation, such secondary markets do not operate in the same manner as the secondary markets in stocks, in that Option positions are not actually transferred from one holder or writer to another in a closing transaction. However, the effect is much the same from the point of view of the liquidating holder or writer whose position with the Clearing Corporation is cancelled in the closing transaction. Closing transactions are placed and executed in the same manner as opening transactions, but must be placed through the broker who maintains the account in which the position to be closed is held. A closing transaction may be executed only on an Exchange which provides a market for Options having identical terms to the Option held or written in the position to be liquidated. In addition to closing transactions, which are executed on the floor of one of the Exchanges, a customer may, under certain circumstances, transfer an Option position to his broker or another person in a transaction off the floor of the Exchange.

Each of the Exchanges has advised the Clearing Corporation that, although that Exchange's trading mechanism is designed to provide market liquidity for the Options traded on that Exchange, it must be recognized that there can be no assurance that a liquid secondary market on that Exchange will exist for any particular Options, or at any particular time, and for some Options no secondary market on that Exchange may exist at all. Among the reasons why a secondary market might not exist are the following: (i) there may be insufficient trading interest in certain Options; (ii) restrictions may be imposed on opening transactions or closing transactions or both, (iii) trading halts, suspensions or other restrictions may be imposed with respect to particular classes or series of Options or underlying securities; (iv) unusual or unforeseen circumstances may interrupt normal Exchange operations; (v) the facilities of an Exchange or the Clearing Corporation may not at all times be adequate to handle current trading volume; or (vi) one or more Exchanges could, for economic, regulatory or other reasons decide or be compelled at some future date to discontinue the trading of Options (or a particular class or series of Options), in which event the secondary market on that Exchange (or on that Exchange in that class or series of Options) would cease to exist, although outstanding Options that had been issued by the Clearing Corporation as a result of trades on that Exchange would continue to be exercisable in accordance with their terms (subject to the imposition of exercise restrictions by that Exchange or the Clearing Corporation).

In any of the foregoing events, it might not be possible to effect closing transactions in particular Options, with the result that a holder would have to exercise his Option (requiring the holder to pay for the underlying security or meet margin requirements in connection with its purchase) in order to realize any profit, and a writer would be unable to terminate his writer's obligation until the Option expires or he performs upon being assigned an exercise notice. In addition, in the event of circumstances (e.g., a tender offer for an underlying security) that have the effect of impairing liquidity in the market for an underlying security, or for other reasons, an Exchange might suspend or restrict trading in a class of Options. Such circumstances might also cause an Exchange or the Clearing Corporation to impose exercise restrictions on the affected class of Options. If trading is suspended or restricted at the same time that exercise restrictions are imposed, holders and writers of Options of the affected class would be unable to liquidate their positions in closing transactions and such Options could not be exercised. In lieu of exercise, the Clearing Corporation might fix daily settlement values during the ten business days prior to expiration. It should also be noted that a secondary market will not be beneficial to the holder of an Option that has lost all of its value.

Closing Sale Transactions

So long as a secondary market in Options remains available on an Exchange, the holder of an Option traded on that Exchange ordinarily may realize any gain in the market price of his Option by selling it in a closing sale transaction. For example, a holder might have purchased an XYZ July 50 Call in January (when XYZ stock was selling at 51) for a premium of $600 (plus transaction costs). Three months later XYZ stock is selling at 57 and XYZ July 50 Calls are selling at 8½ (or $850 per Call). In this situation, the holder could realize the $250 gain in the Call price (less applicable transaction costs) in a closing sale transaction. Similarly, the holder of a Put may realize in a closing sale transaction any gain in the Put price resulting from a decline in the market price of underlying security. However, it may sometimes be advisable for a holder of a profitable Option, after taking into account the relative market prices of the Option and the underlying security, as well as the applicable transaction costs, margin requirements, tax considerations, investment objectives and other relevant considerations, to exercise the Option rather than to sell it in the secondary market.

735

When the closing sale order is executed, the holder's Option position will (except as noted below) be deemed to be extinguished and he will no longer be able to exercise his Option. In the event a certificate has been issued to evidence an Option, the certificate must be surrendered to the Clearing Corporation when the Option position is to be extinguished in a closing sale transaction. If the certificate is not surrendered, the transaction will be treated by the Clearing Corporation as an opening sale transaction, will result in the creation of a new writer's position, and will not extinguish the pre-existing holder's position.

The clearance of a closing sale transaction is, like all other Options transactions, subject to the receipt by the Clearing Corporation of a report of a matched trade and to the acceptance of the transaction by the Clearing Corporation. The premium will be credited to the account of the Clearing Member acting for the seller by 8:00 A.M. Pacific Time, 10:00 A.M. Central Time, 11:00 A.M. Eastern Time, of the business day following the day on which the Clearing Corporation receives a report of a matched trade from an Exchange, subject to being charged back in the event that the transaction is rejected by the Clearing Corporation.

Closing Purchase Transactions

So long as a secondary market in Options remains available on an Exchange, the writer of an Option traded on that Exchange ordinarily may terminate his writer's obligation by entering into a closing purchase transaction. In such a transaction, the writer "buys" an Option in the same series as the Option he previously wrote. However, instead of the transaction resulting in the issuance of an Option, it has the effect of cancelling the writer's pre-existing obligation.

Closing purchase transactions may be illustrated by the following:

1. A holder of 100 shares of XYZ stock might have written an XYZ July 50 Call in January when XYZ stock was selling at 51 and received a premium of, say, $600 (less transaction costs) in the transaction. Three months later, XYZ stock is selling at 47 and XYZ July 50 Calls are selling at 2½ (or $250 per Call), and the writer anticipates a further decline in the price of the stock. Since his Call

736

has three months to run, selling his stock to eliminate any further loss would put him in the position of an uncovered writer (requiring that he maintain margin to cover his position) and expose him to unlimited upside risk should the stock price rise. To avoid this risk the writer might enter into a closing purchase transaction, paying a premium of $250 plus transaction costs. This closes out his writer's position, leaving him free to sell the XYZ stock.

2. The uncovered writing of an XYZ July 50 Call occurred in January at a premium of $600, and three months later XYZ stock is selling at 57, XYZ July 50 Calls are selling at 8½ (or $850 per Call) and the writer anticipates a further increase in the price of the stock. If the writer does not wish to commit his capital to the purchase of 100 shares of XYZ at 57 to cover his position, he might, in a closing purchase transaction, pay $850 to purchase a July XYZ 50 Call and will have incurred a loss of $250 plus transaction costs.

3. An XYZ July 50 Put may have been written in January at a premium of $500 and three months later XYZ stock is selling at 46, XYZ July 50 Puts are selling at 7 ($700 per Put), and the writer anticipates a further decline in the price of the stock. The writer may sell short 100 shares of XYZ stock at 46 to hedge against a further stock price decline, but this may require an additional margin requirement on account of the stock position and would expose the writer to the risks of the short stock position should the price of the stock increase. An alternative might be to purchase an XYZ July 50 Put for $700 in a closing purchase transaction, incurring a net loss of $200 plus transaction costs. Similarly, an investor who sold stock short at the same time that he wrote a Put representing that stock, in the event the stock subsequently increases in price, might wish to "buy in" the Put in a closing purchase transaction and then to cover the short stock position and not be left with any market risk on account of either the Put position or the short stock position.

A closing purchase transaction becomes effective at 10:00 A.M. Pacific Time, Noon Central Time, 1:00 P.M. Eastern Time, on the business day following the trade if the Clearing Corporation has received a report of a matched trade from an Exchange and the transaction has been accepted by the Clearing Corpora-

that brokers not bound by such times may fix earlier cut-off times for their customers. Each customer should determine from his broker the applicable cut-off time, since a customer's failure to instruct his broker to exercise an Option prior to that time will mean that the Option may not be exercised.

In unusual circumstances (as, for example, exceptional circumstances preventing a customer from communicating with an Exchange member or preventing the member from receiving exercise instructions), exceptions may be made to an Exchange member's cut-off time, but any such exception is subject to Exchange review. Writers of Options should be aware that the exercise cut-off time established by a broker, pursuant to Exchange rules or otherwise, does not affect the validity of an exercise notice filed in proper form with the Clearing Corporation before the Clearing Corporation's expiration time, and such exercise notice will be treated by the Clearing Corporation as valid and effective, and will be assigned by the Clearing Corporation regardless of whether the exercise notice was submitted in violation of the rules of an Exchange or a broker's procedures with respect to cut-off times.

If the Clearing Corporation is unable to follow the procedures provided in its rules for the receipt of exercise instructions from Clearing Members on the expiration date, the deadline for the submission of exercise instructions by Clearing Members may be extended past the expiration time in accordance with the Clearing Corporation's by-laws, and exercise instructions submitted during such an extension will be deemed to have been submitted before the expiration time. No such extension will have any effect on the exercise cut-off time prior to which a customer must instruct his broker to exercise an Option. The Clearing Corporation has authority to accept exercise instructions after the expiration time only in situations where the Clearing Corporation itself is unable to follow its normal procedures for the receipt of exercise instructions on the exercise date; except in those circumstances, the Clearing Corporation does not have authority to extend the expiration time of any Option.

The preceding paragraphs describe time limits for exercise immediately prior to the expiration of an Option. On business days other than the expiration date, Clearing Members may tender exercise notices to the Clearing Corporation between the hours of 7:00 A.M. and 1:30 P.M. Pacific Time, 9:00 A.M. and 3:30 P.M. Central Time, and 10:00 A.M. and 4:30 P.M. Eastern Time in order for the exercise to be assigned on the following business day. Brokers will generally fix their own time limits within which a customer must give instructions to tender an exercise notice in order that these time limits at the Clearing Corporation may be met.

In order to exercise an outstanding Option, proper notice of exercise must be given to the Clearing Corporation by the Clearing Member in whose account with the Clearing Corporation the Option is held. This means that a holder of an Option may only exercise it through the broker handling the account in which the Option is held. In the event a certificate has been issued to evidence an Option, notice of exercise with respect to that Option generally must be accompanied by the certificate. Otherwise the exercise may be rejected by the Clearing Corporation.

The Clearing Corporation assumes no responsibility for the timely or proper tender to it of exercise notices by Clearing Members. The failure of a Clearing Member (or of any broker) to transmit an exercise notice within the required time or in proper form will not result in any obligation on the part of the Clearing Corporation. If an Option is not properly exercised prior to its expiration, it will become worthless.

Every notice of exercise properly submitted to the Clearing Corporation is irrevocable. Upon the proper and timely submission of an exercise notice, the exercising Clearing Member (and his customer, if the exercise was pursuant to a customer's authorization) will be under a contractual obligation to deliver the underlying security covered by the Option in the case of a Put, or to pay the aggregate exercise price for the underlying security in the case of a Call, on the "exercise settlement date," even though the underlying security may change in value after the exercise notice has been submitted. When a Call is exercised, the exercising holder becomes subject to all of the risks of a holder of the underlying security and to the applicable margin requirements.

Because brokers may have lower transaction costs than public customers, a broker may find it profitable to exercise an Option that would not be profitable for a public customer to exercise. Some brokers may, in their customer account agreements or otherwise, reserve the right to exercise for their own accounts expiring Options that customers have elected not to exercise. The Clearing Corporation understands that brokers' practices with respect to the compensation of customers in such circumstances may vary. A customer may determine from his broker the broker's practices in that respect.

Assignment of Exercise Notices

An exercise notice that is properly submitted to the Clearing Corporation will be assigned by the Clearing Corporation on the following business day, and all assignments will be dated and effective as of such following business day. Thus an exercise notice filed on a given day may be assigned to a writer position resulting from an opening writing transaction executed on the same day. If the Clearing Corporation is unable to make assignments on the business day following any day on which exercise notices are submitted, the Clearing Corporation will make such assignments as soon as practicable thereafter. In the event of any such delayed assignments, the Clearing Corporation will fix such assignment and exercise settlement dates as it deems fair and reasonable in the circumstances.

The exercise notice will be assigned to a randomly selected Clearing Member account with the Clearing Corporation that reflects the writing of an Option or Options of the same series as the exercised Option. The Clearing Corporation has the authority under its rules to classify writer positions of Clearing Members by the types of margin deposited in respect of such positions, and to apply its random selection procedures separately to positions for which different types of margins have been deposited. As of the date of this writing, however, the Clearing Corporation does not do so.

If the Clearing Corporation assigns an exercise notice to a Clearing Member's customers' account, the Member is required to allocate the exercise notice to a customer maintaining a position as a writer in the account. Under the rules of each Exchange at the date of this writing, this allocation by the member may be upon a random selection basis, a "first-in, first-out" basis, or any other method chosen by the member that is fair and equitable to its customers. Customers may request that their brokers inform them of the method used in allocating exercise notices to the accounts of writers. Writers should be aware that they may receive notification from their brokers that an exercise notice has been allocated to them one or more days following the date of the initial assignment by the Clearing Corporation. If an exercise notice is assigned to the writer of a Put, that writer becomes subject to all of the risks of a holder of the underlying security and to the applicable margin requirements.

Experience has shown that Options may be exercised at any time during their lives, including times when they are only marginally "in the money" or even out of the money. In that connection, it should be noted that some holders of Options, such as Exchange members and other brokers and dealers, may have lower transaction costs than the average public customer, and may find it advantageous to exercise an Option at a time when it would not be profitable for a public customer to do so. The writer of an Option must therefore assume that he may be assigned an exercise notice at any time during the life of that Option.

Delivery and Payment

Once an exercise notice has been assigned to the writer of an Option, the writer may no longer effect a closing purchase transaction in respect of the exercised Option, but must purchase (in the case of a Put) or sell (in the case of a Call) the underlying security pursuant to the exercise. If an exercise notice is properly tendered to the Clearing Corporation prior to the ex-dividend date for a distribution for which there is no adjustment to the terms of the Option (such as an ordinary cash dividend), the distribution will go to the assigned writer of a Put, or to the exercising holder of a Call, notwithstanding that notice of the assignment may be received by the writer on or after the ex-dividend date. This means that the assigned writer of a Call or the exercising holder of a Put may be required to deliver the underlying security together with the property included in a distribution at a time when the underlying security may be acquired only on an ex-dividend basis.

Settlement for the purchase or sale of underlying securities resulting from the exercise of an Option is ordinarily made through correspondent clearing corporations with which the Clearing Corporation has made arrangements for exercise settlement in the manner described below. As of the date of this writing, such arrangements have been made with Midwest Clearing Corporation, Stock Clearing Corporation, American Stock Exchange Clearing Corporation, Pacific Clearing Corporation and Stock Clearing Corporation of Philadelphia. Each of these correspondent clearing corporations is registered with the Securities and Exchange Commission as a "clearing agency" pursuant to the provisions of the Securities Exchange Act of 1934, as amended, and the rules of each and certain other documents pertaining to them are required to be filed with the Commission.

Under these arrangements and the rules of the Clearing Corporation in force on the date of this writing, each Clearing Member must maintain a special account ("exercise settlement account") and a regular account with at least one correspondent clearing corporation. Exercising Clearing Members effect delivery of and payment for underlying securities through their exercise settlement accounts, and assigned Clearing Members effect such delivery and payment through their regular accounts, with the correspondent clearing corporation. As of the opening of business on the "exercise settlement date" (which is defined below) in respect of an exercise, appropriate bookkeeping entries are made in the respective accounts maintained by the exercising and assigned Clearing Members at correspondent clearing corporations, and thereafter delivery of the underlying security and payment therefor is made by the Clearing Members in accordance with the then effective rules of their respective correspondent clearing corporations. To the extent set forth below under "Remedies," the Clearing Corporation will indemnify Clearing Members exercising Calls against certain losses which they might sustain in the event of defaults or delays by a correspondent clearing corporation in delivering securities which have not yet been fully paid for by such Clearing Members, and will indemnify Clearing Members exercising Puts against certain losses which they might sustain in the event of default by a correspondent clearing corporation in paying for or in receiving delivery of securities. With these exceptions, the Clearing Corporation is discharged and has no further responsibility in respect of any exercise settlement through a correspondent clearing corporation from and after the opening of business on the exercise settlement date.

Although the Clearing Corporation anticipates that exercise settlements will ordinarily be made through the facilities of

743

correspondent clearing corporations, the Clearing Corporation may require that particular exercises or exercises generally be settled between the assigned Clearing Member and the exercising Clearing Member directly, in which event the exercise must be settled on or before 10:00 A.M. Pacific Time, 12:00 noon Central Time, 1:00 P.M. Eastern Time, on the "exercise settlement date." Under the rules of the Clearing Corporation in force on the date of this writing, the exercise settlement date is the fifth business day following the date when the exercise notice is properly tendered to the Clearing Corporation except that (a) the Clearing Corporation may fix a different exercise settlement date for property that is deliverable as a result of an adjustment to an Option and (b) the Clearing Corporation may postpone an exercise settlement date whenever in its opinion such action is required in the public interest or to meet unusual conditions. Where settlement is made directly between Clearing Members, the obligations of the Clearing Corporation are completely discharged when the aggregate exercise price in the case of a Put, or the underlying security in the case of a Call, is delivered to the exercising Clearing Member.

Once its obligations are discharged, the Clearing Corporation has no responsibility if the exercising Clearing Member should fail to pay the aggregate exercise price or to deliver the underlying security to or upon the order of the exercising holder, or if a correspondent clearing corporation should fail to pay the aggregate exercise price or to deliver fully paid-for securities to the Clearing Member.

Remedies

If an exercising or an assigned Clearing Member is suspended by the Clearing Corporation, with the result that a pending exercise will not be settled in the ordinary course, the other party to the exercise may (unless the Clearing Corporation provides for settlement in some other manner) buy in or sell out the underlying securities involved in the exercise in the best available market. Gains on any such transactions are required to be paid over to the Clearing Corporation for the account of the suspended Clearing Member. Losses on such transactions constitute senior claims against certain assets of the suspended Clearing Member in the possession of the Clearing Corporation, and are compensable out of the Clearing Fund to the extent that those assets are insufficient. In addition, if the suspended Clearing Member was the assigned Clearing Member, losses sustained by the exercising Clearing Member would constitute claims against the general assets of the Clearing Corporation. Once an exercise reaches settlement, however, the assigned Clearing Member has no further rights against the Clearing Corporation or any assets in its possession, and the rights of the exercising Clearing Member are limited to those described in the following two paragraphs.

If a Clearing Member which has exercised a Call (the "Receiving Clearing Member") requests delivery of underlying securities credited to its exercise settlement account with a correspondent clearing corporation which have not yet been paid for, and fails to receive the securities within thirty days thereafter, or if the correspondent clearing corporation becomes insolvent, or if underlying securities are not delivered on the exercise settlement date in cases where settlement is made directly between the exercising and assigned Clearing Members, the Receiving Clearing Member may issue a "buy-in" notice in accordance with the Rules of the Clearing Corporation and purchase the undelivered securities in the best available market. The Clearing Corporation is obligated to pay the Receiving Clearing Member an amount equal to the excess (if any) of the price paid in such buy-in over the price which would have been payable by the Receiving Clearing Member to the correspondent clearing corporation or to the Clearing Member that failed to make delivery initially, as the case may be.

If a Clearing Member which has exercised a Put (the "Delivering Clearing Member") delivers or seeks to deliver the underlying securities into its exercise settlement account with a correspondent clearing corporation, and the correspondent clearing corporation fails to receive or to pay for such securities or becomes insolvent, or in cases where settlement is made directly between the exercising and assigned Clearing Members, if the assigned Clearing Member fails to receive or to pay for underlying securities tendered by the Delivering Clearing Member on the exercise settlement date, the Delivering Clearing Member may sell out the underlying securities (or, where the underlying securities have been delivered to a correspondent clearing corporation but not recovered, securities of the same description and quantity) in the best available market. The Clearing

Corporation is obligated to pay the Delivering Clearing Member an amount equal to the excess (if any) of the price which the Delivering Clearing Member was entitled to receive on delivery of the underlying securities from the correspondent clearing corporation or the assigned Clearing Member, as the case may be, over the price received on such sell-out. Any loss resulting from a Delivering Clearing Member's inability to recover underlying securities delivered into its exercise settlement account with a correspondent clearing corporation or to an assigned Clearing Member and not paid for must be borne by the Delivering Clearing Member.

The Back-Up System

The settlement procedures of the Clearing Corporation are designed so that for every outstanding Option there will be a writer—and a Clearing Member representing the writer (unless the Clearing Member is also the writer)—of an Option of the same series who has undertaken to perform the obligations of the Clearing Corporation in the event an exercise notice for the Option is assigned to him. As a result, no matter how many Options of a given series may be outstanding at any time, there will always be a group of writers of Options of the same series who, in the aggregate, have undertaken to perform the Clearing Corporation's obligations with respect to such Options.

Once an exercise notice for an Option is assigned to a particular writer, that writer is contractually obligated to his broker to pay the aggregate exercise price, in the case of a Put, or to deliver the underlying security in the case of a Call, in accordance with the terms of the Option. This contractual obligation of the writer is secured by the securities or other margin which the writer is required to deposit with his broker with respect to the writing of all Options.

The Clearing Member representing the writer is also contractually obligated, whether or not his customer performs, to perform the Clearing Corporation's obligations on an assigned Option. Standing behind a Clearing Member's obligations are (1) the Clearing Member's net capital, (2) the Clearing Member's margin deposits with the Clearing Corporation, (3) the Clearing Corporation's lien on certain of the Clearing Member's assets, and (4) the Clearing Fund.

746

1. *The Clearing Member's net capital.* Every Clearing Member must be a member of an Exchange and must have an initial net capital (as defined in the Clearing Corporation's rules) of $150,000 or more, depending on the nature and magnitude of its assets and obligations. The Clearing Member may not permit the withdrawal of any funds from any subordinated loan account or any account of partners, or pay any dividends, if the effect of such withdrawal or payment would be to reduce its net capital below $150,000 or a greater amount determined by the application of a formula in the rules of the SEC prescribing minimum net capital requirements for bokers and dealers generally. A Clearing Member's net capital may fall to less than that amount as a result of transactions in the regular course of business, but a Clearing Member may not engage in or clear any Options transaction whenever its net capital falls below $100,000 or a greater amount determined by the application of a formula in the rules of the Clearing Corporation.

The Clearing Corporation obtains certain financial reports from each Clearing Member on a monthly basis, and the Clearing Corporation may require more frequent reports. A Clearing Member whose net capital falls below a prescribed "early warning" level must promptly notify the Clearing Corporation of that fact. The financial books and records of each Clearing Member must be audited at least once annually by independent public accountants and a report of such audit must be filed with the Clearing Corporation in a form prescribed by the Clearing Corporation.

Although the Clearing Corporation seeks to achieve compliance with its net capital requirements by all Clearing Members, neither the Clearing Corporation nor any of the Exchanges is liable for any damages suffered as a result of any Clearing Member's failure to comply.

2. *The Clearing Member's margin deposits.* Each Clearing Member is required with respect to each Option for which it represents the writer (such positions in Options are referred to as "short" positions) either, in the case of a Call, to deposit the underlying security represented by the Call or, in the case of a Put or a Call, to deposit and maintain specified margin with the Clearing Corporation by 7:00 A.M. Pacific Time, 9:00 A.M. Central Time, 10:00 A.M. Eastern Time, of the business day following the day on which the Option was

written. The deposit of the underlying security intended to serve in lieu of cash margin in the case of a Call is made with a bank, trust company or other depository satisfactory to the Clearing Corporation under agreements requiring the delivery of the underlying security against payment of the aggregate exercise price specified in the Call. Such deposits may be made by a Clearing Member as a commingled deposit (called a "bulk deposit") of securities of a number of customers or as a specific deposit for a particular customer. Clearing Members are not permitted, under applicable law, to make bulk deposits of fully paid or excess margin securities (as those terms are defined in the rules of the SEC). At the present time, the Clearing Corporation has approved The Depository Trust Company, Midwest Securities Trust Company, Pacific Securities Depository Trust Company, and Stock Clearing Corporation of Philadelphia as depositories for bulk and specific deposits made by Clearing Members. Clearing Members may also file with the Clearing Corporation escrow receipts from approved banks. An escrow receipt is a representation by the issuing bank to the Clearing Corporation that a particular customer's securities are on deposit with the bank and will be delivered upon exercise of the Call for which the receipt was issued. The Clearing Corporation has approved certain banks having capital and surplus of at least $20,000,000 at the time of approval as issuers of escrow receipts, and each bank may issue escrow receipts for securities having a market value not exceeding 10% of its capital and surplus. Although the Clearing Corporation has no reason to believe that any approved bank or depository will not promptly deliver the underlying securities in accordance with the terms of its agreement with the Clearing Corporation, there can be no assurance that a bank or depository will not default under the terms of such agreement, and a default could adversely affect the Clearing Corporation's ability to perform its obligations as the issuer of Options.

If the Clearing Member does not deposit the underlying security in the case of a Call, or in any event in the case of a Put, it must maintain each day with the Clearing Corporation margin with respect to Options held in a short position in the form of cash, U.S. Government securities or bank letter of credit. The amount of such margin must generally be equal to 100% or such greater percentage as the Clearing Corporation prescribes (which at the date of this writing is 130%) of the closing asked quotation for the Option on the Exchanges on the preceding business day, except that in the case of certain accounts of the Clearing Member the amount of such margin may be reduced to the extent a Clearing Member is permitted to pledge to the Clearing Corporation certain Options carried in a long position. Options carried in a long position in customers' and firm non-lien accounts may be so pledged only if they are treated as part of a "spread" under the customer margin rules of the Exchanges. Except for such pledged Options, all Options for which the premium has been fully paid to the Clearing Corporation and which are carried in long positions in customers' and firm non-lien accounts will be held by the Clearing Corporation free of any lien.

If an exercise notice has been assigned to a Clearing Member in respect of an Option held in a short position, it is required (in the event the underlying security represented by the Option is not on deposit) to deposit and maintain margin with respect to the assigned Option. The amount of such margin depends upon whether Options of the same series as the assigned Option continue to be traded on one or more of the Exchanges. In the event such Options are so traded, the amount of margin required with respect to assigned Options is the same as described in the preceding paragraph with respect to unassigned Options held in short positions. In the event such Options are not so traded, the amount of such margin is equal to the amount by which the closing price for the underlying security in the primary market during the preceding business day (or, if it was not traded on the preceding day, the closing asked quotation on such day) is less than, in the case of a Put, or exceeds, in the case of a Call, the exercise price of the Option.

The Clearing Corporation is authorized to require any Clearing Member to deposit higher margins at any time in the event it deems such action necessary and appropriate in the circumstances to protect the interests of the other Clearing Members, the Clearing Corporation or the public.

On June 30, 1978 margin deposited with the Clearing Corporation totaled approximately $9,193,000 in cash, $49,146,000 in U.S. Government securities and $784,946,000 in letters of credit issued by 16 banks. It should be understood that the amount of margin on deposit with the Clearing Corporation will vary substantially from time to time, depending on such factors as prevailing premium levels and the number of Options outstanding. It should also be understood that margin deposited by a Clearing Member may be applied only to the obligations of that Clearing Member to the Clearing Corporation (and, under certain circumstances, to other Clearing Members), and may not be applied to the obligations of other Clearing Members or the obligations of the Clearing Corporation itself.

3. *The Clearing Corporation's lien.* With the exception noted below, the Clearing Corporation has a lien on all securities (including customers' securities in bulk deposits), margins and funds maintained in each Clearing Member's accounts with the Clearing Corporation. In the event a Clearing Member does not perform its obligations to the Clearing Corporation, these assets may be sold or converted to cash and the proceeds applied to the performance of the Clearing Member's obligations on Options. Such lien does not apply to Options in the Clearing Member's customers' or firm non-lien accounts for which the premium has been fully paid to the Clearing Corporation except to the extent such Options may be pledged to the Clearing Corporation, and the proceeds of customers' securities in bulk deposits may be used only to satisfy the obligations of the Clearing Member arising out of the customers' accounts.

4. *The Clearing Fund.* Each Clearing Member, upon admission to membership, must make a minimum initial deposit to the Clearing Fund of $10,000, plus such additional amount as may be fixed by the Clearing Corporation, and this deposit must be maintained for three calendar months following the date of admission. Thereafter, each Clearing Member's Clearing Fund deposit is redetermined on a monthly basis pursuant to a formula prescribed in the rules of the Clearing Corporation, but in no event can a Clearing Member's Clearing Fund deposit be less than $10,000. All Clearing Fund deposits must be made in cash or by the deposit of securities issued or guaranteed by the United States government and having a maturity of ten years or less.

If a Clearing Member fails to discharge any obligation to the Clearing Corporation, that Clearing Member's Clearing Fund deposit may be applied to the discharge of that obligation. If there is a deficiency in its Clearing Fund deposit, the Clearing Member is liable to the Clearing Corporation for the full amount of that deficiency.

If a Clearing Member's obligation to the Clearing Corporation exceeds its total Clearing Fund deposit, and if it fails to pay the deficiency within 24 hours, the amount of the deficiency is charged pro rata by the Clearing Corporation against all other Clearing Members' deposits to the Clearing Fund. Whenever any amount is paid out of the Clearing Fund as a result of any such pro rata charge, every other Clearing Member is required promptly to make good any deficiency in its own deposit resulting from such payment, except that no Clearing Member is required to pay more than an additional 100% of the amount of its prescribed Clearing Fund deposit if within five business days following the pro rata charge it notifies the Clearing Corporation that it is terminating its membership and closes out or transfers all of its clearing positions.

In addition, under certain limited circumstances specified in its rules, the Clearing Corporation may borrow against the Clearing Fund to meet obligations arising out of the suspension of a Clearing Member and related actions taken by the Clearing Corporation.

The Clearing Fund was established for the protection of the Clearing Corporation and is not a general indemnity fund available to other persons (including customers of Clearing Members). As of June 30, 1978 there were 143 Clearing Members with total Clearing Fund deposits aggregating $63,977,000. It should of course be understood that Clearing Fund deposits, like margin deposits, are based on a formula and may vary substantially over time. Accordingly, the amount on deposit at any particular date is not necessarily representative of the amount that will be on deposit at any other date.

The Clearing Corporation will also have available its own assets in the event the Clearing Fund is deficient.

Neither any Exchange nor any member of any such Exchange (except as such member may be the writer or a Clearing Member representing the writer to whom an exercise notice has been assigned) has an obligation for the performance of any Option upon the exercise thereof.

MARGIN REQUIREMENTS

Separate and apart from the requirement that Clearing Members maintain margin with the Clearing Corporation, the rules of the Exchanges, as well as the rules of the NASD and other self-regulatory organizations of which a broker may be a member, impose margin requirements with respect to a customer's position as an Options writer, and these rules also impose requirements as to the minimum amount of margin that must be constantly maintained by a customer in his margin account. Further, Regulation T of the Federal Reserve Board (the "FBR") governs the amount of credit (if any) which may be initially extended by a broker or dealer at the time a customer enters into any securities transaction. The margin requirements of the self-regulatory organizations are in addition to, and do not replace or modify, the requirements imposed by Regulation T. Accordingly, when any transaction occurs in a margin account (including the purchase, writing or exercise of an Option or the assignment of an exercise notice to an Option writer), the status of the account as a whole must be tested against the requirements of Regulation T. *It should be emphasized that the margin requirements of Regulation T and of the various self-regulatory organizations are minimum requirements, and many brokers impose more stringent requirements upon their customers.*

The margin requirements of Regulation T (including the interpretations thereof by the FRB) and the margin requirements of the Exchanges and of other securities exchanges are very complex and are subject to change from time to time. In addition, special margin requirements may be imposed from time to time with respect to particular Options, or particular positions in Options (such as certain spread positions), or particular accounts or customers. Moreover, under the current provisions of Regulation T, Options have no loan value in a margin account. Customers should determine the margin obligations that will be imposed upon them by their brokers before engaging in any Option transaction.

As a result of the applicable margin requirements, Option writing transactions are required to be conducted in a margin account, and Option writers are generally required to enter into margin agreements which give their broker a lien on securities and other assets held in the account.

An exception to the requirement that Option writing be conducted in a margin account is contained in FBR interpretations of Regulation T that permit transactions in Options to be effected in a special cash account under certain circumstances.

Changes in applicable margin requirements or in the availability of certain margin provisions may occur after an investor has purchased or written an Option and while he continues to hold the resulting position of holder or writer, and such changes could have a significant effect on an investor's opportunities and risks. Accordingly, it is again emphasized that investors should assure themselves that they have sufficient available capital for margin in case such changes occur.

TRANSACTION COSTS

Commissions

Brokers may charge their customers commissions upon the purchase or writing of Puts and Calls and upon the exercise of either type of Option. Accordingly, the buyer of an Option may be required to pay a commission at the time of his opening purchase transaction and another commission if he should elect to liquidate his position in a closing sale transaction or if he should exercise the Option. Writers similarly may be required to pay a commission for the opening sale transaction and another commission if they either engage in a closing purchase transaction or are required to purchase or deliver the underlying security upon exercise. Commissions on Options transactions, including exercise transactions, are as agreed upon between each customer and his broker, although it should be noted that many brokers may be unwilling to negotiate modifications in commission rates established by them.

Because Exchange members may purchase, writer or exercise Options without paying commissions (although such transactions may involve other costs), and broker-dealers who are not Exchange members may be able to negotiate lower commission rates than those typically charged to public customers, an Option transaction that would not be profitable for a customer may be profitable for an Exchange member or broker-dealer. For example, if an expiring Option is "in the money" by an amount smaller than the commission that a customer would be required to pay upon exercise, it might nonetheless be profitable for an Exchange member or a broker to exercise such an Option.

Other Charges

Under the Exchange Act, each Exchange is required to pay to the SEC a fee amounting to one three hundredth of one percent of the dollar amount of sales of securities transaction on that Exchange. The Exchanges pass on this fee to their members and most members in turn pass on the fee to their customers.

BENEFITS OF BUYING OPTIONS

BUYING OPTIONS

There are a number of possible uses of Options by buyers (holders). Each of these uses involves risk, in varying degrees, and not every use is suitable for every investor. Some uses of Options and attendant risks are illustrated below. (As in previous examples, transaction costs and tax consequences are not considered in these descriptions, but may be significant in determining the net gain or loss in Options transactions.

Purposes and Risks of Call Buying

1. *Using Calls for leverage potential.* Because the premium of a Call is considerably less than the cost of the underlying security covered by the Call, a given amount of funds may purchase Calls covering a much larger quantity of such security than could be purchased directly. By so leveraging his funds, the purchaser of Calls has the opportunity to benefit from any significant increase in the price of the security to a greater extent than had he purchased the security outright. However, if the Call is not sold while it has remaining value, and if the security does not appreciate during the life of the Call, the Call purchaser may lose his entire investment in the Call, whereas had he purchased the security directly he might have had no loss or only a paper loss.

This risk of purchasing Calls may be illustrated by comparing Investor A, who for a total investment of $5,000 (plus transaction costs) buys 100 shares of XYZ stock at $50 per share, with Investor B, who invests $5,000 (plus transaction costs) in Calls covering 1,000 shares of XYZ at an exercise price of $50 per share. Both A and B anticipate a rise in the market price of XYZ, but should their expectations not be realized, A's loss would be quite different from B's. If by the expiration of the

Call XYZ stock has fallen to $45 per share (and assuming XYZ has paid no dividends), A will have suffered a paper loss of $500 (plus being out-of-pocket the transaction costs), and his investment will be worth $4,500. He will not be required to realize this loss, and may recover it should XYZ later rise in price while he still owns the 100 shares. Investor B, on the other hand, if he has not sold the Calls in an Exchange's secondary market, will have suffered the loss of his entire $5,000 (plus transaction costs) with no possibility for recovery. Indeed, in the above example Investor A would have had no gain or loss (other than transaction costs paid) if the market price of XYZ had remained at $50, but Investor B would have lost his entire investment. Moreover, if XYZ had paid dividends, they would have been received by A as a stockholder, but not by B as the holder of Calls.

Further, except where the value of the remaining life of a Call may be realized in the secondary market, for a Call purchase to be profitable the underlying security must appreciate in value by more than the premium and transaction costs paid in connection with the purchase and sale (or exercise) of the Call. For example, if a Call covering 100 shares of XYZ stock at an exercise price of $50 per share is purchased for a premium of $600 (plus transaction costs), and if the Call has no value which may be realized on account of its remaining life (i.e., its only value depends upon the exercise price being below the market price of the underlying security), before the Call can be exercised or sold at a profit the price of the underlying security must increase so that the difference between the market value of the shares covered by the Call and the aggregate exercise price is insufficient to cover the premium of $600, the initial transaction costs and the transaction costs payable on the sale or exercise of the Call. Accordingly, this use of Calls is extremely risky, and is unsuitable for investors who do not have the financial capability to withstand large losses.

2. *Using Calls as an alternative to investing in the underlying security.* This use of Calls assumes an investor who anticipates a rise in the price of XYZ stock, but does not think it prudent to expose himself to the risk of a severe price decline by buying the stock outright. Through the purchase of a Call on 100 shares of XYZ as an alternative to the purchase of 100 shares of the stock, the investor may put

himself in a position to realize the hoped for profit (less the premium paid for the Call and less transaction costs) but to limit his losses to the premium (and transaction costs) should the stock decline in value. *This use of Calls anticipates the investment of the entire difference between the cost of the Call and the cost of the underlying security in a relatively risk-free manner (such as a savings account or Treasury bills), the income from which helps offset the cost of the Call.* (To the extent that an investor departs from this risk limiting use of Calls by failing to invest in a relatively risk-free manner the entire difference between the cost of the Call and the cost of the underlying security, the Call investment becomes more of a leverage device as described under example 1 above, and the investor becomes subject to the risks specified thereunder.)

Although generally considered to be among the more conservative uses of Call buying, the use of Calls described in this example 2 still involves significant risks that are not present in an ordinary stock purchase. Unlike the stock investor, the Call purchaser must not only predict *whether* the price of the stock is going to rise, but *when* it will rise. If the stock price does not rise above the exercise price during the life of the Call, the Call purchaser will lose his entire Call investment (unless he is able to recover a portion of the premium in a closing sale transaction) whereas the stock investor will have suffered no loss (disregarding transaction costs) or if the stock price has declined, only a paper loss, until he chooses to sell the stock. Thus a Call investor does not have the choice of "waiting out" an unexpected downturn in the stock price beyond the expiration date of the Call. Obviously, the shorter the term of the Call, the greater is this risk.

Further, the very stock which might be considered more conservative from the standpoint of a direct purchase could be more risky as a Call investment. For example, a stable stock might be considered a safer investment than a more volatile stock because its price is less likely to fall, but the same stability factor also may mean that the stable stock's price is less likely to rise significantly during the relatively short duration of a Call. If the stock price does not rise during that period, the Call holder stands to lose his entire investment in such Calls.

3. *Hedging a short position against a price increase.* Because a Call gives the holder the right to acquire the underlying

security at a fixed price, it may be used by one intending to sell a security short in anticipation of a decline in the price of the security to hedge against a rise in the price of the security. If the security price remains the same, the investor will have lost the amount of the Call premium (and transaction costs). If it declines, any profit made in the short-selling transaction will be reduced by the amount of the premium (and transaction costs). However, should the price of the security rise, the short seller may be protected against a substantial loss he would otherwise have had to incur if he had to cover his short security position at the increased market price. Such hedged short selling, although less risky than unhedged short selling, involves complex considerations which make such transactions suitable only for sophisticated investors.

4. *Fixing the price of a future security purchase.* If an investor anticipates the purchase of a security at some point in the future, such as when funds become available, and finds the present price attractive, he may fix that price (plus the premium) as the purchase price of the security by buying a Call which does not expire until after the time the purchase is anticipated. At that time, he can merely exercise the Call to acquire the security (unless the market price of the security has declined to below the exercise price, in which event the security could be bought in the open market and the Call allowed to lapse).

Purposes and Risks of Put Buying

1. *Buying Puts in anticipation of a price decline in the underlying security.* This use contemplates the purchase of Puts by an investor who does not own the underlying security. The Put buyer, like the short seller, seeks to benefit from a decline in the market price of the underlying security. Unlike the short seller, the Put buyer is not subject to margin calls nor to the theoretically unlimited risk of the short seller should the price of the underlying security increase. On the other hand, if the Put is not sold when it has value prior to its expiration, and if at expiration the market price of the underlying security is equal to or greater than the exercise price, the Put buyer will lose his entire investment in the Option. As the Put buyer acquires Puts covering a greater

757

number of shares than he might have sold short directly, he is in a more highly leveraged position and is subject to the increased risks of that position. Accordingly, the use of Puts for leverage is extremely risky and is unsuitable for investors who do not have the financial capability to withstand large losses.

The risk of losing one's entire investment in the purchase of Puts may be illustrated by comparing Investor C, who does not own any shares of XYZ, and who, at a time when the market price of XYZ is $50 per share, purchases a Put giving him the right to sell 100 shares of XYZ at $50 per share, paying an aggregate premium of $500 (plus transaction costs) for the Put, with Investor D, who sells short 100 shares of XYZ at $50 per share. Both C and D anticipate a decline in the market price of XYZ, but should their expectations not be realized, C's results would be different from D's. If at the time the Put expires XYZ is trading at $50 or above, C will have lost his entire $500 investment in the Put (plus transaction costs), unless he had previously sold the Put in an Exchange's secondary market. D, on the other hand, will have a paper loss (and will have to maintain increased margin on his short position) only to the extent XYZ moves above 50. Thus while the short seller's potential loss, exclusive of transaction costs, can range from zero to the theoretically unlimited amount by which XYZ may move above 50, the Put buyer will lose the total amount he paid for the Put (plus transaction costs), but no more than that amount, whenever XYZ is at 50 or above at the time the Put expires.

2. *Buying Puts to hedge a long stock position against a price decline.* Puts may be purchased to protect the profits in an existing long position in an underlying security, or to protect a newly acquired position in an underlying security against a substantial decline in its market value. In either case, the protection is provided only during the life of the Put, when the holder of the Put is able to sell the underlying security at the Put exercise price regardless of any decline in the underlying security's market price. An investor using Puts in this manner will have reduced any profit he might otherwise have realized in his long security position by the premium paid for the Put and by transaction costs.

Writer Call Options

The writer of a Call assumes an obligation to deliver the underlying security represented by the Call against payment of the aggregate exercise price upon the assignment to him of an exercise notice. This obligation continues until the writer closes out his position in the Option. Once a writer has been assigned an exercise notice in respect of an Option, he will thereafter be unable to effect a closing purchase transaction in that Option. Accordingly, a person who is or may be legally prohibited from selling an underlying security should not write Calls on that underlying security.

A principal reason for writing Calls on a securities portfolio is to attempt to realize, through the receipt of premium income, a greater return than would be earned on the securities alone. The covered Call writer who owns the underlying security has, in return for the premium, given up the opportunity for profit from a price increase in the underlying security above the exercise price so long as his writer obligation continues, but has retained the risk of loss should the price of the security decline. Unlike one who owns securities not subject to a Call, the covered Call writer has no control over when he may be required to sell his securities, since he may be assigned an exercise notice at any time prior to the expiration of his obligations as a writer. Indeed, he must assume that he may be assigned an exercise notice at any time, and that in such circumstances a loss may be incurred.

The risks of uncovered Call writing depend in large part upon the purpose of the writing transaction and whether the writer has a securities position related to the underlying security. For example, in order to accomplish a spread or arbitrage transaction, one may write a Call on XYZ stock while he holds not the stock itself but a warrant or option to buy XYZ or a security convertible into XYZ. Such a writer, though not a holder of the underlying security itself, may actually be in a risk position more like that of a writer who holds the underlying security, depending upon the terms of the Call compared with the terms upon which he is able to acquire the underlying security.

Where the writer of a Call owns neither the underlying security nor a security entitling him to acquire the underlying security, his position is extremely risky, and he may incur larger losses. Such an uncovered Call writer generally hopes to realize income from the writing transaction, but without the necessity of committing capital to the purchase of the underlying security. As distinguished from the covered Call writer, he stands to incur an out-of-pocket loss if and to the extent the price of the underlying security increases above the exercise price. The extent to which the current market value of the underlying security exceeds the aggregate exercise price (which theoretically can be without limit), reduced by the premium and increased by transaction costs, represents the uncovered Call writer's loss.

Because of the potentially large (theoretically unlimited) losses which may be incurred and the complexity of uncovered Call writing, such transactions are only suitable for sophisticated investors having the financial capacity to sustain such losses. Further, uncovered writers should have the financial capacity and liquid assets available to meet margin calls and (unless they are engaged in arbitrage or hedge transactions) to cover by purchasing the underlying security.

As discussed, to the extent that a secondary market in particular Calls is available either the covered or the uncovered Call writer may liquidate his position prior to the assignment of an exercise notice by purchasing in a closing purchase transaction a Call of the same series as the Call previously written. Of course, the cost of such a liquidating purchase plus transaction costs may be greater than the premium received upon writing the original Call, in which event the writer will have incurred a loss in the transaction.

Unless a restriction on uncovered writing is in effect, the covered Call writer may with the consent of his broker at any time uncover his position by selling the underlying security or the Call serving as cover, and concurrently depositing the margin required. The uncovered Call writer may cover at any time by depositing the underlying security or the appropriate Calls in his account with his broker (or by purchasing such securities in his account), in which case he may be able, depending on the overall status of the account under applicable margin requirements, to withdraw the deposited margin in respect of the previously uncovered position. A covered writer who becomes uncovered is, of course, subject to the risks of uncovered Call writing, discussed above. Similarly, the formerly uncovered Call writer who covers is, so long as he remains a covered writer, subject to the risks of that position.

Purposes and Risks of Put Writing

As with the writer of a Call, a Put writer generally hopes to realize premium income. If such a Put writer does not have a short position in the underlying security or a long position in another Put covering the same underlying security that expires no sooner than the expiration of the Put written and has an exercise price not less than the exercise price of the Put written, he must maintain margin with his broker on account of writing the Put, and he stands to incur a loss if and to the extent the price of the underlying security falls below the exercise price of the Put written. Any such loss incurred would be reduced by the premium received by the Put writer and increased by transaction costs. For example, assume an investor writes a January XYZ 50 Put when the market price of XYZ is 50, and receives an aggregate premium of $600. If the market price of XYZ stock does not fall below $50 per share, it is unlikely that the Put will be exercised, and the $600 premium, less transaction costs, will represent the investor's return on the margin he has had to put up in order to maintain his position as a Put writer. On the other hand, if XYZ stock falls below 50 to, say 45, the Put will be exercised and the investory will be required to purchase XYZ at $50 per share. His net cost (exclusive of transaction costs) of buying the stock, however, is reduced to $44 per share after reflecting $6 per share premium.

Apart from the realization of premium income, Puts may be written by investors as a means of acquiring the underlying security at a price which is less than the current market price. If the Put is exercised, the Put writer's cost of acquiring the underlying security would be the exercise price less the premium. If the Put is not exercised, the Put writer will not have to acquired the underlying security, but will nonetheless have earned the premium for writing the Put. For example, if the writer of the January XYZ 50 Put discussed in the preceding paragraph is assigned an exercise notice in respect of that Put, he will have acquired XYZ stock at a cost of $44 per share, which is less than the assumed $50 market price prevailing at the time the Put was written. As noted above, however, the net cost to the Put writer of acquiring the stock may be substantially above the market price prevailing at the time the Put is exercised.

761

If an investor writes a Put covering an underlying security that he has sold short, the investor still hopes to realize premium income in the writing transaction, but his risk position is different from that of the Put writer without such a short position. Such an investor may still incur a loss in his Put writing transaction if the price of the underlying security falls below the exercise price, but this loss may be offset by a profit realized in the related short stock position. For example, an investor may write a January XYZ 50 Put when the market price of XYZ is 50, and receive a premium of $300. At the same time, he may sell short 100 shares of XYZ for $5,000. Ignoring all transaction costs, if XYZ falls to 45, the investor may be required to purchase 100 shares of XYZ at 50 pursuant to an exercise of the Put he wrote, or he may be able to close out his Put writer's position prior to exercise in a closing purchase transaction, paying a premium of $500. If exercised, the Put writer may use the stock "put" to him to cover his short stock position, in which case his profit will be the $300 originally received in the writing transaction. If the Put position is closed out, there will be a net loss of $200 in the Put transaction by itself, since the $500 paid in the closing transaction will be offset in part by the $300 premium originally received. However, the short stock position could be covered at a profit of $500 if 100 shares of XYZ could be purchased for their market price of $4,500. Thus, in this situation the net gain to the Put writer would also be $300.

Of course, the Put writer who is also a short seller of the underlying security bears the risk of his short stock position. Thus if the price of the underlying security should increase, such an investor stands to incur a loss in covering his short stock position, offset to the extent of the premium received in the Put writing transaction. Potential losses which may be incurred in short selling transactions are limited only by the extent of the increase in the price of the security sold short. Accordingly, writing Puts against short positions in the underlying security is risky, and is suitable only for sophisticated investors who have the means to meet margin calls and to sustain large losses.

As the above example illustrates, a Put writer may liquidate his position prior to the assignment of an exercise notice by purchasing a Put of the same series as the Put previously written. To the extent that the cost of such a liquidating

762

purchase plus transaction costs exceeds the premium initially received, the Put writer will have incurred a loss in the Put transaction.

Every writer of a Put is subject to being assigned an exercise notice at any time prior to the expiration of his obligations as a writer, in which event the writer is obligated to pay for the underlying security at the exercise price. Accordingly, Put writing transactions are only suitable for investors having the financial capacity and liquid assets available to pay for the underlying security in the event of exercise.

Spreads

A spread position is one in which an investor is the holder of one or more Options of a given class and concurrently maintains a position as a writer of one or more Options of different series within that same class. An example of a spread position is one in which the investor is the holder of an XYZ April 35 Call and the writer of an XYZ January 35 Call. Spread positions may involve holding an Option with a different expiration date from that of the Option written, as in the above example, or holding and writing Options with different exercise prices but with the same expiration date, or both the expiration date and the exercise price may differ. Spread positions may be undertaken to fulfill a variety of investment strategies, and they are among the most complicated of all Options transactions. No investor should establish spread position unless he thoroughly understands the mechanics and risks involved and is financially able to bear the risks.

Spread positions are subject to the same risks that are involved in the purchase and writing of Options as described throughout this writing. In addition, they are subject to certain special risks, including the following:

1. *Difficulty of Execution.* Because spread orders require the execution of both a purchase and a writing transaction at or about the same time, spread orders are often difficult to execute and there can be no certainty that any such order can be executed within the limits designated by the investor, or at all.

2. *Risk of Exercises.* The writing side of a spread position is subject to being exercised at any time prior to the Option's

expiration, and an investor who is assigned an exercise notice must purchase or deliver the underlying security in accordance with the terms of the Option. Such an investor will then no longer be in a spread position but will continue to hold the Option on the other side of the spread and will be subject to the risks of that position, unless the investor exercises the Option held either to obtain the underlying security for delivery in the case of a Call spread, or to dispose of the underlying security in the case of a Put spread. If the market value of the Option held in the spread reflected significant time value, exercise of the Option would result in loss of that value. Further, if an exercise notice assigned to the writing side of a Call spread position was tendered to the Clearing Corporation prior to an ex-date for an ordinary cash dividend or other distribution for which no adjustment to the terms of the Call is made, the assigned writer will be required to deliver such distribution to the exercising holder notwithstanding that the writer receiving notice of such assignment on or after the ex-date will himself not be entitled to such distribution upon exercise of the other side of his Call spread position.

3. *Closing Out One Side of a Spread Transaction May Significantly Increase Risk.* Certain of the advantages of maintaining a spread position may be eliminated if the investor liquidates either side of the spread in a closing purchase or sale transaction, after which the investor will remain at risk on the other side of the spread. If as a result of such a partial liquidation of a spread the investor becomes the uncovered writer of an Option, a margin call may be issued by the investor's broker in respect of that position, since the investor will no longer be able to avail himself of the special margin requirements applicable to certain spread positions.

Straddles

A straddle is an equivalent number of Puts and Calls covering the same underlying security and having the same exercise price and expiration date. (Similar combinations of Puts and Calls covering the same underlying security but differing as to exercise price or expiration date or both do not come within the definition of a straddle, but they involve much the same risks as are described below with respect to straddles.) An investor may buy a straddle or he may write a straddle; an example of the former is the purchase of an XYZ April 35 Put and the purchase of an XYZ April 35 Call. As with spreads, straddle orders are more difficult to execute than orders for Puts or Calls alone, because they require the execution of orders covering different series of Options at or about the same time.

An investor who buys a straddle generally anticipates relatively large price fluctuations in the underlying security, but does not know in which direction the price may move. Through the purchase of a straddle, the investor is in a position to profitably exercise or sell the Call component of the straddle if the underlying security increases in value, and to profitably exercise or sell the Put component if the underlying security declines in value. Because the purchase of a straddle represents the purchase of two Options, the premium for a straddle is greater than that for a Put or a Call alone. This means that the price of the underlying security must rise or fall enough to permit the investor to recover the premium paid for the straddle and transaction costs before a profit may be realized. Thus a straddle involves all of the risks of the purchase of a Put or a Call alone, plus the added risk that the underlying security must change in value to a greater degree in order for the transaction to be profitable. Of course, as with the purchase of Puts or calls alone, timing is important for an investor to realize any profit through the purchase of a straddle. That is, not only must the value of the underlying security move upwards or downwards for a straddle to become profitable, but the investor must correctly determine when to exercise or sell one or both components of the straddle in order to realize a profit.

An investor who writes a straddle generally wishes to earn more premium income that he would earn from writing a Put or a Call alone. Of course, since a straddle writer is the writer of both a Put and a Call, he is subject to the risks of both such writing positions. It should be noted that if the underlying security both rises and falls during the life of a straddle, both the Put and the Call could be exercised, resulting in substantial losses. These risks may be somewhat moderated if the investor buys the underlying security at the same time as he writes a straddle covering that security, which serves to cover his obligation as a writer of the Call component of the straddle. Of course, such an investor must be willing to assume the risk of holding the underlying security, not only in respect of the shares purchased at the time he wrote the straddle, but also in respect of the additional shares which he may be required to purchase in the event the Put component is exercised.

As in the case of all other Options transactions, the purchasers and writers of straddles are subject to applicable margin requirements.

The following additional benefits indicate some of the tax considerations in using options.

Perhaps the single most important new tax change is that, pursuant to Internal Revenue Code Section 1234 (as amended by the Tax Reform Act of 1976), an option writer no longer has ordinary gain or loss upon entering into a closing purchase transaction *for options written on or after September 2, 1976.*

The character of income realized in connection with puts and calls depends on the character of the underlying property in the hands of the investor. Since the underlying property (stock) is generally a capital asset to an investor, the option is treated as a capital asset and any gain or loss would be capital gain or loss. Investors may enter the CBOE market either as writers (sellers) or as buyers (holders). Tax consequences to investors are, for the most part, deferred until the option position is disposed of in one way or another. However, writing or buying an option may have tax ramifications. Option transactions can affect transactions in the underlying property; for instance, by operation of the wash sale or short sale rules.

TAX RULES APPLICABLE TO OPTION HOLDERS

An investor for whom the underlying stock is or would be a capital asset becomes the holder of a capital asset when a put or call is purchased. The cost of the put or call is its basis, and its holding period is measured from the date of purchase. In view of the extension of the holding period to more than nine months for long-term capital gain treatment, effective for sales in taxable years beginning after December 31, 1976, and to more than twelve months for sales in years beginning after December 31, 1977, there will be few long-term gains in future years in connection with CBOE options unless options with terms longer than the current standard term of nine months are issued.

A put or call may be disposed of by the older through
1. exercise,
2. sale; or
3. expiration unexercised.

Exercise

CALLS

If a call is exercised, the call holder becomes the owner of the underlying stock. The basis for the stock includes the cost of exercising the option and the original cost of purchasing the option. There is a brokerage commission when the call is exercised in addition to the commission on purchase of the call. Both commissions are part of the cost basis. The holding period of the stock is measured from the exercise date. *It does not include the holding period of the call.* Exercise is a way to take a long position in the stock.

Example:

An XYZ Co. July 50 call is purchased on April 3 at a premium of $5 per share. At expiration, the stock is selling at $58 per share and the option premium is $8. If the call is exercised on July 14, the tax basis of 100 shares of XYZ Co. is calculated as follows: (excluding commissions)

1 call purchased @ $5	$ 500.00
Exercise @ $50	5,000.00
Total Cost	$5,500.00

The date of the beginning of the holding period is July 14. (*Note:* Technically, the holding period excludes the date of purchase and includes the date of sale. Until December 31, 1976, long-term status results if the option is held at least until the next calendar day in the sixth subsequent month or, if there is no next day in the latter month, the first day of the seventh month. Thereafter, the extended holding periods previously delineated begin to take effect.)

PUTS

As with a call, exercise of a put is at the discretion of the holder. Exercise of a put by a put holder involves delivery of the underlying stock against receipt of the strike price. A capital gain or loss is realized on the sale of underlying stock. The cost of the put is treated as a reduction in the proceeds of the sale, as is the commission on the sale.

Example:

An ABC Co. July 50 put is purchased on April 3 at a premium of $5 per share. By expiration, the ABC Co. stock is selling at $42 and the put premium is $8. If the put is exercised on July 14, the proceeds of the sale, for tax purposes, are calculated as follows: (excluding commissions)

Proceeds—exercise of put at $50	$5,000.00
Less—cost of put	500.00
Total Proceeds excluding commissions	$4,500.00

The $4,500.00 proceeds are compared to the tax basis of ABC shares delivered against the sale to determine capital gain or loss.

The acquisition of a put is generally treated as a short sale. However, except to the extent the holder owns or acquires substantially identical property while holding the put, the short sale rules do not apply. If substantially identical property is held short-term at the time a put is acquired, or is acquired during the period such put is held, special rules apply. Their application can result in treating any gain on the disposition of such put as short-term capital gain, and gain on the sale of substantially identical property (even if otherwise held long-term) as short-term capital gain.

The acquisition of a put is not treated as a short sale if the following conditions are met:

(1) the put and stock identified on the holder's records as intended to be used in connection with the exercise of the put are acquired on the same day ("married" put), *and*

(2) the put is not exercised or, if exercised, the put is exercised by the delivery of the identified stock.

In the case of a put "married" with particular shares of stock, the normal stock holding period rules apply in determining whether gain or loss on exercise is long-term or short-term.

Additional complexities arise if exercise of a put is effectuated with borrowed stock or if a "married" put is exercised with other than identified stock. These complex rules are discussed more fully in connection with tax strategies.

Sale

CALLS

If a call is sold, the holder realizes capital gain or loss determined by comparison of the sale proceeds with the cost basis of the call, long-term or short-term depending on the period for which the call was held.

Example:

The July 50 call purchased at a $5 premium in the first example is sold rather than being exercised. Gain is figured as follows: (excluding commissions)

Proceeds (7/14/–)	
1 XYZ/July 50 call @ 8	$800.00
Cost (4/3/–trade date)	
1 XYZ/July/50 call @ 5	500.00
Net Short-Term Capital Gain (Note)	$300.00

Note: As a method of acquiring the stock, selling the previously purchased call and buying the stock on the market could require a little less cash than would acquisition through exercise. In these examples, selling the call would also result in recognized gain. If the call were worth less when sold than its cost basis, sale would give rise to a currently deductible capital loss. The wash sale rule may not apply to the sale of a call at a loss and the more or less simultaneous purchase of underlying stock. If the wash sale rule does apply to calls, the stock acquired should not be considered substantially identical with the call. Revenue Ruling 58-384 so holds for short sale purposes and should also apply to the wash sale rule.)

PUTS

If a CBOE put is sold, the holder realizes capital gain or loss determined by comparison of the sale proceeds with the cost basis of the put. Once the new holding period rules are fully effective, that gain or loss will always be short-term.

The IRS now holds that sale of a put by a holder is the closing of a short sale (if substantially identical property was held *short-term* at the time of the acquisition of the put or was acquired subsequent thereto). Therefore, any gain on sale of a put is short-term if substantially identical property is held during the period such put is held.

The IRS position with respect to sale of a "married" put is not entirely clear. The statute provides that "if the option (put) is *not exercised,* the cost of the option shall be added to the basis of the property (underlying stock) with which the option is identified." Trying to apply this language to determine gain on sale of a "married" put and the basis of the underlying stock after sale of the put leads to many anomalies.

Expiration

CALLS

If a call is allowed to expire unexercised, the loss to the holder is a capital loss measured by the cost basis of the call, and long or short-term depending on the holding period from acquisition to expiration.

PUTS

If a put is allowed to expire unexercised, the loss to the holder is a capital loss as with a call; but, if the put was "married" to stock, the cost of the put is added to the basis of the stock. Expiration of a put closes any short sale deemed made by its acquisition.

HOLDER'S TAX STRATEGY

While puts and calls are both options and both capital assets, a *put* gives the holder an option to *sell* stock at the strike price, whereas a *call* gives the holder an option to *buy* stock at the strike price. In addition, as the acquisition of a put is treated as a short sale, it is clear that not only market action but also tax consequences dictate very different strategies with respect to puts and calls.

Call Holders

The call holder's principal tax strategy has been to make any gains long-term and any losses short-term. Longer holding periods for long-term treatment make it impractical to hold a

CBOE option for long-term gain, even in 1977, except in those few cases where the nominally nine month life of an option runs a few days over nine months as measured for federal income tax purposes.

When a call is first traded, its price reflects both the value of the right to purchase the underlying stock at a fixed price (the strike price) for a period of time, and the difference between the market value of the stock and the strike price. The time value declines as the call approaches its expiration date. At any time, the underlying stock may be selling for less than the strike price, in which case the call is considered as "out-of-the-money"; or, the underlying stock may be selling above the strike price, in which case the call is "in-the-money" and has value even when it is about to expire.

PROFITABLE CALLS

The holder of a call may have a potential profit, whether the call is in-the-money or out-of-the-money. For example, if there is still time before expiration, an out-of-the-money call purchased when the underlying stock was selling considerably below the strike price will increase in value as the price of the underlying stock rises toward the strike price. This profit can be captured only by sale of the call. The gain will be long-term or short-term depending on the actual holding period and the applicable rules for long-term at the time of sale. If a call is in-the-money, exercise may be a viable alternative to sale of the call. However, because of the added commissions, a higher net profit usually results from selling the call, rather than exercising the call and selling the stock. If the call holder wishes to acquire the stock for investment, it may be less costly to sell the call and acquire the stock on the market, rather than to acquire the stock through exercise of the call. The holding period of the stock will begin with its acquisition, and will not include the holding period of the call in either case.

Any holder who is about to exercise a profitable call should consider the loss of holding period that exercise entails, particularly if gain on sale of the call could still be long-term.

At year-end, various techniques are available to lock-in gain and defer realization to the following year. For example, a call holder can buy a put, write a call or exercise the call and sell the stock short. The third possibility is appropriate for calls expiring in October but, obviously, involves both substantial commission costs and available funds. The second possibility is viable due to the change in treatment of gain on writing calls from ordinary income on expiration or closing purchase to short-term capital gain. However, this strategy is subject to the risk that the writer position might be cancelled-out through unwelcome exercise before year-end which increases costs substantially. The acquisition of a put is the safest and most efficient technique for this purpose once trading in puts is authorized. The locking in of a gain is only one example of the mixed strategies involving puts.

UNPROFITABLE CALLS

The holder of a call that has declined in value has two ways of establishing loss for tax purposes:

(1) permit the call to expire unexercised, or

(2) sell the call.

In either case, the holder will have a capital loss. If a calendar year taxpayer purchases a call more than six months before its expiration date, expiration in 1976 results in long-term capital loss.

However, if in 1976 the call is sold before it is held for more than six months after purchase, the loss is short-term. If a call has been held for more than six months but does not expire until January, 1977, it may be held until January, 1977 at which time the longer (nine month) holding period is applicable and the loss on the sale is short-term. Holders of calls that appear to be worthless as the expiration date nears should, in most cases, dispose of them by bona-fide sale before they are held long-term. Loss on such a sale, even at a nominal price, is, in our opinion, a short-term capital loss.

Where the call has value (because the underlying stock is selling above the striking price), but that value is less than the original cost of the call, a holder who already has a long-term holding period for the call has an interesting opportunity to turn potential long-term loss on sale of the option into a short-term loss by exercising the call and immediately selling the stock. The cost of the call becomes part of the basis of the stock, but the holding period of the stock does not include the holding period of the call. However, such a procedure incurs two full commissions based on the stock, one on the acquisition through exercise of the call and one on sale of the stock. This added expense could outweigh the tax benefit. Beginning after December 31, 1977, this is entirely academic since nine month call holder losses are all short-term.

As with profitable calls and gains, year-end planning may require deferring losses. Buying puts, writing calls and combining exercise with short sales are techniques which may be used to fix losses and defer recognition until the following year.

PURCHASE OF A CALL IN COMBINATION WITH SHORT SALE

The Internal Revenue Code contains rules that effectively preclude converting a potential short-term gain into long-term by selling stock short and closing the short sale, after the long stock has been held for more than the requisite period. A short sale by a seller who holds long-term stock prevents any *subsequent* appreciation from giving rise to long-term gain and short-term loss by classifying as long-term and loss on closing the short sale. These complicated provisions apply if the long and short positions involve substantially identical property.

A call, according to the IRS, is not substantially identical to the underlying stock for the purposes of the short sale rules. Therefore, through a short sale of underlying stock the potential profit on a call could be protected while it was still short-term and, to the extent subsequently realized on the sale of the call, be taxed as long-term. Indeed, subsequent appreciation could increase the long-term gain on the sale of the call and produce a short-term loss on closing the short position. This will no longer be possible once the new holding period rules are fully effective because no call will be outstanding for a sufficient period of time to qualify for long term capital gain.

WASH SALE RULE

The wash sale rule applies to call option transactions, at least to a limited extent. Under the wash sale rule a loss on the sale of a security is deferred if the seller reacquires (or enters into a contract or option to reacquire) the security within a period beginning 30 days before the sale and ending 30 days thereafter. A call may not be a security, but it is an option. Thus, a loss on the sale of a call may not be subject to the wash sale rule; but the purchase of a call clearly brings the wash sale rule into operation to defer loss on a sale of underlying stock if the sale and the purchase of the call fall within the wash sale period. Security dealers, with respect to dealer securities, and non-corporate security traders are exempt from the wash sale rules. A trader is one who, though not a dealer, is in the business of buying and selling securities for a speculative profit.

If a "wash sale" call is exercised, the basis of the stock acquired through the exercise is the basis of the stock on which the loss was disallowed under the wash sale rule, adjusted for any difference between the proceeds of the wash sale and the cost of the new stock. (The cost of the new stock, of course, includes both the call premium and the strike price plus commissions.) The holding period of the new stock includes the holding period of the wash sale stock. Apparently, the holding period of the call disappears without a trace.

There is no provision in the Code or the Regulations for subsequent allowance of the wash sale loss, if the call is *not* exercised. In view of the general purpose of the wash sale rule to *defer* losses only until economically realized, we are of the opinion that the Treasury would rule that where loss on a sale of stock is deferred under the wash sale rule because of the purchase of a call option within the prescribed sixty-one day period and the call is subsequently sold or allowed to expire unexercised, the loss is allowed on the date of sale or expiration of the call. It is uncertain whether that loss should be treated as long-term or short-term, based only on the holding period of the stock sold at a loss, only on the holding period of the call or on the combined holding periods. This no-man's land should be avoided, if at all possible.

The Internal Revenue Code does not define securities for wash sale purposes. There is a risk, therefore, that the rule applies to the sale and reacquisition, within the statutory period, of calls with the same striking price and expiration date. We believe that this risk does not exist with respect to CBOE calls where there is a difference in either category as it is our opinion such calls are not substantially identical.

Put Holders

The put holder's principal tax strategies are, for the most

part, defensive—protecting gains on stock or calls and avoiding various tax traps in the short-sale rules which can convert long-term gain into short-term gain, convert short-term loss into long-term loss, and reduce holding periods. The holding period rule is probably the most difficult. Generally, if underlying stock is held short-term at any time from the date a put is purchased to the time the put is disposed of, the holding period of that stock *does not begin* until after disposition of the put. The earliest acquired short-term stock is the first affected and only to the extent not in excess of the amount sold short. If the affected stock is sold after the put is acquired, it appears that no other stock's holding period is tainted under Sec. 1233.

Example:

Acquisition of stock (100 shs.)	July 15, 1976
Acquisition of stock (100 shs.)	July 16, 1976
Acquisition of put (100 shs.)	January 12, 1977
Sale of put	April 6, 1977
Sale of stock (200 shs.)	June 8, 1977

Gain or loss on sale of shares purchased July 15, 1976 is short-term since the holding period runs only from April 6, 1977 to June 8, 1977 for tax purposes since when the put, which is treated as a short sale, was acquired, the stock had not been held long-term. Gain or loss on sale of shares purchased July 16, 1976 is long-term since the holding period runs from July 16, 1976 to June 8, 1977. (*Note:* The holding period of stock is not affected if the holding period of other earlier acquired stock equal in amount to that sold short is affected.)

At the time of this writing, trading in puts on the CBOE has not yet begun. We assume that put prices will reflect both the value of the right to sell stock at a fixed price (the strike price) for a period of time, and the difference between the market value of the stock and the strike price. The time value will decline as the put approaches its expiration date. The underlying stock may be selling for *less than the strike price* of the put, in which case the put is "in-the-money." Since any holder of the put can capture the difference between the cost of buying the stock and the strike price, an "in-the-money" put has value even when it is about to expire. If the underlying stock is selling for *more than* the strike price, the put is "out-of-the-money" and its value will progressively decline as the expiration date approaches. Note that this relationship of put value to stock price is the exact opposite of a call.

PROFITABLE PUTS

The simplest way for a put holder to realize gain on a put if the market value of the underlying stock declines, is to sell the put. Gain will be long-term or short-term capital gain, depending on the period the put was held. If the put holder exercises the option, the exercise is a sale. Exercise requires delivery of underlying stock by the put holder for the strike price. The gain is long-term or short-term depending on when the stock was acquired.

If the delivered stock was purchased more than the requisite period prior to the acquisition of the put and no other substantially identical stock was purchased in the interim, any gain or loss on exercise is long-term. If any stock was purchased less than the requisite period before the put was purchased or was acquired after the put was purchased, any gain on the exercise is short-term; but loss on exercise is short-term unless substantially identical stock was held short-term at the time the put was acquired.

If the stock was acquired on the same day the put was acquired and the put and the stock were "married" on the put holder's records by identifying the stock to be used in the exercise of the put, then exercise of the put with that stock results in long-term or short-term gain or loss depending on the period for which the stock was held.

Sale of the "married" put at a gain, or its exercise with other stock, dissolves the marriage. The acquisition of the put is treated as a short sale, and the tax consequences follow the short sale rules. Since our present hypothesis is that the value of the put has increased, the price of the stock has probably declined. In such a situation it is usually preferable to deliver the married stock when the put is exercised, probably with a small net short-term loss. However, there is an opportunity to realize a short-term gain on sale of the put and hold the stock for a short-term loss at a later date, or vice-versa. Such year-end transactions must take into consideration the investor's tax position and both the tax consequences and costs. The decision to exercise involves the economic analysis of costs, of tax benefits or detriments and use of money considerations that can be quite complicated.

UNPROFITABLE PUTS

The holder of a put that has declined in value has two ways of establishing loss for tax purposes:

(1) permit the put to expire unexercised, or

(2) sell the put.

In either case, the holder will have capital loss which will, in most cases, be short-term when the new holding period rules are in effect.

In the case of a put "married" to stock, sale of the put is necessary to establish the loss. The cost of a married put upon exercise is added to the basis of the stock. It is unclear whether a loss due to sale of the put would be treated in a similar fashion. If it is not, the sale of the put might terminate the holding period of the underlying stock. Since the stock has, by assumption, appreciated in most cases, it is wiser to accept the addition to basis and hold the stock a little longer for long-term gain and not sell the put.

TAX RULES APPLICABLE TO OPTION WRITERS

The investor who writes (sells) a put or a call is in a very different economic position from the buyer; but, under the new tax rules for options the tax treatment is much more similar than it was. Previously, expiration or a closing purchase transaction led to ordinary income or loss to the writer. Now, the gain or loss is short-term capital gain or loss. The tax treatment of the premium received by the option writer is still held in suspense until the obligation is terminated by performance on exercise, by expiration or by a closing purchase transaction.

Writing with the same strike price and expiration date of a put and a call (if simultaneous, known as a straddle) has quite different results. The Tax Reform Act of 1976 has repealed the previous tax rules regarding straddles and their tax treatment. Under that Act CBOE listed puts and calls do not have a basis allocation problem and, it appears that the put and call are not substantially identical. *Therefore, there is no short sale or wash sale problem unless the call is exercised prior to disposition of the put.*

Exercise

CALLS

Exercise is initiated by the holder, not the writer. When the Options Clearing Corporation (OCC) is notified that a CBOE call holder has elected to exercise an option to buy, the OCC "assigns" the call to a firm who assigns it to a writer. When the writer delivers stock pursuant to the assignment against payment of the strike price specified in the call, a capital gain or loss is realized. The transaction is treated as a sale of the stock delivered.

The premium previously held in suspense is part of the proceeds of sale. Total proceeds (the premium plus the payment of the exercise price) are compared with the basis of the stock delivered to determine the amount of the gain or loss. The holding period of the stock delivered determines whether the gain or loss is long or short-term.

Example:

The writer of the XYZ/July/50 call in the first example elects to buy stock in the market to cover the obligation when a call is exercised and assigned. (excluding commissions)

Proceeds of Sale:	
Premium received on 1 XYZ/July/50 call	$ 500.00
Strike price received 100 XYZ at 50	5,000.00
Total proceeds excluding commission:	$ 5,500.00
Cost:	
100 XYZ @ 58	$ 5,800.00
Short-term capital (loss)	$ (300.00)

PUTS

As with calls, exercise of a put is initiated by the holder. On the settlement day, the put writer will pay for and receive the stock. The transaction is treated by the writer as a purchase of stock. The premium, received for writing the put and carried in suspense, is subtracted from the cost basis for the stock. The acquisition date for the stock would appear to be the settlement date, but may be the earlier date of exercise or assignment. The use of trade date for stock transactions is an exception to the more general rule that date of payment for, and receipt of, property marks date of acquisition. Nevertheless, if the stock is to be sold to realize a loss before it becomes long-term, it would be prudent to use the earlier date. If the stock has appreciated and long-term gain is sought, the later date should be used in measuring the requisite period.

Expiration
CALLS
If the holder allows the call option to expire unexercised, the writer treats the premium as short-term capital gain realized at the expiration date.

PUTS
If the holder of a put allows it to expire unexercised, the writer will, under the new law, realize short-term capital gain, as with a call.

Closing Purchase Transaction
CALLS
At any time before exercise, the writer can enter into a closing purchase transaction; that is, a "purchase" can be made of an equivalent call on the CBOE designated as a closing transaction. As with expiration, any gain (or loss) is measured by the difference between the net amount previously received and the amount paid for the closing purchase, and is short-term and capital in nature for options written on or after September 2, 1976.

Example:
Again using the same call example, if the writer of the XYZ/July/50 call unwinds the position by making a closing purchase at $8, the loss is: (excluding commissions)

$5 premium received on call	$ 500.00
Cost of calls purchased @ 8	800.00
Short-term capital (loss)	$ (300.00)

Previously, the writer of a call in a rising market *had* the opportunity to have long-term capital gain on the long side, either by owning the stock or a different call on the same stock, and an ordinary deduction by the closing out of the writer's obligation.

PUTS

As with calls, the writer of a put can enter into a closing purchase transaction at any time before exercise and any gain or loss realized will be treated as short-term capital gain or loss. In our opinion, a put closing purchase transaction will not be treated as the acquisition of a put for short sale purposes.

TAX STRATEGIES FOR OPTION WRITERS

Since under the new law writers of puts and calls have only short-term capital gain or loss on expiration or on termination through closing purchase transactions, opportunities for effective tax planning are somewhat reduced but by no means entirely eliminated.

Calls

A CBOE call is not treated as substantially identical with the underlying stock. Therefore, a holder of stock may write a call against stock without bringing the short sale rules into play. If a CBOE call is written against a long position (covered writing) and the call is exercised, the stock held can be delivered with the tax consequences previously indicated. The holding period of the stock is not affected by the existence of the call writer obligation.

The covered call writer has another alternative on exercise. The long position can be sold at the market and a new purchase of stock can be made for delivery against the call. These transactions create a greater long-term gain and a short-term loss resulting in a tax saving if the investor has other short-term gains and the short sale rules do not apply.

Suppose, instead, that a closing purchase transaction is made with respect to the call before it is exercised. The long-term gain on selling the long position is the same, but there is a short-term loss with respect to the call. This loss offsets the investor's other short-term gains, if any, and the long-term gain is entitled to its usual tax benefits. In view of the various commission costs involved in any extra stock transactions, this alternative might be preferable.

While the tax advantages in a rising market are considerable, the pendulum swings in the other direction when prices decline. In this situation, premiums on expired calls are short-term capital gain, but capital losses incurred on the long positions may be long-term. The covered writer who owns stock that is not yet long-term may wish to realize loss while it is still short-term. Alternatively, the investor may be willing to maintain the stock position in anticipation of at least a partial recovery, particularly if any loss ultimately realized can be short-term. The purchase of a put accomplishes this. On a short sale, it erases the accumulated holding period of an equal amount of short-term stock. That stock is not long-term until the requisite period for long-term gain or loss has passed *after* disposing of the put. This leads to consideration of tax strategies involving puts.

Puts

The risk in writing a put is not the same as the risk in writing a call. The risks and rewards of writing puts are the reverse of those of writing naked calls. If the market price of the underlying stock drops below the strike price by more than the put premium, the put writer has a cost basis in excess of market value for the stock acquired when the put is exercised.

Example:
An XYZ July 50 put is written at 8. The put is exercised when XYZ is at 41. (excluding commissions)

Purchase of 100 XYZ at 50 on exercise	$ 5,000.00
Less: premium on writing put @ 8	800.00
Cost basis, excluding commissions	$ 4,200.00
Fair market value @ 41	$ 4,100.00

If the market rises and stays above the strike price, the put writer realizes short-term capital gain when the put expires unexercised.

To protect against the risk of a falling market, a put writer can sell stock short at the same time a put is written. This, however, leaves the writer exposed to the usual short-seller's risk in a rising market. Buying a call covers this risk. However, the combined cost of all these various transactions might exceed any possible economic benefit. All the gains and losses in this situation are usually short-term capital gains and losses.

After exercise, the put writer is left with an investment position in the underlying stock. The basis of that stock is the strike price plus commission less the net premium on writing the put, and the holding period begins with the exercise. In our opinion, writing a put is not the acquisition of an option to acquire stock, even though it results in acquisition by the writer on exercise. Therefore, it does not fall within the wash sale rules, and the stock acquired is subject only to the usual tax rules for investments in stock.

Between the poles of exercise and expiration, the writer of a put has an option to make a closing purchase transaction. Since the costs of a closing purchase transaction are substantially less than those of acquisition and disposition of stock on exercise, the writer of a put faced with the likelihood of unwelcome exercise is generally well-advised to enter into a closing purchase transaction. Likewise, a closing purchase transaction is a possibility when a potential gain exists because the price of the stock has advanced, but the put will not expire for some time. Gain or loss on a closing purchase transaction is now a short-term capital gain or loss for options written on or after September 2, 1976.

Spreads

A call spread position involves writing and holding calls on the same underlying security, but with a difference in expiration date, strike price or both. Spreads are used in trading against price differences based on expiration date or strike price. These differences vary with time and with changes in the price of the underlying stock. Even with the same expiration date, the relative price movements of options with different strike prices are sufficiently different, as price changes of the underlying stock bring one or the other of the options in or out of the money, to provide potential economic gain or loss.

With the change in treatment of gain or loss on expiration or on execution of a closing purchase transaction and with the holding period changes, a spread transaction usually results in short-term capital gain or loss. Each option in a spread is treated separately for tax purposes and can be closed out (or replaced) at different times.

A put spread involves writing and holding puts on the same underlying stock, but with different expiration dates, strike prices or both. The economics should be similar to those of call spreads. A put spread also results in short-term capital gains and losses.

A final caution with respect to tax strategies: While the investor is a buyer or a writer of CBOE options, incidental purchases and sales of the underlying stock should be made only after wash sale and short sale consequences have been considered.

Identical Options

There are strategies for the simultaneous writing and purchase of calls for the same stock with the same strike price and the same expiration similar to spreads, but the tax consequences differ. There is a risk that such a position would be treated as involving a single combined transaction for tax purposes, particularly if both sides of the spread position are closed out on the same day. However, this risk is progressively reduced as the time between the closing of the two sides widens. If a spread is treated as involving a single combined transaction, any loss on the closing purchase is added to the basis of the purchased option instead of being a short-term capital loss in its own right. Of course, if this is the case, consistency would appear to require that a closing purchase gain should merely reduce the basis of the purchased option, instead of being a separate short-term capital gain. In 1970, prior to the start of the CBOE operations, the IRS issued a "single transaction" ruling with respect to a taxpayer's simultaneous purchase of stock and writing of a call, which was followed a month later by a simultaneous sale of the stock and repurchase of the call (in a transaction analagous to a

CBOE closing purchase transaction). While the writer doubts the correctness of this ruling and does not think that it applies to CBOE transactions, it has not been withdrawn by the IRS and is one of the causes for concern in the particular case described in this paragraph.

Unwelcome Exercise

The exercise of a call is not within the control of the call writer. Exercise becomes more likely as the market price of the stock rises above the strike price; and, as the call approaches its expiration date, if the market price of the underlying stock is above the call exercise price, exercise becomes more and more nearly certain. Which writer will be called upon to deliver stock as the result of a particular holder's election to exercise his call option is largely a matter of random chance because of the assignment procedures adopted by the Options Clearing Corporation. Some brokers have adopted a FIFO system (first in as writer, first out when calls are exercised) to make a decision as to which of their customers to call first. Other brokers use random selection.

A covered writer generally hopes an exercise notice will not be received until the underlying stock has been held the requisite period for long-term gain. The opposite is true for potential losses.

The exercise of a call becomes more and more likely the higher the price of the stock and the closer the expiration date. If the call is "in-the-money," a covered writer seeking to convert short-term into long-term capital gain is well-advised to enter into a closing purchase transaction as soon as it becomes evident that the call is likely to be exercised and continue to hold the underlying stock.

Alternatively, the covered writer could purchase additional stock and identify it for delivery against the exercise. If the purchase was more than 31 days after the first purchase, no wash sale problem exists and the holding period continues to run on the original stock.

To protect the long-term gain possibility in the above situation, it is important that the exercise of the call not result in a short sale. If it did, the writer would have to hold the long stock for more than the requisite period after closing the short sale with newly purchased stock to produce a long-term gain. A short sale for tax purposes might result if, upon exercise of the call, stock not owned by the writer must be delivered by the broker.

Experience shows that exercise can occur as a result of arbitrage transactions and other professional trading by call holders even when stock price movements are minimal and there is substantial time remaining before expiration of the call period. Thus, the risk of untimely exercise (untimely from the point of view of the writer of the call) should not be ignored.

The simultaneous purchase of stock and writing of a call gives some economic protection (to the extent of the call premium) against down-side risk. Any gain on exercise or expiration of the call will now generally be short-term.

When the extended holding period rules are fully operational, it may be necessary to use two or more calls routinely in order to secure long-term capital gain on stock appreciation when the stock is acquired at the same time the first call was written.

While unwelcome exercise of a put is always a possibility when the price of the stock is at or below the put strike price, the resultant acquisition by exercise is basically an investment problem—whether to keep or sell the stock—and thus outside the scope of this brochure. However, a put writer acquires stock by purchase at exercise and as previously discussed, *this* might create wash sale for short sale problems.

SPECIAL TAX PROBLEMS

Individuals

The income or loss realized by an option writer when an option written on or after September 2, 1976 expires unexercised, or when a closing purchase transaction terminates the position, is short-term capital gain to be reported on Schedule D of Form 1040. For an individual investor, ordinary income or loss realized on such transactions on options written before that date is usually reported as other income on page 2 of Form 1040. However, the IRS has not ruled in this area.

Short-term capital gain option premium income plays a positive role in permitting the deduction of investment interest expense. Since the Tax Reform Act otherwise tightened limitations on investment interest expense deductions, this may be significant. For both wash sale and net operating loss computations, the question of whether the income is derived from a trade or business is also important. An investor, active enough to be classed as a trader, would not have wash sale problems; on the other hand, treatment of such income as business income in connection with a net operating loss carry-back could be less beneficial than if the income is considered non-business.

Other investors have different income classification problems which either may preclude their acting in the CBOE market or may excite their interest.

Personal Holding Companies

A personal holding company might now find option writing less advantageous than before because option premium income, as short-term capital gain, is neutral so far as personal holding company income is concerned.

To be subject to the 70% tax on undistributed personal holding company income, a corporation must be closely-held (more than 50% owned by not more than 5 individuals) and must have at least 60% of its "adjusted ordinary gross income" fall into the category of "personal holding company income" (largely dividends, interest, rents and royalties). *Capital gains* are excluded from adjusted ordinary gross income and from personal holding company income so neither gains from buying and selling options, not income for writing options, realized either on expiration or through a closing transaction, play a part in personal holding company status determination.

Tax-Exempt Organizations

For tax-exempt organizations, option premiums are no longer unrelated business income. Even when the IRS held, in 1966, that option premium income could be taxable to an exempt organization, option writing was regarded as part of investment management.

Tax-exempt organizations are commonly subject to supervision by government authorities and their tax status often depends on operating within approved guidelines. Any tax-exempt entity considering writing options should first determine the official position of its supervisory authorities before engaging in this activity.

Private charitable foundations should be aware that the purchase of puts and calls is among the investment methods that, although not "per se" prohibited, will be closely scrutinized to determine whether requisite standards of care and prudence are being met.

Uncovered put and call writing, even in the CBOE market, might jeopardize the tax-exempt status of a private foundation, and possibly result in imposition of heavy taxes on both the foundation and its managers. Therefore, each organization should satisfy itself as to the proper course of action in this regard.

The Pension Reform Act of 1974 extended the "prudent man" rule to trustees and other fiduciaries of pension trusts, profit-sharing trusts and the like. As with private charitable foundations, fiduciaries of such trusts should exercise caution in entering into put or call transactions.

Regulated Investment Companies

Regulated investment companies, despite an IRS ruling that call premium income is other than dividends, interest and gains from the sale or other disposition of stock or securities, may take considerable comfort from the Committee on Ways and Means Report on the meaning of the recent changes in the tax treatment of option writers. Therein, it is stated that this change is intended to result in treatment of income on lapse or on termination other than through exercise as income from the sale or other disposition of a stock or security for regulated investment company purposes (the "90-10" rule), and that the "holding period" of the writer position (for purposes of the 30%–3 month requirement of Section 851 (b) (3) of the Code) be measured from the time of writing the option. It is to be hoped that the regulations will soon reflect this interpretation even though the new statutory language in Section 1234 (b) refers to treatment of the writer's gain or loss as a gain or loss "from the sale or exchange of a capital asset" rather than to gains "from the sale or other disposition of stock or securities" which is the language of Section 851 (b).

There is a relatively recent revenue ruling dealing with the effect of the application of short sale rules on the characterization of gain by regulated investment companies for purposes of the 30%–3 month rule. In our opinion, this ruling is erroneous in a number of respects. Nevertheless, it must be taken into account by any regulated investment company buying puts, since the acquisition of a put is a short sale for tax purposes.

Section 1244

Investors in a small business corporation which meets the definitional requirements of Section 1244 of the Internal Revenue Code may be entitled to treat losses on their investment as ordinary rather than capital loss. One of the requirements is that the corporation not derive more than 50% of its aggregate gross receipts from "royalties, rents, dividends, interest, annuities, and sales or exchanges of stock or securities" to the extent of any gain. A holder's gain falls into a tainted category and, in our opinion, the same is true of a writer's capital gains. This is almost identical to the problem in the subchapter "S" area and is discussed below in greater detail. Briefly, capital gains from option transactions might jeopardize an otherwise proper Section 1244 election, but ordinary gain would not.

Subchapter "S" Corporations

A Sub-S corporation retains its special status only if it does not receive more than 20% of its gross receipts as passive investment income. Passive investment income includes interest, dividends and *gain* from sale of stock or securities. To a holder, what is the effect of selling or failure to exercise an option or sale of the underlying stock at a gain or loss? Clearly, the gain on the sale of stock falls into the passive investment income category. A loss cannot be used to offset other included gains. Does the same rule hold true for options? It appears that it does. Even if one takes the position that an option is not a security, the gain or loss is to be considered as having the same character as if the underlying stock had been disposed of. To the writer, the result is somewhat different. If the option is exercised, it is clear that a sale of stock has taken place and therefore the above rules would apply. However, if the option either expires or a closing purchase transaction takes place, it appears that the gain is not passive investment income for options written prior to September 2, 1976 since no sale or exchange has taken place. However, it is possible that the change in Section 1234 mandates a contrary result for options written on or after September 2, 1976. Therefore a Sub-S corporation involved in options should be very aware of its tax position before realizing gain or loss.

Non-Resident Aliens and Foreign Corporations

Characterization of income or loss on expiration or termination of an option writer's position (for options written on or after September 2, 1976) as short-term capital gain or loss eliminates any uncertainty as to the United States tax liability of non-resident aliens and foreign corporations with respect to such income and the duty of United States persons dealing with foreigners to withhold United States tax at source with respect to such income. The House Ways and Means Committee Report indicates that option lapse income (and income from closing transactions) treated as capital gains is not subject to the 30% withholding tax at source, and that brokers and dealers as withholding agents have no liability for failing to withhold on writer premiums.

Dividend Received Deduction

In general, a corporation receiving dividend income from other domestic corporations is entitled to at least an 85% deduction with respect to such income.

There are, however, various limitations on the availability of this deduction under Section 246 of the Code. In particular, if the receiving corporation is under an obligation to make a corresponding payment with respect to substantially identical stock or securities, no dividend deduction is allowed. This is the case where stock has been sold short "against the box" and short dividend payments are due to the lender. This limitation will be avoided with CBOE puts, since (unlike over-the-counter puts) there will be no short dividend adjustment. However, there is another limitation which will be brought into play by purchase of a put by a corporation. That is the rule that requires that a corporation hold stock

789

"naked" (without having at the same time an option to sell, being under an obligation to sell, or having made and not closed a short sale of, substantially identical stock or securities) for at least 15 days not counting any days more than 15 days after the ex-dividend date. Since a put is an option to sell, a corporation will not be accumulating holding period for purposes of the dividend received deduction for dividends on any underlying stock during the time it holds a put on such stock.

Estate and Gift Tax Considerations

The estate and gift tax aspects of options are quite complicated but a few general observations are in order. The following is not intended to be a complete discussion of all of the considerations in this area.

To the holder of an option, the option will be valued for estate tax purposes at market value on the appropriately selected valuation date. The Tax Reform Act of 1976 drastically changed the estate tax area in a number of ways that are beyond the scope of this brochure. However, one important change was the denial of a step-up in basis for property acquired from a decedent dying after December 31, 1976. There is a limited relief from this provision including a clause concerning property owned by the decedent prior to January 1, 1977. This is a complicated provision which should allow an increase in basis up to fair market value at December 31, 1976 for purposes of determining gain. This part of the provision will have no application to options after 1977. However, this same section also allows an increase in basis limited to fair market value for any federal and state inheritance taxes. The rule for increasing basis for gift tax is similar but is limited to the federal gift tax only. Any gain or loss from disposition of the option acquired from a decedent is treated as long-term capital gain or loss even though the holding period requirements are or cannot be satisfied.

The estate and gift tax consequences to a writer are more unsettled. The cash premium received by a writer is obviously included in the gross estate. But, what is the treatment of the obligation at the time of death? It is an opinion that this obligation is measured by the fair market value of the option and not the underlying price of the stock.

This position represents either unrealized gain or loss. It is unclear whether this unrealized gain or loss is income in respect of decedents.

For estates of persons dying after December 31, 1976, this particular question is moot since the gain will be taxable when the option is disposed of at a profit except for the limited step-up in basis discussed above.

There are also very involved questions as to the tax treatment of transfers of options by gift. While it is clear that the holder's position is generally a capital asset, the effect of a transfer of a writer's position, and whether or not such a transfer, in fact, can be made, is unclear. It is an opinion that such transfers of the writer's obligation should be avoided. The assistance of the Chicago Board Options Exchange in the preparation of the above tax considerations is gratefully acknowledged.

RISKS OF EXCHANGE TRADED PUT AND CALL OPTIONS

Before an investor purchases or writes an Option, he should inform himself of the risks involved, including the particular risks pertaining to the business and financial condition of the issuer of the underlying security, and should determine whether such a transaction is appropriate for him in light of his financial situation and investment objectives.

Since the value of an Option largely depends upon the likelihood of favorable price movements in the underlying security in relation to the exercise price during the life of the Option, historical price and volume information concerning the underlying security may be significant in evaluating the risks of an Option transaction. Historical price information is required under the Exchange Act to be included in the annual reports of issuers of underlying securities. Such information and volume information is also available through various financial publications, in the financial press and elsewhere. In addition, each exchange has agreed with the Clearing Corporation to prepare a brochure showing for each underlying security with respect to which Options are traded on that Exchange the high and low prices for each calendar quarter during the past five calendar years and to make its brochure available upon request. The Exchanges have advised that many of their members may also make such brochures available to their customers.

1. The purchaser of a Put or a Call runs the risk of losing his entire investment in a relatively short period of time.

Should the market price of the underlying security not rise above the exercise price in the case of a Call or fall below the exercise price in the case of a Put, the Option will become entirely worthless at its expiration. Further, unless the Put or Call may be sold in the secondary market on one of the Exchanges, in order for the purchase of an Option to become a profitable investment, the value of the underlying security must move sufficiently above (in the case of a Call) or below (in the case of a Put) the aggregate exercise price to cover the premium and transaction costs. This risk is particularly great where the exercise price of a Call is considerably above, or the exercise price of a Put is considerably below, the market price of the underlying security, or where the Option is approaching its expiration. In these circumstances, there may be little likelihood that the Option will increase in value, and anyone purchasing such an Option must expect to lose the amount paid for it and the related transaction costs. Accordingly, no investor should commit any amount of money to the purchase of Puts or Calls unless he is able to withstand the loss of the amount so committed.

This risk of purchasing Calls may be illustrated by comparing Investor A, who for a total investment of $5,000 (plus transaction costs) buys 100 shares of XYZ stock at $50 per share, with Investor B, who invests $5,000 (plus transaction costs) in Calls covering 1,000 shares of XYZ at an exercise price of $50 per share. Both A and B anticipate a rise in the market price of XYZ, but should their expectations not be realized, A's loss would be quite different from B's. If by the expiration of the Call XYZ stock has fallen to $45 per share (and assuming XYZ has paid no dividends), A will have suffered a paper loss of $500 (plus being out-of-pocket the transaction costs), and his investment will be worth $4,500. He will not be required to realize this loss, and may recover it should XYZ later rise in price while he still owns the 100 shares. Investor B, on the other hand, if he has not sold the Calls in an Exchange's secondary market, will have suffered the loss of his entire $5,000 (plus transaction costs) with no possibility for recovery. Indeed, in the above example Investor

A would have had no gain or loss (other than transaction costs paid) if the market price of XYZ had remained at $50, but Investor B would have lost his entire investment. Moreover, if XYZ had paid dividends, they would have been received by A as a stockholder, but not by B as the holder of Calls.

The risk of losing one's entire investment in the purchase of Puts may be illustrated by comparing Investor C, who does not own any shares of XYZ, and who, at a time when the market price of XYZ is $50 per share, purchases a Put giving him the right to sell 100 shares of XYZ at $50 per share, paying an aggregate premium of $500 (plus transaction costs) for the Put, with Investor D, who sells short 100 shares of XYZ at $50 per share. Both C and D anticipate a decline in the market price of XYZ, but should their expectations not be realized, C's results would be different from D's. If at the time the Put expires XYZ is trading at $50 or above, C will have lost his entire $500 investment in the Put (plus transaction costs), unless he had previously sold the Put in an Exchange's secondary market. D, on the other hand, will have a paper loss (and will have to maintain increased margin on his short position) only to the extent XYZ moves above 50. Thus while the short seller's potential loss, exclusive of transaction costs, can range from zero to the theoretically unlimited amount by which XYZ may move above 50, the Put buyer will lose the total amount he paid for the Put (plus transaction costs), but no more than that amount, whenever XYZ is at 50 or above at the time the Put expires.

2. The uncovered writer of a Call is subject to a risk of loss should the price of the underlying security increase, and the uncovered writer of a Put who does not have a short position in the underlying security equivalent to the number of shares covered by the Put is subject to a risk of loss should the price of the underlying security decrease.

The type of Option writing described in this caption is extremely risky, and an investor engaging in such Option writing may incur large losses. Therefore, only very sophisticated investors having substantial capital should engage in these types of transactions. Even such persons must expect to incur substantial losses in many of their writing transactions. Specifically, the writer of a Call who does not own the underlying security, upon being assigned an exercise notice, is required to sell the underlying security at an exercise price which may be less than the price he must pay to acquire the underlying security. The writer of a Put, upon exercise, must purchase the underlying security at a price which is likely to be greater than its current market price.

For example, assume the writing of a Call covering 100 shares of XYZ at an exercise price of $50 per share for a premium of $500. In addition to paying his broker the transaction costs applicable to the writing transaction, the writer who does not own 100 shares of XYZ stock will have to maintain a specified amount of margin on deposit in his account. Further, he may be assigned an exercise notice at any time, in which event he may be called upon by his broker at any time to purchase the 100 shares at their then current market price in order to be able to deliver them at the $50 per share exercise price. If this occurs, the writer will be required to pay transaction costs upon his purchase of the underlying stock and additional transaction costs upon his delivery of the underlying stock to the exercising holder. Thus, if an exercise notice is assigned to him when the stock price is $70 per share, the writer will have a loss of $2,000 on the purchase and sale of the shares and will have paid the transaction costs of three transactions offset in part by the $500 premium received at the time he wrote the Call.

Similarly, the writer of an XYZ 50 Put who does not have a short position in 100 shares of XYZ stock is subject to the margin requirements applicable to his Put writer's position, and to risk of loss upon assignment of an exercise notice. If an exercise notice is assigned to such a writer when the marekt price of XYZ stock is $40 per share, the writer will be required to purchase 100 shares of XYZ stock in the exercise transaction and to pay for this stock at the exercise price of $50 per share. If the Put writer then chooses to sell the XYZ stock so acquired, he will have to do so at the market price of $40 per share, thus incurring a loss of $1,000 on the purchase and sale of the stock. He will also have paid the transaction costs of the original Put writing transaction and the two stock transactions, offset in part by the premium received at the time he wrote the Put.

It should be emphasized that the writer of an Option has no control over when he might be required to respond to an exercise notice; indeed, he must assume that he may be assigned an exercise notice at any time when exercise of the Option is advantageous to a holder, and that in such circumstances a loss may be incurred.

3. The writer of a Call who owns the underlying security deliverable upon exercise of the Call, and the writer of a Put who has a short position in the underlying security purchasable upon exercise of the Put are subject to the full risk of their respective positions in the underlying security; in exchange for the premium, so long as such persons remain the writer of an Option they have given up the opportunity for gain resulting from, in the case of a Call writer, an increase in the price of the underlying security above the exercise price, or, in the case of a Put writer, a decrease in the price of the underlying security below the exercise price.

Assume that A has purchased 100 shares of XYZ at $50 per share (plus transaction costs), and has written a Call covering those shares at an exercise price of $50, receiving a premium of $500 (less transaction costs). Should XYZ fall to $40 per share, the Call is not likely to be exercised and A will have suffered a paper loss of $1,000 in his stock position (in addition to having paid transaction costs), offset in part by the $500 premium he received (and any dividend that may have been paid on XYZ). On the other hand, should XYZ rise to $60 per share, the Call will likely be exercised (costing A additional transaction costs) and A will not have participated in any of the $1,000 paper profit in his stock position, having foregone this opportunity in exchange for the premium.

Similarly, in the case of a Put, assume that B sells short 100 shares of XYZ at $50 per share, and writes a Put covering the same number of shares at an exercise price of $50, receiving a premium of $500 (less transaction costs). Should XYZ increase to $60 per share, the Put will not likely be exercised, and B will have suffered a paper loss of $1,000 in his short stock position and will have paid transaction costs, offset in part by the $500 premium. Should XYZ fall to $40 per share, the Put will likely be exercised (costing B additional transaction costs) and B will not have participated in the potential $1,000 paper profit in his short stock position, having foregone this opportunity in exchange for the premium received at the time he wrote the Put.

4. Risks pertaining to secondary market.

Some of the above risks of Options transactions may be

moderated to the extent that a secondary market in particular Options is available on one or more of the exchanges on which those Options are traded. This would ordinarily permit holders and writers in the appropriate circumstances to limit their losses by closing out positions in those Options prior to the time trading in such Options ceases. At the date of this writing, Options covering many underlying securities are not generally traded on more than one Exchange, and Puts will not initially be traded in all of the underlying securities that are the subject of Call trading. An Option position may be closed out only on an Exchange which provides a market for Options having identical terms to the Options in the position being closed out.

Each of the Exchanges has advised the Clearing Corporation that, although that Exchange's trading mechanism is designed to provide market liquidity for the Options traded on that Exchange, it must be recognized that there can be no assurance that a liquid secondary market on that Exchange will exist for any particular Options, or at any particular time, and for some Options no secondary market on that Exchange may exist, as a result of the following factors: (i) there may be insufficient trading interest in certain Options; (ii) restrictions may be imposed on opening transactions or closing transactions or both; (iii) trading halts, suspensions or other restrictions may be imposed with respect to particular classes or series of Options or underlying securities; (iv) the Exchanges and the Clearing Corporation have had only limited experience with Options trading, and the facilities of an Exchange or the Clearing Corporation may not at all times be adequate to handle current trading volume (see paragraph 5 below); or (v) one or more Exchanges could, for economic or other reasons decide or be compelled at some future date to discontinue the trading of Options (or a particular class or series of Options), in which event the secondary market on that Exchange (or on that Exchange in that class or series of Options) would cease to exist, although outstanding Options that had been issued by the Clearing Corporation as a result of trades on that Exchange would continue to be exercisable in accordance with their terms. In any of these events, it might not be possible to effect closing transactions in particular Options, with the result that a holder would have to exercise his Option in order to realize any profit, and a writer would be unable to terminate his writer's obligation until the Option expires or he performs upon being assigned an exercise notice. It should also be noted that a secondary market will not be beneficial to the holder of an Option that has lost all of its value.

5. Additional Risks.

Investors should be aware that the experience of the Clearing Corporation and the Exchanges has been limited to trading in Calls which commenced on April 26, 1973 on CBOE, January 13, 1975 on AMEX, June 25, 1975 on PHLX, and April 9, 1976 on PSE. Neither the Exchanges nor the Clearing Corporation have had any experience with Puts. Further, although the Clearing Corporation believes, based on forecasts provided by the Exchanges, that its facilities are adequate to handle the volume of Options transactions reasonably anticipated for the period covered by this prospectus, and although each Exchange has advised the Clearing Corporation that it believes its facilities will also be adequate to handle anticipated volume, there can be no assurance that higher than anticipated trading activity or order flow or other unforeseen events might not, at times, render certain of these facilities inadequate and thereby result in the institution of special procedures, such as trading rotations and restriction on certain types of orders.

Investors should also be aware that, although the Clearing Corporation has developed a system of safeguards which stands behind its obligations with respect to exercises, the capital of the Clearing Corporation may not, by itself, be sufficient to permit the Clearing Corporation to honor exercises, and it might be unable to honor exercises if its system of safeguards were to fail. Further, because exercise notices are assigned on a random basis, an exercising holder has no way of knowing the amount of capital of the particular Clearing Member obligated to perform on the exercised option. In addition, the insolvency of a Clearing Member or other broker might affect the ability of its customers (including customers who are brokers and the customers of such brokers) who hold Options to sell or exercise their Options during the pendency of any insolvency proceeding. Further, the writers' positions (other than certain covered Call writing positions) of customers of an insolvent Clearing Member or other broker may be closed out. Additional risk is present in

797

Options transactions by virtue of the fact that trading may be stopped in the underlying security, in which event the holder of an Option may not be able to ascertain the current market price of the underlying security in making a decision whether or not to exercise the Option, and may not be able to purchase the underlying security required to be delivered in order to exercise a Put, or to sell the underlying security acquired upon exercise of a Call. Similarly, an Exchange or the Clearing Corporation may restrict the exercise of an Option or the Clearing Corporation may impose a restriction on delivery of the underlying security by a holder of a Put or by an uncovered writer of a Call. The uncovered Call writer in such circumstances would be unable to cover his writer's position by purchasing the underlying security for delivery, and such a writer, as well as the writer of a Put who does not receive delivery of the underlying security upon exercise, may be required to pay a prescribed settlement value in lieu of the ordinary delivery or payment upon exercise. An added risk of Options trading is that the issuer of an underlying security may not be or may cease to be in compliance with reporting requirements, or the underlying security may cease to meet the Exchanges' guidelines applicable to the initial selection and continued listing of underlying securities.

FEDERAL TAX ASPECTS OF OPTIONS TRANSACTIONS

The Internal Revenue Service has published rulings setting forth the Federal income tax consequences to holders and writers of Options on one of the Exchanges. See Revenue Ruling 78-182, 1978-20 Internal Revenue Bulletin, p. 13. The substance of certain of the rulings is set forth below under the caption "Published Tax Rulings."

The discussions which follow under "Published Tax Rulings" and "Summary of Holding Period Requirement" are based upon the assumptions that, with respect to the tax consequences to the holder of Options, the securities which are the subject of the Options are capital assets in the hands of the holder or would be if acquired by the holder, and with respect to the tax consequences to the writer of Options, the Options are not granted in the ordinary course of the writer's trade or business

798

of writing options. These discussions are presented for the general information of investors, and do not cover certain more complicated transactions such as transactions involving the purchase and/or writing of more than one Option in the same underlying stock, or dealings in both Options and underlying stocks. Investors are urged to consult their own professional tax advisers before engaging in any such transactions. The discussions also do not cover transactions involving Options where the underlying securities are other than common stocks. At the date of this writing. Options covering underlying securities other than common stocks are not available on the Exchanges.

Published Tax Rulings

A. With respect to the holder of an Option, the Internal Revenue Service has ruled as follows:

1. The cost of the Option is a nondeductible capital expenditure.

2. If the Option is sold prior to exercise, any gain or loss recognized to the holder constitutes capital gain or loss, and is short-term or long-term, depending upon the holding period of the Option.

3. If the Option is allowed to expire unexercised, the expiration is treated as a sale or exchange of the Option on the expiration date. The resultant loss is a capital loss, and is short-term or long-term, depending upon the holding period of the Option.

4. If the Option is exercised, its cost is treated as an addition to the basis of the stock purchased (in the case of a Call), or as a reduction in the amount realized upon the sale of the underlying stock (in the case of a Put). Gain or loss on such sale is capital gain or loss, and is short-term or long-term, depending upon the holding period of the stock involved.

5. For purposes of Section 1233(b) of the Internal Revenue Code, the acquisition of a Put constitutes a short sale, and the exercise, sale, or expiration of the Put is a closing of the short sale. If the Put is acquired at a time when the underlying stock has been held by the taxpayer for a period shorter than the applicable long-term holding period, or if shares of the underlying stock are acquired after acquisition of the Put and before its exercise, sale, or expiration, any gain on exercise, sale, or expiration of the Put is short-term capital gain, and the holding period of the underlying stock begins to run on the earliest of

(1) the date such stock is disposed of, (2) the date the Put is exercised, (3) the date the Put is sold, or (4) the date the Put expires.

6. If a Put and stock identified to be used in its exercise are acquired on the same day, the acquisition of the Put does not constitute a short sale for purposes of Section 1233(b) of the Internal Revenue Code. If the Put is exercised and if the identified stock is delivered pursuant to the exercise, the premium for the Put reduces the amount realized on the sale. If the Put is not exercised, the premium paid for the Put is added to the basis of the identified stock.

B. With respect to the writer of an Option, the Internal Revenue Service has ruled as follows:

1. The premium received for writing the Option is not included in income at the time of receipt, but is carried in a deferred account until the writer's obligation expires through the passage of time, until the writer sells the underlying stock pursuant to the exercise of a Call or purchases the underlying stock pursuant to the exercise of a Put, or until the writer engages in a closing transaction.

2. If the obligation of a writer of an Option expires through the passage of time, the premium constitutes short-term capital gain upon such expiration.

3. If the Option is exercised, the premium received is treated as a reduction in the cost of the underlying stock (in the case of a Put), or as part of the proceeds of the sale of the underlying stock (in the case of a Call). Gain or loss on such sale is capital gain or loss, and is short-term or long-term, depending upon the holding period of the stock involved.

4. If the writer of an Option engages in a closing transaction by payment of an amount equivalent to the value of the Option at the time of such payment, the difference between the amount so paid and the premium received constitutes short-term capital gain or loss.

5. Section 1233(b) of the Internal Revenue Code does not apply where an Option is written, but applies only where stock is sold short or a Put is purchased. Consequently, if a Call is written at a time when the underlying stock (or a Call thereon) has been held by the taxpayer for a period shorter than the applicable long-term holding period, or if the underlying stock (or a Call thereon) is acquired after a Call is written and before

exercise or expiration of the Call so written, the writing of the Call does not affect the holding period of the underlying stock (or of the Call thereon).

Summary of Holding Period Requirement

The holder of an Option or the underlying stock is entitled to long-term capital gain or loss treatment on disposition of such Option or underlying stock only if, among other requirements, he satisfies the applicable long-term holding period requirement of the Internal Revenue Code. With respect to a disposition of property in a taxable year beginning in 1977, a taxpayer is entitled to long-term capital gain or loss treatment if the property has been held for more than nine months as of the date of disposition. If the disposition occurs in a taxable year beginning in 1978 or thereafter, a taxpayer is entitled to such treatment if the property has been held for more than one year as of the date of disposition. Since the maximum term of Options presently traded on the Exchange is approximately nine months, the holder of an Option is unlikely to be able to obtain long-term capital gain or loss treatment on disposition of an Option in a taxable year beginning in 1977, and will be unable to obtain such treatment on disposition of an Option in a taxable year beginning in 1978 or thereafter.

GLOSSARY OF TERMS

Exchange Traded Options; Put Options; Call Options—The Options discussed in this writing are Put Options and Call Options ("Puts" and "Calls") traded (or, in the case of Puts, proposed to be traded) on one or more of the Exchanges. These Options (subject to certain exceptions summarized under "Limitations on Exercise") give a holder the right to buy from the Clearing Corporation in the case of a Call, or to sell to the Clearing Corporation in the case of a Put, the number of shares or other units of the underlying security covered by the Option at the stated exercise price by the proper filing of an exercise notice prior to the fixed expiration time of the Option. The designation of an Option includes the underlying security, the expiration month, the exercise price and whether the Option is a Put or a Call (e.g., an "XYZ July 50 Call" means a Call covering a unit of trading (typically 100 shares) of XYZ stock and having an exercise price of $50 per share and expiring in July).

Underlying Security—The security subject to being purchased or sold upon the exercise of an Option.

Class of Options—Options of the same type (i.e., Put or Call) covering the same underlying security.

Series of Options—Options of the same class having the same exercise price and expiration time and the same unit of trading.

Unit of Trading—The number of units of the underlying security designated by the Clearing Corporation as the subject of a single Option. In the absence of any other designation, the unit of trading for a common stock is 100 shares, subject to adjustment in certain events.

Exercise Price—The price per unit at which the holder of an Option may purchase or sell the underlying security upon exercise. The exercise price is sometimes call the "striking price."

Expiration Time—The latest time in the expiration month when an Option may be exercised at the Clearing Corporation. (Holders of Options should determine from their brokers the earlier exercise cutoff time, which is the latest time a customer may instruct his broker to exercise an Option so that the exercise notice may be received *at the Clearing Corporation* prior to the expiration time.)

Premium—The aggregate price of an Option agreed upon between the buyer and writer or their agents in a transaction on the floor of an Exchange.

Opening Purchase Transaction—A transaction in which an investor intends to become the holder of an Option.

Opening Sale Transaction—A transaction in which an investor intends to become the writer of an Option.

Closing Purchase Transaction—A transaction in which an investor who is obligated as a writer of an Option intends to terminate his obligation as a writer. This is accomplished by "purchasing" in a closing purchase transaction an Option of the same series as the Option previously written. Such a transaction has the effect, upon acceptance by the Clearing Corporation, of cancelling the investor's pre-existing position as a writer, instead of resulting in the issuance of an Option to the investor.

802

Closing Sale Transaction—A transaction in which an investor who is the holder of an outstanding Option intends to liquidate his position as a holder. This is accomplished by "selling" in a closing sale transaction an Option of the same series as the Option previously purchased. Such a transaction has the effect of liquidating the investor's pre-existing position as a holder of the Option, instead of resulting in the investor assuming the obligation of a writer.

Covered Put Writer—A writer of a Put who, so long as he remains obligated as a writer, holds on a share-for-share basis a Put of the same class as the Put written where the exercise price of the Put held is equal to or greater than the exercise price of the Put written.

Covered Call Writer—A writer of a Call who, so long as he remains obligated as a writer, owns the shares or other units of underlying security covered by the Call, or holds on a share-for-share basis a Call of the same class as the Call written where the exercise price of the Call held is equal to or less than the exercise price of the Call written.

Uncovered Writer—A writer of an Option who is not a covered writer.

Clearing Member—A member of an Exchange who has become a clearing member of the Clearing Corporation.

COMMODITY OPTIONS

Commodity options are growing in interest along with call and put options. Domestic commodity options involving metals, such as copper, gold and silver may soon be available. Commodity options were introduced in 1971 to America, from England, where people have invested in them for over 100 years. Because they offer leverage with protection against margin calls and forced liquidations, they have been growing in popularity in America.

Some investors are attracted to commodity futures because their leverage offers enormous profit potential. A sugar futures contract, for example, moves $1120 each time the price of sugar moves a penny.

So it's not unheard of for an investor to double, triple, or even quadruple his or her money, trading commodity futures, in just a few months.

The problem is that the leverage of commodity futures can work against you as well. If the market moves against you, you are subject to margin calls, and, if you can't meet them, you're subject to forced liquidations. Indeed you can end up losing far more than your original investment. So even if your long-term assessment of the market is right, an adverse short-term fluctuation can force you to close out your position with a severe loss.

Commodity options give you most of the profit potential of commodity futures, but without the risks of margin calls or forced liquidations.

There are risks in commodity options, just as in any other investment. Before you can show a profit, you must earn back the premium you pay for the option, and this limits the likelihood of profits. But on the other hand all you can lose is your relatively modest initial investment. *Unlike commodity futures*—and other margin investments—*you can never lose more than you put up in the beginning.* So your risk is fixed and known in advance. Moreover, because you can never get a margin call, you're assured that you can stay in the market regardless of short-term fluctuations.

Because commodity options offer profit potential with an

absolute limit on losses, they can help you to hedge against inflation . . . to attain short-term profits while strictly limiting your risk . . . or to make substantial long-term capital gains.

A commodity option gives you the right—though not the obligation—to buy or sell a commodity at a specified price, on or before a given time and date.

A one-year sugar call option, for example, would give you the right to buy a sugar futures contract—at the now current market price—at any time between today and about a year from now. The price specified in the option is called the "striking price." The cost of the option itself is called the "premium."

Here's how the option works: If, during the life of the option, the price of the commodity moves the way you think it will, you can make some nicely leveraged profits—two, three, or even four times your initial investment. This is because your option gives you the *right* to buy the commodity at the striking price and sell it at the current, higher price.

On the other hand, if its price moves against you, you can lose only the premium because you have no *further obligations*. In time your option will simply expire and that's the end of it—no fees, no charges, no paperwork.

You can choose between the two basic types of commodity options: a "call" option and a "put" option.

A call (buy) option gives you the right to *buy* the commodity at the striking price at any time before expiration. If you think a commodity is going to rise in price, buy a call option. This will let you participate, with leverage, in any price rise, and will limit your loss to your initial investment should things go wrong.

A put (sell) option gives you the right to *sell* the commodity at the striking price, at any time before expiration. If you think a commodity is going to fall in price, buy a put option. This will let you profit from declining prices and will limit your loss should the price go up.

Moreover, a combination commodity option is also available. As its name indicates, a combination option is both a call option and a put option, together. With a combination option, you can either buy or sell the commodity at the striking price, or do both. Since a combination option costs about double the price of either a put or a call, it takes twice as large a price movement to break even. On the other hand, a combination option gives you the potential for making money whichever way the market moves.

Commodity options are usually available for cocoa, coffee, copper, lead, rubber, silver, sugar, and zinc.

A cocoa option covers 22,046 pounds (10 metric tons) of cocoa. Thus each penny per pound the price of cocoa changes represents $220. For example, if the price of cocoa goes up 2¢, that represents $440 on a cocoa call option.

A coffee option covers 11,023 pounds (5 metric tons) of coffee. Thus each penny per pound that the price of coffee moves represents $110 to an option holder.

A copper option covers 55,115 pounds (25 metric tons) of copper. Thus each penny per pound that the price of copper moves represents $551 to an option holder.

A lead option covers 55,115 pounds (25 metric tons) of lead. Each penny per pound that the price of lead moves represents $551 to an option holder.

A rubber option covers 33,069 pounds (15 metric tons) of rubber. Each penny per pound that the price of rubber moves represents $330 to an option holder.

A silver option covers 10,000 Troy ounces of silver. Each penny per ounce that the price of silver moves represents $100 to an option holder.

A sugar option covers 112,000 pounds (50 long tons) of sugar. Each penny per pound that the price moves represents $1,120.

A zinc option covers 11,025 pounds (5 metric tons) of zinc. Each penny per pound the price moves represents $110.

Cocoa, coffee, rubber, and sugar are traded on or by members of the London commodity exchanges, and each option you buy is an option on a commodity futures contract. Copper, lead, silver, and zinc are traded on or by members of the London Metal Exchange, and each option you buy is an option on the physical commodity.

Commodity options, in general, run between 3 and 14 months. This means you can use them to meet both short and long-term investment objectives.

The shorter the option, the less time you have for a favorable price move. Conversely, the longer the option, the more time.

There are only two possibilities—either you exercise your option or you don't. If you don't exercise the option, it simply runs out and that's the end of it. If you *do* exercise it, there are simple standard procedures for liquidating your position into cash.

In general, you can expect to get between 2-to-1 leverage and 10-to-1 leverage. The precise amount of leverage depends on the premium: the lower the premium, the higher the leverage.

In general, the shorter the option runs, the lower the premium. So shorter options usually offer greater leverage than longer ones.

But whatever the leverage it's important to note that unlike commodity futures contracts, the leverage of a commodity option works only one way—for you. If the market stands still or goes against you, you will lose the premium. But no matter how perversely the market acts, you can never lose more than your initial investment.

On the other hand, there's virtually no limit on your profits. In 1974, for instance, when sugar moved from 13¢ per pound to 66¢ a $4,500 1-year sugar call (buy) option would have brought you more than $51,000 in profits—a 1130% profit. Later, the price of sugar went back down to 13¢. If, when sugar was near the top of its price movement, you had misread the market and bought a call option, you would have lost only your relatively modest premium. On the other hand, if you had read the market correctly and bought a put (sell) option, you would have made another enormous profit.

Of course, this was an extraordinary situation and we may never again see such enormous profits, but you can aim for substantial profits.

If you think a commodity is going to rise in price, but you want "insurance" against a down move, invest in a combination option. The call (buy) option will pick up value if the price rises. The put (sell) option is your protection against an unexpected decline, because it will pick up value if the price drops.

The same strategy works if you think the market's going to tumble, but want protection against an unexpected rise.

In the sugar option example above, a combination option would have yielded smaller profits than a single option since, of course, it costs more. Nonetheless, your profits on either the up or down sides of the move would have been a substantial $46,000, or 510%.

Moreover, in a volatile, up-and-down market like that *you can sometimes profit from both sides of a combination option.*

Once you have paid the premium for the commodity option, there can be no margin calls or further assessments of any kind against you for the option—no matter what the market does. Thus your risk on a commodity option is limited to your initial investment, the premium.

Since there can be no margin calls, you can stay in the market for the duration of the option, no matter what the short-term fluctuations are. This means that even if the market goes against you in the beginning, it can still come back and give you a substantial profit later on.

If you own a call (buy) option and the price of the commodity has risen and you want to cash it in, you simply tell your Account Executive, who then exercises the option for your account. This gives you the commodity at the striking price specified in the option. Simultaneously, your Account Executive sells the commodity at the current market price. The difference, minus the premium, is your profit.

For example, as this is being written, in June 1976, a 1-year rubber call option costs about $3,750 and the striking price is 54¢ per pound. Let's say the price rises to 75¢ per pound and you want to cash in. Just tell your Account Executive who will simultaneously:

(A) Exercise the option giving you a rubber futures contract—33,069 pounds of rubber—at the striking price, 54¢ per pound, or $17,857.

(B) Sell the rubber futures contract at the then current market price, 75¢ per pound, or $24,801.

(C) The difference, $6,944 minus the premium, $3,750, is the profit, $3,194.

The following are examples of a call option, a put option, and a combination option.

Call Option. Let's take, for example, a 12-month sugar call option. It costs about $6,000. The striking price is about 15¢.

The option covers 112,000 pounds of sugar so each penny the price of sugar rises yields $1,120. So if, over the next 12 months, the price of sugar rises 5.4¢, you'll break even. Anything over that is profit. In recent years, the price of sugar has moved more than 9 times that much so it's not unreasonable to aim for substantial profits.

Put Option. Let's take, for example, a 12-month cocoa put option. It costs about $3,600; the striking price is about 75¢.

The option covers 22,046 pounds of cocoa so each penny the price of cocoa drops yields $220. To break even the price must drop 16.4¢ over the next 12 months. Any greater drop is profit.

In recent years, the price of cocoa has on occasion dropped several times that within a year so, again, it's not unreasonable to aim for substantial profits.

Combination Option. Let's take, for example, a 12-month rubber combination option. It costs about $7500; the striking price is about 54¢.

The option covers 33,069 pounds of rubber so each penny the price of rubber rises above or falls below 54¢ yields $330. To break even, the price must move 22.7¢ in either direction over the next 12 months. Any greater move is profit. Since rubber has moved over 45¢ up and down in the past two years, we see that once again substantial profits are a reasonable goal.

Options for cocoa, coffee, rubber, and sugar are written by members of the International Commodity Clearing House which guarantees the performance of its members. Options for copper, lead, silver, and zinc are written through member firms of the London Metal Exchange. The London Metal Exchange has no clearing house so the member firms back their options themselves.

The Internatonal Commodity Clearing House was established in London in the 1880's; the London Metal Exchange in the 1960's. Every option guaranteed by the International Commodity Clearing House or written by members of the London Metal Exchange—during their entire existence—has been fully and promptly honored.

As with any other investment, commodity options have both advantages and disadvantages.

The main disadvantages are as follows:

a. Before you can show a profit, you must earn back the premium. This can limit the likelihood of profits.

b. If the market doesn't move or moves against you, you can lose the entire premium.

c. The options have a definite expiration date, so if the move you expect in a commodity comes after the option expires, it won't benefit you.

The advantages are as follows:

a. Powerful leverage. In general, commodity options offer you between 2-to-1 and 10-to-1 leverage.

b. Enormous profit potential. You can double, triple, or quadruple your money. Sometimes, in exceptional cases, you can do even better.

c. Limited, predetermined risk. You can lose the premium

you pay for the option, but never a penny more. This allows you to control, in advance, the maximum amount you can possibly lose—a critically important advantage if you're seeking a diversified, balanced portfolio.

d. No additional charges. Other than the 1-time, upfront premium to pay for the option, there are no other charges, fees, interest payments, or whatever.

e. No margin calls. No matter which way the market moves, there can be no margin calls or further assessments against you.

f. No forced liquidations. You can't be forced out of the market, so even if the market goes against you in the beginning, it can still come back and give you a substantial profit later on.

g. Peace of mind. With a commodity option you can watch the market without worry about minute-to-minute decisions to prevent or minimize loss—because there can be no margin calls or forced liquidations, and you know the most you can possibly lose is your initial investment.

h. Hedge against inflation and deflation. Commodity prices tend to rise during inflations so commodity call options can be used to preserve capital against inflation. Similarly, put options can be used to hedge against deflation.

A long-term combination option generally runs less than $10,000 and more than $3,000. Short-term, one-way options may cost as little as $1,000.

How much you invest and in what options depends on factors such as age, income, assets, financial responsibilities, marital status, emotional make-up, and investment objectives. Many people prefer a diversified portfolio. You should invest in commodity options only in an amount you can afford to lose.

The assistance of International Trading Group Ltd., in the preparation of this material on commodity options, is gratefully acknowledged. Its telephone number is 1-800-521-0102.

Glossary of Terms

ACTUALS: The physical commodities—also referred to as 'physicals.'

BEAR: One who believes prices will move lower.

BULL: One who expects prices to rise.

CALL OPTION: A call option gives you the right to buy a commodity or commodity futures contract of a particular commodity, at a guaranteed price, on or before a given time and date. You would buy a call option if you expected the price to rise.

CASH IN AN OPTION: You cash in a call option by having your Account Executive buy the underlying commodity futures contract at the striking price and, simultaneously, sell another contract at the current price. The difference in value between the two contracts less the premium is your profit. You cash in a put option in the same way.

CLEARING HOUSE: The separate agency associated with a futures exchange through which futures contracts are offset or fulfilled and through which financial settlement is made (also Clearing Association).

COMBINATION OPTION: A combination option is both a put option and a call option. You'd buy a combination option if you think the price is going to rise but want "insurance" against a down move, or vice versa.

COMMODITY OPTION: A commodity option is an enforce-able contract that gives you the right—though not the obligation—to take a specified position in (either to buy or sell) a commodity futures contract of a particular commodity, at a guaranteed price, on or before a given time and date.

DECLARATION DATE: The date and time when the option expires.

DELIVERY MONTH: The month in which the futures contract matures and within which delivery of the physical commodity can be made.

EXERCISE: Liquidating an option.

EXERCISE AN OPTION: You exercise a call option by buying the underlying commodity futures contract at the guaranteed price. You exercise a put option by selling the underlying commodity futures contract.

EXPIRATION DATE: The time and date when the option expires. You may exercise your option at any time until the expiration date. The expiration date is also sometimes called the "declaration date."

FORCED LIQUIDATION: If you buy a commodity futures contract, and receive a margin call, you must forward the demanded additional funds promptly, or your broker may close out your position, whether or not you wish him to. Forced liquidations, like margin calls, are impossible with commodity options.

COMMODITY FUTURES CONTRACT: A commodity futures contract is an enforceable contract to buy a commodity and take delivery at a specified time in accordance with the rules of the commodity exchange.

HEDGE: The establishment of an opposite position in the futures market from that held in an Option or in physicals. Call Options can be hedged with a short futures position; Put Options can be hedged with a long futures position. Hedging can be used to "lock in" an accumulated value in an Option.

LEVERAGE: The use of a relatively small amount of money to control a larger investment.

LONG: You are "long" in a commodity when you buy a commodity futures contract in it, in the expectation of higher prices.

MARGIN CALL: A demand by a broker for additional funds sufficient to raise your deposit on a commodity futures contract above the minimum acceptable level. Margin calls are possible only on commodity futures contracts, not commodity options.

MARKET ORDER: When you place a market order, you're instructing your broker to buy or sell a commodity futures contract or commodity option at whatever price can be obtained at that time in the market.

OPTION GRANTOR: The originator of a commodity option, usually a member of one of the London commodity exchanges. An option grantor is sometimes called an option writer.

PREMIUM: The premium is the amount you pay for your option. When you invest in a commodity option you can lose the entire premium, but never more.

PUT OPTION: A put option gives you the right to sell a commodity futures contract of a particular commodity, at a guaranteed price, on or before a given time and date. You would buy a put option if you expected the price to go down.

SHORT: You are "short" in a commodity when you sell a commodity futures contract in it, in the expectation of lower prices.

STOP LOSS ORDER (OR "STOP"): An order which becomes a market order to *sell* if the market declines to a specified level. Or an order which becomes a market order to *buy* if the market rises to a specified level. Used to protect profits, limit losses, or to initiate new positions.

STRIKING PRICE: The striking price is the price that is guaranteed in your option. It is the price of the underlying commodity futures contract at the time the option is granted. The striking price is sometimes called the "basis" price, the "base" price, or the "starting" price.

INSURED TAX-FREE MUNICIPAL BONDS

Sophisticated investors have been using minicipal bonds to their advantage for years. They offer attractive yields; they help communities finance public projects; and the interest is exempt from all Federal income taxes.

The Fund is a $16,500,000 insured portfolio of interest-bearing obligations (including delivery statements relating to contracts for the purchase of certain such obligations and cash and an irrevocable letter of credit providing funds for such purchases), issued by or on behalf of municipalities and other governmental authorities, the interest on which is, in the opinion of recognized bond counsel to the issuing governmental authority, exempt from all Federal income taxes under existing law.

Insurance has been obtained from an independent company guaranteeing the payments of principal and interest on the Bonds in the portfolio of the Fund. Such insurance relates only to the Bonds in the Fund and not to the Units offered hereby or to the market value thereof. As a result of such portfolio insurance, the Units of the Fund have received a rating of "AA."

No representation is made as to the Insurer's ability to meet its commitments.

Estimated Current Return to Unit holders under the monthly distribution plan was 6.66% per annum. Estimated current return is calculated by dividing the net annual interest income per Unit by the Public Offering Price. Interest income per Unit will vary with changes in fees and expenses of the Trustee and the Evaluator and with the redemption, maturity, exchange or sale of Bonds; Public Offering Price will vary with changes in the offering price of the underlying Bonds; therefore, there is no assurance that the estimated current return will be realized in the future.

The Objectives of the Fund are federally tax-exempt income and conservation of capital through an investment in an insured portfolio of tax-exempt bonds. The payment of interest and the preservation of principal are, of course, dependent upon the continuing ability of the issuers and/or obligors of Bonds and of the Insurer to meet their respective obligations.

The Public Offering Price of the Units is equal to the aggregate offering price of the Bonds in the portfolio of the Fund divided by the number of Units outstanding, plus a sales charge equal to 4½% of the Public Offering Price (4.712% of the amount invested).

Each Unit represents a 1/16,500 undivided interest in the principal and net income of the Fund in the ratio of one Unit for each $1,000 principal amount of Bonds deposited in the Fund.

Distributions of interest, pro rated on an annual basis, received by the Fund will be made monthly unless the Unit holder elects to receive them quarterly or semi-annually.

The Sponsor, although not obligated to do so, intends to maintain a market for the Units at prices based upon the aggregate offering price of the Bonds in the portfolio of the Fund. If such a market is not maintained, a Unit holder **will be able to dispose of his Units only through redemption at prices based upon the bid prices of the underlying Bonds.** Neither the bid nor offering prices of the underlying Bonds or of the Units include any value attributable to the insurance.

The Fund was created pursuant to a Trust Indenture and Agreement (the "Indenture"), dated the Date of deposit, with Jefferson, as Sponsor, Adams, as Trustee, and Monroe, as Evaluator. On the Date of Deposit, the Sponsor deposited with the Trustee $16,500,000 principal amount of interest-bearing obligations, including delivery statements relating to contracts for the purchase of certain such obligations and cash, cash equivalents and/or an irrevocable letter of credit issued by a major commercial bank in the amount required for such purchases (the "Bonds"). The Trustee thereafter delivered to the Sponsor a registered certificate for 16,500 Units, representing the entire ownership of the Fund, which Units are being offered hereby.

The objectives of the Fund are federally tax-exempt income and conservation of capital through an investment in an insured portfolio of interest-bearing obligations issued by or on behalf of states, counties, territories or municipalities of the United States, or authorities or political subdivisions thereof, the interest on which is, in the opinion of recognized bond counsel to the issuing governmental authorities, exempt from all Federal income tax under existing law. The Fund has obtained insurance guaranteeing the timely payment, when due, of all

815

principal and interest on such obligations. There is, of course, no guarantee that the Fund's objectives will be achieved.

In selecting Bonds, the following facts, among others, were considered: (i) the Standard & Poor's Corporation rating of the Bonds was in no case less than "BBB,"[1] or the Moody's Investors Service, Inc. rating of the Bonds was in no case less than "Baa" including provisional or conditional ratings, respectively (see "Description of Bond Ratings"), (ii) the prices of the Bonds relative to other bonds of comparable quality and maturity, (iii) the availability and cost of insurance of the principal and interest on the Bonds, and (iv) the diversification of Bonds as to purpose of issue and location of issuer. Subsequent to the Date of Deposit, a Bond may cease to be rated or its rating may be reduced below the minimum required as of the Date of Deposit. Neither event requires elimination of such Bond from the portfolio, but may be considered in the Sponsor's determination as to whether or not to direct the Trustee to dispose of the Bond (see "How May Bonds Be Removed from the Fund"?). Two issues of Bonds in the Fund are general obligations of or guaranteed by a governmental entity. The remaining issues are payable from the income of a specific project or authority. The portfolio is divided by purpose of issue as follows: Housing, 5; Hospitals, 4; Public Utilities, 4; Universities and Schools, 4; Miscellaneous, 4. The Bond Portfolio consists of 21 Bond issues in 17 states. Two Bond issues have received provisional ratings. See "Description of Bond Ratings."

Approximately 10% of the aggregate principal amount of Bonds in the Fund are general obligations of or guaranteed by a governmental entity and are backed by the taxing power of such entity. The remaining Bonds are payable from the income of a specific project or authority and are not supported by the issuer's power to levy taxes.

Some of these latter issues may also have the additional benefit of a moral commitment (but not legal obligation) of a governmental entity to satisfy any deficiency in debt service requirements if the issuer is not able to meet its obligations. There is no assurance that in the event of a default in payment of principal or interest on bonds backed by such moral obligations such default will be cured. However, the principal and interest payments due on any "moral obligation" Bonds in the Fund's portfolio are provided for by the same non-cancellable insurance covering all Bonds in the portfolio.

Because certain of the Bonds may from time to time under certain circumstances be sold or redeemed or will mature in accordance with their terms and because the proceeds from such events will be distributed to Unit holders and will not be reinvested, no assurance can be given that the Fund will retain for any length of time its present size and composition. Neither the Sponsor nor the Trustee shall be liable in any way for any default, failure or defect in any Bond. In the event that any contract for the purchase of Bonds shall not be completed, the Trustee will distribute from the Principal Account the amounts deposited in respect of any such contract and the Sponsor will refund to Unit holders the sales charge attributable to such contract.

Bond issues in the Fund may consist of school district bonds. In *Rodriguez v. San Antonio Independent School District*, the Supreme Court of the United States upheld the constitutionality under the Federal Constitution of the Texas system of financing public education in part from ad valorem property taxes. The plaintiff in that case had argued that the variation in taxable wealth among school districts which resulted in substantial disparities in expenditures per pupil and in local school tax rates among school districts violated the equal protection clause of the Federal Constitution. Other litigation of the same nature challenging the validity under state constitutions of present systems of levying taxes and applying funds for public school purposes has been pending in a number of states. Some decisions have been reached holding such school financing systems violative of state constitutions. In addition, legislation to effect changes in school financing has been introduced in a number of states. The Supreme Court's decision in *Rodriguez*, which was based on the Federal Constitution, is not controlling on the issue whether school financing systems violate state constitutions. The course and outcome of pending and future litigation and legislation in this area and any resulting change in the sources of funds including property taxation applied to the support of public schools may affect school bonds in the Fund.

To the best knowledge of the Sponsor, there is no other litigation pending as of the Date of Deposit in respect of any Bonds which might reasonably be expected to have a material adverse effect upon the Fund. At any time after the Date of Deposit, litigation may be initiated on a variety of grounds with respect to Bonds in the Fund. Such litigation, as, for example, suits challenging the issuance of pollution control revenue bonds under recently-enacted environmental protection statutes, may affect the validity of such Bonds or the tax-free nature of the interest thereon. While the outcome of litigation of such nature can never be entirely predicted, the Fund has received opinions of bond counsel to the issuing authorities of each Bond on the date of issuance to the effect that such Bonds have been validly issued and that the interest thereon is exempt from Federal income tax. In addition, other factors may arise from time to time which potentially may impair the ability of issuers to meet obligations undertaken with respect to the Bonds.

Each Unit initially offered represents a 1/16,500 undivided interest in the Fund. To the extent that any Units are redeemed by the Trustee, the fractional undivided interest in the Fund represented by each unredeemed Unit will increase, although the actual interest in the Fund represented by such fraction will remain unchanged. Units will remain outstanding until redeemed upon tender to the Trustee by any Unit holder, which may include the Sponsor, or until the termination of the Trust Agreement.

What Are Annual Unit Income and Estimated Current Return? Return?

The average weighted interest rate of Bonds in the Fund was 7.13% at the Date of Deposit, computed by dividing the total annual interest income to the Fund by the principal amount of the Bonds therein. After deducting the estimated annual fees and expenses, including current insurance costs, of the Trustee and the Evaluator, the net annual interest rate was 6.88%, 6.92% and 6.95% under the monthly, quarterly and semi-annual distribution plans, respectively, which reflects the lower expenses resulting from the fewer distributions required under the quarterly and semi-annual plans. "Estimated Annual Unit Income" is calculated by multiplying the net average weighted interest rate by $1,000 (the principal amount of Bonds underlying each Unit at the Date of Deposit). The weighted average interest rate of the Bonds in the Fund as well as the "Estimated Annual Unit Income", will change as Bonds are exchanged in certain refundings, redeemed, paid or sold, or as the expenses of the Fund change.

Tax-exempt bonds are customarily offered to investors on a "yield price" basis (as contrasted to a "dollar price" basis) at the lesser of the yield as computed to maturity of the bonds or to an earlier redemption date. Since Units of the Fund are offered on a dollar price basis, the estimated rate of return on an investment in Units of the Fund is stated in terms of "Estimated Current Return", computed by dividing the Estimated Annual Unit Income (determined as described above) by the Public Offering Price. If the average price of the Bonds is less than par, the yield to maturity will be greater than the Estimated Current Return; if the average price of the Bonds is greater than par, the yield to maturity will be less than the Estimated Current Return. Any change in either the Estimated Annual Unit Income or the Public Offering Price will result in a change in the Estimated Current Return. The Public Offering Price will vary in accordance with fluctuations in the prices of the underlying Bonds and the Estimated Annual Unit Income will change as Bonds are redeemed, paid, sold or exchanged in certain refundings or as the expenses of the Fund change. For example, as of the Date of Deposit, Estimated Annual Unit Income of $68.75 divided by the Public Offering Price of $1,032.53 results in an Estimated Current Return of 6.66% to Units under the monthly distribution plan. The Estimated Current Return under the quarterly and semi-annual distribution plans are 6.70% and 6.73%, respectively, based upon Estimated Annual Unit Income of $69.16 and $69.45, respectively.

Record Dates for the distribution of interest under the monthly distribution plan are the fifteenth day of each month with the Distribution Dates being the first day of the month following each Record Date. It is anticipated that an amount equal to approximately one-twelfth of the amount of net annual interest income per unit will be distributed on or shortly after each Distribution Date to Unit holders of record on the preceding Record Date.

Record Dates for quarterly distributions are the fiteenth day of March, June, September and December and Record Dates for semi-annual distributions are the fifteenth day of June and December. The Distribution Dates for distributions of interest under the quarterly and semi-annual distribution plans are the first day of the month following that in which the related Record Date occurs. All Unit holders will receive the first distribution of interest regardless of the plan of distribution chosen and all Unit holders will receive distributions from the Principal Account as of the Record Dates for the months of June and December of each year.

Why and How are the Bonds Insured?

In an effort to protect Unit holders against any delay in payment of interest and against principal loss, insurance has been obtained guaranteeing prompt payment of interest and principal, when due, in respect of the Bonds. The insurance policy is non-cancellable and will continue in force so long as the Fund is in existence, the Insurer and/or the reinsurer referred to below are still in business and the Bonds described in the policy continue to be held by the Fund. Non-payment of premiums will not result in the cancellation of insurance but will force the Insurer to take action against the Trustee to recover premium payments due it.

The insurance guarantees the timely payment of principal and interest on the Bonds as they fall due. It does not guarantee the market value of the Bonds or the value of the Units. The insurance is only effective as to Bonds owned by and held in the Fund. In the event of a sale of any Bond by the Trustee, the insurance terminates as to such Bond on the date of sale. Consequently, the insurance has no recognizable market value or other effect on the price or redemption value of Units. Therefore, the price which an individual pays on acquisition of Units, or receives on redemption or resale of Units, does not include any element of value for the insurance. As a result, a Unit holder who redeems or sells his Units at a time when a Bond or Bonds in the portfolio of the Fund are in default (or when the market price of such Bond or Bonds reflects a significant risk of default) may receive a lesser amount than if he retained the Units until after such Bond or Bonds mature and the principal and interest thereon have been paid by the Insurer (or the obligor). A Unit holder should recognize that in order to receive any benefit from the portfolio insurance he must be an owner of the Units at the time the Trustee becomes entitled to receive payment from Indemnity.

The policy was issued by Indemnity Corporation ("Indemnity"), a subsidiary of Investment Corporation. Indemnity was organized as a stock insurance company. In addition to insurance for the portfolio of the Fund, Indemnity insures the prompt payment of the interest and principal of new issues of municipal bonds and municipal bond portfolios of individuals, banks, trust companies, corporations and insurance companies. It also writes lease guaranty insurance in three states, mobile home credit insurance in 49 states and directors' and officers' liability insurance for banks, savings and loan associations and life insurance companies in all states. The total assets of Indemnity are $900,000,000 with a capital and surplus of $300,000,000.

Indemnity has a reinsurance agreement with Municipal Bond Insurance Corporation ("MBAC"), another subsidiary of Investment Corporation, under which Indemnity cedes to MBAC 95% of the risks it writes on BBB/Baa and higher rated bonds in its municipal bond insurance programs. This reinsurance agreement is applicable to the insurance on the Bonds in the Fund. MBAC was organized as a stock insurance company. MBAC writes only policies of insurance for new issues and portfolios of municipal bonds. The total assets of MBAC are $400,000,000 and its capital and surplus was $200,000,000.

In order to be in the portfolio, Bonds must be eligible for the insurance being obtained from Indemnity. In determining eligibility, Indemnity has applied its own standards which correspond generally to the standards it normally uses in establishing the insurability of new issue municipal bonds and which are not necessarily the same as the criteria used in regard to the selection of Bonds by the Sponsor. This decision is made prior to the Date of Deposit, as Bonds not eligible for such insurance are not deposited in the Fund. Thus all Bonds in the portfolio are subject to the insurance.

The contract of insurance relating to the Bond Portfolio and the negotiations in respect thereof represent the only relationship between Indemnity and the Fund. Otherwise neither Indemnity nor its parent, Investment Corporation, or any associate thereof has any significant relationship, direct or indirect, with the Fund or the Sponsor, except that the Sponsor has in the past and may from time to time in the future, in the normal course of its business, participate as sole underwriter or as manager or as a member of underwriting syndicates in the distribution of new issues of municipal bonds for which a policy of insurance guaranteeing the timely payment of interest and principal has been obtained from Indemnity or MBAC. Neither the Fund, the Units nor the portfolio is insured directly or indirectly by Investment Corporation.

Because the Bonds are insured by Indemnity as to the timely payment of principal and interest, Monroe has assigned to the Fund its "AA-High Grade" investment rating. This is next to the highest rating assigned to securities by Monroe, which is

"AAA-Prime" (see "Description of Bond Ratings"). Approximately 44.3% of the aggregate principal amount of the Bonds in the portfolio already had a "AA" rating on the Date of Deposit. The obtaining of this rating by the Fund should not be construed as an approval of the offering of the Units by Monroe or as a guarantee of the market value of the Fund or the Units.

At the date of this writing, the weighted average interest rate on the Bonds in the portfolio was 7.03%, after payment of the insurance premium. The average weighted interest rate on an identical, but uninsured, portfolio would have been 7.13% on such date.

In the event of nonpayment of interest or principal when due in respect of a Bond, Indemnity shall make such payment not later than 30 days after it has been notified that such nonpayment has occurred or is threatened (but not earlier than the date such payment is due). Indemnity, as regards any payment it may make, will succeed to the rights of the Trustee in respect thereof.

Indemnity recently obtained a letter ruling from the Internal Revenue Service which holds in effect that insurance proceeds representing maturing interest on defaulted municipal obligations paid by Indemnity to municipal bond funds substantially similar to the Fund, under policy provisions substantially identical to the policy described herein, will be excludable from Federal gross income under Section 103(a)(1) of the Internal Revenue Code. Holders of the Units should discuss with their tax advisors the degree of reliance which they may place on this letter ruling. However, Counsel for the Sponsor has given an opinion to the effect such payment of proceeds would be excludable from Federal gross income if, and to the same extent as, such interest would have been so excludable if paid by the issuer of the defaulted obligations. See "What Is the Tax Status of Unit Holders?".

Indemnity is subject to regulation by the department of insurance in each state in which it is qualified to do business. Such regulation, however, is no guarantee that it will be able to perform its contract of insurance in the event a claim should be made thereunder at some time in the future. At the date hereof it is reported that no claims have been submitted to Indemnity or its affiliate, Municipal Bond Insurance Corporation, pursuant to any contract of bond or portfolio insurance.

The information relating to Indemnity, MBAC and Investment Corporation contained above has been furnished by such corporations. The financial information contained herein with respect to Indemnity and MBAC is unaudited but appears in reports filed by the respective companies with state insurance regulatory authorities and is subject to audit and review by such authorities. No representation is made herein as to the accuracy or adequacy of such information or as to the absence of material adverse changes in such information subsequent to the date hereof.

What is the Tax Status of Unit Holders?

In the opinion of Counsel for the Sponsor, under existing law:

(1) the Fund is not an association taxable as a corporation for Federal income tax purposes and interest on Bonds which is exempt from Federal income tax under the Internal Revenue Code of 1954 will retain its status as tax-exempt interest, for Federal income tax purposes, when distributed to a Unit holder;

(2) exemption of interest on any bonds for Federal income tax purposes does not necessarily result in tax exemption under the laws of the several states as such laws vary with respect to the taxation of such securities and in many states all or a part of such interest may be subject to tax;

(3) each Unit holder is considered to be the owner of a pro rata portion of the Fund under Section 676(a) of the Internal Revenue Code of 1954 and will have a taxable event when the Fund disposes of a Bond, or when the Unit holder redeems or sells his Units. The tax cost reduction requirements of said Code relating to amortization of bond premium may, under some circumstances, result in the Unit holder realizing a taxable gain when his Units are sold or redeemed for an amount equal to his original cost. A Unit holder will realize a taxable gain when his Units are sold or redeemed for an amount greater than his original cost;

(4) any proceeds paid under the insurance policy issued to the Trustee by Indemnity which represent maturing interest on defaulted obligations held by the Trustee will be excludable from Federal gross income if, and to the same extent as, such interest would have been so excludable if paid by the issuer of the defaulted obligations.

In the opinion of Special Counsel to the Fund for reality tax matters, under existing law, the Fund is not an association taxable as a corporation and the income of the Fund will be treated as the income of the Unit holder under the income tax laws of the State and City of reality.

All statements in the Prospectus concerning exemption from Federal, state or other taxes are the opinion of Counsel and are to be so construed.

At the respective times of issuance of the Bonds, opinions relating to the validity thereof and to the exemption of interest thereon from Federal income tax are rendered by bond counsel to the respective issuing authorities. Neither the Sponsor nor Counsel have made any special review for the Fund of the proceedings relating to the issuance of the Bonds or of the basis for such opinions.

From time to time proposals have been introduced before Congress the purpose of which is to restrict or eliminate the Federal income tax exemption for interest on debt obligations similar to the Bonds in the Fund, and it can be expected that similar proposals may be introduced in the future. The Fund cannot predict what additional legislation, if any, in respect of the tax status of interest on debt obligations may be proposed by the present Administration or by members of Congress, nor can it predict which proposals, if any, might be enacted or whether any legislation, if enacted, would apply to the Bonds in the Fund.

What are the Expenses and Charges?

The Sponsor will not charge the Fund an advisory fee. At no cost to the Fund, the Sponsor has borne all the expenses of creating and establishing the Fund, including the cost of the initial preparation, printing and execution of the Indenture and the certificates for the Units, legal and accounting expense, expenses of the Trustee and other out-of-pocket expenses.

For each valuation of the Bonds in the Fund, the Evaluator will receive a fee of $35 plus $.25 for each issue of Bonds in excess of 50 issues (treating separate maturities as separate issues). The Trustee will receive for its ordinary recurring services to the Fund an annual fee computed at $1.08, $.85 and $.60 per annum per $1,000 principal amount of underlying Bonds, for those portions of the Fund representing monthly,

824

quarterly and semi-annual distribution plans, respectively. For example, if all Unit holders elected the monthly distribution plan, the Trustee's initial annual fee would be $17,820. For a discussion of the services performed by the Trustee pursuant to its obligations under the Indenture, reference is made to the material set forth under "Rights of Unit Holders". The Trustee's and Evaluator's fees are payable monthly on or before each Distribution Date from the Interest Account to the extent funds are available and then from the Principal Account. Both fees may be increased without approval of the Unit holders by amounts not exceeding proportionate increases under the category "All Services Less Rent" in the Consumer Price Index published by the United States Department of Labor.

The cost of the portfolio insurance to the Fund is $18,053.75 per annum so long as the Fund retains its original size and composition. Premiums are payable monthly by the Trustee on behalf of the Fund. As Bonds in the portfolio are redeemed by their respective issuers or are sold by the Trustee, the amount of the premium will be reduced in respect of Bonds no longer owned by and held in the Fund.

The following additional charges are or may be incurred by the Fund: all expenses (including legal and auditing expenses) of the Trustee incurred in connection with its responsibilities under the Indenture, except in the event of negligence, bad faith or willful misconduct on its part; the expenses and costs of any action undertaken by the Trustee to protect the Fund and the rights and interests of the Unit holders; fees of the Trustee for any extraordinary services performed under the Indenture; indemnification of the Trustee for any loss, liability or expense incurred by it without negligence, bad faith or willful misconduct on its part, arising out of or in connection with its acceptance or administration of the Fund; indemnification of the Sponsor for any loss, liability or expense incurred without gross negligence, bad faith or willful misconduct in acting as Depositor of the Fund; all taxes and other governmental charges imposed upon the Bonds or any part of the Fund (no such taxes or charges are being levied or made or, to the knowledge of the Sponsor, contemplated); and expenditures incurred in contacting Unit holders upon termination of the Fund. The above expenses and the Trustee's annual fee, when paid or owing to the Trustee, are secured by a lien on the Fund. In addition, the Trustee is empowered to sell Bonds in order to make funds

825

available to pay all these amounts if funds are not otherwise available in the Interest and Principal Accounts.

PUBLIC OFFERING

How is the Public Offering Price Determined?

The price of the Units as of the Date of Deposit was determined by adding to the Evaluator's determination of the aggregate offering price of the Bonds per Unit an amount of 4.712% thereof, equal to a sales charge of 4½% of the Public Offering Price which is equivalent to 4.712% of the net amount invested. A proportionate share of accrued and undistributed interest on the Bonds at the date of delivery of the Units to the purchaser is also added to the Public Offering Price. The Public Offering Price will vary in accordance with fluctuations in the prices of the underlying Bonds.

The aggregate price of the Bonds in the Fund is determined by the Evaluator, on the basis of bid prices or offering prices as is appropriate, (1) on the basis of current market prices for the Bonds obtained from dealers or brokers who customarily deal in bonds comparable to those held by the Fund; (2) if such prices are not available for any of the Bonds, on the basis of current market prices for comparable bonds; (3) by determining the value of the Bonds by appraisal; or (4) by any combination of the above. The Evaluator will not attribute any value to the insurance on the Bonds as such insurance will terminate as to any Bond on its disposition by the Fund.

The Division of Investment Management Regulation of the Securities and Exchange Commission has questioned whether the above described method of evaluation is inappropriate in not allowing any value to be attributed to the portfolio insurance under certain circumstances, particularly when a bond is in default or danger of imminent default. In a letter, among other things, the staff of such Division stated: "In our view, the insurance is an asset of the trust, which must be considered in the computation of net asset value by the trust". In response to the request of the staff of the Commission, the Sponsor submitted in writing its position with regard to the appropriateness of continuing to use its present method of evaluation. The Sponsor has received a second letter from the staff which stated that the question had been submitted to the Commission and that "The Commission believes that the views of the

Division [of Investment Management Regulation] as expressed in its letter are not unreasonable interpretations of the applicable law." The Sponsor is continuing its discussions with the staff of the Commission in order to satisfy the staff as soon as reasonably possible as to the Sponsor's compliance with applicable law. Although it is impossible to predict at this time what changes, if any, in the operations of the Fund may be necessary, under certain circumstances the Sponsor might apply to the Commission for an order permitting a full or partial suspension of the right of Unit holders to redeem their Units if a significant portion of the Bonds in the portfolio is in default or danger of imminent default. In any event, even if it is ultimately agreed after further discussions with the staff and/or the Commission that the insurance feature of the Fund should be considered in the computation of the net asset value of the Fund under certain circumstances, particularly when a bond is in default or danger of imminent default, it is the Sponsor's position that the insurance has no value as of the date of this prospectus.

During the initial public offering period, such a determination is made, at the expense of the Sponsor, on an offering price basis as of the close of trading on the New York Stock Exchange on each day on which it is open, effective for all sales made subsequent to the last preceding determination. For secondary market purposes, the Evaluator will be requested to make such a determination as of the close of business on the last business day of the preceding week which will be effective for transactions during the following week.

The Evaluator shall also determine the aggregate value of the Fund as of the close of trading on the New York Stock Exchange (i) on each June 30 and December 31 (or the last business day prior thereto), (ii) on the day on which any Unit is tendered for redemption and (iii) at such other times as may be necessary.

The Public Offering Price of the Units is equal to the *offering* price per Unit of the Bonds in the Fund plus the applicable sales charge and interest accrued to the date of settlement. The *offering* price of Bonds in a Fund may be expected to average approximately 1-1½% more than the *bid* price of such Bonds.

Although payment is normally made five business days following the order for purchase, payment may be made prior thereto. However, delivery of Certificates representing Units so ordered will be made five business days following such order or shortly thereafter. (See "Rights of Unit Holders—How May Units be Redeemed?" for information regarding the ability to redeem Units ordered for purchase.)

How are Units Distributed?

Until the primary distribution of the 16,500 Units offered is completed, Units will be offered to the public at the Public Offering Price computed as described above by the Underwriters, including the Sponsor (see "**Underwriting**") and through dealers. Upon completion of the initial offering, Units which are repurchased in the secondary market (see "*Will There be a Secondary Market?*") may be offered at the secondary market public offering price determined in the manner described above.

It is the intention of the Sponsor to qualify Units of the Fund for sale in a number of states by the Underwriters and by dealers who are members of the National Association of Securities Dealers, Inc. Sales initially will be made to dealers at prices which represent a concession of $25 per unit, but the Sponsor reserves the right to change the amount of the concession to dealers from time to time.

What are the Sponsor's Profits?

The Underwriters, including the Sponsor, will receive a gross sales commission equal to 4½% of the Public Offering Price of the Units (equivalent to 4.712% of the net amount invested). In addition, the Sponsor and the other Underwriters may be considered to have realized a profit or the Sponsor may be considered to have sustained a loss, as the case may be, in the amount of any difference between the cost of the Bonds to the Fund (which is based on the Evaluator's determination of the aggregate offering price of the underlying bonds on the Date of Deposit) and the cost of such Bonds to the Sponsor. Such profits or losses may be realized or sustained by the Sponsor and the other Underwriters with respect to Bonds which were acquired by the Sponsor from underwriting syndicates of which it and the other Underwriters were members. During the initial offering period, the Underwriters also may realize profits or sustain losses as a result of fluctuations after the Date of Deposit in the offering prices of the Bonds and hence in the Public Offering Price received by the Underwriters.

The Sponsor has participated as sole underwriter or manager or member of underwriting syndicates from which approximately 46% of the aggregate principal amount of the Bonds in the portfolio were acquired. An underwriter or underwriting syndicate purchases bonds from the issuer on a negotiated or competitive bid basis as principal with the motive of marketing such bonds to investors at a profit.

In maintaining a market for the Units, the Sponsor will also realize profits or sustain losses in the amount of any difference between the price at which Units are purchased (based on the offering prices of the Bonds in the Fund) and the price at which Units are resold (which price includes a sales charge of 4½%) or redeemed (based on the bid prices of the Bonds in the Fund). The secondary market public offering price of Units may be greater or less than the cost of such Units to the Sponsor.

Will There be a Secondary Market?

Although it is not obligated to do so, the Sponsor intends to maintain a market for the Units and continuously to offer to purchase Units at prices, subject to change at any time, based upon the aggregate offering price of the Bonds in the portfolio of the Fund plus interest accrued to the date of settlement. All expenses incurred in maintaining a secondary market, other than the fees of the Evaluator and the costs of the Trustee in transferring and recording the ownership of Units, will be borne by the Sponsor. If the supply of Units exceeds demand, or for some other business reason, the Sponsor may discontinue purchases of Units at such prices. In the event that a market is not maintained for the Units, a Unit holder desiring to dispose of his Units may be able to do so only by tendering such Units to the Trustee for redemption at the Redemption Price, which is based upon the aggregate bid price of the Bonds in the portfolio of the Fund. The aggregate bid price of the underlying Bonds is expected to be less than the aggregate offering price. *If a Unit Holder wishes to dispose of his Units, he should inquire of the Sponsor as to current market prices prior to making a tender for redemption to the Trustee.*

RIGHTS OF UNIT HOLDERS

How are Certificates Issued and Transferred?

The Trustee is authorized to treat as the record owner of Units that person who is registered as such owner on the books of the Trustee. Ownership of Units is evidenced by registered certificates executed by the Trustee and the Sponsor. Delivery of certificates representing Units ordered for purchase is normally made five business days following such order or shortly thereafter. Certificates are transferable by presentation and surrender to the Trustee properly endorsed or accompanied by a written instrument or instruments of transfer. Certificates to be redeemed must be properly endorsed or accompanied by a written instrument or instruments of transfer. A Unit holder must sign exactly as his name appears on the face of the certificate with the signature guaranteed by an officer of a commercial bank or trust company, a member firm of either the New York, American, Midwest or Pacific Stock Exchange, or in such other manner as may be acceptable to the Trustee. In certain instances the Trustee may require additional documents such as, but not limited to, trust instruments, certificates of death, appointments as executor or administrator or certificates of corporate authority. Record ownership may occur before settlement.

Certificates will be issued in fully registered form, transferable only on the books of the Trustee in denominations of one Unit or any multiple thereof, numbered serially for purposes of identification. Certificates for Units will bear an appropriate notation of their face indicating which plan of distribution has been selected in respect thereof. When a change is made, the existing certificate must be surrendered to the Trustee and a new certificate issued to reflect the then currently effective plan of distribution. There will be no charge for this service.

Although no such charge is now made or contemplated, a Unit holder may be required to pay $2.00 to the Trustee per certificate reissued or transferred, and to pay any governmental charge that may be imposed in connection with each such transfer or exchange. For new certificates issued to replace destroyed, stolen or lost certificates, the Unit holder may be required to furnish indemnity satisfactory to the Trustee and pay such expenses as the Trustee may incur. Mutilated certificates must be surrendered to the Trustee for replacement.

How are Interest and Principal Distributed?

Interest from the Fund will be distributed on or shortly after the first day of each month on a pro rata basis to Unit holders of record as of the preceding Record Date who are entitled to distributions at that time under the plan of distribution chosen. All distributions will be net of applicable expenses.

The pro rata share of cash in the Principal Account will be computed as of the semi-annual Record Date, and distributions to the Unit holders as of such Record Date will be made on or shorly after the first day of the following month. Proceeds received from the disposition of any of the Bonds after such Record Date and prior to the following Distribution Date will be held in the Principal Account and not distributed until the next Distribution Date. The Trustee is not required to make a distribution from the Principal Account unless the amount available for distribution shall equal at least $1.00 per Unit.

The Trustee will credit to the Interest Account all interest received by the Fund, including that part of the proceeds (including insurance proceeds) of any disposition of Bonds which represents accrued interest. Other receipts will be credited to the Principal Account. The distribution to the Unit holders as of each Record Date will be made on the following Distribution Date or shortly thereafter and shall consist of an amount substantially equal to such portion of the holders' pro rata share of the estimated annual income to the Interest Account after deducting estimated expenses as is consistent with the distribution plan chosen. Because interest payments are not received by the Fund at a constant rate throughout the year, such interest distribution may be more or less than the amount credited to the Interest Account as of the Record Date. For the purpose of minimizing fluctuations in the distributions from the Interest Account, the Trustee is authorized to advance such amounts as may be necessary to provide interest distributions of approximately equal amounts. The Trustee shall be reimbursed, without interest, for any such advances from funds in the Interest Account on the ensuing Record Date. Persons who purchase Units between a Record Date and a Distribution Date will receive their first distribution on the second Distribu-

831

tion Date after the purchase, under the applicable plan of distribution.

As of the fifteenth day of each month, the Trustee will deduct from the Interest Account and, to the extent funds are not sufficient therein, from the Principal Account, amounts necessary to pay the expenses of the Fund. The Trustee also may withdraw from said accounts such amounts, if any, as it deems necessary to establish a reserve for any governmental charges payable out of the Fund. Amounts so withdrawn shall not be considered a part of the Fund's assets until such time as the Trustee shall return all or any part of such amounts to the appropriate account. In addition, the Trustee may withdraw from the Interest Account and the Principal Account such amounts as may be necessary to cover redemption of Units by the Trustee.

Purchasers of Units who desire to receive distributions on a quarterly or semi-annual basis may elect to do so at the time of purchase during the initial public offering period. Those indicating no choice will be deemed to have chosen the monthly distribution plan. However, all Unit holders purchasing Units during the initial public offering period and prior to the first Record Date will receive the first distribution of interest. Thereafter, record dates for monthly distributions will be the fifteenth day of each month, record dates for quarterly distributions will be the fifteenth day of March, June, September and December, and record dates for semi-annual distributions will be the fifteenth day of June and December. Distributions will be made on the first day of the month subsequent to the respective Record Dates.

The plan of distribution selected by a Unit holder will remain in effect until changed. Unit holders purchasing Units in the secondary market will initially receive distributions in accordance with the election of the prior owner. Each year, approximately six weeks prior to the end of November, the Trustee will furnish each Unit holder a card to be returned to the Trustee not more than 30 nor less than 10 days before the end of such month. Unit holders desiring to change the plan of distribution in which they are participating may so indicate on the card and return same, together with their certificate, to the Trustee. If the card and certificate are returned to the Trustee, the change will become effective as of December 16 of that year. If the card is not returned to the Trustee, the Unit holder will be deemed to have elected to continue with the same plan for the following twelve months.

What Reports Will Unit Holders Receive?

The Trustee shall furnish Unit holders in connection with each distribution a statement of the amount of interest, if any, and the amount of other receipts, if any, which are being distributed, expressed in each case as a dollar amount per Unit. Within a reasonable time after the end of each calendar year, the Trustee will furnish to each person who at any time during the calendar year was a Unit holder of record, a statement (1) as to the Interest Account: interest received (including amounts representing interest received upon any disposition of Bonds), the percentage of such interest by states or territories in which the issuers of the Bonds are located, the amount of such interest representing insurance proceeds, deductions for payment of applicable taxes and for fees and expenses of the Fund, redemption of Units and the balance remaining after such distributions and deductions, expressed both as a total dollar amount and as a dollar amount representing the pro rata share of each Unit outstanding on the last business day of such calendar year; (2) as to the Principal Account: the dates of disposition of any Bonds and the net proceeds received therefrom (excluding any portion representing interest), deductions for payment of applicable taxes and for fees and expenses of the Fund, redemptions of Units, and the balance remaining after such distributions and deductions, expressed both as a total dollar amount and as a dollar amount representing the pro rata share of each Unit outstanding on the last business day of such calendar year; (3) a list of the Bonds held and the number of Units outstanding on the last business day of such calendar year; (4) the Redemption Price per Unit based upon the last computation thereof made during such calendar year; and (5) amounts actually distributed during such calendar year from the Interest Account and from the Principal Account, separately stated, expressed both as total dollar amounts and as dollar amounts representing the pro rata share of each Unit outstanding.

In order to comply with Federal and State tax reporting requirements, Unit holders will be furnished, upon request to the Trustee, evaluations of the Bonds furnished to it by the Evaluator.

Each distribution statement will reflect pertinent information in respect of all plans of distribution so that Unit holders may be informed regarding the results of other plans of distribution.

How May Units be Redeemed?

A Unit holder may redeem all or a portion of his Units by tender to the Trustee at its corporate trust office of the certificates representing the Units to be redeemed, duly endorsed or accompanied by proper instruments of transfer with signature guaranteed as explained above (or by providing satisfactory indemnity, as in connection with lost, stolen or destroyed certificates), and payment of applicable governmental charges, if any. No redemption fee will be charged. On the seventh calendar day following such tender, or if the seventh calendar day is not a business day, on the first business day prior thereto, the Unit holder will be entitled to receive in cash an amount for each Unit equal to the Redemption Price per Unit next computed after receipt by the Trustee of such tender of Units. The "date of tender" is deemed to be the date on which Units are received by the Trustee, except that as regards Units received after the close of trading on the New York Stock Exchange, the date of tender is the next day on which such Exchange is open for trading and such Units will be deemed to have been tendered to the Trustee on such day for redemption at the redemption price computed on that day. Units so redeemed shall be cancelled.

Accrued interest paid on redemption shall be withdrawn from the Interest Account or, if the balance therein is insufficient, from the Principal Account. All other amounts paid on redemption shall be withdrawn from the Principal Account.

The Redemption Price per Unit will be determined on the basis of the bid price of the Bonds in the Fund, while the Public Offering Price of Units will be determined on the basis of the offering price of the Bonds, as of the close of trading on the New York Stock Exchange on the date any such determination is made. On the Date of Deposit the Public Offering Price per Unit (which is based on the *offering* prices of the Bonds in the Fund and includes the sales charge) exceeded the Unit Value at which Units could have been redeemed (based upon the current *bid* prices of the Bonds in the Fund) by the amount shown above.

The Redemption Price per Unit is the pro rata share of each Unit determined by the Trustee on the basis of (1) the cash on hand in the Fund or moneys in the process of being collected, (2) the value of the Bonds in the Fund based on the bid prices of the Bonds and (3) interest accrued thereon, less (a) amounts representing taxes or other governmental charges payable out of the Fund and (b) the accrued expenses of the Fund. The Evaluator may determine the value of the Bonds in the Fund (1) on the basis of current bid prices of the Bonds obtained from dealers or brokers who customarily deal in bonds comparable to those held by the Fund, (2) on the basis of bid prices for bonds comparable to any Bonds for which bid prices are not available, (3) by determining the value of the Bonds by appraisal, or (4) by any combination of the above. In determining the Redemption Price per Unit no value will be assigned to the Portfolio insurance maintained on Bonds in the Fund. (See "Why and How are the Bonds Insured?")

The difference between the bid and offering prices of such bonds may be expected to average 1-1½% of principal amount. In the case of actively traded bonds, the difference may be as little as ½ of 1% and, in the case of inactively traded bonds, such difference usually will not exceed 3%. Therefore, the price at which Units may be redeemed could be less than the price paid by the Unit holder. On the Date of Deposit the aggregate current offering price of such Bonds per Unit exceeded the Redemption Price per Unit (based upon current bid prices of such Bonds) by $11.52 per Unit.

The Trustee is empowered to sell underlying Bonds in order to make funds available for redemption. To the extent that Bonds are sold, the size and diversity of the Fund will be reduced. Such sales may be required at a time when Bonds would not otherwise be sold and might result in lower prices than might otherwise be realized. Under the provisions for insurance of the principal and interest payments on the Bonds, the insurance may not be transferred by the Fund. Accordingly, any such Bonds must be sold on an uninsured basis.

The right of redemption may be suspended and payment postponed for any period during which the New York Stock Exchange is closed, other than for customary weekend and holiday closings, or during which the Securities and Exchange Commission determines that trading on that Exchange is restricted or an emergency exists, as a result of which disposal or evaluation of the Bonds is not reasonably practicable, or for such other periods as the Securities and Exchange Commission may by order permit.

How May Units be Purchased by the Sponsor?

The Trustee shall notify the Sponsor of any tender of Units for redemption. If the Sponsor's bid in the Secondary Market at that time equals or exceeds the Redemption Price per Unit, it may purchase such Units by notifying the Trustee before the close of business on the second succeeding business day and by making payment therefor to the Unit holder not later than the day on which the Units would otherwise have been redeemed by the Trustee. Units held by the Sponsor may be tendered to the Trustee for redemption as any other Units, provided that the Sponsor shall not receive for Units purchased as set forth above a higher price than it paid, plus accrued interest.

The offering price of any Units acquired by the Sponsor will be in accord with the Public Offering Price described in the then currently effective prospectus describing such Units. Any profit resulting from the resale of such Units will belong to the Sponsor which likewise will bear any loss resulting from a lower offering or redemption price subsequent to its acquisition of such Units.

How May Bonds be Removed from the Fund?

The Sponsor is empowered, but not obligated, to direct the Trustee to dispose of Bonds in the event of advanced refunding or when certain other events occur that adversely affect the value of Bonds, including default in payment of interest or principal, default in payment of interest or principal of other obligations of the same issuer, institution of legal proceedings, default under other documents aversely affecting debt service, decline in price or the occurrence of other market or credit factors, or decline in projected income pledged for debt service on revenue Bonds that, in the opinion of the Sponsor, may be detrimental to the interests of the Unit holders. Because the portfolio insurance is applicable only while Bonds are held by the Fund, the price received by the Fund upon the disposition of a Bond will reflect a value placed upon it as an uninsured bond by the market rather than a value resulting from the insurance. Since the portfolio is thus insured, it is the present intention of the Sponsor not to direct the Trustee to dispose of Bonds merely because of a deterioration of the credit behind them but to retain the Bonds in the portfolio so that if a default occurs, the Fund may realize the benefits of the related insurance. Nevertheless, under unusual circumstances the Sponsor may deem it to be in the best interests of Unit holders to dispose of a deteriorated Bond. In making such a determination, the Sponsor will balance the benefits of such a sale to the Unit holders against the need to preserve continuing payments of interest and principal. While it cannot state in advance the exact factors that will be deemed controlling in such determination, the Sponsor will consider the following: (a) the objectives of the Fund, to wit, federally tax-exempt income and conservation of capital; (b) the ability of the insurer to meet its insurance commitments; and (c) the present value of the proceeds of such a sale to Unit holders as compared with the ultimate receipt of principal at, and interest to, the maturity of such Bond (or insurance payments in respect thereto).

If any default in the payment of principal or interest on any Bond occurs and no provision for payment is made therefor either pursuant to the portfolio insurance, or otherwise, within thirty days, the Trustee is required to notify the Sponsor thereof. If the Sponsor fails to instruct the Trustee to sell or to hold such Bond within thirty days after notification by the Trustee to the Sponsor of such default, the Trustee may, in its discretion, sell the defaulted Bond and not be liable for any depreciation or loss thereby incurred.

The Trustee is also empowered to sell, for the purpose of redeeming Units tendered by any Unit holder, and for the payment of expenses for which funds may not be available, such of the Bonds in a list furnished by the Sponsor as the Trustee in its sole discretion may deem necessary. The Sponsor would place a deteriorated Bond on such a list only under unusual circumstances after balancing the need to maintain the liquidity of the Fund for purposes of redemption and marketability of outstanding Units against the need to preserve continuing payments of interest and principal. To the extent that Bonds are sold which are current in payment of interest in order to meet redemption requests and defaulted Bonds are retained in the portfolio in order to preserve the insurance protection applicable to said Bonds, the overall quality of the

Bonds remaining in the Fund's portfolio will tend to diminish.

The Sponsor shall instruct the Trustee to reject any offer made by an issuer of any of the Bonds to issue new obligations in exchange and substitution for any Bonds pursuant to a refunding or refinancing plan, except that the Sponsor may instruct the Trustee to accept such an offer or to take any other action with respect thereto as the Sponsor may deem proper if the issuer is in default with respect to such Bonds or in the written opinion of the Sponsor the issuer will probably default in respect to such Bonds in the foreseeable future.

Any obligations so received in exchange or substitution will be held by the Trustee subject to the terms and conditions of the Indenture to the same extent as Bonds originally deposited thereunder. Within five days after the deposit of obligations in exchange or substitution for underlying Bonds, the Trustee is required to give notice thereof to each Unit holder, identifying the Bonds eliminated and the Bonds substituted therefor. Except as stated in this paragraph and in the preceding paragraph, the acquisition by the Fund of any securities other than the Bonds initially deposited is prohibited.

INFORMATION AS TO SPONSOR, TRUSTEE AND EVALUATOR

Who is the Sponsor?

Jefferson, the Sponsor, has specialized in the underwriting and disbribution of tax-exempt securities since its formation.

The total stockholders' equity (unaudited) of Jefferson is $8,588,000. (Note: This paragraph relates to the Sponsor only. The information is included herein only for the purpose of informing investors as to the financial responsibility of the Sponsor and its ability to carry out its contractual obligations. More comprehensive financial information may be obtained from the Sponsor upon request.)

Who is the Trustee?

The Trustee is Adams. Adams has, since its establishment, engaged primarily in the management of trust and agency accounts for corporations. The Trustee is subject to supervision and examination by the Superintendent of Banks of the State of reality and the Federal Deposit Insurance Corporation.

The Trustee, whose duties are ministerial in nature, has not participated in the selection of the portfolio. For information relating to the responsibilities of the Trustee under the Indenture, reference is made to the material set forth under "Rights of Unit Holders".

The Trustee and any successor trustee may resign by executing an instrument in writing and filing the same with the Sponsor and mailing a copy of a notice of resignation to all Unit holders. Upon receipt of such notice, the Sponsor is obligated to appoint a successor trustee promptly. If the Trustee becomes incapable of acting or becomes bankrupt or its affairs are taken over by public authorities, the Sponsor may remove the Trustee and appoint a successor as provided in the Indenture. If upon resignation of a trustee no successor has accepted the appointment within 30 days after notification, the retiring trustee may apply to a court of competent jurisdiction for the appointment of a successor. The resignation or removal of a trustee becomes effective only when the successor trustee accepts its appointment as such or when a court of competent jurisdiction appoints a successor trustee.

Any corporation into which a Trustee may be merged or with which it may be consolidated, or any corporation resulting from any merger or consolidation to which a Trustee shall be a party, shall be the successor Trustee. The Trustee must be a banking corporation organized under the laws of the United States or any State and having at all times an aggregate capital, surplus and undivided profits of not less than $5,000,000.

Limitations on Liabilities of Sponsor and Trustee.

The Sponsor and the Trustee shall be under no liability to Unit holders for taking any action or for refraining from taking any action in good faith pursuant to the Indenture, or for errors in judgment, but shall be liable only for their own willful misfeasance, bad faith, gross negligence or reckless disregard of their obligations and duties. The Trustee shall not be liable for depreciation or loss incurred by reason of the sale by the Trustee of any of the Bonds. In the event of the failure of the Sponsor to act under the Indenture, the Trustee may act thereunder and shall not be liable for any action taken by it in good faith under the Indenture.

The Trustee shall not be liable for any taxes or other governmental charges imposed upon or in respect of the Bonds or upon the interest thereon or upon it as Trustee under the Indenture or upon or in respect of the Fund which the Trustee may be required to pay under any present or future law of the United States of America or of any other taxing authority having jurisdiction. In addition, the Indenture contains other customary provisions limiting the liability of the Trustee.

If the Sponsor shall fail to perform any of its duties under the Indenture or become incapable of acting or become bankrupt or its affairs are taken over by public authorities, then the Trustee may (a) appoint a successor Sponsor at rates of compensation deemed by the Trustee to be reasonable and not exceeding amounts prescribed by the Securities and Exchange Commission, or (b) terminate the Indenture and liquidate the Fund as provided therein, or (c) continue to act as Trustee without terminating the Indenture.

Who is the Evaluator?

The Evaluator is Monroe. The Evaluator may resign or may be removed by the Sponsor and the Trustee, in which event the Sponsor and the Trustee are to use their best efforts to appoint a satisfactory successor. Such resignation or removal shall become effective upon the acceptance of appointment by the successor Evaluator. If upon resignation of the Evaluator no successor has accepted appointment within 30 days after notice of resignation, the Evaluator may apply to a court of competent jurisdiction for the appointment of a successor.

The Trustee, Sponsor and Unit holders may rely on any evaluation furnished by the Evaluator and shall have no responsibility for the accuracy thereof. Determinations by the Evaluator under the Indenture shall be made in good faith upon the basis of the best information available to it, provided, however, that the Evaluator shall be under no liability to the Trustee, Sponsor or Unit holders for errors in judgment. This provision shall not protect the Evaluator in any case of willful misfeasance, bad faith, gross negligence or reckless disregard of its obligations and duties.

OTHER INFORMATION

How May the Indenture be Amended or Terminated?

The Sponsor and the Trustee have the power to amend the Indenture without the consent of any of the Unit holders when such an amendment is (1) to cure any ambiguity or to correct or supplement any provision of the Indenture which may be defective or inconsistent with any other provision contained therein, or (2) to make such other provisions as shall not adversely affect the interest of the Unit holders (as determined in good faith by the Sponsor and the Trustee), provided that the Indenture is not amended to increase the number of Units issuable thereunder or to permit the deposit or acquisition of securities either in addition to or in substitution for any of the Bonds initially deposited in the Fund, except for the substitution of certain refunding securities for such Bonds. In the event of any amendment, the Trustee is obligated to notify promptly all Unit holders of the substance of such amendment.

The trust may be liquidated at any time by consent of 100% of the Unit holders or by the Trustee when the value of the Fund, as shown by any Semi-Annual Evaluation, is less than $3,300,000 and will be liquidated by the Trustee in the event that Units not yet sold aggregating more than 9,900 Units are tendered for redemption by the Underwriters, including the Sponsor. If the trust is liquidated because of the redemption of unsold Units by the Underwriters, the Sponsor will refund on request to each purchaser of Units the entire sales charge paid by such purchaser. The Indenture will terminate upon the redemption, sale or other disposition of the last Bond held thereunder, but in no event shall it continue beyond December 31, 2025. In the event of termination, written notice thereof will be sent by the Trustee to all Unit holders. Within a reasonable period after termination, the Trustee will sell any Bonds remaining in the Fund, and, after paying all expenses and charges incurred by the Fund, will distribute to each Unit holder (including the Sponsor if it then holds any Units), upon surrender for cancellation of his Certificate for Units, his pro rata share of the balances remaining in the interest and Principal Accounts, all as provided in the Indenture. Because the portfolio insurance is applicable only while Bonds are held by the Fund (and does not apply to Bonds which are disposed of), the price to be received by the Fund upon the disposition of any Bond which is in default (by reason of nonpayment of principal or interest) or whose market value has deteriorated because of a fear of default will not reflect any value based on the insurance. Therefore, in connection with any liquidation of the Fund, it shall not be necessary for the Trustee to dispose of any Bond or Bonds if retention of such Bond or Bonds, until due, shall be deemed to be in the best interests of Unit holders including, but not limited to, situations in which a Bond or Bonds are in default and situations in which a Bond or Bonds reflect a deteriorated market price resulting from a fear of default. All proceeds received, less applicable expenses, from insurance on defaulted Bonds not disposed of at the date of termination will ultimately be distributed to Unit holders of record as of such date of termination as soon as practicable after the date such defaulted Bond or Bonds become due and applicable insurance proceeds have been received by the Trustee.

UNDERWRITING

The Underwriters, including the Sponsor, have severally purchased Units.

On the Date of Deposit, the Underwriters became the owners of the Units and entitled to the benefits thereof, as well as the risks inherent therein.

The Agreement Among Underwriters provides that a public offering of the Units will be made at the Public Offering Price described in the Prospectus. Units may also be sold to dealers who are members of the National Association of Securities Dealers, Inc. at prices representing a concession of $25 per Unit. However, resales of Units by such dealers to the public will be made at the Public Offering Price described in the Prospectus. The Sponsor reserves the right to change the amount of the concession to dealers from time to time.

In addition to any other benefits that the Underwriters may realize from the sale of the Units, the Agreement Among Underwriters provides that the Sponsor will share with the other Underwriters a portion of the aggregate gain, if any, represented by the difference between the Sponsor's cost of the Bonds in connection with their acquisition and the evaluation thereof on the Date of Deposit.

DESCRIPTION OF BOND RATINGS*

Standard & Poor's Corporation. A brief description of the applicable Standard & Poor's Corporation rating symbols and their meanings follow:

AAA—PRIME. These are obligations of the highest quality. They have the strongest capacity for timely payment of debt service.

> *General Obligation Bonds.* In a period of economic stress, the issuers will suffer the smallest declines in income and will be least susceptible to autonomous decline. Debt burden is moderate. A strong revenue structure appears more than adequate to meet future expenditure requirements. Quality of management appears superior.

> *Revenue Bonds.* Debt service coverage has been and is expected to remain substantial. Stability of the pledged revenues is also exceptionally strong, due to the competitive position of the municipal enterprise or to the nature of the revenues. Basic security provisions (including rate covenant, earnings test for issuance of additional bonds, debt service reserve requirements) are rigorous. There is evidence of superior management.

AA—HIGH GRADE. The investment characteristics of general obligation and revenue bonds in this group are only slightly less marked than those of the prime quality issues. Bonds rated "AA" have the second strongest capacity for payment of debt service.

A—GOOD GRADE. Principal and interest payments on bonds in this category are regarded as safe. This rating describes the third strongest capacity for payment of debt service. It differs from the two higher ratings because:

> *General Obligation Bonds.* There is some weakness, either in the local economic base, in debt burden, in the balance between revenues and expenditures, or in quality of management. Under certain adverse circumstances, *any one such weakness* might impair the ability of the issuer to meet debt obligations at some future date.

> *Revenue Bonds.* Debt service coverage is good, but not exceptional. Stability of the pledged revenues could show some variations because of increased competition or eco-

*As published by the rating companies.

nomic influences on revenues. Basic security provisions, while satisfactory, are less stringent. Management performance appears adequate.

BBB—MEDIUM GRADE. This is the lowest investment grade security rating.

General Obligation Bonds. Under certain adverse conditions, several of the above factors could contribute to a lesser capacity for payment of debt service. The difference between "A" and "BBB" ratings is that the latter shows *more than one fundamental weakness, or one very substantial fundamental weakness*, whereas the former shows only one deficiency among the factors considered.

Revenue Bonds. Debt coverage is only fair. Stability of the pledged revenues could show substantial variations, with the revenue flow possibly being subject to erosion over time. Basic security provisions are no more than adequate. Management performance could be stronger.

In order to provide more detailed indications of credit quality, Standard & Poor's bond letter ratings described above may be modified by the addition of a **plus** or a **minus** sign, when appropriate, to show relative standing within the major rating categories (except for the AAA-Prime category).

Provisional Ratings. The letter "p" following a rating indicates the rating is provisional, where payment of debt service requirements will be largely or entirely dependent upon the timely completion of the project.

Moody's Investors Service, Inc. A brief description of the applicable Moody's Investors Service, Inc. rating symbols and their meanings follow:

Aaa—Bonds which are rated Aaa are judged to be the best quality. They carry the smallest degree of investment risk and are generally referred to as "gilt edge." Interest payments are protected by a large, or by an exceptionally stable margin, and principal is secure. While the various protective elements are likely to change, such changes as can be visualized are most unlikely to impair the fundamentally strong position of such issues. With the occasional exception of oversupply in a few specific instances, the safety of obligations of this class is so absolute that their market value is affected solely by money market fluctuations.

Aa—Bonds which are rated Aa are judged to be of high quality by all standards. Together with the Aaa group they comprise what are generally known as high grade bonds. They are rated lower than the best bonds because margins of protection may not be as large as in Aaa securities or fluctuations of protective elements may be of greater amplitude or there may be othe elements presesent which make the long-term risks appear somewhat larger than in Aaa securities. These Aa bonds are high grade, their market value virtually immune to all but money market influences, with the occasional exception of oversupply in a few specific instances.

A—Bonds which are rated A possess many favorable investment attributes and are to be considered as higher medium grade obligations. Factors giving security to principal and interest are considered adequate, but elements may be present which suggest a susceptibility to impairment sometime in the future. The market value of A-rated bonds may be influenced to some degree by credit circumstances during a sustained period of depressed business conditions. During periods of normalcy, bonds of this quality frequently move in parallel with Aaa and Aa obligations, with the occasional exception of oversupply in a few specific instances.

A 1 and Baa 1—Bonds which are rated A 1 and Baa 1 offer the maximum in security within the A and Baa groups respectively. They can be bought for possible appreciation.

Baa—Bonds which are rated Baa are considered as lower medium grade obligations, i.e., they are neither highly protected nor poorly secured. Interest payments and principal security appear adequate for the present but certain protective elements may be lacking or may be characteristically unreliable over any great length of time. Such bonds lack outstanding investment characteristics and in fact have speculative characteristics as well. The market value of Baa-rated bonds is vulnerable to changes in economic circumstances as well as money market influences. Aside from occasional speculative factors and the aforementioned economic circumstances applying to some bonds of this class, Baa market valuations move in parallel with Aaa, Aa and A obligations during periods of economic normalcy, except instances of over-supply.

Con. (—)—Bonds for which the security depends upon the completion of some act or the fulfillment of some condition are rated conditionally. These are bonds secured by (a) earnings of projects under construction, (b) earnings of projects unseasoned in operating experience, (c) rentals which begin when facilities are completed, or (d) payments to which some other limiting condition attaches. Parenthetical rating denotes probable credit stature upon completion of construction or elimination of basis of condition.

Insured municipal bonds give the investor two major advantages. One is diversification. Each unit of the trust represents ownership of a share in the trust's full portfolio of professionally selected municipal bonds. Bonds in the portfolio are diversified in ratings, geography, maturity dates, and projects. The trust's investment objective is to provide the maximum tax-exempt return consistent with relative security and stability. The second is additional protection. The bonds in the trust's portfolio are insured against default in the timely payment of interest and principal. As a result of the insurance, the trust is able to include higher yield bonds in its portfolio and at the same time receive a Standard & Poor's "AA" rating. The insurance does not remove market risk and relates only to the bonds in the portfolio and not to the units of the Trust.

As more taxpayers climb into higher tax brackets, more of them find tax-exempt bonds attractive.

---

[1]This is Standard & Poor's lowest investment grade security rating. It indicates there is some weakness, either in the local economic base, in debt burden, in the balance between revenues and expenditures, or in quality of management. Under certain adverse conditions, several of the above factors could contribute to a lesser capacity for the payment of debt service. The difference between A and BBB ratings is that the latter shows more than one fundamental weakness, or one very substantial fundamental weakness, whereas the former shows only one deficiency among the factors considered. In the case of Revenue Bond, the rating indicates that debt coverage is only fair and stability of the pledged revenues could show substantial variations and possibly be subject to erosion over time. Basic security provisions are no more than adequate. Management performance could be stronger.

DIVERSIFIED VARIABLE ANNUITIES

The individual variable annuity contracts are designed to provide payments for life, or for a selected number of years, to the Owner, who will be the Annuitant unless another Annuitant is designated on the date of issue. These contracts may be categorized as periodic payment deferred contracts, single payment deferred contracts, and single payment immediate contracts.

Payments, after deductions, under deferred contracts are allocated to the Growth Division or Income Division of Variable Annuity Account IV, or to both divisions, as selected by the Owner. If payments are allocated to both divisions, an accumulation account is maintained under the contract with respect to each separate account division. Under immediate contracts, payments, after deductions, are allocated to the Growth Division. Amounts allocated to the Growth Division or Income Division are applied to purchase shares of Growth Fund or Income Fund, Inc., respectively, at their net asset values. Each Fund pays its investment advisor a monthly fee equal to an effective annual rate of 0.35% based upon the average daily net asset value of such Fund.

Under periodic payment contracts, a sales and administration charge is deducted from each payment. This charge is 12.50% during the first contract year, 8.50% during the second through fourth contract years and 5.50% for the fifth and subsequent contract years. In each case, 1.00% of the charge is for administration expenses and the balance is for sales expenses. In addition, an annual administration charge is deducted from each accumulation account on each June 1 and on the date such account is cancelled to effect an annuity or a complete redemption of that account. The charge deducted from each account will not exceed $18. If during the first contract year, a minimum annual payment of $600 is made, the total charge would amount to $93, or 18.34% of the payment made less the sales and administration charge and the annual administration charge.

Under single payment contracts, a sales and administration charge is deducted from the payment. This charge depends on the amount of the payment and grades downward from 7.50% (6.30% sales and 1.20% administration expenses). In addition, an administration charge of $75 is deducted from the single payment. If a minimum payment of $2,000 is made, the total charge would amount to $225, or 12.68% of the payment made less the total sales and administration charge.

Under all contracts, Life Insurance Company deducts from each accumulation account at the end of each valuation period for assuming mortality and expense risks 0.85% and 0.25%, respectively, on an annual basis for a total of 1.10%. A deduction may also be made from each accumulation account at the end of each valuation period to provide for a 30% tax reserve established for any realized and unrealized capital gains. Any premium taxes payable with respect to a variable annuity contract will be deducted when due. Such taxes presently range from 0% to 3% in the various jurisdictions. The deductions for mortality and expense risks and premium taxes are not reflected in the above calculations of total charges.

The minimum and maximum annual payments for periodic payment contracts are, respectively, $600 ($1,200 if payments are allocated to both separate account divisions) and 200% of the annual payment initially selected by the Owner. The minimum payment for single payment contracts is $2,000 to either separate account division (or more under certain circumstances in the case of single payment immediate contracts).

Any person who purchases a periodic payment contract has the right to surrender his contract for any reason within 45 days after the mailing to him of a notice of that right and to receive in cash the value of his accounts plus an amount equal to the difference between the gross payments made and the net amount invested. Such notice will be mailed within 60 days after issuance of the contract and will contain a statement of charges to be deducted from the projected payments and notice of the right of withdrawal.

The Life Insurance Company also has individual variable annuity contracts designed for use in connection with (1) pension and profit-sharing plans or annuity plans qualified under either Section 401 or 403(a) of the Internal Revenue Code of 1954, as amended (the "Code") including plans established by persons entitled to the benefits of the Self-Employed Individuals Tax Retirement Act of 1962, as amended, commonly called "HR-10 Plans," (2) annuity purchase plans adopted by public school systems and certain tax exempt organizations pursuant to Section 403(b) of the Code, and (3) Individual Retirement Account Plans adopted by or on behalf of individuals pursuant to Section 408 of the Code. These contracts are part of Variable Annuity Account V and differ from those under Variable Annuity Account IV as follows:

Payments, after deductions, under deferred contracts are allocated to the Growth Division or Income Division of Variable Annuity Account V, or to both divisions, as selected by the Owner. If payments are allocated to both divisions, an accumulation account is maintained under the contract with respect to each separate account division. Under immediate contracts, payments, after deductions, are allocated to the Growth Division. Amounts allocated to the Growth Division or Income Division are applied to purchase shares of Companion Fund, Inc. or Companion Income Fund, Inc., respectively, at their net asset values. Each fund pays its investment advisor a monthly fee equal to an effective annual rate of 0.35% based upon the average daily net asset value of such Fund.

Under periodic payment contracts, a sales and administration charge is deducted from each payment. This charge is 12.50% during the first contract year, 8.50% during the second through fourth contract years and 5.50% for the fifth and subsequent contract years. In each case, 1.00% of the charge is for administration expenses and the balance is for sales expenses. In addition, an annual administration charge is deducted from each accumulation account on each June 1 and on the date such account is cancelled to effect an annuity or a complete redemption of that account. The charge deducted from each account will not exceed the lesser of $18 or 5.00% of the annual rate at which payments, before deductions, were last made with respect to that account. If during the first contract year, a minimum annual payment of $120 is made, the total charge would amount to $21, or 21.21% of the payment made less the sales and administration charge and the annual administration charge.

Under single payment contracts, a sales and administration charge is deducted from the payment. This charge depends on the amount of the payment and grades downward from 7.50% (6.30% sales and 1.20% administration expenses). In addition, an administration charge of $75 is deducted from the single payment. If a minimum payment of $2,000 is made, the total charge would amount to $225, or 12.68% of the payment made less the total sales and administration charge.

Under all contracts, Life Insurance Company deducts from each accumulation account at the end of each valuation period for assuming mortality and expense risks 0.85% and 0.25%, respectively, on an annual basis for a total of 1.10%. Any premium taxes payable with respect to a variable annuity contract will be deducted when due. Such taxes presently range from 0% to 3% in the various jurisdictions. The deductions for mortality and expense risks and premium taxes are not reflected in the above calculations of total charges.

The minimum and maximum annual payments for periodic payment contracts are, respectively, $120 ($240 if payments are allocated to both separate account divisions) and 200% of the annual payment initially selected by the Owner. The minimum payment for single payment contracts is $2,000 to either separate account division (or more under certain circumstances in the case of single payment immediate contracts).

Any person who purchases a periodic payment contract has the right to surrender his contract for any reason within 45 days after the mailing to him of a notice of that right and to receive in cash the value of his accounts plus an amount equal to the difference between the gross payments made and the net amount invested. Such notice will be mailed within 60 days after issuance of the contract and will contain a statement of charges to be deducted from the projected payments and notice of the right of withdrawal.

The Objective

The objective of these contracts is to provide payments which will tend to reflect changes in the cost of living after the date of issue. Life Insurance Company seeks to accomplish this by investing net payments made under the contracts in shares of Growth Fund, or Income Fund, (the "Fund" or "Funds"). Growth Fund's principal objective is a long-term growth of capital and it is intended that such Fund's assets will consist principally of a portfolio of common stocks. Since historically the value of a diversified portfolio of common stocks held for an extended period of time has tended to rise during periods of inflation, shares of Growth Fund are made available as an

850

investment medium. However, since for some periods the values of common stocks have declined while the cost of living was rising, an alternative investment medium is available through shares of Income Fund, whose principal objective is to provide as high a level of income as is consistent with safety of principal. It is intended that Income Fund's assets will consist principally of a portfolio of debt securities. There is no assurance that the objective of the contracts will be attained through either investment medium, since the values under the contracts will increase or decrease to reflect the current values of the underlying securities which are subject to the risks of changing economic conditions and the risks inherent in the ability of management to anticipate changes in such investments necessary to meet changes in economic conditions.

The Separate Account

All payments received under the contracts, less authorized deductions, are credited to Variable Annuity Account IV ("VAA-IV"), a separate account established by Life Insurance Company and registered as a unit investment trust under the Investment Company Act of 1940, as amended ("1940 Act"). Such registration does not involve supervision of the investments or investment policies of the separate account. Amounts allocated to the Growth Division of VAA-IV are used to purchase shares of Growth Fund and amounts allocated to the Income Division of VAA-IV are used to purchase shares of Income Fund, in both cases at the net asset value of such shares. Each Fund is an open-end investment company organized by Life Insurance Company and registered under the 1940 Act. Additional information concerning each Fund, including information as to expenses paid by such Fund, is given in the applicable Fund prospectus.

Your Options

The Owner of a deferred contract selects whether payments are to be allocated to the Growth Division (for investment in Growth Fund shares), the Income Division (for investment in Income Fund shares), or both. If payments are allocated to both divisions, the allocation to each division must be a whole percentage of the payment and may not be less than $50 a month, or its equivalent. Whenever payments are allocated to both divisions the annual administration charge will be twice as large as when payments are allocated to only one division. The allocation may be changed from time to time by the Owner, subject to the above conditions, and the Owner may direct that all or a part (usually at least $500) of the accumulation account value attributable to one separate account division be transferred to the other, subject to certain limitations and a $5 transfer charge.

Upon the commencement of annuity payments, the value of the accumulation account maintained with respect to the Growth Division will be applied to effect a variable annuity, and the value of the accumulation account maintained with respect to the Income Division will be applied to effect a fixed-dollar annuity. The Owner of a deferred contract may select the form of variable and fixed annuities which he wishes to receive and the date annuity payments are to begin, except that payments must begin no later than age 85. Prior to the first annuity payment date the Owner of a deferred contract may change the date the annuity payments are to begin or elect another form of annuity.

The Payments

The initial variable annuity payment is based upon the annuity rates set forth in the contract in the case of deferred contracts and is based upon the annuity rates published by Life Insurance Company in the case of immediate contracts. Subsequent payments will increase or decrease to reflect the investment performance of Growth Fund.

Your Rights

An Owner of a deferred contract may, at any time prior to the date the annuity payments begin, elect to redeem all or a portion of either or both accumulation accounts. However, certain tax consequences may result from any such election.

In the event of the Annuitant's death prior to the start of annuity payments, the Beneficiary will receive a cash payment equal to the total value of both accumulation accounts less the annual administration charge deducted from each account or may elect to have such value applied to effect a variable or fixed annuity. The contracts provide certain voting rights in relation to the shares of the Funds held in VAA-IV.

Contract Changes

Life Insurance Company may, at any time, make any change in a contract to the extent that such change is required in order to make the contract conform with any law or regulation issued by any government agency to which Life Insurance Company is subject.

If shares of either Fund should not be available, or, if in the judgment of Life Insurance Company, investment in shares of either Fund is no longer appropriate in view of the purposes of VAA-IV, shares of another registered, open-end investment company may be substituted for such Fund shares or in the case of periodic payment contracts, net payments received after a date specified by Life Insurance Company may be applied to the purchase of shares of another registered, open-end investment company in lieu of Fund shares. In either event, approval of the Securities and Exchange Commission and approval by a majority of the votes entitled to be cast with respect to the shares held by the separate account division affected shall be obtained.

Variable Annuity Account IV

Variable Annuity Account IV ("VAA-IV") was established pursuant to a resolution of Life Insurance Company. The income, gains or losses of VAA-IV are credited to or charged against the assets of VAA-IV without regard to the other income, gains or losses of Life Insurance Company. These assets are held with relation to the contracts described herein and such other variable annuity contracts as may be issued by Life Insurance Company and designated by it as participating in VAA-IV. Although the assets maintained in VAA-IV will not be charged with any liabilities arising out of any other business conducted by Life Insurance Company, all obligations arising under the variable annuity contracts, including the promise to make annuity payments, are general corporate obligations of Life Insurance Company. Accordingly, all of Life Insurance Company's assets are available to meet its obligations and expenses under the variable annuity contracts participating in VAA-IV.

Any and all distributions made by each Fund with respect to shares held by VAA-IV will be reinvested in additional shares of such Fund, at net asset value. Deductions and redemptions from

VAA-IV, will, in effect, be made by redeeming Fund shares at net asset value. The Fund shares held in VAA-IV are in the custody of Bank and Trust Company, which is acting as custodian pursuant to an Agreement of Custodianship.

THREE TYPES OF CONTRACTS

Forms of Individual Variable Annuity Contracts

Life Insurance Company offers three forms of individual variable annuity contracts as follows:

(1) The periodic payment deferred contract—The purchase price of the contract is paid prior to the annuity commencement date through periodic payments. The contract provides for a life annuity to begin at some selected future date with a provision that annuity payments will be made for at least 120 or 180 months, as elected. The Owner may elect one of the optional modes of settlement.

(2) The single payment deferred contract—The purchase price of the contract is paid in one sum as of the date of issue of the contract. The contract provides for a life annuity to begin at some selected future date with a provision that annuity payments will be made for at least 120 or 180 months, as elected. The Owner may elect one of the optional modes of settlement.

(3) The single payment immediate contract—The purchase price of the contract is paid on one sum as of the date of issue of the contract. The contract provides for a life annuity to begin immediately. The Owner may elect: (a) a variable life annuity, (b) a variable life annuity with monthly payments certain for 120 or 180 months, or (c) a last survivor variable annuity. These annuities are identical to Options 1, 2 and 3 as set forth herein.

THE ACCUMULATION PERIOD—GROWTH IS THE GOAL

The Accumulation Account

During the accumulation period—the period before the commencement of annuity payments—there is maintained for each deferred contract an accumulation account with respect to each separate account division.

After deducting the sales and administration charge, each

payment is allocated to either the Growth Division, the Income Division, or both, and credited in the form of accumulation units to an accumulation account or accounts. The number of accumulation units credited is determined by dividing the balance of the payment allocated to a division by the applicable accumulation unit value as of the end of the valuation period in which the payment is received. The number of accumulation units so determined will not be changed by any subsequent change in the accumulation unit value but will be reduced, in the case of periodic payment contracts, as a result of the deduction for the annual administration charge.

Valuation Date and Valuation Period

Accumulation unit values and annuity unit values and the value of Fund shares are determined as of each day on which the New York Stock Exchange is open for unrestricted trading. Under the variable annuity contract each such day is a valuation date and the period from one valuation to the next is a valuation period.

Accumulation Unit and Accumulation Account Values

The accumulation unit values for both separate account divisions were initially set at $10.00. The accumulation unit value for each separate account division is redetermined on each valuation date and is equal to the accumulation unit value determined on the preceding valuation date multiplied by the applicable net investment factor for the current valuation period. The accumulation unit value for a valuation period is the value determined at the end of such period. An accumulation account value at any time is equal to the total number of accumulation units credited to that account multiplied by the then current value of the applicable accumulation unit.

Net Investment Factor

The net investment factor with respect to each separate account division is a quantitative measure of the investment performance of that division. Such net investment factor for any valuation period is determined by dividing the sum, after any taxes, of (a) the net asset value of a share of the Fund held by that division determined as of the end of such valuation period and (b) the per share amount of any dividends and other distributions made by such Fund during the valuation period, by the net asset value of a share of such Fund determined as of the end of the immediately preceding valuation period, and subtracting from this result the mortality and expense risks charge and a deduction to provide for the 30% reserve established for realized and unrealized capital gains.

Hypothetical Example of Calculation of Accumulation Unit Value

The computation of the accumulation unit value for one of the separate account divisions may be illustrated by the following hypothetical example. Assume that the net asset value of a Fund share determined as of the end of the current valuation period is $14.80; that there are no dividends or other distributions made by the Fund during the current valuation period; that the net asset value of a Fund share determined as of the end of the immediately preceding valuation period was $14.78; and that the accumulation unit value for the preceding valuation period was $10.185363. To determine the net investment factor with respect to that division for the current valuation period, divide $14.80 by $14.78 which produces 1.001353 and deduct from this amount the mortality and expense risks charge of .000030 which is the rate for one day that is equivalent to an annual rate of 1.10%. The result, 1.001323, is the net investment factor for the current valuation period. The accumulation unit value for the preceding valuation period ($10.185363) is then multiplied by the net investment factor for the current valuation period (1.001323) which produces an accumulation unit value of $10.198838 for the current valuation period. (The above assumes no deduction for taxes.)

THE ANNUITY PERIOD—MONTHLY INCOME

The Annuity Period

The variable annuity payments under the contracts will vary in amount either up or down to reflect the investment experience of Growth Fund. Variable annuity payments will commence on the annuity payment date selected by the Owner. An Owner of a deferred contract may elect to change the

856

annuity payment date to any date (other than the 29th, 30th or 31st day of any month) which is at least two months after such election but not beyond the first day of the month following the Annuitant's 85th birthday. Variable annuity payments are made monthly (except for special provisions concerning minimum payments) on a specified day of each month, called the annuity payment date. Each contract sets forth the annuity payment date applicable under that contract.

Upon the commencement of annuity payments, the value of the accumulation account maintained with respect to the Growth Division will be applied to effect a variable annuity, and the value of the accumulation account maintained with respect to the Income Division will be applied to effect a fixed-dollar annuity. By notifying Life Insurance Company at least 30 days prior to the first annuity payment date, an Owner may elect to have funds held in the Income Division applied to effect a variable annuity or funds held in the Growth Division applied to effect a fixed-dollar annuity. By giving similar notice, an Owner may also elect one of the variable annuity options specified below and one of the fixed-dollar annuity options specified in the contract in lieu of receiving the annuity payments as initially provided in the contract. Unless otherwise provided by the Owner, such options may also be elected by a Beneficiary for himself, or with Life Insurance Company's consent, his nominee. Such options are available only with Life Insurance Company's consent if the payee is a corporation, partnership, association, trustee or assignee or if the amount available to provide either fixed or variable annuity payments is less than $2,000 or is not sufficient to provide annuity payments of $20 a month on each basis selected. The term "annuitant" referred to in the options described herein means the Annuitant under the contract or a Beneficiary entitled to elect an annuity option or such Beneficiary's nominee. Once variable annuity payments have commenced, the annuitant cannot redeem his variable annuity for a cash payment, except as provided in Option 4 herein.

Option 1—Variable Life Annuity—A variable annuity which provides monthly payments during the lifetime of the annuitant with no monthly payments or other benefits payable subsequent to the date his death occurs. This option offers a higher level of monthly payments than options 2 or 3 because no further payments are payable after the death of the annuitant. It would be possible under this option for the annuitant to receive only one annuity payment if he died prior to the due date of the second payment, two if he died prior to the due date of the third payment, etc.

Option 2—Variable Life Annuity with Monthly Payments Certain for 120 or 180 Months—A variable annuity which provides monthly payments during the lifetime of the annuitant and further provides that if, at the death of the annuitant, payments have been made for less than the elected period certain, which may be 120 or 180 months, the annuity payments will be continued during the remainder of such period.

Option 3—Last Survivor Variable Annuity—A variable annuity payable during the joint lifetime of two annuitants and continued during the lifetime of the surviving annuitant. All monthly payments will cease at the death of the last surviving annuitant.

Option 4—Period Certain Variable Annuity—A variable annuity which provides payments for 36, 60, 120 or 180 months, whichever period is elected. At any time during the period certain, the annuitant may elect that (1) any future payments to which he is entitled be commuted and paid in one sum or (2) such commuted amount, provided that the value thereof is at least $2,000 and will provide annuity payments of at least $20 per month, be applied to effect a variable annuity under one of the other options described herein. Since there is a right to elect an annuity involving a life contingency, a deduction is made under option 4 as it is under the other options described herein for mortality and expense risks. Such deduction is reflected in the Annuity Unit Value. If the annuitant dies during the period certain, payments will be continued to his designated beneficiary for the balance of the period certain. No payments are payable after the end of the period certain either to the annuitant or the beneficiary. It is therefore possible under this option for an annuitant to outlive the variable annuity payments.

Other forms of variable annuities, not in conflict with this prospectus or the contracts, may be effected with the consent of Life Insurance Company.

Variable Annuity Purchase Rates

The deferred contracts contain a schedule of annuity rates for the form of variable annuity initially selected and for each

858

form of variable annuity described in Options 1 through 4 above. The annuity rates for the forms of immediate variable annuities are published by Life Insurance Company. The annuity rates show how much the first monthly variable annuity payment will be for each $1,000 applied to effect the annuity. The rates vary with the form of annuity, the date of birth and sex of the Annuitant and the Joint Annuitant, if any, and the date on which the annuity is effected. The annuity purchase rates for annuities involving payments for life are based on the Individual Annuitant Mortality Table and an assumed investment return of 4% and include a table for determining the adjusted age to be used. The adjusted age involves a decrease from actual age depending upon the date annuity payments commence, such decrease being one year for annuity payment dates commencing before 1980 and one *additional* year for each decade from 1980 to the year 2000. Because of this age adjustment, it may be advantageous for the Owner to designate an annuity payment date that precedes the year in which an age adjustment would occur under the contract and disadvantageous to designate an annuity payment date in or after such a year.

The annuity purchase rates for all variable annuity contracts described herein are based on, among other things, an annual interest rate, referred to as the assumed investment return. Under the contracts, if the net investment return (which reflects dividends and market value changes with respect to Fund shares, any adjustment to the tax reserve and the mortality and expense risks charge) on the shares of Growth Fund in VAA-IV were the same as the assumed investment return, the variable annuity payments would remain level. If the net investment return exceeded the assumed investment return, the variable annuity payments would increase and, conversely, if it were less than the assumed investment return the payments would decrease. The rates applicable to all contracts described herein are based upon an assumed investment return of 4% except that a lower assumed investment return will be used in connection with contracts issued in any state or jurisdiction which requires the use of a lower assumed investment return. When the assumed investment return is 4%, the variable annuity payments will (i) remain level during periods when the net investment return is 4% on an annual basis, (ii) increase during periods when the net investment return exceeds an annual rate of 4%,

859

and (iii) decrease during periods when the net investment return is less than an annual rate of 4%. If the assumed investment return is lower than 4% the initial variable annuity payment will be smaller but subsequent payments will increase more rapidly and will decline more slowly.

Determining the Amount of the First Monthly Annuity Payment

Under deferred contracts, on the date on which a variable annuity is effected, the accumulation account maintained with respect to the Growth Division is cancelled and the number of accumulation units credited thereto on such date is multiplied by the applicable accumulation unit value on the last valuation date preceding the annuity payment date by at least 20 calendar days. From the amount so determined, the annual administration charge and any applicable premium tax are deducted and the balance is applied to effect the variable annuity by dividing such balance by 1000 and by multiplying the result by the appropriate annuity purchase rate. The first variable annuity payment is paid on the date the variable annuity is effected. The first monthly annuity payment, divided by the annuity unit value on the date when an annuity is effected, equals the number of annuity units credited to the contract.

For immediate contracts, the amount of the first monthly annuity payment is determined by dividing the single payment, less deductions, by 1000 and multiplying the result by the appropriate annuity purchase rate. Such single payment cannot be less than the greater of $2,000 or such amount necessary to provide a first monthly annuity payment of $20. Such monthly annuity payment will be made one month subsequent to the date of issue. If the amount available under a deferred contract to provide either fixed or variable annuity payments is less than $2,000 or is not sufficient to provide annuity payments of $20 a month on each basis selected, Life Insurance Company at its option may pay such amount to the Owner in lieu of annuity payments. If, after annuity payments have commenced, the amount of the monthly variable annuity payments under a deferred or immediate contract should fall below $20, Life Insurance Company reserves the right to change the frequency of such payments to intervals that will result in payments of at least $20.

APPENDIX

Determining the Amount of the Second and Subsequent Monthly Annuity Payments

The amount of the second and subsequent variable annuity payments will be equal to the amount determined by multiplying the number of annuity units credited to the contract by the annuity unit value for the valuation period in which the annuity payment date occurs.

The Annuity Unit and Annuity Unit Value

On the date as of which an annuity is effected, the contract is credited with the number of annuity units computed by dividing (i) the amount of the first monthly annuity payment by (ii) the annuity unit value for the current valuation period. The number of annuity units so credited remains unchanged throughout the period in which annuity payments are received and serves as the basis for determining the amount of the second and subsequent annuity payments payable.

The annuity unit value was set at $1.00. The annuity unit value is redetermined on each valuation date thereafter and is equal to the annuity unit value determined as of the preceding valuation date multiplied by the annuity change factor for the last valuation period ending at least 20 calendar days prior to the current valuation date. The annuity unit value for a valuation period is the value determined as of the end of such period. The annuity change factor for any valuation period is equal to the amount determined by dividing (i) the net investment factor with respect to the Growth Division for such valuation period by (ii) an amount equal to one (1) plus the interest rate for such valuation period at an effective annual rate equal to the assumed investment return. The annuity change factor for the last valuation period ending at least 20 calendar days prior to the current annuity payment date is used in order to permit calculation of amounts of annuity payments and mailing of checks in advance of the due date.

CALCULATING YOUR PAYMENTS

Hypothetical Example of Calculation of Annuity Payments

The determination of the first monthly annuity payment, the number of annuity units and the annuity unit value may be

861

illustrated by the following hypothetical example. Assume that a male Owner who is also the Annuitant resides in a state where there are no applicable premium taxes and elects to have a variable annuity effected on his 65th birthday, selecting a life annuity with 120 monthly payments certain. Assume that on the date the annuity is effected the Owner has credited to the accumulation account maintained with respect to the Growth Division 2,650 accumulation units; and that the accumulation unit value on the last valuation date preceding the annuity payment date by at least 20 calendar days was $10.923047 producing a total value of $28,946 (2,650X $10.923047). From this amount the annual administration charge (assumed at $18.00) is deducted, leaving a balance of $28,928 as the total amount to be applied to effect the annuity. Assuming that the applicable annuity purchase rate is equal to $6.48 per $1,000 applied, the first montly annuity payment is equal to $6.48 multiplied by 28.928 or $187.45.

Assuming an annuity unit value of $1.120290 on the date the annuity was effected, the number of annuity units to be credited to the Owner is determined by dividing the amount of the first annuity payment ($187.45) by $1.120290 and is equal to 167.323. The amount of each subsequent annuity payment will be equal to the amount determined by multiplying the number of annuity units (167.323) by the annuity unit value for the valuation period in which such payment is due.

To determine the amount of the second monthly payment, assume that the annuity unit value for the preceding valuation period is 1.126387 and that the net investment factor with respect to the Growth Division for the last valuation period ending at least 20 calendar days prior to the annuity payment date on which the second payment is due is 1.001475. The annuity change factor for such valuation period is determined by dividing the net investment factor of 1.001475 by 1.000107 (which is equal to 1.000000 plus interest for one day equivalent to an assumed investment return of 4%) and is equal to 1.001368. This factor is then multiplied by the annuity unit value for the preceding valuation period ($1.126387) producing an annuity unit value for the valuation period in which the second payment is due of $1.127928. The second payment is equal in amount to the fixed number of annuity units (167.323) multiplied by the current annuity unit value ($1.127928) or $188.73.

A LOOK AT THE COSTS

Deductions Under the Individual
Variable Annuity Contracts

A. Sales and Administration Charges

Charges will be made, as described below, for sales and administration expenses including such items as salaries, rent, postage, telephone, travel, office equipment, legal fees and expenses of audit of VAA-IV. The administration charges under the contracts are designed only to reimburse Life Insurance Company for its actual administration expenses and Life Insurance Company does not expect to recover from these charges any amount above its accumulated expenses in administering these contracts. The charges are as follows:

(1) Under single payment contracts, a deduction of $75 is made from the single payment, as partial compensation for administration expenses. In addition, a sales and administration charge is deducted from the single payment as indicated by the following table:

Amount of Payment		Percentage of Deduction	Portion Representing Sales Charge	Portion Representing Administration Charge	Total Charge as a Percentage of the Net Amount Invested*
$ 2,000 but less than $	10,000	7.50%	6.30%	1.20%	12.68%
10,000 but less than	25,000	6.00	5.40	.60	7.24
25,000 but less than	50,000	5.00	4.50	.50	5.60
50,000 but less than	100,000	4.00	3.60	.40	4.33
100,000 but less than	250,000	3.00	2.70	.30	3.17
250,000 but less than	500,000	2.00	1.80	.20	2.07
500,000 but less than	1,000,000	1.50	1.35	.15	1.54
1,000,000 of more		1.00	.90	.10	1.02

*Assuming the payment to be the minimum shown in each bracket in the column entitled "Amount of Payment" and, also assuming no applicable state premium taxes. The total charge includes both the percentage deduction and the $75 deduction.

(2) If the single payment consists of proceeds payable under insurance contracts issued by Life Insurance Company (the death benefit under life insurance policies, the maturity value of endowment contracts, the cash value of fixed-dollar life

insurance and annuity contracts and lump sum cash options available to beneficiaries), a deduction of $75 shall be made from such single payment, as partial compensation for administration expenses. In addition, a sales and administration charge is deducted from the single payment as indicated by the following table:

Amount of Payment		Percentage of Deduction	Portion Representing Sales Charge	Portion Representing Administration Charge	Total Charge as a Percentage of the Net Amount Invested*
$ 2,000 but less than	$ 10,000	5.25%	4.05%	1.20%	9.89%
10,000 but less than	25,000	4.20	3.60	.60	5.21
25,000 but less than	50,000	3.50	3.00	.50	3.95
50,000 but less than	100,000	2.80	2.40	, .40	3.04
100,000 but less than	250,000	2.10	1.80	.30	2.22
250,000 but less than	500,000	1.40	1.20	, .20	1.45
500,000 but less than	1,000,000	1.05	.90	, .15	1.08
1,000,000 or more		.70	.60	.10	.71

*Assuming the payment to be the minimum shown in each bracket in the column entitled "Amount of Payment" and, also assuming no applicable state premium taxes. The total charge includes both the percentage deduction and the $75 deduction.

(3) Under periodic payment contracts a sales and administration charge is deducted from each payment, as follows:

Contract Year	Total Percentage Deduction	Portion Representing Sales Charge	Portion Representing Admin. Charge
1st	12.50%	11.50%	1.00%
2nd through 4th	8.50	7.50	1.00
5th and subsequent	5.50	4.50	1.00

The effect of these deductions and the annual administration charge (described below) under the periodic payment contracts is illustrated in the following table.

$50 Monthly Payments	Total Payments	Deduction for the Sales & Adminis- tration Charge	Sales & Adminis- tration Charge as a Percent- age of Total Payments	Total Charge as a Percent- age of Aggregate Net Annual Payments*
1 yr.	$ 600	$ 75.00	12.50%	18.34%
6 yrs.	3,600	294.00	8.17	12.57
12 yrs.	7,200	492.00	6.83	10.91
$500 Monthly Payments				
1 yr.	$ 6,000	$ 750.00	12.50%	14.68%**
6 yrs.	36,000	2,940.00	8.17	9.25
12 yrs.	72,000	4,920.00	6.83	7.68

*The total charge includes both the sales and administration charge and the annual administration charge. The aggregate net annual payments are equal to total payments less the total charge. No assumption has been made for any applicable state premium taxes.

**If payments are allocated to both divisions, the percentage figures for the first, sixth, and twelfth years would be 15.07%, 9.61%, and 8.03%, since both accumulation accounts will be subject to the annual administration charge.

An annual administration charge is deducted by Life Insurance Company under periodic payment contracts as compensation for administration expenses. The charge is deducted from each accumulation account and will be the amount, based upon the frequency of payment, as shown below:

Frequency of Payment	Annual Administration Charge
Annually	$10
Semiannually	11
Quarterly	13
Monthly	18

If during any 12-month period immediately preceding a June 1 no payment has been allocated to a separate account division or no redemption has been made from the accumulation account maintained with respect to such division, or if the accumulation account value as of the first June 1 following the issuance of the contract is less than $100, the annual administration charge shall be $5.

The annual administration charge is deducted from each accumulation account on each June 1 and on the date an accumulation account is cancelled in order to effect an annuity or as a result of a complete redemption of that account. The charge is effected by cancelling the number of accumulation units credited to such account equal in value to the charge. No charge will be made on the date the accumulation account is cancelled if such cancellation occurs on or prior to the first valuation date which follows a June 1.

B. Premium Taxes

At the time any premium taxes are payable by Life Insurance Company, the amount thereof will be deducted either from the payment or from the applicable accumulation account together with any interest thereon. Premium taxes (which presently range from 0% to 3%) are charged by various jurisdictions but in many of these jurisdictions no premium tax is currently charged with respect to annuities such as those described in this writing.

C. Mortality and Expense Risks Charge

While variable annuity payments will reflect the investment performance of Growth Fund, they will not be affected by adverse mortality experience or by any excess in the actual sales and administration expenses over the expense deductions provided for in the contract. Life Insurance Company (1) assumes the risk that annuity payments will continue for a longer period than anticipated because the Annuitant lives longer than expected, and (2) assumes the risk that the sales and administration charge and the annual administration charge may be insufficient to cover the actual cost of these items. Life Insurance Company assumes these risks for the duration of the contract and the charges set forth herein will not be increased regardless of mortality or expense experience.

For assuming these risks Life Insurance Company, in determining the accumulation unit values and annuity unit value, makes a deduction at the end of each valuation period from the current market value of each account. The amount of this deduction for each valuation period is the rate for the number of calendar days in such period which is equivalent to an annual rate of 1.10% (0.85% for mortality risks and 0.25% for expense risks).

A LOOK AT THE FUNDS' PORTFOLIOS

Growth Fund

Cash and Cash Equivalent
Common Stock of Manufacturing and Chemical Companies
Common Stock of Oil, Oil Service and Mining Companies
Common Stock of Wholesale and Service Companies
Common Stock of Public Utility Companies
Common Stock of Merchandising Companies
Common Stock of Office and Business Companies and Electrical Equipment Companies
Common Stock of Food and Beverage Companies
Common Stock of Financial Services Companies
Common Stock of Health Care Companies

Income Fund

Cash and Cash Equivalent
Corporate Bonds of Consumer Goods and Service Companies
Corporate Bonds of Industrial Energy Related Companies
Corporate Bonds of Financial Service Companies
Corporate Bonds of Foreign Companies
Corporate Bonds of Manufacturing Companies
Corporate Bonds of Chemical Companies
Corporate Bonds of Office Equipment Companies
Corporate Bonds of Food and Beverage Companies
Corporate Bonds of Merchandising Companies
Corporate Bonds of Public Utility Electric Companies
Corporate Bonds of Public Utility Telephone Companies

The Distribution of Variable Annuity Contracts

The individual variable annuity contracts will be sold primarily by persons who are insurance agents of or brokers for Life Insurance Company, authorized by applicable law to sell life and other forms of personal insurance and who are similarly authorized to sell variable annuities. In addition, these persons will for the most part be registered representatives of Equity Sales Company, a broker-dealer registered under the Securities Exchange Act of 1934 and a member of the National Association of Securities Dealers, Inc. The variable annuity contracts may be sold through other broker-dealers registered under the Securities Exchange Act of 1934 whose representatives are authorized by applicable law to sell variable annuity contracts.

The Custodian

Life Insurance Company has an agreement with Bank and Trust Company, a trust company, pursuant to which Fund shares and other assets credited to VAA-IV will be held in the custody of Bank and Trust Company.

The Agreement of Custodianship provides that Bank and Trust Company will purchase Fund shares at their net asset value with net payments received from Life Insurance Company. Purchases will be made by the Custodian at the net asset value of Fund shares determined as of the end of the valuation period in which the payments are received by Life Insurance Company. Bank and Trust Company will reinvest all cash distributions of the Funds, effect redemptions of Fund shares in accordance with instructions from Life Insurance Company, and will execute proxies for the voting of Fund shares in accordance with instructions from persons having voting rights in respect of Fund shares. In addition, Bank and Trust Company will be responsible for maintaining appropriate records with respect to all transactions in Fund shares relative to VAA-IV.

The agreement requires Bank and Trust Company to have at all times an aggregate capital, surplus, and undivided profits of not less than $2,000,000 and prohibits resignation by Bank and Trust Company until (a) VAA-IV has been completely liquidated and the proceeds of such liquidation properly distributed or (b) a successor custodian bank having the qualifications enumerated above shall have agreed to serve as custodian. Subject to these conditions the Agreement of Custodianship may be terminated by either party upon 30 days written notice. For its services as custodian, Bank and Trust Company will be paid a fee to be agreed upon from time to time by Bank and Trust Company and Life Insurance Company. The fee shall be paid by Life Insurance Company and in no event may Bank and Trust Company charge or collect against or from the property held by it pursuant to the Agreement of Custodianship any of its fees or expenses without the prior written consent of Life

Insurance Company. In addition, Life Insurance Company has agreed to indemnify Bank and Trust Company for any liability arising in connection with its services as custodian so long as such liability is not attributable to the negligence or bad faith of Bank and Trust Company.

Voting Rights

The Custodian of VAA-IV shall vote Fund shares held in each division of VAA-IV at regular and special meetings of shareholders of such Fund, but will follow voting instructions received from the person having the voting interest in such Fund shares as determined by the variable annuity contract.

The number of Fund shares as to which a person has the voting interest will be determined as of a date to be chosen by Life Insurance Company not more than ninety days prior to the meeting of such Fund, and voting instructions will be solicited by written communication at least ten days prior to such meeting.

During the accumulation period, the Owner is the person having the voting interest in the Fund shares attributable to his accumulation accounts. The number of Fund shares held in each division of VAA-IV which is attributable to each accumulation account is determined by dividing that accumulation account value by the net asset value of one Fund share.

During the annuity period, the person then entitled to variable annuity payments has the voting interest in the Fund shares attributable to such variable annuity. The number of Fund shares held in the Growth Division of VAA-IV which is attributable to each variable annuity is determined by dividing the reserve for such variable annuity by the net asset value of one Fund share.

Fund shares held in each division of VAA-IV as to which no timely instructions are received will be voted in proportion to the instructions with respect to shares of such Fund which are received under other contracts, whether group or individual, providing benefits on a variable basis as may be designated by Life Insurance Company in VAA-IV.

All Fund proxy material will be mailed to the last known address of each person having the voting interest in such Fund shares together with an appropriate form which may be used to give voting instructions to the Custodian.

If Life Insurance Company determines pursuant to applicable law that Fund shares held in VAA-IV need not be voted pursuant to instructions received from persons otherwise having the voting interest as provided above, then Life Insurance Company may vote Fund shares held in VAA-IV in its own right. However, until the applicable law is changed, the voting rights will remain as described in this writing.

Transfer of Account Values

At any time prior to 30 days before the commencement of annuity payments, the Owner of a deferred contract may, subject to certain conditions, direct that all or part of the accumulation account value attributable to one separate account division be transferred to the other division. The minimum amount which may be transferred is $500 or the entire accumulation account value, if less. Life Insurance Company will deduct a transfer charge of $5 from any amount transferred, and such transfer will be made on the basis of the accumulation unit values next determined after receipt of a notice to transfer by Life Insurance Company at its Home Office.

When considering a transfer shortly before the commencement of annuity payments, the Owner should bear in mind that by giving Life Insurance Company notice at least 30 days prior to the first annuity payment date, he may elect to have funds held in the Income Division applied to effect a variable annuity or funds held in the Growth Division applied to effect a fixed-dollar annuity as of the annuity payment date without paying a transfer charge.

Life Insurance Company reserves the right to limit the number of transfers to which the transfer charge applies to two in any one-year period. In addition to reserving the right to itself impose a limitation, Life Insurance Company has also undertaken to provide periodically to the board of directors of each Fund information necessary to evaluate the effect of such transfers on such Fund and to limit the number of such transfers that may be made from an accumulation account in any one-year period to any number, not less than two, recommended by a majority of the directors of the Fund with respect to which such accumulation account is maintained or a majority of the directors of such Fund who are not interested persons of such Fund and to retain any such limitation until its removal or modification is approved by a similar vote. Life

Insurance Company also reserves the right to limit the maximum amount that may be transferred in any calendar month. At present this limit is $250,000.

Redemption

At any time before the annuity payment date the Owner of a deferred contract may elect to receive a cash payment from either or both accumulation accounts. Upon the receipt by Life Insurance Company of such election, the accumulation account will be reduced by the number of accumulation units calculated by dividing the amount of the requested cash payment from that account by the accumulation unit value for such account for the valuation period in which the election becomes effective. The election must specify the accumulation account from which the payment is to be paid, or if the payment is to be paid from both accumulation accounts, the election must specify the amount of the payment to be paid from each accumulation account.

Any cash payment to be made from the deferred contracts will be paid within seven days after the date the request for such payment becomes effective, except as Life Insurance Company may be permitted to defer such payment under the provisions of the 1940 Act. Deferment is currently permissible only (1) for any period (a) during which the New York Stock Exchange is closed other than customary weekend and holiday closings or (b) during which trading on the New York Stock Exchange is restricted; (2) for any period during which an emergency exists as a result of which (a) disposal of securities held in the Funds is not reasonably practicable, or (b) it is not reasonably practicable to determine the values of the Funds' net assets; or (3) for such other periods as the Commission may by order permit for the protection of security holders. A request for payment becomes effective when received in writing by Life Insurance Company at its Home Office. The tax consequences of a cash redemption should be carefully considered.

If, at the time the request for a cash payment becomes effective, the accumulation account value reduced by an amount equal to the annual administration charge does not exceed the cash payment requested from that account by $500, the accumulation account will be cancelled and the balance, if any, of the accumulation account value reduced by the annual administration charge will be paid in addition to the amount of cash payment requested. If both accumulation accounts are cancelled as the result of one or more redemption elections, the final cash payment will be paid in lieu of all other rights and benefits under the contract. No redemption is permitted once variable annuity payments commence, except as provided under Option 4.

DEATH PAYMENTS

Death Payments Prior to the Commencement of Annuity Payments

Upon the death of the Annuitant before annuity payments have commenced, the Beneficiary will receive a cash payment equal in amount to the accumulation account values less any annual administration charge determined as of the date due proof of death is received by Life Insurance Company. In lieu of such payment, the Beneficiary may elect prior to such date that the payment of all or, with Life Insurance Company consent, a part of the accumulation account values less the annual administration charge be deferred to a date which is not later than the date on which the Annuitant's annuity payments were to commence. A Beneficiary (other than an executor, administrator, corporation, association, partnership, or trustee) may elect at any time to have all or a portion of the value of either or both accumulation accounts, less any annual administration charge, applied to effect a variable or fixed annuity for himself or, with the consent of Life Insurance Company, his nominee. For purposes of this election, the accumulation accounts will be valued as of the date the election and all information reasonably required by Life Insurance Company has been received by it or the date Life Insurance Company receives due proof of death, whichever is later, and the first annuity payment will be made on the date which is two months after the date of valuation.

Death Payments After Annuity Payments Commence

Upon the death of the Annuitant on or after the date his annuity payments commence no payments will be payable under the contract except as may be provided under the form of annuity effected. The Owner may, prior to the Annuitant's death, elect that any variable annuity payments to which the Beneficiary may become entitled will be commuted and paid in one sum; or in the absence of such election and unless otherwise provided by the Owner, a Beneficiary who becomes entitled to variable annuity payments may elect that the remainder of such payments be commuted and paid in one sum. Any such commutation will be equal to the value, in a single sum, of the remaining variable annuity payments, discounted from their respective due dates to the date of determination of the single sum at the rate of 4% per annum compounded annually, assuming that the annuity unit value applicable to the payments on the date of determination will remain unchanged thereafter. A Beneficiary (other than an executor, administrator, corporation, association, partnership or trustee) who is entitled to receive the commuted value may elect, prior to the date such value is paid, to have it applied to provide a variable or fixed annuity in the manner described above.

OTHER CONTRACTUAL PROVISIONS

Payment Limits and Issue Ages

For periodic payment contracts, the minimum payment is $600 annually ($1200 if payments are allocated to both separate account divisions) which may be paid in annual, semiannual, quarterly or monthly installments. Payments in excess of 200% of the initial annual payment selected by the Owner may be made only with the consent of Life Insurance Company. For single payment deferred contracts the minimum payment is $2,000 to either separate account division and for single payment immediate contracts the minimum payment with respect to the Growth Division is the greater of (a) $2,000 or (b) such amount necessary to provide an initial monthly variable annuity payment of $20. Since variable annuity payments must commence no later than the first day of the month following the Annuitant's 85th brithday, the maximum issue age is 80 for periodic payment contracts.

Transfer of Ownership

An Owner may transfer all the rights and privileges provided by the contract, such transfer to take effect in accordance with the terms of such contract.

Discontinuance of Payments Under Periodic Payment Contracts

A grace period of one year is allowed for the submission of every payment after the first. For a period of two years following the grace period, the contract, unless it has been surrendered for cash, will be reinstated, and a new grace period commenced, upon written application by the Owner and the submission of a payment for allocation to a separate account division of not less than $50.00. Subsequent to such reinstatement period the contract, unless it has been reinstated or surrendered for cash, will be continued as a paid-up deferred annuity and no further payments will be accepted without the consent of Life Insurance Company. At any time prior to the annuity payment date the Owner may elect to exercise the redemption privilege, or the transfer privilege.

Periodic Reports

Life Insurance Company will send to each Owner, at least once in each calendar year after the first, a statement showing the number of accumulation units in each of the accumulation accounts and the accumulation unit values. In addition, every person having voting rights in VAA-IV will receive the semi-annual and annual reports of the Funds.

FEDERAL TAX STATUS

Life Insurance Company is taxed as a life insurance company under the Life Insurance Company Income Tax Act of 1959, as amended. The operations of VAA-IV are part of the total operation of Life Insurance Company and are not taxed separately, although the operations of VAA-IV are treated separately for accounting and financial statement purposes and must be considered separately in computing Life Insurance Company's tax liability. Under existing Federal income tax law, no taxes are payable on the investment income of VAA-IV; realized capital gains, however, are subject to tax. Life Insurance Company maintains a reserve within each division of VAA-IV for realized and unrealized capital gains based upon the 28% rate currently applicable to corporate taxpayers. If there is a net realized capital gain as to a separate account division on which tax would be payable (if such division were separately taxed), the amount of the tax payable will be transferred to

874

Life Insurance Company from VAA-IV. A transfer of taxes would be made even though Life Insurance Company by reason of losses in its other operations pays no capital gains tax. Conversely, if there is a net realized loss as to a separate account division in VAA-IV, a corresponding transfer will be made from Life Insurance Company to VAA-IV. VAA-IV is not affected by Federal income taxes paid by Life Insurance Company with respect to its other operations. Life Insurance Company reserves the right to charge the variable annuity contracts proportionately with any Federal income tax liability which may result from maintenance of VAA-IV or the variable annuity contracts.

The variable annuity contracts described in this writing are considered annuity contracts taxable under Section 72 of the Code. Under the existing provisions of the Code, an increase in the accumulated value of a contract is not taxable to the Owner until received by him, either in the form of variable annuity payments or as the result of a redemption.

When variable annuity payments commence, a portion of each payment is excluded from gross income as a return of the investment in the contract. The portion of each payment to be excluded is determined by dividing the investment in the contract by the annuitant's life expectancy. Such "excludable amount" requires adjustment for annuity features such as payments certain and refund guarantees. The variable annuity payments in excess of this amount are taxable as ordinary income.

In the event of a complete redemption prior to the annuity payment date, any gain on the termination of the contract will be taxed as ordinary income. Under certain circumstances, the Owner may be eligible for the tax treatment accorded by Sections 1301-1305 of the Code dealing with income averaging. Partial redemptions, which in the aggregate exceed the investment in the contract, may be taxed as ordinary income. No payment by Life Insurance Company under the contracts described in this writing is eligible for capital gains treatment under existing law.

The operations of VAA-V are part of the total operation of Life Insurance Company and are not taxed separately, although the operations of VAA-V are treated separately for accounting and financial statement purposes and must be considered separately in computing Life Insurance Company's tax liability. Under present law, investment income and capital gains attributable to VAA-V and used in determining the value of accumulation units and the value of annuity units are not taxed. VAA-V is not affected by Federal income taxes paid by Life Insurance Company with respect to its other operations. Life Insurance Company reserves the right, however, to charge the variable annuity contract proportionately with any Federal income tax liability which may in the future result from maintenance of VAA-V or the variable annuity contracts. To the best of Life Insurance Company's knowledge, there is no current prospect of any such liability.

Investment gains of the Funds credited to VAA-V are not taxable to an Owner until received in the form of a cash redemption from an accumulation account or in the form of variable annuity payments. Cash redemptions will generally be taxed as ordinary income in the year received, but may be eligible for the income averaging provisions of the Internal Revenue Code (Secs. 1301-1305). Variable annuity payments are taxed as ordinary income in accordance with Section 72 of the Code. This section also provides that, to the extent of the Owner's investment in the contract (if any), a portion of each payment is excluded from gross income as a result of the investment in the contract. As a general rule, however, an Owner who receives variable annuity payments at the time of retirement will be in a lower income tax bracket due to reduced income and a larger exemption.

Public School Systems and Certain Tax-Exempt Organizations

Under Section 403(b) of the Code, employees of public school systems or certain tax-exempt organizations (See Section 501(c)(3) of the Code) are able to exclude from their gross income payments made under individual variable contracts. Such payments are excludable by the employees in the year made to the extent that the aggregate payments per year for such employees do not exceed the exclusion allowance set forth in Section 403(b)(2) of the Code.

Qualified Pension and Profit-Sharing Plans or Annuity Plans

Under present law, including the Employee Retirement Income Security Act of 1974, if an employee or his beneficiary receives a cash distribution equal to the total amount payable with respect to the employee, and such distribution is received after the employee has attained age 59½, or on the occasion of his death, retirement or other separation from the employer's service, or on the occasion of his death after separation from such service, the taxable portion of such distribution attributable to pre-1974 service will be taxed as a long-term capital gain. The balance of such taxable portion shall be taxable as ordinary income, subject to special income-averaging provisions or the employee may elect to apply the special income-averaging to the entire distribution.

If an employee's contract is surrendered and the preceding paragraph does not apply, the taxable portion would be includable in income for that year and, to the extent so included, would be taxed at ordinary rates, subject to possible benefits of income-averaging provisions available to taxpayers generally.

Should a qualified pension or profit-sharing plan or a qualified annuity plan lose its qualification or, in the case of a trust, its tax exemption, the employees may lose some of the tax benefits described in this writing.

Self-Employed Individuals Tax Retirement Act of 1962 ("HR-10")

The Self-Employed Individuals Tax Retirement Act of 1962, as amended, (popularly known as "HR-10") allows self-employed individuals to establish qualified pension and profit-sharing trusts and annuity plans to provide benefits for themselves and their employees.

Self-employed individuals, as well as their employees, are entitled to the same general tax treatment as employees under "Qualified Pension and Profit-Sharing Plans or Annuity Plans" in the case of a distribution equal to the total amount payable with respect to the employee. However, such treatment is not available with respect to self-employed individuals for distributions prior to age 59½, except in the case of death or disability.

The Code requires that HR-10 plans must prohibit payment to owner-employees prior to age 59½ (other than in the event of death or total disability) and such payment before age 59½ may generate certain penalties under the Code. Stipulated payments by, or on behalf of self-employed persons in excess of certain limitations may also result in certain penalties under the Code.

Under the Employee Retirement Income Security Act of 1974, defined benefit (as an alternative to defined contribution) plans may be used in HR-10 situations for tax years beginning after December 31, 1975, within limits prescribed under the applicable provisions of the Code, as amended.

Individual Retirement Account Plans

Under the Employee Retirement Income Security Act of 1974, an individual who is not an active participant under any of the types of plans described above or under a government pension plan, may establish an individual retirement account plan for the accumulation of retirement savings on a tax-deferred basis. The individual may himself establish and make payments into such a plan or this may be done for him by his employer or his union. The assets of such a plan may be invested in, among other things, annuity contracts including the variable annuity contracts offered by this writing. Annual contributions under such a plan are limited to the lesser of $1,500 or 15% of annual earned income ($1.750 if there is a nonworking spouse).

All distributions under these plans will be taxed as ordinary income (subject to possible benefits resulting from the income-averaging provisions available to taxpayers generally under the Code). Thus, these distributions will not be eligible for capital gains treatment or the special averaging rules applicable to lump sum distributions from some types of qualified plans. Moreover, any distribution (or other payment deemed to be a distribution under the Code) made before the individual attains age 59½ (except in the event of death or disability) will be a premature distribution and may result in certain adverse tax consequences. In addition, distributions must begin not later than the end of the year in which the individual attains age 70½.

It should be recognized that the above description of the Federal income tax status of amounts received under the individual variable annuity contracts is not exhaustive and does not purport to cover all situations. A qualified tax advisor should be consulted for complete information.

BENEFITS OF DIVERSIFIED VARIABLE ANNUITIES

You may put your money into your annuity either in one lump sum or through periodic payments. Then, depending on whether or not your retirement plan qualifies for special IRS tax treatment, your investment is placed in one of two pooled accounts: VA Account V or VA Account IV.

You choose where you want your money invested to best accommodate your objectives: in the Income Division, Growth Division, or any combination of both. If your objectives change, you can alter your investment mix at will.

At the end of your accumulation period, you choose how you'd like to receive your annuity (fixed payments or fluctuating monthly payments which will vary depending upon the performance of the Growth Division). These payments can extend for the rest of your life.

There are a number of specific benefits available outlined as follows:

1. Professional Investment Management which means sufficient knowledge of the market to select stocks or bonds for certain investment goals and to make crucial buy and sell decisions, the research capacity to constantly monitor securities markets, various industries and the economy, the resources and the quick reactions to trade in short-term money market instruments when necessary, and a full-time, qualified investment manager.

2. Tax Deferral, Partial Tax Relief to protect you from unnecessary current taxation; insulate you from future taxes; and make it possible to completely avoid many taxes.

Some tax savings are as follows:

A. Postpone paying current income tax on investment income.
   Switch investment portfolio as your objectives change . . . without paying taxes.

C. Take advantage of qualified retirement plan tax provisions in planning for your investment and tax objectives.

D. Help your beneficiaries keep more of your deferred investment income and net investment gains (subject, of course, to federal estate taxes).

E. Use your lower retirement tax bracket to pay tax on investment income and gains.

F. Convert a maturing endowment or annuity contract to an investment vehicle with ongoing tax advantages . . . without paying tax on the exchange.

G. If necessary, withdraw money you've invested in assets

that may have grown . . . without triggering current taxes on your gains.

H. Make sure your heirs avoid the high cost of probate and also reduce administration fees at your death.

3. Choice of Portfolios to Accomodate Different Investment Objectives so that you can deposit money into either the Growth Division, the Income Division, or a combination of both. Subsequently, you can change your investment mix at will for only five dollars.

INCOME DIVISION

OBJECTIVE: Current or deferred income

You might concentrate your contributions into the Income Division if your objectives call for:

1. A conservative long-range accumulation vehicle.
2. A bond-based portfolio to fund a long-term objective or a trust.
3. An investment vehicle geared to a qualified retirement plan's need for conservative investments.
4. A conservative product to invest for your long-term needs. One which avoids current taxes inherent in corporate bonds, certificates of deposit, savings accounts, etc.
5. A way to invest for any long-range financial objective where a generous level of current income and reasonable concern for the conservation of capital is important.

Through its investment in Income Fund, the Income Division seeks to provide a high level of current income by investing in a diversified portfolio of marketable debt securities. It is primarily concerned with securing a high return consistent with good management. Thus, the majority of the portfolio will consist of long-term debt securities.

GROWTH DIVISION

OBJECTIVE: Growth of capital

You might concentrate your contributions into the Growth Division if your objectives call for:

1. A possible long-term hedge against inflation.

2. An investment that is designed to grow as much as possible (given a reasonable risk) prior to retirement.
3. An investment in which to place either corporate dollars to fund the growth needs of a qualified retirement plan, or personal dollars for an Individual Retirement Account.
4. A deferred compensation investment for a corporation which seeks to enhance the total benefit package of its key executives.
5. A way to invest for any financial objective where growth of capital is important.

The Growth Division—through its investment in Growth Fund—invests in those securities which hold potential for long-term growth of capital. Common stocks are selected if they have shown a capacity for growth and flexibility. In addition, special emphasis is placed upon investing in corporations which are currently plowing back earnings with the purpose of producing greater sales and earnings over a longer period of time.

4. Flexibility to change direction if your investment objectives change is an important privilege.

Because your investment objectives could change, you've got to keep your options open. An Exchange Privilege from the Growth Division to the Income Division, and vice versa, provides this essential flexibility.

For only five dollars, you can exchange assets within the Annuity. This privilege enables you to avoid commissions, odd lot charges and transfer fees involved in converting securities, as well as any current capital gains or income taxes.

In addition, you can select a fixed annuity at any point, thus purchasing a product which guarantees your principal.

Finally, at the time you begin to receive annuity payments, you can tailor the size and duration of income payments to your specific needs.

5. Diversification to reduce the risk to your assets is also important.

For this reason, the Annuity invests in securities which represent a number of different industries, companies and geographic locations. These portfolio selections are purposely varied in an attempt to reduce risk and increase stability. It would be difficult—if not impossible—to obtain this type of broad diversification by yourself.

6. A retirement income you cannot outlive is critical because your assets should last as long as you do. With the Annuity, no matter how long you live, your annuity payments will continue. Retirement can be far more enjoyable when you know that you will have an income as long as you live.

RISKS OF A DIVERSIFIED VARIABLE ANNUITY

When you purchase a variable Annuity, you are investing in securities. With any security, an element of risk is involved, regardless of the underlying investment portfolio (bond or common stock), and no rate of return is guaranteed. Although units may be redeemed at any time, the redemption value may be more or less than the investor's cost.

TAX ASPECTS OF A DIVERSIFIED VARIABLE ANNUITY

The Annuity enables you to defer federal income taxation on ordinary income, dividends, and interest until you choose to receive them sometime in the future. (Long-term realized capital gains will be taxed at the insurer's tax rate, currently 28%.)

1. Defer paying income tax on investment income until you are in a lower tax bracket.

Example: An older investor in a high tax bracket selects the Income Division of the Annuity as the investment vehicle for his conservative investments. At retirement, his earned income drops substantially and he receives the deferred income from his investment at a new lower rate.

2. Name a person much younger than yourself as annuitant. If you die before he begins to receive annuity payments, you avoid paying income tax on investment income generated in the Annuity.

Example: A grandfather in a high income tax bracket purchases an Annuity, names his grandson as annuitant and retains ownership himself. Due to the difference in ages, the grandfather should die before his grandson is required to begin receiving annuity payments (at his age 85). The grandfather avoids current income taxation. And, as long as he maintains ownership, no gift tax liability is created.

3. Invest in conservative investments—such as corporate bonds—which let you reduce the risk assumed in your long-term investment portfolio. The yield from a conservative tax-deferred

882

investment may be just as attractive as that of a high-risk taxable investment.

Example: An investor in a 60% tax bracket requires a higher net rate of return than what is available—after taxes—on taxable investments. Previously, he had been forced to turn to growth investments. Now he can select conservative tax-deferred investments in the Annuity.

The Annuity permits the switch from its relatively conservative bond portfolio (Income Division) to its more aggressive common stock portfolio (Growth Division) or vice versa—without triggering current capital gains taxation.

4. Reduce the risk to long-term gains by shifting to the Income Division before you reach your objectives. (The Income Division's bond portfolio should fluctuate less than the Growth Division's equity-based portfolio).

Example: An investor deposits $50,000 in the Growth Division of the Annuity which, over the years, grows to $100,000. At this point, his objectives change and he decides to transfer his $100,000 into the more conservative Income Division of the Annuity. Such an exchange using any similar common stock investment vehicle would incur a substantial capital gains tax. But, with the Annuity, absolutely no tax is due at the time of transfer.

5. Transfer your assets logically and on a tax-deferred basis according to your changing objectives. Avoid having the concern of taxation make your investment decisions for you.

Example: An investor who has substantial assets in the Income Division (which has increased due to tax deferral on income and interest dividends) begins to feel more comfortable about long-term market and economic conditions. So he transfers all his assets to the Growth Division. With the Annuity, the investor is able to adjust his portfolio without any current cost in tax dollars.

6. To gain investment balance, deposit contributions into both the Income and Growth Divisions of the Annuity. Then transfer Income Division assets into the Growth Division by dollar cost averaging on a periodic basis. This transfer again avoids all current ordinary income taxation.

Example: An investor starts out conservatively, investing $3,000 a year, split equally between the Income and Growth Divisions. Five years pass and the account grows. He then periodically moves the entire Income Division account into the Growth Division. The dividends and interest (which would normally be taxed on an annual basis) are transferred to the Growth Division, and taxes continue to be deferred.

Qualified retirement plans may be invested in the Annuity, permitting assets to accumulate tax-deferred and be distributed on a tax-preferred basis.

7. When leaving a qualified retirement plan, either through termination or retirement, have the proceeds distributed into the Annuity . . . without generating taxes. Orient these assets towards specific short and long-term investment objectives.

Example: A high-salaried executive, age 48, leaves his employer. He has $120,000 in fully vested pension and profit-sharing benefits which he wants to take with him. In addition, he'd like to redirect their investment mix. So he asks the trustee of the plan to purchase an Annuity on his life, dividing his assets between the Growth and Income Divisions.

8. During working years, postpone receiving taxable income and continue to alter your investment mix to meet your personal needs.

Examples: A corporation creates a profit-sharing plan in which employees (both young and old) can select the Annuity's Growth and/or Income Divisions. The corporation takes a current tax deduction and the assets in the Annuity accumulate on a tax-deferred basis.

An employee not covered by a corporate qualified retirement plan decides to purchase an Individual Retirement Annuity. He invests the maximum $1,500 a year into a combination of both the Growth and Income Divisions of the Annuity.

If you die before you begin to receive your annuity, your beneficiary will not pay income tax on it until it is paid to him.

9. Invest in the Annuity with the sole purpose of accumulation, and leave assets to named heirs at death.

Example: A 50-year-old contractholder in a 70% tax bracket has an Annuity worth $250,000 at his death. $60,000 of income taxes on the Income Division have been deferred. His beneficiary completely avoids paying any current income tax on net proceeds until paid to him. (Especially opportune since he is in a 50% tax bracket.)

10. Reduce the size of your estate by liquidating assets, but at the same time, leave your Annuity intact. Dollars earned in

the Annuity during your high tax bracket years may be given to a beneficiary at your death and will usually be taxed at a lower estate tax bracket.

Example: A contractholder in poor health gradually liquidates his common stock portfolio to meet income needs and gives other real property to his family and charity. He does not touch his Annuity. These dollars, which were tax deferred during the years he was in a 60% bracket, will most likely be taxed at a much lower estate tax rate after his death. (Thus, his beneficiaries will receive a much larger asset.)

The total amount of your Annuity contributions will be returned to you—tax free—during your annuity period (assuming you live out your normal life expectancy and the underlying investments in the Annuity maintain their value). Taxable income will be spread out during your lifetime as an annuitant, taking advantage of the probability of a lower income tax bracket. In addition, if you live beyond your normal life expectancy, you will receive a portion of your continuing annuity payments tax free.

11. Defer high tax dollars to lower future brackets.

Example: An Annuity contractholder, age 60, elects to retire. The earnings on his Annuity contract—which were deferred during his 50% tax bracket years—can now be taxed in his 30% retirement tax bracket and spread out over the course of his lifetime.

12. Tailor specific annuity payout options to specific tax and income needs.

Example: Having purchased an Annuity contract many years ago, an investor reaches retirement with the Annuity and other investments generating taxable income. Now, because he is anxious to reduce his income tax liability and the overall size of his estate, he makes gifts of income-yielding securities. In addition, he puts the Annuity on a joint and survivor basis to provide the bulk of the required income needs for both himself during his lifetime and his spouse thereafter. In this way, the tax impact of deferred income and net gains is now spread over two lifetimes.

An Annuity can be purchased . . . without current tax . . . with the proceeds from a maturing endowment contract, annuity contract, insurance contract in which the cash value exceeds the face value, or any combination of these products.

Normally, gains from these products are taxed upon liquidation or transfer.

13. Adapt maturing assets to meet current investment and tax goals, while maintaining the tax-deferred build-up inherent in fixed insurance products.

Example: An investor notes that an endowment contract which he purchased many years ago will soon mature. This means he must pay income tax on everything above his investment in the contract. (Assuming a $10,000 gain and a 50% tax bracket, a $5,000 tax bill would be due.) However, he avoids constructive receipt—and therefore current taxation—by exchanging his maturing endowment for an Annuity. (The original income tax basis remains the same.)

14. Combine various insurance-created assets under one tax-deferred vehicle; thereby avoiding current taxation on any of these assets.

Example: An elderly investor has several deferred fixed annuities which he needs to convert to maximum income-producing vehicles. Assuming a $20,000 gain, a 25% tax bracket would trigger a $5,000 tax bill if these contracts were surrendered. Realizing this, the investor exchanges his contracts for a diversified Annuity. This entire procedure occurs without tax incidence, and enables the investor to generate income by receiving the annuity or by withdrawing from his basis. (The original income tax basis remains the same.)

15. Convert maturing endowment contracts into investment assets without being taxed at a growing tax bracket.

Example: An investor with an endowment contract about to mature needs capital for investing in a new business. Yet he wishes to keep his remaining assets in a growth-oriented position. First, he withdraws the original basis in the endowment contract and invests this in the business. Then, without constructive receipt, he transfers any gains to an Annuity and invests them in the Growth Division.

16. Transfer accumulated assets which are no longer generating insurance coverage to the Annuity, and then defer them until the owner's death. In this way, you avoid income tax on these assets during both the insurance and investment stages.

Example: A successful retired individual, age 65, with a high ordinary income tax bracket due to deferred compensation, retirement income and investment income, has an Insurance Income at age 65 contract with $80,000 in accumulated values and a tax basis of $50,000. His 40% tax bracket would normally generate a $12,000 tax on constructive receipt of his insurance income assets. One way he avoids this tax bill is to transfer his assets to the Annuity. By doing this, he continues to defer income taxes.

Before you begin receiving annuity payments, you may make withdrawals from your Annuity up to the amount of your original investment (your basis) . . . without any current tax whatsoever . . . even if your assets have grown. (Amounts in excess of your basis would be taxable if taken.)

17. Withdraw the basis of your investment at will without triggering a current taxable event.

Example: An investor with both education and ultimate estate accumulation objectives periodically deposits a total of $50,000 into an Annuity, naming his son as annuitant. During the 15 years prior to the education need, his Annuity assets grow to $80,000. Because naming a younger annuitant enables him to defer receiving income until age 85 or longer, he can withdraw up to $50,000 (his basis) without taxation during the educational period, and leave the rest of his Annuity assets to accumulate for ultimate distribution to his heirs.

18. With the Annuity, choose when you want to receive cash. (Unlike municipals and corporate bonds which give you no choice and automatically generate non-deferrable income.)

Example: A highly-paid salaried executive, having accumulated significant assets through deferral of income tax in an Annuity, wishes to take advantage of an investment opportunity in vacation real estate property. In his 60% tax bracket, he cannot afford to trigger any tax on unearned income. Without tax cost, he withdraws $50,000 worth of basis from his Annuity, leaving the remaining values on a tax-deferred basis.

19. Use corporate assets with maximum efficiency to increase corporate tax deductions, while providing tax benefits to key corporate executives.

Example: A corporation has accumulated $100,000 in the Annuity's Income Division for a senior executive about to retire. Due to the tax deferral nature of the contract, the corporation has been sheltered from high corporate taxes during the accumulation phase. Now the corporation must pay the retired executive a stipulated sum over a 10-year period of time.

Because of the corporation's high current tax bracket, it elects not to trigger an annuity option. Instead, it withdraws its basis over the course of a few years; thereby generating a current corporate tax deduction without triggering any tax on the dollars withdrawn, and deferring corporate income tax on the remaining assets. Even during the ultimate payout years when the corporation will be receiving taxable income from the contract in order to pay the executive, any corporate tax liability caused by these assets being paid out is offset by an immediate tax deduction.

20. Stagger the withdrawal of basis to coincide with high and low taxable years to permit the maximum utilization of investment assets.

Example: In good years, a manufacturer's representative with extremely cyclical earnings puts away a significant percentage of his compensation into the Annuity. In poor years, non-taxable withdrawals of his basis support his standard of living and keep his taxable income low.

Because of its unique insurance-investment nature, the Annuity allows a beneficiary designation. At your death, this avoids the high cost of probate and reduces administration fees, which combined, normally range between 3% and 10%. This designation also eliminates delay in receiving proceeds and provides heirs with cash assets during the probate period.

21. Increase tax deductions with non-taxable dollars... without decreasing your standard of living.

Example: An investor in a high income tax bracket who has $200,000 invested in an Annuity wants to maximize his tax deductions during his peak earning years. During high tax years, he reaches into his Annuity, withdraws up to 30% of his taxable income, and donates it to a local charity. His standard of living has not been reduced and his income has not been depleted by taxes.

22. Avoid probate and provide liquidity and income for beneficiaries.

Example: An Annuity contractholder, age 74, dies, leaving most assets in a form which will pass through probate. An exception is the Annuity which has a beneficiary designation. Because the Annuity can be drawn upon by the beneficiary at will, it provides maximum liquidity and an immediate

income. Assuming a 5% probate fee on a $100,000 invest-
ment, the Annuity saves the beneficiary $5,000.

23. Provide beneficiaries with instant income to prevent
them from being forced to increase their personal income tax
by switching from personal growth oriented assets to income
producing assets.

Example: Having purchased an Annuity over the years
leading up to retirement, an uninsurable investor dies, leaving
his wife, age 60, as beneficiary. Most assets of the estate were
originally very aggressively invested. If converted to income
producing investments, they would generate taxable yields to
the wife. As the beneficiary of the Annuity, the wife can
choose to receive Annuity income payments (largely return
of principal), or withdraw assets from the contract to meet
living expenses—without any current income tax liability.

OTHER TAX CONSIDERATIONS

No tax planning tool works perfectly for every investor . . .
the Annuity is no exception. It can work well for you only if
you understand its advantages and limitations.

Before investing in the Annuity, you should consider the
following:

1. The Annuity is best used as a retirement tool or as an
investment that will be passed on to the heirs, *not* as an
accumulation investment that will be totally liquidated for a
specific need at a specific date. When cashed in totally, the
contract generates ordinary income tax liability on any realized
net capital gains, as well as on all ordinary income which has
been deferred during the accumulation period. To counter this
disadvantage, the Annuity investor may either cash in the
contract in a year when personal taxes are reduced, or simply
withdraw the basis of the contract. Of course, income averaging
is available, and for many investors, will reduce the tax impact
significantly.

2. Any capital gains in either the growth or income division
of the non-qualified Annuity are paid at the insurance company's tax rate of 28%.

3. Withdrawals up to the basis in an Annuity can be achieved
without taxable incidence. However, a pattern of partial
periodic withdrawals over a period of time may be viewed as a
payment of an annuity within the meaning of Section 72 of the
Internal Revenue Code, and therefore, may be taxed as normal

annuity payments, with part of the income being excludable as a return of basis and part of the income being received as ordinary income. Therefore, a specific withdrawal to meet a personal need as it arises is desirable.

APPROPRIATE IRS TAX REFERENCES

The following tax references support the tax advantages illustrated in this writing.
A. I.R.C. Sec. 801-820; I.R.C. Sec. 72.
B. I.R.C. Sec. 1031; I.R.C. Sec. 1035; Reg. Sec. 1.1031(d)-1.
C. I.R.C. Sec. 402, 403; Reg. Sec. 1.402(a)-1; I.R.C. Sec. 408(b).
D. I.R.C. Sec. 72; Rev. Rul. 70-143, 1970-1 C.B. 167; I.R.C. Sec. 1014; Reg. Sec. 1.1014-1.
E. I.R.C. Sec. 72; Reg. Sec. 1.72-4.
F. I.R.C. Sec. 1035(a); Rev. Rul. 68-235, 1968-1 C.B. 360; Rev. Rul 72-358, 1972-2 C.B. 473; I.R.C. Sec. 1031; Reg. Sec. 1.1031(d)-1; Reg. Sec. 1.1035-1: Rev. Rul. 73-124, 1973-1 C.B. 200.
G. I.R.C. Sec. 72.
H. Individual State Probate exclusions.

A diversified variable annuity can be important because most people eventually retire. At that time, some other source or sources of income will be required to fill the void created when our *earned income* stops. Savings accounts, pensions and life insurance will help us to accomplish this by providing a fixed amount of income.

Although there may be periods when the opposite will occur, the variable annuity has the potential for matching rising costs over the years. What is more, it's an investment vehicle designed to provide an income which can't be outlived.

GLOSSARY OF TERMS

ACCUMULATION UNIT—A measure used to determine the value of an accumulation account.

ANNUITANT—Any natural person for whom a variable annuity has been effected under the individual variable annuity contract.

ANNUITY PAYMENT DATE—The date an annuity is effected and the same day of each month thereafter.

ANNUITY PAYMENTS—Periodic payments made to an annuitant pursuant to an annuity contract.

DEFERRED CONTRACT—A variable annuity which provides for annuity payments to commence at some future date. Included are periodic payment deferred contracts and single payment deferred contracts.

FIXED-DOLLAR ANNUITY—A series of periodic payments, the amounts of which do not vary with investment experience.

FUND SHARES—Shares of Growth Fund, or Income Fund, or shares of any other registered open-end investment company substituted therefor.

GROWTH DIVISION—The division of a Variable Annuity Account the assets of which are invested in shares of Growth Fund (or any investment company substituted therefor).

IMMEDIATE CONTRACT—A variable annuity contract which provides for annuity payments to commence immediately rather than at some future date.

INCOME DIVISION—The division of a Variable Annuity Account the assets of which are invested in shares of Income Fund (or any investment company substituted therefor).

PERIODIC PAYMENT CONTRACT—A variable annuity contract which requires that payments be made in periodic installments rather than in a single sum.

SEPARATE ACCOUNT—The separate account (Variable Annuity Account) established by Life Insurance Company for payments under the contracts offered herein.

SINGLE PAYMENT CONTRACT—A variable annuity contract which requires that the total payment be paid in a single sum rather than in periodic installments. Included are single payment immediate contracts and single payment deferred contracts.

VALUATION DATE—Each date as of which the accumulation unit values and annuity unit value are determined.

VALUATION PERIOD—The period from the time the accumulation unit values and the annuity unit value are determined as of one valuation date to the time such values are determined as of the next valuation date.

VARIABLE ANNUITY—A series of periodic payments, the amounts of which will increase or decrease to reflect the investment experience of the Growth Division of a Variable Annuity Account.

INVESTMENT ANNUITY

An interesting tax shelter which is under close IRS scrutiny is the Investment Annuity.

The Investment Annuity is an insurance contract which consists of wrapping an annuity contract around a separate portfolio created by the contract holder. Generally, the portfolio consists of liquid investments such as stocks, bonds, savings accounts and money market instruments. This annuity differs from the traditional fixed or variable annuity in which the assets backing up the insurance contract are assets held and managed by the insurance company. The Investment Annuity has been structured as a variable annuity where the contract holder constructs the investment portfolio. Typical annuity taxation applies to this product with ordinary income tax deferred due to the special tax status of life insurance companies on interest, dividends and short-term gains. Long-term realized capital gains are taxed, and unrealized gains are reserved for at the insurance company rate. During the accumulation phase, the insurance company receives a sales load and specified percentage of the assets in the contract holder's asset fund.

Pros — Choice of investment vehicle—an advantage to a very sophisticated investor.
  — Tax deferred features.
  — Ability to choose own assumed investment return from the range of 3.5 to 9%.
Cons — No professional management.
  — An asset charge during accumulation even though the insurance company does not provide asset management.
  — IRS risk, Inside tax deferred build up is based on an IRS private ruling.
  — Limited mortality expense guarantees.
  — Long-term gains still taxed at insurance company rate.

THE INVESTMENT ANNUITY CONCEPT

The development of the Investment Annuity has put a whole new perspective on the formulation of financial and retirement plans. It offers all the recognized tax advantages and other benefits of traditional annuities, but overcomes the one major drawback that has restricted their use—the lack of investment flexibility available to individual policyowners.

Under the Investment Annuity each policyowner directs his individual investment program within the favorable tax framework of an annuity, and can change investments at any time during the policy term to take advantage of new opportunities or meet changing personal requirements. The value of each annuitant's benefits reflects directly the performance of his individual Investment Annuity custodian account.

This has been achieved by separating the responsibility for the two components technically essential to the provision of all annuities. Under the Investment Annuity the insurance company provides the annuity framework and operations plus the actuarial mechanism for pooling the risks of annuitant longevity. However, the funds used to support (and determine the value of) annuitant benefits are separated from the insurance company and held by a third party custodian and invested according to the policyowner's instructions.

The Investment Annuity is as relevant to those seeking the most efficient way of accumulating their savings and investments as to those wanting to provide income for themselves or their dependents. It can, in many cases, be used to increase or enhance the value of existing arrangements and investments.

The Investment Annuity is taxed as a new form of variable annuity for Federal Tax purposes.

HOW THE INVESTMENT ANNUITY WORKS

Types of Policies

The Investment Annuity is available as both "qualified" and "non-qualified" policies—and in immediate and deferred form. The qualified policies enjoy full tax-sheltered status, thus accounts can be managed strictly on investment considerations. In the case of non-qualified policies interest and dividends

893

accumulate tax-deferred within each annuitant's custodian account; however, if and when capital gains are realized a deduction is made at the insurance company's corporate rate.

The Role of the Custodian

The Custodian, who must be a Bank or Trust Company, plays a fundamental role without which the Investment Annuity could not exist. Upon receipt of annuity purchase contributions to an Investment Annuity the Custodian sets up an individual custodian account for each annuitant and, after payment of relevant policy premiums to the insurance company, invests the monies according to the policyowner's instructions.

The investments purchased are held by the Custodian for individual annuitants in a nominee name. The Custodian's other responsibilities include the collection and retirement of dividends and income, regular valuation of annuitants' accounts, the provision of periodic reports and normal accounting functions.

Periodically, the Custodian pays premiums to the insurance company from this custodian account. The premiums and the annuitant's benefits are based on the market value of the account, and will reflect changes in its value.

Custodian fees on a published schedule, which can be revised with three months' notice but not more often than annually, are paid out of individual accounts.

Investment Flexibility

At all times while an Investment Annuity remains in force, the policyowner (or his advisor) controls and can change the investments in the Investment Annuity custodian account. Assets to be held are selected from the very broad insurance company Accepted Assets List.

The policyowner may already hold suitable assets such as Mutual Funds, quoted Securities, Savings and Loan Accounts, so that he can still follow the investment program which he may have already chosen.

It is important to recognize, however, that the time taken to handle transactions is longer than the time expected for such transactions handled independently by stockbrokers or savings institutions. This is due to the necessary custodian controls and the additional processing involved. Thus, the Investment Annuity custodian account is not suitable for rapid trading.

Investment Control. The simplest and most popular method used to direct investments is the Investment Designation. Under this, the Custodian is given instructions to invest in asset(s) pre-selected by the policyowner. These instructions can be altered simply by filing a change of Investment Designation with the insurance company, for forwarding to the Custodian.

Under the alternative method—the Trading Authorization, the Custodian is directed by the policyowner to open a cash account with a brokerage firm and to notify that firm whenever a pre-established cash balance becomes available. It is used primarily for assets such as stocks and bonds where the policyowners or his broker wishes to exercise more control over the timing of particular transactions.

Transactions are carried out as soon as a minimum amount of money established by the Custodian becomes available.

The Deferred or Accumulation Period

During this period all investments accumulate within the custodian account and the annuitant receives no income payments. However, the Investment Annuity can be surrendered in whole or in part at any time.

If the annuitant dies during this period, the beneficiary may receive (or elect to receive) either a lump sum benefit or any of the annuity options outlined on the next page. Investment Annuity contracts, like other insurance contracts, bypass the expenses, delays and publicity of probate when a beneficiary, other than the annuitant's estate, is named.

The Immediate or Income Payment Period

The age when the annuitant can start receiving benefits varies depending on the provisions of each particular contract. Income payments are paid monthly by the insurance company and increase or decrease annually to reflect the investment performance of each annuitant's individual custodian account—hence the ruling that the Investment Annuity is a series of one year term, fixed-dollar annuities, renewing annually for life.

Choice of three types of income payment. There are basically three types of income payment from which annuitants can choose to suit their individual circumstances.

1. A Period Certain. Under this option the annuitant elects to withdraw the value of his Investment Annuity account over a period of years selected by himself. If death occurs before the end of the chosen period, the remaining monthly benefits are paid to the beneficiary.
2. A Life Annuity. Income payments are guaranteed for the life of the annuitant. In addition, a minimum number of payments is normally guaranteed so that if death occurs before receipt of the guaranteed number of payments the beneficiary receives the remaining payments.
3. A Joint Life and Last Survivor Annuity. This is similar to option 2 except that payments are guaranteed for the annuitant's lifetime and also for the added lifetime of someone else such as a spouse.

Taxation. The taxation of income payments depends on the individual plan. The general principle is that all contributions paid out of previously taxed dollars are recovered without further taxation. All other payments are taxed as income in the year of receipt.

There may be a liability for Federal Estate and/or Federal Gift Tax depending on individual plans and circumstances.

TYPES OF INVESTMENT ANNUITY OFFERED

Non-Qualified Plans

The Investment Annuity Policy is available to the general public both as a deferred and immediate contract. It can be a particularly important part of an individual's financial planning. Interest and dividends earned within the custodian account accumulate without deduction of current income taxes. Benefits can be taken in a lump sum or as a number of partial surrenders during the accumulation period—or as one of the annuity options in the income payment period.

Qualified Plans

401 Plan Distributions. The Investment Annuity can be used most attractively for annuity policy distributions from existing "tax-qualified" pension, profit sharing and thrift plans. Rather than experience the tax consequences arising from a lump sum cash distribution at retirement or termination of employment, employees may elect to receive their funds as an Investment Annuity. The employee gains investment control and investment growth accumulates under a full tax-shelter. There may be Gift and Estate Tax advantages too.

Tax-Sheltered Annuities. The Tax-Sheltered Investment Annuity offers to full and part-time employees of certain employees) all the benefits that have made Tax-Sheltered Annuities under Section 403(b) a popular method of providing for future income plus the investment control that is a feature of our Investment Annuity plans.

Keogh or HR-10 Plans

The insurance company has developed a variety of plans which have been pre-approved by the IRS for ease of adoption. With the change in tax deductible limits in 1974, the adoption of HR-10 Plans will be even more attractive.

THE INSURANCE COMPANY'S ACCEPTED ASSETS LIST

Subject to meeting the standards of acceptability set out below, investments in the following classes of assets are normally acceptable for an Investment Annuity account.

1. Securities listed and traded on the New York Stock Exchange, the American Stock Exchange or regional stock exchanges.
2. Securities listed on the NASDAQ System.
3. Shares of an investment company registered pursuant to the Investment Company Act of 1940 (mutual funds).
4. Obligations of or guaranteed by the United States government, the Canadian government, any state, or municipality or governmental subdivision of a state. Except Series E and H Bonds.
5. Certificates of Deposit. (Only in U.S. Banks or Savings & Loan Associations.)
6. Savings Accounts. (Only in U.S. Banks or Savings & Loan Associations.)
7. New bond or debt issues which may reasonably be expected to be listed on an exchange regulated by the Securities Exchange Act of 1934 or which otherwise comply with standards of acceptability set down below.

8. Commercial Paper and Bankers Acceptances.
9. Credit Union accounts.
10. Term Life Insurance.
11. Cash, temporarily, pending a choice of investments by the annuitant.
12. Such other classes of assets which meet the standards of acceptability set out below as determined by the insurance company.

A. A Regular Market

There must be a regular market in the asset. This requires the asset to have a readily ascertainable market available to the insurance company from reports of regular market trading, or established by recurring commercial transactions not involving trading in the asset.

B. Administrative Compatibility

The administrative requirements for each asset, are where relevant, for the institution managing the asset, will be reviewed to insure comptability with the administrative procedures established by the insurance company with the Custodian for investing in and accounting for the asset.

Licensed Agents. The purchase of an Investment Annuity may be made only through a licensed life insurance agent. Purchase of such an annuity and the investment of account assets are separate transactions.

The life insurance company does not sell investments, nor offer investment advice, endorse any investment within the Accepted Assets List, practice law, give tax advice or act as an accountant.

Tax Treatment

Insurance Companies are taxed under Subchapter L of the Internal Revenue Code. In general insurance companies do not pay federal income tax on ordinary income earned on Life Insurance Reserves as defined in Section 801(b) of the code. Specifically this policy qualifies for the favorable tax treatment under 801(g) of the code. However, long term capital gains are taxed at the insurance companies' corporate rate.

Opinion varies as to how short term capital gains will be treated. Most authorities interpret 801(g)(4): "Investment yield

. . . if . . . the net short-term capital gains exceeds the net long-term capital loss, such excess shall be allocated between clauses (i) and (ii) of subparagraph (a) in proportion to the respective contributions to such excess of the items taken into account under each such clause" to mean that short term capital gains will be excluded from taxation. It is the insurance company's intention to not pay this tax unless directed to do so by the IRS. In such case the tax will be paid and the appropriate deduction will be made from the custodian account. Section 802 should also be studied by tax advisors contemplating this policy.

When payments under the contract begin they will be taxed to the annuitant under Section 72 of the code. In general the investment in the contract is returned without tax consequence. Annuity payments are taxed as ordinary income (with a dividend exclusion) and the net taxable amount will be computed by dividing "the investment in the contract" by the "expected return" (the undiscounted aggregate of the amounts expected to be received).

Ownership under the policy can be multiple. This makes the policy ideal for gifting both to individuals and charities: for example, a remainder interest could go to a charity with income accruing to an individual for a fixed period or life.

The placing of assets belonging to an owner into the account is a sale of the asset to the insurance company and will trigger a gain or a loss. An exception to this is the treatment of copyrights: the sale of a copyright by the creator generates ordinary income.

Every case is different. But as a general set of rules the following usually apply:

Every asset should be examined to see if it is divisible. Equities should normally remain outside the annuity especially if they are likely to be sold at a gain during the owner's lifetime. Items with intangible write offs, depreciation and depletion should not normally be included. Dividends, interest, rents, royalties and leasehold payments should go into the annuity.

This tax shelter is valuable to the investor who desires to control the choice of investment vehicle in an annuity. If the IRS permits the present favorable tax situation to continue, more sophisticated investors will be drawn to the Investment Acnuity.

INDIVIDUAL RETIREMENT ACCOUNTS

In the Pension Reform Act of 1974 Congress sought to expand the benefits of pensions to people who had no pension or profit sharing plan. The result was the Individual Retirement Account. The following questions and answers deal with the specifics of this benefit.

What Is an "IRA"?

An IRA is an Individual Retirement Annuity or an Individual Retirement Account. The "annuity" phrase is used only when life insurance company contracts are being purchased by the individual, while the "account" term comes into play with programs funded through mutual funds, savings banks, and government bonds.

Who Can Buy IRA's?

Anyone who has earned income and is not having contributions made for him or her during the taxable year by a qualified plan or tax-sheltered annuity. Participants who are 'excessed' out of a plan are eligible, unless that plan is a profit sharing or target benefit plan.

What Can Be Used for IRA's?

Fixed annuities, variable annuities, endowment-type contracts, special US government retirement bonds, savings accounts and mutual funds. Savings accounts and mutual funds must be held in trust or custodial arrangement carrying the legally required strictures, while annuities and endowment contracts may be used without this requirement, if the restrictions are incorporated into the contract.

Are Earnings on the Contributions Tax Free?

As in other retirement plans, contributions are deductible and earnings on the contributions accumulate tax free until retirement or distribution.

How Much Can Be Contributed to, and Deducted for, IRA's?

The maximum contribution and deduction is 15% of earned income or $1,500, whichever is less, except for rollover situations, and regular annual contributions in excess of the maximum cannot be accepted. Regular, annual contributions must be in cash. An individual with earned income can contribute up to a total of $1,750 to separate IRA's for each spouse ($875 to each IRA) or to an IRA which has one subaccount for the husband and another for the wife.

What Happens If an Excess Contribution Should Occur?

The excess amount is subject to a 6% nondeductible, Federal excise tax, additional to normal income taxation, payable each year that the excess is not corrected. Correction may be made by having the excess returned within time for filing the return or by reducing the subsequent year's contribution, *in which latter case the excise tax is still imposed for that first year.*

Where Do "Rollovers" Come Into the Picture?

Essentially, rollovers are a means of deferring taxation; effectively, they are the distributed assets which had accumulated in another qualified plan, and which are then recontributed to an IRA within 60 days of distribution to be a nontaxable event for the recipient. The rollover assets must represent only employer monies not previously taxed (zero basis dollars) and, except for the mutual funds, will be accepted only in cash. Although making a regular, annual contribution and rollover contribution during the same year is all right, each type of contribution must be made to a separate IRA plan. The product being purchased might be the same, but the plans have to be distinct and the assets must be held in separate accounts or contracts.

Rollovers between IRA's are permissible, but may occur only once every three years, if the tax-sheltered status is to be maintained. Rollovers are permitted from terminated pension and profit sharing plans while the individual is still employed.

May the IRA Assets Be Withdrawn?

Yes, but unless the IRA assets are rolled-over or the individual dies or becomes disabled, any such distribution will be considered a premature distribution if occurring prior to an individual's reaching Age 59 1/2. Also, IRA assets borrowed, or used as collateral, will constitute a premature distribution to the extent of the amount of the loan.

What's the Penalty for Premature Distributions?

A 10% nondeductible, Federal excise tax will be imposed on the amount deemed distributed, in addition to the normal income taxation.

Is There a Point at Which Distributions Must Begin?

Yes, the law requires that distributions begin no later than the end of the tax year in which the participant attains Age 70 1/2, but there is no requirement that a lump sum distribution be made at this point. Distributions, so long as they begin at the required time, may be extended over the life of the individual or the individual and spouse, or over a period not longer than the life expectancy of the individual or of the individual and spouse.

What's the Penalty for Not Initiating Distributions by 70 1/2?

A 50% nondeductible, Federal excise tax is imposed on the difference between what should have been paid out and what actually was distributed.

Can Contributions Continue After Age 70 1/2?

No contributions may be made after the beginning of the year in which the individual attains Age 70 1/2.

Can an Employer Elect to Sponsor an IRA?

Yes, employer sponsored IRA's are permitted in lieu of another plan, but it should be noted that many of the new fiduciary and reporting and disclosure requirements then apply. A trust arrangement must also be used for *all* such plans.

Can an Individual File his Own IRA for IRS Determination?

An individual is not permitted to do so, but employers sponsoring IRA's may apply for determination, and institutional sponsors (such as insurance companies), may file for determination on prototype plans.

The 1976 Tax Reform Act provides an exclusion from the gross estate for the value of an annuity receivable by a beneficiary under an individual retirement account or an individual retirement annuity, to the extent an income tax deduction was allowable when the contribution to such account or annuity, was made. The 1976 Tax Reform Act provides comparable exclusions for gift tax purposes. However, the exclusion from the estate tax for these items and all qualified plans will not apply to lump-sum distributions. This provision applies to the estates of decedents dying after December 31, 1976, and to transfers by gift made after December 31, 1976.

"Any person" includes employees as individuals, sole proprietors and their employees, partners and the partnership's employees, and corporate employees.

"Compensation" is defined as wages, salaries, professional fees, commissions, tips, bonuses, or earned income that is based on a percentage of the profits. It also includes the income earned by self-employed individuals.

An "active participant" is one for whom, at any time during the taxable year, (1) benefits are accrued under a qualified plan on his/her behalf, or (2) an employer is obligated to contribute to a qualified plan on his/her behalf, or (3) an employer would have been obligated to contribute to a qualified plan on his/her behalf if any contributions were made to the plan (i.e., as in a Profit Sharing plan).

"Qualified Plan" includes any of the following: a qualified pension or profit sharing plan; an HR-10; a qualified annuity plan; a qualified bond purchase plan; a governmental retirement plan (e.g., the Federal Civil Service Retirement Plan is considered a government plan, but Social Security and railroad retirement plan are not.)

"Retirement Age" an individual may fund for a retirement benefit commencing at any age from 59 1/2 to 70 1/2.

Formulae

— Total compensation is used for IRA's.
— Compensation may be figured on a calendar year basis only.

– An individual may vary the amount of his contribution from year to year.

– An individual may skip contributions in any year.

Vesting

– The entire interest of an individual in his account is nonforfeitable.

Eligibility

– An individual is eligible if he/she is a wage earner and covered by a qualified retirement plan.

When an Individual Changes Employers

– As long as the individual is not covered by a qualified retirement plan, he/she may continue contributions to the IRA.

– If the individual is later included in another retirement plan, the IRA plan stays intact and any earnings accumulate tax free—even though he/she is no longer eligible to make annual contributions to it.

– If at some future time the individual covered by an employer's retirement program leaves that employer— he/she may transfer the vested benefits tax free to an IRA if done within 60 days after receipt.

He/she may change investment vehicles within IRA without penalty not more frequently than once every three years.

Individual Retirement Account Technical Changes under The Revenue Act of 1978.

Extension of period for making individual retirement plan contributions.

Prior law

Prior law allowed an individual a deduction from gross income for certain contributions to an IRA (an individual retirement account, an individual retirement annuity, or a retirement bond) secs. 219 and 229). Under the Employee Retirement Income Security Act of 1974 (ERISA) the contributions for a particular taxable year, in order to be deductible, had to be made by the close of the year. The Tax Reform Act of 1976 extended the time for making deductible contributions and establishing an IRA for a year to 45 days after the close of the year.

Reasons for change

The Congress concluded that it is reasonable to allow an individual to establish an IRA and to make contributions to that IRA up to the due date for filing the tax return for the year in question. This rule will allow greater flexibility in planning and will give individuals more time to obtain needed information. (Since IRA contribution limits are based on 15 percent of an individual's compensation includible in gross income, the individual will have to ascertain this amount before he can know his contribution limit.)

Explanation of provision

The Act extends the date by which an individual can make deductible contributions to an IRA for a taxable year. Under the Act such contributions will be deductible for a year if they are made on account of that year and on or before the date prescribed by law for filing the individual's Federal income tax return for that year (including extensions). As under prior law, the individual will be permitted to establish an IRA on the same date on which he or she made the contribution, so the extension of the time for making a contribution to an IRA applies to the establishment of the IRA as well as to deductions.

Effective date

The provision applies to taxable years beginning after December 31, 1977.

Deduction of excess contributions in subsequent year for which there is an unused limitation.

Prior law

An individual is allowed a deduction from gross income for certain contributions to an IRA (secs. 219 and 220). The maximum deduction allowable for a taxable year generally is the lesser of 15 percent of compensation includible in gross income or $1,500. In the case of an individual who has a nonworking spouse, the maximum deduction allowable is the lesser of 15 percent of compensation includible in gross income or $1,750 provided the individual shares the contribution equally with his or her spouse. An amount contributed which does not qualify as a rollover contribution and which is in excess of the maximum deduction allowable is an "excess contribution."

An excess contribution is subject to an annual 6 percent excise tax unless corrected. In order to correct an excess contribution, an individual must either (1) receive a distribution of the excess amount, or (2) contribute an amount in a future year which falls short of the maximum deduction allowable for that year, in which case the excess contribution is deemed to be corrected to the extent of the shortfall. However, under prior law, the deduction for the year did not include the amount of the shortfall.

Reasons for change

If an individual is entitled to contribute $1,000 to an IRA in each of two years and does so, the individual is allowed a $1,000 tax deduction for each of those two years, for a total deduction of $2,000. However, under prior law, if the individual contributed $1,500 in the first year, then corrected this mistake by contributing only $500 in the second year (instead of the $1,000 he was entitled to contribute), his total deduction was only $1,500 ($1,000 for year one and $500 for year two). The Congress believed that this result was inappropriate. Therefore, the Act allows the individual a make-up deduction (of $500 under the facts given above) for the year the excess contribution is corrected.

Explanation of provision

The Act allows an individual a deduction from gross income for a taxable year where he corrects a previous excess contribution to an IRA by contributing less than the maximum amount allowable as a deduction for the year. The maximum deduction allowed by the Act for a correcting an undercontribution is the amount of the previous excess contribution. For example, if an individual was entitled to make a contribution of $1,000 for 1978 and 1979, an excess contribution of $400 for 1978 could be corrected by making a contribution of only $600 for 1979 ($400 less than the individual's maximum permissible contribution) and the individual would be entitled to a $1,000 deduction for 1978 and for 1979.

If the individual erroneously took a deduction in a previous year for any part of the excess contribution and the period for assessing a deficiency for the previous year has expired, the amount allowed as a deduction under the Act would be correspondingly reduced.

The Act provides a transitional rule with respect to amounts of excess contributions made up by undercontributions for years prior to 1978. The rule allows a one-time catchup deduction from gross income for those amounts for 1978 rather than requiring amended returns to be filed for each year of undercontribution. For example, if an individual entitled to make a $1,500 contribution for 1978 had made an excess contribution of $800 for 1976, and $300 for 1977, he could correct both excess contributions (totaling $1,100) by making only a $400 contribution for 1978 and would be entitled to a $1,500 deduction for that year.

Effective date

The provision applies to taxable years beginning after December 31, 1975.

Additional period to rectify certain excess contributions.

Prior law

A 6-percent excise tax is imposed annually on an excess contribution to an IRA. An excess contribution is a contribution which exceeds the maximum deductible contribution and which does not qualify as a rollover contribution. Under prior law, however, the 6-percent excise tax was not imposed on the excess contributed in a year if (1) such amount did not exceed the excess of $1,500 ($1,750 in the case of a spousal IRA) over the amount allowable as a deduction for the year, (2) such amount, and the earnings thereon, were withdrawn on or before the filing date for the individual's income tax return (including extensions) for the year, and (3) the individual did not take a deduction for such amount.

If the excess contributed for a year was withdrawn after the date for filing the individual's return, (1) it was subject to the 6-percent excise tax for each year for which the excess remained in the IRA, (2) it was subject to a 10-percent early distribution tax if the individual was not at least age 59½ or disabled, and (3) it was includible in the individual's gross income for the year it was withdrawn.

Reasons for change

Under prior law, an individual who made an excess contribution to an IRA and who failed to catch and correct the excess contribution by the due date for filing his tax return could not correct the situation by withdrawing the excess contribution without paying ordinary income tax on the amount of the withdrawal (even though he was not allowed to deduct the excess contribution when he put it into the IRA) and also had a 10-percent additional income tax for making an early withdrawal from the IRA unless the individual was at least 59½ years old or disabled.

The Congress concluded that these rules were overly harsh. Most excess contributions are inadvertent and may not be detected for a substantial period of time. While some individuals may be in a position to correct the excess contribution by making an undercontribution for a later year (as described in the previous section), this alternative is not open to those who have lost their eligibility for IRA participation (as, for example, those who have become active participants in qualified retirement plans).

Explanation of provision

The Act allows an individual who has made a total contribution for a year which does not exceed $1,750 to an IRA, all or part of which is an excess contribution, and who does not correct the excess contribution prior to the due date for filing his or her tax return for the year, later to withdraw the excess contributed for the year without (1) incurring a 10-percent early distribution tax, and (2) being required to include the amount withdrawn in gross income.[1] (In order to avoid administrative and computational problems, the taxpayer is not required to withdraw any earnings attributable to the excess contribution; if such earnings were withdrawn they would be subject to tax, as under prior law.) The provision applies only to the extent that a deduction was not allowed for the amount of the excess contribution withdrawn. (A deduction would be treated as not having been allowed if the taxpayer did not claim the deduction, or if IRS disallowed the deduction upon audit. If a deduction was claimed and allowed for a year for which the period of limitations has not expired, a taxpayer could come under these provisions by filing an amended return for the year for which the excess contribution was made.)

---

[1] As under prior law, the 6-percent excess contribution tax would not apply to the year of withdrawal.

The Act provides a transitional rule for excess contributions to IRAs for taxable years beginning before January 1, 1978. For such excess contributions, the provisions of the Act would apply without regard to the $1,750 limitation. Thus, an individual could withdraw all such excess contributions, regardless of amount, to the extent deductions were not previously allowed for the excess contributions.

The Act also allows an individual to withdraw an excess contribution (regardless of the amount) made with respect to a rollover contribution (including an attempted rollover contribution) in any case in which the excess contribution occurred because the individual making the contribution reasonably relied on erroneous information required to be supplied by the plan, trust, or institution making the distribution which was the subject of the rollover.

The Act applies to distributions from IRAs in taxable years beginning after December 31, 1975. Thus, under the Act, the IRS is to refund to taxpayers all penalties and income taxes based on distributions from IRAs after that date which correct previous excess contributions.

Effective date

The provision applies to distributions from IRAs in taxable years beginning after December 31, 1975.

Addition of requirement that premiums on individual retirement annuity contracts must be flexible.

Prior law

An individual is allowed a deduction from gross income for certain contributions to an individual retirement annuity. To qualify as an individual retirement annuity, an annuity contract must meet certain statutory specifications (sec. 408(b)). Under prior law, a fixed premium contract (e.g., a contract which requires fixed payments over a fixed period of time) which met these specifications qualified as an individual retirement annuity.

Reasons for change

If an individual funded an IRA through a fixed premium contract, he had to continue to make the premium payments (or face substantial forfeitures under the contract) even though his circumstances changed so that all or a portion of the fixed premium payments became nondeductible. Ordinarily this would happen when the individual joined a qualified plan and thereby lost his eligibility for IRA participation. For this reason, the Congress concluded that the fixed premium contract is not appropriate for use as an IRA funding vehicle. Those who wish to fund their IRAs through insurance contracts may use the flexible premium contract.

Explanation of provision

The Act requires that an annuity contract provide for the flexible payment of premiums in order to qualify as an individual retirement annuity.

The Act provides a transitional rule under which the exchange before January 1, 1981, of any fixed premium individual retirement annuity issued on or before November 6, 1978, for a flexible premium annuity contract will, at the election of the individual, be treated as a nontaxable exchange. The exchange of annuity contracts is optional. An individual retirement annuity contract issued before November 7, 1978, will not fail to qualify merely because it provides for fixed premiums.

Effective date

The provision applies to contracts issued or exchanged after November 6, 1978.

Clarification of dollar limit in the case of individual retirement annuities and retirement bonds.

Prior law

The Employee Retirement Income Security Act of 1974 (ERISA) permitted individuals to make deductible contributions to IRAs in an amount equal to the lesser of 15 percent of compensation includible in gross income, or $1,500. The Tax Reform Act of 1976 raised the dollar limitation for such contributions to $1,750 when the individual has a nonworking spouse with whom he or she shares the contribution equally (spousal IRA). Certain provisions of the Code defining an individual retirement annuity and a retirement bond were not amended by the 1976 Act to reflect the change in the dollar limitation from $1,500 to $1,750 for spousal IRAs.

Reasons for change

This provision of the Act corrects a technical oversight in prior law.

Explanation of provision

The Act modifies the definitions of an individual retirement annuity and a retirement bond to make it clear that the maximum dollar limitation for deductible contributions to a spousal IRA is $1,750.

Effective date

The provision applies to taxable years beginning after December 31, 1976.

Rollover of proceeds from sale of property.

Prior law

Under prior law, a participant in a qualified plan who received a lump sum distribution from the plan or a complete distribution upon termination of the plan could avoid current tax by making a rollover contribution to an IRA or to another qualified plan within 60 days after the date of the distribution. If the individual received property other than cash in the distribution, the actual assets received had to be contributed to the IRA or to the other qualified plan in order to qualify for tax-free rollover treatment. If the individual sold any asset received in the distribution and contributed the proceeds from the sale to an IRA or to a qualified plan as part of an attempted rollover contribution, the entire contribution failed to qualify as a rollover. Also, if the unsuccessful rollover was made to an IRA, the amount contributed was treated as an excess contribution. Accordingly, (1) a 6-percent excise tax was imposed for each year for which the excess contribution remained in the IRA, (2) the excess contribution and the earnings thereon were included in gross income when distributed from the IRA, and (3) the excess contribution and earnings thereon were subject to a 10-percent penalty tax if distributed before age 59½ (except in disability cases).

Reasons for change

The Congress concluded that the rules of prior law, requiring property received from a plan to be recontributed in kind in order to constitute a valid rollover, were needlessly restrictive. Hardship could result if the plan participant had difficulty finding a trustee who was willing to accept the property in kind. (Many institutional trustees are reluctant to manage certain kinds of property.)

Explanation of provision

The Act permits the recipient of a lump sum distribution from a qualified plan or a complete distribution upon termination of a qualified plan, which consists in whole or in part of property other than cash, to receive tax-free rollover treatment by contributing the proceeds from the *bona fide* sale of the property, rather than the property itself, to an IRA or to another qualified plan within 60 days from the date of the distribution.

For example, assume that on September 1, 1980, an individual receives a lump-sum distribution consisting of $50,000 in cash and $50,000 worth of Corporation A stock (valued as of September 1, 1978). Assume further that on September 30, 1980, the individual sells all of the stock for $60,000. His maximum rollover contribution (to be completed within 60 days of the September 1, 1980 distribution date) would be $110,000 ($50,000 of cash, plus the $60,000 proceeds received on the sale of the stock). If the individual made a full $110,000 rollover, no gain would be recognized on the sale of the stock. (This is the same result which would have occurred if the property had been rolled over immediately before the sale.)

The same rule would apply in the case of a loss on the sale of the stock. If, on September 30, 1980, the individual sold the Corporation A stock for $40,000, then his maximum rollover contribution would be $90,000, and if the rollover were completed within the 60-day rollover period, no loss would be recognized on the sale of the stock.

Generally, under prior law (and under the Act) where an employee received a distribution of property from a qualified plan, and this distribution is not rolled over, then the employee is required to treat the fair market value of the property as ordinary income, and the amount taken into income becomes the employee's basis in the property.[1] Gain or loss subsequently

---

[1]There is a limited exception to this rule under certain circumstances where the employee receives a lump-distribution of stock in his employer. In this case, the

realized on the sale of the stock is generally treated as capital gain or loss.

These same principles apply where there is a partial rollover of the proceeds of the sale of property, except that it will generally be necessary to allocate the retained proceeds between the ordinary income and capital gains portion of the retained amount. For purposes of these rules, the amount of ordinary income is determined by multiplying the fair market value of the property on the date of distribution by a fraction, the numerator of which is the amount of proceeds retained, and the denominator of which is the total proceeds of the sale. The amount of capital gain or loss is determined by multiplying the difference between the fair market value of the property on the date of sale, and the fair market value on the date of distribution by this same fraction (retained proceeds over total proceeds).

In some cases, where the individual receives both cash and property, or several pieces of property, it will be necessary to determine the extent to which the individual has rolled over cash (or proceeds from the sale of one piece of property as opposed to another) and to what extent he has rolled over proceeds. The Act permits the individual to make an election in this regard (not later than the date for filing his tax return for the year in question) by filing a written designation with the IRS. Once made, this designation is irrevocable. If no designation is made, the rollover amount is to be allocated pro rata between the cash distribution received from the plan and the value of any property received (determined as of the date of the distribution).

Thus, in the case of a partial rollover involving proceeds from the sale of property, the rollover amount will be tax free (until it is distributed from the IRA, at which point it will be treated as ordinary income) and the retained portion will be taxed partly as ordinary income, and partly as capital gain or loss, in accordance with the computation outlined above.

For example, assume that on September 1, 1980, an individual employed by Corporation B receives a lump sum

---

employee is generally not required to include in gross income the unrealized appreciation in the value of the stock which occurred after the stock was contributed to the plan. Of course, when the stock is sold, the employee will recognize capital gain or loss.

913

distribution consisting of $50,000 in cash and $50,000 worth of Corporation A stock (valued as of September 1, 1980). Assume that on September 30, 1980, that individual sells all of the stock for its then fair market value of $60,000. The maximum rollover contribution (to be completed within 60 days of the September 1, 1980, distribution date) would be $110,000 ($50,000 of cash, plus the $60,000 of proceeds received on the sale of the stock). As discussed above, if the individual made a full $110,000 rollover, no gain would be recognized on the sale of the stock. But, assume that the individual makes a rollover of only $80,000. He now may designate irrevocably on his tax return for the year of the rollover the extent to which he has rolled over cash from the plan and the extent to which he has rolled over proceeds from the sale of the stock.[2] Assume the individual designates the rollover as $30,000 of cash from the plan and $50,000 of proceeds. He then will have retained $20,000 ($50,000-$30,000) of cash from the plan and $10,000 ($60,000-$50,000) of proceeds from the sale of the stock, and will be taxed as follows:

Ordinary income:

Cash	$20,000
Portion of value of stock included in distribution which is considered retained ($10,000/$60,000 x $50,000)	8,333
Total amount of distribution retained	28,333
Gain attributable to stock distributed the proceeds from which are considered retained ($10,000/ $60,000 x $10,000)........................	1,667
Total amount retained	$30,000

All of the foregoing discussion assumes that the employee had made no contributions to the plan. If the employee had made contributions to the plan, the employee is permitted to designate (by the due date for filing his tax return) which portion of the lump-sum distribution was attributable to employee contributions, and which portion of the money and property distributed and not rolled over was attributable to employer contributions to the plan. If the employee fails to make this

[2]The property must actually be sold for such a designation to be available.

designation, (1) first, the ordinary income portion of the property received and not rolled over will, to the extent thereof, be treated as being attributable to the employee's contributions to the plan on a pro-rata basis, and (2) second, the remainder of the property not rolled over will be treated as being attributable to the rest of the employee's contributions on a pro-rata basis.

Effective date

The provision applies to qualifying rollover distributions completed after December 31, 1978, in taxable years ending after December 31, 1978.

Rollover contribution to individual retirement plan of distribution to spouse from qualified plan or annuity.

Prior law

A participant in a qualified plan who receives a lump-sum distribution from the plan may avoid current tax by making a rollover contribution to an IRA or to another qualified plan within 60 days after the date of the distribution. However, under prior law, the recipient of a lump-sum distribution on account of the death of a plan participant was not eligible to engage in a tax-free rollover.

Reason for change

The Congress concluded that a spouse should have the same IRA rollover privilege which would have been available to the plan participant had the participant survived. Accordingly, the Act permits the spouse of a plan participant to completely or partially roll over a lump-sum distribution recieved from a plan on account of the participant's death into an IRA.

Explanation of provision

Under the Act, if a married individual participating in a qualified plan dies and his or her spouse receives a distribution from the plan which qualifies as a lump-sum distribution, the spouse may, within 60 days of the date of the distribution, make a tax-free rollover contribution to an IRA of the assets distributed from the qualified plan.

Effective date

The provision applies to lump-sum distributions completed after December 31, 1978.

Removal of certain restrictions on rollovers.

Prior law

If an individual receives a lump sum distribution from a qualified plan or a complete distribution upon termination of a qualified plan, the individual may avoid current tax by making a rollover contribution of the amount of cash plus the property distributed (less any amount allocable to employee contributions) to an IRA or to another qualified plan. Under prior law, for a distribution to qualify as a lump sum distribution, the individual had to have been a participant in the qualified plan for five or more full taxable years before the taxable year of the distribution.

An individual is permitted to make a rollover contribution of a distribution from an IRA to another IRA without including the amount of the distribution in gross income, providing the rollover occurs within 60 days after the date of the distribution. Under prior law, an individual could engage in this type of rollover only one time during any three-year period.

Reasons for change

The Congress concluded that the restrictions on rollovers as outlined above are unnecessarily restrictive and could inhibit both protability and the opportunity of the plan participant to shift his or her investment medium, or to change IRA trustees, as circumstances warrant. Thus, the Act eliminates the 5-year requirement with respect to rollovers from qualified plans, as outlined above, and permits rollover contributions between IRAs once a year (instead of once every three years, as under prior law).

Explanation of provision

The Act removes the requirement that an individual must participate in the qualified plan from which he or she receives a lump sum distribution for 5 or more years in order to be eligible for a tax-free rollover of the distribution to an IRA or to another qualified plan. For individuals who received lump sum distributions in a taxable year beginning in 1978, but who could not engage in a tax-free rollover because of the five-year participation rule, the Act extends the time period for making such rollovers to December 31, 1978. The Act does not modify the 5-year requirement for 10-year averaging or capital gain treatment with respect to a lump-sum distribution.

The Act also reduces the 3-year limitation on rollovers between IRAs to once each year. An individual is allowed to make rollover contributions of amounts from one IRA to another once each year.

Effective date

The provision applies to taxable years beginning after December 31, 1977.

Waiver of excise tax on certain accumulations in individual retirement accounts or annuities.

Prior law

An individual who has established an individual retirement account or an individual retirement annuity is required to begin receiving distributions of a certain minimum amount from the account or annuity not later than the end of the taxable year in which the individual reaches age 70½. If an individual fails to make a required minimum distribution, the individual is subject to an accumulation penalty tax equal to 50 percent of the amount which was required to be distributed, but was not distributed. Under prior law, the Secretary of the Treasury was not given the authority to waive this penalty tax.

Reasons for change

Prior law automatically imposed a flat 50 percent tax on excess accumulations in an IRA. There are circumstances where these accumulations (or underdistributions) may occur through no fault of the plan participant. The Congress concluded that the Internal Revenue Service should be allowed to waive the penalty tax where it is shown that the excess accumulation was due to reasonable error and that reasonable steps are being taken to correct the situation.

Explanation of provision

The Act gives the Secretary of the Treasury the power to waive the 50-percent accumulation penalty tax in circumstances where the individual subject to the tax establishes to the satisfaction of the Secretary that (1) the shortfall in the amount distributed was due to reasonable error, and (2) the individual is taking reasonable steps to remedy the shortfall.

917

Effective date

The provision applies to taxable years beginning after December 31, 1975.

Removal of certain limitations on provision allowing correction of excess contributions.

Prior law

A 6-percent excise tax is imposed on an excess contribution to an IRA. Under prior law, if for a taxable year an individual made an excess contribution to an IRA but withdrew the amount of the contribution, and any earnings thereon, on or before the date prescribed by law for filing his or her tax return for the year, the 6-percent excise tax was not imposed if (1) the excess contribution resulted either from employer contributions to a qualified plan, governmental plan, or tax-sheltered annuity, or from the failure of the individual to earn sufficient compensation for the year to make him eligible for the full amount of the contribution, and (2) the total amount withdrawn from the IRA did not exceed the excess of $1,500 ($1,750 in the case of a spousal IRA) over the amount allowable as a deduction for the year for a contribution to an IRA.

Reasons for change

Prior law permitted an individual to correct an excess contribution to an IRA by withdrawing that excess before the due date for filing his tax return, but imposed a dollar limitation which restricted the usefulness of this correction technique where the excess amount was made in connection with a rollover contribution. The Act corrects this situation by removing the dollar limitation. Under the Act, the full amount of the excess contribution, plus any earnings thereon, are includible in the gross income of the individual for the year for which the excess contribution was made.

Explanation of provision

Under the Act, the dollar limitation is removed. Thus, an individual who makes an excess contribution to an IRA, withdraws the full amount of the excess contributed, and any earnings thereon, on or before the date prescribed by law for filing the tax return for the year (including extensions) and does not take a deduction for the excess contribution, will be treated as not having made an excess contribution for the year. Accordingly, no 6-percent excise tax will be imposed for the year with respect to the excess contributed. The earnings on the excess contributed up to the date of withdrawal will be includible in the gross income of the individual for the year for which the excess contribution was made, but will not be subject to a 10-percent early distribution tax.

Effective date

The provision applies to contributions made for taxable years beginning after December 31, 1977.

Simplification of return requirement with respect to individual retirement plans.

Prior law

Under prior law, an individual who established an IRA was required to file a tax return with respect to the IRA for each year of its existence irrespective of whether, in any particular year, the individual contributed to the IRA, made withdrawals or received distributions from the IRA, engaged in a prohibited transaction with respect to the IRA, or incurred a penalty tax with respect to the IRA.

Reasons for change

The Congress concluded that a taxpayer should not be required to file a separate tax form in connection with the IRA for years where there is no activity other than making allowable contributions to, or receiving permissible distributions from, the IRA. Thus, the Act eliminates the separate filing requirement under these circumstances.

Explanation of provision

Under the Act, an individual does not have to file a tax return for an IRA for any taxable year (1) for which no penalty tax is imposed with respect to the IRA, and (2) for which no activity is engaged in with respect to the IRA other than making deductible contributions to, and permissible distributions from, the IRA. (Under the Act, separate reporting may still be required with respect to rollover contributions.) Information with respect to a deductible contribution or a permissible distribution will be included on the regular Form 1040. (Presently this information is reported both on the Form 1040 and on a separate form.)

Effective date

The provision applies to taxable years beginning after December 31, 1977.

Whoever is not a participant in a qualified pension or profit sharing plan should strongly consider an IRA as an investment can accumulate much faster in a tax-exempt trust compared to regular investing outside such trusts.

EMPLOYEE STOCK OWNERSHIP PLANS

Louis Kelso was a pioneer for Employee Stock Ownership Plans also known as Employee Stock Ownership Trusts, Stock Bonus Plans and Kelso plans. He wrote the Two Factor Theory in which he described the benefit to the individual and our nation for an employee to receive both wages and capital to increase his opportunity for economic independence. Kelso also pointed out that American industry needed capital in addition to internal financing and preferably capital that could be borrowed and repaid on a tax-deductible basis.

ESOP's are defined as an eligible individual account plan which is a qualified stock bonus plan, or a stock bonus plan and a money purchase plan, both of which are qualified under Section 401 of the Internal Revenue Code of 1954, and which are designed to invest primarily in qualified employer securities. The term "eligible individual account plan" is defined by Section 407(d)(3)(a) of the Employee Retirement Income Security Act of 1974 (ERISA) to mean an individual account plan which is:

1. a profit sharing, stock bonus, thrift, and/or savings plan; or

2. an employee stock ownership plan.

Like a profit sharing plan the basic deduction limit for contributions to a stock bonus plan is 15% of compensation. Annual additions, including contribution carry-overs to a participant's account, may not exceed the lesser of $25,000+ or 25% of a participant's compensation. There are two distinguishing features of the stock bonus plan that separate it from profit sharing plans:

1. under a stock bonus plan, the company contributions need not be dependent on profit, and

2. benefits must be distributed in the form of employer stock.

Therefore, an ESOP is a tax-exempt trust created under Section 401 which gives the trustee the power to invest in stock of the employer company. In effect, it is a stock bonus plan. An ESOP may be created by amending an existing profit sharing

921

plan or by installing a new plan. In either case, the trust must provide:

1. that the trustee has the power to accept or purchase, as a trust investment, stock of the employer corporation,

2. that the stock of the employer corporation is to be valued each year (based on a formula which has been approved by the Internal Revenue Service) at the time that the employer corporation makes its contribution to the plan,

3. that the stock of the employer corporation is to be valued at any time stock is distributed, or purchased by the trustee (based on an approved formula),

4. that the cost of any appraisal be borne by the employer corporation or selling shareholder and not the trust,

5. that a distribution from the plan shall be only in stock of the employer corporation,

6. that individual accounts shall be maintained for each participant and the balance in the account shall be the employee's allocated share, less any plan indebtedness, and

7. that the employer corporation may agree to purchase any shares of the employer corporation stock offered by retired or terminated employees if there is no public market for their stock, and if the trustee does not elect to purchase such shares.

Profit Sharing Plan Conversion

Since the great majority of rules pertaining to profit sharing plans also apply to stock bonus plans, the Service has accepted the concept that existing profit sharing plans may be converted to stock bonus plans. However, this route does present a more difficult path and involves more risk than does the creation of a stock bonus plan from the beginning. It would, therefore, be prudent to obtain a pre-conversion ruling from the Local District IRS Office before proceeding with a plan conversion.

Some plans have been aimed at the conversion of an existing profit sharing plan which has in it large amounts of accumulated contributions, with the idea of using those funds to purchase new stock from the corporation. Thus, dollars previously deducted are used to fund the current expansion of the corporation. An alternate procedure is to maintain separate investment accounts for preconversion trust assets. This requires substantially more accounting for the qualified plan.

922

ESOP's Special Status

ERISA has had a great negative impact on many qualified retirement plans. With regard to the ESOP, however, the effect is very positive. It specifically authorizes investment in employer stock, instead of excluding such investments, as is the case in other types of qualified plans. It also excludes ESOP's from the new rules regarding minimum funding and from the requirement for coverage under the new Pension Benefit Guaranty Corporation. In addition, it outlines the exceptions of such plans from areas of new "prohibited-transaction-rules," giving specific approval to the trust to borrow funds for the acquisition of employer stock. This approval includes provisions for loans and extensions of credit from "parties-in-interest" to the trust. Although Section 407(a) of the act specifically prohibits ordinary pension and profit sharing plans from acquiring or holding more than 10% of the fair market value of plan assets in employer securities and employer real property, and requires such plans to dispose of at least 50% of their excess holdings by December 31, 1979, this rule does not apply to the ESOP. Section 407(b) specifically exempts an individual account plan, as defined in Section 407(d)(3), from this diversification requirement. Section 408(b) of ERISA provides nine exceptions to the prohibited transaction rules. Unfortunately, these exceptions are almost entirely technical in nature or are useful only to a limited number of situations. They do very little to reestablish any of the investment opportunities that were closed by the passage of Section 406 of ERISA. The only broad exceptions to these restrictions are those granted to the Employee Stock Ownership Plans.

Corporate Financing Applications

The advantages, uses and variations of ESOP are extensive. First, they can facilitate corporate growth by contributing to cash flow through stock purchase with funds on hand or borrowed money. Thus, the ESOP's highlight the close relationship between finance and the cost of providing employee benefits. Other qualified plans, for example, necessarily involve making a choice between the conflicting goals of providing for future corporate growth and of providing employee benefits. With an ESOP the situation is reversed and the corporation is enabled simultaneously to facilitate corporate growth while providing employee benefits which have a direct impact on incentive and are at least equal to, and frequently greater than, the benefits otherwise provided.

Second, an ESOP permits a business to contribute stock or other assets to the trust and get tax credit for the market value of the asset. Current income may then be directed to meet capital requirements while taxation of that income is defined until the retirement of plan participants.

The ESOP can also be used to refinance existing debt, and in some situations can cause a recapture of all or a substantial portion of the Federal income taxes paid during the prior three years. This occurs when the current company contribution creates a loss to the corporation.

Another interesting use of the ESOP is for spinning off a subsidiary company or an operating division, due either to a change in policy or because of a government-directed divestiture. In such a case, the holding or parent company becomes the selling shareholder, and the employees of the subsidiary or division become the owner.

The acquisition of stock of a corporation by an outside entity can be made deductible in good part. Using this approach, the acquiring entity arranges for "Acquired Company, Inc." (the entity being acquired) to create an ESOP. The acquiring entity then purchases a small portion of the outstanding stock of Acquired Company, Inc. (e.g., 10%) and thereafter arranges for the acquisition of the balance of Acquired Company, Inc.'s stock by the ESOP, usually guaranteeing that purchase. In the following years, the contributions from Acquired Company, Inc., to the ESOP, as deductible items, fund the retirement of the loan used to purchase the remaining 90% of the stock. The acquiring entity has used after-tax dollars to acquire only a small portion of the ownership, now the only outside stock, and thus it can control the corporation.

There are no published rulings which approve this technique, but it seems generally in line with the concept of the ESOP's borrowing money and using those funds to purchase the capital stock of the corporation.

Employee Benefit Uses

The ESOP is an employee incentive plan as well as an executive compensation plan. By allowing employees to acquire

924

an ownership interest in the employer, the ESOP provides employees with a direct vested interest in the success of *their* corporation. Because the trust benefits are allocated in proportion to compensation, the ESOP favors the highly compensated key employee more than the rank and file employees, thereby complementing any executive compensation plan. Since the ESOP enables employees to acquire stock ownership with pre-tax funds, requires no employee contributions, avoids the necessity for employees to use accumulated savings or individually borrowed funds in order to purchase stock, and makes it possible for the corporation to deduct the full cost of these benefits, the ESOP is frequently superior as an executive compensation device. Stock option plans, stock purchase plans, restricted stock purchase plans and other similar executive compensation programs result in reduced employee take-home pay.

As an employee retirement plan, the ESOP is equally beneficial. Trust benefits are distributed at retirement, and therefore, the ESOP functions like a conventional qualified plan in relating retirement benefits to compensation and to length of service. There is an additional advantage under ERISA: the Act phases out capital gain treatment for the portion of a lump sum distribution attributable to earnings of the trust, but it does continue capital gains treatment for the unrealized appreciation of employer securities. Moreover the capital gains tax is not incurred until the employee subsequently sells the stock, and capital gains taxation is available whether the shareholder sells all or part of a stock.

Repurchase of Employee Stock

Most District Pension Trust Offices will not allow a plan that forces the employee to sell his stock back to the Trust or Corporation. The obvious intention here is to safeguard the purpose of the plan which is to make the employee a capital owner.

In many plans the stock does not pay dividends and will have no outside market, therefore, there should be a means whereby the employee can sell his stock for cash. As a result, most plans provide the employee with a right (but not an obligation) to sell his stock to the trust at a price determined by the same valuation formula established for other transactions.

925

Personal and Estate Planning Value to Major Stockholders

In the closely held corporation, there are a variety of possible applications to benefit the existing majority stockholders of the corporation. Major stockholders of non-public corporations often have problems which may be solved by the utilization of an ESOP. When a business owner has accumulated most of his wealth in the form of non-marketable stock in his own firm, and for various reasons he objects to the alternatives of selling out to another firm or selling his stock to the public, he may elect to sell part or all of his stock to the trust, instead of having the company issue stock to be purchased by the ESOP. The transaction can be funded by a bank or other lender just as in the typical ESOP transaction. But if there is difficulty in obtaining such a loan, the selling shareholder can carry the note himself. He may elect to do this anyway, for by receiving his payments over a period of years, the transaction becomes eligible for a favorable capital gains tax treatment as an installment sale. The selling shareholder receives instant liquidity for his closely held stock and obtains a market value for Estate Tax purposes.

ESOP in Publicly Held Corporations

The safest method of going forward for the public corporation is to accept the necessity for obtaining a "no action" letter from the S.E.C. with regard to stock issued to a plan and also with regard to the purchase of stock by the trust in circumstances where the trust may be considered by the S.E.C. to be "controlled" by the corporation or affiliated persons.

No registration is required when the employer company stock goes into the trust by purchase, as this is not considered a public offering. On the distribution from the trust to separated participant employees, however, the public corporation (or the reporting company) must file a Form S-8.

Valuation of Employer Stock

The proper valuation of employer stock is most important to the success of the ESOP from at least two standpoints. The first is whether to contribute cash or stock initially. Although, at first blush, it may appear better for an employer to make a cash contribution to the trust and then have the trust use the cash to purchase stock from the employer, it seems clear that in the long run this is the more dangerous approach. Where the employer contributes stock directly, it is possible for the Internal Revenue Service to later make a determination that the valuation placed on the stock may be higher than the actual stock value, in which event, the amount of contribution to the ESOP may be reduced. However, if cash is contributed to the trust and that cash is later used to purchase stock at a price which the Service finds to be unwarranted, the entire plan may be disqualified.

Since stock will be held by the trustee, it is obvious that the valuation of closely held stock for purposes of an ESOP transaction is of vital importance. The price paid must be fair and reasonable, but need not meet with prior IRS approval. Often a professional valuation service is advisable. Usually the plan provides for valuations to be made periodically by the plan committee appointed by the Board of Directors. Because the problem of stock valuation is a continuing aspect of the ESOP, it has received a substantial amount of time from those practitioners who have been involved with the plans. One practitioner feels that the valuation is so important that it should be performed by a C.P.A. firm not involved in any other aspect of the corporation's activities. The Appeals Section of the National Office of the Pension Trust Division agrees that the proper basis for valuation is that basis set forth (in multiple form) with regard to determination of value of closely held corporations for purposes of estate taxation.[1] Where there is not an annual need for valuation of the stock, it may be appropriate to submit to IRS, before any purchase, a request for determination of the propriety of the investment. This may be the most effective means of assuring that the participants of the plan obtain the benefits anticipated.[2]

Funding of an ESOP

The funding of the ESOP need not, and should not, be only by corporate stock. The ESOP is so designed that it can accept contributions in the form of cash, corporate stock, and other corporate securities. These privileges should be taken into

[1] Revenue ruling, 59-60, 1 CB 237.
[2] I.R.S. Form 4575, Application for Determination, Investment of Trust Fund in Stock or Securities of the Employer.

account when considering the overall amount and type of contributions being made to the plan. Such planning is necessary when one considers the prospect of redeeming the outside stock of current stockholders of redeeming the stock of a retired employee.

To the extent that there is funding planned for the acquisition of stock of an existing stockholder who is also an employee, one must take into consideration both the value of the stock that the person holds outside of the trust (if the trust intends to buy the stock) and the valuation of the employee's vested interest in the plan. Since the plan may pay out stock to the employee upon the employee's termination, it is necessary also to consider purchasing this amount of "inside" stock. Thus, there are really two value areas ("outside" and "inside") which must be considered in planning the overall acquisition of stock from an employee shareholder.

The ESOP could authorize the employee to direct that a portion of his or her account be used to purchase incidental life insurance, payable to a personal beneficiary. Under IRS regulations, up to 49.9% of the participant's account can be invested in permanent insurance (24.9% in the case of term insurance). In addition to incidental life insurance for participants, key employee insurance owned by and payable to the plan's trustee could be an appropriate plan investment.

Stock Dilution

A question often raised by an astute observer is that of dilution of corporate control and value. In the classic ESOP transaction, where the company issues new stock and uses the proceeds of sales to purchase capital goods or new equipment, the increased profits from the new or improved production should, in time, more than exceed any dilution factor. Additionally, there is the earning power that can be generated from the substantial savings to the company in borrowing costs through an ESOP as related to conventional methods of financing. There is no major problem of dilution where the ESOP is used to purchase stock from a majority stockholder, since no new issues are being issued. When contributions to the plan are made in the form of other securities (bonds, commercial paper, equipment notes, etc.), dilutions can be avoided completely.

Trustee Responsibility

Although the quality of stock should be of no real concern from the view of fiduciary responsibility, the strength of a company is vital to the ultimate success or failure of the ESOP, and may well be the all important consideration to a bank in deciding whether to serve as trustee and/or lender.

CORPORATION PROFILE FOR PROSPECTIVE EMPLOYEE STOCK OWNERSHIP PLAN AND TRUST

The following items should be taken into account in evaluating potential candidates for the Stock Ownership Plan and Trust:

1. Company must be a domestic business corporation reporting income and paying taxes under normal corporate tax provisions of the Internal Revenue Code (The "Code").

   (Sub-chapter S corporations do not qualify.)

2. Corporation should be operating profitably and be in the full federal tax bracket (48%). With a minimum of $50,000 in net after tax income. The company should have the potential for going public sometime in the future or at present be a public corporation.

   (There should be reasonable prospects for a continuing profitable operation.)

3. The gross compensation paid to all employees in the form of salaries, wages, and commissions should be in excess of $250,000 annually.

4. The corporation may be a "private" or a "public" company.

   (Normally, a private company is considered to be one where the stock is held by a relatively small number of stockholders, and no public market exists for the purchase and sale of such stock.)

   A stock ownership trust may be employed to create a market for the stock of public corporations.

5. An existing profit-sharing plan is an extremely desirable factor.

   (If the program is properly designed, an existing profit-sharing plan may be converted into a Stock Ownership Plan, thereby freeing the funds for investment in the company.)

6. A corporation where one or more stockholders desires to liquidate their holdings is also an ideal candidate.

> (By employing proper techniques, the selling shareholder may realize a price on a par with that of a comparable equity in a public company. This stock may be purchased by the Stock Ownership Trust from corporate contributions, which are deductible from corporate pre-tax earnings.)

7. Corporations with substantial borrowings.

> (Corporate borrowings can be arranged or refinanced through the Stock Ownership Trust and repaid from company contributions to the Trust so that the principal payments are deductible from pre-tax earnings, i.e., for a loan of $1,000,000 only $1,000,000 of *pre-tax income* is required to service the principal payments, whereas $2,000,000 of pre-tax earnings are required to amortize such a loan in a conventional transaction if the corporation is in a 50% tax bracket. Raising corporate capital via issue of debt securities which are contributed to ESOP is also possible.)

8. Acquisition-minded corporations.

> (Acquisitions may be facilitated through the use of Stock Ownership Trust as the acquiring vehicle. Acquisitions may be arranged so that purchase payments come from corporate contributions to a Trust, which are deductible from pre-tax income.)

9. Corporations involved in fights for control.

> (Although this problem occurs most frequently in public companies, management can defend against take-overs by use of a Stock Ownership Trust. Shares issued to such Trust are voted at the direction of management.)

10. The key stockholders prefer to sell out to their employees rather than the public.

The 1976 Tax Reform Act reaffirms congressional intent with respect to employee stock ownership plans and expresses concern that administrative rules and regulations may frustrate congressional intent. It has come to the attention of Congress, however, that proposed regulations issued by both the Department of the Treasury and the Department of Labor on July 30, 1976, may make it virtually impossible for ESOP's, and especially leveraged ESOP's, to be established and function

930

effectively. The following areas are of specific concern to the conferees: (1) independent third parties, (2) "put" options, (3) stock subject to lien, (4) allocation of stock, (5) voting rights, (6) dividend restrictions, (7) right of first refusal, (8) treatment of sale as redemption, (9) nonvoting common stock (10) prepayment penalty, (11) calls and other options, (12) contingent contributions, (13) comparability, and (14) inferences.

Under prior law, an employer is entitled to an additional percentage point of investment credit (11 percent rather than 10 percent) if it contributes employer securities equal in value to the additional credit to an employee stock ownership plan (ESOP). The additional 1 percent credit expires after December 31, 1976.

The 1976 Tax Reform Act extends through December 31, 1980, the additional percentage point of investment credit for employers who contribute employer securities equal in value to the additional credit to an ESOP. An additional one-half percentage point of investment credit (11½ percent rather than 11 percent) is available only to the extent of the amount of employee matching contributions to the ESOP. These provisions apply for taxable years beginning after 1976. The conference agreement also makes a number of technical modifications in the investment tax credit ESOP provisions of the Internal Revenue Code and the Tax Reduction Act of 1975. These technical amendments apply generally to taxable years beginning after December 31, 1974.

An employee stock ownership plan is a technique of corporate finance designed to build beneficial equity ownership of shares in the employer corporation into its employees substantially in proportion to their relative incomes, without requiring any cash outlay on their parts, any reduction in pay or other employee benefits, or the surrender of any rights on the part of the employees. The employee generally is not taxed on employer contributions to an employee stock ownership plan until they are distributed under the plan.

Under an employee stock ownership plan, a trust generally acquires common stock of the employer. (The trust may also acquire other equity securities of the employer, as well as certain bonds, debentures, notes and other evidences of indebtedness.) Generally, stock is acquired either through direct employer contributions or with the proceeds of a loan made to the plan (sec. 4975(e)(7)). Under prior law this type of plan was generally called an ESOP or leveraged ESOP.

Under prior law, regulations required that if a plan participant received employer securities from an ESOP, the employee was also to receive a "put option" (i.e., an option to require the employer to repurchase the stock at a specified price) if the stock was not publicly traded.

TRASOPs

Under prior law, an employee stock ownership plan to which an employer contributed stock (or cash) in order to qualify for additional investment tax credit was generally called a TRASOP. The TRASOP provisions were to expire after December 31, 1980.

All TRASOPs have to meet certain statutory requirements. Under prior law, an employee who participated in a TRASOP at any time during the year for which an employer contribution was made was entitled to have a share of the employer contribution credited to his or her TRASOP account based upon the amount of the employee's compensation from the employer.[1] Also, a plan participant was entitled to direct the voting of employer stock allocated to his or her account under a TRASOP, whether or not such stock was registered under Federal securities laws.[2]

In addition to these requirements, which had to be met by all TRASOPs, a TRASOP could be a tax-qualified plan only if it met the other requirements applicable to tax-qualified retirement plans. However, TRASOPs were not required to be tax-qualified under prior law. Even if a TRASOP was not a tax-qualified plan it had to satisfy special rules with respect to employee participation and limitations on contributions and benefits which were the same as those for tax-qualified plans.

A TRASOP had to be established within the taxable year for which the additional investment tax credit was claimed in order to be considered a tax-qualified plan for that year. However, a TRASOP could be established as late as the date for filing the employer's tax return for a year (including extensions) in order for the additional investment tax credit to be claimed for the

---

[1] Only the first $100,000 of an employee's compensation is considered for this purpose.

[2] Under prior law, there were no voting requirements with respect to stock held by an ESOP or any other type of qualified plan other than a TRASOP.

year. Therefore, under prior law, a TRASOP might have been nonqualified for its first plan year and qualified thereafter.

The employer's contribution to a TRASOP must be in the form of employer securities or cash (provided the cash is used by the TRASOP to acquire employer securities). Under prior law, the securities contributed to (or purchased by) a TRASOP were required to be common stock with voting power and dividend rights no less favorable than the voting power and dividend rights of other common stock of the issuing corporation. Securities convertible into such common stock could also be contributed.

An employer could contribute stock of another corporation to a TRASOP, provided that the two corporations were under at least 80 percent common control. However, gain or loss may have been recognized where a corporation made a TRASOP contribution in other than its own stock.

The amount of additional investment tax credit contributed to a TRASOP reduces an employer's income tax liability. Under prior law, this reduction in income tax could result in an increased minimum tax liability, even though the employer's income tax savings was offset by its contribution to the TRASOP.

Under prior law, where an investment tax credit amount for a year was recaptured with the result that the credit originally claimed for the year was later decreased, the employer had three alternatives with respect to adjusting the TRASOP contribution: (1) the amount of the decrease could be applied to offset employer contributions for other years; (2) the amount of the decrease could be deducted; or (3) the decrease could be used as the basis for a withdrawal from the TRASOP.

Under prior law, the type of distribution that could be made from a leveraged ESOP or a TRASOP depended on the nature of the particular plan (i.e., profit sharing, stock bonus, etc.).

Reasons for change

The ESOP provisions and the TRASOP provisions have been part of the tax laws for several years. Experience in the operation of these provisions indicated that several changes were appropriate. In addition, based on experience since the Tax Reduction Act of 1975, the Congress determined that the TRASOP provisions should be extended and should be made a part of the Code.

Statutory and administrative rules developed with respect to TRASOPs which were different from those rules which apply to tax-qualified plans in general. The Congress believed that the interests of uniformity would best be served if, in general, TRASOPs were required to become tax-qualified under the same standards generally applicable to tax-qualified plans. This requirement also should help employers maintaining TRASOPs to obtain interpretations of statutory provisions, since long-standing interpretations are available with respect to many of the rules governing tax-qualified plans.

Often, an employer does not establish a TRASOP until the time prescribed by law for filing its return for the year (including extensions), since the TRASOP does not have to be established before that time for the employer to claim the additional investment tax credit. Because of the requirement that a tax-qualified plan be established by the close of a taxable year in order to be tax-qualified for that year, many TRASOPs are not tax-qualified for their initial plan year. Since tax qualification for TRASOPs for all future years is required under the Act, the Congress believes that a TRASOP established on or before the due date for an employer's tax return for a year (including extensions), and which otherwise qualifies, should be treated as tax-qualified for that year. The Congress does not intend, however, to change the prior law rule requiring that tax-qualified plans other than TRASOPs be established before the close of a taxable year to be tax-qualified for that year. Consequently, no deduction is allowed for a taxable year for contributions to a plan which was not in existence at the close of that year.

The Congress believes that undue complexity has resulted from the prior law provision requiring that contributions to a TRASOP for a plan year be allocated to all plan participants irrespective of their service with the employer for that plan year. The Act therefore replaces this provision with the general rule for tax-qualified plans for determining which participants are required to share in a contribution for a plan year.

The Congress recognized that giving participants in leveraged ESOPs and TRASOPs full voting rights with respect to shares allocated to their accounts may be unduly burdensome in the case where the corporation issuing the employer securities is closely held. However, the Congress also recognized the general need of leveraged ESOP and TRASOP participants for voting rights on closely held employer securities with respect to major corporate issues (such as mergers, acquisitions, consolidations, or sales of all or substantially all of the assets of a corporation).

Many subsidiary corporations were unable to establish TRASOPs with the stock of their parent corporations because the parent corporations did not meet the 80-percent stock ownership requirement of prior law. The Congress concluded that this 80-percent requirement was unduly restrictive and that the interests of the public in broader employee stock ownership would better be served by a 50-percent stock ownership requirement. At the same time, a 50-percent requirement will provide a sufficient identity of interests between a parent corporation and a subsidiary corporation to make it reasonable to consider the stock of the parent corporation as employer securities of the subsidiary corporation.

The TRASOP provisions of prior law permitted subsidiary corporations to make contributions to TRASOPs of stock of their parent corporations. However, under prior law, it was not clear whether gain or loss was recognized with respect to such contributions. The Congress believed that it is inappropriate for the benefit of the additional investment tax credit to be offset by tax on gain recognized under these circumstances.

In certain cases, the additional investment tax credit attributable to TRASOP contributions could have increased an employer's minimum tax liability under prior law. The Congress concluded that this result was not appropriate because the benefit of the credit is offset by the contribution of the employer.

The Congress decided that any participant (or beneficiary) who receives a benefit distribution from a leveraged ESOP or a TRASOP should be able to dispose of the distributed employer securities for cash. The Congress recognized that in some cases this conversion occurs almost simultaneously with the actual distribution. The Congress concluded that the administrative paperwork and expense which is required for the leveraged ESOP or TRASOP to make a distribution in employer securities and then immediately repurchase the securities for cash is unwarranted in these cases. Accordingly, the Congress believed that this process should be simplified when the leveraged ESOP or TRASOP wants to distribute benefits in cash. However, if a participant wishes to receive this benefit in securities of the employer, and retain ownership of these securities, he should be able to do so, and he should have the future right to convert the securities to their cash equivalent through a "put option" to the employer if the securities are not readily tradeable on an established market.

Explanation of Provisions

General

The Revenue Act of 1978 changes the meaning of the term "ESOP." The type of plan previously referred to as a TRASOP (or investment tax credit ESOP) is designated as an ESOP. The type of plan previously referred to as an ESOP or leveraged ESOP is designated as a leveraged employee stock ownership plan. For purposes of this explanation the new terminology is used.

The Act (1) made several amendments to the provisions of law which deal with ESOPs and with leveraged employee stock ownership plans, (2) made the ESOP provisions as amended by the Act, part of the Code for the first time, and (3) extended the expiration date of the ESOP provisions to December 31, 1983.

Qualification requirements for ESOPs

Under the Act, all ESOPs are required to be tax-qualified plans. This represents a departure from the prior law provision which allowed ESOPs to be nonqualified provided that they met certain specified statutory standards. The Congress expects that the regulations which generally apply to tax-qualified plans will henceforth also apply to ESOPs, and that the Treasury Department will not write separate regulations regarding the application of the tax-qualification standards to ESOPs, except where ESOPs are distinguished from other qualified plans by statute.

Under the Act, an ESOP may be treated as tax-qualified from its effective date even though the ESOP is not actually established until the date for filing the employer's tax return for its taxable year (including extensions).

Allocation of ESOP contributions

Because ESOPs are now subject to the qualification requirements generally applicable to tax-qualified plans, employer contributions to an ESOP for a plan year generally are to be allocated in accordance with the rules governing the allocation of contributions under tax-qualified defined contribution plans.

However, the Act retains the requirement that the allocation of employer contributions to an ESOP for a year must be made in proportion to the total compensation of all participants sharing in the allocation for the plan year, taking into account only the first $100,000 of compensation for an employee.

Provisions relating to employer securities

The Act provides that if a leveraged employee stock ownership plan or an ESOP holds employer securities issued by a corporation the stock of which is registered under Federal securities laws, the plan must provide that the plan participants are entitled to exercise voting rights with respect to such employer securities. The Act also provides that if a leveraged employee stock ownership plan or an ESOP holds employer securities issued by a corporation the securities of which are not registered under Federal securities laws, the plan must provide that the plan participants are entitled to exercise voting rights with respect to such employer securities on any corporate issue which must by law (or charter) be decided by more than a majority vote of outstanding common shares voted on the issue.

The Act provides that, in the case of an ESOP, the only types of employer securities which may be acquired and held by the plan are (1) common stock of the issuing corporation and (2) preferred stock of the issuing corporation which is readily convertible into its common stock. The shares acquired by an ESOP, other than shares which are readily tradeable on an established securities market, must, in the aggregate, have a combination of (1) voting rights equivalent to rights possessed by shareholders of the class of common stock of the issuing corporation having the greatest voting rights, and (2) dividend rights equivalent to rights possessed by shareholders of any other class of stock of the issuing corporation having the greatest dividend rights. Thus, an ESOP or a leveraged employee stock ownership plan could satisfy this requirement if it holds a mixture of employer securities which reasonably reflects the outstanding securities of the employer.

The Act modifies the definition of employer securities for purposes of the ESOP provisions by applying a 50-percent test in lieu of the present law 80-percent test in determining whether corporations are members of the same parent-subsidiary controlled group of corporations. Under the Act, the stock of a parent corporation in a parent-subsidiary controlled group of corporations (determined by applying the 50-percent test) may be contributed as employer securities by a subsidiary to its ESOP. The Act does not disturb the present law rule under which an 80-percent test is applied in determining whether corporations are members of the same brother-sister controlled group for purposes of defining employer securities.

The Act provides that in a case where a parent corporation controls a subsidiary corporation (including a second tier subsidiary) under an 80-percent test for control, the subsidiary corporation will not recognize gain or loss on a contribution of stock of the parent corporation to an ESOP maintained by the subsidiary. The Act does not affect prior law applicable to other transactions.

Minimum tax

The Act provides that in any case where an employer claims additional investment tax credit as a result of an ESOP contribution, the additional credit will not result in the imposition of additional minimum tax on the employer. The Act makes no change in the present law provision under which each dollar of investment tax credit (other than investment tax credit attributable to ESOP contributions) may increase the base for computing the minimum tax.

Prohibition of withdrawal of ESOP contributions on recapture

The Act repeals the prior law permitting an employer to withdraw from an ESOP a contribution attributable to additional investment tax credit which is recaptured. Under the Act, an ESOP contribution made with respect to a particular qualified investment may not be withdrawn if all or a portion of the credit is later recaptured due to an early disposition of the property which gave rise to the credit. Under the Act, as under prior law, an employer may either (1) deduct the amount of the contribution attributable to the recaptured additional investment tax credit for the taxable year in which the recapture occurs, or (2) apply the amount of the contribution attributable to the recaptured additional investment tax credit against its obligation for a future ESOP contribution.

Distributions from ESOPs and leveraged employee stock ownership plans

Under the Act, a participant in a leveraged employee stock ownership plan or an ESOP who is entitled to a distribution under the plan is given the right to demand that the distribution be made in the form of employer securities rather than in cash (or other property). Subject to a participant's right to demand a distribution of employer securities, the plan may elect to distribute the participant's interest to him in cash, in employer securities, or partially in cash and partially in employer securities. Each participant should be advised in writing of the right to require a distribution of employer securities, before the leveraged employee stock ownership plan or the ESOP makes a distribution.

Put option on stock distributed from ESOP or leveraged employee stock ownership plan

Under the Act, any participant who receives a distribution of employer securities from an ESOP or a leveraged employee stock ownership plan must be given a "put option" on the distributed employer securities if the employer securities are not readily tradeable. The put option which a participant receives should have the following terms:

1. Upon receipt of the employer securities, the distributee must be given up to six months to require the employer to repurchase the securities at their fair market value. Although the obligation to repurchase securities under the put option would apply to the employer, and not the ESOP or the leveraged stock ownership plan, it is permissible for the ESOP or leverage stock ownership plan to make the purchase in lieu of the employer. If the distributee does not exercise the initial put option within the six-month period, the option would temporarily lapse.

2. After the close of the employer's taxable year in which the temporary lapse of a distributee's option occurs and following a determination of the value of the employer securities (determined in accordance with Treasury regulations) as of the end of that taxable year, the employer is required to notify each distributee who did not exercise the initial put option in the preceding year of the value of the employer securities as of the close of the taxable year. Each such distributee must then be given up to three months to require that the employer repurchase his or her employer securities. If the distributee does not exercise this put option, the option permanently lapses.

3. At the option of the party repurchasing employer securities under the put option, securities can be repurchased on an installment basis over a period of not more than five years. If

the distributee agrees, the repurchase period can be extended to a period of ten years. As security for an installment repurchase, the seller must be given a promissory note (or a secured obligation), the full payment of which could be required by the seller if the repurchaser defaults on any scheduled installment payment. In addition, if the term of the installment obligation exceeds five years, the employee must be given adequate security during the years in excess of the five years for the outstanding amount of the note.

4. Because a participant might wish to contribute a distribution from an ESOP or a leveraged employee stock ownership plan to an IRA in a "tax-free" rollover and because the contribution would have to be made before the expiration of the first six-month put option period, an IRA trustee or custodian must be able to exercise the same put option as the participant.

Effective date

The provisions generally apply with respect to qualified investments made after December 31, 1978.

As the need grows for making employees more financially independent and for increasing the amounts of capital available to industry, Employee Stock Ownership Plans will be formed in greater numbers.

ESOPs and TRASOPs—An Explanation for Employees

Introduction

Since 1974, the United States Congress has by legislation created two programs which are designed to give employees the chance to acquire a stock ownership in their employer. In the Employee Retirement Income Security Act of 1974, Congress first defined the employee stock ownership plan, or "ESOP" as it is usually called. In the Tax Reduction Act of 1975, and the Tax Reform Act of 1976, Congress implemented, and expanded, a different form of employee stock ownership plan, usually called a "TRASOP." The ESOP and TRASOP provide stock ownership for each employee without requiring the employee to spend any of his own money; his investment is the time and effort he puts into his job to make his employer profitable. Although some ESOPs and TRASOPs permit or require employees to put money into the ESOP or TRASOP, most provide that the employer will make all necessary ESOP and TRASOP payments.

What Is An ESOP or TRASOP?

An ESOP or TRASOP is an employee benefit plan which is "qualified" under the Internal Revenue Code. That is, it has been written in such a way that it satisfies the requirements of the Internal Revenue Code. As a qualified plan, the ESOP or TRASOP is required to be operated for the "exclusive benefit" of participating employees (and their beneficiaries).

How Does an ESOP Work?

The ESOP is designed to acquire stock of an employer for the benefit of employees. To do so, the ESOP may borrow money from a bank or other lender (including the employer). The stock is bought directly from the employer or from shareholders. When the ESOP borrows money, the employer guarantees to the lender that the ESOP will repay the loan. Employees are never required to assume any obligation for the repayment of the money borrowed by the ESOP. The employer is required to make annual payments to the ESOP in an amount at least equal to the amount the ESOP must pay on the money it borrowed. These amounts are then paid by the ESOP to the lender each year.

941

The employer is also permitted to make additional payments of cash or stock to the ESOP each year. The amount of these additional payments is usually decided by the board of directors of the employer. Because the ESOP is "qualified," the employer gets a tax deduction for all payments to the ESOP, up to a maximum limitation established by the Internal Revenue Code. This tax deduction is available for the required employer payments and any additional payments, and its effect is to reduce the annual cost of the ESOP to the employer. Cash put into the ESOP by the employer will be used primarily to purchase employer stock. In addition, this cash may be invested temporarily in savings accounts or certain other permitted investments.

How Does a TRASOP Work?

An employer which adopts a TRASOP may claim a tax credit against its Federal income taxes if it makes payments of its stock, or cash which is used to purchase its stock, to the TRASOP. The amount of the credit which the employer may claim is limited by law, and part of it may only be claimed if the employees make payments to the TRASOP which match the payments made by the employer. Only employers which buy things like equipment and machinery are generally able to adopt a TRASOP, because the tax credit is based upon the amount spent for things like capital equipment and machinery.

What Do Employees Get as Part of the ESOP or TRASOP?

Each year, all amounts of cash and employer stock paid by the employer and employees to the ESOP, and employer stock bought with cash held in the ESOP, are allocated among the accounts of employees who are participating in the ESOP. This allocation is usually done on a formula related to each employee's salary or wages as compared to the salaries or wages of all other participating employees. Take as an example an employee who earns $10,000 per year from a company where the total salaries of all participating employees equal $500,000. That employee's salary or wages is 2 percent of the total, and so his share of allocations of cash and employer stock under the ESOP for that year would be 2 percent. If the employer contributed $100,000 to the ESOP during the year, the employee's share would be $2,000.

A trust will be established (under the ESOP) to hold the cash and employer stock paid to the ESOP for the benefit of employees (and their beneficiaries). It is created by a separate written trust agreement and will be administered by a trustee. This is done to assure that each employee's interest in ESOP assets will be protected.

Under a TRASOP, allocations to employees' accounts is done in the same way as under an ESOP, except that the maximum of any employee's salary or wages which can be taken into account under a TRASOP is $100,000 each year.

What Do I Own in the ESOP or TRASOP?

An ESOP, like most employee benefit plans, is designed to benefit employees who remain with the employer the longest and contribute most to the employer's success. Therefore, an employee's ownership interest in cash and employer stock held in the ESOP is usually based on his number of years of employment with the employer. The employee's ownership interest in the ESOP is called his "vested interest," and the language in the ESOP which determines his vested interest is called a "vesting schedule." Although there are many vesting schedules which may be used by an ESOP, most vesting schedules are set up so that the longer an employee stays with the employer, the greater his vested interest becomes.

If an employee terminates employment with the employer for any reason other than his retirement, or, in some cases his death, his vested interest will be determined by looking at the vesting schedule and measuring how many years he has worked for the employer. All cash and employer stock in which he does not have a vested interest because he has not worked for the employer for enough years will be treated as a "forfeiture," to which the former employee will not be entitled. Forfeitures are usually allocated among the ESOP accounts of the remaining employees on the same basis as employer payments to the ESOP are allocated.

The vesting schedule applies only where an employee does not end his employment because of retirement or, in some cases death. If an employee retires, or, in some cases if he dies, he will immediately have a 100-percent vested interest in all ESOP assets held for him.

Under a TRASOP, each employee automatically has a 100 percent vested interest in all amounts which he or his employer contribute to the TRASOP and which are allocated to his account. Therefore, there are never any forfeitures under a TRASOP.

When Do I Receive What I Own From the ESOP or TRASOP?

Even though employer stock and cash are usually put into the ESOP or TRASOP for an employee each year, and put into a special account under his name, he will normally not be able to actually get any employer stock and cash from the ESOP or TRASOP until after his employment with the employer terminates and he ceases to be a participant in the ESOP or TRASOP.

After an employee's participation in the ESOP or TRASOP ends, he (or his beneficiary) will be eligible to receive a payment of his vested interest.

There are many permissible times and methods for making the payment to him from the ESOP or TRASOP. For example, it may provide that payment will be made as soon as possible after an employee's termination of employment. On the other hand, it may require that any payment be deferred until some later time, such as the employee's death or his normal retirement date. However, payment of a former employee's vested benefit must start soon after his death or attainment of age 65. Payment may be made to a former employee (or his beneficiary) in a lump sum, or it may be made in installments.

Payment of an employee's vested interest from an ESOP or TRASOP may be made in cash or employer stock, as determined under the ESOP or TRASOP, subject to the right of the former participant (or his beneficiary) to demand a distribution of his benefit in shares of employer stock.

What Can I Do With My Shares of Employer Stock From the ESOP or TRASOP?

Once a former employee (or his beneficiary) gets his shares of employer stock from the ESOP or TRASOP, they are his property and he can do what he wants with them. He can vote the shares of employer stock at shareholders' meetings, receive any dividends paid on the stock by the employer, and he may keep the stock as long as he wishes.

However, if he wishes to sell or otherwise transfer ownership of the stock to a third party, he may be required by the terms of the ESOP or TRASOP to first offer to sell the stock to the employer and the ESOP or TRASOP. This requirement is called a "right of first refusal" for the employer and the ESOP or TRASOP; they can exercise this right and purchase the employer stock at its fair market value. Generally, the price offered by the prospective buyer or the price at which the stock is publicly traded would establish the fair market value for the stock. The purpose of this right of first refusal is to protect the employees or the employer by preventing the stock from being acquired by outside parties who have no interest in the employer or the ESOP or TRASOP and to protect the employer whose stock is closely held from violating any Federal law as a result of having its stock sold when it does not satisfy certain Government rules.

In addition, at the time the former employee (or his beneficiary) receives employer stock which is not publicly traded from the ESOP or TRASOP, he must be given a "put option," the right to demand that the employer buy his shares of employer stock at their fair market value. In such a case, the

ESOP or TRASOP may provide that the ESOP or TRASOP may buy the employer stock, although the ESOP or TRASOP may not be required to buy the stock under the put option. The purpose for including a put option is to assure that each former employee (or his beneficiary) will have someone available to buy his shares of employer stock if he wishes to sell.

How Does the ESOP or TRASOP Help My Employer?

The employer benefits primarily from the favorable tax treatment it receives for all payments made to the ESOP or TRASOP. As explained before, an employer receives a tax credit for amounts paid to a TRASOP and a tax deduction for amounts paid to an ESOP. This is very important when the employer uses the ESOP as a means of borrowing money. In order to understand how the use of the ESOP to raise money benefits the employer, a comparison must be made with the usual method of borrowing money.

If an employer which does not have an ESOP wishes to borrow money to build a new building, expand production, or for any other reason, the employer would go to a bank to borrow money. When the employer repays the loan, it will also pay interest on the loan, just like an individual person would do with a charge account. Although the interest payments would be tax deductible, the principal payments on the loan would not. This means that the employer would first figure its taxable income, then pay its income taxes, and then make its payment on the loan.

The use of an ESOP for this purpose greatly helps the employer because of the effect it has on the employer's taxes.

945

In this situation, the ESOP borrows the money from a bank, and signs a promissory note for the money:

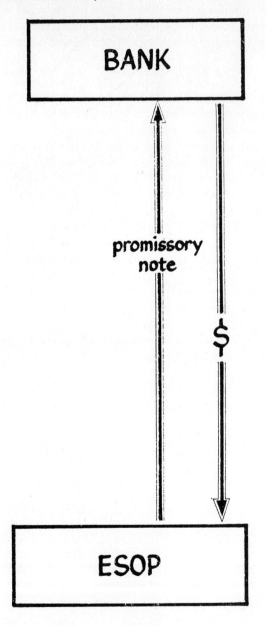

As part of the ESOP loan, the employer gives a written guarantee to the bank, promising that the ESOP will repay the loan and that each year the employer will pay to the ESOP enough money to permit the ESOP to make its annual repayment of the loan:

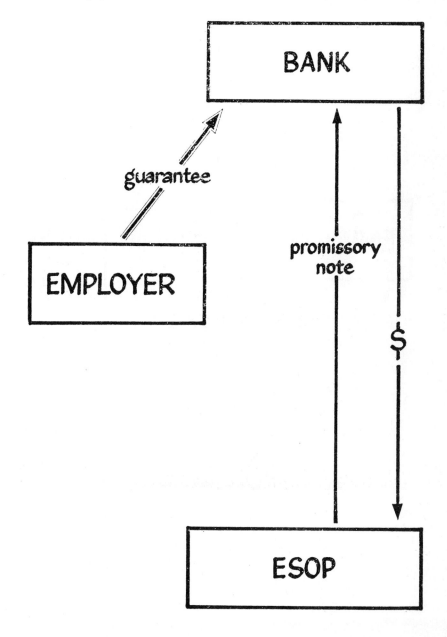

The ESOP then uses the money from the loan to buy stock from the employer:

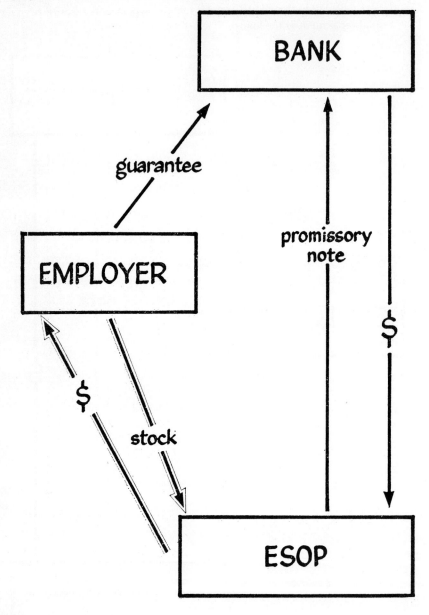

Each year, the employer makes a tax-deductible payment to the ESOP, sufficient to let the ESOP make its annual debt repayment to the bank:

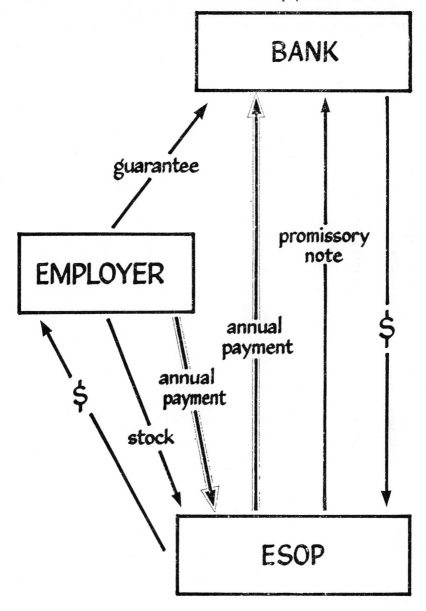

The effect of this transaction is to allow the employer to borrow money from a lender and repay the loan with tax-deductible dollars. Since the principal and interest repayments are deducted before the employer's taxable income is determined, the taxable income is lower than through regular borrowing and the employer's taxes are reduced.

Since the major portion of the ESOP or TRASOP assets are used to buy employer stock, the value of each employee's ESOP or TRASOP benefit is directly tied to the financial success of the employer. Also, the employer, as a result of the use of an ESOP or TRASOP, benefits because employees understand that their work performance directly affects the financial success of the employer and the value of ESOP or TRASOP assets. After all, they now own part of the company. This should encourage employees to work more productively and increase the profitability of their employer.

Another benefit to the employer is that the ESOP provides its shareholders with a buyer for their stock if they wish to sell. For stockholders of a small employer, this is a tremendous advantage, and it could also assist the employer in attracting additional investors.

Summary

The adoption of an ESOP or a TRASOP provides benefits for the employer, its shareholders and its employees. Our tax laws encourage the establishment and use of ESOPs and TRASOPs. Congress has passed seven laws in the past 6 years to encourage employers to consider ESOP and TRASOP. Will it continue? Senator Russell B. Long, chairman of the Senate Finance Committee, has repeatedly stated: "Just as in 1862, when Congress passed a law to allow Americans who had very little money to own and develop up to 160 acres of land, we should now give Americans the opportunity to become owners of our growing frontier of new capital (stock). The way to do this is through laws which encourage the development of programs like ESOP."

O

THE SECTION 79 PLAN

Over the last several years there has been continued interest in the sale of so-called "Section 79 Plans." These programs involve the use of permanent life insurance in conjunction with employee group-term insurance plans in order to combine tax advantages of group-term coverage with the features of a permanent policy.

The Section 79 Plan derives its name from section 79 of the Internal Revenue Code, which provides that as long as the employer is neither a direct or indirect beneficiary of the policy, an employee need not report the cost of the first $50,000 of group-term life insurance provided directly or indirectly by an employer, and that the amounts in excess of $50,000 are taxed in accordance with Table I rates established by the IRS. If the insured employee becomes disabled or retires, even the cost for the term coverage in excess of $50,000 need not be reported.

Section 79 does not, however, answer many questions concerning the proper tax treatment of group insurance plans. The Treasury Department accordingly has issued proposed regulations, which are expected to be finalized sometime in 1979 and which should resolve most of the current uncertainty.

The proposed regulations take a two-pronged approach to valuing a permanent life insurance contract issued under a group-term plan. The amount of group-term in any permanent life insurance contract is to be determined on the basis of the total death benefit minus the amount of paid-up insurance available at the year end. This amount, when added to other group-term benefits provided to the employee and reduced by the $50,000 group-term exemption, is the total benefit which is taxed to the employee at Table I rates. The premium for the permanent portion is computed by means of a complex actuarial formula which can be understood as an amount equal to the greater of the increase in "statutory" reserves or cash values.

Because the regulations utilize the greater of reserve or cash value in determining the employee's taxable benefit, there is no longer the potential "windfall" for the employee which was available under the prior regulations. Section 79 is no longer a *reason* to buy life insurance; rather it is a *method* of purchasing it.

It should be pointed out that Section 79 Plans must meet the reporting (summary plan description) and disclosure requirements set forth by ERISA for welfare-benefit plans. In addition, the amounts of coverage for each employee must be based on a formula which precludes individual selection. Thus, a schedule may refer to salary or position as a basis for determining face amounts, but the program as a whole must present a balanced plan of coverage.

Where Section 79 May Be Useful. An appropriate application for Section 79 Plans is where an employee does not meet the requirements for insurance at standard rates. In this case, the employee need not report the cost of the extra premium which might be charged for the coverage. The employee is taxed on the protection enjoyed based on Table I rates rather than the actual premium cost of the insurance. Since the employer can continue to deduct the *full* premium for the plan under section 162 of the Code, this ability to have the cost of the additional premium paid on a deductible basis without any charge to the employee can be an ideal solution where health or other factors are involved.

Another situation where section 79 may be used to advantage is in the case of the older employee. Since the taxable cost for the term coverage ceases at retirement, only the charge for the permanent portion must be reported after retirement, if the employer continues to pay the entire premium.

RETIRED LIVES RESERVE
(PREFUNDING POST-RETIREMENT GROUP
LIFE INSURANCE)

Group term life insurance is perhaps one of the most common of employee fringe benefits. The gradual elimination of state regulations restricting amounts of group life has led to the issuance of high amounts of coverage for executive employees. Such employees tend to rely heavily on this protection to provide for their families and to create liquidity for their estates.

Unfortunately, most group life plans either stop at retirement or provide for substantially reduced amounts, often for only a limited period of time. While an employee has the right to convert group term insurance to an individual permanent policy at retirement, the premium may be prohibitive. Furthermore, conversion of large amounts of group insurance will result in significant "experience charges" to the employer, possibly resulting in increased rates for the whole group.

A Possible Solution: Retired Lives Reserve. Retired Lives Reserve (RLR) *may* be the answer by providing a way for employers to prefund the cost of post-retirement group life insurance for employees on a favorable tax basis. This is achieved by the employer making actuarially determined deposits to a reserve fund which will be used to continue the employees' insurance protection beyond retirement. While neither the employer nor employee will be able to use the reserve funds for any other purpose as long as the plan is in effect, the accumulated funds will permit the continuation of the employees' group life insurance indefinitely.

TAX ASPECTS OF RETIRED LIVES RESERVE

Proponents of the RLR concept claim the tax results listed below. However, it should be recognized that other practitioners feel that some of these tax results are not settled and may be challenged by the IRS. These concerns stem from the fact that the IRS has not yet issued final regulations for section 79 of the Code—the section dealing with taxation of group life insurance benefits. Additionally, questions have been raised about the discriminatory nature of many RLR plans and the possibility that the large reserve deposits required for older employees may not be considered "reasonable compensation" and could, therefore, be subjected to less favorable tax treatment. Finally, there are indications that the IRS is concerned about the significant loss of revenue that would result if RLR plans become more popular.

(1) Contributions by an employer to the Retired Lives Reserve are fully deductible assuming the plan has been properly established, the contributions are actuarially determined and the employees' total compensation, including the RLR payment, is reasonable.

(2) Earnings on funds in the Retired Lives Reserve often will accumulate free of federal income taxation.

(3) Employer contributions to the RLR do not constitute taxable income to the employees if the funds are not made available to them.

(4) Employees will not incur tax liability for the economic value (Table I) of group term life insurance protection provided after retirement.

(5) The payment of accumulated RLR funds to either employer or employee will be taxed as ordinary income.

FUNDING THE RLR PROGRAM

There are two basic elements in the complete RLR program: (1) the group term life insurance protection, and (2) the actual reserve or accumulation fund. Let's examine the funding of each separately.

(1) *Group Term Life Insurance.* Depending on the size of the basic group, the number of executives to be covered by the RLR program, and the group carrier's willingness to continue term coverage into the post-retirement period, the post-retirement benefits can be provided either by the continuation of the basic group coverage or through the use of individual term policies written as part of the overall plan of group insurance.

(2) *The Retired Lives Reserve Fund.* This is typically funded through one of the following methods.
  a. *Tax-Exempt Trust.* Under this approach a voluntary employees' association trust is created for the purpose of providing the group life insurance and other selected benefits. In order to obtain the tax exemption under Code section 501(c)(9) required of such associations, no part of the net earnings of the trust can inure to the benefit of any private shareholder or individual. Further, benefits must be offered to employees on a basis that does not discriminate in favor of shareholders or other highly compensated employees.
  Since most firms adopting a Retired Reserve program wish to provide benefits primarily for their executive group, the exempt trust usually will not be an appropriate vehicle.

b. *Taxable Trust.* A non-exempt (taxable) trust can also be used to prefund the cost of post-retirement group term life insurance. Because of the taxation of regular trust income, it is generally advantageous for such trusts to accumulate the funds through annuity contracts. The build-up of cash values of annuities is not subject to income taxation until such time as annuity benefits commence. Proponents claim that a properly designed trust used with the RLR concept should not have any current taxable income.

c. *Reserve Maintained by A Life Insurance Company.* One of the simpler methods used for prefunding post-retirement group life benefits is to have the same company which is providing the group term insurance also hold the RLR fund. Traditionally used with larger plans, some companies are now applying this concept to smaller plans through the use of multi-employer trusts.

COMPARISON OF RETIRED LIVES RESERVE WITH SECTION 79 PERMANENT

Section 79 of the Code deals with the taxation of group life insurance provided to employees. In that respect, it affects both RLR and the so-called "Section 79" insurance policies that include permanent (cash value) benefits. Group term life insurance, under both approaches, is taxed in the same way, i.e., a uniform premium table issued by the IRS is used to compute the value of group term insurance protection enjoyed by the employee. The cost of the first $50,000 of such protection is tax free, as are all amounts provided after retirement.

The taxation and ownership of the permanent or cash value portions of the two programs is quite different. Under the Section 79 permanent plan, the employee usually owns and pays (directly or indirectly) for the permanent portion of the plan. The employee pays income tax on the permanent portion of the premium and may use the permanent values for personal needs such as educational expenses, retirement income, estate liquidity, etc. In the event the employee terminates employment, the policy is portable and may be continued on a personal basis with premiums based on the original age of issue.

The deposits made by the employer to the Retired Lives Reserve may not be used by either the employer or employee so long as any active or retired participant is alive. Consequently, proponents of the plan suggest that the employee is not currently taxed on monies accumulated in the reserve. In the event the plan is ultimately discontinued and distribution of the reserve made to either the employer or employee, any amounts received will then be subjected to income taxation.

GEOTHERMAL ENERGY

Just as the oil industry has developed terms like wildcat well and abbreviations like Mcf (gas), the geothermal industry is now evolving a new language with words such as magma and reference codes such as lbs/sq in/hr (steam).

In order to arrive at an understanding of geothermal energy, the first concept is steam. Steam is created by heat. Except for hydroelectric, all methods of manufacturing electric power commercially involve steam-operated turbines. The steam is manufactured by heat derived from uranium, gas, oil, coal, and magmatic (geothermal) sources. Steam pressure is measured in *pounds per square inch (lbs/sq in) or kilograms per square centimeter (kg/cm^2).* Steam volume is measured in *pounds per hour (lbs/hr) or kilograms per hour (kg/hr).* An electric power plant uses the steam to manufacture electricity which is measured in *kilowatts per hour (kw/hr or kwh or simply kw)* — a kilowatt is 1,000 watts and could operate ten 100-watt light bulbs for one hour.

An electric company often computes its kwh charges on the basis of mils. A mil is 1/10 of a cent. In the Geysers Geothermal Field in California, the Pacific Gas and Electric Company currently (July 1978) pays the companies producing dry steam at a rate of approximately 16.02 mils (1.602 cents) per kwh.

According to the Pacific Gas and Electric Company ("The Geysers" Folder of September 1974), it requires slightly less than 20 pounds of dry steam to produce one kwh of electricity. *Thus, about 20 pounds of dry steam from a geothermal well in the Geysers Field will produce one kwh of electricity with a current (July 1978) value of approximately 16.02 mils.*

Some power plants constructed in the Geysers Field have a capacity of 55,000 kwh (55 MW) of electricity. A plant of this size would require over one million pounds of steam per hour for full operation at rated capacity.

QUESTIONS AND ANSWERS
ABOUT GEOTHERMAL ENERGY

Q. WHAT IS GEOTHERMAL ENERGY?

A. It is steam or high temperature water derived from within the earth. Its principal use, at present, is in generating electricity.

Q. WHERE IS GEOTHERMAL ENERGY BEING USED?

A. Italy, New Zealand, Russia, Japan, Mexico and the United States all have geothermally-powered electric generating plants. The number of these installations is presently small but worldwide interest is developing rapidly.

Q. WHERE AND HOW DO YOU EXPLORE FOR IT?

A. The most obvious places are in the vicinity of thermal springs, geysers, and areas of recent volcanic activity. Many of the sophisticated geophysical techniques developed in the search for oil and gas are also used in detecting these "hot spots". The actual presence of a geothermal reservoir can only be determined by drilling.

Q. DO THE DRILLING METHODS DIFFER FROM OIL?

A. No. Drilling for geothermal energy employs comparable techniques to those used in drilling for oil and gas.

Q. WHAT DOES GENERAL PARTNER KNOW ABOUT GEOTHERMAL?

A. Like other oil companies that are beginning to engage in geothermal exploration, General Partner has a staff of professional geologists, geophysicists and engineers who are broadly skilled in the earth sciences — and much of the knowledge used to explore for oil and gas can also be used to explore for geothermal energy. In addition, General Partner is retaining geothermal consultants, and working with another Company that is experienced in geothermal operations.

Q. WHY HASN'T GEOTHERMAL POWER BEEN
DEVELOPED EARLIER?

A. Italy began developing its geothermal resources in the late 1930's but with oil, gas and coal being generally cheap and abundant throughout the world, there was little reason to seek other forms of energy until recently.

Q. IS STEAM THE ONLY USABLE FORM OF
GEOTHERMAL ENERGY?

A. Dry natural steam, or superheated waters which flash into steam, are currently the only practical applications of geothermal energy used to generate electric power. Other methods of commercially utilizing geothermal energy are in the research and pilot-plant stages.

Q. HOW FAR CAN YOU TRANSPORT THE STEAM OR
HEATED FLUIDS?

A. Present technology requires that a generating plant be located within about one mile of the wells.

Q. IS A PARTICIPATION ASSESSABLE?

A. No, participations are not assessable. However, Participants in a geothermal exploratory discovery well will have pre-emptive rights to invest in development drilling on the discovery block.

GENERAL CONSIDERATIONS

Nature of Geothermal Energy

Geothermal Energy is energy created by the heat which is derived from the molten rock beneath the earth's surface. Normally, temperature within the earth increases as depth increases. Occasionally, through geologic anomaly, extremely hot molten rock or magma approaches the surface of the earth or, as in the case of a volcano, may actually surface. In some instances, the magma penetrates near the surface of the earth under conditions which create reservoirs of heat. Under ideal conditions these reservoirs may contain accumulations of superheated water or steam which may be extracted and employed to drive electrical generating turbines. Hot springs, geysers and other thermal surface manifestations indicate shallow-lying heat reservoirs. The production of geothermal fluids from a sub-terranean reservoir is comparable to the production of oil and gas, but its technology and knowledge of reservoir mechanics is at this time significantly less developed. The extractive system is basically a well, drilled to a depth sufficient to encounter geo-thermal fluids, cased and completed to provide a stable conduit through which the fluids can flow to the surface, and furnished with the facilities necessary to control and transport the fluids to their point of utilization.

Geothermal fluids are found to exist either in liquid water or as gaseous steam. In this writing, such fluids are included in the term "Geothermal Energy". The energy in a geothermal reservoir consists of heat, largely stored in rocks, and to a lesser extent, in liquid water and/or steam filled pores and fractures. The water and steam provide the means by which heat from deep sources is transferred by convection to depths shallow enough to be tapped by drilling. Water and steam also serve as the agent by which geothermal heat escapes at the surface in hot springs. For a geothermal reservoir to have appreciable potential for exploration, generally it must meet the following requirements: (1) relatively high temperature (preferably more than 400° Fahrenheit, depending on the processing technology), (2) a depth shallow enough to permit drilling (generally 10,000 feet or less), (3) sufficient rock permeability and porosity to allow the heat transfer agent such as water or steam to flow continuously at a high rate and (4) sufficient water supply to maintain production over many years.

In a dry steam Geothermal Energy resource as utilized for the production of electricity, Magma, the molten rock that is underlying the geothermal area, is the heat source. It radiates heat energy (wavy arrows) through the reservoir rock above it, converting fluids in open fractures of the rock into steam. Most open fractures don't extend to the surface, but when they do hot springs or fumaroles occur. A drilling rig bores down into the rock, cutting through several fractures to tap the natural steam supply After the drilling is completed, the steam is piped from the steam well to an electrical generating station.

While the Partnerships may seek dry steam reservoirs, they may also explore for other forms of Geothermal Energy. The Partnerships will confine their activities to the search for dry steam or superheated water, and will not attempt to explore for superheated rocks not found in association with a heat transfer agent, such as dry steam or superheated water. The technology required to economically exploit such superheated rocks is not believed to be sufficient.

The primary use of Geothermal Energy to date is for the generation of electricity. Under existing technology, geothermal fluids are expanded into a low-pressure turbine which drives a conventional electric generator. In some areas, the geothermal reservoir produces natural dry steam that can be brought to the surface and introduced directly into the turbine. In other areas, geothermal fluids, under pressure and heated beyond the boiling point, are brought to the surface. A portion of this fluid flashes into steam which is used to drive the generator turbine.

Such Geothermal Energy might be kept under pressure and passed in liquid form through a heat exchanger to heat a secondary lower boiling point fluid to produce a vapor for use in driving the generator turbine.

The technology exists for utilizing hot dry steam for the generation of electric power and is being employed. The flashing of very hot water into steam at the surface also is being used, but only a portion of the heat value of the fluid is utilized. Technology for passing hot water through a heat exchanger has been developed and utilized in pilot plant operations and larger systems are being planned.

The Geysers Geothermal Field in Sonoma County, California, at present is the only Geothermal Energy producing area in the United States, and in 1977 the total power output from this field was the largest of any Geothermal Energy field in the world.

The estimation of Geothermal Energy reserves is yet to be accepted as a proven procedure. The length of time that Geothermal Energy can be withdrawn from a given reservoir and the possible life of the steam wells drawing therefrom are very speculative. Presently, the procedures for estimating geothermal reserves are drawn from the methods and principles utilized in estimating petroleum reserves. These include considerations of the subsurface fluid pressure, temperatures, reservoir rock porosity and steam volumes produced over a period of time. These methods, however, lack the precision of oil and gas reserve estimates because of the complexity of geothermal reservoirs. The Geysers Geothermal Field has been producing steam in commercial quantities since 1960. The Larderello Geothermal Fields in Italy have produced steam for electric power generation as early as 1913, the Wairakei Field located in New Zealand has been producing steam for electric power generation since 1952, and the Cerro Prieto Field in Mexico, approximately 20 miles south of the California border, has been producing Geothermal Energy in commercial quantities since 1964.

Exploration and Confirmation Activities

Because of the relatively long period of time which must elapse between the discovery of a commercial accumulation of Geothermal Energy and the extraction of that energy for use in generating electrical power, it is not believed to be feasible for a Partnership to fully develop each Area of Interest on which it will conduct activities. Accordingly, the Partnerships will adhere to the following procedure with respect to their exploratory operations.

Initially, an Area of Interest will be defined by a Partnership. An Area of Interest will generally be an area large enough to include several Geothermal Blocks, each of which will be designated with a view toward production of sufficient Geothermal Energy to support one generating station. Thus, while an Area of Interest may include several thousand acres, a Geothermal Block generally will include less than 1,000 acres, and probably about 400 or 500 acres.

The first Well drilled on an Area of Interest will be classified as an Exploratory Well as will all subsequent wells until it is established that commercial accumulations of Geothermal Energy are indicated to be present in the Area of Interest.

After the existence of commercial accumulations of Geothermal Energy has been indicated by an Exploratory Well, the first well drilled thereafter on any other Geothermal Block within that Area of Interest will generally be classified as a New Block Confirmation Well, since, generally, the possibilities of encountering commercial accumulations of Geothermal Energy on those Geothermal Blocks will be greater than in a purely exploratory situation. Subsequent wells drilled on a Geothermal Block on which there is a New Block Confirmation Well will be classified as either Confirmation Wells or Development Wells, the former classification being distinguished from the latter by whether the wells previously drilled on that Geothermal Block have indicated sufficient Geothermal Energy to warrant a utility company or industrial end-user to agree to commence the construction of a generating station.

962

General Partner will approve all prospects acquired by a Partnership, will oversee the drilling and completion of all wells and may operate some or all of such wells. General Partner does not intend to act as drilling contractor. Accordingly, no contracts for drilling or well services will exist between General Partner and the Partnerships; all such contracts will be with independent third parties. Should General Partner or an Affiliate enter into an agreement with a Partnership to provide such services, such contracts would be terminable upon sixty days written notice by the Partnership without penalty. Although it is not anticipated that any Leases will be acquired directly from General Partner, any Leases acquired by a Partnership from General Partner will be acquired at General Partner's Lease Acquisition and Maintenance Cost which includes an interest charge equal to 2% above the prime rate offered by Bank at the date of the Partnership's acquisition computed from the later of the date of General Partner's expenditure or three years. The Partnerships will not be charged with any Lease Acquisition and Maintenance Costs with respect to the Francisco Geothermal Block.

Utility Purchase

Unlike oil or gas, which may be used at great distances from where they are produced, Geothermal Energy must be used near its place of extraction since in transportation heat is lost and the fluid loses its heat energy. Therefore, a power generating station must be constructed on or near the productive Geothermal Block. A utility company or an industrial end-user will construct one of these stations (which stations cost several million dollars) only if it can be assured that sufficient Geothermal Energy can be produced to power the station for a period sufficient to permit recovery of the high investment and a profit. To minimize the risk that a Partnership will drill wells which indicate the existence of commercially producible steam and for which no market exists, before commencing the drilling of an Exploratory Well, General Partner will attempt to secure from a utility or an industrial end-user an indication of interest to construct a generating station and purchase Geothermal Energy. However, any such indication of interest will not be binding.

If commercial accumulations of Geothermal Energy are indicated by Confirmation Wells drilled by a Partnership, General

Partner will endeavor to interest a utility or an industrial end-user in committing to the construction of a generating station. Should it be unable to do so, it is unlikely that development will occur, and the investment in the producible Geothermal Block will probably be lost.

In many instances, there may be only one company that is in a position to purchase Geothermal Energy from a particular area. In such instances, the purchaser may be able to dictate the sales price of Geothermal Energy and thereby pay less for Geothermal Energy than it would be required to pay in situations wherein several purchasers were competing for such Geothermal Energy. Additionally, it is possible that the federal government may enter the utility field and that such would result in a reduced price for Geothermal Energy.

Revenue Sharing Among Partnerships

Since the Partnerships are not expected to be in a position to fully develop any Geothermal Blocks which are indicated to be commercially productive, it is anticipated that development of Geothermal Blocks will be undertaken by other programs which may be organized by General Partner. In an effort to ensure that there is an equitable disposition of any revenues which may be obtained by the programs jointly involved in the exploration, confirmation and development of a Geothermal Block, the following formula has been established which will govern revenue sharing among those partnerships. Partnerships that participate in the drilling of an Exploratory Well or incur Geophysical Costs in such a Geothermal Block will receive 25% of the revenues attributable to the joint partnership interests, those that participate in the drilling of Confirmation Wells will receive 25% of the revenues attributable to the joint partnership interests and the Related Program that has drilled the Development Wells will receive 50% of the revenues attributable to the joint partnership interests. If the initial well drilled in a Geothermal Block is a New Block Confirmation Well (which is classified as a Confirmation Well), Partnerships that participate in the drilling of Confirmation Wells or incur Geophysical Costs will receive 50% of the revenues attributable to the joint partnership interests and the Related Program or Partnership that has drilled the Development Wells will receive 50% of the revenues attributable to the joint partnership interests in the Geothermal

964

Block. This division of revenues will continue until such time as the total cost to acquire, explore, develop and operate that Geothermal Block has been recovered by the partnerships jointly, at which time the revenues will be divided among the classes of partnerships described above in a manner which approximates the respective costs borne in that Geothermal Block by each partnership. The division of revenues among the partnerships prior to payout will not necessarily reflect the respective costs borne by each partnership.

If more than one partnership participates in the drilling of a single well, or a single type of well, on a Geothermal Block, they will share in the revenues allocated to that class of well in a manner which approximates their share of such well costs. Partnerships incurring Geophysical Costs shall share in revenues applicable to Partnerships drilling Exploratory Wells.

If more than one General Partner Program drills a Development Well on the Francisco Geothermal Block they would receive, in the aggregate, not more than 50% of the joint program revenues from the Block until payout of total costs of the partnerships has occurred.

For purposes of the above sharing arrangement, Lease Acquisition and Maintenance Costs shall be considered a cost of drilling a well.

Development

Because of the time lag involved in constructing a generating station, several years may lapse between the completion of Confirmation Well drilling and the completion of drilling of Development Wells in any Geothermal Block. In view of this fact, development of Geothermal Blocks is intended to be undertaken by programs organized exclusively for that purpose (Related Programs) and in which all Participants that have borne a portion of the costs of drilling Exploratory Wells or incurred Geophysical Costs may be afforded an opportunity to participate in other General Partner Programs. The Limited Partnership Agreement provides that General Partner's interest (excluding any interests which it may purchase on the same basis as Participants) cannot exceed 40% of the revenues of the Related Program computed without regard to investment. Thus, while the interest of General Partner in a Related Program may be different than its interest in one of the Partnerships, excluding any interest it may purchase, General Partner may not obtain an interest in any well of a Related Program which exceeds the interest in such a well obtainable by it hereunder. It is possible that General Partner will not organize a Related Program, in which case General Partner is permitted to perform the functions of a Related Program. However, General Partner's intention is to organize Related Programs and it will undertake such activities itself only if it is reasonably determined not to be feasible to organize such a program and not in the best interests of the Partnership to farmout its Geothermal Blocks or enter into joint ventures with third parties.

Because of the substantial costs incurred in developing any Geothermal Block, it is possible that Related Programs organized in the future by General Partner to perform such development work will not raise sufficient public funds to complete all of the development work necessary to supply a power generating station. To minimize (but not eliminate) the risk that development will not be completed because of insufficient Related Program funds, once a determination has been made by General Partner to form a Related Program, General Partner will provide sufficient drilling funds in addition to those provided by the Related Program as may be necessary to fully develop the Geothermal Block. Such funds will be provided on a proportionate working interest basis with the Related Program. If through a Related Program only 50% of the funds necessary to fully develop a Geothermal Block are raised, General Partner will provide the funds necessary for the additional 50% share and will retain a 50% working interest in the Related Program's share of revenues from the Geothermal Block. General Partner is unlimited in the manner it chooses to provide such funds. For example, General Partner may, if it desires, employ its own corporate funds to pay its share of development costs, may borrow such funds employing its interest in the Geothermal Block as security, may sell a portion of the Geothermal Block attributable to its interest, enter into industry arrangements with respect to such interest or form a Related Program. Consequently, any losses attributable to the interest retained by General Partner (and any profits) will be attributable solely to General Partner and not to the programs. In this respect, General Partner may have a conflict of interest.

Geophysical Operations

A Partnership may conduct Geophysical activities in areas throughout the Western United States. At this time, the areas in which such activities would be undertaken is not known. Expenditures for such activities will be limited to 10% of available drilling funds.

Geophysical activities may be conducted in areas where General Partner believes geothermal anomalies might exist, but where additional exploration work is required to confirm the existence of a drillable prospect. Generally, these areas will not be defined as an Area of Interest unless General Partner believes that it is probable, although not assured, that a Geothermal Block will be formed and a well drilled therein. In some cases leases will have previously been acquired on acreage covering parts or all of a potential Area of Interest and exploration work may have been previously conducted. As a result of the Partnership's efforts, General Partner may determine that the area merits further evaluation, a well should be drilled thereon or that further work is not warranted in the area. In either of the first two cases, others, including General Partner Programs, may conduct the additional Geophysical work or drilling operations in the area.

The type and number of surveys conducted will vary from area to area but may consist of one or more of the following:

1. Surface geologic and hydrologic mapping to determine the surface configuration of the rock layers and to locate surface signs of geothermal activity.

2. Acquisition and analysis of Earth Satellite imagery mapping.

3. Geophysical surveys of various sorts to measure indirectly the various physical parameters at depth such as temperature, electrical conductivity, propagation, velocity of elastic waves, density, magnetic susceptibility, seismic noise, Microearthquake measurements, all of which can be used to determine the likelihood of presence of geothermal anomalies.

4. Gravity surveys to aid in determining the regional geologic model.

5. Geochemical surveys to analyze the chemical content of surface waters, sub-surface waters, surface soils and sub-surface soils to determine the presence of geochemical indications of thermal anomalies.

6. Shallow drill holes to measure thermal gradients and other properties indicative of thermal anomalies.

Participants will recover 400% of such Geophysical Costs on the Geothermal Block prior to General Partner sharing in revenues as a general partner on such Block.

THE PROGRAM

The Geothermal Energy Program will consist of a series of not more than six limited partnerships which will engage in the drilling of wells for Geothermal Energy. Partnership operations will be conducted within one or more Areas of Interest which may contain several Geothermal Blocks, which are basically areas of land sufficient in size to support an electrical generating plant. It is not anticipated that a Partnership will have sufficient funds to test or develop an entire Area of Interest. However, each Partnership may have sufficient funds to test one or more Geothermal Blocks. The first well drilled by a Program in an Area of Interest will be an Exploratory Well. If commercial accumulations of Geothermal Energy are indicated by an Exploratory Well, subsequent wells drilled in the Geothermal Block in which the Exploratory Well is located will be classified as Confirmation Wells until a commitment has been obtained from a utility company or industrial end-user to build a generating station. Thereafter, wells in that Geothermal Block will be classified as Development Wells.

General Partner and affiliates have previously organized geothermal programs which have completed exploratory and confirmation drilling at the Francisco Geothermal Block in the North Geysers Area of Interest. An agreement has been entered to construct a generating station on the Francisco Geothermal Block. Therefore, all further wells drilled on the Francisco Geothermal Block shall be considered Development Wells.

Approximately 40% of the available drilling funds in Partnership will be used for the drilling of Development Wells in the Francisco Geothermal Block. General Partner has scheduled approximately $2,900,000 of development drilling within the next year on the Francisco Geothermal Block. General Partner estimates that an additional $16,555,000 expenditure will be required to complete development operations on the Francisco Geothermal Block to a stage at which a generating station may commence operations. Further development will be financed through additional development partnerships, through funds provided by General Partner or affiliates, through borrowings, including loans guaranteed by the Federal Department of Energy or through arrangements with other companies.

It is intended (although not assured) that approximately 50% of the available drilling funds in Partnership will be utilized for Exploratory drilling or Confirmation drilling or a combination thereof. Approximately 10% of available drilling funds may be expended for Geophysical Costs.

While General Partner will endeavor to observe the preceding ratio of expenditures for Partnership, unexpected difficulties may be encountered in the drilling of a well which would increase the cost from that estimated, or actual drilling may cost less than budgeted. Accordingly, that ratio is an objective and not a limitation.

Size of the Partnerships

The maximum aggregate amount of this offering of Units in Partnership is $7,000,000 (7,000 Units) and the minimum amount necessary to form Partnership is $1,000,000 (1,000 Units). General Partner will purchase sufficient Units to ensure such minimum capitalization with respect to Partnership. An investor must make a minimum purchase of 5 Units ($5,000) and may purchase additional Units in $1,000 increments. No fractional Units may be purchased.

General Partner will purchase at least 1% of all Units purchased in each Partnership offered and may purchase additional Units in any Partnership.

If, after formation of a Partnership, additional funds are required to permit it to complete operations which it has commenced, General Partner may contribute such additional funds as required for such purpose. Such contribution will permit General Partner to share in revenues on the same basis as the Participants with respect to funds so contributed.

COMPENSATION

General Partner will receive a single non-recurring management fee of 10% of the purchase price of all Units purchased. General Partner will be reimbursed for a portion of all expenditures and expenses attributable to the acquisition and maintenance of its geothermal Lease inventory with respect to Geothermal Blocks acquired by a Partnership, determined in accordance with generally accepted accounting principles, and shall include Lease bonuses, delay rentals and such portion of General Partner's direct and indirect expenses for exploration, geological, land engineering, drafting, accounting, legal and other services as is allocated to the property. The price of any Leases acquired from General Partner by a Partnership will also include an interest charge, which will not exceed 2% above the prime rate which prevails on the date of the sale. In addition, if General Partner operates one or more wells of the Partnership, General Partner will receive a payment to reimburse it for its district and camp expense.

The Participants will bear all Offering Costs (other than underwriting commissions) up to 2.5% of the gross proceeds from the sale of Units. The gross amount of such expenses is estimated to be $138,700. If such expenses exceed 2.5% of the gross proceeds from the sale of Units, the excess will be borne by General Partner. Offering Costs will be apportioned between the Partnerships on a basis which approximates their respective capital. Geologic, engineering and other data will remain the property of General Partner. Participants who have purchased Units in a Partnership will bear a portion of General Partner's General and Administrative Expenses chargeable to the operation of such Partnership in the same proportions as revenues are shared. Other entities in which General Partner or its affiliates possess an interest may participate in the exploration and development of Geothermal Blocks in which a Partnership also possesses an interest.

PARTICIPATION IN COSTS AND REVENUES

Costs and revenues of each Partnership will be shared on a "Geothermal Block" basis. The Participants will bear the costs of acquiring and maintaining all Leases in the Area of Interest in which they drill an Exploratory Well. The Participants will also bear all Partnership costs of acquiring, maintaining, exploring, confirming and operating each Geothermal Block. The Participants will receive 100% of a Partnership's share of any revenues from each Geothermal Block until they have been credited with revenues from such Geothermal Block equal to:

970

(i)   400% of all of the Partnership's Recoverable Drilling Costs of any Exploratory Wells and Geophysical Costs in such Geothermal Block,

(ii) 200% of all of the Partnership's Recoverable Drilling Costs of any Confirmation Wells in such Geothermal Block.

(iii) 100% of the Partnership's share of all Operating Charges and 100% of all Replacement Charges,

(iv) 100% of the Partnership's Recoverable Drilling Costs of any Development Wells in such Geothermal Block, and

(v)   100% of the Partnership's Lease Acquisition and Maintenance Costs theretofore charged to the Partnership with respect to the Area of Interest in which such Geothermal Block is located.

Thereafter, the Participants will bear 60% of the Partnership's costs and be credited with 60% of the Partnership's revenues from such Geothermal Block and General Partner will be charged with 40% of the Partnership's costs and receive 40% of the Partnership's revenues from such Geothermal Block.

Participants will also be credited with a portion of the Net Profits attributable to General Partner's interest in all Geothermal Blocks in an Area of Interest in which such Participants are charged with the costs of an Exploratory Well or Geophysical Costs except the Geothermal Block in which such activities take place. The amount of such Net Profits will be either 10% or 50%.

Preemptive Rights

To limit the dilution of a Participant's interest in a productive Geothermal Block, if Development Wells are to be drilled by a Related Program, the Limited Partnership Agreement grants each Participant that contributed to the drilling of a productive Exploratory Well or incurred Geophysical Costs thereon a preemptive right to subscribe to the purchase of Units in any Related Program organized exclusively to develop such Geothermal Block. No right to purchase Units on a preemptive basis in a Related Program is granted to a Participant who is in a program which drills only a Confirmation or Development Well on a Geothermal Block, and his interest in such Block is therefore subject to dilution. To maintain his full preemptive right, a Participant must purchase the maximum number of Units offered him in all Related Programs, since the failure to exercise such right to the full extent available terminates the preemptive right as to the unexercised portion in all future Related Programs. To the extent that a Participant fails to exercise his preemptive rights, the activities contemplated for the Related Program may be offered through General Partner Programs open to other investors.

No assurance may be given that a Related Program will be formed or that if formed applicable law will permit interests therein to be offered to Participants.

BENEFITS OF A GEOTHERMAL ENERGY PROGRAM

1. Recovery of Investment: On successful geothermal blocks, exploratory well Participants recover 400% of exploratory well drilling costs, confirmation well Participants receive 200% of the drilling costs and development well Participants receive 100% of all costs before General Partner shares in any revenues.

2. Tax Advantages: Reduce current-year taxable income with allowable deductions from drilling costs.

3. After Participants' Payout in a geothermal block, Participants share revenues with General Partner 60/40%.

4. Future Geothermal Blocks: Participants in exploratory wells will receive 10% to 50% of General Partner's future net profits from any and all successful geothermal blocks, excepting the first geothermal block, developed within an Area of Interest — without additional investment.

RISKS OF A GEOTHERMAL ENERGY PROGRAM

A prospective Participant should consider the following factors before subscribing:

Time of Production and Sale. Prior to commencing the drilling of an Exploratory Well, General Partner generally will have received an indication of interest from a utility or industrial end-user. After completion of an Exploratory Well, if commercially producible quantities of Geothermal Energy are indicated, General Partner will endeavor to enter into a contract under which a utility company or other user will agree to purchase the production from the Geothermal Block. After obtaining regulatory agency approval, if necessary, the construction by such utility or other user of a generating plant capable of profitable generation of electric power using currently applied production techniques will require at least three years. At that point, revenues from the sale of Geothermal Energy may commence. In considering whether to assume the risk of construction, a utility company or industrial end-user may be expected to consider various factors, including anticipated production. Two years after the completion of a Partnership's drilling activities, General Partner will solicit bids for the sale of Participants' interests in Partnerships which have drilled a producible Exploratory Well. No assurance may be given that General Partner will be able to obtain such bids. A Participant should not anticipate that distributions will be made by a Partnership for at least four years after drilling an Exploratory Well.

Geothermal Exploration. Both exploration for and development of Geothermal Energy involves a high degree of risk and uncertainty. There can be no assurance that Geothermal Energy will be found in commercially producible quantities or in kinds susceptible to the generation of electric power. While exploration for Geothermal Energy is similar in many respects to exploration for oil or gas, the technology of Geothermal Energy exploration and production is less developed. Additionally, while a single oil well may be economically productive, more than one Geothermal Energy well is required to produce sufficient energy flow to supply a generating unit.

Taxation — Special Allocation. A Participant's federal income tax deductions resulting from Partnership activities may be spread over more than one calendar year since it is probable that all of the funds provided by Participants will not be expended during a Partnership's initial calendar year of operations. In an attempt to accelerate deductions resulting from expenditures for deductible costs, such costs will be allocated first to the Participants (other than General Partner) until the funds invested by such Participant which remain available for the payment of such costs have been exhausted; thereafter such costs will be charged to General Partner, and General Partner shall thereupon furnish funds to the Partnerships as needed. There is

973

no assurance that the IRS will observe this allocation. While this arrangement may permit Participants to claim larger deductions for federal income tax purposes during the first calendar year of a Partnership's operations than might otherwise be available to them, it will defer the time at which General Partner pays for certain of its Units. General Partner will, however, receive the share of revenues attributable to the Units for which it has subscribed even though it has not paid for them.

Taxation — Certain Risks. The Partnerships intend to treat the cost of drilling Geothermal Energy wells as intangible drilling costs and intend to claim depletion with respect to any Geothermal Energy produced and sold by them. There is a high risk that the Internal Revenue Service ("IRS") will disallow any such deductions, in which case litigation may be required to determine whether such deductions are allowable. Despite Tax Court decisions permitting deduction of intangible drilling and development costs on geothermal wells, the IRS has continued to assert that costs of geothermal energy wells are not intangible drilling costs and that depletion is not allowable. The economic burden of establishing the validity of any such deductions (including the cost of litigation, if any) may fall upon an individual Participant if the deductions allocated to and claimed by him are disallowed by the IRS. There is limited reported judicial authority respecting the allowability of these deductions, and it is possible that they may be allowed for certain types of Geothermal Energy and not for other types or that they may be disallowed in their entirety. Thus, no assurance may be given that any of such deductions if claimed will be allowed.

Year-End Drilling. If a Partnership pays drilling costs in a taxable year prior to the actual expenditure of such funds by the drilling contractor no assurance can be given that deductions with respect to such prepaid expenses will be allowed by the Internal Revenue Service.

Deductions. Due to the nature of the activities contemplated, a significant portion of the Participants' funds probably will not be expended during the current year and therefore available deductions will probably be spread over at least two years.

Prior Geothermal Experience. General Partner's staff has limited experience in the exploration for Geothermal Energy. General Partner has drilled geothermal wells for its own account and has organized the Programs which have participated in the drilling of geothermal wells, which appear to have encountered commercial accumulations of Geothermal Energy. To supplement its staff, General Partner intends to utilize the services of geothermal consultants some of whom may possess interests in the Leases explored or developed by the Partnerships.

Commercial Geothermal Production. Geothermal Energy was produced commercially in foreign areas as early as 1913. One producing area exists in the United States, the Geysers Geothermal Field in Sonoma and Lake Counties, California. Efforts to commercially produce Geothermal Energy elsewhere in the United States are being made. While many of these efforts have not yet been abandoned, to the date hereof none have reached a stage of profitability.

Additional Financing May Be Required. The Units are not assessable and the proceeds of this offering may not be sufficient to fully develop any productive Geothermal Blocks of a Partnership. Accordingly, General Partner has the authority to farm out or joint venture the further development of such Geothermal Blocks with others. General Partner intends to undertake the development of productive Geothermal Blocks through other programs organized by General Partner. Subject to applicable law, Participants have preemptive rights to acquire interests in programs organized by General Partner to drill Development Wells in Geothermal Blocks in which their Partnership has drilled a productive Exploratory Well or incurred Geophysical Costs. However, to maintain such preemptive rights, a Participant must continuously invest in such programs. Although General Partner will endeavor to permit the Participants, under such circumstances, to invest in such subsequent programs, there is no assurance that development will be undertaken by a program organized by General Partner or that if such a program is organized the Participants will be able to exercise their rights to acquire interests therein. Therefore, there is a risk that Participants may not receive any benefits they otherwise would receive by investing in such program. There is a risk that a Participant's interest in a productive Geothermal Block will be diluted. Moreover, because it cannot be determined precisely what interest a Partnership will ultimately possess in any Geothermal Block, it is anticipated that such interest may be only a small fraction of the working interest.

Market for Geothermal Energy. Since the principal market for Geothermal Energy appears to be its use as a source of energy for the generation of electric power, a Partnership will not explore a Geothermal Block unless it has received from a utility company or industrial end-user an indication of interest to purchase Geothermal Energy from the Geothermal Block. While such an indication of interest will not be binding, it will reduce the risk (which is present) that a market will not exist for any Geothermal Energy which may be discovered. General Partner has entered into an agreement for the construction of a power plant to utilize Geothermal Energy from the Francisco Geothermal Block in which present Partnership, and possibly subsequent Partnerships, will drill Development Wells. However, prior to construction of the power plant it will be necessary to demonstrate the development of sufficient quantities of steam to operate the power plant. Numerous permits will be required before full field development can be undertaken and before the power plant can be constructed and operated. No assurances can be given that such permits will be forthcoming.

Technology. Knowledge of the characteristics and parameters of individual geothermal systems in the United States is highly limited. Techniques for effectively utilizing the energy produced from geothermal wells are relatively new and less is known about the subject than is known about exploration for, and utilization of, more conventional energy resources such as hydrocarbons. Geothermal Energy must be of acceptable quality and producible in substantial quantities at required pressures and temperatures to warrant commercial production. Certain Geothermal Energy reservoirs may contain highly corrosive particles which render utilization of the Geothermal Energy difficult and costly. Particulates may, under certain conditions, render use of the Geothermal Energy uneconomic under present technology. If waste materials from a generating facility are re-injected into the ground, as may be required, the reservoir temperature and corresponding energy potential may decrease.

Design Limitations. The characteristics of individual Geo-thermal Energy reservoirs and the Geothermal Energy produced therefrom may vary greatly. Power generation facilities must be designed and constructed to meet such characteristics if they are to function optimally and thus produce maximum revenues to the seller of Geothermal Energy, since the sales price of the Geothermal Energy may be based upon the electrical output of the facility, rather than the amount of Geothermal Energy consumed. The Partnerships will have little, if any, control over design of a facility and, thus, will not be in a position to ensure that their revenues are maximized.

Revenues From Production. In general, as to each Geo-thermal Block, the costs and risks of drilling will be borne by the Participants. However, after Participants' Payout, the sharing of costs and revenues will be 60% by the Participants and 40% by General Partner. Such sharing will bear no relation to the relative investments of the Participants and General Partner with respect to the Geothermal Block. Since Participants' Payout is determined on a Geothermal Block basis, General Partner may receive substantial revenues before the Participants have recovered their total investment in the Partnership, Participants in a Partnership which drills an Exploratory Well or incurs Geophysical Costs will share in a portion of the Net Profits attributable to General Partner's interests in other Geothermal Blocks in the Area of Interest. This interest does not burden Geothermal Blocks in which Exploratory Wells are drilled or Geophysical Costs incurred.

Government Regulation and Environmental Controls. In most states, before a utility company may construct an electrical generating plant and purchase Geothermal Energy, the approval of a state commission is required. The Partnerships will endeavor to obtain informal indications that necessary approvals, if required, will be granted before spending substantial amounts of money on a Geothermal Block. Since the approval may be a matter of discretion, there can be no assurance that Geothermal Energy from commercially productive Geothermal Blocks will be sold. Additionally, the Partnerships will be required to comply with various laws and regulations designed to protect the environment. Damage to the environment including contamination of ground water reservoirs whether or not caused by negligence, may be the responsibility of the Partnerships. These factors may limit the number of Leases which can be acquired and explored and increase present and future production costs. Prior to the commencement of the drilling of a well for Geothermal Energy it will be necessary to obtain drilling permits and environmental clearances.

Transferability of Units. Units will not be marketable. In general, Units may be transferred only with the consent of General Partner. Preemptive rights are not transferable and will terminate upon a transfer of the Units to which they appertain.

Competition. Competition for well-situated geothermal prospects is intense; it is not always possible to obtain desirable acreage at reasonable prices. Because other companies may have greater financial resources than the Partnerships, the Partnerships may be at a disadvantage in this competition.

Conflicts of Interest. A Partnership engaging in exploratory or geophysical activity may acquire Leases from General Partner covering sufficient acreage to constitute a Geothermal Block. General Partner may retain Leases in the Area of Interest not acquired by a Partnership and General Partner intends to develop those Leases through programs similar to the Partnerships. Information gained through the Partnership's activities may enhance the value of the retained Leases. However, should General Partner not organize such programs, it is permitted to develop those Leases for its own account. Participants in programs which have drilled an Exploratory Well or incurred Geophysical Costs in this Area of Interest will, however, possess a 50% Net Profits interest in General Partner's interest in the Area of Interest and may thus benefit through General Partner's efforts.

Material and Equipment Shortage. Materials and equipment necessary for the drilling of wells have been in short supply in recent periods. This situation could result in a delay in operations and consequently a delay in the tax deductions which may be generated through operations.

Limited Capitalization. The capitalization of a Partnership may not be sufficient to enable the Partnership to participate in the drilling of numerous wells. Therefore, the risks of loss to an investor will be greater than if the Partnerships were able to diversify their activities through participation in numerous ventures.

Limited Liability. Certain states in which the Partnerships may conduct their operations have not established if limited partnerships formed under the laws of another state possess limited liability. However, assuming compliance with the Limited Partnership Agreement and applicable law, the liability of Participants will be limited to their Participations, and any wrongfully distributed assets. The Partnership may be dissolved at the election of General Partner. In the event a Partnership is liquidated, the Participants may receive their interest in Partnership assets in kind. As direct owners of such assets, Participants would not have the shield from liability provided by the Partnership. In such event, the Participants may desire to undertake the normal protections of working interest owners including obtaining liability insurance which normally does not insure against all risks of operations. In certain states the Participants' ability to exercise their voting rights with respect to certain basic Partnership matters may jeopardize the status of the Partnership as a limited partnership under state law.

TAX ASPECTS OF A GEOTHERMAL ENERGY PROGRAM

1. Each partner is required to take into account his distributive share of the partnership's income, whether or not such income is distributed to him, retained by the partnership or used to repay loans.
2. Costs of lease acquisition must be capitalized and recovered through depletion or deducted when the property is abandoned. Geological and geophysical expenses which relate to an area of interest in which property is retained or acquired must be capitalized and recovered through depletion or deducted when the property is abandoned. If no leases are acquired within the area of interest to which such costs relate, such expenditures may be deducted.
3. Subject to the qualifications set forth below, assuming a proper election is made by a partnership, each partner is entitled to deduct his distributive share of the partnership's allowable intangible drilling and development costs. Such costs include such items as wages, fuel, hauling and supplies incident to and

979

necessary for the drilling of wells and the preparation of wells for the production of Geothermal Energy. They do not include expenditures incurred for the acquisition of tangible property ordinarily considered as having a salvage value such as the cost of pipe, casing, tubing and machines.

The Tax Court of the United States, affirmed by the United States Court of Appeals for the Ninth Circuit, has held that geothermal steam produced from The Geysers field is a "gas" entitled to cost or percentage depletion under Sections 611 and 613 of the Internal Revenue Code and that intangible costs of drilling and developing geothermal steam wells are deductible under Section 263(c) of the Internal Revenue Code. *Arthur E. Reich,* 52 T.C.700(1969), aff'd *Reich v. Commissioner,* 454 F. 2d 1157(9th Cir.1972). The Tax Court also held in the related case of *George D. Rowan,* T.C.Memo 1969-160, 28 T.C.M.797 (1969), that intangible costs of drilling geothermal steam wells at The Geysers are deductible under Section 263(c) of the Internal Revenue Code. There is no assurance that, if other courts are faced with the issue of the deductibility of intangible drilling and development costs or if the Tax Court or Ninth Circuit are again confronted with the issue only with respect to a Geothermal Energy field in which gaseous steam is not the heat transfer agent, such courts would not render adverse decisions on these matters. Furthermore, there is no assurance that the Internal Revenue Service will not issue published interpretations or rulings which would deny the deductibility of intangible drilling and development costs or that legislation will not be enacted which would deny such deductibility.

Notwithstanding these decisions, the Internal Revenue Service has continued to assert that costs of Geothermal Energy wells are not intangible drilling costs and that depletion is not allowable with respect to Geothermal Energy. If costs which would otherwise be deductible as intangible drilling and development costs for oil and hydrocarbon gas drilling are held to be nondeductible, such costs must be capitalized. These expenditures may be recovered through depreciation to the extent they relate to equipment which is subject to the allowance for depreciation under applicable provisions of the Internal Revenue Code, through the allowance for depletion, if permitted under applicable laws, or as a reduction of any gain or increase in any loss upon sale, abandonment or other taxable disposition.

980

4. If a partnership pays drilling costs in a taxable year prior to the actual expenditure of such funds by the drilling contractor, the partnership will be allowed to deduct in the year of payment the amount paid if and to the extent that (i) such amount is reasonable, (ii) such amount is paid pursuant to *bona fide* contract entered into for valid business reasons and (iii) the drilling contractor actually commences drilling or performs preliminary work with respect thereto in the year of payment. Since the foregoing factors involve a factual determination, no assurance can be given that any deductions with respect to prepaid expenses will be allowed by the Internal Revenue Service.

5. Each partner is entitled to deduct his distributive share of a partnership's depreciation and amortization with respect to expenditures which may not be currently deducted but which must be capitalized and depreciated or amortized pursuant to applicable provisions of the Code, as well as any investment credit upon the acquisition of any property qualifying therefor. When a partnership sells property on which depreciation has been claimed, any gain on the sale attributable to the depreciation may be treated as ordinary income rather than capital gain. In addition, disposition, whether by sale or abandonment, of property with respect to which an investment credit has been claimed before the expiration of the useful life which was taken into account in computing the credit may result in a tax equal to all or part of the credit previously claimed. If any lease is abandoned, each partner is entitled to his distributive share of the partnership's loss deduction, if any, with respect thereto. Such deduction will generally be treated as ordinary loss.

6. Under the *Reich* and *Rowan* cases, if production of geothermal steam which is considered to be a gas, rather than vaporized water, is obtained by a partnership, each partner is entitled to deduct his distributive share of the partnership's depletion allowance. In general, the depletion allowance is based upon either a percentage of the income from or the cost of the property from which production is obtained. Depletion based upon income is 22% of the annual gross income received from a domestic producing property, but not more than 50% of the taxable income therefrom (before deduction for depletion from such property). Depletion based upon the cost of the property allows writing off the capitalized cost (bonus, exploratory charges, legal fees and the like) of a producing property over its life by an annual deduction computed by dividing the

amount of unrecovered capitalized costs at the end of the year by estimated recoverable reserves at the beginning of such year and by multiplying the quotient by the number of units of production sold during the year.

7. The excess of the deduction for depletion of each property, if allowed, over the adjusted basis of such property at the end of each year (determined without regard to the depletion deduction for the year) is an item of "tax preference". A "minimum tax" of 15% will be imposed on the amount, if any, by which such excess, together with all other items of "tax preference" for the year, exceeds the greater of $10,000 or one-half the non-corporate partner's regular federal income tax liability for the year. Items of tax preference for individuals include one-half of net long term capital gains, itemized deductions (other than medical and casualty deductions) in excess of 60% of adjusted gross income, intangible drilling and development costs of producing wells, if otherwise deductible, to the extent they exceed the amount deductible if such costs were capitalized, the excess of the deduction for depletion over the adjusted basis of the property at the end of the taxable year and certain accelerated depreciation on real property and on personal property subject to a lease. A partner's regular federal income tax is his federal income tax computed without regard to the minimum tax for tax preferences, the accumulated earnings tax and the personal holding company tax and reduced by the foreign tax credit, the investment credit and certain other credits.

8. Generally, gain on the sale of one or more partnership interests by a partner who has held such interests for the period required by the Tax Reform Act of 1976 will be long-term capital gain. However, to the extent that the proceeds of sale are attributable to such partner's share of a partnership's substantially appreciated inventory or unrealized receivables, the gain will be treated as ordinary income. A partner's share of a partnership's unrealized receivables will include his distributive share of a partnership's potential depreciation recapture determined as though a partnership had sold its depreciable property at its fair market value on the date of the sale of a partnership interest. Gain on the sale of an interest in a geothermal property, including a partnership interest, is treated as ordinary income rather than as capital gain to the extent of deductions taken for intangible drilling and development expenditures made after December 31, 1975, reduced by the amount of intangible drilling

and development expenditures which would have been deductible had they been capitalized and deducted through cost depletion. Although intangible drilling and development expenses of geothermal wells are not expressly included within this provision, it appears that if otherwise allowed as deductions they will be so included. Generally, loss on the sale of one or more partnership interests by a partner will be a capital loss. Under certain circumstances a sale of a partnership interest may result in recapture by a selling partner of any investment credit previously credited against his tax liability. The holding period for entitlement for long-term capital gain and loss treatment is twelve months for 1978 and following years. The amount of ordinary income against which capital loss may be offset is increased to $3,000 for 1978 and thereafter.

9. The deduction by a partner of his distributive share of the loss (including capital loss) of a partnership is allowed only to the extent of his adjusted basis in his partnership interest at the end of the partnership's taxable year in which the loss occurs. Excess losses may be allowed as deductions in subsequent years to the extent the partner then has basis in his partnership interest. Generally, the tax basis of any partnership interest is equal to its cost, reduced by the partner's share of partnership distributions and losses and increased by his share of partnership income. In addition, in certain instances the tax basis of a partner's partnership interest may be increased by his proportionate share of liabilities to which partnership assets are subject, but for which neither any partner nor the partnership is liable (such as mortgage indebtedness not assumed by the partnership or any of its partners). The partner's proportionate share of such liabilities for tax-basis purposes is determined on the same basis as his proportionate share in the profits of the partnership. However, under the provisions of the Tax Reform Act of 1976, the amount of otherwise allowable loss which may be deducted in any taxable year with respect to a partner's interest may not exceed the amount with respect to which the partner is at risk in the partnership. For this purpose, a limited partner is not considered at risk with respect to non-recourse liabilities of a partnership. A decrease in a partner's share of such liabilities (e.g., by reason of repayment) is treated for tax purposes as though it were a cash distribution to such partner. Any loans made by General Partner to a Partnership will not augment the adjusted bases of the Participants of their interests in such Partnership.

10. If the cash distributions to a partner by the partnership in any year exceed his share of the partnership's taxable income for that year, the excess will constitute a return of capital to the partner. A return of capital will not be reportable as taxable income by a recipient for federal income tax purposes but it will reduce the tax basis of his partnership interest. Any return of capital in excess of basis, such as a case where the tax basis of a partner's partnership interest is reduced to zero and his share of any cash distributions for any year exceeds his share of partnership taxable income, will be taxable to him as though it were a gain on the sale or exchange of his partnership interest. If a distribution is made to a partner in liquidation of the partnership, gain is recognized to the extent that cash received exceeds the partner's tax basis of his interest in the partnership immediately before the distribution. His basis in the remaining assets distributed shall be the basis of his interest immediately before the distribution reduced by the amount of monies received. Under certain circumstances, if in a distribution a partner receives other property in return for all or part of his share of unrealized receivables or substantially appreciated inventory, to the extent of the receipt of such other property, the partner shall be regarded as having sold such unrealized receivables or substantially appreciated inventory, thereby producing ordinary income to the extent of the gain. Gain will be recognized as ordinary income if other property is received for a partner's interest in a productive well to the extent of recapturable intangible drilling and development costs.

11. Certain of the Partnerships' deductions and credits resulting from the payment of Partnership costs and expenses with the contributions of the Participants, and any recapture thereof, are allocated to the Participants. As a result, the allocation of such deductions and credits, and any recapture thereof, is made in a ratio which is disproportionate to the Participants' interest in the Partnerships. The capital accounts of the Participants are adjusted to reflect such disproportionate allocations and the capital accounts, as adjusted, of General Partner and the Participants will be given effect in distributions made to the Partners in the event of dissolution of a Partnership. Under the Tax Reform Act of 1976, the Internal Revenue Service will recognize such a special allocation if it has "such substantial economic effect." If upon audit, the Internal Revenue Service should take the position that such disproportionate allocation lacks "substantial

economic effect," the disproportionate part of the deductions allocated to the Participants (i.e., the excess over 60%) would not be allowable to them if such position were ultimately sustained by the Internal Revenue Service. The Internal Revenue Service has on occasion taken the position that revenue sharing arrangements involving reversionary interests (such as those possessed by General Partner) result in a loss of a portion of the intangible expense deductions allocated by the governing partnership agreement to the persons bearing such expenses.

The Internal Revenue Service has not yet issued regulations or other administrative guidelines interpreting the partnership allocation provisions of the Tax Reform Act of 1976. No assurance can be given that when such regulations or other guidelines are promulgated they will not adopt a more restrictive interpretation of these positions than that in effect for the corresponding provisions of prior law. Should the Internal Revenue Service adopt such a restrictive interpretation, no assurance can be given that the allocations made in the Partnership Agreement for federal income tax purposes would be upheld if challenged by the Internal Revenue Service.

Moreover, an additional provision of the Tax Reform Act of 1976 requires that the basis of oil and gas properties owned by a partnership be allocated to the partners in accordance with their interest in the capital or profits of the partnership. Presumably, if other provisions relating to oil and gas are held to be applicable to geothermal energy, such provision would also be applied. While, again, no regulations or guidelines have been promulgated, it is possible that this provision will be interpreted by the Internal Revenue Service as preventing an allocation of any losses or deductions computed with respect to the basis of an oil or gas property (such as cost depletion or abandonment losses) to the Partners in a manner disproportionate to their respective interests in the capital or profits of a Partnership or as preventing an allocation of gain or loss on the sale or other disposition of an oil or gas property (such as that portion of any gain treated as recapture of intangible drilling and development costs) to the Partners in a manner disproportionate to their respective interests in the capital or profits of a Partnership.

12. The maximum rate of federal income tax on an individual's "personal service taxable income" for 1977 and subsequent years is limited to 50%. The maximum tax is now of greater significance in that the Tax Reform Act of 1976 has expanded

the categories of income eligible for the maximum 50% tax rate to include pensions, annuities and deferred compensation. However, personal service taxable income must be reduced, for purposes of applying the 50% limit, by the total amount of the taxpayer's items of tax preference in the taxable year, including a Participant's share of a Partnership's items of tax preference. To the extent that personal service taxable income is reduced, such income is subject to a tax at normal rates applicable to ordinary income. Thus, items of tax preference generated by a Partnership which are allocable to a Participant will decrease the amount of that Participant's personal service taxable income qualifying for the 50% maximum rate on a dollar for dollar basis. Moreover, it is not anticipated that a Participant's distributive share of the net income of a Partnership or any gain realized on the sale, exchange or liquidation of an interest in a Partnership will be "personal service income" within the meaning of this provision.

13. Fees for the organization and syndication of a partnership must be capitalized. Organization fees paid or incurred in taxable years beginning after December 31, 1976, may be amortized over a five-year period. General Partner intends to treat the 10% management fee as an organizational cost and amortize it over a five-year period. There is a risk that the Internal Revenue Service will challenge such amortization on the basis that such fee should properly be characterized as a syndication expense.

Numerous states have proposals pending which could eliminate depletion and certain other tax incentives which may be applicable to the activities of the Partnerships. The adoption of such proposals could reduce or eliminate any such incentives available under state laws.

Allocation of Costs

General Partner is obligated to acquire a minimum of 1% of the total number of Units purchased in each Partnership. With respect to such 1%, General Partner shall contribute the applicable purchase price to the capital of the Partnership at the time the interest is acquired. As to additional Units purchased by General Partner, capital shall be contributed and applied to Partnership costs as needed after Participants' contributions have been exhausted. The Limited Partnership Agreement allocates Partnership costs to the partner who furnishes the funds with which an expenditure is made. Accordingly, it is anticipated that in current Participants, other than General Partner, may be allocated a larger proportion of Partnership deductions than their percentage interest of the Units in a Partnership. Consequently, in subsequent periods, General Partner would be allocated a disproportionately increased share of Partnership costs. There is a significant risk that the Internal Revenue Service will not accept this allocation. The impact upon the Participants of such an action by the Internal Revenue Service would be to cause a portion of the deductions claimed in the current taxable year to be deferred to a subsequent period.

National Audit Program

Although it is customary for the Internal Revenue Service to audit businesses in general, in late 1973 the Commissioner of Internal Revenue announced publicly that a National Audit Program would be instituted to audit virtually all "tax shelter" programs, both public and private, aimed at curtailing certain "abuses" which the IRS feels are prevalent in the "tax shelter" area.

General Partner has been advised that the Internal Revenue Service has audited oil and gas drilling programs organized by certain unrelated companies and has disallowed certain intangible drilling costs, where such costs were prepaid prior to the end of a given calendar year and where the well was not spudded prior to the end of such calendar year. The apparent theory of the Internal Revenue Service is that such prepayments were instigated solely by the drilling partnership involved and not by the supplier of services, and therefore, there was no "business purpose" for the prepayment. The effect of such disallowance of prepayment is to shift the deduction from the year of prepayment to the following year when the services are rendered. It is expected that some drilling funds may litigate this question in the courts.

Any audit of a Partnership may lead to adjustments, in which event the Participants may be required to file amended personal federal income tax returns. Any such audit could also lead to an audit of a Participant's tax return which may, in turn, lead to adjustments other than those relating to investment in a

987

Partnership. Furthermore, President Carter proposed in his January 21, 1978 tax message to Congress the enactment of legislation which would authorize the Internal Revenue Service to determine a partner's taxable income or deductible loss upon audit at the partnership level. If such legislation were enacted, it could have the practical effect of preventing direct participation by a limited partner or his representative in the Internal Revenue Service's determination of his tax consequences as a partner.

State Income Taxes

Operations of a Partnership may also be subject to income tax assessed by states where a Participant is a resident or domiciled and where the operations of a Partnership are conducted.

Proposed Treasury Regulations

On January 5, 1977, proposed regulations were published for comment by the Treasury Department which, if adopted, would be effective as of that date. In effect, these regulations would revise existing regulations covering the classification of organizations as partnerships for federal income tax purposes or as associations taxable as corporations. Under the proposed regulations, organizations such as the Partnerships would probably be taxable as corporations rather than as partnerships, in which case none of the contributions made by the Participants would generate immediate deductions, but would be treated as the purchase price of stock in a corporation. Similarly, distributions from the Partnership to the Participants would be taxed as dividend income to the extent of current and accumulated earnings and profits. Income of the Partnerships would be treated as income of corporations, and the Partnerships would be entitled to depletion to the extent available to the exclusion of General Partner and the Participants.

On January 6, the proposed regulations were withdrawn. It is impossible to predict whether and to what extent the regulations governing the classification of the Partnerships for federal income tax purposes may be modified. Prospective investors are advised that there is a risk that the proposed regulations or similar such regulations may in fact be promulgated, in which case, the Partnership may not be classifiable as such for federal income tax purposes.

Proposed Legislation

On January 21, 1978, proposals for tax reform were submitted to the Congress by the Carter Administration. Amplification of certain of the proposals has come from the Treasury Department. Included in the proposals is one which would treat all limited partnerships with more than 15 limited liability members other than certain housing partnerships as associations taxable as corporations. Partnerships formed before January 1, 1979, would not be affected by the proposal unless on or after such date a limited liability member makes a contribution to the partnership (other than a contribution made pursuant to a binding commitment existing before the enactment of the provisions). If adopted, Partnerships formed after December 31, 1978 would be treated as corporations for tax purposes.

Additional proposals submitted to Congress by the Carter Administration would eliminate the deduction against items of tax preference of one-half the noncorporate taxpayer's regular income tax and would eliminate the availability of the benefit of the 25% alternative tax rate on capital gains of noncorporate taxpayers.

Provisions of the Energy Production and Conservation Tax Incentive Act, H.R. 5263, which has been passed by the House and Senate and referred to a Conference Committee consisting of members of both Houses of Congress to resolve differences, could materially affect investors in geothermal properties if they are enacted. The House version would provide a 10% allowance for percentage depletion limited to adjusted cost basis of the property. The Senate version would permit percentage depletion at the rate of 22% through 1980, 20% for 1981, 18% for 1982, 16% for 1983 and 15% for all years thereafter. No limitation would be imposed on the total allowable depletion Excess depletion would be subject to the minimum tax, as under present law.

A deduction would be allowed for intangible drilling and development costs of geothermal wells. Costs in excess of the amount allowable as a deduction if such costs were capitalized and which also exceed geothermal income would constitute an item of tax preference for individuals subject to the 15% minimum tax.

The Revenue Act of 1978 (H.R. 13511), as passed by both Houses of Congress and referred to the President for his approval, does not contain President Carter's proposal regarding partnership classification. Such Act contains provisions which could favorably impact a taxpayer investing in a geothermal partnership. It would reduce the tax on capital gains. The current 50% exclusion would be increased to 60%. While it would eliminate the 25% alternative rate on the first $50,000 of long-term capital gains, capital gains (and excess itemized deductions) would be removed from the list of tax preferences which are subject to the 15% minimum tax and which reduce the income eligible for the 50% maximum tax on personal service income. In order to assure that some minimum rate of tax is paid on all capital gains, a new type of minimum tax would be added applicable to the excluded 60% of capital gains. The alternative minimum tax would apply to taxable income plus the excluded 60% of capital gains and excess itemized deductions. After subtracting a $20,000 exemption, the alternative minimum tax would be 10% on the first $40,000; 20% on the next $40,000; and 25% on amounts above that. The alternative minimum tax then would be compared to regular tax liability (including the 15% minimum tax on the other items of tax preference), and the taxpayer would pay whichever is higher. The impact of the legislation will be to reduce the maximum effective tax rate on capital gains (including the 15% minimum tax and 50% maximum tax) from 49.125% to 28%.

The legislation would also require the inclusion of intangible drilling and development cost deductions of producing oil and gas wells as an item of tax preference only to the extent such deductions exceed oil and gas income (before reduction for the drilling costs of dry holes). Presumably, if drilling costs of geothermal wells are currently deductible as intangible drilling and development costs, this provision will apply to geothermal wells as well as to conventional oil and gas wells.

GOVERNMENT REGULATION

The exploration for, drilling and production of Geothermal Energy subjects the Partnerships to laws and regulations relating to drilling procedures, safety precautions, employee health and safety, air quality standards, pollution of stream and fresh water sources, odor, noise, dust and other environmental protection controls adopted by Federal, state and local governmental authorities. The Partnerships may be required to prepare and present to Federal, state and local authorities statements of the effect or impact that any proposed exploration or drilling for geothermal resources on either public or private land might have upon the environment. Such statements, if required, must be presented and approved prior to the commencement of drilling operations. Such requirements may delay commencement or continuation of exploration or drilling operations.

Environmental problems known to exist at this time and compliance with regulations that may be enacted in the future could have a substantial impact upon the capital expenditures required in order to deal with such problems, could reduce net revenues and, in the event the Partnership could not comply with such regulations and problems, the competitive position of the Partnership could be substantially impaired.

The Nation's energy crisis forces us to search for more sources of energy. Geothermal energy is a logical area to pursue but a high risk for the investor.

DEFINITIONS

Area of Interest. An area containing one or more Leases designated as an Area of Interest by General Partner. The Area designated shall be the largest of any of the three following geographical areas: (i) The acreage actually acquired by a Partnership under an agreement with a person solely by the Partnership's drilling of an Exploratory Well thereon, but not an amount of acreage in excess of the area covered by (iii) below; (ii) The area as to which Lease Acquisition and Maintenance Costs are charged to the Participants in a Partnership; (iii) The area covering the geothermal anomaly tested by an Exploratory Well drilled by one of the Partnerships. General Partner's determination as to the lands included within the Area of Interest shall be conclusive upon the Participants as long as the determination is made in good faith.

Exploratory Well. A well drilled by a Partnership in an Area of Interest in which no person (other than a prior General Partner Program) has drilled and completed a well which, in the judgment of General Partner, has possibilities of producing Geothermal Energy in commercial quantities. In general, Exploratory Wells will be those that are drilled for the purpose of ascertaining the existence of Geothermal Energy within an Area of Interest.

Confirmation Well. A well (other than an Exploratory Well), including a New Block Confirmation Well, drilled in a Geothermal Block prior to the time that a utility company or user enters into an agreement with a Partnership to construct a generating station on that Geothermal Block; such well must be one drilled after a Partnership has drilled a well in the Area of Interest in which such Geothermal Block is located, which, in the judgment of General Partner, indicates the existence of commercial accumulations of Geothermal Energy.

Development Well. A well in a Geothermal Block other than an Exploratory or a Confirmation Well or a New Block Confirmation Well which is intended to be drilled into a formation capable of being productive in a known producing area. Development Wells shall include only those wells commenced after an agreement with a utility or industrial end-user for the construction of a generating plant has been entered with respect to a Geothermal Block.

Geophysical Costs. Costs of surface and subsurface geological, hydrological, geochemical and geophysical testing, evaluation or interpretation which are incurred by the Partnership in determining whether an area merits further evaluation by drilling an Exploratory Well (as opposed to bore holes drilled to perform surface and shallow temperature measurements, geothermal gradient surveys, heat flow determinations and similar geophysical evaluation techniques) and which are incurred prior to the drilling of the first well by a General Partner Program in the Area of Interest designated as a result of such work.

Geothermal Block. A geographical area designated in writing as a Geothermal Block by General Partner containing one or more Leases (or parts thereof) suitable in the judgment of General Partner for the drilling of at least one Exploratory or New Block Confirmation Well therein, and if such Exploratory or New Block Confirmation Well indicates commercial production, a sufficient number of Confirmation and Development Wells to permit the commercial extraction of Geothermal Energy therefrom. Geothermal Blocks shall be designated with a view to establishing the necessary "block of power" to provide sufficient Geothermal Energy to operate a generating unit of sufficient output capacity to render the operation commercial, considering the area of operation, present and anticipated price of the Geothermal Energy and other factors which General Partner deems relevant. A Geothermal Block may contain lands under lease which are not intended for near term development operations. The designation of an area as a Geothermal Block does not require a Partnership to drill a well therein. A Geothermal Block may have any configuration deemed reasonable by General Partner, and its size or configuration may be increased by General Partner at any time.

Geothermal Energy. Geothermal steam and associated geothermal resources including (i) all products of geothermal processes, embracing indigenous steam, hot water and hot brines; (ii) steam and other gases, hot water and hot brines resulting from water, gas or other fluids artifically introduced into geothermal formations; (iii) heat or other associated energy found in geothermal formations; and (iv) any by-product derived from them. By-product includes any mineral or minerals which are found in solution or in association with Geothermal Energy.

Lease. All leases, licenses, contracts, concessions, interests in real property and rights in or affecting such leases, licenses, contracts, concessions or interests which permit the exploration for or production of Geothermal Energy, or the receipt of such production or the proceeds thereof.

Lease Acquisition and Maintenance Costs. All of General Partner's costs of acquiring, screening, investigating, or maintaining any Lease of a Partnership or Lease in an Area of Interest of a Partnership, including delay rentals, ad valorem taxes, geological, geophysical and geochemical costs, accounting, legal and other services allocated to such Lease, plus interest on funds employed by General Partner to acquire or maintain such Lease, but excluding any drilling or equipment costs and Geophysical Costs incurred directly by the Partnership. Costs incurred more than three years prior to formation of a Partnership will not be charged as Lease Acquisition and Maintenance Costs.

General Partner Program. A Geothermal Energy program formed as a partnership, venture, or association in which interests therein are offered to the public, in which General Partner or an Affiliate is a general partner or manager, and which is formed for the sole purpose of the drilling for Geothermal Energy. General Partner Programs include Related Programs.

Net Profits. Revenues received by General Partner from the sale of Geothermal Energy derived from wells located in an Area of Interest after deducting from such revenues all expenditures made or liabilities incurred by General Partner in producing such revenues, including the costs of such wells, gathering lines, compressors, a portion of corporate overhead and other charges related to the production of such revenues. Net Profits are calculated separately for each Area of Interest. Net Profits do not include revenues received as a result of General Partner's purchase of interests in a program on the same basis as public investors.

New Block Confirmation Well. The first well drilled by a Partnership in a previously undrilled Geothermal Blcok, which well, because of its close proximity to one or more other producible or producing geothermal wells and because of the similarity of geological, geochemical and geophysical characteristics of the Geothermal Block in which such well is located to that in which such producible or producing well is located, is classified as a Confirmation Well by General Partner.

Operating charges. All customary expenses of operation and production incurred on a recurring basis in connection with the production and marketing of the Geothermal Energy of a Partnership, including ad valorem and severance taxes, and costs of acquisition and maintenance of access roads.

Participants' Payout. The time at which a Partnership's share of the revenues from all wells, including Development Wells, bottomed within a Geothermal Block equals the sum of (i) 400% of all of the Partnership's Recoverable Drilling Costs of Exploratory Wells and Geophysical Costs in such Geothermal Block, (ii) 200% of all of the Partnership's Recoverable Drilling Costs of Confirmation Wells in such Geothermal Block, (iii) 100% of all Operating Charges and 100% of all Replacement Charges theretofore charged to the Partnership with respect to such Geothermal Block, (iv) 100% of all of the Partnership's Recoverable Drilling Costs of Development Wells in such Geothermal Block, and (v) 100% of all Lease Acquisition and Maintenance Costs paid by the Partnership and charged to such Geothermal Block with respect to the Area of Interest in which such Geothermal Block is located.

Participation. With respect to each Partnership, the total cost of the Units which a Participant has agreed to purchase in such Partnership.

Recoverable Drilling Costs. All costs of a Partnership paid or incurred in exploring and developing a Geothermal Block, which costs include drilling costs and any other costs (including overhead) which have been allocated to such Geothermal Block by General Partner, and are not Lease Acquisition and

Maintenance Costs, Geophysical Costs, Operating Charges, Replacement Charges, or General and Administrative Expenses.

Related Program. A Geothermal Energy Program formed as a partnership, venture or association in which interests are offered to the public, in which General Partner or an Affiliate is general partner or manager, and which is formed for the exclusive purpose of drilling one or more Development Wells on a Geothermal Block or Blocks of the Partnership.

Replacement Charges. All costs of the replacement of equipment at periodic intervals as a result of the corrosive nature of the gaseous or other products transmitted there through and all costs of drilling, redrilling, completing and equipping a well (including injection and disposal wells) in a Geothermal Block, which well is required to maintain or augment the flow of Geothermal Energy in an operative generating unit or to dispose of effluent therefrom.

GOVERNMENT VIEWS ON TAX SHELTERS

Tax shelters have been studied by the Government for many years, and recently, papers were issued setting forth some of its thoughts. The first deals with the reaction of the Securities and Exchange Commission to fraudulent practices in connection with oil and gas interests. The second examines the I.R.S. analysis of various tax shelters such as real estate, oil and gas drilling, farm operations, and movie films.

SECURITIES AND EXCHANGE COMMISSION
Washington, D.C.

Securities Exchange Act of 1934
Release No. 11992 / January 8, 1976

FRAUDULENT PRACTICES IN CONNECTION WITH OIL AND GAS FRACTIONAL INTERESTS

The energy crisis has focused attention upon oil and gas exploration and in public offerings of fractional undivided interests in oil and gas leases. Such offerings are frequently made pursuant to a claim of exemption from registration under the Securities Act of 1933 ("the Act"). One such claimed exemption is that provided by Regulation B and Schedule D thereunder. In 1974, the approximate dollar amount of such offerings filed with the Commission increased from $20 million to $30 million. About $20 million in offerings have been filed with the Commission in the first six months of 1975. Other such claimed exemptions are those provided by Section 4(2) of the Act, and Rule 146 thereunder, for private offerings and Section 3(a)(11), and Rule 147 thereunder, for intrastate offerings.

The demand for oil and gas coupled with the speculative nature of such offerings have fueled widespread individual-investor interest. Tax advantages that accrue to investors make the offerings even more attractive. While a number of oil and gas fractional interests which are offered throughout the country are legitimate in their conception, business-like in their

marketing and prudent in their operation, unscrupulous promoters have taken advantage of the investor attention to engage in
a number of fraudulent marketing practices. As a result, the
Commission and State authorities have within the past two
years instituted an increasing number of enforcement actions.
Accordingly, the Commission wishes at this time to alert
investors to some of the fraudulent marketing practices that
have recently come to its attention.

Fraudulent promoters have revived the "boiler-room" techniques employed in the 1920's and again in the 1950's.
Salesmen with little or no background in oil and gas (but a great
deal in selling) are hired to make high-pressured sales over the
phone to strangers. Mimeographed sales pitches, WATS lines
and name-lists are employed. Typically, unfounded claims or
suggestions of potentially spectacular profits are made. The
only sobering element is the occasional reference to the
speculative risk involved, usually couched in gambling context.
In addition to fraudulent marketing practices, unscrupulous
promoters have also padded expenses.

In an effort to assist prospective investors in guarding against
fraudulent offerings of fractional undivided working interests in
oil and gas leases, the Commission suggests the following
precautions:

(1) Be particularly wary of unsolicited phone calls from
strangers;

(2) Be skeptical of suggestions of possible spectacular
profits;

(3) Resist pressures to make hurried, uninformed investment decisions;

(4) Be cautious of any representations regarding the
accomplishments of the offeror in drilling other wells
since prior success is not necessarily indicative of
future results.

(5) Consider the risks in relation to your own financial
position and needs. Ask yourself if you can afford the
potential loss of the entire investment.

More specifically, pose the following questions and requests
to the person(s) making the offering:

(1) In the instance of an unsolicited call or letter how did
the caller/writer obtain your name?;

(2) Is the offering filed with the SEC? (If so then you are
entitled to a copy of a prospectus or offering sheet);

(3) Is the offering filed with the Securities Commission of your State?;

(4) Is the salesmen licensed to sell securities in your State?;

(5) Is the company or any of its principals subject to any Federal or State injunctive or cease and desist orders?;

(6) Ask for a copy of any geological report that may have been made; however keep in mind that such reports are not assurances of the presence or amount of oil and gas. Review the report or survey with someone who is knowledgeable and unaffiliated with the company.

If you believe that you may have been the victim of a fraud, you should consult your attorney to determine what steps to take to assert and protect your rights. Also, contact your State Securities Commission or the nearest SEC Regional Office at any of the following locations: Manhattan, New York; Boston; Atlanta; Chicago; Fort Worth; Denver; Los Angeles; Seattle; and Arlington, Virginia. Although the SEC cannot intervene on your behalf or provide legal representation to obtain redress of your individual rights, your complaint to the SEC may prevent others from being defrauded.

INVESTIGATE *BEFORE* YOU INVEST

OVERVIEW OF TAX SHELTERS

Overview of Tax Shelters

1.0
Introduction

A tax shelter, as used here, denotes a means of
providing certain tax advantages to an investor.
Regardless of the type of shelter, a common concept prevails, namely (1) deferral, (2) leverage,
and (3) conversion.

The deferral concept involves the postponement
of income which essentially results in a tax-free
Federal loan. The leverage concept involves the
use in investments of borrowed funds resulting in
accelerated deductions. Here are favored nonrecourse borrowings for which the borrower is not
personally liable. For this reason, limited
partnership arrangements are generally used as the
vehicle. The conversion concept provides tax
advantages by converting otherwise ordinary income
to capital gain on the disposition of an asset.

The taking of accelerated deductions also
results in a conversion of tax rates if the taxpayer is in a lower tax bracket in later years.

Many tax shelters result from congressional
intent for legislation, assuring certain social-
economic benefits. The audit effort is not directed against these legitimate shelters. Tax
shelters of many kinds are being actively promoted
and, from volume alone, we can expect that some
will be abusive shelters.

The nature of tax shelters gives rise to tax
considerations not ordinarily encountered.
Investors engage in transactions, individually, or
through partnerships, with little or no promise of
gain apart from the anticipated income tax benefits. The manipulations of many promoters and
investors are at the brink of acceptability, for
tax purposes, and are to be scrutinized. The
Commissioner has expressed interest in the tax
shelter program and his concern for those shelters
"...stretching, bending, or breaking the provisions of the tax law." /1/

It should be kept in mind that a loss return,
in and of itself, is not indicative of tax shelter
"ABUSE".

Perhaps a strata classification of loss returns
will place the tax shelter "ABUSE" problem in
perspective:

> CLASS I   GOOD SHELTERS: Loss returns
>   which are perfectly legiti-
>   mate in all respects:
>   economic, form, substance,
>   etc.
>
> CLASS II   PROBLEM SHELTERS: Loss
>   returns which may contain on
>   their face "elements" or
>   items which were incorrectly
>   handled, i.e., capitalizable
>   items claimed as current
>   deductions, etc., but in
>   other respects are economi-
>   cally viable.
>
> CLASS III   ABUSIVE SHELTERS: Loss
>   returns which lack economic
>   reality or viability in
>   varying degrees. For defining
>   this area, any transaction
>   that fails to produce a
>   return relative to the risk
>   involved is suspect. Many
>   factors interact in this
>   determination.

An indepth analysis of returns that appear to
be merely Class I (Good Shelters) or Class II
(Problem Shelters) often reveals them to be, in
fact, Class III (Abusive Shelters). Illustrations
of the three classes are provided in Exhibits I-A,
I-B, and I-C.

Coordinated audit programs are being implemented in the following shelter areas:

(1) Real estate.
(2) Oil and gas drilling.
(3) Farm operations.
(4) Movie films.

An overview of each program is provided here.
In addition, agents are encouraged to submit
unusual situations or problems for technical
advice. For this reason Rev. Proc. 73-8, providing procedures for obtaining technical advice, is
also included in this booklet, along with a suggested request format.

A brief summary of revenue procedures and
revenue rulings that are tax-shelter related is
supplied as a quick reference. /2/ Additionally,
certain key words underlined throughout this text
are included in a glossary following the summaries
of the revenue rulings.

Exhibit I-A

CLASS I -Economically and legally viable

Formation date: 1-1-74

Sales price	$500,000	FMV $500,000
Lease - rent (yr.)	$ 60,000	FMV $ 60,000
Investment return	15%	Risk rate 15%(a)

Claimed deductions:
Real estate tax paid
Interest paid 1st year
Management fees (actual services)

(a) or prevailing rate relative to risk involved.

Exhibit I-B

Class II - Usually deduction vs. capitalization

Formation Date: 6-30-74

Sales price $500,000 FMV $550,000
Lease - rent (yr.) $ 60,000 FMV $ 60,000
Investment return 15% Risk Rate 15% (a)
Claimed deductions:
    Interest prepaid (b)
    Interest on wrap-around mortgages (c)
    Real estate taxes
    Payments to general partners (d)
    Management fees (Disguised Commissions)
    Commissions
    Organization fees
    Loan fees
    Appraisal fees (e)
    Commitment fees (f)
    Construction loan items (g)
    Points
    Pre-opening expenses
    Timing factor of loans

(a)   or prevailing rate relative to risk involved.
(b)   Rev. Rul. 75-152, 1975-1 C.B. 144 (distortion).
(c)   Rev. Rul. 75-99. 1975-1 C.B. 197.
(d)   Rev. Rul. 75-214, 1975-1 C.B. 185 (organization expense).
(e)   Rev. Rul. 74-104, 1974-1 C.B. 70.
(f)   Rev. Rul. 75-172, 1975-1 C.B. 145.
(g)   Rev. Rul. 74-395, 1974-2 C.B. 45 (one-loan concept).

Exhibit I-C

CLASS III - Lacking economic reality or viability

Formation date: 12-28-75

Sales price $1,000,000 (a) FMV $500,000
Lease - rent (yr.) $ 60,000   FMV $120,000
Return on investment   3%   Risk Rate 15%
Deductions:
    Interest prepaid (b)
    Interest on wrap-around mortgages (c)
    Real estate taxes
    Payments to general partners (d)
    Management fees (disguised commissions)
    Commissions
    Organization fees
    Loan fees
    Appraisal fees
    Commitment fees (e)
    Construction Loan Items (f)
    Points
    Pre-opening expenses
    Timing factor of loans

(a)   Apparent excessive price, standing alone, does
       not establish "abuse"; other factors must be
       considered.
(b)   Rev. Rul. 75-152, 1975-1 C.B. 144.
(c)   Rev. Rul. 75-99, 1975-1 C.B. 197
(d)   Rev. Rul. 75-214, 1975-1 C.B. 185 (organization
       expense).
(e)   Rev. Rul. 75-172, 1975-1 C.B. 145.
(f)   Rev. Rul. 74-395, 1974-2 C.B. 45 (one-loan con-
       cept).

2.0
Real estate

The real estate industry requires the
commitment of large sums of capital over a
long period of time. In order to provide
capital for the construction of apartment
buildings, shopping centers, office buildings, etc., a number of investment vehicles
have been used which allow the pooling of
financial resources by investors. This is
generally referred to as real estate syndication. Various legal forms can be used for
this purpose—the joint venture, real estate
investment trust, corporation, and, most
often, the partnership. These various forms
differ with respect to right of control,
participation in management, personal liability, etc.

In general, a real estate tax shelter is
an investment in which a significant portion
of the investor's return is derived from
"pass-through" deductions which offset ordinary income, thus creating significant tax
benefits. The shelters encourage investments
by higher income taxpayers because of our
progressive tax structure. Hence, benefits
increase as the tax bracket increases. The
taxpayer is allowed, in effect, to postpone
the payment of tax. This deferral is the
equivalent of an interest-free loan from the
Government, the economic benefits of which
can be significant.

The limited partnership is the most common
vehicle of the real estate tax shelter. This
type of ownership enables partner-investors
to offset their ordinary income with pass-
through deductions, while limiting personal
liability through nonrecourse financing.

2.01
Economic benefit

A real estate investment decision involves
an analysis of benefits to be received. Such
analysis includes evaluation of the following:

(1) Potential risks involved.
(2) Overall rate of return.
(3) Potential for appreciation.
(4) Potential tax benefits.

Generally, losses are generated in the
first years of existence and pass through to
investors, who sometimes achieve a complete
return of their original investment through
tax savings.

An investor must weigh the advantages of
tax savings against other risks involved.
The savings in tax are principally achieved
by taking current deductions for costs attributable to later years, such as accelerated
depreciation, and deducting interest and tax
paid during the construction period.

In addition, individual partner's risk of
loss is diminished by the use of the limited
partnership in conjunction with debt financing through nonrecourse loans.

2.02
Leverage

A partner, including a limited partner,
can deduct losses only to the extent of the
basis in his or her partnership interest.
However, if none of the partners has any
personal liability (nonrecourse loan), then
all partners, including limited partners, are
considered as sharing such liability in
proportion to their share of profits. /3/
The partner's share of nonrecourse liabilities is added to the adjusted basis in determining the limitation on the partner's share
of partnership losses.

Nonrecourse financing is extremely important to the real estate tax shelter since
such debt financing (leverage) increases the
tax benefits to the limited partners and
permits them to deduct losses which exceed
the amount they have at risk

Example 1

If a partner invested
$5,000 in a partnership in
return for a 10 percent interest, and the partnership
borrowed $50,000 in the form
of a nonrecourse loan, the
partner's basis in the
partnership would be $10,000
($5,000 of contributions to
the partnership, plus 10
percent of the $50,000 nonre-
course loan).

Accelerated methods of depreciation provide the taxpayer with methods to deduct depreciation at a more rapid rate than that allowed under the straight-line method. The tax Reform Act of 1969 limited the extent to which accelerated depreciation is allowed for real property. The use of the accelerated methods depends upon the class of property involved, new or used residential, new or used nonresidential, or low income property.

The interaction of the depreciation provisions and nonrecourse financing, which, in effect, increases the amount of tax benefits in proportion to the risks involved, gives the real estate tax shelter its tremendous popularity. The following example will illustrate.

Example 2

An apartment building, constructed on leased land, is to be purchased at a cost of $600,000.

Situation 1. Partner A invests $100,000 of his or her own money and a nonrecourse mortgage of $500,000 is obtained. (The mortgage is secured solely by property.)

Situation 2. Partner B borrows $500,000 on his or her personal signature and invests $100,000 of his or her own money.

The only difference in the above situations is the risk involved. Partner A can lose only $100,000 since the remainder is financed by a nonrecourse mortgage. On the other hand, Partner B can lose $600,00, since he or she is personally liable for $500,000 plus his or her investment of $100,000.

Further, the depreciable basis in the property to both A and B is $600,000. Partner A can conceivably deduct depreciation in excess of his or her investment and thereby obtain significant tax benefits.

2.04
Capital gain
treatment

When a building is sold, any realized gain may be eligible for capital gains treatment to the extent accelerated depreciation is not recaptured as ordinary income. However, there is no recapture with respect to the construction period interest and taxes. As a result, the deductions for construction period interest and taxes that are taken against ordinary income enable the taxpayer to, in effect, convert ordinary income into capital gains.

2.05
Construction period

During the construction period, the interest paid on the construction loan and the real estate taxes are currently deducted even though there is no income from the property, except to the extent the taxpayer elects to capitalize these items as carrying charges. If such an election is made, the amount capitalized will be amortized over the useful life of the building. The deduction for interest during the construction period includes "points" or loan-processing fees so long as these fees are paid by the borrower before the receipt of the loan funds and are not paid for specific services.

The deduction for taxes includes sales and real estate taxes paid or accrued on real or personal property during the construction period.

The allowance of a deduction for construction period interest and taxes has contributed to the development of real estate tax shelters. Since the rental income from the building occurs substantially later than the time when the construction period interest and taxes are actually deducted, this results in losses which the investors are permitted to offset against their other income, thereby sheltering that income from taxes and providing a substantial deferral of tax liability.

2.06
Prepaid interest

In certain cases, prepaid interest may also be deducted, but the availability of a deduction for certain prepaid interest is not peculiar to the real estate tax shelter.

2.07
Expenses of
syndication

A limited partnership's payments to one of its general partners for services he or she rendered in organizing the partnership constitute capital expenditures and are not deductible currently. /4/

3.0
Oil and gas drilling

Most oil and gas drilling tax shelters are
organized as a limited partnership with an
oil company or promoter (often a corporation)
as the general partner. The investor's or
limited partner's share of gain or loss
(mostly loss) is reported on Schedule E and
R, Form 1040. Examiners of individual returns are often the first Internal Revenue
Service employees to encounter tax shelter
deductions. These usually appear as a
partnership loss in excess of $5,000.

The principal features of the oil and gas
tax shelter include:

(1) The use of a limited partnership to
pass through the deduction for intangible drilling costs;

(2) The use of leverage through nonrecourse loans (that is none of the
limited partners are liable for that
debt) so that limited partners are
able to deduct expenses in excess of
their actual equity investment; and

(3) Conversion of ordinary income into
capital gains.

Another feature of this tax shelter is the
immediate writeoff of organizational expenses.

3.01
Individual
returns

It should be noted that it is seldom
possible to determine whether a partnership
loss is from an abusive tax shelter without
an examination of the partnership return;
however, certain facts developed during an
individual examination may aid in identifying
potential abuse situations.

3.011
Potential
abuse

Listed below are some situations that may
be encountered during examinations of individual returns that could indicate a potential abuse situation:

1013

(1) Investments made late in the year (for example, November or December) indicate there may be a deduction for prepaid drilling expenses on the partnership return.

(2) A large portion of the investment is written off during the first year.

(3) The taxpayer's loss exceeds his or her investment, indicating the possibility of a nonrecourse loan. This determination cannot be made without an examination of the partnership return.

In these situations, consideration should be given to a request for a collateral examination of the partnership return. This is especially true for larger losses, although even a $5,000 loss could be just part of a return showing a $2,000,000 loss and when scrutinized could result in the identification of other returns that would otherwise escape examination. There is a possibility that the partnership returns may not be examined due to staff limitations or other reasons, but the Internal Revenue Service will at least have had the opportunity to inspect the return.

3.012
Charitable
contributions

Another possible abuse area that may surface during an examination of an individual return is the donation of the partnership interest in oil properties to qualified charitable organizations at a greatly inflated value.

Engineers will provide taxpayers with an engineering report showing that the oil properties have considerable reserves. These reserves are often not proven by drilling.

Example 3

Investor A acquired an interest in an oil program for $20,000 in 1973. The entire investment was deducted as intangible drilling costs in 1973. In 1974, the taxpayer contributed the entire inter-

est to a qualified charitable
organization. A then claimed
a contribution equal to his
1973 investment based on the
erroneous engineering report.

It is obvious that taxpayers in the
60-percent bracket can actually make money on
their taxes regardless of the outcome of the
oil and gas program.

The examining agent should request an
engineering report on large contributions of
oil interests, especially if little or no oil
income has been reported by the investor.

3.02 Partnership returns

As indicated earlier, it is seldom possible to determine a tax abuse situation without an examination of the partnership return.
There are a number of issues common to the
oil and gas tax shelter area and each issue
will be discussed in detail for the benefit
of the agent examining the partnership returns.

3.021 Nonrecourse financing

The use of nonrecourse financing can
usually be identified from the inspection of
Schedule M, Reconciliation of Partners'
Capital Account, Form 1065. If it is an
initial return and the amount of ordinary
loss, column c, exceeds the capital contributed during the year, column b, there is a
strong possibility of financing through the
use of nonrecourse borrowing.

It will be necessary for the examining
agent to determine the source of additional
funds and to make appropriate inquiry into
the circumstances surrounding the loan. The
inquiry must go beyond the entries on the
partnership books. If the loan is made by a
financial institution, review the collateral
securing the loan, being especially watchful
for guarantees made by the general partner or
related companies. If the loan is secured by
assets other than assets of the partnership,
it may be treated as a capital contribution

and the bases of the partners' capital accounts are not increased for the purpose of
claiming a loss. /5/

Example 4

The "loan" made by a financial institution may have been
repaid through check swapping
or circular financing among
the fund, this bank, and
others.

Financing arrangements sometimes are
merely the simultaneous exchange of checks
among the parties. The examining agent must
carefully analyze all transactions among the
lending agency, the fund, and the other
parties.

Sometimes investors may recoup part of
their initial investment by a nonrecourse
loan made by companies related to the general
partner or program operator. These amounts
will not be recorded on company records, but
may be disclosed by reading the prospectus,
interviewing an investor, or directly questioning the program operator.

The timing of nonrecourse loans is a vital
factor in determining their validity. It is
extremely difficult, if not impossible, to
secure a nonrecourse loan, secured only by
undeveloped properties, from a responsible
lending institution. After properties have
been drilled and reserves proven, it is not
uncommon for future development to be financed by loans secured by the property.
This is a legitimate, recurring method of
financing.

3.022
Prepaid drilling
expense

Current law permits deductions for
drilling costs before actual drilling of the
hole, provided certain conditions are met.
/6/ However, partnerships are interpreting
the law to say that if the contract requires
payment before December 31 of the tax year,
and such payment is made, the deduction is
allowable.

The examining agent should:

(1) Review each drilling contract to insure that it is legal and binding. Determine if payment represents a bona fide payment or a deposit.

(2) Determine the relationship between the parties. If parties deal at less than arm's length, the validity of the contract should be established.

> Example 5
>
> Corporation X is the general partner of A, an oil fund. Corporation Y is a drilling operator who may or may not own drilling rigs. Corporations X and Y are owned by corportion Z. X enters into a drilling contract with Z to drill wells for A, the oil fund. Z requires that X pay the drilling costs before the end of the taxable year. Investigation discloses that Z arranges for drilling in subsequent years and does not pay until the drilling is completed.
>
> The Internal Revenue Service takes the position that the primary reason for payment of the drilling costs is to obtain a current deduction for investors in A, the oil fund.

(3) Determine the progress of work done and when the actual drilling began and was completed.

(4) Develop all the facts concerning the need for prepayment. Contact the driller to see who instigated the contract. Determine if the driller had free and unrestricted use of the funds. Determine how the driller treated the payment; was it reported as income, treated as a deposit, or deferred income? Consider an adjustment on the driller's tax return if the facts warrant such action.

(5) Consider a request for technical advice in situations when no precedent has been established.

3.023
Management fees

This issue arises from payments made by
the limited partnership to the general
partner. In most instances this is a flat
percentage ranging from 5 to 15 percent of
the original subscription and is usually paid
immediately after the subscription price is
paid to the partnership. The partnership
contends that this is a guaranteed payment to
the general partner and as such is deductible
under Code § 707(a) or 707(c). Code § 707(a)
provides that if a partner engages in a
transaction with a partnership other than in
the capacity of a member of such partnership,
the transactions shall be considered as
occurring between the partnership and one who
is not a partner. Code § 707(c) provides
that to the extent determined without regard
to the income of the partnership, payments to
a partner for services or the use of capital
shall be considered as made to one who is not
a member of the partnership, but only for
purposes of § 61(a) (relating to gross income) and § 162(a) (relating to trade or
business expenses).

These expenses must first meet the requirements of Code § 162 as ordinary and
necessary business expenses to be deductible.
Any part of the expenditure that is attributable to the organization of the partnership,
selling units of participation, purchasing
capital assets, or payments for services to
be performed after the close of the partnership's current year, does not qualify as a
current deduction.

Example 6

Investment by each limited partner	$	10,000
Limited partners		x 100
Total subscrip- tion price	$	1,000,000
Management fee at 15%		x .15
Total paid to general partner		$150,000.00

```
           Disbursements by general partner:
             Legal fees (organizational
             matters, etc.)                   $ 50,000
             Selling expenses for units
             of participation                   35,000
             Future services (to be
             performed after close of
             current tax year)                  50,000
             Current services                   15,000
             Total disbursements              $150,000
```

As can be seen from this example, $135,000 of the "management fee" would not be considered as deductible in the current year. The legal fees and selling expenses represent capital expenditures and as such are not deductible by virtue of Code § 263. The payment for future services to be performed after the close of the current year does not qualify as a current deduction.

The examining agent should determine what services were rendered to the partnership for this payment and determine what portion meets the requirements of Code § 162. An analysis of the prospectus may provide help in making the determination. If it is determined that a portion of this payment is reimbursement for organizational expenses, selling expenses, etc., that portion does not qualify as an ordinary and necessary business expense. It may be necessary to determine how this payment was treated on the recepient's records.

3.024
Income distortion

Operators of oil or gas wells who drill the wells themselves, providing their own labor and machinery, can elect to treat certain intangible drilling and development costs as a current expense, deductible in the year paid or incurred instead of a charge to the capital account. /7/ These intangible drilling and development costs include labor, fuel and power, material and supplies, tool rental, truck and auto hire, repairs to drilling equipment, and depreciation of drilling equipment.

The Service has previously considered the question of clearly reflecting income in the area of prepaid interest and prepaid feed. Prepaid interest deductions for a period in excess of 12 months beyond the end of the current year is considered as materially distorting income. /8/ Deductions for pre-paid feed expense are allowable if: (1) the expenditure is for the purchase of feed rather than a deposit, (2) the prepayment is made for a business purpose and not for tax avoidance, and (3) the deduction will not result in a material distortion of income. /9/

The examining agent should determine how much time has elapsed between the payment and the completion of drilling. If it extended for more than a 12-month period, considera-tion should be given to proposing Code § 446 as an alternative issue.

3.025
Taxable entity

Most tax shelters are organized as limited partnerships and many have requested and received rulings stating that they qualify as limited partnerships. When rulings have not been requested, the fund relies on the opin-ion of counsel that it is qualified as a limited partnership. This statement will be in the prospectus.

The examining agent should make sufficient inquiry into the actual operations to deter-mine the correct taxable status of the en-tity. While these are not all inclusive, the following items should be considered:

(1) Transferability of interest.
(2) Personal liability of partners.
(3) Centralized management.
(4) Continuity of business.
(5) Requirements of the Uniform Limited Partnership Act. (Have the necessary registration documents been filed with the proper State authorities?)

3.026
Excessive charges

Another area of abuse involves excessive amounts charged to the fund for drilling costs. This is especially true if the driller has a close relationship with the general partner. The Tax Court has held that amounts paid for intangible drilling costs in excess of the going rates for drilling in the area could constitute amounts paid for items other than intangible drilling costs. /10/

The examining agent should compare costs charged the fund with the costs charged other parties for similar work in the same area.

Because limited investors have no voice in management and are often unfamiliar with the operations of gas and oil programs, the operator of the fund may charge unreasonable amounts for general, administrative, and operating expenses.

The agent should determine what services are rendered for payment by the fund and the reasonableness of such payments. Also, the examining agent should make sure that no deduction is taken in the first year of the fund, for services to be performed in succeeding years.

Amounts charged for supervision of drilling operations and lease operating expenses should be reasonable for the operating area.

4.0
Farm operations

Farm operations generally involve the raising of animals and plants for consumption as food. The operations vary in size from small family farms to large multi-unit organizations. The types of ownership also vary from sale proprietorships to large corporations and nationally syndicated limited partnerships with passive investors.

For brevity, the discussion of farm operations will be restricted to the cattle tax shelter.

The publicly offered farm tax shelters and similar private plans are designed to make money for the promoters, and to gain tax advantages for the <u>investor</u> through the deduction of <u>noneconomic losses</u> and the conversion of ordinary deductions into long-term capital gains.

The first year losses as usually the result of yearend deductions for such items as prepaid management fees as well as bonus depreciation and investment credit. The use of <u>nonrecourse</u> loans often results in little or no net cash outlay by the investor in the first year because the tax deferred may equal or exceed the investment.

4.01
Partnership--
feeder cattle

The limited partnership is formed late in the year when non-recourse financing may be obtained to pay for prepaid feed in an amount that often exceeds the partner's initial equity. Cattle purchased in the initial year and early in the second year will ordinarily be sold the second year of the partnership. Some partnerships then terminate, leaving the investor with a 1-year deferral and the opportunity to continue the deferral by investing in another similar partnership. Most feeder cattle shelters have a longer life and perpetuate the deferral of income by continuing to prepay feed for a number of years.

4.011
Prepaid feed

    (1) Determine that funds were available and that payment was actually made by year-end.

    (2) The prepaid feed deduction must meet ALL THREE criteria of Rev. Rul. 75-152. /11/ These tests—deposit, business purpose, and material distortion—are explained in detail in the revenue ruling which cites the cases related to each test. The facts related to each test must be fully developed. Rev. Rul. 75-152 emphasizes distortion of income (which is also an issue in other types of tax shelters that emphasize prepaid interest and management fees).

4.012
Prefed feed

    Some limited partnerships have erroneously deducted purchases of feed that the cattle consumed before the partnership was formed.

Example 7

The promoter, a general partner, purchased the following on November 1:

Item	Cost
Feed	$2,000
Cattle	3,000
Total	$5,000

On December 1 of the same year, a limited partnership was formed. The partnership records show the following purchases:

Feed	$2,000
Cattle	$3,000

The partnership deducts feed cost of $2,000 for December although the cattle actually consumed $1,000 before the formation of the partnership. The records should show purchases of:

```
                    Cattle          $4,000
                    Feed             1,000
                    Total           $5,000
```

The cattle cost is not deductible until they are sold.

4.02
Partnership—
breeder feeder

A number of publicly offered cattle tax shelters are limited partnerships which invest in both feeder cattle and breeding stock. The emphasis on either activity can vary from year to year.

The guidelines that pertain to partnerships in general and to feeder partnerships also apply to these operations. Some of the integrated cattle operations claim substantial prepayments in addition to the tax benefits that result from ownership of a breeding herd.

The issues that pertain more specifically to breeding stock follow.

4.021
Breeding herd

The breeding herd often is purchased from the general partner or an affiliate. This, of course, gives the taxpayer control of the transaction and also makes historical information on the animals easier to obtain during the audit.

4.022
Investment
credit

Original use or first use of the livestock must begin with the partnership for the breeding stock to qualify as new property. /12/

Verification that breeding stock is or is not new property is an important item in the examination because the $50,000 limitation on used property is at the partnership level. Thus, used livestock acquired in a particular year in excess of $50,000 does not qualify. /13/ The age of the animals is an indication

1025

of prior use. The registration records of
purebred herds should substantiate prior use.

4.023
Depreciation

An unreasonable portion of the price of
animals purchased in group lots might be
allocated to older animals which would give a
faster writeoff.

Determine whether the property qualifies
for additional first-year and accelerated
depreciation.

4.024
Code § 1231

One of the primary objectives of farm tax
shelters is the attempt to convert ordinary
deductions to long-term capital gains. Some
are more fanciful in their determination of
Code § 1231 qualifications.

Some shelter operators held most heifers
to little over 2 years, apparently relying
primarily on age and holding period as determinative of Code § 1231 qualifications.

Actual use is the best indication of
intent. Culls, those unfit for the breeding
herd, would be identified as not being part
of the breeding herd in many operations well
before the animals reach 2 years.

When the taxpayer claims § 1231 classification for heifers sold at 2 years of age,
the animals are not old enough to have been
used in the herd and may be merely culls
retained to meet the 24-month holding period
requirement.

Price can be an indication of intent to
include animals in the herd. A price significantly higher than ordinarily received
for culls is an indication that it is a
quality animal. The failure to use it in the
herd then indicates that it was held primarily for sale, not use.

Some herd owners have claimed herd status
for large numbers of male calves; more than
could or would be used in any normal breedng
operation. Others have reported bull sales
in the same manner when the operator utilized

artificial insemination and required a minimal number of bulls. Verify that the breeder
had available for sale, the number of animals
sold or for which payment was received. The
determination of intent requires a full
development of the facts. /14/

4.025
Code § 1245

Livestock depreciation after 1969 is
subject to recapture. Determination of the
recapture should present little problem when
the animals are specifically identified in
the purchase and sale transactions. Because
Code § 1245 applies only to gains on the sale
of each item, it is important that losses be
eliminated from transactions in which gains
and losses are netted. Code § 1245 gains are
includible in distributable ordinary income
as determined on page one of the partnership
return, Form 1065.

Losses from the sale of breeding stock
held 2 years are Code § 1231 losses that must
be grouped with § 1231 gains and reported as
a distributable Code § 1231 gain or loss on
Schedule K-1 of Form 1065.

4.03
Breeding--managed
herds

Cases involving cattle breeder herd tax
shelters are generally promoted by a pro-
moter-operator corporation. Breeding herds,
usually consisting of units (herds) of 10
female animals, are offered for sale through
offering memorandums or prospectuses.

4.031
Characteristics

Characteristics of these plans are:

(1) The promoter purchases the cattle at
    market prices, then sells to the
    investors at inflated prices.

(2) The investors enter into a maintenance
    contract with the promoter who will
    feed, breed, and care for the cattle.

(3) The investors take additional first-
    year and accelerated depreciation, and

1027

the investment credit based on the
inflated purchase price.

Example 8

(1) An investor purchases 10
purebred cows, 1 to 4
years old for $35,000.

(2) The 7-year maintenance
contract with the seller
provides for feeding,
breeding, and caring for
the herd in exchange for
all the bull calves and 10
percent of the heifer
calves.

(3) The promoter estimates
that at the end of 7 years
the herd will consist of
67 animals (averaging
$600) worth approximately
$40,000.

(4) The return to the investor
is 2 percent a year,

(a) Total dollar return:
$40,000
-35,000
$ 5,000

(b) Return per year:
$5,000 ÷ 7 years =
$714.29

(c) Percent of return:
$714.29 ÷ $35,000 = 2
percent.

(5) The investor uses accelerated depreciation, addi-
tional first-year depre-
ciation and claims the
investment credit (10%) on
the $35,000 investment.
The paper tax loss is
applied against the investor's other taxable in-
come.

4.032
Potential issues

(1) The inflated purchase price of the
    herd is allocated to the breeding
    animals, it will result in excessive
    depreciation deductions and an invest-
    ment credit for the investor. One
    position is that, without specific
    reasonable evidence identifying its
    nature, the premium paid for the
    cattle should be a capital expenditure
    which is recovered when the investment
    is terminsited.

(2) Another position is that this is not a
    transaction entered into for profit.
    /15/

(3) The investors sell the female progeny
    at different times. Many apparently
    operate on the premise that all
    2-year-old heifers qualify as Code §
    1231 property. At times, when progeny
    are sold to the management company,
    the 2-year holding period may be
    questionable.

(4) Some investors renegotiate their plans
    and, for example, may exchange a
    "purebred" herd for a "commercial"
    herd, or they may sell the original
    herd to the management company and
    purchase another. Some, in this
    instance, fail to correctly compute
    investment credit at the acquisition
    of substantially identical livestock.
    /16/

(5) The sale of bull calves, though not a
    factor in many shelters, have, in some
    instances, been reported as Code §
    1231 property when the animals were
    barely 2 years old and when the number
    far exceeded that which could have
    been intended for inclusion in the
    herd. /17/

(6) In a number of reported instances,
    sometimes at the time the management
    company became bankrupt, the investor
    has claimed a contribution for the
    fair market value of purchased and
    raised animals. In addition to the
    valuation problems, of Code § 170

regarding stock-in-trade, appreciated
Code § 1231 property, and Code § 1245
property are numerous.

(7) The age of the cows in the herds
purchased by investors often varies
from 2 to 7 years. This creates an
identification problem of "new" or
"used" cows for the purpose of investment credit, accelerated depreciation
methods, and first-year depreciation.

(8) In the few instances when the Code §
1251(b) Excess Deductions Account
applies to the investor, it is clear
that the recapture applied to Code §
1231 breeding livestock.

5.0
Movie films

Movie film tax shelters generally involve
two basic forms. In one, a <u>limited partner-
ship</u> is formed to purchase the rights to an
already completed film (may be either domestic or foreign). In the film purchase
shelter, the purchase price is often unrealistically inflated and heavily encumbered.
Additionally, the partners benefit from
substantial depreciation deductions and
investment credit.

The second form again involves a limited
partnership. This partnership is formed as a
production company commonly referred to as a
service company. This service company uses
the cash basis and writes off production
costs as they are paid with borrowed funds.
Income realization is subsequently spread
over the period of distribution of the film.

5.01
Film purchase
tax shelter

In the film purchase transaction, a syndicate of investors, usually formed as a limited partnership, purchases a completed film
for a cash downpayment, plus a <u>nonrecourse
note</u>. It is not uncommon for the <u>leverage
factor</u> in this type of transaction to be 3 or
4 to 1 (that is, 3 or 4 dollars of borrowing
for each dollar of equity investment) and
sometimes even higher.

The partnership usually turns over the
function of distributing the picture to a
major studio-distributor (sometimes the same
entity that sold the film to the
partnership), which makes prints, arranges
showings, and handles advertising and promotion in return for a percentage of the gross
receipts.

The income from showing the film is divided between the theater owners who show the
film, and the distributor who receives a
distribution fee. In addition, it is common
for the producer and/or the stars of the film
to share the income. The limited partnership, as the owner of the film, has the
<u>negative interest</u> which is also a right to a
certain share of the gross receipts. The

1031

negative interest is often heavily mortgaged and the nonrecourse note is to be liquidated from the film's receipts. Some agreements provide that the nonrecourse note must be liquidated before the limited partners recover any of their own equity capital or realize a profit. Other arrangements provide for some form of prorated payoff, under which each dollar allocated to the negative interest is divided between the noteholder and the limited partners on some predetermined basis.

5.011
Characteristics

The following characteristics of the film purchase shelter indicate a potential for tax issues:

(1) Purchase of film at an inflated value.

(2) Nonrecourse note for 70-80 percent of purchase price.

(3) Investment tax credit on investment.

(4) Depreciation deduction based on the income forecast method, which uses the following formula:

Purchase price x Current year's income/Total estimated income = Depreciation deduction /18/

(5) Classification of film as a capital asset or Code § 1231 property.

5.012
Potential issues

The film-purchase limited partnership may include conditions that disqualify the partnership from benefiting from favorable depreciation deductions and investment tax credit. Some of these conditions are discussed on the following pages.

5.0121
License or joint
venture v. purchase

The purchase agreement should be carefully scrutinized to determine if a seller retains rights as a licensor or retains an equity interest in the venture.

1032

Some licensor characteristics are:

(1) The retention of a continuing interest by the seller in the revenue generated by the film.

(2) Substantial restrictions placed by the seller on the distribution of the film.

In a joint venture, the seller receives payments from film profits after the payment of the principal and interest on the note. The seller retains the right to contribute management services and the purchaser (investor) advances the funds.

In either the license or joint venture situation, the partnership's basis in the film may be limited to the initial cash investment by the partners, thereby resulting in a lower depreciable basis. This could result in the failure of property to qualify for investment tax credit purposes.

5.0122
Film appraisal

Verification of the reasonable fair market value of the film is one essential and critical point in determining whether the organization of the partnership for tax purposes has substance as well as form. This fair market value is the basis for which depreciation, investment credit, and gain or loss is computed on disposition of either the film or partner's interests.

The partnership should provide the required information concerning the determination of the fair market value of the film. The following factors should be considered for valuation purposes:

(1) Relationship of fair market value to purchase price.

(2) Potential for audience acceptance (well-known story or star, favorable review of negative, etc.).

(3) Restrictions placed on distribution of film.

(4) Were any of the above factors considered in making the appraisal and
was the appraiser qualified and independent?

5.0123
Promissory note

The promissory note must represent a true
debtor-creditor relationship, including a
fixed time and amount due. Clauses in a
nonrecourse promissory note granting the
lender the option, at any time, to convert
debt into an equity interest in the partnership or participate in the profits may be
deemed a contribution to the partnership's
capital whether the lender is a general
partner /19/ or an unrelated party /20/.

The portion of the promissory note deemed
to be a contribution of capital reduces the
amount of partnership loss by disallowing
interest on the equity portion of the nonrecourse loan and decreasing the depreciation
deduction.

Also, attention should be given to the
term of the loan and its relationship to the
projected income from the film. A mortgage
term longer than the period of projected
income usually indicates that the loan is not
expected to be repaid. In this situation,
the film was probably overvalued so that the
basis for computing depreciation and the
investment credit is thereby overstated.

5.0124
Investment credit

In order for property to qualify as Code §
38 investment property, it must be of a type
subject to depreciation under Code § 167.
Depreciation under this section permits a
writeoff of the cost of an asset over its
useful life by various acceptable methods.
Determination of useful life for a film is
difficult, since the income forecast method
of depreciation (Purchase price x Current
year's income/Total estimated income = Depreciation deduction) does not easily lend
itself to a term stated in years, which is
required to determine amount of the cost
subject to investment credit. Therefore,
interpolation of the depreciation computation
is necessary.

In 1971, the conference committee addressed the issue, and developed specific guidelines. If projected accumulated depreciation at intervals of 3, 5, and 7 years does not exceed 20 percent of accumulated depreciation using the most favorable of the other depreciation methods (such as the double declining balance), the useful life of the asset under the income forecast method will be assumed to be 7 years.

The question arises, what is total estimated income? It is net receipts, not gross receipts, based on conditions known to exist at the end of the period. Net receipts exclude receipts from television on U.S.-produced film.

In determining whether a film is qualified investment tax credit property, attention should be given to whether the film was produced in the U.S. and whether the film was exhibited in a foreign country (thus perhaps qualifying as used property) and whether the film was primarily used outside U.S. (nonqualifying property).

Finally, one must remember that the recapture provisions apply to partnerships and partners when property ceases to be Code § 38 property.

A partner would be required to recapture the full amount of investment tax credit upon the sale of his or her interest to another in less than 3 years from the date the film was placed in service.

5.0125
Dispositions

When a sale or other disposition occurs, the question arises whether the gain or loss is ordinary or capital gain or loss? Since the partnership purchased the film and it derives its income from distribution rights to theaters and television stations, the film would be a Code § 1231 asset used in a trade or business. Therefore, Code § 1245 would be applicable in determining the amount of ordinary and capital gain. Gain on foreclosure should be investigated since it may represent a foregiveness of indebtedness. One should not only look to Code § 61, but also Code § 752(b) (tax treatment where there

is a decrease in a partner's liability), Code
§ 731 (recognition of gain or loss in distribution), and Code § 735 (character of gain or
loss or disposition).

5.02
Production service
tax shelter

Film service partnerships use a combination of the cash method of accounting and
nonrecourse loans to achieve high-leverage
losses for their partners. The typical
amount of loss is three or four times the
capital contribution for the first year. The
partnership finances and actually produces a
film, although it maintains the form of
providing "services" instead of a product.
The partnership contends that title to the
film at all times remains with another entity
(owner/distributor); therefore, the partnership has no inventory and the cash method of
accounting is proper.

In this type of arrangement, the limited
partnership enters into an agreement with the
owner or a distributor of a film to produce a
motion picture. The owner and distributor
may be the same entity. The distributor's
requirements are generally outlined in detail
and include rights as to quality control.
The production work is often subcontracted to
an independent producer. This independent
producer may in fact be the owner or distributor.

Financing for the production costs is
provided by capital contributions by the
limited partners and the balance from a
nonrecourse loan from a bank, which is guaranteed by the distributor, leveraged in a
ratio of 3 to 4 to 1. The limited partnership does not have an ownership interest in
the film, so income equals costs plus potential profit payable over several years.
Financing agreements generally provide for
guaranteed payments of the bank loan from
initial income. There may be additional
income in the form of a percentage of film
receipts (often with a ceiling) that may be
payable over a period of 6 to 7 years.

Many high-income individuals use grantor
trusts in such a way that the initial loss is
deducted on their individual tax returns, and

the income reported in subsequent years is taxable to multiple trusts at a relatively nominal tax rate; thus, these partners receive a tax deferral, and when income is realized, it is taxed to another entity at a lower tax rate.

5.021
Characteristics

(1) Nonrecourse loan of 70-80 percent of production costs.

(2) Cash method of accounting; therefore, current expensing of all production costs, which are generally incurred within 1 year.

(3) No obvious interest in film, although income may include a percentage of film receipts.

5.022
Potential issues

A service/production company may operate under conditions that preclude it from the favorable deduction of expenses. Some of these conditions are discussed here.

5.0221
Nonrecourse loan

A nonrecourse loan from the owner or distributor indicates that an owner or distributor entered into a joint venture as a general partner with the partnership /21/ and the proceeds from the loan are considered a contribution to capital by the lender as a general partner. Therefore, the expense of producing the film is not deductible as a current expense. The fees received under the service agreement would be considered repayment of the loan principal and only any excess would be considered interest.

A nonrecourse loan from an unrelated third party may be deemed an equity purchase /22/ if:

(1) There is an unrealistic prospect that the loan will be repaid.

Example 9

Loan is due and payable in 10
years, yet the fees from
service contract will cease at
end of 7th year.

(2) If at any time, the lender has the
right to convert the debt into an
equity interest of partnership profits.

5.0222
Method of accounting

Any accounting method is acceptable as
long as it clearly reflects income; however,
the Service may prescribe another method if
the method employed by the taxpayer distorts
income. /23/ Consideration to changing a
taxpayer's method should be given if, under
State law, films in production are considered
inventory of the service company.

Cost of production should be capitalized
if it is determined that a joint venture
exists between the service company and the
owner of the film.

5.0223
Corporation v.
limited partnership

The limited partnership service company
may be taxable as a corporation if it has
more corporate than noncorporate characteristics. /24/ Whether a tax entity has corporate characteristics is a factual determination that should be guided by the intent and
conduct of the parties to the service contract. Centralized control may indicate that
a corporation exists. In this instance, a
corporation may exist in which the owner of
the film possesses the centralized control.
Centralized control is indicated when, for
instance:

(1) The owner of the film has hiring
authority or approval privileges as to the
producer, director, actors, and subcontrac-
tors of the film.

(2) The owner reviews and corrects the
film during production rather than providing
mere quality control of the film.

(3) Potential losses of the service company are limited to the cash investment and the owner is a full guarantor of nonrecourse loans. (In this instance, the characteristics of the limited partnership are voided since local law usually requires at least one member to hold unlimited liability for debts of the partnership.)

4. The service company's only real function is the raising of risk capital because actual production of the film is sub-contracted to the owner of the film.

5.0224
Transactions not
for profit--
Code § 183

If the partnership fails to show a profit in at least 2 of 5 consecutive years, it will be deemed to have entered into a transaction not engaged in for profit. The nonprofit issue is likely to occur when the service company continues to acquire service contracts of a 1-2 year duration and the cost of production is greater for each subsequent production, thereby offsetting income of initial production with production expense of subsequent productions.

6.0
Technical advice

Form 4463, Request for Technical Advice,
is used for requesting technical advice and
transmitting necessary supporting documents
and data (see Exhibit 6-A). The request must
contain sufficient information for the technical employee to properly analyze and develop the issue or issues. Present the
information to Technical in broad, clear, and
concise language, making certain that all
alternative issues are properly identified
and developed. The care you take in preparing the request will reduce handling delays
resulting from vague or ambiguous information
(see Exhibit 6-B).

Exhibit 6-C of this booklet contains Rev.
Proc. 73-8 in its entirety. Footnotes were
supplied as a reference to the various procedures provided in the Internal Revenue Manual. Exhibit 6-D provides a **suggested** format
for the written statement.

Using the written statement format should
provide uniformity and clarity to insure a
practicable method for requesting technical
advice. The format, adopted from section
7.03 of Rev. Proc. 73-8, is not intended to
restrict the originality of the writer or to
prohibit appropriate deviation.

Request for Technical Advice

Please submit original and two copies - Complete all applicable boxes

1. TO: Internal Revenue Service, Washington, D. C. 20224 ATTENTION: T:PS:T		6. DATE OF REQUEST
2. FROM	DISTRICT	7. PRINCIPAL CODE SECTION
SIGNATURE	TITLE	8. YEAR(S) INVOLVED
3. (a) NAME AND TELEPHONE NUMBER OF DISTRICT OFFICE CONTACT		9. STATUTORY PERIOD EXPIRES
(b) NAME AND TELEPHONE NUMBER OF AUDIT GROUP MANAGER		
4. NAME AND ADDRESS OF TAXPAYER OR ORGANIZATION		10. TAXPAYER IDENTIFICATION NO.
5. NAME AND ADDRESS OF TAXPAYER'S REPRESENTATIVE	AREA CODE AND TELEPHONE NO.	11. ATTACHED: POWER OF ATTORNEY AND DECLARATION ☐ YES ☐ NO / ☐ YES ☐ NO

ITEM	(Check) YES	NO	AT-TACHED	ITEM	(Check) YES	NO	AT-TACHED
12. GENERAL INFORMATION				13. ADDITIONAL ITEMS IN CERTAIN CASES			
a. Was taxpayer informed Technical Advice is being requested and did you explain procedures?. If not, please state reason:				a. Is an inter vivos trust involved?............ If Yes, please attach a copy of the trust instrument.....................................			
				b. Is a testamentary trust or an estate involved?................................... If Yes, please attach a copy of the Will....			
b. Does taxpayer desire a National Office conference if adverse decision is indicated?................................				c. Is revocation or modification of exemption or determination letter in the exempt organization or pension trust area involved?................................			
c. Did you give taxpayer a statement of facts and questions as your office sees them?.....				If Yes:			
If Yes, please attach copy .... If not, please state reason:				(1) Recommended effective date of revocation or modification_____ .			
				(2) Attach statement of reasons for recommended effective date of revocation or modification................................			
d. Does taxpayer agree with statement? .... If not, please attach taxpayer's statement of facts and questions				(3) Is the organization a private foundation?...................................			
e. If you have prepared a statement of applicable law, argument, and conclusion, please attach copy................................				d. Is sensitive case involved? .... If Yes, please attach copy of sensitive case report			
f. If taxpayer has submitted a protest, brief, response, or other information, please attach copy				e. Is Controlled Large Case Program involved?			

INSTRUCTIONS

A. This form is used by District Directors in transmitting requests for technical advice to the National Office in accordance with the procedures in IRM 4550. Supporting documents and all pertinent material should be included and not necessarily limited to that called for by this form and instructions. This form is not used in transmitting requests for rulings, technical assistance, or general technical information.

B. Information with respect to the following matters should be included in the file, if applicable:

    1. Prior Ruling or Determination Letter. Give date of letter, if related to issue involved in this Request for Technical Advice, and if determination letter, please furnish a copy.

2. Taxpayer Previously Examined. State disposition of prior case if issue involved in this Request for Technical Advice was also involved in prior case.

3. Pension, Profit-Sharing, Stock Bonus, or Bond Purchase Plan. Enclose plan file, reporting forms, supporting schedules, actuarial reports, and any other pertinent information.

4. Employer-Employee Determination. Furnish information from both parties (See Form SS-8). If taxpayer has 4 or more workers, attempt to obtain information from at least 4.

5. Partnership. Furnish copy of partnership agreement.

6. Credit for Foreign Taxes. State whether standards of Revenue Ruling 67-308, 1967-2, C.B. 254, have been met.

Form **4463** (Rev. 4-73)

Department of the Treasury - Internal Revenue Service

INTERNAL REVENUE SERVICE
NATIONAL OFFICE TECHNICAL ADVICE MEMORANDUM
(Original and copies date stamped by T:PS:T)

District Director
(Name of District Office)

    Taxpayer's Name:
    Taxpayer's Address:
    Taxpayer's Identification No.:
    Years Involved:
    Date of Conference: (*OR* No Conference Held)

Issues

State the issues as presented by the District. Also, whenever appropriate, state in clear, precise language any additional issues that have been identified that were not specifically raised by the incoming correspondence, or restate the issue presented by the District to pinpoint the real question to be decided.

Facts

The statement of facts incorporated in the technical advice memorandum should be set out concisely but without any sacrifice of clarity. The essential facts should be fully presented. Short quotations from the incoming statement may be used as an aid in definitely pinning down particular areas when the conclusion depends on the interpretation of such language. However, lengthy quotations from documents contained in the file are to be avoided wherever practicable.

Applicable Law

This part of the document should set forth clearly and concisely the pertinent law, regulations, published rulings of the Service, and case law or other precedent. Care should be taken that all citations are directly in point. Quotations which are helpful may be used judiciously, but lengthy ones are to be avoided wherever practicable.

Rationale

Sufficient rationale must be provided to bridge any gaps between the issue, law, and conclusion reached.

Conclusion

A specific statement as to the conclusion reached with respect to each issue is the final important step. These conclusions must be written to leave no doubt as to their meaning and to make it clear they are based solely on the facts presented.

(If a copy of the technical advice memorandum is not to be given to the taxpayer, that fact should be noted here.)

In summary, it is our function to promote uniformity, clarity, and responsiveness and, to the extent practicable, to insure an orderly method of approaching a technical advice problem. It is not intended in any way to restrict originality or ingenuity on the part of the writer, nor is it intended to prevent necessary or desirable deviation from the pattern where proper.

Exhibit 6-C

Rev. Proc. 73-8
1973-1 C.B. 754

Section 1. Purpose

.01 The purpose of this Revenue Procedure is to supersede
Revenue Procedure 72-2, 1972-1 C.B. 695, by providing revised
procedures for furnishing technical advice to District Directors
of Internal Revenue. It is also intended to inform taxpayers of
their rights when a District Director requests such advice from
the National Office.

.02 Sections 4.03, 4.04, 5.02, 5.03, 6.01 and 6.04, as revised indicate the time a taxpayer has to reply to the Service,
the time within which a National Office conference is to be held,
the procedure in obtaining extensions of time, and the Service
official who must approve such extensions. Section 6.02, as
revised, allows the examining officer to attend the National
Office conference in appropriate cases.

.03 For purposes of this Revenue Procedure any reference to
District Director or district office, also includes the office of
the Director, Office of International Operations, where appropriate.

Sec. 2. Definition and Nature of Technical Advice

.01 "Techical advice", as used herein, means advice or guidance as to the interpretation and proper application of internal
revenue laws, related statutes, and regulations, to a specific
set of facts, furnished by the National Office upon request of a
district office in connection with the examination of a taxpayer's return or consideration of a taxpayer's claim for refund
or credit. It is furnished as a means of assisting Sevice personnel in closing cases and establishing and maintaining consistent holdings in the several districts. /25/ It does not include
memorandums on matters of general technical application furnished
to district offices where the issues are not raised in connection
with the examination of the return of a specific taxpayer.

.02 The consideration or examination of the facts relating to
a request for a determination letter is considered to be in
connection with the examination or consideration of a return of
the taxpayer. Thus, a District Director may, in his discretion,
request technical advice with respect to the consideration of a
request for a determination letter.

.03 If a District Director is of the opinion that a ruling
letter previously issued to a taxpayer should be modified or

Exhibit 6-C (cont.)

revoked, and he requests the National Office to reconsider the ruling, the reference of the matter to the National Office is treated as a request for technical advice and the procedures specified in section 4 should be followed in order that the National Office may consider the District Director's recommendation. Only the National Office can revoke a ruling letter. Before referral to the National Office, the District Director should inform the taxpayer of his opinion that the ruling letter should be revoked. The District Director, after development of the facts and consideration of the taxpayer's arguments, will decide whether to recommend revocation of the ruling to the National Office. For procedures relating to a request for a ruling, see Revenue Procedure 72-3, 1972-1 C.B. 698.

.04 The Assistant Commissioner (Technical), acting under a delegation of authority from the Commissioner of Internal Revenue, is exclusively responsible for providing technical advice in any issue involving the establishment of basic principles and rules for the uniform interpretation and application of tax laws other than those under the jurisdiction of the Bureau of Alcohol, Tobacco and Firearms. This authority has been largely redelegated to subordinate officials.

.05 The provisions of this Revenue Procedure apply only to a case under the jurisdiction of a District Director. They do not apply to a case under the jurisdiction of the Bureau of Alcohol, Tobacco and Firearms or to a case under the jurisdiction of a regional Appellate Division, including a case previously considered by Appellate. A case remains under the jurisdiction of the District Director even though a regional Appellate Division has the identical issue under consideration in the case of another taxpayer (not related within the meaning of section 267 of the Code) in an entirely different transaction. Technical advice may not be requested with respect to a taxable period if a prior Appellate disposition of the same taxable period of the same taxpayer's case was based on mutual concessions (ordinarily with a Form 870-AD, Offer of Waiver of Restrictions on Assessment and Collection of Deficiency in Tax and of Acceptance of Overassessment). Technical advice may not be requested by a district office on issues previously considered in a prior Appellate disposition, not based on mutual concessions, of the same taxable periods of the same taxpayer, unless Appellate concurs in the request.

Sec. 3. Areas in Which Technical Advice May Be Requested

.01 District Directors may request technical advice on any technical or procedural question that develops during the audit or examination of a return, or claim for refund or credit, of a taxpayer. These procedures are applicable as provided in section 2.

Exhibit 6-C (cont.)

.02 District Directors are encouraged to request technical advice on any technical or procedural question arising in connection with any case of the type described in section 2, at any stage of the proceedings in the district office, which cannot be resolved on the basis of law, regulations, or a clearly applicable Revenue Ruling or other precedent published by the National Office.

Sec. 4. Requesting Technical Advice /26/

.01 It is the responsibility of the district office to determine whether technical advice is to be requested on any issue before that office. However, while the case is under the jurisdiction of the District Director, a taxpayer or his representative may request that an issue be referred to the National Office for technical advice on the grounds that a lack of uniformity exists as to the disposition of the issue, or that the issue is so unusual or complex as to warrant consideration by the National Office. While taxpayers are encouraged to make written requests setting forth the facts, law, and argument with respect to the issue, and reasons for requesting National Office advice, a taxpayer may make the request orally. If, after considering the taxpayer's request, the examining officer or conferee is of the opinion that the circumstances do not warrant referral of the case to the National Office, he will so advise the taxpayer. (See section 5 for taxpayer's appeal rights where examining officer or conferee declines to request advice.)

.02 When technical advice is to be requested, whether or not upon the request of the taxpayer, the taxpayer will be so advised, except as noted in section 4.07. If the examining officer or the conferee initiates the action, the taxpayer will be furnished a copy of the statement of the pertinent facts and the question or questions proposed for submission to the National Office. The request for advice submitted by the District Director should be so worded as to avoid possible misunderstanding, in the National Office, of the facts or of the specific point or points at issue.

.03 After receipt of the statement of facts and specific questions from the district office, the taxpayer will be given 10 calendar days in which to indicate in writing the extent, if any, to which he may not be in complete agreement. An extension of time must be justified by the taxpayer in writing and approved by the Chief, Audit Division. Every effort should be made to reach agreement as to the facts and the specific point at issue. If agreement cannot be reached, the taxpayer may submit, within 10 calendar days after receipt of notice from the district office, a statement of his understanding as to the specific point or points at issue which will be forwarded to the National Office with the request for advice. An extension of time must be justified by

Exhibit 6-C (cont.)

the taxpayer in writing and approved by the Chief, Audit Division.

.04 If the taxpayer initiates the action to request advice, and his statement of the facts and point or points at issue are not wholly acceptable to the district officials, the taxpayer will be advised in writing as to the areas of disagreement. The taxpayer will be given 10 calendar days after receipt of the written notice to reply to the district official's letter. An extension of time must be justified by the taxpayer in writing and approved by the Chief, Audit Division. If agreement cannot be reached, both the statements of the taxpayer and the district official will be forwarded to the National Office.

.05 If the taxpayer has not already done so, he may submit a statement explaining his position on the issues, citing precedents which he believes will bear on the case. This statement will be forwarded to the National Office with the request for advice. If it is received at a later date, it will be forwarded for association with the case file.

.06 At the time the taxpayer is informed that the matter is being referred to the National Office, he will also be informed of his right to a conference in the National Office in the event an adverse decision is indicated, and will be asked to indicate whether he desires such a conference.

.07 The provisions of this section, relating to the referral of issues upon request of taxpayer, advising taxpayers of the referral of issues, and the granting of conferences in the National Office, are not applicable to matters primarily of internal concern or in instances where it would be prejudicial to the interests of the Internal Revenue Service (as for example in cases involving fraud or jeopardy assessments).

.08 Form 4463, Request for Technical Advice, should be used for transmitting requests for technical advice to the National Office. /27/

Sec. 5. Appeal by Taxpayers of Determinations Not to Seek Technical Advice

.01 If the taxpayer has requested referral of an issue before a district office to the National Office for technical advice, and after consideration of the request the examining officer or conferee is of the opinion that the circumstances do not warrant such referral, he will so advise the taxpayer.

.02 The taxpayer may appeal the decision of the examining officer or conferee not to request technical advice by submitting to that official, within 10 calendar days after being advised of

Exhibit 6-C (cont.)

the decision, a statement of the facts, law, and arguments with respect to the issue, and the reasons why he believes the matter should be referred to the National Office for advice. An extension of time must be justified by the taxpayer in writing and approved by the Chief, Audit Division.

.03 The examining officer or conferee will submit the statement of the taxpayer through channels to the Chief, Audit Division, accompanied by a statement of his reasons why the issue should not be referred to the National Office. The Chief, Audit Division, will determine, on the basis of the statements submitted, whether technical advice will be requested. If he determines that technical advice is not warranted, he will inform the taxpayer in writing that he proposes to deny the request. In the letter to the taxpayer the Chief, Audit Division, will (except in unusual situations where such action would be prejudicial to the best interests of the Government) state specifically the reasons for the proposed denial. The taxpayer will be given 15 calendar days after receipt of the letter in which to notify the Chief, Audit Division, whether he agrees with the proposed denial. The taxpayer may not appeal the decision of the Chief, Audit Division, not to request technical advice from the National Office. However, if he does not agree with the proposed denial, all data relating to the issue for which technical advice has been sought, including taxpayer's written request and statements, will be submitted to the National Office, Attention: Director, Audit Division, for review. After review in the National Office, the district office will be notified whether the proposed denial is approved or disapproved.

.04 While the matter is being reviewed in the National Office, the district office will suspend action on the issue (except where the delay would prejudice the Government's interests) until it is notified of the National Office decision. This notification will be made within 30 calendar days after receipt of the data in the National Office. The review will be solely on the basis of the written record and no conference will be held in the National Office.

Sec. 6. Conference in the National Office /28/

.01 If, after a study of the case file, it appears that advice that is adverse to the taxpayer should be given and a conference has been requested, the taxpayer will be notified of the time and place of the conference. If conferences are being arranged with respect to more than one request for advice involving the same taxpayer, they will be so scheduled as to cause the least inconvenience to the taxpayer. The conference will be arranged by telephone, if possible, and must be held within 21 calendar days after contact has been made. Extensions of time will be granted only if justified in writing by the taxpayer and approved by the appropriate Technical branch chief.

Exhibit 6-C (cont.)

.02 A taxpayer is entitled, as a matter of right, to only one conference in the National Office unless one of the circumstances discussed in this section exists. This conference will usually be held at the branch level in the appropriate division (Income Tax Division or Miscellaneous and Special Provisions Tax Division) in the office of the Assistant Commissioner (Technical), and will usually be attended by a person who has authority to act for the branch chief. In appropriate cases the examining officer may also attend the conference to clarify the facts in the case. If more than one subject is discussed at the conference, the discussion constitutes a conference with respect to each subject. At the request of the taxpayer or his representative, the conference may be held at an earlier stage in the consideration of the case than the Service would ordinarily designate. A taxpayer has no "right" of appeal from an action of a branch to the director of a division or to any other National Office official.

.03 In the process of review in Technical of a holding proposed by a branch, it may appear that the final answer will involve a reversal of the branch proposal with a result less favorable to the taxpayer. Or it may appear that an adverse holding proposed by a branch will be approved, but on a new or different issue or on different grounds than those on which the branch decided the case. Under either of these circumstances, the taxpayer or his representative will be invited to another conference. The provisions of the Revenue Procedure limiting the number of conferences to which a taxpayer is entitled will not foreclose inviting a taxpayer to attend further conferences when, in the opinion of National Office personnel, such need arises. All additional conferences of the type discussed in this paragraph are held only at the invitation of the Service.

.04 It is the responsibility of the taxpayer to furnish to the National Office, within 21 calendar days after the conference, a written record of any additional data, line or reasoning, precedents, etc., that were proposed by the taxpayer and discussed at the conference but were not previously or adequately presented in writing. Extensions of time will be granted only if justified in writing by the taxpayer and approved by the appropriate Technical branch chief. Any additional material and a copy thereof should be addressed to and sent to the National Office which will forward the copy to the appropriate District Director. The District Director will be requested to give the matter his prompt attention. He may verify the additional facts and data and comment upon it to the extent he deems it appropriate.

.05 A taxpayer or his representative desiring to obtain information as to the status of his case may do so by contacting the following offices with respect to matters in the areas of their responsibility:

Exhibit 6-C (cont.)

Official	Telephone Numbers (Area Code 202)
Director, Income Tax Division	964-4504 or 964-4505
Director, Miscellaneous and Special Provisions Tax Division	964-3767 or 964-3788

Sec. 7. Preparation of Technical Advice Memorandum by the National Office /29/

.01 Immediately upon receipt in the National Office, the technical employee to whom the case is assigned will analyze the file to ascertain whether it meets all requirements of section 4. If the case is not complete, appropriate steps will be taken to complete the file.

.02 If the taxpayer has requested a conference in the National Office, the procedures in section 6 will be followed.

.03 Replies to request for technical advice will be addressed to the District Director and will be drafted in two parts. Each part will identify the taxpayer by name, address, identification number, and year or years involved. The first part (hereafter called the "Technical Memorandum") will contain (1) a recitation of the pertinent facts having a bearing on the issue; (2) a discussion of the facts, precedents, and reasoning of the National Office; and (3) the conclusions of the National Office. The conclusions will give direct answers, whenever possible, to the specific questions of the district office. The discussion of the issues will be in such detail that the district officials are apprised of the reasoning underlying the conclusion.

.04 The second part of the reply will consist of a transmittal memorandum. In unusual cases it will serve as a vehicle for providing the district office administrative information or other information which, under the nondisclosure statutes, or for other reasons, may not be discussed with the taxpayer.

.05 It is the general practice of the Service to furnish a copy of the technical memorandum to the taxpayer, upon his request, after it has been adopted by the District Director. However, where no definitive answer is given to the specific question presented, where the factual submission is such as to indicate that the issue should be decided by the district office, or where it would not be in the interest of a wise administration of the tax laws, a copy of the technical memorandum will not be furnished the taxpayer. The National Office will specifically advise the District Director in those cases where it is determined that a copy of the technical memorandum is not to be made available to the taxpayer.

Exhibit 6-C (cont.)

Sec. 8. Action on Technical Advice in District Offices /30/

.01 Unless the District Director feels that the conclusions reached by the National Office in a technical advice memorandum should be reconsidered and promptly requests such reconsideration, his office will proceed to process the taxpayer's case on the basis of the conclusions expressed in the technical advice memorandum.

.02 Unless advised otherwise by the National Office as provided in section 7.05, the district office will furnish to the taxpayer, upon his request, a copy of the technical memorandum described in section 7.03, for his information as to the holding of the Service on the issue.

.03 In those cases in which the National Office advises the District Director that he should not furnish a copy of the technical memorandum to the taxpayer, the District Director will so inform the taxpayer if he requests a copy.

Sec. 9. Effect of Technical Advice

.01 A technical advice memorandum represents an expression of the views of the Service as to the application of law, regulations, and precedents to the facts of a specific case, and is issued primarily as a means of assisting district officials in the examination and closing of the case involved.

.02 Except in rare or unusual circumstances, a holding in a technical advice memorandum that is favorable to the taxpayer is applied retroactively. Moreover, since technical advice, as described in section 2.01 of this Revenue Procedure, is issued only on closed transactions, a holding in a technical advice memorandum that is adverse to the taxpayer is also applied retroactively unless the Assistant Commissioner (Technical) exercises the discretionary authority under section 7805(b) of the Code to limit the retroactive effect of the holding. Likewise, a holding in a technical advice memorandum that modifies or revokes a holding in a prior technical advice memorandum will also be applied retroactively, with one exception. If the new holding is less favorable to the taxpayer, it will generally not be applied to the period in which the taxpayer relied on the prior holding in situations involving continuing transactions of the type described in sections 13.07 and 13.08 of Revenue Procedure 72-3.

.03 Technical advice memorandums often form the basis for Revenue Rulings. For the description of Revenue Rulings and the effect thereof, see section 2.01 and section 6.01 of Revenue Procedure 72-1, 1972-1 C.B. 693.

Exhibit 6-C (cont.)

.04 A District Director may raise an issue in any taxable period, even though he may have asked for and been furnished technical advice with regard to the same or a similar issue in any other taxable period.

Sec. 10. Effect of Other Documents

Revenue Procedure 72-2 is superseded by this Revenue Procedure.

Sec. 11. Effective Date

This Revenue Procedure is effective April 2, 1973, the date of its publication in the Internal Revenue Bulletin. Requests for technical advice received prior to April 2, 1973, will be processed under the provisions of Revenue Procedure 72-2.

Exhibit 6-D

SUGGESTED WRITTEN STATEMENT FORMAT

(A) Issues

In your writing, present the issue or issues in precise language. Questions should be broadly framed with alternative
issues identified and sufficiently developed. Pinpoint the real
question or questions to be decided.

(B) Statement of facts

State the facts clearly and concisely, but without any sacrifice of clarity. The pertinent and essential facts should be
fully presented showing both the district's and taxpayer's view,
if available. Refer to supporting documents and key them to
relevant facts.

(C) Applicable law

Clearly and concisely state the pertinent law, regulations,
published rulings of the Service, case law, or other precedent.
Direct all references to the related facts or points at issue.

(D) Conclusion

Write a specific statement describing the impact of the issue
or issues and the district's reason for presenting them.

7.0
Tax Shelters--Partial Listing of Applicable Revenue Procedures and
Revenue Rulings

Revenue Procedures

   Rev. Proc. 72-9, 1972-1 C.B. 718

      An up-to-date list of areas in which the Revenue Service
   will or will not ordinarily issue rulings or determination
   letters because of the inherently factual nature of the
   problems involved, or for other reasons, is set forth.
   Amplified by Rev. Proc. 74-22. Rev. Procs. 69-6 and 71-31
   superseded. (Sec. 601.201, S.P.R.)

   Rev. Proc. 72-13, 1972-1 C.B. 735

      Conditions under which advance rulings will be issued
   concerning the classification of an organization as a limited partnership where a corporation is the sole general
   partner. §301.7701-3. (Sec. 601.201, S.P.R.; Sec. 7701,
   '54 Code.)

   Rev. Proc. 73-8, 1973-1 C.B. 754

      Procedures have been revised effective April 2, 1973, for
   the National Office furnishing of requested technical advice
   to District directors and the time period within which
   taxpayers may exercise their related rights. Rev. Proc.
   72-2 superseded. (Sec. 601.105, S.P.R.)

   Rev. Proc. 74-17, 1974-1 C.B. 438

      Conditions are set forth under which an organization
   formed and operated as a limited partnership will ordinarily
   be issued an advance ruling concerning its classification as
   a partnership under section 7701 of the Code. §301.7701-3.
   (Sec. 601.201, S.P.R.; Sec. 7701, '54 Code.)

   Rev. Proc. 75-21, 1975-1 C.B. 715

      Guidelines are given for determining whether, for advance
   ruling purposes, certain purported leases of property commonly called "leveraged leases" are to te considered leases
   for income tax purposes. §§1.38-1, 1.61-1, 1.162-1,
   1.167(a)-1. (Sec. 601.201, S.P.R.; Secs. 38, 61, 162, 167,
   '54 Code.)

Rev. Proc. 75-28, 1975-1 C.B. 752

Guidelines set forth the information and representation to be furnished by a taxpayer requesting an advance ruling with respect to a transaction purporting to be a leveraged lease. Rev. Proc. 72-3 modified. §§1.38-1, 1.61-1, 1.162-1, 1.167(a)-1. (Sec. 601.201, S.P.R.; Secs. 38, 61, 162, 167, '54 Code.)

Revenue Rulings

Rev. Rul. 57-318, 1957-2 C.B. 362

Where a partner, whose capital account has a deficit which he is obligated to repay, sells his partnership interest to the other partner, the basis of his interest for determining gain or loss on the transaction is zero. The sale proceeds will be considered as gain from the sale or exchange of a capital asset. If, in addition, the deficit is cancelled, the obligor partner is considered to have received a distribution, at the time of the cancellation, of an amount which would be taxable as a capital gain. Clarified by Rev. Rul. 73-301. §§1.705-1, 1.722-1, 1.731-1, 1.741-1, 1.752-1. (Secs. 705, 722, 731, 741, 752; '54 Code.)

Rev. Rul. 68-79, 1968-1 C.B. 310

Where stock held by a partnership as an investment for more than six months is sold at a gain, a partner's distributive share is long term capital gain notwithstanding that he held his partnership interest for not more than six months. §1.702-1. (Sec. 702, '54 Code.)

Rev. Rul. 68-643, 1968-2 C.B. 76

The deduction of prepaid interest in the year of payment by a cash-basis taxpayer may not clearly reflect income. Accordingly, deduction on each indebtedness for a period not in excess of 12 months of the taxable year immediately following the taxable year in which the prepayment is made will be considered on a case-by-case basis. Where a material distortion of income has been found to result from the deduction of prepaid interest for a period of more than 12 months, the taxpayer will be required to change his accounting method. Modified by Rev. Rul. 69-582 with respect to a loan processing fee paid by a mortgagor. §§1.163-1, 1.446-1, 301.7805-1. (Secs. 163, 446, 7805; '54 Code.)

Rev. Rul. 69-77, 1969-1 C.B. 59

The Manuel D. Mayerson decision, which held that the purchase of depreciable property in exchange for a long-term purchase-money mortgage created a bona fide purchase and valid debt obligation and the purchasers were entitled to include in the depreciable basis of the property the debt obligation created by the mortgage, will not necessarily be relied on in the disposition of other cases. §1.167(a)-1. (Sec. 167, '54 Code.)

Rev. Rul. 69-223, 1969-1 C.B. 184

A provision of a limited partnership agreement whereby the limited partner agrees to indemnify the general partners, for payments exceeding their pro rata share of partnership liabilities, does not obligate the limited partner to make additional contributions to the limited partnership beyond his initial contribution of capital. Such limited partner, therefore, may not increase the basis of his partnership interest therein by any part of a mortgage liability assumed by the partnership. Instead, the general partner will increase the basis of his partnership interest by the full amount of the mortgage liability assumed. §§1.705-1, 1.722-1, 1.752-1. (Secs. 705, 722, 752; '54 Code.)

Rev. Rul. 70-333, 1970-1 C.B. 38

The Revenue Service will not follow the decision of the Tax Court in Perry A. Nichols which held that a taxpayer was entitled to a theft loss deduction for his out-of-pocket expenses incurred in connection with a tax avoidance scheme entered into in reliance upon misrepresentations that he would realize a tax "bonanza," in the form of an interest deduction, from such transaction. §1.163-1, 1.165-8. (Secs. 163, 165; '54 Code.)

Rev. Rul. 70-355, 1970-2 C.B. 51

A limited partner may deduct as an ordinary loss the adjusted basis amount of his partnership interest upon bankruptcy of the partnership, even though it exceeds the amount of his capital account on the books of the partnership and the partnership agreement limits the distribution of losses to limited partners to the extent of their capital account. §1.165-1. (Sec. 165, '54 Code.)

Rev. Rul. 70-356, 1970-2 C.B. 68

Insurance and storage costs incurred during the aging process of whiskey purchased as an investment are capital expenditures to be treated as part of the acquisition costs of the whiskey. §§1.212-1, 1.263(a)-1, 1.1012-1. (Secs. 212, 263, 1012; '54 Code.)

Rev. Rul. 70-626, 1970-2 C.B. 158

A donation to a charitable organization of appreciated securities, which have been held for more than six months and are pledged as collateral for an outstanding loan that is in excess of the donor's basis, constitutes partly a sale and partly a gift. Therefore, the donor realizes a long-term capital gain of the difference between the amount of the loan and his basis in the securities. He is also entitled to a charitable contributions deduction in the amount of the excess of the fair market value of the securities over the loan. §§1.61-6, 1.170-1, 1.1001-1. (Secs. 61, 170, 1001; '54 Code.)

Rev. Rul. 71-252, 1971-1 C.B. 146

Intangible drilling and development costs incurred and paid, pursuant to a contract, by a cash basis taxpayer, who had elected in a prior year to treat such costs as expenses, are deductible in the year paid even though the work is performed in the following year. This Ruling will not be applied for taxable years ending on or before June 7, 1971, to require adjustment where such costs were treated in accordance with Rev. Rul. 170. Rev. Rul. 170 revoked; distinguished by Rev. Rul. 71-579. §§1.263(c)-1, 1.461-1, 1.612-4, 301.7805-1. (Secs. 263, 461, 612, 7805; '54 Code.)

Rev. Rul. 71-579, 1971-2 C.B. 225

Intangible drilling and development costs paid by a cash basis taxpayer in a taxable year prior to the year in which payment was required under the drilling contract and before any work was performed under the contract are not deductible in that year. Rev. Rul. 71-252, distinguished. §§1.263(c)-1, 1.461-1, 1.612-4. (Secs. 263, 461, 612; '54 Code.)

Rev. Rul. 72-135, 1972-1 C.B. 200

A nonrecourse "loan" made by a general partner of a limited partnership to a partnership or to limited partners on the basis of their subscription interest is a contribution to capital to be added to the basis of the general partner's interest in the partnership. §1.722-1. (Sec. 722, '54 Code.)

Rev. Rul. 72-205, 1972-1 C.B. 37

Income attributable to the discharge of indebtedness incurred in the trade or business of a partnership may be excluded from income of the partnership by filing a consent to the regulations under section 1017 of the Code. The discharge of the indebtedness including the amount of the liability reduction excluded from the partnership's gross income is considered a distribution to the partners that reduces their partnership interests. §§1.61-12, 1.108(a)-1, 1.752-1, 1.1017-1. (Secs. 61, 108, 752, 1017; 54 Code.)

Rev. Rul. 72-350, 1972-2 C.B. 394

A so-called "loan" to a limited partnership by a nonmember, secured by partnership properties and the right to convert the loan for an interest in the partnership profits, is a capital investment in the venture representing the lender's equity interest. It is not considered a bona-fide debt but is an equity interest in the venture belonging to the lender. The advance of the funds will have no effect on the bases of the partnership interests of the other parties. §1.705-1. (Sec. 705, '54 Code.)

Rev. Rul. 73-211, 1973-1 C.B. 303

A taxpayer's investment in an oil and gas venture under a contract designating a dollar amount as intangible drilling and development costs is deductible pursuant to an election under section 263(c) of the Code only to the extent that such costs would have been incurred in an arms-length transaction with an unrelated drilling contractor. The remainder of the total investment is the basis of the taxpayer's working interest. §§1.263(c)-1, 1.612-4. (Secs. 263, 612; '54 Code.)

Rev. Rul. 73-301, 1973-2 C.B. 215

An unrestricted progress payment received by a partnership, reporting its income on the completed contract method, during its performance on a two-year construction contract did not constitute a partnership liability or add to the partners' interests within the meaning of section 752(a) of the Code. Further, one partner's cash withdrawals that created a deficit in his capital account did not constitute loans from the partnership under section 707(a) when no unconditional and legally enforceable obligation existed requiring him to repay the money; the withdrawals are to be treated as partnership distributions to a partner. Rev. Rul. 57-318 clarified. §§1.707-1, 1.731-1, 1.751-1, 1.752-1. (Secs. 707, 731, 751, 752; '54 Code.)

Rev. Rul. 73-410, 1973-2 C.B. 53

The component method of computing depreciation may be utilized to depreciate an office building that was thirty years old at the time of acquisition if the cost is properly allocated to the various components based on their value, useful lives are assigned to the component accounts based on the condition of such components at the time of acquisition, and provided the Class Life (ADR) System is not elected. Rev. Rul. 66-111 modified. §1.167(a)-7. (Sec. 167, '54 Code.)

Rev. Rul. 73-482, 1973-2 C.B. 44

Interest deducted in advance from the amount of a life insurance policy loan, or due and unpaid interest added to the principal of the loan, is deductible as "interest paid" by a calendar-year, cash-method taxpayer only for the taxable year in which actual payment is made. Rev. Rul. 67-258 distinguished. §§1.163-1, 1.461-1. (Secs. 163, 461; '54 Code.)

Rev. Rul. 74-40, 1974-1 C.B. 159

Federal income tax consequences to a limited partner from the sale or exchange of his partnership interest and to a limited partner who withdraws from the partnership in cases where no personal liability has been assumed either by the partnership or by any of the partners with respect to the limited partner's share of partnership liabilities. §§1.731-1, 1.741-1, 1.752-1. (Secs. 731, 741, 752; '54 Code.)

Rev. Rul. 74-104, 1974-1 C.B. 70

Evaluation expenditures incurred by a domestic corporation in connection with the acquisition of existing residential property for renovation and resale are capital expenditures that must be taken into account as part of the cost of acquiring the property. However, if such expenditures do not result in the acquisition of property they are deductible as losses in the taxable year the corporation decides not to acquire the property. §§1.165-1, 1.263(a)-1. (Secs. 165, 263; '54 Code.)

Rev. Rul. 74-290, 1974-1 C.B. 41

A leasing arrangement under which a municipality will issue bonds for the financing of equipment to be acquired by a manufacturing corporation and leased, for the term of the bonds plus one day, to the city which will sublease it to the corporation for the term of the bonds for subrentals sufficient to retire the bonds, is a financing arrangement entitling the corporation as owner of the equipment to the tax treatment contained in Rev. Rul. 68-590. §1.162-1. (Sec. 162, '54 Code.)

Rev. Rul. 74-320, 1974-2 C.B. 404

Limited partnerships formed under the California Uniform
Limited Partnership Act, as amended by section 15520.5
thereof, or those limited partnerships formed prior to the
amendment that elect to be governed by that section, will
lack the corporate characteristic of "continuity of life",
as defined in section 301.7701-2(b) of the regulations, from
the date they elect to be governed thereby and so long as
section 15520.5 remains effective. §301.7701-2. (Sec.
7701, '54 Code.)

Rev. Rul. 74-395, 1974-2 C.B. 45

A commitment fee, paid by a lending bank to the Federal
National Mortgage Association in connection with the assumption of an accrual method taxpayer's construction loan and
withheld by the bank from the face amount of the loan proceeds received by the taxpayer, is deductible by the taxpayer as interest. If the loan instrument is silent as to
what portion of each loan payment is discounted interest,
the fee must be deducted ratably by the taxpayer over the
entire period of the loan unless the loan instrument requires that prepaid interest is subject to the "Rule of
78's." Rev. Rul. 56-136 distinguished. §§1.163-1, 1.461-1.
(Secs. 163, 461; '54 Code.)

Rev. Rul. 75-19, 1975-1 C.B. 382

A partnership formed under a statute corresponding to the
Uniform Partnership Act by a domestic corporation's four
domestic subsidiaries, each with business reasons for independent existence outside the partnership, for the purpose
of purchasing a crude oil storage barge and chartering it to
an unrelated corporation, and not to avoid tax, is classified as a partnership. §301.7701-2. (Sec. 7701, '54 Code.)

Rev. Rul. 75-31, 1975-1 C.B. 10

Determination of whether a limited partnership formed
under New York State law is to be treated as the owner of
the project and whether each partner may include a portion
of a loan made by the New York Housing Finance Agency in the
basis of his partnership interest. §§1.61-1, 1.752-1,
1.761-1, 301.7701-2. (Secs. 61, 752, 761, 7701; '54 Code.)

Rev. Rul. 75-43, 1975-1 C.B. 383

A corporate feed lot operator and an individual cattle owner enters into a 5-year service agreement under which the cattle owner makes a cash commitment, supplies cattle for fattening, purchases feed from the feed lot operator, and independently markets the cattle. The feed lot operator furnishes insurance, labor, accommodations, equipment for the separate care and feeding of the cattle, and guarantees the owner a return of a certain percentage of his cash commitment. The feed lot operator received a percentage of the owner's net profit in exchange for his services. The arrangement will not be classified as a partnership. §301.7701-3. (Sec. 7701, '54 Code.)

Rev. Rul. 75-99, 1975-1 C.B. 197

The portion of payments received by a real estate investment trust from a borrower on a "wrap-around" mortgage loan and paid by the trust on the senior obligation are considered made on behalf of the borrower; the portion attributable to interest on the amount of cash advanced by the trust is includible in the trust's gross income and constitutes interest. §1.856-2. (Sec. 856, '54 Code.)

Rev. Rul 75-152, 1975-1 C.B. 144

A cash-method farmer may deduct in the year of payment the amounts paid for feed to be consumed by his own livestock in a following taxable year provided (1) the expenditure is for the purchase of feed rather than a deposit, (2) the prepayment is made for a business purpose and not for tax avoidance, and (3) the deduction will not result in a material distortion of income. §§1.162-12, 1.446-1, 1.461-1. (Secs. 162, 446, 461; '54 Code.)

Rev. Rul. 75-172, 1975-1 C.B. 145

The nonrefundable fee a corporation paid, under a loan agreement for construction and permanent mortgage financing and on or before initial receipt of funds, as compensation for the cost of specific legal, architectural, and engineering services incurred by the lender is a cost to be deducted ratably over the duration of the loan. §1.461-1. (Sec. 461, '54 Cde.)

Rev. Rul. 75-194, 1975-1 C.B. 80

Income tax consequences are given for a limited partner's charitable contribution of his entire interest in a limited partnership having liabilities that were not personally assumed by the partnership or any of the partners. §§1.170A-1, 1.170A-4, 1.741-1, 1.752-1, 1.1011-2. (Secs. 170, 741, 752, 1011; '54 Code.)

Rev. Rul. 75-214, 1975-1 C.B. 185

A limited partnership's payment to one of its general partners for services he rendered in organizing the partnership are payments described in section 707 of the Code, constitute capital expenditures under section 263, and are not deductible under section 162. §§1.162-1, 1.263(a)-1, 1.707-1. (Secs. 162, 263, 707; '54 Code.)

8.0
Glossary

economic reality—from an economic standpoint, an
abusive tax shelter is in substance one where
the present value of all future incomes is
less than the present value of all the investments and associated costs in the
shelter, i.e., the investment is for noneconomic purposes. In abusive tax shelters the
"primary" gain is from the tax advantage.

income forecast method of depreciation—the amount
of depreciation allowed or allowable determined by the following formula: purchase
price x **current year's income**
total estimated income

intangible drilling cost—these costs include
labor, fuel and power, material and supplies,
tool rental, truck and auto hire, repairs to
drilling equipment, and depreciation on
drilling equipment.

investor—one who invests in a limited partnership; used interchangeably with limited
partner.

leverage—the use of borrowed funds to finance a
business venture.

limited partnership—a partnership composed of at
least one general partner who assumes the
liabilities of the partnership and one or
more limited partners who have a limited
liability to partnership creditors.

negative interest—also referred to as negative
pick-up. The terms describe a situation when
a partner or partnership acquires, by purchase, an interest in a completed film before
copies of the film are distributed for exhibition at theaters or on television, with the
intent to sell distribution rights.

noneconomic loss—tax losses in excess of an
individual's investment (cash plus assumed
liabilities); also known as an artificial
loss.

nonrecourse—a type of loan, secured by a partnership, for which none of the limited partners
assume personal liability.

promoter--may be an individual or business entity
that actively secures funds by locating
interested investors. Quite often the promoter is the general partner in the limited
partnership.

real estate syndication--a legal form of business,
such as a corporation, partnership, joint
venture, etc., which allows the pooling of
financial resources to acquire real property.

FOOTNOTES

/1/   Commissioner's speech before the Cleveland
       Tax Institute, Cleveland, Ohio (November 15,
       1973).

/2/   The summaries extracted from Pub. 641,
       Bulletin Index - Digest System, are not
       intended to be a complete listing.

/3/   Treas. Reg. § 1.752-1(e).

/4/   Rev. Rul. 75-214, 1975-1 C.B. 185.

/5/   Rev. Rul. 72-135, 1972-1 C.B. 200;
       Rev. Rul. 72-350, 1972-2 C.B. 394.

/6/   Rev. Rul. 71-252, 1971-1 C.B. 146.   See also
       Barbara Jeanne Pauley v. U.S., 63-1,
       U.S.T.C. 9280 (D.C. Calif); Edwin W. Pauley
       v. U.S., 72-1, U.S.T.C. 9396 (D.C. Calif).

/7/   Code § 263(c).

/8/   Rev. Rul. 68-643, 1968-2 C.B. 76.

/9/   Rev. Rul. 75-152, 1975-1 C.B. 144.

/10/   Bernuth v. Commissioner, 57 T.C. 225 (1971),
       aff'd 73-1, U.S.T.C. 9132.

/11/   Rev. Rul. 75-152, 1975-1 C.B. 144.

/12/   Treas. Reg. § 1.167(c)1-(a)(1) and 2; Treas.
       Reg. § 1.48-1(e(4).

/13/   Treas. Reg. § 1.48-3(c)(3), (4) and (5).

/14/   Treas. Reg. § 1.1231-2.

/15/   Code § 183.

/16/   Treas. Reg. § 1.48-1(1); Walter S. Fox v.
       Commissioner (CA-4) 198 F.2d 719, 52-2
       U.S.T.C. 9423.

/17/   Treas. Reg. § 1.1231-2.

/18/   Other accelerated methods of depreciation
       may also be used.

/19/   Rev. Rul. 72-135, 1972-1 C.B. 200.

/20/   Rev. Rul. 72-350, 1972-2 C.B. 394.

/21/   Rev. Rul. 72-135, 1972-1 C.B. 200.

/22/   Rev. Rul. 72-350, 1972-2 C.B. 394.

/23/   Code § 446(b).

/24/   Treas. Reg. § 301.7701.

/25/   Field offices are encouraged to seek advice
        from the National Office. See Policy State-
        ment P-4-81, IRM, 1218, Policies of the
        Internal Revenue Service Handbook.

/26/   Information concerning "Request Procedures"
        is included in IRM 4551.1, 4551.2, and
        IRM(11)721. Policy Statement P-4-82, IRM
        1218, Policies of the Internal Revenue
        Service Handbook, contains information
        respecting taxpayer's request for technical
        advice.

/27/   Request for Technical Advice Form 4463, is
        shown in Exhibit 6-A of this booklet.

/28/   IRM 4551.3 contains information pertaining
        to "Conferences in Washington".

/29/   Information concerning "Memoranda of Techni-
        cal Advice" is included in IRM 4551.4 and
        Exhibit 6-B of this booklet.

/30/   Information regarding "Differences of Opin-
        ion between District and National Office" is
        provided in IRM 4551.5.

✿U.S. GOVERNMENT PRINTING OFFICE: 1976-211-015/179

Examination of Tax Shelters

CONTENT

amount at-risk--for purposes of the at-risk loss limitation rule, the amount at-risk in any one activity is:

(1) the amount of money and the adjusted basis of property contributed to the activity, and

(2) any amounts borrowed for use in the activity where the taxpayer is personally liable for repayment of the loan or has pledged property other than that used in the activity as security (but only to the extent of the net FMV of his or her interest in the property).

Certain borrowed amounts are excluded from consideration as being at risk if:

(1) borrowed from someone who

(a) has an interest (other than as a creditor) in the activity, or

(b) is related to the taxpayer as defined in Code § 267(b).

(2) the taxpayer is protected against loss through nonrecourse financing, guarantees, stop-loss agreements, or other similar arrangements.

conduit--a conduit is an information return through which the elements of a partnership's activity are passed through to the partners.

economic reality--from an economic standpoint, an abusive tax shelter is one in which the present value of all future incomes is less than the present value of all the investments and associated costs in the shelter: that is, the investment is for noneconomic purposes. In abusive tax shelters the "primary" gain is from the tax advantage.

front end load (fee), etc.--industry slang or jargon for the total of organizational and offering expenses plus management fee.

general partner--a member of the organization who, except as provided in Reg. § 301.7701-2(d)(2) is personally liable for the obligations of the partnership.

general partnership--a partnership composed only of general partners.

income forecast method of depreciation--amount of depreciation for motion picture films allowed or allowable determined by the following formula:

$$\text{purchase price} \times \frac{\text{current year's income}}{\text{total estimated income}}$$

intangible drilling costs--labor, fuel and power, material and supplies, tool rental, truck and auto hire, repairs to drilling equipment, depreciation on drilling equipment, etc. (Code § 263 (c))

investor--as used in the coursebook, an investor is one who invests in a limited partnership; used interchangeably with limited partner.

leverage--the use of borrowed funds to finance a business venture.

limited partner--one who may not be held responsible for partnerhip debts, and whose potential personal liability is confined to the amount of money or other property that the partner contributed or is required to contribute to the partnership.

limited partnership--a partnership composed of at least one general partner who assumes the liabilities of the partnership and one or more limited partners who have a limited liability to partnership creditors.

negative pick-up--describes a situation when a person acquires, by purchase, an interest in a completed film before copies of the film are reproduced or distributed for exhibition at theaters or on television, with the intent to sell distribution rights.

net net net lease (triple net lease)--a lease under which the lessee pays all expenses (taxes, utilities, and upkeep) except mortgage payments (principal and interest).

noneconomic loss--tax losses in excess of an individual's investment (cash plus assumed liabilities); also known as an artificial loss.

nonrecourse loan--in this context, any borrowing by a tax-sheltered partnership or other entity, structured in such a way that lenders can look only to specific assets pledged for repayment, and not to the individual assets of the various participants.

partnership--includes a limited partnership, syndicate, group, pool, joint venture, or other unincorporated organization, through or by means of which any business, financial operation, or venture is carried on, and which is not, within the meaning of the Internal Revenue Code, a corporation, trust, estate, or sole proprietorship.

present value--the discounting of an amount at a fixed rate of interest over a fixed period of time. Example: The present value of $10,000, 10 years from today using a 4% simple interest rate is $7,142.90. (Reg. § 1.483-1(g)(1))

private program (see "public program" also)--a tax-sheltered partnership
    which is offered and sold pursuant to the private offering exemption
    available under the Securities Act of 1933 or some registration
    exemption granted by the securities authorities of one or more
    states; that is, a program which is not registered with the Securi-
    ties and Exchange Commission.

promoter--an individual or business entity that actively secures funds by
    locating interested investors. Quite often the promoter is the
    general partner in the limited partnership.

public program--a tax-sheltered partnership which is registered with the
    Securities and Exchange Commission and distributed in a public offer-
    ing by broker-dealers or employees of the general partner. The
    principal difference between a public program and a private program
    relates to the number of investors, which may be several hundred in a
    public program, but is limited to 35 in a private program.

    In addition to the SEC laws, the various states often have their own
    statutes and regulations defining the type of partnerships requiring
    registration with state administrative bodies.

real estate syndication--a legal form of business, such as a corporation,
    partnership, joint venture, etc., which allows the pooling of finan-
    cial resources to acquire real property.

tier--in its basic form an arrangement in which an interest in an entity
    is vested in another entity held by the taxpayer. This can take
    different forms involving multiple levels or tiers of ownership to
    secure whatever advantage is desired.

turn-around or crossover--the point in the operations of a tax shelter
    when it starts to produce taxable income but often fails to provide
    sufficient cash flow to the partners to pay the accompanying tax due.

wraparound mortgage--a mortgage subordinate to but inclusive of an exist-
    ing mortgage on a property. In general, a third party lender refi-
    nances the property by assuming the existing mortgage (and its debt
    service) and "wraps around" a new (junior) mortgage. The wraparound
    lender extends to the borrower an amount equal to the difference
    between the balance outstanding on the existing mortgage and the face
    amount on the new mortgage.

LESSON 1

INTRODUCTION TO TAX SHELTERS

CONTENT

¶1.01   Course Objective
¶1.02   Basic Concept of a Shelter

¶1.03   General Content of Course
  .031   Excluded
  .032   Included
¶1.04   Layout of Coursebook
Figures 1-A through 1-E

¶1.01
Course Objective

       After completing the assigned lessons in this module, you
will be able to identify and examine abusive tax shelters.

¶1.02
Basic Concept of a Shelter

       Taxpayers who reduce their tax base in any manner are said
to have "sheltered" their income. The method or transaction used for this purpose is termed a "tax shelter".
Thus a wage earner purchasing a personal residence has, in
effect, created a tax shelter by using the mortgage interest and real property tax deductions to shelter the income
earned from wages. A more sophisticated tax shelter would
provide for greater deductions as early as possible without the usual cash outlay.   An example of this is the
taxpayer who purchases a rental property (heavily mortgaged) and offsets the rental receipts by the lawful
deductions for interest, taxes, and depreciation (maximum
allowed).   Generally the Internal Revenue Code is structured to allow the use of tax shelters to insure certain
social and economic benefits intended by Congress.

       Many promoters are involved with creating tax shelters of
one kind or another. You probably have some ·tax shelter
cases in your inventory. Fortunately the vast majority of
these shelters are in full compliance with the tax laws
and do not abuse the congressional intent. Although
certain business or industrial endeavors (for example,
motion picture, farm, coal, real estate, oil and gas) are
generally associated with tax shelters, you can expect

many new variations to replace those outmoded by recent laws, rulings, and court decisions. Unfortunately some will be abusive and thus subject to your scrutiny. Certain tax entites (such as the limited partnership arrangement) are widely used as tax shelter vehicles.

For the record, let's clarify a point at this time. Although the audit effort for partnership examinations has been expanded, the Internal Revenue Service is not "after" any particular classification of tax entity or business form. The Service, however, is taking an aggressive stance against abusive tax shelters whether in real estate, commodity straddles, phonograph records, ping-pong balls, or whatever. You must also be alert to identifying and examining tax entities other than partnerships being used by abusive shelter promoters.

¶1.03
General Content of Course

¶1.031
Excluded

This module is not intended to provide in-depth partnership training. Other training courses are available for that purpose and will not be duplicated here. However, for those examiners who were exposed to partnership training some time ago, certain partnership topics have been identified as problem areas on the job and are included here for refresher training. To reacquaint you with the many areas of partnership tax law, glance briefly at the contents of Unit II of the Revenue Agent Training Program (Course 3125). This material, comprising about 3 1/2 days of classroom study, has been updated by supplements to keep it as current as possible. See Figure 1-A at the end of this lesson.

Neither is it the intent of this brief course to provide in-depth shelter training or training in specific tax shelter business or industrial classifications. At the time of this writing, audit tax shelter guidelines are being developed which will include detailed information in four specific shelter areas: motion pictures, real estate, oil and gas, and farm operations. An idea of the scope of the shelter material to be provided in the guideline handbook can be had from the contents listed in figures 1-B through 1-E. The lists of contents were taken from manuscripts in draft form and are subject to change.

¶1.032
Included

This course was designed to provide examiners with the general tools needed to recognize the abusive elements of a tax shelter regardless of its business nature or reporting form. Throughout this coursebook the limited partnership arrangement was used as the basic reporting form only because of its wide-spread use. (Although the Tax Reform Act of 1976 placed some restrictions on the partnership as a shelter vehicle, many partnerships have been and will remain in existence for a long time.)

Some news items report that the Tax Reform Act of 1976 and recent releases of tax shelter rulings have all but destroyed tax shelters (with the exception of real estate shelters). Other news items claim that the wealthy are receiving more tax advantages than ever through tax shelters. We can always expect imaginative promoters to seek ways to circumvent the letter and spirit of the law. (Your job is to determine if either is being abused.) Publicity regarding the numerous tax advantages available through the use of shelters will provide incentive for some high-bracket investors to seek out such promoters.

If you need technical assistance regarding unclear law or regulations, or if you wish to report on problems caused by existing statutes, you are encouraged to request needed advice or submit problem areas to the National Office. Technical reports are also discussed in this coursebook.

All Code references, unless otherwise identified, are to the Internal Revenue Code of 1954. Regulation references, unless otherwise noted, are to final regulations under the Internal Revenue Code of 1954.

¶1.04
Layout of Coursebook

Take a few minutes at this point to note the glossary at the beginning of this coursebook. Look over the terms. They are generally identified and footnoted throughout the text. Synopses of tax shelter-related procedures and rulings are also included for reference at the end of the coursebook. Some lessons have questions included in the text. Answers are provided before the footnotes at the end of each applicable lesson.

Figure 1-A

Revenue Agent Training Program-Unit II

Partnership Training Material-Text 3125-154

Table of Contents

Figure 1-B

Draft Stage Guidelines

Motion Picture Tax Shelters

Table of Contents

Foreign Entities and Individuals

Figure 1-C

Draft Stage Guidelines

Real Estate Tax Shelters

Table of Contents

3178-02

Figure 1-D

Draft Stage Guidelines

Oil and Gas Tax Shelters

Table of Contents

Figure 1-E

Draft Stage Guidelines

Farm Operations Tax Shelters

Table of Contents

LESSON 2

PARTNERSHIP AS A CONDUIT

CONTENT

¶2.01
Introduction

> Without a knowledge of the partnership conduit [1] princi-
> ple, it is impossible to properly examine a partnership
> return and compute the tax of the partners. Because a
> partnership is a conduit and not a taxable entity, various
> items of income flow through the partnership to the
> partners. "Once [a partnership's] income is ascertained
> and reported, its existence may be disregarded since each
> partner must pay a tax on a portion of the total income as
> if the partnership were merely an agent or conduit * * *
> ."[2]

> To determine the amount and nature of each partner's share
> of the partnership income, you must be aware of the char-
> acter of the separate items to be included. After com-
> pleting this lesson, you will be able to compute the
> amount of partnership income, credits, or deductions
> flowing through to the partners.

¶2.02
Separate Identity

> The Code identifies the items which are to be treated as
> though the partner realized them directly from the source.
> The items of individual character and amount are easy to
> identify as they flow through to a partner.

EXTRACT
Code § 702(a)(1)-(7).

(1) gains and losses from sales or exchanges of capital assets held for not more than 9 months,

(2) gains and losses from sales or exchanges of capital assets held for more than 9 months,

(3) gains and losses from sales or exchanges of property described in section 1231 (relating to certain property used in a trade or business and involuntary conversions),

(4) charitable contributions (as defined in section 170(c)),

(5) dividends with respect to which there is provided an exclusion under section 116 or a deduction under part VIII of subchapter B,

(6) taxes, described in section 901, paid or accrued to foreign countries and to possessions of the United States,

(7) other items of income, gain, loss, deduction, or credit, to the extent provided by regulations prescribed by the Secretary, * * *

Certain restrictions, limitations, or other adjustments may be required at the partner's level when the items listed in Code § 702(a) and the underlying regulations are combined with the partner's similar nonpartnership items.

An eighth item must be added to the list of items in the preceding extract: the partnership's taxable income (or loss). This item, Code § 702(a)(8), differs from the others and in examinations requires more attention. It is computed without the previous items, which keep their separate identity as they pass through to the partners. A further variation from the usual individual income computation exists. This is discussed in the next paragraph.

¶2.03
Taxable Income

Generally, a partnership's taxable income is computed like an individual's, with the following two groups of exceptions.

The first group contains the first seven items listed under Code § 702(a). (See the extract in ¶2.02.) These items retain their identity and are separately stated in Schedule K (Form 1065), Partners' Shares of Income, Credits, Deductions, Etc. Each partner's individual share of

the Schedule K item is similarly recorded on Schedule K-1
(Form 1065) for reporting on the partner's income tax
return.

The second group of exceptions contains individual deductions not allowed on a partnership return.

> EXTRACT
> Code § 703(a)(2)(A)-(F).
>
>   (A) the deductions for personal exemptions
> provided in section 151,
>   (B) the deduction for taxes provided in sec-
> tion 164(a) with respect to taxes, described in
> section 901, paid or accrued to foreign countries
> and to possessions of the United States,
>   (C) the deduction for charitable contributions
> provided in section 170,
>   (D) the net operating loss deduction provided
> in section 172,
>   (E) the additional itemized deductions for
> individuals provided in part VII of subchapter B
> (Sec. 211 and following), and
>   (F) the deduction for depletion under section
> 611 with respect to oil and gas wells.

The additional itemized deductions mentioned in item (E)
in the extract are the following:

> Expenses for production of income (Code § 212).
> Medical expenses (Code § 213).
> Alimony payments (Code § 215).
> Deductions by cooperative housing corporation tenant-
> stockholder (Code § 216).
> Moving expenses (Code § 217).
> Contributions to candidates for public office (Code §
> 218).
> Retirement savings (Code §§ 219 and 220).

The concept of a separate standard deduction for individuals was eliminated for taxable years beginning after
December 31, 1976, and is, therefore, not listed in the
above extract.[3/] For taxable years before 1977, however,
Code § 703(a) also included the standard deduction as an
individual item not allowed on a partnership return.

Code § 702(a) and the income tax regulations require
separate accounting (on Schedule K, Form 1065) for these
items because if they were included in the ordinary income
or loss account (line 26, Form 1065, 1976), they could

result in a distortion of the partners' tax liability. Separate accounting is also required for those items which according to the partnership agreement have a different allocation among the partners than does the general partnership income.[4/] Additionally, each partner must combine the partnership items with like nonpartnership items when computing limitations.

EXTRACT
Reg. § 1.702-1(a)(8)(iii).

* * * [P]artner A has individual domestic exploration expenditures of $300,000. He is also a member of the AB partnership which in 1971, in its first year of operation has foreign exploration expenditures of $400,000 [the maximum overall limitation under Code § 617(h)(i)]. A's distributable share of this item is $200,000. However, the total amount of his distributable share that A can deduct as exploration expenditures under section 617(a) is limited to $100,000 in view of the limitation provided in section 617(h). Therefore, the excess of $100,000 ($200,000 minus $100,000) is not deductible by A. [The Code §617(a) limitation is $400,000.]

Example 1

Partner A has qualifying used § 38 property of $75,000. He is also a member of AB partnership which in 1976, its first year of operation, has qualifying used § 38 property of $100,000. A's distributive share of this item is $50,000.

In combining A's qualified § 38 property of $75,000 with his $50,000 from the partnership, A now has exceeded his total overall limitation of $100,000 to the extent of $25,000 ($75,000 + $50,000 - $100,000 limitation = $25,000 excess). Investment credit can only be claimed on the $100,000 of used property and A cannot claim investment credit on the $25,000 excess.

¶2.04
Business v. Nonbusiness
Deductions

A "business" partnership is one which is actively conducting a trade or business. A "nonbusiness" partnership is one which is not actively conducting a trade or business. Examples of nonbusiness partnerships are those which operate as investment clubs.

The taxable income or loss computed for Form 1065 is determined under Code § 702(a)(8). This is reflected on a partner's Form 1040 as a <u>net item</u> added to or subtracted from gross income, for the purpose of determining the partner's individual adjusted gross income.

Question 1

The ABC <u>business</u> partnership reported the following items on page 1 of its Form 1065 for 1976:

Line 11, L/T capital gain		$ 75,000
Line 13, Wages	$100,000	
Line 16, Interest	50,000	
Line 17, Taxes	25,000	
Line 24, Contributions	10,000	
Line 24, Supplies	5,000	(190,000)
Line 26,		$(115,000)

To ensure proper reporting by the partners, what reporting changes would you recommend?

See answer 1.

Question 2

Where should the ABC partnership items in question 1 be properly reported on the partners' Forms 1040?

See answer 2.

A partnership may be nonbusiness, in which case the Code treats the items of income and expense differently than those resulting from a trade or business. A nonbusiness

partnership may not deduct items under Code § 162, but
rather must use Code § 212 and others. Thus, the
partners' treatment of elements is governed by the character of the partnership: trade or business v. nonbusiness. Expenses of a partnership during its preoperating
period are not deductible.

Example 2

Partnership A paid out the same amounts during its ongoing
business period as did Partnership B during its preoperating period. The items will be passed through to the
partners as shown below:

Expenses incurred by both A Partnership and B Partnership

Depreciation	$110,000
Labor	50,000
Utilities	10,000
Total loss	$170,000

(A) The Partners in A (business) partnership may claim
their proportional share of the $170,000 loss as an ordi-
nary loss.

(B) Partnership B (preoperating partnership) must capitalize all its expenses so that no loss is passed through to
its partners.

Parnership A will pass through $170,000 to its partners on
line 1(b) of Schedule K-1. Partnership B will have no
deductions to pass through.

Expenses incurred during the prebusiness period but improperly claimed as partnership business expenses could
result in a distortion of income to the partners.

This improper deduction could generate a net operating
loss on the partner's individual 1040. On examination,
the improper deduction is adjusted from a component of the
taxpayer's NOL to itemized deductions. If the taxpayer
has no nonoperating income for the taxable year the deduction will be lost. Had the taxpayer properly claimed the
deductions when preparing the return, part of the unused
deduction could have been saved by capitalizing it under
Code § 266 (or § 189 if real property). However, § 266
capitalization must be elected at the time of filing the
return.5/

The taxpayer's improper deduction of the item as a NOL
probably precludes a valid Code § 266 election at the time
of the examination adjustment.   Further, the itemized
deductions would become a possible element of tax preference for the minimum tax.6/ This is discussed in detail in
lesson 3.

Question 3

The DEF investment partnership (nonbusiness) listed the
following items on page 1 of its Form 1065 for 1977:

Line 11, L/T capital gain		$ 75,000
Line 13, Wages	$100,000	
Line 16, Interest	50,000	
Line 17, Taxes	25,000	
Line 24, Contributions	10,000	
Line 24, Supplies	5,000	190,000
Line 26,		$(115,000)

To ensure proper reporting by the partners, what changes
would you recommend?

See answer 3.

Question 4

Where should the DEF partnership items in question 3 be
properly reported on the partners' Forms 1040?

See answer 4.

¶2.05
Tax Preference Items

Congress recognized that large amounts of individual
income legally escaped taxation, resulting in an unfair
distribution of the tax burden.   A partnership is one
means through which such items as accelerated depreciation, depletion, or intangible drilling costs allow the
partners to shield other income from taxation.   Beginning
in 1969, Congress passed a number of laws to correct this
inequity.7/
          The result is Code § 56 which imposes a
minimum tax on items of tax preference as defined by Code
§ 57.

1101

A partner's share of tax preference items is subject to the minimum tax provisions.[8/] Code §§ 56 and 58 provide for the imposition of the minimum tax and give the rules for its application. A partner will take into account his distributive share of the partnership's items of tax preference. These items are then combined with the individual partner's other tax preference items for the computation of minimum tax.

¶2.06
Summary

(1) A partnership is merely a conduit and not a taxable entity.

(2) Many or all partnership items (income, credits, deductions, etc.) retain their separate identities when passed through to the partners.

(3) Identical items in a partnership business setting could receive different treatment in a partnership nonbusiness (or pre-business) setting.

(4) Proper application of the law requires a determination of the partnership setting based on the facts in each situation.

(5) Items of tax preference on the partnership return flow through to the individual partners for minimum tax purposes.

1. Contributions, $10,000, and L/T capital gains,
    $75,000, should be reported in Schedule K as separate
    items instead of being computed as a net figure for
    line 26 on page 1. The ordinary loss for line 26
    would then be reported as ($180,000).

2. The L/T capital gains of $75,000 should be totaled
    with other Schedule D items and included in gross
    income. The $10,000 contributions should be totaled
    with the other contributions on Schedule A of the Form
    1040. The ABC partnership's ordinary loss of
    $180,000 (line 26, Form 1065) should be included in
    Schedule E on Form 1040.

3. By virtue of Code § 703(a)(2)(E), all such deductions
    should not be netted, but should be separately stated
    to pass through their individual identity.

    The deductibility or proper treatment should be deter-
    mined by the partners under Code § 212 or other appli-
    cable Code sections: Interest, Code § 163; Taxes,
    Code § 164; Capitalization, Code § 263; etc.

4. The investment partnership, DEF, is not carrying on a
    trade or business; the deductions must be separately
    stated and cannot qualify under Code § 162. The L/T
    capital gain, $75,000, should be totaled with the
    other gains on Schedule D. The other items would be
    claimed as itemized deductions from adjusted gross
    income:

Wages (if they meet Code § 212)	$100,000
Supplies (if they meet Code § 212)	5,000
Interest (Code § 163)	50,000
Contributions (Code § 170)	10,000
Taxes (Code § 164)	25,000

    Note the different results to the partners by compar-
    ing the results of the DEF pass-through in this answer
    with the ABC pass-through shown in answer 2.

Footnotes

<u>1/</u> This term is explained in the glossary in front of the coursebook.

<u>2/</u> <u>United States v. Basye</u>, 410 U.S. 441 (1973); 31 A.F.T.R.2d 73-802, 73-805; 73-1 U.S.T.C. 80,473 at 80,476.

<u>3/</u> Code § 63 as amended by Act § 102(a) of the Tax Reduction and Simplification Act of 1977, Public Law 95-30, 95th Cong., 1st Sess. (1977), 1977-1 C.B. 451.

<u>4/</u> Reg. § 1.702-1(a)(8).

<u>5/</u> Reg. § 1.266-1(c)(3).

<u>6/</u> Code § 57(a)(1) and (b).

<u>7/</u> The Tax Reform Act of 1969, Public Law 91-172, 91st Cong., 1st Sess. (1969), 1969-3 C.B. 10; later modified by the Tax Reform Act of 1976, Public Law 94-455, 94th Cong., 2nd Sess. (1976), 1976-3 C.B. Vol. 1, 1; and the Tax Reduction and Simplication Act of 1977, Public Law 95-30, 95th Cong., 1st Sess. (1977), 1977-1 C.B. 451.

<u>8/</u> Reg. § 1.58-2(b) (Proposed).

LESSON 3

DETERMINATION OF BUSINESS, NONBUSINESS, OR PREBUSINESS STATUS

CONTENT

¶3.01
Introduction

The mere filing of a tax return with income and/or expenses claimed does not necessarily mean the items were incurred in carrying on a trade or business. If the items were incurred during a nonbusiness or prebusiness status, their tax treatment is substantially different from that of items incurred while carrying on a trade or business. This lesson will cover the criteria used in determining the proper status.

After completing this lesson you will be able to identify nonbusiness or prebusiness items and determine the proper tax treatment of the various items.

¶3.02
Richmond Television Case

A potential issue in all audits is whether and when an entity is carrying on a trade or business.

An entity not involved in a trade or business is either in a nonbusiness or a prebusiness status. An example of nonbusiness status appears in Rev. Rul. 75-523 1/ dealing with investment club partnerships. The ruling states that when investment activities are undertaken jointly, the community of operation does not transform investing activities into business activities insofar as Code § 162 is concerned. The ruling concludes that the expenses incurred by the partnership during the taxable year for postage, stationery, safe deposit box rentals, bank charges, fees for accounting and invesment services, rent, and utility charges are deductible by the partnerships under Code § 212.

Richmond Television Corp. v. United States 2/ defines prebusiness status. Its principle of law applies to all entities including partnerships and corporations. To be deductible, an expenditure must first satisfy the test of Code § 162(a). The deduction must be for "ordinary and necessary expenses paid or incurred during the taxable year in carrying on any trade or business." Neither the Code nor the income tax regulations provide any explicit definition of what is meant by "carrying on a trade or business." Not all partnerships qualify as trade or business entities. Whether and when a partnership meets the required "carrying on a trade or business" test of Coe § 162 must be determined based on the facts.

Making this determination requires the answer to at least two vital questions:

(1) Is the taxpayer (or partnership) indicating to the public that it is engaged in selling goods or services?

(2) Is the taxpayer actually carrying on a trade or business?

The first question has been defined and reiterated in Deputy v. Du Pont3/. The second question is discussed in the Richmond Television case. Read the extracted Richmond Television case, figure 3-A.

The point of law which applies equally to all entities is that expenses of the entity are not deductible as trade or business expenses until the entity has begun to perform those activities for which it is organized. For example, a partnership formed to own and operate one office building does not incur trade or business expenses during construction of the building; the trade or business expense begins when the building is ready for rental. The building cannot be legally held out for rental until construction has been sufficiently completed to permit the State to issue a "Certificate of Use and Occupancy." Before such a certification, the owner's claim that it is "carrying on a trade or business" would be subject to question. The lack of an active pursuit after certification (no tenants) would likewise subject the carrying on of a trade or business to question.

An important distinction must be noted. Recent judical decisions in the bank credit card field4/ are not contrary to the principle of law just reviewed. The expansion of

1106   3178-02

an existing business does not negate the use of Code §
162(a). Because the taxpayer was expanding an existing
business and not establishing a new business, startup
expenses were allowed as expenses incurred in carrying on
a trade or business.

¶3.03
Effect of Determination

During each examination the examiner must verify that the
entity is in fact carrying on a trade or business. The
classification of the items of income and expense of a
partnership have direct impact on each partner because the
conduit principle as reflected in Code §§ 702 and 703
requires different treatment for business and nonbusiness
(or prebusiness) items. A finding that the partnership is
in fact carrying on a trade or business allows the examiner to direct the examination into areas other than the
nonbusiness or prebusiness status.

A finding that a partnership is in a nonbusiness or prebusiness status results in the expenses becoming nonbusiness expenses or capital expenditures. The conduit rules
when applied to nonbusiness and prebusiness partnership
expenses result in the following treatment:

(1) Interest and taxes flow through directly to the
    partners as itemized deductions per Code §§ 163 and
    164 (provided there is no Code § 266 election and
    subject to Code § 189).

(2) Code § 212 expenses flow through directly to the
    partners as itemized deductions.

(3) All other expenses are Code § 263 capital expenditures
    which are added to the basis of the underlying assets.

NOTE: Partnerships that incur real property construction
       period interest and taxes are affected by Code §
       189 enacted by the Tax Reform Act of 1976:   Under
       the Code § 702 conduit rules, the interest and
       taxes flow through to the individual partners as
       before.

       The partner's partnership interest is in real
       property that incurred construction period interest
       and taxes, thus Code § 189 overrides Code § 163 and
       Code § 164 and requires that the interest and taxes
       be capitalized during the construction period and
       then amortized over the period specified in Code §
       189.

3178-02

Partnership AB has a loss of $300,000. The loss is com-
posed of interest and taxes. The partnership has not
commenced the trade or business for which it was organized. Partners A and B are 50 percent partners. The
column captioned "per return" indicates how the partners,
who felt the partnership was engaged in a trade or business, reported the partnership items. The partnership is
not constructing real property. Using the format in
handout 3-C fill in the blank spaces to show the proper
treatment of the partnership items for each partner on
their individual returns. There is no Code § 266 election
or Code § 263 expenditure. Code § 189 does not apply.

Summary of Partner A's Tax Return:

	Per Return
Salaries and wages	$100,000
Dividends and interest	5,000
Partnership loss	(150,000)
(Interest and taxes)	
Adjusted gross income	$(45,000)
Itemized deductions	(25,000)
(No casualty loss)	
Exemptions	(3,000)
Negative taxable income per return	$(73,000)

Loss year modifications

(1) Add back personal exemptions $ 3,000

(2) Add back excess of nonbusiness expenses
over nonbusiness income.

nonbusiness expense	$25,000		
nonbusiness income	5,000	20,000	23,000

NOL available for carryback or carryforward. $(50,000)

Summary of Partner B's Tax Return:

	Per Return
Salaries and wages	$ -0-
Dividends and interest	105,000
Partnership loss	(150,000)
(Interest and taxes)	_____
Adjusted gross income	$(45,000)
Itemized deductions	(25,000)
(No casualty loss)	
Exemptions	(3,000)
Negative taxable income per return	$(73,000)

Loss year modifications

(1) Add back personal exemptions $ 3,000

(2) Add back excess of nonbusiness expenses
    over nonbusiness income.

nonbusiness expense	$25,000		
nonbusiness income	105,000	-0-	3,000

NOL available for carryback or carryforward. $(70,000)

See answer 1.

(1) Nonbusiness or prebusiness status results in expenses not allowed as deductions under Code § 162.

(2) The Richmond Television case covers the deduction of certain prebusiness expenses: Code § 162 expenses are not incurred by the taxpayer before carrying on a trade or business. The application of this principle could materially affect the tax results for partners of a prebusiness partnership. In this situation, partners may not have a net operating loss.

(3) The nonbusiness or prebusiness expenses could be deductible under the following Code sections depending on the entity claiming the expenses:

(a) Code § 163, Interest
(b) Code § 164, Taxes
(c) Code § 212,. . .Management; conservation; or maintenance of investment, determination of tax . . . .

(4) The nonbusiness or prebusiness expenditures could be capitalized under the following Code sections:

(a) Code § 189, Construction period interest and taxes.

(b) Code § 263, Capital assets
(c) Code § 266, Voluntary election for carrying charges and taxes with respect to property.

¶3.05
Answers

1. **Partner A**

	Per Audit
Salaries and wages	$100,000
Dividends and interest	5,000
Partnership loss	-0-
(Interest and taxes)	
Adjusted gross income	$105,000
Itemized deductions	(175,000)
(No casualty loss)	
Exemptions	(3,000)
Negative taxable income per return	$(73,000)

Loss year modifications

(1) Add back personal exemptions		$ 3,000	
(2) Add back excess of nonbusiness expenses over nonbusiness income.			
nonbusiness expense	$175,000		
nonbusiness income	5,000	170,000	173,000
NOL available for carryback or carryforward.			$ -0-

3178-02

Answer 1. (Cont.)

Partner B

	Per Audit
Salaries and wages	-0-
Dividends and interest	105,000
Partnership loss	-0-
(Interest and taxes)	_____
Adjusted gross income	$105,000
Itemized deductions	(175,000)
(No casualty loss)	
Exemptions	(3,000)
Negative taxable income per return	$(73,000)

Loss year modifications

(1) Add back personal exemptions		$ 3,000	
(2) Add back excess of nonbusiness expenses over nonbusiness income.			
nonbusiness expense	$175,000		
nonbusiness income	105,000	70,000	73,000
NOL available for carryback or carryforward.			$ -0-

3178-02

Answer 1. (Cont.)

Narrative:

Because the partnership is in a nonbusiness or prebusiness
state, the expenses are deductible by the partner as
itemized deductions. The items as defined in the question
meet the requirements of Code §§ 163 and 164. The expenses do not meet the requirements of carrying on a trade
or business under Code § 162(a). Therefore, the loss
cannot be used in computing adjusted gross income. As a
result, the partnership loss for partner A or B cannot be
used to create a net operating loss.

Footnotes

1/ 1975-2 C.B. 257.

2/ 345 F.2d 901 (4th Cir. 1965); 15 A.F.T.R.2d 880; 65-1 U.S.T.C. 95,421.

3/ 308 U.S. 488 (1940), 1940-1 C.B. 118; 23 A.F.T.R. 808; 40-1 U.S.T.C. 67. Also see Snow v. Commissioner, 416 U.S. 500 (1974); 1974-1 C.B. 62; 33 A.F.T.R.2d 74-1251; 74-1 U.S.T.C. 84,082.

4/ First National Bank of South Carolina v. United States, 413 F. Supp. 1107 (D.S.C. 1976); 37 A.F.T.R. 2d 76-1378; 76-1 U.S.T.C. 84,028.

Figure 3-A

Richmond Television Case

EXTRACT

Richmond Television Corp. v. U.S., 345F.2d 901 (4th Cir. 1965); 15
A.F.T.R.2d 880; 65-1 U.S.T.C. 95421.

Before Sobeloff, Chief Judge,
and Bryan and J. Spencer Bell, Circuit judges.

[1] Sobeloff, Chief Judge: The taxpayer, Richmond Television
Corporation, owns and operates a television station which
broadcasts over Channel 12 in Richmond, Virginia. In February,
1963, it brought suit in the United States District Court for
the Eastern District of Virginia, seeking a refund of
$21,378.27 in income taxes which it paid after the Commissioner
of Internal Revenue disallowed $35,129.19 of the deductions
claimed on its tax returns for 1956 and 1957.[1/] Its theory is
that the amounts in question are deductible as "ordinary and
necessary expenses of commencing Plaintiff's business and/or of
managing, conserving and maintaining property held for production of income." It claims in the alternative that, if the
total amounts are not deductible as expense items, it is entitled to "amortize them over the life of the construction permit
plus the life of its first regular license from the Federal
Communications Commission (FCC)."

[2] The Judge submitted the case to the jury on special interroga-
tories which asked whether these were ordinary and necessary
business expenses and, if so, in what amount. The jury was
also asked whether the television broadcasting license has a
useful life of limited or indefinite duration and, if the
former, of what duration. The jury found its verdict for the
taxpyaer, answering that the entire $53,129.19 was an ordinary
and necessary business expense and that the license had a
useful life of three years. The United States moved for judgment n.o.v. and, in the alternative, for a new trial. Both
motions were denied.

[3] The Government has appealed, urging that the taxpayer is entitled to no deduction for the amount in question or any part of
it. It contends first that these were capital expenditures as
a matter of law, and that the District Court erred in submitting to the jury the issue of whether these were ordinary and
necessary business expenses. The second contention of the
Government is that there is no evidence to support the jury's
finding that these were capital assets having a definite duration.

1117

3178-02

[4] I. The taxpayer was organized in 1952, and among its stated corporate purposes was the operation of a television station. On December 22, 1952, it submitted an application to the FCC for a construction permit to operate Channel 12. There were at the time two other applicants competing for the license, Larus Brothers & Company (Larus), the owner and operator of radio station WRVA in Richmond, and Richmond Newspapers, Inc.

[5] Larus had submitted its application for the Channel 12 license as early as 1948. In anticipation of success, it designated Samuel S. Carey, a member of its radio station staff to conduct a training program so that if it obtained the license it would have immediately available a trained staff capable of operating a television broadcasting station enabling it to produce income at an early stage.

[6] The training program, organized in the 1948-1949 period, attained full scope during 1951 and 1952. Approximately fifty persons were under training by Carey, twenty-six of them full-time employees of WRVA, Larus' radio station. Twenty were part-time students in local area schools who received no compensation from WRVA. Some members of this group, however, later went to work for the taxpayer. During the training program, Larus purchased equipment and films and set up the beginnings of a television broadcasting studio.

[7] On November 23, 1953, Larus and Richmond Television entered into an agreement described as a merger[2/], which embodied the following provisions: Larus would dismiss its pending application for a television construction permit, leaving the taxpayer's application unopposed except by Richmond Newspapers, Inc., not deemd a serious contender. Larus subscribed to 4500 shares of Richmond Television's common stock, which was sixty percent of its maximum authorized voting stock, at $100 per share, or the total price of $450,000, and it promised to subscribe at a later date to $450,000 worth of capital notes of Richmond Television. The parties agreed that representation on Richmond Television's Board of Directors would be proportional to their stock ownership, thereby assuring Larus of control.

[8] Pursuant to the November, 1953, agreement, Richmond Television also paid Larus $25,799.19 as reimbursement for costs previously incurred in the training program. This amount is described on the tax return as payment for "Retention Personnel--per agreement," and is part of the $53,129.19 which Richmond Television claims it is entitled to deduct as an ordinary and necessary business expense. Following the agreement, Larus continued the training program for the benefit and convenience of Richmond Television. Larus' trainees remained on its payroll, and under the terms of the "Personnel Retention Agreement," Richmond Television reimbursed Larus for the additional $27,330, expense it incurred thereafter in the training of

1118

personnel. This arrangement continued until Richmond Television began broadcasting.

[9] The FCC granted the construction permit on November 30, 1955, and in 1956 it issued a three-year license to the taxpayer which then commenced broadcasting.

[10] Although Richmond Television had no receipts from television broadcasting prior to 1956, it undertook, in its original returns for 1952 through 1956, to claim deductions in the aggregate sum of $114,708 for the cost of the training program as well as the cost of obtaining an operating license from the FCC. In 1956, however, after the Internal Revenue Service issued Revenue Ruling 56-520, holding that certain costs incurred in obtaining a television broadcasting license from the FCC were not deductible from gross income, the taxpayer voluntarily capitalized $58,165.79 of the sum previously deducted for its expenses in obtaining the license from the FCC. The remaining $56,552.01 it continued to treat as deductible. Of that amount, the Internal Revenue Service later allowed $3,422.82, and disallowed $53,129.19, the cost of the training program, both before and after the November, 1953, agreement. These are the items here in dispute.

[11] II. For reasons to be stated, we hold that the taxpayer is not entitled to the claimed refund.

[12] Section 162(a) of the Internal Revenue Code of 1954, 26 U.S.C.A. § 162(a) (1955), provides:

> "There shall be allowed as a deduction all the ordinary and necessary expenses paid or incurred during the taxable year in carrying on any trade or business * * *."

[13] To qualify under this section, expenses must be (a) incurred in carrying on a trade or business, (b) ordinary and necessary, and (c) paid or incurred within the taxable year.[3/] The Government concedes that the expenses in question were ordinary and necessary, and it does not suggest that the expenses were incurred in taxable years other than those claimed. It is the Government's position, however, that as a matter of law the sums expended by the taxpayer in training prospective employees in the techniques of television broadcasting in years prior to receipt of its FCC broadcasting license are not ordinary business expenses but capital expenditures. The argument is that the District Court erred in failing to rule as a matter of law that the taxpayer was not "carrying on any trade or business" during the taxable years, and hence is not entitled to a deduction under section 162(a).

[14] The taxpayer maintains that these were "ordinary and necessary start-up expenses," and asserts that no case or ruling has ever denied a deduction for such expenses. The taxpayer, however, fails to deal with the point that to qualify for the deduction the expenses must have been incurred in "carrying on * * * [a] trade or business."

[15] The precise question is the deductibility of "pre-opening" expenses incurred between the decision to establish a business and the actual beginning of business operations.4/ During the three-year period under consideration, Richmond Television had indeed been incorporated for the purpose of conducting a television station but it had not yet obtained a license or begun broadcasting. The issue therefore is at what point of time did its business begin, and whether at this doubtful, prefatory stage it was to carrying on a business. While decisions are to be found holding that particular taxpayers were or were not engaged in a trade or business, there is little discussion of the question of when, in point of time, a trade or business actually, begins. This is usually a factual issue, but the resolution of the issue must have an evidentiary basis. It is therefore helpful to turn to several cases presenting analogous circumstances. While these did not formally articulate a general rule, the manner in which the facts in those cases were treated may furnish a guide.

[16] In Frank B. Polachek v. Commissioner, 22 T.C. 858 (1954), the taxpayer during the latter part of 1947 devoted his time to planning a new business investment advisory service. The business was never formally organized, but the taxpayer spent $544 for advertising, travelling expenses, secretarial help, printing, mailing, etc. In 1948, the taxpayer abandoned the project. The Tax Court found as a fact that

> "the expenses incurred in planning and organizing of petitioner's proposed investment advisory service were not incurred in carrying on a trade or business,"

and held that the expenses were not deductible in 1947 as trade or business expenses.

> "The petitioner had no business in 1947. At most, * * * he merely had plans for a potential business * * *. Regardless of the time he may have devoted to the project, or the expense in attempting to attract associates and capital and solicit prospective clients, we think that petitioner's idea was still in its formative stages when it was finally abandoned."

[17] The same principle was applied in Radio Station WBIR v. Commissioner, 31 T.C. 803 (1959). Taxpayer, an AM-FM radio station

in operation since the early 1940's, applied to the FCC in 1951
for a television station construction permit. The permit was
granted in 1955, and the taxpayer began broadcasting in 1956.
In its tax returns for 1953, the taxpayer sought to deduct
$37,000 it had spent for legal and engineering fees, travel and
other expenses of prosecuting its application for the license.
The Tax Court held:

> "Prior to the taxable year petitioner was engaged in
> the operation of an AM and an FM radio station. It
> was not engaged in the operation of a TV or televi-
> sion station and had no facilities for such an opera-
> tion. Consequently the expenses incurred in 1953 for
> the purpose of acquiring a television construction
> permit and eventually a television license were not
> paid or incurred 'in carrying on' a 'trade or busi-
> ness' in which petitioner was then engaged so as to
> make such expenditures deductible as ordinary and
> necessary business expenses * * *." (emphasis sup-
> plied)

[18] Even closer in factual context is KWTX Broadcasting Co. v.
Commissioner, 31 T.C. 952 (1959), aff'd per curiam, 272 F.2d
406 (5th Cir. 1959). There a radio station incorporated in
1946 incurred certain expenses in the prosecution of its 1954
application for a television license. It paid $8,000 in legal
fees for counsel to represent it at the FCC hearing and $4,000
for the travelling expenses of its representatives and wit-
nesses. Significantly, it paid $45,000 additional to reimburse
a competitor for its expenses in seeking the license, and
received in exchange the promise of the competitior to dismiss
its application for the license. The competitor withdrew its
application and on December 2, 1955, the taxpayer obtained its
license and began broadcasting.

[19] In its 1954 tax return, KWTX sought no deduction for the legal
fees and travelling expenses but claimed the $45,000 reimburse-
ment as an expense. The Tax Court held that the payment of the
$45,000 was not an ordinary and necessary expense, but was in
the nature of a capital expenditure in connection with the
television permit and license which the petitioner was
seeking.[5] The court held that the $45,000 expenditure was of
the same nature as attorney's and engineering fees and related
expenses, which in WBIR were held to be capital expenditures.

[20] Again, in Petersburg Television Corp. v. Commissioner, 20
T.C.M. 271 (1961), the taxpayer was incorporated in 1953 and
shortly thereafter it filed an application for a television
license. A construction permit was granted on September 29,
1954, and broadcasting began on August 15, 1955. In the tax
return for its fiscal year ending on August 31, 1955, taxpayer
sought deduction for salary, travel expenses, and professional

fees paid in seeking the license. A letter it sent to Internal
Revenue Service requesting an audit contained the following:

> "This is a new corporation that had for the year
> ended 1955 its first year of operation."

Judge Arundell found as an ultimate fact that

> "petitioner began business activity in the fiscal
> year ended August 31, 1955,"

and held that $40,000 of taxpayer's expenditures were unallow-
able "pre-business" expenses since they were "incurred prior to
the time petitioner began business operations."

[21] While Cohn, et al. v. United States, 57-1 U.S.T. Cases 9456
(D.C.W.D. Tenn. 1957), aff'd on other grounds 259 F.2d 371 (6th
Cir. 1958), did not deal with a television broadcasting station, the case is instructive because of the principle it
followed. In December, 1940, taxpayers contracted with the
United States to operate several flying schools for the training of pilots for the Army Air Corps. The schools began their
operations on March 22, 1941. In preparing for the opening of
the schools, taxpayers had spent large sums in training in-
structors, for legal fees and expenses connected with the
negotiations of the lease for the airfield, and in dedication
ceremonies. The District Court held that these expenses of
opening the schools were nonrecurrent capital expenditures, not
deductible from income. The proper treatment of such items
will be considered in Section V of this opinion.

[22] The uniform 6/ teaching of these several cases is that, even
though a taxpayer has made a firm decision to enter into business and over a considerable period of time spent money in
preparation for entering that business, he still has not "engaged in carrying on any trade or business" within the intend-
ment of section 162(a) until such time as the business has
begun to function as a going concern and performed those activities for which it was organized.7/

[23] Applying this rule, we are of the view that there was no basis
in the evidence for a charge permitting the jury to find that
the taxpayer was in business during the period in question. We
are of the opinion, therefore, that the District Court was in
error in failing to hold as a matter of law that Richmond
Television was not in business until 1956, when it obtained the
license and began broadcasting. Until then there was no certainty that it would obtain a license, or that it would ever go
on the air. Since all of the expenditures underlying the
disputed deductions were made before the license was issued and
broadcasting commenced, they are "pre-operating expenses," not
deductible under section 162(a).

[24] III. There is yet another and related reason why the $25,000 is not a current business expense. Our system of income taxation attempts to match income and expenses of the taxable year so as to tax only net income. A taxpayer may, therefore, not deduct as a current business expense the full cost of acquiring an asset, tangible or intangible, which benefits the taxpayer for more than one year. The concept has been explained in United States v. Akin, 248 F.2d 742, 744 (10th Cir. 1957).8/

> "[A]n expenditure should be treated as one in the nature of a capital outlay if it brings about the acquisition of an asset having a period of useful life in excess of one year, or if it secures a like advantage to the taxpayer which has a life of more than one year."

[25] Here, the $25,000 was paid to acquire a staff already trained by Larus in the techniques and skills of television broadcasting. This was in all regards the acqustion of a capital asset whose value to the taxpayer would continue for many years, even though from time to time individual staff members could be expected to leave its employ. The $25,000 therefore could not be taken as a current expense.

[26] The remaining $27,000 was spent between 1953 and 1955, a period when the taxpayer was nearer in point of time to the commencement of its business operation. Had these same sums been expended after 1956 they might have qualified under section 162. But because the taxpayer was not yet in business when these sums were paid, they were not deductible as expenses of "carrying on any trade or business."

[27] IV. The taxpayer further claims that, apart from any question of its being in trade or business, the expenditures are deductible under section 212 of the Internal Revenue Code of 1954, 26 U.S.C.A. § 212 (1955). That section, however, by its terms is applicable only to individuals, and not to corporate taxpayers.9/ Iowa Southern Utilities Co. v. CIR, 333 F.2d 382, 385 (8th Cir. 1964).

[28] V. In its amended complaint, taxpayer advances an alternative theory, namely, that if the expenditures for the training program were costs of acqustion of a capital asset, it is entitled to amortize these costs over the life of the asset and to take the depreciation deduction authorized by section 167 of the Internal Revenue Code of 1954, 26 U.S.C.A. § 167 (1955).10/ Not all intangible property, however, qualifies for the section 167(a)(1) deduction. Treasury Regluation 1.167(a)-3 provides:

> "If an intangible asset is known from experience or
> other factors to be of use in the business or in the
> production of income for only a limited period, the
> length of which can be estimated with reasonable
> accuracy, such an intangible asset may be the subject
> of a depreciation allowance. * * * An intangible
> asset, the useful life of which is not limited, is
> not subject to the allowance for depreciation. * * *"

[29] Richmond argues that the $53,000 spent for the training program
secured to it an advantage with a useful life coextensive with
the combined terms of the FCC construction permit (22 months)
and the first regular broadcasting license (3 years). The
taxpayer contends that, since the useful life of this asset is
of limited duration, its cost may be depreciated.

[30] The United States answers that the jury's finding that the
broadcasting license has a useful life of three years' duration
is unsupported by the evidence. It maintains that while FCC
license are issued for three-year periods the license renewal
policies of the FCC are such that the taxpayer could safely
anticipate renewal for an indefinite period.11/

[31] However, in the view which we take, it is unnecessary to decide
whether a television license is an asset of definite or indefinite duration. Section 167(a)(1) by its terms is applicable
only to "property used in the trade or business." Since, as we
have shown, Richmond was not in business during the taxable
years with which we are concerned, it cannot be said to have
used its trained television broadcasting staff in its "business." Hence, it is not entitled to a depreciation deduction
for the years for which it is claimed.12/

[32] This principle is illustrated in Radio Station WBIR v. Commissioner, 31 T.C. 803 (1959).13/ There a radio station applied
in 1951 for a television station construction permit which was
not granted until 1956. It sought to amortize the cost of
obtaining the permit and to deduct part of that cost for its
1953 taxable year. The Tax Court denied the deduction, stating:

> "The television license for which the expenditures
> were made was not in existence in 1953 and had not as
> yet been granted by the FCC when this case was heard
> in 1958, due to the pendency of the litigation re-
> garding the construction permit. Under the circum-
> stances, any claim by the petitioner for amortization
> of the cost of acquiring a television license is
> premature and it is unnecessary for us to determine
> whether the useful life of a television license, for
> depreciation purposes, is limited to the three year
> period contended for by the petitioner or is indeter-
> minate as argued by the respondent. In any event it

is clear that the petitioner is not entitled to any deduction in 1953 for amortization of the costs of acquiring a television license." (emphasis supplied)

Conclusion

[33] Because Richmond Television was not in business until it obtained its license and began broadcasting operations, the District Court erred in permitting the jury to answer any of the issues pertaining to section 162(a) or section 167(a)(1).

The judgment of the District Court entered upon the jury's findings must therefore be

Reversed and judgment entered for the United States.

Case Footnotes (for Figure 3-A)

1/ The taxpayer deducted this amount on its 1956 and 1957 income tax returns on account of its claimed right to carry over net operating losses from the taxable years 1953 through 1955. The right to these 1956 and 1957 deductions thus depends on the deductibility of the expenditures in the taxable years 1953 through 1955, the years in which they were originally claimed.

2/ Although thus referred to at the trial, the agreement was not a merger in a strict legal sense, since Richmond's corporate existence was unaffected and there was no sale to Larus of Richmond's assets. There is no merger merely because one corporation acquires control over another through majority ownership of its stock. Finance Corporation v. Keystone Credit Corp., 50 F.2d 872 (4th Cir. 1931); 15 Fletcher, Cyclopedia of Corporations (1961 Revised Edition) § 7046, at n. 80.

3/ Hill v. Commissioner, 181 F.2d 906, 908 (4th Cir. 1950); Mertens, Law of Federal Income Taxation, Code Commentary Volume, p. 152.

4/ Of course, expenses incurred prior to and for the purpose of reaching a decision whether to establish a business are indisputably capital expenditures. See Westervelt v. Commissioner, 8 T.C. 1248 (1947); Frank v. Commissioner, 20 T.C. 511 (1953); Mid-State Products v. Commissioner, 21 T.C. 696 (1954); and Walet, Jr. v. Commissioner, 31 T.C. 461 (1958), aff'd per curiam, 272 F.2d 694 (5th Cir. 1959). See also Fleischer, "The Tax Treatment of Expenses Incurred in Investigation for a Business or Capital Investment," 14 Tax L. Rev. 567 (1959).

5/ The parties in the case at bar agree that the tax consequences of the $25,000 lump sum reimbursement to Larus and the subsequent payments totalling $27,000 are indistinguishable. Furthermore, the record does not suggest that the $25,000 was paid for some other purpose in addition to reimbursement. To the extent, however, that it may have been in consideration of Larus' promise to withdraw its application, it would constitute a capital expenditure. KWTX, supra; Houston Natural Gas Corp. v. Commissioner, 90 F. 2d 814, 816 (4th Cir. 1937), cert. denied, 302 U.S. 722 (1937); 4 Mertens, Law of Federal Income Taxation, § 25.37, p. 131.

<u>6/</u> Southeastern Express Co., 19 B.T.A. 490 (1930), the
only authority contra, has not been followed or even
mentioned in later Tax Court cases.

<u>7/</u> Compare concurring opinion of Mr. Justice Frankfurter,
<u>Duputy v. DuPont</u>, 308 U.S. 498, 499 (1940), "'* * *
carrying on any trade or business,' * * * involves
holding one's self out to others as engaged in the
selling of goods or services." See also the following
cases construing the terms "trade or business" as used
in section 174(a)(1), Internal Revenue Code of 1954,
26 U.S.C.A. § 174(a)(1) (1955), dealing with research
and experimental expenses; <u>Koons v. Commissioner</u>, 35
T.C. 1092 (1961), "'trade or business' presupposes an
existing business with which the taxpayer is directly
connected"; <u>Mayrath v. Commissioner</u>, 41 T.C. 582
(1964), "'trade or business,' is used in the practical
sense of a going trade or business."

<u>8/</u> Relied on in <u>Radio Station WBIR, Inc.</u>, 31 T.C. 803,
812-13 (1959).

<u>9/</u> "<u>In the case of an individual</u>, there shall be allowed
as a deduction all the ordinary and necessary expenses
paid or incurred during the taxable year--
"(1) for the production or collection of income.
"(2) for the management, conservation, or maintenance
of property held for the production of income * * *."
(emphasis supplied)

<u>10/</u> "§ 167, Depreciation.
"(a) General rule--There shall be allowed as a depreciation deduction a reasonable allowance for the
exhaustion, wear and tear (including a reasonable
allowance for obsolescence)--
"(1) of property used in the trade or business * * *."

<u>11/</u> In <u>KWTX</u>, supra, the Commissioner introduced considera-
ble evidence on renewal of television licenses. The
Tax Court found as a fact that:
"In the past a large number of these applications for
renewal of television licenses has been granted and
none ever denied," and concluded that:
"While it is doubtless true that it will be within the
power of the F.C.C. to refuse to grant a renewal of
petitioner's television license * * * nevertheless we
think * * * that it is altogether unlikely that the
F.C.C. will deny petitioner's application for a renewal of its license."

12/ Treasury Regulation 1.167(a)-10(b), which provides
that "[t]he period for depreciation of an asset shall
begin when the asset is placed in service," answers
the question of when a taxpayer who is in business may
begin to depreciate an asset. See also Hillcone
Steamship Co. v. Commissioner, 22 T.C.M. 1096 (1963);
Nulex, Inc. v. Commissioner, 30 T.C. 769 (1958).
These authorities indicate that the taxpayer here is
not entitled to the section 167(a)(1) deduction for
the further reason that the television staff did not
begin to serve Richmond until 1956 when broadcasting
began.

13/ Discussed supra, p. 8, as to the section 162(a)(1)
trade or business expense deduction.

LESSON 4

PARTNER'S ADJUSTED BASIS AND CAPITAL ACCOUNT

CONTENT

¶4.01
Introduction

A partnership has a basis in the assets that it owns and the partners have a basis in their interest in the partnership. The partners must adjust their basis in the partnership interest to account for a variety of partnership transactions and their transactions with the partnership.

After completing this lesson you will be able to:

(1) Compute the partner's basis for property transferred to a partnership.

(2) Determine the effect on the basis of the partner's interest of:

(a) A partner's distributive share of partnership taxable income and losses.

(b) Partnership nontaxable income and nondeductible expenditures.

(c) Partnership distributions.

(d) Increases or decreases in partnership liabilities, or in a partner's liabilities when assumed from or by a partnership.

1129

(3) Compute the partner's adjusted basis.

(4) Compute the partner's capital account.

(5) Distinguish between the partner's capital account and adjusted basis.

¶4.02
Basis on Formation of Partnership

The partner's contribution of property to a partnership is generally a tax free exchange. The partner gives up his or her assets in exchange for an interest in the partnership.

On the transfer of property to a partnership in exchange for a partnership interest the partner acquires a basis in the partnership interest equal to the amount of money and the adjusted basis of the other property exchanged. In effect, the basis of what is received is equal to the basis of what is given up. This is necessary to prevent a partner from escaping tax forever on any increase in value of property from the time he or she acquires it until it is contributed to a partnership.

Example 1

Partner A contributed $100,000 in cash (property) to the ABC partnership for a partnership interest. A's adjusted basis in the partnership is $100,000.

Example 2

Partner B contributed to a partnership $100,000 in cash and a machine having an adjusted basis in B's hands of $200,000. On the date of contribution the machine had a fair market value of $500,000. B's basis in the partnership is $300,000.

Cash	$100,000
Adjusted basis of property	200,000
	$300,000

¶4.03
Adjustments to Basis

> The partner's adjusted basis is continually changing - the operations of the partnership increase or decrease the adjusted basis.

> EXTRACT
> Regs. § 1.705-1(a)(1)

> > * * * A partner is required to determine the adjusted basis of his interest in a partnership only when necessary for the determination of his tax liability or that of any other person. The determination of the adjusted basis of a partnership interest is ordinarily made as of the end of a partnership taxable year.* * *

> For various reasons computation of a partner's adjusted basis may be required before the close of the taxable period.

> The computation of a partner's basis would be necessary for the determination of the partner's tax liability upon:

> (1) The sale or exchange of the partnership interest

> (2) A termination of the partnership

> (3) The distribution to a partner of property in a nonliquidating distribution

> (4) The event of a partnership loss.

¶4.031
Partner's Distributive Share of
Taxable Income or Loss

> The partnership is a conduit. The income or loss passes through to the partners. The partners are required to reflect the income or loss on their tax returns; they must also use the income or loss to compute the adjusted basis in their partnership interests.

Example 3

Partner C has an adjusted basis of $150,000 in ABC partnership. The partnership has ordinary income of $100,000 of which C's share is $25,000. C's new adjusted basis is $175,000.

Beginning adjusted basis	$150,000
Income	25,000
Ending adjusted basis	$175,000

Example 4

B invested $100,000 in a partnership. The partnership has a $150,000 loss of which B's distributive share is $50,000. B's adjusted basis is $50,000.

Beginning adjusted basis	$100,000
Loss	50,000
Ending adjusted basis	$ 50,000

A partner is allowed to deduct partnership losses only to the extent of adjusted basis of the partnership interest.[1/]

Example 5

Partner A's partnership interest has an adjusted basis of $25,000 at the beginning of the taxable year. The partnership has a loss of which A's share is $50,000. Partner A is allowed to claim only a $25,000 loss on her individual return.

Beginning adjusted basis	$25,000
Loss	(50,000)
Ending adjusted basis	$ -0-

The adjusted basis cannot be reduced below zero nor can the balance of a loss be deducted currently. If the partner contributes more property to the partnership in a subsequent year, a loss will be allowed to the extent of the adjusted basis of the property contributed. The adjusted basis cannot be reduced below zero, but the partner's capital account can show a negative balance.

M is a partner in MNO partnership. M's partnership interest has an adjusted basis of $75,000 as of January 1,
1975. The partnership has a $300,000 loss for the taxable
year 1975; of which M's share is $100,000. In 1976 M
contributes $50,000, and for 1976 the partnership incurs a
small loss of which M's share is $25,000.

Compute M's loss deduction for the taxable years 1975 and
1976.

See answer 1.

Generally the partners' losses are limited by Code §§ 465
for years beginning after December 31, 1975, or 704(d) for
years beginning after December 31, 1976. The partners are
required to keep a record of their capital accounts, their
adjusted basis accounts, and their "at risk" 2/ accounts.
The only function of the "at risk" account is to limit
losses. The "at-risk" provisions of § 465 and § 704(d)
will be discussed in Lessons 5 and 6.

¶4.032
Nontaxable Income and
Nondeductible Expenditures

The partners are allowed to increase their adjusted basis
by the partnership's nontaxable income, such as tax-exempt
interest. The partners are required to reduce their
adjusted basis by nondeductible expenditures. Such expenditures include life insurance premiums and interest
expense for carrying tax-exempt bonds or political contributions.

¶4.033
Nonliquidating Distributions

Since the partners have been previously taxed on their
distributive shares of partnership income, they are entitled to receive certain distributions from the partnership
tax free. The receipt of property from the partnership
reduces the adjusted basis of the partnership interest. A
partner may withdraw cash or other property from the
partnership at its adjusted basis without any tax effect
until the adjusted basis of the partnership interest
reaches zero. After the adjusted basis of the interest
reaches zero, any withdrawal of cash will result in a
taxable event. In a nonliquidating distribution, the

withdrawal of property, in addition to cash, will not result in a taxable event. The property withdrawn may have a zero adjusted basis.

Example 6

Partner C has a partnership interest with an adjusted basis of $10,000 before any distributions. C withdraws $9,000 in cash which reduces C's adjusted basis to $1,000. This is not a taxable event to C.

C's Beginning adjusted basis	$10,000
Distribution (cash withdrawal)	9,000
C's Ending adjusted basis	$ 1,000

Example 7

If in example 6, $11,000 in cash is withdrawn, C <u>does</u> have a taxable event. In that case C's adjusted basis <u>will</u> be reduced to zero and any subsequent withdrawals are fully taxable.

Adjusted basis	$10,000
Withdrawal of cash	10,000
Adjusted basis to zero	$ -0-

$10,000 of the $11,000 withdrawal reduced C's basis to zero. The balance, $1,000, is capital gain income. The distribution of cash in excess of the adjusted basis is treated as a sale of a partnership interest.

Question 2

Partner B's partnership interest has an adjusted basis of $10,000. B's share of the partnership ordinary income is $2,000. The partnership has received tax-exempt interest income and has paid life insurance premiums. B's share of the tax-exempt interest is $500 and for the life insurance premium expense, $750. B withdraws $7,000 in cash from the partnership. Calculate the adjusted basis of B's partnership interest.

See answer 2.

3178-02

¶4.034
Effect of Liability on
Partner's Adjusted Basis

Each general partner[3] is liable for his or her share of partnership liabilities. A limited partner[4] is generally liable only to the extent of his or her investment. If a partnership has one or more limited partners, it is defined as a limited partnership.[5] When a partnership incurs a full recourse liability, the partners can increase their adjusted bases in regard to these liabilities in the same proportion as they share losses. The limited partners cannot use these liabilities to increase their bases beyond the remaining amount they are obligated to contribute.

Example 8

General partners A and B each have a 25% interest in the ABC partnership. The remaining 50% is owned by 50 limited partners. The partnership incurs a $200,000 full recourse liability. A and B would each increase their adjusted basis by $100,000.

¶4.04
Effect of Nonrecourse Debt
on Adjusted Basis

In the normal operations of a partnership, only the general partners can use the partnership liabilities to increase their adjusted basis. However, when nonrecourse debt[6] is involved, all partners, general and limited, can share in the liability.

EXTRACT
Regs. § 1.752-1(e)

* * *In the case of a limited partnership, a limited partner's share of partnership liabilities shall not exceed the difference between his actual contribution credited to him by the partnership and the total contribution which he is obligated to make under the limited partnership agreement. However, where none of the partners have any personal liability with respect to a partnership liability, * * * *then all partners, including limited partners, shall be considered as sharing such liability under section 752(c) in the same proportion as they share the profits.* * *

This increase in adjusted basis using nonrecourse debt will not be used to determine allowable loss.$\underline{7/}$

¶4.05
Reconciliation of Partner's
Capital Account

Schedule M, of the partnership return provides for the reconciliation of the partners' capital accounts. On it are explained the differences between the partners' capital accounts at the the beginning of the tax year and at the end of the tax year. The beginning and ending capital accounts should agree with the amounts shown on Schedule L, Balance Sheet.

Example 9

Schedule L—BALANCE SHEETS (See General Instruction K)

12 Other assets		
13 Total assets		
LIABILITIES AND CAPITAL		
14 Accounts payable	$ 100,000	$ 125,000
15 Mortgages, notes, and bonds payable in less than 1 year	25,000	15,000
16 Other current liabilities (attach schedule)	5,000	7,500
17 Mortgages, notes, and bonds payable in 1 year or more	1,000,000	900,000
18 Other liabilities (attach schedule)	-0-	-0-
19 Partners' capital accounts	(250,000)	(550,000)
20 Total liabilities and capital	$ 880,000	$ 497,500

Schedule M—RECONCILIATION OF PARTNERS' CAPITAL ACCOUNTS (See Instruction for Schedule M)
(Show reconciliation of each partner's capital account on Schedule K-1)

Number of partners	a. Capital account at beginning of year	b. Capital contributed during year	c. Ordinary income (loss) from line 26, page 1	d. Income not included in column c, plus non-taxable income	e. Losses not included in column c, plus unallowable deductions	f. Withdrawals and distributions	g. Capital account at end of year
25	(250,000)	-0-	(300,000)	-0-	-0-	-0-	(550,000)

Schedule N—COMPUTATION OF NET EARNINGS FROM SELF-EMPLOYMENT (See Instruction for Schedule N)

Ordinary income

¶4.06
Capital Account v.
Adjusted Basis

The capital account fulfills an accounting function, whereas the adjusted basis fulfills a tax function. For that reason, rarely, if ever, will a partner's capital account equal the amount of the adjusted basis. A set of financial records serves many purposes, only one of which is determining tax liabilities. In the case of a contribution of property other than cash to a partnership, the partners for financial statement purposes may elect to

1136

value the property at fair market value. In this event
the contributing partner's capital account would be credited with the fair market value of the property, not the
adjusted basis in the property. The regulations state
that a partner's adjusted basis in a partnership is determined without regard to any amount shown on the books as
the partner's capital, equity, or similar account.[8/]

Example 10

A contributes equipment with an adjusted basis in A's
hands of $10,000 and a fair market value of $20,000. B
contributes $20,000 in cash. Both A and B have a balance
of $20,000 in their capital accounts. The adjusted basis
of B's interest in the partnership is $20,000, while A's
adjusted basis is $10,000.

––––––––––

Although changes in partners' capital accounts do not in
themselves give rise to taxable events, you should not
ignore these accounts.

¶4.07
Summary

(1) When property is exchanged for a partnership interest,
    the partner's basis in the interest is equal to the
    adjusted basis of the property contributed.

(2) A partner's basis in his or her partnership interest
    must be:

    (a) Increased by the partner's distributive share of
        partnership taxable income and tax-exempt income.

    (b) Decreased by distributions to the partner.

    (c) Decreased by the partner's distributive share of
        partnership losses and nondeductible expenses.

    (d) Increased by additional contributions to the
        partnership.

(3) A partner is considered to have contributed money to a
    partnership when his or her:

    (a) Share of partnership liabilities increases; or

    (b) Personal liabilities increase because of the
        assumption of partnership liabilities.

When such liabilities decrease, a partner is considered to have received a distribution of money from the partnership.

(4) A partner's distributive share of partnership losses is deductible only to the extent of the partner's adjusted basis in his or her partnership interest computed before reduction for the loss (limited by Code §§ 465 and 704).

(5) A partner's capital account is reflected on Schedule M.

(6) A partner's capital account generally does not reflect the same amount as the adjusted basis of the partnership interest.

1. M's allowable loss deduction for 1975 is limited by M's adjusted basis in the partnership or $75,000.

Beginning adjusted basis	$ 75,000
Share of partnership loss	(100,000)
M's ending adjusted basis	$ -0-

   M's allowable loss deduction for 1976 is $50,000, the sum of the 1975 carryover loss and M's share of the 1976 partnership loss. Carryover losses are allowed in a subsequent year to the extent of the adjusted basis of contributed property.

Beginning adjusted basis	$ -0-
Capital contribution	50,000
1976 loss	(25,000)
Adjusted basis before 1975 loss	$ 25,000
1975 loss carryover	(25,000)
M's ending adjusted basis	$ -0-

2. $4,750, computed as follows:

Beginning adjusted basis		$10,000
Add: Distributive share of partnership		
taxable income	$2,000	
Tax-exempt interest	500	2,500
		$12,500
Less: Deduction not allowed		
on partnership return	$ 750	
Cash distribution	7,000	7,750
B's ending adjusted basis		$ 4,750

Footnotes

1/ For taxable years beginning after December 31, 1975, see Code §§ 465 and 704(d) for details on limitation of losses.

2/ This term is explained in the glossary in front of the coursebook.

3/ Glossary term.

4/ Glossary term.

5/ Glossary term.

6/ Glossary term.

7/ See footnote 1.

8/ Reg. § 1.705-1(a)(1).

LESSON 5

AT-RISK LIMITATIONS OF § 465

CONTENT

¶5.01
Introduction

Before the Tax Reform Act of 1976, tax shelter investors were able to include in their adjusted bases, for loss purposes, liabilities for which they were not personally liable. Through nonrecourse financing, the investors were able to deduct losses in excess of their actual capital "amount at risk"[1] in the venture. Code § 465 was enacted to limit the amount of these deductions under certain conditions.

After completing this lesson, you will be able to compute the amount at-risk and apply the at-risk provisions to tax returns.

¶5.02
Limitation

Code § 465 prevents **taxpayers** from deducting losses above the amount they have at-risk in an activity. Generally applying to tax years beginning after 1975,[2] it negates some advantages of nonrecourse financing by overriding other loss deduction provisions.

The at-risk provisions apply to losses sustained by noncorporate taxpayers, tax option (Sub S) corporations, and personal holding companies. Regular corporations are not affected by Code § 465. The new at-risk provisions cover only four specific types of activity:

(1) farming

(2) equipment leasing,

(3) oil and gas exploration and exploitation, and

(4) motion picture production and distribution.

The rules under Code § 465 apply only to limiting the deductibility of losses to amounts at risk and do not apply for other tax purposes, such as the determination of basis. Also, they apply separately to each activity of the taxpayer, not on an aggregated basis for all activities. Thus, a taxpayer must apply the rules separately to each farming activity, to each equipment leasing activity, to oil and gas property, and to each motion picture activity. Losses from one activity cannot be used to offset income from another activity.

For purposes of computing separate activities a partner's interest in a partnership or a shareholder's interest in a subchapter S corporation, conducting an activity will be considered a single activity. For example, if a partnership leases several items of unrelated equipment, its entire leasing activity will be treated as one activity. On the other hand, if a partnership conducts activities in more than one category, such as farming and equipment leasing, it will be considered to be conducting more than one activity (in this case two activities) and a separate application of the at risk rule must be made for each category.

¶5.03
Determination of Amount

Taxpayers are "at-risk" in an activity to the extent of the money they contribute to the activity and their adjusted basis of other property they contribute to the activity.³/ If certain requirements are met, taxpayers are also at risk for amounts borrowed to finance the activity.⁴/ These loan requirements apply both to loans obtained by the entity conducting the activity and to those obtained by the taxpayers in order to raise the money or obtain the property to be used in the activity.

Taxpayers are at-risk on <u>recourse</u> loans. Specifically, they are at-risk on the proceeds of a loan to finance the activity to the extent they are personally liable to repay the loan from their personal funds.⁵/ However, taxpayers are generally not at risk on the proceeds of <u>nonrecourse</u> loans used to finance the activity or acquire the property used in the activity.

¶5.031
Pledged Property

Whether taxpayers are at risk on the proceeds of nonrecourse loans depends upon the nature of the property pledged as security. The taxpayers are not at risk if the pledged property is used in the activity or any other § 465 activity.[6/] Generally, however, the taxpayers are at risk to the extent of the net FMV of their interest in pledged property not used in the activity or any other § 465 activity. For example, taxpayers are at risk on the proceeds of a loan to finance an equipment leasing activity to the extent of the net FMV of their interest in the property in personally owned real estate that they have pledged as security. The net FMV of a taxpayer's interest in the property (determined on the date the property is pledged) is the FMV of the property less any prior (or superior) claims against the property. If property used in one Code § 465 activity is pledged to secure a loan having proceeds that are used in another § 465 activity, the taxpayer may not be at risk on the proceeds of the loan. Examiners should be expecially careful to detect these arrangements when taxpayers are engaged in more than one § 465 activity. There is no published Service position on this issue as of February 8, 1978.

¶5.032
Cross-Collateralization

A special rule prevents taxpayers from artifically increasing at risk amounts through cross-collateralization. Using this device, taxpayers start with the property that is used in the same activity that will ultimately be financed. They pledge this property as security for a nonrecourse loan and use the loan proceeds to purchase property not used in the activity. This property is then pledged as security for a second nonrecourse loan whose proceeds are then used to finance the activity. Under the general rule, these nonrecourse loan proceeds would be included in the at-risk amount since the nonrecourse loan is secured by property not used in the activity. However, the new law provides that no property is counted as security, for at-risk purposes, if it is directly or indirectly financed by indebtedness secured by property used in the activity.[7/] The effect of this rule is that the final loan, which was used to finance the activity, will be treated as unsecured as well as nonrecourse. Therefore, the taxpayer will not be at risk on it.

Under another special rule, a taxpayer is not at risk for amounts borrowed to finance an activity if the loan is obtained from a party who has an interest in that activity (other than an interest as a creditor)$\underline{8/}$ or if the loan is obtained from a person "related" to the taxpayer under Code § 267(b).$\underline{9/}$

¶5.033
Computation

The amount at risk is computed on the basis of the facts at the end of each taxable year. Thus, if a partnership obtains a loan upon which the partners are initially personally liable, but which will later become nonrecourse, the partners are at risk during the period they are personally liable. They cease to be at risk from the time that the loan becomes nonrecourse.

To avoid the at-risk limitations of Code § 465, many shelters are being structured with full recourse indebtedness by the investors, which converts to nonrecourse indebtedness after a short period of time. They are thus attempting to claim the flow-through of large losses in early years. The Service is presently formulating a position with respect to this type of transaction.

Examiners should be alert to the "substance v. form" issue, such as that posed in the following example:

Example 1

ABC, a calendar-year cash-basis oil drilling partnership, was formed December 30, 1976. Capitalization for the $2,000,000 drilling program included cash of $1,000,000 and borrowing of $1,000,000, for which the investors were personally liable. The loan arrangement converts the full recourse debt to a nonrecourse debt on January 1, 1977. ABC elected to treat the intangible drilling costs (IDC), which were paid in full in 1976, as an expense for 1976, although the drilling program was not physically completed until July 1, 1977.$\underline{10/}$ The 1976 IDC writeoff resulted in an operating loss of $1,900,000 which passed through the partnership to the individual partners. _In form_, the at-risk limitation of Code § 465 would not apply since as of December 31, 1976, all indebtedness was full recourse. The Service position on this transaction is not yet formulated.

Proper analysis of the facts could reveal a situation completely different in substance than that displayed in

form. One of these loan transactions is described in Rev.
Rul. 77-398, 1977-44 I.R.B. 8, corrected by Ann. 77-157,
1977-47 I.R.B. 21. In such a case, a loss similar to the
one shown in the example could be decreased or eliminated.

¶5.034
Stop-Loss Agreements

The new rules provide that taxpayers are not at risk, even
for money or property they contributed, to the extent they
are protected against loss through nonrecourse financing,
guarantees, stop-loss agreements, or other similar
arrangements.11/ Investors are not at risk if they arrange insurance or other compensation that will be paid to
them after the loss is sustained. They are also not at
risk if a binding agreement between themselves and other
persons entitles them to reimbursement for part of all of
any loss.

It is assumed that the insurance,/ guarantees, stop-loss
orders, etc., will be fully honored and that the taxpayer
will actually be reimbursed under them. Even if there is
a chance that the guarantor will not be able to fulfill
the agreement because of insolvency or other financial
difficulty, the agrement will reduce the taxpayer's at
risk amount until the taxpayer actually becomes uncondi-
tionally entitled to payment and demonstrates that he or
she cannot recover.

Under a stop-loss agreement, the investor is at risk only
on the portion of the investment that will not be reimbursed. Under a repurchase agreement, the investor is at
risk only to the extent the investment exceeds the buy
back price.

Investors may also separately obtain insurance to reimburse any economic loss suffered. For example, Taxpayer A
may obtain insurance to compensate for any payments she
might have to make under personal liability on a mortgage.
Here the taxpayer is at risk only on the uninsured portion
of her liability. If A pays the insurance premiums from
her personal assets, she may add them to her at risk
amount. Casualty insurance or insurance to protect A
against tort liability would not reduce A's at risk
amount.

On the other hand, a normal buy-sell agreement between
partners, to be carried out if a partner dies or retires,
does not reduce the amount the partner is at risk. Also,
governmental price support programs (such as provided by
the Agriculture and Consumer Protection Act of 1973) do
not reduce the taxpayer's at risk amount if there are no
agreements limiting the taxpayer's costs.

3178-02

¶5.04
Application of Limitation

> As with most tax law changes, the computation of the amount affected differs before and after the change. Thus for Code § 465 we have one set of rules for losses incurred before January 1, 1976 and a different set of rules for losses incurred after December 31, 1975.

¶5.041
Years Before January 1, 1976

> If a taxpayer was engaged in farming, equipment leasing, the oil and gas industry, or the motion picture industry in a taxable year beginning before January 1, 1976, the Temporary Regulations require the taxpayer to compute an at risk amount in the activity as of the first day of the first taxable year beginning after December 31, 1975.[12/] Essentially, the taxpayer must calculate the at risk amounts for the pre-1976 years as if the new rules were in effect for those years. Thus, the taxpayer determines an initial at risk amount for the first year the taxpayer engaged in the activity. This initial at risk amount is the taxpayer's initial basis modified by disregarding borrowed amounts which are not at risk due to the rules discussed above.[13/] For each pre-1976 taxable year, the taxpayer adjusts the at risk amount to properly reflect changes in the taxpayer's basis, again disregarding borrowed amounts not deemed to be at risk.[14/] The amounts deducted for the taxable years beginning before that date are considered to first reduce the portion of the taxpayer's basis that is not at risk. If the taxpayer withdrew assets from the activity during the taxable years before January 1, 1976, the withdrawals reduce the amount the taxpayer has at risk.[15/] The initial (1976) amount at risk is never reduced below zero.

Example 2

> On January 1, 1975, A and B formed the AB Partnership, each contributing $100,000 in cash. On July 1, 1975, the partnership borrowed $800,000 under a nonrecourse financing arrangement secured only by new leasable equipment purchased for $1,000,000 ($200,000, cash; plus $800,000, nonrecourse loan). On December 31, 1975, each partner received a $30,000 cash distribution and the partnership has a $400,000 loss. A's amount at risk as of December 31, 1975, is $70,000.

```
Initial amount at risk                              $100,000
Plus:   Items which increase basis other than
        amounts described in § 465(b)(3) or (4)            0
                Total                               $100,000
Less:   Distribution                                 (30,000)
        Portion of loss ($200,000) in excess of
        basis not at risk ($400,000)                    -0-
A's amount at risk as of 12/31/75                   $ 70,000
```

Note: In this example, A's distributive share of the 1975 loss reduces the basis of the portion of A's interest in the partnership which is not at risk.

_____

Example 3

Assume the same facts as in example 2, except that the partnership loss is $900,000. A's amount at risk as of December 31, 1975 is $20,000.

```
Initial amount at risk                              $100,000
Plus items which increase basis other than
amounts described in § 465(b)(3) or (4)                 -0-

Total                                               $100,000
Less:   Distribution                                ( 30,000)
        Portion of loss ($450,000) in excess of
        basis not at risk ($400,000)                ( 50,000)
A's amount at risk as of 12/31/75                   $ 20,000
```

Note: Pre-1/1/76 losses reduce basis not at risk first. Any excess of pre-1/1/76 loss over amount of basis not at risk reduces amount at risk.

_____

Question 1

Given the following facts, determine the at-risk portion of A's basis in the AB partnership as of December 31, 1975.

a. AB Partnership was formed on 1/1/75; A & B are general partners.

b. A contributed $200,000 in cash for a 50% interest in the partnership.

c. The partnership arranged for $2,000,000 nonrecourse financing, secured only by new equipment to be leased.

d. A contributed to the partnership a building having an adjusted basis of $50,000, a fair market value of $60,000, and an outstanding mortgage liability of $40,000. The partnership assumed the $40,000 mortgage liability.

e. The partnership incurred a $2,150,000 loss for the year 1975.

f. A had partnership withdrawals of $20,000 in 1975.

See answer 1.

¶5.042
Years After
December 31, 1975

If a taxpayer is engaged in farming, equipment leasing, the oil and gas industry, or motion pictures after December 31, 1975, the amount at risk is the limiting factor in determining how much of a loss may be deducted. For the first year of loss a taxpayer must determine the at-risk amount at the end of the year and compare that amount to the amount of loss. If the loss is less than the at-risk amount, the entire loss is deductible and the at-risk amount is reduced by the loss deducted. If the loss is greater than the at-risk amount, the deductible loss is limited to the amount at risk at year-end. The at-risk amount is reduced to zero and the excess is carried forward until such time as the taxpayer can increase his or her at-risk amount. A taxpayer's at-risk amount at year-end is determined by first subtracting any withdrawals or distributions.

Example 4

On January 1, 1976, A and B formed the AB Partnership, each contributing $100,000 in cash. The partnership borrowed $800,000 under a nonrecourse financing arrangement secured only by the new leasing equipment purchased for $1,000,000 ($200,000, cash; $800,000, nonrecourse loan). On December 31, 1976, each partner received a $30,000 cash distribution and the partnership had a $400,000 loss. A's amount at risk as of 12/31/76 is:

Initial amount at risk	$100,000
Plus: Items which increase basis other than amounts described in § 465(b)(3) or (4)	-0-
Total	$100,000

Less:	Distribution	(30,000)
	A's amount at risk as of 12/31/76 before application of 1976 loss	$ 70,000
	A's portion of loss ($200,000) limited to A's at-risk amount as of 12/31/76	(70,000)
A's amount at-risk after allowance of loss		$ -0-

Note: A's loss deduction for 1976 is limited to $70,000. The excess loss of $130,000 is carried forward until A's amount at risk is increased.

Question 2

Given the following facts, determine the at-risk portion of A's basis in the AB Partnership as of December 31, 1976.

a. AB Partnership was formed on 1/1/76; A and B are both general partners.

b. A contributed $200,000 in cash for a 50% partnership interest.

c. The partnership obtained a $2,000,000 nonrecourse loan, secured only by the new equipment to be leased.

d. A contributed a building to the partnership with an adjusted basis of $50,000, a fair market value of $60,000, and an outstanding mortgage liability of $40,000. The partnership assumed the $40,000 mortgage liability.

e. The partnership incurred a $2,150,000 loss for the year 1975.

f. A had partnership withdrawals of $20,000 in 1976.

See answer 2.

3178-02

¶5.05
Summary

(1) With the exception of regular corporations, the at-risk rules apply to all taxpayers engaged in four specific activities (farming, equipment leasing, oil and gas, and motion pictures).

(2) The at-risk rules apply <u>separately</u> to <u>each</u> activity, not on an aggregated basis for all the taxpayer's activities.

(3) The amount a taxpayer has at risk is generally the sum of cash and other contributions to the activity, plus the taxpayer's share of the proceeds of any indebtedness <u>for which the taxpayer has unlimited liability</u>.

(4) Taxpayers are <u>not</u> considered to have amounts at risk to the extent they are protected against losses through nonrecourse financing, guarantees, stop-loss agreements, or other similar arrangements.

(5) Losses incurred before January 1, 1976, are treated differently than are losses incurred after December 31, 1975, so it is necessary to determine the amount at risk as of January 1, 1976 for activities begun before then.

1.

Computation of At-Risk as of 12/31/75

Initial amount at-risk (cash)		$200,000
Plus: Items which increase basis other than amounts described in § 465(b)(3) or (4)		30,000
Contribution of building:		
A's adjusted basis	$50,000	
Less: 50% of liability assumed by B	20,000	
Increase in A's partnership basis	$30,000	
Total		$230,000
Less: A's partnership withdrawals		(20,000)
Portion of A;s loss ($1,075,000) in excess of basis not at risk ($1,000,000)		(75,000)
A's amount at risk as of 12/31/75		$135,000

2. The amount at risk as of December 31, 1976, is zero and A's allowable loss for 1976 is $210,000. The loss in excess of the allowable loss of $210,000 is carried forward until A has sufficient at-risk capital to use the loss. In this problem the loss carried forward is $865,000.

Computation of Amount At-Risk as of 12/31/76
and Allowable Loss

Initial amount at risk (cash)		$200,000
Plus: Items which increase basis other than amounts described in § 465(b)(3) or (4)		30,000
Contribution of building:		
A's adjusted basis	$50,000	
Less: 50% of liability assumed by B	20,000	
Increase in A's partnership basis	$30,000	
Total		$230,000
Less: A's partnership withdrawals		(20,000)
A's amount at risk as of 12/31/76 before application of the 1976 loss		$210,000
A's portion of loss ($1,075,000) limited to A's amount at risk as of 12/31/76		(210,000)
A's amount at risk after allowance of loss		$ -0-

3178-02

Footnotes

1/   Glossary term.

2/   Act § 204(c)(1), Tax Reform Act of 1976, Public Law 94-455, 94th Cong., 2d Sess. (1976), 1976-3 C.B. Vol. 1,1.

3/   Code § 465(b)(1)(A).

4/   Code § 465(b)(1)(B).

5/   Code § 465(b)(2)(A).

6/   Code § 465(b)(2).(B).

7/   Code § 465(b)(2)

8/   Code § 465(b)(3)(A).

9/   Code § 465(b)(3)(B).

10/   Rev. Rul. 71-252, 1971-1 C.B. 146.

11/   Code § 465(b)(4).

12/   Temp. Reg. § 7.465-1.

13/   Code § 465(b)(3) and (4).

14/   Temp. Reg. § 7.465-2.

15/   See footnote 14.

LESSON 6

AT-RISK LIMITATIONS OF § 704(d)

CONTENT

¶6.01 Introduction
¶6.02 Determining the Existence of a Partnership
¶6.03 Includible Activities and Entities
¶6.04 Amount At Risk
¶6.05 Summary

¶6.01
Introduction

> In the previous lesson you studied the at-risk limitations
> of Code § 465 which preclude certain taxpayers from claim-
> ing losses in excess of their respective amounts at risk.
> This lesson incorporates the § 465 limitations with the
> at-risk limitations of Code § 704(d). After completing
> this lesson you will be able to identify the activities
> and entities covered by the at-risk limitations of Code §
> 704(d) and apply these limitations.

¶6.02
Determining the Existence of a Partnership

> Code § 704(d) applies only to partnerships. Therefore, it
> is necessary to recognize when a partnership exists. With
> the enactment of the limitation on loss provisions of §
> 704(d), many tax shelter activities ostensibly will be
> structured other than as partnerships. In form, the tax
> shelter may look like something other than a partnership,
> while in substance it may in fact be a partnership and
> fall under § 704(d).

> The term "partnership" for tax purposes is not limited to
> the common law meaning of partnership, but is broader in
> scope. For tax purposes the term partnership "includes a
> syndicate, group, pool, joint venture, or other unincorpo-
> rated organization, through or by means of which any
> business, financial operation, or venture is carried on,
> and which is not * * * a corporation or a trust or
> estate."[1]   Essentially, a partnership is an association
> of two or more persons [2] to carry on, as co-owners, a
> business for profit and divided the gains therefrom. The
> term "co-owners" is significant in that if a person does
> not own part of the business, he or she would not be a

1153

3178-02

partner. In addition to "co-ownership," the term "carry
on * * * a business for profit" is significant in that
co-owners owners of real or personal property who do not
use the property for profit are not partners. A commin-
gling of funds or assets by two or more persons for a
common business purpose with the earnings being shared
usually satisfys the two criteria just mentioned. If the
arrangement under which two or more persons operate has
the characterics of a partnership, it will be classified
as a partnership and Code § 704(d) will apply, even though
no formal partnership agreement exists.

¶6.03
Includible Activities and Entities

Code § 704(d) applies to all partnerships except: (1) to
the extent activities are covered by Code § 465 (farming,
oil and gas, equipment leasing, and motion pictures) and
(2) those the principal activity of which is investing in
real property (other than mineral property). To the
extent Code § 704(d) applies to a partnership, it covers
all partners of the partnership regardless of their form
(individuals, corporations, estates, trusts, etc.). In
Code § 465, regular corporations are excluded from the
at-risk limitations, if they are engaged in one of the
four specific activities (farming, oil and gas, equipment
leasing, and motion pictures). Since Code § 704(d) applies to all activities except real estate investment and
the four specific activities to which § 465 applies, it is
possible that a regular corporation, as a partner, could
deduct losses in excess of its amount at risk if engaged
in one of these activities. If a corporate partner was
engaged in any activity other than real estate investment
or the Code § 465 activities, the at-risk limitations of
Code § 704(d) would, of course, apply.

¶6.04
Amount At Risk

The criteria used in determining whether a partner has
personal liability for purposes of Code § 704(d) are the
same as those used for § 465. If the partner is insulated
from economic loss through nonrecourse financing, guarantees, stop-loss agreements, or other similar arrangements,
these amounts are considered not at risk. The effective
date for determining the amount at risk is a basic difference between Code § 465 and § 704(d). Code § 465 applies
to all nonrecourse financing, agreements, stop-loss, or
other similar arrangements regardless of when they were
entered into. There is, however, special treatment for
pre-1976 bases. See Temp. Regs. § 7.465-let seq. Code §
704(d) applies to all nonrecourse financing arrangements,

guarantees, stop-loss agreements,, or other similar arrangements entered into after December 31,1976. It is possible that a partnership engaged in two activities could be subject to both Code § 465 and § 704(d) .

If a partnership was formed and secured its nonrecourse financing before January 1, 1977, Code § 704(d) would not apply to that financing. However, any nonrecourse financing, guarantees, stop-loss agreements, or other similar arrangements entered into after December 31, 1976, would be subject to the at-risk provisions of Code § 704(d).

Insofar as Code § 465 is applicable, the taxpayer-partner's loss deduction is limited to the amount the partner has at risk. However, for computing the partner's adjusted basis other than for losses, the partner's share of nonrecourse partnership loans is included. Insofar as Code § 704(d) is applicable, the partner's loss is limited to the partner's adjusted basis excluding the partner's allocable share of nonrecourse partnership loans.

When Code § 704(d) applies to a partnership having both operating and capital losses in excess of the partner's adjusted basis (as computed for purposes of Code § 704(d)), the losses must be allocated for deduction purposes.

Example

As of December 31, 1977, Partner A's adjusted basis in the ABC partnership (before applying a December 31, 1977 loss) is $200,000. The adjusted basis includes cash, $50,000, and A's share of nonrecourse financing entered into after December 31,1976, $150,000. ABC is an activity to which Code § 704(d) applies and the distributive loss to Partner A is as follows:

a.   Operating loss from the activity, $40,000

b.   Long-term capital loss, $35,000

c.   Short-term capital loss, $5,000

Computation of A's Allowable Losses for Period Ending December 31, 1977:

Adjusted basis (before 1977 losses)	$ 200,000
Less: nonrecourse financing	150,000
Modified adjusted basis as per § 704(d)	$ 50,000

Losses:	from operating	$40,000
	from long-term	35,000
	from short-term	5,000
	Total losses	$80,000

Since A's adjusted basis is only $50,000, and the total loss is $80,000, A is allowed to deduct 5/8ths of each category of loss as follows:

Operating loss	(5/8ths x $40,000) =	$25,000
Long-term loss	(5/8ths x $35,000) =	21,875
Short-term loss	(5/8ths x $5,000) =	3,125
Total losses deductible		$50,000

The total capital loss available to A, $25,000, is not automatically deductible, due to the limits of Code § 1211. Rather, this loss is available to A to offset A's capital gains from other sources. Any remaining capital loss may be deducted against ordinary income only to yjr extent of § 1211 limits. The balance would be carried over under the rules of Code § 1212. This carried over capital loss would be available to A for future years whether or not A's partnership basis increased. In addition to any § 1212 carryforwards, A would have loss carryforwards of $15,000 (ordinary), $13,125 (long-term), and $1,875 (short-term) which could be used only when A's basis was increased enough to absorb them.

¶6.05
Summary

(1) Code § 704(d) loss limitations apply only to partnerships.

(2) When examining tax returns factually determine whether the entity is a partnership; if so, the at-risk limitations of Code§ 704(d) would apply.

(3) In general, the amount which is considered not to be at risk follows the same rules as those in Code § 465.

(4) A partner who is insulated from loss or has no personal liability for repayment will not be considered to be at risk for such amounts.

(5) The adjusted basis of a partner's interest for loss purposes cannot be reduced below zero; losses in

3178-02

excess of the partner's adjusted basis are not allowable.

(6) If a partner has more than one type of loss (that is, operating and capital loss) and the total loss exceeds adjusted basis (as computed for purposes of Code § 704(d)), the losses must be allocated in proportion to their total. Any unused amount of the loss is carried forward until the taxpayer has sufficient basis to absorb the loss.

(7) Code § 704(d) limitation applies only to not at-risk amounts when the arrangements were entered into after December 31, 1976.

(8) The at-risk limitations of Code § 704(d) apply to all partnership activities except those covered by Code § 465 (farming, oil and gas, equipment leasing, and motion pictures) and investments in real estate (other than mineral property).

(9) If the partnership is engaged in an activity to which Code § 465 applies, Code § 465 takes precedent over § 704(d).

(10) Losses from a Code § 465 activity must be kept separate from other partnership activities.

(11) A partnership will be subject to both Code § 465 and Code § 704(d) if it engages in a Code § 465 activity and a non-Code § 465 activity. In this case, separate computations are necessary for the activities.

Footnotes

<u>1</u>/   Code § 761(a); see also Code § 7701(a)(2).

<u>2</u>/   Code § 7701(a)(1).

LESSON 7

CHARACTERISTICS OF TAX SHELTERS

CONTENT

¶7.01
Introduction

The country's economy requires the commitment of huge sums of money, often over long periods of time, for leasing, drilling for gas and oil, mining, farming, building tankers, and constructing apartment buildings, shopping centers, office buildings, etc. This combination of time and money lends itself to operations which result in tax avoidance, both proper and improper. Participants use different investment vehicles to pool financial resources and accumulate financial benefits. These vehicles differ not only in form but in right of control, participation in management, personal liability, flexibility, and a vast array of elements involved in carrying out their operations or functions. It is because of the many different variations available for structuring financial and tax arrangements that most tax shelters are created.

Whether the tax shelter has any economic merit can be determined by using the profit motive, not taxes, as an evaluating factor. This determination should be made over many years, not merely the tax year or years under examination.

After completing this lesson, you will be able to recognize the general characteristics of a tax shelter.

Various types of business entities are used to achieve the goals of the tax shelter. Limited partnerships [1] have been the most commonly used vehicle for abuse in the structuring of tax shelters. Limited partnerships enable participants to secure pass-through deductions in excess of risk capital (while limiting their personal liability through nonrecourse financing)[2]. These deductions can be used to offset the participants' other ordinary income. A limited partnership is vulnerable to being characterized as an association, taxable as a corporation (Code § 7701), thus losing its conduit [3] advantages.

An examiner must distinguish between two types of benefits--economic and tax.

Normally, in a non-abusive tax shelter, the economic benefits predominate and the tax benefits are only a secondary consideration. However, many tax shelters lack economic reality and are structured primarily for tax avoidance purposes. It is these abusive tax shelters, which have veered away from providing true economic benefits, that the Service will challenge.

The flow-through of tax benefits is a material factor, whether the entity is organized as a limited partnership, joint venture, or Subchapter S corporation, and whether it is offered to investors [4] as a private program [5] or a public program.[6] The most common forms of tax-sheltered investments include: cattle and other livestock breeding, cattle feeding, equipment leasing, motion pictures, farming, oil and gas, real estate, and timber. Although some types of business are conducive to sheltering taxes, tax shelters can not be recognized by names, business or industrial classifications. All tax shelters are not cast in the same mold. They can, however, be recognized by their characteristics.

With the enactment of the Tax Reform Act of 1976, [7] which places limitations on certain partnership activities (see, for example, Code § 704(d)), the current trend is to syndicate tax shelters (except those involved in real property) in forms "other than partnerships." These shelters are structured and packaged so that the entire ownership interest passes to the investing entity which may be an individual, a trust, a corporation, etc. This is a "private tax shelter" because there is no co-ownership of the underlying asset. If there is co-ownership, it may possibly be considered a partnership, and thus fall within the new partnership restrictions on loss and basis.8/ Generally, private tax shelters will be found in areas other than real estate because real estate is not covered by the new restrictions on partnership activities.

¶7.03
Losses

In recent years, many tax shelters have been formed primarily for their tax advantages. High bracket taxpayers are participants in "transactions structured for a loss" with little or no profit motivation other than the gain realized through tax avoidance. Note that while the Code allows deductions for losses arising from transactions entered into for profit, losses are not allowed from transactions entered into for loss (losses for tax avoidance).9/

Common in many tax shelters is a turnaround or crossover 10/ feature by which, after generating tax losses for several years, a shelter begins to generate taxable income. The mere prospect of eventual profitable years does not of itself indicate that the transaction is economically realistic.

> EXTRACT
> Benz v. Commissioner, 63 T.C. 375, 384 (1974).
>
> *   *   *   *   *   *   *
>
> While losses often occur during the formative years of a business * * * the goal must be to realize a profit on the entire operation, which presupposes not only future net earnings but also sufficient net earnings to recoup the losses which have meanwhile been sustained in the intervening years.* * *
>
> *   *   *   *   *   *   *

Not all tax shelters involve losses. Even an investment that has an expectation of profit could be an attractive tax shelter because of the timing of the profit or the way it is taxed. Generally such an investment has some or all of the following characteristics:

(1) Deferral of taxes

(2) Conversion of ordinary deductions to future capital gains

¶7.04
Deferral

Deferral used in this context is a characteristic of tax
shelters resulting in the postponement of income taxes.
In general, the tax shelter is a structure in which a
significant portion of the investor's return is derived
from "pass-through" deductions used to offset ordinary
income from other sources--thus creating significant tax
benefits. The tax shelter allows the taxpayer, in effect, to postpone 11/ the payment of tax or even avoid
payment of tax. The deferral of tax payment is the
equivalent of an interest-free loan from the Government,
the economic benefits of which can be significant.

¶7.041
Cattle Feeding

Cattle feeding is one of the most widely used tax deferral
shelters. 20/ Typically, the investment is organized as a
limited partnership or as an agency relationship (under a
management contract) in which a commercial feedlot or a
promoter agrees to act as an agent for the investor in
buying, feeding, and managing cattle. After being fed a
specialized diet for 4 to 6 months, the fattened cattle
are sold at public auction to meat packers or food companies. A venture of this kind is normally formed in November or December, and by using leverage 12/ and the cash
method of accounting, taxpayers with income from other
sources in that year defer taxes otherwise due on that
income by deducting expenses for prepaid feed, interest,
and other costs incurred in the feeding venture. Income
is realized in the following year when the fattened cattle
are sold. At that time, the bank loans are repaid and any
unpaid fees due the feedlot are repaid. The balance is
distributed to the investors. Since feeder cattle are
held for sale to customers, sales of the animals produce
ordinary income. If the investors were to reinvest their
profits from one feeding cycle into another one, they
could theoretically defer one year's taxes indefinitely on
the nonfarm income they originally sheltered.

Since most investors in cattle feeding shelters buy in at
the end of the calendar year, current deductions for
prepaid feed for the cattle were central to the creation
of tax losses in that year.

¶7.042
Egg Sales

Another deferral shelter involves the production and sale
of eggs. In egg shelters, almost the entire amount invested and borrowed can be spent on items for which deductions are claimed in the first year. These items include
poultry flocks, prepaid feed, and (to some extent) management fees to the person who operates the program for the
investors. Under prior law (before the Tax Reform Act of
1976), amounts paid for egg-laying hens, which are commonly kept for only one year from the time they start
producing, are allowable deductions in the year the hens
are purchased. In the case of farming syndicates, the
hens are now capitalized in accordance with new Code §
464.

¶7.043
Investment Credit

The investment credit is another feature of certain arrangements structured is tax shelters. Qualified assets
13/ are sometimes acquired with nonrecourse financing at
excessive prices to create an excessive investment credit.
Also if an entity terminates or assets are disposed of
early (depending on the length of time held), the investment credit may have to be recaptured.14/ Depending on
the termination point, recapture could range from 100%
(held less than 3 years) to 0% (held over 7 years).

Examiners are cautioned to give consideration to possible
issues involving overpricing arrangements.

¶7.05
Conversion

Conversion is another major characteristic of tax
shelters. As used here this is the obtaining of current
tax deductions against ordinary income, while the underlying asset will be sold at a later date with more favorable
capital gains which are taxed at more favorable rates.
Many variations of this characteristic exist. Illustrations of some are shown in the following paragraphs.

¶7.051
Constructed Property

A common conversion problem exists in the construction field. Builders have placed into partnerships constructed property (held for sale in the ordinary course of business of the builder) and upon sale of their partnership interest (after the long-term capital gain holding period) claimed long-term capital gain. This is an attempt to convert ordinary income into capital gain.

¶7.052
Silver Straddles

The commodity tax straddle is a method used to artificially create losses to negate the tax effects of short-term capital gain and convert short-term capital gain to long-term capital gain. This practice involves an investor who simultaneously buys and sells future contracts for different delivery months. Commodity tax straddles require little original cash outlay thus providing the advantage of high leverage. The availability of quick and relatively easy liquidation coupled with short time periods (usually not more than six months) are other sought after advantages of a tax shelter. Although the price of silver can fluctuate sharply, the price spread between the involved contract months is generally very low. For this reason silver straddles are a popluar form of tax shelter.

Example 1

On February 3, 1976, A, a calendar-year, high-bracket taxpayer realized a short-term capital gain of $35,000 from the sale of X Corporation stock. To soften the tax effect of the short-term gain, A, on February 5, 1976, arranged to buy 50 contracts of silver for delivery in December, 1976 (long) and on the same date A arranged to sell 50 contracts of silver at the same price in January, 1977 (short). Later, the price of silver increased by an amount equal to the X Corporation stock gain ($35,000). By closing out both legs of the silver straddle, A was able to offset the short-term stock gain by a short-term commodity futures contract and generate a long-term silver commodity futures gain: 21/

Short-term gain from X stock	$35,000
Short-term loss from Jan., 77 commodity futures contract closed out in July, 1977	35,000
Net short-term capital gain	$ -0-

Long-term gain from Dec. 76 commodity	$35,000
futures contract closed out	
in December, 1977	

For those artificial losses created to offset capital gains which are taxed at more favorable, the Service takes the position that when no real economic loss results, no deduction would be allowed under Code § 165(a). The same is true for related out-of-pocket expenses incurred in creating the loss.[15]

¶7.053
Real Estate

A real estate tax shelter, unaffected by the Tax Reform Act of 1976, [16] is a complex area for tax analysis. This is true because a real estate tax shelter actually represents an investment in a complex aggregate of interrelated but essentially different assets or elements. Land value may be a substantial component in one investment; while in an office building or store, valuable leases, or other elements may significantly contribute to overall value.

Usually such investments involve interests in a combination of:

    Land
    Buildings and their structural components
    Various items of personal property
    Leases
    Financing (both long-term and short-term)

The sum total of these factors represents the value of the investment.

When securing valuation assistance for appraising elements of a tax shelter, the examiner should explain, in detail, the structure of the transaction pointing out economic interests, for example, leasebacks and delayed delivery dates. To expedite the return of information, the examiner should specifically request details regarding both the economic reality of the transaction and the apparent fair market value. For this purpose, two requests for valuation assistance are needed.

The following examples illustrate the basic deferral and conversion characteristics of a real estate tax shelter.

Example 2

ABC partnership purchased a rental building on January 1, 1975, for $10,000,000 (minimum fair market value). The purchase was made by borrowing $10,000,000, as a mortgage on the property to be repaid over 10 years at an interest rate of 10%. No amount was paid on the principal in the first year. ABC reported the following transactions for 1975:

Rental computation:

Rental income (cash)		$1,000,000
Less:		
"Interest" paid (cash)	$1,000,000	
"Depreciation"	500,000	1,500,000
Ordinary loss for 1975		$(500,000)

Balance Sheet:

	1/1/1975	12/31/75
Building	$10,000,000	$10,000,000
Less depreciation	-0-	500,000
Total assets	$10,000,000	$ 9,500,000
Mortgage payable	$10,000,000	$10,000,000
Partner's capital	-0-	(500,000)
Total liabilities	$10,000,000	$ 9,500,000

Summary: The ABC partners would try to claim a $500,000 ordinary loss deduction for 1975.

Example 3

ABC partnership (example 2) sold the rental property on January 12, 1976 for the amount of the unpaid mortgage on the property.

Selling price	$10,000,000
Adjusted basis ($10,000,000 - $500,000)	9,500,000
Long-term capital gain reported on partners individual returns	$500,000
Less Code § 1202 deduction on partners' individual returns	250,000
Taxable gain	$250,000

Summary: Assuming no other capital transactions the ABC partners would report a $250,000 gain for 1976.

```
1975 - ordinary loss deduction   $500,000
1976 - ordinary income            250,000
Net income offset                $250,000
```

If in example 3, the property sale did not qualify for a §
1202 deduction, the transaction would result only in a
deferral of ordinary income. As shown, the transaction
involves both deferral and conversion (ordinary income to
capital gain).

Example 4

If the property (Examples 2 and 3) was acquired for
$10,000,000 and a sales commission of $50,000, you might
see it on the return as:

```
Rental income                                   $1,000,000
Less:
Management fee (sales commission)$  50,000
Interest                          1,000,000
Depreciation                        500,000   1,550,000
Ordinary loss                                 $(550,000)
```

Analysis (50% ordinary income tax bracket):

```
Loss claimed per return                         $(550,000)
Less commission erroneously claimed as
   management fee                                   50,000
                                                  $500,000

Add depreciation on capitalized commission
   (1/20 of $50,000)                                 2,500
Corrected loss                                   $(502,500)

Value of tax savings from
 1975 loss (50% tax bracket)                      $251,250
```

Summary: Assuming that there is a long-term capital gain
of $502,500 on disposition of the property in 1976, the
net tax savings from the investment, prior to considering
minimum tax would be as follows:

```
Tax savings attributable to 1975
  loss (50% of $502,500)                          $251,250

Less tax on long-term capital gain on
  sale of the property in 1976:
```

3178-02

```
First $50,000 net long-term capital
  gain taxed at 25%                          12,500
Capital gain in excess of $50,000
  taxed at 35% ($502,000-$50,000)
  x 35%                                     158,375     170,875
Net tax savings attributable to
  investment                                          $ 80,375
```

Note: The 35% maximum rate assumes that the taxpayer is using the alternative tax--there would be no §1202 deduction but 50% of net long-term capital gain would still be an item of tax preference. This assumes that in the computation of the minimum tax, the taxpayer had a liability for minimum tax prior to consideration of 50% of the net long-term capital gain. If the taxpayer did not have a liability for minimum tax prior to consideratin of 50% of the net long-term capital gain, the sum of 50% of the net long-term capital gain and any other items of tax preference If it is assumed that there was a 7 year deferral of tax, rather than one year as in the example above, the value of the tax savings attributable to the transaction would be as follows:

```
Tax savings attributable to deduction               $251,250
  of 1975 loss of $502,500

Deferred tax on net long-term capital     $170,875
  gain (see a above)
Present value of deferred tax
  liability if the tax is de-
  ferred 7 years and an interest
  rate of 10% is assumed
  ($170,875 x .5133).  This is
  the amount of money that would
  have to be put at interest at
  10% today to
  accumulate $170,875 in 7 years.                      87,710

Value of tax savings attributable                    $163,540
  to investment
```

Unless other issues are involved, regardless of the tax legally avoided, real estate tax shelters should generally not be examined when the participants acquired ownership at a true fair market value and possess the rights and obligations relative to the prevailing open market.

Coal shelters are usually structured around payment (or prepayment) of royalties and immediate deduction for the payments. The payments are usually made with small cash amounts and leveraged with amounts of nonrecourse notes.

Example 5

The ABC partnership was formed to acquire coal rights for advance royalty payments of $500,000. The transaction was structured as shown:

Cash	$ 50,000
Nonrecourse note (9 to 1 leverage)	450,000
Total	$500,000

The entire $500,000 was then claimed as a deduction on the partnership return.

New final regulations[17] were issued on advance mineral royalties curtailing the practice shown in example 5. The regulations make it clear that partners who invest after October 28, 1976, do not qualify for the deduction of advance royalty payments even though contracted by the partnership before October 29, 1976. The final regulations also limit the deductions for all other applicable provisions of the Internal Revenue Code. Specific mention was mad of Code §461 dealing with the deductibility of expense. Rev. ul. 77-489[18] (published December 19, 1977) further clarified this issue.

Vast numbers of coal shelters were formed late in 1976. Examiners should be alert to situations where after October 28, 1976, partners join partnerships having coal contracts acquired prior to that date. Possible back dating of documents should not be overlooked and fraud referral should be considered in those cases involving back-dating practices.

To avoid the Code §704(d) at-risk provisions, attempts are sometimes made to have the organization elect out from the application of the provisions of Subchapter K of the Code. This practice should not be permitted if the organization was formed under State law as a partnership.

¶7.06

Leverage

Leverage as used in the context of tax shelters is the practice of increasing the ratio of borrowed funds to risk capital. In the past, investors (in certain circumstances) were permitted deductions for interest, management fees, depreciation, etc., on the amount invested, and also for a prorated share of the amount the partnership borrows, even on a nonrecourse basis. 19/ Any loans, therefore, served to increase basis. Code § 704(d) as modified by the Tax Reform Act of 1976, limits partners' deductions with respect to partnerships other than those whose principal activity is investing in real estate to the amount the investor has a risk in the activity. Real estate offers leverage possibilities, as do cattle breeding and equipment leasing, although the latter two categories were severely restricted by the Tax Reform Act of 1976. The leverage characteristic is further discussed in the next lesson.

¶7.07
Summary

(1) A tax shelter will generally provide both economic and tax benefits--economic benefits will always exist.

(2) The limited partnership arrangement is most commonly used for tax shelters; however, other forms are also used.

   (a) General partnership

   (b) Subchapter S corporation

   (c) Joint venture

   (d) Trust

   (e) Corporation

(3) Unrealistic tax shelters are conducive to losses, although, not all tax shelters involve losses.

(4) Tax shelters come in many different forms; however, most will include some or all of these characteristics:

   (a) Deferral of taxes

   (b) Conversion (current ordinary deductions to future capital gains)

(c) Leverage

3178-02

Footnotes

1/ This term is explained in the glossary in front of the coursebook.

2/ Glossary term.

3/ Glossary term.

4/ Glossary term.

5/ Glossary term.

6/ Glossary term.

7/ Public Law 94-55, 94th Cong., 2nd Sess. (1976) 1976-3 C.B. Vol. 1, 1.

8/ Code § 761.

9/ Knetsch v. United States, 364 U.S. 361 (1960); 6 A.F.T.R.2d 5851; 60-2 U.S.T.C. 78,203, See also Goldstein v. Commissioner, 364 F.2d 734 (2d Cir. 1966); 18 A.F.T.R.2d 5328; 66-2 U.S.T.C. 86, 792; and Rothschild v. United States, 407 F.2d 404 (Ct. Cl. 1969); 23 A.F.T.R. 2d 69-637; 69-1 U.S.T.C. 84,016.

10/ Glossary term.

11/ Many deferral types of shelters were closed with the enactment of the Tax Reform Act of 1976.

12/ Glossary term.

13/ Code § 48, Definitions: Special Rules.

14/ Code § 47, Certain Dispositions, etc., of Section 38 Property.

15/ Rev. Rul. 77-185, 1977-1 C.B. 48.

16/ Code § 704(d).

17/ Reg. §1.612-3(b)(3) (T.D. 7523, 1978-5 I.R.B. 11).

18/ 1977-52 I.R.B. 11.

19/ It should be noted that Code § 752(c) limits to the fair market value the amount to be considered as a liability of the owner of the property.

20/ During 1974-1976, however, many feedlot operations suffered severe losses (real losses) and either ceased operations or significantly reduced their scale of operations. Stop-loss arrangements with investors were responsible for many of the real losses. See Code § 464.

21/ A would have to close the January, 1977 contract within 6 months of the acquisition and close the December, 1976 contract after the holding period requirements for long-term capital gain treatment had been satisfied.

LESSON 8

TAX SHELTER TRANSACTIONS

CONTENT

¶8.01
Introduction

From your previous training or experience, you know that a variation in any item, element, or factor can create a completely different picture. For example, variations in the participants' tax brackets can create different values in their minds.

There are many elements that can interact in structuring tax shelters. A few of the major areas conducive to examination will be discussed in this lesson.

After completing this lesson, you will be able to identify the more common tax shelter transactions.

Overpricing is one of the most common devices used in abusive tax shelters. The examiner should always keep in mind that the form of payment is usually critical in any shelter. What a person promises to pay is of little consequence if the person is not truly obligated to carry out the promise. It is a completely different situation when hard cash or binding obligations are placed at risk.

Valuation is a prime consideration in the audit of any tax shelter.

All elements of a transaction have some value (tangible and/or intangible). The crux of a good tax shelter audit is to properly evaluate each of those elements in their respective positions and to total their values in the open market (the true economic market as contrasted to the market for tax avoidance devices).

Keep in mind that seldom in today's market are major transactions consummated without extensive consideration being given to the tax effect. Therefore, the prime concern of the Service is not merely that there are extensive tax benefits flowing from transactions but that those benefits have their roots in true economic substance, taxes aside. When that economic substance is lacking, or minute, the sole purpose or prime purpose of the transaction is to evade or avoid Federal income tax.

In this area, where form and substance have undefined borders, continuous alertness of mind and direction is of the utmost importance. What is at first perceived as "simple" may in light of all the facts, prove to be merely "fragmentary" or a device to conceal.

Often property will appear to be overpriced; however, overpriced assets can and often do take on more subtle forms when they are used in a tax shelter. Often examiners will require engineering assistance in the evaluation of property: be sure to advise the engineer if there are any carved-out economic interests against the property, such as leases, extended delivery dates, or similar restrictions. A completely different analysis is required to determine an asset's fair market value within a transaction as contrasted to a mere "bricks and mortar" evaluation of the asset itself.

When and what the purchaser is to receive must be evaluated: Examiners should "present value"[1] each element from the time of future events back to the starting date of the transaction, using the current interest rate at the time of the transaction. In complexly structured transactions, the calculations are difficult and are better calculated by computer.

¶8.03
Leverage

Leverage as a tax shelter characteristic was mentioned in the preceding lesson. The transaction features of leveraging will be discussed here.

Leverage is defined as the ratio of debt financing to equity capital. The ideal leverage situation is where a party enters into a transaction for no cash contribution whatsoever, buying the property completely on credit. An even better situation is where there is <u>no personal liability</u>, with the creditors looking only to the underlying property as security. (This is known as nonrecourse financing.)

<u>Example 1</u>

Assuming a $1,000,000 purchase:

	Leverage
All cash, no credit	-0-
$500,000 cash, $500,000 credit	1 to 1
$1.00 cash, $9,999,999	999,999 to 1
No cash, $1,000,000 credit	Infinite

Overevluation and leverage (nonrecourse) are elements of most class III tax shelters.

¶8.04
Nominee

To bypass state usury laws, taxpayers often form corporations to enable them to obtain the necessary financing for their developments. Even though the assets are usually transferred by the partnership to the corporation (to satisfy the lender), some partnerships attempt to deduct the interest, depreciation, etc., on the theory that the corporation is merely a <u>nominee</u>. The Tax Court in such a case held that the <u>corporation</u>, not the partnership, sustained the loss, and thus could not be disregarded.

3178-02

Strong v. Commissioner, 66 T.C.12,21 (1976)
aff'd, 77-1 U.S.T.C. 86, 441 (2nd Cir. 1977).

* * * * * * *

The use of sham or dummy corporations to avoid
application of the usury laws is a recognized
practice in New York.*** There is no doubt that
petitioners sought to do business in partnership
form and that the corporation was, at least in
their eyes, a mere tool or conduit. Their argument is not without some appeal, but we conclude
that it should not be accepted.

* * * * * * *

¶8.05
Noncash Deductions

Deductions such as depreciation, amortization, and depletion are allowed without there being any cash expenditures. These deductions alone may provide the asset's
owner with profitable income offsets. In many instances
Congress has seen fit to accelerate these benefits (accelerated depreciation, etc.) as incentives to accomplish
various social goals. Whether the assets were purchased
for cash or on credit does not alter their beneficial use.
Because these deductions result from ownership, rather
than payment, extensive manipulations are found in this
area. An example of this is the structuring of the appearance of ownership by transfer of bare legal title
without transferring the burdens and benefits of ownership
but still seeking to claim ownership based deductions.
Excessive deductions are also often attempted by overstat-
ing asset costs or setting expected lives over too short a
period.

¶8.06
Accounting Methods

The accounting method of a partnership is determined by
the entity without regard to the partners.2/ The accounting period of the partnership is determined with reference
to the partners.3/ In multitiered partnerships it is not
unusual to observe cash and accrual methods of accounting
interspersed throughout the tiering structure. In such
arrangements the examiner should scrutinize all facts and
circumstances for possible distortions in income caused by
such reporting.

¶8.07
Timing

Timing is a tax shelter area often neglected by examiners. If an examiner views a tax shelter benefit as a tax-free loan from the Government, the time the taxpayer can defer tax is an important element in an overall economic evaluation of a tax shelter transaction.

Example 2

$100,000 tax-deferred for 1 year during a period when the going interest rate is 10% would draw interest of $10,000; for 2 years, $21,000, and for 3 years, $33,100, etc. It is apparent that over a period of time the value of the use of avoided or deferred tax can be of greater value than the tax itself.

A different use of timing is to be found in situations when an attempt is made to postpone a short-term capital gain for a sufficient period of time to transform it into a long-term capital gain. This is often attempted in straddle situations in, for instance, silver futures. Rev. Rul. 77-185 [4] gives the Service's position on this problem in the context of silver straddles.

¶8.08
Retroactive Allocations

Examiners should be aware of the prohibition against allocating, to a new partner, losses based on transactions which occurred before the new partner's entry into the partnership.

Although new amendments to Code §§ 704, 706(c), and 761 prohibit these retroactive allocations for taxable years beginning after December 31, 1975, the Service's position prohibits these allocations for tax purposes in years preceding 1976.

Relying on Rodman v. Commissioner[5] and the "assignment of income" doctrine of Helvering v. Horst,[6] Rul. 77-119 states that the new partner's distributive share of the partnership's items of income, gain, loss, deduction, or credit may not include any part of such items realized or sustained before entering the partnership.[7]

¶8.09
Services Exchanged

In many instances, some of the partners contribute cash or other assets, while others (often the general partners) receive a partnership interest <u>for services rendered</u>. The interest may be equal to that of the cash-partners, or it may be <u>limited</u> in some respect. Examples might be interests in losses only, or in profits upon sale of the underlying assets only after a percentage distribution to the limited partners.

Examiners should watch the capital accounts for inconsistent contributions by the partners. Some partners may have zero contributions, while others will have contributed the total capital in cash or other assets. It has been observed that, in some instances, the value of the services has been credited to the partner's capital account by the <u>accrual method of accounting</u> which was used <u>for capital account purposes only</u> and not reported by the partner as income.

¶8.10
Self-Destructing Shelters

Many instances have been observed where syndicator-promoters have been marketing transactions that convert ordinary income to capital gains. With the help of nonrecourse financing, the syndicator will acquire assets even though they are on the verge of bankruptcy or foreclosure, for the purpose of securing large ordinary losses for its investors, with subsequent capital gains upon termination and distribution of the assets to them. The transaction is geared to "self-destruct" by virtue of the probability (or inevitability) of foreclosure or bankruptcy and accordingly should be challenged on the basis that the transaction was not entered into "for profit," but was structured for tax avoidance. Additionally, examiners should not overlook the possibility of <u>tax evasion</u> in this area. Examiners should look for partners who "walk away" from their partnership as in Rev. Rul. 74-40.<u>8/</u>

¶8.11
Misclassification of Items

In tax shelters, as in all other audit areas, the factual determination of the classification of specific items must be based upon the facts and circumstances in each case.

¶8.111
Initial Costs

Partnerships (as well as other tax shelter vehicles) often
attempt to deduct large payments in the year of organization which are paid either to the general partner or to
"outsiders," and are actually capital in nature. Examiners should note that the classification given to the
payment is often misleading, thus requiring a strict
analysis of the substance. Since the payments may require
different tax treatment, Rev. Rul. 75-214 9/ and Code §
709 should be consulted for guidance in this area. A
synopsis of Rev. Rul. 75-214 is included at the end of
this coursebook. Additionally, in Richmond Television
Corp. v. United States 10/ an excellent dissertation is
given on "pre-opening expenses" incurred before becoming a
trade or business.

Taxpayers often label commissions (a proper Code § 263
capital item) as management fees, interest, or any other
classification that would make them appear to be deductible. Often, when the commission is substantial, it is
not unusual to see it fractionalized into any number of
classifications and amounts and spread out so as to appear
deductible.

¶8.112
Interest Expense

Examiners should be aware that various types of nondeductible payments may be couched under the term "interest."
When the transaction under scrutiny calls for a nominal
downpayment, examiners should consider whether the facts
warrant disallowing all or part of the "interest expense,"
under the theory that it is, in reality, a downpayment on
principal, or a deposit. 11/

Additionally, when "interest" is paid to a related entity,
care should be taken to insure that a valid indebtedness
exists, and that funds have actually been advanced by the
lender.

The "material distortion of income" approach, discussed in
Rev. Rul. 68-643, 12/ should be considered when examining
prepaid interest transactions by cash basis taxpayers.
Examiners should also be aware that the "distortion" test
is applied at the partnership level, rather than at the
individual partner level. 13/ Code § 461(g) requires prepayments of interest by cash basis taxpayers after December 31, 1975, to be deducted over the period to which it
is allocable.

Interest paid on a <u>contingent liability</u> is not true interest "for the use or forbearance of money." If it appears unlikely that the balance of the loan will ever be paid off, consideration should be given to disallowance of the deduction.14/

An examiner might find this type of problem in transactions in which properties are acquired through nonrecourse loans at unrealistic prices and the properties are being operated (as contrasted to passive investments such as net net net leases 15/) while losses are passed through to participants.

¶8.12
Evaluation Considerations

The examiner must be familiar with the industry of the shelter area. Each industry has its peculiarities and jargon, the characteristics of which lend to manipulation for tax avoidance or even tax evasion. Just to name a few:

Farming   -- Special accounting methods
Gas and oil -- IDC (Intangible Drilling Costs), capital gains conversion
Real estate
investment   -- Exempt from new Code § 465 (lesson 5) and § 704(d) (lesson 6) limitations.

Consider whether the tax shelter is structured on a reasonable economic basis. Because tax shelters are usually an extended financial venture they must be viewed beyond specific time frames. To the extent possible, the ideal would be to consider every facet from the initial formation through the final windup of its existence.

¶8.121
Prudent Person Approach

The tax shelter examination must be viewed through the eyes of a prudent investor. This does not necessarily mean as viewed by the personal standards of the examiner.

First and foremost, did the shelter have (aside from its potential for tax avoidance) a reasonable economic basis for existence? Could the structure actually at least carry itself? There is no question that a prudent person would not go into a transaction with the intent to lose money. However, a prudent person might well consider a lesser return on an investment which has beneficial tax aspects.

¶8.122
Burdens and Benefits of Ownership

Many abuses in tax shelters are based on bare legal ownership of assets. Legal ownership, in and of itself, does
not necessarily constitute ownership for tax purposes.
The salient points to consider are the "burdens and benefits." Thus ownership for tax purposes looks through the
form to substance. Ownership, in name but not in substance, is not ownership.

Example 3

Taxpayer A purports to purchase a depreciable asset (building) but at the end of 5 years the property must be
deeded back to the seller. Taxpayer A deducts depreciation during the 5 years. Under the terms of the transaction, A pays only interest for 5 years.

Facts in form:

A had title to the property.
A made "interest" payments on purchase paper for which
deductions were claimed.
A claimed 5 years' depreciation.

Facts in substance:

A had a 5 year "lease," which A calls a deed.
A had 5 years of rent payments which incorrectly were
reported as interest expense.
The seller retained the burdens and benefits of ownership
through the contractual obligation.
The seller, therefore, has the right to the depreciation,
not A.

¶8.123
Form

It is important that examiners recognize the substance of
the transaction, no matter how it is cast. Make sure the
transaction is in substance what it purports to be.

The following transactions, among others, in the context
of tax shelters often take on characteristics befitting
the desired tax results:

3178-02

Financing arrangement

Lease   Security

Purchase   Option

Sale   Loan

It is not at all unusual to observe transactions couched
in the form of sales and leasebacks when they are, in
fact, merely financing arrangements in which bare legal
title is transferred only for investment credit or depreciation purposes.

Also look for arrangements in which the end result essentially remains as if no transfer were made.16/

¶8.124
Front End Deductions

High front and deductions 17/ relative to the size of the
transaction usually justify questioning by any examiner.

Tax shelters often tend to bunch many items into deductible categories at the very start of the transaction.
This increases the early deductions of the participant who
may then benefit from the use of funds that would otherwise be paid in taxes.

¶8.125
Unreasonable Value

In the true world of economics, seldom will anyone part
with something of value for nothing. But sometimes, due
to circumstances, such could be the case. For example,
someone gets overextended and cannot make mortgage payments. Here it is possible to lose a true equity because,
within the limited time frame of a foreclosure sale, there
are no buyers.

A low equity and high debt to asset ratio, in and of
itself, is not necessarily indicative of tax shelter
abuse. It could possibly be the financing ideal, that is
everyone's goal, and still be structured upon true value
and reasonable economics. The examiner should verify all
facets of a transaction to determine whether or not it is
what it purports to be. The "true" equity (as previously
discussed in ¶8.02) should be determined relative to the
open market at the time of the transaction, not relative
to the purported purchase price and the related papers.

When the open market value does not appear to have a reasonable relationship to the outstanding debt (the debt is too high relative to the market value), the examiner should always determine why.

Many instances have been noted in which transactions between related parties were not arm's-length dealings. Even between unrelated parties, "phony paper" is often created to attempt to reach other objectives.

¶8.13
Summary

(1) Primarily, the elements used in abusive tax shelters are those which tend to produce noneconomically structured situations. Examples include: overvaluations (in any form), mishandling, misclassification, misrepresentation of specific items, interplayed with or separate from such items as depreciation, amortization, depletion, accounting methods, timing, and leverage through use of both recourse and nonrecourse loans.

(2) Analysis is perhaps the first and foremost consideration in evaluating tax shelters. Primarily, the analysis must start with an overall view of the total transaction based on reasonable economic reality (taxes aside). The analysis must be viewed through a prudent investor's eyes. The characterization of each facet must be determined not by the title it carries, but by the facts and circumstances in which that facet exists. The examiner should determine, for example, whether a deed is a deed or whether it is an option, a lease, a security, etc.

Footnotes

1/ This term is explained in the glossary in front of the coursebook.

2/ Code §446.

3/ Code § 706 -- usually calendar years.

4/ 1977-1 C.B. 48. Silver straddles were discussed in ¶7.052 of the previous lesson.

5/ 542 F.2d 845 (2nd Cir. 1976); 38 A.F.T.R.2d 76-5840; 76-2 U.S.T.C. 85,258.

6/ 311 U.S. 112(1940); 24 A.F.T.R. 1058; 40-2 U.S.T.C. 989.

7/ 1977-1 C.B. 177.

8/ 1974-1 C.B. 159.

9/ 1975-1 C.B. 185.

20/ 345F.2d 901 (4th Cir. 1965); 15 A.F.T.R.2d 880; 65-1 U.S.T.C. 95,421.

11/ La Croix v. Commissioner, 61 T.C. 471 (1974).

12/ 1968-2 C.B. 76.

13/ Resnik v. Commissioner, 66 T.C. 74 (1976).

14/ Marcus v. Commissioner, 30 C.C.H. Tax Ct. Mem. 1263 (1971).

15/ Glossary term.

16/ Frank Lyon Co. v. United States, 536F.2d 746 (8th Cir. 1976); 38 A.F.T.R.2d 76-5060; 76-1 U.S.T.C. 84,205.

Commissioner v. F. & R. Lazarus Co., 308 U.S. 252 (1939); 23 A.F.T.R. 778; 39-2 U.S.T.C. 989.

Franklin v. Commissioner, 554F.2d 1045 (9th Cir. 1976); 38 A.F.T.R.2d 76-6164; 76-2 U.S.T.C. 85,513.

17/ Glossary term.

LESSON 9

CLASSIFICATION OF TAX SHELTERS

CONTENT

¶9.01
Introduction

In recent years the term "tax shelter" has almost become "X-rated." We would do well to understand that the legality for tax shelters has been well established. Tax shelters were not only sanctioned by law but created by law predicated upon a basis of economic reality (business purpose).

What people can create, people can alter and abuse. It is in the area of abuse that we will focus our attention.

A classification of loss returns will place the tax shelter "abuse" problem in perspective: Class I (non-abusive shelters), Class II (abuses within the shelters), and Class III ((abuses of the shelter itself).

An in-depth analysis of returns that appear to be Class I or Class II shelters often reveals them to be Class III, shelters.

The examiner must always remember that the facts and circumstances within any specific framework will dictate the classification of that tax shelter. After completing this lesson, you will be able to recognize the principal characteristics of a Class I, Class II, and Class III tax shelter and determine its classification.

¶9.02
Class I (Non-abusive Shelters)

Class I tax shelters are those having losses which are perfectly legitimate in all respects: economic, form, substance, etc. A Class I shelter is illustrated in the following example:

Example 1

The investment return represents the return on the investor's out-of-pocket cash investment. The risk rate is the prevailing rate relative to the risk involved.

Formation date: 1-1-74 (Operating Entity)

Purchase price	$500,000	FMV	$500,000
Lease - rent (year)	60,000	FMV	60,000
Investment return	15%	Risk rate	15%

Claimed deductions (first year):

    Real estate tax paid
    Interest paid first year
    Management fees (actual services)

¶9.03
Class II (Abuses Within the Shelter)

Class II tax shelters are those which are economically viable but have abuses within the shelter. The abuses can be elements or items which were incorrectly handled, such as capital items claimed as ordinary deductions or mischaracterization of other specific elements. A Class II shelter is illustrated in the next example.

Example 2

The risk rate is a reasonable projection of the prevailing rate relative to the risk involved.

Formation date: 6-30-74 (Operational in 1975)

First year

Purchase price	$550,000	FMV	$500,000
Lease - rent (year)	60,000	FMV	60,000
Investment return	15%	Risk rate	15%
Claimed deductions: (first year)			
Interest prepaid (a)			

Interest on wrap-around mortgages (b)/1/
Real estate taxes
Payments to general partners (c)
Management fees (disguised commissions)
Commissions
Organization fees (d)
Loan fees
Appraisal fees (e)
Commitment fees (f)
Construction loan items (g)
Points
Pre-opening expenses (h) (d)
Timing factor of loans

(a) Rev. Rul. 75-152, 1975-1 C.B. 144 (distortion)

(b) Rev. Rul. 75-99, 1975-1 C.B. 197 (interest tax consequences to a real estate investment trust)

(c) Rev. Rul. 75-214, 1975-1 C.B. 185 (capitalization of organizational expense)

(d) Richmond Television Corp. v. U.S.2/

(e) Rev. Rul. 74-104, 1974-1 C.B. 70 (evaluation expenditures)

(f) Rev. Rul. 75-172, 1975-1 C.B. 145 (amortization: commitment fee)

(g) Rev. Rul. 74-395, 1974-2 C.B. 45 (one-loan concept)

(h) Commissioner v. Idaho Power Co.3/

The returns for examination should be considered on a number of points. To name a few:

(1) Is it a trade or business? An entity in the formation stage of its development is not a trade or business.4/

(2) The income relative to the formation date of the entity is often an indicator of when business started.

(3) Look for heavy deductions packed into the formation period. Often these items are properly capitalizable under Code § 263.

(4) Know your industry. Items that appear quite permissible as deductions in one industry might very well not
be proper in another. For example, a $25,000 yearly
management fee on a $10,000,000 real estate complex
(operating as rental units) might well be proper. The
same fee would be highly questionable on a triple net
lease$^{5/}$ on a $10,000,000 computer.

(5) Look for and identify those items that are improperly
handled in the context in which they are placed.

Placed in a different context, the same item could
well be proper. For example, expenses not allowable
as pre-opening expenses might well be allowable in the
context of an operating business.

.04
ass III (Abuses of the Shelter Itself)

Unlike Class II shelters having abuses __within__ the shelter;
the Class III shelter standing alone is abusive. Abusive
shelters are often very sophisticated, requiring broad
analysis of intricate interrelationships. In examining
them, the basic question is: What criteria will be used
in determining if a tax shelter was structured primarily
for tax avoidance, that is, did it otherwise lack economic
reality?

A financial analysis can reveal whether or not a tax
shelter investment is abusive. The key to this determination is a computation that compares the "present value"$^{6/}$
of all future incomes, with the "present value" of all the
capital invested and the cost associated with the shelter.
If the present value of all future incomes is less than
the present value of the money invested, the tax shelter
__may__ be abusive; that is, it was entered into for other
than economic purposes, such as tax purposes. In an
abusive tax shelter, the "primary" gain is the tax advantage.

Since investments are commonly entered into for purposes
of generating an economic return (profit), the tax shelter
venture should offer a profit that is at least equal to,
if not higher than, a risk-free rate of return. Such
return on alternative investments may range from the
conservative rates banks pay on savings accounts--or
interest on public or industrial bonds--to a "portfolio
rate of return." An examiner should study the validity of
the tax shelter venture and compare the economic return
generated with the available rates of return on alternative investments. For example, if 6 percent is an average
rate of return on investments and the tax shelter invest-

ments generate less than 6 percent, the investor's profit motive must be questioned.

Inflated prices, either direct or indirect (discussed in lesson 8), are at the base of many of the "structured loss" transactions in tax shelters. On the surface, the prices appear to be for fair value. However, upon proper detailed analysis of all interrelated factors, this often proves to be erroneous. Inflated prices reflected in the current basis of depreciable property give an excessive current depreciation deduction and often excessive investment credits.

Inflated prices (payable well into the future) are accepted by the investors not because of the value of the underlying property, but for the current tax effect that can be obtained. The arrangement is structured to make the value **appear** to be in the property, but the real value is in the tax avoided.

The parallel to the inflated price (in essence with the same effect) can occur when the income returned on an item is too small. Stated another way, the price was too high relative to the return. Often these arrangements produce an overall loss.

The question then asked is: "Why would such an arrangement be made?"

The answer is: To make a profit. A profit from loss: profit from tax avoidance.

Losses are claimed as tax deductions which, in turn, reduce what would otherwise be paid as taxes. Not having to pay tax is the equivalent of a profit.

Examples of Class III tax shelters follow.

Example 3

Formation date: 12-28-75 (Operational entity)

Sales price	$1,000,000(a)	FMV	$500,000
Lease - rent (year)	$60,000	FMV	$120,000
Return on investment	3%	Risk rate	15%

Claimed first year deductions:

    Interest prepaid (b)
    Interest on wrap-around mortgages (c)
    Real estate taxes
    Payments to general partners (d)

Management fees (disguised commissions)
Commissions
Organization fees
Loan fees
Appraisal fees
Commitment fees (e)
Construction loan items (f)
Points
Pre-opening expenses
Timing factor of loans

(a) Apparent excessive price, standing alone, does not establish "abuse"; other factors must be considered.

(b) Rev. Rul. 75-152, 1975-1 C.B. 144 (Distortion)

(c) Rev. Rul. 75-99, 1975-1 C.B. 197 (interest-tax consequences to a real estate investment trust)

(d) Rev. Rul. 75-214, 1975-1 C.B. 185 (organization expense)

(e) Rev. Rul. 75-172, 1975-1 C.B. 145 (amortization: commitment fee)

(f) Rev. Rul. 74-395, 1974-2 C.B. 45 (one-loan concept)

Also see Rev. Rul. 77-110, 1977-1 C.B. 58.

Example 4

Facts:

Syndicator purchased property for: $ 600,000 (FMV)
(1st mortgage only - no down payment)

Syndicator sells Bldg. only for: $1,800,000
(Wrap-around financing subject to
1st mortgage)

Gain: (Installment) $1,200,000

Terms: Payment by purchasers: $140,000 per year composed of $126,000 interest on wrap-around mortgage (7% of $1,800,000) and principal payment of $14,000 (claimed equity).

- Balloon payment on mortgage at lease end -

```
Payment    by seller on 1st mortgage:
           Interest - $600,000 x 6% = $36,000
           Principal -                  4,000
                                      $40,000
```

Profit: 66-2/3% on installment sale method

Leaseback from purchaser to seller: 10-year lease
at $140,000 per year.

Depreciation by purchasers: 20 year S/L

Purchaser's
Capital Account

```
Start                      $    -0-
Loss for the year          (   76,000)
Balance                    $(  76,000)
```

Purchaser's
Basis
```
Start (nonrecourse note)   $1,800,000
Loss for the year          (   76,000)
Balance                    $1,724,000*
```

```
*Asset basis               $1,800,000
Less: depreciation         (   90,000)
Adjusted asset basis       $1,710,000
Add:  claimed equity           14,000
(principal payment)
Basis balance              $1,724,000
```

A purchaser would pay a substantial front-end fee[7/] to
secure a shelter as shown in example 4. Incentive: to
avoid tax. The effects of a simple abusive tax shelter
structure are illustrated in the next example.

To avoid complicating the example, the fee was deleted.
It would usually be reflected by taxpayers as a "wash"
(additional deduction to purchaser; additional income to
seller). Other interacting factors such as expenses,
appreciation, actual economic depreciation, inflation,
etc., have also been deleted for simplicity.

3178-02

All activity relative to the lease and wrap mortgage payments are mere book entries.

Example 5

Purchaser (Lessor)
- Title Owner -

Rent Income		$140,000
Interest expense	$126,000	
Depreciation (5% x $1,800,000)	90,000	
		216,000
Net tax loss		($ 76,000)

Mortgage	$1,800,000	
Principal pmt.	14,000	Claimed equity
Balance	1,786,000	
FMV	600,000	
True equity	$ -0-	

Seller (Lessee)
- Beneficial Owner -

Rent expense	$140,000	
Interest income		$126,000
Interest exp. (1st Mtg.)	36,000	
Installment gain (2/3 x $14,000)		9,333
Totals	$176,000	135,333
Net tax loss	$ 40,667	

1st mortgage	$600,000	
Principal pmt.	4,000	True equity
Balance	$596,000	
FMV	600,000	
True equity	$ 4,000	

Cash Flow

Purchaser	Seller	
None	Payments on 1st mortgage	$40,000

1194

($4,000 of which relices 1st mtg.)

¶9.041
Intent of Parties

It is a well-established rule that the <u>substance</u> of a transaction, rather than its form, controls tax liability. "Form" is the pattern, method, or scheme which appears on the face of the transaction. Substance is the reality itself which underlies this outward appearance. The latitude of this area is as broad as the ingenuity of man. It is suggested that examiners not hesitate to take each bare element of the transaction, strip it of the title given by the taxpayer, and re-title it after evaluation. Often a completely different picture appears. As an example, a so-called "deed" transferring title to property with a provision for re-transfer in a few years may very well not be a deed in the common sense, but may in fact represent an <u>option</u>, a <u>lease</u>, or a <u>mere security device</u>.

A Class III shelter is one that lacks economic reality when viewed in its entirety. To prove lack of economic reality, an in-depth financial analysis is required. In a sale-leaseback, for example, present valuing at each of the lease payment dates of the income stream and residual over the life of the transaction would be the desirable method. Examiners should rely on engineering valuations <u>only if</u> all related variables (leases, leasebacks, carved out economic interests of any nature, etc.) were considered in the engineer's evaluation. The key question is, "Was the transaction entered into <u>primarily for tax avoidance?</u>" To help answer this question, the examiner must first gain a complete understanding of the transaction <u>in its entirety</u>. It is suggested that the following approach be used:

In <u>extreme</u> cases in which economic reality is lacking the issue often is relatively easy to pinpoint. However, the entire tax shelter area is one of continuing variation, and, therefore, the degree of variation can affect the economic reality (or lack of reality). In any transaction, the examiner should ascertain the answer to the following questions:

(1) Does the price, together with all of its related elements, bear a relationship to fair market value?

(2) Does the transaction provide any true equity buildup, thus creating a value to forfeit upon possible termination?

1195

(3) Does the transaction transfer the __burdens__ and __benefits__
of ownership?

Inquiry should be made as to whether, based on all the
facts and circumstances, the parties intended that ownership of the property pass at the time of the alleged sale.
The absence of such intent, however, is not established
merely by the use of nonrecourse financing, even though
the buyer can "walk away" from a transaction without
personal liability.8/

On the other hand, the fact that a sales price is to be
partially amortized should not automatically establish the
conclusion that purported buyers are building equity which
they stand to forfeit if they fail to complete the transaction.   If the sales price is unrelated to the fair
market value of the property, such equity may be illusory
and a mere bookkeeping entry. Conceivably, the equity
could also represent part of the price paid for an
option.9/

¶9.042
Pertinent Documents

To help determine the presence or absence of an "abusive"
tax shelter, the examiner should secure copies of all
pertinent documents regarding the transaction.   Examples
of pertinent documents are listed below.

(1) Copy of partnership agreement and any amendments.

(2) Copy of recorded certificate of partnership agreement
and amendments.

(3) Prospectus, if available.

(4) Projections presented to the limited partners.

(5) Sales circulars, advertisements, brochures of general
partner-syndicator, or any other representations made
as inducements to enter into the transaction.

(6) Appraisals, valuation reports, opinions, etc.

(7) Property tax bill and assessments (real and
personal).

(8) Escrow documents or abstract documents:

Instructions	Abstract of title
Amendments	Title policies
Closing statements	Commission agreements

1196

3178-02

Agreements   Other

(9) Purchase agreements, contracts, liens of any nature,
    etc.:

    All existing trust deeds and notes

    All-inclusive deeds of trusts (wrap-around mort-
    gages) and notes

    Land contracts

    Other

(10) Subordination agreements of any nature.

(11) Documentation on insurance coverage relative to
     claimed value.

(12) Construction documents, including building permits.

(13) Lease agreements/sub-lease agreements:

     Date   Terms
     Rent   Balloon payments

(14) Side agreements:

     Secure copies, if available. If there were agree-
     ments, and copies are not available, summarize in a
     narrative the essential elements. If there were no
     such agreements, a statement to that effect should be
     made in the workpapers.

(15) Options (to extend lease, to re-purchase, etc.).

(16) All documentation pertaining to the last arm's-length
     sale or sales prior to syndication. In this context,
     "arm's-length" means true third-party participation.
     The examiner must be alert to the possibility that
     though the parties appear to be at "arms-length," they
     may actually have side agreements or "understandings."

     Date   Terms
     Price   Other

¶9.043
Examining Procedures

        After obtaining the pertinent documents (and any others
        that may be relevant) the examiner should use them to
        determine the facts.

3178-02

(1) Trace all intervening transactions from the last arm's-length sale to the subject syndication sale, keeping in mind the relationship of all parties in the transactions.

(2) Check file with applicable governmental agencies: State Corporation Commissioner, State Department of Real Estate, SEC, etc. The Private Placement Memorandum on file with the SEC may contain many of the adverse tax consequences.

(3) Verify payments (by date) made by limited partners to the partnership. Verify partnership formation date, watching for backdating.

(4) Ascertain (usually from the partnership agreement) whether guarantees were made by the general partner. Examples:

Guaranteed profits to limited partners

Indemnification of limited partners from loss

Guaranteed return on cash investment

(5) Determine percentage of ownership by general partner:

Capital ownership
Profit participation
Loss participation
Liquidation participation

(6) Determine methods of payments, and by whom paid or owed:

Property liens - 1st trust deed, 2nd trust deed, etc.

All-inclusive trust deed (wrap-around) notes

Payments by cash

Payments by gross credits, (that is, lease payments applied to mortgage payments)

Methods of funding of limited partner contributions to partnership[10] Consider relationship between general partner and lender.

¶9.044
Economic Considerations for Leases

After analyzing the pertinent documents, the examiner should determine whether the transaction "makes sense" from an economic standpoint.

(1) What is the cash return on the investment relative to the risk? Does this return compare favorably with the "going rate"? It is suggested that the agent contact mortgage investment brokers, brokerage firms, insurance companies, and bank trust departments to ascertain the "going rate" on various types of investments.

(2) If the transaction involves leased land, what happens at the end of the lease? Does the building revert to the lessor, leaving a partnership with no assets?

(3) What are the provisions in the partnership agreement regarding subsequent "balloon payments"? Is it reasonable to expect the investors on nonrecourse financing to pay off a large balance which is far in excess of the asset's value at that time? Has the partnership provided funds for this purpose?

(4) Is the partnership insuring the asset for less than its "purchase price"?

(5) Are the lease payments to the partnership unrealistically low when compared to the purchase price? Are the lease payments similar or equal to the mortgage payments, so that little or no money flows?

(6) Does the seller lessee have complete control over the property, thus being, in effect, the beneficial owner (as contrasted to the purchaser, who retains bare legal ownership)?

If after examining the necessary documents, and answering the above questions, the examiner feels that the transaction lacks economic reality, consider requesting <u>computer assistance</u> to help in analyzing the present value of the lease income stream, taking into account all payment dates and all related data. A computer program has been developed by the Service for this purpose. If the final analysis reveals a transaction lacking in economic substance, examiners should consider disallowing <u>all</u> deductions, on the basis that the taxpayer has no equity investment in the property, and, at best, is only contingently liable for the debts. Alternatively, depending upon the facts, it may be that the taxpayer-investor has purchased an <u>option</u>, which might be written off at expiration. If the taxpayer has simply entered into the transaction for mere tax avoidance, the out-of-pocket expenses would not be allowable as a deduction should the partnership "fold."<u>11/</u>

(1) Not all tax shelters are abusive. As a matter of fact, most tax shelters are perfectly legitimate. In most areas of finance today, tax consequences play an importance role in decision making. The tax role is secondary to the basic economics underlying the transactions.

(2) Many of the tax laws have been designed to allow legal sheltering. Therefore, transactions entered into for profit and carried out in substance as well as form but producing a loss (tax shelter) are valid Class I tax shelters.

(3) When alterations of the elements or items are made (changing the name of commissions to interest or management fee, or any other name to make an item appear deductible) but the transaction still maintains a realistic economic base, such a shelter would be a Class II tax shelter.

(4) Regardless of how legitimate a transaction appears, how conservative the deductions may appear, or how extensively items are capitalized that would otherwise appear deductible, if the basis of the transaction could never reasonably produce a profit over its overall existence, it is a Class III abusive tax shelter.

Footnotes

1/ This term is explained in the glossary in front of the coursebook.

2/ 345 F.2d 901 (4th Cir. 1965); 15 A.F.T.R.2d 880; 65-1 U.S.T.C. 95,421.

3/ 418 U.S. 1 (1974); 34 A.F.T.R.2d 74-5244; 74-2 U.S.T.C. 84,596.

4/ Previously discussed with the Richmond Television case in lesson 3, ¶3.04.

5/ Glossary term

6/ Present value describes the discounted value of an income stream if it were to be obtained by investing money at the current inflation rate rather than in the activity. The present value is the amount of the investment required to generate the expected income. This computation compares the amounts invested with the income received or to be received, in terms of current dollars absent any distortion caused by inflation.

7/ Glossary term

8/ See Mayerson v. Commissioner, 47 T.C. 340 (1966), acq., 1969-1 C.B. 21; Rev. Rul. 69-77, 1969-1 C.B. 59.

9/ See Franklin v. Commissioner, 64 T.C. 752 (1975).

10/ Refer to Rev. Rul. 72-135, 1972-1 C.B. 200, and Rev. Rul. 72-350, 1972-2 C.B. 394.

11/ See Rev. Rul. 70-333, 1970-1 C.B. 38.

LESSON 10

CONSIDERATIONS BEFORE EXAMINING TAX SHELTERS

CONTENT

¶10.01
Introduction

In previous lessons you studied various problems in dealing with partnerships and the characteristics of tax
shelters, such as deferral, conversion, and leverage.
Previous lessons also discussed the features of the different classes of shelters: Class I (good shelters),
Class II (abuses within the shelter), and Class III
(abuses of the shelter). Knowledge of these areas is
needed to properly prepare the preaudit analysis of a
potential tax shelter return. In particular, care must be
taken in considering the substance (v. form) of the entity
and its transactions as well as in analyzing income,
expense, and balance sheet items.

After completing this lesson you will be able to determine
the practicality of examining the tax shelter return and
its related entities.

¶10.02
Analysis of Return

The steps taken to complete the preaudit analysis of a
corporate return must similarly be taken to analyze for
audit potential the income, expense, and balance sheet
sections of the partnership return.

The partnership is a conduit and not all income or expense
items are used to compute the ordinary income or loss
(line 26, Form 1065). Significant adjustments are often
required because the capital gains, contributions, etc.

1203

3178-02

are not properly passed through to the partners on Schedule K, Form 1065. When large amounts are involved, the failure to separately identify the items could significantly distort the partners' tax liability. Both the source of the income and the amount of the income should be determined. The determination would provide helpful information for ascertaining the business or nonbusiness classification of the partnership. The entity may be erroneously identified as a manufacturing concern when in fact the source of the income places the partnership in the leasing business.

An analysis of expense items could help determine the type of industry.

Expenses, such as depreciation or depletion, may require mandatory engineering referrals, based on the dollar amount of the deduction (see IRM 4216).

The balance sheet or capital account could reflect a significant increase or decrease in an asset or liability account. Negative capital accounts on the formation of a partnership would indicate an unusual situation to be questioned.

The analysis of the partnership must include an analysis of the partnership's Schedule K. The Schedule K will show the items of income or expense that were not reflected in the calculation of ordinary income or loss. The Schedule K will also show any disproportionate distribution of income or expense, for example, a 1 percent limited partner may be claiming 10 percent of the partnership loss. Many disproportionate distributions have a tax avoidance motive.

Any apparent contradiction between the income/expense portion of the return and the balance sheet portion must be noted. The balance sheet could show a depreciable asset while at the same time the expense section shows no depreciation (only other expense). In the pre-completion stage of building, expenses are generally not allowed and the examiner should consider correcting any deducted expense amounts.

¶10.03
Status of Return

Knowledge regarding the status of the return would help determine the examination steps to be taken, additional information needed, related returns required, referrals, etc. Is this a tax shelter return? If it is, what class of shelter is it? Is this a first year return, intervening year return, or final year return? Answers to these questions might be obtained from information entered on the return.

(1) Name on the return.

(2) Principal business activity.

(3) Principal product or service.

(4) Business code.

(5) Type of income or expense:

   (a) Royalties, rents, farm income, leasing income, etc.

   (b) Depletion, amortization, depreciation, intangible drilling cost, etc.

(6) Balance sheet items:

   (a) Buildings (Schedule L, line (8)), depletable assets (line (9), intangible assets (line (10)), etc.

   (b) Large liabilities in relationship to capital.

(7) Amount of nonrecourse loans.

   The methods of determining the tax shelter classification are explained in lesson 9. The Class II shelter is difficult to identify unless you have the initial return; the Class II shelter generally has the characteristic of a Class I shelter in the intervening years.

   The tax return assigned to you can represent a business activity in various stages of operation. The return could be an initial return, a final return, or an intervening year return. Example 1 shows a typical initial return with 6 areas to consider; example 2 shows a typical final return with 5 areas to consider. The intervening years' returns are readily identifiable.

Example 1

① (INITIAL RETURN)
U.S. Partnership Return of Income
FOR CALENDAR YEAR 1976 or other taxable year beginning
③ December 1 _____, 1976, and ending December 31 _____ 19 76

1976

A Principal business activity (See page 2 of instructions)	Name ABC Company ④	D Employer identification no. Pending
B Principal product or service (See page 2 of instructions)	Number and street 1 Apple Street	E Business code no. (See page 2 of instructions)
C Enter total assets from line 13, column (D), Schedule L $	City or town, State, and ZIP code Cherry, Virginia 22091 ⑦	F Date business commenced Dec. 1, 1976

IMPORTANT—Fill in all applicable lines and schedules. If the lines on the schedules are not sufficient, see Instruction Q. Enter any items specially allocated to the partners on Schedule K, line 15, instead of the numbered lines on this page or in Schedules D through J. (See General Instruction P.)

☐ If this is a final return
☐ If th~~is~~ ⟋⟍⟋⟍⟋⟍⟋⟍ ...truction S(3).)

Form 1065 (1976)   Page **4**

Schedule L—BALANCE SHEETS (See General Instruction K) ⑤

ASSETS	Beginning of taxable year (A) Amount	(B) Total	End of taxable year (C) Amount	(D) Total
1 Cash				100,000
2 Trade notes and accounts receivable				
(a) Less allowance for bad debts				50,000
3 Inventories				
4 Gov't obligations: (a) U.S. and instrumentalities				
(b) State, subdivisions thereof, etc.				
5 Other current assets (attach schedule)				25,000
6 Mortgage and real estate loans				
7 Other investments (attach schedule)				
8 Buildings and other fixed depreciable assets . .			1,000,000	
(a) Less accumulated depreciation			100,000	900,000
9 Depletable assets				
(a) Less accumulated depletion				
10 Land (net of any amortization)				
11 Intangible assets (amortizable only)				
(a) Less accumulated amortization				
12 Other assets (attach schedule)				1,075,000
13 Total assets				
LIABILITIES AND CAPITAL				
14 Accounts payable				
15 Mortgages, notes, and bonds payable in less than 1 year . .				
16 Other current liabilities (attach schedule) . . .				
17 Mortgages, notes, and bonds payable in 1 year or more . .				
18 Other liabilities (attach schedule)				
19 Partners' capital accounts				
20 Total liabilities and capital				

Schedule M—RECONCILIATION OF PARTNERS' CAPITAL ACCOUNTS (See Instruction for Schedule M)
(Show reconciliation of each partner's capital account on Schedule K-1)

Number of partners	a. Capital account at beginning of year	b. Capital contributed during year	c. Ordinary income (loss) from line 26, page 1	d. Income not included in column c, plus nontaxable income	e. Losses not included in column c, plus unallowable deductions	f. Withdrawals and distributions	g. Capital account at end of year
50	-0-	100,000	(200,000)	-0-	-0-	-0-	(100,000)

Schedule N—COMPUTATION OF NET EARNINGS FROM SELF-EMPLOYMENT (See Instruction for Schedule N)

⟋⟍⟋⟍ ...dinary income (loss) . . . . ⟋⟍⟋⟍

Example 2

① (FINAL RETURN)

Form 1065
Department of the Treasury
Internal Revenue Service

U.S. Partnership Return of Income
FOR CALENDAR YEAR 1976 or other taxable year beginning
③ January 1 , 1976, and ending **June 10** , 19 76

1976

A Principal business activity (See page 8 of instructions)	**Name** DEF Company
B Principal product or service (See page 8 of instructions)	**Number and street** 1 Orange Street
C Enter total assets from line 13, column (D), Schedule L $	**City or town, State, and ZIP code** Lemon, Virginia 22091

D Employer Identification no.

E Business code no. (See page 8 of instructions)

F Date business commenced 1/1/74

IMPORTANT—Fill in all applicable lines and schedules. If the lines on the schedules are not sufficient, see Instruction Q. Enter any items specially allocated to the partners on Schedule K, line 15, instead of the numbered lines on this page or in Schedules D through J. (See General Instruction P.)

② Check here ▶ ☒ If this is a final return.
☐ If this is a limited partnership. (See General Instruction B(3).)

1a Gross receipts or sales $ .... 1b Less returns and allowances $
Less: Cost .... line 34, Sch...

Form 1065 (1976)

Page **4**

Schedule L—BALANCE SHEETS (See General Instruction K) ④

ASSETS	Beginning of taxable year (A) Amount	(B) Total	End of taxable year (C) Amount	(D) Total
1 Cash		100,000		
2 Trade notes and accounts receivable				
(a) Less allowance for bad debts				
3 Inventories				
4 Gov't obligations: (a) U.S. and instrumentalities				
(b) State, subdivisions thereof, etc.				
5 Other current assets (attach schedule)				
6 Mortgage and real estate loans				
7 Other investments (attach schedule)				
8 Buildings and other fixed depreciable assets	2,000,000			
(a) Less accumulated depreciation	500,000	1,500,000		
9 Depletable assets				
(a) Less accumulated depletion				
10 Land (net of any amortization)		250,000		
11 Intangible assets (amortizable only)				
(a) Less accumulated amortization				
12 Other assets (attach schedule)				
13 Total assets		1,850,000		
LIABILITIES AND CAPITAL				
14 Accounts payable		50,000		
15 Mortgages, notes, and bonds payable in less than 1 year		50,000		
16 Other current liabilities (attach schedule)				
17 Mortgages, notes, and bonds payable in 1 year or more		2,000,000		
18 Other liabilities (attach schedule)				
19 Partners' capital accounts		(250,000)		
20 Total liabilities and capital		1,850,000		

Schedule M—RECONCILIATION OF PARTNERS' CAPITAL ACCOUNTS (See Instruction for Schedule M) ⑤
(Show reconciliation of each partner's capital account on Schedule K–1)

Number of partners	a. Capital account at beginning of year	b. Capital contributed during year	c. Ordinary income (loss) from line 24, page 1	d. Income not included in column c, plus non-taxable income	e. Losses not included in column c, plus unallowable deductions	f. Withdrawals and distributions	g. Capital account at end of year
	(250,000)	--	550,000	--		300,000	-0-

Schedule N—COMPUTATION OF NET EARNINGS FROM SELF-EMPLOYMENT (See Instruction for Schedule N)

1 Ordinary income (loss) (page 1...
Payments to...

1207

3178-02

The stage of operations is important for at least two reasons:

(1) Initial year returns involve frontend loading--the bunching of expenses in the first year of operation. At a minimum, the examiner should make needed adjustments for the Class II items.

(2) Final year returns may trigger the conversion feature of the tax shelter. The conversion of ordinary income to capital gain sometimes occurs on the termination of the partnership.

¶10.04
Effect on Partners

A partner investing in a tax shelter hopes to receive various tax benefits from the investment. The partner can derive benefits in several ways:

(1) The passthrough of losses.

(2) Preferential tax treatment (§ 1231 or capital gains).

(3) Investment and other tax credits.

(4) Any combination of (1), (2), or (3).

By effectively using the tax shelter for tax avoidance, investors in the 70 percent tax bracket can lower their tax to zero. They can even place themselves in a negative tax bracket (carryback of losses to prior years).

Example 3

Ignoring applicable credits, a married taxpayer with taxable income of $52,000 has a partnership loss of $50,000 in 1976.

	Taxable income	Income tax
Before loss	$52,000	$18,060
From partnership	(50,000)	
After loss	$ 2,000	$ 288

Before applying the partnership loss, the taxpayer had an effective tax rate of 34.7% on the $52,000; after applying the loss, the effective tax rate was reduced to less than 1%.

Example 4

Ignoring applicable credits other than an investment credit generated by ABC partnership, the married taxpayer's tax for 1976 on $40,000 taxable income is shown.

	Income tax	Effective tax rate
Applied to $40,000 before credit	$12,140	30.4%
Partnership credit	(10,000)	
Applied to $40,000 after credit	$ 2,140	5.4%

With the partnership investment credit, the taxpayer's effective tax rate on $40,000 was reduced from 30.4% to 5.4%.

The conversion of ordinary income to capital gains can also be an attractive feature of the tax shelter. The investors can offset capital losses generated from other sources or they can use the preferential tax rate. The maximum tax on capital gains is 35 percent.

¶10.05
Examination Decision

The decision to examine tax shelter returns is based on different factors:

(1) Class of tax shelter (if determinable).

(2) Tax potential.

(3) Administrative factors.

(4) Compliance factors.

The class of tax shelter is not always apparent on the face of the return. However, by now you should be able to identify the different classifications (these were discussed in lesson 9).

Class I shelters generally do not warrant examination. On the other hand, Class II shelters generally do warrant examination, and Class III tax shelters always warrant examination.

Adjustments, when made on tax shelter returns, may range from hundreds of thousands of dollars to several million dollars. The adjustments are then passed through to the partners, who are generally taxpayers in the higher tax brackets. Based on the large dollar amounts of the adjustments and the taxpayers' high tax brackets, these returns have high audit potential.

Each examiner is aware of the number of cases in his or her inventory and the priority that each is given. Several administrative factors must be considered before undertaking the examination of a potential tax shelter return. Shelter examinations often require detailed examination of the books and records. The examiner must analyze many lengthy (and often complex) contracts and agreements. Before undertaking the examination, sufficient time should be planned for this purpose. Other problems, such as audit plans, age of the return, or availability of specialist assistance (engineers, computer audit specialist, or evaluation personnel) should be considered before contacting the taxpayer.

Many identified tax shelters are controlled cases and, as such, an examination may be procedurally required. Before surveying a tax shelter return check with your group manager to determine whether the survey is permitted.

Public attention to a return or items on the return in clear opposition to announced policies or rulings are other compliance factors to consider before surveying or examining a return. Consult your supervisor if you believe an assigned return may have intentional opposition features.

¶10.06
Preaudit Analysis

The preaudit analysis is a significant part of the tax shelter examination and should be done with full consideration of the job ahead. The examiner must be prepared to analyze the basic structure of the tax shelter itself with emphasis on its total composition as opposed to checking isolated items. Because of the substance v. form consideration in most tax shelter cases, it is essential to question the activities of the promoter. Inspect the return and note unusual items following the usual preaudit steps for the partnership return. After the overall initial analysis, consider the specifics on the return.

If your analysis of the return identifies it as being a specific type of shelter, review the guidelines for that particular kind of operation. (Pending issuance of IRM guidelines for specific tax shelters, refer to Overview of Tax Shelters, Training 3147-01 (2-76). The "Overview" discusses general issue areas and other problems dealing with oil and gas, real estate, movies, and farming tax shelters.)

After becoming familiar with the specific shelter and the overall operation of the business, specific items worthy of attention should be considered (IDC, income forecast for movies, etc.).

Each shelter is tailored or structured to give maximum tax benefit to its investors. Investors seeking shelters that defer a large income tax liability may invest in a farm shelter or a cattle feeding shelter. The income tax is deferred to a subsequent year or years when the tax rates are lower. An investor with a large capital loss may wish to invest in a conversion shelter. The conversion of ordinary income to capital gain will offset the capital loss. The examiner must not only consider the usual income and expense adjustment possibilities on these returns, but must also be aware of the substance of the transactions involved. The return provides the form of the transaction; the substance must be determined during the examination. What is the economic reality? What was given up and what was received? These are questions that should be asked and answers obtained.

An integral part of the examination involves reading and interpreting various legal documents and agreements. Without properly interpreting such documents, the verification of income or expenses would not be complete. Whenever possible the documents should be requested before the initial interview with the taxpayer. This will help the examiner formulate relevant questions. For the convenience of the examiner, a checklist of documents is provided in lesson 9. The examiner may be able to use the services of other Federal or State agencies, such as the State registration commissions, licensing bureaus, the real estate boards, or the SEC (Securities and Exchange Commission). To assist in securing various documents, you should become familiar with the sources of information available.

¶10.07
Control Procedures

Initiate control over related returns at the beginning of the examination. Intra-district tax returns will be controlled based on district and regional policies. The out-of-district taxpayers must be controlled through the procedures set forth in IRM 4220 and IR MS 42G-376. It is important that these control procedures be implemented immediately.

To briefly review the procedures, the examiner must issue a Form 918-A, Notice of Examination of Fiduciary, Partnership, or Small Business Corporation, for all out-of-district taxpayers. If there are less than 100 partners the examiner forwards the Forms 918-A to the proper district office. If there are over 100 partners, the examiner will prepare one 918-A per district with a list of taxpayers in that district. If there are 500 or more partners from one region, the examiner will send one 918-A to the Assistant Regional Commissioner (ARC_Audit) of that region. The 918-A will be accompanied by a separate list for each district offce. In all the above cases, the examiner will send a copy of Schedule K-1, Form 1065.

Figure 10-A

**Control Procedure
(Form 918-A/ Form 918-B)**

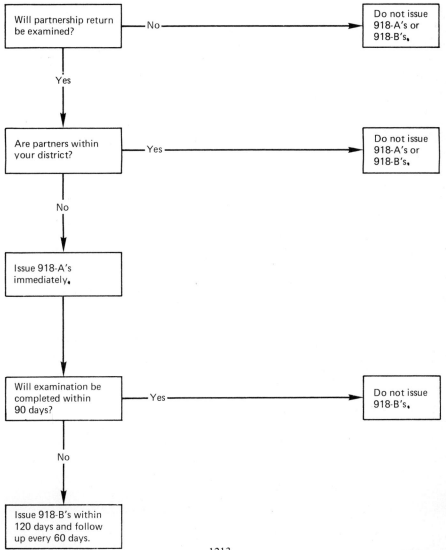

(1) Preaudit analysis is vital to tax shelter audits.

(2) The substance v. form aspects should always be considered.

(3) The status of the return can often be determined from the information provided on the return.

(4) A partner (related entity) can be affected by any of the following partnership items:

    (a) Passthrough losses.

    (b) Tax credits.

    (c) Capital gains and § 1231 gains.

    (d) Additional first-year depreciation.

    (e) Tax preference items.

(5) Decision to audit:

    (a) Class of shelter.

    (b) Audit potential.

    (c) Compliance factors.

    (d) Administrative factors.

(6) Preaudit of a tax shelter:

    (a) Usual areas of examination.

    (b) Special areas of examination.

    (c) Documents required.

    (d) Concept of "total" v. "parts" and "substance v. form".

(7) Form 918-A procedures must be followed for out-of-district taxpayers.

LESSON 11

EXAMINATION PROCEDURES FOR TAX SHELTERS

CONTENT

¶11.01
Introduction

In lesson 7 you reviewed the characteristics of a tax shelter and how to evaluate the significance of each characteristic. Lesson 8 dealt with the grouping of transactions common to tax shelters. Lesson 9 classified the tax shelters as a Class I (good shelters), II, (abuses within the shelter), or III (abuses of the shelter). Lesson 10 discussed the elements or considerations needed to make an examination decision and prepare a preexamination analysis. Lessons 5 and 6 discussed the effects of the Tax Reform Act of 1976[1]/ with its tax shelter limiting provisions--the § 465 "at risk" provisions and § 704(d) limitation on allowance of partnership losses. This lesson brings the preceding lessons together in the context of an ongoing examination.

After completing this lesson you will be able to expand the preaudit analysis to meet the needs of a tax shelter examination.

¶11.02
Audit Techniques

The examination of a tax shelter requires a __multi-dimensional audit__. The examiner reviews the overall operation of the entity. The segments of the entity are reviewed to determine how each relates to the other. Finally, the relationships and dealings of the shelter with other entities are reviewed for their __factual__ content. Review of all these elements often results in a substance v. form issue.

To perform a tax shelter audit, the examiner must revise the examination technique from a Code section-by-Code section determination of line items on the return to an evaluation of the overall structure of the shelter.

First the examiner must become oriented to the industry in which the shelter operates. The orientation is the foundation of the audit, for without it the examiner will not be able to properly evaluate the techniques used in designing the shelter.

The transactions described in lesson 8 are the elements a shelter many use to gain tax benefits. They include such elements as:

(1) Overvaluation.

(2) Leverage.

(3) The use of nominees.

(4) The advantage of noncash deductions such as depreciation, amortization, and depletion.

(5) Accounting methods.

(6) Timing.

(7) Retroactive allocations.

(8) Services exchanged.

(9) Self-destruction.

(10) Misclassification of items.

This partial listing should not be routinely applied; rather you should expand upon it as you uncover other transactions during your tax shelter examinations. Your familiarity with the operation of the particular industry being examined will prove helpful. Industrial operations material is available in most libraries and a wealth of current information is available in a variety of informative tax periodicals.2/ The Internal Revenue Manual also includes helpful information providing insight into the operational activity of different industries.3/ Examiners who are proficient in the industry within which the tax shelter operates will also be able to help you.

Lesson 9 includes a list of documents that you should examine before your first meeting with the taxpayer. When you meet, be certain the taxpayer or representative ex-

plains to your satisfaction each unfamiliar term or transaction. If the transaction appears difficult for you to
understand--perhaps it was designed that way. The more
complicated transactions often result in productive
issues. The time taken to completely understand the
transaction is time well spent. Ask questions.

Each industry has its time-honored methods of operating.
The tax shelter organizer blends the industry methods with
the provisions of the Code to structure a tax shelter.
Familiarity with the industrial vocabulary is very helpful
when examining a tax shelter.

¶11.03
Analyzing the Partnership Agreement

Generally the partnership agreement is the first document
to be reviewed. The agreement contains the partnership
intentions, which, of course, are meaningless unless they
are carried out. Paragraph 11.04 discusses the need for
objectively viewing events for what they are as opposed to
passively accepting the label provided by the taxpayer.

In your analysis you will:

(1) Note the term, activities, and structure of the
    partnership.

    (a) "Term" refers to the life or duration.

    (b) "Activities" refers to the industry in which the
        partnership will operate and the manner of opera-
        tion.

    (c) "Structure of the partnership" refers to the
        general or limited nature of the partnership and,
        in addition, whether it is part of a tier
        arrangement.4/

(2) Note the presence of any corporate characteristics to
    consider whether the entity meets the partnership
    classification requirements set forth in the
    regulations.5/

    EXTRACT
    Reg. § 301.7701-2(a)(1)

    ***There are a number of major character s-
    tics found in a pure corporation which, ta en
    together, distinguish it from other organi a-
    tions. These are: (i) Associates, (ii) an
    objective to carry on business and divide the

gains therefrom, (iii) continuity of life, (iv) centralization of management, (v) liability for corporate debts limited to corporate property, and (vi) free transferability of interests. Whether a particular organization is to be classified as an association must be determined by taking into account the presence or absence of each of these corporate characteristics. The presence or absence of these characteristics will depend upon the facts in each individual case. In addition to the major characteristics set forth in this subparagraph, other factors may be found in some cases which may be significant in classifying an organization as an association, a partnership, or a trust. An organization will be treated as an association if the corporate characteristics are such that the organization more nearly resembles a corporation than a partnership or trust. See Morrissey et al. v. Commissioner (1935) 296 U.S. 344.5/

*   *   *   *   *   *   *

(3) Consider the means by which the partnership is to be funded; determine whether the contributions from partners were by cash, loans, property, or services.

(4) Determine the proper method of accounting (vital to the timing of income recognition and expense deduction).

(5) Note any statements about or provisions for dealings with partners or affiliated or related entities.

(6) Note any reference to legal or tax opinions and obtain the opinions for examination.

(7) Determine whether the partnership agreement contains a completeness or similar type of clause indicating that it is the entire agreement.

(8) Note any provisions or references to modifications, amendments, schedules, or indebtedness.

This paragraph covers only partnership agreements. Other documents, such as the Prospectus or offering circular, should be similarly examined but will not be discussed in this lesson. Your study here concerns the determination of what the agreement truly depicts.

The examiner must consider questions concerning both partnership and partner aspects of the partnership agreement.

¶11.031
Partnership Level

At the partnership level other factors enter into the analysis of the agreement. The examiner must be able to determine what occurred at the partnership level. For this purpose the answers are needed for these questions:

(1) What did the partnership purchase, lease, or receive and when did these transactions occur?

(2) What was the consideration and what were the methods of payment?

(3) What did the other parties to the transaction part with in return?

(4) Is the transaction part of a tier in which a party (mentioned in item (3)) was only an intermediary?

The answers to these questions will help determine the scope and depth of the examination.

You may not need to ask all these questions, or you may need to modify them as you gain more tax shelter examining experience. For example, you may find that the tax shelter is a tier arrangement and you have an intermediate tier. The tier arrangement requires a decision on whether to start the examination at the first tier level.

A questionable transaction between related parties may be noted and a decision may have to be made about making third-party inquiries regarding the handling of the transaction in a true market place context. The possibility of disclosure must also be considered before questioning persons other than the taxpayer or an acknowledged representative.

¶11.032
Partner Level

The partners' questions asked at the level are similar in objective to the reasonable economic basis consideration given to the operation as a whole. At this level, answers are needed for such questions as (1) What tax benefits flow to the partner? and (2) What other economic benefits did the partner receive? Answers to these questions will help in maintaining an <u>unbiased view</u> of whether the exami-

1219   3178-02

nation is really necessary. When additional facts negate
a Class III shelter issue leaving only a Class I shelter,
the examiner should objectively conclude that additional
examination effort is not warranted.

¶11.04
The Future of Tax Shelters

The Tax Reform Act of 1976 revised Code § 704(d) to restrict the losses allowed to the amount of basis. For
that purpose, a partner is not allowed any basis or liabilities for which she is not personally liable. Leverage through use of debt is not really affected. New Code
§ 465 with its limitations applying to four activity
groupings irrespective of structure dictates that tax
shelters must constantly seek new methods to exist.

To cope with the undetermined future of tax shelters, the
successful examiner must keep abreast of the current
practices in shelter areas of various industries, whether
they relate to Form 1065 or to Forms 1040, 1041, 1120, or
1120-S. For all practical purposes, the multidimensional
audit techniques, and document identification review and
analysis discussed for Forms 1065 in this course, can be
modified and used for examining other tax shelter structures regardless of the form used.

Tax shelters have been around since the first Revenue Act
of 1913 and even though many known tax shelters were
curtailed by the Tax Reform Act of 1976 new shelters
appear, indicating that "* * *some promoters are pushing
harder and harder against the edges of the tax law to
produce new shelter products and in some cases may be
passing the bounds of tax avoidance and entering the world
of tax evasion."7/

¶11.05
Summary

(1) The examination of a tax shelter requires a multidimensional audit.

(2) The audit of a tax shelter is of the overall structure
rather than a line-by-line item Code section review of
the return.

(3) The examiner must be familiar with the industry vocabulary and methods of operation.

(4) The partnership agreement should be reviewed to determine the intentions of the partnership and for leads
or references to other documents.

(5) The tax shelter has to be evaluated in terms of reasonable economic basis.

(6) The partnership examination material covered in this course can be fitted to the examination of future tax shelters within any context.

Footnotes

1/ Public Law 94-455, 94th Cong., 2nd Sess. (1976), 1976-3 C.B. Vol. l, l.

2/ Non-Recourse Loans to Partnerships in Oil Deals (Journal of Taxation, May 1972).

Use of Non-Recourse Loans in Tax Planning: The Possiblities and Pitfalls. (Journal of Taxation, November 1973).

Real Estate Tax Shelters - Everything you wanted to know but did not know what to ask. (Taxes, The Tax Magazine, December 1973).

Motion Pictures as a Tax Shelter: A Current Analysis of the Technique and the Problems. (Journal of Taxation, May 1974).

Special Real Estate Financing Techniques Hybrid Financing - "Kickers and Sweetners" (Journal of Real Estate Tax, November 1974).

The Strategy of a Tax Shelter. (Journal of Accountancy, November 1975).

Earmarks of Profit Motiviation in Tax Shelters. (Journal of Taxation, November 1976).

A comprehensive listing is available in libraries having a periodical reference service published by Commerce Clearing House titled Federal Tax Articles. See also Index to Federal Tax Articles, complied by Gersham Goldstein and published by Warren, Gorham, & Lamont.

3/ IRM 4232, Techniques Handbook for Specialized Industries; also see Overview of Tax Shelters, Training 3147-01 (2-76).

4/ This term is explained in the glossary in front of the coursebook. See also partnership loss allocations involving tier arrangements: Rev. Rul. 77-309, 1977-35 I.R.B. 19; Rev. Rul. 77-311, 1977-35 I.R.B. 21.

5/ Reg. §301.7701-1 through 301.7701-3.

6/ XV-1 C.B. 264; 16 A.F.T.R. 1274; 36-1 U.S.T.C. 47.

7/ IRS News Release: Remarks of Jerome Kurtz, Commissioner of Internal Revenue, at the 30th Annual Federal Tax Conference, The University of Chicago Law School, Chicago, Illinois, October 26, 1977.

3178-02

Figure 11-A
MacRae v. Commissioner, 34 T.C. 20(1960).

[1] GORDON MACRAE AND SHEILA MACRAE, PETITIONERS, V.
OF INTERNAL REVENUE, RESPONDENT.

ALBERT GORDON MACRAE AND SHEILA MACRAE, PETITIONERS, V.
COMMISSIONER OF INTERNAL REVENUE, RESPONDENT.

Docket Nos. 61091, 67789. Filed April 12, 1960.

Held, on the facts, petitioners did not purchase various amounts of United States Treasury notes and Land Bank bonds, did not borrow large sums of money, and did not pay any amount deductible as interest.

Bernard Speisman, Esq., and Jerald S. Schutzbank, Esq., for the petitioners.

Mark Townsend, Esq., and Michael P. McLeod, Esq., for the respondent.

FORRESTER, Judge: Respondent has determined deficiencies and an addition in the income tax of petitioners for the calendar years 1952 and 1953 as follows:

Year	Deficiency	Addition Sec. 294(d)(2)
1952 ---	$23,998.38	---------
1953 ---	109,768.42	$6,172.19

Petitioners raise no separate contentions with respect to the addition for 1953; consequently, the sole issue remaining is the deductibility of certain purported interest payments.

FINDINGS OF FACT.

[2]   The stipulated facts are so found.

At all times material petitioners have been husband and wife residing in Beverly Hills, California. Their joint income tax returns for the calendar years 1952 and 1953 were filed on the cash basis with the director of internal revenue at Los Angeles. Gordon MacRae, also known as Albert Gordon MacRae, will be referred to as the petitioner.

[3]   Petitioner is a well-known entertainer. Prior to the years in question he had made no substantial investments in securities. His business and financial matters were handled for him by his attorneys.

1225

[4]   B. Gerald Cantor has at all times material been president of
Cantor, Fitzgerald & Co., Inc. (hereinafter called C-F),
brokers and dealers in securities. In December 1952, Cantor
and petitioner's attorneys discussed the possibility that some
of the latters' clients might purchase substantial face amounts
of United States Treasury notes (hereinafter called notes) with
a minimal downpayment, using borrowed funds for the bulk of the
purchase price.

[5]   Shortly thereafter, one of petitioner's attorneys advised
him that he could purchase $1 million in notes primarily with
borrowed money, and that the interest on the loan would be a
"good tax deduction."   Petitioner was further advised that a
profit reportable as a capital gain was possible, and that the
loan could be made on a nonrecourse basis.

[6]   Petitioner did not seek further details. He did not know
nor did he inquire as to the interest rate required on the
loan, the rate of return on the notes, or the possiblity of
profit or loss on the entire transaction apart from tax considerations. His principal purpose in agreeing thereto was the
creation of a deduction for tax purposes.

[7]   On December 19, 1952, with settlement date of December 26,
petitioner placed with C-F an order to purchase for his account
1 3/8 percent notes, maturing March 15, 1954, in the face
amount of $1 million. The confirmation slip of C-F showed the
price as $992,500, with accrued interest of $3,874.31.   Thereupon, petitioner (1) issued a check in the amount of $3,874.31,
which C-F received on or about December 26, 1952, and (2)
executed and delivered to C-F his promissory note in the amount
of $992,500, dated December 26, 1952, and due March 15, 1954,
with interest at 2 1/2 percent per annum.

[8]   Petitioner's note was without personal liability.   It was
limited to the collateral security, consisting of the notes.
It provided that petitioner might sell the notes at any time,
and discharge the indebtedness by payment of the net proceeds
received. He might also anticipate payment by paying additional interest of one-half percent per annum prorated to the
maturity date of March 15, 1954. The note contained the following provision:

[9]   The undersigned has paid the interest, due and to be due
hereunder, concurrently with the execution hereof, and hereby
gives obligee a lien against the securities pledged for the
principal amount of the indebtedness set forth herein, and
obligee may re-hypothecate or borrow the said securities,
provided, however, that such re-hypothecation or borrowing
shall not be inconsistent in any manner with the ownership by
the undersigned of said securities. Undersigned shall have the
right to obtain the return of said securities in kind at any

time upon tender of payment of the principal indebtedness due hereunder.

[10]   When petitioner placed his above order with C-F, the latter had no notes in inventory. On December 26, 1952, C-F went through the mechanics of both buying and selling $2 million in such notes, which amount included the $1 million ordered by petitioner. At the close of business on December 26, 1952, C-F's inventory did not include any notes.

[11]   The transaction whereby C-F bought and sold the notes was as follows: C-F arranged a purchase from and sale to C. F. Childs (hereinafter called Childs), a dealer in securities, to be effected the same day. Carl M. Loeb Rhoads & Co., Inc. (hereinafter called Rhoads), acted as clearance agent. Pursuant to instructions from C-F, Rhoads received the notes against payment to Childs, and on the same day redelivered them to Childs against payment from the latter. C-F was charged a clearance fee and any differential between the purchase and sale prices.

[12]   The sale to Childs constituted a "borrowing" by C-F of the notes in accordance with the above-quoted provision of petitioner's note, a common practice among dealers and brokers in securities.

[13]   On December 26, 1952, petitioner issued to C-F a check in the amount of $30,257.42, purportedly as interest to March 15, 1954.

[14]   The Gibraltar Financial Corporation (hereinafter called Gibraltar) was incorporated on or about December 24, 1952. Initial working capital consisted of $1,500 in borrowed money and $2,000 of capital investment paid in on December 29, 1952. No further capital was invested in Gibraltar at any time pertinent.

[15]   For the period December 24 to December 31, 1952, Gibraltar's records reflect loans to customers in the amount of $17 million, with another $17 million in such loans for the following month. The first such loan, in the amount of $1,020,000, is recorded as being made December 26, 1952. All "loans" listed on Gibraltar's books during the period here in issue arose through transactions similar to those of petitioner, as hereinafter described.

[16]   Gibraltar's balance sheet was as follows on the dates shown below:

The Gibraltar Financial Corporation Balance Sheet

	Dec. 24, 1952 (date of incorporation)	Dec. 1, 1953
Assets:		
Cash in banks................	$2,000	$23,913.88
Notes and accounts receivable..............		126,609,919.61
Securities owned-long......................		20,158.68
Other assets..............................		1,084.53
Total......................	2,000	126,655,076.70
Liabilities:		
Accounts payable...........................		15,706.75
Accrued expenses-taxes......................		17,058.42
Securities borrowed........................		126,623,456.20
Capital stock................	2,000	2,000.00
Deficit...................................		(3,144.67)
Total......................	2,000	126,655,076.70

[17]   On or about January 26, 1953, petitioner's purported loan owing to C-F was refinanced through Gibraltar, petitioner executing a new note. Under its terms, Gibraltar was substituted for C-F as payee, the nonrecourse feature was eliminated, the interest rate was reduced from 2.5 percent to 2.42 percent, the amount of the "loan" was increased from $992,500 to $1,020,000 (face value of the notes plus interest coupons), and the right to a refund of a portion of interest upon prepayment was eliminated.

[18]   On the same day, petitioner issued his check to C-F, as correspondent for Gibraltar, in the amount of $27,930.11, purportedly as interest to March 15, 1954, on the new note. At the same time, he received a check from C-F in the amount of $28,082.08, as refund of interest on cancellation of the old note.

[19]   Under the terms of the new note, the $1 million in notes was pledged as collateral security. In accordance with this arrangement, petitioner directed C-F to deliver the notes to Gibraltar against payment of $1,020,000. C-F did not then have the notes, and the transfer of the notes and liability was accomplished by book entries of C-F and Gibraltar.

[20]   On August 12, 1953, petitioner purported to sell the notes to C-F at a total price of $1,001,891.98, including accrued interest in the amount of $5,641.98. He authorized C-F to receive the notes from Gibraltar against payment, and on the same day instructed Gibraltar to deliver the notes to C-F against payment.

[21]   Pursuant to petitioner's instructions, Gibraltar placed an order with Guaranty Trust Company of New York (hereinafter called Guaranty) dated August 12 with settlement date of August 13, 1953, for $1 million in notes at a total purchase price, including accrued interest, in the amount of $1,002,204.48, to be delivered to Irving Trust Company (hereinafter called Irving) as clearance agent. At the same time, Gibraltar instructed Irving to receive the notes from Guaranty against payment of $1,002,204.48, and to deliver $1 million in notes to the Chemical Bank & Trust Company (hereinafter called Chemical) as clearance agent for C-F against payment of $1,001,891.98.

[22]   At the same time as it agreed to purchase $1 million in notes from petitioner, C-F also arranged to sell the notes to Chemical in two lots of $500,000 each. C-F instructed Chemical as clearance agent to receive $1 million in notes from Irving, which was acting as Gibraltar's clearance agent, against payment of $1,001,891.98, and to deliver the same amount in notes to the bond department of Chemical against payment of $1,002,126.36.

[23]   As a result of the foregoing, Gibraltar and C-F were charged by their respective clearance agents with the clearance fee and the difference between the buy and sell prices. The only substantial moneys or credit utilized belonged to the clearance agents, whose willingness to use their funds or credit was attributable to the fact that they held instructions to deliver as well as to receive against payment, and that, apart from the comparatively nominal clearance fee and difference between buy and sell prices, no risk existed.

[24]   On March 10, 1953, petitioner entered into a transaction as follows:

On March 10, with settlement date of March 11, petitioner ordered C-F to purchase for his account $2 million face amount 1 3/4 percent Federal Land Bank bonds (hereinafter called bonds), due October 1, 1955-1957, and to deliver them to Gibraltar against payment of $1,925,555.56, the price of C-F's purchase. Thereupon, petitioner executed and delivered to Gibraltar his full-recourse promissory note in the amount of $2,104,000, bearing interest at the rate of 4 1/4 percent per annum, payable October 1, 1955, and renewable to October 1, 1957, with interest at the rate of 2 1/4 percent per annum for any such extended period.

[25]   The note recited that petitioner had pledged the bonds with Gibraltar as collateral security, and that $178,444.44 of the principal amount of the note would be withheld as security for interest, to be released as interest payments were made. Prepayment to September 1, 1955, was permitted at the rate of 1 1/2 percent from date of prepayment to maturity.

[26]   On March 10, 1953, C-F arranged a purchase of $2 million face amount of bonds from Childs with settlement date of March 11, at a price of $1,924,305.56, and instructed Chemical as clearance agent to receive the bonds against payment. On the same day, C-F instructed Chemical to deliver the bonds against payment in the amount of $1,925,555.56 to Irving as clearance agent for Gibraltar. In turn, Gibraltar instructed Irving to receive the bonds from Chemical against payment of $1,925,555.56 and to deliver them on the same day to Childs against payment of $1,923,680.56.

[27]   As a result of the foregoing, C-F and Gibraltar were charged clearance fees and the difference between the respective buy and sell prices. Two million dollars face amount of bonds were bought from and sold to Childs on the same day, and neither C-F nor Gibraltar ever actually received possession thereof.

[28]   On August 13, 1953, and October 30, 1953, petitioner entered into essentially similar transactions involving $1 million face amount United States Treasury notes 1 3/4 percent due December 15, 1955, and $1 million face amount United States Treasury notes 1 1/2 percent due April 1, 1958, respectively. Petitioner executed and delivered to Gibraltar full-recourse notes similar to that covering the bond transaction, in the respective principal amounts of $1,043,250 with interest at 2 7/8 percent and an interest reserve of $54,178.96, and $1,067,000 with interest at 2 3/4 percent and an interest reserve of $94,554.95. Subsequent to the taxable years in issue petitioner closed out these transactions as well as that respecting the bonds in essentially the same manner as already described with respect to the notes.

[29]   During 1952 and 1953, petitioner issued checks to C-F, purportedly as interest payments, as follows:

Checks Issued by Petitioner, Gordon MacRae, During the Years 1952 and 1953 to Cantor, Fitzgerald & Co., Inc. and Deducted in the 1952 and 1953 Income Tax Returns.

Date	Check No.	Total amount	Alleged loans dated					Miscel- laneous
			Dec. 26, 1952	Jan. 26, 1953	Mar. 11, 1953	Aug. 13, 1953	Oct. 30, 1953	
1952								
Dec. 26............	2079	$30,257.42	$30,257.42..	....	....	....	....	......
Total claimed in return.................	......	30,257.42	30,257.42..	....	....	....	....	......
1953								
Jan. 26............	2259	27,930.11..	....	$27,930.11..	....	....	....	......
Jan. 26............	Refund	(28,082.08)	(28,082.08).	....	....	....	....	......
Mar. 9............	2396	11,599.77..	....	....	$11,599.77..	....	....	......
June 4............	2735	11,599.77..	....	....	11,599.77..	....	....	......
Aug. 12............	3034	28,474.29..	....	....	....	$28,474.29..	....	......
Aug. 12............	Refund	(14,285.34).	....	(14,285.34).	....	....	....	......
Aug. 26............	3079	11,599.77..	....	....	11,599.77..	....	....	......
Dec. 4............	3420	11,599.77..	....	....	11,599.77..	....	....	......
Dec. 17............	3464	69,598.62..	....	....	69,598.62..	....	....	......
Dec. 23............	3491	2,631.43..	....	....	....	....	$2,631.43..	......
Miscellaneous adjustment..........	......	(33.99).	....	....	....	....	....	($33.99)
Total claimed in return.................	......	132,632.12	(28,082.08)	13,644.77	115,997.70	28,474.29	2,631.43	(33.99)

The first check, in the amount of $30,257,42, dated December 26, 1952, was received by C-F for its own account. The remaining checks were received for the account of Gibraltar.

[30]   In 1953 petitioner received various amounts from C-F, both on its own and on Gibraltar's account, purportedly as interest, a refund of interest, the balance due on a sale of notes, and a refund of excess loan funds.

[31]   Petitioner reported $34,094.82 in his 1953 return as interest income, and $1,562.50 as 50 percent of capital gain upon sale of the notes.

[32]   The original note of petitioner dated December 26, 1952, was without recourse because petitioner was concerned over a note of such size. Thereafter his legal and business advisers were able to assure him that in reality no risk existed, and all later notes were with recourse. This recourse feature permitted a slightly lower rate of interest, but its principal purpose was to strengthen petitioner's legal position in the event the deductibility of purported interest payments should be challenged.

[33]   Gibraltar did not at any time have possession of any notes or bonds, and consequently did not receive interest thereon. Its books do not reflect such interest receipts, but do credit petitioner with the amount of interest which he would have received as a holder.

[34] Petitioner at no material time intended to borrow money from C-F or Gibraltar, or to purchase securities with their assistance. Nor did C-F or Gibraltar ever intend to lend any amount to petitioner. The intent and purpose of all parties concerned was the creation of a deduction for tax purposes, through a transaction which in form would appear to create an indebtedness but which in fact was lacking in substance.

OPINION.

[35] After careful review of the foregoing facts, we find the instant proceeding indistinguishable in principle from Eli D. Goodstein, 30 T.C. 1178, aff'd. 267 F.2d 127 (C.A. 1). Cf., also, Knetsch v. United States, 272 F.2d 200 (C.A. 9), certiorari granted (Feb. 23, 1960); Danny Kaye, 33 T.C. 511, on appeal (C.A. 9); George G. Lynch, 31 T.C. 990, aff'd. 273 F.2d 867 (C.A. 2); W. Stuart Emmons, 31 T.C. 26, affirmed sub nom. Weller v. Commissioner, 270 F.2d 294 (C.A. 3); Broome v. United States, 170 F.Supp. 613 (Ct.Cl., 1959); Haggard v. United States, an unreported case (D. Ariz., Feb. 17, 1959).

[36] To be sure, formal appearances have been given more artistic attention in the instant case than in any prior proceeding, and petitioners rely heavily on this greater perfection of form. We discern no difference in substance, however. The results in the cited cases were obtained because the substance of each of the respective transactions differed from its form; petitioners here are not aided because this divergence is even greater in their case.

[37] Petitioners may prevail only if the payments in question were in fact and in substance interest, i.e., consideration paid for the use or forbearance of money. Cf. Deputy v. DuPont, 308 U.S. 488. The only money used here belonged to the banks acting as clearance agents. These funds were used for a short period (less than one day), and the banks were paid in full therefore, when they received their clearance fees. Gibraltar, the alleged recipient of most of the so-called interest payments, had no money, and neither it nor C-F forbore or permitted the use thereof, as a result of the "financial round robins" in which the parties engaged. Cf. Broome v. United States, supra.

[38] To be sure, each step taken, if viewed separately, constituted a normal business activity, similar to many real and substantial transactions consummated on any given business day. But we may not thus fragmentize the transactions here under consideration and view each step thereof as though independent of those which went before and those which followed.

[39] On any normal day of business some persons will buy and others will sell securities. Persons will borrow to effect

purchases, and dealers and brokers will hold securities as
collateral and, when necessary, borrow securities so held to
cover short sales. Lending institutions normally lend many
times their actual capital.

[40]   But these observations lose significance in the context of
the transactions now before us. The steps taken, each in
itself a legitimate commercial operation, were here each mirror
images, and add up to zero. The various purchases and sales,
each real without the other, neutralize one another and fairly
shout to the world the essential nullity of what was done.   No
purchase and no sale is essentially identical and with what was
done here, i.e., identical and virtually simultaneous purchases
and sales. The choice of the more complicated and involved
method of doing nothing had no purpose, save the erection of
the facade upon which petitioners now seek to rely.

[41]   We think appropriate here the following language from the
opinion of the Court of Appeals for the First Circuit affirming
our decision in Goodstein, supra, at page 131:

> Moreover, we are convinced that following the transac-
> tions of October 27, 1952, there existed no indebtedness
> from the taxpayer to Seaboard. Despite the transitory
> possession by the Guaranty Trust Company of the Treasury
> notes for Livingstone's account who was acting as the
> taxpayer's agent, there was never in substance either a
> purchase of the notes by the taxpayer or borrowing of the
> purchase funds from Seaboard. However, it would seem that
> these transactions did create a legal relationship between
> the taxpayer and Seaboard, but it was not one of borrower
> and lender.   Rather the net result of these transactions
> was the exchange of promises of future performances be-
> tween the taxpayer and Seaboard. The taxpayer promised to
> pay Seaboard a certain preascertained sum of money on
> March 15, 1954 or at any time before that which he
> may select. Seaboard in return promised to acquire and
> deliver to the taxpayer on the date so selected
> $10,000,000 face value of 1 3/8 percent United States
> Treasury notes maturing on March 15, 1954 with interest
> accrued from the date of the contract.

[42]   Petitioners urge that they had no actual knowledge of the mechanics of the transactions as undertaken by C-F and Gibraltar, and we
believe this to be true. We disposed of this point in the Goodstein
case by the following language at page 1188:

[43]   We think it obvious from the whole record that all the
steps taken were pursuant to a preconceived plan which
lacked substance and which was entered into solely to form
the basis for a claimed tax benefit. The actual purchase
by Livingstone of $10,000,000 face amount of Treasury

notes was consummated only to give color to the transaction, and, as pointed out, these notes were disposed of immediately. We think it apparent that it was the intention of all the three participants that the petitioner would not purchase the Treasury notes, that there would be no actual loan to the petitioner, and that he would not pay any interest. He did not risk any borrowed money. The only amount he actually paid out and risked was the $15,000.

[44]   The petitioner, in an attempt to show that he was not party to a prearranged plan, testified that he did not give an order for the sale of the Treasury notes, and that he did not know of the sale at the time it occurred. However, the evidence shows that he did, in preliminary conferences, discuss the proposed transaction with M. Eli Livingstone, including the tax consequences, and that in his note given to Seaboard he authorized Seaboard to use the securities. Accordingly, any action taken must be considered to have been at least with his acquiescence.

[45]   In any event, regardless of the petitioners' ignorance of the actual steps taken, they may deduct the amounts in question as interest only if they were in fact paid as interest on an existing indebtedness, which they intended in good faith to create. These payments do not fit such description. They were in reality the net consideration paid not for a loan, but for a tax deduction, and so viewed are plainly outside of the statute permitting a deduction for interest paid on an indebtedness. Cf. W. Stuart Emmons, supra, where we said at page 31:

[46]   In the case at bar we might well paraphrase some of the statements of the Supreme Court in the Gregory case. Thus, section 23(b) requires a payment for the use of forbearance of money, and not a payment in pursuance of a plan (the creation of an interest deduction) having no relation to the purported result, the purchase of an annuity. The real payment here was not the alleged interest; it was the net consideration, i.e., the first year's premium plus the advance payment of future premiums plus the purported interest, less the "cash or loan" value of the policy. And the benefit sought was not an annuity contract, but rather a tax deduction of that part of the gross outlay designated for that purpose as "interest." Petitioner did not seek an annuity, and in fact gave up all substantial rights of an annuitant in order to reach his true goal, deductions in an amount large enough to reduce his taxes in a sum greater than the net consideration or cost to him of the entire operation.

[47]   Petitioners correctly note that the interest deduction does not require a business or profit motive or purpose. It does, however,

1234

require a payment of interest on an existing indebtedness, and the contention thus begs the very point in issue.

[48]   Had petitioners in fact borrowed money for a vacation, or for any other purely personal purpose, they would clearly be entitled to a deduction for any interest paid on such loan, and we do not understand respondent to contend otherwise. We must first, however, determine whether petitioners in fact incurred a bona fide indebtedness regardless of their reasons for doing so. We are forced to conclude in the light of the entire record that they did not.

[49]   Petitioners did not purport to borrow funds for personal reasons, but rather in respect of hardheaded commercial transactions for profit. They acted within the formal framework of such premise, and it is in the light of the nature of the transactions as claimed by them that we must determine the reality or lack of it in what they did.

[50]   Petitioners here purported to enter into a profit-seeking transaction. Yet under the circumstances, no reasonable chance existed of realizing a profit, apart from the "tax gimmick" feature of the transactions, the very aspect in which they were originally presented to and found acceptable by petitioners. It is for this reason that we conclude that the transactions in question, the reality of which may be sustained only on the theory that they were commercial undertakings for profit, were shams, and must be disregarded for tax purposes. Accordingly, respondent's determination is here sustained. Cf. L. Lee Stanton, 34 T.C. 1.

[51]   Petitioners now seek, in the alternative, deductions for their net expenditures as losses under section 23(e)(2) of the Internal Revenue Code of 1939.1/

                        As authority, they cite the Court of Appeals in the Goodstein case, which reversed our decision on this issue.

[52]   In Goodstein the fourth paragraph of the petition reads in part as follows:

          c. If the said interest payments are not deductible, the Commissioner erred in failing to allow the sum of $14,722.02 as a loss deduction in the computation of petitioners' taxable income for 1952.

[53]   No such provision appears in either of the petitions filed here. The point was first raised in petitioners' supplemental brief. Manifestly, the issue was not properly pleaded, and we may not now consider it.

[54]   Respondent's present position with respect to the principal issue is to ignore the disputed transactions entirely for tax purposes, both as to income and expense. For protective purposes, he did not in the notice of deficiency delete from petitioners' income certain

items which should be eliminated under his present theory, which we believe sound. Accordingly,

Decisions will be entered under Rule 50.

Footnote

1/   SEC. 23.   DEDUCTIONS FROM GROSS INCOME.

In computing net income there shall be allowed as deductions:

*   *   *   *   *

(e) Losses by individuals--In the case of an individual, losses sustained during the taxable year and not compensated for by insurance or otherwise--

*   *   *   *   *

(2) if incurred in any transaction entered into for profit, though not connected with the trade or business; ***

Figure 11-B

Franklin v. Commissioner, 554 F.2d 1045 (9th Cir. 1976); 38 A.F.T.R.2d 76-6164; 76-2 U.S.T.C. 85,513.

[1]   Estate of Charles T. Franklin, Deceased, Southern California First National Bank, Trust Department, Executor, and Margaret A. Franklin, Petitioners-Appellants v. Commissioner of Internal Revenue, Respondent-Appellee.

Before: BARNES, TRASK and SNEED, Circuit Judges.

[2]   SNEED, Circuit Judge:

This case involves another effort on the part of the Commissioner to curb the use of real estate tax shelters.[1] In this instance he seeks to disallow deductions for the taxpayers' distributive share of losses reported by a limited partnership with respect to its acquisition of a motel and related property. These "losses" have their origin in deductions for depreciation and interest claimed with respect to the motel and related property. These deductions were disallowed by the Commissioner on the ground either that the acquisition was a sham or that the entire acquisition transaction was in substance the purchase by the partnership of an option to acquire the motel and related property on January 15, 1979. The Tax Court held that the transaction constituted an option exercisable in 1979 and disallowed the taxpayers' deductions. Estate of Charles T. Franklin, 64 T.C. 752 (1975). We affirm this disallowance although our approach differs somewhat from that of the Tax Court.

[3]   The interest and depreciation deductions were taken by Twenty-Fourth Property Associates (hereinafter referred to as Associates), a California limited partnership of which Charles T. Franklin and seven other doctors were the limited partners. The deductions flowed from the purported "purchase" by Associates of the Thunderbird Inn, an Arizona motel, from Wayne L. Romney and Joan E. Romney (hereinafter referred to as the Romneys) on November 15, 1968.

[4]   Under a document entitled "Sales Agreement," the Romneys agreed to "sell" the Thunderbird Inn to Associates for $1,224,000. The property would be paid for over a period of ten years, with interest on any unpaid balance of seven and one-half percent per annum. "Prepaid interest" in the amount of $75,000 was payable immediately; monthly principal and interest installments of $9,045.36 would be paid for approximately the first ten years, with Associates required to make a balloon payment at the end of the ten years of the difference between the remaining purchase price, forecast as $975,000, and any mortgages then outstanding against the property.

[5]   The purchase obligation of Associates to the Romneys was nonrecourse; the Romneys' only remedy in the event of default would be forfeiture of the partnership's interest. The sales agreement was

1237

recorded in the local county. A warranty deed was placed in an escrow account, along with a quitclaim deed from Associates to the Romneys, both documents to be delivered either to Associates upon full payment of the purchase price, or to the Romneys upon default.

[6]   The sale was combined with a leaseback of the property by Associates to the Romneys; Associates therefore never took physical possession. The lease payments were designed to approximate closely the principal and interest payments with the consequence that with the exception of the $75,000 prepaid interest payment no cash would cross between Associates and Romneys until the balloon payment. The lease was on a net basis; thus, the Romneys were responsibile for all of the typical expenses of owning the motel property including all utility costs, taxes, assessments, rents, charges, and levies of "every name, nature and kind whatsoever." The Romneys also were to continue to be responsible for the first and second mortgages until the final purchase installment was made; the Romneys could, and indeed did, place additional mortgages on the property without the permission of Associates. Finally, the Romneys were allowed to propose new capital improvements which Associates would be required to either build themselves or allow the Romneys to construct with compensating modifications in rent or purchase price.

[7]   In holding that the transaction between Associates and the Romneys more nearly resembled an option than a sale, the Tax Court emphasized that Associates had the power at the end of ten years to walk away from the transaction and merely lose its $75,000 "prepaid interest payment." It also pointed out that a <u>deed</u> was never recorded and that the "benefits and burdens of ownership" appeared to remain with the Romneys. Thus, the sale was combined with a leaseback in which no cash would pass; the Romneys remained responsible under the mortgages, which they could increase; and the Romneys could make capital improvements.[2/] The Tax Court further justified its "option" characterization by reference to the nonrecourse nature of the purchase money debt and the nice balance between the rental and purchase money payments.

[8]   Our emphasis is different from that of the Tax Court. We believe the characteristics set out above can exist in a situation in which the sale imposes upon the purchaser a genuine indebtedness within the meaning of section 167(a), Internal Revenue Code of 1954, which will support both interest and depreciation deductions.[3/] They substantially so existed in <u>Hudspeth v. Commissioner</u>, 509 F.2d 1224 (9th Cir. 1975) in which parents entered into sales-leaseback transactions with their children. The children paid for the property by executing nonnegotiable notes and mortgages equal to the fair market value of the property; state law proscribed deficiency judgments in case of default, limiting the parents' remedy to foreclosure of the property. The children had no funds with which to make mortgage payments; instead, the payments were offset in part by the rental payments, with the difference met by gifts from the parents to their children. Despite these characteristics this court held that there

1238

was a bona fide indebtedness on which the children, to the extent of the rental payments, could base interest deductions. See also *American Realty Trust v. United States*, 498 F.2d 1194 (4th Cir. 1974); *Manuel D. Mayerson*, 47 T.C. 340 (1966).

[9]   In none of these cases, however, did the taxpayer fail to demonstrate that the purchase price was at least approximately equivalent to the fair market value of the property. Just such a failure occurred here. The Tax Court explicitly found that on the basis of the facts before it the value of the property could not be estimated.   64 T.C. at 767-768.[4/]   In our view this defect in the taxpayer's proof is fatal.

[10]   Reason supports our perception. An acquisition such as that of Associates if at a price approximately equal to the fair market value of the property under ordinary circumstances would rather quickly yield an equity in the property which the purchaser could not prudently abandon. This is the stuff of substance.   It meshes with the form of the transaction and constitutes a sale.

[11]   No such meshing occurs when the purchase price exceeds a demonstrably reasonable estimate of the fair market value. Payments on the principal of the purchase price yield no equity so long as the unpaid balance of the purchase price exceeds the then existing fair market value. Under these circumstances the purchaser by abandoning the transaction can lose no more than a mere chance to acquire an equity in the future should the value of the acquired property increase. While this chance undoubtedly influenced the Tax Court's determination that the transaction before us constitutes an option, we need only point out that its existence fails to supply the substance necessary to justify treating the transaction as a sale *ab initio*. It is not necessary to the disposition of this case to decide the tax consequences of a transaction such as that before us if in a subsequent year the fair market value of the property increases to an extent that permits the purchaser to acquire an equity.[5/]

[12]   Authority also supports our perception. It is fundamental that "depreciation is not predicated upon ownership of property but rather upon an investment in property. *Gladding Dry Goods Co.*, 2 BTA 336 (1925)." *Mayerson, supra* at 350. (italics added). No such investment exists when payments of the purchase price in accordance with the design of the parties yield no equity to the purchaser. Cf. *Decon Corp.*, 65 T.C. 71 (1976); *David F. Bolger*, 59 T.C. 760 (1973); *Edna Morris*, 59 T.C. 21 (1972). In the transaction before us and during the taxable years in question the purchase price payments by Associates have not been shown to constitute an investment in the property. Depreciation was properly disallowed. Only the Romneys had an investment in the property.

[13]   Authority also supports disallowance of the interest deductions. This is said even though it has long been recognized that the ab-

sence of personal liability for the purchase money debt secured by a
mortgage on the acquired property does not deprive the debt of its
character as a bona fide debt obligation able to support an interest
deduction. Mayerson, supra at 352. However, this is no longer true
when it appears that the debt has economic significance only if the
property substantially appreciates in value prior to the date at
which a very large portion of the purchase price is to be discharged. Under these circumstances the purchaser has not secured
"the use or forbearance of money." See Norton v. Commissioner, 474
F.2d 608, 610 (9th Cir. 1973). Nor has the seller advanced money or
forborne its use. See Bornstein v. Commissioner, 334 F.2d 779, 780
(1st Cir. 1964); Lynch v. Commissioner, 273 F.2d 867, 871-872 (2d
Cir. 1959). Prior to the date at which the balloon payment on the
purchase price is required, and assuming no substantial increase in
the fair market value of the property, the absence of personal
liability on the debt reduces the transaction in economic terms to a
mere chance that a genuine debt obligation may arise. This is not
enough to justify an interest deduction. To justify the deduction
the debt must exist; potential existence will not do. For debt to
exist, the purchaser, in the absence of personal liability, must
confront a situation in which it is presently reasonable from an
economic point of view for him to make a capital investment in the
amount of the unpaid purchase price. See Mayerson, supra at 352.[6/]
Associates, during the taxable years in question, confronted no such
situation. Compare Crane v. Commissioner, 331 U.S. 1,11-12 (1947).

[14]   Our focus on the relationship of the fair market value of the
property to the unpaid purchase price should not be read as premised
upon the belief that a sale is not a sale if the purchaser pays too
much. Bad bargains from the buyer's point of view--as well as
sensible bargains from buyer's, but exceptionally good from the
seller's point of view--do not thereby cease to be sales. See
Commissioner v. Brown, 380 U.S. 563 (1965); Union Bank v. United
States, 285 F.2d 126,128 (Ct. Cl. 1961). We intend our holding and
explanation thereof to be understood as limited to transactions
substantially similar to that now before us.

        AFFIRMED.

_____

Footnotes:

1/ An early skirmish in this particular effort appears in Manuel D.
    Mayerson, 47 T.C. 340 (1966), which the Commissioner lost. The
    Commissioner attacked the substance of a nonrecourse sale, but
    based his attack on the nonrecourse and long-term nature of the
    purchase money note, without focusing on whether the sale was
    made at an unrealistically high price. In his acquiescence to
    Mayerson, 1969-2 Cum. Bull. xxiv, the Commissioner recognized
    that the fundamental issue in these cases generally will be
    whether the property has been "acquired" at an artifically high

1240

price, having little relation to its fair market value. "The Service emphasizes that its acquiescence in <u>Mayerson</u> is based on the particular facts in the case and will not be relied upon in the disposition of other cases except where it is clear that the property has been acquired at its fair market value in an arm's length transaction creating a bona fide purchase and a bona fide debt obligation." Rev. Rul. 69-77, 1969-1 Cum. Bull. 59.

2/ There was evidence that not all of the benefits and burdens of ownership remained with the Romneys. Thus, for example, the lease-back agreement appears to provide that any condemnation award will go to Associates. Exhibit 6-F, at p. 5.

3/ Counsel differed as to whether the Tax Court's decision that the transaction was not a sale, but at best only an option, is reviewable by this court as a question of law or of fact. We agree with other circuits that, while the characteristics of a transaction are questions of fact, whether those characteristics constiute a sale for <u>tax purposes</u> is a question of law. See <u>American Realty Trust v. United States</u>, 498 F.2d 1194, 1198-1199 (4th Cir. 1974); <u>ABKCO Industires, Inc. v. Commissioner</u>, 482 F.2d 150, 154-155 (3rd Cir. 1973); <u>Union Planters Nat's Bank v. United States</u>, 426 F.2d 115, 117-118 (6th Cir.) <u>cert. denied</u>, 400 U.S. 827 (1970). Cases cited by the Commissioner to the effect that the decision before us is essentially factual are inapposite. All of the cited cases deal with purely factual questions to which the legal conclusion is clear. See <u>Warren Jones Co. v. Commissioner</u>, 524 F.2d 788 (9th Cir. 1975); <u>Clodfelter v. Commissioner</u>, 426 F.2d 1391,1392 (9th Cir. 1970) (whether a contract had an ascertainable fair market value); <u>Muheim v. United States</u>, 524 F.2d 773,775 (9th Cir. 1975); <u>Northwestern Acceptance Corp. v. Commissioner</u>, 500 F.2d 1222 (9th Cir. 1974) (what the intent of the parties was in signing a purported lease agreement). In the instant decision, the factual issues were generally undisputed with only the legal implications uncertain. As stated in <u>Lundgren v. Commissioner</u>, 376 F.2d 623,627 (9th Cir. 1967), our duty is to decide "whether the Tax Court correctly applied the statute to the factual situation found by the Tax Court."

4/ The Tax Court found that appellants had "not shown that the purported sales price of $1,224,000 (or any other price) had any relationship to the actual market value of the motel property...." 64 T.C. 767.

<u>Petitioners spent a substantial amount of time at trial attempting to establish that, whatever the actual market value of the property, Associates acted in the good faith belief that the market value of the property approximated the selling price. However, this evidence only goes to the issue of sham and does not supply substance to this transaction.</u> "Save in those instances where the statute itself turns on intent, a matter so

real as taxation must depend on objective realities, not on the varying subjective beliefs of individual taxpayers." [emphasis supplied] Lynch v. Commissioner, 273 F.2d 867,872 (2d Cir. 1959). See also Bornstein v. Commissioner, 334 F.2d 779 (1st Cir. 1964); MacRae v. Commissioner, 294 F.2d 56 (9th Cir. 1961).

In oral argument it was suggested by the appellants that neither the Tax Court nor they recognized the importance of fair market value during the presentation of evidence and that this hampered the full and open development of this issue. However, upon an examination of the record, we are satisfied that the taxpayers recognized the importance of presenting objective evidence of the fair market value and were awarded ample opportunity to present their proof; appellants merely failed to present clear and admissible evidence that fair market value did indeed approximate the purchase price. Such evidence of fair market value as was relied upon by the appellants, viz. two appraisals, one completed in 1968 and a second in 1971, even if fully admissible as evidence of the truth of the estimates of value appearing therein does not require us to set aside the Tax Court's finding. As the Tax Court found, the 1968 appraisal was "error-filled, sketchy" and "obviously suspect." 64 T.C. at 767 n. 13. The 1971 appraisal had little relevancy as to 1968 values. On the other side, their existed cogent evidence indicating that the fair market value was substantially less than the purchase price. This evidence included (i) the Romney's purchase of the stock of two corporations, one of which wholly-owned the motel, for approximately $800,000 in the year preceding the "sale" to Associates ($660,000 of which was allocable to the sale property, according to Mr. Romney's estimate), and (ii) insurance policies on the property from 1967 through 1974 of only $583,200, $700,000, and $614,000. 64 T.C. at 767-768.

Given that it was the appellants' burden to present evidence showing that the purchase price did not exceed the fair market value and that he had a fair opportunity to do so, we see no reason to remand this case for further proceedings.

5/ These consequences would include a determination of the proper basis of the acquired property at the date the increments to the purchaser's equity commenced.

6/ Emphasis on the fair market value of the property in relation to the apparent purchase price animates the spirit, if not the letter, of Rev. Rul. 69-77, 1969-1 Cum. Bull. 59.

LESSON 12

TECHNICAL ADVICE AND REPORTS

CONTENT

¶12.01
Introduction

The attention given abusive tax shelters reflects congressional concern regarding the diversion of capital from
legitimate investments.

EXTRACT
News Release: Remarks of Jerome Kurtz, Commissioner of Internal Revenue.1/

        *   *   *   *   *   *   *

Any tax shelter reduces the equity of the tax
system by reducing the taxes of those able to
make such investments -- upper income taxpayers.
In some cases Congress has concluded that this
loss of equity is a tolerable side effect of a
special tax provision designed to encourage
particular investments. But in many cases -- the
abusive ones -- the loss of equity produces no
contemplated benefit to society or the contemplated tax benefits are magnified beyond that
anticipated. When such abuses become widespread,
respect for the fairness of the tax system decreases and voluntary compliance levels may
suffer. It is therefore essential for the Ser-

1243

vice to be vigorous in pursuing abuses that disturb the fairness of the system. The fact that many of these transactions are extremely complex and present substantial administrative problems to the Service cannot be allowed to interfere with the fair administration of the tax laws. New abuses may call for new responses.

*   *   *   *   *   *   *

The Tax Reform Act of 1976 made extensive changes in the treatment of many of the most common tax shelters and resolved a number of controversial issues. One of the consequences of this legislation has been the proliferation of tax shelters in novel areas of investment. In addition, the adoption of unusual business forms is being tried as a means of avoiding specific rules contained in the Act.

We are making a concerted effort to learn of new schemes as they are developed and to confront them as quickly as we can. It is important to give this guidance to investors who might otherwise be misled as to the Service's position.

*   *   *   *   *   *   *

To help in this effort, the National Office in formulating its operating and technical programs will be depending on you for information on changes in the tax shelter picture. New issues may arise on which the Service has never taken a position. This ever-changing environment requires communication between you and the National Office. This lesson will cover two types of such communication.

In addition, because of the nature of tax shelters, the closing conference and report differ in some respects from those for other cases. This lesson will point out the special requirements for the tax shelter closing conference and report.

After completing this lesson you will be able to:

(1) Prepare a request for technical advice

(2) Prepare a Technical Coordination Report and

(3) Identify tax shelter features of closing conferences and report writing.

¶12.02

Technical Advice Memorandum

       A Technical Advice Memorandum is a formal Service position
furnished by the National Office at the request of a
district office on a specific issue or issues in connection with the examination of a taxpayer's return or consideration of a taxpayer's claim for refund or credit.
The purpose of a Technical Advice Memorandum is to assist
district personnel in closing cases and to establish and
maintain consistent positions among the various districts.

       A Technical Advice Memorandum gives guidance for the
interpretation and proper application of the Internal
Revenue Code, Income Tax Regulations, and case law with
respect to a specific set of facts. It can be compared
with a revenue ruling, and in certain situations can
result in the publication of a revenue ruling or revenue
procedure, thereby promoting uniformity in the treatment
of issues on a nationwide basis.

       The form on which you will receive a Technical Advice
Memorandum is illustrated in figure 12-A. Unless you feel
that the National Office conclusions should be reconsidered and promptly request such reconsideration, you
must process the taxpayer's case on the basis of the
conclusions reached in the memorandum. Except in rare
cases the conclusions reached in a Technical Advice Memorandum (favorable or adverse to the taxpayer) are applied
retroactively.[2/]

¶12.021
When To Request Advice

       In general, the National Office encourages requests for
technical or procedural advice from field offices in the
interest of good administration, especially when the
district office believes a lack of uniformity exists in
the disposition of an issue.[3/] The Internal Revenue
Manual lists several situations in which technical advice
should be requested.

       EXTRACT
       IRM 4551.1(1)

       * * *[T]echnical advice or guidance should be
requested in every case in which any of the
following conditions exist.

       (a) The law and regulations are not clear on
the issue being considered and there is no published precedent for determining the proper
treatment of the issue.

(b) There is reason to believe that nonuniformity in the treatment of the issue exists between districts.

(c) A doubtful or contentious issue is involved in a number of cases.

(d) The issue is so unusual or complex as to warrant consideration by the National Office.

(e) The District Director believes that securring technical advice from the National Office would be in the best interest of the service.

During the examination of a tax shelter, you may recognize and develop an issue which fits into category (a). Due to the careful planning that often goes into the structuring of a tax shelter, your success in the examination may well depend on developing just such an issue. This will require imagination and creativity on your part as well as a thorough knowledge and interpretation of the law.. Before requesting technical advice, research known sources of information for proper treatment of the issue. If you find any indication of a Service position in regulations, revenue rulings, revenue procedures, Treasury decisions, or any other precedent published by the National Office, a request probably will not be appropriate. The following is an illustration of an issue which would have been an appropriate issue on which to request technical advice before the issue was clarified by the issuance of Rev. Rul. 75-214 $\underline{4/}$ and the passing of the Tax Reform Act of 1976.

Example 1

You are examining a limited partnership which you have identified as a tax shelter. On the first page of the return, under Deductions, is the item "Payments to partners - Salaries and interest." $120,000. You examine the item and determine the entire amount was paid to one general partner for services he rendered in organizing the partnership. Because you believe this amount should be capitalized and not expensed, you research this issue.

Code § 707(c) covers this situation, providing in part (as it did before the Tax Reform Act of 1976) that payments to a partner for services are to be considered as made to one who is not a member of the partnership, but only for the purposes of Code §§ 61(a) and 162(a). You interpret § 707(c) as meaning that to be deductible the payment must qualify as an ordinary and necessary business expense under § 162(a), and, in addition, that it would be subject

3178-02

to § 263 (dealing with capital expenditures). If this interpretation is correct, the payment would be a capital expenditure under § 263 and therefore not deductible. The problem is that neither the Code nor the regulations are clear on the interpretation. You research the issue thoroughly, but can find no Service position. The taxpayer holds that § 707(c) allows the partnership to deduct all guaranteed payments to partners for services rendered by the partner for the partnership. In accordance with IRM 4551.1(1), you determine that technical advice should be requested for guidance as to the deductibility of the payments.

The taxpayer or taxpayer's representative may initiate the action for requesting technical advice on the grounds that a lack of uniformity exists as to the disposition of the issue, or that the issue is so unusual or complex that it warrants consideration by the National Office.[5] In this instance, you still have the responsibility of determining whether technical advice is warranted. If you determine it is not warranted, you must notify the taxpayer of your decision, whereupon the taxpayer has the right to appeal your decision to the Chief, Audit Division, of your district.[6]

¶12.022
How To Request Advice

Generally, requests for technical advice are submitted on Form 4463, which is illustrated in figure 12-B. You must attach a written statement setting forth the issues, facts, law, and conclusion. See figure 12-C for a suggested format for this statement.

Except in matters of internal concern or fraud, jeopardy assessments, etc., notify the taxpayer of your decision to request technical advice. Also, furnish the taxpayer with a copy of the statement of the issues, facts, law, and conclusions that are to be submitted with the Form 4463 to the National Office. The taxpayer will be given 10 calendar days to indicate in writing any area of disagreement with the statement. It is particularly important to reach agreement with the taxpayer as to the facts and specific issues in question. If agreement cannot be reached, the taxpayer must be given the opportunity to submit a statement presenting the facts and issues as interpreted by the taxpayer. You must then submit both statements to the National Office for consideration. Taxpayers should also be informed of their right to a conference in the National Office in the event that an adverse decision is reached.

If you do not agree with the conclusion reached by the National Office, you may present your views on the matter with a request for reconsideration. You should not inform the taxpayer of the conclusions reached by the National Office until you receive the final determination.

After it has been adopted by the district office, a copy of the technical memorandum received from the National Office should generally be given to the taxpayer. When a copy is not to be given to the taxpayer, the National Office will provide specific instructions that you should not do so.$\underline{7/}$

If it is lacking information required to resolve the issue, the National Office may return a request for technical advice to you for further development. For this reason, you should forward with the request copies of any and all records and documents having a bearing on the issue.

The Tax Reform Act of 1976 added Code § 6110 requiring that (except for certain deletions) Technical Advice Memorandums must be open to public inspection. Advise the taxpayer to submit to you a statement of suggested deletions to be made to the Technical Advice Memorandum as required by Code § 6110(c). You must then submit this statement with the request for technical advice.$\underline{8/}$

Question 1

During the course of an examination, you identify a potential issue which you discuss with the taxpayer. The taxpayer expresses a desire to obtain a determination on the issue by the National Office. What actions would you take?

See answer 1.

¶12.03
Technical Coordination Report

A Form 3558, Technical Coordination Report, is a report on facts, conditions, practices, or developments resulting in significant tax abuses, inequities, and administrative problems caused by existing statutes and regulations. These reports are sources of information to assist the National Office in establishing or improving nationwide operating and technical programs relating to legislation, regulations, tax forms, rulings, and related activities.

¶12.031
When To Submit the Report

Submit a Technical Coordination Report whenever you identify a situation lending itself to tax abuse, inequity, or
difficulties in applying the administrative provisions of
the Internal Revenue Code.

Class III tax shelters provide examples of tax abuse
situations. By adding Code § 465, Congress has attempted
to close four abusive types of tax shelters. Other types
of tax shelters will continue to exist and some of these
will be abusive. Be alert to this possibility.

Tax shelters often combine various elements to produce
their desired results. Analyze each element of a tax
shelter to determine what effect that element has on the
whole. Standing alone, each element may be perfectly
legitimate, but combined with all other elements it may
produce an unintended benefit.

If you discover such a situation, not previously identified, submit a Technical Coordination Report.

An example of a tax shelter element that standing alone is
(or was in some situations before the Tax Reform Act of
1976) perfectly legitimate, but that combined with other
elements produces unintended benefits is the nonrecourse
liability situation. In some situations when combined
with overvaluation of the property, this principle produces excessive depreciation deductions and excessive
investment credit. Before this situation became so widely
known it would have been an appropriate subject for a
Technical Coordination Report.

Of particular significance are situations having any of
the following characteristics:

(1) A large number of taxpayers are affected.

(2) A large amount of potential revenue is involved.

(3) The matter relates to a key policy of the President,
    the Secretary of the Treasury, or the Congress.

(4) The matter is causing or may cause a significant
    amount of adverse publicity or public controversy.

(5) The matter is creating significant problems in the
    examination of returns, appeals, or litigation.

When warranted, you should submit Technical Coordination Reports on all actual cases, even though the problem area has been identified in previous reports. This is because a stronger case can be made for amending a regulation, statute, or ruling when a large number of reports on a specific problem are on hand. This will also assist the National Office in determining the scope of the problem.

¶12.032
How To Submit the Report

Technical Coordination Reports are submitted by using Form 3558, illustrated in figures 12-C. Look over this form and read the instructions for its preparation. Pay particular attention to item 11 in the instructions. Remember that in describing how a particular Code or regulation section, ruling, or court decision operates to create a tax abuse, be sure to explain how this item interacts with the other elements of the tax shelter. Coordinate your efforts in preparing the report with the District Technical Coordinator in your district.

¶12.04
Closing Conference

Because of the complexity of tax shelter issues, considerable preparation is needed for the closing conference. Class III tax shelters will generally contain several alternative issues as well as the primary issue. Be prepared to discuss the alternative issues as well as the primary issue.

Before the closing conference, update your research, checking current matters in the various tax services. This is particularly important in the tax shelter area since law in this area is continually being developed.

Present the law and argument to support your issues just as you would in any other case. If the taxpayer will not agree with the principal issue, attempt to reach accord on any of the alternative issues. Based on how strong your primary issue is, how the issue has been decided in other cases, and the differences in the tax effects between the primary and alternative issues, it may be to the Service's advantage to get an agreement on an alternative issue.

Assuming the partnership case is unagreed and you also have one or more of the partner's returns, give each individual partner an opportunity to agree with the issue or issues on a separate basis. Even though the partnership case is unagreed, some partners for different reasons may wish to agree with the adjustment to their own returns. Of course, they will have the right to file a claim for refund at a later date. Follow 918-A procedures for the out-of-district partners. Record the taxpayer's position on all the issues as completely and accurately as possible. Ask the taxpayer to give you his or her position in writing. Even if you obtain an agreement to your principal issue, you should obtain the taxpayer's position on all other issues. The general partner may agree to the adjustments at the partnership level. Later, the partners may file claims for refund on an individual basis. For this reason, document all tax shelter cases as though they were unagreed.

In many tax shelter cases, taxpayers obtain legal opinions from private attorneys. If a taxpayer has obtained such an opinion, ask for a copy. It will assist you in understanding the taxpayer's position.

¶12.05
Examiner's Case Report

Concerning your examination report on a tax shelter, certain points need to be emphasized. Agreed and unagreed cases should be treated alike for purposes of writing the report. With certain restrictions taxpayers may file claims for refund after the case is initially agreed. Full explanations for all issues, principal and alternative, should be included in the initial report (agreed or unagreed). For each alternative issue having a different tax effect on the partners, prepare a separate Form 4605-A, Audit Changes-Partnerships, Fiduciaries, and Small Business Corporations, and separate Forms 886-S, Partners Shares of Income, Deductions, and Credits.

If your tax shelter case comes under the "Tax Shelter Program" (involves oil and gas drilling funds, farm operations, real estate, and motion pictures), follow the precedures provided in MS 42G-350.

In general, follow the principles of good report writing. A full and complete report covering all the issues, pertinent facts, authority, taxpayer's position, and conclusions may result in an agreement when the taxpayer receives the 30-day letter. At the least, it will help to create a more professional atmosphere during the appeals procedures.

(1) A Technical Advice Memorandum is a formal Service position furnished by the National Office at the request of a district office on a specific issue or issues in connection with the examination of a taxpayer's return or consideration of a taxpayer's claim for refund or credit.

(2) Request technical advice when the law and regulations are not clear on an issue being considered and there is no published precedent by the National Office for determining the proper treatment of the issue.

(3) With the request for technical advice, forward copies of all records and documents which have a bearing on the issue.

(4) A Technical Coordination Report is a report on facts, conditions, practices, or developments which result in significant tax abuses, inequities, and administrative problems caused by existing statutes and regulations.

(5) Submit a Technical Coordination Report whenever you identify a situation lending itself to tax abuse, inequity, or difficulties in applying the administrative provisions of the Internal Revenue Code.

(6) Be alert to identify new tax shelter issues and tax abuse situations.

(7) Both principal and alternative issues must be fully developed, discussed with the taxpayer, and included in the report.

(8) Agreed and unagreed cases should be treated the same for purposes of writing the report.

3178-02

1. a. Inform the taxpayer that you will consider the request and make a determination whether technical advice is warranted or not.

    b. Study the appropriate Code and regulation sections. Search for revenue rulings, revenue procedures, other material published by the National Office, and court decisions which indicate a Service position on the issue. Make your decision based on the provisions in IRM 4551.1.

    c. Discuss the situation and your decision with your group manager. Find out the district procedures.

    d. Inform the taxpayer of your decision. If you determine technical advice is warranted, you may ask the taxpayer to prepare the written statement. Advise the taxpayer to prepare a statement of suggested deletions (Code § 6110(c)).

    e. Inform the taxpayer of the right to a conference in the National Office should an adverse decision be reached.

    f. Come to agreement with the taxpayer on the content of the written statement.

    g. Prepare Form 4463, attach the written statement, and forward with copies of all records and documents which have a bearing on the issue through channels to the National Office.

Figure 12-A
Technical Advice Memorandum

INTERNAL REVENUE SERVICE
NATIONAL OFFICE TECHNICAL ADVICE MEMORANDUM
(Original and copies date stamped by T:PS:T)

District Director
(Name of District Office)

Taxpayer's Name:
Taxpayer's Address:
Taxpayer's Identification No.:
Years Involved:
Date of Conference: (*OR* No Conference Held)

Issues

State the issues as presented by the District. Also, whenever appropriate, state in clear, precise language any additional issues that have been identified that were not specifically raised by the incoming correspondence, or restate the issue presented by the District to pinpoint the real question to be decided.

Facts

The statement of facts incorporated in the technical advice memorandum should be set out concisely but without any sacrifice of clarity. The essential facts should be fully presented. Short quotations from the incoming statement may be used as an aid in definitely pinning down particular areas when the conclusion depends on the interpretation of such language. However, lengthy quotations from documents contained in the file are to be avoided wherever practicable.

Applicable Law

This part of the document should set forth clearly and concisely the pertinent law, regulations, published rulings of the Service, and case law or other precedent. Care should be taken that all citations are directly in point. Quotations which are helpful may be used judiciously, but lengthy ones are to be avoided wherever practicable.

Rationale

Sufficient rationale must be provided to bridge any gaps between the issue, law, and conclusion reached.

Conclusion

A specific statement as to the conclusion reached with respect to each issue is the final important step. These conclusions must be written to leave no doubt as to their meaning and to make it clear they are based solely on the facts presented.

(If a copy of the technical advice memorandum is not to be given to the taxpayer, that fact should be noted here.)

> In summary, it is our function to promote uniformity, clarity, and responsiveness and, to the extent practicable, to insure an orderly method of approaching a technical advice problem. It is not intended in any way to restrict originality or ingenuity on the part of the writer, nor is it intended to prevent necessary or desirable deviation from the pattern where proper.

Request for Technical Advice

Figure 12-B

Please submit original and two copies - Complete all applicable boxes

1. TO: Internal Revenue Service, Washington, D. C. 20224 ATTENTION: T:PS:T	6. DATE OF REQUEST
2. FROM	DISTRICT	7. PRINCIPAL CODE SECTION
SIGNATURE	TITLE	8. YEAR(S) INVOLVED
3. (a) NAME AND TELEPHONE NUMBER OF DISTRICT OFFICE CONTACT	9. STATUTORY PERIOD EXPIRES
(b) NAME AND TELEPHONE NUMBER OF AUDIT GROUP MANAGER	
4. NAME AND ADDRESS OF TAXPAYER OR ORGANIZATION	10. TAXPAYER IDENTIFICATION NO.
5. NAME AND ADDRESS OF TAXPAYER'S REPRESENTATIVE	AREA CODE AND TELEPHONE NO.	11. ATTACHED: POWER OF ATTORNEY ☐ YES ☐ NO AND DECLARATION ☐ YES ☐ NO

ITEM	(Check)			ITEM	(Check)		
	YES	NO	AT-TACHED		YES	NO	AT-TACHED
12. GENERAL INFORMATION				**13. ADDITIONAL ITEMS IN CERTAIN CASES**			
a. Was taxpayer informed Technical Advice is being requested and did you explain procedures?........... If not, please state reason:				a. Is an inter vivos trust involved? .... If Yes, please attach a copy of the trust instrument .... b. Is a testamentary trust or an estate involved?........................... If Yes, please attach a copy of the Will			
b. Does taxpayer desire a National Office conference if adverse decision is indicated?...........................				c. Is revocation or modification of exemption or determination letter in the exempt organization or pension trust area involved?...........................			
c. Did you give taxpayer a statement of facts and questions as your office sees them?..... If Yes, please attach copy .... If not, please state reason:				If Yes: (1) Recommended effective date of revocation or modification_____ .			
				(2) Attach statement of reasons for recommended effective date of revocation or modification...................			
d. Does taxpayer agree with statement? .... If not, please attach taxpayer's statement of facts and questions				(3) Is the organization a private foundation?			
e. If you have prepared a statement of applicable law, argument, and conclusion, please attach copy...................				d. Is sensitive case involved? .... If Yes, please attach copy of sensitive case report			
f. If taxpayer has submitted a protest, brief, response, or other information, please attach copy				e. Is Controlled Large Case Program involved?			

INSTRUCTIONS

A. This form is used by District Directors in transmitting requests for technical advice to the National Office in accordance with the procedures in IRM 4550. Supporting documents and all pertinent material should be included and not necessarily limited to that called for by this form and instructions. This form is not used in transmitting requests for rulings, technical assistance, or general technical information.

B. Information with respect to the following matters should be included in the file, if applicable:

1. **Prior Ruling or Determination Letter.** Give date of letter, if related to issue involved in this Request for Technical Advice, and if determination letter, please furnish a copy.

2. **Taxpayer Previously Examined.** State disposition of prior case if issue involved in this Request for Technical Advice was also involved in prior case.

3. **Pension, Profit-Sharing, Stock Bonus, or Bond Purchase Plan.** Enclose plan file, reporting forms, supporting schedules, actuarial reports, and any other pertinent information.

4. **Employer-Employee Determination.** Furnish information from both parties (See Form SS-8). If taxpayer has 4 or more workers, attempt to obtain information from at least 4.

5. **Partnership.** Furnish copy of partnership agreement.

6. **Credit for Foreign Taxes.** State whether standards of Revenue Ruling 67-308, 1967-2, C.B. 254, have been met.

Form **4463** (Rev. 4-73)

Department of the Treasury - Internal Revenue Service
3178-02

Figure 12-C

TECHNICAL COORDINATION REPORT

To be completed in accordance with Audit Reports Handbook of the Internal Revenue Manual and forwarded
through the Regional Technical Coordinator to the National Office in triplicate

(See instructions on reverse)

ax Forms and Publications Division, National Office; Attention: T:FP:T

Audit Division, National Office; Attention: CP:A:S:E

☐ Employee Plans Division, National Office; E:EP

☐ Exempt Organizations Division, National Office; E:EO

2. FROM	Name of Originator *(Print or type)*		Region	District	Division

3. Type of Problem

☐ Tax Abuse ☐ Inequity ☐ Administrative ☐ Other

4. Name and Address of Taxpayer	5. Taxable Years	
	6. Type of Tax	7. Approx. Effect on Revenue

8. Primary provisions of law involved (including Regulations, Court Decision, and Revenue Rulings)

9. Action taken and present status of case

10. Recommendation in brief

11. Facts and discussion *(Continue on reverse side)*

12. Signature of originator	Title	Date

13. For Use of District Technical Coordinator	14. For Use of Regional Technical Coordinator
☐ Concur ☐ Do not concur } In The above Recommendation	☐ Concur ☐ Do not concur } In The Above Recommendation
Comments: *(Attach sheet, if necessary)*	Comments: *(Attach sheet, if necessary)*
Signature Date	Signature Date

11. Facts and Discussion Continued

(Attach Additional Sheets if Necessary)

INSTRUCTIONS
(Numbers Correspond to Item Numbers on Form)

1. Indicate the National Office division to which the Regional Technical Coordinator should forward the Technical Coordination Report. Reports involving compliance or procedural matters only should be routed to the Audit Division, National Office, Attention: CP:A:S:E. Reports concerning Employee Plans should be routed to the Employee Plans Division, E:EP. Reports concerning Exempt Organizations should be routed to the Exempt Organization Division, E:EO. All other reports, including those which propose amendments to the law, regulations or tax forms, or modification of Revenue Rulings, etc., should be routed to the Tax Forms and Publications Division, National Office, Attention: T:FP:T.

2. The name in item 2 should be printed or typed so as to insure correct identification of the originator. Fill in appropriate boxes only. The space for the district should be left blank when a report originates in a regional office.

3. Check box in item 3 which best describes the type of problem encountered.

4. Give taxpayer's name and address if a particular taxpayer is involved; if not write "none".

6. State type of tax: income, estate, gift, excise or employment. Submit a separate report for each type of tax.

8. Specify I.R.C. or regulations section, tax form, court decision, Revenue Ruling, etc., which is primarily involved in the problem. Omit reference to wording of the statutory or other provision.

10. The recommendation, when one is made, should be stated concisely, e.g., "amend I.R.C. section 1031." Technical wording or detail need not be given here but may be included under item 11. Although completion of item 10 is desirable, a report should be submitted regardless of whether a precise recommendation can be offered.

11. Item 11 is intended to constitute the main body of the report. It may be continued on the back of this report form and additional sheets or exhibits may be attached as necessary. Give all facts and background information essential to an understanding of the problem. Describe in detail just how a particular code or regulations section, tax form, ruling or decision operates to create a tax abuse, inequity, administrative or other problem for the Service. Specific recommendation to eliminate the problem (e.g., proposed statutory language), while not required, will be helpful to the National Office.

13. Items 13 and 14 are not intended to burden District and Regional
& Technical Coordinators. However, some indication of their think-
14. ing on a report, as well as the thinking of other field personnel with whom the report may be discussed, is needed by the National Office to help in evaluating the overall importance of the subject matter.

YOUR COOPERATION IN SUBMITTING THIS REPORT IS APPRECIATED

1260

Form 3558 (Rev. 11-76)

3178-02

Footnotes

1/ 30th Annual Federal Tax Conference, the University of Chicago Law School, Chicago, Illinois, October 26, 1977.

2/ Rev. Proc. 73-8, 1973-1 C.B. 754 (Sec. 9.02).

3/ IRM 1218, Policies of the Internal Revenue Service Handbook, P-4-81.

4/ 1975-1 C.B. 185; also a phrase added to Code § 707(c) made guaranteed payments subject to Code § 263 for purposes of § 162(a). Rev. Rul. 75-214 stated the Service position that payments to a general partner for services rendered in organizing the partnership constitute capital expenditures under Code § 263 and are not deductible under § 162.

5/ Rev. Proc. 73-8, 1973-1 C.B. 754 (Sec. 4.01).

6/ Sec. 5 of Rev. Proc. 73-8.

7/ Sec. 7.05 of Rev. Proc. 73-8.

8/ MS 456-281.

SYNOPSES OF TAX SHELTER RELATED PROCEDURES AND RULINGS

Note: This is intended to be only a partial listing of the many avail-
       able tax shelter related procedures and rulings.

Revenue Procedures:

   Rev. Proc. 72-9, 1972-1 C.B. 718.

        An up-to-date list of areas in which the Revenue Service
        will or will not ordinarily issue rulings or determination
        letters because of the inherently factual nature of the prob-
        lems involved, or for other reasons, is set forth. Amplified
        by Rev. Proc. 76-13, Rev. Proc. 76-19, Rev. Proc. 76-1, and
        Rev. Proc. 74-22. Modified by Rev. Proc. 77-27. Rev. Procs.
        69-6 and 71-31 superseded.

   Rev. Proc. 72-13, 1972-1 C.B. 735.

        Conditions under which advance rulings will be issued con-
        cerning the classification of an organization as a limited
        partnership where a corporation is the sole general partner.

   Rev. Proc. 73-8, 1973-1 C.B. 754.

        Procedures have been revised effective April 2, 1973, for
        the National Office furnishing of requested technical advice to
        District directors and the time period within which taxpayers
        may exercise their related rights. Rev. Proc. 72-2 superseded.

   Rev. Proc. 74-17, 1974-1 C.B. 438.

        Conditions are set forth under which an organization formed
        and operated as a limited partnership will ordinarily be issued
        an advance ruling concerning its classification as a partner-
        ship under section 7701 of the Code.

   Rev. Proc. 75-21, 1975-1 C.B. 715.

        Guidelines are given for determining whether, for advance
        ruling purposes, certain purported leases of property commonly
        called "leveraged leases" are to be considered leases for
        income tax purposes. Modified by Rev. Proc. 76-30.

   Rev. Proc. 75-28, 1975-1 C.B. 752.

        Guidelines set forth the information and representation to
        be furnished by a taxpayer requesting an advance ruling with
        respect to a transaction purporting to be a leveraged lease.
        Rev. Proc. 72-3 modified.

Rev. Proc. 77-11, 1977-1 C.B. 568.

As a condition to issuing a ruling that lessors of coal and iron ore may treat bonuses or advanced royalties as received from a sale of coal or iron ore under section 631(c), the lessors will be required to enter into a closing agreement with respect to their tax liability.

Revenue Rulings:

Rev. Rul. 57-318, 1957-2 C.B. 362.

Where a partner, whose capital account has a deficit which he is obligated to repay, sells his partnership interest to the other partner, the basis of his interest for determining gain or loss on the transaction is zero. The sale proceeds will be considered as gain from the sale or exchange of a capital asset. If, in addition, the deficit is cancelled, the obligor partner is considered to have received a distribution, at the time of the cancellation, of an amount which would be taxable as a capital gain. Clarified by Rev. Rul. 73-301.

Rev. Rul. 68-79, 1968-1 C.B. 310.

Where stock held by a partnership as an investment for more than six months is sold at a gain, a partner's distributive share is long term capital gain notwithstanding that he held his partnership interest for not more than six months.

Rev. Rul. 68-643, 1968-2 C.B. 76.

The deduction of prepaid interest in the year of payment by a cash-basis taxpayer may not clearly reflect income. Accordingly, deduction on each indebtedness for a period not in excess of 12 months of the taxable year immediately following the taxable year in which the prepayment is made will be considered on a case-by-case basis. Where a material distortion of income has been found to result from the deduction of prepaid interest for a period of more than 12 months, the taxpayer will be required to change his accounting method. Modified by Rev. Rul. 69-582 with respect to a loan processing fee paid by a mortgager. John D. Fackler, 39 B.T.A., Court Holding Co., 2 T.C. 531, Nonacq. 1968-2 C.B. 3.

Rev. Rul. 69-77, 1969-1 C.B. 59.

The Manuel D. Mayerson decision, which held that the purchase of depreciable property in exchange for a long-term purchase-money mortgage created a bona fide purchase and valid debt obligation and the purchasers were entitled to include in the depreciable basis of the property the debt obligation created by the mortgage, will not necessarily be relied on in the disposition of other cases.

Rev. Rul. 69-180, 1969-1 C.B. 183.

Examples illustrate the proper method for computing, in accordance with the partnership agreement, the partners' distributive shares of the partnership's ordinary income and capital gain, where a partner also receives a guaranteed payment.

Rev. Rul. 69-223, 1969-1 C.B. 184.

A provision of a limited partnership agreement whereby the limited partner agrees to indemnify the general partners, for payments exceeding their pro rata share of partnership liabilities, does not obligate the limited partner to make additional contributions to the limited partnership beyond his initial contribution of capital. Such limited partner, therefore, may not increase the basis of his partnership interest therein by any part of a mortgage liability assumed by the partnership. Instead, the general partner will increase the basis of his partnership interest by the full amount of the mortgage liability assumed.

Rev. Rul. 70-333, 1970-1 C.B. 38.

The Revenue Service will not follow the decision of the Tax Court in Perry A. Nichols which held that a taxpayer was entitled to a theft loss deduction for his out-of-pocket expenses incurred in connection with a tax avoidance scheme entered into in reliance upon misrepresentations that he would realize a tax "bonanza," in the form of an interest deduction, from such transaction.

Rev. Rul. 70-355, 1970-2 C.B. 51.

A limited partner may deduct as an ordinary loss the adjusted basis amount of his partnership interest upon bankruptcy of the partnership, even though it exceeds the amount of his capital account on the books of the partnership and the partnership agreement limits the distribution of losses to limited partners to the extent of their capital account.

Rev. Rul. 70-356, 1970-2 C.B. 68.

Insurance and storage costs incurred during the aging process of whiskey purchased as an investment are capital expenditures to be treated as part of the acquisition costs of the whiskey.

Rev. Rul. 70-626, 1970-2 C.B. 158.

A donation to a charitable organization of appreciated securities, which have been held for more than six months and are pledged as collateral for an outstanding loan that is in excess of the donor's basis, constitutes partly a sale and partly a gift. Therefore, the donor realizes a long-term capital gain of the difference between the amount of the loan and his basis in the securities. He is also entitled to a charitable contributions deduction in the amount of the excess of the fair market value of the securities over the loan.

Rev. Rul. 71-252, 1971-1 C.B. 146.

Intangible drilling and development costs incurred and paid, pursuant to a contract, by a cash basis taxpayer, who had elected in a prior year to treat such costs as expenses, are deductible in the year paid even though the work is performed in the following year. This Ruling will not be applied for taxable years ending on or before June 7, 1971, to require adjustment where such costs were treated in accordance with Rev. Rul. 170, 1953-2 C.B. 141. Rev. Rul. 170 revoked; distinguished by Rev. Rul. 71-579, 1971-2 C.B. 225.

Rev. Rul. 71-579, 1971-2 C.B. 225.

Intangible drilling and development costs paid by a cash basis taxpayer in a taxable year prior to the year in which payment was required under the drilling contract and before any work was performed under the contract are not deductible in that year. Rev. Rul. 71-252, distinguished.

Rev. Rul. 72-135, 1972-1 C.B. 200.

A nonrecourse "loan" made by a general partner of a limited partnership to a partnership or to limited partners on the basis of their subscription interest is a contribution to capital to be added to the basis of the general partner's interest in the partnership.

Rev. Rul. 72-205, 1972-1 C.B. 37.

Income attributable to the discharge of indebtedness incurred in the trade or business of a partnership may be excluded from income of the partnership by filing a consent to the regulations under section 1017 of the Code. The discharge of the indebtedness including the amount of the liability reduction excluded from the partnership's gross income is considered a distribution to the partners that reduces their partnership interests.

Rev. Rul. 72-350, 1972-2 C.B. 394.

A so-called "loan" to a limited partnership by a nonmember, secured by partnership properties and the right to convert the loan for an interest in the partnership profits, is a capital investment in the venture representing the lender's equity interest. It is not considered a bona-fide debt but is an equity interest in the venture belonging to the lender. The advance of the funds will have no effect on the bases of the partnership interests of the other parties.

Rev. Rul. 72-352, 1972-2 C.B. 395.

Termination of a trust and distribution of its interest in a partnership to a remainderman does not terminate the partnership's taxable year but the trust must include in gross income its distributive share of partnership items to the date of termination. Tax consequences affecting the trust and its beneficiaries are set forth.

Rev. Rul. 73-211, 1973-1 C.B. 303.

A taxpayer's investment in an oil and gas venture under a contract designating a dollar amount as intangible drilling and development costs is deductible pursuant to an election under section 263(c) of the Code only to the extent that such costs would have been incurred in an arms-length transaction with an unrelated drilling contractor. The remainder of the total investment is the basis of the taxpayer's working interest.

Rev. Rul. 73-301, 1973-2 C.B. 215.

An unrestricted progress payment received by a partnership, reporting its income on the completed contract method, during its performance on a two-year construction contract did not constitute a partnership liability or add to the partners' interests within the meaning of section 752(a) of the Code. Further, one partner's cash withdrawals that created a deficit in his capital account did not constitute loans from the partnership under section 707(a) when no unconditional and legally enforceable obligation existed requiring him to repay the money; the withdrawals are to be treated as partnership distributions to a partner. Rev. Rul. 57-318 clarified.

Rev. Rul. 73-410, 1973-2 C.B. 53.

The component method of computing depreciation may be utilized to depreciate an office building that was thirty years old at the time of acquisition if the cost is properly allocated to the various components based on their value, useful lives are assigned to the component accounts based on the condition of such components at the time of acquisition, and provided the

Class Life (ADR) System is not elected. Rev. Rul. 66-111 modified. Clarified by Rev. Rul. 75-55.

Rev. Rul. 73-482, 1973-2 C.B. 44.

Interest deducted in advance from the amount of a life insurance policy loan, or due and unpaid interest added to the principal of the loan, is deductible as "interest paid" by a calendar-year, cash-method taxpayer only for the taxable year in which actual payment is made. Rev. Rul. 67-258 distinguished.

Rev. Rul. 74-40, 1974-1 C.B. 159.

Federal income tax consequences to a limited partner from the sale or exchange of his partnership interest and to a limited partner who withdraws from the partnership in cases where no personal liability has been assumed either by the partnership or by any of the partners with respect to the limited partner's share of partnership liabilities.

Rev. Rul. 74-104, 1974-1 C.B. 70.

Evaluation expenditures incurred by a domestic corporation in connection with the acquisition of existing residential property for renovation and resale are capital expenditures that must be taken into account as part of the cost of acquiring the property. However, if such expenditures do not result in the acquisition of property they are deductible as losses in the taxable year the corporation decides not to acquire the property.

Rev. Rul. 74-290, 1974-1 C.B. 41.

A leasing arrangement under which a municipality will issue bonds for the financing of equipment to be acquired by a manufacturing corporation and leased, for the term of the bonds plus one day, to the city which will sublease it to the corporation for the term of the bonds for subrentals sufficient to retire the bonds, is a financing arrangement entitling the corporation as owner of the equipment to the tax treatment contained in Rev. Rul. 68-590.

Rev. Rul. 74-320, 1974-2 C.B. 404.

Limited partnerships formed under the California Uniform Limited Partnership Act, as amended by section 15520.5 thereof, or those limited partnerships formed prior to the amendment that elect to be governed by that section, will lack the corporate characteristic of "continuity of life", as defined in section 301.7701-2(b) of the regulations, from the date they elect to be governed thereby and so long as section 15520.5 remains effective.

Rev. Rul. 74-395, 1974-2 C.B. 45.

A commitment fee, paid by a lending bank to the Federal National Mortgage Association in connection with the assumption of an accrual method taxpayer's construction loan and withheld by the bank from the face amount of the loan proceeds received by the taxpayer, is deductible by the taxpayer as interest. If the loan instrument is silent as to what portion of each loan payment is discounted interest, the fee must be deducted ratably by the taxpayer over the entire period of the loan unless the loan instrument requires that prepaid interest is subject to the "Rule of 78's." Rev. Rul. 56-136 distinguished.

Rev. Rul. 75-19, 1975-1 C.B. 382.

A partnership formed under a statute corresponding to the Uniform Partnership Act by a domestic corporation's four domestic subsidiaries, each with business reasons for independent existence outside the partnership, for the purpose of purchasing a crude oil storage barge and chartering it to an unrelated corporation, and not to avoid tax, is classified as a partnership.

Rev. Rul. 75-31, 1975-1 C.B. 10.

Determination of whether a limited partnership formed under New York State law is to be treated as the owner of the project and whether each partner may include a portion of a loan made by the New York Housing Finance Agency in the basis of his partnership interest. Distinguished by Rev. Rul. 76-26.

Rev. Rul. 75-43, 1975-1 C.B. 383.

A corporate feed lot operator and an individual cattle owner enters into a 5-year service agreement under which the cattle owner makes a cash commitment, supplies cattle for fattening, purchases feed from the feed lot operator, and independently markets the cattle. The feed lot operator furnishes insurance, labor, accommodations, equipment for the separate care and feeding of the cattle, and guarantees the owner a return of a certain percentage of his cash commitment. The feed lot operator received a percentage of the owner's net profit in exchange for his services. The arrangement will not be classified as a partnership.

Rev. Rul. 75-99, 1975-1 C.B. 197

The portion of payments received by a real estate investment trust from a borrower on a "wrap-around" mortgage loan and paid by the trust on the senior obligation are considered made on behalf of the borrower; the portion attributable to interest on the amount of cash advanced by the trust is includible in the trust's gross income and constitutes interest.

Rev. Rul 75-152, 1975-1 C.B. 144.

A cash-method farmer may deduct in the year of payment the amounts paid for feed to be consumed by his own livestock in a following taxable year provided (1) the expenditure is for the purchase of feed rather than a deposit, (2) the prepayment is made for a business purpose and not for tax avoidance, and (3) the deduction will not result in a material distortion of income.

Rev. Rul. 75-172, 1975-1 C.B. 145.

The nonrefundable fee a corporation paid, under a loan agreement for construction and permanent mortgage financing and on or before initial receipt of funds, as compensation for the cost of specific legal, architectural, and engineering services incurred by the lender is a cost to be deducted ratably over the duration of the loan.

Rev. Rul. 75-194, 1975-1 C.B. 80.

Income tax consequences are given for a limited partner's charitable contribution of his entire interest in a limited partnership having liabilities that were not personally assumed by the partnership or any of the partners.

Rev. Rul. 75-214, 1975-1 C.B. 185.

A limited partnership's payment to one of its general partners for services he rendered in organizing the partnership are payments described in section 707 of the Code, constitute capital expenditures under section 263, and are not deductible under section 162.

Rev. Rul. 75-523, 1975-2 C.B. 257.

A member of an investment club partnership, formed solely to invest in securities and whose income is derived solely from taxable dividends, interest, and gains from security sales, may deduct that member's distributive share of the partnership's reasonable operating expenses incurred in its taxable year.

Rev. Rul. 75-525, 1975-2 C.B. 350.

A member's distributive share of income from an investment club partnership whose activities are limited to investment in, and collection of interest on, savings certificate for its member's accounts is not net earnings from self-employment for purposes of section 1402(a) of the Code.

Rev. Rul. 76-111, 1976-1 C.B. 214.

The transfer of cattle to the seller in consideration of cancellation of indebtedness to the seller, for which the herd was pledged as security, is equivalent to a sale and the excess of the indebtedness cancelled over the adjusted basis of the cattle transferred or the excess of the adjusted basis over the indebtedness cancelled represents, respectively, gain or loss from the sale of assets under section 1001 of the Code regardless of the fair market value of the cattle.

Rev. Rul. 76-189, 1976-1 C.B. 181.

The termination of a partnership that sustained a loss from operations during the taxable year and terminated at the end of the year having no assets or liabilities remaining is treated, under the provisions of section 731, as if an actual distribution had taken place. A partner who purchased a partnership interest at the beginning of the year must reduce the adjusted basis of the interest by the share of the partnership loss and the share of the section 1231 loss, and any remaining basis is a capital loss.

Rev. Rul. 77-110, 1977-1 C.B. 58.

The liability on a nonrecourse interest bearing note given as a part of the purchase price of film distribution rights, whose value could not be shown to approximate the amount of the note, may not be included in the basis of the rights for depreciation purposes and no deduction is allowable for interest accrued on the note.

Rev. Rul. 77-119, 1977-1 C.B. 177.

The retroactive modification of a partnership agreement that allocates to a purchasing partner the partnership loss sustained prior to the new partner's entry into the partnership, will not be recognized and the new partner's distributive share of income, gains, losses, deductions or credits may not include such items realized or sustained prior to the partner's entry.

Rev. Rul. 77-125, 1977-1 C.B. 130.

The tax treatment is shown for motion picture film production service partnership costs, with respect to a limited partnership.

Rev. Rul. 77-137, 1977-1 C.B. 178.

An assignee acquiring substantially all of the dominion and control over the interest of a limited partner is treated as a substituted limited partner for Federal income tax purposes.

Rev. Rul. 77-176, 1977-1 C.B. 77.

The proper treatment is shown for an arrangement under which, in consideration for drilling an oil and gas well at a designed location on a leased tract of land, the driller receives from the lessee of the land an assignment of the entire working interest in the drill site and an undivided fraction of the working interest in the remainder of the tract.

Rev. Rul. 77-185, 1977-1 C.B. 48.

Neither a short-term capital loss created to minimize the tax consequences of an unrelated short-term capital gain through a series of transactions in silver futures contracts, which result in no real economic loss, nor the related out-of-pocket expenses incurred in connection with creating the loss are deductible under section 165(a) of the Code.

Rev. Rul. 77-220, 1977-1 C.B. 263.

A single business operated by 30 individuals was transferred to the three separate corportions for the principal purpose of being able to make the election under section 1372(a) of the Code to be treated as small business corporations. The three corporations will be considered a single corporation with 30 shareholders solely for purposes of making the section 1372(b) election, and any election made will not be valid.

Rev. Rul. 77-254, 1977-30 I.R.B. 6.

An individual may deduct, in accordance with section 165(c)(2) of the Code, expenses incurred in the unsuccessful attempt to acquire a specific business, such as legal expenses incurred in drafting purchase documents. However, expenses incurred in the course of a general search for or preliminary investigation of a business, such as expenses for advertisements and travel to search for a new business, are not deductible. Announcement 77-160, 1977-45 I.R.B. 27 corrects a printing error and an omission of words that occur in the third sentence of the seventh paragraph of this ruling.

Rev. Rul. 77-309, 1977-35 I.R.B. 19.

For purposes of determining the deductibility of a limited partner's distributive share of losses from a limited partnership, the limited partner's adjusted basis of the interest in the limited partnership, which is itself a limited partner of a second limited partnership, is not restricted to nonrecourse liabilities of the first limited partnership, but includes an allocable share of the second limited partnership's nonrecourse liabilities allocated to the first partnership.

Rev. Rul. 77-310, 1977-35 I.R.B. 20.

Allocation of a partnership loss among the partners according to their profit and loss sharing percentages as of the end
of a taxable year in which the percentages were substantially
changed one month before the end of the taxable year due to the
contribution of additional capital by some of the partners is
not a proper method of allocation for purposes of section
706(c)(2)(B) of the Code. An example of an acceptable method
of allocation is provided.

Rev. Rul. 77-311, 1977-35 I.R.B. 21

Allocation of a partnership loss among the members of a
second-tier partnership in accordance with their profit and
loss sharing percentages as of the end of a taxable year in
which the percentages were substantially changed one month
before the end of the taxable year by the entry of a new
partner is not a proper method of allocation for purposes of
section 706(c)(2)(B) of the Code. An example of an acceptable
method of allocation is provided.

Rev. Rul. 77-395, 1977-44 I.R.B. 6.

A taxpayer must capitalize as leasehold acquisition costs
both money paid to a filing service company to file application
to lease Federal lands under the noncompetitive simultaneous
offer procedure and an additional amount paid for an option to
sell an interest in any leases acquired with a concurrent
guarantee by the company that if no leases are so acquired it
will assign a lease and buy it back. If a lease is assigned
and repurchased by the filing service company, the taxpayer's
loss, subject to treatment under section 1231(a) of the Code,
is the difference between the total amount paid to the company
and the amount received on the repurchase.

Rev. Rul. 77-396, 1977-44 I.R.B. 6.

The minimum tax for tax preferences imposed by section 56 of
the Code is a nondeductible Federal income tax under section
275 rather than a deductible excise tax under section 162.

Rev. Rul. 77-397, 1977-44 I.R.B. 7.

An individual, who purchases a master recording of songs in
an arm's length transaction for a cash downpayment and a nonrecourse note and then grants the right to use and exploit the
master recording for a limited period to another individual in
exchange for royalties on the records sold by the second individual, is subject to the loss limitation provisions of section
465 of the Code.

Rev. Rul. 77-398, 1977-44. I.R.B. 8.

An individual who purchases a used motion picture film under an agreement providing for payment of 20 percent of the purchase price in cash and the balance by a 10-year recourse note to be reduced by payments from distribution receipts, and who also enters into another agreement with a third party providing for a loan at the end of the 10-year period to pay any balance due on the original note in exchange for a one-year nonnegotiable note renewable each year at the individual's option, is considered to have at risk under section 465 of the Code only the amount of the cash downpayment.

Rev. Rul. 77-399, 1977-44 I.R.B. 8.

A so-called "tax-sheltered trust" organized under State law as a corporation and registered with the Securities and Exchange Commission as a management open-end investment company that accumulates income from investing in securities in order to avoid income tax on its shareholders is a mere holding or investment company subject to the accumulated earnings tax.

Rev. Rul. 77-400, 1977-44 I.R.B. 9.

Advanced royalties paid or accrued by a lessee under a timber cutting contract are not deductible under the provisions of section 1.612-3(b)(3) of the regulations, but are to be added to the lessee's depletable basis in the timber.

Rev. Rul. 77-401, 1977-44 I.R.B. 10.

A cash basis roadbuilding partnership, formed in January 1977 and adopting a taxable year ending September 30, 1977, that gave cash and a nonrecourse note in payment for roadbuilding machinery and equipment and also gave cash and a full recourse note for medium to short-term U.S. Government obligations used to secure the note, had at risk under section 465 of the Code only the cash downpayments and no portion of either note is includible in the adjusted basis of the partners' interests in the partnership under section 704(d) for the taxable year ended September 30, 1977.

Rev. Rul. 77-402, 1977-44 I.R.B. 10.

An individual who creates an irrevocable trust classified as a grantor trust, purchases, as trustee, an interest in a partnership generating losses derived from accelerated depreciation deductions that reduce the basis of the partnership interest almost to zero, and who renounces the powers that cause the grantor trust classification just before the partnership begins generating income, has recognized gain or loss under section 741 of the Code measured by the difference between the trust's adjusted basis of the partnership interest and its share of the partnership's liabilities.

Rev. Rul. 77-403, 1977-44 I.R.B. 11.

A cash payment for a covenant not to compete that a taxpayer primarily engaged in managing real property made in addition to the purchase price of a newly constructed rental building acquired from a real estate developer who had no desire or ability to compete must be added to the basis of the property pursuant to section 1012 of the Code and may not be amortized over the life of the covenant.

Rev. Rul. 77-489, 1977-52 I.R.B. 11.

A taxpayer who pays or accrues advance minimum royalties in connection with the lease of mineral property may currently deduct only that portion of the minimum royalties due over the term of a lease that is properly atttributable to the current tax year; Rev. Ruls. 70-20 and 74-214 revoked.

Rev. Rul. 78-28, 1978-4 I.R.B. 6.

Payments earned by a limited partnership and not included in the partnership's gross income are not includible in the numerator of the fraction used under the "income forecast" method to compute allowable depreciation of the cost of a motion picture. Further, the denominator in the fraction cannot be less than the amount of the nonrecourse loan secured by the property.

Rev. Rul. 78-29, 1978-4 I.R.B. 7.

The liability created by a nonrecourse interest bearing note given by a corporation as part of the purchase price of a patent, whose value could not be shown to at least approximate the amount of the note, may not be included in the basis of the patent for depreciation purposes, and no deduction is allowable for interest paid or accrued on the note.

Rev. Rul. 78-30, 1978-4 I.R.B. 9.

A cash method individual who pays the dredging costs of a developer's beach front property with his own funds and the proceeds of a nonrecourse loan from a financial institution that will be paid a portion of the sale price of each lot until the loan is repaid with interest, after which the individual will receive the same portion of the sale price of the remaining lots, may deduct only the portion of the dredging costs paid with his own funds. Further, such costs are deductible only in the year payments are received and only in the ratio that the amount received bears to the total amount expected to be received.

1275

As the Treasury continues its search for more revenue. the I.R.S. will undoubtedly keep scrutinizing tax shelters to determine which ones fulfill socio-economic goals of America and those structured to abuse the tax system. It pays to have an expert study whatever investment you are considering in order to minimize the risk of later trouble with the I.R.S.

TAX REFORM ACT OF 1976

The Tax Reform Act of 1976 made changes in some tax shelters which taxpayers used to create deductions to offset their regular income.

These ventures include real estate, farming, oil and gas, movies, equipment leasing and sports franchises.

Investors in oil and gas will be limited to deducting losses from amounts they personally invest. This "at risk" rule will eliminate the use of nonrecourse loans, or loans the investor isn't liable to repay. When an investor sells a well, the Internal Revenue Service will "recapture" as ordinary income—rather than as a capital gain—all deductions for intangible drilling costs to the extent they exceeded the deductions that would have been allowed if the costs had been capitalized and amortized.

Farming operations—except those involving trees other than fruit or nut trees—will likewise be subject to a new at-risk requirement. Farming syndicates will be required to hold off deducting expenses for feed, seed, fertilizer and other farm supplies until they're used, which eliminates the practice of deducting these expenses when incurred. Syndicates will also have to capitalize costs of poultry and costs of groves, orchards or vineyards incurred before the year when the property begins producing a crop.

The new rules apply both to public syndicates, which register their stock with the Securities and Exchange Commission, and to private unregistered syndicates where at least 35% of the deductions go to "passive" partners. But anyone who helps manage the farm, or lives there, or belongs to the family that owns it, or feeds his own cattle in a feedlot, is considered an "active" partner and isn't subject to this new restriction.

Syndicates whose securities were approved for sale by the SEC prior to January 1, 1976, will have one year of grace under the current rules.

Finally, farms organized as corporations will have to use accrual accounting, rather than cash accounting, and will have to capitalize expenses incurred in preproductive periods. But these new requirements won't apply to Subchapter S corporations, which are corporations where a family owns at least 50%

of the stock, or to any other corporation with gross annual receipts of less than $1 million.

Deductions for movie ventures will also be limited to the amount for which the investor is at risk. This change applies generally to amounts paid or incurred starting September 11, 1975. Individuals and Subchapter S corporations that produce films, books, records and similar property will have to capitalize production and display costs, and deduct them over the life of the property rather than at the start.

The same at-risk provision applies to equipment-leasing shelters. For "operating" leases, the change will be retroactive to May 1, 1976; binding contracts in effect before then aren't affected. For "net" leases, the at-risk rule is effective as of January 1, 1976.

The law requires that when a sports franchise is sold, the purchaser can't allocate any more to player contracts than does the seller. And unless the taxpayer can persuade the IRS otherwise, a maximum of 50% of the price can be allocated to player contracts. Finally, at the time of the sale, the government will recapture as ordinary income any previously unrecaptured depreciation on player contracts.

Many tax shelters are organized as limited partnerships. The law requires that fees paid in connection with syndicating a partnership be capitalized, while organization fees can be amortized over five years. Current law is unclear here, but many taxpayers have been taking immediate deductions for these fees.

The law will also put a stop to the practice of allocating a full share of partnership losses for the entire year to a partner who waits until the end of the year to make his tax-shelter investment. The new rule is that a partner's share of income or losses will correspond to the portion of the year he belongs to the partnership.

The assistance of the Wall Street Journal in the foregoing analysis is gratefully acknowledged.

Tax Reform rarely satisfies all glaring tax problems on any particular item, and the 1976 law did little to help capital formation desperately needed by American industry and which the Ford administration considered a critical area for reform. However many noteworthy changes were made in one of the most extensive tax revisions in American history.

A brief summary of the Tax Reform Act of 1976 follows.

TAX REFORM ACT OF 1976
CONTENTS OF SUMMARY

I. **INDIVIDUALS**
   - A. New tax benefits for individuals
     1. Retirement plans for self-employed individuals
     2. Individual retirement plans
     3. Child care expense
     4. Income averaging for lump-sum pension distributions
     5. Moving expense deduction
     6. Alimony deduction
     7. Sale of residence, persons 65 or over
     8. Retirement income credit
   - B. Extension of tax reductions
     1. Personal tax credit
     2. Standard deduction
     3. Earned income credit

II. **CORPORATIONS**
   - A. Extension of corporate tax reductions
   - B. Subchapter S corporation changes

III. **PROVISIONS AFFECTING BOTH INDIVIDUALS AND CORPORATIONS**
   - A. Investment tax credit
   - B. Net operating losses
   - C. Capital gains and losses

IV. **MINIMUM AND MAXIMUM TAX CHANGES**
   - A. Minimum tax changes
     1. Individuals
     2. Corporations
   - B. Maximum tax changes

V. **CHANGES AFFECTING TAX-SHELTERED INVESTMENTS AND OTHER TAX DEDUCTIONS**
   - A. "At risk" limitation (shelters other than real estate)
   - B. Deferred deduction of expenses
   - C. Partnership deductions
   - D. Depreciation recapture
   - E. Interest expense deductions
   - F. Home office deductions
   - G. Vacation home rental expenses
   - H. Ordinary income treatment—Sales between related parties

HIGHLIGHTS OF THE TAX REFORM ACT OF 1976

The Tax Reform Act of 1976 has altered numerous provisions of our existing tax laws. This legislation has extended recently enacted tax reductions for both individuals and corporations, significantly tightened up the rules for so-called "tax shelters" and other tax write-offs, toughened the existing minimum tax for both individuals and corporations, and completely revamped the present estate and gift tax structure. Summarized below are *most* of the major provisions of this new law. Effective dates of particular provisions are noted where the provisions could have a significant impact on your tax planning.

I.   INDIVIDUALS

    A.   NEW TAX BENEFITS FOR INDIVIDUALS

        1. *Retirement Plans for Self-employed Individuals*—Effective for 1976 and future years, self-employed individuals whose adjusted gross income does not exceed $15,000, and who have HR-10 retirement plans may make a minimum contribution to the plan of up to $750 of self-employment income without regard to the percentage limitations on contributions which would otherwise be applicable.

        2. *Individual Retirement Plans*—For calendar year 1977 and future years, a married taxpayer who is eligible to establish an individual retirement account (IRA) (generally these are employed or self-employed individuals who are not covered by an HR—10 or corporate retirement plan) may establish a second separate account (or separate

sub-account) for an unemployed spouse and increase the maximum deductible amount of contributions from $1,500 to $1,750. The deduction may not exceed 15% of the individual's gross compensation, however.

3. *Child Care Expense*—Effective for 1976, an individual will be entitled to a credit against regular taxes of up to 20% of certain child and dependent care expenses which were previously available only as a deduction from income. Payments made to a relative for such purposes will generally qualify for the new credit, and it will be available to a married couple even though one spouse works only part-time or is a full-time student. There will be no upper income limit on individuals eligible for the credit (as under prior law) and, in the case of divorced or separated parents, the custodial parent will be eligible for the credit even though his or her spouse is entitled to the dependency exemption for the child or children. The maximum credit will be $400 for one child or dependent and $800 for two or more.

4. *Income Averaging for Lump-Sum Pension Distributions*—Effective January 1, 1976, the entire amount of certain lump-sum pension distributions may qualify for a special ten-year income averaging break.

5. *Moving Expense Deduction*—For 1977, the moving expense deduction will be slightly liberalized.

6. *Alimony Deduction*—Alimony will be deductible as an adjustment to gross income rather than as an itemized deduction.

7. *Sale of Residence, Persons 65 or Over*—After 1976, the gain attributable to the first $35,000 of proceeds from the sale of a principal residence by an individual age 65 or over will escape tax completely.

8. *Retirement Income Credit*—This credit available for persons 65 and older has been liberalized for 1976 and future years.

B.   EXTENSION OF TAX REDUCTIONS

1.   *Personal Tax Credit*—For individual taxpayers, the personal tax credit has been extended through December 31, 1977. For calendar years 1976 and 1977, the credit will be equal to the greater of $35 for each individual for which a taxpayer is entitled to claim a personal exemption or 2% of taxable income up to $9,000.

2.   *Standard Deduction*—The standard deduction for 1976 and future years will be based on 16% of adjusted gross income as in 1975. The lower and upper limits for the deduction will be $1,700 and $2,400, respectively, for single individuals and $2,100 and $2,800 for couples filing joint returns.

3.   *Earned Income Credit*—The refundable earned income credit for low-income families with children has been extended through 1977. The credit is equal to 10% of the first $4,000 of earned income, but is phased out as taxable income increases from $4,000 to $8,000.

II.   CORPORATIONS

A.   EXTENSION OF CORPORATE TAX REDUCTIONS
Corporate tax reductions were extended through December 31, 1977 by the new Act. In general, the first $25,000 of corporate income will be taxed at 20%, and the second $25,000 at 22%. Income in excess of $50,000 will be taxed at the regular 48% rate.

B.   SUBCHAPTER S CORPORATION CHANGES
For calendar year 1977 and later years, a Subchapter S corporation will, *under certain circumstances*, be permitted to have as many as 15 shareholders, as opposed to the maximum number of ten under current rules. Grantor trusts and voting trusts will be eligible shareholders in 1977 and later years; and a Subchapter S election will be terminated only by a new shareholder who affirmatively refuses to consent to the election within ten days.

III. PROVISIONS AFFECTING BOTH INDIVIDUALS AND CORPORATIONS

    A.   INVESTMENT TAX CREDIT

The 10% investment credit will be extended through 1980. In addition, for tax years beginning on or after January 1, 1976, all taxpayers will be able to use investment tax credits on a first-in, first-out basis. This means that a taxpayer may use investment credit carryforwards from prior years (which may be about to expire) before using current year credits. (Credits not utilized in the current year may still be carried back three years and forward five.) Finally, the increased $100,000 limit on used investment credit property will continue to apply through December 31, 1980.

Corporations which have established employee stock ownership plans (ESOPS) will still be eligible for an additional 1% investment credit through 1980, and may be eligible for a 1-1/2% credit for years beginning after December 31, 1976.

    B.   NET OPERATING LOSSES

Net operating losses incurred by either individuals or corporations for years ending after December 31, 1975 will be eligible for two additional carryforward years (seven years versus five). In addition, taxpayers will be able to forego the three-year carryback and use the entire loss as a carryforward.

    C.   CAPITAL GAINS AND LOSSES

The holding period required to qualify for long-term capital gains will be increased to nine months for taxable years beginning in 1977, and to twelve months for years beginning in 1978 and thereafter.

Another factor to consider is the increased deduction available for capital losses. Previously they could be used to offset a maximum of $1,000 of ordinary income. For years beginning in 1977, this limitation will be raised to $2,000, and finally to $3,000 for years beginning in 1978 and thereafter.

IV. MINIMUM AND MAXIMUM TAX CHANGES

    A.   MINIMUM TAX CHANGES

        1.   *Individuals*—For individuals, the minimum tax

on tax preferences (one-half of net long-term capital gain, accelerated depreciation on certain types of property and several other items) will be increased from 10% to 15% for 1976; and the deduction of $30,000 *plus* the amount of a taxpayer's regular income taxes has been reduced to the *greater of* $10,000 *or* one-half of the regular taxes paid for the year (with no carryover of "excess" regular taxes as in prior years). Finally, several new items have been added as tax preferences, including itemized deductions (other than medical and casualty loss deductions) in excess of 60% of adjusted gross income, certain intangible drilling costs of oil and gas wells, and accelerated depreciation on all leased personal property. As a result of these changes, a great many more individual taxpayers will be subject to the minimum tax, and those already subject to the tax will incur a larger tax.

2. *Corporations*—Corporations will generally be subject to an increased minimum tax on the same basis as individuals except that the new tax preference items will not apply to corporations and the exemption is the greater of $10,000 or the full amount of regular income tax. Only one-half of the minimum tax increase will be imposed for taxable years beginning in 1976.

B. MAXIMUM TAX CHANGES

Pension and annuity income will qualify for the 50% maximum tax rates beginning in 1977 and future tax years. However, all items of tax preference income will offset, dollar for dollar, the amount of income qualifying for maximum tax rates.

V. CHANGES AFFECTING TAX-SHELTERED INVESTMENTS AND OTHER TAX DEDUCTIONS

A. "AT RISK" LIMITATION (SHELTERS OTHER THAN REAL ESTATE)

The taxation of certain tax-sheltered investments has been significantly altered by the 1976 Tax Reform Act. In general, beginning in 1976, all investors (other than corporations which are not Subchapter S corporations) in ventures involving farming, oil and gas production, equipment leasing and movie production and/or distribution will be permitted to deduct losses only to the extent that their money is "at risk." In addition, a general "at risk" rule will apply to losses generated by partnerships engaged in all other types of activities (with the exception of real estate investment). This means that, in general, "nonrecourse" loans (loans for which an investor is not personally liable) will not be included in a taxpayer's basis of an investment so as to increase the amount of deductions which he may claim with respect to that property. Under rather complex transitional provisions, however, some existing movie and equipment leasing tax-shelters will be exempted from these rules.

B. DEFERRED DEDUCTION OF EXPENSES

Many expenditures which were previously deductible when paid or incurred will have to be capitalized under the new Reform Act rules, or deferred until subsequent periods. Some of the major items affected include prepaid feed expense and preproductive period expenses of farming syndicates, production costs incurred by noncorporate taxpayers in connection with films, books, records and similar properties, real estate taxes and mortgage interest incurred by noncorporate taxpayers during construction of buildings or other real estate improvements and all partnership syndication and organization costs.

C. PARTNERSHIP DEDUCTIONS

Partnerships will also have considerably less leeway in allocating income and deductions among partners, and a partnership will be limited to $2,000 of additional first-year bonus depreciation annually.

D. RECAPTURE OF ACCELERATED DEPRECIATION OF REAL PROPERTY

Effective for years ending after December 31, 1975, gains realized from dispositions of nongovernment-subsidized residential real estate will be taxable as ordinary income to the full extent that post-1975 depreciation deductions actually claimed with respect to the property exceed straight-line depreciation. With respect to government-subsidized housing, post-1975 accelerated depreciation will be subject to full "recapture" (as described above) during the first 100 months. Recapture will be gradually phased out over the second 100 months, and there will be no recapture on dispositions after that time. Recapture rules for accelerated depreciation claimed for periods prior to 1976 are not affected by the new provisions. These rules are another reason (in addition to the revised minimum tax) you should reconsider the use of accelerated depreciation methods.

E.   INTEREST EXPENSE DEDUCTIONS

Interest which is prepaid on or after January 1, 1976, will have to be deducted over the period of the loan, and will not be deductible currently as was sometimes the case in the past for cash-basis taxpayers.

Also for 1976 and future years, the total deduction for interest incurred to finance investment or net lease rental property will generally be limited to $10,000 plus the amount of investment income generated by the property. Interest on debts for a specific period which were incurred prior to September 11, 1975, in connection with a specific item of property will still be subject to the higher ceiling in effect under prior law.

F.   HOME OFFICE DEDUCTIONS

For 1976 and future years, no deductions will be permitted in connection with a home office or other business use of a personal residence unless an office or area is used exclusively for business purposes and either constitutes the taxpayer's principal place of business, or is used on a regular basis in meeting or dealing with patients, clients or customers. Even in the limited circumstances where a deduction will still be allowable under these rules, it may not exceed the gross income derived from the use of the home less deductions allocable to such use which are otherwise deductible (such as interest and taxes). These rules apply to partnerships and Subchapter S corporations as well as to individuals.

G.   VACATION HOME RENTAL EXPENSES

Stricter limits are also placed on deductions for expenses connected with rentals of homes or vacation homes for 1976 and future years. If a taxpayer uses a dwelling unit for more than 10% of the number of days during which the unit is rented at a fair rental value, any deductions for maintenance, insurance, depreciation or other expenses allocable to the rental use of the dwelling will not be permitted to exceed the gross rental income less the expenses allocable to such rental use which are otherwise deductible (such as interest and taxes). An individual may use the property for a period not to exceed 14 days (even though the 10% personal use limitation is exceeded) without becoming subject to these limitations, however. Furthermore, where personal use of the property exceeds both the 14-day and 10% tests, no rental deductions will be allowed unless the property is rented for at least 15 days. In this latter situation, however, the taxpayer need not report the associated rental income. These provisions apply to partnerships and Subchapter S corporations as well as to individuals.

H. ORDINARY INCOME TREATMENT OF GAIN ON SALES OF DEPRECIABLE PROPERTY BETWEEN RELATED PARTIES

Under prior law, the entire gain on sales of depreciable property between certain related parties was treated as ordinary income rather than as capital gain. With respect to any transactions entered into after the date the Reform bill was enacted, the definition of related parties has been expanded to include commonly controlled corporations. In addition, expanded attribution rules will apply to determine whether a corporation is indirectly controlled by an individual so as to be treated as a party related to that individual or to another corporation.

I. OTHER PROVISIONS

The tax treatment of income derived from foreign sources has been significantly revised, and the tax benefits available to domestic international sales corporations have been reduced substantially.

Deductions related to attendance at business conventions in foreign countries will be subject to stricter rules in 1977 and future years.

With respect to options granted on or after September 1, 1976, gains (or losses) resulting from closing transactions or the lapse of options will be treated as short-term capital gains (or losses) and not as ordinary income or loss, as was possible under prior law.

The use of partnership "swap funds" to diversify an appreciated stock portfolio without incurring current tax on the gains will be curtailed under the new law. Excepted are a handful of funds already in existence operating with IRS or SEC approval.

Qualified employee stock options issued after May 20, 1976, will be taxed under the same rules that apply to nonqualified options. Consequently, the value of the option when granted will generally be taxed as ordinary income.

For 1977 and future years ending before January 1, 1982, group legal services supplied to employees under a company plan will be nontaxable to the employee.

Gain arising from future condemnations or other involuntary conversions of real property will not be taxable if the proceeds are reinvested within three years (versus two years under prior law).

VI. ESTATE AND GIFT TAX REFORM
    A. UNIFIED ESTATE AND GIFT TAX SYSTEM

Effective January 1, 1977, the taxation of estate and lifetime gift transfers will be unified. A single graduated rate structure will be applied to both lifetime transfers and estates; and lifetime gifts made after December 31, 1976, will be taken into consideration in determining the tax bracket to be applied to the taxable estate of an individual at his death.

The $60,000 estate tax exemption and the $30,000 gift tax exemption will be eliminated and replaced by a single *tax credit* which will offset both lifetime gift taxes and estate taxes until it has been completely used. The initial *credit* for 1977 will be $30,000 (equivalent to an exemption of $120,667) and will gradually increase to $47,000 for 1981 and future years (equivalent to an exemption of $175,625).

Despite a general increase in estate and gift tax rates, taxes will actually be reduced for many estates due to the tax credit available under the new law.

B. SPECIAL RULES FOR FARMS AND CLOSELY HELD BUSINESSES

Special valuation rules for real property used in connection with a closely held business or farm will be available, in some circumstances, to reduce a decedent's gross estate by as much as $500,000. It will also be possible to pay estate taxes over a 15-year period when a farm or closely held business comprises at least 65% of a decedent's adjusted gross estate. In addition, a greater number of estates will be able to utilize the ten-year payment plan which is presently available.

C. INCREASED MARITAL DEDUCTIONS

The first $100,000 of gifts made to a spouse will be deductible in computing the gift tax, and one-half of such gifts in excess of $200,000 will also be deductible. The estate tax marital deduction (for certain property transferred to a spouse) will be increased to the greater of $250,000, or one-half of the adjusted gross estate. The deduction will be reduced, however, by the amount by which deductible lifetime transfers to a spouse exceed one-half of the aggregate of such transfers.

D. CARRYOVER BASIS RULES

Under present law, the tax basis of property acquired from a decedent by inheritance is generally "stepped up" to its fair market value at the date of the decedent's death. Under the new rules, a decedent's cost basis will generally *carry over* to his heirs. A partial step up in basis will still be permitted, for purposes of determining taxable gains, for assets whose carryover basis would otherwise relate back to periods preceding December 31, 1976. For readily marketable securities, basis will be stepped up to fair market value on December 31, 1976. For other property, basis is stepped up by the amount of appreciation deemed to be attributable to pre-1976 periods. This amount is calculated on a pro rata basis taking into account the number of days the property was held before and after December 31, 1976.

E. TAXATION OF GENERATION-SKIPPING TRANSFERS

In the past, it was possible to avoid having assets taxed in the estates of beneficiaries of your property by restricting their interest to a lifetime or income interest and providing for the remainder or corpus to pass to their children or heirs. In the future, such transfers which pass through one or more "generations," will be subjected to a tax upon the termination of the interest of the life or income beneficiary. The tax will be computed just as if the property had been given to the life or income beneficiary outright. Transfers through a grantor's spouse are not subject to the tax, however, and a limited exception is provided for generation skipping transfers to a grandchild of the grantor, but the maximum amount that can be transferred "tax free" under this exemption through each of a grantor's children is $250,000. Generally, these provisions will apply to transfers occurring after April 30, 1976, unless made pursuant to a trust which was irrevocable on that date (but only to the extent that the transfer is not made from corpus added to the trust after that date). Transfers made pursuant to a will or revocable trust in existence on April 30, 1976 will also escape these rules if the will or trust instrument is not revised after that date and the grantor dies before 1982.

F. NEW STOCK REDEMPTION RULES

If certain tests are met, redemptions of shares in a closely held corporation which are included in a decedent's estate, and which would otherwise be taxed as dividend distributions, will presently qualify for capital gains treatment. New rules severely limiting the opportunities for this favorable treatment will apply to redemptions from estates or beneficiaries of decedents dying after December 31, 1976.

G. ESTATE PLANNING UNDER THE NEW LAW

Because of these changes, you should review your present estate plan to make sure that you take full advantage of newly enacted tax breaks where appropriate, and avoid the pitfalls of the new rules where possible. In particular, you should consider making use of the enlarged marital deduction that may be available under the new law if your present will does not accomplish this.

REVENUE ACT OF 1978

Table of Contents

8. Simplified Employee Pensions – Code Sections 219(b)(7) And 408(j)

9. Qualified Cash Or Deferred Profit-Sharing And Stock Bonus Plans – Code Section 401(k)

10. Reform In Individual Retirement Account Rules
    A. Correcting Excess Contributions – Code Sections 219, 220, 408, And 4973
    B. Rollover Opportunities Expanded – Code Sections 402(a), 403(b)(8) And 408(d)(3)
    C. New Rules On Contributions, Returns And Excess Accumulations – Code Sections 219(c), 408(b), 4974 And 6058
    D. Estate And Gift Tax Rules Clarified For Spousal IRA's – Code Sections 2039(c) And 2503(d)

11. Employee Stock Ownership Plans
    A. Tax Credit And Leveraged ESOP's Receive New Names, New Life And Many New Rules – Code Sections 46, 48, 56(c), 401(a)(21), 409(A), 4975 And 6699
    B. Other Employee Stock Ownership Plan Developments

12. Other Qualified Plans Developments
    A. Passthrough Of Stock Voting Rights For All Qualified Plans – Code Section 401(a)(22)
    B. Distributions From Mutual Fund TSA's – Code Section 403(b)(7)
    C. Benefit Limit Changes For Collectively Bargained Plans – Code Section 415(b)(7)
    D. Maximum Tax Treatment For Plan Benefits – Code Section 1348(b)(1)(A)
    E. Clarification Of Definition Of Lump-Sum Distributions For Estate Tax Purposes – Code Section 2039(c)
    F. Bankruptcy Priority For Employer Contributions Owed To Plans – Bankruptcy Reform Act Section 507

INTRODUCTION

The Revenue Act of 1978, signed by the president on November 6, 1978, is by no means a tax reform measure. The primary impact of the Act is an over-18 billion dollar tax cut for both businesses and individuals. The Act, however, contains a number of substantive provisions affecting business, estate and pension planning. It also incorporates a myriad of clerical and clarifying amendments to the Tax Reform Act of 1976. Finally, accompanying the Revenue Act proper were several other bills, similarly passed in the last week of the Ninety-Fifth Congress, which also involved income and estate taxation. As a result, the following is presented as a summary analysis of the topics covered in these acts.

1. TAX REDUCTIONS FOR INDIVIDUALS

A. Rates - Code Section 1

The Revenue Act of 1978 amends Internal Revenue Code section 1 to introduce new individual income rate tables effective for tax years beginning after December 31, 1978. The new rate schedules widen the taxable income brackets to which the rates apply and reduce rates for several income brackets. The number of brackets is reduced from 25 to 16 for single persons and from 25 to 15 for joint filers, with the top and bottom rates of 14% and 70%, respectively, remaining the same.

To illustrate these changes, a portion of the brackets from both the 1978 and new 1979 schedules for married individuals filing joint returns is shown on the next page.

A married couple with a taxable income of $14,000 filing a joint return for 1978 will have a tax of $1,996 before any tax credits. In 1979, on the same taxable income, the couple's tax before any credit will be $1,845 or $151 less than in 1978.

TAXABLE INCOME		TAX	

1978

Over	But Not Over	Tax on Col. 1	Rate on Excess of Col. 1
$11,200	$15,200	$ 1,380	22%
15,200	19,200	2,260	25
19,200	23,200	3,260	28
23,200	27,200	4,380	32
27,200	31,200	5,660	36
31,200	35,200	7,100	39
35,200	39,200	8,660	42
39,200	43,200	10,340	45
43,200	47,200	12,140	48
47,200	55,200	14,060	50
55,200	67,200	18,060	53

1979

Over	But Not Over	Tax on Col. 1	Rate on Excess of Col. 1
$11,900	$16,000	$ 1,404	21%
16,000	20,200	2,265	24
20,200	24,600	3,273	28
24,600	29,900	4,505	32
29,900	35,200	6,201	37
35,200	45,800	8,162	43
45,800	60,000	12,720	49

B. Increased Zero Bracket Amount — Code Section 63

In a further effort to give some relief to the individual tax-payer, the Revenue Act of 1978 has increased the "zero bracket amount" (ZBA). Under prior law, the standard deduction already had been replaced, for 1977 and later years, by the zero bracket amount in order to reduce calculation errors by tax-payers. Basically, the ZBA is a flat-amount standard deduction which is built into the tax tables by giving the lowest tax bracket a zero tax rate.

Revenue Act section 101(b), amending Code section 63(d), provides that beginning in 1979, the zero bracket amount is increased from $3,200 to $3,400 for married couples filing joint returns. For single persons and heads of households, it has been upped $100 to $2,300. If a married couple files separately, the zero bracket amount will be $1,700 each, rather than $1,600.

These new bracket amounts also apply in calculating the amount of excess itemized deductions an individual may deduct. As under prior law, if a taxpayer itemizes his deductions, he may deduct only the excess of his itemized deductions over the ZBA [section 63(b)].

C. Increased Personal Exemption — Code Section 151

Congress has also increased the personal exemption. In amended Code section 151, the exemption for a taxpayer, his spouse and dependents is increased from $750 to $1,000 each. The additional exemptions for a person age 65 or more and for blind persons are also increased to $1,000. Finally, the Revenue Act changes the gross income level at which an individual (other than the taxpayer's child who is a student or younger than 19) loses qualification as a dependent for exemption purposes from $750 to $1,000.

D. Capital Gains Deduction Increased — Code Sections 170(e) And 1202

Individual taxpayers have been greatly benefited by the reduced tax on long-term capital gains. Specifically, the size of the section 1202 deduction has been increased by the Revenue Act of 1978 to 60% of net long-term capital gains in excess of net short-term capital losses. (The former figure is one half of gains in excess of losses.) This translates into a maximum ordinary income tax rate of 28% on capital gains (40% multiplied by the top marginal rate of 70%), a sizable reduction from the former ceiling of 35% (50% of the top marginal rate of 70%). The decrease in the amount of realized capital gains subject to tax, however, was coupled with repeal of the alternate 25% tax on the first $50,000 of net capital gains.

The increased capital gains deduction has been carried over to Code section 170(e), for a favorable effect on the charitable contributions deduction limitations. Corresponding to the changes in section 1202, deductions for charitable contributions of appreciated tangible personal (long-term capital gain) property now need to be reduced only by 40% of the property's value, rather than 50%, in order to avoid realization of capital gain by the donor.

These changes are effective for capital transactions completed after October 31, 1978, but also apply to installment payments received after the same date regardless of when the underlying transaction was completed. In the case of capital transactions in tax years straddling the October 31, 1978 cutoff, a proration rule has been laid down. The deduction is (1) 60% of the lesser of the net capital gain for the year *or* of the transactions taking place in the same tax year after the cutoff plus (2) 50% of the total net capital gain for the year which is in excess of (1).

E. $100,000 Capital Gain Exclusion For Sale Of A Personal Residence — Code Section 121

In Code section 121, the Revenue Act introduces a new, one-time only exclusion for the first $100,000 of gain realized from the disposition of principal residence as a substitute for the prior section 121. The exclusion must be elected by the taxpayer. This change is effective for sales or exchanges made after July 26, 1978.

Prior elections under former section 121(a) do not prevent one under new section 121. The taxpayer must have attained age 55 prior to the date of the sale although only one married taxpayer need be age 55, and the exclusion is only available to the extent of $50,000 each for married couples filing separately.

Additionally, the same residence must have been owned and used as a principal residence for a total of three out of the last five years immediately preceding the sale (unless the taxpayer's previous dwelling were condemmed or otherwise involuntarily converted). For sales through July 25, 1981, a taxpayer over the age of 65 can elect to use the five-out-of-last-eight-years test of prior law.

F. Rollover Of Gain On Sale Of Principal Residence — Code Section 1034

Section 1034 allows the deferral of gain upon the sale of a principal residence if the gain is reinvested in a new principal residence. This nonrecognition, however, was not available on a second sale of a principal residence made within 18 months of the first sale.

The Act added section 1034(d)(2) which provides that the deferral is still permitted for a second sale within 18 months if the sale is in connection with the commencement of work by the taxpayer as an employee or as a self-employed individual at a new principal place of work. To qualify, the 35-mile-move and the length-of-employment tests for moving expense deductions under section 217 must be satisfied. The new rule is effective for sales of residences made after July 26, 1978.

G. Minimum Tax On Preference Items — Code Sections 55 And 57

The minimum tax on "tax preference items" of Code section 57(a) is a tax of 15% on preference items to the extent their total exceeds the greater of one-half of the taxpayer's regular income tax or $10,000. Prior to the Revenue Act, net long-term capital gain deductions were a tax preference item and had the potential of triggering the minimum tax. Thus, it was quite conceivable that the sale of a closely held business upon the death of a major stockholder would result in the realization of a substantial amount of capital gain which in turn would activate the 15% minimum tax and thereby compound the estate shrinkage problem.

Now section 57(a) has been amended to have a more favorable impact on long-term capital gains (and adjusted itemized deductions). The Act has removed capital gains from the list of tax preference items under section 57 and enacted a new "alternative minimum tax" with the introduction of Code section 55. The new minimum tax is expressed in the form of an add-on triggered whenever it is greater than the combined regular income tax and the section 57(a) minimum tax. The new tax is computed on the amount of "alternative minimum taxable income" with a graduated percentage, which is zero for amounts of $20,000 and under, 10% for above $20,000 through $60,000, 20% for above $60,000 through $100,000, and 25% for above $100,000.

The alternative tax preference items which comprise alternative minimum taxable income are (1) gross income less allowable deductions and accumulation distributions from trusts, (2) capital gains deductions, and (3) adjusted itemized deductions (the excess of itemized deductions — not including the four following deductions — over 60% of deductions for medical expenses, casualty losses, estate taxes, and state and local taxes). The capital gain realized from the sale of a principal residence, however, is not an item of tax preference. The new provisions are effective for tax years beginning in 1979.

H. Maximum Tax On Personal Service Income — Code Section 1348

The capital gains changes have also been favorably extended to taxpayers using the Code section 1348 maximum tax on personal service income. The deductible portion of the capital gains realized is no longer an item of tax preference for purposes of section 1348(b)(2)(B) and thus no longer reduces the amount of personal service income eligible for the maximum tax rate of 50%. This amendment applies to sales and exchanges made after October 31, 1978.

Another potentially helpful modification was in section 1348(b)(1)(A), which limited personal service income for tax purposes to 30% of an individual's share of net profits if capital were a material income-producing factor in the trade or Now this arbitrary limit has been removed and personal service income, according to the conference committee report, will be all reasonable compensation for personal services actually rendered. This amendment is effective for tax years beginning in 1979.

The maximum and minimum tax changes should be particularly meaningful to business owners who sell their businesses at retirement — realizing large capital gains - who also may be in a position to benefit from section 1348 through a combination of employment agreements and qualified and nonqualified deferred compensation plans.

2. CORPORATE INCOME TAXES

A. Corporate Rate Reduction — Code Section 11

A major change effected by the Revenue Act of 1978 is in the corporate income tax provisions of the Internal Revenue Code. The former structure of normal tax, surtax and surtax exemption is completely replaced by a graduated rate structure which includes rate reductions. Revenue Act of 1978 section 301 amends Code section 11 by inserting rates for corporations as follows:

TAXABLE INCOME		TAX	
Over	But Not Over	Tax on Col. 1	Rate on Excess of Col. 1
$ 0	25,000	$ 0	17%
25,000	50,000	4,250	20
50,000	75,000	9,250	30
75,000	100,000	16,750	40
100,000		26,750	46

Comparing the new rate structure to the old system, it is readily apparent that the new rates are more favorable than those in existence for 1978 (20% on the first $25,000 of taxable income, 22% on the next $25,000 and 48% above $50,000). For the first $100,000 of taxable corporate income, there is a total tax reduction in 1979 of $7,750 compared to 1978 taxes: the 1978 rates would produce a tax of $34,500 before credits, while the 1979 rates will result in $26,750 in taxes before credits. For taxable corporate income greater than $100,000, there is a 2% reduction, from 48% to 46%.

Members of controlled corporate groups under Code section 1561 will have to share the sub-46% rates as they did the surtax exemption of prior law. This is to be done by equal division of the brackets among the group members or if they elect, by an unequal allocation plan (including proration according to incomes) designed to utilize all of the sub-46% brackets.

The Revenue Act of 1978's rate reductions certainly make nondeductible nonqualified deferred compensation plans and split dollar arrangements more attractive than in the past. This is especially significant when taxable income is in the $50,000 to $100,000 range because the new rates are 30% and 40% rather than 48%, a total savings of $6,500 for income between $50,000 and $100,000.

B. Investment Tax Credit Changes — Code Section 46

Sections 311-313 of the 1978 Revenue Act have amended section 46 of the Internal Revenue Code in several ways. The new law permanently sets the investment credit rate at 10%. It had been scheduled to decrease to 7% on January 1, 1981.

Also, the limit on the cost of used property eligible for the investment credit, which was set at $100,000 and scheduled to decrease on January 1, 1981, has been permanently fixed at $100,000.

Finally, the Act increases the tax liability limitation, the maximum amount of credit a taxpayer may use to offset tax liability in any one year, from 50% to 90% of tax liability over the first $25,000. The increase to 90% is to be phased in by 10% a year beginning in 1979. Thus, the limit for tax years ending in 1979 is $25,000 plus 60% of tax liability over the first $25,000.

C. Capital Gains Alternative Tax Reduction — Code Section 1201

Corporate taxpayers never have had a capital gains deduction like the section 1202 deduction available to individuals. They do, however, have a corporate capital gain alternative tax which was reduced by the Revenue Act of 1978 from a flat 30% to 28%. The change is effective for tax years beginning in 1979 and, allowing for the different cutoff date and direct application of the alternative rate (rather than a deduction), the calculation method for tax years straddling the cutoff is the same as it is for individuals, as described above in article 1 D.

D. Minimum Tax — Code Sections 57(a) And 58(i)

In general, the corporate minimum tax has not been changed by the Revenue Act. Under it, however, personal holding and Subchapter S corporations will be treated as corporations, rather than as individuals as they were previously. Consequently, their minimum tax is the greater of 15% of the excess of their tax preferences over $10,000 or their total tax liability. This change is effective for tax years beginning in *1976*.

3. NONQUALIFIED DEFERRED COMPENSATION

A. Deferred Compensation In Taxpaying Entities — Revenue Act Section 132

Section 132 of the Act provides specific congressional approval for nonqualified deferred compensation plans maintained by taxpaying entities. Under this section, the tax treatment of of deferred compensation is to be determined in accordance with the principles set forth in regulations, rulings and judicial decisions which were in effect on February 1, 1978. This date is especially important since it means that Congress has directly overruled the proposed Treasury regulations under Code section 61 on deferred compensation which were issued on February 3, 1978. Under the proposed regulations, an employee would have been currently taxable on any compensation he or she chose to defer pursuant to an individual option.

It should be noted that the new law does contain an important exception to the general rule of noncurrent taxability. Specifically, any plan falling under Code section 83 will continue to be taxed according to the rules for that section. Thus, for example, if the deferred compensation were placed in an irrevocable trust, the employee would be taxed currently on the funds unless the employee's rights were not transferable and were subject to a substantial risk of forfeiture.

Quite clearly, the legislative sanction represented by this portion of the new legislation (which is effective for tax years ending after February 1, 1978) comes as good news to fringe benefit planners and signals deferred compensation as an increasingly important component of an employer's fringe benefit package.

B. Public Employees' Deferred Compensation — Code Section 457

Act Section 131 adds new Code section 457 and specifically authorizes deferred compensation plans for states, local governments, and their political subdivisions. Under this section, both employees and independent contractors who provide services are eligible to participate in a plan.

Section 457 does place a limit on the amount that can be deferred. Under it, the maximum annual deferral is equal to the lesser of $7,500 or one third of the participant's includible compensation from the governmental unit. For example, if an individual is earning $20,000, the maximum which may be deferred is $5,000 (this represents one third of the $15,000 includible compensation). The new law does contain a limited "catch-up" provision for participants approaching retirement. Subject to a maximum total annual deferral of $15,000, during the three-year period immediately preceding the participant's normal retirement age, he or she will be permitted to defer in excess of

$7,500 annually in order to make up for prior years in which the actual deferrals were less than the permitted ceiling.

It should be noted that if a participant in the deferred compensation plan is also participating in a section 403(b) plan (*i.e.*, a tax-sheltered annuity), the amount deferred under each plan is taken into account in determining the maximum that can be deferred under the other plan. Thus, an individual will be unable to defer an amount in excess of $7,500 simply by participating in two plans.

Many public employers, especially states, already have plans which have been in operation for several years, but which do not conform to the new law. In addressing this problem, the Act provides a transitional rule so that, until January 1, 1982, participants in existing plans will continue to avoid taxation on any deferred amounts (to a maximum of $7,500 or one third of includible compensation). As of January 1, 1982, a plan which is not administered in accordance with the requirements of the law will lose its eligible status on the first day of the plan year beginning *more than* 180 days after notification by the Secretary of the Treasury that the requirements are not being met, unless satisfactory corrective action is taken by the first day of that plan year. If a plan loses its status as an eligible plan, amounts deferred by participants will be includible in income when they were deferred, unless they were subject to a substantial risk of forfeiture. In other words, the rules of Code section 83 will apply.

C. Pension Reserve Credit Extended To Contracts Issued For Governmental Retirement Plans, Including Deferred Compensation — Code Section 805(d)

Under the Code, favorable tax treatment is given to income relating to life insurance company reserves attributable to contracts issued for individual retirement annuities, tax-sheltered annuities and qualified retirement plans.

The Act amended this Code provision so that reserves for contracts issued for public employees' deferred compensation arrangements and to governmental retirement plans that are not qualified under Code section 401(a) can be accorded this tax advantage for tax years beginning on or after January 1, 1979.

D. Deferred Compensation In Tax-Exempt Organizations To Be Clarified

One major area which was not covered by the Revenue Act is the tax treatment of deferred compensation for tax-exempt organizations, *i.e.,* organizations falling under Code section 501. Although the Senate version of the bill would have covered these plans by subjecting them to the same rules as apply to taxpaying employers, this provision was deleted in conference and Act section 132 (applicable to taxpaying entities) clearly excludes them from its coverage. Thus, such plans are in a state of limbo and further clarification must be awaited.

Unfortunately, it appears that some authorities are adopting the view that Congress's failure to cover tax-exempts in any explicit manner signals its disapproval of plans in such organizations. If a tax-exempt organization is considering a plan and wishes to minimize the tax exposure to its participants, it is suggested that annuities and/or life insurance with a high early cash value be used as the informal funding vehicle. In this way, if the plan does ultimately receive negative tax consequences, the underlying contracts probably could be transferred to the participant so that his or her loss would be relatively small.

E. New Law Clarifies Timing Of Deferred Compensation Deductions For Independent Contractors — Code Section 404(d)

Under the prior law, there existed some question as to the proper timing of deductions when the participant in a non-qualified deferred compensation plan was an independent contractor. Code section 404(a)(5) generally indicated that the employer's deductions should coincide with the employee's taxability. Since, however, this section dealt only with employer-employee relationships, some authorities had maintained that the section had no application when the deferred compensation plan ran between a corporation and an independent contractor. In such instances, it was argued, an accrual basis corporation could take current deductions for a deferred compensation liability accruing to an independent contractor when the latter's right to the benefit was nonforfeitable. The new law rejects this position and makes it clear that the deduction and corresponding reportable income shall occur in the same year.

4. OTHER FRINGE BENEFITS

A. Sick Pay Exclusion Rules For Married Couples — Code Section 105(d)

The Code now restricts the sick pay exclusion for sick pay plans established under section 105 to taxpayers who retire on permanent and total disability and have not attained age 65. Further, when the employee's adjusted gross income before the exclusion exceeds $15,000, the maximum amount of sick pay which the employee can exclude from gross income is phased out on a dollar-for-dollar basis for any excess over $15,000. It was not clear, however, whether this income phase-out with respect to a married couple applied separately or jointly to their combined adjusted gross income. It was equally unclear how the maximum exclusion amount of $5,200 applied in such a situation.

Section 701(c)(1) of the Revenue Act clarifies these ambiguities by amending Code section 105(d) to provide that the $5,200 maximum exclusion is to applied separately to each spouse and the $15,000 adjusted gross income limit for phase-out purposes is to be applied to a couple's total adjusted gross income. These technical clarifications are effective for tax years beginning after 1975.

B Medical Reimbursement Plans — Code Section 105(h)

Prior to the Revenue Act of 1978, medical expense reimbursement plans allowed taxpayers to exclude from gross income any amounts received under a plan designed to reimburse employees, their spouses and/or other dependents for expenditures for medical care. The primary problem was being certain that a plan was for the benefit of employees rather than stockholders. If not, payments to stockholders under the plan would be deemed dividends.

The law now requires that a plan not discriminate in favor of the "highly compensated," defined as (1) the five highest paid officers, (2) stockholders owning directly or indirectly more than 10% of the shares of the employer, and (3) the highest paid 25% of all employees.

The nondiscrimination tests are similar to those enacted by ERISA under Code section 410(b) — a plan must meet either the 70%-80% tests or the nondiscriminatory classification test.

For purposes of applying these tests, certain employees may be excluded: those who have less than three years of service, those under age 35, part-time or seasonal workers, those who are covered under a collective bargaining agreement, and non-resident aliens who receive no U'S' earned income.

In addition, the benefits provided to the highly compensated under the plan must be the same as those for all other participants. On the other hand, offsetting of benefits by those under other health and accident plans, including federal and state, is allowed.

The penalty for disqualification of a plan is the treatment of benefits as taxable compensation. If a type of benefit is not available to "a broad cross-section of employees," the compensation is the amount of the reimbursement. If the plan as a whole is discriminatory, the taxable compensation is the same proportion of the reimbursement as the benefits of the highly compensated are of all benefits paid under the plan.

These new rules apply only to self-insured plans, i.e., those plans for which reimbursement is not provided under a "policy of accident and health insurance." They are effective for tax years beginning in 1980.

C. Cafeteria Plans – Code Section 125

Act section 134 introduces new Code section 125 and provides rules with regard to the taxation of benefits received under a "cafeteria plan." Under such a plan, an employee is generally permitted to choose from a package of employer-provided fringe benefits some of which may not be taxable (*e.g.,* group-term life insurance under $50,000).

Under the new rules, effective for tax years beginning after 1978, employer contributions to a written cafeteria plan will not generate taxable income for the employee to the extent that nontaxable benefits are chosen, *provided* the plan does not discriminate in favor of highly compensated individuals in eligibility for participation, contributions and benefits.

In determining whether the plan is nondiscriminatory, several tests are provided. Regarding eligibility, a plan will not be considered discriminatory if:

    (1) The eligible class satisfies the general antidiscrimination rule of Code section 410(b)(1)(B) which is applicable to qualified plans;

(2) There is a maximum three-year service requirement for participation; and

(3) Participation commences on the first day of the plan year after the service requirement has been satisfied.

In connection with contributions and benefits, a plan will not be considered discriminatory if nontaxable benefits and total benefits (or employer contributions allocable to nontaxable benefits and employer contributions for total benefits) do not discriminate in favor of highly compensated participants. In this regard, the Senate report states that a plan is not discriminatory if the total benefits and nontaxable benefits attributable to highly compensated employees (as a percentage of compensation) are not significantly greater than total benefits and nontaxable benefits attributable to other employees. Further, a cafeteria plan providing health benefits will not be considered discriminatory if:

(1) Contributions on behalf of each participant include an amount which equals either (a) 100% of the cost of health benefit coverage under the plan of the majority of highly compensated participants who are similarly situated (*e.g.,* same family size), or (b) are at least equal to 75% of the cost of the most expensive health benefit coverage elected by any similarly situated participant; and

(2) Other contributions or benefits other than those set forth in (1) above bear a uniform relationship to the compensation of plan participants.

Finally, the new law states that any cafeteria plan maintained pursuant to a collective bargaining agreement will automatically be considered to be nondiscriminatory.

D. Educational Assistance Programs — Code Section 127

In an effort to assist employees in obtaining a higher education, the Revenue Act introduced "educational assistance programs." Under this concept, which is set forth in new Code section 127, an employee will be able to exclude from gross income amounts paid by an employer for educational assistance to the employee if it is furnished pursuant to a program which meets specific requirements.

According to the requirements, the plan must be in writing and must not discriminate in favor of employees who are officers, owners, or highly compensated (or dependents of any of the foregoing). Further, not more than 5% of the amounts paid by the employer during a year may be provided for the class of individuals who are shareholders or owners and each of whom owns more than 5% of the stock (after application of the attribution rules of Code section 1563).

In connection with the types of expenses that can be covered under the program, the Revenue Act is fairly generous. Specifically, it includes tuition, fees, books, supplies, and equipment. It does not, however, include payment for tools or supplies which the employee may retain after completion of the course of instruction. Also excluded are expenses relating to sports, games or hobbies.

It should be noted that this new provision of the Code is effective for tax years beginning after 1978, but it is only a temporary provision. According to the Act, it is scheduled to expire for tax years beginning after 1983.

5. BUSINESS PLANNING

A. Congress Abolishes The Section 357(c) Accounts-Payable Trap

Section 365 of the Revenue Act of 1978 addresses a problem which has existed with regard to tax-free incorporations under Code section 351 and which has often been called the "accounts-payable tax trap" of section 357(c). Basically, if a cash-basis taxpayer incorporates, the transaction is tax free (*i.e.,* no gain or loss is recognized) if the transferor owns at least 80% of the corporation's stock immediately after the transaction. Code section 357, however, does provide that gain is to be recognized to the extent that the basis of the property transferred to the corporation is less than the sum of the liabilities assumed by the corporation and the liabilities to which the property is subject.

Generally, the Internal Revenue Service has given the term "liabilities" a very broad definition so that it includes the transferor's accounts payable. The effect of this definition was that a transferor would recognize gain in an otherwise tax-free incorporation if the new corporation assumed the transferor's accounts payable when such accounts exceeded the transferor's basis in the property.

1309

The new law makes it clear that if a cash-basis transferor transfers assets to a corporation pursuant to an otherwise tax-free incorporation, any accounts payable which are transferred will not be considered "liabilities" if the transferor would have received a deduction if he had paid them. Thsi provision codifies the Tax Court decision in *Focht v. Comm'r,* 68 T.C. 223 (1977). Thus, a potential tax trap often facing proprietors and partners who wish to incorporate has been removed and such incorporations should be facilitated.

B. Section 1244 Stock Limits Raised

Section 1244 allows an individual who suffers a loss on the sale or exchange of stock to deduct it (subject to a maximum amount) as an ordinary instead of capital loss if the corporation qualifies as a "small business corporation" under the section. Any gain realized upon the sale of section 1244 stock would, nonetheless, be capital gain.

Under prior law, the small business corporation could issue no more than $500,000 worth of stock under a section 1244 plan. The Act raises this to $1,000,000. Further, prior to amendment, the statute also limited small business corporations to those with no more than $1,000,000 of equity capital. This restriction has been eliminated, but the amount of existing capital is to be subtracted from the $1,000,000 limit for section 1244 stock. In other words, $500,000 of existing capital means only $500,000 of section 1244 stock can be issued, while $1,000,000 of existing capital means none can be issued.

Under the statute, the maximum deductible loss is now $50,000 (raised from $25,000) per individual taxpayer and is $100,000 (from $50,000) for spouses filing joint returns. Finally, a written plan no longer need be adopted prior to issue of section 1244 stock if the overall capital stock does not exceed $1,000,000. The new rules apply to stock issued after November 6, 1978, and tax years beginning in 1979.

C. Subchapter S Shareholder Rules Liberalized — Code Section 1371

Formerly, the rules for tax-option (Subchapter S) corporations allowed a varying number of shareholders. Ten were allowed for corporations within the first five years of existence, but increases of up to fifteen were permitted as the result of inheritance. Fifteen was also the maximum number permissible after the first five years. Now fifteen is the permissible maximum at all times.

The Revenue Act also liberalizes the rules on who is a shareholder. A husband and wife will in all cases be treated as a single shareholder. The Tax Reform Act of 1976 had expanded the list of permissible shareholders to include grantor trusts. The Revenue Act further expands this exception to include a grantor trust which is no longer such by reason of the grantor's death. The exception lasts 60 days if the trust corpus is not includible in the grantor's gross estate and two years if the entire trust corpus is includible.

There was also a change in the time when the Subchapter S election can be made. Under old law, the election had to be made just prior to the beginning of the corporation's tax year. The Act liberalizes this to include (1) *any* time during the preceding tax year or (2) during the first 75 days of the current tax year.

6. ESTATE TAXATION OF BUSINESS INTERESTS

A. Section 306 Stock, Carryover Basis And Section 303

Section 306 was introduced into the Internal Revenue Code in order to prevent taxpayers from obtaining long-term capital gains treatment on the sale of certain stock received in nontaxable stock dividends and thus bailing out corporate earnings without ordinary income taxation. The section 306 "taint" triggers dividend tax treatment for section 306 stock upon its disposition to the same extent a cash distribution would have been a dividend at the time the stock was issued. This taint, however, was removed if the section 306 stock were held until death. The introduction of the carryover basis system, though, altered this result and created confusion over its relationship with section 303 since the decedent's estate or heirs now took the decedent's basis (subject to certain adjustments).

The Revenue Act of 1978 clarifies this area with the addition of Code section 306(a)(3). If section 303 is applicable to the redemption, then section 306 does not apply. On the other hand, disposition of section 306 stock distributed before 1977 receives a basis of its December 31, 1976 adjusted basis plus any increase in basis under section 1035(h) of the carryover basis rules (see article 7A, below).

B. Restrictions On Retention Of Voting Rights In Stock Slightly Eased — Code Section 2036(a)

In the case of *United States v. Byrum,* 408 U.S. 125 (1972), the Supreme Court held that the value of closely held corporate stock given to a trust was not includible in the donor's estate even though the donor personally retained the right to vote the shares. This decision was amplified by *Estate of Gilman v. United States,* 547 F.2d 32 (2nd Cir. 1977), *aff'g* 65 T.C. 296 (1975), nonacq. 1978-45 I.R.B. 5, which extended the holding of *Byrum* to a situation in which the donor could vote the stock only as one of three trustees.

As a result of these two cases, many owners of closely held corporations transferred their stock to trusts while retaining voting control. Since this type of stock often pays no dividends, the motivation behind the transfers appears to have been merely estate tax avoidance as the donors were giving up in reality little or nothing because they still could control the actions of their corporations (including the setting of their own salaries). Since in many cases dividends were either small or nonexistent, loss of the right to receive them was considered a small enough price to pay in order to have the value of the stock removed from the donors' estates.

Both *Byrum* and *Gilman* were criticized by many tax experts and the IRS. This criticism was based on the contention that the retention of voting rights in closely held corporate stock constitutes a retained life interest. As such, it was argued that the value of the stock should be includible in the donor's estate under Internal Revenue Code section 2036(a).

The Tax Reform Act of 1976 overruled the *Byrum* and *Gilman* cases. It amended section 2036(a) to provide that the retention of voting rights in stock is retention of the lifetime enjoyment of the stock. Therefore, any donor who retains voting control in stock that is given away will have the value of that stock includible in his estate for federal estate tax purposes as a transfer with a retained life interest. Any transfers made after June 22, 1976, are subject to the new law.

The Revenue Act of 1978 limits this amendment to the transfer of stock in a "controlled corporation," which is defined to be a corporation in which the decedent owned or could vote at least 20% of the stock within three years of his death. The Code section 318 attribution rules apply in determining whether the ownership tests have been violated.

C. Special Use Valuation Changes — Code Sections 2032A And 6325(d)

The Tax Reform Act of 1976 provided special valuation methods to be used for qualifying real estate used in farming or in a closely held family business. The valuation permitted by section 2032A of the Internal Revenue Code is based on the present use of the property, as opposed to its highest and best use, if the property is passed to "qualified heirs" (categories of family members specified by the statute). This provision was added to permit some tax relief for owners of qualifying property and to make it easier for persons owning such property to keep it within their families following their deaths.

Section 702 of the Revenue Act addresses various aspects of this special use valuation election. Under the Tax Reform Act, it was ambiguous whether the portion of farm or business realty in excess in value of the limitations of the election should nonetheless have had special use valuation applied to it when it did not pass to a qualified heir. The new law provides that the special valuation rules apply only to real property actually passing to a qualified heir.

The Revenue Act further amends the special valuation provision by permitting qualified real property distributed to a qualified heir from an estate or trust in satisfaction of a pecuniary bequest to be valued under section 2032A. Under prior law, such distributions were ineligible for special use valuation because they were treated as taxable events and not considered to have been passed or acquired from a decedent.

Also, the provisions for special use valuation under the Tax Reform Act did not deal with community property restrictions; the new law, however, provides for equal treatment of community property and separately owned property. Thus, the full value of the property will be considered in determining whether the rules are met.

In addition, under the original statute, when an election is made, any tax benefits gained are subject to recapture if, within 15 years after the death of the decedent, the property is disposed of to nonfamily members or is no longer used for farming or closely held business purposes. The qualified heir is personally liable for the recapture tax attributed to his interest in the qualified property. The Revenue Act of 1978 now allows the qualified heir to be relieved of this personal liability by furnishing a bond.

For the case of involuntary dispositions of special use property, Public Law 95-472 has further amended section 2032A to eliminate the tax benefit recapture if the property is involuntarily converted. This amendment, though, is only effective if the proceeds of the conversion are invested in property used for the same purpose as the original property.

Finally, in conjunction with the recapture tax rules, a special lien under section 6324B attaches to the qualified property to secure the tax. Under prior law, the IRS had authority to subordinate a tax lien to another lien if subordination would enhance the value of the property and facilitate collection of the tax [section 6325(d) of the Internal Revenue Code]. Revenue Act section 517 has amended section 6325(d) to specifically permit, in case of a lien imposed by section 6324B, subordination if the IRS determines that the United States will be adequately secured after the subordination. In this way, the Revenue Act attempts to help owners of real property that has been valued according to its actual use to obtain credit when the farm or business property must be put up as security.

D. Expansion Of Right Of Decedents' Families To Use The Extension Of Time To Pay Estate Taxes On Farms And Closely Held Businesses — Code Section 6166

The Revenue Act of 1978 makes it possible for more estates to utilize the 15-year extension of time for paying estate taxes attributable to holdings in farm or other closely held businesses provided for by Code section 6166. Basically, if such an interest is included in the decedent's gross estate and is greater than 65% of the adjusted gross estate, the election can be made.

The election permits a deferral of the first payment for up to five years, during which no installments have to be made and only interest (currently 4%) on the unpaid taxes is due. Then the ten-year payout period applies. For a partnership or corporation to qualify as an interest in a closely held business for purposes of the 65% rule, either (1) at least 20% of the total capital interest or voting stock must be included in the gross estate or (2) there must be no more than 15 partners or shareholders.

There is no need requirement in this provision; the tests revolve around the nature and size of the property interest in relation to the estate. Consequently, section 6166 can be used as an indirect source of working capital at low interest rates if the funds to pay the estate taxes are already available through life insurance proceeds or otherwise.

Under the new law, stock or partnership interests held by the decedent's family within the meaning of section 267(c)(4), including brothers and sisters, spouse, grandparents (ancestors) and children and grandchildren (lineal descendants), are taken into account and treated as held by the decedent for the purposes of meeting the requirements of section 6166. It should be noted that these attribution rules can only be used to meet the 20% test of section 6166 if the stock has no market on a stock exchange or in over-the-counter trade. Also in such a case, when the attribution rules are used, there is only a ten-year extension to pay taxes, without the five-year delay before the first payment and with interest at the regular rate, currently 7%. This is the so-called "Gallo Wine" amendment, because it was inspired by the needs of the Gallo vinting family, and applies beginning in 1979.

E. Estate Tax Lien Changes For Elections Under Code Sections 6166 And 6166A — Code Section 6324A

Under the Tax Reform Act of 1976, if either sections 6166 or 6166A, extensions of time to pay estate taxes, is elected, an executor's personal liability can be discharged and under section 6324A, a lien attaches to real property or other assets with long useful lives. The lien is equal to the deferred taxes plus the total amount of interest which will be payable on the deferred taxes.

The Revenue Act of 1978, section 702(e), changes the amount of the lien to be equal to the deferred taxes plus the total interest for the first four years of the deferral period. The law also provides that a bond can be given for any difference not covered by the property. This amendment applies to estates of decedents dying after December 31, 1976.

7. ESTATE PLANNING

A. Postponement Of The Carryover Basis System — Code Sections 1014, 1016, 1023 And 2614

Prior to the Tax Reform Act of 1976, Code section 1014 gave assets includible in a decedent's estate a stepped-up basis equal to the estate tax valuation of each asset. Thus, when these assets were subsequently sold by taxpayers who received them from the decedent, any gain would be determined by reference to this stepped-up basis rather than to the decedent's original basis. The effect, of course, was to reduce, usually significantly, the income tax payable.

Elimination of the Stepped-Up Basis. The Tax Reform Act introduced section 1023, which eliminated the full step-up and replaced it, for decedents dying after December 31, 1976, with a "carryover" of the decedent's basis. The carryover was subject to certain adjustments based on the property's value as of December 31, 1976, state and federal taxes, and certain other statutory increases to basis dependent on the type of property or the total value of the decedent's estate.

Carryover Basis is Postponed and Clarified. The Revenue Act of 1978 postpones the effective date of carryover basis to January 1, 1980. The old section 1014 rules will govern retroactively the estates of all decedents dying prior to this date.

The Revenue Act has also clarified some of the more difficult mechanics of the carryover basis and has provided interim guidelines to coordinate the carryover basis rules with related Code provisions. For example, if a special valuation election is made under section 2032A, which allows real property used in connection with a farm or closely held business (and also satisfying other statutory tests) to be valued at less than its highest and best use for estate tax purposes before 1980, the property will receive a basis equal only to its special use valuation – not its full fair market value. In addition, the Act outlines a mechanical test which will allow an executor to arrive at the decedent's basis for items of personal property.

As one of its adjustments, the carryover basis system provides an increase in basis for that portion of the death taxes attributable to post-1976 appreciation. If there were an outstanding debt against the property, either the full fair market value of the property would have been includible if the decedent were personally liable or only the decedent's equity if the note were nonrecourse. The Act now provides for the apportionment of death taxes on the basis of full value regardless of the character of the debt.

There were also several straightforward but unanswered questions which now are resolved:

1. There is only one "fresh start" adjustment unless the property were jointly held and only a portion were includible in the estate of the first to die.
2. Property received from a decedent will be deemed to have satisfied the holding period for long-term capital gains treatment.
3. State death taxes will provide a basis increase whether or not there is a federal estate tax payable even if technically assessed against the estate as long as they are actually paid by the heir.

B. Transfers In Contemplation Of Death And The Gift Tax Annual Exclusion Clarified — Code Section 2035

Under law applicable prior to 1977, there was a *rebuttable* presumption that any gift made within three years of death was made in contemplation of death. If this presumption were not successfully rebutted, the gift would be includible in the donor's estate under Internal Revenue Code section 2035. If, however, the estate could prove living motives for the gift, there would not have to be inclusion of the gift in the estate of the donor.

Whether there were living motives behind a gift made within three years of death is a question whose determination depends on the facts and circumstances of each case. This lack of an objective standard made this issue often litigated. Consequently, under section 2035 as amended by the Tax Reform Act of 1976, the presumption was made irrebuttable. In other words, all gifts made within the three-year period prior to a decedent's death will be includible in his or her estate regardless of the motives involved. This absolute rule should eliminate litigation of this question. The rule applies to gifts made after December 31, 1976.

Nevertheless, under section 2035(b)(2) gifts made within three years of death which qualified for the $3,000 annual exclusion will not be includible in the decedent's estate up to the amount of the exclusion. This exception, unfortunately, proved hard to administer. The Revenue Act of 1978 modifies this rule so that gifts made within three years of death are excludible from the transferor's gross estate as long as a gift tax return did not have to be filed with respect to the transfer. The amendment is effective for transfers taking place after 1976.

The Revenue Act specifically makes section 2035(b)(2) *not applicable* to the gift of a life insurance policy. According to the Senate report, however, the exclusion is available for gifts of premiums if the underlying policy would not have been includible under prior law because of the premium payments.

C. Fractional Interest Rule For Husband And Wife Joint Tenants Extended to Pre-1977 Tenancies — Code Sections 2040(b) And 2515(c)

Under law prior to 1977, the entire value of any assets held in joint tenancy would have been includible in the estate of the first joint tenant to die except to the extent the survivor could prove a contribution to the consideration paid for the property. The Tax Reform Act modified this rule for husbands and wives who are joint tenants. Under the added section, section 2040(b), if certain conditions are met, only one half of the value of the assets held in joint tenancy will be includible in the decedent's gross estate regardless of which spouse contributed the consideration for the original acquisition of the assets. (Correlative changes were made in federal gift tax section 2515(c).)

The conditions are:
1. The joint tenancy must have been created by one or both of the joint tenants; joint tenancies received by inheritance or gift will not qualify.
2. Creation of the joint tenancy must have been a completed gift for gift tax purposes in the case of personal property.
3. If a joint tenancy is in real estate, the donor must have elected to treat the creation of the joint tenancy as a gift at the time it was made.
4. The only joint tenants are the decedent and the decedent's spouse.

If these requirements are met, it is possible to have only one-half the value of assets held in joint tenancy includible in the estate of the decedent. It should be kept in mind, however, that due to the nature of the joint property, the entire interest will pass to the survivor and will be fully includible in the survivor's estate at his or her death.

Since section 2040(b) was only available for joint tenancies created after 1976, there was much confusion over whether prior joint tenancies would have to be severed and recreated to qualify. This charade seemed unnecessary and the Revenue Act of 1978 now provides that it is not necessary to sever and re-create these tenancies. Instead section 2040(b) treatment will be available if for any quarter in 1977, 1978 or 1979, an election to fall under this section is made by filing a gift tax return. The amount of the gift is deemed to be the appreciation attributable to the gift portion of the consideration furnished by the donor-spouse at the time the tenancy was created.

D. Certain Interspousal Gifts No Longer Reduce Estate Tax Marital Deduction — Code Section 2056(c)(1)(B)

Under the Tax Reform Act of 1976, section 2056(c)(1)(B) mandated an adjustment to be made in the amount of the maximum estate tax marital deduction to the extent a decedent obtained an excess benefit from the 100% gift tax marital deduction provided by section 2523 for the first $100,000 in gifts between spouses. For example, if an individual decides to transfer $100,000 to his spouse during his lifetime, this amount will be totally free from gift taxation. Should the individual then die with an adjusted gross estate of more than $400,000 designed to transmit to his wife an amount equal to the maximum marital deduction, that amount would have to be adjusted to offset the "excess" gift tax marital deduction that had been taken.

The amendments made by the Revenue Act change this result in two situations. First, annual interspousal gifts of $3,000 or less, that is, those covered by the gift tax annual exclusion, do not reduce the estate tax marital deduction. Second, if a lifetime gift to the spouse were includible by reason of section 2035, *i.e.,* it was made within three years of death, no reduction in the estate tax marital deduction would be required. The two provisions are effective for estates of decedents dying after December 31, 1976, but the first does not apply to transfers made before January 1, 1977.

E. Minors' Trusts Permitted Under Orphan's Exclusion — Code Section 2057

Internal Revenue Code section 2057 allows a deduction from a decedent's gross estate for certain property passing to the decedent's minor children if the decedent is not survived by a spouse. Essentially, the law allows a deduction equal to $5,000 times the difference between a child's actual age and age 21.

Thus an orphan child, 16 years of age, whose last surviving parent died without a surviving spouse would provide the decedent's estate with a deduction of up to $25,000 for property included in the decedent's estate which passed to him (21 − 16 = 5; 5 x $5,000 = $25,000). If more than one minor child survives, additional deductions, calculated in the same manner as above, would be allowed to the extent of property passing to them.

The law, however, does require that the property interest passing to the minor children (1) be includible in the decedent's gross estate, and (2) not be a "terminable interest" as defined for purposes of the marital deduction in section 2056. The Revenue Act of 1978, however, now permits an orphan's interest to terminate before age 23 if because of his death.

The Act also amplifies section 2057 to include a "qualified minors' trust," which can singly cover more than one child. Such a trust can accumulate income and is deemed not to violate the terminable-interest requirement of section 2057 if:

1. All beneficiaries of the trust are minor children of the decedent;
2. The corpus of the trust has passed from the *decedent* to the trust;
3. All distributions to beneficiaries are pro rata or in accordance with an ascertainable standard based on their health, education, support or maintenance;
4. A beneficiary's interest can be maintained for other trust beneficiaries or be directed to third parties if death occurs before the youngest beneficiary attains age 23; and
5. Upon termination each beneficiary must receive a pro rata share of corpus and accumulated income.

These changes thus allow for the standard "pot trust" distribution whose validity was questionable in light of language contained in the Tax Reform Act of 1976. They are effective for estates of decedents dying in 1977 and later.

F. Qualified Disclaimers Cannot Be Directed By Disclaimants — Code Section 2518

The Tax Reform Act of 1976 added section 2518 to the Code in an attempt to codify the treatment of disclaimers for federal estate, gift and generation-skipping tax purposes. The effect of the new law was to provide that if a qualified disclaimer was made, the property disclaimed would be treated as if never transferred to the person making the disclaimer.

Unfortunately it was not clear whether any property disclaimed by a spouse could validly pass under the statute to a nonmarital trust in which the spouse had an income interest. The existence of such an income interest could be interpreted to mean the disclaimed property had not passed to someone other than the disclaimant.

The Revenue Act now makes it clear that an income interest in the disclaimed property will not disqualify the disclaimer as long as the income interest does not arise from any direction by the surviving spouse. The clarification is effective for transfers taking place after 1976 that create an interest in the disclaimant.

8. SIMPLIFIED EMPLOYEE PENSIONS – CODE SECTIONS 219(b)(7) AND 408(j)

Beginning January 1, 1979, a new employer-sponsored alternative to a qualified retirement plan called "simplified employee pensions" has been made available by the Revenue Act of 1978. Like the employer-sponsored IRA's introduced by the Pension Reform Act, this arrangement uses individual retirement accounts or annuities as the funding vehicles. If, however, certain requirements are met, a maximum contribution limit of the lesser of 15% of the employee's compensation or $7,500 applies to simplified employee pensions, rather than the regular 15%/$1,500 limits.

An employer may adopt a simplified pension arrangement even though it already sponsors a qualified pension or profit-sharing plan. In addition, employees may be included in such a plan while participating in a qualified plan sponsored by the same or another employer. The contributions provided under the simplified pension, however, must be considered in determining whether the Code section 415 maximum limits for qualified plan benefits and contributions are being observed. These contributions must also be aggregated with other employer contributions to qualified plans for purposes of deduction limits under Code section 404.

Requirements For Simplified Employee Pensions

To qualify as a simplified employee pension plan, Code section 408(j), added by the Act, specifies four requirements that must be met. First, the employer must contribute to the plan on behalf of *each* employee who has attained age 25 and has performed service for the plan sponsor during at least three of the immediately preceding five calendar years. It currently appears that no minimum number of hours may be imposed in determining whether this service requirement has been met. Accordingly, part-time employees will have to be included. This contrasts with qualified corporate and Keogh plans, in which only employees with a minimum number of hours of service need be included, and with regular employer-sponsored IRA's, in which the employer can pick and choose the employees who will participate.

Under the second requirement, the employee must have unrestricted control of his or her IRA and the entire account must be nonforfeitable as with any IRA. In addition, the employer may not require that contributions be retained in the account as a condition of making the contribution. Thus, the employee may withdraw employer contributions *at any time,* but the penalty taxes on IRA premature withdrawals will apply. Employer contributions in qualified plans, on the other hand, may not be withdrawn solely at the employee's option.

In order to qualify as a simplified employee pension plan, the Act requires that contributions to the plan may not discriminate in favor of officers, more-than-10% shareholders, self-employed individuals and the highly compensated. In making this determination, employees covered by a collective bargaining agreement may be disregarded.

To satisfy the nondiscrimination provision, the contributions must bear a uniform relationship to the total compensation of each employee, but only the first $100,000 of compensation will be counted for this purpose. While a maximum earnings limit is used to determine contributions for owner-employees in Keogh plans, it should be remembered that there is no such limit on earnings considered for qualified corporate plans unless a Subchapter S election is in force. In determining the plan contribution, the Act does allow the employer to take into account the employer's portion of the social security tax paid for each employee, as long as the entire self-employment tax of the self-employed individual is also considered. For example, the employer contribution may be set at 15% of the employee's compensation, less the amount of employer social security tax paid. For 1979, this would mean that the employer would contribute only 8.87% (15% − 6.13%) of the first $22,900 of each employee's compensation.

Finally, contributions to the simplified employee pension plan must be made under a written allocation agreement specifying what requirements an employee must satisfy to share in the allocation, and the method for determining the amounts allocated. (Note: Since these plans are covered under Title 1 of the Pension Reform Act, *all* provisions regarding the plan must be included in a written document.) Because these plans are not subject to the Code section 412 minimum funding standards, it appears contributions to the plan may vary from year to year. Accordingly, a discretionary formula or one based on the profits of the business should be acceptable.

Contribution Limits

Under the simplified pension approach, the employer may deduct contributions of 15% of the employee's compensation during the calendar year ending within the employer's tax year, up to a maximum of $7,500. Employer contributions that exceed these limits may be deductible in succeeding tax years, subject to a maximum deduction of 15% of compensation in any one year. Contributions made within 3½ months after the close of the calendar year may be treated as if made on the prior December 31.

If the employer's contribution to a simplified employee pension plan is less than 15% of an employee's compensation *and* no more than $1,500, the participant may contribute and deduct the difference between the employer contribution and the regular IRA limits, provided he or she is not also a participant in a qualified retirement plan, a governmental plan, or a tax-sheltered annuity.

For example, if the employer contributes $1,000 for an employee whose compensation is $10,000, the employee may, but is not required to, contribute the difference between $1,000 and the lesser of 15% of his compensation or $1,500, which in this case would equal $500. (Officers, shareholders, or owner employees, however, must reduce the amount that may be contributed under this provision by the amount of employer social security tax paid if this were considered in determining the employee's contribution.)

Because these employee contributions are considered amounts contributed to an IRA, and thus deductible, the simplified employee pension arrangements can offer a distinct advantage to a participant over participation in a qualified retirement plan, provided the employer contribution is less than $1,500. With a 15% or $1,500 employer contribution, though, an employer-sponsored IRA will yield the same advantage to the participating employee.

It appears that the employee must recognize the employer contributions and any employee contributions as gross income for federal income tax purposes, and then claim a deduction for these amounts under Code section 219. Accordingly, under the terms of section 220(b)(2), it seems that the employee may not deduct contributions to a spousal IRA in any year in which contributions to a simplified employee pension plan are made on his or her behalf.

Other Provisions

The Act indicates that the Code section 414 rules for controlled groups apply to employers adopting a simplified pension plan. In complying with these rules and the nondiscrimination requirements for qualified plans under section 401(a), the Act allows the employer to take into account all simplified pension plans to which *only* the employer contributes. Because all employees who meet the age and service requirements must be included in a simplified plan, it is likely that the section 401(a) nondiscrimination requirements will be a consideration in only two situations. The first will occur if the employer sponsors a qualified retirement plan covering only a portion of the employees included in the simplified plan. A second possibility will arise when members of a controlled group of employers are required to provide a retirement plan for their employees because of plans sponsored by other group members.

As employee benefit plans, simplified employee pensions are subject to the reporting and disclosure requirements included in the Pension Reform Act. The Revenue Act, however, indicates that "simplified" reporting will be specified in regulations by the Treasury Department.

9. QUALIFIED CASH OR DEFERRED PROFIT-SHARING AND STOCK BONUS PLANS — CODE SECTION 401(k)

Until 1972, the Internal Revenue Service granted qualified tax status to "cash or deferred profit-sharing plans," under which an employee could choose to receive his or her profit share in cash currently or have it contributed to the plan by the employer. As long as such plans met certain antidiscrimination requirements, any amounts the employee chose to have contributed to the plan were not currently taxed.

Late in 1972, the IRS issued proposed regulations eliminating tax deferral on the amounts actually contributed to the profit-sharing plan under this arrangement. In the Pension Reform Act and other legislation, Congress acted to prohibit the IRS from making these regulations final and allowed continuation of the favorable tax treatment for plans in existence on January 27, 1974. Employee contributions to new plans under a cash or deferred approach, however, would be taxed as current income.

In the Revenue Act of 1978, Congress has now extended the pre-1972 favorable tax treatment to all cash or deferred profit-sharing arrangements, as long as the requirements of new section 401(k) are met. This new option is available for plan years beginning on or after January 1, 1980, but under transitional rules, those plans in existence on January 27, 1974, may continue to rely on the IRS's pre-1972 position (as stated in Revenue Rulings 56-497, 1956-2 C.B. 284, 63-180, 1963-2 C.B. 189, and 68-89, 1968-1 C.B. 402) until such time as the new rules are effective.

To qualify under the new rules, the plan must meet all of the requirements of Code section 401(a) and must provide that benefits derived from the employee contributions made under the cash or deferred option are nonforfeitable. The benefits attributable to these contributions may not be distributed earlier than retirement, death, disability, separation from service, attainment of age 59½, or hardship. Distribution after a fixed period of time or a period of participation, generally allowable in profit-sharing plans, cannot be available under this approach.

In addition to these requirements, the Act specifies that the plan must meet one of two tests regarding the percentage of compensation deferred by highly compensated employees relative to that deferred by other employees in each year in order to satisfy the Code section 410 and 401(a) participation and nondiscrimination standards. For purposes of these tests, "highly compensated employee" is defined as an employee who is more highly compensated than two-thirds of all eligible employees.

The actual deferral percentage for a group of employees is determined by using the average of the deferral ratios for each employee in the group. An individual's ratio for a plan year is the employer contributions made to the trust under the cash or deferral option divided by the employee's compensation. Only the compensation used to determine the employer plan contribution made on behalf of this employee for the plan year is used for purposes of these determinations.

Under the first test, the actual deferral percentage for the highly compensated group may not be more than the actual deferral percentage for all other employees, multiplied by 1.5. For example, if the deferral percentage for the highly compensated group is 8% while for all others it is 6%, the first test will be satisfied because 8% is less than 6% x 1.5 (which equals 9%).

The second test will be met if the *excess* of the actual deferral percentage for the highly compensated group is not more than three percentage points over the actual deferral percentage for all other employees, *and* the actual percentage for the highly paid group is not more than the actual deferral percentage for all other employees multiplied by 2.5. For example, if the deferral for the highly compensated group is 4.2% and for all other employees it is 1.8%, the second test will be satisfied because (1) 4.2% minus 1.8% equals 2.4%, which is less than three percentage points difference, and (2) 4.2% is less than 2.4% x 2.5 or 4.25%.

10. REFORM IN INDIVIDUAL RETIREMENT ACCOUNT RULES

Since being introduced by ERISA, the individual retirement account (IRA) has created many opportunities and many problems for taxpayers. The Revenue Act of 1978 has expanded the opportunities and has substantially eliminated the problems. (See article 8, above, for a discussion of "simplified employee pensions.")

A. Correcting Excess Contributions — Code Sections 219, 220, 408 And 4973

Excess Can Be Corrected By Undercontributing

One of the most serious IRA problems involved penalty taxes on excess contributions. If a taxpayer contributes to an IRA more than the lesser of 15% of compensation or $1,500, he incurs a 6% nondeductible excise tax. The tax is charged every year until the excess is corrected. Under prior law, the taxpayer could correct the excess contribution in a subsequent year and eliminate the recurring penalty by not making the maximum allowable contribution. When he did this, however, he was not permitted to take a new deduction for the excess amount that was absorbed.

For example, assume that in 1977 the maximum permissible deduction for taxpayer A was $800. By mistake he put $1,000 into his IRA but only deducted $800. A's excess contribution of $200 would cost him $12 in penalty taxes. He could correct the $200 in 1978 and avoid the recurring $12 tax by putting in $200 less than his maximum permissible deduction for 1978. Under prior law, A would not have been allowed to deduct the $200 in 1978. The Revenue Act of 1978 corrects the problem by permitting A to deduct the $200 in 1978.

It must be emphasized that the deduction will be allowed in a subsequent year only if the taxpayer did not previously deduct the excess amount. If taxpayer A in this example had deducted the $200 excess in 1977, he could not have deducted the $200 when he undercontributed in 1978. If A had deducted half of the excess in 1977, he could have deducted only half ($100) when he corrected the excess in 1978.

In drafting the new law, Congress recognized that many taxpayers have already erased excess contributions made in 1975 and 1976. Rather than requiring multiple amended returns to permit deductions for past years, the new law allows taxpayers to claim a one-time catch-up deduction on the 1978 return. If the taxpayer does not take advantage of the catch-up rule in the 1978 return, he may still save the deduction by timely filing an amended return for the particular year involved.

Withdrawing the Excess After Tax Filing Date

A second method for correcting excess contributions involves withdrawing excess amounts from the IRA. Withdrawals under prior law, however, could only be made up to the date for filing the tax return. If a withdrawal were made after that date, the taxpayer not only incurred a 6% penalty tax for each year the excess remained in the plan, but he also had to pay a 10% premature distribution penalty tax if he were under age 59½. Furthermore, the amount withdrawn was includible in his gross income.

Under the Act, a withdrawal of an excess contribution after the tax filing date is not subject to the 10% penalty tax and is not includible in gross income. This provision will only apply, however, if a deduction were not allowed for the excess contribution and if the total contribution, including the excess, did not exceed $1,750. The $1,750 limit may be disregarded for withdrawals of excess contributions made in pre-1978 tax years and it may be disregarded when excess rollover contributions are caused by erroneous information furnished by the plan or the institutions responsible for making a distribution (such as a bank or insurance company).

The old law also required that any income earned on the excess contribution had to be withdrawn at the same time. Not only was the earned income taxable, but it was also sometimes difficult to calculate. Now the income does not have to be withdrawn. Finally, Congress recognized that some taxpayers have already paid penalty taxes on excess contributions and have paid income taxes on distributions which were made to correct excess contributions. For those persons, the new law offers relief in the form of refunds.

Withdrawing The Excess Before The Tax Filing Date

While taxpayers could withdraw excess contributions up to the tax filing date (including extensions) under prior law, there were certain restrictions which often caused problems. First, such a withdrawal could only be made if the taxpayer had improperly made an IRA contribution while he was also an active participant in a qualified pension plan or if he had failed to earn enough to be entitled to the full deduction. Second, he could only withdraw the excess if the total contributions had not exceeded $1,500 (or $1,750 for spousal IRA's). For example, if a taxpayer had contributed $1,500 when his allowable deduction was $800, he could have withdrawn the excess $700 and avoided the 6% penalty. If, however, he had contributed $1,600, the $800 excess would have been subject to the penalty whether or not it was withdrawn. For tax years beginning after 1977, all these restrictions are removed. The excess does not have to be caused solely by active participation in a qualified plan or by a shortfall in income, and the $1,500 ($1,750) limit has been deleted. Furthermore, earnings on the excess portion need not be withdrawn, as discussed above under withdrawals after the tax filing date.

B. Rollover Opportunities Expanded – Code Sections 402(a), 403(b)(8) And 408(d)(3)

One of the most heralded provisions of ERISA was the IRA rollover. Sponsors of the Act claimed that the rollover was the answer to the problem of portability between qualified plans and the problem of tax sheltering plan distributions. While the IRA rollover did offer some welcome relief, several requirements and restrictions were written into the law which severely curtailed its use. The Revenue Act of 1978 has removed many of those requirements and restrictions.

Partial Rollovers Now Permitted

One of the most restrictive provisions of the old law was the requirement that a taxpayer had to roll over the entire amount of a lump-sum distribution (less his own contributions) if he wished to take advantage of the rollover approach. Under the Revenue Act of 1978, taxpayers no longer have to roll over the full amount. Any portion not rolled, however, is ineligible for ten-year averaging or capital gains treatment.

Same-Property Test Modified

Another roadblock to the use of IRA rollovers under prior law was the same-property rule. Under that rule, if a taxpayer had received property other than cash from a plan, he could have only rolled over that same property to an IRA. The new law now permits the taxpayer to sell the property and roll over the proceeds. This provision can only be used for distributions made after December 31, 1978. Furthermore, the sale and subsequent rollover must still be made within the sixty-day period after receipt of the distribution.

Not only has the same-property requirement been dropped, but the taxpayer can even shelter the gain made on the sale of property. For example, if taxpayer A receives a $200,000 distribution consisting of $100,000 in cash and $100,000 in property, and he sells the property for $150,000, he can roll the full $250,000 into the IRA and not recognize the $50,000 gain (losses on sales are likewise not recognized). If the rollover is partial (as discussed above), the taxpayer is given the flexibility of designating how much will be considered a contribution of cash and how much will be considered a contribution of property.

Assuming taxpayer A in the example only wanted to roll over $175,000 of his distribution, he could designate $75,000 of the amount rolled over as cash and $100,000 as proceeds from the sale; $25,000 of the total cash and $50,000 ($150,000 minus $100,000) of the proceeds would be retained, and would be immediately taxable, part as ordinary income and part as capital gain. If the distribution is made from a contributory plan, the taxpayer can even designate the portion of the sale proceeds he wants treated as attributable to his own contributions. If no designation is made, the law states that the apportionment will be made on a "ratable basis." All taxpayer designations must be made by the tax return filing date (including extensions) and once made, they are irrevocable.

Five-Year Participation Requirement And Three-Year Restriction On Rollovers Between IRA's Eliminated

Under prior law, a taxpayer could only have rolled over a distribution upon termination of employment if he had been a plan participant for at least five years. This rule severely restricted portability for the employee who really needed it the most. In view of this problem, the five-year participation requirement was deleted.

The old law also permitted rollovers between IRA's only once every three years. This provision, Congress recognized, unfairly and unnecessarily locked individuals into funding vehicles they did not want. The Revenue Act of 1978 now permits rollovers between IRA's once a year. These provisions are effective for tax years beginning after 1977.

Rollovers By Surviving Spouses Now Allowed

An oversight in ERISA concerned rollovers for surviving spouses. Under a literal interpretation of the phrase "the balance to credit of an employee" in the old law, payments made on account of death would not qualify for rollover treatment. The Act corrects this oversight by permitting a surviving spouse to roll over all or part of a lump-sum distribution received on account of the employee's death. As with all other rollovers, such a rollover must be made within 60 days of receipt of the funds. The only restriction is that the spouse cannot subsequently roll the assets from the IRA to a qualified plan in which she may be a participant.

Furthermore, it appears that under Revenue Ruling 68-287, 1968-1 C.B. 174, liquidation of the IRA in a later year will not qualify as a lump-sum distribution. Consequently, the estate tax exclusion should be available for a distribution rolled over by a spouse as long as the IRA is not liquidated in the same year as the rollover. Even if it is, the exclusion may still be preserved if the spouse irrevocably waives the ten-year averaging privilege. (See article 12E, below.) The new rules for surviving-spouse rollovers apply to distributions completed after December 31, 1978 in tax years ending after that date.

TSA Rollovers

Under the new law, lump-sum distributions from tax-sheltered annuities can either be rolled into an IRA or through a conduit IRA to another TSA or IRA (but not into a qualified plan). For purposes of determining whether the distribution is a lump-sum distribution, all TSA contracts purchased for the employee will be treated as a single contract. Again, as in all other rollover situations, all or any portion of the distribution may be rolled, and the transfer to the IRA must be completed within 60 days of receipt of the lump sum. When an IRA is being used as a conduit, the transfer from the IRA to the new TSA must be completed no later than 60 days after receipt of the distribution from the old TSA and the entire amount in the conduit must be rolled into the new TSA.

It appears that TSA rollovers may have limited appeal even with the possibility of greater variety in funding vehicles. Once the funds are transferred to the IRA, the IRA distribution restrictions and penalties apply, and the estate tax exclusion will only be preserved if the payout is made in 36 equal installments as required by Code section 2039(e), rather than the more flexible provisions of section 2039(c). Furthermore, exchange of TSA annuity contracts was already allowed under Code section 1035(a). Consequently, little seems to have been gained. The TSA rollover is available for transfers made after December 31, 1978, in tax years beginning after that date.

C. New Rules On Contributions, Returns, And Excess Accumulations

Period For Establishing IRA And Making Contributions Extended — Code Section 219(c)

Many individuals are not in a position to establish an IRA until they know exactly what they have earned in a tax year. By looking back on a tax year that has ended, a taxpayer can also better determine what he should contribute and deduct for tax planning purposes. Under prior law, a taxpayer had a grace period of 45 days after the close of his tax year in which to establish an IRA and make the contribution. The Revenue Act of 1978 has extended that period an additional two months. For tax years beginning after 1977, a taxpayer will be allowed a deduction for contributions made up to the due date for filing his tax return (including extensions). The IRA, likewise, may also be established any time on or before his new due date.

Flexible Premiums Now Required For Individual Retirement Annuities — Code Section 408(b)

In drafting the Revenue Act of 1978, Congress recognized some of the most serious IRA problems involved the use of fixed premium annuity and retirement income endowment life insurance (RIE's) contracts. Taxpayers who purchased fixed premium contracts found themselves in trouble when their allowable contributions decreased due to a drop in earnings or when no contributions at all could be made because of active participation in a qualified plan. Taxpayers had to choose between forfeitures imposed by the contract carrier or the 6% penalty tax imposed by the Code.

To prevent taxpayers from getting into this dilemma, the new law now prohibits the use of fixed premium contracts, including RIE's, after November 6, 1978.

Those individuals who did purchase fixed premium annuity contracts before November 7, 1978 can exchange them for flexible premium contracts before January 1, 1981, and not have the exchange be treated as a taxable event. The new law also makes it clear that for tax years beginning after December 31, 1976, the dollar limit on spousal individual retirement annuities and individual retirement bonds is $1,750.

Penalty Tax On Excess Accumulations Can Be Varied — Code Section 4974

One of the most severe penalty taxes that can be imposed on IRA participants is the 50% excise tax on excess accumulations — the result of not fulfilling the minimum distribution rules of section 4974 for participants age 70½ and older. The 50% penalty is applied to the difference between what has been paid to the participant and what should have been paid. In recognition of an insufficient distribution's sometimes being caused by a mistake, Congress has given the Secretary of Treasury the power to waive the tax if the taxpayer can satisfy the Secretary that (1) the shortfall in the distribution was due to a reasonable error, and (2) that reasonable steps are being taken to correct the situation. Taxpayers who can satisfy these two conditions may file for refunds if they paid penalty taxes in tax years beginning after 1975.

IRA Returns Simplified — Code Section 6058

Previously, a taxpayer was required to file an annual return (Form 5329) with his Form 1040 for each year he maintained an IRA, regardless of whether he made contributions to the IRA during that year. In response to criticism of such reporting as unncecssary, the Revenue Act of 1978 significantly reduces the number of annual returns that will have to be filed. For tax years beginning after 1977, a taxpayer will not have to file a Form 5329 if no penalty tax has been imposed during the year and if there has been no plan activity *other than* making contributions or receiving permissible distributions. Information concerning deductible contributions and permissible distributions will apparently be entered on the Form 1040. The new law provides that an annual return will have to be filed if there has been a rollover to the IRA during the year.

D. Estate And Gift Tax Rules Clarified For Spousal IRA's — Code Sections 2039(e) And 2503(d)

While the Tax Reform Act of 1976 permitted individuals to establish IRA's for nonworking spouses, there was some question on whether the estate tax exclusion applied to only the working spouse's IRA or to both spouses' IRA's. The Revenue Act of 1978 makes it clear that the exclusion will apply to an annuity paid from a nonworking spouse's IRA for the estate of a decedent dying after December 31, 1978.

The Tax Reform Act of 1976 was also unclear on whether a contribution to a nonworking spouse's IRA qualified as a present interest gift eligible for the $3,000 gift tax annual exclusion. Under a typical nonworking spouse IRA arrangement, a working spouse will make contributions to the IRA for the benefit of the nonworking spouse, but the nonworking spouse will not receive the IRA benefits until age 59½. The new law makes it clear that contributions made after December 31, 1976, will be considered present interest gifts which qualify for the annual exclusion.

11. EMPLOYEE STOCK OWNERSHIP PLANS

A. Tax Credit And "Leveraged" ESOP's Receive New Names, New Life, And Many New Rules

The most positive highlight of the Revenue Act of 1978's work on employee stock ownership plans (ESOP's) was the three-year life extension, to December 31, 1983, for investment tax credit (Tax Reduction Act of 1975) ESOP's (TRASOP's). Congress, however, also chose to add numerous rules, as well as some benefits, and to change officially the names of both ESOP's and TRASOP's. Under Code section 4975(e)(7), the garden-variety employee stock ownership plan will now be termed a "leveraged employee stock ownership plan," presumably in deference to its frequently promoted utilization for financed acquisitions of employer securities. Under new Code section 409(A), a TRASOP now will be known simply as an "ESOP."

New Rules For Leveraged ESOP's —
Code Sections 4975 and 409A

Under the law, the notable characteristics of a leveraged ESOP are still that if it is a stock bonus plan (or a combination of a stock bonus and money purchase plan), qualified under section 401(a), which is "designed to invest primarily in qualifying employer securities," a loan to it by a disqualified person is exempt from the prohibited transaction rules. Under section 4975(d)(3), of course, such a loan must be primarily for the benefit of participants and at a reasonable rate of interest, and its only collateral must be employer securities.

The Revenue Act, though, has added two new conditions for leveraged ESOP's — subsections (e) and (h) of new section 409(A), the "TRASOP" section. The first new condition, section 409(A)(e), concerns the participants' voting rights in the employer securities. If the employer's securities are publicly traded, the participants must be allowed to vote the stock allocated to their accounts. On the other hand, if the securities are stock of a closely held corporation, the participants only need be able to direct how they will be voted on matters which are legally required to be decided by *more* than a majority of the outstanding common stock. (Under regulation section 54.4975-7, the voting right passthrough requirement had been deleted for leveraged ESOP's.)

Under section 409(A)(h), participants are also given extensive rights in the distribution of employer securities from a plan. While a distribution may be made in cash, a participant must be entitled to demand distribution in kind and must be notified in writing of his right to do so before any distributions are made.

When distributed securities are not readily tradable on an established market, the participant must have the right to sell the stock to the employer under a "fair valuation formula." According to the Senate committee report, this repurchase right may also be fulfilled by the plan and an IRA trustee which has received a rollover consisting of employer securities must also be able to exercise the option. The Senate report also states that a put option should last for six months after receipt of the securities and become available again, after a valuation of the stock, for three months after the end of the employer's tax year in which the six months expires. (This requirement is somewhat different than that specified in regulation sections 54.4975-7(b)(4), (10), (11) and (12), see article 11B, below.) The leveraged ESOP provisions are effective for tax years beginning in 1979.

(Tax Credit) ESOP's Now Must Be Qualified Plans —
Code Sections 401(a)(21) and 409A

The Senate committee report on employee stock ownership plans states:

[A]ll TRASOPs are required to be tax-qualified plans.

. . . The committee expects that the regulations which generally apply to tax-qualified plans will henceforth also apply to TRASOPs, and that the Treasury Department will not write separate regulations regarding the application of the tax-qualification standards to TRASOPs, except where TRASOPs are distinguished from other qualified plans by statute.

The consequences of this change in attitude in regard to ESOP's (*i.e.*, TRASOP's), which is a little surprising in that their extra investment tax credit is due to expire at the end of 1983, are that they now must adhere to the rules of section 401(a), but also they probably will be able to make leveraged-ESOP-style loans. The cost of this change is an extensive list of requirements, in addition to the voting and distribution rights described above for leveraged ESOP's, which must be conformed to under section 409(A). Even so, under new section 401(a)(21), ESOP's do not violate the section 401(a) permanency test simply because they base contributions on the allowable additional investment tax credit they generate.

While ESOP's must be qualified plans, one may be established after the end of the employer's tax year if this is done prior to the filing date (including extensions) for the employer's tax return. In connection with establishing and administering the plan under section 409(A)(i), the employer may withhold from plan contributions (otherwise required under the rules for the additional tax credit) specifically limited amounts actually paid for expenses. Under section 409A(j), an employer may condition plan contributions on obtaining IRS approval. To do so, though, the employer must file for a determination letter within 90 days of claiming an ESOP tax credit and the contribution must be returned to the employer within one year after an unfavorable determination is given.

One aspect of employee stock ownership plans which has been problematic is the method of allocating these employer securities to the participants' accounts. All allocation formulae seem to have deficiencies if viewed from the right perspective. In the case of ESOP's, this dilemma is resolved by section 409(A)(b), which requires that all stock transferred to a plan as a consequence of section 48(n)(1)(A) in a plan year be allocated in that year to the accounts of all participants who are entitled to share in the allocation. The allocation must have the result that the stock allocated to a participant's account is in essentially the same proportion to all stock being allocated as is his compensation to compensation paid to all plan participants during that year. For purposes of the allocation, a participant's compensation in excess of $100,000 a year must be disregarded, and the compensation considered must be limitation year compensation as defined by Code section 415(c)(3) and Revenue Ruling 75-41, 1975-2 C.B. 188. In light of section 415, however, an allocation to a participant's account may be suspended for whatever period is necessary to avoid exceeding the contribution limits for that participant.

Once the employer securities are allocated, under section 409(A)(c) participants must be immediately 100% vested in them. On the other hand, under section 409(A)(d), except for separation from service, death or disability, a participant may not be permitted to withdraw employer securities allocated to his account "before the end of the 84th month beginning after the month" in which they were allocated.

Notwithstanding the allocation rules, under section 409(A)(k), neither the ESOP vesting rules nor the exclusive-benefit rule of section 401(a) will be violated if employer contributions intended for matching by employee contributions (see the discussion of the investment tax credit rules, below) are withdrawn because they were not matched or they were in excess of the section 415 limitations. Such withdrawals will also be deemed permitted by section 403(c)(1) of the Employee Retirement Income Security Act of 1974. Apart from this exception, though, under section 409(A)(g), employer contributions must remain in the plan and stay allocated, if they were allocated, even if the tax credit is recaptured or redetermined.

Sections 409(A)(l) and (m) specify the types of employer securities permitted for an ESOP. In addition to common stock readily tradable on an established market, an ESOP may receive employer stock that is not readily tradable if it has voting power and dividend rights at least equal to that of the employer's common stock with greatest voting power and of the stock of any class with the greatest dividend rights. Noncallable preferred stock can be used if it is convertible into readily tradable common stock at a price which is reasonable as of the date of acquisition by the ESOP. Stock of subsidiaries may also be used in a parent corporation's ESOP. For purposes of this provision, the existence of a subsidiary is determined by the controlled group rules of Code section 1563(a), except that a parent need only directly own 50% or more of the stock of a "first tier subsidiary." Finally, a subsidiary may contribute to its own ESOP stock of its parent without recognition of gain or loss if the parent owns at least 80% of the stock of the subsidiary.

Investment Tax Credit Rules For ESOP's —
Code Sections 46, 48, 56(c) And 6699

As related at the beginning of this article, the additional one-percent investment tax credit under Code section 46(a)(2) for transfers of employer's securities to an ESOP has been extended to the end of 1983. In addition, ESOP tax credits will no longer be considered tax preference items under section 56(c) which increase the employer's minimum tax. (In general the changes made by the Revenue Act to employer stock ownership plans are effective for tax years beginning in 1979, except this elimination of the effect of the minimum tax, which is effective retroactively.)

Accompanying these liberalizations of the ESOP tax credit rules are numerous revisions in and additions to conditions for receiving the credit — not the least of which is section 409(A), discussed above. Under section 48(n), to receive the additional one-percent tax credit in any tax year, the employer must agree on his tax return to transfer to the ESOP, not later than 30 days after the filing date for his tax return (including extensions), employer securities equal in value to the credit. A tax credit ESOP contribution can be made in cash rather than in employer securities if the cash is used within 30 days to purchase employer securities.

If the overall investment tax credit is required to be carried over (because of the tax liability rules — see article 2B above), the employer securities equal in value to the portion of the ESOP tax credit which must be carried over need not be transferred earlier than 30 days after the filing date (including extensions) of the tax return for the tax year in which the carryover is allowed. In determining whether the ESOP tax credit must be carried over, a carryover (or carryback) is first applied against the regular investment tax credit. If it is not then exhausted, it is next applied against the basic (one-percent) ESOP credit. If this fails to exhaust it, it is last applied against the matching ESOP tax credit.

In general, because ESOP contributions under section 48(n)

receive a full tax credit, no additional tax deduction is allowed for them. Nevertheless, if any portion of the ESOP tax credit is recaptured or reduced by the IRS, the employer has the choice of reducing current or future amounts to be transferred by the recapture or reduction, *or* to deduct the recapture or reduction under section 404. (Of course, contributions to qualified employee stock ownership plans are generally deductible under the rules of section 404 and may be made in addition to the contributions receiving a tax credit.)

Matching of employee contributions to ESOP's can make the employer eligible for an additional one-half percent tax credit. When the employer is already eligible for the one-percent credit, the additional one-half percent can be obtained if the employer agrees to transfer additional employer securities to the ESOP equal in value to the total matching contributions made by the employees for that tax year. Timing of the transfer must be the same as for the basic one percent.

The actual matching rules are as follows: (1) each employee who is entitled to an allocation of securities under the basic one-percent ESOP credit must be entitled to make a matching contribution; (2) the participant must designate his contribution as one to be matched; (3) he must pay the employer or the plan administrator his contribution in cash within 24 months after the close of the tax year; (4) the contribution must be immediately invested in employer securities; and (5) the plan must provide for allocation of the employer matching contributions and employer securities for each participant's account in an amount equal to the participant's matching contribution for the year.

The employer cannot require participation in the matching ESOP as a condition of employment and the ESOP cannot require matching employee contributions as a condition of participation. Finally, the employee contributions under the ESOP cannot discriminate in favor of the prohibited group as defined in section 401(a)(4).

Penalties are specified under new Code section 6699 for employers who fail to observe the time limits of section 48(n) or to meet the requirements of section 409(A). A penalty can be avoided if the employer corrects the failure in the manner determined by the IRS within 90 days of being notified of it by the IRS. The amount of the penalty is the "amount involved" in the failure to meet the ESOP rules. The penalty amount, however, cannot be greater than the value of the tax-credit investment for the tax year multiplied times the ESOP tax credit percentage claimed by the employer, nor less than one-half percent of the maximum penalty times the number of months in which the failure continued.

B. Other Employee Stock Ownership Plan Developments

Amendments to Revenue Procedure 77-30

Revenue Procedure 77-30, 1977-2 C.B. 539, gave a guide on receiving an advance ruling by the IRS on whether a proposed sale of employer securities to a defined contribution plan (which would include both ESOP's and leveraged ESOP's) will be treated as a redemption rather than a capital transaction. During 1978, two additional revenue procedures were issued to clarify Revenue Procedure 77-30.

Revenue Procedure 78-18, 1978-30 I.R.B. 13, clarifies when restrictions on dispositions on ESOP-held or -distributed stock are not more onerous than those on the majority of shares held by other stockholders. Specifically, the stock proposed for sale may be subject to a right of first refusal on part of the employer or the plan if the stock is not publicly traded at the time the right is exercised and the right does not provide prices and terms less favorable than the greater of (1) fair market value or (2) the price and terms of a buyer (other than the employer or the plan) actually making a good faith offer to purchase the stock. The right of first refusal must lapse within 14 days after the seller gives notice to the holders of the right that he has received from a third party an offer to purchase the stock.

Revenue Procedure 78-23, 1978-34 I.R.B. 30, deals with the stipulation in Revenue Procedure 77-30 that the direct and indirect beneficial interest in the plan of the person selling the stock to it not exceed 20%. According to Revenue Procedure 78-23, any "separately managed fund or account within the plan . . . will not be taken into account in determining whether the combined beneficial interest in the employee plan of the selling shareholder and all related persons exceeds 20%" if that account will never receive employer stock.

Final Leveraged ESOP Regulations On Distribution Protections And Integration

On November 17, 1978, too soon to reflect the Revenue Act of 1978, final regulations were issued which deal with the requirement of regulation sections 54.4975-7(b)(4), (10), (11) and (12) that a participant receiving a distribution of employer securities which were acquired with the proceeds of an exempt loan must be given a put option exercisable for at least 15 months after the distribution. Under new regulation section 54.4975-11(a)(3), the put option protections required by the regulations cannot terminate merely because the loan is repaid or the plan ceases to be a leveraged ESOP. Furthermore, these rights must be specifically spelled out in the plan.

It should be noted that the leveraged ESOP protections and rights of regulation sections 54.4975-7(b)(4), (10), (11) and (12) are quite similar to, though perhaps a little more rigorous than, those required for them under new Code section 409(A)(h) and the Senate committee report discussed above in article 11A. What revisions to the regulations, if any, will be made by the IRS in response to the Revenue Act of 1978 remain to be seen.

As noted by the Senate committee report, ESOP's (formerly known as TRASOP's) are not permitted to integrate with social security. under regulation section 54.4975-11(a)(7)(ii), no plan designated as a leveraged ESOP after November 1, 1977, may be integrated directly or indirectly with social security. Plans established and integrated before that date may remain integrated but cannot be amended to increase the integration level or percentage. The integration level, however, may continue to increase if the increase "is limited by reference to a criterion existing apart from the plan," such as the taxable wage base.

12. OTHER QUALIFIED PLANS DEVELOPMENTS

A. Passthrough Of Stock Voting Rights For All Qualified Plans – Code Section 401(a)(22)

In addition to the elaborate stock voting rights rules for ESOP's and leveraged ESOP's, the Revenue Act of 1978 has mandated a voting rights passthrough for all defined contribution plans. The Act has added Code section 401(a)(22) which requires section 409(A)(e) to be observed by defined contribution plans investing more than 10% of total plan assets in employer securities if the stock of the employer is not publicly traded. That is, plans with such stock will have to allow the participants to vote the stock on matters legally required to be decided on by *more* than a majority vote of the outstanding common stock.

The effective date of this section is ambiguous in that Act section 143(b) states that it "shall apply to acquisitions of securities after December 31, 1979." Some commentators have interpreted this as meaning that section 401(a)(22) applies only to stock the plan acquires after 1979. The intent, however, appears to be that if the plan has more than 10% of its assets in employer securities after 1979, the passthrough will have to be given no matter when they were acquired.

B. Distributions From Mutual Fund TSA's — Code Section 403(b)(7)

The Pension Reform Act and the Tax Reform Act of 1976 made it possible for contributions for tax-sheltered annuities to be made to custodial accounts representing open-end and closed-end investment company stock. The Internal Revenue Service had proposed regulations which stated that custodial agreements for such mutual fund TSA's must prohibit distributions to an employee or his beneficiary prior to age 55, death, disability, or termination of service *after* age 55.

Congress believed these provisions too restrictive and amended Code section 403(b)(7) to allow distributions on account of death, obtaining age 59½, termination of service, disability, or financial hardship. Mutual fund TSA's, however, are still subject to the penalty tax on excess contributions under Code section 4973(a)(2) while regular TSA contracts, *i.e., actual annuities, are* neither subject to early distribution restrictions nor excess contribution penalty taxes. The amendment to section 403(b)(7) is effective for tax years beginning in 1979.

C. Benefit Limit Changes For Collectively Bargained Plans — Code Section 415(b)(7)

Under Code section 415(b), the maximum pension a participant in a defined benefit plan may receive is limited to the lesser of 100% of the highest three years' average compensation or $75,000 (adjusted annually for cost-of-living changes, therefore $90,150 for 1978). Code section 415(b)(7), added by the Revenue Act, permits collectively bargained plans with at least 100 participants to disregard the 100%-of-compensation maximum if its requirements are met.

To qualify, the plan must require no more than 60 days of service for eligibility and no more than four years of service for full vesting. The pension benefit must be a specific dollar amount (the same for all participants) for each year of service, and cannot exceed one half of the section 415(b) maximum dollar limitation (for 1978, this reduced dollar limit is $40,075).

Even though a plan may satisfy all of these requirements, the 100% of compensation limit will *not* be lifted for an individual participant if his or her average compensation in any three of the ten years preceding separation from service exceeds the average compensation for all other plan participants for the same period, or, apparently, if he or she is covered by another qualified plan sponsored by an employer contributing to the collectively bargained plan. This option for collectively bargained plans is available for tax years beginning on or after January 1, 1979.

D. Maximum Tax Treatment For Plan Benefits — Code Section 1348(b)(1)(A)

The Tax Reform Act of 1976 liberalized the definition of "earned income" for purposes of the maximum tax rate under Code section 1348 and changed its designation to "personal service income." A major intent of the liberalization was to accord maximum tax treatment to periodic payments received under qualified and nonqualified deferred compensation plans (but not including lump-sum distributions receiving ten-year averaging or capital gains treatment).

Unfortunately, the Tax Reform Act amendment merely stipulated that amounts "received as a pension or annuity" were personal service income; this simple statement could be interpreted to include any annuity a taxpayer might purchase or otherwise obtain without any connection to an employer-sponsored or tax-qualified retirement plan. The Revenue Act of 1978 has eliminated this danger by amending Code section 1348(b)(1)(A) to define personal service income as including amounts "received as a pension or annuity which arises from an employer-employee relationship or from tax-deductible contributions to a retirement plan.

E. Clarification Of Definition Of Lump-Sum Distributions For Estate Tax Purposes — Code Section 2039(c)

The Tax Reform Act of 1976 amended Code section 2039(c) so as to prevent simultaneous use of section 402(e) "ten-year" income averaging and the estate tax exclusion for qualified plan death benefits. Since the Internal Revenue Service has not yet issued relevant regulations, the change generated considerable unease over what would be deemed sufficient to qualify a death benefit for the exclusion.

In the hope of alleviating this unease, Congress substituted in section 2039(c), for the previous specification of lump-sum distributions "described in section 402(e)(4)," a reference to new subsection (f). Section 2039(f) is ambiguously written, but it is apparent that it permits the estate tax exclusion when the recipient *irrevocably* elects *not* to make the ten-year averaging election. Use of this election will also deny capital gains treatment for the distribution. In other words, a recipient making the required irrevocable election can receive the distribution in a single sum (or in one tax year) without losing the estate tax exclusion, but this is done at the cost of no income averaging other than five-year averaging under section 1301, if available.

It is not clear that this latest amendment of section 2039(c) represents real progress. It was possible that the Internal Revenue Service would have issued regulations permitting the estate tax exclusion if ten-year averaging were in fact not elected. Even without such regulations, it seems clear that the exclusion can be easily obtained by making the distribution, in any proportion, in two or more tax years of the recipient. Furthermore, distribution of a nontransferable annuity appears superior since such an annuity will be excluded from the participant's estate and the beneficiary will only pay income taxes on it as payments are received, normally over his or her life expenctancy; that is, both income and estate tax advantages are obtained. Finally, under the proposed income tax regulations for lump-sum distributions [section 1.402(e)-2(c)(1)(i)], it seems certain that a distribution can be made a combination of a nontransferable annuity and lump-sum cash, in any proportion, and the annuity portion will receive the estate tax exclusion while the lump sum will qualify for ten-year averaging.

Another shortcoming of the Revenue Act's amendment of section 2039(c) is that it provides no guidance on the estate taxation of tax-sheltered annuities or military death benefits paid in single sums, neither of which were ever eligible for ten-year averaging. In short, clarifying regulations are still needed for the qualified plan estate tax exclusion.

F. Bankruptcy Priority For Employer Contributions Owed To Plans — Bankruptcy Reform Act Section 507

Signed the same day as the Revenue Act of 1978 was the Bankruptcy Reform Act of 1978, which represents a complete revision of the federal bankruptcy law under Title 11 of the United States Code. Section 507 of the Act deals with the priority to be given various types of claims in bankruptcy matters.

Previously, employer contributions owed to employee benefit plans were given no priority. Under the Bankruptcy Reform Act, these unpaid contributions are now given the fourth priority, preceded only by (1) administrative expenses, fees, and charges assessed against the bankruptcy estate, (2) claims arising in the ordinary course of a debtor's business between the beginning of an involuntary bankruptcy action and appointment of the trustee, and (3) allowed unsecured wage claims of no more than $2,000 per individual earned within 90 days before the date of the bankruptcy petition or the cessation of the business, whichever occurs first.

Priority for claims for employee benefit plan contributions is limited to those arising from services rendered by the employees within 180 days before the filing of the bankruptcy petition or the date of the cessation of the business, whichever occurs first, and the amount can be no more than $2,000 times the number of employees covered by the plan. Furthermore, this maximum claim must be reduced by the amount paid to the employees under the third priority category as well as by amounts paid by the bankruptcy estate on behalf of the employees to any other employee benefit plans maintained by the debtor.

This creation of bankruptcy priority for employee benefit plan contribuitons is welcome but does not necessarily provide full protection. The amounts owed by an employer to an underfunded pension plan, even measured only by Pension Benefit Guaranty Corporation standards, could be well in excess of the amount allowed under priority four. For the balance, then, the plan would be on equal footing with other unsecured, priorityless creditors of the bankrupt.

INDEX

The following index cites broad concepts for the most part, but includes more specific references to concepts in the General Introduction and Part Four, and cites all words and terms included in the definitions' sections (indicated by quotation marks) and most assets listed in the appendixes. More precise indexing throughout the text of such terms as "accelerated depreciation," "minimum tax," etc., has not been undertaken since entries such as these are introduced in each chapter, example and discussion of benefits, risks and taxes as applicable, and are to be approached in the content of the chapter or example in which they are included.